S0-BCA-577

Gleim Publications, Inc., offers five university-level study systems:

Auditing & Systems Exam Questions and Explanations with Test Prep Software
Business Law/Legal Studies Exam Questions and Explanations with Test Prep Software
Federal Tax Exam Questions and Explanations with Test Prep Software
Financial Accounting Exam Questions and Explanations with Test Prep Software
Cost/Managerial Accounting Exam Questions and Explanations with Test Prep Software

The following is a list of Gleim examination review systems:

CIA Review: Part 1, The Internal Audit Activity's Role in Governance, Risk, and Control
CIA Review: Part 2, Conducting the Internal Audit Engagement
CIA Review: Part 3, Business Analysis and Information Technology
CIA Review: Part 4, Business Management Skills
CIA Review: A System for Success

CMA Review: Part 1, Financial Planning, Performance, and Control
CMA Review: Part 2, Financial Decision Making
CMA Review: A System for Success

CPA Review: Financial
CPA Review: Auditing
CPA Review: Business
CPA Review: Regulation
CPA Review: A System for Success

EA Review: Part 1, Individuals
EA Review: Part 2, Businesses
EA Review: Part 3, Representation, Practices, and Procedures
EA Review: A System for Success

Use the order form provided at the back of this book or contact us at www.gleim.com or (800) 874-5346.

Visit www.gleim.com for the latest updates and information on all of our products.

REVIEWERS AND CONTRIBUTORS

Garrett W. Gleim, B.S., CPA (not in public practice), received a Bachelor of Science degree from The Wharton School at the University of Pennsylvania. Mr. Gleim coordinated the production staff, reviewed the manuscript, and provided production assistance throughout the project.

Grady M. Irwin, J.D., is a graduate of the University of Florida College of Law, and he has taught in the University of Florida College of Business. Mr. Irwin provided substantial editorial assistance throughout the project.

John F. Rebstock, B.S.A., is a graduate of the Fisher School of Accounting at the University of Florida. He has passed the CPA and CIA exams. Mr. Rebstock reviewed portions of the manuscript.

A PERSONAL THANKS

This manual would not have been possible without the extraordinary effort and dedication of Jacob Brunny, Julie Cutlip, Eileen Nickl, Teresa Soard, Joanne Strong, Candace Van Doren, Jennifer Vann, and Eleanor Wilson, who typed the entire manuscript and all revisions, and drafted and laid out the diagrams and illustrations in this book.

The authors also appreciate the production and editorial assistance of Melissa Del Valle, Chris Hawley, Katie Larson, Cary Marcous, Shane Rapp, Drew Sheppard, Katie Wassink, and Martha Willis.

The authors also appreciate the critical reading assistance of Ellen Buhl, Reed Daines, Stephanie Garrison, Devin Grief, Daniela Guanipa, Alyssa Hagerty, and Jerry Mathis.

Finally, we appreciate the encouragement, support, and tolerance of our families throughout this project.

2013 Q1-Q2 EDITION
CPA REVIEW

Auditing

by

Irvin N. Gleim, Ph.D., CPA, CIA, CMA, CFM, RTRP

and

William A. Hillison, Ph.D., CPA, CMA

The AICPA formal title of this section is *Auditing and Attestation*, and the AICPA acronym is AUD.

ABOUT THE AUTHORS

Irvin N. Gleim is Professor Emeritus in the Fisher School of Accounting at the University of Florida and is a member of the American Accounting Association, Academy of Legal Studies in Business, American Institute of Certified Public Accountants, Association of Government Accountants, Florida Institute of Certified Public Accountants, The Institute of Internal Auditors, and the Institute of Management Accountants. He has had articles published in the *Journal of Accountancy*, *The Accounting Review*, and *The American Business Law Journal* and is author/coauthor of numerous accounting books, aviation books, and CPE courses.

William A. Hillison is a Professor Emeritus of Accounting at Florida State University. His primary teaching duties included graduate and undergraduate auditing and systems courses. He is a member of the Florida Institute of Certified Public Accountants, American Accounting Association, and Institute of Certified Management Accountants. He has had articles published in many journals, including the *Journal of Accounting Research*, the *Journal of Accounting Literature*, the *Journal of Accounting Education*, *Cost and Management*, *The Internal Auditor*, *ABACUS*, the *Journal of Accountancy*, *The CPA Journal*, and *The Journal of Forecasting*.

Gleim Publications, Inc.
P.O. Box 12848
University Station
Gainesville, Florida 32604
(800) 87-GLEIM or (800) 874-5346
(352) 375-0772
Fax: (352) 375-6940
Internet: www.gleim.com
Email: admin@gleim.com

For updates to this 2013 Q1-Q2 printing of
CPA Review: Auditing

Go To: www.gleim.com/updates

Or: Email update@gleim.com with
CPA AUD 2013-Q1Q2 in the subject
line. You will receive our current
update as a reply.

Updates are available until the next edition is
published.

ISSN: 1547-8033

ISBN: 978-1-58194-266-8 *CPA Review: Auditing*
ISBN: 978-1-58194-271-2 *CPA Review: Business*
ISBN: 978-1-58194-272-9 *CPA Review: Financial*
ISBN: 978-1-58194-273-6 *CPA Review: Regulation*
ISBN: 978-1-58194-292-7 *CPA Review: A System for Success*

ACKNOWLEDGMENTS

Material from *Uniform CPA Examination, Selected Questions and Unofficial Answers*, Copyright
© 1974-2012 by the American Institute of Certified Public Accountants, Inc., is reprinted and/or adapted
with permission. Visit the AICPA's website at www.aicpa.org for more information.

The author is indebted to the Institute of Certified Management Accountants for permission to use
problem materials from past CMA examinations. Questions and unofficial answers from the Certified
Management Accountant Examinations, copyright by the Institute of Certified Management
Accountants, are reprinted and/or adapted with permission.

The authors are grateful for permission to reproduce Certified Internal Auditor Examination
Questions, Copyright © 1991-2008 by The Institute of Internal Auditors, Inc.

This publication was printed and bound by Corley Printing Company, St. Louis, MO, a registered
ISO-9002 company. More information about Corley Printing Company is available at
www.corleyprinting.com or by calling (314) 739-3777.

TABLE OF CONTENTS

Gleim Publications' Customer Service Procedures

To continue providing our customers with first-rate service, we request that questions about the content of our materials be sent to us via email or mail. The appropriate author, consultant, or staff member will give each question thorough consideration and a prompt response.

Questions concerning orders, prices, shipments, or payments will be handled via telephone, email, Internet, or mail by our competent and courteous customer service staff.

For Test Prep Online technical support, you may use our automated technical support service at www.gleim.com/support/, email us at support@gleim.com, or call us at (800) 874-5346.

Thank you.

DETAILED TABLE OF CONTENTS

PREFACE FOR CPA CANDIDATES

The purpose of this Gleim *CPA Review* study book is to help YOU prepare to pass the Q1 or Q2 version of the 2013 Auditing and Attestation (referred to throughout the rest of this text as Auditing) section of the CPA examination. Our overriding consideration is to provide an inexpensive, effective, and easy-to-use study program. This book

1. Explains how to optimize your grade by focusing on the Auditing section of the CPA exam.

2. Defines the subject matter tested on the Auditing section of the CPA exam.

3. Outlines all of the subject matter tested on the Auditing section in 20 easy-to-use-and-complete study units.

4. Presents multiple-choice questions from recent CPA examinations to prepare you for questions in future CPA exams. Our answer explanations are presented to the immediate right of each question for your convenience. Use a piece of paper to cover our answer explanations as you study the questions.

5. Presents several task-based simulations in each study unit to acquaint you with simulation task formats. Answer the simulations in your book. The answers and grading instructions follow each simulation.

The outline format, the spacing, and the question and answer formats in this book are designed to facilitate readability, learning, understanding, and success on the CPA exam. Our most successful candidates use the entire Gleim CPA Review System,* which includes books, Test Prep Online, Audio Review, Gleim Online, Simulation Wizard, Practice Exam, and access to a Personal Counselor; or a group study CPA review program. (Check our website for live courses we recommend.) This review book and all Gleim *CPA Review* materials are compatible with other CPA review materials and courses that follow the AICPA Content and Skill Specification Outlines (CSOs/SSOs).

To maximize the efficiency and effectiveness of your CPA review program, augment your studying with *CPA Review: A System for Success*. This booklet has been carefully written and organized to provide important information to assist you in passing the CPA examination.

Thank you for your interest in the Gleim *CPA Review* materials. We deeply appreciate the thousands of letters and suggestions received from CIA, CMA, EA, RTRP, and CPA candidates during the past 5 decades.

If you use the Gleim materials, we want YOUR feedback immediately after the exam and as soon as you have received your grades. The CPA exam is NONDISCLOSED, and you will sign an attestation including, "I hereby agree that I will maintain the confidentiality of the Uniform CPA Examination. In addition, I agree that I will not divulge the nature or content of any Uniform CPA Examination question or answer under any circumstance..." We ask only for information about our materials, i.e., the topics that need to be added, expanded, etc. Our approach has AICPA approval.

Please go to www.gleim.com/feedbackAUD to share your suggestions on how we can improve this edition.

Good Luck on the Exam,

Irvin N. Gleim
William A. Hillison
December 2012

OPTIMIZING YOUR AUDITING SCORE

CBT-e Exam

	Auditing	Business	Financial	Regulation
Gleim Section Title	**Auditing**	Business	Financial	Regulation
AICPA Formal Title	**Auditing & Attestation**	Business Environment & Concepts	Financial Accounting & Reporting	Regulation
Acronym	**AUD**	BEC	FAR	REG
Exam Length	**4 hours**	3 hours	4 hours	3 hours
Testlets:				
Multiple-Choice	**3, 30 questions each**	3, 24 questions each	3, 30 questions each	3, 24 questions each
Simulations	**1 with 7 tasks**	0	1 with 7 tasks	1 with 6 tasks
Written Communication	**0**	1 with 3 tasks	0	0

The Auditing Standards Board Clarity Project

In an effort to make U.S. GAAS easier to read, understand, and apply, the Auditing Standards Board is redrafting all of the auditing sections into a new Codification of Statements on Auditing Standards. Under this clarity project, each standard will present the requirement paragraphs separate from an addendum of the application and example material. The new standards will also converge as much as possible with the International Auditing Standards. In addition, material has been reorganized and redundancies removed. Standards will be given a new three-digit identification number. Virtually all the standards will become effective at one time for audits on or after December 15, 2012.

What does this mean to you, the candidate? Not too much. First, the new material will not be tested until July 2013, so you have time to complete the exam before the material is effective. You will use this Q1-Q2 edition of *CPA Review: Auditing*. Second, audit concepts and requirements will not change significantly even after the implementation. We at Gleim are on top of this change and will release a Q3-Q4 edition of this text to ensure that you have the appropriate information and study materials to be successful in passing the exam.

ALLOW GLEIM TO GUIDE YOU THROUGH THE STUDY PROCESS AND PASS THE EXAM

1. Read this **Introduction** to familiarize yourself with the content and structure of the Auditing section of the exam. In the following pages, you will find

    a. An **overview of the Auditing section** and what it generally tests, including

        1) The AICPA's Content Specification Outlines (CSOs) for Auditing, cross-referenced with the Gleim study units that contain each topic
        2) The AICPA's Skill Specification Outlines (SSOs) for Auditing
        3) The AICPA's suggested references for Auditing

    b. A detailed plan with **steps to obtain your CPA license**, including

        1) The order in which you should apply, register, and schedule your exam
        2) The studying tactics on which you should focus
        3) How to organize your study schedule to make the most out of each resource in the Gleim CPA Review System (i.e., books, Test Prep Online, Audio Review, Gleim Online, Simulation Wizard, etc.)

    c. Tactics for your **actual test day**, including

        1) Time budgeting so you complete each testlet with time to review
        2) Question-answering techniques to obtain every point you can in both the multiple-choice and simulation testlets
        3) An explanation of how to be in control of your CPA exam

2. Scan the Gleim *CPA Review: A System for Success* booklet and note where to revisit later in your studying process to obtain a deeper understanding of the of the CPA exam.

    a. *CPA Review: A System for Success* has seven study units:

        Study Unit 1: The CPA Examination: An Overview and Preparation Introduction
        Study Unit 2: AICPA Content Specification Outlines and Skill Specification Outlines
        Study Unit 3: Content Preparation, Test Administration, and Performance Grading
        Study Unit 4: Multiple-Choice Questions
        Study Unit 5: Task-Based Simulations and Written Communication Questions
        Study Unit 6: Preparing to Pass the CPA Exam
        Study Unit 7: How to Take the CPA Exam

    b. If you feel that you need even more details on the test-taking experience, watch our **Free Tutorial** at www.gleim.com/accounting/cpa/basics.php.

        1) This tutorial is best for candidates who have little or no experience with the basic computer skills required for the CPA exam (e.g., copy/paste, search, etc.).

    c. Additionally, the AICPA requires that all candidates review the tutorial and sample tests at www.aicpa.org.

3. Before you begin studying, take a **Diagnostic Quiz** at www.gleim.com/cpadiagnosticquiz or use our Gleim Diagnostic Quiz App for iPhone, iPod Touch, and Android.

    a. The Diagnostic Quiz includes a representative sample of 40 multiple-choice questions and will determine your weakest areas in Auditing.

    b. When you are finished, one of our **Personal Counselors** will consult with you to better focus your review on any areas in which you have less confidence.

4. Follow the steps outlined on page 11, "How to Study an Auditing Study Unit Using the Gleim CPA Review System." This is the **study plan** that our most successful candidates adhere to. Study until you have reached your **desired proficiency level** (e.g., 75%) for each study unit in Auditing.

    a. As you proceed, be sure to check any **Updates** that may have been released.

        1) Gleim Online, Simulation Wizard, and Test Prep Online are updated automatically.

    2) Book updates can be viewed at www.gleim.com/updates, or you can have them emailed to you. See the information box in the top right corner of page iv for details.

   b. **Review the *CPA Review: A System for Success* booklet** and become completely comfortable with what will be expected from you on test day.

5. Shortly before your test date, take a **Practice Exam** (complimentary with the CPA Review System) at www.gleim.com/cpapracticeexam.

   a. The Gleim Practice Exam is designed to exactly emulate the CPA test-taking experience at Prometric.

   b. This timed, scored exam tests you not only on the content you have studied, but also on the question-answering and time-management techniques you have learned throughout the Gleim study process.

   c. When you have completed the exam, consult with your Personal Counselor to discuss where you should **focus your review during the final days before your exam** (question-answering techniques, time management, specific content areas, etc.).

6. **Take and PASS** the Auditing section of the CPA exam!

   a. When you have completed the exam, please contact Gleim with your **suggestions, comments, and corrections**. We want to know how well we prepared you for your testing experience.

OVERVIEW OF AUDITING

Auditing is scheduled for 4 hours (240 minutes).

AICPA title:	Auditing and Attestation
AICPA acronym:	AUD
Gleim title/acronym:	Auditing/AUD
Question format:	90 multiple-choice questions in three testlets of 30 questions each One testlet with seven Task-Based Simulations
Areas covered:	I. (14%) Engagement Acceptance and Understanding the Assignment II. (18%) Understanding the Entity and Its Environment (including Internal Control) III. (18%) Performing Audit Procedures and Evaluating Evidence IV. (18%) Evaluating Audit Findings, Communications, and Reporting V. (14%) Accounting and Review Services Engagements VI. (18%) Professional Responsibilities

The Auditing and Attestation section tests knowledge and understanding of the following professional standards: Auditing standards promulgated in the United States of America [related to audits of an "Issuer" (a public company), a "Nonissuer" (an entity that is not a public company), governmental entities, not-for-profit entities, and employee benefit plans], standards related to attestation and assurance engagements, and standards for performing accounting and review services.

Candidates are expected to demonstrate an awareness of (1) the International Auditing and Assurance Standards Board (IAASB) and its role in establishing International Standards on Auditing (ISAs), (2) the differences between ISAs and U.S. auditing standards, and (3) the audit requirements under U.S. auditing standards that apply when they perform audit procedures on a U.S. company that supports an audit report based upon the auditing standards of another country, or the ISAs.

This section also tests knowledge of professional responsibilities of certified public accountants, including ethics and independence. Candidates are also expected to demonstrate an awareness of (1) the International Ethics Standards Board for Accountants (IESBA) and its role in establishing requirements of the International Federation of Accountants (IFAC) *Code of Ethics for Professional Accountants* and (2) the independence requirements that apply when they perform audit procedures on a U.S. company that supports an audit report based upon the auditing standards of another country, or the ISAs.

In addition to demonstrating knowledge and understanding of the professional standards, candidates are required to demonstrate the skills required to apply that knowledge in performing auditing and attestation tasks as certified public accountants.

According to the AICPA, candidates will be expected to perform the following inclusive list of tasks to demonstrate such knowledge and skills:

- Demonstrate an awareness and understanding of the process by which standards and professional requirements are established for audit, attestation, and other services performed by CPAs, including the role of standard-setting bodies within the U.S. and those bodies with the authority to promulgate international standards.
- Differentiate between audits, attestation and assurance services, compilations, and reviews.
- Differentiate between the professional standards for issuers and nonissuers.
- Identify situations that might be unethical or a violation of professional standards, perform research and consultations as appropriate, and determine the appropriate action.
- Recognize potentially unethical behavior of clients and determine the impact on the services being performed.
- Demonstrate the importance of identifying and adhering to requirements, rules, and standards that are established by licensing boards within their states, and which may place additional professional requirements specific to their state of practice.
- Appropriately apply professional requirements in practice, and differentiate between unconditional requirements and presumptively mandatory requirements.
- Exercise due care in the performance of work.
- Demonstrate an appropriate level of professional skepticism in the performance of work.
- Maintain independence in mental attitude in all matters relating to the audit.
- Research relevant professional literature.

AICPA CONTENT SPECIFICATION OUTLINES (CSOs)

In the Uniform CPA Examination Alert newsletter of Spring 2009, when it was first unveiling the new CBT-e exam, the AICPA indicated that the content specification outlines have several purposes, including

1. *Ensure that the testing of entry-level knowledge and skills that are important to the protection of the public interest is consistent across examination administrations*
2. *Determine what kinds of questions should be included on the CPA Examination so that every version of the examination reflects the required distribution and balance of knowledge and skill components*
3. *Provide candidates preparing for the examination with information about the subject matter that is eligible to be tested*

For your convenience, we have reproduced verbatim the AICPA's Auditing CSOs. We also have provided cross-references to the study units and subunits in this book that correspond to the CSOs' coverage. If one entry appears above a list, it applies to all items.

AICPA CONTENT SPECIFICATION OUTLINE

Auditing and Attestation

I. **Engagement Acceptance and Understanding the Assignment (14%)**

   A. Determine Nature and Scope of Engagement - 1.1-1.4

   B. Consider the Firm's Policies and Procedures Pertaining to Client Acceptance and Continuance - 1.5

   C. Communicate with the Predecessor Auditor - 3.1

   D. Establish an Understanding with the Client and Document the Understanding Through an Engagement Letter or Other Written Communication with the Client - 3.1

   E. Consider Other Planning Matters

   1. Consider using the work of other independent auditors - 3.2, 17.1
   2. Determine the extent of the involvement of professionals possessing specialized skills - 3.2, 4.2
   3. Consider the independence, objectivity, and competency of the internal audit function - 4.1

   F. Identify Matters Related to Planning and Prepare Documentation for Communications with Those Charged with Governance - 9.2

II. **Understanding the Entity and Its Environment (including Internal Control) (18%)**

   A. Determine and Document Materiality Levels for Financial Statements Taken as a Whole - 3.2, 3.3

   B. Conduct and Document Risk Assessment Discussions Among Audit Team, Concurrently with Discussion on Susceptibility of the Entity's Financial Statement to Material Misstatement Due to Fraud - 3.3

   C. Consideration of Fraud - 3.6

   1. Identify characteristics of fraud
   2. Document required discussions regarding risk of fraud
   3. Document inquiries of management about fraud
   4. Identify and assess risks that may result in material misstatements due to fraud

   D. Perform and Document Risk Assessment Procedures

   1. Identify, conduct and document appropriate inquiries of management and others within the entity - 3.4

   2. Perform appropriate analytical procedures to understand the entity and identify areas of risk - 3.5

   3. Obtain information to support inquiries through observation and inspection (including reading corporate minutes, etc.) - 3.4

   E. Consider Additional Aspects of the Entity and its Environment, including: Industry, Regulatory and Other External Factors; Strategies and Business Risks; Financial Performance - 3.4

   F. Consider Internal Control

   1. Perform procedures to assess the control environment, including consideration of the COSO framework and identifying entity-level controls - 5.1-5.4

   2. Obtain and document an understanding of business processes and information flows - 5.1-5.4

   3. Determine the effect of information technology on the effectiveness of an entity's internal control - 5.5

   4. Perform risk assessment procedures to evaluate the design and implementation of internal controls relevant to an audit of financial statements - 5.3

   5. Identify key risks associated with general controls in a financial IT environment, including change management, backup/recovery, and network access (e.g., administrative rights) - 5.5, 8.3

6. Identify key risks associated with application functionality that supports financial transaction cycles, including: application access control (e.g., administrative access rights); controls over interfaces, integrations, and e-commerce; significant algorithms, reports, validation, edit checks, error handling, etc. - 5.5, 6.4, 7.5, 8.3

7. Assess whether the entity has designed controls to mitigate key risks associated with general controls or application functionality - 5.5

8. Identify controls relevant to reliable financial reporting and the period-end financial reporting process - SU 6, SU 7

9. Consider limitations of internal control - 5.1

10. Consider the effects of service organizations on internal control - 9.4

11. Consider the risk of management override of internal controls - 3.6

G. Document an Understanding of the Entity and its Environment, including Each Component of the Entity's Internal Control, in Order to Assess Risks - 5.3, 5.4

H. Assess and Document the Risk of Material Misstatements - SU 8

1. Identify and document financial statement assertions and formulate audit objectives including significant financial statement balances, classes of transactions, disclosures, and accounting estimates

2. Relate the identified risks to relevant assertions and consider whether the risks could result in a material misstatement to the financial statements

3. Assess and document the risk of material misstatement that relates to both financial statement level and specific assertions

4. Identify and document conditions and events that may indicate risks of material misstatement

I. Identify and Document Significant Risks that Require Special Audit Consideration

1. Significant recent economic, accounting, or other developments - 3.4
2. Related parties and related party transactions - 4.3
3. Improper revenue recognition - 3.6, 11.1
4. Nonroutine or complex transactions - 3.4
5. Significant management estimates - 4.4
6. Illegal acts - 3.7

III. Performing Audit Procedures and Evaluating Evidence (18%)

A. Develop Overall Responses to Risks

1. Develop overall responses to risks identified and use the risks of material misstatement to drive the nature, timing, and extent of further audit procedures - 8.2

2. Document significant risks identified, related controls evaluated, and overall responses to address assessed risks - 8.2

3. Determine and document level(s) of tolerable misstatement - 3.3, 8.2

B. Perform Audit Procedures Responsive to Risks of Material Misstatement; Obtain and Document Evidence to Form a Basis for Conclusions

1. Design and perform audit procedures whose nature, timing, and extent are responsive to the assessed risk of material misstatement - 10.1

2. Integrating audits: in an integrated audit of internal control over financial reporting and the financial statements, design and perform testing of controls to accomplish the objectives of both audits simultaneously - 9.3

3. Design, perform, and document tests of controls to evaluate design effectiveness - 8.1, 9.3, 10.1

4. Design, perform, and document tests of controls to evaluate operating effectiveness - 8.1, 9.3, 10.1

5. Perform substantive procedures - SU 11, SU 12, SU 13

6.   Perform audit sampling - SU 15

7.   Perform analytical procedures - 3.5

8.   Confirm balances and/or transactions with third parties - 10.2

9.   Examine inventories and other assets - 10.2

10. Perform other tests of details, balances, and journal entries - SU 11, SU 12, SU 13

11. Perform computer-assisted audit techniques (CAATs), including data query, extraction, and analysis - 10.4

12. Perform audit procedures on significant management estimates - 4.4

13. Auditing fair value measurements and disclosures, including the use of specialists in evaluating estimates - 4.4, 13.2

14. Perform tests on unusual year-end transactions - SU 11, SU 12, SU 13

15. Audits performed in accordance with International Standards on Auditing (ISAs) or auditing standards of another country: determine if differences exist and whether additional audit procedures are required - See "ISA Differences" boxes in relevant study units.

16. Evaluate contingencies - 13.3, 14.1

17. Obtain and evaluate lawyers' letters - 14.1

18. Review subsequent events - 14.2

19. Obtaining and placing reliance on representations from management - 14.4

20. Identify material weaknesses, significant deficiencies, and other control deficiencies - 9.1

IV. **Evaluating Audit Findings, Communications, and Reporting (18%)**

A.   Perform Overall Analytical Procedures - 3.5

B.   Evaluate the Sufficiency and Appropriateness of Audit Evidence and Document Engagement Conclusions - 10.3

C.   Evaluate Whether Audit Documentation is in Accordance with Professional Standards - 10.3

D.   Review the Work Performed by Others, including Specialists and Other Auditors, to Provide Reasonable Assurance that Objectives are Achieved - 17.1

E.   Document the Summary of Uncorrected Misstatements and Related Conclusions - 10.3

F.   Evaluate Whether Financial Statements are Free of Material Misstatements - 16.1

G.   Consider the Entity's Ability to Continue as a Going Concern - 14.5, 17.3

H.   Consider Other Information in Documents Containing Audited Financial Statements (e.g., Supplemental Information and Management's Discussion and Analysis) - 19.1-19.9

I.   Retain Audit Documentation as Required by Standards and Regulations - 10.3

J.   Prepare Communications

1.   Reports on audited financial statements - SU 16, SU 17
2.   Reports required by government auditing standards - SU 20
3.   Reports on compliance with laws and regulations - 19.13
4.   Reports on internal control - 9.3
5.   Reports on the processing of transactions by service organizations - 9.4
6.   Reports on agreed-upon procedures - 19.10
7.   Reports on financial forecasts and projections - 19.11
8.   Reports on pro forma financial information - 19.12
9.   Special reports - 18.4
10. Reissue reports - 14.3, 17.4
11. Communicate internal control related matters identified in the audit - 9.1
12. Communications with those charged with governance - 9.2
13. Subsequent discovery of facts existing at the date of the auditor's report - 14.2, 14.3
14. Consideration after the report date of omitted procedures - 4.5

V.   Accounting and Review Services Engagements (14%)

   A.   Plan the Engagement

      1.   Determine nature and scope of engagement - 18.1, 18.2

      2.   Decide whether to accept or continue the client and engagement including determining the appropriateness of the engagement to meet the client's needs and consideration of independence standards - 18.1-18.3

      3.   Establish an understanding with the client and document the understanding through an engagement letter or other written communication with the client - 18.1, 18.2

      4.   Consider change in engagement - 18.3

      5.   Determine if reports are to be used by third parties - 18.1, 18.2

   B.   Obtain and Document Evidence to Form a Basis for Conclusions

      1.   Obtain an understanding of the client's operations, business, and industry - 18.1, 18.2

      2.   Obtain knowledge of accounting principles and practices in the industry and the client - 18.1, 18.2

      3.   Perform analytical procedures for review services - 18.2

      4.   Obtain representations from management for review services - 18.1, 18.2

      5.   Perform other engagement procedures - 18.1, 18.2

      6.   Consider departures from generally accepted accounting principles (GAAP) or other comprehensive basis of accounting (OCBOA) - 18.1, 18.2

      7.   Prepare documentation from evidence gathered - 18.1, 18.2

      8.   Retain documentation as required by standards - 18.1, 18.2

      9.   Review the work performed to provide reasonable assurance that objectives are achieved - 18.1, 18.2

   C.   Prepare Communications

      1.   Reports on compilations - 18.1, 18.3
      2.   Reports on reviews - 18.2, 18.3
      3.   Restricted use of reports - 18.1, 18.2
      4.   Communicating to management and others - 18.1, 18.2
      5.   Subsequent discovery of facts existing at the date of the report - 18.1, 18.2
      6.   Consider degree of responsibility for supplementary information - 18.1, 18.2

VI.   Professional Responsibilities (18%)

   A.   Ethics and Independence

      1.   Code of Professional Conduct (AICPA) - 2.1-2.6
      2.   Requirements related to issuers, including the PCAOB, the SEC and the Sarbanes-Oxley Act of 2002, Titles II and III, Section 303 - 2.7
      3.   Government Accountability Office (GAO) - 20.1
      4.   Department of Labor (DOL) - 2.7
      5.   Code of Ethics for Professional Accountants (IFAC) - 2.7

   B.   Other Professional Responsibilities

      1.   A firm's system of quality control - 1.5
      2.   General role, structure, and requirements of the PCAOB (Title I and Title IV of the Sarbanes-Oxley Act of 2002) - 2.7

AICPA SKILL SPECIFICATION OUTLINES (SSOs)

The SSOs identify the skills that will be tested on the CPA exam. The following table explains the skills tested, the weight range assigned to each skill category (approximate percentage of CPA exam that will use skills in the category) in Auditing, the question format that will be used to test the skill in Auditing, and the resources that will be available to the candidates to demonstrate proficiency in each skill.

Skills Category	Weight	Question Format	Resource(s)
Knowledge and Understanding	60%	Multiple-choice questions	Calculator
Application of the Body of Knowledge	40%	Task-based simulations	Authoritative literature, calculator, spreadsheets, etc.
Written Communication*	--	--	--

*The Written Communication category is tested through essays, which are not present in the Auditing section of the CPA exam.

REFERENCES

The AICPA suggests that the following publications will be sources of questions for Auditing. Our outlines and answer explanations are based on these publications and are organized into meaningful, easy-to-use, common-sense study units to facilitate your exam preparation via the Gleim Knowledge Transfer System.

- AICPA Statements on Auditing Standards and Interpretations
- Public Company Accounting Oversight Board (PCAOB) Standards (SEC-Approved) and Related Rules, PCAOB Staff Questions and Answers, and PCAOB Staff Audit Practice Alerts
- U.S. Government Accountability Office Government Auditing Standards
- Single Audit Act, as amended
- Office of Management and Budget (OMB) Circular A-133
- AICPA Statements on Quality Control Standards
- AICPA Statements on Standards for Accounting and Review Services and Interpretations
- AICPA Statements on Standards for Attestation Engagements and Interpretations
- AICPA Audit and Accounting Guides
- AICPA Auditing Practice Releases
- AICPA *Code of Professional Conduct*
- IFAC *Code of Ethics for Professional Accountants*
- Sarbanes-Oxley Act of 2002
- Department of Labor Guidelines and Interpretive Bulletins re: Auditor Independence
- SEC Independence Rules
- Employee Retirement Income Security Act of 1974
- The Committee of Sponsoring Organizations of the Treadway Commission (COSO): Internal Control – Integrated Framework
- Current textbooks on auditing, attestation services, ethics, and independence
- International Standards on Auditing (ISAs)

STEPS TO BECOME A CPA

1. Become knowledgeable about the exam, and decide which section you will take first.

2. Purchase the Gleim CPA Review System to thoroughly prepare for the CPA exam. Commit to our systematic preparation for the exam as described in our review materials, including *CPA Review: A System for Success*.

3. Communicate with your Personal Counselor to design a study plan that meets your needs. Call (800) 874-5346 or email CPA@gleim.com.

4. Determine the board of accountancy (i.e., state) to which you will apply to sit for the CPA exam.

5. Obtain, complete, and submit your application form, including transcripts, fees, etc., to your State Board or NASBA. You should receive a Notice To Schedule (NTS) from NASBA in 4 to 6 weeks.

    a. Do not apply for a section of the exam until you are ready to take it. An NTS is valid for a specific period established by the boards of accountancy, and you will forfeit any fees you paid for sections not taken.

    b. Remember, the following testing windows are available for test taking: January/February, April/May, July/August, and October/November.

6. Schedule your test with Prometric (online or by calling your local Prometric testing site). Schedule at least 45 days before the date you plan to sit for the exam.

7. Work systematically through the study units in each section of the Gleim CPA Review System (Auditing, Business, Financial, and Regulation).

8. Use the Gleim CPA Test Prep Online: Thousands of questions, all updated to current tax law, Accounting Standards Codification, etc. Listen to CPA Audio Review as a supplement.

9. Sit for and PASS the CPA exam while you are in control.

10. Enjoy your career and pursue multiple certifications (CIA, CMA, EA, RTRP, etc.), recommend Gleim to others who are also taking these exams, and stay up-to-date on your continuing professional education with Gleim CPE.

More specifically, you should focus on the following **system for success** on the Auditing section of the CPA exam:

1. **Understand the exam, including its purpose, coverage, preparation, format, administration, grading, and pass rates.**

    a. The better you understand the examination process from beginning to end, the better you will perform.

    b. Study the Gleim *CPA Review: A System for Success*. Please be sure you have a copy of this useful booklet. (*CPA Review: A System for Success* is also available online at www.gleim.com/sfs.)

2. **Learn and understand the subject matter tested.** The AICPA's CSOs and SSOs for the Auditing section are the basis for the study outlines that are presented in each of the 20 study units that make up this book.* You will also learn and understand the Auditing material tested on the CPA exam by answering numerous multiple-choice questions from recent CPA exams. Multiple-choice questions with the answer explanations to the immediate right of each question are a major component of each study unit.

*Please fill out our online feedback form (www.gleim.com/feedbackAUD) IMMEDIATELY after you take the CPA exam so we can adapt to changes in the exam. Our approach has been approved by the AICPA

3. **Practice answering actual exam questions to perfect your question-answering techniques.** Answering recent exam questions helps you understand the standards to which you will be held. This motivates you to learn and understand while studying (rather than reading) the outlines in each of the 20 study units.

    a. Question-answering techniques are suggested for multiple-choice questions and task-based simulations in Study Units 4 and 5 of *CPA Review: A System for Success*.

    b. Our **CPA Test Prep Online** contains thousands of additional multiple-choice questions that are not offered in our books. Additionally, CPA Test Prep Online has many useful features, including documentation of your performance and the ability to simulate the CBT-e exam environment.

    c. Our **CPA Gleim Online** is a powerful Internet-based program that allows CPA candidates to learn in an interactive environment and provides feedback to candidates to encourage learning. It includes multiple-choice questions and task-based simulations in Prometric's format. Each CPA Gleim Online user has access to a Personal Counselor, who helps organize study plans that work with busy schedules.

    d. Additionally, all candidates are required by the AICPA to review the tutorial and sample tests at www.aicpa.org. According to the AICPA, failure to follow the directions provided in the tutorial and sample tests, including the directions on how to respond, may adversely affect your scores.

4. **Plan and practice exam execution.** Anticipate the exam environment and prepare yourself with a plan: When to arrive? How to dress? What exam supplies to bring? How many questions and what format? Order of answering questions? How much time to spend on each question? See Study Unit 7 in *CPA Review: A System for Success*.

    a. Expect the unexpected and adjust! Remember, your sole objective when taking an examination is to maximize your score. You must outperform your peers, and being as comfortable and relaxed as possible gives you an advantage!

5. **Be in control.** Develop confidence and ensure success with a controlled preparation program followed by confident execution during the examination.

HOW TO STUDY AN AUDITING STUDY UNIT USING THE GLEIM CPA REVIEW SYSTEM

To ensure that you are using your time effectively, we recommend that you follow the steps listed below when using all of the CPA Review System materials together (books, Test Prep Online, Audio Review, Gleim Online, and Simulation Wizard). Before you begin the steps, take the Gleim CPA Diagnostic Quiz. The Gleim CPA Diagnostic Quiz provides a representative sample of 40 multiple-choice questions for each exam part to identify your preliminary strengths and any weaknesses before you start preparing in earnest for the CPA exam.

1. (30 minutes, plus 10 minutes for review) In the **CPA Gleim Online** course, complete Multiple-Choice Quiz #1 in 30 minutes. It is expected that your scores will be lower on the first quiz in each study unit than on subsequent quizzes.

    a. Immediately following the quiz, you will be prompted to review questions you flagged and/or answered incorrectly. For each question, analyze and understand why you were unsure or answered it incorrectly. This step is an essential learning activity.

2. (30 minutes) Use the online audiovisual presentation for an overview of the study unit. **CPA Audio Review** can be substituted for audiovisual presentations and can be used while driving to work, exercising, etc.

3. (45 minutes) Complete the 30-question online True/False quiz. It is interactive and most effective if used prior to studying the Knowledge Transfer Outline.

4.   (60 minutes) Study the Knowledge Transfer Outline, particularly the troublesome areas identified from the multiple-choice questions in the Gleim Online course. The Knowledge Transfer Outline can be studied either online or from the books.

5.   (30 minutes, plus 10 minutes for review) Complete Multiple-Choice Quiz #2 in the Gleim Online course.

   a.   Immediately following the quiz, you will be prompted to review questions you flagged and/or answered incorrectly. For each question, analyze and understand why you were unsure or answered it incorrectly. This step is an essential learning activity.

6.   (60 minutes) Complete two 20-question quizzes while in Test Mode from the **CPA Test Prep Online**. Review as needed.

7.   (90 minutes) Complete and review the simulation section of the Gleim Online course.

When following these steps, you will complete all 20 study units in about 120 hours. Then spend about 10-20 hours taking customized tests in the CPA Test Prep Online until you approach your desired proficiency level, e.g., 75%+. To get immediate feedback on questions in your problem areas, use Study Sessions. You should also complete all of the simulation tasks in the Simulation Wizard for extra practice on this difficult aspect of the exam.

CPA FINAL REVIEW

Final review is the culmination of all your studies and topics and should occur one week prior to when you sit for your exam. All study units in Gleim Online should be completed by this time.

Step 1: Take the CPA Practice Exam under exam conditions at the beginning of your final review stage. The Practice Exam is 4 hours (240 minutes) long and contains three testlets with 30 multiple-choice questions each and one testlet with seven task-based simulations, just like the CPA exam. This will help you identify any weak areas for more practice. Discuss your results with your Personal Counselor for additional guidance.

Step 2: Work in Gleim CPA Test Prep Online, focusing on your weak areas identified from your Practice Exam. Also, be sure to focus on all the material as a whole to refresh yourself with topics you learned at the beginning of your studies. View your performance chart to make sure you are scoring 70% or higher.

CPA GLEIM ONLINE

CPA Gleim Online is a versatile, interactive, self-study review program delivered via the Internet. It is divided into four courses (one for each section of the CPA exam).

Each course is broken down into 20 individual, manageable study units. Completion time per study unit will average out to 5 hours. Each study unit in the course contains an audiovisual presentation, 30 true/false study questions, 10-20 pages of Knowledge Transfer Outlines, and two 20-question multiple-choice quizzes. Task-based simulations are also included with each study unit in Auditing, Financial, and Regulation, while written communication tasks are in each study unit of Business. Downloadable PDFs with additional information, such as Core Concepts, are also included with each study unit.

CPA Gleim Online provides you with access to a Personal Counselor, a real person who will provide support to ensure your competitive edge. CPA Gleim Online is a great way to get confidence as you prepare with Gleim. This confidence will continue during and after the exam.

GLEIM SIMULATION WIZARD FOR AUDITING, FINANCIAL, AND REGULATION

The Gleim Simulation Wizard for Auditing is a training program that focuses on the task-based simulations that appear in the Auditing, Financial, and Regulation sections of the CPA exam. This online course provides one simulation per study unit, as well as test-taking tips from Dr. Gleim to help you stay in control.

GLEIM BOOKS

This edition of the CPA Auditing Review book has the following six features to make studying easier:

1. **Examples:** Illustrative examples, both hypothetical and those drawn from actual events, are set off in shaded, bordered boxes.

EXAMPLE

If financial statement materiality was set at $50,000, performance materiality for the audit of accounts receivable might be set at $3,000 to compensate for the possibility of multiple undetected or uncorrected misstatements in this and other accounts on the balance sheet.

---

2. **Backgrounds:** In certain instances, we have provided historical background or supplemental information. This information is intended to illuminate the topic under discussion and is set off in bordered boxes with shaded headings. This material does not need to be memorized for the exam.

Background

The Sarbanes-Oxley Act of 2002 authorized the Public Company Accounting Oversight Board to establish auditing and related professional practice standards to be used by **registered public accounting firms**. The PCAOB has adopted, as **Interim Auditing Standards** on a transitional basis, the GAAS established by the AICPA as of April 16, 2003. Since then, the PCAOB has issued various pronouncements applying to audits by registered public accounting firms of public companies (issuers).

---

3. **Gleim Success Tips:** These tips supplement the core exam material by suggesting how certain topics might be presented on the exam or how you should prepare for an issue.

There has been a recent emphasis on quality control, and you should recognize its importance in your study for the exam. Be familiar with the role of practice monitoring, and make sure that you understand the six elements of the AICPA's Statements on Quality Control Standards. Note that each element requires the CPA firm to have "policies and procedures" in place to ensure the standards are met.

---

4. **Auditing Review Checklist:** This appendix to the 20 study units contains a complete listing of all study units and subunits in the Gleim Auditing Review. Use this list as a study aid to mark off your progress and to provide jumping-off points for review.

5. **ISA Differences:** When international standards differ significantly from U.S. auditing standards, we note the differences.

ISA Difference

Under the ISAs, if the **terms of the engagement** are changed, for example, from an audit to a review, the auditor and client may not be able to agree to the change. In these circumstances, the auditor should withdraw and consider whether to report to others

---

6. **Auditing Authoritative Pronouncements Cross-References:** This section at the end of the Introduction lists all Authoritative Pronouncements and cross-references them to the Gleim study unit(s) in which they are discussed.

CPA TEST PREP ONLINE

Twenty-question tests in the **CPA Test Prep Online** will help you to focus on your weaker areas. Make it a game: How much can you improve?

Our CPA Test Prep Online (in Test Mode) forces you to commit to your answer choice before looking at answer explanations; thus, you are preparing under true exam conditions. It also keeps track of your time and performance history for each study unit, which is available in either a table or graphical format.

STUDYING WITH BOOK AND TEST PREP ONLINE*

Simplify the exam preparation process by following our suggested steps listed below. DO NOT omit the step in which you diagnose the reasons for answering questions incorrectly; i.e., learn from your mistakes while studying so you avoid making similar mistakes on the CPA exam.

1. In test mode of CPA Test Prep Online, answer a 20-question diagnostic test before studying any other information.

2. Study the Knowledge Transfer Outline for the corresponding study unit in your Gleim book.

   a. Place special emphasis on the weaker areas that you identified with the initial diagnostic quiz in Step 1.

3. Take two or three 20-question tests in test mode after you have studied the Knowledge Transfer Outline.

4. Immediately following each test, you will be prompted to review the questions you flagged and/or answered incorrectly. For each question, analyze and understand why you were unsure or answered it incorrectly. This step is an essential learning activity.

5. Continue this process until you approach a predetermined proficiency level, e.g., 75%+.

6. Modify this process to suit your individual learning process.

   a. Learning from questions you answer incorrectly is very important. Each question you answer incorrectly is an **opportunity** to avoid missing actual test questions on your CPA exam. Thus, you should carefully study the answer explanations provided until you understand why the original answer you chose is wrong as well as why the correct answer indicated is correct. This learning technique is clearly the difference between passing and failing for many CPA candidates.

   b. Also, you **must** determine why you answered questions incorrectly and learn how to avoid the same error in the future. Reasons for missing questions include

      1) Misreading the requirement (stem)
      2) Not understanding what is required
      3) Making a math error
      4) Applying the wrong rule or concept
      5) Being distracted by one or more of the answers
      6) Incorrectly eliminating answers from consideration
      7) Not having any knowledge of the topic tested
      8) Using a poor educated guessing strategy

   c. It is also important to verify that you answered correctly for the right reasons (i.e., read the discussion provided for the correct answers). Otherwise, if the material is tested on the CPA exam in a different manner, you may not answer it correctly.

---

*Gleim does not recommend studying for Auditing using only this book and Test Prep Online. Candidates need to practice the task-based simulations in an exam environment, which means on a computer. Use CPA Gleim Online and CPA Simulation Wizard to become an expert on task-based simulations.

d. It is imperative that you complete the predetermined number of study units per week so you can review your progress and realize how attainable a comprehensive CPA review program is when using the Gleim CPA Review System. Remember to meet or beat your schedule to give yourself confidence.

GLEIM AUDIO REVIEWS

Gleim **CPA Audio Reviews** provide an average of 30 minutes of quality review for each study unit. Each review provides an overview of the Knowledge Transfer Outline in the *CPA Review* book. The purpose is to get candidates started so they can relate to the questions they will answer before reading the study outlines in each study unit.

The audios get to the point, as does the entire **Gleim System for Success**. We are working to get you through the CPA exam with minimum time, cost, and frustration. You can listen to two short sample audio reviews on our website at www.gleim.com/accounting/demos.

TIME BUDGETING AND QUESTION-ANSWERING TECHNIQUES FOR AUDITING

Expect three testlets of 30 multiple-choice questions each and one task-based simulation testlet with seven tasks on the Auditing section with a 240-minute time allocation. See Study Units 4 and 5 in *CPA Review: A System for Success* for additional discussion of how to maximize your score on multiple-choice questions and simulations.

MULTIPLE-CHOICE QUESTIONS

1. **Budget your time.** We make this point with emphasis. Just as you would fill up your gas tank prior to reaching empty, so too would you finish your exam before time expires.

    a. Here is our suggested time allocation for Auditing:

	Minutes	Start Time	
Testlet 1 (MC)	45	4 hours	00 minutes
Testlet 2 (MC)	45	3 hours	15 minutes
Testlet 3 (MC)	45	2 hours	30 minutes
Testlet 4 (TBS)	90	1 hour	45 minutes
***Extra time	15	0 hours	15 minutes

    b. Before beginning your first testlet of multiple-choice questions, prepare a Gleim Time Management Sheet as recommended in Study Unit 7 of *CPA Review: A System for Success*.

    c. As you work through the individual items, monitor your time. In Auditing, we suggest 45 minutes for each testlet of 30 questions. If you answer five items in 7 minutes, you are fine, but if you spend 10 minutes on five items, you need to speed up.

    ***Remember to allocate your budgeted extra time, as needed, to each testlet. Your goal is to answer all of the items and achieve the maximum score possible.

2. **Answer the questions in consecutive order.**

    a. Do **not** agonize over any one item. Stay within your time budget.

    b. Flag for review any questions you are unsure of and return to them later as time allows.

        1) Once you have selected either the Continue or Quit option, you will no longer be able to review or change any answers in the completed testlet.

    c. Never leave a multiple-choice question unanswered. **Make your best educated guess in the time allowed.** Remember that your score is based on the number of correct responses. You will not be penalized for guessing incorrectly.

3. **For each multiple-choice question,**

    a. **Try to ignore the answer choices.** Do not allow the answer choices to affect your reading of the question.

        1) If four answer choices are presented, three of them are incorrect. These choices are called **distractors** for good reason. Often, distractors are written to appear correct at first glance until further analysis.

        2) In computational items, the distractors are carefully calculated such that they are the result of making common mistakes. Be careful, and double-check your computations if time permits.

    b. **Read the question** carefully to determine the precise requirement.

        1) Focusing on what is required enables you to ignore extraneous information, to focus on the relevant facts, and to proceed directly to determining the correct answer.

            a) Be especially careful to note when the requirement is an **exception**; e.g., "Which of the following is **not** a management assertion?"

    c. **Determine the correct answer** before looking at the answer choices.

    d. **Read the answer choices carefully.**

        1) Even if the first answer appears to be the correct choice, do **not** skip the remaining answer choices. Questions often ask for the "best" of the choices provided. Thus, each choice requires your consideration.

        2) Treat each answer choice as a true/false question as you analyze it.

    e. **Click on the best answer.**

        1) You have a 25% chance of answering the question correctly by guessing blindly; improve your odds with educated guessing.

        2) For many multiple-choice questions, two answer choices can be eliminated with minimal effort, thereby increasing your educated guess to a 50-50 proposition.

4. After you have answered all the items in a testlet, consult the question status list at the bottom of each multiple-choice question screen **before** clicking the "Exit" button, which permanently ends the testlet.

    a. Go back to the flagged questions and finalize your answer choices.
    b. Verify that all questions have been answered.

5. **If you don't know the answer,**

    a. Again, guess; but make it an educated guess, which means select the best possible answer. First, rule out answers that you think are incorrect. Second, speculate on what the AICPA is looking for and/or the rationale behind the question. Third, select the best answer or guess between equally appealing answers. Your first guess is usually the most intuitive. If you cannot make an educated guess, read the stem and each answer and pick the best or most intuitive answer. It's just a guess!

    b. Make sure you accomplish this step within your predetermined time budget per testlet.

TASK-BASED SIMULATIONS

In Auditing, Testlet 4 consists of seven short task-based simulations. The following information and toolbar icons are located at the top of the testlet screen.

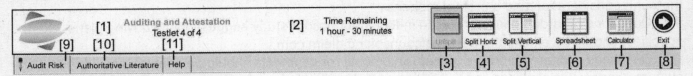

1. **Exam Section and Testlet Number:** For Auditing, this part of the toolbar will always show Auditing and Attestation as the Exam Section and Testlet 4 of 4 as the Testlet Number.

2. **Time Remaining:** This information box displays to the examinee how long (s)he has remaining in the entire exam. Consistently check the amount of time remaining in order to stay on schedule.

3. **Unsplit:** This icon, when selected, will unsplit the screen between two tabs.

4. **Split Horiz:** This icon, when selected, will split the screen horizontally between two tabs, enabling you to see, for example, both the simulation question and the help tab at the same time.

5. **Split Vertical:** This icon, when selected, will split the screen vertically between two tabs, enabling you to see, for example, both the simulation question and the help tab at the same time.

6. **Spreadsheet:** This icon opens a spreadsheet that operates like most others and is provided as a tool available for complex calculations. You may enter and execute formulas as well as enter text and numbers.

7. **Calculator:** The calculator provided is a basic tool for simple computations. It is similar to calculators used in common software programs.

8. **Exit:** There are three options when you choose this icon.

   - You may choose Review Testlet to return to the beginning of the testlet to review your answers. You will be able to change your answers.
   - You may choose Continue Exam to close the current testlet and go on to the next testlet. Once you have chosen Continue, you may not return to that testlet. For Auditing, the choice to Continue will only be relevant after each multiple-choice testlet, since the simulation is the last testlet.
   - Finally, you may choose Quit Exam, which means either that you have completed the exam or that you chose not to complete it. Your exam will end and you will not be able to return to any testlet. If you chose to quit your exam before you have completed it, there are security measures in place to determine that you are intentionally not completing the exam.

9. **Work Tabs:** A work tab requires the test taker to respond to given information. Each task will have at least one work tab (distinguished by a pencil icon), and each work tab will have specific directions that you must read in order to complete the tab correctly. There are different varieties of work tabs; the one in the toolbar above is just an example. You may encounter work tabs that require you to complete forms, fill in spreadsheets, or select an option from multiple choices.

10. **Information Tabs:** An information tab gives the test taker information to aid in responding to work tabs. Each task will have at least one information tab (the Authoritative Literature, as shown in the example above). If your task has additional information tabs, go through each to familiarize yourself with the task's content.

11. **Help:** This tab, when selected, provides a quick review of certain functions and tool buttons specific to the type of task you are working on. It will also provide directions and general information but will not include information related specifically to the test content.

Task-Based Simulation Grading

Remember, on the real exam, you will need to complete seven different tasks, all of which will count toward your final grade. Your score on all of the tasks together will make up **40%** of your total grade. The other **60%** of your grade will be your total score on the multiple-choice testlets.

IF YOU HAVE QUESTIONS

Content-specific questions about our materials will be answered most rapidly if they are sent to us via email to accounting@gleim.com. Our team of accounting experts will give your correspondence thorough consideration and a prompt response.

Questions regarding the information in this Introduction (study suggestions, studying plans, exam specifics) should be emailed to personalcounselor@gleim.com.

Questions concerning orders, prices, shipments, or payments should be sent via email to customerservice@gleim.com and will be promptly handled by our competent and courteous customer service staff.

For technical support, you may use our automated technical support service at www.gleim.com/support, email us at support@gleim.com, or call us at (800) 874-5346.

HOW TO BE IN CONTROL

Remember, you must be in control to be successful during exam preparation and execution. Perhaps more importantly, control can also contribute greatly to your personal and other professional goals. Control is the process whereby you

1. Develop expectations, standards, budgets, and plans
2. Undertake activity, production, study, and learning
3. Measure the activity, production, output, and knowledge
4. Compare actual activity with expected and budgeted activity
5. Modify the activity, behavior, or study to better achieve the expected or desired outcome
6. Revise expectations and standards in light of actual experience
7. Continue the process or restart the process in the future

Exercising control will ultimately develop the confidence you need to outperform most other CPA candidates and PASS the CPA exam! Obtain our *CPA Review: A System for Success* booklet for a more detailed discussion of control and other exam tactics.

Update Service

Visit the GLEIM® website for free updates,
which are available until the next edition is published.

gleim.com/updates

AUDITING AUTHORITATIVE PRONOUNCEMENTS CROSS-REFERENCES

The following listing relates AU and other auditing pronouncements to the Gleim study unit(s) in which they are discussed. Note that the subject matter may be covered without specific reference to the pronouncement. Recall that the CPA exam does not test pronouncement numbers or titles.

AU Sec. No.	Gleim Study Unit	Statements on Auditing Standards
110	1	Responsibilities and Functions of the Independent Auditor
120	1	Defining Professional Requirements in Statements on Auditing Standards
150	1	Generally Accepted Auditing Standards
161	1	The Relationship of Generally Accepted Auditing Standards to Quality Control Standards
201	1	Nature of the General Standards
210	1	Training and Proficiency of the Independent Auditor
220	1	Independence
230	1	Due Professional Care in the Performance of Work
311	1	Planning and Supervision
312	3	Audit Risk and Materiality in Conducting an Audit
314	3	Understanding the Entity and its Environment and Assessing the Risks of Material Misstatement
315	3	Communications between Predecessor and Successor Auditors
316	3	Consideration of Fraud in a Financial Statement Audit
317	3	Illegal Acts by Clients
318	3, 10	Performing Audit Procedures in Response to Assessed Risks and Evaluating the Audit Evidence Obtained
322	3	The Auditor's Consideration of the Internal Audit Function in an Audit of Financial Statements
324	9	Service Organizations
325	9	Communicating Internal Control Related Matters Identified in an Audit
326	10-14	Audit Evidence
328	4	Auditing Fair Value Measurements and Disclosures
329	3	Analytical Procedures
330	10, 11	The Confirmation Process
331	12	Inventories
332	13	Auditing Derivative Instruments, Hedging Activities, and Investments in Securities
333	14	Management Representations
334	4	Related Parties
336	4	Using the Work of a Specialist
337	14	Inquiry of a Client's Lawyer Concerning Litigation, Claims, and Assessments
339	10	Audit Documentation
341	14	The Auditor's Consideration of an Entity's Ability to Continue as a Going Concern
342	4	Auditing Accounting Estimates
350	15	Audit Sampling
380	9	The Auditor's Communication with those Charged with Governance
390	4	Consideration of Omitted Procedures after the Report Date
410	16	Adherence to Generally Accepted Accounting Principles
411	16	The Meaning of *Present Fairly in Conformity with Generally Accepted Accounting Principles* in the Independent Auditor's Report
420	17	Consistency of Application of Generally Accepted Accounting Principles
431	16	Adequacy of Disclosure in Financial Statements
504	16	Association with Financial Statements
508	1, 16, 17	Reports on Audited Financial Statements
530	16	Dating of the Independent Auditor's Report
532	19	Restricting the Use of an Auditor's Report
534	19	Reporting on Financial Statements Prepared for Use in Other Countries
543	17	Part of Audit Performed by Other Independent Auditors
544	16	Lack of Conformity with Generally Accepted Accounting Principles
550	19	Other Information in Documents Containing Audited Financial Statements
551	19	Supplementary Information in Relation to the Financial Statements as a Whole
552	19	Reporting on Condensed Financial Statements and Selected Financial Data
558	19	Required Supplementary Information

AU Sec. No.	Gleim Study Unit	Statements on Auditing Standards
560	14	Subsequent Events
561	14	Subsequent Discovery of Facts Existing at the Date of the Auditor's Report
623	18	Special Reports
625	19	Reports on the Application of Accounting Principles
634	19	Letters for Underwriters and Certain Other Requesting Parties
711	19	Filings Under Federal Securities Statutes
722	19	Interim Financial Information
801	20	Compliance Auditing
901	12	Public Warehouses -- Controls and Auditing Procedures for Goods Held

		Statements on Standards for Attestation Engagements
AT 20	1	Defining Professional Requirements in SSAEs
AT 50	1	SSAE Hierarchy
AT 101	1	Attest Engagements
AT 201	1, 19	Agreed-Upon Procedures Engagements
AT 301	1, 19	Financial Forecasts and Projections
AT 401	1, 19	Reporting on Pro Forma Financial Information
AT 501	1, 9	An Examination of an Entity's Internal Control over Financial Reporting that is Integrated with an Audit of Its Financial Statements
AT 601	1, 19	Compliance Attestation
AT 701	1	Management's Discussion and Analysis
AT 801	9	Reporting on Controls at a Service Organization

		Statements on Standards for Accounting and Review Services
AR 60	18	Framework for Performing and Reporting on Compilation and Review Engagements
AR 80	1, 18	Compilation of Financial Statements
AR 90	1, 18	Review of Financial Statements
AR 200	18	Reporting on Comparative Financial Statements
AR 300	18	Compilation Reports on Financial Statements Included in Certain Prescribed Forms
AR 400	18	Communications Between Predecessor and Successor Accountants
AR 600	18	Reporting on Personal Financial Statements Included in Written Personal Financial Plans

		Statements on Quality Control Standards
SQCS 7	1	A Firm's System of Quality Control

		Standards for Performing and Reporting on Peer Reviews
PR 100	1	Standards for Performing and Reporting on Peer Reviews

		Other Standards and References
	2	Department of Labor: Auditor Independence
	20	*Government Auditing Standards* (Yellow Book)
	2	*IFAC Code of Ethics for Professional Accountants*
	5	The Committee of Sponsoring Organizations (COSO)

		Public Company Accounting Oversight Board
AS No. 1	16	References in Auditor's Reports to the Standards of the PCAOB
AS No. 2		[Superseded by AS No. 5]
AS No. 3	10	Audit Documentation
AS No. 4	9	Reporting on Whether a Previously Reported Material Weakness Continues to Exist
AS No. 5	9	An Audit of Internal Control Over Financial Reporting That is Integrated with an Audit of Financial Statements
AS No. 6	16, 17	Evaluating Consistency of Financial Statements
AS No. 7	1	Engagement Quality Review
AS No. 8	3	Audit Risk
AS No. 9	1	Audit Planning
AS No. 10	1	Supervision of the Audit Engagement
AS No. 11	3	Consideration of Materiality in Planning and Performing an Audit
AS No. 12	3	Identifying and Assessing Risks of Material Misstatement
AS No. 13	3, 10	The Auditor's Responses to the Risks of Material Misstatement
AS No. 14	3	Evaluating Audit Results
AS No. 15	10-14	Audit Evidence

STUDY UNIT ONE
ENGAGEMENT RESPONSIBILITIES

(15 pages of outline)

This study unit begins the consideration of engagement planning for attest and audit engagements. Candidates should understand the types of services performed by CPAs. The differences among compilation, review, examination or audit, and agreed-upon procedures engagements are stressed. The list below is an overview:

Compilation – disclaimer of any assurance
Review – limited assurance
Examination/audit – positive assurance or opinion expressed
Agreed-upon procedures – results of procedures but no assurance

Summarized here are the specific **attestation standards** that have been issued that address a variety of practitioner services. Most are considered in more detail in other study units.

Assurance services also are covered in this study unit. They represent a significant enlargement of the practice of CPAs. An understanding of how these services contrast with others provided by a CPA should be obtained.

Quality control is the final subject in this study unit. The candidate must learn the six specific quality control elements and what each includes. This topic appears to be gaining importance.

1.1 ATTEST ENGAGEMENTS (AT 101)

1. **Applicable Pronouncements**

   a. The AICPA's **Statements on Standards for Attestation Engagements (SSAEs)** are codified in section AT of the professional standards within the framework of the 11 attestation standards (summarized on page 23). The AICPA also issues SASs (auditing services), SSARSs (compilation and review services), and SSCSs (consulting services).

      1) **SAS** = Statement on Auditing Standards issued by the ASB
         SSARS = Statement on Standards for Accounting and Review Services
         SSCS = Statement on Standards for Consulting Services

      2) The **Sarbanes-Oxley Act of 2002** is federal legislation that has had a dramatic effect on the engagement responsibilities of public accounting firms. This act created the **Public Company Accounting Oversight Board (PCAOB)**. The PCAOB has issued 14 currently effective auditing standards (AS No. 1 and AS Nos. 3-15) applicable to audits of issuers (companies required to file with the SEC) by public accounting firms.

2. **Nature of an Attest Engagement**

    a. An **attest engagement** is one in which a practitioner is engaged to issue or does issue an **examination**, a **review**, or an **agreed-upon procedures** report on subject matter, or an assertion about the subject matter, that is the **responsibility of another party**.

    b. A **practitioner** is a CPA in the **practice of public accounting**. This is the performance for a client while holding out as a CPA of accounting, tax, personal financial planning, litigation support, and those professional services for which standards are issued by bodies designated by the AICPA Council.

    c. Because the attestation standards apply **only to attest engagements involving a practitioner as defined above**, it follows that they apply only to the rendering by a CPA in public accounting of those professional services that are considered attest services (attest engagements).

    d. Attest services have traditionally been limited to expressing an opinion on historical financial statements on the basis of an audit in accordance with GAAS.

        1) But CPAs increasingly provide assurance on representations other than historical statements and in forms other than an opinion. For example, positive assurance may be provided on financial forecasts based on an **examination**, and limited (negative) assurance may be provided on historical financial statements based on a **review**.

    e. SSAEs cover only attest engagements, not services to which specific standards apply, for example, SASs, SSARSs, and SSCSs.

        1) Other professional services to which the SSAEs specifically do not apply include engagements in which the practitioner (a) advocates a client's position, (b) prepares tax returns or gives tax advice, (c) has the sole function of assisting the client (e.g., to prepare information other than financial statements), or (d) testifies as an expert witness given certain stipulated facts.

    f. Some of the assurance services developed by the AICPA are considered attestation engagements, for example, **WebTrust** and **SysTrust**.

    g. Compilation engagements, although not an attest service, are defined in the standard addressing prospective financial statements. This service requires a disclaimer of assurance.

3. **Attestation Standards (AT 50)**

    a. The need to provide standards for the growing range of attest services resulted in the issuance of the attestation standards. These standards are a natural extension of the 10 standards that are the basis for GAAS and other standards, but they do not supersede them. Thus, the candidate should master both.

    b. The summary table may be helpful in understanding the similarities and differences.

    c. The mnemonics are helpful for recalling the 10 GAAS and the 11 Attestation Standards. However, learning the order is not necessary for the exam.

SUMMARY COMPARISON OF ATTESTATION STANDARDS AND GAAS	
ATTESTATION (11)	**AUDITING (10)**
General Standards	
1. **Training** and proficiency in attestation	1. **Training** and proficiency in auditing
2. Knowledge of **subject matter**	
3. Suitable and available **criteria**	
4. **Independence** in mental attitude	2. **Independence** in mental attitude
5. Due **professional care**	3. Due **professional care**
Standards of Field Work	
1. **Planning** and supervision	1. **Planning** and supervision
	2. Sufficient understanding of **internal control**
2. Sufficient **evidence**	3. Sufficient appropriate audit **evidence**
Standards of Reporting	
1. **Character** of engagement	
2. **Conclusion** about the subject matter	1. Conformity with **GAAP**
	2. Principles **consistently** observed
	3. Informative **disclosures** reasonably adequate
3. Significant **reservations**	4. Expression of an **opinion**
4. Any **restrictions** on use	

Attestation Standards	Mnemonic
T = Training	Trisha
S = Subject matter	Said
C = Criteria	Chris
I = Independence	Is
P = Professional care	Profane
P = Planning and supervision	Please
E = Evidence	Excuse
C = Character	Cousin
C = Conclusion	Chris's
R = Reservations	Rude
R = Restrictions	Remarks

GAAS	Mnemonic
T = Training	Tammy
I = Independence	Is
P = Professional care	Pretty
P = Planning and supervision	Peter
I = Internal control	Is
E = Evidence	Evil
G = GAAP conformity	Great
C = Consistency	Couple
D = Disclosure	Doing
O = Opinion	Okay

d. **General Standards**

1) *The practitioner must have adequate technical training and proficiency to perform the attestation engagement.*

2) *The practitioner must have adequate knowledge of the subject matter.*

3) *The practitioner must have reason to believe that the subject matter is capable of evaluation against criteria that are suitable and available to users.*

    a) Suitable criteria have the attributes of objectivity, measurability, completeness, and relevance.

        i) For example, an engagement to attest to management's representation that "workers recorded an average of 40 hours per week on a project" could be accepted by a CPA. "Recorded" and "40 hours" are measurable and objectively determinable.

        ii) However, an engagement to attest that "workers worked very hard on the project" could not be accepted. "Very hard" is not measurable or objectively determinable.

    b) Criteria should be available to users in one or more of the following ways:

        i) Publicly available

        ii) Clearly included in the presentation of the subject matter or in the assertion

        iii) Clearly included in the practitioner's report

        iv) Well understood by most users (e.g., 40 hours per week)

        v) Available only to specified parties (in which case the report should be restricted to those parties)

4) *The practitioner must maintain independence in mental attitude in all matters relating to the engagement.*

5) *The practitioner must exercise due professional care in the planning and performance of the engagement and the preparation of the report.*

e. **Standards of Field Work**

1) *The practitioner must adequately plan the work and must properly supervise any assistants.*

2) *The practitioner must obtain sufficient evidence to provide a reasonable basis for the conclusion that is expressed in the report.*

f. **Standards of Reporting**

1) *The practitioner must identify the subject matter or the assertion being reported on and state the character of the engagement in the report.*

2) *The practitioner must state the practitioner's conclusion about the subject matter or the assertion in relation to the criteria against which the subject matter was evaluated in the report.*

3) *The practitioner must state all of the practitioner's significant reservations about the engagement, the subject matter, and, if applicable, the assertion related thereto in the report.*

    4) *The practitioner must state in the report that the report is intended solely for the information and use of the specified parties under the following circumstances:*

        a) *When the criteria used to evaluate the subject matter are determined by the practitioner to be appropriate only for a limited number of parties who either participated in their establishment or can be presumed to have an adequate understanding of the criteria*

        b) *When the criteria used to evaluate the subject matter are available only to specified parties*

        c) *When reporting on subject matter and a written assertion has not been provided by the responsible party*

        d) *When the report is on an attest engagement to apply agreed-upon procedures to the subject matter*

4. Two **levels of attest assurance** are permitted in general-distribution reports:

    a. **Positive** (high level) assurance should be given in reports that express conclusions on the basis of an **examination**.

    b. **Limited** (moderate level) assurance (sometimes termed negative assurance) should be given in reports that express conclusions on the basis of a **review**.

5. **Scope Limitations**

    a. The practitioner may report directly on the subject matter. Nevertheless, as part of the attestation procedures for examinations and reviews, the practitioner ordinarily should obtain a **written assertion provided by the responsible party**.

    b. A failure to obtain a written assertion is considered a **scope limitation** when the responsible party is the client.

    c. In addition, a **representation letter** is typically obtained by the practitioner from the responsible party. A failure of the responsible party or client to provide written representations is normally considered a **scope limitation**.

6. **Attest documentation** (working papers) should be prepared and maintained.

    a. Its form and content will vary with the circumstances and the practitioner's judgment.

    b. The procedures performed, evidence gathered, and the findings reached should be documented.

Stop and review! You have completed the outline for this subunit. Study multiple-choice questions 1 through 4 beginning on page 36.

1.2 AUDIT ENGAGEMENTS

1. The **objective** of an independent, external audit in accordance with **generally accepted auditing standards (GAAS)** is to express an opinion on (attest to) whether an entity's financial statements present fairly, in all material respects, its financial position, results of operations, and cash flows in conformity with generally accepted accounting principles (GAAP).

2. **Assertions**

    a. Financial statements implicitly or explicitly include management's **assertions** about the fair presentation of information, that is, about its recognition, measurement, presentation, and disclosure. Most audit work consists of obtaining and evaluating evidence about these assertions.

b. **Assertions** about classes of **transactions and events** for the period (the income statement and statement of cash flows)

    1) **Occurrence** - Recorded transactions and events actually occurred.

    2) **Completeness** - All transactions and events that should have been recorded were recorded.

    3) **Accuracy** - Amounts and other data were recorded appropriately.

    4) **Cutoff** - Transactions and events were recorded in the proper period.

    5) **Classification** - Transactions and events were recorded in the proper accounts.

c. **Assertions** about **account balances** at period-end (the balance sheet)

    1) **Existence** - Assets, liabilities, and equity interests exist.

    2) **Rights and Obligations** - The entity holds or controls the rights to assets, and liabilities are its obligations.

    3) **Completeness** - All assets, liabilities, and equity interests that should have been recorded were recorded.

    4) **Valuation and Allocation** - Assets, liabilities, and equity interests are included at appropriate amounts, and adjustments are appropriately recorded.

d. **Assertions** about **presentation and disclosure** (notes to the financial statements)

    1) **Occurrence and Rights and Obligations** - Disclosed transactions and events have occurred and pertain to the entity.

    2) **Completeness** - All disclosures that should have been included were included.

    3) **Classification and Understandability** - Financial information is appropriately presented and described, and disclosures are clearly expressed.

    4) **Accuracy and Valuation** - Information is disclosed fairly and at appropriate amounts.

e. The auditor uses the **relevant assertions** to form a basis for the assessment of risks of material misstatement and the design and performance of further audit procedures.

f. Some assertions overlap categories. Thus, only eight separate assertions are included in the model. If these are known, they can easily be assigned to the three categories of assertions. The following mnemonic is helpful for learning the assertions (envision management as a large crocodile emerging from a cave):

    C - Completeness
    A - Accuracy
    V - Valuation and Allocation
    E - Existence

    C - Cutoff
    R - Rights and Obligations
    O - Occurrence
    C - Classification and Understandability

    g.   The PCAOB's AS No. 15, *Audit Evidence*, describes just five assertions to be applied selectively to the financial statement transactions, balances, and disclosures. These are essentially the same as those previously described issued by the ASB.

        1)   **Existence or occurrence** - Assets or liabilities of the company exist at a given date, and recorded transactions have occurred during a given period.

        2)   **Completeness** - All transactions and accounts that should be presented in the financial statements are so included as well as proper cutoff is achieved.

        3)   **Valuation or allocation** - Asset, liability, equity, revenue, and expense components have been included in the financial statements at appropriate amounts.

        4)   **Rights and obligations** - The company holds or controls rights to the assets, and liabilities are obligations of the company at a given date.

        5)   **Presentation and disclosure** - The components of the financial statements are properly classified, described, and disclosed.

    h.   An audit performed by an independent, external auditor provides assurance to external users of the financial statements of the objectivity of the auditor's opinion.

        1)   The auditor may make suggestions about the form or content of the financial statements or draft them based on management's information. However, the auditor's responsibility for the financial statements is confined to the **expression of an opinion**.

    i.   The standard independent auditor's report states, "An audit includes examining, on a test basis, evidence supporting the amounts and disclosures in the financial statements. An audit also includes assessing the accounting principles used and significant estimates made by management, as well as evaluating the overall financial statement presentation" (AU 508).

3. **Auditing Standards**

    a.   Auditing standards address the quality of audit performance and the objectives to be attained. Their nature requires the exercise of judgment in their application. **Auditing procedures** are performed during the audit to comply with the standards. Materiality and audit risk (see Study Unit 3) underlie the application of the standards.

    b.   The three general standards, three standards of field work, and four standards of reporting **(the 10 standards)** were adopted by the AICPA's members (and amended by the ASB).

    c.   **General Standards**

        1)   *The auditor must have adequate technical training and proficiency to perform the audit.*

        2)   *The auditor must maintain independence in mental attitude in all matters relating to the audit.*

        3)   *The auditor must exercise due professional care in the performance of the audit and the preparation of the report.*

    d.   **Standards of Field Work**

        1)   *The auditor must adequately plan the work and must properly supervise any assistants.*

        2)   *The auditor must obtain a sufficient understanding of the entity and its environment, including its internal control, to assess the risk of material misstatement of the financial statements whether due to error or fraud, and to design the nature, timing, and extent of further audit procedures.*

        3)   *The auditor must obtain sufficient appropriate audit evidence by performing audit procedures to afford a reasonable basis for an opinion regarding the financial statements under audit.*

e.   **Standards of Reporting**

1)   *The auditor must state in the auditor's report whether the financial statements are presented in accordance with generally accepted accounting principles (GAAP).*

2)   *The auditor must identify in the auditor's report those circumstances in which such principles have not been consistently observed in the current period in relation to the preceding period.*

3)   *When the auditor determines that informative disclosures are not reasonably adequate, the auditor must so state in the auditor's report.*

4)   *The auditor must either express an opinion regarding the financial statements, taken as a whole, or state that an opinion cannot be expressed, in the auditor's report. When the auditor cannot express an overall opinion, the auditor should state the reasons therefor in the auditor's report. In all cases where an auditor's name is associated with financial statements, the auditor should clearly indicate the character of the auditor's work, if any, and the degree of responsibility the auditor is taking, in the auditor's report.*

4.   **Hierarchy of Pronouncements**

a.   The 10 standards are binding on AICPA members. They also are considered standards of the profession by state boards of accountancy and the courts. Thus, they are binding on non-AICPA members.

b.   The AICPA's *Code of Professional Conduct* includes a rule providing for enforcement of standards issued by the ASB.

c.   **SASs** are standards codified within the framework of the 10 standards and are deemed to have the status of GAAS.

d.   **Interpretive publications** do not have the status of auditing standards, but they provide recommendations on the application of the SASs. These publications include (1) interpretations of the SASs, (2) appendixes to the SASs, (3) AICPA Audit and Accounting Guides, and (4) auditing Statements of Position. An auditor who does not follow an applicable interpretive publication should be prepared to explain how (s)he complied with the relevant SAS.

e.   **Other auditing publications** have no authoritative effect, but they may provide assistance in applying the SASs. They include all other auditing literature, including articles and textbooks.

Background

The Sarbanes-Oxley Act of 2002 authorized the Public Company Accounting Oversight Board to establish auditing and related professional practice standards to be used by **registered public accounting firms**. The PCAOB has adopted, as **Interim Auditing Standards** on a transitional basis, the GAAS established by the AICPA as of April 16, 2003. Since then, the PCAOB has issued various pronouncements applying to audits by registered public accounting firms of public companies (issuers).

Stop and review! You have completed the outline for this subunit. Study multiple-choice questions 5 through 9 beginning on page 37.

1.3 ADDITIONAL PROFESSIONAL SERVICES

1.   **Compilations and Reviews (AR 80 and AR 90)**

a.   The AICPA bylaws designate the Accounting and Review Services Committee as the senior technical committee authorized to issue pronouncements in connection with the unaudited financial statements or other unaudited financial information of a nonissuer (nonpublic entity).

    b.   A **compilation of financial statements** is the presentation in statement form of information that is the representation of management. The accountant expresses **no assurance** in a compilation report. It includes a disclaimer. The accountant need **not** be independent to compile financial statements. (See Study Unit 18, Subunit 1.)

    c.   In a **review** of financial statements, the accountant makes inquiries, applies analytical procedures, and obtains management representations. These procedures provide the accountant with a reasonable basis for expressing **limited assurance** that no material modifications need to be made to the statements for them to be in conformity with GAAP (or, if applicable, with another comprehensive basis of accounting). The accountant **must be** independent to review financial statements. (See Study Unit 18, Subunit 2.)

2.   **Agreed-Upon Procedures (AT 201)**

    a.   Attest engagements include reporting on findings based on **agreed-upon procedures** performed on subject matter. The practitioner is engaged by a client to assist specified parties to evaluate the subject matter or an assertion. The report is restricted to the specified parties who have agreed to the specific procedures and taken responsibility for their sufficiency. (See Study Unit 19, Subunit 10.)

        1)   The practitioner provides **neither positive nor limited assurance**.
        2)   The practitioner must be independent.

3.   **Prospective Financial Statements (PFSs) (AT 301)**

    a.   PFSs consist of financial forecasts or projections, including summaries of significant assumptions and accounting policies. An accountant should examine, compile, or apply agreed-upon procedures to PFSs if they are, or reasonably might be, expected to be used by another (third) party. As with other attest services, the practitioner must be independent. (See Study Unit 19, Subunit 11.)

    b.   A **financial forecast** consists of PFSs that present, to the best of the responsible party's knowledge and belief, an entity's expected financial position, results of operations, and cash flows.

    c.   A **financial projection** differs from a forecast. A projection is based on the responsible party's assumptions reflecting conditions it expects would exist and the course of action it expects would be taken, given one or more **hypothetical assumptions**. A projection is sometimes prepared to present one or more hypothetical courses of action for evaluation, as in response to a question such as, "What would happen if . . .?" A projection may be expressed as a point estimate or a range.

4.   **Pro Forma Financial Information (PFFI) (AT 401)**

    a.   PFFI shows "what the significant effects on historical financial information would have been had a consummated or proposed transaction (or event) occurred at an earlier date."

    b.   Examples of these transactions include (1) a business combination, (2) disposal of a segment, (3) change in the form or status of an entity, and (4) a change in capitalization. An independent accountant may **examine or review** PFFI. (See Study Unit 19, Subunit 12.)

5.   **Examination of Internal Control over Financial Reporting (AT 501)**

    a.   Practitioners may perform an **examination** on a nonissuer's internal control over financial reporting and express an opinion in coordination with the financial statement audit.

    b.   The standard is parallel with the PCAOB's AS No. 5, *An Audit of Internal Control over Financial Reporting that is Integrated with an Audit of Financial Statements*, for issuers.

    c.   This service requires the practitioner to be independent. (See Study Unit 9, Subunit 3.)

6. **Compliance Attestation (AT 601)**

    a. The independent practitioner may perform an **examination** leading to an opinion on whether the entity is in compliance with specified requirements (e.g., covenants of a contract, either financial or nonfinancial) or the effectiveness of the entity's internal control over compliance.

    b. Also, an agreed-upon procedures engagement may be performed but not a review engagement. (See Study Unit 19, Subunit 13.)

7. **Management's Discussion and Analysis (AT 701)**

    a. Management discussion and analysis (MD&A) may be presented in an annual report or other documents filed with the SEC. MD&A constitutes a written assertion that may be examined or reviewed by the practitioner. However, a report on a review engagement report cannot be filed with the SEC.

    b. The practitioner must be independent.

Stop and review! You have completed the outline for this subunit. Study multiple-choice questions 10 through 15 beginning on page 39.

1.4 ASSURANCE SERVICES

1. **Nature of Assurance Services**

    a. Assurance services are independent professional services that improve the quality of information, or its context, for decision makers.

    b. Information might be financial or nonfinancial, historical or prospective, consist of data or relate to systems, or be internal or external to the user.

    c. Assurance services encompass audit and other attestation services but also include nonstandard services.

    d. Unless the services fall under the AICPA's attestation standards, assurance services do not require written assertions.

    e. Assurance services evolved naturally from attestation services, which in turn evolved from audits. The roots of all three are in independent verification.

    f. The form and content of assurance services differ.

        1) Traditional audit-related services are highly structured and considered to be relevant to a large number of users.

        2) The newer assurance services are more customized and targeted and are intended to be highly useful in more limited circumstances.

2. Assurance services can

    a. **Capture information.** Assurance services can capture information by using existing or improved measurement tools.

    b. **Improve information reliability.** Raw information is refined into reliable information. Any raw information can be refined, regardless of whether it is used for decision making.

    c. **Improve decision making.** Decision making can be improved by improving the context, such as decision models, used by the decision maker. This facet of assurance services differs from existing attestation models.

3. Assurance services do not encompass consulting services. However, assurance and consulting services have similarities because they are delivered using a similar body of knowledge and skills.

    a. Assurance services differ from consulting services in two ways:

        1) They focus on improving information rather than providing advice, and

2) They usually involve situations in which one party wants to monitor another (often within the same company) rather than the two-party arrangements common in consulting engagements.

4. The following table contrasts traditional attest, assurance, and consulting services:

	Attestation	Assurance	Consulting
Result	Written conclusion about subject matter or a written assertion of another party	Better information for decision makers. Recommendations might be a byproduct.	Recommendations based on the objectives of the engagement
Objective	Reliable information	Better decision making	Better outcomes
Parties to the engagement	Not specified, but generally three (the third party is usually external). CPA is generally paid by the preparer.	Generally three (although the other two might be employed by the same entity). CPA is paid by the preparer or user.	Generally two; CPA is paid by the user
Independence	Required by standards	Included in definition	Not required
Substance of CPA output	Conformity with established or stated criteria	Assurance about reliability or relevance of information. Criteria might be established, stated, or unstated.	Recommendations; not measured against formal criteria
Form of CPA output	Written	Some form of communication	Written or oral
Critical information developed by	Asserter	Either CPA or asserter	CPA
Information content determined by	Preparer (client)	Preparer, CPA, or user	CPA
Level of assurance	Examination, review, or results of agreed-upon procedures	Flexible. For example, it might be compilation level, explicit assurance about usefulness of the information for intended purpose, or implicit from the CPA's involvement.	No explicit assurance

5. The AICPA has identified six services to date. Some address the needs of existing customers; others are for new customers. Some are based on the types of data CPAs traditionally report on, but others focus on new types of data. There are likely to be many additions in the future.

Assurances about Risks	Assurances about Performance	Assurances about Systems
CPA Risk Advisory ElderCare (PrimePlus)	CPA Performance Review Healthcare Effectiveness	SysTrust WebTrust

a. **CPA risk advisory.** Managers and investors are concerned about whether entities have identified the full scope of various business risks and taken precautions to mitigate them.

b. **ElderCare Services (PrimePlus).** ElderCare services assess whether specified goals regarding care for the elderly are being met by various care givers. Services provided to the elderly include accumulation of information, financial management, and assessment of nursing care.

c. **CPA performance review.** This service evaluates whether an entity's performance measurement system contains relevant and reliable measures for assessing (1) the degree to which the entity's objectives are achieved or (2) how its performance compares with that of its competitors. The review provides investors, managers, or others with a comprehensive information base and a more balanced scorecard.

d. **Healthcare effectiveness.** This service provides assurance about the effectiveness of healthcare services provided by HMOs, hospitals, doctors, and other providers.

e. **SysTrust.** This service assesses whether an entity's internal information systems (financial and nonfinancial) provide reliable information for operating and financial decisions. Information systems address (1) reporting concepts and systems, (2) transaction processing systems, (3) management reporting systems, and (4) risks within a business. SysTrust is an assurance service developed under the AICPA attestation standards. SysTrust is designed to increase the comfort of management, customers, creditors, bankers, and business partners with the systems that support a business or a particular activity.

   1) The practitioner uses suitable **criteria** or benchmarks that are objective, measurable, complete, and relevant to determine whether management's assertions about any or all of the following principles are fairly stated:

      a) **Online privacy.** Personal information obtained is collected, used, disclosed, and retained as committed or agreed.

      b) **Security.** The system is protected against unauthorized access (both physical and logical).

      c) **Processing integrity.** System processing is complete, accurate, timely, and authorized.

      d) **Availability.** The system is available for operation and used as committed or agreed.

      e) **Confidentiality.** Information designated as confidential is protected as committed or agreed.

   2) Practitioners test the **policies, communications, procedures, and monitoring systems** using suitable criteria to assess the fairness of management's assertions about a particular principle. The report may address management's assertions or directly address the system.

f. **WebTrust.** This service, developed under the AICPA attestation standards, provides Internet users, including businesses and Internet service providers, assurance about electronic commerce activities.

   1) The practitioner uses the same **criteria** as outlined for SysTrust in e.1) and 2) above.

Stop and review! You have completed the outline for this subunit. Study multiple-choice questions 16 through 25 beginning on page 40.

1.5 QUALITY CONTROL

There has been a recent emphasis on quality control, and you should recognize its importance in your study for the exam. Be familiar with the role of practice monitoring, and make sure that you understand the six elements of the AICPA's Statements on Quality Control Standards. Note that each element requires the CPA firm to have "policies and procedures" in place to ensure the standards are met.

1. **Practice-Monitoring Programs**

a. To be admitted to or retain membership in the AICPA, practitioners who are engaged in the practice of public accounting are required to practice in firms enrolled in an AICPA-approved **practice-monitoring program** if the services performed by the firm are within the scope of the AICPA's practice-monitoring standards.

b. A firm (or individual) enrolled in the **Center for Public Company Audit Firms Peer Review Program (Center PRP)** or the **AICPA Peer Review Program** (AICPA PRP) is deemed to be enrolled in an approved practice-monitoring program.

c. Quality control over the audits of public companies will be evaluated during periodic inspections of the **Public Company Accounting Oversight Board (PCAOB)**. The Center PRP is designed to review and evaluate those portions of a firm's accounting and auditing practice that are not inspected by the PCAOB.

    d.   Public accounting firms required to maintain a monitoring program, but without public clients, should comply with the AICPA PRP.

2.   An audit firm has a responsibility to adopt a system of quality control and establish policies and procedures to provide reasonable assurance that personnel comply with GAAS.

    a.   GAAS apply to individual engagements, and quality control standards apply to the conduct of a firm's practice as a whole. Thus, quality control may affect audits.

    b.   Nevertheless, deficiencies in, or instances of noncompliance with, the system of quality control do not, by themselves, signify a departure from GAAS in conducting a specific audit (AU 161).

NOTE: Similar rules are stated in SSAEs, SSARSs, and SQCSs.

3.   **Statements on Quality Control Standards (SQCSs)**

    a.   SQCSs require that a CPA firm have a system of quality control.

    b.   Quality control for a CPA firm applies to all audit, attestation, compilation and review, and other services for which standards have been established by the Auditing Standards Board or the Accounting and Review Services Committee. It does not apply explicitly to consulting or tax services.

        1)   A firm is defined broadly to include "a form of organization permitted by law or regulation whose characteristics conform to resolutions of Council of the AICPA that is engaged in the practice of public accounting." This definition includes proprietorships, partnerships, and professional corporations.

    c.   The following are the six elements of a system of quality control:

        1)   **Leadership responsibilities for quality within the firm (the "tone at the top").** The firm should promote an internal culture recognizing that quality is essential in performing engagements. This requires clear, consistent, and frequent actions and messages from all levels of management that emphasize quality control policies and procedures. Emphasis also should be on (a) performing work that complies with all professional standards and legal/regulatory requirements and (b) issuing appropriate reports.

        2)   **Relevant ethical requirements.** Policies and procedures should be established to provide reasonable assurance that the firm and personnel comply with relevant ethical requirements (e.g., the AICPA *Code of Professional Conduct*).

        3)   **Acceptance and continuance of client relationships and specific engagements.** Policies and procedures should be established to provide reasonable assurance that

            a)   The likelihood of association with clients whose managers may lack integrity is minimized,

            b)   The firm undertakes only engagements it expects to complete with professional competence, and

            c)   It appropriately considers the risk of providing services.

        4)   **Human resources.** Policies and procedures should be established to provide reasonable assurance that the firm has sufficient personnel with the capabilities, competence, and commitment to ethical principles to (a) perform engagements in accordance with professional standards and legal/regulatory requirements and (b) issue appropriate reports.

            a)   Matters addressed include recruitment, hiring, determining competencies, assignment of personnel, development of personnel, performance evaluation, compensation, and advancement.

5) **Engagement performance.** Policies and procedures should be established to provide reasonable assurance that engagements are consistently performed in accordance with professional standards and legal/regulatory requirements, and that the firm issues appropriate reports.

a) Matters addressed include responsibilities for performance, supervision, and review.

6) **Monitoring.** Policies and procedures should be established to provide reasonable assurance that the policies and procedures relating to the system of quality control are relevant, adequate, operating effectively, and complied with in practice. Monitoring is an ongoing process and includes inspection and evaluation of prior engagements.

d. **Administration** of a system of quality control requires that

1) Responsibility for designing and maintaining policies and procedures be assigned to appropriate individuals,

2) Those policies and procedures be communicated so as to provide reasonable assurance that they are understood and complied with,

3) Consideration be given to whether and to what extent policies and procedures must be documented for effective communication, and

4) The firm appropriately documents the control policies and procedures as well as compliance with them.

4. **Peer Review**

a. A **peer review** does not substitute for monitoring, but it is a necessary part of the practice-monitoring requirement for AICPA membership. The applicable pronouncements issued by the AICPA Peer Review Board are the Standards for Performing and Reporting on Peer Reviews (PR 100). They govern peer reviews supervised by state CPA societies of firms enrolled in the AICPA Peer Review Program.

b. The portion of a firm's accounting and auditing practice covered by the peer review standards includes engagements under SASs, SSARSs, SSAEs, and Government Auditing Standards.

c. A **system review** is an on-site review required for a firm that performs the highest level of services. It provides the reviewer with a reasonable basis for expressing an opinion on the firm's system of quality control.

d. An **engagement review** is for a firm not required to have a system review but not qualifying for a report review. It provides the reviewer with a reasonable basis for expressing limited assurance on whether the financial statements or information and the accountant's reports submitted materially conform with professional standards and on whether the firm's documentation conforms with the professional standards.

e. A **report review** is for a firm that performs only compilations omitting substantially all disclosures. The report consists of comments and recommendations after review of a sample of engagements. These comments should be based on professional standards.

5. **Sarbanes-Oxley Act of 2002**

a. Under the federal Sarbanes-Oxley Act of 2002, a registered accounting firm must adopt quality control standards. Many of the provisions of Sarbanes-Oxley relate to improving the quality control of the audit and improving the quality of financial reporting. These standards relate to the audits of public companies.

b. A **second partner review and approval** is required of audit reports.

    c.   The **lead auditor** and the **reviewing partner** must be rotated off the audit every 5 years.

    d.   The accounting firm must supervise any **associated person** with respect to auditing or quality control standards.

    e.   **Independence rules have been expanded** by prohibiting the auditor from providing a variety of nonaudit services.

    f.   The client's CEO and CFO must certify the appropriateness of the **financial statements and disclosures**.

    g.   **Penalties** for destroying documents to impede an investigation have been expanded.

    h.   Management must **assess the effectiveness of internal control** and issue a report on its effectiveness.

    i.   The auditor must **audit internal control** and express an opinion on its effectiveness.

6.   **The PCAOB**

    a.   According to AS No. 7, *Engagement Quality Review*, an **engagement quality review (EQR)** and concurring approval of issuance are required for each audit of an issuer.

    b.   The **objective** of the **reviewer** is to evaluate the significant judgments made and the related conclusions reached.

    c.   The reviewer must be an associated person of a registered public accounting firm. The reviewer may be from outside the firm.

        1)   The reviewer must have the competence to serve as a partner on the engagement.

        2)   The reviewer also must have independence, integrity, and objectivity.

        3)   But an engagement partner on either of the two preceding audits ordinarily may not be the reviewer.

    d.   The EQR process in an audit evaluates the **significant judgments** made.

        1)   This involves discussions with the engagement partner and other team members and reviewing whether the documentation supports the conclusions reached and appropriate responses to significant risks.

    e.   The reviewer should evaluate

        1)   Significant judgments about planning matters

        2)   The assessment of, and responses to, significant risks, including those identified by the reviewer

        3)   Corrected and uncorrected identified misstatements and control deficiencies

        4)   The audit firm's independence

        5)   The engagement completion document and whether unresolved matters are significant

        6)   The statements, the internal control report, and the audit report

        7)   Other information filed with the SEC

        8)   Whether consultations have addressed difficult matters

        9)   Whether matters have been communicated to the audit committee, management, and other parties

    f.   In an audit, the reviewer may provide **concurring approval of issuance**, and the client may use the report, only if the reviewer is not aware of a significant engagement deficiency.

Stop and review! You have completed the outline for this subunit. Study multiple-choice questions 26 through 34 beginning on page 43.

QUESTIONS

1.1 Attest Engagements (AT 101)

1. Which of the following is a conceptual difference between the attestation standards and generally accepted auditing standards?

A. The attestation standards provide a framework for the attest function beyond historical financial statements.

B. The requirement that the practitioner be independent in mental attitude is omitted from the attestation standards.

C. The attestation standards do not permit an attest engagement to be part of a business acquisition study or a feasibility study.

D. None of the standards of field work in generally accepted auditing standards are included in the attestation standards.

Answer (A) is correct. *(CPA, adapted)*
REQUIRED: The conceptual difference between the attestation standards and GAAS.
DISCUSSION: Two principal conceptual differences exist between the attestation standards and GAAS. First, the attestation standards provide a framework for the attest function beyond historical financial statements. Second, the attestation standards accommodate the growing number of attest services in which the practitioner expresses assurance below the level that is expressed for the traditional audit (an opinion).
Answer (B) is incorrect. In any attest engagement, the practitioner must be independent in mental attitude. Answer (C) is incorrect. Attestation services may be provided in conjunction with other services provided to clients. Answer (D) is incorrect. The attestation standards and GAAS require that work be adequately planned and that assistants be properly supervised. Both also require sufficient evidence.

2. Which of the following is **not** an attestation standard?

A. Sufficient evidence shall be obtained to provide a reasonable basis for the conclusion that is expressed in the report.

B. The report shall identify the subject matter or the assertion being reported on and state the character of the engagement.

C. The work shall be adequately planned and assistants, if any, shall be properly supervised.

D. A sufficient understanding of internal control shall be obtained to plan the engagement.

Answer (D) is correct. *(CPA, adapted)*
REQUIRED: The item not an attestation standard.
DISCUSSION: No attestation standard mentions internal control. However, the second standard of field work applicable to audits in accordance with GAAS states, "The auditor must obtain a sufficient understanding of the entity and its environment, including its internal control, to assess the risk of material misstatement of the financial statements whether due to error or fraud and to design the nature, timing, and extent of further audit procedures."
Answer (A) is incorrect. The evidentiary requirement is contained in the second attestation standard of field work. Answer (B) is incorrect. The first attestation standard of reporting concerns the character of the engagement. Answer (C) is incorrect. The first attestation standard of field work concerns planning and supervision.

3. Which of the following professional services is considered an attest engagement?

A. A consulting service engagement to provide computer advice to a client.

B. An engagement to report on compliance with statutory requirements.

C. An income tax engagement to prepare federal and state tax returns.

D. The compilation of financial statements from a client's accounting records.

Answer (B) is correct. *(CPA, adapted)*
REQUIRED: The attest service.
DISCUSSION: Attest services have traditionally been limited to expressing an opinion on historical financial statements on the basis of an audit in accordance with GAAS. But CPAs increasingly provide assurance on representations other than historical statements and in forms other than an opinion. Thus, attest services may extend to engagements related to management's compliance with specified requirements or the effectiveness of internal control over compliance.
Answer (A) is incorrect. The attestation standards explicitly do not apply to consulting services in which the practitioner provides advice or recommendations to a client. Answer (C) is incorrect. Tax return preparation is not an attest service according to the attestation standards. Answer (D) is incorrect. A compilation of a financial statement is not an attest service according to the attestation standards.

4. In performing an attest engagement, a CPA typically

- A. Supplies litigation support services.
- B. Assesses control risk at a low level.
- C. Expresses a conclusion about a written assertion.
- D. Provides management consulting advice.

Answer (C) is correct. *(CPA, adapted)*
REQUIRED: The usual CPA's task in an attestation engagement.
DISCUSSION: When a CPA in the practice of public accounting performs an attest engagement, the engagement is subject to the attestation standards. An attest engagement is one in which a practitioner is engaged to issue or does issue an examination, a review, or an agreed-upon procedures report on subject matter, or an assertion about the subject matter, that is the responsibility of another party. Moreover, according to the second attestation standard of reporting, the report shall state the practitioner's conclusion about the subject matter or the assertion in relation to the criteria against which the subject matter was evaluated. However, the conclusion may refer to that assertion or to the subject matter to which the assertion relates. Furthermore, given one or more material deviations from the criteria, the practitioner should modify the report and ordinarily should express the conclusion directly on the subject matter.
Answer (A) is incorrect. Litigation support services are consulting services. Answer (B) is incorrect. The CPA assesses control risk in an audit but not necessarily in all attest engagements. Furthermore, the assessment may not be at a low level. Answer (D) is incorrect. An attest engagement results in a report on subject matter or on an assertion about the subject matter.

1.2 Audit Engagements

5. Who establishes generally accepted auditing standards?

- A. Auditing Standards Board and the Public Company Accounting Oversight Board.
- B. Financial Accounting Standards Board and the Governmental Accounting Standards Board.
- C. State Boards of Accountancy.
- D. Securities and Exchange Commission.

Answer (A) is correct. *(Publisher, adapted)*
REQUIRED: The organization that promulgates generally accepted auditing standards (GAAS).
DISCUSSION: AICPA Conduct Rule 202, *Compliance with Standards*, requires adherence to standards promulgated by bodies designated by the AICPA Council. The Auditing Standards Board (ASB) is the body designated to issue auditing standards. They are in the form of Statements on Auditing Standards (SASs), which are codified within the framework of the 10 standards. The Public Company Accounting Oversight Board (PCAOB) was created by the Sarbanes-Oxley Act of 2002. It establishes by rule auditing, quality control, ethics, independence, and other standards relating to the preparation of audit reports for issuers. The PCAOB is required to cooperate with the AICPA and other groups in setting auditing standards and may adopt their proposals. Nevertheless, the PCAOB is authorized to amend, modify, repeal, or reject any such standards. A number of auditing standards have been issued to date, the most significant requiring opinions on internal control for public companies.
Answer (B) is incorrect. The FASB and the GASB issue financial accounting pronouncements and interpretations. Answer (C) is incorrect. Boards of Accountancy in the states and territories regulate the practice of accounting. They typically grant CPA certificates and licenses. Answer (D) is incorrect. The SEC issues Financial Reporting Releases and Accounting and Auditing Enforcement Releases.

6. Which of the following best describes what is meant by the term "generally accepted auditing standards"?

A. Rules acknowledged by the accounting profession because of their universal application.

B. Pronouncements issued by the Auditing Standards Board.

C. Measures of the audit quality.

D. Procedures to be used to gather evidence to support financial statements.

Answer (C) is correct. *(CPA, adapted)*
REQUIRED: The best definition of "generally accepted auditing standards."
DISCUSSION: An audit should be planned, performed, and reported on in accordance with GAAS. Auditing standards are concerned with audit quality and the objectives to be attained (AU 150).
Answer (A) is incorrect. Auditing standards are not elective guidelines but standards required of all accountants during the performance of an audit. Answer (B) is incorrect. Although Statements on Auditing Standards (SASs) issued by the ASB are now deemed to be GAAS, they do not constitute all GAAS. Additionally, the Public Company Accounting Oversight Board (PCAOB) establishes auditing standards for public companies. Answer (D) is incorrect. Auditing procedures are acts that the auditor performs during the course of an audit to comply with auditing standards (AU 150).

7. The third general standard states that due professional care is to be exercised in the planning and performance of the audit and the preparation of the report. This standard requires

A. Thorough review of the existing safeguards over access to assets and records.

B. Limited review of the indications of employee fraud and illegal acts.

C. Objective review of the adequacy of the technical training and proficiency of firm personnel.

D. Supervision of assistants by the auditor with final responsibility for the audit.

Answer (D) is correct. *(CPA, adapted)*
REQUIRED: The requirement under the third general standard (due professional care).
DISCUSSION: According to AU 230, *Due Professional Care in the Performance of Work*, due professional care imposes a responsibility upon each professional within an independent auditor's organization to observe the standards of field work and reporting. The first standard of field work requires proper supervision of assistants (AU 150). Thus, AU 230 states that the auditor with final responsibility is responsible for the assignment of tasks to, and the supervision of, assistants.
Answer (A) is incorrect. Although a review of safeguards over access to assets and records relates to the conduct of the audit, this procedure is not required specifically by the third general standard. Answer (B) is incorrect. Although a review of the likelihood of employee fraud and illegal acts relates to the conduct of the audit, this procedure is not required specifically by the third general standard. Answer (C) is incorrect. Objective review of the adequacy of the technical training and proficiency of firm personnel relates to the first general standard (adequate technical training and proficiency as an auditor).

8. Which of the following statements is true concerning an auditor's responsibilities regarding financial statements?

A. Making suggestions that are adopted about the form and content of an entity's financial statements impairs an auditor's independence.

B. An auditor may draft an entity's financial statements based on information from management's accounting system.

C. The fair presentation of audited financial statements in conformity with GAAP is an implicit part of the auditor's responsibilities.

D. An auditor's responsibilities for audited financial statements are not confined to the expression of the auditor's opinion.

Answer (B) is correct. *(CPA, adapted)*
REQUIRED: The true statement about the auditor's responsibilities for financial statements.
DISCUSSION: The independent auditor may make suggestions about the form or content of the financial statements or draft them, in whole or in part, based on information from management's accounting system. However, the auditor's responsibility for the financial statements he or she has audited is confined to the expression of his or her opinion on them (AU 110).
Answer (A) is incorrect. Suggestions about the form and content of an entity's financial statements do not impair an auditor's independence as long as management takes responsibility for the financial statements. Answer (C) is incorrect. The presentation of the financial statements in conformity with GAAP is the responsibility of management. Answer (D) is incorrect. The auditor's responsibilities for audited financial statements are confined to the expression of the opinion.

9. An auditor observes the mailing of monthly statements to a client's customers and reviews evidence of follow-up on errors reported by the customers. This test of controls most likely is performed to support management's financial statement assertion(s) of

	Classification and Understandability	Existence
A.	Yes	Yes
B.	Yes	No
C.	No	Yes
D.	No	No

Answer (C) is correct. *(CPA, adapted)*
REQUIRED: The financial statement assertion(s) related to observing the client's follow-up on errors reported on monthly statements.
DISCUSSION: The existence assertion relates to whether the related balance exists at the balance sheet date. Observation of the mailing of monthly statements as well as observing the correction of reported errors provides evidence that controls may be effective in ensuring that client customers are genuine.
Answer (A) is incorrect. The observation of client activities related to customer statements provides little evidence about proper classification and understandability in the financial statements. Answer (B) is incorrect. The procedure provides little evidence about the classification and understandability assertion. Answer (D) is incorrect. The mailing and follow-up procedures provide evidence that controls may be effective in ensuring that client customers are genuine.

1.3 Additional Professional Services

10. North Co., a nonissuer, asked its tax accountant, King, a CPA in public practice, to generate North's interim financial statements on King's personal computer when King prepared North's quarterly tax return. King should not submit these financial statements to North unless, as a minimum, King complies with the provisions of

A. Statements on Standards for Accounting and Review Services.

B. Statements on Standards for Unaudited Financial Services.

C. Statements on Standards for Consulting Services.

D. Statements on Standards for Attestation Engagements.

Answer (A) is correct. *(CPA, adapted)*
REQUIRED: The standards appropriate for an accountant who generates interim financial statements.
DISCUSSION: The Statements on Standards for Accounting and Review Services apply to compilations and reviews performed by practitioners. The AICPA bylaws designate the Accounting and Review Services Committee as the senior technical committee authorized to issue pronouncements in connection with the unaudited financial statements or other unaudited financial information of a nonissuer.
Answer (B) is incorrect. These standards do not exist. Answer (C) is incorrect. The practitioner is providing compilation services, not consulting services. Answer (D) is incorrect. Statements on Standards for Attestation Engagements are appropriate whenever the practitioner is engaged in providing attestation services. A compilation, however, provides no assurance.

11. Which of the following services, if any, may an accountant who is **not** independent provide?

A. Compilations but **not** reviews.

B. Reviews but **not** compilations.

C. Both compilations and reviews.

D. No services.

Answer (A) is correct. *(CPA, adapted)*
REQUIRED: The requirement to be independent.
DISCUSSION: Attest services offer assurance and require the accountant to be independent. However, a compilation provides no assurance; thus, the accountant need not be independent. The report will describe the compilation service and disclaim an opinion or any other form of assurance on the financial statements. The accountant would also state in the report that (s)he was not independent.

12. Which of the following components is appropriate in a practitioner's report on the results of applying agreed-upon procedures?

A. A list of the procedures performed, as agreed to by the specified parties identified in the report.

B. A statement that management is responsible for expressing an opinion.

C. A title that includes the phrase "independent audit."

D. A statement that the report is unrestricted in its use.

Answer (A) is correct. *(CPA, adapted)*
REQUIRED: The component appropriate for an agreed-upon procedures report.
DISCUSSION: In an agreed-upon procedures engagement, the practitioner is engaged to report on the results of performing specific procedures set forth by specified parties. The report would list the procedures performed and provide the results of those procedures but would provide no form of positive or negative assurance.

13.   The party responsible for assumptions identified in the preparation of prospective financial statements is usually

A.   A third-party lending institution.

B.   The client's management.

C.   The reporting accountant.

D.   The client's independent auditor.

Answer (B) is correct.   *(CPA, adapted)*
   REQUIRED: The party usually responsible for assumptions identified in the preparation of prospective financial statements.
   DISCUSSION: Management is usually the responsible party, that is, the person(s) responsible for the assumptions underlying prospective financial statements. However, the responsible party may be a party outside the entity, such as a possible acquirer.

14.   A financial forecast consists of prospective financial statements that present an entity's expected financial position, results of operations, and cash flows. A forecast

A.   Is based on the most conservative estimates.

B.   Presents estimates given one or more hypothetical assumptions.

C.   Unlike a projection, may contain a range.

D.   Is based on assumptions reflecting conditions expected to exist and courses of action expected to be taken.

Answer (D) is correct.   *(Publisher, adapted)*
   REQUIRED: The true statement about a financial forecast.
   DISCUSSION: According to AT 301, a financial forecast consists of prospective financial statements "that present, to the best of the responsible party's knowledge and belief, an entity's expected financial position, results of operations, and cash flows." A forecast is based on "the responsible party's assumptions reflecting conditions it expects to exist and the course of action it expects to take."
   Answer (A) is incorrect. The information presented is based on expected (most likely) conditions and courses of action rather than the most conservative estimate. Answer (B) is incorrect. A financial projection (not a forecast) is based on assumptions by the responsible party reflecting expected conditions and courses of action, given one or more hypothetical assumptions (a condition or action not necessarily expected to occur). Answer (C) is incorrect. Both forecasts and projections may be stated either in point estimates or ranges.

15.   Which of the following presents what the effects on historical financial data might have been if a consummated transaction had occurred at an earlier date?

A.   Prospective financial statements.

B.   Pro forma financial information.

C.   Interim financial information.

D.   A financial projection.

Answer (B) is correct.   *(Publisher, adapted)*
   REQUIRED: The kind of financial data showing what the effects of a consummated transaction would have been if it had occurred at an earlier date.
   DISCUSSION: Pro forma information shows what the significant effects on historical financial information would have been had a consummated or proposed transaction (or event) occurred at an earlier date. Examples of these transactions include a business combination, disposal of a segment, a change in the form or status of an entity, and a change in capitalization.
   Answer (A) is incorrect. Prospective financial statements do not cover periods that have completely expired. Hence, they are not historical statements. Answer (C) is incorrect. Interim financial information states actual results. Answer (D) is incorrect. A financial projection is a prospective statement and therefore is not a presentation of historical information.

1.4   Assurance Services

16.   Assurance services are best described as

A.   Services designed for the improvement of operations, resulting in better outcomes.

B.   Independent professional services that improve the quality of information, or its context, for decision makers.

C.   The assembly of financial statements based on information and assumptions of a responsible party.

D.   Services designed to express an opinion on historical financial statements based on the results of an audit.

Answer (B) is correct.   *(Publisher, adapted)*
   REQUIRED: The description of assurance services.
   DISCUSSION: The AICPA defines assurance services as "independent professional services that improve the quality of information, or its context, for decision makers." Assurance services encompass audit and other attestation services but also include nonstandard services. Assurance services do not encompass consulting services.
   Answer (A) is incorrect. Consulting services are services designed for the improvement of operations, resulting in better outcomes. Answer (C) is incorrect. Compilation services are the assembly of financial statements based on information and assumptions of a responsible party. Answer (D) is incorrect. The traditional audit consists of services designed to express an opinion on historical financial statements based on the results of an audit.

17. The objective of assurance services is to

A. Provide more timely information.

B. Enhance decision making.

C. Compare internal information and policies to those of other firms.

D. Improve the firm's outcomes.

Answer (B) is correct. *(Publisher, adapted)*
REQUIRED: The objective of assurance services.
DISCUSSION: The main objective of assurance services, as stated by the AICPA, is to provide information that assists in better decision making. Assurance services encompass audit and other attestation services but also include nonstandard services. Assurance services do not encompass consulting services.
Answer (A) is incorrect. Providing more timely information is not a stated objective. Answer (C) is incorrect. Assurance services do not involve analysis of other companies. Answer (D) is incorrect. Providing information that results in better outcomes is an objective of consulting services.

18. Assurance services differ from consulting services in that they

	Focus on Providing Advice	Involve Monitoring of One Party by Another
A.	Yes	Yes
B.	Yes	No
C.	No	Yes
D.	No	No

Answer (C) is correct. *(Publisher, adapted)*
REQUIRED: The way(s) in which assurance services differ from consulting services.
DISCUSSION: Assurance services encompass attestation services but not consulting services. Assurance services differ from consulting services in two ways: (1) They focus on improving information rather than providing advice, and (2) they usually involve situations in which one party wants to monitor another rather than the two-party arrangements common in consulting engagements.

19. SysTrust is an assurance service designed to

A. Increase the comfort of management and other stakeholders relative to an information system.

B. Provide an opinion on the fairness of an information system's output.

C. Provide the SEC with information used to administer the securities laws.

D. Allow a CPA to provide a consulting service to management relating to their information system.

Answer (A) is correct. *(Publisher, adapted)*
REQUIRED: The purpose of SysTrust.
DISCUSSION: The objective of SysTrust is an attestation report on management's assertion about the reliability of an information system that supports a business or a given activity. The CPA also may report directly on the reliability of the system. This assurance service is designed to increase the stakeholders' comfort relative to the system's satisfaction of the SysTrust principles: online privacy, security, processing integrity, availability, and confidentiality. The practitioner may provide assurance about any or all of these principles.
Answer (B) is incorrect. SysTrust does not directly address the output of a system. Answer (C) is incorrect. The report is not specifically designed for any one user. Answer (D) is incorrect. Assurance services are not classified as consulting services.

20. The AICPA committee on assurance services has identified a professional service called ElderCare (PrimePlus) services. One fundamental purpose of this assurance service is to assist the elderly and their families by

A. Investing the funds of the elderly person.

B. Reporting whether specified objectives are being met by caregivers.

C. Choosing caregivers.

D. Performing operational audits of healthcare providers.

Answer (B) is correct. *(Publisher, adapted)*
REQUIRED: The fundamental purpose of ElderCare services.
DISCUSSION: The AICPA committee on assurance services has developed business plans for six assurance services, one of which involves elder care. The fundamental purpose of elder care services is to gather evidence and report to concerned parties (e.g., adult children of an elderly parent) as to whether agreed-upon objectives have been met with regard to care delivery, such as medical, household, and financial services. Related services provided directly to the elderly person or to the other concerned parties may include oversight of investment of funds (but not making an investment of funds), assistance in the choice of caregivers, accounting for the elderly person's income and expenses, and arranging for care and services, such as transportation, meal delivery, or placement in a retirement facility.
Answer (A) is incorrect. The CPA might oversee, but not make, investments. Answer (C) is incorrect. The CPA might help in the choice of caregivers but would not make the decision. Answer (D) is incorrect. An operational audit is far beyond the limits of an elder care service.

21. The AICPA assurance service, called CPA Performance Review, attempts to provide users with

   A. A profile of the business risks and the appropriate systems in place to manage those risks.

   B. An opinion on whether the financial statements are fairly stated.

   C. An evaluation of whether an entity has reliable measures of performance beyond the traditional financial statements.

   D. An assessment of management's assertion on internal control and whether the system is meeting the objectives of the organization.

Answer (C) is correct.   *(Publisher, adapted)*
   REQUIRED: The purpose of CPA Performance Review.
   DISCUSSION: CPA Performance Review evaluates whether an entity's performance measurement system contains relevant and reliable measures for assessing the degree to which the entity's goals and objectives are achieved. It attempts to provide a more balanced scorecard than just the traditional financial statements.
   Answer (A) is incorrect. Evaluation and reporting on an entity's business risk describes the CPA Risk Advisory assurance service. Answer (B) is incorrect. An opinion on the financial statements describes the purpose of a financial audit. Answer (D) is incorrect. An assessment of management's assertion on internal control is performed in an attestation engagement to report on internal control.

22. Which of the following is a term for an attest engagement in which a CPA assesses a client's commercial Internet site for compliance with principles, such as online privacy, security, and confidentiality?

   A. ElectroNet.

   B. EDIFACT.

   C. TechSafe.

   D. WebTrust.

Answer (D) is correct.   *(CPA, adapted)*
   REQUIRED: The attest engagement for an Internet site.
   DISCUSSION: The WebTrust seal provides assurance about compliance with the principles of online privacy, security, processing integrity, availability, and confidentiality. It is a modular service that allows the practitioner to express an opinion about compliance with individual principles or combinations of principles. Online privacy is the protection of the collection, use, disclosure, and retention of personal information. Security is the protection against unauthorized access to the system (both physical and logical). Processing integrity is the assurance that system processing is complete, accurate, timely, and authorized. Availability is the assertion that the system is available for operation and used as agreed. Confidentiality is the protection of information from being viewed by non-authorized parties.
   Answer (A) is incorrect. ElectroNet is a nonsense term. Answer (B) is incorrect. EDIFACT (Electronic Data Interchange For Administration Commerce and Transport) is an ISO standard for electronic data interchange (EDI). Answer (C) is incorrect. TechSafe is a nonsense term.

23. An entity engaged a CPA to determine whether the client's web sites comply with defined WebTrust principles and criteria. In performing this engagement, the CPA should apply the provisions of

   A. Statements on Assurance Standards.

   B. Statements on Standards for Attestation Engagements.

   C. Statements on Standards for Management Consulting Services.

   D. Statements on Auditing Standards.

Answer (B) is correct.   *(CPA, adapted)*
   REQUIRED: The pronouncements that apply to WebTrust.
   DISCUSSION: An attest engagement involves reporting on subject matter, or an assurance about subject matter, that is the responsibility of another party. When providing WebTrust assurance, the accountant must address written assertions by management. Thus, Statements on Standards for Attestation Engagements are applicable.
   Answer (A) is incorrect. The AICPA has not issued specific Statements on Assurance Standards. Answer (C) is incorrect. WebTrust is not considered a management consulting service. Answer (D) is incorrect. Statements on Auditing Standards are applicable to audits of financial statements.

24. A WebTrust engagement on processing integrity requires from client management a

   A. Written assertion.

   B. Set of financial statements.

   C. Third-party verification letter.

   D. Statement about the integrity of top management.

Answer (A) is correct.   *(Publisher, adapted)*
   REQUIRED: The requirement of management when a CPA provides the WebTrust service.
   DISCUSSION: WebTrust was developed from the attestation standards and requires a written assertion by management for each principle reported on. When the assertion about a website complies with WebTrust principles, it is granted the CPA WebTrust seal to be displayed on the entity's web page. Consumers may access the examination report and CPA WebTrust principles and criteria through the entity's web page.

25. Under the assurance service WebTrust, the broad principles relating to websites are security, availability, confidentiality, processing integrity, and

    A. Information disclosure.

    B. Website performance.

    C. Online privacy.

    D. Transaction assurance.

Answer (C) is correct. *(Publisher, adapted)*
    REQUIRED: The principle relating to websites under the assurance service WebTrust.
    DISCUSSION: WebTrust provides assurance about compliance with the principles of online privacy, security, processing integrity, availability, and confidentiality. It is a modular service that allows the practitioner to express an opinion and grant the corresponding seal with respect to individual principles or combinations of principles.
    Answer (A) is incorrect. Information disclosure is not included in the list of principles. Answer (B) is incorrect. Website performance is not included in the list of principles. Answer (D) is incorrect. Transaction assurance is not included in the list of principles.

1.5 Quality Control

26. One of a CPA firm's basic objectives is to provide professional services that conform with professional standards. Reasonable assurance of achieving this basic objective is provided through

    A. A system of quality control.

    B. A system of peer review.

    C. Continuing professional education.

    D. Compliance with generally accepted reporting standards.

Answer (A) is correct. *(CPA, adapted)*
    REQUIRED: The means of reasonably assuring that a CPA firm's services meet professional standards.
    DISCUSSION: A CPA firm must have a system of quality control that ensures that its personnel comply with professional standards applicable to its audit and accounting practice. However, a deficiency in an engagement, by itself, does not necessarily indicate that the firm's system of quality control is not sufficient. GAAS apply to individual engagements, and quality control standards apply to the firm's practice as a whole (AU 161).
    Answer (B) is incorrect. A system of peer review is a necessary part of the practice-monitoring requirement for AICPA membership. Answer (C) is incorrect. Continuing professional education is but one element of quality control. Answer (D) is incorrect. Firms must comply with all pronouncements applicable to the services rendered, not just with the reporting standards.

27. The purpose of establishing quality control policies and procedures for deciding whether to accept or continue a client relationship is to

    A. Monitor the risk factors concerning misstatements arising from the misappropriation of assets.

    B. Provide reasonable assurance that personnel are adequately trained to fulfill their responsibilities.

    C. Minimize the likelihood of associating with clients whose management lacks integrity.

    D. Document objective criteria for the CPA firm's responses to peer review comments.

Answer (C) is correct. *(CPA, adapted)*
    REQUIRED: The purpose of policies and procedures for accepting or continuing clients.
    DISCUSSION: The procedures pertaining to client acceptance or continuation should provide reasonable assurance that the likelihood of association with a client whose management lacks integrity is minimized. They include consideration of the business reputation of the client's principal owners, key management, related parties, and those charged with governance.
    Answer (A) is incorrect. The engagement performance element of quality control should monitor the risk factors concerning misstatements arising from the misappropriation of assets. Answer (B) is incorrect. The human resources element of quality control should provide reasonable assurance that personnel will be adequately trained to fulfill their responsibilities. Answer (D) is incorrect. Documenting objective criteria for the CPA firm's responses to peer review comments is not an objective for establishing quality control policies or procedures. However, it is a result of the monitoring aspect of a quality control system.

28. Which of the following is an element of a CPA firm's quality control system that should be considered in establishing its quality control policies and procedures?

A. Complying with laws and regulations.

B. Using statistical sampling techniques.

C. Managing human resources.

D. Considering audit risk and materiality.

Answer (C) is correct. *(CPA, adapted)*
REQUIRED: The element of quality control.
DISCUSSION: The quality control element of human resources requires establishment of policies and procedures to provide reasonable assurance that only qualified persons with the required technical training and proficiency perform the work.
Answer (A) is incorrect. The auditor considers compliance with laws and regulations. However, this consideration is not an element of quality control. Answer (B) is incorrect. An auditing firm may use statistical or nonstatistical sampling techniques in performing audits; a particular sampling technique is not an element of quality control. Answer (D) is incorrect. An auditor must consider audit risk and materiality in performing the audit, but this consideration is not an element of quality control.

29. Which of the following are elements of a CPA firm's quality control that should be considered in establishing its quality control policies and procedures?

	Human Resources	Monitoring	Engagement Performance
A.	Yes	Yes	No
B.	Yes	Yes	Yes
C.	No	Yes	Yes
D.	Yes	No	Yes

Answer (B) is correct. *(CPA, adapted)*
REQUIRED: The elements that should be considered in establishing quality control policies and procedures.
DISCUSSION: The quality control element of human resources relates to ensuring that employees have the skills needed for the responsibilities they are called upon to assume. The quality control element of monitoring is concerned with providing reasonable assurance that procedures related to the other elements are suitably designed and being effectively applied. The quality control element of engagement performance requires the firm to establish policies and procedures to ensure proper planning, performing, supervising, reviewing, documenting, and communicating the results of engagements.

30. A CPA firm should establish procedures for conducting and supervising work at all organizational levels to provide reasonable assurance that the work performed meets the firm's standards of quality. To achieve this goal, the firm most likely would establish procedures for

A. Evaluating prospective and continuing client relationships.

B. Reviewing documentation of the work performed and reports issued.

C. Requiring personnel to adhere to the applicable independence rules.

D. Maintaining personnel files containing documentation related to the evaluation of personnel.

Answer (B) is correct. *(CPA, adapted)*
REQUIRED: The procedure necessary to provide reasonable assurance that the work performed meets the firm's standards of quality relating to supervision.
DISCUSSION: The engagement performance element of quality control includes policies and procedures that cover planning, performing, supervising, reviewing, documenting, and communicating the results of each engagement. Objectives of supervision include establishing procedures for (1) planning engagements, (2) maintaining the firm's standards of quality, and (3) reviewing documentation of the work performed and reports issued.
Answer (A) is incorrect. Evaluating client relationships relates to the quality control element of acceptance and continuance of client relationships and specific engagements. Answer (C) is incorrect. Requiring adherence to independence rules relates to the quality control element of relevant ethical requirements. Answer (D) is incorrect. Evaluation of personnel relates to the quality control element of human resources.

31. The nature and extent of a CPA firm's quality control policies and procedures depend on

	The CPA Firm's Size	The Nature of the CPA Firm's Practice	Cost-Benefit Considerations
A.	Yes	Yes	Yes
B.	Yes	Yes	No
C.	Yes	No	Yes
D.	No	Yes	Yes

Answer (A) is correct. *(CPA, adapted)*
REQUIRED: The factors affecting a CPA firm's quality control policies and procedures.
DISCUSSION: The nature and extent of a firm's quality control policies and procedures depend on a number of factors, such as the firm's size, the degree of operating autonomy allowed, its human resources policies, the nature of its practice and organization, and appropriate cost-benefit considerations.

32. All of the following are audit quality control requirements contained in the Sarbanes-Oxley Act of 2002 **except**

- A. The lead audit partner must rotate off the audit every 5 years.
- B. The audit report must be submitted to the Public Company Accounting Oversight Board prior to issuance.
- C. The audit report must be reviewed and approved by a second partner.
- D. The Public Company Accounting Oversight Board will periodically inspect registered CPA firms.

Answer (B) is correct. *(Publisher, adapted)*
REQUIRED: The quality control issue not addressed in the Sarbanes-Oxley Act.
DISCUSSION: Audit reports must be determined appropriate for issuance by the CPA firm but need not be approved by the PCAOB.

33. According to PCAOB quality control standards applying to an audit, the engagement quality reviewer evaluates

- A. The documentation.
- B. Only the uncorrected misstatements.
- C. The audit report but not the internal control report.
- D. Only the assessment of risks identified by management.

Answer (A) is correct. *(Publisher, adapted)*
REQUIRED: The subject matter evaluated by the EQR.
DISCUSSION: The EQR process in an audit evaluates the significant judgments made. This involves discussions with the engagement partner and other team members and reviewing whether the documentation supports the conclusions reached and appropriate responses to significant risks.
Answer (B) is incorrect. The reviewer evaluates corrected and uncorrected identified misstatements and control deficiencies. Answer (C) is incorrect. The reviewer evaluates the statements, the internal control report, and the audit report. Answer (D) is incorrect. The reviewer evaluates the assessment of, and responses to, significant risks, including those identified by the reviewer.

34. According to PCAOB quality control standards applying to audits, the engagement quality reviewer most likely

- A. May provide concurring approval of issuance of the report even if (s)he is aware of a significant engagement deficiency.
- B. Must be an associate of a registered public accounting firm.
- C. Must have integrity and objectivity but not independence.
- D. May be an engagement partner on a prior audit but not the current audit.

Answer (B) is correct. *(Publisher, adapted)*
REQUIRED: The limit on an engagement quality reviewer.
DISCUSSION: The objective of the reviewer is to evaluate the significant judgments made and the related conclusions reached. (S)he must be an associated person of a registered public accounting firm and may be from outside the firm. Moreover, the reviewer must have the competence to serve as a partner on the engagement and have independence, integrity, and objectivity. But an engagement partner on either of the two preceding audits ordinarily may not be the reviewer.
Answer (A) is incorrect. Awareness of a significant engagement deficiency precludes concurring approval of issuance. Answer (C) is incorrect. The reviewer must be independent. Answer (D) is incorrect. An engagement partner on either of the two preceding audits ordinarily is disqualified from reviewing the current audit.

Use the additional questions in Gleim **CPA Test Prep Online** to create Test Sessions that emulate Prometric!

1.6 PRACTICE SIMULATION

Auditing and Attestation Testlet 4 of 4	Time Remaining 1 hour - 30 minutes	

Unsplit Split Horiz Split Vertical   Spreadsheet   Calculator   Exit

DIRECTIONS

Note: If you believe you have encountered a software malfunction, report it to the test center staff immediately.

Navigation

To navigate from task to task, use the controls at the bottom of the screen. Click on the **Next** button to advance to the next task, or the **Previous** button to go to the previous task. To go directly to any task, click on its number.

⚑ = Reminder		Directions	1 2 3 4 5 6 7		◀ Previous Next ▶

If you would like a reminder to revisit a task, or want to indicate that you are finished with it, click on the reminder flag below the task number. To clear the flag, click on it again. Reminder flags are for your use only – they do not contribute to your score.

Tabs

In this part of the examination, you will be asked to complete various tasks. Every task has one or more **Work Tabs**. Some tasks have one or more **Information Tabs**, others may have none. Every task has a **Help** tab.

If a task has **Information Tabs**, you may use the information in them to complete your responses in the **Work Tabs**.

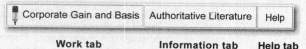

Corporate Gain and Basis | Authoritative Literature | Help

Work tab   Information tab   Help tab

Work Tabs:

- **Work Tabs** are identified with a pencil icon. This is where your responses are expected.
- Each task has one or more **Work Tabs**.
- **Work Tabs** contain directions for completing the task – be sure to read these directions carefully.
- The **Work Tab** name in the example above is for illustration only – yours will differ.
- You must complete all of the **Work Tabs** in each task to receive full credit.

Information Tabs:

- The Authoritative Literature will be provided in all tasks in the AUD, FAR, and REG sections for your reference.
- Your simulation may have one or more additional **Information Tabs**. Like the Authoritative Literature tabs, **Information Tabs** do not have a pencil icon.
- If your task has additional **Information Tabs**, go through each to familiarize yourself with the task content.

Help Tab:

- The **Help Tab** provides assistance with the exam software that is used in this task. For example, if the task is to compose a memorandum, **Help** will provide information about the word processor.

The Toolbar

The toolbar at the top of the screen shows the amount of time remaining for you to complete the tasks. In addition, the following tools are available. Note that only the Exit button is displayed when Directions are visible - the others will appear when you begin the tasks.

Click on these buttons to split or unsplit the screen. You can split the screen vertically or horizontally.

Click on this button to display the calculator; click on it again to hide the calculator. To move the calculator, click on the calculator title bar and drag the calculator to the desired location.

Click on this button to use the spreadsheet; click on it again to hide the spreadsheet. To move the spreadsheet, click on the the spreadsheet title bar and drag the spreadsheet to the desired location.

Click on this button to go on to the next part of the examination. You must complete all of the tasks to receive full credit. Once you click on **Exit** and confirm the action, you will NOT be able to return to this testlet.

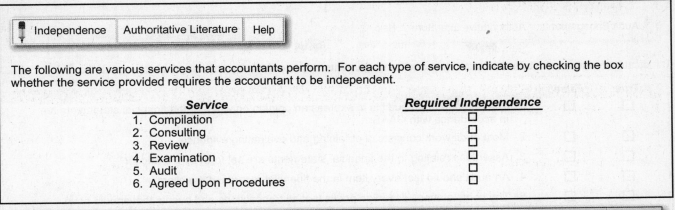

Independence | Authoritative Literature | Help

The following are various services that accountants perform. For each type of service, indicate by checking the box whether the service provided requires the accountant to be independent.

Service	Required Independence
1. Compilation	☐
2. Consulting	☐
3. Review	☐
4. Examination	☐
5. Audit	☐
6. Agreed Upon Procedures	☐

▼ = Reminder	Directions	1 ▽	2 ▽	3 ▽	4 ▽	5 ▽	◀ Previous Next ▶

Quality Control | Authoritative Literature | Help

Select a choice from the list provided to match the related quality control element with the associated description of a typical policy or procedure. Each choice may be used once, more than once, or not at all.

Policy and Procedure	Answer
1. Considering the business reputation of key management and those charged with governance	
2. Emphasizing independence of mental attitude in firm training programs and in supervision and review work	
3. Reviewing engagement working papers and reports	
4. Training and designating individuals within the firm as specialists to serve as authoritative sources	
5. Establishing qualifications and guidelines for evaluating potential entry-level employees	
6. Promoting an internal culture or "tone at the top" recognizing the importance of quality	
7. Inspection	
8. Assuring that current employees have the skills needed for the responsibilities they are called upon to assume	
9. Requiring employees to be honest and candid within the constraints of client confidentiality	

Control Element
A) Leadership responsibilities for quality within the firm
B) Relevant ethical requirements
C) Acceptance and continuance of client relationships and specific engagements
D) Human resources
E) Engagement performance
F) Monitoring

▼ = Reminder	Directions	1 ▽	2 ▽	3 ▽	4 ▽	5 ▽	◀ Previous Next ▶

| Audit Engagements | Authoritative Literature | Help |

Indicate whether each statement relating to audit engagements is true or false by checking the appropriate box.

True **False**

☐ ☐ 1. The purpose of an audit is to express an opinion on whether the financial statements are in accordance with GAAS.

☐ ☐ 2. Most audit work consists of obtaining and evaluating evidence.

☐ ☐ 3. Assertions relating to the financial statements are set forth by the auditor.

☐ ☐ 4. An audit should test every item in the financial records of the client.

☐ ☐ 5. The completeness assertion posits that all transactions and events that should have been recorded were recorded.

☐ ☐ 6. Audits of issuers must follow the standards of the Public Company Accounting Oversight Board.

☐ ☐ 7. The purpose of risk assessment by the auditor is to form a basis to design and perform an audit.

▼ = Reminder   Directions   1 2 [3] 4 5   ◀ Previous Next ▶

| Levels of Assurance | Authoritative Literature | Help |

Select a choice from the list provided to match the level of assurance provided by the various services that CPAs may offer. Each choice may be used once, more than once, or not at all.

Service	Answer
1. Audit	
2. Compilation	
3. Agreed-upon procedures	
4. Review	
5. Examination	

List
A) No assurance
B) Limited assurance
C) Positive assurance

▼ = Reminder   Directions   1 2 3 [4] 5   ◀ Previous Next ▶

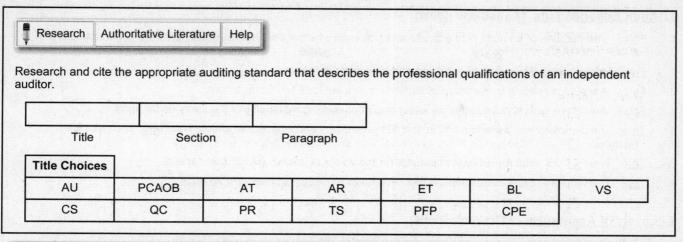

Research and cite the appropriate auditing standard that describes the professional qualifications of an independent auditor.

Title	Section	Paragraph

Title Choices

AU	PCAOB	AT	AR	ET	BL	VS
CS	QC	PR	TS	PFP	CPE	

▼ = Reminder Directions 1 2 3 4 [5] ◀ Previous Next ▶

Unofficial Answers

1. Independence (6 Gradable Items)

1. <u>No.</u> Independence is not required.
2. <u>No.</u> Independence is not required.
3. <u>Yes.</u> Independence is required.
4. <u>Yes.</u> Independence is required.
5. <u>Yes.</u> Independence is required.
6. <u>Yes.</u> Independence is required.

2. Quality Control (9 Gradable Items)

1. <u>C) Acceptance and continuance of client relationships and specific engagements.</u> Policies and procedures should be established for deciding whether to accept a client. The purpose is to minimize the likelihood of association with a client whose management lacks integrity.

2. <u>B) Relevant ethical requirements.</u> Firm-sponsored training programs and supervision can help assure that personnel understand the expectation that they maintain independence both in mental attitude and in appearance.

3. <u>E) Engagement performance.</u> The firm should employ policies and procedures for the conduct and supervision of work at all organizational levels to provide reasonable assurance that the work performed meets professional standards, regulatory requirements, and the firm's standards of quality.

4. <u>E) Engagement performance.</u> Policies and procedures should be established to provide reasonable assurance that personnel assigned to engagements will seek assistance, to the extent required, from persons having appropriate levels of knowledge, competence, judgment, and authority.

5. <u>D) Human resources.</u> The firm should ensure that employees possess the appropriate qualifications and characteristics to enable them to perform competently.

6. <u>A) Leadership responsibilities for quality within the firm.</u> The firm should promote an internal culture based on the recognition that quality is essential in performing engagements and should establish policies and procedures to support that culture.

7. <u>F) Monitoring.</u> Inspection procedures evaluate the adequacy of quality control policies and procedures, employee understanding of them, and the extent of compliance. These procedures relate to monitoring because findings are evaluated and changes considered.

8. <u>D) Human resources.</u> Policies and procedures should be established to provide reasonable assurance that those selected for advancement will have the qualifications necessary for the fulfillment of the responsibilities they will be called on to assume.

9. <u>B) Relevant ethical requirements.</u> Policies and procedures should be established to provide reasonable assurance that personnel perform all professional responsibilities with integrity. Thus, they should be candid except as constrained by the *Code of Professional Conduct.*

3. Audit Engagements (7 Gradable Items)

1. <u>False.</u> The purpose of an audit is to express an opinion on whether the financial statements are in accordance with GAAP, not GAAS.

2. <u>True.</u> Most audit work consists of obtaining and evaluating evidence.

3. <u>False.</u> Assertions relating to the financial statements are set forth by management.

4. <u>False.</u> Audits are typically conducted on a test basis considering materiality of the items under audit.

5. <u>True.</u> The completeness assertion posits that all transactions and events that should have been recorded were recorded.

6. <u>True.</u> The PCAOB establishes audit standards for the audits of issuers (public companies).

7. <u>True.</u> The purpose of risk assessment is to form a basis to design and perform an audit.

4. Levels of Assurance (5 Gradable Items)

1. <u>C) Positive assurance.</u> Positive assurance is provided by the opinion in an audit.

2. <u>A) No assurance.</u> No assurance is provided, as a compilation report contains a disclaimer of opinion.

3. <u>A) No assurance.</u> Agreed-upon procedures engagements provide the results of the procedures but offer no assurance.

4. <u>B) Limited assurance.</u> A review provides limited assurance but offers no opinion.

5. <u>C) Positive assurance.</u> An examination, like an audit, provides positive assurance expressed as an opinion.

5. Research (1 Gradable Item)

Answer: 110.04

AU Section 110 -- *Responsibilities and Functions of the Independent Auditor*

Professional Qualifications

.04 The professional qualifications required of the independent auditor are those of a person with the education and experience to practice as such. They do not include those of a person trained for or qualified to engage in another profession or occupation. For example, the independent auditor, in observing the taking of a physical inventory, does not purport to act as an appraiser, a valuer, or an expert in materials. Similarly, although the independent auditor is informed in a general manner about matters of commercial law, he does not purport to act in the capacity of a lawyer and may appropriately rely upon the advice of attorneys in all matters of law. [Paragraph renumbered by the issuance of Statement on Auditing Standards No. 82, February 1997.]

Gleim Simulation Grading

Task	Correct Responses		Gradable Items		Score per Task
1	_____	÷	6	=	_____
2	_____	÷	9	=	_____
3	_____	÷	7	=	_____
4	_____	÷	5	=	_____
Research	_____	÷	1	=	_____

	Total of Scores per Task	_____
÷	Total Number of Tasks	5
	Total Score	_____ %

Use **CPA Gleim Online** and **Simulation Wizard** to practice more task-based simulations in a realistic environment.

STUDY UNIT TWO
PROFESSIONAL RESPONSIBILITIES

(28 pages of outline)

The Auditing and Attestation section of the CPA exam tests the AICPA *Code of Professional Conduct* and other ethics pronouncements, including an awareness of the *Code of Ethics for Professional Accountants* of the International Federation of Accountants (IFAC). This review is not a manual or guide but an aid to understanding concepts. The issues related to independence are the most challenging. In that section, the rule or interpretation is given followed by insights into ethics concepts and examples derived from questions from prior exams.

Focus your attention on the AICPA *Code of Professional Conduct* (Subunits 1 through 6). The material in Subunit 7, "Other Pronouncements on Professional Responsibilities," parallels the *Code* conceptually in most cases. The specific rule or section numbers need not be memorized for any of the material in this study unit. Professional responsibilities constitute 16-20% of this section of the exam.

2.1 CODE OF PROFESSIONAL CONDUCT

1. **Principles and Rules**

   a. The *Code*, which consists of Principles and Rules of Conduct, applies to professional services performed by AICPA **members**.

   b. The Principles provide the framework for the Rules. They are goal-oriented but **nonbinding**.

   c. The following are the Principles:

      1) **Responsibilities.** All members should exercise sensitive **professional and moral judgments** when carrying out their professional responsibilities.

      2) **The public interest.** All members should act to benefit the public interest, honor the public trust, and demonstrate commitment to professionalism.

         a) The AICPA adopted the ethical standards because a distinguishing mark of a profession is an **acceptance of responsibility to the public**.

      3) **Integrity.** All members should perform all professional responsibilities with the highest sense of integrity to maintain public confidence.

      4) **Objectivity and independence.** All members should maintain objectivity and be free of conflicts of interest. A **member in public practice** should be **independent in fact (mind) and appearance** when providing attestation services.

      NOTE: A member **not** in public practice need not be independent.

      5) **Due care.** All members should follow the profession's technical and ethical standards, strive for improved competence and quality services, and discharge professional responsibility to the best of the member's ability.

         a) All members must adequately plan and supervise any activity for which they are responsible.

      6)   **Scope and nature of services.** A **member in public practice** should follow the Principles of the *Code of Professional Conduct* in determining the nature and scope of services. This principle is for members in public practice only.

   d.   The Rules of Conduct are **mandatory**.

     1.   Rule 101 – Independence
     2. [1]Rule 102 – Integrity and Objectivity
     3. [1]Rule 201 – General Standards
     4. [1]Rule 202 – Compliance with Standards
     5. [1]Rule 203 – Accounting Principles
     6.   Rule 301 – Confidential Client Information
     7.   Rule 302 – Contingent Fees
     8. [1]Rule 501 – Acts Discreditable
     9.   Rule 502 – Advertising and Other Forms of Solicitation
   10. [2]Rule 503 – Commissions and Referral Fees
   11. [1]Rule 505 – Form of Organization and Name

[1] These rules of Conduct apply to **all members**.
[2] Conduct Rule 503 applies in part (Referrals) to **all members** and in part (Commissions) only to **members in public practice**. The remaining Rules apply only to members in public practice.

  2.   **Interpretations and Ethics Rulings**

    a.   AICPA Interpretations provide guidelines for the scope and application of the Rules.

    b.   Ethics Rulings apply the Rules and Interpretations to **specific facts** to determine whether a violation exists. Many rulings appear in examples in the following subunits.

Stop and review! You have completed the outline for this subunit. Study multiple-choice questions 1 and 2 on page 79.

2.2 INDEPENDENCE

  1.   **Rule 101 -- Concepts**

    a.   A member in public practice shall be independent when performing professional services (typically auditing and attestation) as required by standards-setting bodies.

      1)   These bodies include, among others, the AICPA, the IFAC, the Securities and Exchange Commission (SEC), the Public Company Accounting Oversight Board (PCAOB), and the Government Accountability Office (GAO).

      2)   To inspire public confidence, an auditor must not only be independent (intellectually honest) but also recognized as independent (free of any obligation to, or interest in, the client, management, or owners). As defined in the AICPA Conceptual Framework, this is termed "independence in mind (fact)" and "independence in appearance," respectively.

    b.   Independence is impaired if a covered member has certain interests or relationships.

    c.   A **covered member** includes

      1)   An individual on the engagement team or who can influence the engagement,

      2)   A partner or manager who provides nonattest services to a client,

      3)   A partner in the office where the lead engagement partner primarily practices in relation to the engagement, and

      4)   The accounting firm, including the firm's employee benefit plans.

2. **Impairment**

    a. Independence **is impaired** if a covered member **has a direct financial interest** in a client.

CONCEPT

The covered member must have no ownership of equity, debt securities, or other investments in a client. The restriction includes the covered member's immediate family (spouse and dependents).

EXAMPLES

A covered member must not (1) own shares in a mutual fund that is an attest client, (2) participate in a retirement fund or savings plan sponsored by an attest client, (3) own bonds issued by an attest client, or (4) own a prepaid (529) tuition plan administered by an attest client. Even if shares of a client were held in a blind trust for the covered member, independence would be impaired.

An unsolicited financial interest in a client, such as through a gift or inheritance, does not impair independence if disposed of within 30 days.

---

    b. Independence **is impaired** if a covered member **has loans to or from** a client or its officers, directors, or 10% (or greater) owners.

        1) Exceptions. Independence is **not** impaired by

            a) Certain loans from a client financial institution (e.g., bank). These include (1) auto loans and leases collateralized by the auto, (2) loans fully collateralized by the cash surrender value of insurance, (3) loans fully collateralized by cash deposits, and (4) credit cards with a total outstanding balance of $10,000 or less on a current basis by the payment due date.

            b) Certain loans that are considered "grandfathered" because they were in existence before independence rules became more restrictive.

CONCEPT

Loans are considered a direct financial interest. The restriction on loans includes the covered member's immediate family (spouse and dependents).

EXAMPLES

A covered member must not borrow money from an attest client. Also, fees outstanding from an attest client for more than 1 year are considered a loan and would impair independence.

---

    c. Independence **is impaired** if a covered member **has a material indirect financial interest** in a client.

CONCEPT

A covered member (and his/her immediate family) may have some limited financial interests in clients as long as they are not direct and not material to the wealth of the member or the client.

EXAMPLE

A covered member or spouse may own shares in a mutual fund that holds shares of a client as long as the mutual fund investment was not material to the member.

    d.   Independence **is impaired** if a covered member **is a trustee of a trust** or **executor of an estate** that has a direct or material indirect financial interest in a client.

CONCEPT

A covered member must not be in a **position to make decisions** related to a trust or an estate that involves investments or other financial interests in clients.

EXAMPLE

A covered member must not be a trustee of a trust that holds any shares of a client. But (s)he may be a trustee of a trust that holds shares of a mutual fund that has an investment in a client as long as the amount is not material.

    e.   Independence **is impaired** if a covered member **has a material joint, closely held investment** with a client.

CONCEPT

A covered member is prohibited from having a material financial relationship with a client that might cause third parties to question the member's objectivity.

EXAMPLES

A covered member must not join with a client to develop and market a product. A covered member also must not own a vacation home jointly with a key officer or principal shareholder of a client.

    f.   Independence **is impaired** if a firm partner or professional employee **owns more than 5% of a client**.

CONCEPT

This allows some members of a CPA firm, other than covered members, to have some financial interest in clients without affecting the independence of the firm.

EXAMPLES

- A professional employee in the office that conducts an audit, who is not part of the audit team, may own a 5% or less equity interest in a client of the firm.
- However, a partner in that office must not. (S)he is considered a covered member and must have no financial interest in the client.

    g.   Independence **is impaired** if a firm or one of its partners or professional employees **is associated with the client** as an officer, director, manager, employee, promoter, underwriter, etc.

CONCEPT

The individual or firm must not appear to be acting in the capacity of management or employee of the client. This includes having the responsibility to perform any duties of employees or management.

EXAMPLES

A covered member must not (1) sign or cosign client checks, (2) supervise employees, (3) authorize transactions, (4) execute transactions, (5) prepare source documents, or (6) maintain custody of assets for a client.

h.   Independence **may be impaired** if a covered member was **formerly employed by or associated with** the client as an officer, director, promoter, underwriter, etc.

CONCEPT

The covered member must disassociate from the client before becoming a covered member. (S)he also must not (1) participate on the engagement team or (2) be able to influence the engagement when his/her former employment/ association overlaps the period of the engagement.

EXAMPLE

Disassociation includes, among other things, disposing of direct or material indirect financial interests and ceasing to participate in most employee benefit plans.

---

i.   The covered member's immediate family (spouse or dependents) are subject to Rule 101.

CONCEPT

The financial interests, employment relationships, and other circumstances of immediate family members are attributed to the covered member.

EXAMPLES

An immediate family member may be employed by the client in a non-key position. As a result of such permitted employment, the immediate family member may participate in various employee benefit plans under limited circumstances. For example, the immediate family member must not, among other things, (1) participate on the engagement team or be able to influence the engagement or (2) be involved in investment decisions.

---

j.   As a result of his/her permitted employment, an **immediate family member** of a covered member may participate in a **benefit plan** that is an attest client or that is sponsored by an attest client (other than a client's share-based compensation arrangement or nonqualified deferred compensation plan — see item k. on the following page) provided that the plan is offered to all employees in comparable employment positions and the immediate family member does not serve in a position of governance for the plan.

1)   An immediate family member of a covered member may hold a **direct or material indirect financial interest** in an attest client through participation in a plan, provided that the covered member neither participates on the attest engagement team nor is in a position to influence the attest engagement; such investment is an unavoidable consequence of such participation; and in the event that a plan option to invest in a nonattest client becomes available, the immediate family member selects such option and disposes of any direct or material indirect financial interests in the attest client as soon as practicable but no later than 30 days after such option becomes available.

CONCEPT

This covers general benefit plans for immediate family members that may create financial interests in clients and impact the covered member.

EXAMPLE

The spouse of a covered member has a non-key position in a client and, along with other employees, is a part of an employee profit sharing plan in a client.

k.   As a result of his/her permitted employment, an **immediate family member** of a covered member may participate in a **share-based compensation arrangement** that results in him/her holding a beneficial financial interest in an attest client, provided that the covered member neither participates on the attest engagement team nor is in a position to influence the attest engagement and the immediate family member does not serve in a position of governance for the share-based compensation arrangement.

1)   When the beneficial financial interests are distributed or the immediate family member has the right to dispose of the shares, the immediate family member must dispose of the shares as soon as practicable but no later than 30 days after (s)he has the right to dispose of the shares.

CONCEPT

This covers specific stock-based benefit plans for immediate family members that may create financial interests in clients and impact the covered member.

EXAMPLE

The immediate family member may participate in an employee stock ownership plan (ESOP) if the restrictions are maintained.

---

l.   Independence **is impaired** if an individual participating on the engagement (or able to exert influence or that is a partner in the lead partner's office) has a **close relative** (sibling, parent, or non-dependent child) who holds **a key position** with the client or certain financial interests.

CONCEPT

If a close relative has a financial interest in the client that (1) the individual knows or has reason to believe is material to the relative or (2) permits the relative to exert significant influence over the client, independence is impaired. Some latitude is permitted in the application of this rule based on the family relationship.

EXAMPLES

- A sibling may be a salesperson for a client but not the CFO or a director.
- A parent may be a production manager (non-key position), but not the CEO or a director.

---

m.   Independence of the firm **is impaired** if a former partner or professional employee of the firm is **employed by or associated with an attest client** in a key position.

1)   Independence is **not** impaired in this case if the person is no longer associated or active with the CPA firm and any retirement compensation is fixed.

CONCEPT

Third parties may believe that the person is in a position to influence the engagement.

EXAMPLE

A retired partner must not become a CFO of a client while performing consulting duties for the CPA firm or having retirement pay contingent on retaining the client.

n. Independence of the firm **may be impaired** if certain **nonattest services** are performed for an attest client.

CONCEPT

The practitioner appears to be an advocate or a decision maker for the attest client when performing certain nonattest services. In these circumstances, (s)he is not independent.

---

1) Independence **is impaired** by providing to attest clients the following services:

   a) **Appraisal, valuation, or actuarial services**
   b) **Expert witness services**
   c) **Internal audit services**
   d) **Tax advocacy services**
   e) **Recruiting, hiring, firing, or other employment services**

2) Independence is **not impaired** by providing to attest clients the following services:

   a) **Consulting services** (where the client is responsible for the decisions)
   b) **Tax preparation and compliance services**
   c) **Business risk advising services**
   d) **Providing general advice** based on audit findings

EXAMPLES

- Internal audit services must not be outsourced to the audit firm, but the audit firm may provide advice on how to improve the internal audit function.
- The auditor may prepare the client's tax return but must not testify as an advocate of the client in a tax case.

---

3) Independence is **not impaired** for attest engagements of nonissuers by providing bookkeeping, payroll processing, or other conventional recordkeeping functions.

CONCEPT

The AICPA allows practitioners to perform these duties for nonissuers (typically small clients) as long as management functions are not performed. The PCAOB rules do not allow these services to be provided to issuers by their auditors. However, issuers are not likely to request these services. Issuers have their own recordkeeping functions.

EXAMPLE

An auditor of a nonissuer may record transactions in a computer program and generate financial statements but must not provide those services for an issuer.

---

o.   Independence **is impaired** by **actual or threatened litigation** by either the CPA or the client.

1)   Independence is **not impaired** when the litigation issue is **not related to the work product** and is **not material**, for example, a dispute over billing.

2)   Independence is **not necessarily impaired** when shareholders or others bring a class action suit against both the client and the auditor.

CONCEPT

Legal action creates adverse interests between the parties involved. These interests can affect independence.

EXAMPLES

- The client may allege that the member was negligent, or the member may allege that the client's management committed fraud. In these circumstances, the interests of the client and the CPA are opposed, and independence is impaired.
- However, if a creditor or insurer files a suit that alleges reliance on the audited financial statements of a client, independence is not impaired.

p.   Independence is **not impaired** if a member holds an **honorary directorship or trusteeship** of a not-for-profit organization that is a client.

1)   The position must be clearly honorary, and the member must not be able to vote or participate in board or management decisions.

2)   The member must be identified as an honorary director or trustee.

CONCEPT

CPAs may lend their support to charitable organizations without impairing independence. However, they must not have managerial responsibilities.

EXAMPLE

An auditor's name is placed on the letterhead as "Honorary Director" of a not-for-profit charity who is a client. As long as the relationship is purely honorary, the auditor is independent.

q.   Financial interests in, and other relationships with, entities that are related in various ways (**affiliates**) to a financial statement attest client may impair independence. In general, members **should apply the independence provisions** to the attest client's affiliates. There are many relationships typically considered to be the client's affiliates, including

1)   An entity that a client can control

2)   An entity that controls the client

3)   An entity in which a client has a direct financial interest that gives the client the significant influence over such entity

4)   An entity with a direct financial interest in the client

5)   A sister entity of a client

6)   A trustee deemed to control a client's trust that is not an investment company

7)   The sponsor of a single employer employee benefit plan client

8)   Any union or participating employer that has significant influence over a multiple or multiemployer employee benefit plan client

9)   An employee benefit plan sponsored by either a client or an entity controlled by the client

10) An investment adviser, general partner, or trustee of an investment company client (fund)

CONCEPT

Various member involvements with affiliates create an indirect interest in an attest client. Thus, some measure of materiality is considered as with other indirect interests. What should be recognized is that significant mutual interests between a member and client may cause an impairment of independence.

EXAMPLE

A member could not be an investor or be on the board of directors of an attest client's affiliate.

---

r. An **auditor** of the basic financial statements of a **governmental entity must be independent** of the entity.

    1) However, a primary auditor need not be independent in the following circumstances:

        a) With respect to any fund, component unit, or disclosed entity, if the auditor explicitly relies on reports by **other auditors** on such entity

        b) With respect to a disclosed entity, if the reporting entity is **not financially accountable** for it and the required disclosure does not include financial information

    2) Neither the member nor a member of his/her immediate family should occupy a **key position** with the disclosed entity.

    3) An auditor who is not auditing the primary government must be independent only of the statements reported on.

        a) Nevertheless, the covered member or a member of his/her immediate family may not occupy a key position with the primary government.

CONCEPT

Governmental financial statements often display combinations of reporting entities. The basic financial statements may include a fund or entity audited by another auditor. Even if the auditor of the basic financial statements is not independent of the fund, it is acceptable to report on the basic financial statements.

EXAMPLE

The reporting entity is a local government. A state authority with a state-approved board provides temporary fiscal oversight. Because it issues bonds and collects revenues on behalf of the local government, it is included in the reporting entity. Moreover, the primary auditor must be independent of the authority although the reporting entity is not financially accountable for it. The disclosures required for the authority consist in part of financial information. However, the primary auditor need not be independent of the authority if (s)he relies on the report of another auditor.

---

s. **Alternative Practice Structures (APSs)**

    1) Independence rules for an alternative practice structure (APS) apply when the "traditional CPA firm" is closely aligned with another organization that performs other professional services.

    2) In an APS, **direct superiors** of covered members are subject to the same independence rules as covered members.

    3) In an APS, **indirect superiors** (including a spouse or dependents) may not have a material financial interest in an attest client of the new firm. They also should not have significant influence over an attest client.

CONCEPT

Today's business environment has created many alternative structures for CPA firms. Regardless of the structure, relationships that create concern about the influence on the attest function are not permitted.

EXAMPLE

A CPA firm becomes a subsidiary of a non-CPA firm that provides nonattest services (tax, consulting, etc.). The owners and employees of the CPA firm become employees of a subsidiary and may offer nonattest services. The original owners create a **new CPA firm** to offer attest services within the structure. The relationship is represented by the following:

Figure 2-2

Majority ownership in the new firm must be held by CPAs. In this case, employees, offices, and equipment are leased from the parent, which also may provide various other services. The CPA firm (the firm) and any leased or employed persons are potentially **covered members**. Any direct supervisors of activities of the new CPA firm are subject to the independence rules.

t. The practitioner **must be independent** of the **party responsible** for the subject matter of **restricted-use reports**. The Statements on Standards for Attestation Engagements describe certain engagements resulting in restricted-use reports.

1) Restricted-use reports may be issued on (a) agreed-upon procedures, (b) internal control, (c) prospective financial information, (d) compliance, (e) pro forma financial information, and (f) management's discussion and analysis.

CONCEPT

Attest engagements may be performed for many reasons and involve different kinds of clients. Regardless of the nature of the attest service or client, the practitioner must be independent of the party that is responsible for the subject matter of the attest engagement.

EXAMPLE

A bank, in anticipation of making a loan to an entity, engages a practitioner to perform certain agreed-upon procedures on the assets of the entity. The practitioner's report on the agreed-upon procedures would be restricted to the bank's use. The practitioner must be independent from the entity, the party responsible for the subject matter of the procedures.

u. Independence will be **impaired** if, during the period of a professional engagement, a member or his/her firm had any cooperative arrangement with the client that was material to the member's firm or to the client. A cooperative arrangement exists when a member's firm and a client jointly participate in a business activity.

CONCEPT

The relationship may create a conflict of interest between the member and those users of the auditor's services.

EXAMPLE

Cooperative arrangements with a client include

- Prime/subcontractor arrangements to provide services or products to a third party
- Joint ventures to develop or market products or services
- Distribution or marketing arrangements

---

    v.   To enhance their capabilities to provide professional services, firms frequently join larger groups, such as **membership associations (networks)**, that are separate legal entities otherwise unrelated to their members. Whether a firm is part of a network is contingent on the nature of shared goals and resources. A network firm is required to be independent of financial statement audit and review clients of the other network firms.

CONCEPT

Firms that are part of larger attest organizations must be cognizant of the independence requirements and work with other members of the network to achieve independence.

EXAMPLE

ABC Firm is part of a network of five other firms to share audit methodology, audit manuals, technical departments to consult on technical or industry specific issues, training courses, and facilities. They are considered part of the network and are required to be independent of clients of other firms in the network.

---

    w.   Partners or professional employees of a firm may seek employment as an **adjunct faculty member** of a client educational institution. Independence is **not impaired**, provided that the partner or professional employee

        1)   Does not hold a key position at the educational institution;

        2)   Does not participate on the attest engagement team;

        3)   Is not an individual in a position to influence the attest engagement;

        4)   Is employed by the educational institution on a part-time and nontenure basis;

        5)   Does not participate in any employee benefit plans sponsored by the educational institution, unless participation is required; and

        6)   Does not assume any management responsibilities or set policies for the educational institution.

Stop and review! You have completed the outline for this subunit. Study multiple-choice questions 3 through 8 beginning on page 79.

2.3 INTEGRITY AND OBJECTIVITY

    1.   **Rule 102 -- Concepts**

        a.   A member shall maintain objectivity and integrity, be free of conflicts of interest, not knowingly misrepresent facts, and not subordinate his/her judgment to others when performing professional services.

    2.   **Knowing Misrepresentations of Facts**

        a.   These include

            1)   Knowingly making materially false and misleading entries in **financial statements or records**,

            2)   Failing to make **corrections** in materially false or misleading statements or records when the member has such authority, or

            3)   **Signing** a document with materially false and misleading information.

EXAMPLE

The use of the CPA designation by a member not in public practice to imply that the member is independent of his/her employer is an intentional misrepresentation. The member should clearly indicate the employment title in any communication in which (s)he uses the CPA designation.

---

3. **Conflicts of Interest**

    a. A conflict of interest may be permitted in certain circumstances if **disclosure** is made to and consent is obtained from the appropriate parties.

        1) However, an **independence** objection cannot be overcome by disclosure and consent.

EXAMPLES – Possible Conflicts of Interest

- Performing litigation services for the plaintiff when the defendant is a client
- Providing tax or personal financial planning (PFP) services to both parties to a divorce
- Suggesting that a PFP client invest in a business in which the member has an interest
- Providing tax or PFP services to family members with conflicting interests
- Performing consulting services for a client that is a major competitor of a company in which the member has a significant financial interest, occupies a management position, or exercises influence
- Serving on a board of tax appeals that hears matters involving clients
- Providing services in connection with a real estate purchase from a client
- Referring a tax or PFP client to a service provider that refers clients to the member under an exclusive arrangement
- Referring a client to a service bureau in which the member or a partner in the member's firm has a material interest

---

EXAMPLE

A member is a director of a fund-raising organization that distributes funds to local charities that are clients (with significant relationships with the member). If the significant relationship is disclosed and consent is received from the appropriate parties, performance of services not requiring independence is allowed.

---

4. **Obligations to the Employer's External Accountant**

    a. A member must be candid and not knowingly misrepresent facts or fail to disclose material facts.

5. **Subordination of Member's Judgment**

    a. A member and his/her supervisor may disagree about **statement preparation or recording of transactions**. The member should do the following:

        1) The member should do nothing if the supervisor's position is an acceptable alternative and does not materially misrepresent the facts.

        2) If a **material misstatement** would result, the member should consult the appropriate higher level of supervisor and consider documenting relevant matters.

        3) If appropriate action still has not been taken, the member should consider the

            a) Continuing relationship with the employer,
            b) Obligation to communicate with third parties, and
            c) Desirability of consulting legal counsel.

EXAMPLES – Other Issues Related to Integrity and Objectivity

- A member has an obligation to act if a dispute with a supervisor about financial statement presentation would result in a material misstatement.
- A member lacks integrity if (s)he prematurely expresses an opinion on financial statements because of time pressures imposed by the client.
- A member is required to disclose the use of a third-party service provider when offering professional services to a client. If the client objects, the third-party service provider may not be used.
- A member must act with objectivity and integrity when providing educational services, such as teaching and research.
- A member should not accept gifts or entertainment from a client unless acceptance is reasonable in the circumstances. The nature, cost, occasion, frequency, etc., of the gift or entertainment should be considered in the assessment of reasonableness.
- A member should consider the risks to integrity and objectivity when providing services related to client advocacy.

Stop and review! You have completed the outline for this subunit. Study multiple-choice question 9 on page 81.

2.4 PROFESSIONAL STANDARDS

1.   **General Standards – Rule 201**

   a.   A member shall comply with the general standards and interpretations issued by designated bodies (the PCAOB and relevant AICPA committees and boards). The following are the general standards:

   1)   Undertake only those services that the member can reasonably expect to complete with **professional competence.**

   2)   Exercise **due professional care** when performing professional services.

   3)   Adequately **plan and supervise** performance of professional services.

   4)   Obtain **sufficient relevant data** to provide a reasonable basis for conclusions in relation to any professional service.

   NOTE: The following is a helpful mnemonic:

   PC and Double PC. PS and obtain SuRe Data.

   b.   The following is an illustration of the general standards:

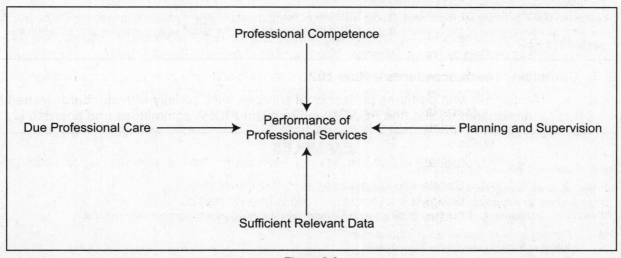

Figure 2-3

c.   **Proficiency.** A member must have the following:

1)   Adequate technical training
2)   Education
3)   Experience
4)   Proper supervision
5)   Objectivity
6)   Seasoned and independent judgment

d.   **Due Professional Care**

1)   An auditor uses due care to plan and perform the audit and prepare the report.

2)   An auditor should have the degree of skill commonly possessed by other auditors and must exercise it with reasonable care and diligence.

3)   An auditor also should exercise **professional skepticism**.

a)   (S)he should have a questioning mind and critically assess audit evidence.

4)   Due care allows the auditor to obtain reasonable assurance.

5)   A member should complete professional services according to professional standards and with reasonable care and diligence.

a)   **Competence** involves technical qualifications and the ability to supervise and evaluate the work. It relates to knowledge of standards, techniques, and technical subject matter and to the ability to exercise sound judgment.

b)   In some cases, **additional research and consultation** is a normal part of performing services. However, if a member cannot gain sufficient competence, (s)he should suggest the engagement of someone competent.

e.   **Consulting Services**

1)   The general standards apply to consulting services.

EXAMPLES

- In a consulting engagement to design and implement an IT application, a member hires a subcontractor to provide additional programming services. The member has a responsibility to ensure that the subcontractor has the professional qualifications and skills needed.
- A member plans to hire a systems analyst as a member of the firm's staff. The member is not required to be able to perform all the services of the systems analyst. But the member must be qualified to supervise and evaluate the specialist's work.

---

2.   **Compliance with Standards – Rule 202**

a.   A member who performs professional services shall comply with standards issued by designated bodies (the PCAOB and relevant AICPA committees and boards).

EXAMPLES

Professional services include the following:

- Audits, reviews, and compilations of financial statements
- Engagements to issue special reports
- Attestation engagements other than traditional audits and reviews, such as engagements to report on

  - Performance of agreed-upon procedures
  - Internal control over financial reporting
  - Compliance with statutes, regulations, or contracts
  - Financial forecasts or projections

- Tax services
- Consulting services
- Valuation services
- Personal financial planning services

---

3. **Accounting Principles – Rule 203**

   a. **Any material departure** from an accounting principle issued by an AICPA-designated standard setter prevents a member from

      1) Expressing an **opinion** (or **stating affirmatively**) that the financial statements (or other financial data) of any entity are presented in conformity with **GAAP**.

         a) Thus, the member provides **positive assurance**.

      2) Stating that (s)he is **not aware** of any **material modifications** that should be made to achieve conformity with **GAAP**.

         a) Thus, the member provides **limited assurance**.

   b. Rule 203 applies to **all members**, whether or not in public practice, regarding any affirmative statement about GAAP conformity.

EXAMPLES

Rule 203 applies

- To members who sign client reports provided to regulatory agencies, creditors, or auditors that contain such representations.
- To members who provide litigation support services. A member provides expert witness testimony that the defendant's financial statements are not fairly stated in conformity with GAAP.
- If the communication states that the financial statements conform with GAAP. A member submits financial statements in his/her capacity as an officer, shareholder, partner, director, or employee to a third party.

---

   c. A departure is **material** if it has a material effect on the **financial statements or data as a whole**.

   d. However, in some cases, a member may be able to provide assurance about conformity with GAAP despite a material departure.

      1) To do so, the member must be able to demonstrate that, due to **unusual circumstances**, the financial statements or data would have been **misleading** without a departure from GAAP. The member must describe

         a) The departure;
         b) Its approximate effects, if practicable; and
         c) The reasons compliance with the principle would be misleading.

      2) Events that may justify departures from established accounting principles are **new legislation** or evolution of a **new form of business transaction**.

      3) An unusual degree of materiality or conflicting industry practices ordinarily does not justify departures.

Stop and review! You have completed the outline for this subunit. Study multiple-choice questions 10 and 11 beginning on page 81.

2.5 RESPONSIBILITIES TO CLIENTS

1. **Confidential Client Information – Rule 301**

    a.   A member in public practice shall not disclose confidential client information without the client's consent. However, this Rule does not affect a CPA's obligations to

    1) Comply with a valid subpoena or summons or with applicable laws and regulations

    2) Discharge his/her professional obligations

    3) Cooperate in an official review of his/her professional practice

    4) Initiate a complaint with or respond to any inquiry made by an appropriate investigative or disciplinary body

---

EXAMPLES

- A member withdrew from an engagement because of fraud on a client's tax return. If contacted by the successor accountant, the member should suggest that the successor obtain permission from the client to reveal the reasons for leaving.
- A member works for a municipality to verify that proper amounts of taxes have been paid by area businesses. The member is prohibited from releasing any confidential information obtained in his/her professional capacity.
- A member reveals a client's name without permission. Disclosure violates Rule 301 if the client is in bankruptcy and the member specializes in bankruptcy cases. Disclosure in this situation constitutes release of confidential information.
- Knowledge and expertise obtained from a prior engagement may be used on behalf of a current client provided that the details of the other engagement are not revealed without permission.

---

    b.   **Review of a Member's Practice**

    1) The rule against disclosure of confidential information does not prohibit the review of a member's practice as part of a purchase, sale, or merger of the practice.

    2) However, appropriate precautions (e.g., a written confidentiality agreement) should be taken so that the prospective buyer does not disclose such information.

2. **Contingent Fees – Rule 302**

    a.   A **contingent fee** is established as part of an agreement under which the amount of the fee is dependent upon the finding or result.

    b.   Nevertheless, fees are **not** considered to be contingent if

    1) They are fixed by **public authorities** (e.g., courts).

    2) In **tax matters**, they are based on

        a) The results of **judicial proceedings** or

        b) The findings of **governmental agencies**.

    c.   A member in **public practice** shall not perform for a contingent fee any professional services for any of the following:

    1) An **audit or review** of a financial statement

    2) A **compilation** of a financial statement if

        a) The member might reasonably expect that a third party will use the statement and

        b) The report does **not disclose** the lack of independence

    3) An **examination** of **prospective financial information** (a financial forecast or projection)

    d.   A member in **public practice** shall not prepare for a contingent fee

        1)   An original tax return
        2)   An amended tax return
        3)   A claim for a tax refund

EXAMPLES

- A member's spouse may provide services to the member's attest client for a contingent fee provided the spouse's activities are separate from the member's practice and the member is not significantly involved. However, a conflict of interest issue may arise.
- A member who provides investment advisory services for an attest client for a percentage of the investment portfolio ordinarily violates Rule 302.
- Providing investment advisory services to the owners, officers, or employees of an attest client for a contingent fee does not violate Rule 302. However, the member should consider the possible conflict of interest and also Rule 301.
- A contingent fee is allowed for representation of a client (1) in an examination by a revenue agent or (2) who is obtaining a private letter ruling. A contingent fee is not allowed for the preparation of an amended income tax return for a client claiming a refund of taxes because of an inadvertent omission of a proper deduction. But a contingent fee is allowed for filing an amended tax return claiming a refund based on a tax issue that is the subject of a test case involving a different taxpayer.

Stop and review! You have completed the outline for this subunit. Study multiple-choice question 12 on page 82.

2.6 OTHER RESPONSIBILITIES

1.   **Acts Discreditable – Rule 501**

    a.   A member shall not commit an act that is discreditable to the profession.

EXAMPLES

- A firm may arrange with a bank to collect notes issued by a client in payment of fees.
- A CPA employed by a firm with one or more non-CPA practitioners must obey the Rules of Conduct. If the CPA becomes a partner, (s)he is responsible for compliance with the Rules of Conduct by all associated practitioners.
- A member not in public practice who is controller of a bank may use the CPA title on bank stationery and in paid advertisements.
- A member who is an attorney and a CPA may use a letterhead with both titles on it.
- A member interviewed by the press should observe the Rules of Conduct and not provide information that the member could not publish.

---

    b.   **Response to Requests for Records**

        1)   Client-provided records and reproductions of such records must be returned after a client request even if (a) fees have not been paid or (b) the state in which the member practices grants a lien on certain records.

           a)   **Client-provided records** are "accounting or other records belonging to the client that were provided to the member by or on behalf of the client."

        2)   **Working papers** are the member's property and need not be made available to the client or others unless required by

           a)   Statute,
           b)   Regulation, or
           c)   Contract.

        3)   **Client records prepared by the member** include accounting and other records (e.g., tax returns, journals, ledgers, and supporting schedules) that the member was engaged to prepare.

           a)   They may be withheld if fees are due or the engagement is incomplete.

4) **Supporting records** contain information produced by the member that is not in the client's records, without which its financial information is incomplete.

   a) They are not otherwise available to the client.

   b) Supporting records for an **issued work product** should be given to the client upon request unless fees are due for that product.

5) The following summarizes the types of records and responsibilities:

Type	Right to Withhold
Client-provided records	None
Working papers	Absolute barring legal or contractual exception
Member-prepared client records	If fees due or engagement incomplete
Supporting records	If fees due or engagement incomplete

6) Records also must be given to a client who suffered a loss because of an **act of war or natural disaster**.

7) The member may

   a) Charge a reasonable fee,

   b) Retain copies, and

   c) Provide records in any format or usable form unless the engagement was to prepare them in the requested format.

8) Compliance with a client's request usually should be within **45 days**.

EXAMPLES

- Individuals associated with a client may be involved in an internal dispute, and each may request records. A member who has provided records to the designated client representative is not obligated to comply with requests for those records by others associated with the client.

- If the relationship of a member who is not an owner of a firm is terminated, (s)he may not take or retain originals or copies from the firm's client files or proprietary information without permission.

---

c. **Discrimination and Harassment**

1) When a court or administrative agency has made a final determination that a member has violated an antidiscrimination law, (s)he is deemed to have committed an act discreditable.

d. **Following the Requirements of Governmental Bodies**

1) A member must follow **GAAP** and the requirements of governmental bodies when preparing **financial statements** for entities subject to their jurisdiction.

2) If the member performs **attest services**, (s)he must follow the requirements of those bodies as well as **GAAS**.

3) A material departure from the requirements is an act discreditable unless the member discloses the reasons.

e. **Governmental Audits**

1) In a governmental audit, failure to adhere to applicable audit standards, guides, procedures, statutes, rules, and regulations is an act discreditable to the profession unless the report discloses the failure and the reasons for it.

f. **CPA Examination**

1) Solicitation or knowing disclosure of CPA examination questions or answers is an act discreditable.

g. **Negligence**

1) It is an act discreditable to be responsible for negligently

a) Making materially false and misleading entries in the financial statements or records,

b) Failing to correct materially false and misleading statements, or

c) Signing a document with materially false and misleading information.

h. **Failure to File a Tax Return or Pay Tax**

1) Failing to comply with laws regarding (a) timely filing of personal or firm tax returns or (b) timely payment of taxes collected for others is an act discreditable.

i. **Regulated Entities and Limitation of Liability**

1) Regulators may prohibit regulated entities from entering into certain kinds of indemnification and **limitation of liability agreements** in connection with **attest services**.

2) Regulators also may prohibit members from providing services under such agreements.

3) Failing to comply with such prohibitions is an act discreditable.

2. **Advertising and Other Forms of Solicitation – Rule 502**

a. A member in public practice shall not seek to obtain clients by advertising or other forms of solicitation done in a false, misleading, or deceptive manner.

b. Solicitation through coercion, overreaching, or harassing conduct is prohibited.

EXAMPLES

- A newsletter, tax booklet, etc., not prepared by the member may be attributed to the member if the member has a reasonable basis to believe the information attributed to the member is not false, misleading, or deceptive.

- The designation "Personal Financial Specialists" may only be used on a letterhead when all partners or shareholders have the AICPA-awarded designation. However, the individual members holding the designation may use it after their names.

---

c. **False, Misleading, or Deceptive Acts**

1) Such acts are prohibited because they are against the public interest. These prohibited activities include the following:

a) Creating **false expectations** of favorable results

b) Implying the **ability to influence** any court, regulatory agency, etc.

c) Representing that specific services will be performed for a **stated fee** when it is likely at the time that the fees will be substantially increased and the client is not advised of the possibility

d) Other representations that would cause a **reasonable person** to misunderstand or be deceived

d. **Obtaining Clients Through Third Parties**

1) Members are permitted to render services to **clients of third parties**.

2) If the third party obtained its clients through advertising, the members must determine that all promotional efforts were within the Rules of Conduct.

a) Members must not do through others what they are prohibited from doing themselves.

3.   **Commissions and Referral Fees – Rule 503**

   a.   **Prohibited commissions** are those received when a **member in public practice**

      1)   Recommends or refers

         a)   **To a client** any product or service or
         b)   Any product or service **to be supplied by a client**.

      2)   **Also performs** for the client

         a)   An audit,
         b)   A review,
         c)   A compilation reasonably expected to be used by a third party if the member's lack of independence is not disclosed, or
         d)   An examination of prospective financial information (PFI).

   b.   A **permitted commission** must be **disclosed** to any person or entity to whom the member recommends or refers a related product or service.

   c.   **Referral fees** are not considered commissions and are permitted if **disclosed** to the client. These include

      1)   Acceptance of a referral fee for recommending or referring any **service of a CPA** to anyone
      2)   Payment of a referral fee to **obtain a client**

EXAMPLES

- A member is permitted to purchase a product and resell it to a client. Any profits collected are not considered a commission because the member had title to the product and assumed the risks of ownership.
- A member may not refer for commissions products to audit clients through distributors and agents when the member is performing any of the services described in Rule 503. A member may not do through others what (s)he cannot do himself or herself. If the services are not being provided by the member, (s)he may refer the products, provided (s)he discloses the commission to the client.

---

4.   **Form of Organization and Name – Rule 505**

   a.   A member may practice public accounting only in a form of organization allowed by law or regulation that conforms with resolutions of the AICPA Council.
   b.   The firm name must not be misleading.
   c.   Names of past owners may be included in the name of the successor firm.
   d.   A firm cannot designate itself as "members of the AICPA" unless all CPA owners are members.
   e.   If a firm **holds itself out as CPAs** or performs audits, reviews, or examination of prospective financial information, it must have certain attributes:

      1)   CPAs own a **majority** of the firm.
      2)   A CPA must be **responsible** for all services.
      3)   A non-CPA owner must be **active** as a member of the firm or its affiliates.
      4)   Non-CPA owners cannot hold themselves out as CPAs.
      5)   A member must not permit a person (s)he **controls** to do what is prohibited to the member by the *Code*.

         a)   The member also may be responsible for the acts of such a person who is an associate in the **practice of public accounting**.

      6)   Non-CPA owners are not eligible to be AICPA members.

   f.   Members may practice not only in corporations and general partnerships but also in limited liability companies, limited liability partnerships, and other forms permitted by state law.

g. **Ownership of a Separate Business**

   1) A member **practicing public accounting** may own an interest in a **separate business** that performs the services for which standards are established.

   2) If the member **controls** the separate business, the entity and all its owners and employees must comply with the *Code*.

      a) Absent such control, only the member is subject to the *Code*.

h. **Alternative Practice Structures (APSs)**

   1) AICPA requirements emphasize that CPAs remain responsible, financially and otherwise for the **attest work** performed to protect the public interest.

   2) However, in an APS, CPAs may own the majority of financial interests in the attest firm, but substantially all revenues may be paid to another entity for services and the lease of employees, equipment, etc.

   3) Nevertheless, given the requirements of state law and the AICPA, if the CPA-owners of the attest firm remain **financially responsible** under state law, they are deemed to be in compliance with the financial-interests requirement.

EXAMPLES

- A partnership may continue to practice using the managing partner's name as the firm name after (s)he withdraws. "And Company" should be added to the partnership name.
- If a CPA forms a partnership with a non-CPA, the CPA is responsible for the non-CPA's violation of the *Code*.
- A CPA in partnership with non-CPAs may sign the firm name to a report and below it affix his/her name with the CPA designation. However, it must be clear that the partnership does not consist entirely of CPAs.
- Although members may share an office, have the same employees, etc., they should not use a letterhead with both their names unless a partnership exists.
- CPA firms that are associated for joint advertising and other purposes should practice under their own names and indicate the association in other ways.

In addition to testing the AICPA *Code of Professional Conduct*, the CPA exam includes ethics and independence questions based on standards of the Securities and Exchange Commission (SEC), the Public Companies Accounting Oversight Board (PCAOB), the Government Accountability Office (these standards are covered in Study Unit 20), Department of Labor (DOL), and the Sarbanes-Oxley Act of 2002. Candidates are also expected to demonstrate an awareness of the International Ethics Standards Board for Accountants (IESBA) and its role in establishing requirements of the International Federation of Accountants (IFAC) *Code of Ethics for Professional Accountants*.

The material may appear imposing at first. However, it is important to recognize that in most cases the standards for independence from the various standard setters are very similar. Thus, use your knowledge of the AICPA *Code of Professional Conduct* as a foundation for your study. For other ethics issues you should focus on those issues that may not be "common sense" to you. With a little effort, you should be able to gain considerable confidence in comprehending the issues.

Stop and review! You have completed the outline for this subunit. Study multiple-choice questions 13 through 17 beginning on page 82.

2.7 OTHER PRONOUNCEMENTS ON PROFESSIONAL RESPONSIBILITIES

1.   Sarbanes-Oxley, PCAOB, and the SEC

Background
The Sarbanes-Oxley Act of 2002 is a response to numerous financial reporting scandals involving large public companies. It contains provisions relating to corporate governance that impose new responsibilities on publicly held companies and their auditors. The Public Company Accounting Oversight Board (PCAOB) was created by the act. The act applies to **issuers** of publicly traded securities subject to federal securities laws. The following section addresses ethical issues of Sarbanes-Oxley, the PCAOB, and the SEC. Most of the independence rules are parallel to the AICPA rules and the focus here is on other issues not addressed in the AICPA *Code of Professional Conduct*.

a.   **Responsibilities and Activities of the Public Company Accounting Oversight Board**

1)   **Register** public accounting firms

2)   **Oversee the audit** of public companies (issuers) that are subject to the securities laws

3)   **Establish or adopt standards** on auditing, quality control, ethics, and independence

4)   **Inspect audit firms** to include three components:

   a)   Examine selected audit and review engagements;

   b)   Evaluate the system of quality; and

   c)   Test audit, supervisory, and quality control procedures.

5)   **Conduct investigations** and disciplinary proceedings concerning, and impose appropriate sanctions upon, registered public accounting firms and associated persons

b.   **Preapproval of Services**

1)   Audit committees ordinarily must preapprove the services performed by accountants (permissible nonaudit services and all audit, review, and attest engagements).

   a)   Approval must be either explicit or in accordance with detailed **policies and procedures**.

   b)   If approval is based on detailed policies and procedures, the audit committee must be informed, and no delegation of its authority to management is allowed.

c.   **Disclosure of Fees**

1)   An issuer must **disclose** in its proxy statement or annual filing **fees paid to the accountant** segregated into four categories:

   a)   Audit,

   b)   Audit-related,

   c)   Tax, and

   d)   All other.

2)   The disclosure is for the 2 most recent years.

d.   **Rotation of Partners**

1)   The lead and concurring (reviewing) audit partners must **rotate** every 5 years, with a 5-year **time-out period**. Other audit partners must rotate every 7 years, with a 2-year time-out.

  e. **Communications with the Audit Committee**

     1) The firm must include

        a) All critical accounting policies and practices;

        b) All material alternative accounting policies and practices within GAAP that were discussed with management; and

        c) Other material written communications with management, such as representations and schedules of unadjusted audit differences.

     2) These communications must be prior to filing the audit report with the SEC.

     3) The firm must discuss the potential effects of the services on the independence and document the discussion.

  f. **Prohibited Nonaudit Services**

     1) The firm is prohibited from offering certain nonaudit services to their attest clients, including

        a) Appraisal and other valuation services

        b) Designing and implementing financial information systems

        c) Internal auditing or actuarial functions

        d) Management services

        e) Human resource services

        f) Bookkeeping

        g) Expert services not pertaining to the audit

        h) Investment banking or advisory services

        i) Broker-dealer services

     2) Preapproved compliance tax engagements are not prohibited.

  g. **Audit Committees**

     1) Each member of the **audit committee** must be an **independent** member of the **board of directors**.

     2) The audit committee must be **directly responsible** for appointing, compensating, and overseeing the work of the auditor.

     3) Audit committees must have at least one member designated as a **financial expert**.

  h. **PCAOB Interim Independence Standards**

     1) The PCAOB adopted AICPA Conduct Rule 101 as well as two pronouncements of the now-defunct Independence Standards Board (ISB). They also issued a number of specific independence rules that apply to registered public accounting firms. However, these are parallel, in most cases, with the AICPA *Code of Professional Conduct*.

  i. **Management's Financial Statement Responsibility**

     1) The CEO and CFO of a public company must provide a statement to accompany the audit report. This statement certifies the appropriateness of the financial statements and disclosures. However, a violation of this requirement must be knowing and intentional.

  j. **Fraud Issues**

     1) Sarbanes-Oxley created a new crime for securities fraud that imposes penalties of fines and imprisonment, extends the statute of limitations on securities fraud claims, and makes it a felony to create or destroy documents to impede a federal investigation.

2.   **Department of Labor**

a.   The DOL requires auditors to be independent for audits of pension funds administered under the Employee Retirement Income Security Act of 1974 (ERISA).

The AICPA Content Specification Outlines (CSOs) require candidates to "demonstrate an awareness" of the international ethics standards. As with other ethics standards, in most cases these parallel the AICPA *Code of Professional Conduct*. The following summary of the standards is presented at the awareness level.

3.   **IFAC *Code of Ethics for Professional Accountants***

a.   Under the auspices of the International Federation of Accountants (IFAC), the **International Ethics Standards Board for Accountants (IESBA)** has issued a *Code of Ethics for Professional Accountants*. This outline addresses fundamental principles followed by standards for accountants in public practice.

b.   **Fundamental Principles**

1)   **Integrity.** A professional accountant must be straightforward and honest in all professional and business relationships.

2)   **Objectivity.** A professional accountant must not allow bias, conflict of interest, or undue influence of others to override professional or business judgments.

3)   **Professional competence and due care.** A professional accountant must maintain professional knowledge and skill at the level required to ensure that a client or employer receives competent professional services based on current developments in practice, legislation, and techniques. (S)he also must act diligently and in accordance with applicable technical and professional standards.

4)   **Confidentiality.** A professional accountant must respect the confidentiality of information acquired as a result of professional and business relationships. Thus, (s)he must not disclose any such information to third parties without proper and specific authority, unless a legal or professional right or duty exists to disclose. Moreover, (s)he must not use the information for the personal advantage of the professional accountant or third parties.

5)   **Professional behavior.** A professional accountant must comply with relevant laws and regulations and avoid any action that discredits the profession.

c.   **Public Practice**

1)   **Threats** to compliance with fundamental principles may arise from many circumstances and relationships. Threats may involve the following:

a)   **Self-interest** (for example, a direct financial interest in the client)

b)   **Self-review** (for example, reporting on the effectiveness of a financial accounting system after designing it)

c)   **Advocacy** (for example, advocating on behalf of a client in litigation)

d)   **Familiarity** (for example, a close or immediate family member of a person on the engagement team is a director of the client)

e)   **Intimidation** (for example, the client states that it will not give a consulting contract to the firm if it disagrees with a choice of an accounting principle)

2)   **Safeguards** eliminate or reduce threats to an acceptable level. Safeguards include the following:

a)   Safeguards created by the profession, legislation, or regulation (for example, education requirements, professional standards, and external review)

b) Safeguards in the work environment (for example, firm-wide safeguards, such as leadership that promotes compliance with fundamental principles, engagement-specific safeguards, such as review of the work by an accountant, and safeguards in the client's systems, such as a governance body that appropriately oversees the firm's work)

d. **Section 210 – Professional Appointment.** Before accepting a new client, a professional accountant must determine whether acceptance would create any threats to compliance with the fundamental principles.

1) The principle of professional competence and due care imposes an obligation on a professional accountant to provide only those services that (s)he is competent to perform.

a) When a professional accountant intends to rely on the advice or work of an expert, (s)he determines whether such reliance is warranted by reputation, expertise, etc.

2) A professional accountant who is asked to replace another must determine whether there are any reasons, professional or otherwise, for not accepting the engagement.

3) An existing accountant may be prevented by confidentiality from discussing the affairs of a client with a proposed accountant.

4) A professional accountant will generally need to obtain the client's permission, preferably in writing, to initiate discussion with an existing accountant.

e. **Section 220 – Conflicts of Interest.** A professional accountant must take reasonable steps to identify circumstances that could pose a conflict of interest.

f. **Section 230 – Second Opinions.** Providing a second opinion on the application of standards or principles to specific circumstances or transactions on behalf of an entity that is not an existing client may create threats to compliance with the fundamental principles.

g. **Section 240 – Fees and Other Types of Remuneration.** Fees should not be so low that it may be difficult to perform the engagement in accordance with applicable technical and professional standards for that price.

1) The client should be aware of the terms of the engagement, the basis on which fees are charged, and which services are covered by the fees.

2) **Contingent fees** may create a self-interest threat to objectivity depending on factors including

a) The nature of the engagement;
b) The range of amounts;
c) The basis for the fee; and,
d) Whether the result is to be reviewed by an independent third party.

3) A contingent fee is prohibited by a firm for an audit engagement or for a nonassurance service provided to an audit client.

4) A professional accountant may receive a **referral fee** or **commission** relating to a client.

a) A professional accountant also may pay a referral fee to obtain a client.
b) Examples of safeguards include

i) Disclosing to the client any such arrangements
ii) Obtaining advance agreement from the client for commission arrangements in connection with the sale by a third party of goods or services to the client

c) Purchasing a firm by making payments to individuals formerly owning the firm does not constitute paying commissions or referral fees.

h. **Section 250 – Marketing Professional Services.** A professional accountant must not bring the profession into disrepute when marketing professional services. (S)he must be honest and truthful and not make exaggerated claims or disparaging references or unsubstantiated comparisons to the work of another.

i. **Section 260 – Gifts and Hospitality.** A professional accountant in public practice, or an immediate or close family member, may be offered gifts and hospitality from a client.

   1) If a reasonable and informed third party would consider them trivial and inconsequential, they may be accepted.

   2) But if the resulting threats to compliance with fundamental principles cannot be eliminated or reduced to an acceptable level through safeguards, a professional accountant must not accept such an offer.

j. **Section 270 – Custody of Client Assets.** A professional accountant must not assume custody of client assets unless permitted by law and in compliance with any additional legal duties imposed on a professional accountant holding such assets.

   1) A professional accountant entrusted with assets belonging to others must

      a) Keep them separate from personal or firm assets
      b) Use them only for the purpose for which they are intended
      c) Be ready to account for them and any income
      d) Comply with all relevant laws and regulations

   2) A professional accountant must make appropriate inquiries about the source of such assets and consider legal and regulatory obligations.

k. **Section 280 – Objectivity–All Services.** A professional accountant must determine when providing any professional service whether there are threats to compliance with the fundamental principle of objectivity resulting from having interests in, or relationships with, a client or its directors, officers, or employees.

l. **Section 290 – Independence: Audits and Reviews**

   1) If a firm is a **network firm**, it must be independent of the audit clients of the other firms within the network.

      a) The judgment as to whether the larger structure is a network is based on all the specific facts and circumstances.

   2) The professional accountant must **document** conclusions regarding compliance with independence requirements and the substance of any relevant discussions that support those conclusions.

   3) Independence from the audit client is required during both the **engagement period** and the **period covered by the financial statements**.

   4) When, as a result of a **merger or acquisition**, an entity becomes a related entity of an audit client, the firm must evaluate interests and relationships with the related entity that could affect its independence and therefore its ability to continue the audit after the merger or acquisition.

   5) If an **inadvertent violation** occurs, it generally does not compromise independence, provided the firm has appropriate quality control policies and procedures and the violation is corrected promptly.

   6) In general, the independence rules for **financial interests**, including loans and guarantees, stated by the IFAC Code of Ethics are similar to those of the AICPA.

   7) A **close business relationship** between a firm, a member of the audit team, or a member of that individual's immediate family and the audit client or its management arises from a commercial relationship or common financial interest and may create self-interest or intimidation threats. Unless any financial interest is immaterial and the business relationship is insignificant, independence is impaired.

a) The **purchase of goods and services** from an audit client by the firm, a member of the audit team, or a member of that individual's immediate family does not generally create a threat to independence if the transaction is in the normal course of business and at arm's length.

8) **Family and personal relationships** between a member of the audit team and a director or officer or certain employees (depending on their role) of the audit client may create self-interest, familiarity, or intimidation threats. The existence and significance of any threats will depend on a number of factors, including the individual's responsibilities on the audit team, the role of the family member or other individual within the client, and the closeness of the relationship.

9) Familiarity or intimidation threats may be created if a director or officer of the client, or an employee in a position to exert significant influence over the preparation of the client's accounting records or the financial statements, has been a **member of the audit team or partner of the firm**.

10) The **lending of staff** by a firm to an audit client may create a self-review threat. Such assistance may be given, but only for a short time and if the firm's personnel do not provide impermissible services or assume management responsibilities.

11) Self-interest, self-review, or familiarity threats may be created if a member of the audit team has **recently served** as a director, officer, or employee of the audit client. This would be the case when, for example, a member of the audit team has to evaluate elements of the financial statements for which the member of the audit team had prepared the accounting records while with the client.

12) **Serving as a director or officer** of an audit client impairs independence.

13) Familiarity and self-interest threats are created by using the same **senior personnel** on an audit engagement over a long period.

14) Firms provide to their audit clients a range of **nonassurance services**. Providing non-assurance services may, however, create threats to the independence of the firm or members of the audit team.

   a) If a firm were to assume **management responsibility** for an audit client, the threats created would be so significant that no safeguards could reduce the threats to an acceptable level.

   b) Providing an audit client with accounting and bookkeeping services, such as preparing accounting records or financial statements, creates a self-review threat when the firm subsequently audits the financial statements.

      i) But accounting and bookkeeping services, which would otherwise not be permitted, may be provided to audit clients in **emergency** or other unusual situations when it is impractical for the audit client to make other arrangements.

15) **Tax return preparation** does not generally create a threat to independence if management takes responsibility for the returns, including any significant judgments made.

   a) **Tax planning or other tax advisory services** may result in a self-review threat if the advice will affect matters to be reflected in the financial statements.

      i) If the effectiveness of the tax advice depends on a material, doubtful accounting treatment or presentation in the financial statements, the self-review threat would be so significant that no safeguards could reduce the threat to an acceptable level.

16) The provision of **internal audit services** to an audit client creates a self-review threat to independence if the firm uses the internal audit work in the course of a subsequent external audit. Performing a significant part of the client's internal audit activities increases the possibility that firm personnel providing internal audit services will assume management responsibility.

17) Providing services to an audit client involving the **design or implementation of IT systems** that (a) form a significant part of the internal control over financial reporting or (b) generate information that is significant to the client's accounting records or financial statements on which the firm will express an opinion creates a self-review threat.

18) **Litigation support services** may include activities such as acting as an expert witness, calculating estimated damages or other amounts that might become receivable or payable, and assistance with document management and retrieval. These services may create a self-review or advocacy threat.

19) Acting in an **advocacy** role for an audit client in resolving a dispute or litigation when the amounts involved are material to the financial statements on which the firm will express an opinion would create advocacy and self-review threats so significant that no safeguards could reduce the threat to an acceptable level.

20) The firm may generally provide such **recruiting services** as reviewing the professional qualifications of a number of applicants and providing advice on their suitability for the post. In addition, the firm may interview candidates and advise on a candidate's competence for financial accounting, administrative, or control positions.

21) Providing **corporate finance services** may create advocacy and self-review threats.

   a) If the effectiveness of corporate finance advice depends on a **material, doubtful accounting treatment or presentation** in the financial statements, the self-review threat would be so significant that no safeguards could reduce the threat to an acceptable level.

22) When the total **fees** from an audit client represent a large proportion of the total fees of the firm expressing the audit opinion (or a partner or office), the dependence on that client and concern about losing the client creates a self-interest or intimidation threat.

   a) A self-interest threat may be created if **overdue fees** remain unpaid for a long time, especially if a significant part is not paid before the issue of the audit report for the following year. Generally, the firm is expected to require payment of such fees before such audit report is issued.

23) A key audit partner must not be **evaluated on or compensated** based on that partner's success in selling non-assurance services to the partner's audit client.

24) Accepting **gifts or hospitality** from an audit client may create self-interest and familiarity threats. If a firm or a member of the audit team accepts gifts or hospitality, unless the value is trivial and inconsequential, the threats created would be so significant that no safeguards could reduce the threats to an acceptable level.

25) When the firm and the client's management are placed in adversarial positions by **actual or threatened litigation**, affecting management's willingness to make complete disclosures, self-interest and intimidation threats are created.

Stop and review! You have completed the outline for this subunit. Study multiple-choice questions 18 through 31 beginning on page 84.

CPA who is **not** in public practice is obligated to
w which of the following rules of conduct?

A. Independence.

3. Integrity and objectivity.

C. Contingent fees.

D. Commissions.

Answer (B) is correct. *(CPA, adapted)*
REQUIRED: The applicable rule of conduct applicable to a CPA not in public practice.
DISCUSSION: Under Conduct Rule 102, *Integrity and Objectivity*, all members must maintain objectivity and integrity, be free of conflicts of interest, not knowingly misrepresent facts, and not subordinate his/her judgment to others when performing professional services.
Answer (A) is incorrect. Conduct Rule 101, *Independence*, applies only to CPAs in public practice. Answer (C) is incorrect. Conduct Rule 302, *Contingent Fees*, applies only to CPAs in public practice. Answer (D) is incorrect. Conduct Rule 503, *Commissions and Referral Fees*, applies only in part (Referrals) to all members and in part (Commissions) to CPAs in public practice.

2. Under the *Code of Professional Conduct* of the AICPA, which of the following is required to be independent in fact and appearance when discharging professional responsibilities?

A. A CPA in public practice providing tax and management advisory services.

B. A CPA in public practice providing auditing and other attestation services.

C. A CPA **not** in public practice.

D. All CPAs.

Answer (B) is correct. *(CPA, adapted)*
REQUIRED: The person(s) required to be independent in fact and appearance.
DISCUSSION: According to the Principles of Professional Conduct, *Article IV – Objectivity and Independence*, "A member in public practice should be independent in fact and appearance when providing audit and other attestation services."
Answer (A) is incorrect. A CPA in public practice providing tax and management advisory services need not be independent unless attestation services also are performed. Answer (C) is incorrect. A CPA not in public practice need not be independent. Answer (D) is incorrect. All CPAs do not provide attestation services in public practice.

2.2 Independence

3. Under the AICPA's conceptual framework for independence, the member-client relationship is evaluated to determine whether independence in fact and appearance is jeopardized. This is considered

A. A sufficiency of safeguards approach.

B. An avoidance approach.

C. A risk-based approach.

D. A professional skepticism approach.

Answer (C) is correct. *(Publisher, adapted)*
REQUIRED: The term associated with the AICPA's conceptual framework approach to considering member independence.
DISCUSSION: The member assesses the risks to independence of the circumstances and then considers the sufficiency of safeguards to mitigate those risks. If the safeguards are sufficient, then the member can maintain independence in both mind and appearance.
Answer (A) is incorrect. Although safeguards mitigate the risk, this is not the term associated with the approach to considering member independence. Answer (B) is incorrect. Although members should avoid the lack of independence where required, this is not the term associated with the approach to considering member independence. Answer (D) is incorrect. Although members should exercise professional skepticism, this is not the term associated with the approach to considering member independence.

4. The concept of materiality is **least** important to an auditor when considering the

A. Adequacy of disclosure of a client's illegal act.

B. Discovery of weaknesses in a client's internal control.

C. Effects of a direct financial interest in the client on the CPA's independence.

D. Decision whether to use positive or negative confirmations of accounts receivable.

Answer (C) is correct. *(CPA, adapted)*
REQUIRED: The item with respect to which materiality is least important.
DISCUSSION: Independence is impaired if a CPA has any direct financial interest in a client. Whether this direct financial interest is material is irrelevant. The test of materiality is applied, however, if the financial interest is indirect.
Answer (A) is incorrect. In considering the effect of an illegal act on the financial statements and its implications for other aspects of the audit, materiality is important. Answer (B) is incorrect. An auditor who is considering internal control in a financial statement audit must make materiality judgments. Answer (D) is incorrect. Materiality is one factor considered when deciding between positive or negative confirmations.

5. According to the profession's ethical standards, an auditor is considered independent in which of the following instances?

A. The auditor is the officially appointed stock transfer agent of a client.

B. The auditor's checking account, which is fully insured by a federal agency, is held at a client financial institution.

C. The client sponsors an employee benefit plan in which the auditor participates.

D. The client is the only tenant in a commercial building owned by the auditor.

Answer (B) is correct. *(CPA, adapted)*
    REQUIRED: The circumstance in which the CPA is considered independent.
    DISCUSSION: A CPA's independence is not impaired w respect to a financial institution if checking accounts, savings accounts, or certificates of deposit are fully insured. Moreove uninsured amounts do not impair independence if they are immaterial.
    Answer (A) is incorrect. Serving as a stock transfer or escrow agent, registrar, general counsel, or its equivalent involves performing management functions or making management decisions for the attest client. Answer (C) is incorrect. The auditor's independence is impaired with regard t the plan and its sponsor. Answer (D) is incorrect. Leasing property to a client results in an indirect financial interest in that client.

6. Under the ethical standards of the profession, which of the following investments by a CPA in a corporate client is an indirect financial interest?

A. An investment held in a retirement plan of which the CPA is a trustee.

B. An investment held in a blind trust.

C. An investment held through a regulated mutual fund.

D. An investment held through participation in an investment club.

Answer (C) is correct. *(CPA, adapted)*
    REQUIRED: The indirect financial interest.
    DISCUSSION: Independence is impaired if, during the period of the professional engagement, a covered member had a direct or material indirect financial interest in the client. Ownership of fund shares is a direct financial interest in the fund. Underlying investments in the fund are indirect interests.
    Answer (A) is incorrect. Participation in a retirement plan constitutes a direct financial interest in the plan. Investments of a plan sponsored by the member's firm are direct interest of the firm. Investments of a plan controlled or supervised by the member (e.g., as a trustee) are the member's direct interests. Otherwise, they are indirect interests of the members. Answer (B) is incorrect. A blind trust and its investments are direct interests of the grantor. The investments will revert to the grantor. Answer (D) is incorrect. One kind of direct financial interest is a financial interest beneficially owned through an intermediary (e.g., and investment club) when the beneficiary has the authority to participate in the intermediary's investment decisions. In an investment club, the members make investment decisions.

7. Kar, CPA, is a staff auditor participating in the audit engagement of Fort, Inc. Which of the following circumstances most likely impairs Kar's independence?

A. During the period of the professional engagement, Fort gives Kar tickets to a football game worth $25.

B. Kar owns stock in a corporation that Fort's 401(k) plan also invests in. These interests are immaterial.

C. Kar's friend, an employee of another local accounting firm, prepares Fort's tax returns.

D. Kar's sibling is the director of internal auditing for Fort.

Answer (D) is correct. *(CPA, adapted)*
    REQUIRED: The circumstances that most likely impair a CPA's independence.
    DISCUSSION: Independence is impaired if an individual participating in the audit engagement has a close relative who has a key position with the client. A close relative is a parent, sibling, or independent child. A key position is one in which an individual has primary responsibility for significant accounting functions that support material components of the financial statements, has primary responsibility for the preparation of the financial statements, or has the ability to exercise influence over the contents of the financial statements. Thus, because Kar's sibling is the director of internal auditing for Fort, Inc., auditor independence is impaired.
    Answer (A) is incorrect. Acceptance of a gift impairs the member's independence unless its value is clearly insignificant to the recipient. However, it is likely that a $25 gift is insignificant to Kar. Answer (B) is incorrect. If the respective investments are not material, independence is not impaired. Answer (C) is incorrect. The position of a friend, in this case, someone who is not in a key position and is not a close relative or member of the immediate family, has no effect on the CPA's independence.

8. A violation of the profession's ethical standards most likely would have occurred when a CPA

   A. Expressed an unmodified opinion on the current year's financial statements when fees for the prior year's audit were unpaid.

   B. Recommended a controller's position description with candidate specifications to an audit client.

   C. Purchased a CPA firm's practice of monthly write-ups for a percentage of fees to be received over a 3-year period.

   D. Made arrangements with a financial institution to collect notes issued by a client in payment of fees due for the current year's audit.

Answer (A) is correct. *(CPA, adapted)*
   REQUIRED: The violation of the ethical standards.
   DISCUSSION: Audit fees that are long past due take on the characteristics of a loan under Conduct Rule 101. Independence is impaired if billed or unbilled fees, or a note arising from the fees, for client services rendered more than 1 year prior to the current year's report date, remain unpaid when the current year's report is issued. However, this ruling does not apply if the client is in bankruptcy. Moreover, long overdue fees do not preclude the CPA from performing services not requiring independence.
   Answer (B) is incorrect. A CPA will not impair independence by recommending job position descriptions. However, the CPA will be in violation if (s)he is responsible for screening candidates or making decisions to hire. Answer (C) is incorrect. No pronouncement prohibits purchase of a bookkeeping firm for a percentage of fees. Answer (D) is incorrect. The AICPA has ruled that this practice does not violate the *Code*.

2.3 Integrity and Objectivity

9. Which of the following acts by a CPA who is **not** in public practice will most likely be considered a violation of the ethical standards of the profession?

   A. Using the CPA designation without disclosing employment status in connection with financial statements issued for external use by the CPA's employer.

   B. A CPA firm indicates on its letterhead that other CPA firms are correspondents rather than members of an association.

   C. A member sells a newsletter bearing his/her name.

   D. Compiling the CPA's employer's financial statements and making reference to the CPA's lack of independence.

Answer (A) is correct. *(CPA, adapted)*
   REQUIRED: The action violating ethical standards.
   DISCUSSION: A member not in public practice who uses the CPA designation in a manner implying that (s)he is independent of the employer has committed a knowing misrepresentation of fact in violation of Conduct Rule 102.
   Answer (B) is incorrect. CPA firms are not allowed to use a firm name indicating an association. The public may believe a partnership exists when it does not. Answer (C) is incorrect. A member may sell a newsletter bearing his/her name if the member writes it and ensures that those promoting it do not make statements about the author or his/her writings that violate the Conduct Rule on advertising and other forms of solicitation. Answer (D) is incorrect. An accountant may compile a nonissuer's financial statements if (s)he issues the appropriate report. The lack of independence should be disclosed.

2.4 Professional Standards

10. According to the standards of the profession, which of the following activities may be required in exercising due professional care?

	Consulting with Experts	Obtaining Specialty Accreditation
A.	Yes	Yes
B.	Yes	No
C.	No	Yes
D.	No	No

Answer (B) is correct. *(CPA, adapted)*
   REQUIRED: The activity(ies) that may be required in exercising due care.
   DISCUSSION: A CPA should undertake only those services that (s)he reasonably expects to complete with professional competence and should exercise due professional care in performing those services. Additional research or consultation with others may be necessary to gain sufficient competence to complete a service in accordance with professional standards. However, professional standards do not require specialty accreditation, although many CPAs choose to specialize in specific services.

11. According to the profession's ethical standards, which of the following events may justify a departure from an established accounting principle?

	New Legislation	Evolution of a New Form of Business Transaction
A.	No	Yes
B.	Yes	No
C.	Yes	Yes
D.	No	No

Answer (C) is correct. *(CPA, adapted)*
REQUIRED: The event(s), if any, that may justify departure from an established accounting principle.
DISCUSSION: In general, strict compliance with accounting principles is required. However, Conduct Rule 203 recognizes that, due to unusual circumstances, adhering to GAAP may cause financial statements to be misleading. New legislation and the evolution of a new form of business transaction are events that may justify departure from an established accounting principle.

2.5 Responsibilities to Clients

12. A CPA is permitted to disclose confidential client information without the consent of the client to

I.   Another CPA firm if the information concerns suspected tax return irregularities

II.   A state CPA society voluntary peer review board

    A. I only.

    B. II only.

    C. Both I and II.

    D. Neither I nor II.

Answer (B) is correct. *(CPA, adapted)*
REQUIRED: The event(s) that allow disclosure of confidential client data without the client's consent.
DISCUSSION: Under Conduct Rule 301, *Confidential Client Information*, a CPA may reveal confidential information without the client's permission for a state board- or state society-sponsored peer review. Identifying information revealed to the review team is precluded from disclosure. However, a CPA may not disclose information to another CPA firm without the client's permission or unless pursuant to a valid subpoena.

2.6 Other Responsibilities

13. According to the ethical standards of the profession, which of the following acts is generally prohibited?

    A. Purchasing a product from a third party and reselling it to a client.

    B. Writing a financial management newsletter promoted and sold by a publishing company.

    C. Accepting a commission for recommending a product to an audit client.

    D. Accepting engagements obtained through the efforts of third parties.

Answer (C) is correct. *(CPA, adapted)*
REQUIRED: The prohibited act.
DISCUSSION: Conduct Rule 503, *Commissions and Referral Fees*, prohibits a member in public practice from recommending any product or service to a client when the firm performs (1) an audit or review of financial statements, (2) a compilation of a financial statement that is reasonably expected to be used by a third party if the report does not disclose the CPA's lack of independence, or (3) an examination of prospective financial information for that client.
Answer (A) is incorrect. Resale of products to clients is permitted. The profit is not a commission. Answer (B) is incorrect. If the CPA reasonably concludes that the newsletter does not contain false, misleading, or deceptive information, the arrangement is not an ethics violation. Answer (D) is incorrect. Rule 502 permits accepting engagements obtained through the efforts of third parties.

14. With respect to records in a CPA's possession, the *Code of Professional Conduct* provides that

   A. An auditor may retain client-provided records, after a demand is made for them, if fees due with respect to a completed engagement have not been paid.

   B. Supporting records that contain journal entries not reflected in the client's records need not be furnished to the client upon request.

   C. Extensive analytical review schedules prepared by the client at the auditor's request are working papers that belong to the auditor and need not be furnished to the client upon request.

   D. The auditor who returns client records must comply with any subsequent requests to again provide such information.

Answer (C) is correct. *(Publisher, adapted)*
REQUIRED: The true statement regarding records in the CPA's possession.
DISCUSSION: A member's working papers are the member's property, not client records, and need not be made available. However, the PCAOB's Auditing Standards No. 3, *Audit Documentation*, relating to public clients is silent on property rights in working papers. Moreover, a statute, regulation, or contract may state otherwise.
Answer (A) is incorrect. After a demand is made for them, client-provided records must be returned even if fees have not been paid. Answer (B) is incorrect. Supporting records containing client financial information not reflected in the client's books must be returned to the client upon request if the engagement is complete. Answer (D) is incorrect. Once the member has complied with the requirements for the return of client records, (s)he has no further obligation to provide such information.

15. Which of the following statements is(are) true regarding a CPA employee of a CPA firm taking copies of information contained in client files when the CPA leaves the firm?

   I. A CPA leaving a firm may take copies of information contained in client files to assist another firm in serving that client.

   II. A CPA leaving a firm may take copies of information contained in client files as a method of gaining technical expertise.

   A. I only.

   B. II only.

   C. Both I and II.

   D. Neither I nor II.

Answer (D) is correct. *(CPA, adapted)*
REQUIRED: The act(s), if any, considered discreditable to the profession.
DISCUSSION: Conduct Rule 501 states that a member shall not commit an act discreditable to the profession. After the relationship of a member who is not an owner of the firm is terminated, the member may not take or retain copies or originals from the firm's client files or proprietary information without permission.

16. According to the ethical standards of the profession, which of the following acts generally is prohibited?

   A. Accepting a contingent fee for representing a client in connection with obtaining a private letter from the Internal Revenue Service.

   B. Retaining client-provided records after the client has demanded their return.

   C. Revealing client tax returns to a prospective purchaser of the CPA's practice.

   D. Issuing a modified report explaining the CPA's failure to follow a governmental regulatory agency's standards when conducting an attest service for a client.

Answer (B) is correct. *(CPA, adapted)*
REQUIRED: The act generally prohibited by the profession's ethical standards.
DISCUSSION: Retention of client-provided records after the client has demanded their return is an act discreditable to the profession. Even if the state in which a member practices grants a lien on certain records, the ethical standard is still applicable.
Answer (A) is incorrect. A contingent fee for representing a client in connection with obtaining a private letter ruling from the IRS is permitted. Answer (C) is incorrect. The disclosure of confidential information in the review of a member's professional practice is not prohibited under a purchase, sale, or merger of the practice. However, appropriate precautions (e.g., a written confidentiality agreement) should be taken so that the prospective buyer does not disclose any confidential client information. Answer (D) is incorrect. Failure to substantially follow such requirements is an act discreditable to the profession, unless the member discloses in his or her report that such requirements were not followed and the reasons therefor. Not following such requirements could require the member to modify his or her report.

17. Which of the following is required for a CPA firm to designate itself as "Members of the American Institute of Certified Public Accountants" on its letterhead?

    A. All CPA owners must be members.

    B. The owners whose names appear in the firm name must be members.

    C. At least one of the owners must be a member.

    D. The firm must be a dues-paying member.

Answer (A) is correct. *(CPA, adapted)*
    REQUIRED: The requirement for a CPA firm to use the designation, "Members of the AICPA."
    DISCUSSION: Conduct Rule 505, *Form of Organization and Name*, states that a firm may not use the quoted designation unless all of its CPA owners are members of the AICPA.
    Answer (B) is incorrect. All CPA owners, not just certain owners, must be AICPA members. Answer (C) is incorrect. All CPA owners must be members. Answer (D) is incorrect. The CPA owners, not the firm, must be members of the AICPA.

2.7   Other Pronouncements on Professional Responsibilities

18. According to SEC independence regulations,

    A. All audit partners must rotate every 5 years.

    B. Preapproval of accountants' services may be in accord with detailed policies and procedures rather than explicit.

    C. The issuer must disclose only those fees paid to the accountant for audit work.

    D. No partner may sell nonaudit services to the client during the audit.

Answer (B) is correct. *(Publisher, adapted)*
    REQUIRED: The true statement about SEC independence regulations.
    DISCUSSION: Audit committees ordinarily must preapprove the services performed by accountants (permissible nonaudit services and all audit, review, and attest engagements). Approval must be either explicit or in accordance with detailed policies and procedures. If approval is based on detailed policies and procedures, the audit committee must be informed, and no delegation of its authority to management is allowed.
    Answer (A) is incorrect. The lead and concurring (reviewing) audit partners must rotate every 5 years, with a 5-year time-out period. Other audit partners must rotate every 7 years, with a 2-year time-out. Answer (C) is incorrect. An issuer must disclose in its proxy statement or annual filing fees paid to the accountant segregated into four categories: (1) audit, (2) audit-related, (3) tax, and (4) all other. Answer (D) is incorrect. An accountant is not independent if, during the audit and the period of the engagement, any audit partner (excluding specialty partners such as tax partners) earns or receives compensation for selling services (excluding audit, review, or attest services) to the client.

19. According to the PCAOB, an accounting firm's independence is **least** likely to be impaired if the firm

    A. Provides a service to the audit client for a contingent fee.

    B. Receives a commission from the audit client.

    C. Has an audit client that employs a former firm professional.

    D. Provides tax services to a person in a financial reporting oversight role at the audit client.

Answer (C) is correct. *(Publisher, adapted)*
    REQUIRED: The circumstances least likely to impair an accounting firm's independence.
    DISCUSSION: Firm independence is impaired by a client's employment of a former firm professional that could adversely affect the audit unless safeguards are established. Pre-change safeguards include removal from the audit of those negotiating with the client, and post-change safeguards include possibly modifying the audit plan.
    Answer (A) is incorrect. A firm is not independent of its client if the firm or any affiliate, during the audit and engagement period, provides any service or product to the client for a contingent fee or a commission, or receives from the client a contingent fee or commission. Answer (B) is incorrect. A firm is not independent of its client if the firm or any affiliate, during the audit and engagement period, provides any service or product to the client for a contingent fee or a commission, or receives from the client a contingent fee or commission. Answer (D) is incorrect. A registered public accounting firm is not independent of its audit client if the firm or any affiliate, during the professional engagement period, provides any tax service to a person in a financial reporting oversight role at the audit client.

20. According to the PCAOB, an accounting firm is most likely to be independent of its audit client if

    A. A reasonable investor would conclude that it is not objective and impartial.

    B. The firm's audit professional is responsible for internal control over financial reporting.

    C. The firm's audit professional implemented the client's internal control over financial reporting.

    D. The firm recommended an aggressive tax position to the client that is more likely than not to be legally allowed.

Answer (D) is correct. *(Publisher, adapted)*
    REQUIRED: The circumstances in which an accounting firm is most likely to be independent.
    DISCUSSION: A firm is not independent of its audit client if, during the audit and engagement period, it provides any nonaudit service related to marketing, planning, or expressing an opinion in favor of the tax treatment of aggressive tax-position transactions for the purpose of tax avoidance. However, this Rule does not apply if the tax treatment is at least more likely than not to be allowable under tax law.
    Answer (A) is incorrect. An auditor is not independent if (s)he is not, or a reasonable investor would conclude that (s)he is not, able to be objective and impartial. Answer (B) is incorrect. Guiding principles regarding independence include whether the auditor assumes a management role or audits his/her own work. Thus, an auditor is not independent if, for example, the auditor is responsible for internal control over financial reporting or had designed or implemented it. Answer (C) is incorrect. Designing or implementing internal control over financial reporting impairs independence.

21. Under the IFAC's *Code of Ethics for Professional Accountants*, fundamental principles include

    I.   Objectivity and independence
    II. Professional behavior
    III. Confidentiality
    IV. The public interest

    A. I and II only.

    B. II and III only.

    C. III and IV only.

    D. I, II, III and IV.

Answer (B) is correct. *(Publisher, adapted)*
    REQUIRED: The fundamental principles of the IFAC's *Code of Ethics for Professional Accountants*.
    DISCUSSION: Professional behavior and confidentiality are fundamental principles. According to the principle of professional behavior, a professional accountant must comply with relevant laws and regulations and avoid any action that discredits the profession. According to the principle of confidentiality, a professional accountant must respect the confidentiality of information acquired as a result of professional and business relationships. Thus, (s)he must not disclose any such information to third parties without proper and specific authority, unless a legal or professional right or duty exists to disclose. Moreover, (s)he must not use the information for the personal advantage of the professional accountant or third parties.
    Answer (A) is incorrect. Objectivity and independence is a principle of the AICPA *Code of Professional Conduct*. All members should maintain objectivity and be free of conflicts of interest. A member in public practice should be independent in fact and appearance when providing attestation services. A member not in public practice need not be independent. Answer (C) is incorrect. The public interest is a principle of the AICPA *Code of Professional Conduct*. All members should act to benefit the public interest, honor the public trust, and demonstrate commitment to professionalism. The AICPA adopted the ethical standards because a distinguishing mark of a profession is an acceptance of responsibility to the public. Answer (D) is incorrect. Objectivity and independence and the public interest are principles of the AICPA *Code of Professional Conduct*.

22. The IFAC's *Code of Ethics for Professional Accountants* considers threats to compliance with fundamental principles and safeguards that eliminate or reduce them. Threats may involve

    A. Self-interest, such as advocacy for a client.

    B. Self-review, such as leadership that promotes compliance.

    C. Familiarity, such as an immediate relative's service as a director of the client.

    D. Intimidation, such as oversight by a governance body.

Answer (C) is correct. *(Publisher, adapted)*
    REQUIRED: The threat to compliance with fundamental principles.
    DISCUSSION: Threats involve self-interest, self-review, familiarity, intimidation, and advocacy. For example, a familiarity threat arises when a close or immediate family member of a person on the engagement team is a director of the client.
    Answer (A) is incorrect. A self-interest threat arises from a direct financial interest in the client. Answer (B) is incorrect. For example, a self-review threat arises when the designer of a financial accounting system reports on its effectiveness. Answer (D) is incorrect. Oversight by a governance body is a safeguard in the client's systems.

23. According to the IFAC's *Code of Ethics for Professional Accountants* section on professional appointment,

    A. The existing accountant must discuss relevant matters with the proposed accountant.

    B. The fundamental principle of integrity requires the accountant to provide only the services for which (s)he has the needed expertise.

    C. The client must not provide a second opinion to an existing client.

    D. An accountant generally needs the client's permission to communicate with the current accountant.

Answer (D) is correct. *(Publisher, adapted)*
    REQUIRED: The ethical obligation related to professional appointment.
    DISCUSSION: Before accepting a new client, a professional accountant must determine whether acceptance would create any threats to compliance with the fundamental principles. Thus, a professional accountant will generally need to obtain the client's permission, preferably in writing, to initiate discussion with an existing accountant.
    Answer (A) is incorrect. An existing accountant may be prevented by confidentiality from discussing the affairs of a client with a proposed accountant. Answer (B) is incorrect. The principle of professional competence and due care imposes an obligation on a professional accountant to provide only those services that (s)he is competent to perform. Answer (C) is incorrect. Providing a second opinion on the application of standards or principles to specific circumstances or transactions on behalf of an entity not an existing client may create threats to compliance with the fundamental principles.

24. According to the IFAC's *Code of Ethics for Professional Accountants*,

    A. A contingent fee arrangement may create a self-interest threat.

    B. An auditor may not receive a referral fee.

    C. An auditor may not receive a commission.

    D. Fees may be too high but not too low.

Answer (A) is correct. *(Publisher, adapted)*
    REQUIRED: The true statement on auditor's compensation.
    DISCUSSION: Contingent fees may create a self-interest threat to objectivity depending on factors including (1) the nature of the engagement, (2) the range of amounts, (3) the basis for the fee, and (4) whether the result is to be reviewed by an independent third party.
    Answer (B) is incorrect. An accountant may receive or pay a referral fee given adequate safeguards, such as disclosure to the client. Answer (C) is incorrect. An accountant may receive a commission obtaining advance agreement from the client for commission arrangements in connection with the sale by a third party of goods or services to the client. The AICPA *Code* prohibits commissions related to audit and attest clients. Answer (D) is incorrect. Fees should not be so low that it may be difficult to perform the engagement in accordance with applicable technical and professional standards for that price.

25. Under the IFAC's *Code of Ethics for Professional Accountants*, independence is most likely impaired when

    A. An immediate family member of a member of the audit team is a director of the client.

    B. The firm and the client have an insignificant business relationship involving an immaterial financial interest.

    C. The firm prepares a client's tax returns.

    D. The firm purchases goods and services from the client.

Answer (A) is correct. *(Publisher, adapted)*
    REQUIRED: The most likely impairment of independence.
    DISCUSSION: When an immediate family member of a member of the audit team is (1) a director or officer of the audit client, (2) an employee in a position to exert significant influence over the preparation of the client's accounting records or financial statements, or (3) in such a position during any period covered by the engagement or the financial statements, the threat to independence can only be reduced to an acceptable level by removing the individual from the audit team.
    Answer (B) is incorrect. A close business relationship between a firm, a member of the audit team, or a member of that individual's immediate family, and the audit client or its management, arises from a commercial relationship or common financial interest and may create self-interest or intimidation threats. Unless any financial interest is immaterial and the business relationship is insignificant, independence is impaired. Answer (C) is incorrect. Tax return preparation does not generally create a threat to independence if management takes responsibility for the returns including any significant judgments made. Answer (D) is incorrect. The purchase of goods and services from an audit client by the firm, or a member of the audit team, or a member of that individual's immediate family, does not generally create a threat to independence if the transaction is in the normal course of business and at arm's length.

26. Under the IFAC's *Code of Ethics for Professional Accountants*,

- A. An accountant, whether or not in public practice, may not accept a gift from a client.

- B. An accountant in public practice may accept an inconsequential gift from a client.

- C. A close relative of an accountant not in public practice may not accept a gift from a client.

- D. An immediate family member of an accountant, whether or not in public practice, may not accept a gift from a client.

Answer (B) is correct. *(Publisher, adapted)*
REQUIRED: The acceptability of a gift from a client.
DISCUSSION: A professional accountant in public practice, or an immediate or close family member, may be offered gifts and hospitality from a client. If a reasonable and informed third party would consider them trivial and inconsequential, they may be accepted. But if the resulting threats to compliance with fundamental principles cannot be eliminated or reduced to an acceptable level through safeguards, a professional accountant must not accept such an offer.

27. Under the IFAC's *Code of Ethics for Professional Accountants*, independence is **least** likely to be impaired when

- A. The firm charges a client a contingent fee for an audit.

- B. The firm charges an audit client a contingent fee for a nonassurance service.

- C. The firm provides financial services that depend for their effectiveness on a material, doubtful accounting treatment.

- D. The firm's overdue fees from an audit client are a small part of the firm's total fees.

Answer (D) is correct. *(Publisher, adapted)*
REQUIRED: The least likely impairment of independence.
DISCUSSION: When the total fees from an audit client represent a large proportion of the total fees of the firm expressing the audit opinion (or a partner or officer), the dependence on that client and concern about losing the client creates a self-interest or intimidation threat. Safeguards include an external quality control review or consulting a third party (e.g., a regulator or a professional accountant) on key audit decisions. A self-interest threat may be created if overdue fees remain unpaid for a long time, especially if a significant part is not paid before the issue of the audit report for the following year. However, a small amount of overdue fees for a short period of time does not likely create a problem.
Answer (A) is incorrect. A contingent fee charged by a firm in respect of (1) an audit engagement or (2) a nonassurance service provided to an audit client creates a self-interest threat that is so significant that no safeguards could reduce the threat to an acceptable level. Answer (B) is incorrect. A contingent fee charged by a firm in respect of (1) an audit engagement or (2) a nonassurance service provided to an audit client creates a self-interest threat that is so significant that no safeguards could reduce the threat to an acceptable level. Answer (C) is incorrect. If the effectiveness of corporate finance advice depends on a material, doubtful accounting treatment or presentation in the financial statements, the self-review threat would be so significant that no safeguards could reduce the threat to an acceptable level.

28. When Congress passed the Sarbanes-Oxley Act of 2002, it imposed greater regulation on public companies and their auditors and required increased accountability. Which of the following is **not** a provision of the act?

- A. Executives must certify the appropriateness of the financial statements.

- B. The act provides criminal penalties for fraud.

- C. Auditors may not provide specific nonaudit services for their audit clients.

- D. Audit firms must be rotated on a periodic basis.

Answer (D) is correct. *(Publisher, adapted)*
REQUIRED: The provision not included in the Sarbanes-Oxley Act.
DISCUSSION: The act requires rotation of the lead audit or coordinating partner and the reviewing partner on audits of public clients every 5 years. However, the act does not require the rotation of audit firms.
Answer (A) is incorrect. The CEO and CFO of a public company must provide a statement to accompany the audit report. This statement certifies the appropriateness of the financial statements and disclosures. However, a violation of this requirement must be knowing and intentional. Answer (B) is incorrect. The act creates a new crime for securities fraud with penalties of fines and imprisonment, extends the statute of limitations on securities fraud claims, and makes it a felony to create or destroy documents to impede a federal investigation. Answer (C) is incorrect. The act makes it unlawful for a registered public accounting firm to perform certain nonaudit services for audit clients, for example, bookkeeping, systems design, management functions, or any other service the Public Company Accounting Oversight Board (PCAOB) determines by regulation to be impermissible.

29. The Sarbanes-Oxley Act of 2002 has strengthened auditor independence by requiring that management of a public company

- A. Include only independent persons on the board of directors.
- B. Report the nature of disagreements with former auditors.
- C. Select auditors through audit committees.
- D. Hire a different CPA firm from the one that performs the audit to perform the company's tax work.

Answer (C) is correct. *(CPA, adapted)*
REQUIRED: The Sarbanes-Oxley requirement that strengthened auditor independence.
DISCUSSION: The audit committee must hire and pay the external auditors. Such affiliation inhibits management from changing auditors to gain acceptance of a questionable accounting method. Also, a successor auditor must inquire of the predecessor before accepting an engagement.
Answer (A) is incorrect. The audit committee must include only independent members. Answer (B) is incorrect. Reporting disagreements with auditors is a long-time SEC requirement. Answer (D) is incorrect. The act does not restrict who may perform tax work. Other engagements, such as outsourcing internal auditing or certain consulting services, are limited.

30. Which of the following most likely is an allowable service that an auditor may provide to a public client?

- A. Internal audit outsourcing.
- B. Legal services.
- C. Management consulting services.
- D. Tax compliance services.

Answer (D) is correct. *(Publisher, adapted)*
REQUIRED: The type of service that an audit firm most likely may provide to an audit client.
DISCUSSION: The Sarbanes-Oxley Act prohibits audit firms from providing consulting, legal, and internal auditing services to public audit clients. However, the PCAOB may, on a case-by-case basis, create exemptions from the prohibition against providing certain nonaudit services at the time of the audit. Audit firms may provide conventional tax planning and compliance services to public audit clients.
Answer (A) is incorrect. Internal audit outsourcing is a service that may not be provided to public audit clients. Answer (B) is incorrect. Legal services are services that may not be provided to public audit clients. Answer (C) is incorrect. Management consulting services are services that may not be provided to public audit clients.

31. Inspections performed by the PCAOB focus on quality control of registered CPA firms that perform audits of public companies (issuers). As required by the Sarbanes-Oxley Act, inspections determine all of the following **except** that

- A. The lead partner of a client is rotated every 5 years.
- B. A second partner review is performed.
- C. Independence is maintained by audit staff.
- D. Only staff with prior experience work on audits.

Answer (D) is correct. *(Publisher, adapted)*
REQUIRED: The issue not considered in a PCAOB inspection.
DISCUSSION: Staff members are required to be trained and supervised in accordance with auditing standards. However, there is no requirement that they have prior experience.
Answer (A) is incorrect. The lead partner must be rotated at least every 5 years. Answer (B) is incorrect. A second partner review is required for each audit engagement of an issuer. Answer (C) is incorrect. Registered firms must have "policies and procedures in place to comply" with applicable independence requirements.

Use the additional questions in Gleim **CPA Test Prep Online** to create Test Sessions that emulate Prometric!

2.8 PRACTICE SIMULATION

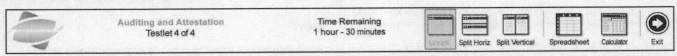

Auditing and Attestation	Time Remaining		
Testlet 4 of 4	1 hour - 30 minutes	Unsplit Split Horiz Split Vertical	Spreadsheet Calculator Exit

DIRECTIONS

Note: If you believe you have encountered a software malfunction, report it to the test center staff immediately.

Navigation

To navigate from task to task, use the controls at the bottom of the screen. Click on the **Next** button to advance to the next task, or the **Previous** button to go to the previous task. To go directly to any task, click on its number.

▼ = Reminder	Directions 1 2 3 4 5 6 7		◀ Previous Next ▶

If you would like a reminder to revisit a task, or want to indicate that you are finished with it, click on the reminder flag below the task number. To clear the flag, click on it again. Reminder flags are for your use only – they do not contribute to your score.

Tabs

In this part of the examination, you will be asked to complete various tasks. Every task has one or more **Work Tabs**. Some tasks have one or more **Information Tabs**, others may have none. Every task has a **Help** tab.

If a task has **Information Tabs**, you may use the information in them to complete your responses in the **Work Tabs**.

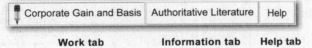

Corporate Gain and Basis	Authoritative Literature	Help
Work tab	**Information tab**	**Help tab**

Work Tabs:
- **Work Tabs** are identified with a pencil icon. This is where your responses are expected.
- Each task has one or more **Work Tabs**.
- **Work Tabs** contain directions for completing the task – be sure to read these directions carefully.
- The **Work Tab** name in the example above is for illustration only – yours will differ.
- You must complete all of the **Work Tabs** in each task to receive full credit.

Information Tabs:
- The Authoritative Literature will be provided in all tasks in the AUD, FAR, and REG sections for your reference.
- Your simulation may have one or more additional **Information Tabs**. Like the Authoritative Literature tabs, **Information Tabs** do not have a pencil icon.
- If your task has additional **Information Tabs**, go through each to familiarize yourself with the task content.

Help Tab:
- The **Help Tab** provides assistance with the exam software that is used in this task. For example, if the task is to compose a memorandum, **Help** will provide information about the word processor.

The Toolbar

The toolbar at the top of the screen shows the amount of time remaining for you to complete the tasks. In addition, the following tools are available. Note that only the Exit button is displayed when Directions are visible - the others will appear when you begin the tasks.

Unsplit Split Horiz Split Vertical

Click on these buttons to split or unsplit the screen. You can split the screen vertically or horizontally.

Calculator

Click on this button to display the calculator; click on it again to hide the calculator. To move the calculator, click on the calculator title bar and drag the calculator to the desired location.

Spreadsheet

Click on this button to use the spreadsheet; click on it again to hide the spreadsheet. To move the spreadsheet, click on the the spreadsheet title bar and drag the spreadsheet to the desired location.

Exit

Click on this button to go on to the next part of the examination. You must complete all of the tasks to receive full credit. Once you click on **Exit** and confirm the action, you will NOT be able to return to this testlet.

▼ = Reminder	Directions 1 2 3 4 5		◀ Previous Next ▶

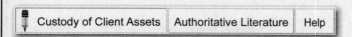

| Custody of Client Assets | Authoritative Literature | Help |

Under the IFAC Code of Ethics, Section 270, a professional accountant must not assume custody of client assets unless permitted by law and must be in compliance with any additional legal duties imposed on a professional accountant. For each situation, select the applicable requirement regarding an accountant entrusted with client assets (Column A) and whether or not that accountant is in compliance with the requirement (Column B). Each answer choice may be selected once, more than once, or not at all.

Situation	Column A	Column B
1. Job CPAs was given $10,000 of cash from their client to use to pay any regulatory fees required to be paid by the client. Although Job kept the cash in a separate checking account, Job pledged the client's money as security for a loan to obtain a lower interest rate.		
2. Fastidious CPAs was entrusted with the inventory of Larry's Lumberyard for the purposes of testing valuation. While in possession of the inventory, inventory was sold, and Fastidious maintained a record of the inventory sold and any related income.		
3. To cut down on paperwork, Easy CPAs deposited client money entrusted to Easy's checking account but made sure to keep accurate records.		

Requirement	Compliance
A) Keep client assets separate from personal or firm assets	A) In compliance with IFAC requirement
B) Use client assets only for purpose(s) for which they are intended	B) Not in compliance with IFAC requirement
C) Account for client assets and any income	
D) Comply with relevant laws and regulations	

| IFAC Issues | Authoritative Literature | Help |

Threats to compliance with fundamental ethics principles may arise from many circumstances and relationships. Select from the list provided the one example that best matches the threats to an accountant in public practice identified in the IFAC standards. Each selection may be used once, more than once, or not at all.

Threat	Example
1. Self-interest	
2. Self-review	
3. Advocacy	
4. Familiarity	
5. Intimidation	

Choices
A) Testifying for a client
B) Ownership in a client
C) Spouse is on the BOD of a client
D) Client threatens to engage a new auditor over a dispute
E) Client offers inconsequential gift
F) Audit of a client control system designed by the auditor

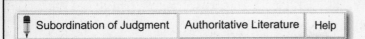

| Subordination of Judgment | Authoritative Literature | Help |

For each situation below, determine whether or not the member acted appropriately or inappropriately (Column A). If the member acted inappropriately, select what the member should have done (Column B). If the member acted appropriately, select N/A for Column B.

Situation	Column A	Column B
1. Altruistic CPA felt that the position taken by the supervisor was not acceptable even though it complied with GAAP. Altruistic notified the client's regulators of this disagreement.		
2. Obedient CPA reasonably believed that the proposed recording of a transaction would result in a material misstatement but did nothing after the supervisor informed Obedient that this was how the client wanted the transaction recorded.		
3. Observant CPA noticed that the client recorded inventory in a way that materially misstated the financial statements. When Observant's supervisor failed to adequately resolve the disagreement, Observant consulted a higher level supervisor.		

Member Action	Suggested Action
A) Appropriate	A) N/A
B) Inappropriate	B) Do nothing
	C) Consult higher level supervisor and consider documenting relevant matters

PCAOB Issues | Authoritative Literature | Help

For each of the following issues, select from the list provided the correct relationship with the Public Company Accounting Oversight Board (PCAOB) for the audit of issuers. Each choice may be used once, more than once, or not at all.

Issues	Relationships		Choices
1. Registration with the PCAOB			A) Required of audit firms by the PCAOB
2. Establishment of generally accepted accounting principles			B) Performance by audit firms prohibited by the PCAOB
3. Disclosure of audit fees			C) Function provided by the PCAOB
4. Provision of internal auditing services			D) Not addressed by the PCAOB
5. Rotation of lead audit partner			
6. Disclosure of fees for tax services			
7. External approval of audit report before issuance			
8. Inspection of public accounting firms			
9. Establishment or adoption of ethics standards			
10. Communication of accounting policies to audit committees			

▼ = Reminder   Directions   1 2 3 [4] 5   ◀ Previous   Next ▶

Research | Authoritative Literature | Help

Research and cite the appropriate ethics standard relating to the application of the Independence Rules to Close Relatives of CPAs.

Title	Section	Paragraph

Title Choices						
AU	PCAOB	AT	AR	ET	BL	VS
CS	QC	PR	TS	PFP	CPE	

▼ = Reminder   Directions   1 2 3 4 [5]   ◀ Previous   Next ▶

Unofficial Answers

1. Custody of Client Assets (6 Gradable Items)

1. Column A: B) Use client assets only for purpose(s) for which they are intended; Column B: B) Not in compliance with IFAC requirement. Job is required to use client assets only for the purpose for which they are intended. Job is not in compliance with the requirement since they pledged the client's cash when the cash was intended to be used only to pay regulatory fees due by the client.

2. Column A: C) Account for client assets and any income; Column A: A) In compliance with IFAC requirement. Fastidious is required to account for client assets and any income. Fastidious is in compliance with the requirement since they maintained a record of the inventory sold and any related income.

3. Column A: A) Keep client assets separate from personal or firm assets; Column B: B) Not in compliance with IFAC requirement. Easy is required to keep client assets separate from firm assets and is in violation of this requirement even if Easy keeps accurate records.

2. IFAC Issues (5 Gradable Items)

1. B) Ownership in a client. Ownership in a client creates a threat of self-interest.

2. F) Audit of a client control system designed by the auditor. Auditors who evaluate their own designed system create a threat of self-review.

3. A) Testifying for a client. Advocating on behalf of a client in litigation creates a threat of advocacy.

4. C) Spouse is on the BOD of a client. Having a close relative on the board of directors of the client creates a threat of familiarity.

5. D) Client threatens to engage a new auditor over a dispute. Being threatened by a client creates a threat of intimidation.

3. Subordination of Judgment (6 Gradable Items)

1. Column A: B) Inappropriate; Column B: B) Do nothing. If the supervisor's position is an acceptable alternative and does not materially misrepresent the facts, the member should do nothing. By notifying the client's regulators of this disagreement, the member acted inappropriately.

2. Column A: B) Inappropriate; Column B: C) Consult higher level supervisor and consider documenting relevant matters. If a material misstatement would result, the member should consult the appropriate higher level of supervisor and consider documenting relevant matters. By doing nothing, the member acted inappropriately.

3. Column A: A) Appropriate; Column B: A) N/A. If a material misstatement would result, the member should consult the appropriate higher level of supervisor and consider documenting relevant matters. Since a material misstatement would result, Observant acted appropriately by consulting a higher level supervisor on the matter.

4. PCAOB Issues (10 Gradable Items)

1. A) Required of audit firms by the PCAOB. The PCAOB registers public accounting firms that audit issuers.

2. D) Not addressed by the PCAOB. The FASB (not the PCAOB) establishes generally accepted accounting principles.

3. A) Required of audit firms by the PCAOB. The PCAOB requires issuers to disclose audit, audit-related, tax, and all other fees paid to their accountants.

4. B) Performance by audit firms prohibited by the PCAOB. Audit firms are prohibited from providing certain internal audit services to their audit clients.

5. A) Required of audit firms by the PCAOB. The PCAOB requires that the lead audit partner be rotated every 5 years.

6. A) Required of audit firms by the PCAOB. The PCAOB requires issuers to disclose audit, audit-related, tax, and all other fees paid to their accountants.

7. D) Not addressed by the PCAOB. The audit report need not be approved by an external party before issuance.

8. C) Function provided by the PCAOB. The PCAOB performs periodic inspections of public accounting firms to evaluate the services that they provide to their clients.

9. C) Function provided by the PCAOB. The PCAOB establishes or adopts standards on auditing, quality control, ethics, and independence.

10. A) Required of audit firms by the PCAOB. The PCAOB requires audit firms to communicate to the audit committee all critical accounting policies and practices used by the client.

5. Research (1 Gradable Item)

Answer: 101.02

ET Section 101 -- *Independence*

.02 101-1 -- Interpretation of Rule 101.

Application of the Independence Rules to Close Relatives

Independence would be considered to be impaired if --

1.   An individual participating on the attest engagement team has a close relative who had

   a.   A key position with the client, or
   b.   A financial interest in the client that

      i)   Was material to the close relative and of which the individual has knowledge or
      ii) Enabled the close relative to exercise significant influence over the client.

2.   An individual in a position to influence the attest engagement or any partner in the office in which the lead attest engagement partner primarily practices in connection with the attest engagement has a close relative who had

   a.   A key position with the client, or
   b.   A financial interest in the client that

      i)   Was material to the close relative and of which the individual or partner has knowledge and
      ii) Enabled the close relative to exercise significant influence over the client.

Gleim Simulation Grading

Task	Correct Responses		Gradable Items		Score per Task
1	_____	÷	6	=	_____
2	_____	÷	5	=	_____
3	_____	÷	6	=	_____
4	_____	÷	10	=	_____
Research	_____	÷	1	=	_____

Total of Scores per Task		_____
÷ Total Number of Tasks		5
Total Score		_____ %

Use **CPA Gleim Online** and **Simulation Wizard** to practice more task-based simulations in a realistic environment.

STUDY UNIT THREE
RISK ASSESSMENT

(21 pages of outline)

In general, the recognition and consideration of risks related to an audit have great significance on the CPA exam. The AICPA appears determined to ensure that successful candidates understand the consequences of those risks. Candidates can expect to be tested on the auditor's consideration of audit risk and its components. An understanding of the interrelationship between risk and materiality is critical.

3.1 PRE-ENGAGEMENT ACCEPTANCE ACTIVITIES

1. **The First Standard of Field Work**

   a. The first standard of field work states,

      The auditor must adequately plan the work and must properly supervise any assistants.

      1) "The auditor has a responsibility to plan and perform the audit to provide reasonable assurance about whether the financial statements are free of material misstatement, whether caused by error or fraud" (AU 110).

2. **Appointment of the Auditor**

   a. AU 311, *Planning and Supervision*, indicates that an early appointment of the auditor is advantageous to the auditor and the client. One advantage is that it permits planning before the balance-sheet date.

   b. Before acceptance of an engagement near or after the close of the fiscal year, an independent auditor should determine whether circumstances permit an adequate audit and expression of an unqualified opinion. If they do not, the auditor and client should discuss the possibility of a qualified opinion or a disclaimer of opinion.

   c. Before significant audit activities begin, the auditor must determine that ethical requirements, including **independence**, can be met.

3. **Client Acceptance**

   a. Client acceptance includes the continued evaluation of existing clients and the evaluation of new clients. Concluding that management **lacks integrity** causes the auditor to **reject** a potential client or to end a relationship with an existing client.

   b. The auditor should **communicate with the predecessor auditor before accepting the engagement** (AU 315).

   c. The auditor is responsible for **initiating** the communication.

   d. Conduct Rule 301, *Confidential Client Information*, protects the confidentiality of client information. Hence, both the auditor and his/her predecessor should **obtain client permission** to have discussions about the integrity of management as well as pertinent audit-related issues.

    e.   Inquiries should include

        1)   Facts that bear on the integrity of management

        2)   Disagreements with management about accounting principles, audit procedures, or other similar matters

        3)   Findings of fraud or illegal acts, or internal control problems that had been communicated by the predecessor auditor to the audit committee (or equivalent)

        4)   The predecessor's **understanding** as to the reason for the change in auditors

    f.   The working papers of the auditor's predecessor normally should be available.

    g.   The **client's refusal to grant permission** or the predecessor auditor's failure to respond fully requires the auditor to consider the implications when deciding whether to accept the engagement.

ISA Difference

Under the ISAs, an auditor may obtain sufficient appropriate evidence about **opening balances** by reviewing the predecessor's **working papers**. In this case, the auditor should consider the competence and independence of the predecessor. Under U.S. GAAS, the auditor may wish to inquire about the predecessor's reputation and standing. But the inquiry is not necessarily related to review of the predecessor's working papers.

---

4.   **Engagement Letter**

    a.   The auditor should establish an **understanding** with the client through a written communication regarding the services to be performed.

    b.   The objectives and limitations of the audit and the responsibilities of the auditor and management should be stated in a contract evidenced by an **engagement letter**.

    c.   The understanding also may address other issues, for example, (1) the overall audit strategy; (2) additional services; (3) limits on liability (auditor or client); (4) involvement of the predecessor auditor, internal auditors, or specialists; (5) access to audit documentation; and (6) fees.

        1)   However, it does not provide details about the audit plan. The client should not be able to anticipate the nature, timing, and extent of audit procedures.

    d.   An engagement letter should be sent by the CPA to the prospective client on each engagement, audit or otherwise. If the client agrees to the terms of the letter by signing a copy and returning it to the CPA, a written contract is created.

    e.   Management is responsible for adjusting the statements to correct material misstatements. Furthermore, management's **representation letter**, which should be distinguished from the engagement letter, must assert that the effects of any uncorrected misstatements are immaterial individually or in the aggregate. An appendix to the letter should be included that summarizes all uncorrected misstatements (see Study Unit 14).

ISA Difference

Under the ISAs, if the **terms of the engagement** are changed, for example, from an audit to a review, the auditor and client may not be able to agree to the change. In these circumstances, the auditor should withdraw and consider whether to report to others.

EXAMPLE – Engagement Letter

SWIFT, MARCH & COMPANY   *Certified Public Accountants*

[Date]
Mr. Thomas Thorp, President
Anonymous Company, Inc.
Route 32
Nowhere, New York 10000

Dear Mr. Thorp:

This will confirm our understanding of the arrangements for our audit of the financial statements of Anonymous Company, Inc. for the year ending [date].

We will audit the company's financial statements of the year ending [date], for the purpose of expressing an opinion on the fairness with which they present, in all material respects, the financial position, results of operations, and cash flows in conformity with generally accepted accounting principles.

We will conduct our audit in accordance with generally accepted auditing standards. Those standards require that we obtain reasonable, rather than absolute, assurance that the financial statements are free of material misstatement, whether caused by error or fraud. Accordingly, a material misstatement may remain undetected. Also, an audit is not designed to detect error or fraud that is immaterial to the financial statements; therefore, the audit will not necessarily detect misstatements less than this materiality level that might exist due to error, fraudulent financial reporting, or misappropriation of assets. If, for any reason, we are unable to complete the audit or are unable to form or have not formed an opinion, we may decline to express an opinion or decline to issue a report as a result of the engagement.

While an audit includes obtaining an understanding of internal control sufficient to plan the audit and to determine the nature, timing, and extent of audit procedures to be performed, it is not designed to provide assurance on internal control or to identify significant deficiencies or material weaknesses. However, we are responsible for ensuring that the audit committee (or others with equivalent authority or responsibility) is aware of any significant deficiencies or material weaknesses that come to our attention.

The financial statements are the responsibility of the company's management. Management is also responsible for (1) establishing and maintaining effective internal control over financial reporting; (2) identifying, and ensuring the company complies with, the laws and regulations applicable to its activities; (3) making all financial records and related information available to us; and (4) providing to us at the conclusion of the engagement a representation letter that, among other things, will confirm management's responsibility for the preparation of the financial statements in conformity with generally accepted accounting principles, the availability of financial records and related data, the completeness and availability of all minutes of the board and committee meetings, and, to the best of its knowledge and belief, the absence of fraud involving management or those employees who have a significant role in the entity's internal control.

Assistance to be supplied by your personnel, including the preparation of schedules and analyses of accounts, is described on a separate attachment. Timely completion of this work will facilitate the completion of our audit.

As part of our engagement of the year ending [date], we will also prepare the federal and state income tax returns for Anonymous Company, Inc.

Our fees will be billed as work progresses and are based on the amount of time required at various levels of responsibility, plus actual out-of-pocket expenses. Invoices are payable upon presentation. We will notify you immediately of any circumstances we encounter that could significantly affect our initial estimate of total fees of $[amount].

If this letter correctly expresses your understanding, please sign the enclosed copy and return it to us.

Very truly yours,

SWIFT, MARCH & COMPANY

| Adapted from a presentation in a January 1998 |
| *Journal of Accounting* article by Gibson, Pany, and Smith. |

_____, *Partner*

APPROVED:

By: _____, *President*
Date: _____

Stop and review! You have completed the outline for this subunit. Study multiple-choice questions 1 through 4 on page 115.

3.2 PLANNING AND SUPERVISION (AU 311, AS NO. 9, AND AS NO. 10)

1. **Audit Strategy**

   a. Planning continues throughout the audit. It initially involves developing an **overall audit strategy**.

   b. The size and complexity of the entity, the auditor's experience with the entity, and the auditor's understanding of the entity and its environment (including internal control) affect planning. The auditor also should consider the following:

      1) Characteristics of the engagement and reporting objectives
      2) Appropriate materiality levels
      3) Areas of high risk of material misstatement
      4) Material client locations and account balances
      5) Whether to seek evidence of the operating effectiveness of controls
      6) Relevant entity-specific, industry, or financial developments
      7) Consideration of the audit resources required

   c. The **engagement partner** is responsible for the engagement and its performance.

2. **Audit Plans in Accordance with GAAS**

   a. An **audit plan** must be developed and documented for all audit engagements. It includes the nature, timing, and extent of procedures expected to reduce audit risk to an acceptably low level.

      1) Thus, the audit plan includes a description of risk assessment procedures directed toward the **risks of material misstatement (RMMs)**.

         a) **Risk assessment procedures** are performed to obtain an understanding of the entity and its environment, including its internal control, to identify and assess the RMMs at the levels of (1) the financial statements as a whole and (2) relevant assertions.

            i) The RMM is the combined assessment of **inherent risk** and **control risk**.

      2) The plan also includes a description of **further procedures** at the relevant assertion levels for material classes of transactions, account balances, and disclosures. These procedures are to be performed in response to assessed risks and evaluations of audit evidence.

         a) This element of the plan is based on (1) the decision whether to test the operating effectiveness of controls and (2) the nature, timing, and extent of planned substantive procedures.

      3) The third element of the plan describes any other procedures required by GAAS or PCAOB standards.

   b. The audit plan will likely be adjusted as the audit progresses. For example, the auditor may change the assessments of control risk and inherent risk as evidence is collected from the performance of risk assessment procedures. As a result, the acceptable level of detection risk may change, and the auditor may need to alter the nature, timing, and extent of further procedures.

   c. Audit plans are part of the **audit documentation**.

   d. Based on the audit strategy, the auditor develops a **detailed audit plan**.

      1) However, the two planning activities are not necessarily discrete or sequential because changes may result.

e. Procedures in planning include the following:

1) Reviewing prior audit documentation
2) Discussing audit matters with the CPA firm's personnel
3) Inquiring about current business developments
4) Reading the current interim financial statements
5) Considering the effects of accounting and auditing pronouncements
6) Coordinating the assistance of entity personnel in data preparation
7) Determining the involvement, if any, of consultants, specialists, and internal auditors
8) Establishing the timing of the work
9) Establishing and coordinating staffing requirements

f. Planning also involves determining whether and to what extent the services of IT, tax, and other **specialists** will be required. The auditor should have supervisory responsibility for specialists. Moreover, the auditor should have sufficient knowledge to

1) Communicate their objectives,
2) Evaluate whether their planned procedures will achieve the objectives, and
3) Evaluate the results.

3. **Communication**

a. The auditor should communicate the **planned scope and timing of the audit** to those charged with governance (e.g., a board of directors or audit committee).

1) But the communication of this overview should not compromise the audit, for example, by making detailed procedures too predictable.

4. **Initial Audits**

a. The following are examples of additional planning considerations for initial audits:

1) Performance of procedures in accordance with the quality control element of acceptance of clients and specific engagements
2) Communication with prior auditor
3) Major issues discussed with management
4) Planned audit procedures regarding opening balances
5) Assignment of firm personnel with appropriate capabilities and competence

5. **Materiality**

a. Materiality should be established for planning purposes.

1) It may be adjusted as audit evidence is collected.
2) Material balances and locations should be determined.

6. **Supervision**

a. Supervision **involves directing the efforts of assistants who are involved in accomplishing the objectives of the audit and determining whether those objectives were accomplished** (AU 311).

1) Among other things, the extent of supervision depends on the qualifications of personnel and the subject matter of the work.

b. The elements of supervision are (1) instructing assistants, (2) keeping informed of significant issues encountered, (3) reviewing the work of each assistant (including documentation) to determine that it is adequately performed and documented and is consistent with conclusions in the report, and (4) resolving differences of opinion.

7. Audit team members should be informed about the susceptibility of the statements to material misstatement due to error or fraud, but especially **fraud**. The **discussion** aids in understanding the entity and its environment, including its internal control, and the risks it confronts.

   a. Moreover, the discussion should emphasize **professional skepticism**.

      1) "Due professional care requires the auditor to exercise professional skepticism" (AU 230). It is an attitude that includes a questioning mind and critical assessment of audit evidence.

8. **Assistants** should be informed about (a) their audit responsibilities, (b) the objectives of procedures, (c) matters affecting those procedures (e.g., the entity's business and accounting and auditing issues), and (d) their duty to report significant auditing and accounting issues and difficulties in audit performance.

9. Procedures should be implemented and followed for **resolution of differences** about auditing and accounting issues. Assistants should be able to document their disagreements, and the final resolution should be documented.

10. **Internal Audit Plans**

    a. Internal audit plans differ from those written by the independent external auditor.

       1) The independent external auditor's purpose is to express an opinion on the fairness of the financial statements, i.e., to evaluate the client's financial reporting.

       2) However, the internal auditor's work is more comprehensive. According to **The Institute of Internal Auditors**, internal auditing is an independent (but not the same as the external auditor), objective assurance **and** consulting function that adds value and improves an organization's operations. Internal auditors evaluate and improve the effectiveness of governance, risk management, and control processes. Accordingly, they evaluate risks and the adequacy and effectiveness of controls regarding (a) the reliability and integrity of financial and operational information; (b) the effectiveness and efficiency of operations; (c) the safeguarding of assets; and (d) compliance with laws, regulations, and contracts.

          a) Consequently, the internal auditor's plans are more detailed and cover areas that normally are not considered by the independent auditor.

Stop and review! You have completed the outline for this subunit. Study multiple-choice questions 5 through 9 beginning on page 116.

3.3 AUDIT RISK AND MATERIALITY (AU 312, AS NO. 8, AND AS NO. 11)

> The CPA exam can be viewed as your ticket into the profession. The AICPA uses the exam as part of its attempt to ensure that you recognize the risks associated with your new career. Thus, many questions relate to risks that accountants face. Alternatively, few questions relate to the rewards that the profession provides. Study appropriately.

1. Audit risk and materiality affect the application of GAAS, especially the field work and reporting standards, and are reflected in the auditor's standard report. The auditor must make judgments about audit risk and materiality in determining the nature, timing, and extent of procedures to apply and in evaluating the results.

2. **Audit Risk**

   a. The characteristics of audit evidence and fraud prevent the auditor from providing more than **reasonable assurance** that material misstatements are detected. Thus, audit risk is implicit in reasonable assurance. **Audit risk is the risk that the auditor expresses an inappropriate audit opinion when the financial statements are materially misstated.**

      1) It should be distinguished from risk of malpractice litigation, adverse publicity, or erroneously concluding that financial statements are materially misstated.

      2) The audit should reduce audit risk to an appropriately low level for expressing an opinion.

3. **Materiality**

   a. The concept of **materiality** recognizes that some but not all matters, evaluated individually or in the aggregate, are important for fair presentation of the financial statements in conformity with GAAP.

      1) The auditor is responsible for planning and performing the audit to obtain reasonable assurance that material misstatements, whether caused by error or fraud, are detected.

      2) Materiality is a matter of **professional judgment** influenced by the needs of reasonable people who use the financial statements.

         a) **Users** are assumed to be those who have a reasonable understanding of business and economic activities and who are willing to study the information with appropriate diligence.

      3) Materiality judgments consider surrounding circumstances and involve **qualitative and quantitative** factors.

         a) It ordinarily is not practical to design audit procedures to detect misstatements that are material based solely on qualitative factors.

      4) For an audit of internal control for an issuer, the auditor should use the same materiality considerations as for the audit of the company's financial statements.

4. **Misstatements**

   a. Misstatements arise in may ways, for example, (1) inaccuracies in data processing, (2) omissions, (3) departures from GAAP, and (4) unreasonable management judgments about accounting estimates or principles. Misstatements may be known or likely. They are caused by errors or fraud.

   b. **Known misstatements** are specifically identified during the audit.

   c. **Likely misstatements** derive from

      1) Differences between the auditor's and management's judgments about accounting estimates or

      2) Extrapolations from audit evidence.

   d. **Errors** are unintentional misstatements.

   e. **Fraud** is an intentional act involving deception to obtain an unjust or illegal advantage.

5. **Audit Risk and Materiality Levels**

   a. Audit risk and materiality are considered at the **overall financial statement level** (statements as a whole) and the **individual balance, transaction class, or disclosure level**.

   b. Risk assessment procedures are performed at both levels.

   c. For the statements as a whole, the auditor considers **RMMs** that may affect many relevant assertions but not be identifiable with specific ones.

      1) Such risks are particularly relevant to the consideration of fraud.

6.   **Overall Financial Statement Level**

    a.   **Audit risk and materiality** should be considered in

        1)   Developing the overall audit strategy,

        2)   Planning the audit,

        3)   Designing risk assessment procedures,

        4)   Identifying and assessing RMMs,

        5)   Designing additional procedures,

        6)   Evaluating results of procedures, and

        7)   Determining whether the financial statements as a whole are fairly presented in all material respects in conformity with GAAP.

7.   **Balance, Transaction Class, or Disclosure Level (BTCDL)**

    a.   **Audit risk and materiality have an inverse relationship.** Thus, the risk of a large misstatement may be low, but the risk of a small misstatement may be high.

    b.   Accordingly, if other factors are constant, decreasing the audit risk judged to be appropriate or the amount of material misstatement for a balance, etc., requires the auditor to do at least one of the following:

        1)   Perform more effective procedures,

        2)   Perform procedures nearer to year-end, or

        3)   Increase the extent of certain procedures.

    c.   At the BTCDL, the auditor's procedures should provide reasonable assurance of detecting misstatements that are material to the **statements as a whole** when **aggregated** with other misstatements.

        1)   The consideration of audit risk for individual items at the BTCDL helps in the design of **further audit procedures** for the relevant assertions.

8.   **Audit Risk Model**

    a.   Audit risk has **three components** that may be assessed in quantitative terms, such as percentages, or in nonquantitative terms that range, for example, from high to low.

    b.   The **RMM** of relevant assertions consists of the following:

        1)   **Inherent risk** is the susceptibility of a relevant assertion to material misstatement in the absence of related controls.

        2)   **Control risk** is the risk that internal control will not prevent or detect on a timely basis a material misstatement that could occur in a relevant assertion.

    c.   **Detection risk** is the risk that the auditor will not detect a material misstatement that exists in a relevant assertion. It is a function of the effectiveness of an audit procedure and its application by the auditor.

        1)   Detection risk relates to substantive procedures and may be changed by the auditor's response to the RMM.

        2)   Detection risk is inversely related to the RMM. Thus, as the RMM increases, the acceptable detection risk decreases.

    d.   Inherent risk and control risk are independent of the audit and cannot be changed by the auditor.

    e.   The audit risk model uses the following terms: **audit risk (AR), detection risk (DR), and risk of material misstatement (RMM)**.

$$AR = RMM \times DR$$

        1)   Because the auditor determines an acceptable AR and assesses the components of the RMM, the equation can be solved for the appropriate DR.

$$DR = \frac{AR}{RMM}$$

EXAMPLE

The auditor determines an acceptable audit risk (AR) at 5% and assesses control risk (CR) and inherent risk (IR) at 30% and 50%, respectively.

$$DR = \frac{5\%}{30\% \times 50\%}$$

$$DR = 33 \ 1/3\%$$

---

    2) An **expanded risk formula** for a given substantive test of details divides detection risk (DR) into the risk for the **test of details (TD)** and the risk for **substantive analytical procedures (AP)**.

$$AR = RMM \times AP \times TD$$

        a) This risk may be solved for the auditor's acceptable risk for TD.

$$TD = \frac{AR}{RMM \times AP}$$

        b) Given the facts in the previous example, assume that the auditor assessed AP at 60%. The acceptable level of risk for TD is

$$TD = \frac{5\%}{30\% \times 50\% \times 60\%}$$

$$TD = 55.5\%$$

9. **Materiality and Planning**

    a. The auditor establishes a materiality level for the statements as a whole when developing the **overall audit strategy**.

        1) But identified misstatements below this level are not necessarily immaterial. **Qualitative considerations** may affect the auditor's professional judgment about whether a misstatement is material to users.

            a) Examples of such considerations are (1) the possible bias of management, (2) the cumulative effect in the future, (3) regulatory or contractual requirements, (4) occurrence of fraud or illegal acts, and (5) whether the misstatement conceals a negative trend in profitability.

10. **Performance Materiality**

    a. Performance materiality is the amount set by the auditor at less than financial statement materiality to reduce to an appropriately low level the probability that the aggregate of uncorrected and undetected misstatements exceeds financial statement materiality.

    b. Tolerable misstatement is the application of performance materiality to a particular sampling procedure.

EXAMPLE

If financial statement materiality was set at $50,000, performance materiality for the audit of accounts receivable might be set at $3,000 to compensate for the possibility of multiple undetected or uncorrected misstatements in this and other accounts on the balance sheet.

---

11. **Revision of Judgments**

    a. Because an audit is a cumulative process, information obtained during the audit may lead to revision of auditor judgments about audit risk and materiality.

12. **Communication of Misstatements**

   a.   Identified known and likely misstatements (unless trivial) must be timely communicated to appropriate managers.

       1)   The auditor should request that management record corrections of **known** misstatements and examine any material **likely** misstatements of a balance, class, or disclosure.

       2)   The auditor also should request management review of assumptions and methods used to develop an **estimate** that is likely misstated.

   b.   The auditor should communicate significant findings to **those charged with governance**.

   c.   The auditor also must communicate to those charged with governance and management any **significant deficiencies or material weaknesses** in internal control identified, including those previously communicated but not remedied.

13. **Evaluating Findings**

   a.   When evaluating audit findings, the auditor considers the individual and aggregate effects of misstatements not corrected by the entity. This consideration addresses qualitative and quantitative factors. Moreover, the consideration and aggregation should include **likely misstatement**, not merely known misstatement.

   b.   The auditor need not consider misstatements that are "clearly trivial" as defined by being inconsequential, whether considered individually or in the aggregate.

Stop and review! You have completed the outline for this subunit. Study multiple-choice questions 10 through 16 beginning on page 118.

3.4 UNDERSTANDING THE ENTITY AND ITS ENVIRONMENT (AU 314 AND AS NO. 12)

1.   The **second standard of field work** states,

> *The auditor must obtain a sufficient understanding of the entity and its environment, including its internal control, to assess the risk of material misstatement of the financial statements whether due to error or fraud, and to design the nature, timing, and extent of further audit procedures.*

   a.   This process, like planning, is continuous throughout the audit.

2.   The following are among the reasons for obtaining the understanding:

   a.   Determining materiality for planning the audit and evaluating it during the audit

   b.   Considering accounting policies and disclosures

   c.   Identifying areas of audit emphasis, e.g., complex financial transactions

   d.   Setting expectations for results of analytical procedures

   e.   Designing further audit procedures

   f.   Evaluating audit evidence, e.g., that related to management's assumptions and representations

3.   **Categories of Risk Assessment Procedures**

   a.   The broad categories of risk assessment procedures performed to obtain the understanding are (1) inquiries of management and others within the entity, (2) analytical procedures, and (3) observation and inspection. The auditor also may perform other appropriate procedures, such as inquiring of external parties (e.g., legal counsel) or reviewing externally generated information (e.g., financial publications).

   b.   **Inquiries within the entity** may be directed to

       1)   Those responsible for financial reporting;

       2)   Those charged with governance;

       3)   Internal auditors;

    4) Legal counsel;

    5) Marketing, sales, and production managers; and

    6) Others with different levels of authority who may have information about RMMs.

  c. An **analytical procedures** outline is in the next subunit.

  d. **Observation and inspection** provide support for inquiries and direct evidence about the entity and its environment. Examples are

    1) Observing activities and operations;

    2) Inspecting documents and records;

    3) Reading reports, e.g., internal audit reports, interim statements, quarterly reports, and minutes of board meetings;

    4) Tours of facilities; and

    5) Tracing financial transactions during a walk-through.

4. Uses of **prior period information** about the entity and its environment (structure, nature of business, controls, and responses to prior misstatements) contributes to the understanding.

  a. But procedures should be performed to evaluate its current relevance.

5. The auditor specifically assesses the RMM due to **fraud**. (S)he considers this assessment in designing auditing procedures. (See Subunit 3.6.)

6. The auditor may consider pertinent information obtained from (a) the auditor's client acceptance (or continuation) procedures, (b) previous engagements for the client, and (c) other sources.

7. **Understanding the Entity**

  a. The understanding extends to such matters as

    1) External factors (e.g., the relevant industry and regulatory issues);

    2) The nature of the entity (operations, governance, ownership, structure, financing, and investments);

    3) Its overall plans (objectives), operational approaches to achieving objectives (strategies), and business risks (which differ from risks of misstatement);

    4) Financial performance measurement and review (an indicator of what the entity considers important); and

    5) **Internal control.** (See Study Unit 5.) The auditor uses the understanding of internal control to

      a) Determine the types of possible misstatements,

      b) Identify what affects the RMMs, and

      c) Design further procedures (tests of controls and substantive procedures).

  b. For an issuer, the auditor should consider

    1) Reading public information about the company

    2) Obtaining information from earnings calls to investors and rating agencies

    3) Gaining an understanding of compensation for senior management

    4) Obtaining information about trading activities in the company's securities

  c. The auditor should consider company performance measures that could create incentives or pressures on management to manipulate the financial information.

8. Basically, the auditor should consider the likely sources of material misstatement and ask "what could go wrong?"

Stop and review! You have completed the outline for this subunit. Study multiple-choice questions 17 through 19 on page 120.

3.5 ANALYTICAL PROCEDURES (AU 329)

Background

The Auditing Standards Board (ASB) recognized that most substantive tests (tests of details of transactions and balances) are fairly narrow in scope. That is, they are directed toward a particular assertion for a specific account. There have been cases in which auditors have failed because they "missed the forest by focusing on the trees." Analytical procedures, however, are much broader in scope. For example, the auditor might ask "Would the client's reported inventory be able to fit into their current warehouse space?" The ASB decided that analytical procedures should be applied in every audit.

---

1. Analytical procedures are evaluations of financial information made by **a study of plausible relationships among financial and nonfinancial data** using models that range from simple to complex.

2. The basic premise is that plausible relationships among data may reasonably be expected to exist and continue in the absence of known conditions to the contrary. The following exhibit represents the decision process:

| Auditor Developed Expectation of Balance or Ratio | ⟶ | Are These Materially Different? | ⟵ | Management Reported Balance or Ratio |

3. **Analytical Procedures**

    a. Should be applied to some extent in **planning** all financial statement audits for risk assessment to assist the auditor in determining the nature, timing, and extent of other auditing procedures.

    b. Used as **substantive tests** may be more effective or efficient than tests of details in achieving an audit objective related to a specific financial statement assertion.

    c. Should be applied to some extent in the **final stage** of the audit as an overall review.

4. **Development**

    a. The auditor develops expectations or predictions of recorded balances or ratios. The candidate should learn **the five sources of information used to develop analytical procedures**. They are frequently tested on the CPA exam.

        1) **Financial Information from Comparable Prior Period(s)**

EXAMPLE

If a client's prior reported sales were $120,000 in Year 1, $130,000 in Year 2, and $140,000 in Year 3, respectively, the auditor likely will predict Year 4 sales to be approximately $150,000 based on the trend. If management's reported sales are materially different, the auditor will increase the assessed RMM and investigate the underlying causes.

---

        2) **Anticipated results**, such as budgets or forecasts prepared by management (or others) prior to the end of the period

---

EXAMPLE

If management prepares a budget at the beginning of the period reporting forecasted cost of sales to be $100,000, the auditor will expect cost of sales to approximate $100,000 at year-end.

The use of standard costs and variance analysis facilitates the application of analytical procedures in this context.

---

        3) **Relationships among data**, such as those among the balances on the financial statements

---

EXAMPLE

If the auditor determines that sales increased by 25% for the year, accounts receivable should increase by approximately that amount.

---

4) **Comparable Information from the Client's Industry**

> ### EXAMPLE
>
> If the usual inventory turnover ratio in the industry is 10 times per year, the auditor will expect the client's turnover ratio to be approximately 10 times.

5) **Related Nonfinancial Information**

> ### EXAMPLE
>
> If the number of hours worked increased by 30%, the auditor will expect an increase in labor costs of approximately 30%.

5. **Significant Differences**

   a. Significant differences between expectations and recorded amounts should be investigated and evaluated. Significance is largely a function of **materiality** and the desired degree of assurance to be provided.

      1) It also considers that individually insignificant items may be **significant in the aggregate**.

   b. Significant differences should result in (1) evaluation of how expectations were developed and (2) inquiries of management.

      1) Responses should be corroborated with other audit evidence.

   c. Absent an explanation of the difference, other procedures should be performed, and the RMM due to **fraud** should be considered.

6. **Planning the Audit**

   a. Analytical procedures applied in planning the audit emphasize (1) improving the understanding of the business and the transactions and events since the last audit and (2) identifying areas that may represent specific audit risks.

   b. The objective of the procedures is to identify such things as the existence of unusual transactions and events, and amounts, ratios, and trends that might indicate matters that have financial statement and audit planning ramifications (AU 329).

   c. Moreover, they ordinarily use highly aggregated data.

7. **Substantive Testing**

   a. Analytical procedures and **tests of details** may be used as substantive tests of management assertions.

      1) The auditor's judgment about expected effectiveness and efficiency in providing the **desired level of assurance** determines the procedures chosen. For some assertions, analytical procedures alone may provide the necessary assurance.

   b. The effectiveness and efficiency of analytical procedures depend on the following factors:

      1) **Nature of the assertion.** Analytical procedures may be effective when tests of details may not indicate potential misstatements. For example, they may be effective for testing the **completeness assertion**.

      2) **Plausibility and predictability of the relationship.** Relationships in stable environments are more predictable than those in unstable environments, and income statement amounts tend to be more predictable than balance sheet amounts.

         a) The reason is that income statement amounts are based on transactions over a period of time, but balance sheet amounts are for a moment in time.

         b) However, amounts subject to management discretion may be less predictable.

3) **Availability and reliability** of the data used to develop the expectation. Reliability is affected by the source of the data and the conditions under which they were gathered. For example, data are considered more reliable when

a) Obtained from **independent sources** outside the entity

b) Obtained from sources **inside the entity independent of those responsible** for the amount being audited

c) Developed under reliable **internal control**

d) Subjected to **audit testing in the current or prior years**

e) Obtained from a variety of sources

4) **Precision of the expectation.** As the expectation becomes more precise, significant differences between the expectation and management's reported number are more likely to be caused by misstatements.

a) Ordinarily, the more detailed the information, the more precise the expectation. For example, monthly data provide more precise expectations than annual data.

c. When an analytical procedure is the **principal test** of a significant assertion, the auditor should document

1) The expectation, if not readily determinable from the documentation of the work

2) The factors used to develop the expectation

3) The results of the comparison of the expectation with the recorded amounts or ratios

4) Any additional auditing procedures performed to resolve differences and their results

8. **Final Review Stage**

a. Analytical procedures used in the overall review assess conclusions and the overall financial statement presentation.

b. They ordinarily include reading the financial statements and notes and considering

1) The adequacy of evidence regarding **unusual or unexpected balances** detected in planning or performing the audit and

2) Such balances or relationships not detected previously.

c. To be effective, analytical procedures in the overall review should be performed by a manager or partner having a comprehensive knowledge of the client's business and industry.

9. **Ratio Analysis**

a. Auditors apply ratio analysis in all stages of the audit as analytical procedures. An auditor should understand not only how to calculate each ratio but also the potential explanations of changes in ratio from period to period.

1) **Current ratio**

$$\frac{Current\ assets}{Current\ liabilities}$$

a) Changes in the ratio may be caused by changes in the components of current assets (typically cash, receivables, and inventory) and current liabilities (typically accounts payable and notes payable).

b) If the current ratio is less than 1.0, a transaction that results in equal increases (decreases) in the numerator and denominator increases (decreases) the ratio.

      i)   However, if the current ratio is more than 1.0, equal increases (decreases) in the numerator and denominator decrease (increase) the ratio.

2) **Quick (acid-test) ratio**

$$\frac{Current\ assets\ -\ Inventory}{Current\ liabilities}$$

   a)   Quick assets are convertible to cash quickly. Auditors ordinarily calculate this ratio as current assets minus inventory. Thus, changes in inventory do not affect the quick ratio, but other components of the current ratio do.

3) **Receivables turnover**

$$\frac{Net\ sales}{Average\ net\ receivables}$$

   a)   Auditors often calculate this ratio using ending net receivables as the denominator because it is the balance being audited. Changes in sales or receivables affect this ratio.

   b)   In principle, the numerator should be net credit sales, but this amount may not be known.

4) **Days' sales in receivables**

$$\frac{365,\ 360,\ or\ 300}{Receivables\ turnover}$$

   a)   This ratio has the same components as receivables turnover and is affected by changes in sales or receivables.

   b)   The number of days in a year may be 365, 360 (a banker's year), or 300 (number of business days).

5) **Inventory turnover**

$$\frac{Cost\ of\ goods\ sold}{Average\ inventory}$$

   a)   Auditors often calculate this ratio using ending inventory as the denominator because it is the balance being audited. Changes in cost of goods sold or inventory affect this ratio.

   b)   A high turnover implies that the entity does not hold excessive inventories that are unproductive and lessen its profitability.

   c)   A high turnover also implies that the inventory is truly marketable and does not contain obsolete goods.

6) **Day's sales in inventory**

$$\frac{365,\ 360,\ or\ 300}{Inventory\ turnover}$$

   a)   This ratio has the same components as inventory turnover and is affected by changes in inventory or cost of sales.

   b)   The number of days in a year may be 365, 360 (a banker's year), or 300 (number of business days).

7) **Total asset turnover**

$$\frac{Net\ sales}{Total\ assets}$$

   a)   This ratio calculates how many times the total assets turn over in sales. It is affected by changes in sales and total assets.

   b)   The denominator also may be average total assets.

8) **Debt-to-equity ratio**

$$\frac{Total\ debt}{Total\ equity}$$

a)   This ratio measures how much external parties contribute to assets relative to owners. Shifts in debt or equity affect this ratio.

b)   The ratios of total assets to total equity and total assets to total debt provide similar analysis and conclusions.

9) **Times interest earned**

$$\frac{Net\ income + Interest\ expense + Income\ tax\ expense}{Interest\ expense}$$

a)   Times interest earned measures the ability of an entity to pay its interest charges. Taxes are added back to net income because interest is paid before taxes. Interest is added back to net income because it is included in the calculation of net income.

b)   An alternative is to exclude interest from the numerator and to add 1.0 to the quotient once the calculation is made.

c)   Changes in interest and net income may affect this ratio.

d)   If earnings decline sufficiently, no income tax expense will be recognized.

10) **Cost of goods sold ratio**

$$\frac{Cost\ of\ goods\ sold}{Net\ sales}$$

a)   This ratio measures the percentage amount of sales consumed by cost of goods sold. Nonproportional changes in either affect the ratio.

11) **Gross margin percentage**

$$\frac{Net\ sales - Cost\ of\ goods\ sold}{Net\ sales}$$

a)   The gross margin percentage measures earnings from the sale of products. Nonproportional changes in net sales and cost of goods sold affect the ratio.

12) **Net operative margin percentage**

$$\frac{Operating\ income}{Net\ sales}$$

a)   Operating income is calculated before subtracting interest and taxes. Nonproportional changes in either operating income or net sales cause a change in the ratio.

13) **Return on equity**

$$\frac{Net\ income}{Total\ equity}$$

a)   This is an overall measure of a rate of return on investment. Changes in net income or changes in equity may affect this ratio.

b)   A return on average total equity or on common equity also may be calculated.

Stop and review! You have completed the outline for this subunit. Study multiple-choice questions 20 through 27 beginning on page 121.

3.6 CONSIDERATION OF FRAUD IN A FINANCIAL STATEMENT AUDIT (AU 316)

1. **Responsibilities**

    a. The auditor should plan and perform the audit to obtain **reasonable assurance** about whether the financial statements are free of material misstatement, whether caused by error or fraud.

    b. **Management** is responsible for programs and controls that prevent, deter, and detect fraud. **Management** and **those charged with governance** (e.g., the board and audit committee) must set the proper tone and maintain a culture of honesty.

        1) **Absolute assurance** is unattainable because of the characteristics of fraud and the limitations of audit evidence. Management may override controls in unpredictable ways or alter accounting records, and fraud may be concealed through collusion, falsifying documentation (including electronic approvals), or withholding evidence.

2. Fraud is intentional. The **three conditions** ordinarily present when fraud exists include **pressures or incentives** to commit fraud, an **opportunity**, and the capacity to **rationalize** misconduct.

3. The types of fraud relevant to the auditor include misstatements arising from

    a. **Fraudulent financial reporting.** These are intentional misstatements or omissions to deceive users, such as altering accounting records or documents, misrepresenting or omitting significant information, and misapplying accounting principles.

    b. **Misappropriation of assets.** These result from theft, embezzlement, or an action that causes payment for items not received.

4. **Professional Skepticism**

    a. Professional skepticism should be maintained in considering the **risk of material misstatement due to fraud** ("fraud risk"). An auditor should critically assess evidence, continually question whether fraud has occurred, and not accept unpersuasive evidence solely because management is believed to be honest.

    b. **Discussion among key engagement personnel** should emphasize professional skepticism and continual alertness to potential fraud. It may occur before or during information gathering, and communication should be ongoing.

        1) The discussion should include **brainstorming** about factors that might create the conditions for fraud, how and where the statements might be misstated, how assets might be misappropriated or financial reports fraudulently misstated, concealment, and how to respond to fraud risk.

5. **Identifying Fraud Risks**

    a. Obtaining information for identifying fraud risks includes inquiring of management, those charged with governance, the internal auditors, and others. It also involves considering the results of **planning-stage analytical procedures** and fraud risk factors.

        1) The auditor should apply analytical procedures to **revenue accounts**, e.g., by comparing recorded sales and production capacity to detect fictitious sales.

        2) **Fraud risk factors** are events or conditions indicating possible fraud. The auditor should judge whether they are present and affect the assessment of fraud risks.

        3) Other information may be derived from (a) discussions among audit team members, (b) procedures related to the acceptance and continuance of clients and engagements, (c) reviews of interim statements, and (d) identified inherent risks at the account-balance or class-of-transactions level.

b.   The information obtained may be considered in terms of the **three conditions**, but an identifiable risk may exist when all conditions have not been observed, especially rationalization. The extent of a condition may by itself create a fraud risk, e.g., pressure to reach an earnings goal.

1)   Fraud risks vary with the entity's size, complexity, ownership, etc.

2)   Fraud risks may relate to specific assertions or to the statements as a whole.

3)   High inherent risk of an assertion about an account balance or transaction class may exist when it is susceptible to management manipulation.

4)   Identifying fraud risks entails considering the type of risk and its significance, likelihood, and pervasiveness.

5)   The auditor must address the risk of **management override** of controls in all audits because of its unpredictability and ordinarily should assume the existence of a fraud risk relating to **improper revenue recognition**. In the latter case, the contrary conclusion must be documented in the working papers.

c.   Identified **fraud risks are assessed** after the auditor's evaluation of **relevant antifraud programs and controls**. As part of the **understanding of internal control**, the auditor should evaluate whether programs and controls have been **suitably designed and implemented**. The auditor then determines whether they mitigate or increase the risks.

6.   **Responses to Fraud Risk**

a.   The responses to the assessment of fraud risks should reflect a critical evaluation of the audit evidence. Responses may have an overall effect on the audit, involve changes in audit procedures performed in response to specific fraud risks, or further address management override.

b.   One **overall effect** is to assign more experienced personnel, or individuals with special skills, or to increase supervision. A second overall effect is to consider **accounting principles**, especially those involving subjective measurements and complex transactions, and whether they indicate a **collective bias**. Another overall effect is to make **unpredictable** choices of audit procedures.

c.   Audit procedures vary with the risks and the balances, transactions, and assertions affected. Procedures may provide more reliable evidence or increased corroboration, be performed at year-end or throughout the reporting period, or involve larger samples or the use of computer-assisted techniques.

d.   The auditor should further address **management override**.

1)   Material misstatements may result from inappropriate **journal entries or adjustments**. The auditor should therefore

a)   Understand the financial reporting process and controls

b)   Identify, select, and test entries and adjustments after considering the risk assessments, effectiveness of controls, nature of the reporting process, and audit evidence (electronic or manual)

c)   Choose whether to test entries during the period

d)   Make inquiries about inappropriate or unusual activity

2)   Fraud may result from intentional misstatement of **significant accounting estimates**. The auditor should perform a retrospective review of estimates in the prior-year statements that are based on sensitive assumptions or significant management judgments.

3)   The auditor should understand **significant unusual transactions**.

7. **Evaluating Audit Evidence**

   a. The assessment of fraud risks should be ongoing because field work may reveal conditions that modify the judgment.

   b. **Analytical procedures** performed in the overall review or as substantive tests may detect previously unrecognized fraud risks. These procedures should be applied to **revenue** through year-end. The auditor also should evaluate **responses to inquiries** about analytical relationships.

   c. At or near the end of field work, the auditor should evaluate **earlier assessments of fraud risk**. The performance of additional procedures may result. Furthermore, the auditor responsible for the audit should determine that information about fraud risks has been properly **communicated** to team members.

   d. The auditor should consider whether **identified misstatements** indicate fraud, with consequent effects on **materiality** judgments. If the fraud is not material, the auditor still should evaluate the implications.

      1) If the possible fraud is material, the auditor should obtain additional evidence; consider the implications for the audit; and discuss the matter with management one level (or more) above those involved, senior management, and those charged with governance.

      2) If fraud risk is great, the auditor may consider withdrawing and communicating the reasons to those charged with governance.

8. **Communications**

   a. Communications about fraud are required given **evidence that fraud may exist**. Inconsequential fraud should be brought to the attention of the appropriate management. Other fraud should be reported directly to those charged with governance.

9. **Documentation**

   a. Documentation of the consideration of fraud should include

      1) Planning-stage discussions
      2) Procedures for identifying and assessing fraud risks
      3) Specific risks identified and the response
      4) Reasons for not identifying improper revenue recognition as a fraud risk
      5) Results of further addressing management override
      6) Responses to other conditions and analytical relationships
      7) Fraud communications

Stop and review! You have completed the outline for this subunit. Study multiple-choice questions 28 through 33 beginning on page 123.

3.7 ILLEGAL ACTS BY CLIENTS (AU 317)

1. **Illegal acts** are violations of laws or governmental regulations that do not include personal misconduct by the client's personnel unrelated to their business activities. Whether an act is illegal is a determination normally beyond the auditor's competence.

2. Illegal acts vary in their relation to the financial statements.

   a. The further removed an illegal act is from the financial statements, the less likely the auditor is to become aware of the act or recognize its illegality.

   b. The auditor should consider laws and regulations recognized as having a **direct and material effect** on the financial statements, such as tax laws.

      1) Examples less likely to have a direct and material effect include laws and regulations relating to environmental protection, food and drug administration, and antitrust.

3. **Auditor's Responsibility**

   a. The auditor's responsibility for detection of misstatements arising from illegal acts having **direct and material effects** is the same as that for **material errors and fraud**. The auditor should specifically **assess the risk of material misstatements due to such illegal acts**.

   b. Other illegal acts "relate more to an entity's operating aspects than to its financial and accounting aspects, and their financial statement effect is indirect."

      1) An audit usually does not include audit procedures specifically designed to detect illegal acts that have **indirect effects**. Because of the nature of such illegal acts, an audit provides no assurance that they will be detected or that any contingent liabilities that may result will be disclosed.

      2) However, an auditor should be aware of the possibility of such illegal acts.

      3) If information comes to the auditor's attention indicating the potential for an illegal act having material but indirect effects, the auditor should apply specific audit procedures.

      4) Although a financial audit does not include audit procedures specifically designed to detect illegal acts having indirect effects, the auditor should **inquire of management** concerning compliance with laws and regulations and obtain written representations about the absence of violations.

      5) However, the auditor considers laws or regulations from the perspective of their known relationship with audit objectives rather than of legality per se.

   c. The following results of normal procedures should raise questions:

      1) Unauthorized or improperly recorded transactions

      2) Investigation by a governmental or enforcement agency

      3) Large unexplained payments to consultants, affiliates, employees, or officials

      4) Large payments in cash or purchases of bank checks payable to bearer, transfers to numbered accounts, and similar transactions

      5) Failure to file tax returns or pay governmental fees

      6) Excessive sales commissions on agents' fees

      7) Violations cited in reports by regulators

ISA Difference

The ISAs do not differentiate between violations of laws and regulations having **direct and indirect effects**.

---

4. **Audit Procedures**

   a. The following procedures respond to a possible illegal act having indirect effects:

      1) Obtaining an understanding of the act, the circumstances in which it occurred, and sufficient other information to evaluate its financial statement effects

      2) Inquiring of management at a level above those involved

      3) Consulting with client's legal counsel

      4) Applying any other appropriate audit procedures

   b. The auditor's response to detected illegal acts is to consider the effects on the financial statements and the implications for other aspects of the audit, especially the reliability of management's representations. The auditor should

      1) Consider the qualitative and quantitative materiality of the act

      2) Consider the adequacy of disclosure

      3) Communicate material problems to those charged with governance

5. **Auditor's Opinion**

   a. If an illegal act having a direct and material effect on the financial statements has not been accounted for properly, the auditor should express a qualified or adverse opinion (see Study Unit 16).

   b. If unable to collect sufficient information, the auditor usually disclaims an opinion.

   c. When the auditor concludes that an illegal act has or is likely to have occurred, (s)he should discuss the matter with the appropriate level of management and request that any necessary remedial actions be taken. If the alleged illegal act has a material effect on the financial statements or the client does not take the remedial action that the auditor considers necessary, the auditor should express a qualified or adverse opinion, depending on the level of materiality, or withdraw from the engagement.

6. **Disclosure to Outside Parties**

   a. Disclosure of possible illegal acts to outside parties ordinarily is not the auditor's responsibility and would violate the duty of confidentiality. However, the auditor may need to

      1) Comply with legal and regulatory requirements. For example, "reportable events" must be disclosed to the SEC, and reports on illegal acts may be required within one business day by the *Private Securities Litigation Reform Act of 1995*.

      2) Communicate with a successor auditor.

      3) Respond to a subpoena.

      4) Report to a funding or other specified agency in accordance with governmental audit requirements, such as those established by the *Single Audit Act*. (See Study Unit 20.)

Stop and review! You have completed the outline for this subunit. Study multiple-choice questions 34 through 38 beginning on page 125.

QUESTIONS

3.1 Pre-Engagement Acceptance Activities

1. Before accepting an audit engagement, an auditor should make specific inquiries of the predecessor auditor regarding the predecessor's

A. Awareness of the consistency in the application of generally accepted accounting principles between periods.

B. Evaluation of all matters of continuing accounting significance.

C. Opinion of any subsequent events occurring since the predecessor's audit report was issued.

D. Understanding as to the reasons for the change of auditors.

Answer (D) is correct. *(CPA, adapted)*
   REQUIRED: The inquiries made by an auditor of a predecessor auditor before accepting an engagement.
   DISCUSSION: According to AU 315, the auditor should make specific and reasonable inquiries of the predecessor auditor regarding issues bearing upon acceptance of the engagement. The inquiries should include specific questions regarding, among other things, the predecessor's understanding as to the reasons for the change of auditors.
   Answer (A) is incorrect. A specific inquiry about consistency of application of GAAP is not necessary. Answer (B) is incorrect. All matters of continuing accounting significance are not applicable to the auditor's decision to accept the engagement. Answer (C) is incorrect. The predecessor is not responsible for events subsequent to his/her report.

2. Which of the following conditions most likely would pose the greatest risk in accepting a new audit engagement?

    A. Staff will need to be rescheduled to cover this new client.

    B. There will be a client-imposed scope limitation.

    C. The firm will have to hire a specialist in one audit area.

    D. The client's financial reporting system has been in place for 10 years.

Answer (B) is correct. *(CPA, adapted)*
    REQUIRED: The condition creating the greatest risk for client acceptance.
    DISCUSSION: A client-imposed scope limitation suggests that management will not be completely forthcoming with all necessary evidence to support the auditor's opinion. This issue may raise doubts about the integrity of management.
    Answer (A) is incorrect. New clients will often require rescheduling of staff to conduct the audit. Answer (C) is incorrect. Recognizing the need for the expertise of a specialist in one particular area prior to acceptance of a client does not create a significant risk to the auditor. Answer (D) is incorrect. Although the system may be dated, it may still meet the needs of the organization and be able to provide the evidence necessary to complete the audit.

3. Hill, CPA, has been retained to audit the financial statements of Monday Co. Monday's predecessor auditor was Post, CPA, who has been notified by Monday that Post's services have been terminated. Under these circumstances, which party should initiate the communications between Hill and Post?

    A. Hill, the auditor.

    B. Post, the predecessor auditor.

    C. Monday's controller or CFO.

    D. The chair of Monday's board of directors.

Answer (A) is correct. *(CPA, adapted)*
    REQUIRED: The party responsible for initiation of communications between the auditor and the predecessor.
    DISCUSSION: AU 315 indicates that the auditor should communicate with the predecessor auditor before accepting the engagement. Initiation of the communication is the responsibility of the successor. Moreover, the auditor should seek permission from the prospective client to inquire of the predecessor before final engagement acceptance. Thus, the auditor should ask the client to authorize the predecessor to make a full response.
    Answer (B) is incorrect. Post, the predecessor auditor, need not initiate the communication. Answer (C) is incorrect. Monday's controller or CFO need not initiate the communication. Answer (D) is incorrect. The chair of Monday's board of directors need not initiate the communication.

4. The scope and nature of an auditor's contractual obligation to a client is ordinarily set forth in the

    A. Management representation letter.

    B. Scope paragraph of the auditor's report.

    C. Engagement letter.

    D. Introductory paragraph of the auditor's report.

Answer (C) is correct. *(CPA, adapted)*
    REQUIRED: The form of the contractual agreement with a client.
    DISCUSSION: The audit scope, audit limitations and expectations, the responsibilities of the parties, and fees for services are required to be set forth in a written communication commonly termed an engagement letter.
    Answer (A) is incorrect. A management representation letter is obtained to assure that management understands its responsibility for the financial statements. Answer (B) is incorrect. The scope paragraph describes the nature of the audit. Answer (D) is incorrect. The introductory paragraph states that the financial statements were audited and the responsibilities of management and the auditor.

3.2 Planning and Supervision (AU 311, AS No. 9, and AS No. 10)

5. Audit plans should be designed so that

    A. Most of the required procedures can be performed as interim work.

    B. Inherent risk is assessed at a sufficiently low level.

    C. The auditor can make constructive suggestions to management.

    D. The audit evidence gathered supports the auditor's conclusions.

Answer (D) is correct. *(CPA, adapted)*
    REQUIRED: The use of audit plans.
    DISCUSSION: The auditor is responsible for collecting sufficient, appropriate audit evidence. Audit plans describe the steps involved in that process. The evidence should support the auditor's conclusions.
    Answer (A) is incorrect. Depending on the assertion, work may be performed at interim dates or in the subsequent events period. Answer (B) is incorrect. The auditor must assess inherent risk based upon the characteristics of the client. Answer (C) is incorrect. Suggestions to management are not required in an audit.

6. In designing written audit plans, an auditor should establish specific audit objectives that relate primarily to the

    A. Timing of audit procedures.

    B. Cost-benefit of gathering evidence.

    C. Selected audit techniques.

    D. Financial statement assertions.

Answer (D) is correct. *(CPA, adapted)*
    REQUIRED: The item to which specific audit objectives primarily relate.
    DISCUSSION: Most audit work consists of obtaining and evaluating evidence about relevant financial statement assertions, which are management representations embodied in financial statement components.
    Answer (A) is incorrect. Timing is important in meeting the objectives of the audit but does not relate to the audit objectives themselves. Answer (B) is incorrect. The cost-benefit of gathering evidence is important to the auditor but is not the primary objective. Answer (C) is incorrect. Audit objectives determine the specific audit techniques.

7. During the initial planning phase of an audit, a CPA most likely would

    A. Identify specific internal control activities that are likely to prevent fraud.

    B. Evaluate the reasonableness of the client's accounting estimates.

    C. Discuss the timing of the audit procedures with the client's management.

    D. Inquire of the client's attorney as to whether any unrecorded claims are probable of assertion.

Answer (C) is correct. *(CPA, adapted)*
    REQUIRED: The activity performed in the initial planning phase of an audit.
    DISCUSSION: The first step in the audit process is the auditor's decision whether to accept a client. After having decided to perform an audit, the auditor enters the initial planning phase. During initial planning, an auditor should, among other things, meet with the client to agree on the type, scope, and timing of the engagement (AU 311).
    Answer (A) is incorrect. Understanding internal control is subsequent to the initial planning phase. Answer (B) is incorrect. Evaluation of estimates would be completed during the evidence collection phase of the audit. Answer (D) is incorrect. Communication with attorneys would be completed during the evidence collection phase of the audit.

8. The senior auditor responsible for coordinating the field work usually schedules a pre-audit conference with the audit team primarily to

    A. Give guidance to the staff regarding both technical and personnel aspects of the audit.

    B. Discuss staff suggestions concerning the establishment and maintenance of time budgets.

    C. Establish the need for using the work of specialists and internal auditors.

    D. Provide an opportunity to document staff disagreements regarding technical issues.

Answer (A) is correct. *(CPA, adapted)*
    REQUIRED: The purpose of a pre-audit conference.
    DISCUSSION: A pre-audit conference is useful to provide guidance to the staff regarding such technical issues as the expected use of client personnel and the expectations of the audit team.
    Answer (B) is incorrect. Time budgets are prepared by supervisors based on the estimates of the time necessary to complete the tasks. Answer (C) is incorrect. The determination of the need for specialists and the use of internal auditors is made by supervisors, not the staff. Answer (D) is incorrect. Disagreements regarding technical issues do not normally arise prior to the audit.

9. The in-charge auditor most likely would have a supervisory responsibility to explain to the staff assistants

    A. That immaterial fraud is not to be reported to the client's audit committee.

    B. Possible accounting issues.

    C. What benefits may be attained by the assistants' adherence to established time budgets.

    D. Why certain documents are being transferred from the current file to the permanent file.

Answer (B) is correct. *(CPA, adapted)*
    REQUIRED: The responsibility of the audit supervisor.
    DISCUSSION: AU 311 indicates that assistants should be informed of their responsibilities and the objectives of the procedures that they are to perform. They should be informed about the matters that affect the nature, timing, and extent of procedures, including possible accounting and auditing issues.
    Answer (A) is incorrect. Immaterial fraud may be reported to those charged with governance, for example, the client's audit committee. Answer (C) is incorrect. Discussion of time budgets is not a responsibility under GAAS. Answer (D) is incorrect. At the end of the audit, supervisors determine which documents are to be transferred to the permanent file. These decisions need not be justified to staff assistants.

3.3 Audit Risk and Materiality (AU 312, AS No. 8, and AS No. 11)

10. The existence of audit risk is recognized by the statement in the auditor's standard report that the

A. Auditor is responsible for expressing an opinion on the financial statements, which are the responsibility of management.

B. Financial statements are presented fairly, in all material respects, in conformity with GAAP.

C. Audit includes examining, on a test basis, evidence supporting the amounts and disclosures in the financial statements.

D. Auditor obtains reasonable assurance about whether the financial statements are free of material misstatement.

Answer (D) is correct. *(CPA, adapted)*
REQUIRED: The statement that recognizes the existence of audit risk.
DISCUSSION: Audit risk is the risk that the auditor expresses an inappropriate audit opinion when the financial statements are materially misstated (AU 312). The high, but not absolute, level of assurance that is intended to be obtained by the auditor is expressed in the auditor's report as obtaining reasonable assurance about whether the financial statements are free of material misstatement (whether caused by error or fraud) (AU 230).
Answer (A) is incorrect. The introductory paragraph of the standard audit report states the degree of the auditor's responsibility. Answer (B) is incorrect. This language indicates the auditor's belief that the statement as a whole are not materially misstated in conformity with GAAP. Answer (C) is incorrect. The scope paragraph of the audit report recognized that examining all items under audit is not feasible. This limitation is one of many inherent in the audit process.

11. The risk that an auditor's procedures will lead to the conclusion that a material misstatement does **not** exist in an account balance when, in fact, such misstatement does exist is

A. Audit risk.

B. Inherent risk.

C. Control risk.

D. Detection risk.

Answer (D) is correct. *(CPA, adapted)*
REQUIRED: The risk that audit procedures will fail to detect a material misstatement.
DISCUSSION: Detection risk is the risk that the auditor will not detect a material misstatement that exists in a relevant assertion. It is affected by the auditor's procedures and can be changed at his/her discretion.
Answer (A) is incorrect. Audit risk includes inherent risk and control risk, which are not affected by the auditor's procedures. Answer (B) is incorrect. Inherent risk is the susceptibility of an assertion to material misstatement in the absence of related controls. Answer (C) is incorrect. Control risk is the risk that a material misstatement will not be prevented or detected by internal control.

12. As the acceptable level of detection risk decreases, an auditor may

A. Reduce substantive testing by relying on the assessments of inherent risk and control risk.

B. Postpone the planned timing of substantive tests from interim dates to the year-end.

C. Eliminate the assessed level of inherent risk from consideration as a planning factor.

D. Lower the assessed level of control risk from a high level to a low level.

Answer (B) is correct. *(CPA, adapted)*
REQUIRED: The action of the auditor as the acceptable level of detection risk decreases.
DISCUSSION: A decrease in the acceptable level of detection risk or in the amount considered material will result in the auditor's modifying the audit plan to obtain greater assurance from substantive testing by (1) selecting a more effective audit procedure, (2) applying procedures nearer to year end, or (3) increasing the extent of particular tests.
Answer (A) is incorrect. Substantive testing would be increased. Answer (C) is incorrect. The auditor should always consider the assessed level of inherent risk in the planning phase of an audit. Answer (D) is incorrect. Control risk is assessed prior to determining the acceptable level of detection risk.

13. The acceptable level of detection risk is inversely related to the

A. Assurance provided by substantive procedures.

B. Risk of misapplying auditing procedures.

C. Preliminary judgment about materiality levels.

D. Risk of failing to discover material misstatements.

Answer (A) is correct. *(CPA, adapted)*
REQUIRED: The relationship between detection risk and the assurance provided by substantive procedures.
DISCUSSION: An auditor considers internal control to assess control risk. (S)he also assesses inherent risk. The greater (lower) the assessed levels of control risk and inherent risk, the lower (greater) the acceptable level of detection risk. Hence, the relationship between performing substantive procedures and detection risk is inverse.
Answer (B) is incorrect. The risk of misapplying auditing procedures is related to the auditor's training and experience. Answer (C) is incorrect. Preliminary judgments about materiality are used by the auditor to determine the acceptable level of audit risk. Detection risk is just one component of audit risk. Answer (D) is incorrect. The acceptable level of detection risk is an inverse function of the assessments of control risk and inherent risk.

14. When expressing an unqualified opinion, the auditor who evaluates the audit findings should be satisfied that the

A. Amount of known misstatement is documented in the management representation letter.

B. Estimate of the total likely misstatement is less than a material amount.

C. Amount of known misstatement is acknowledged and recorded by the client.

D. Estimate of the total likely misstatement includes the adjusting entries already recorded by the client.

Answer (B) is correct. *(Publisher, adapted)*
REQUIRED: The audit findings that support an unqualified opinion.
DISCUSSION: The opinion paragraph of the standard auditor's report explicitly states that the financial statements present fairly, in all material respects, the financial position, results of operations, and cash flows of the entity in conformity with GAAP. It reflects the auditor's judgment that uncorrected misstatements do not cause the financial statements to be materially misstated. The evaluation of whether the financial statements are materially misstated requires the auditor to consider the individual and aggregate effects (qualitative and quantitative) of uncorrected misstatements. This consideration and aggregation should include the best estimate of total misstatement (likely misstatement), not just the amount specifically identified (known misstatement). Moreover, the auditor must document the nature and effect of the aggregated misstatements and the conclusion about whether they cause material misstatement (AU 312).
Answer (A) is incorrect. The auditor's judgment regarding whether the financial statements are fairly presented, in all material respects, relates to his/her evaluation of likely misstatement, not known misstatement. Answer (C) is incorrect. The auditor's judgment regarding whether the financial statements are fairly presented, in all material respects, relates to his/her evaluation of likely misstatement, not known misstatement. Answer (D) is incorrect. Total likely misstatement excludes material misstatements eliminated by, for example, adjusting entries.

15. Which of the following would an auditor most likely use in determining materiality for the statements as a whole when establishing the overall audit strategy?

A. The anticipated sample size of the planned substantive tests.

B. The entity's period-to-date financial results and position.

C. The results of the internal control questionnaire.

D. The contents of the management representation letter.

Answer (B) is correct. *(CPA, adapted)*
REQUIRED: The factor most likely used in determining the preliminary judgment about materiality.
DISCUSSION: The auditor's materiality level might be based on the entity's period-to-date financial results and position or financial statements of one or more prior periods. But recognition should be given to the effect of major changes in the entity's circumstances (for example, a significant merger) and relevant changes in the economy as a whole or the industry in which the entity operates.
Answer (A) is incorrect. The auditor's materiality level is used to determine the sample sizes for substantive tests. Sample sizes are calculated during evidence collection. Answer (C) is incorrect. Results of the internal control questionnaire are considered during the assessment of control risk. Answer (D) is incorrect. The contents of the management representation letter are determined near the end of the audit.

16. A client decides not to make an auditor's proposed adjustments that collectively are not material and wants the auditor to issue the report based on the unadjusted numbers. Which of the following statements is correct regarding the financial statement presentation?

A. The financial statements are free from material misstatement, and **no** disclosure is required in the notes to the financial statements.

B. The financial statements do **not** conform with generally accepted accounting principles (GAAP).

C. The financial statements contain unadjusted misstatements that should result in a qualified opinion.

D. The financial statements are free from material misstatement, but disclosure of the proposed adjustments is required in the notes to the financial statements.

Answer (A) is correct. *(CPA, adapted)*
REQUIRED: The action when a client decides not to make an auditor's proposed adjustments that collectively are not material.
DISCUSSION: If the proposed adjustments are immaterial, by definition the financial statements are free from material misstatement, and an unqualified opinion may be expressed. However, the schedule of proposed adjustments must be included in the management representation letter, and management must assert that these proposed adjustments are individually and collectively immaterial.
Answer (B) is incorrect. The financial statement would be free of material misstatements and would conform with GAAP. Answer (C) is incorrect. An unqualified opinion would be warranted. Answer (D) is incorrect. No disclosure in the notes would be required.

3.4 Understanding the Entity and Its Environment (AU 314 and AS No. 12)

17. Prior to beginning the field work on a new audit engagement in which a CPA does **not** possess expertise in the industry in which the client operates, the CPA should

   A. Reduce audit risk by lowering initial levels of materiality.

   B. Design special substantive procedures to compensate for the lack of industry expertise.

   C. Engage financial experts familiar with the nature of the industry.

   D. Perform risk assessment procedures.

Answer (D) is correct. *(CPA, adapted)*
   REQUIRED: The action taken by an auditor who lacks experience with the client's industry.
   DISCUSSION: The auditor should obtain an understanding of the entity and its environment, including its internal control. For this purpose, the auditor performs the following risk assessment procedures: (1) inquiries of management and others within the entity, (2) analytical procedures, and (3) observation and inspection.
   Answer (A) is incorrect. The auditor cannot make judgments about materiality levels until (s)he has a sufficient understanding of the entity. Answer (B) is incorrect. The auditor cannot design substantive procedures until (s)he has a sufficient understanding of the entity. Answer (C) is incorrect. The use of experts does not relieve the auditor of the responsibility to obtain an understanding of the entity.

18. To obtain an understanding of a continuing client in planning an audit, an auditor most likely would

   A. Perform tests of details of transactions and balances.

   B. Read internal audit reports.

   C. Read specialized industry journals.

   D. Reevaluate the risks of material misstatement.

Answer (B) is correct. *(CPA, adapted)*
   REQUIRED: The procedure used to obtain an understanding of a continuing client.
   DISCUSSION: The auditor performs risk assessment procedures to obtain the understanding of the entity and its environment, including its internal control. These include, for example, reading (1) internal audit reports, (2) interim statements, (3) quarterly reports, and (4) minutes of board meetings.
   Answer (A) is incorrect. Tests of details are used to collect sufficient, appropriate audit evidence to support the opinion. Answer (C) is incorrect. Reading specialized industry journals would provide information about the industry, but not necessarily about the specific client. Answer (D) is incorrect. The auditor reevaluates the RMMs after updating the understanding of a continuing client.

19. A CPA wishes to determine how various issuers have complied with the disclosure requirements of a new financial accounting standard. Which of the following information sources would the CPA most likely consult for this information?

   A. AICPA Codification of Statements on Auditing Standards.

   B. AICPA Accounting Trends and Techniques.

   C. PCAOB Inspection Reports.

   D. SEC Statement 10-K Guide.

Answer (B) is correct. *(CPA, adapted)*
   REQUIRED: The publication most likely consulted for compliance information of a new financial accounting standard.
   DISCUSSION: Practical guidance for conducting accounting and audit engagements can be found in various nonauthoritative publications, such as Accounting Trends and Techniques, which describes current practice regarding corporate financial accounting and disclosure policies. It is a useful source for practitioners in industry and public practice. This annual AICPA publication is based on a survey of the annual financial reports of over 600 public companies.
   Answer (A) is incorrect. The AICPA Codification of Statements on Auditing Standards contains U.S. generally accepted auditing standards (GAAS). Answer (C) is incorrect. Although quality control extends to adherence to GAAP, the PCAOB Inspection Reports do not provide information about prevalent practice regarding compliance with particular disclosure requirements. Answer (D) is incorrect. Consulting the actual Form 10-K filings by public companies, which contain audited financial statements, would be more useful than consulting the guidance information provided by the SEC.

3.5 Analytical Procedures (AU 329)

20. A basic premise underlying analytical procedures is that

A. These procedures cannot replace tests of balances and transactions.

B. Statistical tests of financial information may lead to the discovery of material misstatements in the financial statements.

C. The study of financial ratios is an acceptable alternative to the investigation of unusual fluctuations.

D. Plausible relationships among data may reasonably be expected to exist and continue in the absence of known conditions to the contrary.

Answer (D) is correct. *(CPA, adapted)*
REQUIRED: The basic premise underlying analytical procedures.
DISCUSSION: AU 329 states, "A basic premise underlying the application of analytical procedures is that plausible relationships among data may reasonably be expected to exist and continue in the absence of known conditions to the contrary." Variability in these relationships can be explained by, for example, unusual events or transactions, business or accounting changes, misstatements, or random fluctuations.
Answer (A) is incorrect. For some assertions, analytical procedures alone may provide the auditor with the level of assurance (s)he desires. Answer (B) is incorrect. Analytical procedures, such as simple comparisons, do not necessarily require statistical testing. Answer (C) is incorrect. The objective of analytical procedures, such as ratio analysis, is to identify significant differences for evaluation and possible investigation.

21. The objective of performing analytical procedures in planning an audit is to identify the existence of

A. Unusual transactions and events.

B. Illegal acts that went undetected because of internal control weaknesses.

C. Related party transactions.

D. Recorded transactions that were not properly authorized.

Answer (A) is correct. *(CPA, adapted)*
REQUIRED: The objective of analytical procedures.
DISCUSSION: The objective of analytical procedures "is to identify such things as the existence of unusual transactions and events, and amounts, ratios, and trends that might indicate matters that have financial statement and audit planning ramifications" (AU 329).
Answer (B) is incorrect. The objective of performing analytical procedures to plan the audit is to identify areas of specific risk, not specific illegal acts. Answer (C) is incorrect. Although the auditor should evaluate disclosures about related party transactions, analytical procedures performed to plan the audit do not necessarily detect such transactions. Answer (D) is incorrect. Tests of controls are necessary to determine whether transactions were properly authorized.

22. For audits of financial statements made in accordance with generally accepted auditing standards, analytical procedures should be applied to some extent

	In the Planning Stage	As a Substantive Test	In the Final Review Stage
A.	No	Yes	Yes
B.	Yes	Yes	No
C.	Yes	No	Yes
D.	No	No	No

Answer (C) is correct. *(CPA, adapted)*
REQUIRED: The use of analytical procedures.
DISCUSSION: AU 329 states that analytical procedures should be applied to some extent to assist the auditor in planning other auditing procedures and as an overall review of the financial information in the final review stage of the audit. Analytical procedures may be more efficient or effective than substantive tests of details to achieve certain audit objectives.

23. Which of the following nonfinancial information would an auditor most likely consider in performing analytical procedures during the planning phase of an audit?

A. Turnover of personnel in the accounting department.

B. Objectivity of audit committee members.

C. Square footage of selling space.

D. Management's plans to repurchase stock.

Answer (C) is correct. *(CPA, adapted)*
REQUIRED: The nonfinancial information considered in performing analytical procedures during audit planning.
DISCUSSION: AU 329 states, "Although analytical procedures used in planning the audit often use only financial data, sometimes relevant nonfinancial information is considered as well. For example, number of employees, square footage of selling space, volume of goods produced, and similar information may contribute to accomplishing the purpose of the procedures."
Answer (A) is incorrect. Turnover of personnel in the accounting department is not a measure related to analytical procedures. Answer (B) is incorrect. Objectivity of audit committee members is not a measure related to analytical procedures. Answer (D) is incorrect. Management's plans to repurchase stock is not a measure related to analytical procedures.

24. An auditor's decision either to apply analytical procedures as substantive tests or to perform tests of transactions and account balances usually is determined by the

A. Availability of data aggregated at a high level.

B. Relative effectiveness and efficiency of the tests.

C. Timing of tests performed after the balance sheet date.

D. Auditor's familiarity with industry trends.

Answer (B) is correct. *(CPA, adapted)*
   REQUIRED: The basis for choosing between analytical procedures and tests of details.
   DISCUSSION: The decision is based on the auditor's judgment about the expected effectiveness and efficiency of the available procedures. The auditor considers the level of assurance required to be provided by substantive testing for a particular audit objective related to a particular assertion. (S)he must then decide which procedure or combination of procedures can provide that level of assurance. "For some assertions, analytical procedures are effective in providing the appropriate level of assurance" (AU 329).
   Answer (A) is incorrect. Availability of data is just one factor in evaluating effectiveness and efficiency. Answer (C) is incorrect. The timing of tests is one of many considerations in determining effectiveness and efficiency. Answer (D) is incorrect. Familiarity with trends is one factor among many in determining effectiveness and efficiency.

25. Analytical procedures are most appropriate when testing which of the following types of transactions?

A. Payroll and benefit liabilities.

B. Acquisitions and disposals of fixed assets.

C. Operating expense transactions.

D. Noncurrent debt transactions.

Answer (C) is correct. *(CPA, adapted)*
   REQUIRED: The most appropriate use of analytical procedures.
   DISCUSSION: Audit standards indicate that relationships involving income statement accounts tend to be more predictable than relationships involving only balance sheet accounts because income statement accounts represent transactions over a period of time, whereas balance sheet accounts represent an amount at a moment in time. Thus, operating expense transactions would likely be more predictable than balance sheet accounts.
   Answer (A) is incorrect. Payroll and benefit liabilities are balance sheet accounts and not as predictable as, for example, payroll expense. Answer (B) is incorrect. Acquisitions and disposals of fixed assets relate to balance sheet accounts, which are not typically as predictable as income statement accounts. Answer (D) is incorrect. Noncurrent debt transactions relate to balance sheet accounts, which are not typically as predictable as income statement accounts.

26. The primary objective of analytical procedures used in the final review stage of an audit is to

A. Obtain evidence from details testing to corroborate particular assertions.

B. Identify areas that represent specific risks relevant to the audit.

C. Assist the auditor in assessing the validity of the conclusions reached.

D. Satisfy doubts when questions arise about a client's ability to continue in existence.

Answer (C) is correct. *(CPA, adapted)*
   REQUIRED: The primary objective of analytical procedures used in the final review stage of an audit.
   DISCUSSION: Analytical procedures should be applied to some extent as an overall review in the final review stage of the audit. They are useful in assessing the conclusions reached by the auditor and in evaluating financial statement presentation. Many procedures may be used. These ordinarily should include reading the statements and notes and considering (1) the adequacy of evidence regarding previously identified unusual or unexpected balances and (2) unusual or unexpected balances or relationships not previously noted (AU 329).
   Answer (A) is incorrect. Obtaining evidence to corroborate particular assertions is done before the final review stage. Answer (B) is incorrect. Identifying specific areas of risk is done in the planning stage. Answer (D) is incorrect. Resolving a going concern issue is a secondary objective.

27. Analytical procedures used in the overall review stage of an audit generally include

    A. Considering unusual or unexpected account balances that were not previously identified.

    B. Performing tests of transactions to corroborate management's financial statement assertions.

    C. Gathering evidence concerning account balances that have not changed from the prior year.

    D. Retesting controls that appeared to be ineffective during the assessment of control risk.

Answer (A) is correct. *(CPA, adapted)*
    REQUIRED: The analytical procedure used in the final review stage.
    DISCUSSION: Analytical procedures should be applied to some extent as an overall review in the final review stage of the audit. They are useful in assessing the conclusions reached by the auditor and in evaluating financial statement presentation. Many procedures may be used. These ordinarily should include reading the statements and notes and considering (1) the adequacy of evidence regarding previously identified unusual or unexpected balances and (2) unusual or unexpected balances or relationships not previously noted (AU 329).
    Answer (B) is incorrect. Analytical procedures are not tests of transactions. Answer (C) is incorrect. The lack of change from the prior year may not be unusual or unexpected. Answer (D) is incorrect. Analytical procedures are substantive tests, not tests of controls.

3.6 Consideration of Fraud in a Financial Statement Audit (AU 316)

28. Which of the following statements reflects an auditor's responsibility for detecting errors and fraud?

    A. An auditor is responsible for detecting employee errors and simple fraud, but not for discovering fraudulent acts involving employee collusion or management override.

    B. An auditor should plan the audit to detect errors and fraud that are caused by departures from GAAP.

    C. An auditor is not responsible for detecting errors and fraud unless the application of GAAS would result in such detection.

    D. An auditor should design the audit to provide reasonable assurance of detecting errors and fraud that are material to the financial statements.

Answer (D) is correct. *(CPA, adapted)*
    REQUIRED: The statement reflecting the auditor's responsibility for detecting errors and fraudulent activity.
    DISCUSSION: "The auditor has a responsibility to plan and perform the audit to obtain reasonable assurance about whether the financial statements are free of material misstatements, whether caused by error or fraud" (AU 110). Thus, the consideration of fraud should be logically integrated into the overall audit process in a manner consistent with other pronouncements, e.g., those on planning and supervision, audit risk and materiality, and internal control. This consideration entails (1) understanding fraud, (2) discussing fraud risks with members of the engagement team, (3) obtaining information needed to identify fraud risks, (4) identifying those risks, (5) assessing fraud risks, (6) responding to the assessments, (7) evaluating evidence at the end of the audit, (8) making appropriate communications about fraud, and (9) documenting the consideration.

29. Because of the risk of material misstatement due to fraud, an audit of financial statements in accordance with generally accepted auditing standards should be planned and performed with an attitude of

    A. Objective judgment.

    B. Independent integrity.

    C. Professional skepticism.

    D. Impartial conservatism.

Answer (C) is correct. *(CPA, adapted)*
    REQUIRED: The attitude required for planning and performing an audit.
    DISCUSSION: Due professional care requires the auditor to exercise professional skepticism. Professional skepticism is an attitude that includes a questioning mind and critical assessment of audit evidence. Regardless of past experience with the entity or belief in management's honesty, the audit should be conducted with (1) an awareness that a material misstatement due to fraud may exist and (2) ongoing questioning of whether the evidence suggests that such fraud has occurred (AU 316).
    Answer (A) is incorrect. Although objective judgment is a quality appropriate for practitioners, it is not required to be applied specifically in an audit. Answer (B) is incorrect. Although independent integrity is a quality appropriate for practitioners, it is not required to be applied specifically in an audit. Answer (D) is incorrect. Although impartial conservatism is a quality appropriate for practitioners, it is not required to be applied specifically in an audit.

30. Which of the following statements describes why a properly designed and executed audit may **not** detect a material fraud?

A. Audit procedures that are effective for detecting an unintentional misstatement may be ineffective for an intentional misstatement that is concealed through collusion.

B. An audit is designed to provide reasonable assurance of detecting material errors, but there is no similar responsibility concerning material fraud.

C. The factors considered in assessing control risk indicated an increased risk of intentional misstatements, but only a low risk of unintentional errors in the financial statements.

D. The auditor did not consider factors influencing audit risk for account balances that have effects pervasive to the financial statements taken as a whole.

Answer (A) is correct. *(CPA, adapted)*
REQUIRED: The reason a properly designed and executed audit may not detect a material fraud.
DISCUSSION: Because of the concealment of fraudulent activity, including the fact that fraud often involves collusion or falsified documents, and the need to apply professional judgment in the identification and evaluation of fraud risk factors and other conditions, even a properly planned and performed audit may not detect a material misstatement resulting from fraud.
Answer (B) is incorrect. The auditor's responsibility is the same for fraud as for material errors. Answer (C) is incorrect. If the risk of intentional misstatements is assessed to be high, the auditor would apply additional procedures, and thereby increase the probability of uncovering the fraud. Answer (D) is incorrect. An audit that is properly designed and executed should consider audit risk factors for accounts having pervasive effects on the statements.

31. Which of the following circumstances most likely would cause an auditor to consider whether material misstatements exist in an entity's financial statements?

A. Management places little emphasis on meeting earnings projections.

B. The board of directors makes all major financing decisions.

C. Significant deficiencies and material weaknesses previously communicated to management are not corrected.

D. Transactions selected for testing are not supported by proper documentation.

Answer (D) is correct. *(CPA, adapted)*
REQUIRED: The circumstance most likely to cause an auditor to consider whether material misstatements exist.
DISCUSSION: The planned scope of audit procedures should be reconsidered when conditions differ adversely from expectations. When transactions chosen for testing lack proper documentation or authorization, the likelihood of misstatement increases.
Answer (A) is incorrect. If management places increased emphasis on meeting earnings projections, the likelihood for misstatement increases. Answer (B) is incorrect. The board's involvement in decision making reduces the likelihood of material misstatements. Answer (C) is incorrect. Management should evaluate the cost and benefits of corrections in deciding whether to correct control deficiencies.

32. Which of the following situations represents a risk factor that relates to misstatements arising from misappropriation of assets?

A. A high turnover of senior management.

B. A lack of independent checks.

C. A strained relationship between management and the predecessor auditor.

D. An inability to generate cash flow from operations.

Answer (B) is correct. *(CPA, adapted)*
REQUIRED: The risk factor that relates to misstatements arising from misappropriation of assets.
DISCUSSION: Fraud in financial statements results from either fraudulent financial reporting by management or the misappropriation of assets by employees or others. Misappropriation of assets is mitigated by internal controls, including independent checks.
Answer (A) is incorrect. A high turnover of senior management represents a risk factor that relates to fraudulent financial reporting. Answer (C) is incorrect. A strained relationship between management and the predecessor auditor represents a risk factor that relates to fraudulent financial reporting. Answer (D) is incorrect. An inability to generate cash flow from operations represents a risk factor that relates to fraudulent financial reporting.

33. Disclosure of fraud to parties other than a client's senior management and its audit committee ordinarily is not part of an auditor's responsibility. However, to which of the following outside parties may a duty to disclose fraud exist?

	To the SEC When the Client Reports an Auditor Change	To a Successor Auditor When the Successor Makes Appropriate Inquiries	To a Governmental Agency from Which the Client Receives Financial Assistance
A.	Yes	Yes	No
B.	Yes	No	Yes
C.	No	Yes	Yes
D.	Yes	Yes	Yes

Answer (D) is correct. *(CPA, adapted)*
REQUIRED: The outside parties to whom a duty to disclose fraud exists.
DISCUSSION: According to AU 316, a duty of disclosure to parties other than the client may exist when the entity reports an auditor change to the SEC on Form 8-K, and the fraud (or risk factors) is a reportable event or a source or disagreement. An auditor must also respond in accordance with the requirements for governmental audits, for example, those imposed by Government Auditing Standards. Under AU 315, a predecessor auditor must respond to inquiries by the auditor if the client gives its specific permission.
Answer (A) is incorrect. An auditor responds to a government agency in accordance with the requirements of audits of recipients of government funds. Answer (B) is incorrect. A predecessor auditor responds to inquiries by the auditor if the client gives its specific permission. Answer (C) is incorrect. An auditor responds to the SEC when the entity reports an auditor change on Form 8-K.

3.7 Illegal Acts by Clients (AU 317)

34. Which of the following procedures would **least** likely result in the discovery of possible illegal acts?

A. Reading the minutes of the board of directors' meetings.

B. Making inquiries of the client's management.

C. Performing tests of details of transactions.

D. Reviewing an internal control questionnaire.

Answer (D) is correct. *(CPA, adapted)*
REQUIRED: The procedure least likely to result in the discovery of possible illegal acts.
DISCUSSION: Auditors should design the audit to provide reasonable assurance of detecting illegal acts that have a direct and material effect on the financial statements. Internal control questionnaires document the auditor's understanding of internal control. Reviewing the responses to the questionnaire may reveal control weaknesses but not illegal acts.
Answer (A) is incorrect. Reading the minutes of the board of directors' meetings may provide evidence regarding illegal acts. Answer (B) is incorrect. The auditor should inquire of management about the entity's compliance with laws and regulations. Answer (C) is incorrect. Performing tests of details of transactions may provide information regarding illegal acts.

35. Jones, CPA, is auditing the financial statements of XYZ Retailing, Inc. What assurance does Jones provide that direct-effect illegal acts that are material to XYZ's financial statements and illegal acts that have a material but indirect effect on the financial statements will be detected?

	Direct-Effect Illegal Acts	Indirect-Effect Illegal Acts
A.	Reasonable	None
B.	Reasonable	Reasonable
C.	Limited	None
D.	Limited	Reasonable

Answer (A) is correct. *(CPA, adapted)*
REQUIRED: The auditor assurance provided in connection with a client's potential illegal acts.
DISCUSSION: The auditor has the same responsibility for detecting misstatements arising from illegal acts that have a direct and material effect on the financial statements as for material errors and fraud. Thus, the auditor should plan and perform the audit to obtain reasonable assurance about whether the financial statements are free of material misstatement caused by illegal acts having direct and material effects. However, because of the nature of illegal acts that have an indirect effect, an audit in accordance with GAAS provides no assurance that such illegal acts will be detected or that any resulting contingent liabilities will be disclosed (AU 317).

36. If specific information that implies the existence of possible illegal acts that could have a material but indirect effect on the financial statements comes to an auditor's attention, the auditor should next

    A. Apply audit procedures specifically directed to ascertaining whether an illegal act has occurred.

    B. Seek the advice of an informed expert qualified to practice law as to possible contingent liabilities.

    C. Report the matter to an appropriate level of management at least one level above those involved.

    D. Discuss the evidence with the client's audit committee, or others with equivalent authority and responsibility.

Answer (A) is correct. *(CPA, adapted)*
    REQUIRED: The auditor's responsibility when (s)he becomes aware of an illegal act having a material indirect effect.
    DISCUSSION: The auditor should apply audit procedures specifically directed to ascertaining whether an illegal act has occurred. When the auditor becomes aware of information concerning a possible illegal act, the auditor should obtain an understanding of the nature of the act, the circumstances in which it occurred, and sufficient other information to evaluate the effect on the financial statements.
    Answer (B) is incorrect. The auditor need not consult legal counsel until after determining that an illegal act has occurred. Answer (C) is incorrect. Making inquiries of management is just one possible procedure involved in determining whether an illegal act has occurred. Answer (D) is incorrect. The auditor should not discuss the evidence with those charged with governance until after determining that an illegal act has occurred.

37. During the audit of a new client, the auditor determined that management had given illegal bribes to municipal officials during the year under audit and for several prior years. The auditor notified the client's board of directors, but the board decided to take no action because the amounts involved were immaterial to the financial statements. Under these circumstances, the auditor should

    A. Add an explanatory paragraph emphasizing that certain matters, while **not** affecting the unqualified opinion, require disclosure.

    B. Report the illegal bribes to the municipal official at least one level above those persons who received the bribes.

    C. Consider withdrawing from the audit engagement and disassociating from future relationships with the client.

    D. Issue an "except for" qualified opinion or an adverse opinion with a separate paragraph that explains the circumstances.

Answer (C) is correct. *(CPA, adapted)*
    REQUIRED: The appropriate auditor action.
    DISCUSSION: If the client does not take the remedial action considered necessary by the auditor, the auditor should consider withdrawal from the engagement even when the illegal acts are not material. The auditor should weigh the effects on the ability to rely on management's representations and the possible results of continued association with the client. The auditor may wish to seek legal advice (AU 317).
    Answer (A) is incorrect. The illegal acts may not require disclosure; however, remedial action would be expected by the auditor. Answer (B) is incorrect. The auditor has no responsibility to report this information to the external organization associated with the bribes. Answer (D) is incorrect. Immaterial items do not affect the fairness of the financial statements; thus, a modified opinion is unwarranted.

38. Under the Private Securities Litigation Reform Act of 1995, Baker, CPA, reported certain uncorrected illegal acts to Supermart's board of directors. Baker believed that failure to take remedial action would warrant a qualified audit opinion because the illegal acts had a material effect on Supermart's financial statements. Supermart failed to take appropriate remedial action, and the board of directors refused to inform the SEC that it had received such notification from Baker. Under these circumstances, Baker is required to

    A. Resign from the audit engagement within 10 business days.

    B. Deliver a report concerning the illegal acts to the SEC within 1 business day.

    C. Notify the shareholders that the financial statements are materially misstated.

    D. Withhold an audit opinion until Supermart takes appropriate remedial action.

Answer (B) is correct. *(CPA, adapted)*
    REQUIRED: The requirements under the Private Securities Litigation Reform Act of 1995.
    DISCUSSION: Disclosure of illegal acts to outside parties is not normally the auditor's responsibility. However, under the Private Securities Litigation Reform Act of 1995, accountants must report illegal acts to the appropriate level of management and the audit committee unless they are clearly inconsequential. If senior management and the board fail to take action on reported material illegal acts, and this failure will result in a departure from a standard report or resignation from the audit, the accountants should report their conclusions to the board immediately. The board must then, within 1 business day, notify the SEC. If the accountants do not receive a copy of the notice within the 1-day period, they must furnish the SEC with a copy of their report within 1 business day.
    Answer (A) is incorrect. The auditor is not required to resign from the engagement. Answer (C) is incorrect. A qualified audit opinion states that, except for the effects of the matter to which the qualification relates, the financial statements are presented fairly in all material respects. Any other notice to the shareholders is not required. Answer (D) is incorrect. The auditor should express a qualified opinion if it is justified by the lack of remedial action. GAAS do not provide for a delay in the report until remedial action is taken.

3.8 PRACTICE SIMULATION

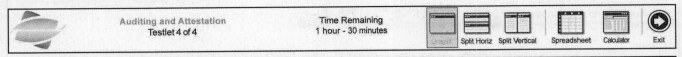

DIRECTIONS

Note: If you believe you have encountered a software malfunction, report it to the test center staff immediately.

Navigation

To navigate from task to task, use the controls at the bottom of the screen. Click on the **Next** button to advance to the next task, or the **Previous** button to go to the previous task. To go directly to any task, click on its number.

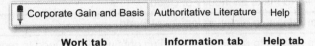

If you would like a reminder to revisit a task, or want to indicate that you are finished with it, click on the reminder flag below the task number. To clear the flag, click on it again. Reminder flags are for your use only – they do not contribute to your score.

Tabs

In this part of the examination, you will be asked to complete various tasks. Every task has one or more **Work Tabs**. Some tasks have one or more **Information Tabs**, others may have none. Every task has a **Help** tab.

If a task has **Information Tabs**, you may use the information in them to complete your responses in the **Work Tabs**.

Corporate Gain and Basis	Authoritative Literature	Help
Work tab	**Information tab**	**Help tab**

Work Tabs:
- **Work Tabs** are identified with a pencil icon. This is where your responses are expected.
- Each task has one or more **Work Tabs**.
- **Work Tabs** contain directions for completing the task – be sure to read these directions carefully.
- The **Work Tab** name in the example above is for illustration only – yours will differ.
- You must complete all of the **Work Tabs** in each task to receive full credit.

Information Tabs:
- The Authoritative Literature will be provided in all tasks in the AUD, FAR, and REG sections for your reference.
- Your simulation may have one or more additional **Information Tabs**. Like the Authoritative Literature tabs, **Information Tabs** do not have a pencil icon.
- If your task has additional **Information Tabs**, go through each to familiarize yourself with the task content.

Help Tab:
- The **Help Tab** provides assistance with the exam software that is used in this task. For example, if the task is to compose a memorandum, **Help** will provide information about the word processor.

The Toolbar

The toolbar at the top of the screen shows the amount of time remaining for you to complete the tasks. In addition, the following tools are available. Note that only the Exit button is displayed when Directions are visible - the others will appear when you begin the tasks.

Click on these buttons to split or unsplit the screen. You can split the screen vertically or horizontally.

Click on this button to display the calculator; click on it again to hide the calculator. To move the calculator, click on the calculator title bar and drag the calculator to the desired location.

Click on this button to use the spreadsheet; click on it again to hide the spreadsheet. To move the spreadsheet, click on the the spreadsheet title bar and drag the spreadsheet to the desired location.

Click on this button to go on to the next part of the examination. You must complete all of the tasks to receive full credit. Once you click on **Exit** and confirm the action, you will NOT be able to return to this testlet.

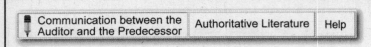

| Communication between the Auditor and the Predecessor | Authoritative Literature | Help |

Client

Adams Company is a firm that has been in operation for 15 years. It produces products for a number of wholesalers and has experienced significant growth over the past several years. The firm has recently replaced its Chief Financial Officer because of questionable practices by the Officer. One problem has been the inability of the firm's control system to keep up with the growth. The client has expressed concern that the auditor did not uncover the CFO's questionable practices and has decided to seek a new auditor.

Predecessor Auditor

Dodd, CPA, has been Adams' auditor for several years and has expressed unqualified opinions on the financial statements for those years, the latest for the year ended December 31, Year 1. Dodd believes that the fault is with Adams' control system and that no audit would have uncovered the CFO's questionable practices.

Potential Auditor

On November 5, Year 2, Adams invited Hall, CPA, to make a proposal for an engagement to audit its financial statements for the year ended December 31, Year 2. Hall has had no previous relations with Adams.

For each procedure below, determine if it should be performed before accepting the engagement, and check the appropriate box.

Procedures	Yes	No
1. Explain to Adams the need to make an inquiry of Dodd.		
2. Request permission from Adams to make an inquiry of Dodd.		
3. Request permission from Adams to disclose information obtained from Dodd to regulatory agencies.		
4. Ask Adams to authorize Dodd to respond fully to Hall's inquiries.		
5. Request personal financial statements from Dodd.		
6. Make inquiries of Dodd concerning the integrity of the management of Adams.		
7. Make inquiries of Dodd concerning the fee arrangements that Dodd had with Adams.		
8. Make inquiries of Dodd concerning disagreements with the management of Adams as to accounting principles and auditing procedures.		
9. Request from Dodd the reasons for the change in auditors.		
10. Demand that Dodd make available the audit documentation prepared in the prior year's audit.		

| Ratios | Authoritative Literature | Help |

Adams Company
Balance Sheet
As of October 31, Year 2

Assets

Cash	$ 240,000
Receivables	400,000
Inventory	600,000
Total current assets	$ 1,240,000
Plant and equipment-net	760,000
Total assets	**$ 2,000,000**

Liabilities and equity

Accounts payable	$ 160,000
Notes payable	100,000
Other current liabilities	140,000
Total current liabilities	$ 400,000
Noncurrent debt	350,000
Common stock	750,000
Retained earnings	500,000
Total liabilities and equity	**$ 2,000,000**

Adams Company
Income Statement
For the 10 Months Ending October 31, Year 2

Sales		$ 3,000,000
Cost of goods sold		
Materials	$800,000	
Labor	700,000	
Overhead	300,000	1,800,000
Gross margin		$ 1,200,000
Selling expenses	$240,000	
General and administrative expenses	300,000	540,000
Operating income		$ 660,000
Minus interest expense		40,000
Income before taxes		$ 620,000
Minus federal income taxes		220,000
Net income		**$ 400,000**

Given the year-to-date financial information, calculate the ratios. Enter the appropriate amounts in the shaded cells in the table below. Calculations should be rounded if necessary to the same number of places as the prior year's ratios, which are provided for comparative purposes only.

Ratio	Adams Company's Ratios for the 10 Months Ending 10/31/Year 2	Adams Company's Ratios for the 10 Months Ending 10/31/Year 1
1. Current ratio		2.5
2. Quick ratio		1.3
3. Accounts receivable turnover		5.5
4. Inventory turnover		2.5
5. Total asset turnover		1.2
6. Gross margin percentage		35%
7. Net operating margin percentage		25%
8. Times interest earned		10.3
9. Total debt to equity percentage		50%

The table below contains the most likely explanation(s) of the auditor's observations of changes in certain financial statement ratios or amounts from the prior year's ratios or amounts. For each observed change, choose one, two, or three explanations (as indicated) by checking the appropriate boxes in the table. Each explanation may be used once, more than once, or not at all.

Observed Changes

1.   Inventory turnover increased substantially from the prior year. **(Choose three explanations.)**
2.   Accounts receivable turnover increased substantially from the prior year. **(Choose three explanations.)**
3.   The allowance for doubtful accounts increased from the prior year, but, as a percentage of accounts receivable, it decreased from the prior year. **(Choose three explanations.)**
4.   Noncurrent debt increased from the prior year, but interest expense increased by an amount that was proportionately greater than the increase in noncurrent debt. **(Choose one explanation.)**
5.   Operating income increased from the prior year, although the entity was less profitable than in the prior year. **(Choose two explanations.)**
6.   The gross margin percentage was unchanged from the prior year, although gross margin increased from the prior year. **(Choose one explanation.)**

1	2	3	4	5	6	*Explanation*
						A) Items shipped on consignment during the last month of the year were recorded as sales.
						B) A significant number of credit memos for returned merchandise that were issued during the last month of the year were not recorded.
						C) Year-end purchases of inventory were overstated by incorrectly including items received in the first month of the subsequent year.
						D) Year-end purchases of inventory were understated by incorrectly excluding items received before year-end.
						E) A larger percentage of sales occurred during the last month of the year, as compared with the prior year.
						F) A smaller percentage of sales occurred during the last month of the year, as compared with the prior year.
						G) The same percentage of sales occurred during the last month of the year, as compared with the prior year.
						H) Sales increased by the same percentage as cost of goods sold, as compared with the prior year.
						I) Sales increased by a greater percentage than cost of goods sold increased, as compared with the prior year.
						J) Sales increased by a lower percentage than cost of goods sold increased, as compared with the prior year.
						K) Interest expensed decreased, as compared with the prior year.
						L) The effective income tax rate increased, as compared with the prior year.
						M) The effective income tax rate decreased, as compared with the prior year.
						N) Short-term borrowing was refinanced on a long-term basis at the same interest rate.
						O) Short-term borrowing was refinanced on a long-term basis at lower interest rates.
						P) Short-term borrowing was refinanced on a long-term basis at higher interest rates.

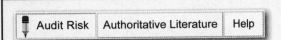

| Audit Risk | Authoritative Literature | Help |

Bestwood Furniture, Inc., a nonissuer that produces wood furniture, is undergoing a Year 2 audit. The situations in the table below describe changes Bestwood made during Year 2 that may or may not contribute to audit risk. For each situation, select from the list provided the impact, if any, that the situation has on a specific component of audit risk for the Year 2 audit. A choice may be used once, more than once, or not at all.

Situation	Effect on component of audit risk
1. During Year 2, the company instituted a new procedure whereby the internal audit department distributes payroll checks to employees for selected payroll cycles.	
2. In Year 2, the auditor noted that the company's newly hired purchasing agent was not obtaining competitive bids for all major purchase requisitions.	
3. Early in Year 2, the company extended its existing warranty program on some of its major products in an effort to increase revenue.	

Choices
A) Decreases control risk
B) Decreases detection risk
C) Decreases inherent risk
D) Increases control risk
E) Increases detection risk
F) Increases inherent risk
G) No effect on audit risk

| ▼ = Reminder | | Directions | 1 ▽ | 2 ▽ | 3 ▽ | 4 ▽ | 5 ▽ | 6 ▽ | | ◀ Previous | Next ▶ |

Analytical procedures consist of evaluations of financial information made by a study of plausible relationships among both financial and nonfinancial data. They range from simple comparisons to the use of complex models involving many relationships and elements of data. They involve comparisons of recorded amounts, or ratios developed from recorded amounts, to expectations developed by the auditors.

Choose three items from List A that describe the broad purposes of analytical procedures.

Purposes
1.
2.
3.

List A
I) To assist the auditor in planning the nature, timing, and extent of other auditing procedures.
II) As a substantive test to obtain audit evidence about particular assertions related to account balances or classes of transactions.
III) To understand relationships between financial and nonfinancial information.
IV) To test details of account balances and transaction classes.
V) As an overall review of the financial information in the final review stage of the audit.

Choose three items from List B that identify the most likely sources of information from which an auditor develops expectations.

Sources
4.
5.
6.

List B
I) Data aggregated at the lowest level.
II) Gross domestic product and other macroeconomic information.
III) Financial information for comparable prior periods giving consideration to known changes.
IV) Anticipated results -- for example, budgets, forecasts, and extrapolations.
V) Company-wide comparisons based on 5-year trend data.
VI) Information regarding the industry in which the client operates.

Choose three items from List C that identify factors that most likely enhance the reliability of audit evidence.

Reliability Factors
7.
8.
9.

List C
I) Data were obtained from sources within the entity that are responsible for the amounts being audited.
II) Data were developed under a reliable system with adequate controls.
III) Data were not subjected to audit testing in the current or prior year.
IV) Expectations were developed using data from a variety of sources.
V) Data were obtained from independent sources outside the entity.

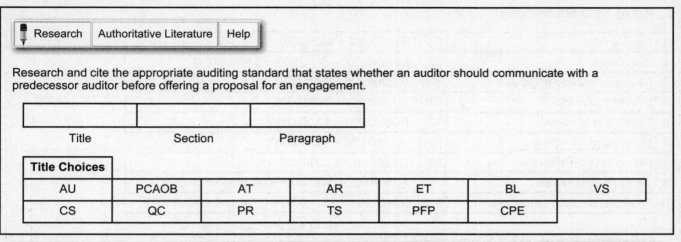

Research and cite the appropriate auditing standard that states whether an auditor should communicate with a predecessor auditor before offering a proposal for an engagement.

Title	Section	Paragraph

Title Choices

AU	PCAOB	AT	AR	ET	BL	VS
CS	QC	PR	TS	PFP	CPE	

▼ = Reminder   Directions   1 2 3 4 5 **6**   ◄ Previous   Next ►

Unofficial Answers

1. Communication between the Auditor and the Predecessor (10 Gradable Items)

1. <u>Yes.</u> Communication by the auditor with the predecessor is necessary so that information can be gathered in determining whether to accept the engagement. The auditor should explain to the prospective client the need to make an inquiry of the predecessor (AU 315).

2. <u>Yes.</u> Because the information to be communicated is considered confidential, permission should be gained by both the auditor and the predecessor prior to the inquiry.

3. <u>No.</u> Normally, the auditor has no obligation to report to parties external to the client. Thus, information obtained from Dodd should not be disclosed by Hall to regulatory agencies.

4. <u>Yes.</u> Because the information obtained by the auditor is confidential, the client should be requested to authorize the predecessor to respond fully to the auditor's inquiries.

5. <u>No.</u> Only information about the client pertinent to the decision to accept the engagement should be requested. Personal financial information about the predecessor is not relevant.

6. <u>Yes.</u> Inquiries by the auditor should include specific questions regarding, among other things, facts that might bear on the integrity of the prospective client's management.

7. <u>No.</u> The fee arrangement with the predecessor is unlikely to provide information that will assist the auditor in determining whether to accept the engagement.

8. <u>Yes.</u> Inquiries should include specific questions regarding facts that might bear on disagreements with the prospective client's management about accounting principles, auditing procedures, and other similarly significant matters.

9. <u>Yes.</u> The auditor's inquiries should include specific questions regarding facts that might bear on the predecessor's understanding about the reason for the change in auditors.

10. <u>No.</u> The current audit may be facilitated by consideration of the prior year's audit documentation. Thus, the auditor may request the client to authorize the predecessor to allow a review of the predecessor's audit documentation, and it is customary for the predecessor to cooperate. However, the auditor cannot demand that Dodd make available all audit documentation prepared during the prior period's audit.

2. Ratios (9 Gradable Items)

1. Current ratio	3.1	($1,240,000 ÷ $400,000)
2. Quick ratio	1.6	[($1,240,000 − $600,000) ÷ $400,000]
3. Accounts receivable turnover	7.5	($3,000,000 ÷ $400,000)
4. Inventory turnover	3.0	($1,800,000 ÷ $600,000)
5. Total asset turnover	1.5	($3,000,000 ÷ $2,000,000)
6. Gross margin percentage	40%	($1,200,000 ÷ $3,000,000)
7. Net operating margin percentage	22%	($660,000 ÷ $3,000,000)
8. Times interest earned	16.5	[($400,000 + $40,000 + $220,000) ÷ $40,000]
9. Total debt to equity percentage	60%	[($400,000 + $350,000) ÷ ($750,000 + $500,000)]

3. Changes in Ratios (13 Gradable Items)

1. A), B), D) Inventory turnover is cost of sales divided by average inventory. Consignment items should still be included in inventory. However, because items shipped on consignment were recorded as sales, the items were removed from inventory. Returned merchandise should increase inventory, but, because the credit memos were not recorded, the inventory was understated. By not including year-end purchases, inventory is also understated. Hence, a lower inventory causes a higher inventory turnover ratio.

2. A), B), E) Accounts receivable turnover is net credit sales divided by average accounts receivable. Goods shipped on consignment are properly included in the consignor's inventory at cost, and sales revenue from such goods should be recognized by the consignor when the merchandise is sold by recording as sales items shipped on consignment but not yet sold.

3. A), B), E) If the allowance for doubtful accounts increased, and allowance for doubtful accounts as a percentage of accounts receivable decreased, accounts receivable must have increased by a greater degree than the allowance decreased. Accounts receivable would have increased if items shipped on consignment were mistakenly recorded as sales, if significant credits for returned goods were not recorded, or if a larger percentage of sales occurred during the month compared with the prior year.

4. P) If short-term debt is refinanced as noncurrent debt at a higher interest rate, noncurrent debt will increase but not as significantly as interest expense will increase. This effect results from applying an increased rate to a greater amount of noncurrent debt.

5. L), P) Operating income minus interest expense and federal income taxes yields net income for the year. If operating income increased from the prior year but net income decreased, interest expense or federal income taxes must have increased. Refinancing short-term debt as noncurrent debt with a higher interest rate or an increase in the effective income tax rate explain this decrease in net income.

6. H) The gross margin percentage is gross margin divided by sales. If it remained constant although gross margin increased, sales also must have increased by the same proportionate amount. Because gross margin is sales minus cost of goods sold, cost of goods sold also must have increased by the same proportionate amount to maintain the relationship between sales and gross margin.

4. Audit Risk (3 Gradable Items)

1. A) Decreases control risk. Generally, the internal audit department should have no ongoing functional responsibilities. However, the internal audit department may randomly select a period to distribute paychecks as part of its evaluation of internal control. Paychecks should be distributed by someone with no other payroll responsibilities.

2. D) Increases control risk. The failure in internal control creates a risk that the purchasing agent may be favoring certain suppliers to gain kickbacks or bribes.

3. F) Increases inherent risk. The extension of the warranty program to increase revenue is a management decision that increases the entity's liability and therefore its inherent risk.

5. Analytical Procedures (9 Gradable Items)*

Purposes

1.   I) The audit standards indicate that auditors should apply analytical procedures to assist the auditor in planning the nature, timing, and extent of other auditing procedures.

2.   II) The audit standards indicate that auditors may apply analytical procedures as a substantive test to obtain audit evidence about particular assertions related to account balances or classes of transactions.

3.   V) The audit standards indicate that auditors should apply analytical procedures as an overall review of the financial information in the final review stage of the audit.

Sources

4.   III) The five sources of information to develop expectations include (a) financial information from comparable prior periods; (b) anticipated results, such as budgets or forecasts prepared by management; (c) relationships among data, such as those among the balances on the financial statements; (d) comparable information from the client's industry; and (e) related nonfinancial information.

5.   IV) The five sources of information to develop expectations include (a) financial information from comparable prior periods; (b) anticipated results, such as budgets or forecasts prepared by management; (c) relationships among data, such as those among the balances on the financial statements; (d) comparable information from the client's industry; and (e) related nonfinancial information.

6.   VI) The five sources of information to develop expectations include (a) financial information from comparable prior periods; (b) anticipated results, such as budgets or forecasts prepared by management; (c) relationships among data, such as those among the balances on the financial statements; (d) comparable information from the client's industry; and (e) related nonfinancial information.

Reliability Factors

7.   II) Data are more reliable when developed under a reliable system with adequate controls.

8.   IV) Expectations are more reliable when developed using data from a variety of sources rather than from a single source.

9.   V) Data are more reliable when obtained from independent sources outside the entity than from inside the entity.

*Note: Your answers need not be in the same order under each subheading. Give yourself a point for each item chosen correctly regardless of the order in which you entered them.

6. Research (1 Gradable Item)

Answer: 315.03

AU Section 315 -- *Communications Between Predecessor and Successor Auditors*

Change of Auditors

.03   An auditor should not accept an engagement until the communications described in paragraphs .07 through .10 have been evaluated. However, an auditor may make a proposal for an audit engagement before communicating with the predecessor auditor. The auditor may wish to advise the prospective client (for example, in a proposal) that acceptance cannot be final until the communications have been evaluated.

Gleim Simulation Grading

Task	Correct Responses		Gradable Items		Score per Task
1	____	÷	10	=	____
2	____	÷	9	=	____
3	____	÷	13	=	____
4	____	÷	3	=	____
5	____	÷	9	=	____
Research	____	÷	1	=	____

Total of Scores per Task	____
÷ Total Number of Tasks	6
Total Score	____%

Use **CPA Gleim Online** and **Simulation Wizard** to practice more task-based simulations in a realistic environment.

Have something to say?

Tell Gleim what's on your mind!

www.gleim.com/feedbackAUD

STUDY UNIT FOUR
STRATEGIC PLANNING ISSUES

(12 pages of outline)

This study unit considers issues that are fundamental to planning an audit. Questions about the internal audit function, related parties, and accounting estimates can be expected on the exam. Moreover, most of the issues considered in this study unit have an effect on other facets of the audit, including evidence collection and reporting. We cover the additional matters here to provide comprehensive and coherent coverage.

4.1 THE AUDITOR'S CONSIDERATION OF THE INTERNAL AUDIT FUNCTION (AU 322)

1. The independent, external auditor ("the auditor") considers the existence of an internal audit function in determining the nature, timing, and extent of audit procedures.

   a. The auditor must be **independent** of the entity.

2. Internal auditors cannot be independent because they are employees of the entity.

Background
According to the **International Standards for the Professional Practice of Internal Auditing (ISPPIA)** issued under the auspices of The Institute of Internal Auditors (IIA), internal auditors must be **objective**, and the internal audit activity (IAA) must be independent. The IAA is independent when it is free from conditions threatening its ability to carry out its responsibilities in an unbiased way.

   a. Internal auditors provide analyses, evaluations, assurances, recommendations, and other information to management and those charged with governance.

3. **Understanding the Internal Audit Function**

   a. An understanding of **internal control** includes an understanding of the internal audit function sufficient to identify activities relevant to audit planning. This function is part of the **monitoring** component.

   b. Inquiries should be made about the internal auditors'

      1) Organizational status
      2) Application of professional standards
      3) Audit plan, including the nature, timing, and extent of audit work
      4) Access to records and limitations on the scope of their work

   c. Inquiring about the internal audit function's charter, mission statement, or similar directive provides information about its objectives.

   d. Certain internal audit activities may not be relevant to an audit of the financial statements, e.g., evaluating certain management decision-making processes.

   e. Relevant internal audit activities provide the following:

      1) Evidence about the design and effectiveness of internal control relating to the ability to initiate, authorize, record, process, and report financial data consistent with relevant assertions in the financial statements

      2) Direct evidence about potential misstatements of financial data

    f.   The following actions are helpful in assessing the relevance of internal audit activities:

        1)   Considering prior-year audits
        2)   Reviewing how the internal auditors allocate their audit resources
        3)   Reading internal audit reports

    g.   If the auditor concludes that the internal auditors' **activities are not relevant**, (s)he need not further consider the function unless the auditor requests their direct assistance.

        1)   The auditor may conclude that considering further the work of the internal auditors would be **inefficient**, even if some of their activities are relevant.

    h.   The auditor may decide that it is **efficient** to consider how the internal auditors' work might affect audit procedures. The auditor then should assess the **competence** and **objectivity** of the internal auditors in relation to the intended effect of their work on the audit.

4. Assessing Competence and Objectivity

    a.   **Assessing competence.** The auditor considers the following:

        1)   Educational level and professional experience
        2)   Professional certification and continuing education
        3)   Audit policies, programs, and procedures
        4)   Practices regarding assignment of internal auditors
        5)   Supervision and review
        6)   Quality of documentation, reports, and recommendations
        7)   Performance evaluation

    b.   **Assessing objectivity.** The auditor considers the following:

        1)   The **organizational status** of the chief audit executive (CAE). This assessment includes whether

            a)   The CAE reports to someone with sufficient status to ensure broad audit coverage and adequate consideration of, and action on, findings and recommendations.

            b)   The CAE has direct access and reports regularly to those charged with governance.

            c)   Those charged with governance oversee employment decisions by the CAE.

        2)   Policies to maintain objectivity about the areas audited. These include prohibitions against auditing areas in which

            a)   Relatives are employed in important or audit-sensitive positions.
            b)   Internal auditors were recently assigned or are scheduled to be assigned.

    c.   Assessing competence and objectivity involves considering information from the auditor's previous experience, discussions with management, and a recent external quality review.

5. Effect of the Internal Auditors' Work

    a.   The internal auditors' work may affect substantive audit procedures and the procedures performed in obtaining the understanding of internal control and assessing risk.

    b.   Because a primary objective of many internal audit functions is to review, assess, and monitor internal control, internal audit procedures may provide useful information.

    c.   Risk assessment at the **financial-statement level** involves an overall assessment of the **risk of material misstatement (RMM)** and thus may affect the overall audit strategy.

1) The internal audit function may affect the overall risk assessment and decisions about audit procedures. For example, the auditor may coordinate work with the internal auditors and reduce the number of locations at which the auditor performs procedures.

    d. Risk assessment at the **account-balance or class-of-transactions level** involves obtaining and evaluating evidence about relevant assertions. The auditor assesses the RMM for each relevant assertion and performs tests of controls to support an expectation of the operating effectiveness of controls.

        1) When testing controls, the auditor may consider the results of internal audit procedures.

    e. Substantive procedures performed by the internal auditors may provide direct evidence about material misstatements in specific relevant assertions.

    f. Obtaining sufficient appropriate audit evidence and reporting on the financial statements are solely the responsibilities of the auditor. They cannot be shared with the internal auditors.

        1) Judgments about (a) assessments of risk, (b) materiality, (c) the sufficiency of tests, (d) the evaluation of estimates, and (e) other matters affecting the report always should be those of the auditor.

    g. The **extent of the effect of the internal auditors' work** depends on the materiality of amounts, RMMs, and the subjectivity involved in evaluating audit evidence.

        1) For assertions related to material amounts for which the RMM or the degree of subjectivity is high, the internal auditors' work alone cannot reduce audit risk to an acceptable level to eliminate direct tests of assertions by the auditor.

        2) For certain assertions related to less material amounts for which the RMM or the degree of subjectivity is low, the auditor may decide that (a) audit risk has been reduced to an acceptable level, and (b) direct testing by the auditor may not be necessary.

6. **Coordination of Audit Work**

    a. If the work of the internal auditors is expected to affect the auditor's procedures, it may be efficient for the auditor and the internal auditors to coordinate their work by

        1) Holding periodic meetings
        2) Scheduling audit work
        3) Providing access to internal auditors' engagement records (documentation)
        4) Reviewing audit reports
        5) Discussing possible accounting and auditing issues

7. **Evaluating and Testing the Internal Auditors' Work**

    a. If the work of the internal auditors significantly affects the auditor's work, the auditor should evaluate the quality and effectiveness of the internal auditors' work. Thus, the auditor tests some of that work relevant to significant assertions.

ISA Difference

The ISAs state that, when specific work of the internal auditors is to be used, it should be **evaluated and tested**.

---

8. **Using Internal Auditors to Provide Direct Assistance**

    a. The auditor may request direct assistance from the internal auditors when performing an audit. When direct assistance is provided, the auditor should assess the internal auditors' competence and objectivity and supervise, review, evaluate, and test the work performed by internal auditors to the extent appropriate.

Stop and review! You have completed the outline for this subunit. Study multiple-choice questions 1 through 8 beginning on page 148.

4.2 USING THE WORK OF A SPECIALIST (AU 336)

1. A **specialist** is a person (or firm) possessing **special skill or knowledge** in a particular field other than auditing or accounting, e.g., actuaries, appraisers, attorneys, engineers, and geologists.

2. **Decision to Use the Specialist**

   a. The auditor is not expected to have the expertise of a person trained for or qualified to engage in the practice of another profession or occupation. The auditor may use the work of a specialist to obtain appropriate audit evidence.

   b. Examples of types of matters for which the auditor may use the work of a specialist include

      1) Valuation (works of art, special drugs, restricted securities)
      2) Determination of physical characteristics relating to quantity or condition (mineral reserves, materials stored in piles above ground)
      3) Determination of amounts by using special techniques or methods (certain actuarial determinations)
      4) Interpretation of technical requirements, regulations, or agreements (the significance of contracts, legal title to property)

3. **Selecting a Specialist**

   a. The auditor should become satisfied about the qualifications and reputation of the specialist. Consideration should be given to the specialist's

      1) Professional certification, license, or other recognition of competence
      2) Reputation and standing
      3) Relationship with the client

   b. The auditor should attempt to obtain a specialist who is unrelated to the client. However, circumstances may permit using the work of a specialist having a relationship with the client.

ISA Difference

Under the ISAs, the auditor need not evaluate the capabilities and competence of an expert **for each audit** if the expert is **employed by the audit firm** and is therefore subject to its recruitment and training systems.

---

4. **Understanding the Specialist's Work**

   a. The auditor should have an understanding of the nature of the work to be performed by the specialist. The understanding should be documented and cover

      1) The objectives and scope of the work
      2) The specialist's relationship, if any, with the client
      3) The methods or assumptions to be used and a comparison with those used in the preceding period
      4) The appropriateness of using the specialist's work
      5) The form and content of the specialist's report that will enable the auditor to evaluate whether the findings support the assertions

5. **Using the Findings of the Specialist**

   a. The auditor should (1) obtain an understanding of the methods or assumptions used to determine whether the findings may serve as corroboration, (2) consider whether the findings support the assertions, and (3) test the data provided by the client.

   b. If the specialist is related to the client, the auditor should consider performing additional procedures to determine that the findings are not unreasonable or engage an outside specialist for that purpose.

6. **Effect of the Specialist's Work on the Auditor's Report**

    a.   If the specialist's findings support the assertions, the auditor may reasonably conclude that sufficient appropriate evidence has been obtained.

    b.   If the specialist's findings and the assertions differ materially, the auditor should apply additional procedures.

        1)   If (s)he is then unable to resolve the matter, the auditor should seek the opinion of another specialist unless the matter cannot be resolved.

            a)   An unresolved matter is a scope limitation that will usually result in a **qualified opinion or a disclaimer of an opinion** (see Study Unit 16).

        2)   If the auditor concludes after additional procedures that the assertions are not in conformity with GAAP, (s)he should express a **qualified or adverse opinion**.

7. **Reference to the Specialist in the Auditor's Report**

    a.   When expressing an **unqualified opinion**, the auditor ordinarily should not refer to the work or findings of the specialist. This reference might be misunderstood to be a qualification of the opinion or a division of responsibility.

    b.   In certain circumstances, however, the auditor may express an unqualified opinion and refer to the specialist. A specialist may be referred to and identified in the report if the auditor believes the reference will facilitate an understanding of the reason for an explanatory paragraph, for example, when

        1)   Describing a substantial doubt about the entity's ability to continue as a going concern

        2)   Emphasizing a matter

    c.   The auditor also may refer to the work of a specialist if (s)he departs from an unqualified opinion.

ISA Difference

If the work of an expert results in a modified report and a reference to or description of the work, the auditor obtains the **permission** of the expert.

Stop and review! You have completed the outline for this subunit. Study multiple-choice questions 9 through 13 beginning on page 150.

4.3 RELATED PARTIES (AU 334)

1. **Accounting Considerations**

    a.   Accounting principles ordinarily do not require transactions with related parties to be accounted for differently from those with unrelated parties.

    b.   Primary emphasis should be on the **adequacy of disclosure**.

    c.   Furthermore, the auditor should understand that the substance of a transaction could differ significantly from its form. Financial statements should recognize substance, not legal form.

    d.   Transactions indicative of the existence of related parties include the following:

        1)   Borrowing or lending interest-free or at a rate significantly different from prevailing market rates at the time of the transaction

        2)   Selling real estate at a price significantly different from appraised value

        3)   Making nonmonetary exchanges of similar property

        4)   Making loans with no scheduled terms for repayment

2.   **Audit Procedures**

a.   An audit cannot provide assurance that all related party transactions will be detected, but the auditor should be aware of the possible existence of material related party transactions and of certain relationships that must be disclosed, even in the absence of transactions.

1)   Many of the procedures listed in this outline are normally performed in an audit, even if the auditor has no reason to suspect that related party transactions exist.

b.   The auditor should obtain an understanding of management responsibilities and the relationship of each component to the total entity. Consideration should be given to

1)   Internal controls relevant to management activities,
2)   The business purpose served by the components of the entity, and
3)   Whether business structure and operating style are designed to obscure related party transactions.

c.   In the absence of contrary evidence, transactions with related parties should not be assumed to be outside the ordinary course of business. But such transactions may have been motivated solely or largely by any of the following:

1)   Lack of sufficient working capital or credit to continue the business
2)   A desire for favorable earnings to support the entity's stock price
3)   An overly optimistic earnings forecast
4)   Dependence on one or a few products, customers, or transactions for success
5)   A declining industry with many business failures
6)   Excess capacity
7)   Significant litigation, especially between shareholders and management
8)   Significant obsolescence because the entity is in a high-technology industry

d.   **Determining the existence of related parties.** Emphasis should be on known related party transactions. Certain relationships, such as parent-subsidiary or investor-investee, may be clearly evident. Determining the existence of others requires specific audit procedures, which may include the following:

1)   Evaluating the entity's procedures for identifying and properly accounting for related party transactions
2)   Requesting from management the names of all related parties and inquiring whether transactions occurred with them
3)   Reviewing filings with the SEC and other regulatory agencies for the names of related parties and for other businesses in which officers and directors occupy directorship or management positions
4)   Determining the names of all pensions and other trusts established for employees and the names of their officers and trustees
5)   Reviewing shareholder listings of closely held entities to identify principal shareholders
6)   Reviewing prior years' audit documentation for the names of known related parties
7)   Inquiring of predecessor, principal, or other auditors of related entities concerning their knowledge of existing relationships and the extent of management involvement in material transactions
8)   Reviewing material investment transactions during the period to determine whether they have created related parties

e. **Identifying related party transactions.** The following procedures may identify material transactions with known related parties or indicate the existence of previously unknown related parties:

1) Provide personnel performing all segments of the audit with the names of known related parties.
2) Review the minutes of meetings of the board and committees.
3) Review filings with the SEC and other regulatory agencies.
4) Review conflict-of-interest statements obtained by the entity from its management.
5) Review business transacted with major customers, suppliers, borrowers, and lenders for indications of undisclosed relationships.
6) Consider whether unrecognized transactions are occurring, such as receiving or providing accounting, management, or other services at no charge or a major shareholder absorbing entity expenses.
7) Review accounting records for large, unusual, or nonrecurring transactions or balances, especially those near the end of the period.
8) Review confirmations of compensating balance arrangements for indications that balances are or were maintained for or by related parties.
9) Review invoices from law firms.
10) Review confirmations of loans receivable and payable for guarantees.

f. **Examining related party transactions**

1) After identifying related party transactions, the auditor should become satisfied about their purpose, nature, extent, and effect. The following should be considered:

   a) Obtain an understanding of the business purpose of the transaction.
   b) Examine invoices, executed copies of agreements, contracts, and other documents.
   c) Determine whether the transaction has been approved by those charged with governance.
   d) Test for reasonableness the compilation of amounts to be disclosed or considered for disclosure.
   e) Arrange for the audits of interentity balances to be performed as of concurrent dates, even if the fiscal years differ, and for the examination of specified, important, and representative related party transactions by the auditors for each of the parties, with appropriate exchange of relevant information.
   f) Inspect or confirm and obtain satisfaction concerning the transferability and value of collateral.

2) To fully understand a particular transaction, the auditor may

   a) Confirm the transaction amount and terms, including guarantees and other significant data, with the other parties.
   b) Inspect evidence in possession of the other parties.
   c) Confirm or discuss significant information with intermediaries, such as banks, guarantors, agents, or attorneys.
   d) Refer to financial publications, trade journals, and credit agencies.
   e) With respect to material uncollected balances, guarantees, and other obligations, obtain information about the financial capability of the other parties from audited financial statements, unaudited financial statements, income tax returns, and reports issued by credit agencies.

3.   **Disclosure**

a.   For transactions or relationships for which GAAP requires disclosure, the auditor should consider whether (s)he has obtained sufficient appropriate evidence to understand the relationships and the effects of the transactions.

1)   The auditor should evaluate the transactions or relationships and become satisfied on the basis of professional judgment that they are adequately disclosed in the notes to the financial statements.

b.   Except for routine transactions, determining whether a transaction would have occurred if the parties had not been related or what the terms and manner of settlement would have been is ordinarily not possible. Accordingly, representations by management that a transaction was consummated on terms equivalent to those that prevail in **arm's-length transactions** are difficult to substantiate.

1)   If the auditor believes that a representation is unsubstantiated, (s)he should express a qualified or adverse opinion because of a departure from GAAP, depending on materiality.

Stop and review! You have completed the outline for this subunit. Study multiple-choice questions 14 through 20 beginning on page 152.

4.4 ACCOUNTING ESTIMATES AND FAIR VALUE (AU 342 AND AU 328)

 The more you study accounting, the more you will realize the importance of estimates. Most significant values in financial statements involve estimates in some manner. Be sure to understand the importance of estimates and auditors' concerns with them.

1.   Auditors should obtain and evaluate sufficient appropriate evidence to support significant accounting estimates.

a.   An **accounting estimate** in historical financial statements approximates an element, item, or account by measuring the effects of past transactions or events or the current status of an asset or liability.

1)   Examples include (a) net realizable values of inventory and accounts receivable, (b) property and casualty insurance loss reserves, (c) revenues from contracts accounted for by the percentage-of-completion method, and (d) pension and warranty expenses.

b.   Such estimates often are necessary because

1)   Measurement or valuation may be uncertain pending future events.
2)   Relevant data for past events cannot be accumulated on a timely, cost-effective basis.

2.   **Management is responsible** for making the judgments about accounting estimates.

a.   These judgments are normally based on subjective as well as objective factors, including knowledge about past and current events and assumptions about future conditions and courses of action.

3.   The auditor should evaluate the **reasonableness of accounting estimates** in the context of the financial statements taken as a whole.

a.   Even when the estimation process involves competent personnel using relevant and reliable data, **potential bias exists** in the subjective factors, and control may be difficult to establish.

1) When planning and performing procedures to evaluate accounting estimates, the auditor should adopt an attitude of **professional skepticism** toward both the subjective and objective factors.

2) According to AU 312, *Audit Risk and Materiality in Conducting an Audit*, the difference between the estimate best supported by the evidence and the estimate in the financial statements must be reasonable.

   a) If the amount in the financial statements is not reasonable, it should be treated as a likely misstatement and aggregated with other likely misstatements.

   b) If the differences are individually reasonable but collectively indicate possible bias (for example, when the effect of each difference is to increase income), the auditor should reconsider the estimates as a whole.

4. **Developing Accounting Estimates**

   a. Management's process of preparing accounting estimates, whether or not documented or formally applied, normally consists of the following:

   1) Determining when estimates are required
   2) Identifying the relevant factors
   3) Accumulating relevant, sufficient, and reliable data
   4) Developing assumptions regarding the most likely circumstances and events with respect to the relevant factors
   5) Determining the estimated amount based on the assumptions and other relevant factors
   6) Determining that presentation and disclosure conform with applicable accounting principles

5. The **risk of material misstatement** of accounting estimates varies with the

   a. Complexity and subjectivity of the process
   b. Availability and reliability of relevant data
   c. Number, significance, and degree of uncertainty of the assumptions

6. **Internal Control Related to Accounting Estimates**

   a. Internal control may reduce the probability of material misstatements of accounting estimates. Specific aspects of internal control relevant to the process of arriving at estimates include the following:

   1) Management communication of the need for proper estimates
   2) Accumulation of relevant, sufficient, and reliable data
   3) Preparation of estimates by qualified personnel
   4) Adequate review and approval by proper authority of

      a) Sources of relevant factors
      b) Development of assumptions
      c) Reasonableness of assumptions and resulting estimates

   5) Consideration by proper authority of the need to use the work of specialists
   6) Consideration by proper authority of changes in methods
   7) Comparison of prior estimates with results to assess the reliability of the process
   8) Consideration by management of whether the resulting estimate is consistent with operational plans

7.   **Evaluating Accounting Estimates**

   a.   The auditor's objective is to obtain sufficient appropriate evidence to provide reasonable assurance that

      1)   All material accounting estimates have been developed.
      2)   Those estimates are reasonable (free from bias).
      3)   Presentation and disclosure conform with applicable accounting principles.

8.   **Circumstances Requiring Accounting Estimates**

   a.   In evaluating whether all material accounting estimates have been developed, the auditor considers the entity's industry, its business methods, new accounting pronouncements, and other external factors. Possible procedures include the following:

      1)   Considering financial statement assertions to determine the need for estimates
      2)   Evaluating information obtained from other procedures

         a)   Changes in the entity's business and its industry indicative of the need for an accounting estimate
         b)   Changes in the methods of accumulating information
         c)   Litigation, claims, and assessments
         d)   Available minutes
         e)   Regulatory or examination reports, supervisory correspondence, and similar materials from regulatory agencies

      3)   Inquiring of management about circumstances indicating the need for an estimate

9.   **Evaluating Reasonableness**

   a.   The evaluation concentrates on key factors and assumptions that are

      1)   Significant to the estimate
      2)   Sensitive to variations
      3)   Different from historical patterns
      4)   Subjective and susceptible to misstatement and bias

   b.   The auditor normally also should consider

      1)   The entity's experience in making past estimates
      2)   The auditor's experience in the industry
      3)   Any changes that may cause factors different from those previously considered to become significant
      4)   The possible need to obtain written representations from management regarding the key factors and assumptions

   c.   The auditor should understand how management developed the estimate and then use one or more of the following approaches:

      1)   **Review and test the process used by management.** Procedures for this purpose may include the following:

         a)   Identifying any controls over the process that might be useful in the evaluation
         b)   Identifying the sources of data and factors used in forming the assumptions and considering whether they are relevant, reliable, and sufficient in light of information from other audit tests
         c)   Considering whether other key factors or alternative assumptions exist
         d)   Evaluating whether the assumptions are consistent with each other and with relevant data

e) Analyzing historical data used to develop assumptions to assess comparability, consistency, and reliability

f) Considering whether business or industry changes cause other factors to become significant to the assumptions

g) Reviewing documentation of the assumptions and inquiring about plans and objectives that might relate to them

h) Using the work of a specialist

i) Testing calculations used to translate assumptions and key factors into the estimate

2) **Develop an independent expectation of the estimate** to corroborate management's estimate by using other key factors or alternative assumptions.

3) **Review subsequent events or transactions** occurring after the date of the balance sheet but prior to the date of the auditor's report that are important in identifying and evaluating the reasonableness of accounting estimates, key factors, or assumptions.

10. **Fair Value Measurement**

a. **AU 328**, *Auditing Fair Value Measurements and Disclosures*, states that FVMD arise from initial recording or from later changes in value reflected in net income or other comprehensive income.

b. **Fair value** is the amount at which an asset (liability) can be bought (or incurred) or sold (or settled) in a current transaction between willing parties, not in a forced sale. An **observable market price** is the preferable measure of fair value when it is available (SFAC 7).

c. **Management's responsibility** is to establish a process for (1) determining FVMD, (2) selecting proper valuation methods, (3) identifying significant assumptions, and (4) ensuring conformity with GAAP.

d. Absent observable market prices, **assumptions** (preferably those used in the market) must be included in **valuation methods** (e.g., discounted cash flows).

e. The auditor should **understand the entity's process** for making FVMD and the **relevant controls**. This understanding is used to assess the RMM and determine the nature, timing, and extent of audit procedures.

f. An auditor may use the work of a **specialist** as evidence when evaluating FVMD.

g. The auditor evaluates internal and external evidence to determine whether **significant assumptions**, individually and in the aggregate, form a reasonable basis for FVMD.

h. The auditor's responsibility relative to a **valuation model** is not to act as an appraiser but to evaluate the reasonableness of the assumptions and the appropriateness of the model in the circumstances.

i. **Tests of the data** used to prepare the FVMD are performed to verify that they are accurate, complete, and relevant.

j. The evaluation of whether **fair-value disclosures conform with GAAP** is based on the same kinds of procedures as those applied to measurements in the statements. The auditor determines the **adequacy** of disclosures and assesses whether they are sufficiently informative about measurement **uncertainty**.

k. **Written management representations** about FVMD normally should concern the reasonableness of assumptions and whether they properly reflect the ability and intent to carry out specific relevant actions.

l. The auditor should **communicate with those charged with governance** about the process used to develop especially sensitive fair value estimates.

Stop and review! You have completed the outline for this subunit. Study multiple-choice questions 21 through 27 beginning on page 154.

4.5   CONSIDERATION OF OMITTED PROCEDURES AFTER THE REPORT DATE (AU 390)

1.   An auditor may determine, subsequent to the date of the report, that (a) auditing procedures considered necessary at the time of the audit were omitted, but (b) nothing indicates that the financial statements are materially misstated.

   a.   However, an auditor has no responsibility to review the work once (s)he has reported.

2.   When the auditor decides that a necessary procedure was omitted, (s)he should assess its importance to his/her current ability to support the previously expressed opinion.

   a.   The results of other procedures applied or audit evidence obtained in a later audit (possibly at an interim date) may compensate for an omitted procedure.

3.   The auditor may determine that the omission impairs his/her current ability to support the opinion. If (s)he believes persons are currently relying, or are likely to rely, on the report, the auditor should promptly undertake to apply the omitted procedure or alternative procedures that would provide a satisfactory basis for the opinion.

4.   If the auditor is unable to apply the previously omitted procedure or alternative procedures, (s)he should consult an attorney.

Stop and review! You have completed the outline for this subunit. Study multiple-choice questions 28 through 30 beginning on page 157.

QUESTIONS

4.1   The Auditor's Consideration of the Internal Audit Function (AU 322)

1.   In assessing the competence and objectivity of an entity's internal auditor, an independent auditor would **least** likely consider information obtained from

A.   Discussions with management personnel.

B.   External quality reviews of the internal auditor's activities.

C.   Previous experience with the internal auditor.

D.   The results of analytical procedures.

Answer (D) is correct. *(CPA, adapted)*
   REQUIRED: The least likely procedure in assessing the competence and objectivity of an entity's internal auditor.
   DISCUSSION: Analytical procedures are evaluations of financial information made by a study of plausible relationships among both financial and nonfinancial data, using models that range from simple to complex. They are substantive tests used by the auditor to gather evidence about the fairness of the financial statements.
   Answer (A) is incorrect. AU 322 identifies discussions with management as a procedure appropriate for assessing competence and objectivity of an internal auditor. Answer (B) is incorrect. AU 322 identifies quality reviews as a procedure appropriate for assessing competence and objectivity of an internal auditor. Answer (C) is incorrect. AU 322 identifies consideration of previous experience as a procedure appropriate for assessing competence and objectivity of an internal auditor.

2.   In assessing the competence of an internal auditor, an independent CPA most likely would obtain information about the

A.   Quality of the internal auditor's documentation.

B.   Organization's commitment to integrity and ethical values.

C.   Influence of management on the scope of the internal auditor's duties.

D.   Organizational levels to which the internal auditor reports.

Answer (A) is correct. *(CPA, adapted)*
   REQUIRED: The information needed to assess the competence of an internal auditor.
   DISCUSSION: In assessing the competence of an internal auditor, the auditor should consider such factors as educational level and professional experience; professional certification and continuing education; audit policies, programs, and procedures; supervision and review of the internal auditor's activities; departmental practices regarding assignments; quality of documentation, reports, and recommendations; and evaluation of the internal auditor's performance.
   Answer (B) is incorrect. The organization's commitment to integrity and ethical values relates to objectivity rather than competence. Answer (C) is incorrect. The influence of management on the scope of the internal auditor's duties relates to objectivity rather than competence. Answer (D) is incorrect. The organizational levels to which the internal auditor reports relate to objectivity rather than competence.

3. In assessing the objectivity of internal auditors, an independent auditor should

A. Evaluate the quality control program in effect for the internal auditors.

B. Examine documentary evidence of the work performed by the internal auditors.

C. Test a sample of the transactions and balances that the internal auditors examined.

D. Determine the organizational level to which the internal auditors report.

Answer (D) is correct. *(CPA, adapted)*
REQUIRED: The procedure performed to assess an internal auditor's objectivity.
DISCUSSION: If the auditor decides that it is efficient to consider how the internal auditors' work may affect the nature, timing, and extent of audit procedures, the competence and objectivity of the internal auditors should be assessed. Assessing objectivity includes obtaining information about (1) organizational status (the level to which the internal auditors report, access to those charged with governance, and whether these individuals oversee employment decisions related to the internal auditors) and (2) policies to maintain internal auditors' objectivity concerning the areas audited (AU 322).
Answer (A) is incorrect. Evaluating quality control pertains to competence, not objectivity. Answer (B) is incorrect. Examining internal auditors' engagement records (documentation) pertains to competence, not objectivity. Answer (C) is incorrect. Testing details examined by internal auditors pertains to competence, not objectivity.

4. For which of the following judgments may an independent auditor share responsibility with an entity's internal auditor who is assessed to be both competent and objective?

	Assessment of Inherent Risk	Assessment of Control Risk
A.	Yes	Yes
B.	Yes	No
C.	No	Yes
D.	No	No

Answer (D) is correct. *(CPA, adapted)*
REQUIRED: The judgment(s) that an auditor may share with an entity's internal auditor.
DISCUSSION: The auditor may use the internal auditor to provide direct assistance in the audit as long as the auditor supervises, reviews, evaluates, and tests the work of the internal auditor. However, an internal auditor, regardless of his/her competence and objectivity, should never make judgments about the audit work being conducted. All judgments should be made by the auditor.

5. For which of the following judgments may an independent auditor share responsibility with an entity's internal auditor who is assessed to be both competent and objective?

	Materiality of Misstatements	Evaluation of Accounting Estimates
A.	Yes	No
B.	No	Yes
C.	No	No
D.	Yes	Yes

Answer (C) is correct. *(CPA, adapted)*
REQUIRED: The judgment(s) for which an auditor may share responsibility with an internal auditor.
DISCUSSION: The responsibility to report on financial statements rests solely with the auditor and cannot be shared with internal auditors. Because the auditor has the ultimate responsibility to express an opinion on the financial statements, judgments about (1) assessments of inherent and control risk, (2) materiality of misstatements, (3) sufficiency of tests performed, (4) evaluation of significant accounting estimates, and (5) other matters affecting the auditor's report always should be those of the auditor.

6. During an audit, an internal auditor may provide direct assistance to an independent CPA in

	Obtaining an Understanding of Internal Control	Performing Tests of Controls	Performing Substantive Tests
A.	No	No	No
B.	Yes	No	No
C.	Yes	Yes	No
D.	Yes	Yes	Yes

Answer (D) is correct. *(CPA, adapted)*
REQUIRED: The types of direct assistance an internal auditor may provide to an independent CPA.
DISCUSSION: The auditor may request direct assistance from the internal auditor when performing the audit. Thus, the auditor may appropriately request the internal auditor's assistance in obtaining the understanding of internal control, performing tests of controls, or performing substantive tests (AU 322). The internal auditor may provide assistance in all phases of the audit as long as (1) the internal auditor's competence and objectivity have been tested, and (2) the independent auditor supervises, reviews, evaluates, and tests the work performed by the internal auditor to the extent appropriate.

7. An internal auditor's work would most likely affect the nature, timing, and extent of an independent auditor's auditing procedures when the internal auditor's work relates to assertions about the

A. Existence of contingencies.

B. Valuation of intangible assets.

C. Existence of fixed asset additions.

D. Valuation of related party transactions.

Answer (C) is correct. *(CPA, adapted)*
REQUIRED: The assertion most likely affected by the internal auditor's work.
DISCUSSION: Assertions may relate to material financial statement amounts for which the risk of material misstatement or the degree of subjectivity involved in the evaluation of the audit evidence is high. In these cases, reliance on the internal auditor is less effective. However, certain assertions may relate to less material financial statement amounts for which the risk of material misstatement or the degree of subjectivity involved is low. For example, the auditor may be able to rely on the internal auditor's work regarding assertions about the existence of cash, prepaid assets, and fixed asset additions.
Answer (A) is incorrect. The auditor is less likely to rely on the internal auditor's work regarding subjective issues such as existence of contingencies. Answer (B) is incorrect. The auditor is less likely to rely on the internal auditor's work regarding subjective issues such as valuation of intangible assets. Answer (D) is incorrect. The auditor is less likely to rely on the internal auditor's work regarding subjective issues such as valuation of related party transactions.

8. Miller Retailing, Inc., maintains a staff of three full-time internal auditors. The independent auditor has found that they are competent and objective. Moreover, the work of the internal auditors is relevant to the audit, and it is efficient to consider how that work may affect the audit. The independent auditor most likely will

A. Nevertheless need to make direct tests of assertions about material financial statement amounts for which the risk of material misstatement is high.

B. Decrease the extent of the tests of controls needed to restrict detection risk to the acceptable level.

C. Increase the extent of the procedures needed to reduce control risk to an acceptable level.

D. Not evaluate and test the work performed by the internal auditors.

Answer (A) is correct. *(CPA, adapted)*
REQUIRED: The true statement about the effect of the work of the internal auditors.
DISCUSSION: The auditor has the sole reporting responsibility and makes all judgments about matters affecting the report. When amounts are material and the risk of material misstatement or the subjectivity of the evaluation of the evidence is high, the consideration of the internal auditors' work cannot alone reduce audit risk to an acceptable level. Thus, direct testing of those assertions by the auditor cannot be eliminated (AU 322).
Answer (B) is incorrect. The auditor performs substantive tests, not tests of controls, to restrict detection risk to the acceptable level. Answer (C) is incorrect. Control risk can be assessed but not restricted by the auditor. Answer (D) is incorrect. The auditor should evaluate the quality and effectiveness of the work of the internal auditors that significantly affects the nature, timing, and extent of the audit procedures.

4.2 Using the Work of a Specialist (AU 336)

9. In using the work of a specialist, an auditor referred to the specialist's findings in the auditor's report. This would be an appropriate reporting practice if the

A. Auditor is not familiar with the professional certification, personal reputation, or particular competence of the specialist.

B. Auditor, as a result of the specialist's findings, adds an explanatory paragraph emphasizing a matter regarding the financial statements.

C. Specialist understands the auditor's corroborative use of the specialist's findings in relation to the assertions in the financial statements.

D. Auditor, as a result of the specialist's findings, decides to indicate a division of responsibility with the specialist.

Answer (B) is correct. *(CPA, adapted)*
REQUIRED: The instance in which an auditor may refer to a specialist's findings.
DISCUSSION: An auditor ordinarily should not refer to the work or findings of a specialist. However, the auditor may, as a result of the report or findings of the specialist, decide to add explanatory language to his/her standard report or depart from an unqualified opinion. The specialist may be identified if the auditor believes the reference will facilitate an understanding of the reason for the explanatory paragraph or the departure from the unqualified opinion (AU 336). Emphasizing a matter is a basis for adding an explanatory paragraph that may justify referring to a specialist.
Answer (A) is incorrect. The auditor is required to evaluate the professional qualifications of the specialist. Answer (C) is incorrect. The specialist's awareness of the use of his/her work is independent of the decision to refer to the specialist. Answer (D) is incorrect. A division of responsibility with the specialist is inappropriate.

10. When using the work of a specialist, an auditor may refer to and identify the specialist in the auditor's report if the

    A. Auditor wishes to indicate a division of responsibility.

    B. Specialist's work provides the auditor greater assurance of reliability.

    C. Auditor expresses a qualified opinion as a result of the specialist's findings.

    D. Specialist is not independent of the client.

Answer (C) is correct. *(CPA, adapted)*
    REQUIRED: The instance when an audit report may refer to and identify a specialist.
    DISCUSSION: The auditor may refer to the specialist if (s)he departs from an unqualified opinion (AU 336). An auditor also may express an unqualified opinion and refer to a specialist if, as a result of the work of the specialist, (s)he adds an explanatory paragraph.
    Answer (A) is incorrect. An auditor may divide responsibility with other independent auditors, not with a specialist. Answer (B) is incorrect. The reference is solely to clarify the reason for the modification of the report. Answer (D) is incorrect. The specialist's lack of independence is not a basis for the reference.

11. Which of the following statements is true about the auditor's use of the work of a specialist?

    A. The specialist should not have an understanding of the auditor's corroborative use of the specialist's findings.

    B. The auditor is required to perform substantive procedures to verify the specialist's assumptions and findings.

    C. The client should not have an understanding of the nature of the work to be performed by the specialist.

    D. The auditor should obtain an understanding of the methods and assumptions used by the specialist.

Answer (D) is correct. *(CPA, adapted)*
    REQUIRED: The true statement about the auditor's use of the work of a specialist.
    DISCUSSION: The auditor should obtain an understanding of the methods and assumptions used to determine whether the findings are suitable for corroborative purposes. The auditor should (1) consider whether the specialist's findings support the assertions and (2) test the accounting data provided by the client to the specialist.
    Answer (A) is incorrect. The specialist should have an understanding about the nature of the work to be performed. Answer (B) is incorrect. If the specialist's findings support the assertions, the auditor may reasonably conclude that sufficient appropriate evidence has been obtained. Answer (C) is incorrect. The client should have an understanding about the nature of the work to be performed.

12. Which of the following statements is true concerning an auditor's use of the work of a specialist?

    A. The auditor need not obtain an understanding of the methods and assumptions used by the specialist.

    B. The auditor may not use the work of a specialist in matters material to the fair presentation of the financial statements.

    C. The reasonableness of the specialist's assumptions and their applications are strictly the auditor's responsibility.

    D. The work of a specialist who has a contractual relationship with the client may be acceptable under certain circumstances.

Answer (D) is correct. *(CPA, adapted)*
    REQUIRED: The true statement about use of a specialist.
    DISCUSSION: A related specialist may be acceptable, but the auditor should assess the risk of impairment of objectivity. If the specialist's objectivity may be impaired, the auditor performs additional audit procedures regarding his/her assumptions, methods, and findings to determine whether the findings are reasonable.
    Answer (A) is incorrect. The auditor should obtain an understanding of the methods or assumptions used to determine whether the findings are suitable for corroborative purposes. Answer (B) is incorrect. The auditor may use the work of a specialist in helping to collect sufficient appropriate evidence. Answer (C) is incorrect. Although the auditor should evaluate the assumptions and their usefulness for the auditor's purpose, the reasonableness of the specialist's assumptions and their application is the responsibility of the specialist.

13. In using the work of a specialist, an understanding should exist among the auditor, the client, and the specialist as to the nature of the specialist's work. The documentation of this understanding should cover

A. A statement that the specialist assumes no responsibility to update the specialist's report for future events or circumstances.

B. The conditions under which a division of responsibility may be necessary.

C. The specialist's understanding of the auditor's corroborative use of the specialist's findings.

D. The auditor's disclaimer as to whether the specialist's findings corroborate the representations in the financial statements.

Answer (C) is correct. *(CPA, adapted)*
REQUIRED: The matter covered in the understanding about the work of the specialist.
DISCUSSION: The understanding should be documented and should cover (1) the objectives and scope of the work, (2) the specialist's representations as to his/her relationship to the client, (3) the methods or assumptions to be used, and (4) a comparison with those used in the preceding period. It also should cover the (1) specialist's understanding of the auditor's corroborative use of the findings in relation to the assertions in the financial statements and (2) the form and content of the specialist's report that would enable the auditor to evaluate the specialist's work (AU 336).
Answer (A) is incorrect. The understanding need not contain a disclaimer about the specialist's responsibility to update the report. Answer (B) is incorrect. The auditor may in some cases refer to a specialist but may not divide responsibility with him/her. Answer (D) is incorrect. The understanding need not contain a disclaimer about whether the findings corroborate the representations.

4.3 Related Parties (AU 334)

14. When auditing related party transactions, an auditor places primary emphasis on

A. Confirming the existence of the related parties.

B. Verifying the valuation of the related party transactions.

C. Evaluating the disclosure of the related party transactions.

D. Ascertaining the rights and obligations of the related parties.

Answer (C) is correct. *(CPA, adapted)*
REQUIRED: The primary concern of the auditor about related party transactions.
DISCUSSION: The auditor's primary emphasis with regard to related party transactions should be on the presentation and disclosure assertion with respect to their nature and their effect on the financial statements. However, the FASB requires that transactions with related parties be accounted for on the same basis as would be appropriate if the parties were not related.
Answer (A) is incorrect. In an audit of related party transactions, the auditor places no special emphasis on existence assertions. Answer (B) is incorrect. In an audit of related party transactions, the auditor places no special emphasis on valuation assertions. Answer (D) is incorrect. In an audit of related party transactions, the auditor places no special emphasis on rights and obligations assertions.

15. An auditor searching for related party transactions should obtain an understanding of each subsidiary's relationship to the total entity because

A. This may permit the audit of intercompany account balances to be performed as of concurrent dates.

B. Intercompany transactions may have been consummated on terms equivalent to arm's-length transactions.

C. This may reveal whether particular transactions would have taken place if the parties had not been related.

D. The business structure may be deliberately designed to obscure related party transactions.

Answer (D) is correct. *(CPA, adapted)*
REQUIRED: The reason for understanding parent-subsidiary relationships when searching for related party transactions.
DISCUSSION: AU 334 states that the auditor should obtain an understanding of management responsibilities and the relationship of each component to the total entity. The auditor also should consider internal control and the business purpose of each component of the entity. The auditor should be aware that business structure and operating style are occasionally deliberately designed to obscure related party transactions.
Answer (A) is incorrect. A concurrent audit is not required. Answer (B) is incorrect. The auditor's concern is that related party transactions were not at arm's-length. Answer (C) is incorrect. Except for routine transactions, determining whether a transaction would have occurred and what the terms would have been if the parties were unrelated is ordinarily not possible.

16. Which of the following procedures most likely could assist an auditor in identifying related-party transactions?

- A. Performing tests of controls concerning the segregation of duties.
- B. Evaluating the reasonableness of management's accounting estimates.
- C. Reviewing confirmations of compensating balance arrangements.
- D. Scanning the accounting records for recurring transactions.

Answer (C) is correct. *(CPA, adapted)*
    REQUIRED: The procedure most likely used to identify related-party transactions.
    DISCUSSION: The auditor performs procedures to identify material transactions that may be indicative of previously undetermined relationships. These procedures include reviewing confirmations of compensating balance arrangements for indications that balances are or were maintained for or by related parties (AU 334).
    Answer (A) is incorrect. Testing segregation of duties of entity personnel is unlikely to identify related-party transactions. Answer (B) is incorrect. Evaluating the reasonableness of accounting estimates has little relevance to related-party transactions. The auditor should concentrate on transactions of a kind that tend to be entered into with related parties. Answer (D) is incorrect. Scanning the accounting records for recurring transactions are not by their nature indicative of related-party transactions.

17. Which of the following events **least** likely would indicate the existence of related party transactions?

- A. Making a loan with **no** scheduled date for the funds to be repaid.
- B. Exchanging property for the benefit of a principal stockholder.
- C. Borrowing funds at an interest rate significantly below prevailing market rates.
- D. Writing off obsolete inventory to net realizable value just before year end.

Answer (D) is correct. *(CPA, adapted)*
    REQUIRED: The event that least likely indicates the existence of related party transactions.
    DISCUSSION: The following suggest possible related party transactions: (1) exchanging property for similar property in a nonmonetary transaction, (2) borrowing or lending at rates significantly above or below market rates, (3) selling realty at a price materially different from its appraised value, and (4) making loans with no scheduled repayment terms (AU 334).

18. Which of the following statements is true about related party transactions?

- A. In the absence of evidence to the contrary, related party transactions should be assumed to be outside the ordinary course of business.
- B. An auditor should determine whether a particular transaction would have occurred if the parties had not been related.
- C. An auditor should substantiate that related party transactions were consummated on terms equivalent to those that prevail in arm's-length transactions.
- D. The audit procedures directed toward identifying related party transactions should include considering whether transactions are occurring but are not being given proper accounting recognition.

Answer (D) is correct. *(CPA, adapted)*
    REQUIRED: The true statement about related party transactions.
    DISCUSSION: The audit procedures directed toward identifying related party transactions should include considering whether transactions are occurring, but are not being given proper accounting recognition. An example is receiving or providing accounting, management, or other services at no charge or a major shareholder's payment of corporate expenses (AU 334).
    Answer (A) is incorrect. In the absence of contrary evidence, related party transactions are assumed to be in the ordinary course of business. Answer (B) is incorrect. Determining whether a particular transaction would have occurred if the parties had not been related is ordinarily not possible unless it is routine. Answer (C) is incorrect. Related party transactions need not be consummated on terms equivalent to those that prevail in arm's-length transactions.

19. After determining that a related party transaction has, in fact, occurred, an auditor should

   A. Add a separate paragraph to the auditor's standard report to explain the transaction.

   B. Perform analytical procedures to verify whether similar transactions occurred, but were not recorded.

   C. Obtain an understanding of the business purpose of the transaction.

   D. Substantiate that the transaction was consummated on terms equivalent to an arm's-length transaction.

Answer (C) is correct. *(CPA, adapted)*
   REQUIRED: The procedure performed after determining that a related party transaction has occurred.
   DISCUSSION: After identifying related party transactions, the auditor should become satisfied about their purpose, nature, extent, and effect. Among other things, the auditor should obtain an understanding of the business purpose of the transaction (AU 334).
   Answer (A) is incorrect. If the related party transaction has been accounted for properly, no modification of the standard report is necessary. However, in some cases, the auditor may wish to add a separate paragraph emphasizing that the entity has had significant related party transactions (AU 508). Answer (B) is incorrect. Analytical procedures are not likely to identify similar, unrecorded transactions. Answer (D) is incorrect. The auditor normally cannot determine whether a transaction was consummated on terms equivalent to an arm's-length transaction. The auditor's primary concern is with disclosure of related party transactions.

20. An auditor most likely would modify an unqualified opinion if the entity's financial statements include a note on related party transactions

   A. Disclosing loans to related parties at interest rates significantly below prevailing market rates.

   B. Describing an exchange of real estate for similar property in a nonmonetary related party transaction.

   C. Stating that a particular related party transaction occurred on terms equivalent to those that would have prevailed in an arm's-length transaction.

   D. Presenting the dollar volume of related party transactions and the effects of any change from prior periods in the method of establishing terms.

Answer (C) is correct. *(CPA, adapted)*
   REQUIRED: The note most likely resulting in a modified opinion.
   DISCUSSION: Stating that a particular related party transaction occurred on terms equivalent to those that would have prevailed in an arm's-length transaction is difficult to substantiate. If such a representation is included in the statements and the auditor believes that it is unsubstantiated, (s)he should modify the opinion because of the departure from GAAP.

4.4   Accounting Estimates and Fair Value (AU 342 and AU 328)

21. Which of the following procedures would an auditor ordinarily perform first in evaluating the reasonableness of management's accounting estimates?

   A. Review transactions occurring prior to the date of the auditor's report that indicate variations from expectations.

   B. Compare independent expectations with recorded estimates to assess management's process.

   C. Obtain an understanding of how management developed its estimates.

   D. Analyze historical data used in developing assumptions to determine whether the process is consistent.

Answer (C) is correct. *(CPA, adapted)*
   REQUIRED: The first procedure ordinarily performed in evaluating the reasonableness of accounting estimates.
   DISCUSSION: Auditors should obtain and evaluate sufficient appropriate evidence to provide reasonable assurance that (1) all material estimates have been developed, (2) they are reasonable in the circumstances, and (3) they are presented in accordance with GAAP and properly disclosed. To evaluate reasonableness, the auditor obtains an understanding of the development of the estimates. That understanding is the basis for the approach(es) used to evaluate reasonableness: (1) reviewing and testing the process used, (2) developing an independent estimate to corroborate the estimate, and (3) reviewing events or transactions occurring after the date of the balance sheet but prior to the date of the auditor's report (AU 342).
   Answer (A) is incorrect. The auditor should review transactions only after an understanding of how management developed the estimate is gained. Answer (B) is incorrect. The auditor should compare independent expectations and reported estimates after an understanding of how management developed its estimates is obtained. Answer (D) is incorrect. The auditor should analyze historical data after it is understood how management developed its estimates.

22. In evaluating the reasonableness of an entity's accounting estimates, an auditor normally is concerned about assumptions that are

   A. Susceptible to bias.

   B. Consistent with prior periods.

   C. Insensitive to variations.

   D. Similar to industry guidelines.

Answer (A) is correct. *(CPA, adapted)*
   REQUIRED: The auditor's normal concern about assumptions used in making accounting estimates.
   DISCUSSION: AU 342 states that in evaluating the reasonableness of an estimate, the auditor normally concentrates on key factors and assumptions that are (1) significant to the accounting estimate, (2) sensitive to variations, (3) deviations from historical patterns, and (4) subjective and susceptible to misstatement and bias.
   Answer (B) is incorrect. Assumptions consistent with those of prior periods are of less concern to the auditor. Answer (C) is incorrect. Assumptions insensitive to variations are of less concern to the auditor. Answer (D) is incorrect. Estimates that are similar to industry guidelines are more likely to be reasonable.

23. The auditor's evaluation of the reasonableness of accounting estimates

   A. Should be in the context of individual transactions.

   B. Considers that management bases its judgment on both subjective and objective factors.

   C. Will be unfavorable if the estimates in the financial statements are based on assumptions about future events and transactions.

   D. Should be based on an attitude of conservatism.

Answer (B) is correct. *(Publisher, adapted)*
   REQUIRED: The true statement about the auditor's evaluation of the reasonableness of accounting estimates.
   DISCUSSION: Estimates are based on both subjective and objective factors. Hence, control over estimates may be difficult to establish. Given the potential bias in the subjective factors, the auditor should adopt an attitude of professional skepticism toward both the subjective and objective factors.
   Answer (A) is incorrect. The evaluation should be in the context of the financial statements as a whole. Answer (C) is incorrect. Estimates are often based on assumptions about the future. Answer (D) is incorrect. Estimates should be based on assumptions regarding the most likely circumstances and events. The auditor should evaluate those assumptions with professional skepticism.

24. Auditors should obtain and evaluate sufficient appropriate evidence to support significant accounting estimates. Differences between the estimates best supported by the evidence and those in the financial statements

   A. Are per se unreasonable and should be treated as material misstatements.

   B. May be individually reasonable but collectively indicate possible bias.

   C. May be individually unreasonable, but if they collectively indicate no bias, aggregation of the differences with other likely misstatements is not required.

   D. Should arouse concern only when estimates are based on hypothetical assumptions or subjective factors.

Answer (B) is correct. *(Publisher, adapted)*
   REQUIRED: The true statement about differences between the estimates best supported by the evidence and those in the financial statements.
   DISCUSSION: If the amount in the financial statements is not reasonable, it should be treated as a likely error or fraud and aggregated with other likely misstatements. If the differences between the best estimates and those in the financial statements are individually reasonable but collectively indicate possible bias (for example, when the effect of each difference is to increase income), the auditor should reconsider the estimates as a whole.
   Answer (A) is incorrect. No estimate is considered accurate with certainty. Hence, differences may be reasonable and not considered to be likely material misstatements. Answer (C) is incorrect. An unreasonable difference should be considered a likely misstatement and aggregated with other likely misstatements. Answer (D) is incorrect. Estimates are based on subjective as well as objective factors.

25. George Karl, an auditor with extensive experience in the retail industry, is assigned to audit the reasonableness of accounting estimates in the Year 1 financial statements of Haas Company. Haas, which was formed in Year 1, markets fishing lures. Which of the following is the **least** important consideration for Karl's audit of the reasonableness of accounting estimates?

A. An inexperienced employee at Haas prepared the financial statements and was entirely responsible for the accounting estimates.

B. Karl has never been involved in an audit of a company that sells fishing lures.

C. The accounting estimates in the financial statements of Haas Company are based on numerous significant assumptions.

D. The accounting estimates in the financial statements are susceptible to bias.

26. During the audit of fair value measurements and disclosures (FVMD), the auditor most likely should

A. Understand the components of internal control but need not specifically obtain an understanding of the entity's process for determining FVMD.

B. Use the understanding of the audited entity's process for determining FVMD to assess the risk of material misstatement.

C. Determine that the entity has measured fair values using discounted cash flows whenever feasible.

D. Focus primarily on the initial recording of transactions.

Answer (B) is correct. *(Publisher, adapted)*
REQUIRED: The least important consideration in an audit of the reasonableness of accounting estimates.
DISCUSSION: The auditor evaluates the reasonableness of estimates. Among the factors considered are (1) the entity's experience in making past estimates, (2) the auditor's experience in the industry, (3) any changes that may cause factors different from those previously considered to become significant, and (4) the possible need to obtain written representations from management regarding the key factors and assumptions. Karl has extensive experience in the retail industry and therefore most likely has an acceptable level of competence. If necessary, Karl may seek the help of a specialist before conducting the audit.
Answer (A) is incorrect. Preparation of the statements by an inexperienced employee who may not have the competence necessary to formulate accounting estimates suggests the need for additional audit effort. Answer (C) is incorrect. The significant assumptions underlying accounting estimates are crucial to the audit. The auditor should concentrate on the key factors and assumptions that are significant to the estimates, sensitive to variations and deviations from historical patterns, and subjective and susceptible to misstatement and bias (AU 342). Answer (D) is incorrect. Estimates that are subjective or susceptible to bias require additional consideration by the auditor.

Answer (B) is correct. *(Publisher, adapted)*
REQUIRED: The necessary procedure in an audit of FVMD.
DISCUSSION: To meet its responsibility to make the FVMD included in the financial statements, management may need to adopt an accounting and financial reporting process that consists of (1) choosing valuation methods, (2) identifying significant assumptions, (3) preparing the measurements and disclosures, and (4) ensuring conformity with GAAP. The auditor should obtain an understanding of this process and the relevant controls that are sufficient for an effective audit of FVMD. The understanding is used to assess the risk of material misstatement and to determine the nature, timing, and extent of audit procedures.
Answer (A) is incorrect. The auditor should obtain an understanding of the entity's process for determining FVMD. Answer (C) is incorrect. GAAP do not require a specific method for measuring fair value. However, use of observable market prices is preferable. In their absence, the measurement is based on the best available information, and the entity's process will be more complex. Answer (D) is incorrect. Measurements also are necessary for changes in fair value subsequent to initial recording, e.g., adjustments at the balance sheet date for holding gains or losses on trading and available-for-sale securities.

27. As part of the audit of fair value measurements and disclosures (FVMD), an auditor may need to test the entity's significant assumptions. In these circumstances, the auditor should

A. Verify that the entity has used its own assumptions, not those of marketplace participants.

B. Obtain sufficient evidence to express an opinion on the assumptions.

C. Evaluate whether the assumptions individually and as a whole form a reasonable basis for the FVMD.

D. Identify especially sensitive assumptions.

Answer (C) is correct. *(Publisher, adapted)*
REQUIRED: The necessary step in an audit of FVMD when the auditor tests significant assumptions.
DISCUSSION: Observable market prices are not always available for fair value measurements. In this case, the entity uses valuation methods based on the assumptions that the market would employ to estimate fair values, if obtainable without excessive cost. Accordingly, GAAS require the auditor to evaluate whether the significant assumptions form a reasonable basis for the measurements. Because assumptions often are interdependent and must be consistent with each other, the auditor should evaluate them independently and as a whole. Reasonable assumptions are consistent with (1) economic conditions, (2) existing market data, (3) the entity's plans, (4) past experience, (5) prior-period assumptions, (6) cash flow risks, and (7) other matters (e.g., assumptions used to develop accounting estimates other than FVMD).
Answer (A) is incorrect. Valuation methods should be based on the assumptions that participants in the market would use to estimate fair value without undue cost and effort. Answer (B) is incorrect. The procedures applied to the entity's assumptions are required merely to evaluate whether, in the context of the audit of the financial statements as a whole, the assumptions form a reasonable basis for the measurements. Answer (D) is incorrect. The auditor considers the sensitivity of valuations to changes in assumptions. Accordingly, the auditor considers using procedures to identify especially sensitive assumptions but is not always required to do so.

4.5 Consideration of Omitted Procedures After the Report Date (AU 390)

28. On February 9, Brown, CPA, expressed an unqualified opinion on the financial statements of Web Co. On October 9, during a peer review of Brown's practice, the reviewer informed Brown that engagement personnel failed to perform a search for subsequent events for the Web engagement. Brown should first

A. Request Web's permission to perform substantive procedures that would provide a satisfactory basis for the opinion.

B. Inquire of Web whether persons are currently relying or likely to rely on the financial statements.

C. Take no additional action because subsequent events have no effect on the financial statements that were reported on.

D. Assess the importance of the omitted procedures to Brown's present ability to support the opinion.

Answer (D) is correct. *(CPA, adapted)*
REQUIRED: The first action taken after a subsequent discovery of an omitted procedure.
DISCUSSION: The results of other procedures applied or audit evidence obtained in a later audit (possibly at an interim date) may compensate for an omitted procedure. Furthermore, the auditor should assess the importance of the omitted procedure to the support of the audit opinion in relation to the overall engagement and the circumstances of the audit. The auditor determines whether (1) the omission impairs the current ability to support the opinion, and (2) persons are currently relying or are likely to rely on the report. If these conditions exist, the auditor should promptly undertake to apply the omitted procedure or alternative procedures that would provide a satisfactory basis for the opinion (AU 390).
Answer (A) is incorrect. Brown should decide the importance of the omitted procedures before taking action. Answer (B) is incorrect. Brown must first determine whether the omission is important. Answer (C) is incorrect. Subsequent events may require adjustment of, or disclosure in, the financial statements.

29. An auditor is considering whether the omission of a substantive procedure considered necessary at the time of an audit may impair the auditor's present ability to support the previously expressed opinion. The auditor need **not** apply the omitted procedure if the

    A. Financial statements and auditor's report were not distributed beyond management and the board of directors.

    B. Auditor's previously expressed opinion was qualified because of a departure from GAAP.

    C. Results of other procedures that were applied tend to compensate for the procedure omitted.

    D. Omission is due to unreasonable delays by client personnel in providing data on a timely basis.

Answer (C) is correct. *(CPA, adapted)*
    REQUIRED: The condition under which an auditor need not apply an omitted procedure.
    DISCUSSION: When the auditor decides that a necessary audit procedure was omitted, (s)he should assess its importance to his/her current ability to support the previously expressed opinion. The results of other procedures applied or audit evidence obtained in a later audit, possibly at an interim date, may compensate for the omitted procedure.
    Answer (A) is incorrect. The need to apply procedures to support the audit opinion is independent of the distribution of the audit report. Answer (B) is incorrect. The type of opinion originally expressed is independent of the need to support that opinion. Answer (D) is incorrect. The auditor should assess any scope limitation in determining whether to express an opinion.

30. On March 15, Year 2, Kent, CPA, issued an unqualified opinion on a client's audited financial statements for the year ended December 31, Year 1. On May 4, Year 2, Kent's internal inspection program disclosed that engagement personnel failed to observe the client's physical inventory. Omission of this procedure impairs Kent's present ability to support the unqualified opinion. If the shareholders are currently relying on the opinion, Kent should first

    A. Advise management to disclose to the shareholders that Kent's unqualified opinion should not be relied on.

    B. Undertake to apply alternative procedures that would provide a satisfactory basis for the unqualified opinion.

    C. Reissue the auditor's report and add an explanatory paragraph describing the departure from generally accepted auditing standards.

    D. Compensate for the omitted procedure by performing tests of controls to reduce audit risk to a sufficiently low level.

Answer (B) is correct. *(CPA, adapted)*
    REQUIRED: The appropriate action when an auditor discovers that a necessary audit procedure was not performed during the previous audit.
    DISCUSSION: The auditor determines whether (1) the omission impairs his/her current ability to support the opinion, and (2) persons are currently relying or are likely to rely on the report. If these conditions currently exist, the auditor should promptly undertake to apply the omitted procedure or alternative procedures that would provide a satisfactory basis for the opinion (AU 390).
    Answer (A) is incorrect. Notification of users is only necessary if the auditor could not become satisfied upon applying the procedure. Answer (C) is incorrect. The auditor has followed GAAS in becoming satisfied with the application of the procedure. Answer (D) is incorrect. Tests of controls do not substitute for required substantive tests.

Use the additional questions in Gleim **CPA Test Prep Online** to create Test Sessions that emulate Prometric!

4.6 PRACTICE SIMULATION

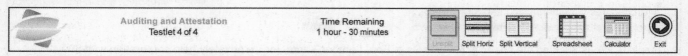

DIRECTIONS

Note: If you believe you have encountered a software malfunction, report it to the test center staff immediately.

Navigation

To navigate from task to task, use the controls at the bottom of the screen. Click on the **Next** button to advance to the next task, or the **Previous** button to go to the previous task. To go directly to any task, click on its number.

If you would like a reminder to revisit a task, or want to indicate that you are finished with it, click on the reminder flag below the task number. To clear the flag, click on it again. Reminder flags are for your use only – they do not contribute to your score.

Tabs

In this part of the examination, you will be asked to complete various tasks. Every task has one or more **Work Tabs**. Some tasks have one or more **Information Tabs**, others may have none. Every task has a **Help** tab.

If a task has **Information Tabs**, you may use the information in them to complete your responses in the **Work Tabs**.

| Corporate Gain and Basis | Authoritative Literature | Help |
| Work tab | Information tab | Help tab |

Work Tabs:
- **Work Tabs** are identified with a pencil icon. This is where your responses are expected.
- Each task has one or more **Work Tabs**.
- **Work Tabs** contain directions for completing the task – be sure to read these directions carefully.
- The **Work Tab** name in the example above is for illustration only – yours will differ.
- You must complete all of the **Work Tabs** in each task to receive full credit.

Information Tabs:
- The Authoritative Literature will be provided in all tasks in the AUD, FAR, and REG sections for your reference.
- Your simulation may have one or more additional **Information Tabs**. Like the Authoritative Literature tabs, **Information Tabs** do not have a pencil icon.
- If your task has additional **Information Tabs**, go through each to familiarize yourself with the task content.

Help Tab:
- The **Help Tab** provides assistance with the exam software that is used in this task. For example, if the task is to compose a memorandum, **Help** will provide information about the word processor.

The Toolbar

The toolbar at the top of the screen shows the amount of time remaining for you to complete the tasks. In addition, the following tools are available. Note that only the Exit button is displayed when Directions are visible - the others will appear when you begin the tasks.

 Click on these buttons to split or unsplit the screen. You can split the screen vertically or horizontally.

 Click on this button to display the calculator; click on it again to hide the calculator. To move the calculator, click on the calculator title bar and drag the calculator to the desired location.

 Click on this button to use the spreadsheet; click on it again to hide the spreadsheet. To move the spreadsheet, click on the the spreadsheet title bar and drag the spreadsheet to the desired location.

 Click on this button to go on to the next part of the examination. You must complete all of the tasks to receive full credit. Once you click on **Exit** and confirm the action, you will NOT be able to return to this testlet.

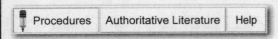

Temple, CPA, is auditing the financial statements of Ford Lumber Yards, Inc., a privately held corporation with 300 employees and five shareholders, three of whom are active in management. Ford has been in business for many years but has never had its financial statements audited. Temple suspects that the substance of some of Ford's business transactions differs from their form because of the pervasiveness of related party relationships and transactions in the local building supplies industry.

The audit procedures Temple should apply to identify Ford's related-party relationships and transactions include some of the following. Determine whether each procedure is appropriate (true) or not (false), and check the appropriate box.

Procedures	True	False
1. Evaluate the company's procedures for identifying and properly reporting related party relationships and transactions.		
2. Request from management the names of all related parties and inquire whether there were any related party transactions.		
3. Review confirmations of accounts receivable, particularly for the small balances.		
4. Review tax returns and filings with other regulatory agencies for the names of related parties.		
5. Review cash receipts for a few days prior to and after year end, particularly for significant amounts of currency.		
6. Review the stock certificate book to identify the shareholders.		
7. Review the minutes of board of directors' meetings.		
8. Review conflict-of-interest statements obtained by the company from its management.		
9. Review the extent and nature of business transacted with major customers, suppliers, borrowers, and lenders.		
10. Request from the client's competitors the names of known related parties.		
11. Review all investment transactions to determine whether the investment created related party relationships.		
12. Review accounting records for large, unusual, or nonrecurring transactions or balances, paying particular attention to transactions recognized at or near the end of the reporting period.		
13. Review invoices from law firms that have performed services for the company for indications of the existence of related party relationships or transactions.		
14. Review accounting records for consistently recurring transactions that, in the aggregate, are considered immaterial.		

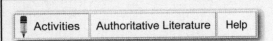

The independent, external auditor decides that it is efficient to consider how the internal auditors' work might affect the nature, timing, and extent of audit procedures. Thus, the independent auditor should assess both the competence and objectivity of the internal auditors. For each of the following procedures, select from the list provided to show whether it is appropriate for assessing competence, objectivity, both, or neither. Each choice may be used once, more than once, or not at all.

Procedures	Answer
1. Update or obtain information about the supervision and review of internal auditors' work.	
2. Update or obtain information about the policies regarding the employment of relatives of internal auditors in audit-sensitive positions.	
3. Evaluate evidence from a recent external quality review of the internal auditors.	
4. Update or obtain information about the audit plans and procedures used by the internal auditors.	
5. Evaluate the personal financial statements of the internal auditors.	
6. Determine whether the internal auditors have direct access to the board of directors.	
7. Update or obtain information about the professional certification of the internal auditors.	
8. Update or obtain information about the continuing education programs provided to the internal auditors.	
9. Consider information obtained in previous audits about the activities of internal auditors.	
10. Consider whether the internal auditors are well paid.	

Choices
A) The independent auditor should perform this procedure to test the competence and objectivity of the internal auditors.
B) The independent auditor should perform this procedure to test the competence but not the objectivity of the internal auditors.
C) The independent auditor should perform this procedure to test the objectivity but not the competence of the internal auditors.
D) The auditor would not perform this procedure.

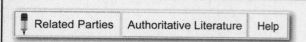

Each of the following describes a possible related party transaction, motive for such a transaction, audit procedure pertinent to related party transactions, or disclosure. Select from the list provided the appropriate choice. Each choice may be used once, more than once, or not at all.

Description	Answer
1. An overly optimistic earnings forecast.	
2. The transaction was consummated on terms equivalent to those that prevail at arm's-length.	
3. Confirm significant information with intermediaries.	
4. Review conflict-of-interest statements obtained by the company for its management.	
5. Making nonmonetary exchanges of similar property.	
6. Interest-free borrowing.	
7. Reviewing shareholder listings of closely held companies.	
8. Excess capacity.	
9. The transaction would have occurred even if the parties were not related.	
10. Determine whether the transaction was approved by the board of directors.	

Choices
A) Transactions indicative of the existence of related parties.
B) Motivation for entering into related party transactions.
C) Specific audit procedure that may uncover related parties.
D) Procedure to gain an understanding of a related party transaction.
E) Appropriate financial statement disclosure by management about related party transactions.
F) Inappropriate financial statement disclosure by management about related party transactions.

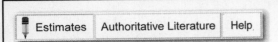

Management and the auditor have certain responsibilities and expectations relative to estimates in the financial statements. Show by checking the appropriate box whether each statement is true or false relative to those responsibilities.

Statements	True	False
1. The auditor is responsible for determining the need for accounting estimates in the financial statements.		
2. The auditor should evaluate the reasonableness of the estimates used in the financial statements.		
3. The auditor should adopt an attitude of professional skepticism toward the financial statement estimates.		
4. Management would be expected to make few, if any, estimates to be used in the financial statements.		
5. The auditor would expect the risk of material misstatement to increase with more subjectivity in the estimation process.		
6. The auditor should communicate with competitors about the reasonableness of the client's estimates.		
7. Management should enlist the auditor to help in making appropriate estimates.		
8. Management should use only objective, not subjective, information in developing estimates.		

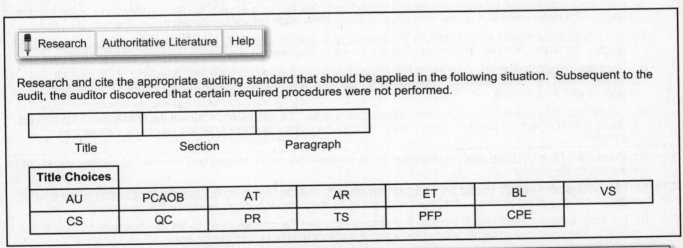

Research and cite the appropriate auditing standard that should be applied in the following situation. Subsequent to the audit, the auditor discovered that certain required procedures were not performed.

Title	Section	Paragraph

Title Choices

AU	PCAOB	AT	AR	ET	BL	VS
CS	QC	PR	TS	PFP	CPE	

Unofficial Answers

1. Procedures (14 Gradable Items)

1. <u>True.</u> It is management's responsibility to identify and report related party transactions. The auditor should evaluate the client's procedures for meeting this responsibility.

2. <u>True.</u> To begin the investigation of potential related party transactions, the auditor should inquire of management concerning the names of parties and types of transactions.

3. <u>False.</u> Accounts receivable confirmations are not likely to disclose related parties because a confirmation request does not ask for such information.

4. <u>True.</u> Filings with the SEC, IRS, and any other agency reported to by the entity should be reviewed for any named related parties.

5. <u>False.</u> Cutoff tests are not likely to disclose related parties.

6. <u>True.</u> Principal shareholders are considered related parties, and transactions with them are subject to disclosure requirements.

7. <u>True.</u> Deliberations of the board of directors should be evaluated for a number of purposes, including the possibility of discussions concerning transactions with related parties.

8. <u>True.</u> Clients often request management to submit statements about conflicts of interest. A conflict of interest by management may result from certain types of related party transactions.

9. <u>True.</u> Significant transactions should be evaluated from many perspectives related to the assertions of management. One issue is the possibility for disclosure of any related party transactions.

10. <u>False.</u> The auditor is not likely to communicate with the client's competitors.

11. <u>False.</u> Only significant (material) investment transactions are evaluated individually.

12. <u>True.</u> Significant transactions should be evaluated for disclosure implications, particularly those at or near year end.

13. <u>True.</u> Contracts and agreements typically result in attorneys' fees represented by invoices. The auditor is interested in this type of information because of the potential for detecting related party transactions.

14. <u>False.</u> Immaterial transactions, in the aggregate, are not typically a concern to the auditor.

2. Activities (10 Gradable Items)

1. <u>B) The independent auditor should perform this procedure to test the competence but not the objectivity of the internal auditors.</u> The supervision and review of internal auditors' work relate to their competence.

2. <u>C) The independent auditor should perform this procedure to test the objectivity but not the competence of the internal auditors.</u> The employment of relatives of internal auditors in audit-sensitive positions relates their objectivity.

3. <u>A) The independent auditor should perform this procedure to test the competence and objectivity of the internal auditors.</u> Evidence from a recent external quality review of the internal auditors provides information about both objectivity and competence.

4. <u>B) The independent auditor should perform this procedure to test the competence but not the objectivity of the internal auditors.</u> Evaluating audit plans and procedures used by the internal auditors provides information about their competence.

5. <u>D) The auditor would not perform this procedure.</u> The personal financial statements of the internal auditors would not be evaluated by the auditor.

6. <u>C) The independent auditor should perform this procedure to test the objectivity but not the competence of the internal auditors.</u> Having direct access to the board of directors by the internal auditors relates to their objectivity.

7. <u>B) The independent auditor should perform this procedure to test the competence but not the objectivity of the internal auditors.</u> The professional certification of the internal auditors relates to their competence.

8. <u>B) The independent auditor should perform this procedure to test the competence but not the objectivity of the internal auditors.</u> The continuing education programs provided to the internal auditors relate to their competence.

9. <u>A) The independent auditor should perform this procedure to test the competence and objectivity of the internal auditors.</u> Information from previous audits about the activities of internal auditors relates to both objectivity and competence.

10. <u>D) The auditor would not perform this procedure.</u> Considering whether the internal auditors are well paid would not be performed by the auditor.

3. Related Parties (10 Gradable Items)

1. B) Motivation for entering into related party transactions. Management may be motivated to enter into related party transactions in order to meet overly optimistic forecasts.

2. F) Inappropriate financial statement disclosure by management about related party transactions. It is inappropriate for management to assert that a transaction was consummated on terms equivalent to those that prevail at arm's-length.

3. D) Procedure to gain an understanding of a related party transaction. Procedures to gain an understanding of a related party transaction would include confirming significant information with intermediaries.

4. C) Specific audit procedure that may uncover related parties. Reviewing conflict-of-interest statements may uncover the existence of related parties.

5. A) Transactions indicative of the existence of related parties. Nonmonetary exchange of similar property is indicative of transactions made with related parties.

6. A) Transactions indicative of the existence of related parties. Interest-free borrowing is indicative of transactions made by related parties.

7. C) Specific audit procedure that may uncover related parties. Reviewing shareholder listings of closely held companies may uncover the existence of related parties.

8. B) Motivation for entering into related party transactions. Attempting to fill excess capacity may motivate management to enter into related party transactions.

9. F) Inappropriate financial statement disclosure by management about related party transactions. It is inappropriate for management to assert that a transaction would have occurred even if the parties were not related.

10. D) Procedure to gain an understanding of a related party transaction. Procedures to gain an understanding of a related party transaction would include determining whether the transaction was approved by the board of directors.

4. Estimates (8 Gradable Items)

1. False. Management is responsible for determining the need for accounting estimates in the financial statements.

2. True. The auditor should evaluate the reasonableness of the estimates used in the financial statements.

3. True. The auditor should adopt an attitude of professional skepticism toward the financial statement estimates.

4. False. The financial statements contain many estimates including allowance accounts, depreciation, and amortization.

5. True. The auditor would expect the risk of material misstatement to increase with more subjectivity in the estimation process.

6. False. The auditor would not communicate with the client's competitors about the reasonableness of estimates.

7. False. Management is responsible for making accounting estimates in the financial statements.

8. False. Accounting estimates are typically subjective by their very nature.

5. Research (1 Gradable Item)

Answer: 390.01

AU Section 390 -- *Consideration of Omitted Procedures after the Report Date*

.01 This section provides guidance on the considerations and procedures to be applied by an auditor who, subsequent to the date of his report on audited financial statements, concludes that one or more auditing procedures considered necessary at the time of the audit in the circumstances then existing were omitted from his audit of the financial statements, but there is no indication that those financial statements are not fairly presented in conformity with generally accepted accounting principles or with another comprehensive basis of accounting. This circumstance should be distinguished from that described in section 561, which applies if an auditor, subsequent to the date of his report on audited financial statements, becomes aware that facts regarding those financial statements may have existed at that date that might have affected his report had he then been aware of them.

Gleim Simulation Grading

Task	Correct Responses		Gradable Items		Score per Task
1	_____	÷	14	=	_____
2	_____	÷	10	=	_____
3	_____	÷	10	=	_____
4	_____	÷	8	=	_____
Research	_____	÷	1	=	_____

Total of Scores per Task	_____
÷ Total Number of Tasks	5
Total Score	_____ %

Use **CPA Gleim Online** and **Simulation Wizard** to practice more task-based simulations in a realistic environment.

STUDY UNIT FIVE
INTERNAL CONTROL CONCEPTS
AND INFORMATION TECHNOLOGY

(16 pages of outline)

Concepts related to the client's internal control are tested extensively. AU 314, *Understanding the Entity and its Environment and Assessing the Risks of Material Misstatement*, provides the basis for consideration of this topic. Emphasis also is placed on technology in the standards. Accordingly, this study unit contains definitions and concepts of great significance for exam preparation. Many of these were developed in the report of the Committee of Sponsoring Organizations of the Treadway Commission **(the COSO report)** and are reflected in AU 314 and other AICPA pronouncements.

Because of the Sarbanes-Oxley Act of 2002, control concepts are crucially important to entities subject to the Securities Exchange Act of 1934. Certain issuers ("accelerated filers" with $75 million in market equity) must include in its annual report an assessment by management of whether internal control over financial reporting is effective. The auditor is required to attest to the effectiveness of internal control as part of the overall audit. However, PCAOB AS No. 5 requires the auditor merely to express an opinion, or disclaim an opinion, on internal control, not on management's assessment of internal control.

The general concepts described in this study unit are applied specifically in the transaction processing cycles considered in Study Units 6 and 7. CPA candidates should master the material in this study unit before continuing.

5.1 INTRODUCTION TO INTERNAL CONTROL

1. **Second Standard of Field Work**

   a. The second standard of field work (GAAS) states:

      The auditor must obtain a sufficient understanding of the entity and its environment, including its internal control, to assess the risk of material misstatement of the financial statements whether due to error or fraud, and to design the nature, timing, and extent of further audit procedures.

2. Internal control is a process -- effected by those charged with governance, management, and other personnel -- designed to provide reasonable assurance regarding the achievement of **objectives** related to the following:

   a. **Reliability of financial reporting**
   b. **Effectiveness and efficiency of operations**
   c. **Compliance with applicable laws and regulations**

3. **Components of Internal Control**

    a. The COSO's internal control framework consists of the following five interrelated components (a useful mnemonic is "Controls stop **CRIME**," with E representing the control environment):

        1) **Control activities** are the policies and procedures that help ensure that management directives are carried out.

        2) **Risk assessment** is the entity's identification and analysis of relevant risks as a basis for their management.

        3) **Information and communication systems** support the identification, capture, and exchange of information in a form and time frame that enable people to carry out their responsibilities.

        4) **Monitoring** is a process that assesses the quality of internal control performance over time.

        5) **Control environment** sets the tone of an organization, influencing the control consciousness of its people.

4. **Relevant Controls**

    a. The relationship between an entity's objectives and the components is direct. Moreover, internal control is relevant to the whole entity (or any operating unit or business function).

    b. However, an entity generally has controls relating to objectives that are not relevant to an audit and need not be considered, for example, a computerized production scheduling system.

    c. Furthermore, understanding internal control relevant to each operating unit or business function may not be needed to perform an audit.

5. **Limitations of Internal Control**

    a. Because of its **inherent limitations**, internal control can be designed and operated to provide only **reasonable assurance** that the entity's objectives are met.

    b. **Human judgment is faulty**, and controls may fail because of simple error or mistake. For example, design changes for an automated order entry system may be faulty because the designers did not understand the system or because programmers did not correctly code the design changes. Errors also may arise when automated reports are misinterpreted by users.

    c. Manual or automated controls can be circumvented by **collusion**.

    d. Management may inappropriately **override** internal control.

Stop and review! You have completed the outline for this subunit. Study multiple-choice questions 1 through 4 beginning on page 183.

5.2 INTERNAL CONTROL COMPONENTS

1. **Control Environment**

    a. This component is the foundation for the other components. It provides discipline and structure. To understand the control environment, the auditor considers programs and controls addressing **fraud risk** that have been implemented by management and those charged with governance. Their absence or inadequacy may be a material weakness. The evaluation of the design of the control environment includes the following factors:

        1) Communication and enforcement of **integrity and ethical values.** These are essential elements of the control environment and influence the effectiveness of the other components. Standards and values should be effectively communicated, e.g., by management example. Management also should remove incentives and temptations for dishonest or unethical acts.

2) **Commitment to competence.** Management must consider the competence levels for particular jobs.

3) **Participation of those charged with governance (board of directors, audit committee, etc.).** Their independence, experience, and stature are among the qualities that affect the entity's control consciousness.

4) **Management's philosophy and operating style.** They relate to management's approach to taking and managing business risks. They also relate to management's attitudes and actions toward (a) financial reporting, (b) information processing, (c) accounting functions, and (d) personnel.

5) **Organizational structure.** Key areas of authority and responsibility and appropriate lines of reporting should be considered. The organizational structure is depicted by an organizational chart. (See Figure 6-1 in Study Unit 6 on page 206.)

6) **Assignment of authority and responsibility.** This factor concerns how authority over and responsibility for operating activities are assigned and how reporting relationships and authorization hierarchies are established.

7) **Human resource policies and practices.** These relate to recruitment, orientation, training, evaluation, counseling, promotion, compensation, and remedial action. Training policies should communicate roles and responsibilities and expected levels of performance and behavior.

2. **Risk Assessment**

   a. Relevant risks include events and circumstances that may adversely affect an entity's ability to initiate, authorize, record, process, and report financial data consistent with financial statement assertions. The following factors affecting risk should be considered:

   1) **Changes in operating environment.** A shift in the regulatory or operating environment may require reconsideration of risks.

   2) **New personnel.** New employees may have a different focus on control issues.

   3) **New or revamped information systems.** Automated systems are important to the risk assessment process because they provide timely information for identifying and managing risks. However, significant and rapid changes in information systems themselves may affect risk.

   4) **Rapid growth.** Significant and rapid expansion may strain controls and increase risk.

   5) **New technology.** Integrating new technology into production or information processes may change risk.

   6) **New business models, products, or activities.** Inexperience with respect to new business areas or transactions may change risk.

   7) **Corporate restructurings.** Staffing and supervision changes may change risk.

   8) **Expanded foreign operations.** Expansion to foreign markets may result in changes in risk, for example, from currency exchange.

   9) **New accounting pronouncements.** Adoption or changes of principles may affect risk in statement preparation.

3. **Control Activities**

   a. These are the policies and procedures helping to ensure that actions are taken to address risks to achievement of objectives. Whether automated or manual, they have various objectives and are applied at various levels.

   1) **Performance reviews** include reviews of actual performance versus budgets and prior performance.

2) **Information processing** requires checks of accuracy, completeness, and authorization of transactions. These controls include general controls and application controls.

3) **Physical controls** involve the safeguarding of assets, records, periodic counts, and reconciliations that creates asset accountability.

4) **Segregation of duties** involves the separation of the functions of authorization, record keeping, and asset custody so as to minimize the opportunities for a person to be able to perpetrate and conceal errors or fraud in the normal course of his/her duties.

4. **Information System and Communication**

a.   An information system consists of physical and hardware elements (infrastructure), software, data, manual and automated procedures, and people that interrelate to achieve a business goal.

b.   For financial reporting, the information system (including the accounting system) encompasses automated and manual procedures and records used to initiate, authorize, record, process, and report transactions, events, and conditions and to maintain accountability for assets, liabilities, and equity.

1) **Initiation** may be automatic through programmed methods. **Authorizing** is management's approval process. **Recording** includes identification and capture of relevant information. **Processing** involves edit and validation, calculation, measurement, valuation, summarization, and reconciliation by manual or automated means. **Reporting** of financial and other information for use in, for example, the monitoring function, may be in a print or electronic medium.

c.   An **information system**

1) Identifies and records all valid transactions
2) Describes transactions sufficiently for proper classification
3) Measures transactions
4) Determines the proper reporting period for transactions
5) Presents transactions and related disclosures properly

d.   **Communication** includes providing an understanding to employees about their roles and responsibilities. For example, communication may be through policy manuals, financial reporting manuals, and memoranda. It also may be by electronic and oral means or by management actions.

5. **Monitoring**

a.   Monitoring is management's timely assessment of internal control and the taking of corrective action so that controls operate as intended and are modified for changes in conditions. **Establishing and maintaining internal control is management's responsibility.**

b.   The monitoring process involves the following:

1) Ongoing activities built into normal recurring actions such as supervision, possibly combined with separate evaluations
2) The actions of internal auditors
3) Consideration of communications from external parties

c.   Monitoring information may be produced by the information system. Hence, the auditor should obtain sufficient knowledge about major monitoring activities, including the sources of related information and the basis for considering it to be reliable.

Stop and review! You have completed the outline for this subunit. Study multiple-choice questions 5 through 14 beginning on page 184.

5.3 UNDERSTANDING INTERNAL CONTROL

1. In all audits, the auditor should obtain an understanding of the five components of internal control sufficient to assess the **risk of material misstatement (RMM)** and to design further audit procedures. A sufficient understanding is obtained by performing **risk assessment procedures** to evaluate the design of controls relevant to the audit and determine whether they have been implemented.

    a. However, the auditor is not obligated to search for deficiencies in internal control, although (s)he **must communicate any significant deficiencies and material weaknesses noted**.

2. The understanding should be used to

    a. Identify types of potential misstatements.
    b. Consider factors that affect the RMMs.
    c. Design tests of controls if appropriate (see Study Unit 8).
    d. Design substantive procedures.

3. **Accounting Policies**

    a. The auditor should obtain an understanding of the selection and application of accounting policies and consider whether they are appropriate. This understanding includes the following:

        1) Significant and unusual transactions
        2) Significant policies applied when there is a lack of guidance or consensus in controversial or emerging areas
        3) Changes in policies
        4) Adoption of new standards and regulations

4. **Relevant Controls**

    a. Relevant controls ordinarily address **objectives** related to the preparation of fairly presented financial statements, including management of RMMs.

        1) But assessing all such controls is not necessary, and the auditor should use **professional judgment** regarding what should be assessed.

    b. For **significant risks**, the auditor should evaluate the **design** of the related controls and determine whether they have been **implemented**. For this purpose, the auditor considers

        1) The control component;
        2) The circumstances;
        3) Materiality;
        4) The size of the entity;
        5) The nature of the business, including organizational and ownership characteristics;
        6) The diversity and complexity of operations;
        7) The nature and complexity of control systems, including the use of service organizations; and
        8) Legal and regulatory concerns.

    c. Controls over the **completeness and accuracy** of information used by the auditor are relevant.

    d. **Identifying** relevant controls is facilitated by

        1) Previous experience with the entity,
        2) The understanding of the entity and its environment, and
        3) Information gathered during the audit.

    e.   Controls over **operations and compliance** may be relevant if they relate to information or data involved in performance of audit procedures.

        1)   Examples are controls related to (a) nonfinancial data used in analytical procedures or (b) noncompliance with tax laws and regulations having a direct and material effect on the statements.

    f.   Controls over **safeguarding of assets** against unauthorized acquisition, use, or disposition may include those relating to financial reporting and operations objectives.

        1)   But the auditor's consideration is usually limited to **controls relevant to financial reporting**, such as controls that limit access to the data and programs (e.g., passwords) that process cash payments.

5.   **Design and Implementation**

    a.   The **evaluation of design** considers whether a control (alone or with others) can effectively prevent or detect and correct material misstatements.

    b.   A control has been **implemented** if it exists and the entity is using it.

        1)   An auditor may decide not to consider implementation if the design is improper.

            a)   An improper design may be a **material weakness** in internal control that the auditor should communicate to management and those charged with governance.

6.   **Risk Assessment Procedures**

    a.   Risk assessment procedures performed to obtain evidence about the design and implementation of relevant controls include (1) inquiries, (2) observation of the application of specific controls, (3) inspection of documents and reports, and (4) tracing transactions.

        1)   Inquiries alone are not sufficient procedures.

7.   **Operating Effectiveness**

    a.   Obtaining the understanding is insufficient to test the operating effectiveness of controls (see Study Unit 8), unless they are automated and subject to effective **IT general controls**.

    b.   Operating effectiveness is concerned with how and by whom the control (manual or automated) was applied and the consistency of application.

8.   **Understanding IT-Based Systems**

    a.   **IT skills** may be required to (1) determine the effect of IT on the audit, (2) understand IT controls, and (3) design and perform tests of IT controls and substantive procedures.

    b.   These skills may be obtained from an audit staff member or an outside professional.

        1)   Whether a professional is needed depends on such factors as (a) the complexity of systems and IT controls, (b) their use in the business, (c) the extent of data sharing among systems, (d) implementation of new systems or changes in old ones, (e) the involvement in electronic commerce, (f) use of emerging technologies, and (g) audit evidence available only electronically.

        2)   An outside professional may make inquiries of the entity's IT personnel, inspect documentation, observe operation of controls, and test IT controls.

        3)   The auditor must have sufficient IT expertise to (a) communicate audit objectives, (b) evaluate whether the IT professional's procedures will meet those objectives, and (c) evaluate the results.

    c.   The auditor should understand the **information system relevant to financial reporting**, that is, (1) the classes of significant transactions; (2) the automated and manual procedures used to initiate, authorize, record, process, and report transactions; (3) the related accounting records, supporting information, and specific accounts; (4) how the system captures other significant events and conditions; and (5) the financial reporting process, including significant accounting estimates and disclosures.

        1)   Thus, the auditor should understand not only the manual procedures but also the IT systems, programs, and controls in the financial reporting process.

9.   **Documentation**

    a.   Documentation of the understanding is required by GAAS. Its form and extent are influenced by the nature and complexity of the controls. For example, a complex information system that electronically initiates, authorizes, records, processes, and reports a large volume of transactions requires extensive documentation. Accordingly, flowcharts, questionnaires, or decision tables may be appropriate for a complex information system, but a memorandum may suffice when little or no use is made of IT or few transactions are processed. In general, the more complex the controls and the more extensive the audit procedures, the more extensive the documentation.

    b.   **Systems (document) flowcharts** are diagrams of the client's system that track the flow of documents and processing. Advantages are that they provide a visual representation of the system and are flexible in construction. Flowcharts are introduced in Subunit 5.4 and are illustrated in Study Units 6 and 7.

    c.   **Questionnaires** consist of a series of interrelated questions about internal control policies and procedures. The questions are typically phrased so that a "Yes" indicates a control strength and a "No" indicates a potential weakness. An area is provided next to the responses for the auditor to explain the responses or cross-reference the answer with other working papers. An advantage of the questionnaire is that it helps identify control concerns and prevents the auditor from overlooking important control considerations.

    d.   A **narrative memorandum** is a written description of the process and flow of documents and of the control points. The advantage is flexibility. However, following the flow from the narrative may be difficult for a complex system.

    e.   A **decision table** identifies the contingencies considered in the description of a problem and the appropriate actions to be taken in each case. Decision tables are logic diagrams presented in matrix form. Unlike flowcharts, they do not present the sequence of the actions described.

    f.   A **checklist** consists of a series of procedures to be performed.

Stop and review! You have completed the outline for this subunit. Study multiple-choice questions 15 through 22 beginning on page 187.

5.4 FLOWCHARTING

Flowcharting is a topic that many CPA candidates try to avoid. However, you should realize that flowcharting is just another auditor's tool. The good news is that it is improbable that you will be required to construct a flowchart. Any questions that you may get will likely require you to interpret a flowchart. Keep an open mind as you begin using the flowcharts in Study Units 6 and 7. Spend enough time to understand the general flow of information and documents. You will likely surprise yourself with the confidence you gain.

1. Flowcharting is a useful tool for systems development as well as for understanding internal control. A flowchart is a pictorial diagram of the definition, analysis, or solution of a problem in which symbols are used to represent operations, data flow, documents, records, etc.

   a. The processing is presented sequentially from the point of origin to the distribution of final output.

      1) Processing usually flows from top to bottom and from left to right in the flowchart.

   b. A **system flowchart** provides an overall view of the inputs, processes, and outputs of a system.

   c. A **program flowchart** represents the specific steps in a computer program and the order in which they will be carried out.

      1) Macro- and microflowcharts describe a program in less or greater detail, respectively.

   d. A **document flowchart** depicts the flow of documents through an entity.

      1) Areas of responsibility (e.g., data processing or purchasing) are usually depicted in vertical columns or areas.

2. Flowcharts are used to understand, evaluate, and document client internal control. Many CPA questions address flowcharting itself. Other CPA questions address specific controls, audit procedures, weaknesses, etc., that are related to or are a part of internal control.

3. Commonly used document flowchart symbols include

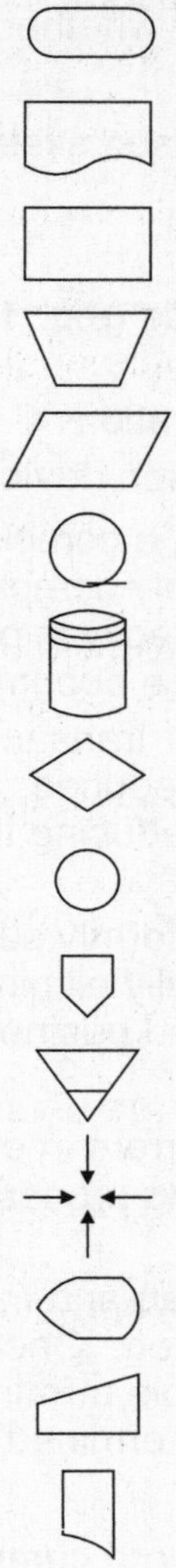

Starting or ending point or point of interruption

Input or output of a document or report

Computer operation or group of operations

Manual processing operation, e.g., prepare document

Generalized symbol for input or output used when the medium is not specified

Magnetic tape used for input or output

Magnetic disk used for storage

Decision symbol indicating a branch in the flow

Connection between points on the same page

Connection between two pages of the flowchart

Storage (file) that is not immediately accessible by computer

Flow direction of data or processing

Display on a video terminal

Manual input into a terminal or other online device

Adding machine tape (batch control)

Figure 5-1

Stop and review! You have completed the outline for this subunit. Study multiple-choice questions 23 through 26 beginning on page 189.

5.5 INTERNAL CONTROL AND INFORMATION TECHNOLOGY

1. The **goals** of a business information system are the same regardless of whether it is manual or computer-based. The **risks**, on the other hand, can be quite different.

   a. **System availability.** The ability to make use of any computer-based system is dependent on

      1) An uninterrupted flow of electricity
      2) Protection of computer hardware from environmental hazards (e.g., fire and water)
      3) Protection of software and data files from unauthorized alteration
      4) Preservation of functioning communications channels between devices

   b. **Volatile transaction trails.** In any computer-based environment, a complete trail useful for audit purposes might exist for only a short time or in only computer-readable form. In online, real-time systems, data are entered directly into the computer, eliminating portions of the audit trail provided by source documents.

   c. **Decreased human involvement.** Because employees who enter transactions may never see the "final results," the potential for detecting errors is reduced. Also, output from a computer system often carries a mystique of infallibility, reducing the incentive of system users to closely examine reports and transaction logs.

   d. **Uniform processing of transactions.** Computer processing uniformly subjects like transactions to the same processing instructions, therefore virtually eliminating clerical error. Thus, it permits consistent application of predefined business rules and the performance of complex calculations in high volume.

      1) However, programming errors (or other similar systematic errors in either the hardware or software) will result in all like transactions being processed incorrectly.

   e. **Unauthorized access.** When accounting records were kept in pen-and-ink format, physical access to them was the only way to carry out an alteration. Once they are computer-based, however, access can be carried out from multiple terminals throughout the organization or from anywhere in the world by determined hackers using the Internet.

      1) Security measures, such as firewalls and user id-and-password combinations, are thus vital to maintaining security over data in an automated environment.

   f. **Data vulnerability.** Destruction of hardware devices or units of storage media could have disastrous consequences if they contain the only copies of crucial data files or application programs.

      1) For this reason, it is vital that an organization's computer files be duplicated and stored offsite periodically.

   g. **Reduced separation of duties.** Many functions once performed by separate individuals may be combined in an automated environment.

EXAMPLE

Receiving cash, issuing a receipt to the payor, preparing the deposit slip, and preparing the journal entry may once have been performed by separate individuals. In a computer-based system, the receipt, deposit slip, and journal entry may be automatically generated by the computer. If the same employee who receives the cash is also responsible for entering the relevant data into the system, the potential for error or fraud is increased.

---

   h. **Reduced individual authorization of transactions.** Certain transactions may be initiated automatically by a computer-based system. This is becoming ever more widespread as an increasing number of business processes become automated.

EXAMPLE

An enterprise resource planning system at a manufacturing concern may automatically generate a purchase order when raw materials inventory reaches a certain level. If the company shares an EDI system with the vendor, the purchase order may be sent to the vendor electronically without any human intervention.

    1) This reduced level of oversight for individual transactions requires careful coding to ensure that computer programs accurately reflect management's goals for business processes.

2. **Two Basic Processing Modes of Data**

    a. **Batch processing.** In this mode, transactions are accumulated and submitted to the computer as a single batch. In the early days of computers, this was the only way a job could be processed.

        1) In batch processing, the user cannot influence the process once the job has begun (except to ask that it be aborted completely). (S)he must wait until processing is complete to see if any transactions in the batch were rejected and failed to be processed.

        2) Despite huge advances in computer technology, this accumulation of transactions for processing on a delayed basis is still widely used. It is very efficient for such applications as payroll, where large numbers of routine transactions must be processed on a regular schedule.

    b. **Online, real-time processing.** In some systems, having the latest information available at all times is crucial to the proper functioning of the system. An airline reservation system is a common example.

        1) In an online, real-time system, the database is updated immediately upon entry of the transaction by the operator. Such systems are referred to as **online transaction processing**, or **OLTP**, systems.

3. The two broad groupings of information systems control activities are general controls and application controls.

    a. **General controls** are the umbrella under which the IT function operates. Because they affect the organization's entire processing environment, the auditor should achieve satisfaction about their proper operation before relying on application controls. They commonly include controls over data center and network operations; systems software acquisition, change, and maintenance; access security; and application system acquisition, development, and maintenance.

        1) Controls over data center and network **operations** ensure efficient and effective operations of the computer activity. These include aspects of the control environment and risk assessment.

        2) Controls over **software acquisition, change, and maintenance** ensure that proper software is available for use.

        3) Controls over **access** encompass access to both computer hardware devices themselves (physical access) and to data and programs through the system (logical access).

    b. **Application controls** are particular to each of the organization's applications. Some features come built-in when applications are acquired from vendors. Software developed by the organization's own programmers must have appropriate controls incorporated in the design. Application controls may be further classified as follows:

        1) **Input controls** provide reasonable assurance that data received for processing have been identified, properly authorized, and converted into machine-sensible form, and that data (including data transmitted over communication lines) have not been lost, added to, suppressed, duplicated, or otherwise improperly changed. Input controls also relate to rejection, correction, and resubmission of data initially incorrect.

2)   **Processing controls** provide reasonable assurance that processing has been performed as intended for the particular application. Thus, all transactions should be processed as authorized, no authorized transactions should be omitted, and no unauthorized transactions should be added.

3)   **Output controls** ensure the accuracy of the processing result (such as account listings, reports, files, invoices, or disbursement checks) and the receipt of output by authorized personnel only.

c.   Both categories of controls are discussed in greater detail in the rest of this subunit.

4.   **General Controls – Controls Over Operations**

a.   From an audit perspective, the most significant of these general controls is the assignment of **authority and responsibility**.

1)   **Separation of duties** is vital because a separation of functions (authorization, recording, and access to assets) may not be feasible in an IT environment. For example, a computer may print checks, record disbursements, and generate information for reconciling the account balance, which are activities customarily segregated in a manual system.

2)   The following are typical jobs within the IT function:

a)   **Database administrators (DBAs)** are responsible for developing and maintaining the organization's databases and for establishing controls to protect their integrity.

b)   **Network technicians** maintain the bridges, hubs, routers, switches, cabling, and other devices that interconnect the organization's computers. They are also responsible for maintaining the organization's connection to other networks, such as the Internet.

c)   The **webmaster** is responsible for the content of the organization's website. (S)he works closely with programmers and network technicians to ensure that the appropriate content is displayed and that the site is reliably available to users.

d)   **Computer (console) operators** are responsible for the moment-to-moment running of the organization's medium- and large-scale computers, i.e., servers and mainframes.

i)   Computers in this size range, unlike desktop computers, require 24-hour monitoring. Operators respond to messages received from the system by consulting run manuals that detail the steps for processing.

e)   **Librarians** maintain control over and accountability for documentation, programs, and data storage media.

f)   **Systems programmers** maintain and fine-tune the operating systems on the organization's medium- and large-scale computers. The operating system is the core software that performs a computer's basic tasks.

g)   A **systems analyst** uses his/her detailed knowledge of the organization's databases and applications programs to determine how an application should be designed to best serve the user's needs.

i)   These duties are often combined with those of programmers. **Applications programmers** design, write, test, and document computer programs according to specifications provided by the end users.

h)   **Help desk** personnel log problems reported by users, resolve minor difficulties, and forward more difficult problems to the appropriate person, such as a database administrator or the webmaster. Help desk personnel are often called on to resolve such issues as desktop computers crashing or problems with email.

b. **Periodic backup and offsite rotation** of computer files is the most basic part of any disaster recovery/business continuity plan.

1) A **typical backup routine** involves duplicating all data files and application programs at least once a month. Incremental changes are then backed up and taken to the offsite location periodically, often once a week. (Application files must be backed up in addition to data since programs change too.)

2) The **offsite location** must be temperature- and humidity-controlled and guarded against physical intrusion. Just as important, it must be geographically remote enough from the site of the organization's main operations that it would not be affected by the same natural disaster. It does the organization no good to have adequate backup files if the files are not accessible or have been destroyed.

3) **Fully protected systems** have generator or battery backup to prevent data destruction and downtime from electrical power disturbances.

4) **Fault-tolerant computer systems** have additional hardware and software as well as a backup power supply.

5) **Hot-site and cold-site backup facilities.** A hot site is a fully operational processing facility that is immediately available (e.g., a service bureau). A cold site is a shell facility where the user can quickly install equipment.

c. Protection against Malicious Software (Malware)

1) **Virus protection.** A virus is a software program that infects another program or a system's primary storage (main memory) by altering its logic. Infection often results in the destruction of data. Once infected, a software program can spread the virus to other software programs. Obtaining software through a shareware network or by downloading from untrustworthy sources is a typical cause of infection. Propagation of viruses through email attachments is also common.

2) To protect against viruses, three types of controls should be implemented:

a) **Preventive controls** include (1) establishing a formal security policy, (2) using only clean and certified copies of software, (3) not using shareware software, (4) checking new software with antivirus software, (5) restricting access, and (6) educating users.

b) **Detective controls** include making file size and date/time stamp comparisons.

c) **Corrective controls** include ensuring that clean backup is maintained and having a documented plan for recovery from a virus.

3) **Worms** are viruses that make copies of themselves with either benign or malignant intent. They ordinarily exist as independent programs and use operating system services as their means of replication.

4) A **Trojan horse** is software that appears to have a legitimate function but performs some destructive or illicit function after it begins to run.

d. Network Security

1) **Local area networks (LANs)** and **wide area networks (WANs)** are defined by the area over which they provide communications.

2) **Intranets and extranets** are defined by who has access. An intranet is a network based on the same technology (connectivity standards and web software) as the Internet, but access is limited to an organization or those with specific authorization. An extranet provides web access for existing customers or specific users rather than the general public.

3) The most important control is to install an entity-wide network security system. **User account management** involves installing a system to ensure that

   a) New accounts are added correctly and assigned only to authorized users.

   b) Old and unused accounts are removed promptly.

   c) **Passwords** are changed periodically, and employees are taught how to choose a password that cannot be easily guessed. A password should consist of at least six diverse characters that do not form a word.

4) **Internet security.** Connection to the Internet presents security issues.

   a) A **firewall** separates an internal from an external network (e.g., the Internet) and prevents passage of specific types of traffic. It identifies names, Internet Protocol (IP) addresses, applications, etc., and compares them with programmed access rules.

   b) Firewall systems ordinarily produce reports on entity-wide Internet use, exception reports for unusual activity patterns, and system penetration-attempt reports. These reports are very helpful to the auditor as a method of continuous monitoring, or logging, of the system.

      i) Firewalls do not provide adequate protection against viruses. Thus, an entity should include one or more of the virus controls listed in its network security policy.

5) **Digital signatures** are a form of **encryption** technology used by businesses to authenticate documents. A plaintext document is sent with an encrypted portion of the same document over the Internet. If the plaintext document is tampered with, the two will not match.

5. **General Controls – Controls Over Software Acquisition, Change, and Maintenance**

   a. **Controls over systems software** ensure that operating systems, utilities, and database management systems are acquired and changed only under close supervision and that vendor updates are routinely installed.

   b. **Controls over application software** ensure that programs used for transaction processing (e.g., payroll and accounts receivable) are cost-effective and stable.

   c. Collectively these controls are termed **"change controls"** and require proper authorization, testing, and acceptance. All changes should be properly documented.

6. **General Controls – Access Controls**

   a. Access controls prevent improper use or manipulation of data files and programs. They ensure that only those persons with a bona fide purpose and authorization have access.

   b. Physical security controls protect against unauthorized access to equipment and information.

   c. **Passwords and ID numbers.** The use of passwords and identification numbers (for example, a PIN used for an ATM) is an effective control in an online system to prevent unauthorized access to files. Lists of authorized persons are maintained online. To avoid unauthorized access, the entity may combine (1) the entry of passwords or identification numbers; (2) a prearranged set of personal questions; and (3) the use of badges, magnetic cards, or optically scanned cards.

   d. **Device authorization table.** This control grants access only to those physical devices that should logically need access. For example, because it is illogical for anyone to access the accounts receivable file from a manufacturing terminal, the device authorization table will deny access even when a valid password is used.

   e. **System access log.** This log records all uses and attempted uses of the system. The date and time, codes used, mode of access, data involved, and interventions by operators are recorded.

    f.   **Encryption.** Encoding data before transmission over communication lines makes it more difficult for someone with access to the transmission to understand or modify its contents. Encryption technology converts data into a code. Unauthorized users may still be able to access the data but, without the encryption key, will be unable to decode the information.

    g.   **Callback.** This feature requires the remote user to call, give identification, hang up, and wait for a call to an authorized number. This control ensures acceptance of data only from authorized modems. However, a call-forwarding device may thwart this control by transferring access from an authorized to an unauthorized number.

    h.   **Controlled disposal of documents.** One method of enforcing access restrictions is to destroy data when they are no longer in use. Thus, paper documents may be shredded, and magnetic media may be erased.

    i.   **Biometric technologies.** These are automated methods of establishing an individual's identity using physiological or behavioral traits. These characteristics include fingerprints, retina patterns, hand geometry, signature dynamics, speech, and keystroke dynamics.

    j.   **Automatic log-off** (disconnection) of inactive data terminals may prevent the viewing of sensitive data on an unattended data terminal.

    k.   **Security personnel.** An entity may hire security specialists. For example, (1) developing an information security policy for the entity, (2) commenting on security controls in new applications, and (3) monitoring and investigating unsuccessful access attempts are appropriate duties of the information security officer.

7.   **Application Controls – Input**

    a.   **Input controls** provide reasonable assurance that data submitted for processing are (1) authorized, (2) complete, and (3) accurate. These controls vary depending on whether input is entered in online or batch mode.

    b.   **Online input controls** can be used when data are keyed into an input screen.

        1)   **Preformatting.** The data entry screen mimics a hardcopy document, forcing data entry in all necessary fields.

        2)   **Edit (field) checks.** The data entry screen prevents certain types of incorrect data from entering the system. For example, the system rejects any attempt to enter numerals in the Name box or letters in the Amount box. Dropdown menus can restrict the user's choices to only valid selections.

        3)   **Limit (reasonableness) checks.** Certain amounts can be restricted to appropriate ranges, such as hours worked less than 10 per day, or invoices over $100,000 requiring supervisor approval.

        4)   **Check digits.** An algorithm is applied to any kind of serial identifier to derive a check digit. During data entry, the check digit is recomputed by the system to ensure proper entry.

        5)   **Closed-loop verification.** Inputs by a user are transmitted to the computer, processed, and displayed back to the user for verification.

    c.   **Batch input controls** can be used when data are grouped for processing in "batches."

        1)   **Management release.** A batch is not released for processing until a manager reviews and approves it.

        2)   **Record count.** A batch is not released for processing unless the number of records in the batch, as reported by the system, matches the number calculated by the user.

        3)   **Financial total.** A batch is not released for processing unless the sum of the dollar amounts of the individual items as reported by the system matches the amount calculated by the user.

4) **Hash total.** The arithmetic sum of a numeric field, that has no meaning by itself, can serve as a check that the same records that should have been processed were processed. An example is the sum of all Social Security numbers.

   a) This number is much too unwieldy to be calculated by the user, but once it is calculated by the system, it can follow the batch through subsequent stages of processing.

8. **Application Controls – Processing**

   a. Processing controls provide reasonable assurance that (1) all data submitted for processing are processed and (2) only approved data are processed. These controls are built into the application code by programmers during the systems development process.

   b. Some processing controls repeat the steps performed by the **input controls**, such as limit checks and batch controls.

   c. **Validation.** Identifiers are matched against master files to determine existence. For example, any accounts payable transaction in which the vendor number does not match a number on the vendor master file is rejected.

   d. **Completeness.** Any record with missing data is rejected.

   e. **Arithmetic controls.** Cross-footing compares an amount to the sum of its components. Zero-balance checking adds the debits and credits in a transaction or batch to assure they sum to zero.

   f. **Sequence check.** Computer effort is expended most efficiently when data are processed in a logical order, such as by customer number. This check ensures the batch is sorted in this order before processing begins.

   g. **Run-to-run control totals.** The controls associated with a given batch are checked after each stage of processing to ensure all transactions have been processed.

   h. **Key integrity.** A record's "key" is the group of values in designated fields that uniquely identify the record. No application process should be able to alter the data in these key fields.

9. **Application Controls – Output**

   a. **Output controls** provide assurance that processing was complete and accurate.

   b. A complete **audit trail** should be generated by each process: batch number, time of submission, time of completion, number of records in batch, total dollars in batch, number of records rejected, total dollars rejected, etc.

      1) The audit trail is immediately submitted to a **reasonableness check** by the user, who is most qualified to judge the adequacy of processing and the proper treatment of erroneous transactions.

   c. **Error listings** report all transactions rejected by the system. These should be corrected and resubmitted by the user.

Stop and review! You have completed the outline for this subunit. Study multiple-choice questions 27 through 47 beginning on page 191.

QUESTIONS

5.1 Introduction to Internal Control

1. The primary objective of procedures performed to obtain an understanding of internal control is to provide an auditor with

A. Knowledge necessary for audit planning.

B. Evidential matter to use in assessing inherent risk.

C. A basis for modifying tests of controls.

D. An evaluation of the consistency of application of management's policies.

Answer (A) is correct. *(CPA, adapted)*
REQUIRED: The objective of procedures performed to obtain an understanding of internal control.
DISCUSSION: The second standard of field work states, "The auditor must obtain a sufficient understanding of the entity and its environment, including its internal control, to assess the risk of material misstatement of the financial statements whether due to error or fraud, and to design the nature, timing, and extent of further audit procedures."
Answer (B) is incorrect. Inherent risk is independent of internal control. Answer (C) is incorrect. The understanding is obtained to plan all aspects of the audit, not merely tests of controls. Answer (D) is incorrect. Evaluating the consistency of application of management's policies is a test of controls.

2. An auditor uses the knowledge provided by the understanding of internal control and the assessed risk of material misstatement primarily to

A. Determine whether procedures and records concerning the safeguarding of assets are reliable.

B. Ascertain whether the opportunities to allow any person to both perpetrate and conceal fraud are minimized.

C. Modify the initial assessments of inherent risk and judgments about materiality levels for planning purposes.

D. Determine the nature, timing, and extent of substantive procedures for financial statement assertions.

Answer (D) is correct. *(CPA, adapted)*
REQUIRED: The auditor's purpose in understanding internal control and assessing the risk of material misstatement.
DISCUSSION: The second standard of field work states, "The auditor must obtain a sufficient understanding of the entity and its environment, including its internal control, to assess the risk of material misstatement of the financial statements whether due to error or fraud, and to design the nature, timing, and extent of further audit procedures." Substantive procedures are intended to detect material misstatements in the financial statements.
Answer (A) is incorrect. Knowledge about operating effectiveness need not be obtained as part of the understanding of internal control. Answer (B) is incorrect. Knowledge about operating effectiveness need not be obtained as part of the understanding of internal control. Answer (C) is incorrect. Inherent risk and materiality are independent of internal control.

3. In an audit of financial statements, an auditor's primary consideration regarding an internal control is whether the control

A. Reflects management's philosophy and operating style.

B. Affects management's financial statement assertions.

C. Provides adequate safeguards over access to assets.

D. Relates to operations objectives.

Answer (B) is correct. *(CPA, adapted)*
REQUIRED: The auditor's primary consideration regarding an internal control.
DISCUSSION: An auditor's primary concern is whether a specific control affects relevant financial statement assertions. Much of the audit work required to form an opinion consists of gathering evidence about the relevant assertions in the financial statements. These assertions are management representations embodied in the components of the financial statements (AU 326). Controls relevant to an audit pertain to the preparation of financial statements that are fairly presented in conformity with GAAP (AU 314).
Answer (A) is incorrect. Management's philosophy and operating style is just one factor in one component (the control environment) of internal control. Answer (C) is incorrect. Restricting access to assets is only one of many physical controls, which constitute one element of one component (control activities) of internal control. Answer (D) is incorrect. Many controls relating to operations objectives are not relevant to an audit.

4. Which of the following most likely would **not** be considered an inherent limitation of the potential effectiveness of an entity's internal control?

    A. Incompatible duties.

    B. Management override.

    C. Faulty judgment.

    D. Collusion among employees.

Answer (A) is correct. *(CPA, adapted)*
    REQUIRED: The item not considered an inherent limitation of internal control.
    DISCUSSION: Internal control has inherent limitations. The performance of incompatible duties, however, is a failure to assign different people the functions of authorization, recording, and asset custody, not an inevitable limitation of internal control. Segregation of duties is a category of control activities.
    Answer (B) is incorrect. Management establishes internal controls. Thus, it can override those controls. Answer (C) is incorrect. Human judgment in decision making may be faulty. Answer (D) is incorrect. Controls, whether manual or automated, may be circumvented by collusion among two or more people.

5.2 Internal Control Components

5. An auditor would most likely be concerned with controls that provide reasonable assurance about the

    A. Efficiency of management's decision-making process.

    B. Appropriate prices the entity should charge for its products.

    C. Decision to make expenditures for certain advertising activities.

    D. Entity's ability to initiate, authorize, record, process, and report financial data.

Answer (D) is correct. *(CPA, adapted)*
    REQUIRED: The controls about which an auditor is most likely to be concerned.
    DISCUSSION: The information system relevant to financial reporting objectives, which includes the accounting system, consists of the procedures, whether automated or manual, and records established to initiate, authorize, record, process, and report entity transactions (as well as events and conditions) and to maintain accountability for the related assets, liabilities, and equity (AU 314).
    Answer (A) is incorrect. The efficiency of certain management decision-making processes is not likely to be relevant to a financial statement audit. Answer (B) is incorrect. Product pricing is not likely to be relevant to a financial statement audit. Answer (C) is incorrect. Decisions about advertising are not likely to be relevant to the auditor's consideration of controls.

6. Which of the following is a management control method that most likely could improve management's ability to supervise company activities effectively?

    A. Monitoring compliance with internal control requirements imposed by regulatory bodies.

    B. Limiting direct access to assets by physical segregation and protective devices.

    C. Establishing budgets and forecasts to identify variances from expectations.

    D. Supporting employees with the resources necessary to discharge their responsibilities.

Answer (C) is correct. *(CPA, adapted)*
    REQUIRED: The management control method most likely to improve supervision.
    DISCUSSION: The control activities component of internal control includes performance reviews. Performance reviews involve comparison of actual performance with budgets, forecasts, or prior performance. Identifying variances alerts management to the need for investigative and corrective actions. Such actions are necessary for effective supervision.
    Answer (A) is incorrect. Management's supervisory responsibilities extend well beyond internal control requirements imposed by regulatory bodies. Answer (B) is incorrect. Access control pertains to the physical controls factor. Answer (D) is incorrect. Supporting employees concerns the human resource policies and practices factor of the control environment component.

7. Which of the following are considered control environment factors?

	Detection Risk	Commitment to Competence
A.	Yes	Yes
B.	Yes	No
C.	No	Yes
D.	No	No

Answer (C) is correct. *(CPA, adapted)*
    REQUIRED: The factor(s), if any, considered part of the control environment.
    DISCUSSION: Commitment to competence is a control environment factor. It relates to the knowledge and skills needed to do the tasks included in a job and management's consideration of required competence levels.

8. Which of the following is **not** a component of internal control?

- A. Control risk.
- B. Monitoring.
- C. Information and communication.
- D. The control environment.

Answer (A) is correct. *(CPA, adapted)*
REQUIRED: The item not a component of internal control.
DISCUSSION: Control risk is one of the elements in the audit risk model. It is the risk that a material misstatement that could occur in an assertion will not be prevented or detected on a timely basis by the entity's internal control. Hence, control risk is a function of the effectiveness of internal control, not a component thereof.

9. Which of the following factors are included in an entity's control environment?

	Audit Committee Participation	Integrity and Ethical Values	Organizational Structure
A.	Yes	Yes	No
B.	Yes	No	Yes
C.	No	Yes	Yes
D.	Yes	Yes	Yes

Answer (D) is correct. *(CPA, adapted)*
REQUIRED: The factors in a control environment.
DISCUSSION: The control environment is the foundation for all other control components. It provides discipline and structure, sets the tone of the organization, and influences the control consciousness of employees. It includes participation of those charged with governance, integrity and ethical values, organizational structure, management's philosophy and operating style, assignment of authority and responsibility, human resource policies and practices, and commitment to competence.

10. Which of the following components of internal control includes development and use of training policies that communicate prospective roles and responsibilities to employees?

- A. Monitoring.
- B. Control environment.
- C. Risk assessment.
- D. Control activities.

Answer (B) is correct. *(Publisher, adapted)*
REQUIRED: The component of internal control that includes the development of training policies.
DISCUSSION: The control environment sets the tone of an organization. It includes human resource policies and practices relative to hiring, orientation, training, evaluating, counseling, promoting, compensating, and remedial actions.
Answer (A) is incorrect. Monitoring assesses the quality of internal control over time. Answer (C) is incorrect. Risk assessment is the identification and analysis of relevant risks. Answer (D) is incorrect. Control activities are the policies and procedures that help ensure that management directives are carried out. They include performance reviews, information processing, physical controls, and segregation of duties.

11. Proper segregation of duties reduces the opportunities to allow persons to be in positions both to

- A. Journalize entries and prepare financial statements.
- B. Record cash receipts and cash disbursements.
- C. Establish internal control and authorize transactions.
- D. Perpetrate and conceal errors and fraudulent acts.

Answer (D) is correct. *(CPA, adapted)*
REQUIRED: The effects of the segregation of duties.
DISCUSSION: Segregation of duties is a category of the control activities component of internal control. Segregating responsibilities for authorization, recording, and asset custody reduces an employee's opportunity to perpetrate an error or fraud and subsequently conceal it in the normal course of his/her duties.
Answer (A) is incorrect. Accountants typically journalize entries and prepare financial statements. Answer (B) is incorrect. Accountants may record both cash receipts and cash disbursements as long as they do not have custody of cash. Answer (C) is incorrect. Management establishes internal control and ultimately has the responsibility to authorize transactions.

12. Proper segregation of functional responsibilities to achieve effective internal control calls for separation of the functions of

    A. Authorization, execution, and payment.

    B. Authorization, recording, and custody.

    C. Custody, execution, and reporting.

    D. Authorization, payment, and recording.

Answer (B) is correct. *(CPA, adapted)*
    REQUIRED: The duties separated to achieve effective internal control.
    DISCUSSION: One person should not be responsible for all phases of a transaction, i.e., for authorization of transactions, recording of transactions, and custodianship of the related assets. These duties should be performed by separate individuals to reduce the opportunities to allow any person to be in a position both to perpetrate and conceal errors or fraud in the normal course of his/her duties (AU 314).
    Answer (A) is incorrect. Payment is a form of execution (operational responsibility). Answer (C) is incorrect. Custody of assets and execution of related transactions are often not segregated. Answer (D) is incorrect. Payments must be recorded when made.

13. Internal control can provide only reasonable assurance of achieving an entity's control objectives. The likelihood of achieving those objectives is affected by which limitation inherent to internal control?

    A. The auditor's primary responsibility is the detection of fraud.

    B. The board of directors is active and independent.

    C. The cost of internal control should not exceed its benefits.

    D. Management monitors internal control.

Answer (C) is correct. *(Publisher, adapted)*
    REQUIRED: The true statement about the limitation of internal control.
    DISCUSSION: It is recognized that the cost of an entity's internal control should not exceed the benefits that are expected to be derived. Although the cost-benefit relationship is a primary criterion that should be considered in designing internal control, the precise measurement of costs and benefits usually is not possible.
    Answer (A) is incorrect. The auditor's responsibility is to plan and perform the audit to obtain reasonable assurance about whether the financial statements are free of material misstatement, whether caused by error or fraud (AU 110). Answer (B) is incorrect. An active and independent board strengthens the control environment. Answer (D) is incorrect. Monitoring strengthens internal control.

14. An independent auditor is concerned with controls designed to safeguard assets that are relevant to the reliability of financial reporting. Adequate safeguards over access to and use of assets means protection from

    A. Any management decision that would unprofitably use company resources.

    B. Only those losses arising from fraud.

    C. Losses such as those arising from setting a product price too low and subsequently realizing operating losses from the product's sale.

    D. Losses arising from access by unauthorized persons.

Answer (D) is correct. *(Publisher, adapted)*
    REQUIRED: The meaning of adequate safeguards over access to and use of assets.
    DISCUSSION: A management objective implicit in internal control is that access to assets be permitted only in accordance with management's authorization. However, elimination of access is not feasible because access to assets is necessary in normal business operations. The extent of access is determined by the nature of the assets and their susceptibility to loss through errors and fraud. Authorization of access entails limitations on both physical access and indirect access.
    Answer (A) is incorrect. Internal control cannot protect against every decision that uses resources unprofitably. Answer (B) is incorrect. The organization should be protected against losses from both errors and fraud. Answer (C) is incorrect. Internal controls concerning the efficiency and effectiveness of certain management decision-making processes, such as those related to product pricing, ordinarily do not relate to a financial statement audit.

5.3 Understanding Internal Control

15. In obtaining an understanding of controls that are relevant to audit planning, an auditor is required to obtain knowledge about the

A. Design of the controls included in the internal control components.

B. Effectiveness of the controls that have been implemented.

C. Consistency with which the controls are currently being applied.

D. Controls related to each principal transaction class and account balance.

Answer (A) is correct. *(CPA, adapted)*
REQUIRED: The knowledge required in gaining an understanding of internal control.
DISCUSSION: In all audits, the auditor should obtain an understanding of each of the five components of internal control sufficient to plan the audit. A sufficient understanding is obtained by performing procedures to understand the design of controls relevant to an audit of financial statements and determining whether they have been implemented (AU 314).
Answer (B) is incorrect. The issue of the effectiveness of controls is required to be addressed when the auditor assesses control risk. Answer (C) is incorrect. The issue of the consistency of application is required to be addressed when the auditor assesses control risk. Answer (D) is incorrect. Audit planning ordinarily does not require understanding every balance and transaction class or every assertion relevant thereto.

16. In obtaining an understanding of internal control in a financial statement audit, an auditor is **not** obligated to

A. Determine whether the controls have been implemented.

B. Perform procedures to understand the design of internal control.

C. Document the understanding of the entity's internal control components.

D. Search for significant deficiencies in the operation of internal control.

Answer (D) is correct. *(CPA, adapted)*
REQUIRED: The step an auditor need not take in obtaining an understanding of internal control.
DISCUSSION: In all audits, the auditor should obtain an understanding of each of the five components of internal control sufficient to plan the audit. A sufficient understanding is obtained by performing procedures to understand the design of controls relevant to an audit of financial statements and determining whether they have been implemented. In addition, the auditor should document the understanding of the entity's internal control components obtained to plan the audit (AU 314). However, in an audit of financial statements, the auditor is not obligated to search for significant deficiencies or material weaknesses (AU 325).
Answer (A) is incorrect. The auditor should determine whether the controls are in operation. Answer (B) is incorrect. The auditor should understand the design of controls. Answer (C) is incorrect. The auditor should document the understanding of the controls.

17. As part of understanding internal control, an auditor is **not** required to

A. Consider factors that affect the risk of material misstatement.

B. Ascertain whether internal controls have been implemented.

C. Identify the types of potential misstatements that can occur.

D. Obtain knowledge about the operating effectiveness of internal control.

Answer (D) is correct. *(CPA, adapted)*
REQUIRED: The step not required in obtaining the understanding of internal control.
DISCUSSION: The understanding is used to identify types of potential misstatements; consider factors affecting the risk of material misstatements; design tests of controls, when applicable; and design substantive procedures. The understanding should include not only the design of relevant controls but also whether they have been implemented. However, operating effectiveness is required to be addressed only when the auditor intends to rely on the controls.
Answer (A) is incorrect. The auditor should consider factors affecting the risk of material misstatement. Answer (B) is incorrect. The auditor should determine whether controls have been implemented. Answer (C) is incorrect. The auditor should determine the types of possible misstatements.

18. In planning an audit of certain accounts, an auditor may conclude that specific procedures used to obtain an understanding of an entity's internal control need **not** be included because of the auditor's judgments about materiality and assessments of

    A. Control risk.

    B. Detection risk.

    C. Sampling risk.

    D. Inherent risk.

Answer (D) is correct. *(CPA, adapted)*
    REQUIRED: The assessed risk that may justify omission of procedures used to obtain the understanding.
    DISCUSSION: The nature, timing, and extent of procedures performed to obtain the understanding vary with the size and complexity of the entity, the auditor's prior experience with the entity, the nature of specific controls used by the entity (including its use of IT), the nature and extent of changes in systems and operations, and the entity's documentation of specific controls. The auditor's assessments of inherent risk and judgments about materiality for various account balances, transaction classes, and disclosures also affect the nature and extent of the procedures performed (AU 314). Thus, if an account has a low assessed level of inherent risk and the amounts involved are not material, specific procedures for obtaining the understanding might be omitted.
    Answer (A) is incorrect. Obtaining the understanding precedes or is concurrent with the assessment of control risk. Answer (B) is incorrect. The assessed level of control risk is used to determine the acceptable level of detection risk. Answer (C) is incorrect. Sampling risk is controllable by the auditor. The auditor assesses inherent risk and control risk, not detection risk or sampling risk.

19. When obtaining an understanding of an entity's internal controls, an auditor should concentrate on their substance rather than their form because

    A. The controls may be operating effectively but may not be documented.

    B. Management may establish appropriate controls but not enforce compliance with them.

    C. The controls may be so inappropriate that the auditor assesses control risk at the maximum.

    D. Management may implement controls whose costs exceed their benefits.

Answer (B) is correct. *(CPA, adapted)*
    REQUIRED: The reason an auditor should concentrate on the substance of controls, not their form.
    DISCUSSION: The auditor must concentrate on the substance rather than the form of controls because management may establish appropriate controls but not act on them. Whether controls have been implemented at a moment in time differs from their operating effectiveness over a period of time. Thus, operating effectiveness concerns not merely whether the entity is using controls but also how the controls (manual or automated) are applied, the consistency of their application, and by whom they are applied (AU 314).
    Answer (A) is incorrect. An auditor is concerned with the actual operating effectiveness of controls, not with a lack of evidence about form (documentation). Answer (C) is incorrect. If controls are so inappropriate that the auditor assesses control risk at the maximum, their substance is irrelevant. Answer (D) is incorrect. When considering internal control in a financial statement audit, the auditor is primarily concerned with the effectiveness of controls, not their cost-benefit relationship.

20. In obtaining an understanding of a manufacturing entity's internal control concerning inventory balances, an auditor most likely would

    A. Review the entity's descriptions of inventory policies and procedures.

    B. Perform test counts of inventory during the entity's physical count.

    C. Analyze inventory turnover statistics to identify slow-moving and obsolete items.

    D. Analyze monthly production reports to identify variances and unusual transactions.

Answer (A) is correct. *(CPA, adapted)*
    REQUIRED: The step in obtaining an understanding of an entity's internal control concerning inventory balances.
    DISCUSSION: The auditor should obtain a sufficient understanding of the internal control components to plan the audit, including knowledge about the design of relevant controls and whether they have been implemented. Reviewing the entity's descriptions of inventory policies and procedures helps the auditor understand their design.
    Answer (B) is incorrect. Performing test counts of inventory is a test of details (a substantive test). Answer (C) is incorrect. Analysis of inventory turnover statistics is an analytical procedure performed as a substantive test. Answer (D) is incorrect. Analysis of monthly production reports to identify variances and unusual transactions is an analytical procedure performed as a substantive test.

21. An auditor should obtain sufficient knowledge of an entity's information system relevant to financial reporting to understand the

A. Safeguards used to limit access to computer facilities.

B. Process used to prepare significant accounting estimates.

C. Procedures used to assure the proper supervision of staff.

D. Policies used to detect the concealment of fraud.

Answer (B) is correct. *(CPA, adapted)*
   REQUIRED: The purpose of obtaining sufficient knowledge of an entity's accounting system.
   DISCUSSION: The auditor should obtain sufficient knowledge of the information system relevant to financial reporting to understand (1) the classes of significant transactions; (2) the procedures, both automated and manual, by which transactions are initiated, authorized, recorded, processed, and reported from their incurrence to their inclusion in the statements; (3) the related accounting records (whether electronic or manual) supporting information, and specific accounts involved; (4) how the information system captures other significant events and conditions; and (5) the financial reporting process used to prepare the entity's financial statements, including significant accounting estimates and disclosures (AU 314).

22. In an audit of financial statements in accordance with generally accepted auditing standards, an auditor should

A. Identify specific controls relevant to management's financial statement assertions.

B. Perform tests of controls to evaluate the effectiveness of the entity's accounting system.

C. Determine whether procedures are suitably designed to prevent or detect material misstatement.

D. Document the auditor's understanding of the entity's internal control.

Answer (D) is correct. *(CPA, adapted)*
   REQUIRED: A procedure in an audit of financial statements in accordance with GAAS.
   DISCUSSION: The auditor should document the understanding of the entity's internal control components obtained to plan the audit. The form and extent of the documentation are influenced by the nature and complexity of the entity's controls (AU 314).

5.4 Flowcharting

23. An auditor's flowchart of a client's accounting system is a diagrammatic representation that depicts the auditor's

A. Assessment of control risk.

B. Identification of weaknesses in the system.

C. Assessment of the control environment's effectiveness.

D. Understanding of the system.

Answer (D) is correct. *(CPA, adapted)*
   REQUIRED: The purpose of an auditor's flowchart.
   DISCUSSION: The auditor should document the understanding of the client's internal control components obtained to plan the audit. The form and extent of this documentation are influenced by the nature and complexity of the entity's controls. For example, documentation of the understanding of internal control of a complex information system in which many transactions are electronically initiated, authorized, recorded, processed, or reported may include questionnaires, flowcharts, or decision tables (AU 314).
   Answer (A) is incorrect. The conclusions about the assessment of control risk should be documented. This is the judgment of the auditor documented in the working papers. Answer (B) is incorrect. The flowchart is a tool to document the auditor's understanding of internal control but does not specifically identify weaknesses in the system. Answer (C) is incorrect. The auditor's judgment is the ultimate basis for concluding that controls are effective.

24. An advantage of using systems flowcharts to document information about internal control instead of using internal control questionnaires is that systems flowcharts

    A. Identify internal control weaknesses more prominently.

    B. Provide a visual depiction of clients' activities.

    C. Indicate whether controls are operating effectively.

    D. Reduce the need to observe clients' employees performing routine tasks.

Answer (B) is correct. *(CPA, adapted)*

    REQUIRED: The advantage of systems flowcharts over internal control questionnaires.

    DISCUSSION: Systems flowcharts provide a visual representation of a series of sequential processes, that is, of a flow of documents, data, and operations. In many instances, a flowchart is preferable to a questionnaire because a picture is usually more easily comprehended.

    Answer (A) is incorrect. A systems flowchart can present the flow of information and documents in a system, but it does not specifically identify the weaknesses. Answer (C) is incorrect. The flowchart does not provide evidence of how effectively controls are actually operating. Answer (D) is incorrect. The flowchart is useful in documenting the understanding of internal control, but it does not reduce the need for observation of employees performing tasks if those tests of controls are deemed necessary.

25. The following is a section of a system flowchart for a payroll application:

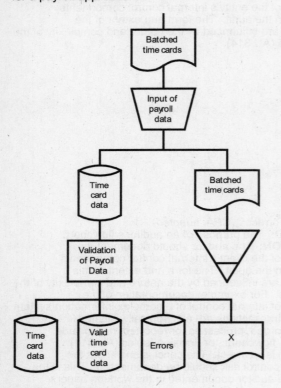

Symbol X could represent

    A. Erroneous time cards.

    B. An error report.

    C. Batched time cards.

    D. Unclaimed payroll checks.

Answer (B) is correct. *(CPA, adapted)*

    REQUIRED: The item represented by Symbol X.

    DISCUSSION: Symbol X is a document, that is, hard copy output of the validation routine shown. The time card data, the validated data, and the errors are recorded on magnetic disk after the validation process. Thus, either an error report or the valid time card information is represented by Symbol X.

    Answer (A) is incorrect. Time cards were stored offline before the validation process. Answer (C) is incorrect. Time cards were stored offline before the validation process. Answer (D) is incorrect. No payroll checks are shown.

26. Which of the following symbolic representations indicates that new payroll transactions and the old payroll file have been used to prepare payroll checks, prepare a printed payroll journal, and generate a new payroll file?

A.

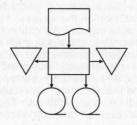

B.

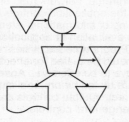

C.

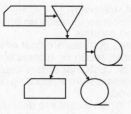

D.

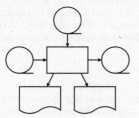

Answer (D) is correct. *(CPA, adapted)*
REQUIRED: The symbolic representation for updating the payroll file and generating checks and a payroll journal.
DISCUSSION: The new payroll transactions and the old payroll file are represented by the magnetic tape symbols. These files are entered into the process function (the rectangle). The output is a new payroll file on magnetic tape and payroll checks and a printed payroll journal represented by the document symbols.
Answer (A) is incorrect. Two magnetically stored payroll files and two offline storage files are produced from a single document form. Answer (B) is incorrect. Two offline storage files and one document are produced (manually) from an offline storage file and a tape file. Answer (C) is incorrect. Two magnetically stored files and a punchcard are produced from the processing of a punchcard and an offline storage file.

5.5 Internal Control and Information Technology

27. Which of the following characteristics distinguishes computer processing from manual processing?

A. Computer processing virtually eliminates the occurrence of computational error normally associated with manual processing.

B. Errors or fraud in computer processing will be detected soon after their occurrence.

C. The potential for systematic error is ordinarily greater in manual processing than in computerized processing.

D. Most computer systems are designed so that transaction trails useful for audit purposes do not exist.

Answer (A) is correct. *(CPA, adapted)*
REQUIRED: The feature that distinguishes computer processing from manual processing.
DISCUSSION: Computer processing uniformly subjects like transactions to the same processing instructions. A computer program defines the processing steps to accomplish a task. Once the program is written and tested appropriately, it will perform the task repetitively and without error. However, if the program contains an error, all transactions will be processed incorrectly.
Answer (B) is incorrect. When an error does occur, for example, in input, it may not be discovered on a timely basis. Ordinarily, much less human intervention occurs once the transaction is processed. Answer (C) is incorrect. Systematic (repetitive) errors will occur in computerized processing if an error exists in the program. Answer (D) is incorrect. Adequately designed systems maintain transaction, console, and error logs that create useful audit trails.

28. An auditor anticipates placing reliance on controls to reduce the risk of material misstatement in an automated environment. Under these circumstances, on which of the following activities would the auditor initially focus?

A. Programmed controls.

B. Application controls.

C. Output controls.

D. General controls.

Answer (D) is correct. *(CPA, adapted)*
REQUIRED: The initial concern when the auditor anticipates placing reliance on controls to reduce the risk of material misstatement in a computer environment.
DISCUSSION: Placing reliance on controls involves identifying specific controls that are likely to prevent or detect material misstatements in specific assertions, performing tests of controls, and reaching a conclusion on the assessed level of control risk. The two broad groupings of information systems control activities are general controls and application controls. General controls commonly include controls over data center and network operations; systems software acquisition and maintenance; access security; and application system acquisition, development, and maintenance. Application controls apply to the processing of individual applications. These controls help ensure that transactions occurred, are authorized, and are completely and accurately recorded and processed (AU 314). General controls apply to mainframe, network, and end-user environments. They support the application controls by helping to ensure the proper functioning of information systems. Thus, they should be tested prior to evaluation of application controls.
Answer (A) is incorrect. Programmed activities relate to application controls, which should be tested for effectiveness once the general controls prove to be effective. Answer (B) is incorrect. General controls are tested before application controls. Answer (C) is incorrect. Output controls are application controls, which are tested after general controls.

29. In which of the following circumstances would an auditor expect to find that an entity implemented automated controls to reduce risks of misstatement?

A. When errors are difficult to predict.

B. When misstatements are difficult to define.

C. When large, unusual, or nonrecurring transactions require judgment.

D. When transactions are high-volume and recurring.

Answer (D) is correct. *(CPA, adapted)*
REQUIRED: The circumstance in which an entity is most likely to implement automated controls.
DISCUSSION: Automated controls are cost effective when they are applied to high-volume, recurring transactions. For example, credit limit checks on customer orders could be automated to relieve management from evaluating each customer order as it is received.
Answer (A) is incorrect. When errors are difficult to predict, judgment may be required and it would be less likely that a control could be automated. Answer (B) is incorrect. When errors are difficult to define, it would be hard to design automated controls to detect them. Answer (C) is incorrect. When judgment is required, it is less likely that automated controls would be effective.

30. Which of the following controls most likely could prevent computer personnel from modifying programs to bypass programmed controls?

A. Periodic management review of computer utilization reports and systems documentation.

B. Separation of duties for computer programming and computer operations.

C. Participation of user department personnel in designing and approving new systems.

D. Physical security of computer facilities in limiting access to computer equipment.

Answer (B) is correct. *(CPA, adapted)*
REQUIRED: The control necessary to prevent computer personnel from modifying programs to bypass controls.
DISCUSSION: Programmers and analysts can modify programs, data files, and controls, so they should have no access to programs used to process transactions. Separation of programming and operations is necessary to prevent unauthorized modifications of programs.
Answer (A) is incorrect. Although periodic management review is appropriate, reports and systems documentation will not prevent or detect unauthorized modifications. Answer (C) is incorrect. User participation relates to new systems, not modification of existing systems. Answer (D) is incorrect. Programmers may have access through data communications. Thus, physical security is not sufficient to prevent unauthorized modifications.

31. For control purposes, which of the following should be organizationally separated from the computer operations function?

A. Data conversion.

B. Surveillance of video display messages.

C. Systems development.

D. Minor maintenance according to à schedule.

Answer (C) is correct. *(CPA, adapted)*
   REQUIRED: The activity that should be separated from computer operations.
   DISCUSSION: Systems analysts survey the existing system, analyze the organization's information requirements, and design new computer systems to meet those needs. These design specifications will guide the preparation of specific programs by computer programmers. The console operator should not be assigned programming duties, much less responsibility for systems design, and thus not have the opportunity to make changes in programs and systems as (s)he operates the equipment.
   Answer (A) is incorrect. Data conversion may be assigned to computer operations. Answer (B) is incorrect. Surveillance of video display messages may be assigned to computer operations. Answer (D) is incorrect. Minor maintenance according to a schedule may be assigned to computer operations.

32. A client is concerned that a power outage or disaster could impair the computer hardware's ability to function as designed. The client desires off-site backup hardware facilities that are fully configured and ready to operate within several hours. The client most likely should consider a

A. Cold site.

B. Cool site.

C. Warm site.

D. Hot site.

Answer (D) is correct. *(CPA, adapted)*
   REQUIRED: The type of off-site backup hardware facility that is an available, fully operational processing facility.
   DISCUSSION: A hot site is a service facility that is fully operational and is promptly available in the case of a power outage or disaster.
   Answer (A) is incorrect. A cold site is a shell facility suitable for quick installation of computer equipment. Installing computer equipment would take more time in a cold site than in a hot site. Answer (B) is incorrect. It is a fabricated term that does not describe actual facilities. Answer (C) is incorrect. A warm site provides an intermediate level of backup and causes more downtime than a hot site.

33. Which of the following procedures would an entity most likely include in its computer disaster recovery plan?

A. Develop an auxiliary power supply to provide uninterrupted electricity.

B. Store duplicate copies of critical files in a location away from the computer center.

C. Maintain a listing of all entity passwords with the network manager.

D. Translate data for storage purposes with a cryptographic secret code.

Answer (B) is correct. *(CPA, adapted)*
   REQUIRED: The most likely procedure to follow in a computer disaster recovery plan.
   DISCUSSION: Off-site storage of duplicate copies of critical files protects them from a fire or other disaster at the computing facility. The procedure is part of an overall disaster recovery plan.
   Answer (A) is incorrect. The use of an uninterruptible power supply assures continued processing rather than recovery from a disaster. Answer (C) is incorrect. Maintaining a safeguarded copy of passwords protects against loss of passwords by personnel. Answer (D) is incorrect. Encrypting stored data files protects them from unauthorized use.

34. Which of the following is a computer program that appears to be legitimate but performs some illicit activity when it is run?

A. Hoax virus.

B. Web crawler.

C. Trojan horse.

D. Killer application.

Answer (C) is correct. *(CPA, adapted)*
   REQUIRED: The apparently legitimate computer program that performs an illicit activity.
   DISCUSSION: A Trojan horse is a computer program that appears friendly, for example, a game, but that actually contains an application destructive to the computer system.
   Answer (A) is incorrect. A hoax virus is a false notice about the existence of a computer virus. It is usually disseminated through use of distribution lists and is sent by email or via an internal network. Answer (B) is incorrect. A web crawler (a spider or bot) is a computer program created to access and read information on websites. The results are included as entries in the index of a search engine. Answer (D) is incorrect. A killer application is one that is so useful that it may justify widespread adoption of a new technology.

35. An Internet firewall is designed to provide adequate protection against which of the following?

    A. A computer virus.

    B. Unauthenticated logins from outside users.

    C. Insider leaking of confidential information.

    D. A Trojan horse application.

Answer (B) is correct. *(Publisher, adapted)*
    REQUIRED: The protection provided by an Internet firewall.
    DISCUSSION: A firewall is a device that separates two networks and prevents passage of specific types of network traffic while maintaining a connection between the networks. Generally, an Internet firewall is designed to protect a system from unauthenticated logins from outside users, although it may provide several other features as well.
    Answer (A) is incorrect. A firewall cannot adequately protect a system against computer viruses. Answer (C) is incorrect. Industrial spies need not leak information through the firewall. Flash drives and CDs are much more common means of sharing confidential information. Answer (D) is incorrect. Like a virus, a firewall cannot adequately protect against a Trojan horse or any other program that can be executed in the system by an internal user.

36. A client communicates sensitive data across the Internet. Which of the following controls would be most effective to prevent the use of the information if it were intercepted by an unauthorized party?

    A. A firewall.

    B. An access log.

    C. Passwords.

    D. Encryption.

Answer (D) is correct. *(Publisher, adapted)*
    REQUIRED: The most effective control for preventing the use of intercepted information.
    DISCUSSION: Encryption technology converts data into a code. Encoding data before transmission over communications lines makes it more difficult for someone with access to the transmission to understand or modify its contents.
    Answer (A) is incorrect. A firewall tries to prevent access from specific types of traffic to an internal network. After someone has obtained information from the site, a firewall cannot prevent its use. Answer (B) is incorrect. An access log only records attempted usage of a system. Answer (C) is incorrect. Passwords prevent unauthorized users from accessing the system. If information has already been obtained, a password cannot prevent its use.

37. A client who recently installed a new accounts payable system assigned employees a user identification code (UIC) and a separate password. Each UIC is a person's name, and the individual's password is the same as the UIC. Users are not required to change their passwords at initial log-in nor do passwords ever expire. Which of the following statements does **not** reflect a limitation of the client's computer-access control?

    A. Employees can easily guess fellow employees' passwords.

    B. Employees are not required to change passwords.

    C. Employees can circumvent procedures to separate duties.

    D. Employees are not required to take regular vacations.

Answer (D) is correct. *(CPA, adapted)*
    REQUIRED: The item not a limitation of the client's computer-access control.
    DISCUSSION: To be effective, passwords should consist of random letters, symbols, and numbers. They should not contain words or phrases which are easily guessed. Proper user authentication by means of passwords requires procedures to ensure that the valid passwords generated are known only by appropriate individuals. Moreover, passwords should be changed frequently so that the maximum retention period (the period during which they may be compromised) is relatively short. However, a minimum retention period should be required so that users cannot change passwords back to their old, convenient forms. Another weakness in access control is that different passwords are not required to perform different functions, e.g., to obtain access, to read certain files, or to update certain files. Use of separate passwords is a means of separating duties. However, the password security system is unrelated to the absence of a requirement to take vacations. Nevertheless, such requirement may be appropriate for personnel in a position to embezzle funds.
    Answer (A) is incorrect. A control deficiency exists if employees can easily guess fellow employees' passwords. Answer (B) is incorrect. A control deficiency exists if employees are not required to change passwords. Answer (C) is incorrect. A control deficiency exists if employees can circumvent procedures to separate duties.

38. An auditor is gaining an understanding of a client's Internet controls. Which of the following would likely be the least effective control?

A. The client requires all users to select passwords that are not easily guessed.

B. The client requires users to share potentially useful downloaded programs from public electronic bulletin boards with only authorized employees.

C. The client uses digital signatures to authenticate transmitted documents.

D. The client uses a firewall system that produces reports on Internet usage patterns.

Answer (B) is correct. *(Publisher, adapted)*
REQUIRED: The least effective control for Internet security.
DISCUSSION: Sharing programs from public electronic bulletin boards with authorized employees would be a futile control. The programs are available to anyone on the public electronic bulletin board.
Answer (A) is incorrect. Passwords can be an effective control against unauthorized access. Answer (C) is incorrect. Digital signatures are a form of encryption technology to authenticate documents. Answer (D) is incorrect. Firewalls separate an internal network from an external network. Reports on Internet usage patterns can help in monitoring the effectiveness of the system.

39. Which of the following is the most serious password security problem?

A. Users are assigned passwords when accounts are created, but they do not change them.

B. Users have accounts on several systems with different passwords.

C. Users copy their passwords on note paper, which is kept in their wallets.

D. Users select passwords that are not listed in any online dictionary.

Answer (A) is correct. *(CPA, adapted)*
REQUIRED: The password technique that poses the greatest security problem.
DISCUSSION: Proper user authentication by means of a password requires password-generating procedures to ensure that valid passwords are known only by the proper individuals. If passwords are assigned, users should change passwords frequently so that they are the only persons with access under those identifiers.
Answer (B) is incorrect. No security issue arises when different passwords are used for accounts on different systems. Answer (C) is incorrect. Although any record of a password is potentially a security problem, storing a password online would be a greater problem. Answer (D) is incorrect. A password should not be an item in an online dictionary.

40. A client installed the sophisticated controls using the biometric attributes of employees to authenticate user access to the computer system. This technology most likely replaced which of the following controls?

A. Use of security specialists.

B. Reasonableness tests.

C. Passwords.

D. Virus protection software.

Answer (C) is correct. *(Publisher, adapted)*
REQUIRED: The control most likely replaced by biometric technologies.
DISCUSSION: The use of passwords is an effective control in an online system to prevent unauthorized access to computer systems. However, biometric technologies are more sophisticated and difficult to compromise.
Answer (A) is incorrect. Biometric technologies do not eliminate the need for specialists who evaluate and monitor security needs. Answer (B) is incorrect. Reasonableness tests are related to input controls, not access controls. Answer (D) is incorrect. Virus protection software prevents damage to data in a system, not access to a system.

41. An entity has many employees who access a database. The database contains sensitive information concerning the customers of the entity and has numerous access points. Access controls prevent employees from entry to those areas of the database for which they have no authorization. All salespersons have certain access permission to customer information. Which of the following is a true statement regarding the nature of the controls and risks?

A. Because there is no separation of duties among the salespersons, risk of collusion is increased.

B. Only one salesperson should be allowed access permission.

C. Sales department personnel should not have access to any part of the database.

D. A salesperson's access to customer information should extend only to what is necessary to perform his/her duties.

Answer (D) is correct. *(Publisher, adapted)*
REQUIRED: The true statement concerning information technology controls and risks.
DISCUSSION: Internal control risks vary with the nature and characteristics of IT usage. Employees should be allowed access to systems only to the extent necessary for them to carry out their responsibilities.
Answer (A) is incorrect. Salespersons carry out the same responsibilities. Thus, no separation of responsibilities is expected. Answer (B) is incorrect. All salespersons may need access to fulfill their responsibilities. Answer (C) is incorrect. Certain information from the database, for example, a customer's credit standing, may need to be accessed.

42. An entity has the following invoices in a batch:

Invoice Number	Product	Quantity	Unit Price
201	F10	150	$ 5.00
202	G15	200	10.00
203	H20	250	25.00
204	K35	300	30.00

Which of the following most likely represents a hash total?

A. FGHK80

B. 4

C. 204

D. 810

Answer (D) is correct. *(CPA, adapted)*
REQUIRED: The example of a hash total.
DISCUSSION: Input controls in batch computer systems are used to determine that no data are lost or added to the batch. Depending on the sophistication of a particular system, control may be accomplished by using record counts, financial totals, or hash totals. The hash total is a control total without a defined meaning, such as the total of employee numbers or invoice numbers, that is used to verify the completeness of data. The hash total of the invoice numbers is 810.
Answer (A) is incorrect. A hash total is ordinarily the sum of a numeric field. Answer (B) is incorrect. The record count is four. Answer (C) is incorrect. The last invoice number is 204.

43. A customer intended to order 100 units of product Z96014 but incorrectly ordered nonexistent product Z96015. Which of the following controls most likely would detect this error?

A. Check digit verification.

B. Record count.

C. Hash total.

D. Redundant data check.

Answer (A) is correct. *(CPA, adapted)*
REQUIRED: The control that would detect a nonexistent product number.
DISCUSSION: Check digit verification is used to identify incorrect identification numbers. The digit is generated by applying an algorithm to the ID number. During input, the check digit is recomputed by applying the same algorithm to the entered ID number.
Answer (B) is incorrect. A record count is a control total of the number of transactions in a batch. Answer (C) is incorrect. A hash total is a control total that is the sum of a field without a defined meaning. Answer (D) is incorrect. A redundant data check searches for duplicate information in a database.

44. Which of the following is an example of a validity check?

A. The computer ensures that a numerical amount in a record does not exceed some predetermined amount.

B. As the computer corrects errors and data are successfully resubmitted to the system, the causes of the errors are printed out.

C. The computer flags any transmission for which the control field value did not match that of an existing file record.

D. After data for a transaction are entered, the computer sends certain data back to the terminal for comparison with data originally sent.

Answer (C) is correct. *(CPA, adapted)*
REQUIRED: The example of a validity check.
DISCUSSION: Validity checks test identification numbers or transaction codes for validity by comparison with items already known to be correct or authorized. For example, a validity check may identify a transmission for which the control field value did not match a preexisting record in a file.
Answer (A) is incorrect. A limit check determines whether a numerical amount exceeds a predetermined amount. Answer (B) is incorrect. An error log or error listing identifies errors that were previously detected and subsequently corrected. Answer (D) is incorrect. A closed-loop verification sends certain data back to the terminal for comparison with data originally sent by the operator.

45. Able Co. uses an online sales order processing system to process its sales transactions. Able's sales data are electronically sorted and subjected to edit checks. A direct output of the edit checks most likely would be a

A. Report of all missing sales invoices.

B. File of all rejected sales transactions.

C. Printout of all user code numbers and passwords.

D. List of all voided shipping documents.

Answer (B) is correct. *(CPA, adapted)*
REQUIRED: The output of edit checks.
DISCUSSION: Edit checks test transactions prior to processing. Rejected transactions should be recorded in a file for evaluation, correction, and resubmission. Edit checks are applied to the sales transactions to test for completeness, reasonableness, validity, and other related issues prior to acceptance. A report of missing invoices, a printout of all user code numbers and passwords, and a list of all voided shipping documents are unlikely to be direct outputs of the edit routine.

46. One of the major problems in a computer system is that incompatible functions may be performed by the same individual. One compensating control is the use of

- A. Echo checks.
- B. A check digit system.
- C. Computer-generated hash totals.
- D. A computer access log.

Answer (D) is correct. *(CPA, adapted)*
REQUIRED: The control compensating for inadequate separation of duties in a computer system.
DISCUSSION: A computer (console) access log is a record of computer and software usage usually produced by the operating system. Proper monitoring of the log is a compensating control for the lack of separation of duties. For instance, the log should list operator interventions.
Answer (A) is incorrect. Echo checks are hardware controls used to determine if the correct message was received by an output device. Answer (B) is incorrect. A check digit system is an input control that tests identification numbers. Answer (C) is incorrect. Hash totals are control totals used to check for losses or inaccuracies arising during data processing or movement.

47. In the accounting system of Acme Company, the amounts of cash disbursements entered at a computer terminal are transmitted to the computer, which immediately transmits the amounts back to the terminal for display on the terminal screen. This display enables the operator to

- A. Establish the validity of the account number.
- B. Verify the amount was entered accurately.
- C. Verify the authorization of the disbursement.
- D. Prevent the overpayment of the account.

Answer (B) is correct. *(CPA, adapted)*
REQUIRED: The effect of displaying the amounts entered at a terminal.
DISCUSSION: The display of the amounts entered is an input control that permits visual verification of the accuracy of the input by the operator. This is termed "closed-loop verification."
Answer (A) is incorrect. Displaying the amounts entered at a terminal does not establish the validity of the account number. Answer (C) is incorrect. Displaying the amounts entered at a terminal does not verify the authorization of the disbursement. Answer (D) is incorrect. Displaying the amounts entered at a terminal does not prevent the overpayment of the account.

Use the additional questions in Gleim **CPA Test Prep Online** to create Test Sessions that emulate Prometric!

5.6 PRACTICE SIMULATION

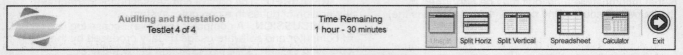

Auditing and Attestation
Testlet 4 of 4

Time Remaining
1 hour - 30 minutes

Unsplit   Split Horiz   Split Vertical   Spreadsheet   Calculator   Exit

DIRECTIONS

Note: If you believe you have encountered a software malfunction, report it to the test center staff immediately.

Navigation

To navigate from task to task, use the controls at the bottom of the screen. Click on the **Next** button to advance to the next task, or the **Previous** button to go to the previous task. To go directly to any task, click on its number.

⚑ = Reminder   Directions | 1 | 2 | 3 | 4 | 5 | 6 | 7 | ◄ Previous   Next ►

If you would like a reminder to revisit a task, or want to indicate that you are finished with it, click on the reminder flag below the task number. To clear the flag, click on it again. Reminder flags are for your use only – they do not contribute to your score.

Tabs

In this part of the examination, you will be asked to complete various tasks. Every task has one or more **Work Tabs**. Some tasks have one or more **Information Tabs**, others may have none. Every task has a **Help** tab.

If a task has **Information Tabs**, you may use the information in them to complete your responses in the **Work Tabs**.

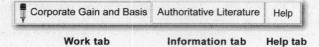

      Corporate Gain and Basis   Authoritative Literature   Help

         Work tab   **Information tab**   **Help tab**

Work Tabs:
- **Work Tabs** are identified with a pencil icon. This is where your responses are expected.
- Each task has one or more **Work Tabs**.
- **Work Tabs** contain directions for completing the task – be sure to read these directions carefully.
- The **Work Tab** name in the example above is for illustration only – yours will differ.
- You must complete all of the **Work Tabs** in each task to receive full credit.

Information Tabs:
- The Authoritative Literature will be provided in all tasks in the AUD, FAR, and REG sections for your reference.
- Your simulation may have one or more additional **Information Tabs**. Like the Authoritative Literature tabs, **Information Tabs** do not have a pencil icon.
- If your task has additional **Information Tabs**, go through each to familiarize yourself with the task content.

Help Tab:
- The **Help Tab** provides assistance with the exam software that is used in this task. For example, if the task is to compose a memorandum, **Help** will provide information about the word processor.

The Toolbar

The toolbar at the top of the screen shows the amount of time remaining for you to complete the tasks. In addition, the following tools are available. Note that only the Exit button is displayed when Directions are visible - the others will appear when you begin the tasks.

Unsplit   Split Horiz   Split Vertical

Click on these buttons to split or unsplit the screen. You can split the screen vertically or horizontally.

Calculator

Click on this button to display the calculator; click on it again to hide the calculator. To move the calculator, click on the calculator title bar and drag the calculator to the desired location.

Spreadsheet

Click on this button to use the spreadsheet; click on it again to hide the spreadsheet. To move the spreadsheet, click on the the spreadsheet title bar and drag the spreadsheet to the desired location.

Exit

Click on this button to go on to the next part of the examination. You must complete all of the tasks to receive full credit. Once you click on **Exit** and confirm the action, you will NOT be able to return to this testlet.

⚑ = Reminder   Directions | 1 | 2 | 3 | 4 | 5 | ◄ Previous   Next ►

| Internal Control Documentation Methods | Authoritative Literature | Help |

An entity may use a variety of methods for documenting internal controls. The same methods may be used by the auditor to document the understanding of the controls in a financial statement audit. Select from the list provided to match the documentation method with the phrase or description with which it is most closely associated. Each choice may be used once, more than once, or not at all.

Phrase or Description	Documentation Method	Choices
1. A written description of a process		A) Flowchart
2. A logic diagram in matrix form		B) Questionnaire
3. A problem and appropriate actions		C) Narrative memorandum
4. Diagram of a series of sequential processes		D) Decision table
5. Visual depiction of the flow of documents		
6. Series of interrelated queries		
7. The most flexible documentation method		
8. Control strength represented by a "Yes"		

| Audit Procedures | Authoritative Literature | Help |

Select from the list provided to match each audit procedure with the most appropriate statement. Each choice may be used once, more than once, or not at all.

Procedures	Answer		Choices
1. The auditor performs tests of controls.		A)	Describes a reason for the auditor to obtain an understanding of the entity and its environment, including its internal control
2. The auditor prepares flowcharts, narratives, questionnaires, or other material.			
3. The auditor considers the factors affecting the risks of material misstatement.			
4. The auditor performs risk assessment procedures to test the operating effectiveness of controls.		B)	Describes what is done when an auditor has an expectation of the operating effectiveness of controls
5. The auditor designs substantive procedures.			
6. The auditor documents the assessed risks of material misstatement but not the basis for the assessment.		C)	Describes the documentation of the understanding of the entity and its environment, including its internal control, and assessment of the risks of material misstatement
7. The auditor records the controls evaluated.			
8. The auditor considers whether substantive procedures alone do not provide sufficient appropriate audit evidence at the relevant assertion level.			
9. The auditor applies limited substantive procedures to determine whether a control is operational.		D)	Describes a procedure that is not performed
10. The auditor identifies the types of potential misstatement.			

▼ = Reminder   Directions   1 [2] 3 4 5   ◀ Previous   Next ▶

| Control Activities | Authoritative Literature | Help |

Select from the list provided to match each management action with the appropriate control activity. Each choice may be used once, more than once, or not at all.

Management's Action	Answer		Choices
1. Investigating performance indicators		A)	Performance reviews
2. Review of documents and transactions		B)	Information processing
3. Safeguarding assets		C)	Physical controls
4. Comparing actual performance with budgeted performance		D)	Separation of duties
5. Reconciliation			
6. Dividing authorization of transactions and record-keeping			
7. Periodic counting of inventory.			
8. Design and use of adequate documents and records			

▼ = Reminder   Directions   1 2 [3] 4 5   ◀ Previous   Next ▶

Control Environment | Authoritative Literature | Help

Smith, CPA, has been engaged to audit the financial statements of Reed, Inc., a publicly held retailing company. Before assessing the risk of material misstatement, Smith is required to obtain an understanding of Reed's internal control.

Identify by checking the appropriate box which of the following are control environment factors that establish, enhance, or mitigate the effectiveness of specific policies and procedures, and which are not.

Factors	Yes	No
1. Internal audit function.		
2. Management's philosophy and operating style.		
3. Participation of those charged with governance.		
4. External influences.		
5. Information and communication systems.		
6. Performance reviews.		
7. Integrity and ethical values.		
8. Human resource policies and practices.		
9. Segregation of duties.		
10. Organizational structure.		
11. Commitment to competence.		

▼ = Reminder   Directions   1 2 3 [4] 5   ◀ Previous   Next ▶

Research | Authoritative Literature | Help

Research and cite the appropriate auditing standard that describes the necessity to understand both the design and implementation of an internal control.

Title	Section	Paragraph

Title Choices

AU	PCAOB	AT	AR	ET	BL	VS
CS	QC	PR	TS	PFP	CPE	

▼ = Reminder   Directions   1 2 3 4 [5]   ◀ Previous   Next ▶

Unofficial Answers

1. Internal Control Documentation Methods (8 Gradable Items)

1. __C) Narrative memorandum.__ A narrative memorandum is a written description of the processing and flow of documents and control points. The advantage of this method is its flexibility.

2. __D) Decision table.__ A decision table identifies the contingencies considered in the description of a problem and the appropriate actions to be taken relative to those contingencies. Decision tables are logic diagrams presented in matrix form.

3. __D) Decision table.__ A decision table identifies the contingencies considered in the description of a problem and the appropriate actions to be taken relative to those contingencies. Decision tables are logic diagrams presented in matrix form.

4. __A) Flowchart.__ A flowchart is a pictorial diagram of a set of sequential processes. It may be a diagram of the documents and processes of a system or of the steps in a computer program.

5. __A) Flowchart.__ A flowchart is a pictorial diagram of a set of sequential processes. It may be a diagram of the documents and processes of a system or of the steps in a computer program.

6. __B) Questionnaire.__ Questionnaires consist of a series of interrelated questions about internal control polices and procedures. The questions are typically phrased so that a "Yes" response indicates a control strength and a "No" indicates a potential weakness.

7. __C) Narrative memorandum.__ A narrative memorandum is a written description of the processing and flow of documents and control points. The advantage of this method is its flexibility.

8. __B) Questionnaire.__ Questionnaires consist of a series of interrelated questions about internal control polices and procedures. The questions are typically phrased so that a "Yes" response indicates a control strength and a "No" indicates a potential weakness.

2. Audit Procedures (10 Gradable Items)

1. __B) Describes what is done when an auditor has an expectation of the operating effectiveness of controls.__ The auditor tests controls when (a) his/her risk assessment is based on an expectation of the operating effectiveness of controls, or (b) substantive procedures alone do not provide sufficient appropriate evidence at the relevant assertion level.

2. __C) Describes the documentation of the understanding of the entity and its environment, including its internal control, and assessment of the risks of material misstatement.__ The auditor documents, among other things, the understanding of the entity and its environment, including its internal control. This documentation extends to the five components of internal control. Also documented are (a) the sources of information, (b) the risk assessment procedures, (c) the assessment of the risks of material misstatement, (d) the basis of the assessments, and (e) the risks identified and related controls evaluated. Flowcharts, questionnaires, decision tables, checklists, and narratives are among the possible forms of documentation.

3. __A) Describes a reason for the auditor to obtain an understanding of the entity and its environment, including its internal control.__ The auditor should obtain an understanding of the components of internal control to assess the risk of material misstatement, whether due to error or fraud, and to design further audit procedures. This knowledge should be used to (a) determine the types of potential misstatement, (b) consider factors affecting the risks of material misstatement, (c) design tests of controls (when applicable), and (d) design substantive procedures.

4. __D) Describes a procedure that is not performed.__ Risk assessment procedures are performed to obtain an understanding of the entity and its environment, including its internal control. Tests of controls evaluate operating effectiveness.

5. __A) Describes a reason for the auditor to obtain an understanding of the entity and its environment, including its internal control.__ The auditor should obtain an understanding of the components of internal control to assess the risk of material misstatement, whether due to error or fraud, and to design further audit procedures. This knowledge should be used to (a) determine the types of potential misstatement, (b) consider factors affecting the risks of material misstatement, (c) design tests of controls (when applicable), and (d) design substantive procedures.

6. __D) Describes a procedure that is not performed.__ The auditor documents (a) the assessed risks of material misstatement at the financial statement and relevant assertion levels and (b) the basis for the assessment.

7. __C) Describes the documentation of the understanding of the entity and its environment, including its internal control, and assessment of the risks of material misstatement.__ The auditor documents the risks identified and the related controls evaluated.

8. __B) Describes what is done when an auditor has an expectation of the operating effectiveness of controls.__ The auditor tests controls when (a) his/her risk assessment is based on an expectation of the operating effectiveness of controls, or (b) substantive procedures alone do not provide sufficient appropriate evidence at the relevant assertion level.

9.   D) Describes a procedure that is not performed. The auditor performs substantive procedures to detect material misstatements. The auditor tests controls to determine their operating effectiveness.

10. A) Describes a reason for the auditor to obtain an understanding of the entity and its environment, including its internal control. The auditor should obtain an understanding of the components of internal control to assess the risk of material misstatement, whether due to error or fraud, and to design further audit procedures. This knowledge should be used to (a) determine the types of potential misstatement, (b) consider factors affecting the risks of material misstatement, (c) design tests of controls (when applicable), and (d) design substantive procedures.

3. Control Activities (8 Gradable Items)

1.   A) Performance reviews. These include reviews of actual performance versus budgets and prior performance.

2.   B) Information processing. This requires checks of accuracy, completeness, and authorization of transactions.

3.   C) Physical controls. These involve the safeguarding of assets, records, periodic counts, and reconciliations that creates asset accountability.

4.   A) Performance reviews. These include reviews of actual performance versus budgets and prior performance.

5.   B) Information processing. This requires checks of accuracy, completeness, and authorization of transactions.

6.   D) Separation of duties. This involves the separation of the functions of authorization, record keeping, and asset custody so as to minimize the opportunities for a person to be able to perpetrate and conceal errors or fraud in the normal course of his/her duties.

7.   C) Physical controls. These involve the safeguarding of assets, records, periodic counts, and reconciliations that creates asset accountability.

8.   B) Information processing. This requires checks of accuracy, completeness, and authorization of transactions.

4. Control Environment (11 Gradable Items)

1.   No. The internal audit function is part of the monitoring component of internal control.

2.   Yes. This is a control environment factor that establishes, enhances, or mitigates the effectiveness of specific policies and procedures.

3.   Yes. This is a control environment factor that establishes, enhances, or mitigates the effectiveness of specific policies and procedures.

4.   No. Existence of external influences, such as a shift in the regulatory or operating environment, is part of the risk assessment component.

5.   No. Information and communication systems are part of the information system and communications control component.

6.   No. Performance reviews are part of the control activities control component.

7.   Yes. This is a control environment factor that establishes, enhances, or mitigates the effectiveness of specific policies and procedures.

8.   Yes. This is a control environment factor that establishes, enhances, or mitigates the effectiveness of specific policies and procedures.

9.   No. Segregation of duties is part of the control activities control component.

10. Yes. This is a control environment factor that establishes, enhances, or mitigates the effectiveness of specific policies and procedures.

11. Yes. This is a control environment factor that establishes, enhances, or mitigates the effectiveness of specific policies and procedures.

5. Research (1 Gradable Item)

Answer: 314.54

AU Section 314 -- *Understanding the Entity and its Environment and Assessing the Risks of Material Misstatement*

.54 Obtaining an understanding of internal control involves evaluating the design of a control and determining whether it has been implemented. Evaluating the design of a control involves considering whether the control, individually or in combination with other controls, is capable of effectively preventing or detecting and correcting material misstatements. Further explanation is contained in the discussion of each internal control component below (see paragraphs 67 through 101). Implementation of a control means that the control exists and that the entity is using it. The auditor should consider the design of a control in determining whether to consider its implementation. An improperly designed control may represent a material weakness in the entity's internal control and the auditor should consider whether to communicate this to those charged with governance and management.

Gleim Simulation Grading

Task	Correct Responses		Gradable Items		Score per Task
1	_____	÷	8	=	_____
2	_____	÷	10	=	_____
3	_____	÷	8	=	_____
4	_____	÷	11	=	_____
Research	_____	÷	1	=	_____

	Total of Scores per Task	_____
÷	Total Number of Tasks	5
	Total Score	_____ %

Use **CPA Gleim Online** and **Simulation Wizard** to practice more task-based simulations in a realistic environment.

STUDY UNIT SIX
INTERNAL CONTROL --
SALES-RECEIVABLES-CASH RECEIPTS CYCLE

(10 pages of outline)

A standard approach to considering internal control as well as to substantive testing is to divide the auditee's transactions, balances, and related control activities into groupings of related items. This cycle approach is consistent with how transactions are recorded in journals and ledgers. Among the relevant accounts considered are cash, trade receivables, other receivables, allowance for bad debts, sales, sales returns, and bad debt expense.

Understanding how information and documents flow through a particular cycle enables an auditor to determine what controls are in place and whether they are effective in safeguarding assets and preventing or detecting and correcting errors and fraud. Auditors must obtain and document an understanding of internal control sufficient to plan the audit. Thus, a knowledge of flowcharts is important in preparing for the CPA exam.

Some candidates may feel that information presented in flowcharts is difficult to master. The study materials presented here provide the foundations of understanding. They have been kept simple and straightforward. Nevertheless, they capture the information most often tested on the CPA exam. CPA candidates in the past have not been required to prepare flowcharts but have been expected to evaluate them. The narrative should be studied in conjunction with the flowcharts. Candidates should understand and not just memorize the various documents, flows, and control points. Although the basic concepts are derived from a manual system, they can be extended to a computer environment. Subunit 6.4 provides candidates with an understanding of the effect of technology on the sales cycle.

6.1 RESPONSIBILITIES/ORGANIZATIONAL STRUCTURE/FLOWCHARTS

1. **Management's Responsibility**

    a. Management is responsible for the establishment of the controls over the sales-receivables-cash receipts cycle to ensure

       1) Proper acceptance of the customer order
       2) Granting of credit approval in accordance with credit limits
       3) Safeguarding of assets associated with the sale
       4) Timely shipment of goods to customers
       5) Billing for shipments at authorized prices
       6) Accounting for and collection of receivables
       7) The recording, safeguarding, and depositing intact of cash (checks) received

Organizational Chart

This is a typical organizational chart. To help you visualize the internal control of this typical organization, the following document flowcharts with explanations are presented for your study:

	Page
Study Unit 6	
Sales-Receivables Manual System Flowchart	208
Cash Receipts Manual System Flowchart	210
Sales-Receivables Computer System Flowchart	213
Study Unit 7	
Purchases Manual System Flowchart	235
Purchases-Payables Computer System Flowchart	239
Payroll Manual System Flowchart	245
Payroll Computer System Flowchart	247

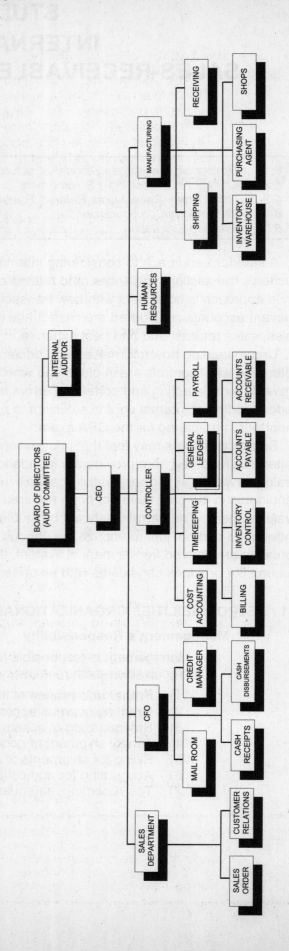

Figure 6-1

2. **The Auditor's Responsibility**

   a. The auditor must obtain an understanding of the entity and its environment, including its internal control, to assess the risk of material misstatement and to design further audit procedures. For this purpose, the auditor performs risk assessment procedures. The plan for further audit procedures reflects (1) the auditor's decision whether to test the operating effectiveness of controls over the sales-receivables-cash receipts cycle and (2) the nature, timing, and extent of substantive procedures.

3. **Separation of Duties**

   a. The organizational structure should separate duties and responsibilities so that an individual is not in the position both to perpetrate and conceal errors or fraud. The ideal separation of duties is

      1) **Authorization** of the transaction

         a) **Specific authorization** may be needed for some transactions, such as unusual credit approvals, but a **general authorization** may suffice for others, such as retail cash sales.

      2) **Recording** of the transaction

      3) **Custody** over the assets (e.g., inventory, receivables, and cash) associated with the transaction

   b. However, **cost-benefit** considerations typically affect the organizational structure and complete separation may not be feasible. Compensating controls will likely be established when the separation of duties is not maintained. Typical compensating controls may include

      1) More supervision

      2) Owner involvement in the process

4. **Responsibilities of Personnel**

   a. The following are the responsibilities of personnel or departments in the sales-receivables-cash receipts cycle:

      1) **Sales** prepares sales orders based on customer orders.

      2) **Credit Manager** authorizes customer credit and initiates write-off of bad debts. The credit manager should report to the CFO.

      3) **Inventory Warehouse** maintains physical custody of products.

      4) **Shipping** prepares shipping documents and ships products based on authorized sales orders.

      5) **Billing** prepares customer invoices based on goods shipped.

      6) **Accounts Receivable** maintains the accounts receivable subsidiary ledger.

      7) **Mail Room** receives mail and prepares initial cash receipts records.

      8) **Cash Receipts** safeguards and promptly deposits cash receipts.

      9) **General Ledger** maintains the accounts receivable control account and records sales. Daily summaries of sales are recorded in a sales journal. Totals of details from the sales journal are usually posted monthly to the general ledger.

      10) **Receiving** department prepares receiving reports and handles all receipts of goods or materials, including sales returns.

 As you are considering the flowcharts in this and subsequent study units, remember that they are simply examples. Instead of assigning importance to the actual number of documents prepared or the document numbers, you should focus on the control provided by the division of duties and responsibilities and the control processes. Your understanding of the issues will help you answer many more CPA exam questions than just those related to flowcharting.

Sales-Receivables Manual System Flowchart

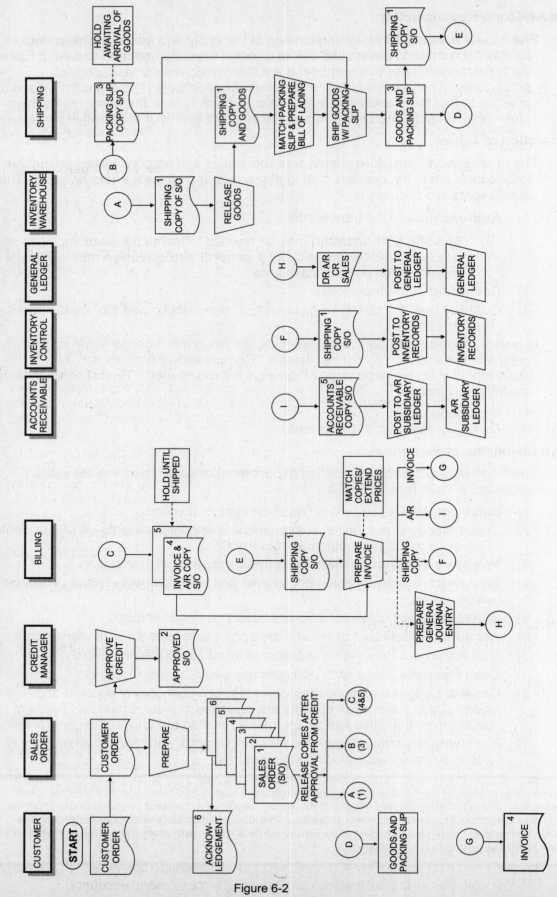

Figure 6-2

5. **Sales-Receivables Flowchart**

    a. Study the flowchart on the previous page. Understand and visualize the sales-receivables process and controls. Read the following description as needed. Note the control activities implemented and listed in item 7. below.

6. **The Document Flow**

    a. The process begins in the upper left corner of the flowchart marked **START**. (To simplify the presentation, the flowchart does not show the disposition of all documents, for example, by filing or other supplemental procedures.)

        1) The Sales Order department receives a customer order and prepares a multipart sales order. Copy 2 of the sales order is sent to the Credit Manager.

        2) The Credit Manager performs a credit check and authorizes the order if appropriate. The approval is conveyed to Sales Order, and an acknowledgment (copy 6) is sent to the customer.

        3) Sales Order then releases the remaining copies of the order. Two copies, the invoice copy and accounts receivable copy (copies 4 and 5), are sent to Billing and held awaiting notification of shipment.

        4) A copy (the packing slip copy 3) is sent to Shipping pending arrival of the goods from the Inventory Warehouse.

        5) A copy (the shipping copy 1) is released to the Inventory Warehouse as authorization to release the goods to be sent to the Shipping department.

        6) When the goods and the shipping copy 1 arrive at the Shipping department, the matching packing slip copy 3 is pulled from the file, and shipping documents (e.g., a bill of lading) are prepared. The goods are packed for shipment along with the packing slip copy 3. The shipping copy 1 is marked "shipped" and forwarded to Billing.

        7) Billing pulls the matching invoice and accounts receivable copies (4 and 5). Prices are checked and extended based on the quantities shipped. The invoice (copy 4) is completed and mailed to the customer. The invoice contains a section (a remittance advice) to be returned with the customer check.

        8) Billing prepares a journal entry to be posted by the General Ledger department (credit to sales and debit to the accounts receivable control account).

        9) The accounts receivable copy 5 is forwarded to Accounts Receivable for posting to the individual account in the accounts receivable subsidiary ledger.

        10) The shipping copy 1 is sent to Inventory Control for reduction of quantities for goods shipped.

7. **Control Activities Implemented**

    a. The division of the duties of the transaction is as follows: authorization, recording, and custody of assets.

    b. Routing the sales order copy through the Credit Manager assures that goods are shipped only to customers who are likely to pay (i.e., properly valued).

    c. Routing the shipping copy through the Inventory Warehouse helps assure that goods are safeguarded and released only upon proper approval of the order.

    d. Matching of the packing slip copy held by Shipping can assure that all goods released from the Inventory Warehouse are received by Shipping on a timely basis.

    e. Matching of the copies held by the Billing department can assure that all goods shipped are invoiced to customers.

    f. Documents are prenumbered to permit detection of unrecorded or unauthorized transactions. For example, sales invoices are prenumbered and accounted for to ensure that all orders are billed.

    g. Periodic reconciliation of the accounts receivable subsidiary ledger with the general ledger can assure that all invoices are recorded in customers' accounts.

8.   **Cash Receipts Flowchart**

a.   Study the flowchart below. Understand and visualize the cash receipts process and
controls. Read the following description as needed. Note the control activities
implemented and listed in item 10. on the next page.

Cash Receipts Manual System Flowchart

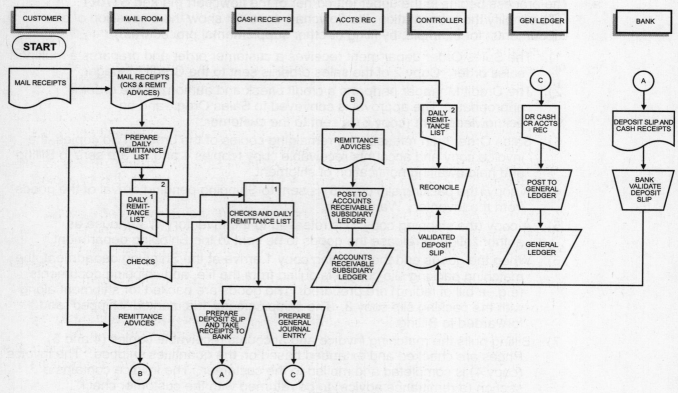

Figure 6-3

9.   **The Document Flow**

a.   This flowchart represents the procedures and documents for cash collections from
credit customers; cash receipts from cash sales are considered in Subunit 2 of this
study unit. (To simplify the presentation, the flowchart does not show the disposition
of documents, for example, by filing or other supplemental procedures.) The process
begins at **START**.

1)   The Mail Room receives all customer receipts, opens the mail, separates the
checks from the remittance advices, and prepares a daily listing of the checks
received (the daily remittance list). If no remittance advice is received, the mail
clerks prepare one. A copy of the daily remittance list is sent to the Controller.

a)   A remittance advice is part of or a copy of the sales invoice sent to a
customer and intended to be returned with the payment. It contains the
customer's name, the invoice number, and its amount.

2)   Cash receipts and copy 1 of the daily remittance list are forwarded to Cash
Receipts for preparation of the deposit ticket and recording in the cash receipts
register.

3)   The receipts are deposited daily by Cash Receipts. The validated (by the bank)
deposit ticket is returned to the Controller. The Controller reconciles the
validated deposit ticket with the daily remittance list of cash received from the
Mail Room.

    4) A journal voucher (entry) prepared by Cash Receipts indicating the debit to cash and credit to accounts receivable is sent to the General Ledger.

    5) The remittance advices are sent to Accounts Receivable for posting the reductions in accounts receivable to the individual customers' accounts.

10. **Control Activities Implemented**

    a. Two clerks should be present in the Mail Room during the opening and recording of the receipts.

    b. Checks are endorsed "For Deposit Only into Account Number XXXX" immediately upon opening the mail.

    c. All cash is deposited intact daily. This procedure assures that the cash received and recorded on the daily remittance list can be reconciled with the deposit ticket validated by the bank.

    d. Periodic reconciliation of the accounts receivable subsidiary ledger and the accounts receivable control account in the general ledger establishes agreement of the total amounts posted. However, the reconciliation cannot determine whether an amount was posted to the wrong account in the subsidiary ledger. Moreover, application of such a control will be ineffective if sales were not recorded in the books of original entry, e.g., the sales journal.

    e. Monthly statements are sent to customers to assure that failure to receive and/or record payments made by customers is detected (not shown on flowchart).

    f. A **lockbox system** (not depicted in the flowchart) can assure that cash receipts are not abstracted by mail clerks or other employees. This system provides for customer payments to be sent to a post office box and collected directly by the bank.

        1) Hence, a lockbox system prevents lapping. **Lapping** occurs when an employee with access to both the accounts receivable subsidiary ledger and customer payments steals a portion of the receipts without recording them in the customer accounts. To conceal the theft, subsequent receipts are posted to the accounts of customers whose payments were stolen. This process of using new receipts to cover a recent theft must continue indefinitely to avoid detection.

Stop and review! You have completed the outline for this subunit. Study multiple-choice questions 1 through 15 beginning on page 215.

6.2 CONTROLS IN A CASH SALE ENVIRONMENT

1. Cash sales cycles often lack the separation of duties necessary for the proper framework of control. For example, the sales clerk often

    a. Authorizes the sale (e.g., acceptance of a check)
    b. Records the sale (i.e., enters it on the sales terminal)
    c. Has custody of the assets related to the sale (i.e., cash and inventory)

2. Compensating controls include

    a. Use of a cash register or sales terminal to record the sale. The terminal makes a permanent record of the event that the clerk cannot erase.

    b. Assignment of one clerk to be responsible for sales recording and cash receipts during a work period. The cash drawer can be reconciled with the record of sales and accountability assigned to the clerk.

    c. Increased supervision. For example, the manager's office may be positioned to observe the clerks' sales recording and cash collection activities.

d.   Customer audit of the transaction. Displaying the recorded transaction and providing a receipt to the customer provide some assurance that the recording process was accomplished appropriately by the clerk.

e.   Bonding of employees responsible for handling cash. Because the bonding company investigates employees before providing the bond, some assurance is provided concerning their integrity. Also, the bond provides insurance against losses.

Stop and review! You have completed the outline for this subunit. Study multiple-choice questions 16 and 17 beginning on page 219.

6.3 OTHER SALES-RECEIVABLES RELATED TRANSACTIONS

1.   Sales returns and allowances should have controls to assure proper approval and processing. The key controls include

a.   Approval by the sales department to return goods

b.   Receipt of the returned goods by the receiving department and preparation of a receiving report

c.   The separate approval of the credit memo related to a sales return or allowance, that is, approval by someone not in the sales department

2.   The write-off of bad debts requires strong controls. The key controls include

a.   Initiation of the write-off by the credit manager and approval by the CFO or other officer. The credit manager will be evaluated, in part, on the amount of bad debts written off and will require significant evidence before initiating a write-off.

b.   Maintenance of a separate accounting ledger for accounts written off.

Stop and review! You have completed the outline for this subunit. Study multiple-choice questions 18 through 21 beginning on page 220.

6.4 TECHNOLOGY CONSIDERATIONS

1.   Computer processing typically replaces the activities of clerks performing recording functions, e.g., recording sales and accounts receivable, updating the inventory file to reflect goods sold, and recording customer receipts by posting the amounts to the accounts receivable subsidiary file.

2.   Periodic reconciliations (weekly or monthly) of the accounts receivable subsidiary file and general ledgers are usually replaced by daily reconciliations.

3.   Sophisticated systems may replace the paper flow with computer control over authorization of the release of goods for packing and shipping.

a.   The use of online systems expedites the response to customer orders.

b.   Batching transactions is useful for processing large volumes of data, especially when the transactions are sorted sequentially. Batch processing is appropriate when an immediate response is not necessary.

4.   Study the flowchart on the next page. Understand and visualize the sales-receivables process and controls in a normative computer environment. Read the following description as needed. Note the control activities implemented and listed in item 6. on page 214.

Sales-Receivables Computer System Flowchart

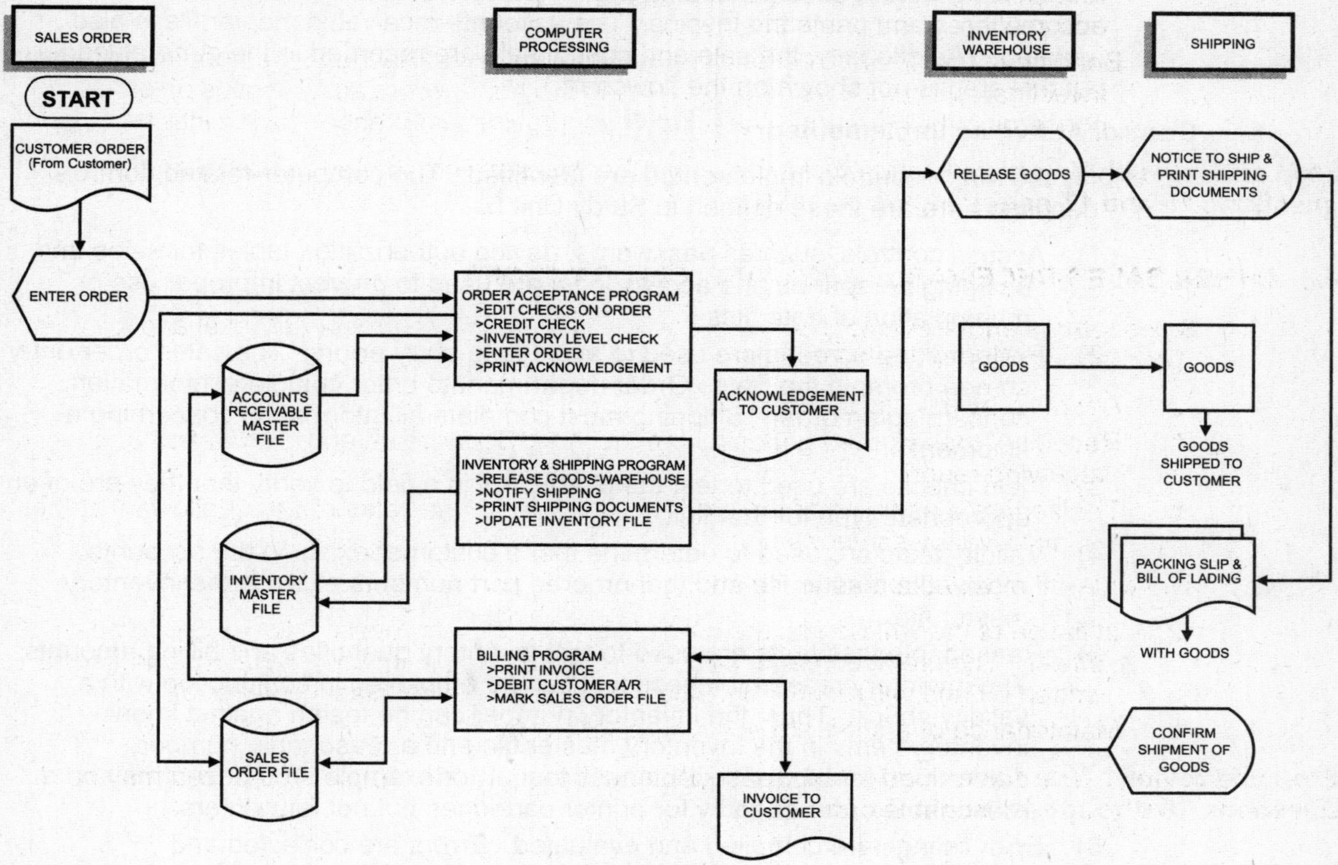

Figure 6-4

5. **The Information Flow**

   a. The sales-receivables computer system flowchart above provides one view of computer processing using online systems. In this case, paper flow is replaced with electronic transmissions, and manual files and ledgers are replaced by computer disk files. The accounting departments (from the previous flowcharts) of Billing, Inventory Control, and Accounts Receivable are replaced by the Computer Processing department. Furthermore, routine credit decisions are replaced by a computer program.

   b. The Sales Order department receives a customer order (beginning at **START** in the flowchart) and records it into the order acceptance program on a preformatted sales entry screen. Edit checks are used to assure proper entry. The accounts receivable master file is checked for current customer information and credit limits. Inventory levels are checked for availability from the inventory master file. The accepted order, along with prices determined from the inventory master file, is entered into the sales order master file, and an acknowledgment is printed and sent to the customer.

   c. Information is passed to the inventory and shipping program that sends a release authorization to the Inventory Warehouse via a computer workstation. Inventory levels are formally updated upon release of the goods from the Inventory Warehouse. An electronic shipping authorization is sent to the Shipping department. The communication also generates a packing slip and shipping documents (e.g., a bill of lading) that are printed in the Shipping department.

    d.   Shipping provides the billing program with the information concerning the shipment. The billing program accesses demographic and price data from the sales order file and prepares and prints the invoice. The accounts receivable master file is also updated. (Additionally, the sale and cost of sale are recorded in the general ledger, but this step is not shown on the flowchart.)

6.   **Control Activities Implemented**

    a.   Only the major controls implemented are identified. The computer-related controls identified here are those defined in Study Unit 5.

        1)   Access controls, such as passwords, device authorization tables for sales and shipping personnel, and access logs, are used to prevent improper use or manipulation of data files.

        2)   Preformatted screens are used to avoid data entry errors. The sales order entry screen prompts the Sales Order department to enter complete information concerning an order. Shipping must complete all information concerning a shipment.

        3)   Field checks are used to test the characters in a field to verify that they are of an appropriate type for that field.

        4)   Validity tests are used to determine that a customer exists in the accounts receivable master file and that ordered part numbers exist on the inventory master file.

        5)   Reasonableness tests are used to test inventory quantities and billing amounts. The inventory reasonableness test can be employed in conjunction with a validity check. Thus, the inventory number can be tested against known inventory items in the inventory master file and a reasonable number determined for the reasonableness test. (For example, 100 dozen may be a reasonable order quantity for printer cartridges but not for printers.)

        6)   Error listings are compiled and evaluated. Errors are corrected and reprocessed.

7.   **E-Commerce Considerations**

    a.   The sales-receivables computer flowchart may be used to envision sales processing for a firm using an Internet website. Likely changes include direct entry of the order by the customer, elimination of the sales order department, and payment by credit card. Thus, accounts receivable will not be maintained. Acknowledgment of the order acceptance would be immediately communicated to the customer via an email or other Internet response. However, shipping department procedures and controls would be largely unaltered.

        1)   Additional controls include

            a)   A **firewall** between the customer and internally stored client data
            b)   **Passwords** for authorized or preferred customers
            c)   **Encryption** procedures for transmission of sensitive information

Stop and review! You have completed the outline for this subunit. Study multiple-choice questions 22 through 27 beginning on page 221.

QUESTIONS

6.1 Responsibilities/Organizational Structure/Flowcharts

1. At which point in an ordinary sales transaction of a wholesaling business is a lack of specific authorization of **least** concern to the auditor in the conduct of an audit?

A. Granting of credit.

B. Shipment of goods.

C. Determination of discounts.

D. Selling of goods for cash.

Answer (D) is correct. *(CPA, adapted)*
REQUIRED: The point in an ordinary sales transaction at which specific authorization is of least concern to an auditor.
DISCUSSION: Selling goods for cash is the consummation of a transaction that would likely be covered by a general authorization. Thus, the risk of loss arising from lack of specific authorization of cash sales is minimal.
Answer (A) is incorrect. Granting of credit in a sales transaction may require specific authorization, i.e., special consideration before approval by the appropriate person. Answer (B) is incorrect. Shipment of goods in a sales transaction may require specific authorization. Answer (C) is incorrect. Determination of discounts in a sales transaction may require specific authorization.

2. During the consideration of a small business client's internal control, the auditor discovered that the accounts receivable clerk approves credit memos and has access to cash. Which of the following controls would be most effective in offsetting this weakness?

A. The owner reviews errors in billings to customers and postings to the subsidiary ledger.

B. The controller receives the monthly bank statement directly and reconciles the checking accounts.

C. The owner reviews credit memos after they are recorded.

D. The controller reconciles the total of the detail accounts receivable accounts to the amount shown in the ledger.

Answer (C) is correct. *(CPA, adapted)*
REQUIRED: The most effective control to compensate for an employee's performance of incompatible functions.
DISCUSSION: The clerk is in a position to both perpetrate and conceal a fraud in the normal course of his/her duties. The clerk has custody of cash, performs the record keeping function for accounts receivable, and authorizes credit memos. Thus, the clerk could conceal a theft of cash collected from customers on account by authorizing sales returns. In a small business, cost-benefit considerations ordinarily preclude establishment of formal control activities. In this situation, effective owner-management involvement may compensate for the absence of certain control activities. Accordingly, the owner should determine that credit memos are genuine.
Answer (A) is incorrect. The clerk could commit a defalcation without errors in billing and postings to the subsidiary ledger. Answer (B) is incorrect. The bank reconciliation will not detect a theft of cash concealed by improper credit memos. Cash abstracted by the clerk would not be recorded. Answer (D) is incorrect. Improper credits to accounts receivable do not cause a discrepancy between the control account and the subsidiary ledger.

3. Which of the following controls most likely would be effective in offsetting the tendency of sales personnel to maximize sales volume at the expense of high bad debt write-offs?

A. Employees responsible for authorizing sales and bad debt write-offs are denied access to cash.

B. Shipping documents and sales invoices are matched by an employee who does not have authority to write off bad debts.

C. Employees involved in the credit-granting function are separated from the sales function.

D. Subsidiary accounts receivable records are reconciled to the control account by an employee independent of the authorization of credit.

Answer (C) is correct. *(CPA, adapted)*
REQUIRED: The control most effective in offsetting the tendency of sales personnel to maximize sales volume at the expense of high bad debt write-offs.
DISCUSSION: Salespeople should be responsible for generating sales and providing service to customers. For effective control, the credit department should be responsible for monitoring the financial condition of prospective and continuing customers in the credit approval process and should report to the CFO.
Answer (A) is incorrect. Denial of access to cash does not address the problem of the incompatibility of the sales and credit granting functions. Answer (B) is incorrect. Matching of shipping and sales documents does not address the issue. Answer (D) is incorrect. Reconciliation of the subsidiary and general ledgers does not address the issue.

4. An auditor tests an entity's policy of obtaining credit approval before shipping goods to customers in support of management's financial statement assertion of

A. Valuation.

B. Completeness.

C. Occurrence.

D. Rights and obligations.

Answer (A) is correct. *(CPA, adapted)*
REQUIRED: The assertion related to the policy of credit approval before shipping goods to customers.
DISCUSSION: The proper approval of credit provides assurance that the account receivable is collectible. Thus, it is related to the valuation assertion that balances are reported at appropriate amounts, e.g., accounts receivable at net realizable value.
Answer (B) is incorrect. The completeness assertion is that all transactions, events, and balances that should have been recorded have been recorded. Answer (C) is incorrect. The occurrence assertion is that recorded transactions and events have occurred and pertain to the entity. Answer (D) is incorrect. Rights and obligations assertions relate to whether assets are rights of the entity and liabilities are obligations of the entity.

5. An auditor is determining whether internal control over the revenue cycle of a wholesaler is operating effectively in minimizing the failure to prepare sales invoices. The auditor most likely will select a sample of transactions from the population represented by the

A. Sales order file.

B. Customer order file.

C. Shipping document file.

D. Sales invoice file.

Answer (C) is correct. *(CPA, adapted)*
REQUIRED: The population sampled to test control over preparation of sales invoices.
DISCUSSION: The auditor should trace shipping document file copies relating to customer shipments to sales invoices (or possibly to the accounts receivable subsidiary ledger) to determine whether shipments were not billed.
Answer (A) is incorrect. The sales order file may contain orders not yet shipped. Answer (B) is incorrect. The customer order file may contain orders that were not approved and shipped. Answer (D) is incorrect. To test for failure to invoice, the auditor should not sample from a file of invoiced orders. Comparing sales invoices with shipping documents provides evidence of actual shipments and therefore occurrence.

6. Which of the following activities most likely would **not** be an internal control activity designed to reduce the risk of errors in the billing process?

A. Comparing control totals for shipping documents with corresponding totals for sales invoices.

B. Using computer programmed controls over the pricing and accuracy of sales invoices.

C. Matching shipping documents with approved sales orders before invoice preparation.

D. Reconciling the control totals for sales invoices with the accounts receivable subsidiary ledger.

Answer (D) is correct. *(CPA, adapted)*
REQUIRED: The procedure not considered an internal control designed to reduce the risk of errors in the billing process.
DISCUSSION: The accounts receivable subsidiary ledger contains all receivables outstanding to date. It would not be practical to attempt to reconcile current sales invoices with the accounts receivable subsidiary ledger. The accounts receivable subsidiary ledger should be reconciled to the general ledger control account periodically, however.
Answer (A) is incorrect. The total amounts shipped should correspond to the sales invoices and can be reconciled on a daily basis. Answer (B) is incorrect. Programmed controls would be appropriate in a computerized environment. Answer (C) is incorrect. The preparation of an invoice should be contingent on the shipment of goods.

7. Which of the following controls most likely would help ensure that all credit sales transactions of an entity are recorded?

A. The billing department supervisor sends copies of approved sales orders to the credit department for comparison to authorized credit limits and current customer account balances.

B. The accounting department supervisor independently reconciles the accounts receivable subsidiary ledger to the accounts receivable control account monthly.

C. The accounting department supervisor controls the mailing of monthly statements to customers and investigates any differences they report.

D. The billing department supervisor matches prenumbered shipping documents with entries in the sales journal.

Answer (D) is correct. *(CPA, adapted)*
REQUIRED: The control to detect unrecorded sales.
DISCUSSION: The sequential numbering of documents provides a standard control over transactions. The numerical sequence should be accounted for by an independent party. A major objective is to detect unrecorded and unauthorized transactions. Moreover, comparing shipments with the sales journal also will detect unrecorded transactions.
Answer (A) is incorrect. Credit approval does not ensure that sales have been recorded. Answer (B) is incorrect. The reconciliation will not detect sales that were never recorded. Answer (C) is incorrect. Customers are unlikely to report understatement of their accounts.

8. Refer to the flowchart below.

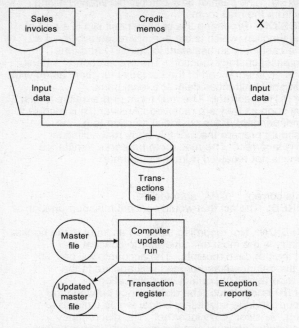

In a credit sales and cash receipts system flowchart, Symbol X could represent

  A. Auditor's test data.

  B. Remittance advices.

  C. Error reports.

  D. Credit authorization forms.

Answer (B) is correct. *(CPA, adapted)*

   REQUIRED: The document in the credit sales and cash receipts flowchart represented by Symbol X.

   DISCUSSION: Remittance advices (Symbol X) are sent with sales invoices to customers to be returned with cash payments. Credit memos are internal documents crediting customer accounts for returns or allowances granted. These documents are processed against the master file in the updating run.

   Answer (A) is incorrect. Auditor's test data are not part of the client's processing of accounts receivable payments. Answer (C) is incorrect. Error reports are an output of the process. Answer (D) is incorrect. Credit authorization forms are documents approving credit sales. They should be distinguished from credit memos.

9. Upon receipt of customers' checks in the mail room, a responsible employee should prepare a remittance listing that is forwarded to the cashier. A copy of the listing should be sent to the

  A. Internal auditor to investigate the listing for unusual transactions.

  B. CFO to compare the listing with the monthly bank statement.

  C. Accounts receivable bookkeeper to update the subsidiary accounts receivable records.

  D. Entity's bank to compare the listing with the cashier's deposit slip.

Answer (C) is correct. *(CPA, adapted)*

   REQUIRED: The use of a copy of the client's remittance listing.

   DISCUSSION: The individuals with record-keeping responsibility should not have custody of cash. Hence, they should use either the remittance advices or a listing of the remittances to make entries to the cash and accounts receivable control account and to the subsidiary accounts receivable records. Indeed, having different people make entries in the control account and in the subsidiary records is an effective control.

   Answer (A) is incorrect. The internal auditors should have no ongoing control responsibilities. The investigation of unusual transactions is first conducted in the CFO's department. Answer (B) is incorrect. The monthly bank statement should be reconciled by someone outside of the treasury function. Answer (D) is incorrect. The entity's bank will supply a validated deposit slip based on the deposit for the day. Company management outside the treasury function will compare the validated deposit slip with the remittance listing.

10. An auditor would consider a cashier's job description to contain compatible duties if the cashier receives remittances from the mail room and also prepares the

A. Prelist of individual checks.

B. Monthly bank reconciliation.

C. Daily deposit slip.

D. Remittance advices.

Answer (C) is correct. *(CPA, adapted)*
REQUIRED: The cashier duty compatible with receiving remittances from the mail room.
DISCUSSION: Preparing the bank deposit slip is a part of the custodial function, which is the primary responsibility of a cashier. The cashier is an assistant to the CFO and thus performs an asset custody function. The preparation of a bank deposit slip is an integral part of the custodial function, along with the depositing of remittances daily at a local bank.
Answer (A) is incorrect. The mail room prepares the prelist of checks as soon as they are received. Answer (B) is incorrect. Someone independent of the custodial function (e.g., the controller) should prepare the monthly bank reconciliation. Answer (D) is incorrect. The mail room prepares remittance advices if one is not received from the customer.

11. Cash receipts from sales on account have been misappropriated. Which of the following acts would conceal this defalcation and be **least** likely to be detected by an auditor?

A. Understating the sales journal.

B. Overstating the accounts receivable control account.

C. Overstating the accounts receivable subsidiary ledger.

D. Understating the cash receipts journal.

Answer (A) is correct. *(CPA, adapted)*
REQUIRED: The act that would conceal misappropriation of cash.
DISCUSSION: Not recording sales on account in the books of original entry is the most effective way to conceal a subsequent theft of cash receipts. The accounts will be incomplete but balanced, and procedures applied to the accounting records will not detect the defalcation.
Answer (B) is incorrect. The discrepancy between the control account and the subsidiary ledger would indicate a misstatement. Answer (C) is incorrect. The discrepancy between the control account and the subsidiary ledger would indicate a misstatement. Answer (D) is incorrect. Cash receipts will not reconcile with the credits to accounts receivable. If accounts receivable are not credited, confirmation will detect the defalcation.

12. Which of the following internal controls most likely would reduce the risk of diversion of customer receipts by an entity's employees?

A. A bank lockbox system.

B. Prenumbered remittance advices.

C. Monthly bank reconciliations.

D. Daily deposit of cash receipts.

Answer (A) is correct. *(CPA, adapted)*
REQUIRED: The control that would reduce the risk of employee misappropriation of cash.
DISCUSSION: A lockbox system assures that cash receipts are not abstracted by mail clerks or other employees. Customer payments are mailed to a post office box and collected directly by the bank.
Answer (B) is incorrect. Prenumbering facilitates control over remittance advices, but it would not prevent diversion of cash. Answer (C) is incorrect. A bank reconciliation reconciles the cash in the bank with the amount recorded. However, if cash is not recorded, the reconciliation does not detect its diversion. Answer (D) is incorrect. If the diversion occurs prior to the deposit, timely deposits do not necessarily reduce the risk of diversion.

13. Evidence concerning the proper segregation of duties for receiving and depositing cash receipts ordinarily is obtained by

A. Completing an internal control questionnaire that describes the control activities.

B. Observing the employees who are performing the control activities.

C. Performing substantive procedures to verify the details of the bank balance.

D. Preparing a flowchart of the duties performed and the entity's available personnel.

Answer (B) is correct. *(CPA, adapted)*
REQUIRED: The procedure testing separation of duties for receiving and depositing cash.
DISCUSSION: Observation is a risk assessment procedure performed to obtain an understanding of the entity and its environment, including its controls. It is also a test of controls. Observation of entity activities and operations supports inquiries of management and provides information about the entity and its environment.
Answer (A) is incorrect. The questionnaire will document the understanding of the controls, not whether they are operating effectively. Answer (C) is incorrect. Substantive procedures directly address financial statement assertions, not controls. Answer (D) is incorrect. The flowchart documents the understanding of the controls, not whether they are operating effectively.

14. Employers bond employees who handle cash receipts because fidelity bonds reduce the possibility of employing dishonest individuals and

    A. Protect employees who make unintentional errors from possible monetary damages resulting from their errors.

    B. Deter dishonesty by making employees aware that insurance companies may investigate and prosecute dishonest acts.

    C. Facilitate an independent monitoring of the receiving and depositing of cash receipts.

    D. Force employees in positions of trust to take periodic vacations and rotate their assigned duties.

Answer (B) is correct. *(CPA, adapted)*
    REQUIRED: The purpose of bonding employees.
    DISCUSSION: Effective internal control, including human resources practices that stress the hiring of trustworthy people, does not guarantee against losses from embezzlement and other fraudulent acts committed by employees. Accordingly, an employer may obtain a fidelity bond to insure against losses arising from illegal acts by the covered employees. Prior to issuing this form of insurance, the underwriters investigate the individuals to be covered. Also, employees should be informed that bonding companies are diligent in prosecuting bonded individuals who commit fraud.
    Answer (A) is incorrect. Bonding insures employers against intentional wrongdoing. Answer (C) is incorrect. Bonding is irrelevant to monitoring the receipt and deposit of cash receipts. Answer (D) is incorrect. Bonding is irrelevant to periodic vacations and rotation of duties.

15. Which of the following internal control activities most likely would deter lapping of collections from customers?

    A. Independent internal verification of dates of entry in the cash receipts journal with dates of daily cash summaries.

    B. Authorization of write-offs of uncollectible accounts by a supervisor independent of credit approval.

    C. Separation of duties between receiving cash and posting the accounts receivable ledger.

    D. Supervisory comparison of the daily cash summary with the sum of the cash receipts journal entries.

Answer (C) is correct. *(CPA, adapted)*
    REQUIRED: The best protection from lapping of collections from customers.
    DISCUSSION: Lapping is the delayed recording of cash receipts to cover a cash shortage. Current receipts are posted to the accounts of customers who paid one or two days previously to avoid complaints (and discovery) when monthly statements are mailed. The best protection is for the customers to send payments directly to the company's depository bank. The next best procedure is to assure that the accounts receivable clerk has no access to cash received by the mail room. Thus, the duties of receiving cash and posting the accounts receivable ledger are separated.
    Answer (A) is incorrect. Lapping delays recording cash receipts so that posting the cash receipts journal and recording in the cash summary occur on the same date and in the same amounts. Answer (B) is incorrect. Lapping involves delayed posting of cash payments, not bad debt write-offs. Moreover, the credit manager should initiate write-offs to be approved by the CFO. Answer (D) is incorrect. Lapping delays recording cash receipts so that posting the cash receipts journal and recording in the cash summary occur on the same date and in the same amounts.

6.2 Controls in a Cash Sale Environment

16. Which of the following procedures would an auditor most likely perform to test controls relating to management's assertion about the completeness of cash receipts for cash sales at a retail outlet?

    A. Observe the consistency of the employee's use of cash registers and tapes.

    B. Inquire about employee's access to recorded but undeposited cash.

    C. Trace the deposits in the cash receipts journal to the cash balance in the general ledger.

    D. Compare the cash balance in the general ledger with the bank confirmation request.

Answer (A) is correct. *(CPA, adapted)*
    REQUIRED: The test of controls for the completeness assertion.
    DISCUSSION: An assertion about completeness of transactions addresses whether all transactions that should be presented are included in the financial statements. To determine that controls are operating effectively to ensure that all cash receipts are being recorded for cash sales in a retail environment, the auditor may observe the activities of the employees. Controls should provide assurance that employees use cash registers that contain internal functions (e.g., tapes) to record all sales.
    Answer (B) is incorrect. Inquiry about employees' access to recorded cash pertains to the existence assertion. Once the sales are recorded, other controls are in place to determine that the existence of cash can be assured. Answer (C) is incorrect. Tracing cash receipts to the ledger is a substantive procedure, not a test of controls. Answer (D) is incorrect. Confirmation of cash with the bank is a substantive procedure, not a test of controls.

17. In a retail cash sales environment, which of the following controls is often absent?

  A. Competent personnel.

  B. Separation of functions.

  C. Supervision.

  D. Asset access limited to authorized personnel.

Answer (B) is correct. *(Publisher, adapted)*
  REQUIRED: The control often absent in a cash sales environment.
  DISCUSSION: In the usual retail cash sales situation, the sales clerk authorizes and records the transactions and takes custody of assets. However, management ordinarily employs other compensating controls to minimize the effects of the failure to separate functions. The cash receipts function is closely supervised, cash registers provide limited access to assets, and an internal recording function maintains control over cash receipts.

6.3 Other Sales-Receivables Related Transactions

18. An auditor noted that the accounts receivable department is separate from other accounting activities. Credit is approved by a separate credit department. Control accounts and subsidiary ledgers are balanced monthly. Similarly, accounts are aged monthly. The accounts receivable manager writes off delinquent accounts after 1 year, or sooner if a bankruptcy or other unusual circumstances are involved. Credit memoranda are prenumbered and must correlate with receiving reports. Which of the following areas could be viewed as an internal control weakness of the above organization?

  A. Handling of credit memos.

  B. Monthly aging of receivables.

  C. Credit approvals.

  D. Write-offs of delinquent accounts.

Answer (D) is correct. *(Publisher, adapted)*
  REQUIRED: The area viewed as an internal control weakness of the organization.
  DISCUSSION: The accounts receivable manager has the ability to perpetrate fraud because (s)he performs incompatible functions. Authorization and recording of transactions should be separate. Thus, someone outside the accounts receivable department should authorize write-offs.
  Answer (A) is incorrect. The procedures regarding credit memoranda are standard controls. Answer (B) is incorrect. Monthly aging is appropriate. Answer (C) is incorrect. Credit approval is an authorization function that is properly segregated from the record-keeping function.

19. Which of the following most likely would be the result of ineffective internal control in the revenue cycle?

  A. Final authorization of credit memos by personnel in the sales department could permit an employee defalcation scheme.

  B. Fictitious transactions could be recorded, causing an understatement of revenues and an overstatement of receivables.

  C. Fraud in recording transactions in the subsidiary accounts could result in a delay in goods shipped.

  D. Omission of shipping documents could go undetected, causing an understatement of inventory.

Answer (A) is correct. *(CPA, adapted)*
  REQUIRED: The most likely result of ineffective internal controls in the revenue cycle.
  DISCUSSION: Ineffective controls in the revenue cycle, such as inappropriate separation of duties and responsibilities, inadequate supervision, or deficient authorization, may result in the ability of employees to perpetrate fraud. Thus, sales personnel should approve sales returns and allowances but not the related credit memos. Moreover, no authorization for the return of goods, defective or otherwise, should be considered complete until the goods are returned as evidenced by a receiving report.
  Answer (B) is incorrect. Recording fictitious sales would overstate revenues. Answer (C) is incorrect. The customers' accounts are not posted until after goods are shipped. Answer (D) is incorrect. If shipping documents are omitted, shipments of goods may not be credited to inventory, thereby overstating the account.

20. Proper authorization of write-offs of uncollectible accounts should be approved in which of the following departments?

  A. Accounts receivable.

  B. Credit.

  C. Accounts payable.

  D. CFO.

Answer (D) is correct. *(CPA, adapted)*
  REQUIRED: The department authorizing write-offs of applicable accounts.
  DISCUSSION: The write-off of uncollectible accounts requires strong controls. The initiation of the write-off is performed by the credit manager. However, authorization should be by an independent party, typically the CFO. The credit manager will be evaluated, in part, on the amount of bad debt written off and should require significant evidence before initiating a write-off.
  Answer (A) is incorrect. Accounts receivable is a recording function and should not authorize transactions. Answer (B) is incorrect. The credit manager should not both initiate and approve the write-off. Answer (C) is incorrect. Accounts payable is a recording function and should not authorize transactions.

21. Sound internal control activities dictate that defective merchandise returned by customers be presented initially to the

A. Accounts receivable supervisor.

B. Receiving clerk.

C. Shipping department supervisor.

D. Sales clerk.

Answer (B) is correct. *(CPA, adapted)*

REQUIRED: The individual to whom customers should return defective merchandise.

DISCUSSION: For control purposes, all receipts of goods or materials should be handled by the receiving clerk. Receiving reports should be prepared for all items received.

Answer (A) is incorrect. The accounts receivable supervisor has a record keeping function incompatible with access to assets. Answer (C) is incorrect. Shipping and receiving should be segregated. Answer (D) is incorrect. All returns of goods should be handled by an independent receiving function.

6.4 Technology Considerations

22. An online sales order processing system most likely would have an advantage over a batch sales order processing system by

A. Detecting errors in the data entry process more easily by the use of edit programs.

B. Enabling shipment of customer orders to be initiated as soon as the orders are received.

C. Recording more secure backup copies of the database on magnetic tape files.

D. Maintaining more accurate records of customer accounts and finished goods inventories.

Answer (B) is correct. *(CPA, adapted)*

REQUIRED: The advantage of an online system over a batch system.

DISCUSSION: An online processing system can handle transactions as they are entered because of its direct connection to a computer network. Thus, shipment of customer orders may be initiated instantaneously as they are received. Batch processing is the accumulation and grouping of transactions for processing on a delayed basis.

Answer (A) is incorrect. Both systems use edit programs. Answer (C) is incorrect. Online systems record information on disk or other direct access memory devices. Answer (D) is incorrect. Online and batch systems provide equivalent accuracy.

23. Mill Co. uses a batch processing method to process its sales transactions. Data on Mill's sales transaction file are electronically sorted by customer number and are subjected to programmed edit checks in preparing its invoices, sales journals, and updated customer account balances. One of the direct outputs of the creation of this file most likely would be a

A. Report showing exceptions and control totals.

B. Printout of the updated inventory records.

C. Report showing overdue accounts receivable.

D. Printout of the sales price master file.

Answer (A) is correct. *(CPA, adapted)*

REQUIRED: The most likely direct output of the creation of a sales transaction file.

DISCUSSION: Batch processing is useful for processing large volumes of data, especially when sorted in sequential order, for example, by customer number. Editing (validation) of data should produce a cumulative automated error listing that includes not only errors found in the current processing run but also uncorrected errors from earlier runs. Each error should be identified and described, and the date and time of detection should be given. The creation of the file will also generate various totals that will serve as controls over the accuracy of the processing.

Answer (B) is incorrect. A batch system is less appropriate for printing records that require up-to-date information. Answer (C) is incorrect. Testing for overdue accounts receivable should be done prior to approving current sales orders. Answer (D) is incorrect. A complete listing of sales prices would not be found in a sales transactions file.

Questions 24 and 25 are based on the following information. A flowchart of a client's revenue cycle appears below.

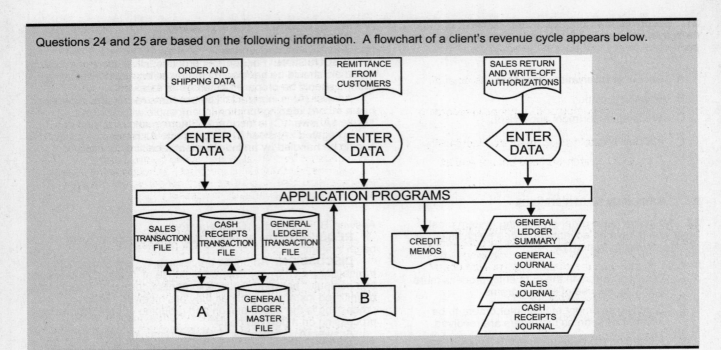

24. Symbol A most likely represents

A. Remittance advice file.

B. Receiving report file.

C. Accounts receivable master file.

D. Cash disbursements transaction file.

Answer (C) is correct. *(CPA, adapted)*
REQUIRED: The file accessed during the processing of a client's revenue transactions.
DISCUSSION: During the processing of sales orders and remittances from customers, as well as sales returns and write-off authorizations, the accounts receivable master file is accessed and updated. Thus, symbol A represents the accounts receivable master file.
Answer (A) is incorrect. The remittance advice file is represented by the cash receipts transaction file. Answer (B) is incorrect. The receiving report file relates to the purchasing cycle. Answer (D) is incorrect. The cash disbursements transaction file relates to the purchasing cycle.

25. Symbol B most likely represents

A. Customer orders.

B. Receiving reports.

C. Customer checks.

D. Sales invoices.

Answer (D) is correct. *(CPA, adapted)*
REQUIRED: The document represented by symbol B.
DISCUSSION: One output of the revenue cycle is the generation of sales invoices to be sent to customers.
Answer (A) is incorrect. Customer orders are entered online and not outputted from the system. Answer (B) is incorrect. Receiving reports are generated from the purchasing cycle, not the revenue cycle. Answer (C) is incorrect. Customer checks are represented by remittances from customers and entered online. However, the customer checks are safeguarded and deposited daily into the bank account.

26. When evaluating internal control of an entity that processes sales transactions on the Internet, an auditor would be most concerned about the

A. Lack of sales invoice documents as an audit trail.

B. Potential for computer disruptions in recording sales.

C. Inability to establish an integrated test facility.

D. Frequency of archiving and data retention.

Answer (B) is correct. *(CPA, adapted)*
REQUIRED: The greatest concern about Internet controls.
DISCUSSION: Processing sales on the Internet (often called e-commerce) creates new and additional risks for clients. The client should use effective controls to ensure proper acceptance, processing, and storage of sales transactions. Threats include not only attacks from hackers but also system overload and equipment failure.
Answer (A) is incorrect. E-commerce sales transactions would not typically result in sales invoice documents. Answer (C) is incorrect. An integrated test facility is just one of many techniques for testing sales processing controls and transactions. Answer (D) is incorrect. Although archival and data retention are disaster recovery concerns, the question relates to controls over sales processing.

27. A CPA is gaining an understanding of the internal controls for a client that sells garden products using an Internet site. Which of the following is **not** likely to be found on the client's organization chart?

A. The sales order department.

B. The shipping department.

C. The warehouse.

D. Computer processing.

Answer (A) is correct. *(Publisher, adapted)*
REQUIRED: The department or process not associated with an e-commerce client.
DISCUSSION: The customer directly communicates the order via the Internet site. Thus, a sales order department is not needed to handle and process the order. Acceptance of the order, collection of payment, and scheduling of products for shipment are largely independent of human involvement.
Answer (B) is incorrect. The products must be stored and subsequently shipped to the customer. Answer (C) is incorrect. The products must be stored and subsequently shipped to the customer. Answer (D) is incorrect. The order processing procedure is handled primarily by computer, and a computer processing department is likely to be found on the organization chart.

Use the additional questions in Gleim **CPA Test Prep Online** to create Test Sessions that emulate Prometric!

6.5 PRACTICE SIMULATION

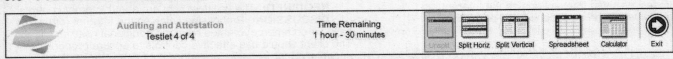

DIRECTIONS

Note: If you believe you have encountered a software malfunction, report it to the test center staff immediately.

Navigation

To navigate from task to task, use the controls at the bottom of the screen. Click on the **Next** button to advance to the next task, or the **Previous** button to go to the previous task. To go directly to any task, click on its number.

| ▼ = Reminder | | Directions | 1 2 3 4 5 6 7 | | ◀ Previous   Next ▶ |

If you would like a reminder to revisit a task, or want to indicate that you are finished with it, click on the reminder flag below the task number. To clear the flag, click on it again. Reminder flags are for your use only – they do not contribute to your score.

Tabs

In this part of the examination, you will be asked to complete various tasks. Every task has one or more **Work Tabs**. Some tasks have one or more **Information Tabs**, others may have none. Every task has a **Help** tab.

If a task has **Information Tabs**, you may use the information in them to complete your responses in the **Work Tabs**.

| Corporate Gain and Basis | Authoritative Literature | Help |

Work tab   **Information tab**   **Help tab**

Work Tabs:
- **Work Tabs** are identified with a pencil icon. This is where your responses are expected.
- Each task has one or more **Work Tabs**.
- **Work Tabs** contain directions for completing the task – be sure to read these directions carefully.
- The **Work Tab** name in the example above is for illustration only – yours will differ.
- You must complete all of the **Work Tabs** in each task to receive full credit.

Information Tabs:
- The Authoritative Literature will be provided in all tasks in the AUD, FAR, and REG sections for your reference.
- Your simulation may have one or more additional **Information Tabs**. Like the Authoritative Literature tabs, **Information Tabs** do not have a pencil icon.
- If your task has additional **Information Tabs**, go through each to familiarize yourself with the task content.

Help Tab:
- The **Help Tab** provides assistance with the exam software that is used in this task. For example, if the task is to compose a memorandum, **Help** will provide information about the word processor.

The Toolbar

The toolbar at the top of the screen shows the amount of time remaining for you to complete the tasks. In addition, the following tools are available. Note that only the Exit button is displayed when Directions are visible - the others will appear when you begin the tasks.

Click on these buttons to split or unsplit the screen. You can split the screen vertically or horizontally.

Click on this button to display the calculator; click on it again to hide the calculator. To move the calculator, click on the calculator title bar and drag the calculator to the desired location.

Click on this button to use the spreadsheet; click on it again to hide the spreadsheet. To move the spreadsheet, click on the the spreadsheet title bar and drag the spreadsheet to the desired location.

Click on this button to go on to the next part of the examination. You must complete all of the tasks to receive full credit. Once you click on **Exit** and confirm the action, you will NOT be able to return to this testlet.

Select from the list provided to match each department or person involved in the sales-receivables-cash receipts cycle with the associated responsibility. Each choice may be used once, more than once, or not at all.

Department or Person	Answer		Responsibilities
1. Inventory warehouse		A)	Prepares sales orders
2. Shipping department		B)	Authorizes customer credit
3. Credit manager		C)	Prepares purchase orders to vendors
4. Sales department		D)	Maintains physical custody of products
5. General ledger		E)	Prepares shipping documents
6. Cash receipts		F)	Prepares customer invoices
7. Mail room		G)	Maintains accounts receivable subsidiary ledger
8. Account receivable clerk		H)	Receives initial customer receipts
9. Billing department		I)	Safeguards and deposits cash receipts
		J)	Maintains the accounts receivable control account

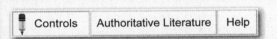

Select from the list provided to match each department or person involved in the sales-receivables-cash receipts cycle with the associated control. Each choice may be used once, more than once, or not at all.

Department or Person	Answer		Controls
1. Inventory warehouse		K)	Safeguards the cash and checks prior to deposit in the bank
2. Shipping department		L)	Releases goods only upon receipt of a valid copy of a sales order
3. Credit manager		M)	Matches copies of documents to ensure that all customers are invoiced
4. Sales department		N)	Checks are immediately endorsed "For Deposit Only" when received
5. General ledger		O)	Only remittance advices are forwarded here for posting to customer accounts
6. Cash receipts		P)	Approved customer orders are required before sales orders are released for processing
7. Mail room		Q)	Goods sent to customers based only on authorized sales orders
8. Account receivable clerk		R)	Goods are paid for only when proper documentation is on hand to support a payment
9. Billing department		S)	Investigates potential customers and their likelihood to pay
		T)	Provides the check balance for the sum of the accounts receivable

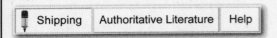

Indicate whether the questions below are likely to be included in the shipping segment of a mail-order retailer's internal control questionnaire by checking the appropriate box.

Questions	Yes	No
1. Are shipping documents prepared from sales orders approved in accordance with management's authorization?		
2. Are sales orders prenumbered?		
3. Are shipping documents periodically accounted for?		
4. Is a sales order copy sent to billing?		
5. Are copies of shipping documents forwarded to the billing and inventory control departments?		
6. Does the credit manager authorize the sales order?		
7. Is the shipping function independent of the warehouse?		
8. Does billing match copies of invoices and sales orders?		
9. Are type and quantities of goods withdrawn and packed for shipping verified by independent counts?		
10. Are receipts from carriers obtained and filed?		

| Internal Controls | Authoritative Literature | Help |

The following flowchart depicts the activities relating to the sales, credit, shipping, billing, and collecting processes used by Newton Hardware, Inc.

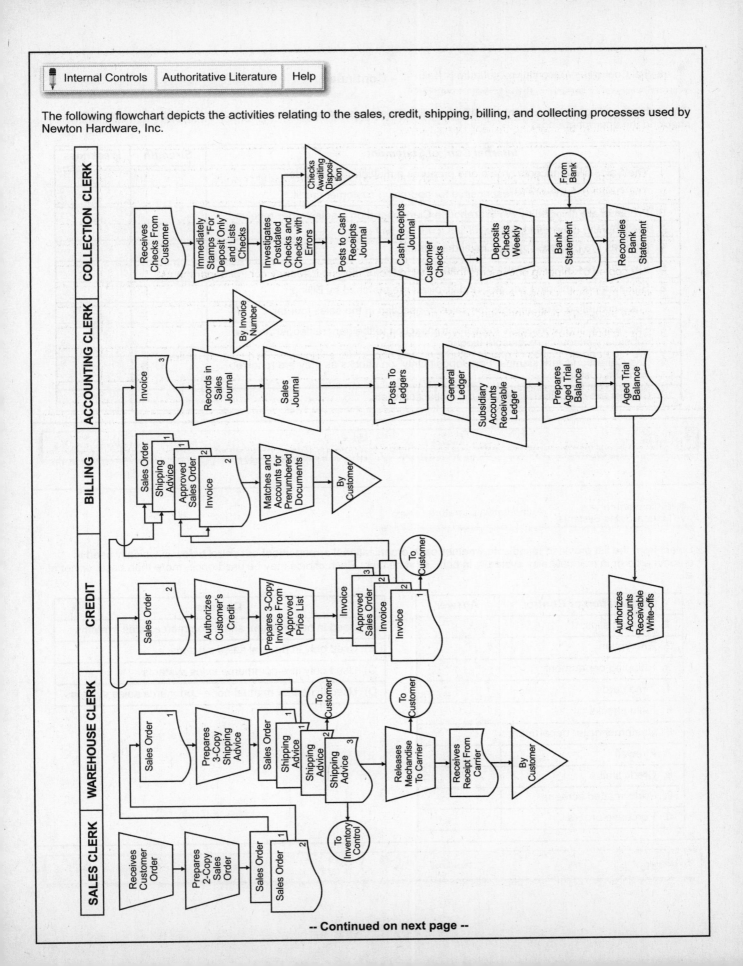

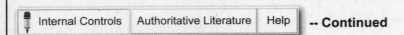

| Internal Controls | Authoritative Literature | Help | -- Continued |

For each internal control statement, classify it as either a strength or weakness in the control system of Newton by checking the appropriate box.

Internal Control Statement	Strength	Weakness
1. The Sales Clerk accepts orders and prepares a multipart sales order.		
2. The Credit department is responsible for approving customer credit.		
3. Products are shipped by the Warehouse Clerk based on a sales order received directly from the Sales Clerk.		
4. Invoices are prepared by the Credit department.		
5. Invoices are prepared based on the approved sales order.		
6. Sales orders, shipping advices, and invoices are matched by Billing.		
7. The Accounting Clerk records the sales transaction in the sales journal.		
8. The Accounting Clerk posts the sales transaction to the general ledger and the subsidiary accounts receivable ledger.		
9. The Collection Clerk stamps "For Deposit Only" on checks as they are received from the customer.		
10. Checks are deposited weekly by the Collection Clerk.		

| E-Commerce vs. Manual Sales Systems | Authoritative Literature | Help |

Select from the list provided to indicate whether each organizational arrangement or control below is typically used in e-commerce or in manual sales systems, in both, or in neither. Each choice may be used once, more than once, or not at all.

Organization or Control	Answer
1. Packing slips	
2. Encryption	
3. Shipping department	
4. Time cards	
5. Field checks	
6. Customer order department	
7. Firewall	
8. Credit limit	
9. Preformatted screens	
10. Purchase orders	

Choices
A) Used in both manual and e-commerce sales systems
B) Used only in manual sales systems
C) Used only in e-commerce sales systems
D) Used in neither manual nor e-commerce sales systems

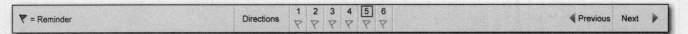

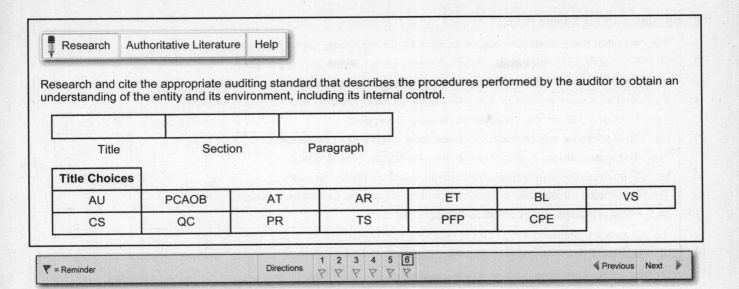

Unofficial Answers

1. Responsibilities (9 Gradable Items)

1. <u>D) Maintains physical custody of products.</u> The inventory warehouse department maintains physical custody of products.

2. <u>E) Prepares shipping documents.</u> The shipping department prepares shipping documents.

3. <u>B) Authorizes customer credit.</u> The credit manager authorizes customer credit.

4. <u>A) Prepares sales orders.</u> The sales department prepares sales orders.

5. <u>J) Maintains the accounts receivable control account.</u> General ledger personnel maintain accounts receivable control account.

6. <u>I) Safeguards and deposits cash receipts.</u> Cash receipts personnel safeguard and deposit cash receipts.

7. <u>H) Receives initial customer receipts.</u> Mail room personnel receive initial customer receipts.

8. <u>G) Maintains accounts receivable subsidiary ledger.</u> Accounts receivable personnel maintain the accounts receivable subsidiary ledger.

9. <u>F) Prepares customer invoices.</u> Billing department personnel prepare customer invoices.

2. Controls (9 Gradable Items)

1. <u>L) Releases goods only upon receipt of a valid copy of a sales order.</u> The inventory warehouse releases goods only upon receipt of a valid copy of a sales order.

2. <u>Q) Goods sent to customers based only on authorized sales orders.</u> The shipping department sends goods to customers based only on authorized sales orders.

3. <u>S) Investigates potential customers and their likelihood to pay.</u> The credit manager investigates potential customers and their likelihood to pay.

4. <u>P) Approved customer orders are required before sales orders are released for processing.</u> The sales department approves customer orders before sales orders are released for processing.

5. <u>T) Provides the check balance for the sum of the accounts receivable.</u> General ledger personnel provide the check balance for the sum of the accounts receivable.

6. <u>K) Safeguards the cash and check prior to deposit in the bank.</u> Cash receipts personnel safeguard the cash and checks prior to deposit in the bank.

7. <u>N) Checks are immediately endorsed "For Deposit Only" when received.</u> Mail room personnel ensure that checks are immediately endorsed "For Deposit Only" when received.

8. <u>O) Only remittance advices are forwarded here for posting to customer accounts.</u> The accounts receivable clerk uses only remittance advices for posting to customer accounts.

9. <u>M) Matches copies of documents to ensure that all customers are invoiced.</u> The billing department matches a suspense copy of the sales order with the shipping copy to ensure that all customers are invoiced.

3. Shipping (10 Gradable Items)

1. <u>Yes.</u> Whether shipping documents are prepared from authorized sales orders pertains to shipping.

2. <u>No.</u> Prenumbering of sales orders does not strictly pertain to the shipping function.

3. <u>Yes.</u> Periodic accounting for shipping documents pertains to shipping.

4. <u>No.</u> Whether a sales order is sent to billing does not strictly pertain to the shipping function.

5. <u>Yes.</u> Forwarding of shipping documents pertains to shipping.

6. <u>No.</u> Credit manager authorization of a sales order is not a shipping function.

7. <u>Yes.</u> The independence of shipping and the warehouse pertains to shipping.

8. <u>No.</u> Billing department matching of documents is not a shipping function.

9. <u>Yes.</u> Verification of quantities of goods packed for shipping is a shipping function.

10. <u>Yes.</u> Filing of receipts from carriers is a shipping function.

4. Internal Controls (10 Gradable Items)

1. <u>Strength.</u> The Sales Clerk should accept customer orders and prepare sales orders for internal processing.

2. <u>Strength.</u> The Credit department should be responsible for approving customer credit.

3. <u>Weakness.</u> Products may be shipped to customers before credit approval. There is no communication between Credit and the Warehouse Clerk.

4. <u>Weakness.</u> Invoices should be prepared by the Billing department.

5. <u>Weakness.</u> Invoices should be prepared based on the products shipped, not ordered.

6. <u>Strength.</u> Matching by the Billing department of the sales orders, shipping advices, and invoices assures that the order was completed and the customer was billed.

7. <u>Strength.</u> Recording is an accounting function and should be separate from authorization and custody.

8. <u>Weakness.</u> Although posting is an accounting function, ideally the general ledger and subsidiary ledger should be maintained by different individuals. The two records should be reconciled periodically.

9. <u>Strength.</u> Stamping "For Deposit Only" (ideally with a bank account number) on checks would help ensure that checks could not be stolen and cashed.

10. <u>Weakness.</u> Receipts should be deposited intact daily.

5. E-Commerce vs. Manual Sales Systems (10 Gradable Items)

1. <u>A) Used in both manual and e-commerce sales systems.</u> Packing slips are used in manual and e-commerce sales systems.

2. <u>C) Used only in e-commerce sales systems.</u> Encryption is used only in e-commerce sales systems.

3. <u>A) Used in both manual and e-commerce sales systems.</u> A shipping department is used in manual and e-commerce sales systems.

4. <u>D) Used in neither manual nor e-commerce sales systems.</u> Time cards are part of the payroll cycle.

5. <u>C) Used only in e-commerce sales systems.</u> Field checks are made only in e-commerce sales systems.

6. <u>B) Used only in manual sales systems.</u> A customer order department is found only in manual sales systems.

7. <u>C) Used only in e-commerce sales systems.</u> A firewall is used only in e-commerce sales systems.

8. <u>A) Used in both manual and e-commerce sales systems.</u> A credit limit is used in manual and e-commerce sales systems.

9. <u>C) Used only in e-commerce sales systems.</u> Preformatted screens are used only in e-commerce sales systems.

10. <u>D) Used in neither manual nor e-commerce sales systems.</u> Purchase orders are part of the purchases-payables-cash disbursements cycle.

6. Research (1 Gradable Item)

Answer: 314.06

AU Section 314 -- *Understanding the Entity and its Environment and Assessing the Risks of Material Misstatement*

Risk Assessment Procedures

.06 The auditor should perform the following risk assessment procedures to obtain an understanding of the entity and its environment, including its internal control:

a. Inquiries of management and others within the entity
b. Analytical procedures
c. Observation and inspection

The auditor is not required to perform all the risk assessment procedures described above for each aspect of the understanding described in paragraph 21. However, all the risk assessment procedures should be performed by the auditor in the course of obtaining the required understanding.

Gleim Simulation Grading

Task	Correct Responses		Gradable Items		Score per Task
1	____	÷	9	=	____
2	____	÷	9	=	____
3	____	÷	10	=	____
4	____	÷	10	=	____
5	____	÷	10	=	____
Research	____	÷	1	=	____

Total of Scores per Task	____
÷ Total Number of Tasks	6
Total Score	____ %

Use **CPA Gleim Online** and **Simulation Wizard** to practice more task-based simulations in a realistic environment.

Update Service

Visit the **GLEIM**® website for free updates,
which are available until the next edition is published.

gleim.com/updates

STUDY UNIT SEVEN
INTERNAL CONTROL --
PURCHASES, PAYROLL, AND OTHER CYCLES

(16 pages of outline)

The initial sections of this study unit describe control concepts in a payment system. Their focus is on a traditional, manual voucher system that requires each payment to be vouched, or supported, prior to payment. This system has many variations, but the objectives and concepts of control are similar. The manual system presented here has most of the elements that are expected to be tested on future CPA exams.

The computer system described eliminates most of the paper flow from the manual system. The objectives of internal control, however, are the same. Only the methods have changed. As always, understanding the concepts rather than attempting to memorize the material is the better approach to learning.

The primary focus of the remainder of this study unit is on payroll. Flowcharts again are used to gain a perspective on the document and information flow. However, the flowcharts are limited to essential points, particularly the payroll computer system flowchart. The narrative should be studied in conjunction with the flowcharts. Candidates should stress gaining an understanding of the objectives of the controls.

Controls related to other accounts, not previously included in the study units, also are covered at the end of this study unit. Only the major controls are addressed, giving consideration to the questions traditionally asked on the CPA exam.

7.1 PURCHASES RESPONSIBILITIES/ORGANIZATIONAL STRUCTURE/FLOWCHART

1. **Management's Responsibility**

    a. Management is responsible for establishing the controls over the purchases-payables-cash disbursements cycle to ensure the following:

    1) Proper authorization of the purchase
    2) Ordering the proper quality and quantity of goods on a timely basis
    3) Acceptance only of goods that have been ordered
    4) Receipt of proper terms and prices from the vendor
    5) Payment only for those goods and services that were ordered, received, and properly invoiced
    6) Payment on a timely basis (e.g., to take advantage of cash discounts)

2. **The Auditor's Responsibility**

    a. The auditor must obtain an understanding of the entity and its environment, including its internal control, to assess the risk of material misstatement and to design further audit procedures. For this purpose, the auditor performs risk assessment procedures. The plan for further audit procedures reflects (1) the auditor's decision whether to test the operating effectiveness of controls over the purchases-payables-cash disbursement cycle and (2) the nature, timing, and extent of substantive procedures.

3.   **Organizational Structure**

    a.   Although some of the following information was presented in Study Unit 6, it has been repeated for your convenience.

    b.   The ideal structure separates duties and responsibilities as follows:

        1)   Authorization of the transaction

        2)   Recording of the transaction

        3)   Custody over the assets (e.g., inventory and cash disbursements) associated with the transaction

    c.   However, cost-benefit considerations may affect the organizational structure, and complete separation may not be feasible. Compensating controls will likely be established when the separation of duties is not maintained. Typical **compensating controls** may include

        1)   More supervision

        2)   Owner involvement in the process

4.   **Responsibilities of Personnel**

    a.   Responsibilities of personnel and departments in the purchases-payables-cash disbursements cycle include the following:

        1)   **Inventory Control** provides authorization for the purchase of goods and performs an accountability function (e.g., Inventory Control is responsible for maintaining perpetual records for inventory quantities and costs).

        2)   **Purchasing Agent** issues purchase orders for required goods.

        3)   **Receiving** department accepts goods for approved purchases, counts and inspects the goods, and prepares the receiving report.

        4)   **Inventory Warehouse** provides physical control over the goods.

        5)   **Accounts Payable** (vouchers payable) assembles the proper documentation to support a payment voucher (and disbursement) and records the account payable.

        6)   **Cash Disbursements** evaluates the documentation to support a payment voucher and signs and mails the check. This department cancels the documentation to prevent duplicate payment.

        7)   **General Ledger** maintains the accounts payable control account and other related general ledger accounts.

5.   **The Document Flow**

    a.   The organizational chart (Study Unit 6) displays the reporting responsibilities of each function in the flowchart. To simplify the presentation, the flowchart does not show the disposition, e.g., the filing of documents, or other supplemental procedures. Some text is added to the flowchart to facilitate understanding of the flow. The flowchart begins at the point labeled **START**. Copies of documents are numbered so they may be referenced through the system.

    b.   Inventory Control, based on the preestablished reorder point, initiates a requisition as authorization for the purchase. The quantity authorized is the economic order quantity (EOQ). One copy of the requisition is sent to the Purchasing Agent (copy 2), and another is sent to Accounts Payable (copy 1). Inventory Control maintains a perpetual inventory by recording both reductions for sales of goods to customers and increases for receipts of goods from vendors.

Purchases Manual System Flowchart

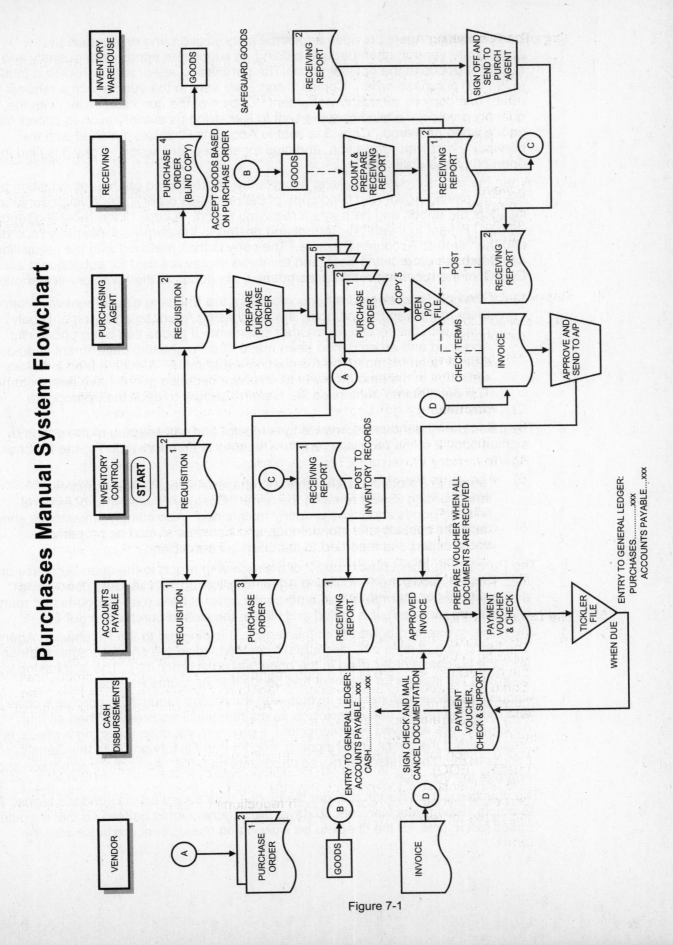

Figure 7-1

c. The Purchasing Agent provides additional authorization and determines the appropriate vendor, often through bidding, to supply the appropriate quantity and quality of goods at the optimal price. The purchasing agent then prepares a multipart (five-part) purchase order. Copies 1 and 2 are sent to the vendor with a request to return one copy as an acknowledgment. Copy 4 of the purchase order (with the quantity omitted -- a blind copy) is sent to Receiving as authorization to accept the goods when delivered. Copy 3 is sent to Accounts Payable, matched with the previously received requisition, and filed for subsequent action. Copy 5 is filed in the open purchase order file.

d. When the goods arrive, Receiving accepts the goods based on the authorization by the Purchasing Agent (the blind copy of the purchase order). Receiving counts and inspects the goods and prepares a receiving report. A copy of the receiving report (copy 1) is sent to Inventory Control and posted to the perpetual inventory records and then sent to Accounts Payable. The copy is then matched with the requisition and purchase order being held, and the three copies are filed for subsequent action. Copy 2 of the receiving report accompanies the goods to the Inventory Warehouse.

    1) If the goods received are nonconforming, the Shipping department will return them to the vendor and notify the Purchasing Agent so arrangements can be made with the vendor for another shipment. If goods had been previously accepted and an entry had been made, the Purchasing department should send a debit memo to the Accounting department. A debit memo indicates a reduction in the amount owed to a vendor because goods have been returned. The debit memo authorizes the General Ledger to debit the appropriate payable.

e. The Inventory Warehouse acknowledges receipt and safekeeping of the goods by signing copy 2 of the receiving report. The copy is then forwarded to the Purchasing Agent.

    1) If goods are produced rather than purchased for resale, the objective of safeguarding assets remains the same. Custody of work-in-process and finished goods should be properly maintained. Accordingly, inventories should be in the custody of a storekeeper, and transfers should be properly documented and recorded to establish accountability.

f. The Purchasing Agent posts copy 2 of the receiving report to the open purchase order file. This file allows the Purchasing Agent to follow up with vendors concerning delivery times and terms. When a purchase order is filled (i.e., all goods and related invoices are received), it is pulled and filed in the closed purchase order file.

g. When the invoice is received from the vendor, it is directed to the Purchasing Agent. The terms (e.g., prices and discounts) from the invoice are checked against those from the purchase order (filed in the open purchase order file). The purchasing agent approves the invoice for payment and sends it to Accounts Payable.

h. Accounts Payable matches the invoice with the related requisition, purchase order, and receiving report, and determines its mathematical accuracy. When all four documents are received and reconciled, a payment voucher, including a check, is prepared (but the check is not signed), and an entry is forwarded to the General Ledger to debit purchases and credit accounts payable. An authorized person should approve the voucher.

i. The voucher is then filed in a tickler file by due date based on the vendor's terms. For example, if the terms were net 30 days, the voucher would be filed so that it would be pulled just in time for the check to be signed and mailed in accordance with the terms.

  j. On the due date, the voucher is pulled from the tickler file and sent to Cash Disbursements. Cash Disbursements makes the determination that the documentation supports the voucher and check. If so, the check is signed and mailed to the vendor. At the time the check is signed, the documentation, (i.e., payment voucher, approved invoice, requisition, purchase order, and receiving report) is canceled so that it cannot be used to support a duplicate payment.

  k. The check is recorded in the cash disbursements journal, and an entry is forwarded to the General Ledger to debit accounts payable and credit cash.

6. **Controls Implemented**

  a. The division of duties for the transaction is as follows: authorization, recording, and custody of assets.

  b. Requisitions, purchase orders, receiving reports, payment vouchers, and checks are prenumbered and accounted for.

  c. Purchases are based only on proper authorizations. Receiving should not accept merchandise unless an approved purchase order is on hand.

  d. Receiving's copy of the purchase order omits the quantity so that employees must count the goods to determine the quantity to record on the receiving report.

  e. The Purchasing Agent compares prices and terms from the vendor invoice with requested and acknowledged terms from the vendor.

  f. Vouchers and the related journal entries are prepared only when goods are received that have been authorized, ordered, and appropriately invoiced.

  g. The tickler file permits timely payments to realize available cash discounts.

  h. Cash Disbursements ascertains that proper support exists for the voucher and check before signing the check.

  i. Two signatures may be required for checks larger than a preset limit.

  j. Cash Disbursements, which reports to the CFO, mails the checks so that no one internal to the entity can gain access to the signed checks.

  k. Cash Disbursements cancels payment documents to prevent their use as support for duplicate vouchers and checks.

  l. Periodic reconciliation of the vouchers in the tickler file with Accounts Payable assures proper recording in the accounts payable control account.

  m. Periodic counts of inventory, independently reconciled with perpetual records, provide assurance that physical controls over inventory are effective.

    1) Internal verification of inventory is independent if performed by an individual who is not responsible for custody of assets or the authorization and recording of transactions.

  n. Accounts Payable examines the vendor invoice for mathematical errors.

  o. Accounts Payable compares the vendor's invoice with the receiving report, the requisition, and the purchase order to assure that a valid transaction occurred.

7. **Other Payment Authorizations**

    a.   This voucher-disbursement system is applicable to virtually all required payments by the entity, not just purchases of inventory as described previously. The following are additional considerations:

        1)   The authorizations may come from other departments based on a budget or policy (e.g., a utility bill might need authorization by the plant manager).

        2)   Accounts Payable would require different document(s) (e.g., a utility bill with the signature of the plant manager) to support the preparation of the payment voucher and check.

        3)   A debit other than purchases (e.g., utilities expense) would be entered on the payment voucher and recorded in the general ledger. Accounts payable would still be credited.

        4)   The use of the tickler file and the functions of Cash Disbursements would not change when other types of payments were made.

Stop and review! You have completed the outline for this subunit. Study multiple-choice questions 1 through 16 beginning on page 249.

7.2 PURCHASES TECHNOLOGY CONSIDERATIONS

1.   Computer processing ordinarily replaces the activities of clerks performing recording functions (e.g., updating the inventory file to record goods received from vendors and updating the open purchase order file). Computer Processing is not shown on the Organizational Chart in Study Unit 6, but it is discussed here.

2.   No physical voucher is prepared, the tickler file is maintained by the computer, and no check is prepared until the due date.

3.   Sophisticated systems may replace the internal paper flows with electronic transmissions.

4.   Ordinarily, the manual files and ledgers are replaced by digital files.

Purchases-Payables Computer System Flowchart

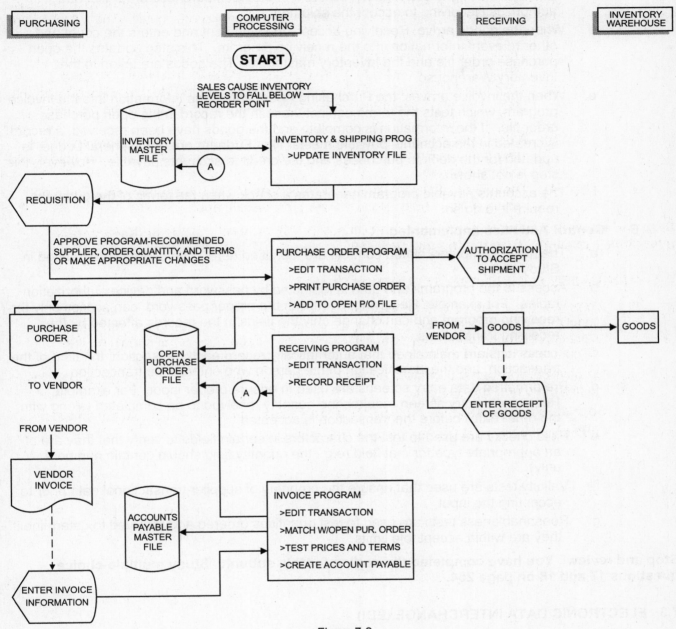

| PURCHASING | COMPUTER PROCESSING | RECEIVING | INVENTORY WAREHOUSE |

Figure 7-2

5.   The Information Flow

a.   This purchases-payables computer system flowchart depicts one example of an online purchasing system. The accounting departments (see the previous flowchart) of Inventory Control and Accounts Payable and the Purchasing Agent's open purchase order file are replaced by Computer Processing. In addition, routine order decisions are replaced by computer programs.

b.   The shipping of inventory for sales orders and the related reduction of inventory on the inventory master file cause inventory levels to fall below the reorder point (beginning at **START** on the flowchart). As a result, a requisition request is transmitted to the Purchasing Agent. The approved vendor, economic order quantity, costs, and other relevant terms are stored in the inventory master file and provided to the Purchasing Agent. The Purchasing Agent can approve the information or make modifications based on current conditions.

    c.   Once the requisition is approved, the purchase order program prints the purchase order for mailing to the vendor, records it in the open purchase order file, and authorizes Receiving to accept the shipment.

    d.   When the goods arrive, Receiving accepts the shipment and enters the count and other relevant information into the receiving program. This step updates the open purchase order file and the inventory master file. The goods are taken to the Inventory Warehouse.

    e.   When the invoice arrives, the Purchasing Agent enters the information into the invoice program, which tests the terms against those in the record in the open purchase order file. If the information is complete and the goods have been received, a record is created in the accounts payable master file. Furthermore, the General Ledger is updated for the debit to purchases and the credit to accounts payable. However, this step is not shown.

    f.   The accounts payable program generates a check when the terms of the purchase require it to do so.

6. **Control Activities Implemented**

    a.   The major computer-related controls are identified here. The controls are defined in Study Unit 5.

    b.   Access to the programs and data is restricted by password and device authorization tables. For example, Receiving, even with the proper password, can access only the receiving program and can change only the fields in the records affected by the receiving transactions.

    c.   Access logs are maintained that automatically record each transaction, the time of the transaction, and the identification of the person who entered the transaction.

    d.   Preformatted data entry screens are used to ensure proper input. For example, Receiving's entry screen requires the quantity received to be completed (along with the other data) before the transaction is accepted.

    e.   Field checks are used to test the characters in certain fields to verify that they are of an appropriate type for that field (e.g., the quantity field should contain numbers only).

    f.   Validity tests are used that ensure the propriety of supplier transactional data prior to accepting the input.

    g.   Reasonableness tests are used to test quantities ordered and received to determine if they are within acceptable limits.

Stop and review! You have completed the outline for this subunit. Study multiple-choice questions 17 and 18 on page 254.

7.3 ELECTRONIC DATA INTERCHANGE (EDI)

1.   EDI is the communication of electronic documents directly from a computer in one entity to a computer in another entity. EDI eliminates the paper documents, both internal and external, that are the traditional basis for many audit procedures.

2.   Advantages include reduction of clerical errors, speed, and the elimination of repetitive clerical tasks. EDI also eliminates document preparation, processing, filing, and mailing costs.

    a.   Moreover, an organization that has **reengineered** its procedures and processes to take full advantage of EDI may eliminate even the electronic equivalents of paper documents.

        1)   For example, the buyer's **point-of-sale (POS) system** may directly transmit information to the seller, which delivers on a JIT (just-in-time) basis.

b. Purchase orders, invoices, and receiving reports are replaced with a **long-term contract** establishing

1) Quantities, prices, and delivery schedules;
2) Production schedules;
3) Advance shipment notices;
4) Evaluated receipts settlements (periodic payment authorizations transmitted to the trading partner); and
5) Payments by **electronic funds transfer (EFT)**.

a) EFT is a process based on EDI that transfers money from one account to another by computer.

3. **Audit Procedures**

a. Accordingly, auditors must seek **new forms of evidence** to support assertions about EDI transactions, whether the evidence exists at the auditee, the trading partner, or a third party (e.g., a value-added network).

1) Examples of such evidence are

a) The EDI long-term contract,
b) An electronic completed production schedule image, and
c) Internal and external evidence of evaluated receipts settlements sent to the trading partner.

b. Auditors should evaluate **electronic signatures and reviews** when testing controls.

c. Auditors may need to consider **other subsystems** when testing a particular system.

1) Thus, production cycle evidence may be needed to test the expenditure cycle.

d. Auditing an EDI application requires consideration of the **audit trail**. In addition to the elements listed above, an essential element of an EDI audit trail is an **activity log**.

1) Because an audit trail allows for the **tracing** of a transaction from initiation to disposition, an activity log provides a key link in the process. Such a log provides information about the

a) Users who have accessed the system,
b) Files accessed,
c) Processing accomplished,
d) Time of access, and
e) Amount of time the processing required.

4. **Value-Added Networks (VANs)**

a. EDI often uses a VAN as a **third-party service provider**, and **controls** provided by the VAN may be critical.

b. VANs are privately owned telecommunications carriers that sell capacity to outside users.

c. Among other things, a VAN provides a **mailbox service** permitting EDI messages to be sent, sorted, and held until needed in the recipient's computer system.

1) **Encryption** of such messages that is performed by physically secure **hardware** is more secure than encryption performed by software.

5. Successful implementation of EDI begins with identifying the work processes and flows that support the entity's objectives.

a. The initial phase of EDI implementation includes understanding the entity's **mission** and an analysis of its **activities** as part of an integrated solution to its needs.

6.   **EDI Terms and Components**

a.   **Standards** focus on procedures to convert written documents into a uniform electronic document-messaging format to facilitate EDI.

b.   **Conventions** are the procedures for arranging **data elements** in specified formats for various accounting transactions, e.g., invoices, materials releases, and advance shipment notices.

1)   To provide standardization and structure for EDI, organizations such as the **American National Standards Institute (ANSI)** have defined virtually every type of business transaction in terms of their fields and information content.

a)   EDI users must **map** their data elements into the standard data fields of each transmission set (e.g., an invoice).

b)   These **transmission sets** facilitate communication between trading partners.

c.   **Transmission protocols** are rules on how each envelope or package of information is structured and processed by the communications devices so that messages are kept separate.

7.   Telephone or other communication lines and modems are used for communication among computers.

a.   **Point-to-point** is the traditional EDI connection. Both parties have fixed computer connections, and the computers are used solely for EDI. The direct connection that is created forces all the computers to be compatible with each other. A point-to-point arrangement is very similar to networks within one company.

b.   **Value-added networks** (VAN) are mailbox-type services in which the sender's and receiver's computers are never directly connected to each other. Instead, both parties to the EDI arrangement subscribe to a third-party VAN provider.

1)   Because of the third-party buffer, the VAN users are not required to conform to the same standards, conventions, and protocols.

2)   Also, VANs can store messages, so the parties can batch outgoing and incoming communications.

c.   The **Internet** is a means of conducting business directly with a trading partner. It can be used in a more open environment in which one firm transmits documents to another.

1)   This approach is often based on less formal agreements between the trading partners than in EDI and requires the sender to reconfigure documents into the format of the recipient.

Background

XML and XBRL will likely change the way we communicate information. Currently, data stored in a database has a structure. For example, the trial balance in Access will have a field for each account, e.g., Cash, with the value stored in the field. When data is taken out of the database, it is difficult to interpret and use without keeping or knowing the structure.

Instead of using a structure, XML and XBRL tag or code each piece of data as it is retrieved from the database so that it can be communicated and then interpreted. For example, the account value may be accessed from the database and tagged as "Cash: $10,000." For now, the CPA exam expects you to understand the uses of XML and XBRL, particularly for financial reporting. Be prepared in the future to gain a much fuller understanding of these languages.

8. **XML (extensible markup language)** was developed by an international group of interested organizations as an open standard usable with many programs and platforms. XML codes all information in such a way that a user can determine not only how it should be presented but also what it is.

   a. Thus, all computerized data may be **tagged with identifiers**. Unlike HTML, XML uses codes that are extensible, not fixed.

      1) Accordingly, if an industry can agree on a set of codes, software for that industry can be written that incorporates those codes.

9. **XBRL (extensible business reporting language)** for Financial Statements is the specification developed by an AICPA-led group for U.S. commercial and industrial companies that report in accordance with U.S. GAAP.

   a. It is a variation of XML that is expected to decrease the costs of generating financial reports, reformulating information for different uses, and sharing business information using electronic media.

   b. The SEC requires issuers, unless specifically excluded, to submit and post their financial statements and financial statement schedules on their corporate websites using XBRL. However, the SEC rules do not require assurance on the XBRL files.

Stop and review! You have completed the outline for this subunit. Study multiple-choice questions 19 through 26 beginning on page 254.

7.4 PAYROLL RESPONSIBILITIES/ORGANIZATIONAL STRUCTURE/FLOWCHART

1. **Management's Responsibility**

   a. Management is responsible for the establishment of the controls to ensure

      1) Proper authorization of the payroll
      2) Appropriate calculation of the payroll
      3) Safeguarding of assets associated with the payment of payroll
      4) Proper distribution of the payroll
      5) Proper accounting for the payroll transactions

2. **The Auditor's Responsibility**

   a. The auditor must obtain an understanding of the entity and its environment, including its internal control, to assess the risk of material misstatement and to design further audit procedures. For this purpose, the auditor performs risk assessment procedures. The plan for further audit procedures reflects (1) the auditor's decision whether to test the operating effectiveness of controls over the payroll cycle and (2) the nature, timing, and extent of substantive procedures.

3. **Organizational Structure**

   a. Although the following information is similar to that in the previous flowchart discussions, it has been repeated for your convenience.

   b. The structure should separate duties and responsibilities as follows:

      1) Authorization of payroll transactions
      2) Recording of payroll transactions
      3) Custody of the assets (e.g., payroll checks) associated with payroll transactions

c.   Duties and responsibilities for payroll have traditionally been appropriately separated. However, cost-benefit considerations may affect the organizational structure, and complete separation may not be feasible. **Compensating controls** will likely be established when separation of duties is not maintained. They may include the following:

   1)   More supervision
   2)   Owner involvement in the payroll process

d.   The following are the responsibilities of organizational subunits in the payroll cycle:

   1)   **Human Resources** provides an authorized list of employees and associated pay rates, deductions, and exemptions.

   2)   **Payroll** is an accounting function responsible for calculating the payroll (i.e., preparing the payroll register) based on authorizations from Human Resources and the authorized time records from Timekeeping.

   3)   **Timekeeping** is an accounting function that oversees the employees' recording of hours on time cards (using the time clock) and that receives and reconciles the job time tickets from Manufacturing.

   4)   **Cost Accounting** is an accounting function that accumulates direct materials, direct labor, and overhead costs on job order cost sheets to determine the costs of production.

   5)   **Accounts Payable** prepares the payment voucher based on the payroll register prepared by Payroll.

   6)   **Cash Disbursements** signs and deposits a check based on the payment voucher into a separate payroll account, prepares individual employee paychecks, and distributes paychecks.

e.   Study the flowchart on the next page. Understand and visualize the payroll process and controls. The organizational chart in Study Unit 6 displays the reporting responsibilities of each function in the flowchart. Read the following description as needed. Note the control activities implemented.

4.   **The Document Flow**

a.   To simplify the presentation, the flowchart does not show the disposition, e.g., the filing of documents, or other supplemental procedures. The process begins at the point labeled **START**.

b.   Human Resources provides authorizations of employees, pay rates, and deductions to Payroll just prior to calculation of the payroll.

c.   Employees punch the time clock with their time cards in Timekeeping before and after each shift.

d.   The shop supervisor assigns employees production-order tasks to be performed, and each employee completes a job time ticket for each task performed. Indirect labor (e.g., down time, cleaning machines, and setup) is also reported on job time tickets. At the end of the shift, the shop supervisor determines that employees have submitted job time tickets to account for all time worked. The job time tickets are then forwarded to Timekeeping.

e.   Timekeeping reconciles the clock cards with the job time tickets to ensure that employees were present and working. Clock cards are approved (e.g., initialed) by Timekeeping.

f.   Clock cards are forwarded to Payroll as authorization of the hours worked. The authorized employees, rates, and deductions from Human Resources, together with the authorized hours from Timekeeping, are used to calculate the payroll for the period. A payroll register is prepared listing each employee, gross pay, all deductions, and net pay. The payroll register is then sent to Accounts Payable.

g.   Accounts Payable uses the payroll register as authorization to prepare a payment voucher and check for the payroll equal to the total of the net pay to employees. (Actually, a number of separate vouchers and checks will be prepared for each required payment generated from the payroll. For example, a check will be prepared with the IRS as payee for withholding taxes, and a check may be prepared with the union as payee for withheld union dues, etc.)

h.   The check, voucher, and supporting documentation will be sent to Cash Disbursements (CFO) for signing. The check for the net payroll drawn on the general cash account is deposited in a separate payroll account. Checks drawn on this special account are prepared for each employee; that is, an imprest payroll checking account is used. The checks are distributed to the employees.

Payroll Manual System Flowchart

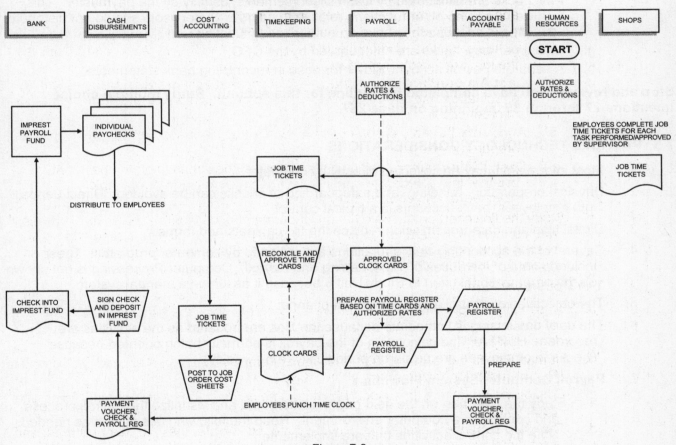

Figure 7-3

i.   The job time tickets, once used by Timekeeping, are sent to Cost Accounting to charge the work-in-process recorded on job cost sheets for the direct labor used in production. The nonproductive labor is accumulated and reported as overhead incurred (not shown on the flowchart).

j.   The accounting entries are forwarded to the General Ledger (not shown on the flowchart). The entry to record the debit to work-in-process is from Cost Accounting. An entry to credit a payable comes from Accounts Payable. When the check based on the payment voucher is signed, Cash Disbursements forwards the entry to the General Ledger to debit accounts payable and credit cash.

5.   **Control Activities Implemented**

a.   Human Resources has no functional responsibility other than authorization of employees, pay rates, and deductions.

b.   Supervisors approve (authorize) work performed (executed) by employees.

c.   The Timekeeping reconciliation of the clock cards and job time tickets ensures that employees are present and working. Punching another person's clock card would be detected because of the absence of job time tickets.

d.   Payroll accounting calculates pay only. It does not authorize transactions or handle (take custody of) assets.

e.   Cash Disbursements signs the check but does not authorize, prepare, or account for the transaction.

f.   Paychecks are distributed by Cash Disbursements, usually by the paymaster. This individual has no other functions relative to payroll. Supervisors should not distribute paychecks because they have an authorization function.

g.   Unclaimed paychecks are safeguarded by the CFO.

h.   A separate payroll account allows for ease in reconciling bank statements.

Stop and review! You have completed the outline for this subunit. Study multiple-choice questions 27 through 35 beginning on page 257.

7.5 PAYROLL TECHNOLOGY CONSIDERATIONS

1.   Most information may be collected directly by computer.

2.   Physical preparation, handling, and safeguarding of checks can be avoided. Direct deposit into employees' bank accounts is a typical control.

3.   Digital files and data transmission replace the file cabinets and forms.

4.   Several of the accounting clerk's functions are replaced by computer programs. These include some of the duties of Timekeeping and Payroll. Computer Processing is not shown on the organizational chart in Study Unit 6 because it assumes a manual system.

5.   The objectives of control, however, do not change.

6.   The daily processing is immediate because the files are updated as the activities are recorded. However, the calculation of the payroll is normally batch oriented because checks to employees are prepared periodically (e.g., weekly).

7.   **Payroll Computer System Flowchart**

a.   Study the flowchart on the next page. Understand and visualize the payroll process and controls in a computer environment. Read the following description as needed. Note the control activities that are implemented.

b.   The payroll computer system flowchart illustrates a system that eliminates virtually all of the paper flow found in the manual system.

c.   Human Resources makes authorized changes in the personnel master file.

d.   As the employee enters the plant, a clock card record is initiated by passing an ID card through a terminal that contains the timekeeping program.

e.   Production orders, based on the production schedule, are released to the shops via terminal. Shop supervisors assign production employees to the tasks. Prior to beginning, the production employee logs in to the system using his/her ID card. When the production job is complete, the employee logs out, thereby updating the production record. Information is passed to the timekeeping program to be reconciled with the time records and to update the payroll master file.

f.   Periodically (e.g., weekly), information from the payroll master file is matched with wage rate, deduction, and exemption information to calculate the payroll. The checks are printed and the general ledger is updated (not shown on flowchart).

Payroll Computer System Flowchart

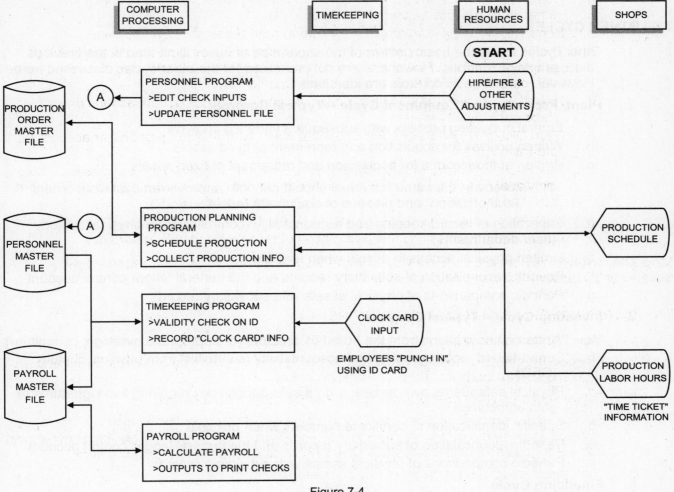

Figure 7-4

8. **Control Activities Implemented**

    a. The major computer-related controls are identified here. The controls are defined in Study Unit 5.

    b. Access controls are used, requiring passwords and identification numbers. Only Human Resources has access to the personnel master file and can make changes. Other departments are limited to the changes that can be made to files. Each shop employee is issued an identification card used as input to initiate timekeeping transactions.

    c. Preformatted data entry screens are used for inputs.

    d. Validity checks are made to ensure that an employee record exists on the personnel file before any transactions are accepted.

    e. Time records from Timekeeping are automatically reconciled with the production time logged in the shops.

    f. Reasonableness tests are made when appropriate, e.g., testing at the end of the week to ensure that total hours recorded for an employee are not in excess of 40 hours or the acceptable limit.

    g. Exception reports are printed, identifying all questionable and potentially incorrect transactions. These transactions are investigated and any corrections are made for reprocessing.

Stop and review! You have completed the outline for this subunit. Study multiple-choice questions 36 through 38 beginning on page 259.

7.6 OTHER CYCLES

1.   Other cycles follow the basic pattern of the separation of duties illustrated in the previous discussions of controls. Flowcharts are not presented for the other cycles discussed here. However, certain basic controls are identified.

2.   **Plant, Property, and Equipment Cycle – Typical Controls**

   a.   Formal budgeting process with subsequent variance analysis

   b.   Written policies for acquisition and retirement of fixed assets

   c.   Written authorizations for acquisition and retirement of fixed assets

      1)   Moreover, the same individual should not both approve removal work orders (authorization) and dispose of equipment (asset custody).

   d.   Separation of record keeping and accountability (controller) from physical custody (user departments)

   e.   Limited physical access to assets when feasible

   f.   Periodic reconciliation of subsidiary records and the general ledger control account

   g.   Periodic comparisons of physical assets with subsidiary records

3.   **Investing Cycle – Typical Controls**

   a.   Written authorizations from the board of directors (or appropriate oversight committee)

   b.   Separation of record keeping and accountability (controller) from physical custody (CFO)

   c.   Physical safeguards over assets, e.g., a safe-deposit box requiring two signatures to gain admittance

   d.   Specific identification of certificate numbers when possible

   e.   Periodic reconciliation of subsidiary records and the general ledger control account

   f.   Periodic comparisons of physical assets with subsidiary records

4.   **Financing Cycle**

   a.   The financing cycle concerns obtaining and repaying capital through noncurrent debt and shareholders' equity transactions. These major transactions are authorized by the board of directors or other ultimate authority.

5.   **Inventory and Warehousing Cycle**

   a.   Transfers of raw materials, finished goods, and costs are subject to cost accounting internal control activities.

   b.   The objectives of internal control include safeguarding assets and promoting the reliability of financial reporting. Thus, internal control includes physical controls over storage, assignment of custody to specific individuals, use of prenumbered documents for authorization of transfers, and perpetual inventory records.

      1)   For example, requisitions and other documents should evidence proper authorizations, quantities, descriptions, and dates, and subsidiary ledgers should be independently reconciled with control accounts.

Stop and review! You have completed the outline for this subunit. Study multiple-choice questions 39 through 50 beginning on page 260.

QUESTIONS

7.1 Purchases Responsibilities/Organizational Structure/Flowchart

1. Which of the following control activities is **not** usually performed with regard to vouchers payable in the accounting department?

A. Determining the mathematical accuracy of the vendor's invoice.

B. Having an authorized person approve the voucher.

C. Controlling the mailing of the check and remittance advice.

D. Matching the receiving report with the purchase order.

Answer (C) is correct. *(CPA, adapted)*
  REQUIRED: The procedure not usually performed with respect to vouchers by the accounting department.
  DISCUSSION: The cash disbursements department, which is responsible to the CFO, has an asset custody function that should be segregated from the recording function of the accounting department. Consequently, checks for disbursements should be signed by a responsible person in that department after necessary supporting evidence has been examined. This individual should also be responsible for canceling the supporting documentation and mailing the signed checks and remittance advices. The documentation typically consists of a payment voucher, requisition, purchase order, receiving report, and vendor invoice.
  Answer (A) is incorrect. The accounting department determines the mathematical accuracy of the vendor's invoice. Answer (B) is incorrect. The accounting department has an authorized person approve the voucher. Answer (D) is incorrect. The accounting department matches the receiving report with the purchase order.

2. When the shipping department returns nonconforming goods to a vendor, the purchasing department should send to the accounting department the

A. Unpaid voucher.

B. Debit memo.

C. Vendor invoice.

D. Credit memo.

Answer (B) is correct. *(CPA, adapted)*
  REQUIRED: The document that purchasing sends to accounting when shipping returns nonconforming goods.
  DISCUSSION: A debit memo indicates a reduction in the amount owed to a vendor because goods have been returned. The debit memo authorizes the accounting department to debit the appropriate payable.
  Answer (A) is incorrect. The purchasing department does not have custody of the unpaid voucher. Answer (C) is incorrect. The purchasing department does not have custody of the vendor invoice. Answer (D) is incorrect. A credit memo is a document indicating a reduction in the amount due from a customer.

3. Which of the following controls would be most effective in assuring that recorded purchases are free of material errors?

A. The receiving department compares the quantity ordered on purchase orders with the quantity received on receiving reports.

B. Vendors' invoices are compared with purchase orders by an employee who is independent of the receiving department.

C. Receiving reports require the signature of the individual who authorized the purchase.

D. Purchase orders, receiving reports, and vendors' invoices are independently matched in preparing vouchers.

Answer (D) is correct. *(CPA, adapted)*
  REQUIRED: The most effective control to assure recorded purchases are free of material errors.
  DISCUSSION: A voucher should not be prepared for payment until the vendor's invoice has been matched against the corresponding purchase order and receiving report (and often the requisition). This procedure provides assurance that a valid transaction has occurred and that the parties have agreed on the terms, such as price and quantity.
  Answer (A) is incorrect. The receiving department should receive a blind copy of the purchase order. Answer (B) is incorrect. It is not as comprehensive as the correct answer. Answer (C) is incorrect. The receiving report is prepared by the receiving department.

4. Which of the following describes a weakness in accounts payable procedures?

A. The accounts payable clerk files invoices and supporting documentation after payment.

B. The accounts payable clerk manually verifies arithmetic on the vendor invoice.

C. The accounts payable system compares the receiving report to the vendor invoice.

D. The accounts payable manager issues purchase orders.

Answer (D) is correct. *(CPA, adapted)*
   REQUIRED: The weakness in accounts payable procedures.
   DISCUSSION: To maintain a proper separation of duties, the purchasing agent, not the accounts payable manager, should issue purchase orders. The accounts payable manager performs a recording function. (S)he should not be able to authorize transactions or have custody of assets.
   Answer (A) is incorrect. The approved vendor invoice and supporting documentation (requisition, purchase order, and receiving report) are retained by the accounts payable function after the payment voucher (and an unsigned check) is prepared and sent to the cash disbursements function. Answer (B) is incorrect. The purchasing agent approves the invoice for payment and sends it to the accounts payable function. The accounts payable clerk matches the invoice with the related requisition, purchase order, and receiving report and determines its mathematical accuracy. Answer (C) is incorrect. The accounts payable clerk matches the invoice with the related requisition, purchase order, and receiving report and determines its mathematical accuracy.

5. For effective internal control, the accounts payable department ordinarily should

A. Obliterate the quantity ordered on the receiving department copy of the purchase order.

B. Establish the agreement of the vendor's invoice with the receiving report and purchase order.

C. Stamp, perforate, or otherwise cancel supporting documentation after payment is mailed.

D. Ascertain that each requisition is approved as to price, quantity, and quality by an authorized employee.

Answer (B) is correct. *(CPA, adapted)*
   REQUIRED: The procedure performed by the accounts payable department.
   DISCUSSION: The accounts payable department is responsible for matching the vendor's invoice against the corresponding purchase order and receiving report. This procedure provides assurance that a valid transaction has occurred and that the parties have agreed on the terms, such as price and quantity.
   Answer (A) is incorrect. The purchasing department is responsible for sending copies of the purchase order to the different departments. Answer (C) is incorrect. The cash disbursements department is responsible for canceling supporting documentation when checks are signed. Answer (D) is incorrect. The purchasing department is responsible for approving each requisition.

6. Which of the following internal control activities is **not** usually performed in the vouchers payable department?

A. Matching the vendor's invoice with the related receiving report.

B. Approving vouchers for payment by having an authorized employee sign the vouchers.

C. Indicating the asset and expense accounts to be debited.

D. Accounting for unused prenumbered purchase orders and receiving reports.

Answer (D) is correct. *(CPA, adapted)*
   REQUIRED: The control not usually performed in the vouchers payable department.
   DISCUSSION: Employees in the vouchers payable department should have no responsibilities related to purchasing or receiving goods. The purchasing department accounts for unused prenumbered purchase orders. The receiving department accounts for unused prenumbered receiving reports.
   Answer (A) is incorrect. Matching the vendor's invoice with the related receiving report, purchase requisition, and purchase order is a function of the vouchers payable department. Answer (B) is incorrect. Signing of vouchers by an authorized employee to signify that information has been verified is a function of the vouchers payable department. Answer (C) is incorrect. Indicating the affected accounts on the voucher is a function of the vouchers payable department.

7. In a well-designed internal control system, the same employee may be permitted to

A. Mail signed checks and also cancel supporting documents.

B. Prepare receiving reports and also approve purchase orders.

C. Approve vouchers for payment and also have access to unused purchase orders.

D. Mail signed checks and also prepare bank reconciliations.

Answer (A) is correct. *(CPA, adapted)*
REQUIRED: The functions the same employee may be permitted to perform in a well-designed control system.
DISCUSSION: The cash disbursements department has an asset custody function. Consequently, this department is responsible for signing checks after verification of their accuracy by reference to the supporting documents. The supporting documents should then be canceled and the checks mailed. Cancelation prevents the documentation from being used to support duplicate payments. Moreover, having the party who signs the checks place them in the mail reduces the risk that they will be altered or diverted.
Answer (B) is incorrect. The receiving department should not know how many units have been ordered. Answer (C) is incorrect. Accounts is responsible for approving vouchers, and purchasing is the only department with access to the purchase orders. The same employee should not approve the purchase and approve payment. Answer (D) is incorrect. The bank reconciliation is performed by someone with no asset custody function.

8. Which of the following questions would most likely be included in an internal control questionnaire concerning the completeness assertion for purchases?

A. Is an authorized purchase order required before the receiving department can accept a shipment or the vouchers payable department can record a voucher?

B. Are purchase requisitions prenumbered and independently matched with vendor invoices?

C. Is the unpaid voucher file periodically reconciled with inventory records by an employee who does not have access to purchase requisitions?

D. Are purchase orders, receiving reports, and vouchers prenumbered and periodically accounted for?

Answer (D) is correct. *(CPA, adapted)*
REQUIRED: The most likely control over the completeness of purchases.
DISCUSSION: The completeness assertion concerns whether all transactions and accounts that should be presented are so included. Thus, management asserts that all purchases are recorded and included in the accounts. A standard control related to the completeness assertion for purchases is the use of prenumbered documents. Items missing from the numerical sequence may represent unrecorded transactions and accounts.
Answer (A) is incorrect. The authorization of purchases concerns the rights and obligations assertion. Answer (B) is incorrect. Purchase orders should be matched with vendor invoices and receiving reports. Answer (C) is incorrect. Reconciliation of the voucher file with the inventory records verifies that recorded liabilities are obligations of the entity.

9. The authority to accept incoming goods in receiving should be based on a(n)

A. Vendor's invoice.

B. Materials requisition.

C. Bill of lading.

D. Approved purchase order.

Answer (D) is correct. *(CPA, adapted)*
REQUIRED: The document on which the authority to accept incoming goods in receiving should be based.
DISCUSSION: A receiving department should accept merchandise only if a purchase order or approval granted by the purchasing department is on hand.
Answer (A) is incorrect. The vendor's invoice does not indicate whether purchase of the goods was properly authorized by someone outside the receiving department. Answer (B) is incorrect. Materials requisition does not indicate whether purchase of the goods was properly authorized by someone outside the receiving department. Answer (C) is incorrect. The carrier's bill of lading does not indicate whether purchase of the goods was properly authorized by someone outside the receiving department.

10. In a well-designed internal control system, employees in the same department most likely would approve purchase orders, and also

    A. Reconcile the open invoice file.

    B. Inspect goods upon receipt.

    C. Authorize requisitions of goods.

    D. Negotiate terms with vendors.

Answer (D) is correct. *(CPA, adapted)*
    REQUIRED: The task appropriately performed by employees who approve purchase orders.
    DISCUSSION: To prevent or detect errors or fraud in the performance of assigned responsibilities, duties are often separated. Approving purchase orders and negotiating terms with vendors are part of the authorization process performed by the purchasing department.
    Answer (A) is incorrect. Reconciling the open invoice file is the accounting department's function. Answer (B) is incorrect. Inspection of goods upon receipt is the receiving department's function. Answer (C) is incorrect. Authorization of the requisition is inventory control's function.

11. Internal control is strengthened when the quantity of merchandise ordered is omitted from the copy of the purchase order sent to the

    A. Department that initiated the requisition.

    B. Receiving department.

    C. Purchasing agent.

    D. Accounts payable department.

Answer (B) is correct. *(CPA, adapted)*
    REQUIRED: The department that should receive a copy of the purchase order from which the quantity of merchandise ordered has been omitted.
    DISCUSSION: A receiving department should accept merchandise only if a purchase order or approval granted by the purchasing department is on hand. A standard control is to delete the quantity from the receiving department's copy of the purchase order. If the receiving clerk does not know the quantity ordered, an independent count is more likely.
    Answer (A) is incorrect. The department that initiated the requisition presumably knows what amount was ordered. Answer (C) is incorrect. The purchasing agent is responsible for authorizing the purchase order. Answer (D) is incorrect. The accounts payable department must compare a duplicate of the original purchase order with the receiving report and other documents before it can prepare a payment voucher.

12. Which of the following situations most likely could lead to an embezzlement scheme?

    A. The accounts receivable bookkeeper receives a list of payments prepared by the cashier and personally makes entries in the customers' accounts receivable subsidiary ledger.

    B. Each vendor invoice is matched with the related purchase order and receiving report by the vouchers payable clerk who personally approves the voucher for payment.

    C. Access to blank checks and signature plates is restricted to the cash disbursements bookkeeper who personally reconciles the monthly bank statement.

    D. Vouchers and supporting documentation are examined and then canceled by the CFO who personally mails the checks to vendors.

Answer (C) is correct. *(CPA, adapted)*
    REQUIRED: The situation that could most likely lead to embezzlement.
    DISCUSSION: Sufficient separation of duties should exist to prevent embezzlement. The cash disbursements bookkeeper has an asset custody function. (S)he signs checks prepared by the accounts payable function after inspecting the supporting documents. (S)he then cancels those documents and mails the checks. The cash disbursements bookkeeper's access to blank checks and ability to reconcile the monthly bank statement are inappropriate. (S)he can perpetrate and conceal fraud.
    Answer (A) is incorrect. An accounts receivable bookkeeper's responsibility is to record entries into the accounts receivable subsidiary ledger. Answer (B) is incorrect. Vendor invoices should be matched with the related requisition, purchase order, and receiving report by the vouchers payable clerk. (S)he then prepares a payment voucher, including a check. The voucher and unsigned check are then placed in the tickler file. Thus, the vouchers payable bookkeeper may approve vouchers as long as (s)he has no access to any other elements of the transaction, for example, approval of purchase orders. Answer (D) is incorrect. Vouchers and supporting documentation should be examined and canceled by the CFO, a person with responsibility for cash payments, to prevent duplicate payments. It is the CFO's duty to have custody of assets. Thus, (s)he should personally mail the checks to vendors.

13. To provide assurance that each voucher is submitted and paid only once, an auditor most likely would examine a sample of paid vouchers and determine whether each voucher is

A. Supported by a vendor's invoice.

B. Stamped "paid" by the check signer.

C. Prenumbered and accounted for.

D. Approved for authorized purchases.

Answer (B) is correct. *(CPA, adapted)*
   REQUIRED: The observation necessary to determine whether a voucher was paid only once.
   DISCUSSION: To assure that voucher documentation is not used to support a duplicate payment, the individual responsible for cash disbursements should examine the voucher and determine the appropriateness of the supporting documents, sign the check, cancel the payment documents, and mail the check to the vendor.
   Answer (A) is incorrect. Each voucher should be supported by a vendor's invoice, but if the invoice is not canceled, it may be recycled to support a second voucher. Answer (C) is incorrect. If additional vouchers are prepared and supported with recycled documentation, accounting for the prenumbered vouchers would not assure that duplicates do not exist. Answer (D) is incorrect. Although vouchers should be approved, unless the documentation is canceled, duplicate payments may be possible.

14. Which of the following internal control activities is **not** usually performed in the CFO's department?

A. Verifying the accuracy of checks and vouchers.

B. Controlling the mailing of checks to vendors.

C. Approving vendors' invoices for payment.

D. Canceling payment vouchers when paid.

Answer (C) is correct. *(CPA, adapted)*
   REQUIRED: The control procedure not usually performed in the CFO's department.
   DISCUSSION: The accounts payable department is responsible for compiling documentation to support an account payable. This approval process is performed in the accounting department.
   Answer (A) is incorrect. Verifying the accuracy of checks and vouchers is a procedure typically performed in the CFO's department. Answer (B) is incorrect. Controlling the mailing of checks to vendors is a procedure typically performed in the CFO's department. Answer (D) is incorrect. Canceling payment vouchers when paid is a procedure typically performed in the CFO's department.

15. Which of the following events occurring in the year under audit would most likely indicate that internal controls utilized in previous years may be inadequate in the year under audit?

A. The entity announced that the internal audit function would be eliminated after the balance sheet date.

B. The audit committee chairperson unexpectedly resigned during the year under audit.

C. The chief financial officer waived approvals on all checks to one vendor to expedite payment.

D. The frequency of accounts payable check runs was changed from biweekly to weekly.

Answer (C) is correct. *(CPA, adapted)*
   REQUIRED: The event indicating that prior-year controls may be currently inadequate.
   DISCUSSION: The CFO's ability to override internal control is a control deficiency. The nature of this action suggests that the CFO may have had this ability in prior years.
   Answer (A) is incorrect. The internal audit function will not be eliminated until the year after the year under audit. Answer (B) is incorrect. The audit committee has not been eliminated or had its functions curtailed. Answer (D) is incorrect. Changing to weekly check runs does not signify that biweekly check runs represent a control deficiency.

16. Which of the following controls most likely would assist in reducing the risk of material misstatement related to the existence or occurrence of manufacturing transactions?

A. Perpetual inventory records are independently compared with goods on hand.

B. Forms used for direct materials requisitions are prenumbered and accounted for.

C. Finished goods are stored in locked limited-access warehouses.

D. Subsidiary ledgers are periodically reconciled with inventory control accounts.

Answer (A) is correct. *(CPA, adapted)*
   REQUIRED: The control most likely to reduce the RMM related to the existence or occurrence assertion.
   DISCUSSION: The recorded accountability for assets should be compared with existing assets at reasonable intervals. If assets are susceptible to loss through errors and fraud, the comparison should be made independently. An independent comparison is one made by persons not having responsibility for asset custody or the authorization or recording of transactions.
   Answer (B) is incorrect. Accounting for prenumbered forms relates more to the completeness assertion than the existence or occurrence assertion. This control provides assurance that all transactions were recorded. Answer (C) is incorrect. Although limitation of access is appropriate for safeguarding certain assets, it does not establish accountability, and locking raw materials and work-in-process inventories in limited-access warehouses may not be feasible. Answer (D) is incorrect. Periodic reconciliation of subsidiary ledgers with control accounts is related to the completeness assertion.

7.2   Purchases Technology Considerations

17. In the accounting system of Apogee Company, the quantities counted by the receiving department and entered at a terminal are transmitted to the computer, which immediately transmits the amounts back to the terminal for display on the terminal screen. This display enables the operator to

- A.   Establish the validity of the account number.
- B.   Verify that the amount was entered accurately.
- C.   Verify the authorization of the disbursement.
- D.   Prevent the overpayment of the account.

Answer (B) is correct. *(CPA, adapted)*
REQUIRED: The effect of displaying the amounts entered at a terminal.
DISCUSSION: The display of the amounts entered is an input control that permits visual verification of the accuracy of the input by the operator. This is termed closed-loop verification.
Answer (A) is incorrect. Displaying the amounts entered at a terminal does not establish the validity of the account number.
Answer (C) is incorrect. Displaying the amounts entered at a terminal does not verify the authorization of the disbursement.
Answer (D) is incorrect. Displaying the amounts entered at a terminal does not prevent the overpayment of the account.

18. A client's program that recorded receiving report information entered directly by the receiving department on vendor shipment receipt included a reasonableness or limit test. Which of the following errors would this test likely detect?

- A.   The receipt was for a shipment from an unauthorized vendor.
- B.   The vendor shipped the wrong item.
- C.   The receiving department clerk entered the quantity of the product received as 0.
- D.   The shipment received from the vendor was past due by 2 weeks.

Answer (C) is correct. *(Publisher, adapted)*
REQUIRED: The error likely to be detected by a reasonableness or limit test.
DISCUSSION: Reasonableness or limit tests are used to test quantities received to determine if they are within acceptable limits. Entry of a product number with 0 received would be identified as probable error.
Answer (A) is incorrect. A validity test should be performed before order acceptance to determine whether the vendor is an authorized vendor. Answer (B) is incorrect. The received products should be compared with the product numbers ordered to determine whether they were ordered. Answer (D) is incorrect. The purchasing department should follow up on past due orders.

7.3   Electronic Data Interchange (EDI)

19. Which of the following statements is correct concerning internal control in an electronic data interchange (EDI) system?

- A.   Preventive controls generally are more important than detective controls in EDI systems.
- B.   Control objectives for EDI systems generally are different from the objectives for other information systems.
- C.   Internal controls in EDI systems rarely permit the risk of material misstatement to be assessed at an acceptably low level.
- D.   Internal controls related to the separation of duties generally are the most important controls in EDI systems.

Answer (A) is correct. *(CPA, adapted)*
REQUIRED: The true statement about EDI controls.
DISCUSSION: In general, preventive controls are more important than detective controls because the benefits typically outweigh the costs. In electronic processing, once a transaction is accepted, the opportunity to apply detective controls is often limited. Thus, preventing errors or fraud before they happen is important.
Answer (B) is incorrect. The basic control objectives are the same regardless of the nature of the processing: to ensure the integrity of the information and to safeguard the assets.
Answer (C) is incorrect. To gather sufficient evidence in a sophisticated computer system, testing controls is often necessary. The RMM may be assessed at an acceptably low level if relevant controls are identified and tested and if the resulting evidence provides the degree of assurance desired regarding operating effectiveness. Answer (D) is incorrect. The level of separation of duties achieved in a manual system is usually not feasible in a computer system.

20. Which of the following is usually a benefit of transmitting transactions in an electronic data interchange (EDI) environment?

A. A compressed business cycle with lower year-end receivables balances.

B. A reduced need to test computer controls related to sales and collections transactions.

C. An increased opportunity to apply statistical sampling techniques to account balances.

D. No need to rely on third-party service providers to ensure security.

Answer (A) is correct. *(CPA, adapted)*
 REQUIRED: The benefit of EDI.
 DISCUSSION: EDI transactions are typically transmitted and processed in real time. Thus, EDI compresses the business cycle by eliminating delays. The time required to receive and process an order, ship goods, and receive payment is greatly reduced compared with that of a typical manual system. Accordingly, more rapid receipt of payment minimizes receivables and improves cash flow.
 Answer (B) is incorrect. Use of a sophisticated processing system increases the need to test computer controls. Answer (C) is incorrect. Computer technology allows all transactions to be tested rather than just a sample. Answer (D) is incorrect. EDI often uses a VAN (value-added network) as a third-party service provider, and reliance on controls provided by the VAN may be critical.

21. Many entities use the Internet as a network to transmit electronic data interchange (EDI) transactions. An advantage of using the Internet for electronic commerce rather than a traditional value-added network (VAN) is that the Internet

A. Permits EDI transactions to be sent to trading partners as transactions occur.

B. Automatically batches EDI transactions to multiple trading partners.

C. Possesses superior characteristics regarding disaster recovery.

D. Converts EDI transactions to a standard format without translation software.

Answer (A) is correct. *(CPA, adapted)*
 REQUIRED: The advantage of using the Internet to transmit EDI transactions.
 DISCUSSION: VAN services have typically used a proprietary network or a network gatewayed with a specific set of other proprietary networks. A direct Internet connection permits real-time computer-to-computer communication for client-server applications, so transactions can be sent to trading partners as they occur.
 Answer (B) is incorrect. The Internet does not automatically batch EDI transactions, although multiple trading partners are possible. Answer (C) is incorrect. The use of the Internet affects the entity's disaster recovery plan. Answer (D) is incorrect. Regardless of the network used to transmit transactions, they first must be translated into a standard format for transmission.

22. Which of the following statements is true concerning the security of messages in an electronic data interchange (EDI) system?

A. When confidentiality of data is the primary risk, message authentication is the preferred control rather than encryption.

B. Encryption performed by physically secure hardware devices is more secure than encryption performed by software.

C. Message authentication in EDI systems performs the same function as separation of duties in other information systems.

D. Security in the transaction phase in EDI systems is not necessary because problems at that level will usually be identified by the service provider.

Answer (B) is correct. *(CPA, adapted)*
 REQUIRED: The true statement about the security of messages in an EDI system.
 DISCUSSION: Physically secure hardware for performing encryption is under the direct control of the client. Software is not easily controlled because it is portable. More control is achieved with the hardware approach. However, in the business environment, most encryption applications rely on software.
 Answer (A) is incorrect. When confidentiality is a concern, encryption and access controls should be used. Answer (C) is incorrect. Authentication relates to authorization, not security issues. Answer (D) is incorrect. Security in the EDI transaction phase is also an issue. The transmission of information to the service provider, such as a VAN, is subject to a variety of problems, for example, interception or alteration, that may not be detected by the service provider.

23. In building an electronic data interchange (EDI) system, what process is used to determine which elements in the entity's computer system correspond to the standard data elements?

A. Mapping.

B. Translation.

C. Encryption.

D. Decoding.

Answer (A) is correct. *(CPA, adapted)*
REQUIRED: The process used in the implementation phase of an EDI system to determine the elements in the entity's computer system corresponding to the standard data elements.
DISCUSSION: Conventions are the procedures for arranging data elements in specified formats for various accounting transactions, e.g., invoices, materials releases, and advance shipment notices. In an attempt to provide standardization and structure for EDI, organizations such as the American National Standards Institute (ANSI) have defined virtually every type of business transaction in terms of their fields and information content. These transmission sets facilitate communication between trading partners. Mapping determines which data elements used by the entity correspond to the standard data elements.
Answer (B) is incorrect. Translation occurs during processing of transactions. Answer (C) is incorrect. Encryption occurs during processing of transactions. Answer (D) is incorrect. Decoding occurs during processing of transactions.

24. Which of the following is usually a benefit of using electronic funds transfer for international cash transactions?

A. Improvement of the audit trail for cash receipts and disbursements.

B. Creation of self-monitoring access controls.

C. Reduction of the frequency of data entry errors.

D. Off-site storage of source documents for cash transactions.

Answer (C) is correct. *(CPA, adapted)*
REQUIRED: The benefit of using EFT for international cash transactions.
DISCUSSION: The processing and transmission of electronic transactions, such as EFTs, virtually eliminates human interaction. This process not only helps eliminate errors but also allows for the rapid detection and recovery from errors when they do occur.
Answer (A) is incorrect. The audit trail is typically less apparent in an electronic environment than in a manual environment. Answer (B) is incorrect. A key control is management's establishment and monitoring of access controls. Answer (D) is incorrect. Source documents are often eliminated in EFT transactions.

25. Which of the following is an essential element of the audit trail in an electronic data interchange (EDI) system?

A. Disaster recovery plans that ensure proper backup of files.

B. Encrypted hash totals that authenticate messages.

C. Activity logs that indicate failed transactions.

D. Hardware security modules that store sensitive data.

Answer (C) is correct. *(CPA, adapted)*
REQUIRED: The essential element in an EDI audit trail.
DISCUSSION: Because an audit trail allows for the tracing of a transaction from initiation to its disposition, an activity log provides a key link in the process. Such a log provides information about users who have accessed the system, the files accessed, the processing accomplished, the time of access, and the amount of time the processing required.
Answer (A) is incorrect. Disaster recovery plans are an important control for any system but do not relate to the audit trail. Answer (B) is incorrect. Encrypted hash totals ensure the integrity of the transmission but do provide for an audit trail. Answer (D) is incorrect. Security of storage is an important control, but it does not relate to the audit trail.

26. Which of the following characteristics distinguishes electronic data interchange (EDI) from other forms of electronic commerce?

A. EDI transactions are formatted using standards that are uniform worldwide.

B. EDI transactions need not comply with generally accepted accounting principles.

C. EDI transactions cannot be processed without the Internet.

D. EDI transactions are usually recorded without security and privacy concerns.

Answer (A) is correct. *(CPA, adapted)*
REQUIRED: The distinguishing characteristic of an EDI system.
DISCUSSION: Organizations such as the American National Standards Institute (ANSI) have defined virtually every type of business transaction in terms of their fields and information content. These definitions are termed transmission sets. When a trading partner sends a transmission set, the receiving computer can expect to receive the specified information in a specified format.
Answer (B) is incorrect. EDI transactions must comply with GAAP. Answer (C) is incorrect. The Internet is frequently used in EDI transactions, but other forms of communication (e.g., telephone lines) can be used. Answer (D) is incorrect. The use of EDI does not eliminate security and privacy concerns.

7.4 Payroll Responsibilities/Organizational Structure/Flowchart

27. The purpose of separating the duties of hiring personnel and distributing payroll checks is to separate the

A. Authorization of transactions from the custody of related assets.

B. Operational responsibility from the record-keeping responsibility.

C. Human resources function from the controllership function.

D. Administrative controls from the internal accounting controls.

Answer (A) is correct. *(CPA, adapted)*

REQUIRED: The purpose of separating the duties of hiring personnel and distributing payroll checks.

DISCUSSION: In principle, the payroll function should be divided into its authorization, recording, and custody functions. Authorization of hiring, wage rates, and deductions is provided by human resources. Authorization of hours worked (executed by employees) is provided by production. Based upon these authorizations, accounting calculates and records the payroll. Based on the calculated amounts, the CFO prepares and distributes payroll checks.

Answer (B) is incorrect. Neither hiring personnel (authorization) nor distributing checks (asset custody) is a record-keeping activity. Answer (C) is incorrect. Controllership is a record-keeping activity. Neither the controller nor the human resources department should distribute checks. Answer (D) is incorrect. The professional standards no longer recognize the distinction between administrative controls and internal accounting controls.

28. In determining the effectiveness of an entity's policies and procedures relating to the existence or occurrence assertion for payroll transactions, an auditor most likely would inquire about and

A. Observe the separation of duties concerning human resources responsibilities and payroll disbursement.

B. Inspect evidence of accounting for prenumbered payroll checks.

C. Recompute the payroll deductions for employee fringe benefits.

D. Verify the preparation of the monthly payroll account bank reconciliation.

Answer (A) is correct. *(CPA, adapted)*

REQUIRED: The audit procedure to test controls relating to the existence or occurrence assertion for payroll transactions.

DISCUSSION: In considering whether transactions actually occurred, the auditor is most concerned about the proper separation of duties between the human resources department (authorization) and the payroll disbursement (custody function).

Answer (B) is incorrect. Accounting for prenumbered payroll checks is related to the completeness assertion. Answer (C) is incorrect. Recomputation of the payroll deductions is related to the valuation assertion. Answer (D) is incorrect. The bank reconciliation is related to the completeness and valuation assertions.

29. The sampling unit in a test of controls pertaining to the occurrence of payroll transactions ordinarily is a(n)

A. Clock card.

B. Employee Form W-2.

C. Employee personnel record.

D. Payroll register entry.

Answer (D) is correct. *(CPA, adapted)*

REQUIRED: The evidence required to verify the existence of payroll transactions.

DISCUSSION: Determining the occurrence of payroll transactions is an internal control objective of the human resources and payroll cycle. The payroll register records each payroll transaction for each employee. Thus, an entry in the payroll register would be reconciled to time cards to test whether the recorded transaction actually occurred.

Answer (A) is incorrect. Clock cards are records of actual hours worked. Using time cards as the sampling unit and tracing them to the payroll register would test the completeness assertion. Answer (B) is incorrect. W-2 forms provide withholding and exemption information. Answer (C) is incorrect. Human resources records contain employment data.

30. Effective internal control activities over the payroll function may include

A. Reconciliation of totals on job time tickets with job reports by employees responsible for those specific jobs.

B. Verification of agreement of job time tickets with employee clock card hours by a timekeeping department employee.

C. Preparation of payroll transaction journal entries by an employee who reports to the supervisor of the human resources department.

D. Custody of rate authorization records by the supervisor of the payroll department.

Answer (B) is correct. *(CPA, adapted)*
REQUIRED: The effective internal control over the payroll function.
DISCUSSION: The total time spent on jobs should closely approximate the total time indicated on time cards. Timekeeping's comparison of these records should provide an independent check of the accuracy of time reported on the time cards.
Answer (A) is incorrect. An independent party should perform the review function. Employees should not review themselves. Answer (C) is incorrect. The payroll department should prepare the payroll transaction journal entries. If the human resources department performed this task, authorization and record keeping would be combined. Answer (D) is incorrect. Human resources authorizes the pay rates used in the payroll calculation.

31. Which of the following internal control activities most likely would prevent direct labor hours from being charged to manufacturing overhead?

A. Periodic independent counts of work in process for comparison to recorded amounts.

B. Comparison of daily journal entries with approved production orders.

C. Use of time tickets to record actual labor worked on production orders.

D. Reconciliation of work-in-process inventory with periodic cost budgets.

Answer (C) is correct. *(CPA, adapted)*
REQUIRED: The control activity to prevent direct labor hours from being charged to manufacturing overhead.
DISCUSSION: Time tickets should specifically identify labor hours as direct or indirect.
Answer (A) is incorrect. Independent counts of work in process for comparison with recorded amounts provide assurance that all inventories are accounted for, but they do not ensure proper classification of the costs within the account. Answer (B) is incorrect. Comparison of daily journal entries with approved production orders only provides assurance that costs are being assigned to production orders. Answer (D) is incorrect. Reconciliation of work-in-process inventory with periodic cost budgets is an analytical procedure that might detect but would not prevent the problem.

32. Which of the following departments most likely would approve changes in pay rates and deductions from employee salaries?

A. Human resources.

B. CFO.

C. Controller.

D. Payroll.

Answer (A) is correct. *(CPA, adapted)*
REQUIRED: The department that most likely would approve changes in pay rates and deductions.
DISCUSSION: The human resources department provides the authorization for payroll-related transactions, e.g., hiring, termination, and changes in pay rates and deductions.
Answer (B) is incorrect. The CFO performs a custody function for payroll-related transactions. Answer (C) is incorrect. The payroll department, which is overseen by the controller, has a record keeping function for payroll-related transactions. Answer (D) is incorrect. The payroll department, which is overseen by the controller, has a record keeping function for payroll-related transactions.

33. In meeting the control objective of safeguarding of assets, which department should be responsible for

	Distribution of Paychecks	Custody of Unclaimed Paychecks
A.	CFO	CFO
B.	Payroll	CFO
C.	CFO	Payroll
D.	Payroll	Payroll

Answer (A) is correct. *(CPA, adapted)*
REQUIRED: The department(s) responsible for the distribution of paychecks and the custody of unclaimed paychecks.
DISCUSSION: Separating paycheck preparation from distribution makes it more difficult for fictitious employees to receive payment. In principle, the payroll function should be divided into its authorization, recording, and custody functions. Authorization of hiring, wage rates, and deductions is provided by human resources. Authorization of hours worked is provided by production. Based upon these authorizations, accounting (the payroll department) calculates and records the payroll and prepares checks. The CFO signs and distributes payroll checks. Consistent with its asset custody function, the CFO should distribute paychecks or cash in a manual system (or make electronic funds transfers in a computerized system) so as to prevent payments to fictitious employees. Furthermore, the CFO, rather than the payroll department, should receive unclaimed paychecks or cash for safeguarding. Moreover, incomplete EFTs should not be returned to any of the other functions.

34. Which of the following activities performed by a department supervisor most likely would help in the prevention or detection of a payroll fraud?

   A. Distributing paychecks directly to department employees.

   B. Setting the pay rate for departmental employees.

   C. Hiring employees and authorizing them to be added to payroll.

   D. Approving a summary of hours each employee worked during the pay period.

Answer (D) is correct. *(CPA, adapted)*
   REQUIRED: The activity performed by a department supervisor to prevent or detect fraud.
   DISCUSSION: The department supervisor is in the best position to determine that employees are present and performing the assigned functions.
   Answer (A) is incorrect. Supervisors should not have a custody function. The paymaster (CFO's department) should be responsible for distribution of paychecks. Answer (B) is incorrect. Human resources should set the appropriate pay rates based on skills and needs. Answer (C) is incorrect. Human resources should identify and hire the appropriate employees and the payroll department (accounting) should add them to the payroll. Human resources may obtain input from supervisors, but the authorization comes from human resources.

35. Which of the following is a control activity that most likely could help prevent employee payroll fraud?

   A. The human resources department promptly sends employee termination notices to the payroll supervisor.

   B. Employees who distribute payroll checks forward unclaimed payroll checks to the absent employees' supervisors.

   C. Salary rates resulting from new hires are approved by the payroll supervisor.

   D. Total hours used for determination of gross pay are calculated by the payroll supervisor.

Answer (A) is correct. *(CPA, adapted)*
   REQUIRED: The control to prevent payroll fraud.
   DISCUSSION: The human resources department should forward personnel changes to payroll promptly to ensure that proper authorizations are used to calculate the payroll.
   Answer (B) is incorrect. Unclaimed payroll checks should be returned to the treasury department (CFO) for safeguarding, not to supervisors. Answer (C) is incorrect. The human resources department, not the payroll supervisor, approves salary rates. Answer (D) is incorrect. The calculation of batch totals in the payroll department is too late in the payroll process to effectively prevent fraud.

7.5 Payroll Technology Considerations

36. Matthews Corp. has changed from a system of recording time worked on clock cards to a computerized payroll system in which employees record time in and out with magnetic cards. The computer system automatically updates all payroll records. Because of this change

   A. A generalized computer audit program must be used.

   B. Part of the audit trail is altered.

   C. The potential for payroll-related fraud is diminished.

   D. Transactions must be processed in batches.

Answer (B) is correct. *(CPA, adapted)*
   REQUIRED: The effect of computerization of a payroll system.
   DISCUSSION: In a manual payroll system, a paper trail of documents would be created to provide audit evidence that controls over each step in processing were operating effectively. One element of a computer system that differentiates it from a manual system is that a transaction trail useful for auditing purposes might exist only for a brief time or only in computer-readable form.
   Answer (A) is incorrect. Use of generalized audit software is only one of many ways of auditing through a computer. Answer (C) is incorrect. Conversion to a computer system may actually increase the chance of fraud by eliminating separation of incompatible functions and other controls. Answer (D) is incorrect. Automatic updating indicates that processing is not in batch mode.

37. In auditing an entity's computerized payroll transactions, an auditor would be **least** likely to use test data to test controls concerning

   A. Overpayment of employees for hours **not** worked.

   B. Control and distribution of unclaimed checks.

   C. Withholding of taxes and Social Security contributions.

   D. Missing employee identification numbers.

Answer (B) is correct. *(CPA, adapted)*
   REQUIRED: The least likely use of test data to test controls.
   DISCUSSION: If wages are not directly deposited into employees' bank accounts, paper checks must be physically distributed by the cash disbursements function. Any unclaimed checks should be turned over to an appropriate custodian for safe storage. Accordingly, the test data approach does not apply to the control and distribution of unclaimed checks. It is a method of testing computerized controls by processing dummy transactions, some of which should result in error listings.
   Answer (A) is incorrect. Test data, some based on false information, may be used to determine whether, for example, hours recorded by the timekeeping function are reconciled with hours logged in the workplace. Answer (C) is incorrect. In the computerized environment, the calculations for withholding of taxes and Social Security contributions are performed by software. Thus, controls over these calculations may be checked by entering test data. Answer (D) is incorrect. Entering information into the computerized payroll transaction system without employee identification numbers is a procedure performed with test data.

38. Which of the following activities most likely would detect whether payroll data were altered during processing?

   A. Monitoring authorized distribution of data control sheets.

   B. Using test data to verify the performance of edit routines.

   C. Examining source documents for approval by supervisors.

   D. Separating duties between approval of hardware and software specifications.

Answer (B) is correct. *(CPA, adapted)*
   REQUIRED: The activity most likely to detect alteration of payroll data during processing.
   DISCUSSION: The test data approach uses the computer to test the processing logic and controls within the system and the records produced. The auditor prepares a set of dummy transactions specifically designed to test the control activities that management claims to have incorporated into the processing programs. The auditor can expect the controls to be applied to the transactions in the prescribed manner. Thus, the auditor is testing the effectiveness of the controls over the payroll data.
   Answer (A) is incorrect. Monitoring authorized distribution of data control sheets detects alteration of data outside the computer, not during processing. Answer (C) is incorrect. Examining source documents for approval by supervisors detects alteration of data outside the computer, not during processing. Answer (D) is incorrect. Separating duties between hardware and software approval will not affect data during processing.

7.6 Other Cycles

39. Equipment acquisitions that are misclassified as maintenance expense most likely would be detected by an internal control activity that provides for

   A. Separation of duties for employees in the accounts payable department.

   B. Independent verification of invoices for disbursements recorded as equipment acquisitions.

   C. Investigation of variances within a formal budgeting system.

   D. Authorization by the board of directors of significant equipment acquisitions.

Answer (C) is correct. *(CPA, adapted)*
   REQUIRED: The control activity to detect misclassification of equipment acquisitions as maintenance expense.
   DISCUSSION: A formal planning and budgeting system that estimates maintenance expense at a certain level will report a significant variance if capital expenditures are charged to the account. Investigation of the variance is likely to disclose the misclassification.
   Answer (A) is incorrect. Accounts payable assembles the required payment documentation but is unlikely to question the classification of the expenditure. Answer (B) is incorrect. Testing the population of recorded equipment acquisitions will not detect items misclassified as maintenance expense. Answer (D) is incorrect. The misclassification would occur subsequent to authorization.

40. Which of the following activities is most likely to prevent the improper disposition of equipment?

A. A separation of duties between those authorized to dispose of equipment and those authorized to approve removal work orders.

B. The use of serial numbers to identify equipment that could be sold.

C. Periodic comparison of removal work orders with authorizing documentation.

D. A periodic analysis of the scrap sales and the repairs and maintenance accounts.

Answer (A) is correct. *(CPA, adapted)*
REQUIRED: The activity most likely to prevent the improper disposition of equipment.
DISCUSSION: Separation of duties reduces the opportunity for an individual both to perpetrate and to conceal errors or fraud. Accordingly, the authorization, recording, and asset custody functions should be separated. Thus, the same individual should not approve removal work orders (authorization) and dispose of equipment (asset custody).
Answer (B) is incorrect. The use of serial numbers to identify equipment that could be sold may detect but will not prevent improper dispositions. Answer (C) is incorrect. Periodic comparison of removal work orders with authorizing documentation may detect but will not prevent improper dispositions. Answer (D) is incorrect. A periodic analysis of the scrap sales and the repairs and maintenance accounts may detect but will not prevent improper dispositions.

41. Which of the following internal control activities most likely would justify a reduced assessed level of control risk concerning plant and equipment acquisitions?

A. Periodic physical inspection of plant and equipment by the internal audit staff.

B. Comparison of current-year plant and equipment account balances with prior-year actual balances.

C. The review of prenumbered purchase orders to detect unrecorded trade-ins.

D. Approval of periodic depreciation entries by a supervisor independent of the accounting department.

Answer (A) is correct. *(CPA, adapted)*
REQUIRED: The internal control activity that would justify reducing an assessed level of control risk.
DISCUSSION: A periodic physical inspection by the internal audit staff is the best activity for verifying the existence of plant and equipment. Direct observation by an independent, competent, and objective internal audit staff helps to reduce the potential for fictitious acquisitions or other fraudulent activities. The result is a lower assessed level of control risk.
Answer (B) is incorrect. Comparing records of assets may not detect nonexistent assets. Answer (C) is incorrect. Reviewing purchase orders is less effective than direct verification. Answer (D) is incorrect. Depreciation is based on recorded amounts. If they are misstated, depreciation will also be misstated.

42. Which of the following questions would an auditor **least** likely include on an internal control questionnaire concerning the initiation and execution of equipment transactions?

A. Are requests for major repairs approved at a higher level than the department initiating the request?

B. Are prenumbered purchase orders used for equipment and periodically accounted for?

C. Are competitive bids solicited for purchases of equipment?

D. Are procedures in place to monitor and properly restrict access to equipment?

Answer (D) is correct. *(CPA, adapted)*
REQUIRED: The question least likely to be included on an internal control questionnaire concerning initiation and execution of equipment transactions.
DISCUSSION: Although access to equipment should be restricted to authorized personnel only, the issue is the initiation and execution of equipment transactions, not custody of the assets.
Answer (A) is incorrect. Approval of major repairs is related to transaction initiation and execution. Answer (B) is incorrect. Use of prenumbered purchase orders is related to transaction initiation and execution. Answer (C) is incorrect. Competitive bidding is related to transaction initiation and execution.

43. Which of the following questions would an auditor most likely include on an internal control questionnaire for notes payable?

A. Are assets that collateralize notes payable critically needed for the entity's continued existence?

B. Are two or more authorized signatures required on checks that repay notes payable?

C. Are the proceeds from notes payable used for the purchase of noncurrent assets?

D. Are direct borrowings on notes payable authorized by the board of directors?

Answer (D) is correct. *(CPA, adapted)*
REQUIRED: The question most likely included on an internal control questionnaire for notes payable.
DISCUSSION: Control is enhanced when different persons or departments authorize, record, and maintain custody of assets for a class of transactions. Authorization of notes payable transactions is best done by the board of directors.
Answer (A) is incorrect. The importance of specific assets to the entity is an operational matter and not a primary concern of an auditor when (s)he is considering internal control. Answer (B) is incorrect. Questions about the payment function are likely to be on the questionnaire relating to cash disbursements. Answer (C) is incorrect. The use of funds is an operating decision made by management and is not a primary concern of the auditor when considering internal control.

44. Which of the following controls would an entity most likely use in safeguarding against the loss of trading securities?

A. An independent trust company that has no direct contact with the employees who have record-keeping responsibilities has possession of the securities.

B. The internal auditor verifies the trading securities in the entity's safe each year on the balance sheet date.

C. The independent auditor traces all purchases and sales of trading securities through the subsidiary ledgers to the general ledger.

D. A designated member of the board of directors controls the securities in a bank safe-deposit box.

Answer (A) is correct.   *(CPA, adapted)*
   REQUIRED: The most likely control over trading securities.
   DISCUSSION: Assigning custody of trading securities to a bank or trust company provides the greatest security because such an institution normally has strict controls over assets entrusted to it and access to its vaults.
   Answer (B) is incorrect. Verification of the existence of securities does not prevent their removal between the verification dates, for example, to be used as collateral for unauthorized loans. Answer (C) is incorrect. The independent auditor's procedures are not part of the client's internal control. Answer (D) is incorrect. Access to a safe-deposit box should require the presence of two authorized persons.

45. Which of the following controls would a company most likely use to safeguard marketable securities when an independent trust agent is **not** employed?

A. The investment committee of the board of directors periodically reviews the investment decisions delegated to the CFO.

B. Two company officials have joint control of marketable securities, which are kept in a bank safe-deposit box.

C. The internal auditor and the controller independently trace all purchases and sales of marketable securities from the subsidiary ledgers to the general ledger.

D. The chairman of the board verifies the marketable securities, which are kept in a bank safe-deposit box, each year on the balance sheet date.

Answer (B) is correct.   *(CPA, adapted)*
   REQUIRED: The control to safeguard marketable securities.
   DISCUSSION: The safeguarding of assets requires physical controls, for example, the use of a safe-deposit box requiring two signatures to gain admittance.
   Answer (A) is incorrect. Proper authorization does not physically safeguard an asset. Answer (C) is incorrect. Independent tracing of purchases and sales to the accounting records ensures proper recording but does not safeguard the asset. Answer (D) is incorrect. Reconciliation once per year is likely to be insufficient to provide adequate control.

46. Which of the following internal control activities would an entity most likely use to assist in satisfying the completeness assertion related to long-term investments?

A. Senior management verifies that securities in the bank safe-deposit box are registered in the entity's name.

B. The internal auditor compares the securities in the bank safe-deposit box with recorded investments.

C. The CFO vouches the acquisition of securities by comparing brokers' advices with canceled checks.

D. The controller compares the current market prices of recorded investments with the brokers' advices on file.

Answer (B) is correct.   *(CPA, adapted)*
   REQUIRED: The control activity to assist in satisfying the completeness assertion for long-term investments.
   DISCUSSION: The items being tested consist of the assets in the safe-deposit box. This population should be compared with the records of the investments to provide assurance that the balance is complete, that is, contains all long-term investments.
   Answer (A) is incorrect. Verification that securities are registered in the entity's name relates to the rights assertion. Answer (C) is incorrect. Comparing canceled checks with brokers' advices pertains to the rights assertion. Answer (D) is incorrect. Comparing market prices with brokers' advices relates most directly to the valuation assertion.

47. An auditor's tests of controls over the issuance of raw materials to production would most likely include

A. Reconciling raw materials and work-in-process perpetual inventory records to general ledger balances.

B. Inquiring of the custodian about the procedures followed when defective materials are received from vendors.

C. Observing that raw materials are stored in secure areas and that storeroom security is supervised by a responsible individual.

D. Examining materials requisitions and reperforming client controls designed to process and record issuances.

Answer (D) is correct. *(CPA, adapted)*
REQUIRED: The tests of controls performed with regard to issuance of raw materials.
DISCUSSION: The internal transfer of raw materials is part of the inventory and warehousing cycle, which encompasses the physical flow of goods and the flow of costs. The transfer of raw materials (and costs) is subject to cost accounting internal controls. These include physical controls over storage, assignment of custody to specific individuals, use of prenumbered documents for authorization of transfers, and perpetual inventory records. Thus, prenumbered materials requisitions should be examined for proper authorizations, quantities, descriptions, and dates. Reperformance of relevant control activities is another possible test. For example, subsidiary ledgers and control accounts should be reconciled by an independent party. The auditor should reperform this control.
Answer (A) is incorrect. Reconciling account balances is a substantive test. Answer (B) is incorrect. Tests of controls over issuance of raw materials do not provide evidence about activities followed when defective materials are received. Answer (C) is incorrect. The question concerns issuance, not storage, of raw materials.

48. In obtaining an understanding of a manufacturing entity's internal control concerning inventory balances, an auditor most likely would

A. Analyze the liquidity and turnover ratios of the inventory.

B. Perform analytical procedures designed to identify cost variances.

C. Review the entity's descriptions of inventory policies and procedures.

D. Perform test counts of inventory during the entity's physical count.

Answer (C) is correct. *(CPA, adapted)*
REQUIRED: The activity for understanding a manufacturer's controls relevant to inventory.
DISCUSSION: The auditor makes inquiries of personnel, observes activities and operations, and reviews an entity's documentation of controls relevant to the management of inventories to obtain an understanding of internal control.
Answer (A) is incorrect. Analytical procedures relate to substantive testing, not the evaluation of controls. Answer (B) is incorrect. Analytical procedures relate to substantive testing, not the evaluation of controls. Answer (D) is incorrect. Test counts relate to substantive testing, not internal controls.

49. Which of the following internal control activities most likely would be used to maintain accurate inventory records?

A. Perpetual inventory records are periodically compared with the current cost of individual inventory items.

B. A just-in-time inventory ordering system keeps inventory levels to a desired minimum.

C. Requisitions, receiving reports, and purchase orders are independently matched before payment is approved.

D. Periodic inventory counts are used to adjust the perpetual inventory records.

Answer (D) is correct. *(CPA, adapted)*
REQUIRED: The internal control activity most useful in maintaining accurate inventory records.
DISCUSSION: The recorded accountability for assets should be compared with existing assets at reasonable intervals. If assets are susceptible to loss through errors or fraud, the comparison should be made independently. Thus, periodic inventory accounts reconciled to the perpetual inventory records provides assurance that the inventory records properly reflect the inventory on hand.
Answer (A) is incorrect. Periodic comparison of inventory records with current cost information may provide assurance that inventories are maintained at lower of cost or market but does not assure the accuracy of the records. Answer (B) is incorrect. A JIT system may provide assurance that inventory levels are maintained at the desired minimum but does not assure the accuracy of the records. Answer (C) is incorrect. This control provides assurance that only goods that are authorized and received are paid for but does not assure the accuracy of the inventory records.

50. Independent internal verification of inventory occurs when employees who

A. Issue raw materials obtain materials requisitions for each issue and prepare daily totals of materials issued.

B. Compare records of goods on hand with physical quantities do not maintain the records or have custody of the inventory.

C. Obtain receipts for the transfer of completed work to finished goods prepare a completed production report.

D. Are independent of issuing production orders update records from completed job cost sheets and production cost reports on a timely basis.

Answer (B) is correct. *(CPA, adapted)*
REQUIRED: The employee functions that permit independent internal verification of inventory.
DISCUSSION: The recorded accountability for assets should be compared with existing assets at reasonable intervals. If assets are susceptible to loss through errors or fraud, the comparison should be made independently. An independent comparison is one made by persons not having responsibility for asset custody or the authorization or recording of transactions. If these functions are separated and an independent reconciliation is made, the opportunity for any person to be in a position to both perpetrate and conceal errors or fraud in the normal course of his/her duties will be reduced.

Answer (A) is incorrect. Employees who have custody of raw materials cannot perform an independent verification of inventory. Answer (C) is incorrect. Employees who have custody of finished goods cannot perform an independent verification of inventory. Answer (D) is incorrect. Employees who maintain inventory records, job cost sheets, and production cost reports are not independent with respect to inventory.

Use the additional questions in Gleim **CPA Test Prep Online** to create Test Sessions that emulate Prometric!

7.7 PRACTICE SIMULATION

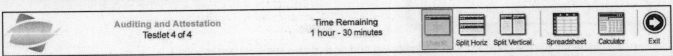

Auditing and Attestation
Testlet 4 of 4

Time Remaining
1 hour - 30 minutes

Unsplit   Split Horiz   Split Vertical   Spreadsheet   Calculator   Exit

DIRECTIONS

Note: If you believe you have encountered a software malfunction, report it to the test center staff immediately.

Navigation

To navigate from task to task, use the controls at the bottom of the screen. Click on the **Next** button to advance to the next task, or the **Previous** button to go to the previous task. To go directly to any task, click on its number.

⚑ = Reminder   Directions |1|2|3|4|5|6|7| ◄ Previous   Next ►

If you would like a reminder to revisit a task, or want to indicate that you are finished with it, click on the reminder flag below the task number. To clear the flag, click on it again. Reminder flags are for your use only – they do not contribute to your score.

Tabs

In this part of the examination, you will be asked to complete various tasks. Every task has one or more **Work Tabs**. Some tasks have one or more **Information Tabs**, others may have none. Every task has a **Help** tab.

If a task has **Information Tabs**, you may use the information in them to complete your responses in the **Work Tabs**.

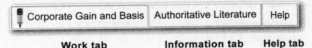

Corporate Gain and Basis | Authoritative Literature | Help

       Work tab   **Information tab**   **Help tab**

Work Tabs:
- **Work Tabs** are identified with a pencil icon. This is where your responses are expected.
- Each task has one or more **Work Tabs**.
- **Work Tabs** contain directions for completing the task – be sure to read these directions carefully.
- The **Work Tab** name in the example above is for illustration only – yours will differ.
- You must complete all of the **Work Tabs** in each task to receive full credit.

Information Tabs:
- The Authoritative Literature will be provided in all tasks in the AUD, FAR, and REG sections for your reference.
- Your simulation may have one or more additional **Information Tabs**. Like the Authoritative Literature tabs, **Information Tabs** do not have a pencil icon.
- If your task has additional **Information Tabs**, go through each to familiarize yourself with the task content.

Help Tab:
- The **Help Tab** provides assistance with the exam software that is used in this task. For example, if the task is to compose a memorandum, **Help** will provide information about the word processor.

The Toolbar

The toolbar at the top of the screen shows the amount of time remaining for you to complete the tasks. In addition, the following tools are available. Note that only the Exit button is displayed when Directions are visible - the others will appear when you begin the tasks.

Unsplit   Split Horiz   Split Vertical

Click on these buttons to split or unsplit the screen. You can split the screen vertically or horizontally.

Calculator

Click on this button to display the calculator; click on it again to hide the calculator. To move the calculator, click on the calculator title bar and drag the calculator to the desired location.

Spreadsheet

Click on this button to use the spreadsheet; click on it again to hide the spreadsheet. To move the spreadsheet, click on the the spreadsheet title bar and drag the spreadsheet to the desired location.

Exit

Click on this button to go on to the next part of the examination. You must complete all of the tasks to receive full credit. Once you click on **Exit** and confirm the action, you will NOT be able to return to this testlet.

⚑ = Reminder   Directions |1|2|3|4|5|6| ◄ Previous   Next ►

Below is a flowchart for the client's current purchasing and cash disbursement transactions.

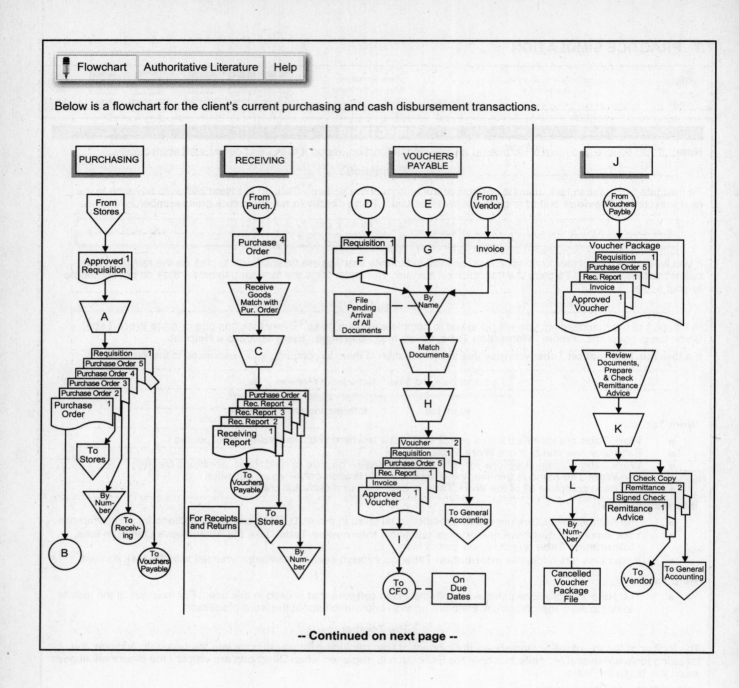

-- Continued on next page --

| Flowchart | Authoritative Literature | Help | -- **Continued** |

Within the flowchart on the previous page are lettered blanks signifying missing information. Select from the list provided the appropriate information for each missing item. Each choice may be used once, more than once, or not at all.

Letter	Answer
A	
B	
C	
D	
E	
F	
G	
H	
I	
J	
K	
L	

Choices
1) Purchase order No. 5
2) Unpaid voucher file, filed by due date
3) Sign checks and cancel voucher package documents
4) File by number
5) Prepare purchase order
6) From Purchasing
7) CFO
8) Stores
9) Receiving report No. 1
10) Canceled voucher package
11) To purchasing agent
12) From Receiving
13) Prepare receiving report
14) Prepare and approve voucher
15) To vendor

| EDI System | Authoritative Literature | Help |

Select the correct phrase from the list provided to complete the sentences relating to a new EDI system and its potential effect on your audit. Each choice may be used once, more than once, or not at all.

Phrases	Answer
1. An EDI system is often used to support the production system of _____.	
2. An advantage of EDI includes _____.	
3. One piece of evidence that the auditor should inspect to assure proper agreements with trading partners is _____.	
4. EDI often uses _____ as a third-party service provider.	
5. Auditing an EDI application requires the consideration of _____.	
6. _____ provides information about users who have accessed the EDI system.	
7. EDI eliminates _____ both internal and external.	
8. EDI messages should be _____ to insure privacy.	
9. Rules on how each "package of information" is structured are referred to as _____.	
10. An open environment would be created when EDI is conducted on _____.	

Choices
A) reduction of errors
B) the Internet
C) transmission protocols
D) a value-added network
E) encrypted
F) the audit trail
G) a written contract
H) paper documents
I) just-in-time
J) an activity log

| Controls Implemented | Authoritative Literature | Help |

Select from the list provided the most specific and appropriate match for each of the following items. Each choice may be used once, more than once, or not at all.

Item	Answer
1. Permits timely payments to realize discounts	
2. Determines that documents support the voucher and check	
3. Examines vendor invoice for errors	
4. Copy of purchase order omits the quantity	
5. Compares vendor invoice with the receiving reports	
6. Cancels payment documents	
7. Mails check to avoid improper access	
8. Required for checks above a preset limit	
9. Assures proper recording in accounts payable control account	
10. Assures effectiveness of physical controls	

Choices
A) Division of duties
B) Prenumbering of documents
C) Purchasing Agent
D) Receiving
E) Cash Disbursements
F) Accounts Payable
G) Periodic reconciliation
H) Periodic counts
I) Dual signatures
J) Tickler file
k) Proper authorization

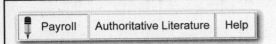

Indicate by checking the appropriate box whether management (column M) or the auditor (column A) is responsible for the following payroll activities.

Payroll Activities	M	A
1. Obtain an understanding of internal control over payroll transactions.		
2. Authorize the payroll.		
3. Calculate the proper amount for the payroll.		
4. Safeguard assets associated with the payment of payroll.		
5. Determine that the controls described in the payroll procedures manual have been implemented.		
6. Assess the risk of material misstatement related to payroll.		
7. Distribute the payroll.		
8. Account for the payroll transactions.		

▼ = Reminder   Directions   1 2 3 [4] 5 6   ◀ Previous   Next ▶

Indicate by checking the appropriate box the responsibility (authorization, recording, or asset custody) of each organizational subunit below.

A) Authorization	B) Recording	C) Asset Custody	Organizational Subunits
			1. Human resources
			2. Payroll
			3. Shops (Supervisor)
			4. Cost accounting
			5. Accounts payable
			6. Cash disbursements

▼ = Reminder   Directions   1 2 3 4 [5] 6   ◀ Previous   Next ▶

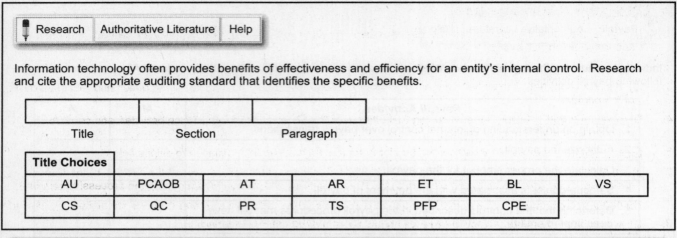

Information technology often provides benefits of effectiveness and efficiency for an entity's internal control. Research and cite the appropriate auditing standard that identifies the specific benefits.

Title	Section	Paragraph

Title Choices

AU	PCAOB	AT	AR	ET	BL	VS
CS	QC	PR	TS	PFP	CPE	

▼ = Reminder   Directions   1 2 3 4 5 6   ◀ Previous   Next ▶

Unofficial Answers

1. Flowchart (12 Gradable Items)

A. **5) Prepare purchase order.** The trapezoid symbol represents a manual (offline) activity. The input is the approved purchase requisition, and the output of this process in Purchasing is the purchase order. Accordingly, the activity is "Prepare purchase order."

B. **15) To vendor.** Purchase order 1 is sent to the vendor of the goods ordered. All other copies of the purchase order are accounted for. The circle is a connection symbol. Thus, copy 1 of the purchase order goes "To vendor."

C. **13) Prepare receiving report.** The goods are received in Receiving, and the output of the manual activity in trapezoid C is the receiving report. Consequently, the activity is "Prepare receiving report."

D. **6) From Purchasing.** Circle D in the vouchers payable section of the flowchart represents documents transferred from some other location. Copy 1 of the requisition and copy 5 of the purchase order came from Purchasing where the documents were previously identified. Hence, circle D is "From Purchasing."

E. **12) From Receiving.** Circle E in the vouchers payable section represents a document transferred from some other location. Copy 1 of the receiving report came from Receiving. Because circle D reflects the transfer of requisition 1 and purchase order 5, the only unidentified document is the receiving report. Thus, circle E is "From Receiving."

F. **1) Purchase order No. 5.** The documents sent from Purchasing to Vouchers Payable are requisition 1 and purchase order 5. Requisition 1 is shown with document F. Document F must therefore be "Purchase order No. 5."

G. **9) Receiving report No. 1.** As noted in the answer to question 5, circle E represents "From Receiving." The document sent from Receiving is "Receiving report No. 1."

H. **14) Prepare and approve voucher.** The responsibility of Vouchers Payable is to assemble documentation appropriate to support a payment voucher. Once the requisition, purchase order, receiving report, and invoice have been matched, a voucher is created.

I. **2) Unpaid voucher file, filed by due date.** The inverted triangle represents a file. The voucher and related supporting documents are filed. The vouchers will be filed by due date, retrieved when due, and sent to the CFO for payment.

J. **7) CFO.** Vouchers Payable sends the voucher and related supporting documentation to the CFO (item J. on the flowchart) on the due date.

K. **3) Sign checks and cancel voucher package documents.** The CFO reviews the documentation in support for the payment. A check is then prepared and signed, and the support for the voucher is canceled so that it cannot be used to support a duplicate payment.

L. **10) Canceled voucher package.** Once the check has been mailed, the supporting canceled voucher documentation is filed.

2. EDI System (10 Gradable Items)

1. <u>I) just-in-time.</u> Just-in-time is a delivery concept where goods or services are delivered only as needed. It is often supported by an EDI system.

2. <u>A) reduction of errors.</u> EDI reduces data entry and typically results in a reduction of errors.

3. <u>G) a written contract.</u> The written contract provides the auditor with an understanding of the duties and responsibilities of the parties.

4. <u>D) a value-added network.</u> An entity using EDI often uses a VAN as a third-party service provider, and controls provided by the VAN may be critical.

5. <u>F) an audit trail.</u> The audit trail allows the auditor to trace a transaction from initiation to disposition.

6. <u>J) an activity log.</u> An activity log provides information about a) users who have accessed the system, b) the files accessed, c) the processing accomplished, d) the time of access, and e) the amount of time the processing required.

7. <u>H) paper documents.</u> The use of EDI eliminates the need for paper documents, as transactions are digitally processed.

8. <u>E) encrypted.</u> To ensure privacy, messages should be encrypted before transmission.

9. <u>C) transmission protocols.</u> Transmission protocols are rules on how each envelope or package of information is structured and processed by the communications devices so that messages are kept separate.

10. <u>B) the Internet.</u> EDI can use private networks or be conducted on the Internet.

3. Controls Implemented (10 Gradable Items)

1. <u>J) Tickler file.</u> Vouchers can be filed in a tickler file by due date based on the vendor's terms and pulled from the file for payment on the due date.

2. <u>E) Cash Disbursements.</u> The Cash Disbursements department should determine that the documentation and voucher support the check before signing and mailing it.

3. <u>F) Accounts Payable.</u> Accounts Payable should compare the vendor invoice with the purchase order to determine that the terms and prices are correct.

4. <u>D) Receiving.</u> The Receiving department's copy of the purchase order should omit the quantities ordered to ensure that the Receiving department counts the goods when received.

5. <u>F) Accounts Payable.</u> Accounts Payable should compare the vendor invoice with the receiving report to determine that the quantity received was the quantity ordered.

6. <u>E) Cash Disbursements.</u> After signing the check, Cash Disbursements should cancel the voucher and documentation so that they cannot be used to support another payment.

7. <u>E) Cash Disbursements.</u> After signing the check, Cash Disbursements should maintain control of the payments until they are placed in the mail.

8. <u>I) Dual signatures.</u> Entities often require large payments to have additional authorization, such as two signatures on one check.

9. <u>G) Periodic reconciliation.</u> Reconciliation of the general ledger accounts payable account with the accounts payable subsidiary ledger helps ensure proper recording.

10. <u>H) Periodic counts.</u> Physical controls to safeguard inventory can be evaluated by periodic counts of the inventory.

4. Payroll (8 Gradable Items)

1. <u>A) Auditor.</u> The auditor is responsible for obtaining an understanding of internal control over payroll transactions.

2. <u>M) Management.</u> Management is responsible for authorizing transactions.

3. <u>M) Management.</u> Management is responsible for calculating the proper amount for the payroll.

4. <u>M) Management.</u> Management is responsible for safeguarding the assets associated with the payment of payroll.

5. <u>A) Auditor.</u> The auditor is responsible for determining that the controls described in the payroll procedures manual have been implemented.

6. <u>A) Auditor.</u> The auditor is responsible for assessing the risk of material misstatement related to payroll.

7. <u>M) Management.</u> Management is responsible for distributing the payroll.

8. <u>M) Management.</u> Management is responsible for accounting for the payroll transactions.

5. Payroll Duties (6 Gradable Items)

1.   A) Authorization. The human resources subunit is responsible for authorization.

2.   B) Recording. The payroll subunit is responsible for recording.

3.   A) Authorization. The shops subunit is responsible for approving job time tickets.

4.   B) Recording. The cost accounting subunit is responsible for recording.

5.   B) Recording. The accounts payable subunit is responsible for recording.

6.   C) Asset Custody. The cash disbursements subunit is responsible for asset custody. It signs the check but does not authorize, prepare, or account for the transaction.

6. Research (1 Gradable Item)

Answer: 314.59

AU Section 314 – *Understanding the Entity and its Environment and Assessing the Risks of Material Misstatement*

Characteristics of Manual and Automated Elements of Internal Control Relevant to the Auditor's Risk Assessment

.59 Generally, IT provides potential benefits of effectiveness and efficiency for an entity's internal control because it enables an entity to:

- Consistently apply predefined business rules and perform complex calculations in processing large volumes of transactions or data.
- Enhance the timeliness, availability, and accuracy of information.
- Facilitate the additional analysis of information.
- Enhance the ability to monitor the performance of the entity's activities and its policies and procedures.
- Reduce the risk that controls will be circumvented.
- Enhance the ability to achieve effective segregation of duties by implementing security controls in applications, databases, and operating systems.

Gleim Simulation Grading

Task	Correct Responses		Gradable Items		Score per Task
1	_____	÷	12	=	_____
2	_____	÷	10	=	_____
3	_____	÷	10	=	_____
4	_____	÷	8	=	_____
5	_____	÷	6	=	_____
Research	_____	÷	1	=	_____

Total of Scores per Task   _____

÷ Total Number of Tasks   6

Total Score   _____%

Use **CPA Gleim Online** and **Simulation Wizard** to practice more task-based simulations in a realistic environment.

STUDY UNIT EIGHT
RESPONSES TO ASSESSED RISKS

(13 pages of outline)

To reduce audit risk to an acceptable level, the auditor makes overall responses to the assessed risks of material misstatement at the financial statement level. At the relevant assertion level, the auditor responds by designing and performing further audit procedures (tests of controls and substantive procedures). These responses must be consistent with the third standard of field work:

> The auditor must obtain sufficient appropriate evidence by performing audit procedures to afford a reasonable basis for an opinion regarding the financial statements under audit.

If the candidate has difficulty understanding the conceptual issues in this study unit, (s)he should review the material in Study Units 5 through 7 before continuing.

8.1 ASSESSING RISKS OF MATERIAL MISSTATEMENT

1. The risk of material misstatement (RMM) is the combined assessment of **inherent risk** and **control risk**.

2. At the financial statement and relevant assertion levels, the auditor should identify **risks and relevant controls**. This occurs while the auditor is obtaining the understanding of the entity and its environment, including its internal control, and considering the classes of transactions, balances, and disclosures.

   a. Risks should be related to the threats at the **relevant assertion level**.

   b. The auditor considers the **magnitude** of the risks and the **likelihood** of material misstatement.

   c. As a basis for the risk assessment, the auditor uses audit evidence gathered from obtaining the understanding, including that from

      1) **Evaluating the design of controls** and
      2) Determining whether they have been **implemented**.

   d. The risk assessment is used to determine the nature, timing, and extent of **further audit procedures**.

   e. If the risk assessment is based on the **expectation** that controls are operating effectively at the relevant assertion level, the auditor **tests suitably designed controls**.

   f. The auditor determines whether the risks relate to

      1) Specific relevant assertions
      2) The statements as a whole

         a) Risks at the statement level often indicate a weak **control environment**.

            i) Such a weakness may affect numerous relevant assertions, and the auditor may need to make an **overall response**.

g. The auditor **identifies controls** related to risks and specific relevant assertions.

1) Some controls may specifically and directly affect an assertion. Others may reduce a risk only indirectly and in conjunction with numerous other controls.

a) For example, controls over handling of cash receipts directly affect the completeness assertion.

i) However, a condensed report on merchandise sales is less directly related to the valuation assertion than requiring credit approval by an appropriate manager.

3. **Significant Risks**

a. As part of the assessment of RMMs, an auditor identifies the risks that require **special audit consideration**.

b. The auditor's professional judgment about significance is based on **inherent risk** prior to considering the effect of identified controls.

c. This judgment also is based on

1) The nature, magnitude, and likelihood of the risk and
2) The potential for pervasive effects.

d. A risk is more likely to be significant when it involves the following:

1) A risk of fraud
2) Recent significant developments (e.g., economic)
3) A complex transaction
4) A related party transaction
5) A high degree of subjectivity or uncertainty in a financial measure
6) A nonroutine (unusual and infrequent) transaction

e. Significant risks frequently arise from nonroutine transactions and judgmental matters. But these are less likely to be governed by routine controls.

1) RMMs related to **significant nonroutine transactions** may be greater if they result from, among other things, the following:

a) Increased manual intervention for data processing
b) Increased management intervention to determine accounting practices
c) Difficult accounting principles
d) Transactions with related parties
e) Transactions for which implementing controls is difficult

2) RMMs related to **significant judgmental matters** may be greater if they involve **accounting estimates** resulting from, among other things, the following:

a) Accounting principles subject to different interpretations
b) Subjective or complex judgments
c) Significant assumptions

f. The auditor responds to a significant risk by performing substantive procedures in addition to evaluating the design of relevant controls and determining whether they have been implemented.

4. **Insufficiency of Substantive Procedures**

a. The auditor may be unable to obtain sufficient appropriate audit evidence about some relevant assertions by applying substantive procedures alone.

1) For example, routine transactions may be highly automated, and audit evidence may not exist in manual form. Thus, **tests of controls** may be essential.

5. The assessment of RMMs at the relevant assertion level may need to be revised as more audit evidence is gathered.

Stop and review! You have completed the outline for this subunit. Study multiple-choice questions 1 through 4 beginning on page 286.

8.2 AUDITOR'S RESPONSE TO RISKS

1. **Financial Statement Level**

   a. **Overall responses** apply to the assessed RMMs at the financial statement level. The following are examples of overall responses:

      1) An emphasis on professional skepticism in evidence gathering and evaluation
      2) Increased supervision
      3) Assignment of staff with greater experience or expertise
      4) Greater unpredictability in the choice of further audit procedures
      5) Performance of substantive procedures at the end of the period

   b. The assessment of the RMMs depends on the understanding of the **control environment**.

      1) An **effective** control environment increases the reliability of internally generated audit evidence.
      2) **Weaknesses** in the control environment lead to a response that may include, for example,

         a) Seeking more evidence from substantive procedures.
         b) Obtaining more persuasive evidence.
         c) Expanding the engagement's scope to audit more locations.

   c. Overall responses relate to the **general approach** to the audit. Thus,

      1) A **substantive audit approach** is based on substantive procedures.
      2) A **combined audit approach** applies tests of controls and substantive procedures.

2. **Relevant Assertion Level**

   a. The nature, timing, and extent of the auditor's **further audit procedures** should respond to the assessed RMMs at the relevant assertion level.
   b. The procedures and the assessed RMMs should be clearly connected.
   c. The most important factor in the response is the nature of the procedures.

      1) Procedures must be relevant to the RMMs and reliable.

   d. The **design** of further audit procedures should consider the following, among other things:

      1) Risk significance
      2) Likelihood of a material misstatement
      3) Characteristics of the transaction class, balance, or disclosure
      4) Nature of the controls (e.g., automated or manual)
      5) Extent of the expectation of obtaining evidence of the effectiveness of controls

3. **Audit Approach**

   a. The assessment of risks is a basis for choosing the audit approach.
   b. For example, the **risk assessment procedures** may not identify effective controls for the relevant assertion, or testing controls may be **inefficient**. The result is that controls are not a factor in the risk assessment.

      1) In these cases, if the auditor adopts the **substantive audit approach**, (s)he needs to be satisfied that it will be effective in reducing **detection risk** to an acceptable level.

         a) For example, the substantive audit approach may not be feasible when the processing of routine transactions is highly automated with little manual intervention. In this case, the **combined audit approach** is chosen.

c.   The auditor should design and perform some **substantive procedures** regardless of the assessment of the RMM or the choice of audit approach.

1)   **Tests of controls** by themselves ordinarily are insufficient to eliminate the RMM.

2)   **Analytical procedures** applied as substantive procedures also may be insufficient.

4.   **Nature of Further Procedures**

a.   The nature of further procedures is a function of purpose and type.

1)   **Purpose** – substantive procedures or tests of controls

2)   **Type** – inspection, observation, inquiry, confirmation, recalculation, reperformance, or analytical procedures

b.   The **choice of audit procedures** depends on the following:

1)   The **Relevant Assertion**

a)   For example, a test of controls may be preferable for the completeness assertion about sales.

2)   The **RMM**

a)   For a high RMM, the evidence must be more appropriate **(relevant and reliable)**. Thus, the auditor may seek external confirmation in addition to inspecting internally generated documents and inquiring of management.

3)   **Reasons for the Assessment of the RMM**

a)   The auditor considers the **inherent risk** (particular characteristics) of each transaction class, balance, or disclosure.

b)   The auditor also considers whether the assessment reflects **control risk**.

i)   For example, a lower RMM for a transaction class because of its characteristics may justify performing only substantive analytical procedures. But if a lower RMM is based on the effectiveness of controls, and substantive procedures are designed accordingly, tests of controls should be performed.

c)   The auditor tests the **accuracy** and **completeness** of information generated by the information system if it is used in applying procedures.

5.   **Timing of Further Procedures**

a.   The greater the RMM, the more likely that procedures will be performed at the **end of the period** or at unpredictable times.

1)   However, **earlier performance of procedures** may identify significant issues in time to permit their resolution with the aid of management or design of an effective audit approach.

b.   Performing procedures before the end of the period should result in consideration of the **additional evidence** needed to address the **remaining period**.

c.   The timing of procedures is based on considerations such as the following:

1)   The relevant period or date
2)   Availability of information
3)   Nature of the risk
4)   The control environment

d.   Some procedures are performed only **at or after** the end of the period, for example, cutoff procedures, comparing financial statement amounts with accounting records, or examining adjustments of the statements.

6.   **Extent of Further Procedures**

    a.   The extent of a procedure is its **quantity**, such as the number of sampled items. The auditor's judgment about extent is based on

        1)   The desired level of assurance,
        2)   The assessed RMM, and
        3)   The tolerable misstatement.

    b.   The use of **computer-assisted audit techniques (CAATs)** may expand the extent of procedures. For example, they may be applied to the whole population of relevant items.

        1)   But **sampling** is often appropriate if statistically sound methods are employed. See Study Unit 15.

7.   **Tests of Controls**

    a.   The auditor tests **suitably designed** controls at the relevant assertion level in two circumstances:

        1)   The risk assessment is based on the **expectation** that controls are operating with some degree of **effectiveness**.

        2)   **Substantive procedures** are inadequate by themselves to obtain sufficient appropriate evidence.

    b.   Accordingly, tests of controls are performed when necessary to reduce **detection risks** to an **acceptably low level**.

        1)   A situation requiring tests of controls is IT processing of routine, high-volume transactions with little manual intervention or hardcopy documentation.

    c.   Performing **risk assessment procedures** to obtain an **understanding** of the entity and its environment involves, among other things, evaluating the **design** of controls and determining whether they have been **implemented**.

        1)   Testing controls takes the additional step of obtaining evidence about their **operating effectiveness**. The evidence addresses such matters as the following:

            a)   How controls were applied at relevant times
            b)   By whom they were applied
            c)   The consistency of their application

    d.   Evaluating design and determining implementation also may serve as a **test of operating effectiveness**.

        1)   For example, if IT general controls are effective, determining that an IT processing control has been implemented also tests effectiveness.

8.   **Nature of Tests of Controls**

    a.   The audit approach may be based primarily on tests of controls. In this case, a **higher level of assurance** of effectiveness should be sought. Tests of controls typically include the following:

        1)   Inquiry
        2)   Inspection (e.g., of electronic files)
        3)   Observation
        4)   Reperformance

    b.   **Inquiry alone** is not a sufficient procedure. Thus, a combination of procedures should be performed.

        1)   A combination of procedures consisting of inquiry and reperformance or inspection normally provides more assurance than inquiry and observation.

    c.   The **nature of the control** affects the selection of a procedure.

        1)   For example, **documentation** may be inspected.

            a)   But in its absence, such as when a control is performed by a computer, inquiry may need to be combined with observation or CAATs.

    d.   The auditor considers obtaining evidence about **direct and indirect controls**.

        1)   For example, the control group's review of an exception report is a direct control over IT processing supported by indirect controls (general controls and application controls).

    e.   The auditor may apply **dual-purpose tests**.

        1)   These meet the objectives of **tests of details of transactions** as well as **tests of controls**.

    f.   Misstatements detected by **substantive procedures** may imply that controls are ineffective.

        1)   But nondetection of misstatements is not evidence of effectiveness.

9.   **Timing of Tests of Controls**

    a.   Timing depends on whether the **objective** is to test controls at a moment in time or for a period.

        1)   For example, a year-end test of controls over property, plant, and equipment may be sufficient.

        2)   However, a test at a moment in time of a programmed control over transactions reported in the income statement ordinarily should be combined with other tests. These include procedures to verify **consistent operation** for the reporting period, e.g., change controls.

    b.   When tests are conducted at an **interim period**, the auditor should determine procedures to be performed during the **remaining period**. The auditor considers the following:

        1)   Assessed RMMs
        2)   Controls tested
        3)   The evidence about operating effectiveness
        4)   The duration of the remaining period
        5)   Any intended reduction of substantive procedures
        6)   The control environment
        7)   Significant changes in internal control

    c.   Procedures should be performed to determine the relevance of audit evidence from **prior audits**.

        1)   For example, the auditor should verify that **changes** in an effective control have not been made that impair its functioning.

        2)   Furthermore, the auditor may not rely on evidence from a prior audit about a control intended to reduce a **significant risk**.

        3)   If the auditor plans to rely on controls that have not changed (other than those related to significant risks), they should be tested **at least once every third year**.

        4)   In determining whether to rely on audit evidence from a prior audit, the auditor considers matters such as the following:

            a)   The RMM and extent of reliance on the control
            b)   Other components of internal control (e.g., the control environment)
            c)   IT general controls

        5)   At least some controls should be **tested every year** when the auditor judges that prior-audit evidence may be used for multiple controls.

10. **Extent of Tests of Controls**

    a.   The following are considered in determining extent:

        1)   Frequency of use
        2)   Expected control deviations
        3)   Relevance and reliability of needed evidence
        4)   Evidence from tests of other controls
        5)   Planned reliance on the control
        6)   Time during the period for which reliance is sought

    b.   **Audit sampling** should be considered when a control is used frequently.

    c.   The extent of tests of controls **increases** with increases in

        1)   Reliance on their operating effectiveness in the assessment of RMMs
        2)   The expected deviation

11. **Substantive Procedures**

    a.   Substantive procedures are performed to detect material misstatements at the relevant assertion level.

        1)   They should respond to the related **assessed RMM** and **planned level of detection risk**.

    b.   The auditor should apply substantive procedures to **all relevant assertions** about material transaction classes, balances, and disclosures.

    c.   The auditor should

        1)   Examine material **entries** and other adjustments made in statement preparation.
        2)   Agree the **statements** to the **accounting records**.

    d.   The auditor should evaluate the qualitative aspects of the company's accounting practices, including

        1)   Selective correction of misstatements
        2)   Proposed additional adjusting entries that offset misstatements accumulated by the auditor
        3)   Bias in the selection of accounting principles or in accounting estimates

    e.   Substantive procedures should be performed that respond specifically and with a high degree of reliability to **significant risks**.

        1)   For example, management may have an incentive to recognize revenue prematurely. The specific response may be to (a) seek external confirmation of the terms of sales agreements (e.g., dates, delivery information, and rights of return) and (b) inquire of nonfinancial employees about changes in such agreements.

12. **Nature of Substantive Procedures**

    a.   They include **tests of details** and **substantive analytical procedures**.

        1)   Tests of details normally should be applied to certain assertions about balances, e.g., **existence** and **valuation**.
        2)   Analytical procedures are most often applied to high-volume, relatively **predictable** transactions.

            a)   For a full outline, see Study Unit 3.

    b.   Analytical procedures alone may suffice to reduce **planned detection risk** to an acceptable level.

        1)   For example, the assessed RMM may have been reduced by **tests of controls**.
        2)   The best responses in other cases may be to perform (a) tests of details only or (b) a combination of the types of procedures.

c. **Existence or occurrence assertion.** The auditor chooses items from a financial statement amount for testing.

d. **Completeness assertion.** The auditor seeks evidence that an item should be and is included in a financial statement amount.

    1) For example, an auditor may compare cash payments with accounts payable to test for unrecorded liabilities.

e. The auditor should consider tests of controls over the **data used** to perform **analytical procedures**.

    1) The risk of **management override of controls** is especially pertinent. It may affect the relationship on which such procedures are based.

        a) Thus, analytical procedures may not be able to detect certain frauds.

    2) The auditor also may consider whether the accuracy and completeness of the data have been audited, especially that generated by the entity's **information system**.

13. **Timing of Substantive Procedures**

a. An auditor who performs procedures at an **interim date** should cover the **remaining period**.

    1) For this purpose, the auditor performs

        a) Further substantive procedures or

        b) A combination of substantive procedures and tests of controls.

    2) If neither option suffices, substantive procedures should be performed at the end of the period.

b. The longer the remaining period, the **greater the detection risk** resulting from performing procedures at an interim date. Accordingly, the auditor should consider, among other things, the following:

    1) Relevant controls, including the control environment
    2) Availability of information at the end of the remaining period
    3) Objective of the procedure
    4) Assessed RMM
    5) Nature of the transaction class or balance and relevant assertions
    6) Ability to reduce detection risk resulting from performing interim-date procedures

c. **Identified RMMs due to fraud.** The auditor may decide that substantive procedures should not be performed at an interim date.

d. **Analytical procedures.** The auditor may compare interim-date and period-end amounts and perform analytical procedures for the remaining period to identify anomalies.

    1) The auditor should consider

        a) The predictability of ending balances.

        b) The entity's procedures for interim-date adjustments and accounting cutoffs.

        c) Whether the information system will produce the information about balances and transactions necessary to an analytical investigation.

e. **Detection of misstatements** at an interim date may result in modification of risk assessments and planned procedures.

f. Audit evidence from performing substantive procedures in a **prior audit** does not suffice to reduce detection risk to an acceptable level.

    1) Moreover, such procedures provide little evidence usable in the current period.

        a) An example to the contrary is evidence of the cost of a fixed asset. But procedures should be performed to determine its current relevance.

g. The auditor also considers the timing issue in the **coordination of procedures**. Examples are

    1) Simultaneous testing of (a) assets temporarily controlled by the auditor (negotiable instruments and cash on hand) and (b) cash in banks, etc., and

    2) Coordinating the audit of cutoffs and related accounts.

14. **Extent of Substantive Procedures**

a. The greater the RMM, the greater the extent of relevant procedures.

    1) The extent of substantive procedures may be reduced if controls are effective.

b. For **tests of details**, the extent is usually a function of **sampling**. See Study Unit 15.

c. For **analytical procedures**, the auditor considers the acceptable variation from the expectation.

    1) This variation relates to the **performance materiality** and the desired **assurance**.

15. **Documentation**

a. The auditor should document the following:

    1) Overall responses

    2) Nature, timing, and extent of further audit procedures and their connection with assessed risks of relevant assertions

    3) Results of audit procedures

    4) Conclusions about use of prior-audit evidence with respect to the operating effectiveness of controls

A lot of detail has been presented in the previous two subunits. However, do not lose sight of the big picture. In planning the audit, the auditor assesses the risk of material misstatement (RMM) by evaluating the client's inherent and control risks. Control risk (and consequently RMM) can be assessed at a lower level if controls are working effectively. Thus, the auditor may perform tests of controls to make this lower assessment. Finally, based on the assessed RMM, the auditor designs appropriate substantive tests to identify potential misstatements. Conceptually, this should make sense to you.

Stop and review! You have completed the outline for this subunit. Study multiple-choice questions 5 through 21 beginning on page 287.

8.3 ASSESSING RISK IN A COMPUTER ENVIRONMENT

1. **Similarities**

a. Assessments of RMMs in a computer environment and in a manual system have many similarities. The candidate should build on these similarities. Most of the terms used here are defined in Study Unit 5.

b. The **objectives** are the same. The RMM is assessed by the auditor to help determine the nature, timing, and extent of the substantive procedures and tests of controls appropriate to support the opinion regardless of the nature of the system.

c. The **concept** is the same. After obtaining an understanding of the entity and its environment, including its internal control, and determining that the controls are implemented, the auditor considers whether testing the effectiveness of the controls and placing reliance on controls is more efficient than forgoing tests of controls. However, the auditee's use of IT requires the auditor to consider whether omitting tests of controls will enable him/her to provide the necessary assurance.

    1) The conventional procedure is first to assess the RMM relative to the control environment (often referred to as the general controls). If the control environment is ineffective, the auditor should not place reliance on individual controls (application controls).

d.   Many **procedures** are the same. Numerous controls in a computer environment are outside the computer system and can be tested using procedures applicable to a manual system. These procedures include the following:

1)   Inquiries of entity personnel
2)   Inspection of documents, reports, and electronic files
3)   Observation of the application of specific controls
4)   Reperformance by the auditor

e.   Computer controls to which traditional tests of controls are applicable include those found in the control environment and control activities components of internal control.

f.   **The Control Environment**

1)   **Organizational structure.** The auditor inspects documentation and observes operations demonstrating that the IT function has no custody of assets or transaction authority and is actually

a)   Operating as a service department independently of users and
b)   Reporting to senior-level management.

2)   **Assignment of authority and responsibility.** The auditor inquires and observes whether the following employees are performing functions consistent with their assigned responsibilities (and have no incompatible responsibilities):

a)   Systems analyst
b)   Programmer
c)   Computer (console) operator
d)   Data conversion (key) operator
e)   Librarian
f)   Data control group

g.   **Control Activities**

1)   **Information processing.** The auditor

a)   Observes the backup copies of files and programs to determine that they are safeguarded;
b)   Inspects the written security policy concerning virus protection and observes the existence of available anti-virus software;
c)   Inspects program acquisition and development requests for the proper authorization, assignment of responsibility for design and coding, testing, and acceptance; and
d)   Inspects program documentation to determine whether it is complete and up-to-date.

2)   The auditor tests **access controls** by

a)   Attempting to sign on to the computer system using various passwords and ID numbers,
b)   Inspecting the system access log for completeness and appropriate use and follow-up (passwords consistent with employees' responsibilities), and
c)   Observing that disposal of sensitive documents and printouts is controlled so that unauthorized persons cannot gain information concerning passwords or ID numbers.

2. **Differences**

    a. Certain controls relating to the input, processing, and output of data are internal to the computer system. They should be tested by procedures that are not traditionally performed in a manual environment. Such techniques have been characterized as auditing around the computer or auditing through the computer.

    b. **Auditing around the computer** is not appropriate when systems are sophisticated or the major controls are included in the computer programs. It may be appropriate for very simple systems that produce appropriate printed outputs.

        1) The auditor manually processes transactions and compares the results with the client's computer-processed results.

        2) Because only a small number of transactions can ordinarily be tested, the effectiveness of the tests of controls must be questioned.

        3) The computer is treated as a black box, and only inputs and outputs are evaluated.

    c. **Auditing through the computer** uses the computer to test the processing logic and controls within the system and the records produced. This approach may be accomplished in several ways, including

        1) Processing test data
        2) Parallel simulation
        3) Creation of an integrated test facility
        4) Programming embedded audit modules

3. **Test Data Approach**

    a. The auditor prepares a set of dummy transactions specifically designed to test the control activities that management claims to have incorporated into the processing programs. The auditor can expect the controls to be applied to the transactions in the prescribed manner. Thus, the auditor is testing the effectiveness of the controls.

EXAMPLE

Management may have represented that the following edit checks were included in the payroll processing program:

1) Field checks for all numeric and alphabetic fields
2) Reasonableness test of hours worked over 40 hours
3) Validity check of employee numbers compared with known employees in the personnel master file
4) Error listings of all transactions that fail a test

The auditor's test transactions include some that should pass the edit checks and be processed and some that should fail the edit checks and be printed on the error listing. Because processing is uniform, only one transaction for each control tested needs to be included.

---

    b. The primary advantage of this method is that it directly tests the controls.

    c. The primary disadvantage is that it tests processing at only one moment in time. That is, the auditor does not have assurance that the program tested is the one used throughout the year to process client transactions.

d. The following illustrates a test data approach in flowchart form:

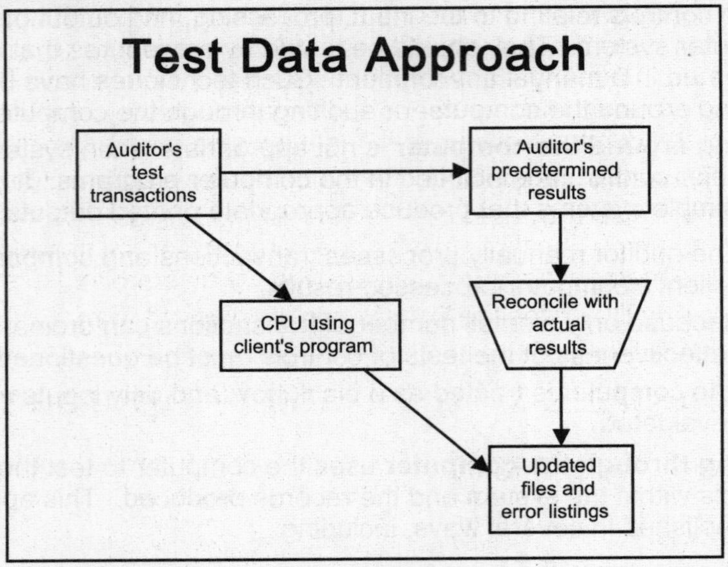

Test Data Approach

Auditor's test transactions → Auditor's predetermined results

Auditor's test transactions → CPU using client's program

Auditor's predetermined results → Reconcile with actual results

CPU using client's program → Updated files and error listings

Reconcile with actual results → Updated files and error listings

Figure 8-1

4. **Parallel Simulation**

a. Parallel simulation uses a controlled program to reprocess sets of client transactions and compares the auditor-achieved results with those of the client. The key is for the auditor's program to include the client's edit checks. Thus, the client's results of processing, rejected transactions, and error listing should be the same as the auditor's.

b. The auditor's controlled program may be a copy of the client's program that has been tested. An expensive alternative is for the auditor to write a program that includes management's controls. Also, a program may be created from generalized audit software.

c. The primary advantage of parallel simulation is that transactions from throughout the period may be reprocessed. The results can then be compared with the client's results to provide assurance that the edit checks (controls) have been applied during the period.

d. The primary disadvantages of this method are the cost of obtaining the program and the coordination effort required to obtain transactions to reprocess.

e. The following illustrates the parallel simulation method in flowchart form:

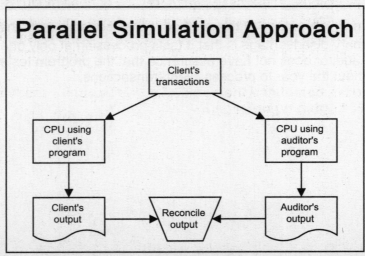

Figure 8-2

5. **Integrated Test Facility Method**

   a. Using the **integrated test facility (ITF)** method, the auditor creates a dummy record within the client's actual system (e.g., a fictitious employee in the personnel and payroll file). Dummy and actual transactions are processed (e.g., time records for the dummy employee and for actual employees). The auditor can test the edit checks by altering the dummy transactions and evaluating error listings.

   b. The primary advantage of this method is that it tests the actual program in operation.

   c. The primary disadvantages are that the method requires considerable coordination, and the dummy transactions must be purged prior to internal and external reporting. Thus, the method is not used extensively by external auditors.

   d. The following illustrates the ITF method in flowchart form:

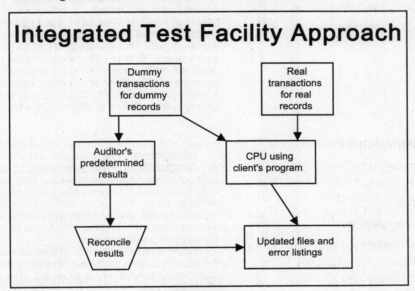

Figure 8-3

6. **Embedded Audit Module**

   a. An embedded audit module is an integral part of an application system that is designed to identify and report actual transactions and other information that meet criteria having audit significance.

   b. An advantage is that it permits continuous monitoring of online, real-time systems.

   c. A disadvantage is that **audit hooks** must be programmed into the operating system and applications programs to permit the use of audit modules.

   d. Upon completion of the tests of computer controls, the auditor assesses computer control risk and relates it to specific financial statement assertions. This risk assessment is a primary factor in determining the appropriate substantive procedures.

Stop and review! You have completed the outline for this subunit. Study multiple-choice questions 22 through 32 beginning on page 292.

QUESTIONS

8.1   Assessing Risks of Material Misstatement

1.   The ultimate purpose of understanding the entity and its environment and assessing inherent risk and control risk is to contribute to the auditor's assessment of the risk that

- A.   Tests of controls may fail to identify procedures relevant to assertions.
- B.   Material misstatements may exist in the financial statements.
- C.   Specified controls requiring separation of duties may be circumvented by collusion.
- D.   Entity policies may be inappropriately overridden by senior management.

Answer (B) is correct.   *(CPA, adapted)*
    REQUIRED: The purpose of understanding the entity and its environment and assessing inherent risk and control risk.
    DISCUSSION: The ultimate purpose of understanding the entity and its environment and assessing inherent risk and control risk is to contribute to the auditor's evaluation of the risk that material misstatements exist in the financial statements. The assessment of inherent risk and control risk (the risk of material misstatement) provides evidence about this risk. The auditor uses the evidence as part of the reasonable basis for an opinion (AU 314).
    Answer (A) is incorrect. An auditor must identify specific controls relevant (directly or indirectly) to specific relevant assertions before (s)he can obtain evidence about the effectiveness of their design and whether they have been implemented. This evidence is part of the basis for the risk assessment. If the auditor then decides to rely on the controls, (s)he will test their operating effectiveness. Answer (C) is incorrect. Collusion is an inherent limitation of internal control. Answer (D) is incorrect. Inappropriate management override is an inherent limitation of internal control.

2.   The risk of material misstatement (RMM) should be assessed in terms of

- A.   Specific controls.
- B.   Types of potential fraud.
- C.   Financial statement assertions.
- D.   Control environment factors.

Answer (C) is correct.   *(CPA, adapted)*
    REQUIRED: The approach used in assessing the RMM.
    DISCUSSION: The auditor should identify risks and relevant controls at the financial statement and relevant assertion levels. The identification occurs while the auditor obtains the understanding of the entity and its environment, including its internal control, and considering the transaction classes, balances, and disclosures. Risk should be related to threats at the relevant assertion level.
    Answer (A) is incorrect. Relevant controls should relate to the identified risks, and risks should relate to the relevant assertions. Answer (B) is incorrect. The auditor should use knowledge obtained from the understanding to identify types of potential misstatements. Answer (D) is incorrect. The auditor considers the control environment in assessing risk but does not assess risk in terms of control environment factors.

3.   The auditor should perform tests of controls when

- A.   Substantive procedures alone do not provide sufficient appropriate audit evidence at the relevant assertion level.
- B.   Tests of details and substantive analytical procedures provide sufficient appropriate audit evidence to support the assertion being evaluated.
- C.   The auditor is not able to obtain an understanding of internal controls.
- D.   The owner-manager performs virtually all the functions of internal control.

Answer (A) is correct.   *(Publisher, adapted)*
    REQUIRED: The basis for performing tests of controls.
    DISCUSSION: The auditor may determine that it is not possible or practicable to reduce the detection risk at the relevant assertion level to an acceptably low level with audit evidence obtained only from substantive procedures. In this case, tests of controls should be performed to obtain audit evidence about their operating effectiveness.
    Answer (B) is incorrect. The auditor need not rely on internal controls when tests of details and substantive analytical procedures provide sufficient appropriate audit evidence to support the assertion being evaluated. Answer (C) is incorrect. The auditor must obtain an understanding of the entity and its environment, including its internal control (Second Standard of Field Work). Answer (D) is incorrect. In small organizations, the owner-manager may perform many or most of the control procedures. However, this circumstance does not dictate tests of controls. Rather, the auditor should consider whether (s)he can obtain sufficient appropriate audit evidence.

4. When assessing the risk of material misstatement at a low level, an auditor is required to document the auditor's

	Understanding of the Entity's Control Environment	Overall Responses to Assessed Risks
A.	Yes	No
B.	No	Yes
C.	Yes	Yes
D.	No	No

Answer (C) is correct. *(CPA, adapted)*
REQUIRED: The item(s) that should be documented when assessing control risk at a low level.
DISCUSSION: The understanding of the components of internal control, including the control environment, should be documented regardless of the risk of material misstatement (AU 314). The overall responses to the assessed risks of material misstatement at the financial statement level also should be documented (AU 318).

8.2 Auditor's Response to Risks

5. Which of the following is a step in an auditor's decision to test controls?

A. Analytical procedures have detected conditions that may indicate weak controls.

B. Tests of details of transactions and account balances have identified potential errors and fraud.

C. The risk assessment includes an expectation of the effectiveness of controls.

D. Document that the additional audit effort to perform tests of controls exceeds the potential reduction in substantive procedures.

Answer (C) is correct. *(CPA, adapted)*
REQUIRED: The step necessary to test controls.
DISCUSSION: The auditor tests controls when the assessment of the risk of material misstatement includes an expectation of the effectiveness of controls. Reliance on controls is necessary when substantive procedures alone do not provide sufficient appropriate audit evidence.
Answer (A) is incorrect. Controls are less likely to be tested when risk assessment procedures provide evidence that relevant controls are ineffective. Answer (B) is incorrect. Identification of errors and fraud may provide an inference that relevant controls are ineffective. Answer (D) is incorrect. The inefficiency of testing controls may result in selecting the substantive audit approach.

6. An auditor may decide to perform only substantive procedures for certain assertions because the auditor believes

A. Controls are not relevant to the assertions.

B. The entity's control components are interrelated.

C. Sufficient appropriate audit evidence to support the assertions is likely to be available.

D. More emphasis on tests of controls than substantive tests is warranted.

Answer (A) is correct. *(CPA, adapted)*
REQUIRED: The reason an auditor may decide to perform only substantive procedures.
DISCUSSION: The auditor's risk assessment procedures may not have identified any suitably designed and implemented controls that are relevant to the assertions. Another possibility is that testing of controls may be inefficient. But the auditor needs to be satisfied that performing only substantive procedures will be effective in reducing detection risk to an acceptable level.
Answer (B) is incorrect. The integration of control components may be a valuable consideration in performing tests of controls as well as substantive procedures. Answer (C) is incorrect. The auditor tests controls when sufficient appropriate audit evidence is not provided by substantive procedures. Answer (D) is incorrect. The auditor's decision to perform only substantive procedures is a decision not to perform procedures to obtain evidence about the effectiveness of controls.

7. A nonissuer audit client failed to maintain copies of its procedures manuals and organizational flowcharts. What should the auditor most likely do in an audit of financial statements?

A. Express a qualified opinion on the basis of a scope limitation.

B. Document the auditor's understanding of internal controls.

C. Perform substantive procedures only.

D. Restrict the auditor's responsibility to assess the effectiveness of controls in the audit engagement letter.

Answer (C) is correct. *(CPA, adapted)*
REQUIRED: The effect on the audit when the client fails to maintain copies of its procedures manuals and organizational flowcharts.
DISCUSSION: When risk assessment procedures do not identify suitably designed and implemented controls that are relevant to the audited assertions, the auditor will perform substantive procedures only.
Answer (A) is incorrect. The auditor may be able to express an unqualified opinion given sufficient appropriate audit evidence obtained by performing substantive procedures. Answer (B) is incorrect. There would be little understanding to document. Answer (D) is incorrect. The auditor need not assess the effectiveness of internal controls for a nonissuer.

8. Which of the following tests of controls most likely will help assure an auditor that goods shipped are properly billed?

    A. Scan the sales journal for sequential and unusual entries.

    B. Examine shipping documents for matching sales invoices.

    C. Compare the accounts receivable ledger to daily sales summaries.

    D. Inspect unused sales invoices for consecutive prenumbering.

Answer (B) is correct. *(CPA, adapted)*
    REQUIRED: The test of controls most likely to assure that goods shipped are properly billed.
    DISCUSSION: The proper starting point to determine whether all goods shipped were properly billed is the shipping documents. Tracing the shipping documents to the matching sales invoices provides assurance that controls worked effectively to ensure that all goods shipped were billed.
    Answer (A) is incorrect. Scanning the sales journal provides evidence concerning shipments that were billed but no evidence about unbilled shipments. Answer (C) is incorrect. The accounts receivable ledger represents shipments that were billed. Answer (D) is incorrect. Unbilled shipments do not create gaps in the prenumbered sales invoices.

9. An auditor is **least** likely to test controls that provide for

    A. Approval of the purchase and sale of trading securities.

    B. Classification of revenue and expense transactions by product line.

    C. Separation of the functions of recording disbursements and reconciling the bank account.

    D. Comparison of receiving reports and vendors' invoices with purchase orders.

Answer (B) is correct. *(CPA, adapted)*
    REQUIRED: The controls that are least likely to be tested.
    DISCUSSION: The independent auditor is primarily concerned with the fairness of external financial reporting. (S)he is less likely to test controls over records used solely for internal management purposes than those used to prepare financial statements for external distribution. Assertions about the presentation of transactions by product line are not typically made. Thus, the independent auditor is unlikely to expend significant audit effort in testing such classifications.
    Answer (A) is incorrect. A basic management objective is proper authorization of transactions. Answer (C) is incorrect. A basic management objective is to compare recorded accountability with existing assets at reasonable intervals, such as by reconciling the bank account and the accounting records. Reconciliations should be performed by an independent employee. Answer (D) is incorrect. Comparison of receiving reports, vendors' invoices, and purchase orders is a control over purchasing.

10. After obtaining an understanding of a client's internal control, an auditor may decide not to test the effectiveness of the computer control procedures. Which of the following is **not** a valid reason for choosing to omit tests of controls?

    A. The controls duplicate operative controls existing elsewhere in the system.

    B. There appear to be major weaknesses that would preclude relying on the controls.

    C. The time and dollar costs of testing exceed the time and dollar savings in substantive testing if the tests of controls show the controls to be operative.

    D. The operating effectiveness of controls appears to support a reduced assessment of the risk of material misstatement.

Answer (D) is correct. *(CPA, adapted)*
    REQUIRED: The invalid reason for omitting tests of controls.
    DISCUSSION: Although controls appear to be operating effectively based on the understanding of internal control, the auditor should perform tests of controls for those assertions for which the risk of material misstatement is to be assessed at a level that allows the auditor to rely on the controls. The risk assessment affects the acceptable level of detection risk used in determining the nature, timing, and extent of substantive procedures.
    Answer (A) is incorrect. Compensating controls may appropriately limit risk. Answer (B) is incorrect. If the auditor intends to place no reliance on the controls, tests of controls are unnecessary, but the auditor must be satisfied that performing only substantive tests will be effective and more efficient in restricting detection risk to an acceptable level. Furthermore, when a significant amount of information supporting assertions is electronically initiated, authorized, recorded, processed, or reported, the auditor may determine that it is not possible to design substantive procedures that by themselves provide sufficient appropriate evidence that the assertions are not materially misstated. Answer (C) is incorrect. If tests of controls are not efficient, the auditor should expand substantive testing.

11. To test the effectiveness of controls, an auditor ordinarily selects from a variety of techniques, including

    A. Inquiry and analytical procedures.

    B. Reperformance and observation.

    C. Comparison and confirmation.

    D. Inspection and verification.

Answer (B) is correct. *(CPA, adapted)*
    REQUIRED: The procedures associated with tests of controls.
    DISCUSSION: According to AU 318, the auditor selects tests of controls from a variety of techniques such as inquiry, observation, inspection, and reperformance of a control that pertains to an assertion. No one specific test of controls is always necessary, applicable, or equally effective in every circumstance.
    Answer (A) is incorrect. Analytical procedures are more closely associated with substantive procedures. Answer (C) is incorrect. Comparison and confirmation are more closely associated with substantive procedures. Answer (D) is incorrect. Inspection and verification are more closely associated with substantive procedures.

12. Which of the following is true related to the auditor's consideration of controls?

    A. Misstatements detected by the auditor's substantive procedures should be considered when testing the effectiveness of related controls.

    B. The absence of misstatements detected by an auditor's substantive procedures should be considered evidence that controls related to the relevant assertion being tested are effective.

    C. A material misstatement detected by the auditor, but not detected by the entity, should be considered a material weakness in internal control.

    D. The auditor should consider testing and documenting the efficiency of the entity's controls related to relevant assertions.

Answer (A) is correct. *(Publisher, adapted)*
    REQUIRED: The true statement related to the consideration of controls.
    DISCUSSION: Misstatements detected by the auditor's substantive procedures should be considered when testing the effectiveness of related controls. The auditor may need to assess the risk of material misstatement at a higher level if errors or frauds are detected that should have been detected by the entity's controls.
    Answer (B) is incorrect. The absence of misstatements during substantive testing does not normally provide sufficient evidence as to control effectiveness. The samples may not be appropriate for that purpose. Answer (C) is incorrect. A material misstatement detected by the auditor, but not detected by the entity, should be considered a significant deficiency and may be indicative of a material weakness in control. Answer (D) is incorrect. The auditor should test and document the effectiveness, not the efficiency, of the entity's controls related to relevant assertions.

13. An auditor generally tests the separation of duties related to inventory by

    A. Personal inquiry and observation.

    B. Test counts and cutoff procedures.

    C. Analytical procedures and invoice recomputation.

    D. Document inspection and reconciliation.

Answer (A) is correct. *(CPA, adapted)*
    REQUIRED: The audit test of the separation of duties for inventory.
    DISCUSSION: The separation of duties reduces the opportunity for an individual to perpetrate and conceal errors or fraud in the normal course of his/her duties. Authorization of transactions, recording of transactions, and custody of assets should be separated. The best evidence that controls based on separation of duties are operating as planned is provided by the auditor's own observation and inquiries.
    Answer (B) is incorrect. Test counts and cutoff procedures are substantive procedures, not tests of controls. Answer (C) is incorrect. Analytical procedures and recomputations are substantive procedures, not tests of controls. Answer (D) is incorrect. Although document inspection may be useful as a test of controls, it is not effective to test the separation of duties.

14. Which of the following procedures concerning accounts receivable is an auditor most likely to perform to obtain evidential matter in support of the effectiveness of controls?

A.   Observing an entity's employee prepare the schedule of past due accounts receivable.

B.   Sending confirmation requests to an entity's principal customers to verify the existence of accounts receivable.

C.   Inspecting an entity's analysis of accounts receivable for unusual balances.

D.   Comparing an entity's uncollectible accounts expense with actual uncollectible accounts receivable.

Answer (A) is correct. *(CPA, adapted)*
REQUIRED: The procedure used in support of the effectiveness of controls.
DISCUSSION: To test the effectiveness of controls, an auditor performs procedures such as inquiry, observation, inspection, and reperformance of a control. Thus, observing an entity's employee prepare the schedule of past due accounts receivable provides evidence of the effectiveness of certain controls over accounts receivable.
Answer (B) is incorrect. Sending confirmation requests to verify the existence of accounts receivable is a test of the details of balances, a substantive procedure. Answer (C) is incorrect. Inspecting an entity's analysis of accounts receivable for unusual balances is a test of the details of balances, a substantive procedure. Answer (D) is incorrect. Comparing uncollectible accounts expense with actual uncollectible accounts receivable is a form of analytical procedure. It is used to determine whether the auditor's expectation is supported by client data.

15. The objective of tests of details of transactions performed as tests of controls is to

A.   Monitor the design and use of entity documents such as prenumbered shipping forms.

B.   Determine whether internal controls have been implemented.

C.   Detect material misstatements in the account balances of the financial statements.

D.   Evaluate whether internal controls operated effectively.

Answer (D) is correct. *(CPA, adapted)*
REQUIRED: The objective of tests of details of transactions performed as tests of controls.
DISCUSSION: The auditor may use tests of details of transactions concurrently as tests of controls (i.e., as dual-purpose tests). As substantive procedures, their objective is to support relevant assertions or detect material misstatements in the financial statements. As tests of controls, their objective is to evaluate whether a control operated effectively.
Answer (A) is incorrect. The client's controls should monitor the use of entity documents. Answer (B) is incorrect. Determination of whether controls have been implemented is made in conjunction with the auditor's understanding of internal control. Answer (C) is incorrect. The objective of substantive procedures is to support relevant assertions or detect material misstatements in the account balances.

16. When an auditor increases the planned assessed risk of material misstatement because certain controls were determined to be ineffective, the auditor will most likely increase the

A.   Extent of tests of details.

B.   Assessed inherent risk.

C.   Extent of tests of controls.

D.   Acceptable detection risk.

Answer (A) is correct. *(CPA, adapted)*
REQUIRED: The effect of an increase in the planned assessed RMM.
DISCUSSION: An auditor must obtain an understanding of internal control to assess the RMM. The greater (lower) the assessed RMM, the lower (greater) the acceptable detection risk. In turn, the acceptable detection risk affects substantive testing. For example, as the acceptable detection risk decreases, the auditor changes the nature, timing, or extent of substantive procedures to increase the reliability and relevance of the evidence they provide.
Answer (B) is incorrect. Inherent risk is not affected by the auditor's procedures. Answer (C) is incorrect. Once controls are determined to be ineffective, further tests of controls are unnecessary. Answer (D) is incorrect. The acceptable detection risk decreases when the assessed RMM increases.

17. When numerous property and equipment transactions occur during the year, an auditor who plans to assess the risk of material misstatement at a low level usually performs

A.   Tests of controls and extensive tests of property and equipment balances at the end of the year.

B.   Analytical procedures for current year property and equipment transactions.

C.   Tests of controls and limited tests of current-year property and equipment transactions.

D.   Analytical procedures for property and equipment balances at the end of the year.

Answer (C) is correct. *(CPA, adapted)*
REQUIRED: The procedures performed when an auditor plans to assess the RMM at a low level.
DISCUSSION: The auditor usually performs tests of controls and substantive procedures (the combined audit approach). The auditor must make decisions about the nature, timing, and extent of substantive procedures that are most responsive to the assessed detection risk. These decisions are affected by whether the auditor has tested controls. Thus, the extent of relevant substantive procedures may be reduced when control is found to be effective.
Answer (A) is incorrect. The extent of substantive procedures may be reduced. Answer (B) is incorrect. When numerous transactions are subject to controls and the RMM is low, the auditor may rely on tests of controls. Answer (D) is incorrect. When numerous transactions are subject to controls and the RMM is low, the auditor may rely on tests of controls.

18. A client maintains perpetual inventory records in both quantities and dollars. If the assessed risk of material misstatement is high, an auditor will probably

    A. Apply gross profit tests to ascertain the reasonableness of the physical counts.

    B. Increase the extent of tests of controls relevant to the inventory cycle.

    C. Request the client to schedule the physical inventory count at the end of the year.

    D. Insist that the client perform physical counts of inventory items several times during the year.

Answer (C) is correct. *(CPA, adapted)*
    REQUIRED: The auditor's action if the RMM for inventory is high.
    DISCUSSION: If the RMM is high, the acceptable detection risk decreases. The auditor should change the nature, timing, or extent of substantive procedures to increase the reliability and relevance of the evidence they provide. Thus, extending work done at an interim date to year-end might be inappropriate. Observation of inventory at year-end would provide more reliable and relevant evidence.
    Answer (A) is incorrect. Comparing the gross profit test results with those of the prior year provides evidence about sales and cost of goods sold but not inventory. Answer (B) is incorrect. If the auditor believes controls are unlikely to be effective, e.g., because the RMM is high, tests of controls may not be performed. However, the auditor needs to be satisfied that performing only substantive procedures will be effective in restricting detection risk to an acceptable level. Answer (D) is incorrect. The risk is that year-end inventory is misstated.

19. An auditor may compensate for a high assessed level of control risk by increasing the

    A. Level of detection risk.

    B. Extent of tests of controls.

    C. Preliminary judgment about audit risk.

    D. Extent of substantive analytical procedures.

Answer (D) is correct. *(CPA, adapted)*
    REQUIRED: The method an auditor may use to compensate for a high assessed level of control risk.
    DISCUSSION: The higher the assessed level of control risk, the higher the risk of material misstatement, and the lower the acceptable level of detection risk. As the acceptable level of detection risk decreases, the auditor should change the nature, timing, or extent of substantive procedures to increase the reliability and relevance of the audit evidence they provide. These procedures may include more extensive analytical procedures.
    Answer (A) is incorrect. The acceptable level of detection risk decreases when the assessed level of control risk increases. Answer (B) is incorrect. The auditor should change the nature, timing, or extent of substantive procedures. Answer (C) is incorrect. The auditor plans the audit so as to reduce the risk of material misstatement of financial statement assertions to an appropriate level. This risk is not necessarily changed because of a high assessed level of control risk.

20. Regardless of the assessed risk of material misstatement, an auditor should perform some

    A. Tests of controls to determine their effectiveness.

    B. Analytical procedures to verify the design of controls.

    C. Substantive procedures to restrict detection risk for significant transaction classes.

    D. Dual-purpose tests to evaluate both the risk of monetary misstatement and preliminary control risk.

Answer (C) is correct. *(CPA, adapted)*
    REQUIRED: The procedures performed regardless of the assessed risk of material misstatement.
    DISCUSSION: Regardless of the assessed risk of material misstatement (thus, regardless of the effectiveness of the controls), the auditor should design and perform substantive procedures for all relevant assertions related to each material transaction class, account balance, and disclosure.

21. Which of the following explanations best describes why an auditor may decide to reduce tests of details for a particular audit objective?

    A. The audit is being performed soon after the balance sheet date.

    B. Audit staff are experienced in performing the planned procedures.

    C. Analytical procedures have revealed **no** unusual or unexpected results.

    D. There were many transactions posted to the account during the period.

Answer (C) is correct. *(CPA, adapted)*
    REQUIRED: A reason to reduce tests of details.
    DISCUSSION: Analytical procedures in the planning stage of the audit help the auditor to assess the risk of material misstatement. When those procedures indicate expected results, the risk of RMM may be assessed lower and allow the auditor to reduce tests of details.
    Answer (A) is incorrect. Timing of audit procedures is a response to the assessed risk, not part of the assessment. Answer (B) is incorrect. The experience of the audit staff is a response to the RMM, not part of the assessment of the risk. Answer (D) is incorrect. Significant activity in an account typically increases the risk of material misstatement in the balance and would require increased tests of details.

8.3 Assessing Risk in a Computer Environment

22. A client maintains a large data center where access is limited to authorized employees. How may an auditor best determine the effectiveness of this control activity?

A. Inspect the policy manual establishing this control activity.

B. Ask the chief technology officer about known problems.

C. Observe whether the data center is monitored.

D. Obtain a list of current data center employees.

Answer (C) is correct. *(CPA, adapted)*
REQUIRED: The best procedure to determine the effectiveness of a control activity.
DISCUSSION: Physically observing that the data center is being monitored provides direct evidence that the control is in place and is being utilized effectively. The auditor will be able to see, first hand, if the control is preventing unauthorized access.
Answer (A) is incorrect. Inspecting the policy manual will ensure that a control has been established, but not test the effectiveness of this control. Answer (B) is incorrect. Inquiry will help the auditor understand the control but will not test its effectiveness. Answer (D) is incorrect. Obtaining a list of current employees does not provide evidence of who has been accessing the data center.

23. To obtain evidence that online access controls are properly functioning, an auditor most likely will

A. Create checkpoints at periodic intervals after live data processing to test for unauthorized use of the system.

B. Examine the transaction log to discover whether any transactions were lost or entered twice because of a system malfunction.

C. Enter invalid identification numbers or passwords to ascertain whether the system rejects them.

D. Vouch a random sample of processed transactions to assure proper authorization.

Answer (C) is correct. *(CPA, adapted)*
REQUIRED: The procedure an auditor will most likely use to obtain evidence that user online access controls are functioning as designed.
DISCUSSION: Employees with access authority to process transactions that change records should not also have asset custody or program modification responsibilities. The auditor should determine that password authority is consistent with other assigned responsibilities. The auditor can directly test whether password controls are working by attempting entry into the system by using invalid identifications and passwords.
Answer (A) is incorrect. Checkpoints are used as a recovery procedure in batch processing applications. Answer (B) is incorrect. Testing for missing or duplicate transactions will not determine whether online access controls were functioning effectively. Answer (D) is incorrect. Unauthorized transactions may be entered by someone having knowledge of valid passwords, etc.

24. When an accounting application is processed by computer, an auditor **cannot** verify the reliable operation of automated controls by

A. Manually comparing detail transaction files used by an edit program with the program's generated error listings to determine that errors were properly identified by the edit program.

B. Constructing a processing system for accounting applications and processing actual data from throughout the period through both the client's program and the auditor's program.

C. Manually reperforming, as of a moment in time, the processing of input data and comparing the simulated results with the actual results.

D. Periodically submitting auditor-prepared test data to the same computer process and evaluating the results.

Answer (C) is correct. *(CPA, adapted)*
REQUIRED: The procedure that would not verify the reliable operation of automated controls.
DISCUSSION: This procedure describes what is termed auditing around the computer. The computer is treated as a black box, and only the inputs and outputs are evaluated. Because the actual controls may not be understood or tested, the technique is ordinarily inappropriate if the effectiveness of automated controls is important to the understanding of internal control and the assessment of control risk. Moreover, the auditor is concerned with the reliable operation of the controls throughout the audit period, not at a single moment in time.
Answer (A) is incorrect. A manual comparison of the computer generated output of an auditor-controlled edit program with the error listings generated by the client's program provides evidence that the client's automated controls were operating as planned. Answer (B) is incorrect. Parallel simulation can be an effective method of testing the reliability of controls. Answer (D) is incorrect. Submitting auditor-prepared test data to the client's computer process is an effective method of assessing the reliability of controls.

25. To obtain evidence that user identification and password controls are functioning as designed, an auditor should

A. Review the online transaction log to ascertain whether employees using passwords have access to data files and computer programs.

B. Examine a sample of password holders and access authority to determine whether they have access authority incompatible with their other responsibilities.

C. Extract a random sample of processed transactions and ensure that transactions are appropriately authorized.

D. Observe the file librarian's activities to discover whether other systems personnel are permitted to operate computer equipment without restriction.

Answer (B) is correct. *(CPA, adapted)*
REQUIRED: The procedure an auditor should use to obtain evidence that user identification and password controls are functioning as designed.
DISCUSSION: Employees with access authority to process transactions that change records should not also have asset custody or program modification responsibilities. The auditor should determine that password authority is consistent with other assigned responsibilities. In addition, the auditor can directly test whether password controls are working by attempting entry into the system by using invalid identifications and passwords.
Answer (A) is incorrect. Password assignment properly provides employees with access to files and programs. Answer (C) is incorrect. Testing transactions for proper authorization does not ensure that user identification controls were functioning effectively. Answer (D) is incorrect. The file librarian oversees the physical protection of files, programs, and documentation, not the operation of computer equipment.

26. An auditor most likely should test for the presence of unauthorized computer program changes by running a

A. Program with test data.

B. Check digit verification program.

C. Source code comparison program.

D. Program that computes control totals.

Answer (C) is correct. *(CPA, adapted)*
REQUIRED: The method used to test for the presence of unauthorized computer program changes.
DISCUSSION: The best way to test for unauthorized computer program changes is to examine the program itself. By comparing a program under his/her control with the program used for operations, the auditor can determine whether unauthorized changes have been made.
Answer (A) is incorrect. The test data may not trigger the unauthorized changes. Answer (B) is incorrect. Check digit verification tests the accuracy of data transcription, not programs. Answer (D) is incorrect. Control totals test the reasonableness and accuracy of processing but will not necessarily detect program changes.

27. Which of the following statements is **not** true of the test data approach to testing an accounting system?

A. Test data are processed by the client's computer programs under the auditor's control.

B. The test data need consist of only those valid and invalid conditions that interest the auditor.

C. Only one transaction of each type need be tested.

D. The test data must consist of all possible valid and invalid conditions.

Answer (D) is correct. *(CPA, adapted)*
REQUIRED: The false statement about the test data approach.
DISCUSSION: The test data approach includes preparation of dummy transactions by the auditor. These transactions are processed by the client's computer programs under the auditor's control. The test data consist of one transaction for each valid and invalid condition that interests the auditor. Consequently, the test data need not consist of all possible valid and invalid conditions.
Answer (A) is incorrect. The test data are processed by the client's computer programs under the control of the auditor. Answer (B) is incorrect. Only those controls deemed important to the auditor need be tested. Answer (C) is incorrect. The computer processes all similar transactions in the same way. Accordingly, only one transaction needs to be tested to determine whether a control is working effectively.

28. An auditor who is testing computer controls in a payroll system will most likely use test data that contain conditions such as

A. Deductions not authorized by employees.

B. Overtime not approved by supervisors.

C. Time tickets with invalid job numbers.

D. Payroll checks with unauthorized signatures.

Answer (C) is correct. *(CPA, adapted)*
REQUIRED: The most likely conditions in test data used in a test of computer controls over payroll.
DISCUSSION: The auditor will most likely test computer controls for detection of time tickets with invalid job numbers. The validity of codes can be determined by the computer system. Testing of approvals, authorizations, and signatures usually require manual procedures.
Answer (A) is incorrect. Testing of authorizations usually requires manual procedures. Answer (B) is incorrect. Testing of approvals usually requires manual procedures. Answer (D) is incorrect. Testing of signatures usually requires manual procedures.

29. In parallel simulation, actual client data are reprocessed using an auditor software program. An advantage of using parallel simulation, instead of performing tests of controls without a computer, is that

A. The test includes all types of transaction errors and exceptions that may be encountered.

B. The client's computer personnel do not know when the data are being tested.

C. There is no risk of creating potentially material errors in the client's data.

D. The size of the sample can be greatly expanded at relatively little additional cost.

Answer (D) is correct. *(CPA, adapted)*
REQUIRED: The advantage of using parallel simulation.
DISCUSSION: Parallel simulation uses a controlled program to reprocess sets of client transactions and compares those results with those of the client. The primary disadvantages are the initial cost of obtaining the software and the need for coordination with client personnel to gain access to transactions. However, the auditors have the freedom to process transactions (1) at their convenience, (2) using their own equipment, and (3) taking as long as necessary. Thus, the auditors can greatly increase the sample size at relatively little marginal cost.
Answer (A) is incorrect. Parallel simulation tests for errors and exceptions that occur only as a result of the software being tested. Answer (B) is incorrect. Whether the computer personnel know when the data are tested is not a concern when the test is at the auditor's own facilities. Answer (C) is incorrect. Use of actual data poses some risk of contamination.

30. Which of the following computer-assisted auditing techniques allows fictitious and real transactions to be processed together without the knowledge of client operating personnel?

A. Integrated test facility (ITF).

B. Input controls matrix.

C. Parallel simulation.

D. Data entry monitor.

Answer (A) is correct. *(CPA, adapted)*
REQUIRED: The technique that processes fictitious and real transactions without the knowledge of client personnel.
DISCUSSION: The ITF or minicompany technique is a development of the test data method. It permits dummy transactions to be processed at the same time as live transactions but requires additional programming to ensure that programs will recognize the specially coded test data. The test transactions may be submitted without the computer operators' knowledge.
Answer (B) is incorrect. Input controls matrix is not a method typically used by auditors to test a client's computer systems. Answer (C) is incorrect. Parallel simulation reprocesses only real, not fictitious, transactions. Answer (D) is incorrect. Data entry monitor is not a method typically used by auditors to test a client's computer systems.

31. An auditor who wishes to capture an entity's data as transactions are processed and continuously test the entity's computerized information system most likely would use which of the following techniques?

A. Snapshot application.

B. Embedded audit module.

C. Integrated data check.

D. Test data generator.

Answer (B) is correct. *(CPA, adapted)*
REQUIRED: The technique that captures an entity's data as transactions are processed and continuously tests the information system.
DISCUSSION: Continuous monitoring and analysis of transaction processing can be achieved with an embedded audit module. An audit module embedded in the client's software routinely selects and abstracts certain actual transactions and other information with audit significance. They may be tagged and traced through the information system. A disadvantage is that audit hooks must be programmed into the operating system and applications. An alternative is recording in an audit log, that is, in a file accessible only by the auditor.

32. The following flowchart depicts

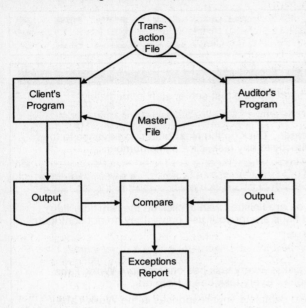

A. Program code checking.

B. Parallel simulation.

C. Integrated test facility.

D. Test data approach.

Answer (B) is correct. *(CPA, adapted)*

REQUIRED: The audit technique depicted by the flowchart.

DISCUSSION: Parallel simulation is a test of the controls in a client's application program. An auditor-developed program is used to process actual client data and compare the output and the exceptions report with those of the client's application program. If the client's programmed controls are operating effectively, the two sets of results should be reconcilable.

Answer (A) is incorrect. Program code checking refers to checking the client's application program code to determine if it contains the appropriate controls. Answer (C) is incorrect. An ITF introduces dummy records into the client's files and then processes dummy transactions to update the records. The auditor can test the controls by including various types of transactions to be processed. Answer (D) is incorrect. Using the test data approach, the auditor prepares a set of dummy transactions specifically designed to test the control activities.

Use the additional questions in Gleim **CPA Test Prep Online** to create Test Sessions that emulate Prometric!

8.4 PRACTICE SIMULATION

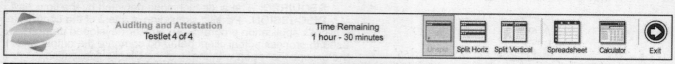

DIRECTIONS

Note: If you believe you have encountered a software malfunction, report it to the test center staff immediately.

Navigation

To navigate from task to task, use the controls at the bottom of the screen. Click on the **Next** button to advance to the next task, or the **Previous** button to go to the previous task. To go directly to any task, click on its number.

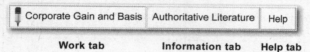

If you would like a reminder to revisit a task, or want to indicate that you are finished with it, click on the reminder flag below the task number. To clear the flag, click on it again. Reminder flags are for your use only – they do not contribute to your score.

Tabs

In this part of the examination, you will be asked to complete various tasks. Every task has one or more **Work Tabs**. Some tasks have one or more **Information Tabs**, others may have none. Every task has a **Help** tab.

If a task has **Information Tabs**, you may use the information in them to complete your responses in the **Work Tabs**.

	Corporate Gain and Basis	Authoritative Literature	Help
	Work tab	Information tab	Help tab

Work Tabs:

- **Work Tabs** are identified with a pencil icon. This is where your responses are expected.
- Each task has one or more **Work Tabs**.
- **Work Tabs** contain directions for completing the task – be sure to read these directions carefully.
- The **Work Tab** name in the example above is for illustration only – yours will differ.
- You must complete all of the **Work Tabs** in each task to receive full credit.

Information Tabs:

- The Authoritative Literature will be provided in all tasks in the AUD, FAR, and REG sections for your reference.
- Your simulation may have one or more additional **Information Tabs**. Like the Authoritative Literature tabs, **Information Tabs** do not have a pencil icon.
- If your task has additional **Information Tabs**, go through each to familiarize yourself with the task content.

Help Tab:

- The **Help Tab** provides assistance with the exam software that is used in this task. For example, if the task is to compose a memorandum, **Help** will provide information about the word processor.

The Toolbar

The toolbar at the top of the screen shows the amount of time remaining for you to complete the tasks. In addition, the following tools are available. Note that only the Exit button is displayed when Directions are visible - the others will appear when you begin the tasks.

Click on these buttons to split or unsplit the screen. You can split the screen vertically or horizontally.

Click on this button to display the calculator; click on it again to hide the calculator. To move the calculator, click on the calculator title bar and drag the calculator to the desired location.

Click on this button to use the spreadsheet; click on it again to hide the spreadsheet. To move the spreadsheet, click on the the spreadsheet title bar and drag the spreadsheet to the desired location.

Click on this button to go on to the next part of the examination. You must complete all of the tasks to receive full credit. Once you click on **Exit** and confirm the action, you will NOT be able to return to this testlet.

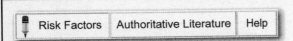

Bond, CPA, is considering the risk of material misstatement (RMM) at the financial statement level for Toxic Waste Disposal (TWD) Company for the year ended December 31, Year 6. TWD is a privately owned entity that contracts with municipal governments to remove environmental wastes. RMM at the financial statement level is influenced by a combination of factors related to management, the industry, and the entity.

Based only on the information in the table, indicate by checking the appropriate box whether each factor below would most likely increase, decrease, or have no effect on RMM.

Factor	Increase RMM	Decrease RMM	No Effect
1. This was the first year TWD operated at a profit since Year 2 because the municipalities received increased federal and state funding for environmental purposes.			
2. TWD's board of directors is controlled by Mead, the majority shareholder, who also acts as the chief executive officer.			
3. The internal auditor reports to the controller, and the controller reports to Mead.			
4. The accounting department has experienced a high rate of turnover of key personnel.			
5. TWD's bank has a loan officer who meets regularly with TWD's CEO and controller to monitor TWD's financial performance.			
6. TWD's employees are paid biweekly.			
7. Bond has audited TWD for 5 years.			
8. During Year 6, litigation filed against TWD in Year 1 alleging that TWD discharged pollutants into state waterways was dropped by the state. Loss contingency disclosures that TWD included in prior years' financial statements are being removed for the Year 6 financial statements.			
9. During December Year 6, TWD signed a contract to lease disposal equipment from an entity owned by Mead's parents. This related party transaction is not disclosed in TWD's notes to its Year 6 financial statements.			
10. During December Year 6, TWD increased its casualty insurance coverage on several pieces of sophisticated machinery from historical cost to replacement cost.			

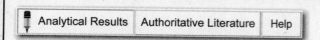

The table below presents some ratios that were considered significant by an auditor in the current and prior year's audit of a client. Select from the list provided the most likely explanation for the analytical results. Each choice may be used once, more than once, or not at all.

Ratio	Year 2	Year 1	Answer
1. Debt to equity	1.99	4.61	
2. Gross profit percentage	38%	41%	
3. Quick	2.00	1.50	

Explanations
A) Sales decreased as compared to the prior year.
B) Cost of goods sold increased during the year at a smaller rate than sales increased.
C) Proceeds from the issuance of noncurrent debt were used to pay payables on a more current basis.
D) Capital stock was issued during the year.
E) The company may have accumulated excess and obsolete inventory.
F) Cost of goods sold decreased less than sales decreased during the year.

An auditor has chosen to increase attention on the financial statement assertion about valuation of account balances. Procedures that might be used in an audit are listed below. Indicate by checking in the boxes which two procedures would be most appropriate to perform in an audit that is giving increased attention to the **valuation assertion** about balances. Only **two** procedures may be chosen.

Procedures	
1. Observing the client count the physical inventory.	☐
2. Inspecting shipping and receiving transactions near year-end for recording in the proper period.	☐
3. Obtaining confirmation from lenders regarding inventories pledged under loan agreements.	☐
4. Examining paid vendors' invoices.	☐
5. Obtaining confirmation of inventories at locations outside the entity.	☐
6. Examining an analysis of inventory turnover.	☐
7. Examining the inventory listing for inclusion of test counts recorded during the physical inventory observation.	☐

Computer Environment | Authoritative Literature | Help

The following are descriptions related to the computer environment. For each one, select from the list provided the one term or phrase that best fits the description. Each choice may be used once or not at all.

Description	Answer
1. A methodology that is not appropriate when systems are sophisticated or the major controls are included in the computer programs.	
2. The auditor prepares a set of dummy transactions specifically designed to test the control activities that management claims to have incorporated into the processing programs.	
3. The inappropriate duty assigned to the IT function.	
4. The auditor attempts to sign on to the computer system using various passwords and ID numbers.	
5. Controls that relate to the client's input, processing, and output.	
6. The auditor uses a controlled program to reprocess sets of client transactions and compares the auditor-achieved results with those of the client.	
7. The auditor should test first.	
8. The auditor inspects this to determine whether it is complete and up-to-date.	
9. A methodology that uses the computer to test the processing logic and controls within the system and the records produced.	
10. May be included in the payroll processing program.	

Term or Phrase
A) Application controls
B) Test data approach
C) Reasonableness test
D) Service department
E) Auditing around the computer
F) Auditing through the computer
G) Parallel simulation
H) Test of access controls
I) Programming
J) General controls
K) Program documentation
L) Asset custody

▼ = Reminder   Directions   1 2 3 [4] 5   ◀ Previous   Next ▶

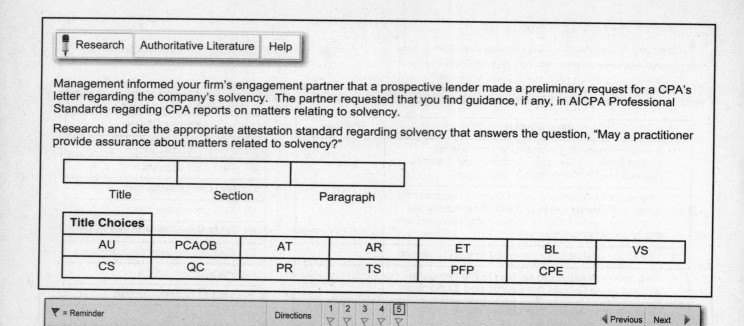

Unofficial Answers

1. Risk Factors (10 Gradable Items)

1.   Decrease RMM. Continued losses indicate an increase in risk. However, the turnaround into a profitable organization will likely decrease the risk of material misstatement in the financial statements for the auditor.

2.   Increase RMM. One set of opportunity risk factors for misstatements arising from fraudulent financial reporting involves ineffective monitoring of management. One such risk factor is domination of management by a single person or small group (in a non-owner managed business) without compensating controls. A compensating control in that circumstance is effective oversight by the board or audit committee of the financial reporting process and internal control.

3.   Increase RMM. Ideally, the internal auditor should report to the audit committee of the board of directors. If the internal auditor reports to operating management, the risk of material misstatement is increased.

4.   Increase RMM. When management turnover is high, particularly of senior accounting personnel, the risk of material misstatement is increased.

5.   Decrease RMM. Oversight by external parties, for example, a bank loan officer, provides some assurance to the auditor and decreases the risk of material misstatement.

6.   No effect. Paying employees biweekly likely has little effect on the risk of material misstatement.

7.   Decrease RMM. A continuing engagement in which the auditor has had experience with management is likely to be less risky than a first-time audit.

8.   Decrease RMM. The settlement of lawsuits filed against the client likely decreases the risk that the financial statements are misstated.

9.   Increase RMM. A set of opportunity risk factors for misstatements arising from fraudulent financial reporting involves the nature of the industry or the entity's operations. One such risk factor is the existence of significant related-party transactions not in the ordinary course of business or with entities not audited or audited by another firm.

10.   No effect. The change in insurance coverage for specific assets will not likely change the risk of material misstatement.

2. Analytical Results (3 Gradable Items)

1. <u>D) Capital stock was issued during the year.</u> The debt-to-equity ratio equals total liabilities divided by total equity. It compares the resources provided by creditors with the resources provided by shareholders. The decrease in the debt-to-equity ratio could be explained by the issuance of capital stock.

2. <u>F) Cost of goods sold decreased less than sales decreased during the year.</u> The gross profit percentage (gross profit margin) equals gross profit (net sales – cost of goods sold) divided by net sales. The smaller gross profit percentage could be explained by larger cost of goods sold relative to sales.

3. <u>C) Proceeds from the issuance of noncurrent debt were used to pay payables on a more current basis.</u> The quick ratio is current assets less inventory divided by current liabilities. Paying current liabilities with noncurrent debt could explain an increase in the quick ratio.

3. Substantive Procedures (7 Gradable Items)

1. <u>Incorrect.</u> Observing the physical count of inventory is a substantive procedure relating to the completeness assertion about balances.

2. <u>Incorrect.</u> Inspecting shipping and receiving transactions near year-end for recording in the proper period is a substantive procedure relating to the rights and obligations and completeness assertions.

3. <u>Incorrect.</u> Obtaining confirmation of inventories pledged under loan agreements is a substantive procedure relating to the rights and obligations assertions.

4. <u>Correct.</u> The valuation assertion about account balances addresses whether assets, liabilities, and equity items have been reported in the statements at appropriate amounts. For example, an assertion related to valuation of the inventory balance is that inventories are properly stated at the lower of cost or market. A substantive procedure for testing that assertion is to examine paid vendors' invoices.

5. <u>Incorrect.</u> Obtaining confirmation of inventories at locations outside the entity is a substantive procedure relating to the existence, completeness, and rights and obligations assertions.

6. <u>Correct.</u> Another consideration related to valuation of the inventory balance is that slow-moving, excess, defective, and obsolete inventory items are identified. A substantive procedure for testing that assertion is to analyze inventory turnover (AU 318).

7. <u>Incorrect.</u> Examining the inventory listing for inclusion of test counts recorded during the physical inventory observation is a substantive procedure relating to the completeness assertion.

4. Computer Environment (10 Gradable Items)

1. <u>E) Auditing around the computer.</u> Auditing around the computer is not appropriate when systems are sophisticated or the major controls are included in the computer programs.

2. <u>B) Test data approach.</u> In the test data approach, the auditor prepares a set of dummy transactions specifically designed to test the control activities that management claims to have incorporated into the processing programs.

3. <u>L) Asset custody.</u> The IT function is primarily recordkeeping and should not be assigned asset custody.

4. <u>H) Test of access controls.</u> In testing access controls, the auditor attempts to sign on to the computer system using various passwords and ID numbers.

5. <u>A) Application controls.</u> Application controls are those that are related to the client's information input, processing, and output.

6. <u>G) Parallel simulation.</u> Parallel simulation is a technique where the auditor uses a controlled program to reprocess sets of client transactions and compares the auditor-achieved results with those of the client.

7. <u>J) General controls.</u> Before testing application controls, the auditor should be satisfied that general controls are designed properly and operating effectively.

8. <u>K) Program documentation.</u> The auditor inspects program documentation to determine whether it is complete and up-to-date.

9. <u>F) Auditing through the computer.</u> Auditing through the computer is a methodology that uses the computer to test the processing logic and controls within the system and the records produced.

10. <u>C) Reasonableness test.</u> A reasonableness test is an application control that may be included in the payroll processing program.

5. Research (1 Gradable Item)

Answer: AT 9101.25

2. Responding to Requests for Reports on Matters Relating to Solvency

.25 *Interpretation*–No. For reasons set forth below, a practitioner should not provide any form of assurance, through examination, review or agreed-upon procedures engagements, that an entity

- Is not insolvent at the time the debt is incurred or would not be rendered insolvent thereby.
- Does not have unreasonably small capital.
- Has the ability to pay its debts as they mature.

In the context of particular transactions other terms are sometimes used or defined by the parties as equivalents of or substitutes for the terms listed above (e.g., fair salable value of assets exceeds liabilities). These terms, and those matters listed above, are hereinafter referred to as "matters relating to solvency." The prohibition extends to providing assurance concerning all such terms.

Gleim Simulation Grading

Task		Correct Responses		Gradable Items		Score per Task
1		_____	÷	10	=	_____
2		_____	÷	3	=	_____
3		_____	÷	7	=	_____
4		_____	÷	10	=	_____
Research		_____	÷	1	=	_____

	Total of Scores per Task	_____
÷	Total Number of Tasks	5
	Total Score	_____ %

Use **CPA Gleim Online** and **Simulation Wizard** to practice more task-based simulations in a realistic environment.

Success story!

I passed all 4 sections with scores greatly exceeding 75. The main thing I liked about Gleim Review Systems for passing the CPA exam was how the information was broken down into 20 separate study units. Each unit covered a small selection of material at a time which made it easier to study it. I felt my personal counselor was a useful asset. There was one instance when I do not think I would have been able to get past my issue without my counselor's guidance. I have already recommended Gleim to others.

- Kyle Boehnlein, CPA

STUDY UNIT NINE
INTERNAL CONTROL COMMUNICATIONS AND REPORTS

(18 pages of outline)

This study unit concerns various auditor communications and reports, most involving internal control. During the conduct of an audit, the auditor may observe control deficiencies. If so, the auditor has a responsibility to communicate significant deficiencies and material weaknesses to management and those charged with governance (*Communicating Internal Control Related Matters Identified in an Audit*). Other issues relating to the conduct of the audit also should be communicated to management and those charged with governance. Some of these issues are closely related to internal control, but others relate to the audit in general (AU 380, *The Auditor's Communication with Those Charged with Governance*). Public companies (issuers) are required by the Sarbanes-Oxley Act of 2002 to provide a management assessment of the effectiveness of internal control over financial reporting in annual reports. The PCAOB's Auditing Standard No. 5, *An Audit of Internal Control over Financial Reporting That is Integrated with An Audit of Financial Statements*, provides guidance on the required process and reporting. For example, it requires the auditor to express an opinion, or disclaim an opinion, on internal control, not on management's assessment. For other entities (nonissuers), the CPA may be engaged to provide a report on the effectiveness of an entity's internal control over financial reporting. This service and the reports issued are governed by the AICPA's AT 501, *An Examination of an Entity's Internal Control over Financial Reporting that is Integrated with an Audit of Its Financial Statements*. The CPA may be either a user or a preparer of a report prepared in accordance with AU 324, *Service Organizations*, and AT 801, *Reporting on Controls at a Service Organization*. Such a report may affect the user CPA's assessment of a client's risk of material misstatement.

9.1 COMMUNICATING INTERNAL CONTROL RELATED MATTERS IDENTIFIED IN AN AUDIT (AU 325)

1. The financial statement auditor is **not** required to perform procedures specifically to identify deficiencies in internal control or to express an opinion on internal control.

2. But, in each audit, the auditor should report **significant deficiencies** and **material weaknesses** in internal control over financial reporting that have been identified.

3. The communication should be **in writing** and directed to **management** and **those charged with governance** (e.g., a board of directors).

4. A **deficiency** in internal control exists when the **design or operation** of a control does not allow management or employees, in the normal course of their assigned functions, to prevent misstatements or detect and correct them on a timely basis.

5. A **significant deficiency** is a deficiency, or combination of deficiencies, in internal control that is less severe than a material weakness, but merits attention by those charged with governance.

6. A **material weakness** is a deficiency, or combination of deficiencies, in internal control that results in a **reasonable possibility** that a **material misstatement** of the financial statements will not be prevented or timely detected and corrected.

    a. A reasonable possibility means that the event is **reasonably possible** or **probable**.

7. **Evaluating Control Deficiencies**

    a. The auditor should evaluate each deficiency to determine whether, individually or in combination, it is a significant deficiency or a material weakness. The **severity of a deficiency** depends on

        1) The magnitude of the potential misstatement and
        2) Whether a reasonable possibility exists that the controls will fail.

    b. Severity does not depend on actual occurrence of a misstatement.

    c. The **magnitude** of a misstatement depends on, among other things,

        1) The financial statement amounts or transactions involved and
        2) The activity in the relevant balance or transaction class.

    d. The maximum **overstatement** ordinarily is the recorded amount, but the **understatement** may be greater.

        1) The auditor need not quantify the **probability** of misstatement.
        2) A small misstatement often is more likely than a large misstatement.

    e. **Risk factors** may indicate whether a reasonable possibility exists that a deficiency(ies) will result in a misstatement. The following are examples of risk factors:

        1) Accounts, transaction classes, disclosures, and assertions involved (e.g., overstatement of revenues and understatement of expenses)
        2) Susceptibility of the related asset or liability to loss or fraud
        3) Degree of judgment required to determine the amount involved
        4) Relationship of the control with other controls
        5) Interaction among deficiencies
        6) Possible consequences of the deficiency

    f. Effective **compensating controls** may limit the severity of a deficiency and prevent it from being reportable (a significant deficiency or a material weakness). However, they do not eliminate the deficiency.

        1) The auditor may consider the effects of compensating controls related to a **deficiency in operation**.

            a) But the auditor must have tested them for operating effectiveness.

    g. **Indicators of material weaknesses** include the following:

        1) Identification of any fraud by senior management
        2) Restatement of financial statements to correct a material misstatement due to fraud or error
        3) Identification by the auditor of a material misstatement that would not have been detected by internal control
        4) Ineffective oversight of financial reporting and internal control by those charged with governance

    h. The auditor considers whether prudent officials, having the same knowledge, would agree with the auditor that a deficiency(ies) is **not** a material weakness.

i. The following are examples of possible deficiencies, significant deficiencies, or material weaknesses related to **design**:

1) Inadequate design of internal control over financial statement preparation
2) Inadequate design of controls over a significant account or process
3) Inadequate documentation of the components of internal control
4) Insufficient control consciousness
5) Absent or inadequate separation of duties
6) Absent or inadequate controls over the safeguarding of assets
7) Inadequate design of IT general and application controls
8) Employees or management who lack the proper qualifications and training
9) Inadequate design of monitoring controls
10) The absence of an internal process to report deficiencies on a timely basis

j. The following are examples of deficiencies, significant deficiencies, or material weaknesses related to **operational failures**:

1) Failures in the operation of effectively designed controls over a significant account or process
2) Failure of the information and communication component of internal control to provide timely, complete, and accurate information
3) Failure of controls designed to safeguard assets
4) Failure to perform reconciliations of significant accounts
5) Undue bias or lack of objectivity by those responsible for accounting decisions
6) Misrepresentation by client personnel to the auditor
7) Management override of controls
8) Failure of an application control caused by deficient design or operation of an IT general control
9) An excessive observed deviation rate in a test of controls

8. **Communication**

a. The auditor should **communicate in writing** significant deficiencies and material weaknesses to management and those charged with governance.

b. The communication is best made at the **audit report release date**, but **no later than 60 days** after.

c. Communication of **significant and urgent matters** during the audit need not be in writing. But the auditor ultimately should communicate significant deficiencies and material weaknesses in writing even if they have been corrected.

d. Management or those charged with governance may **consciously decide to accept the risk** of significant deficiencies or material weaknesses. However, the auditor should communicate them regardless of such decisions.

e. The auditor may communicate other matters to the entity (such as deficiencies that are not significant deficiencies or material weaknesses), which may be made orally or in writing.

f. The **written communication** should

1) State that the purpose of the audit was to express an opinion on the financial statements.
2) State that the auditor is not expressing an opinion on the effectiveness of internal control.
3) State that the auditor's consideration of internal control was **not** designed to identify all deficiencies that might be significant deficiencies or material weaknesses.

4) Include the definition of a material weakness and, if relevant, the definition of a significant deficiency.
5) Identify significant deficiencies and material weaknesses.
6) Limit the use of the communication to management, those charged with governance, and others within the entity (and possibly governmental agencies).

EXAMPLE – Communications of Significant Deficiencies and Material Weaknesses

In planning and performing our audit of the financial statements of ABC Company as of and for the year ended December 31, Year 1, in accordance with auditing standards generally accepted in the United States of America, we considered the Company's internal control over financial reporting (internal control) as a basis for designing our auditing procedures for the purpose of expressing our opinion on the financial statements, but not for the purpose of expressing an opinion on the effectiveness of the Company's internal control. Accordingly, we do not express an opinion on the effectiveness of the Company's internal control.

Our consideration of internal control was for the limited purpose described in the preceding paragraph and was not designed to identify all deficiencies in internal control that might be significant deficiencies or material weaknesses. Therefore, there can be no assurance that all deficiencies, significant deficiencies, or material weaknesses have been identified. However, as discussed below, we identified certain deficiencies in internal control that we consider to be material weaknesses *[and other deficiencies that we consider to be significant deficiencies]*.

A deficiency in internal control exists when the design or operation of a control does not allow management or employees, in the normal course of performing their assigned functions, to prevent, or detect and correct misstatements on a timely basis. A material weakness is a deficiency, or a combination of deficiencies, in internal control, such that there is a reasonable possibility that a material misstatement of the entity's financial statements will not be prevented, or detected and corrected on a timely basis. *[We consider the following deficiencies in the Company's internal control to be material weaknesses:]*

[Describe the material weaknesses that were identified.]

[A significant deficiency is a deficiency, or a combination of deficiencies, in internal control, that is less severe than a material weakness, yet important enough to merit attention by those charged with governance. We consider the following deficiencies in the Company's internal control to be significant deficiencies:]

[Describe the significant deficiencies that were identified.]

This communication is intended solely for the information and use of management, *[identify the body or individuals charged with governance]*, others within the organization, *[identify any specified governmental authorities]* and is not intended to be and should not be used by anyone other than these specified parties.

---

g. A client may ask the auditor to issue a written communication for the client to submit to governmental authorities stating that **no material weaknesses** were identified. A communication similar to the above example is appropriate, with the following paragraph added:

EXAMPLE

Our consideration of internal control was for the limited purpose described in the first paragraph and was not designed to identify all deficiencies in internal control that might be deficiencies, significant deficiencies, or material weaknesses. We did not identify any deficiencies in internal control that we consider to be material weaknesses, as defined above.

---

h. An auditor should **not** issue a written communication stating that **no significant deficiencies** were identified.

Stop and review! You have completed the outline for this subunit. Study multiple-choice questions 1 through 10 beginning on page 320.

9.2 THE AUDITOR'S COMMUNICATION WITH THOSE CHARGED WITH GOVERNANCE (AU 380)

1. Those charged with governance are responsible for oversight of the entity's strategic direction and accountability, including the **financial reporting process**. The **board of directors** and the **audit committee** are typical governance bodies.

   a. **Two-way communication** is expected and should provide those charged with governance with information about matters relevant to their responsibilities, including an overview of the audit process and of the auditor's responsibilities.

      1) It also should allow the auditor to obtain information relevant to the audit.

   b. Communication may be either **oral or in writing** and should be **documented**.

      1) The auditor communicates significant findings from the audit in writing when (s)he judges that oral communication is inadequate.

         a) A written communication should indicate that it is for the **sole use** of those charged with governance.

   c. Communication should take place on a **timely basis** to enable those charged with governance to meet their responsibilities for oversight of financial reporting (e.g., those relating to planning should take place early in the engagement).

   d. It may be appropriate for **management** to communicate certain matters to those charged with governance, and the auditor should be satisfied that such communication has occurred.

      1) Many matters are discussed with management during the audit. But certain discussions may be inappropriate, e.g., those related to management's integrity.

2. **Matters to be communicated** include the auditor's responsibilities under GAAS, an overview of the audit, and significant findings.

3. **Auditor's Responsibilities under GAAS**

   a. The auditor may provide a copy of the **engagement letter** (see Study Unit 3, Subunit 1) to those charged with governance, indicating that, among other things,

      1) The auditor is responsible for forming and expressing an opinion about whether the financial statements are presented fairly.

      2) The audit does not relieve management or those charged with governance of their responsibilities for fair reporting.

4. **Planned Scope and Timing of the Audit**

   a. An **overview** should be provided, but should in no way compromise the effectiveness of the audit. The auditor should never discuss details of procedures to be used. Issues to be addressed include

      1) How the auditor proposes to address the risks of material misstatement, due to error or fraud;

      2) Issues related to internal control and the internal audit function; and

      3) The concept of materiality in planning and executing the audit.

5. **Qualitative Aspects of the Entity's Significant Accounting Practices**

   a. The auditor should inform those charged with governance about

      1) Management's selection of, changes in, and application of significant accounting policies

      2) Management's methods used to account for significant, unusual transactions

      3) The effects of significant accounting policies in controversial or emerging areas that lack authoritative guidance or consensus, such as revenue recognition, off-balance-sheet financing, and accounting for equity investments

6. Those charged with governance should be informed of **significant difficulties** encountered in dealing with management, such as delays in providing required information and unnecessary time constraints on the audit. Other significant problems may include unavailability of information and management-imposed restrictions.

7. All known and likely misstatements, other than those judged trivial, must be communicated to management. **All uncorrected misstatements** should be communicated to those charged with governance, along with their potential effect.

   a. The auditor should discuss with those charged with governance the implications of not correcting misstatements.

8. Management and the auditor may disagree about (a) the application of accounting principles, (b) the basis for accounting estimates, (c) the scope of the audit, (d) disclosures, and (e) the audit report.

   a. The auditor and those charged with governance should discuss any disagreements about matters significant to the statements or the audit report.

9. When the auditor is aware of consultations between management and other accountants, (s)he should discuss with those charged with governance his/her views about the significant matters involved.

10. The auditor and those charged with governance should discuss such issues as (a) business conditions affecting the entity, (b) plans and strategies affecting the RMMs, (c) the initial or recurring retention of the auditors, and (d) the application of accounting principles.

11. Discussions may be appropriate about circumstances or relationships (e.g., financial interests, business or family relationships, or nonaudit services) that, in the auditor's professional judgment,

   a. May reasonably bear on independence and
   b. Were given significant consideration by the auditor in reaching the conclusion that independence has not been impaired.

12. Events or conditions may, when examined in the aggregate, indicate **substantial doubt about the entity's ability to continue as a going concern for a reasonable period of time**.

   a. If, after considering management's plans in response to the events or conditions identified, the auditor concludes that the substantial doubt remains, the auditor should communicate the following to those charged with governance:

      1) The possible effect on the financial statements and the adequacy of related disclosures contained in them
      2) The effects on the auditor's report

13. **Sarbanes-Oxley Act of 2002**

   a. The act requires the auditor to report the following to those charged with governance:

      1) All critical accounting policies and practices to be used
      2) All material alternative treatments of financial information within GAAP discussed with management
      3) Ramifications of the use of alternative disclosures and treatments
      4) The treatment preferred by the auditor

Stop and review! You have completed the outline for this subunit. Study multiple-choice questions 11 through 18 beginning on page 323.

9.3 REPORTING ON AN ENTITY'S INTERNAL CONTROL

1. The PCAOB's **Auditing Standard No. 5 (AS No. 5)**, *An Audit of Internal Control over Financial Reporting that is Integrated with an Audit of Financial Statements*, provides guidance on the required process and reporting for **issuers**.

2. AT 501, *An Examination of an Entity's Internal Control over Financial Reporting that is Integrated with an Audit of Its Financial Statements*, describes the service for **nonissuers**. It is consistent with AS No. 5.

    a. The basic differences are that it is **not a required part** of the financial statement audit, and the required reports refer to AICPA standards rather than PCAOB standards.

    b. The outline beginning below covers the **audit** of internal control under AS No. 5, but it also applies to **examinations** under AT 501.

3. A company subject to the reporting requirements of the Securities Exchange Act of 1934 (an "issuer") with a market equity value of at least $75 million (an "accelerated filer") must include in its annual report **management's assessment** of the design and effectiveness of **internal control over financial reporting**.

    a. The assessment should be performed using suitable **control criteria**, such as *Internal Control – Integrated Framework* published by the Committee of Sponsoring Organizations (COSO) (recall the components of internal control from Study Unit 5, Subunit 1, Controls stop **CRIME**).

        1) The same framework used by management should be used by the auditor.

4. The **auditor's objective** in an audit of internal control over financial reporting ("audit of internal control") is to express an opinion on the effectiveness of the company's internal control over financial reporting ("internal control") based on the control criteria. However, internal control is not effective if a material weakness exists.

    a. Accordingly, the auditor must plan and perform the audit to obtain competent evidence sufficient to obtain **reasonable assurance** about whether **material weaknesses** exist at the date of management's assessment.

    b. AS No. 5 applies when an auditor audits management's assessment of the effectiveness of internal control over financial reporting.

        1) However, the auditor expresses an opinion directly on internal control, not on management's assessment.

            a) If a material weakness exists, the auditor expresses an adverse opinion.

                i)   If management's assessment does not include the material weakness, the report is modified to state that the material weakness was not included in the assessment.

    c. Under AT 501, the auditor may express an opinion directly on internal control or on whether management's assertion about internal control is fairly stated.

5. The **general standards** (included in the 10 GAAS) are applicable to an audit of internal control. Those standards require (a) technical training and proficiency as an auditor, (b) independence, and (c) the exercise of due professional care, including professional skepticism.

    a. AS No. 5 establishes **field work and reporting standards** for the audit of internal control.

6. **Integrating the Audits**

    a. The audit of internal control should be integrated with the audit of the financial statements. The integrated audit should achieve the objectives of both.

1) The auditor should design **tests of controls** to obtain sufficient appropriate evidence to support the auditor's opinion on internal control over financial reporting

    a) At a moment in time (e.g., at year-end)

    b) Taken as a whole (i.e., addressing the effectiveness of selected controls over all relevant assertions)

2) The audit (examination) of internal control typically involves testing controls not tested in a financial statement audit.

7. **Planning the Audit**

    a. The integrated audit should be properly planned, and assistants, if any, should be properly supervised. The auditor should evaluate how the following affect the audit procedures:

        1) Knowledge of internal control obtained during other engagements

        2) Client industry issues, such as financial reporting practices, economic conditions, laws and regulations, and technological changes

        3) Matters related to the business, e.g., operating characteristics, capital structure, and organization

        4) Recent changes in operations or in internal control

        5) Preliminary judgments about materiality, risk, and other factors relating to the determination of material weaknesses

        6) Control deficiencies previously communicated to the audit committee or management

        7) Legal or regulatory matters

        8) The type and extent of available evidence related to the effectiveness of internal control

        9) Preliminary judgments about internal control

        10) Public information relevant to the likelihood of material misstatements and the effectiveness of internal control

        11) The relative complexity of operations

        12) Knowledge about risks obtained from the client acceptance and retention evaluation

8. A direct relationship exists between the degree of risk that a material weakness could exist and the amount of audit attention that should be devoted to that area.

9. The size and complexity of the company, its business processes, and business units may affect the way in which the company achieves many of its **control objectives**. Size and complexity also affect risks and related controls.

    a. Thus, **scaling** is an extension of the risk-based approach.

10. **Addressing the Risk of Fraud**

    a. The auditor should (1) consider the results of the fraud risk assessment and (2) evaluate (a) whether controls sufficiently address the identified risks of material fraud and (b) controls over the risk of management override. The following controls address these risks:

        1) Controls over significant, unusual transactions, particularly those that result in late or unusual journal entries

        2) Controls over journal entries and adjustments made in the period-end financial reporting process

        3) Controls over related-party transactions

          4)   Controls related to significant management estimates

          5)   Controls that mitigate incentives for, and pressures on, management to falsify or inappropriately manage financial results

11. **Using the Work of Others**

    a.   The auditor may use the work performed by, or receive direct assistance from, internal auditors, company personnel, and third parties working under the direction of management or the audit committee that provides evidence about the effectiveness of internal control.

    b.   The auditor should assess the competence and objectivity of the persons whose work the auditor plans to use. The higher the degree of competence and objectivity, the greater use the auditor may make of the work.

12. The same **materiality** considerations apply in the audit of internal control as in planning the audit of the annual financial statements.

13. **Using a Top-Down Approach**

    a.   The auditor begins at the financial statement level by understanding overall risks. (S)he then focuses on **entity-level controls** and works down to significant accounts and disclosures and their relevant assertions. Examples of entity-level controls are controls

          1)   Related to the control environment
          2)   Over management override
          3)   To monitor results of operations
          4)   Over the period-end financial reporting process
          5)   To monitor other controls
          6)   Constituting the entity's risk assessment process

    b.   The auditor should evaluate the **control environment** by assessing whether

          1)   Management's philosophy and operating style promote effective internal control.
          2)   Sound integrity and ethical values, particularly of management, are developed and understood.
          3)   The board or audit committee understands and exercises oversight responsibility over financial reporting and internal control.

    c.   The auditor should evaluate the **period-end financial reporting process**, including procedures

          1)   Used to enter transaction totals into the general ledger;
          2)   Related to the selection and application of accounting policies;
          3)   Used to initiate, authorize, record, and process journal entries;
          4)   Used to record recurring and nonrecurring adjustments to the annual and quarterly financial statements; and
          5)   For preparing annual and quarterly financial statements and related disclosures.

14. **Identifying Significant Accounts and Disclosures and Their Relevant Assertions**

    a.   The auditor may use assertions other than those in AS No. 5 if (s)he has tested controls over the pertinent risks. The following are risk factors related to accounts and disclosures:

          1)   Size and composition of the account
          2)   Susceptibility to misstatement due to errors or fraud
          3)   Volume of activity, complexity, and homogeneity of the transactions
          4)   Nature of the account or disclosure
          5)   Accounting and reporting complexities
          6)   Exposure to losses in the account

       7)   Possibility of significant contingent liabilities arising from the activities reflected in the account or disclosure

       8)   Existence of related-party transactions in the account

       9)   Changes from the prior period or disclosure characteristics

15. Performing **walkthroughs** (following transactions through the process) will frequently be the most effective way of achieving the following objectives

    a.   Understanding the flow of transactions related to relevant assertions

    b.   Identifying the points within the company's processes at which a material misstatement – including a misstatement due to fraud – could arise

    c.   Identifying the controls that management has implemented to address these potential misstatements

    d.   Identifying the controls that management has implemented over the prevention or timely detection of unauthorized acquisition, use, or disposition of assets

16. **Testing Controls**

    a.   **Testing Design Effectiveness**

       1)   The auditor should determine whether controls, if they are operated as prescribed by persons with the necessary authority and competence to perform them effectively, (a) satisfy the control objectives and (b) can effectively prevent or detect errors or fraud that could result in material misstatements in the financial statements.

       2)   Procedures include (a) inquiry of appropriate personnel, (b) observation of operations, and (c) inspection of relevant documentation. Walkthroughs that include these procedures ordinarily are sufficient to evaluate design effectiveness.

    b.   **Testing Operating Effectiveness**

       1)   The auditor should determine whether (a) a control is operating as designed and (b) the person performing the control possesses the necessary authority and competence to perform the control effectively.

       2)   Procedures the auditor performs to test operating effectiveness include a mix of (a) inquiry of appropriate personnel, (b) observation of the company's operations, (c) inspection of relevant documentation, and (d) reperformance of the control.

    c.   **Relationship of Risk to the Evidence to Be Obtained**

       1)   More risk requires more testing and more competent evidence.

       2)   Generally, a conclusion that a control is not operating effectively can be supported by less evidence than is necessary to support a conclusion that a control is operating effectively.

       3)   Different combinations of the **nature, timing, and extent of testing** may provide sufficient evidence.

          a)   **Nature** of tests of controls. The following tests are presented in order of the evidence that they ordinarily would produce, from least to most: (1) inquiry, (2) observation, (3) inspection of relevant documentation, and (4) reperformance of a control. Inquiry alone does not provide sufficient evidence to support a conclusion about the effectiveness of a control.

          b)   **Timing** of tests of controls. Testing controls over a greater period of time provides more evidence of the effectiveness of controls than testing over a shorter period of time. Moreover, testing closer to the date of management's assessment provides more evidence than testing earlier in the year.

        c) **Extent** of tests of controls. The more extensively a control is tested, the greater the evidence obtained from that test.

        d) **Roll-forward procedures.** To roll forward the results of interim work, the auditor should consider (1) the specific controls, their associated risks, and the test results; (2) the sufficiency of evidence obtained at the interim date; (3) the length of the remaining period; and (4) the possibility of changes.

17. **Evaluating Identified Deficiencies**

    a. The auditor should evaluate the severity of each **deficiency** in internal control to determine whether the deficiencies, individually or in combination, are **material weaknesses** as of the date of management's assessment.

       1) A **deficiency** exists when the design or operation of a control does not allow management or employees, in the normal course of performing their assigned functions, to prevent or detect misstatements on a timely basis.

       2) A **significant deficiency** is a deficiency, or a combination of deficiencies, in internal control that is less severe than a material weakness yet important enough to merit attention by those responsible for oversight of the company's financial reporting.

       3) A **material weakness** is a deficiency, or a combination of deficiencies, in internal control such that there is a **reasonable possibility** that a material misstatement of the annual or interim financial statements will not be prevented or detected on a timely basis.

> Note that the definitions of control deficiency, significant deficiency, and material weakness are the same as those used in AU 325 (which requires auditor communication with those charged with governance), discussed in Subunit 9.1. Also, these definitions are the same as those used to describe control deficiencies in governmental audits presented in Study Unit 20. Make sure you know these definitions, as they are popular topics for questions on the CPA exam.

    b. The auditor is not required to search for deficiencies that, individually or in combination, are **less severe than a material weakness**.

    c. The **severity of a deficiency** does not depend on whether a misstatement actually has occurred but rather on whether there is a reasonable possibility that the controls will fail to prevent or detect a misstatement.

18. The following are **indicators of material weaknesses** in internal control:

    a. Identification of fraud, whether or not material, on the part of senior management

    b. Restatement of previously issued financial statements to reflect the correction of a material misstatement

    c. Identification by the auditor of a material misstatement of financial statements in the current period in circumstances that indicate that the misstatement would not have been detected by internal control

    d. Ineffective oversight of the company's external financial reporting and internal control by the audit committee

19. The auditor should **form an opinion** on the effectiveness of internal control by evaluating evidence obtained from all sources, including (a) the auditor's testing of controls, (b) misstatements detected during the financial statement audit, and (c) any identified control deficiencies.

20. The auditor should **obtain written representations** from management.

    a.   Acknowledging management's responsibility for establishing and maintaining effective internal control.

    b.   Stating that management has performed an evaluation and made an assessment of the effectiveness of the internal control and specifying the control criteria (e.g., the COSO model).

    c.   Stating that management did not use the auditor's procedures performed during the audits of internal control or the financial statements as part of the basis for management's assessment of the effectiveness of internal control.

    d.   Stating management's conclusion about the effectiveness of internal control based on the control criteria at a specified date.

    e.   Stating that management has disclosed to the auditor all deficiencies in internal control identified in its evaluation.

    f.   Describing any material fraud and any other fraud involving senior management or management or other employees who have a significant role in internal control.

    g.   Stating whether control deficiencies identified and communicated to the audit committee during previous engagements have been resolved.

    h.   Stating whether there were, subsequent to the date being reported on, any changes in internal control or other factors that might significantly affect internal control.

21. **Communicating Certain Matters**

    a.   The auditor should communicate, in writing, to management and the audit committee all **material weaknesses** and **significant deficiencies** identified during the audit.

    b.   The auditor should communicate to management, in writing, **all deficiencies** in internal control in addition to material weaknesses and significant deficiencies.

    c.   The written communication should be made prior to the issuance of the auditor's report.

22. **Reporting on Internal Control**

    a.   See the example report on the next page for the components of the auditor's report on internal control.

        1)   The report may be a separate report, or it may be combined with the opinion on the financial statements as in the example report.

        2)   The auditor should date the audit report no earlier than the date on which the auditor has obtained sufficient competent evidence to support the auditor's opinion. The dates of the report on the financial statements and the report on internal control should be the same.

        3)   For an examination based on AT 501 for nonissuers, the report refers to AICPA Statements on Standards for Attestation Engagements in the scope paragraph.

EXAMPLE – **Combined Report on the Financial Statements and on Internal Control**

Report of Independent Registered Public Accounting Firm

To: <----------- Addressed to the Board of Directors and/or Stockholders

[Introductory paragraph]

We have audited the accompanying balance sheets of W Company as of December 31, Year 2 and Year 1, and the related statements of income, stockholders' equity and comprehensive income, and cash flows for each of the years in the 3-year period ended December 31, Year 2. We also have audited W Company's internal control over financial reporting as of December 31, Year 2, based on *Internal Control – Integrated Framework Issued by the Committee of Sponsoring Organizations of the Treadway Commission (COSO).* W Company's management is responsible for these financial statements, for maintaining effective internal control over financial reporting, and for its assessment of the effectiveness of internal control over financial reporting, included in the accompanying [title of management's report]. Our responsibility is to express an opinion on these financial statements and an opinion on the company's internal control over financial reporting based on our audits.

[Scope paragraph]

We conducted our audits in accordance with the standards of the Public Company Accounting Oversight Board (United States). Those standards require that we plan and perform the audits to obtain reasonable assurance about whether the financial statements are free of material misstatement and whether effective internal control over financial reporting was maintained in all material respects. Our audits of the financial statements included examining, on a test basis, evidence supporting the amounts and disclosures in the financial statements, assessing the accounting principles used and significant estimates made by management, and evaluating the overall financial statement presentation. Our audit of internal control over financial reporting included obtaining an understanding of internal control over financial reporting, assessing the risk that a material weakness exists, and testing and evaluating the design and operating effectiveness of internal control based on the assessed risk. Our audits also included performing such other procedures as we considered necessary in the circumstances. We believe that our audits provide a reasonable basis for our opinions.

[Definition paragraph]

A company's internal control over financial reporting is a process designed to provide reasonable assurance regarding the reliability of financial reporting and the preparation of financial statements for external purposes in accordance with generally accepted accounting principles. A company's internal control over financial reporting includes those policies and procedures that (1) pertain to the maintenance of records that, in reasonable detail, accurately and fairly reflect the transactions and dispositions of the assets of the company; (2) provide reasonable assurance that transactions are recorded as necessary to permit preparation of financial statements in accordance with generally accepted accounting principles, and that receipts and expenditures of the company are being made only in accordance with authorizations of management and directors of the company; and (3) provide reasonable assurance regarding prevention or timely detection of unauthorized acquisition, use, or disposition of the company's assets that could have a material effect on the financial statements.

[Inherent limitations paragraph]

Because of its inherent limitations, internal control over financial reporting may not prevent or detect misstatements. Also, projections of any evaluation of effectiveness to future periods are subject to the risk that controls may become inadequate because of changes in conditions, or that the degree of compliance with the policies or procedures may deteriorate.

[Opinion paragraph]

In our opinion, the financial statements referred to above present fairly, in all material respects, the financial position of W Company as of December 31, Year 2 and Year 1, and the results of its operations and its cash flows for each of the years in the 3-year period ended December 31, Year 2, in conformity with accounting principles generally accepted in the United States of America. Also in our opinion, W Company maintained, in all material respects, effective internal control over financial reporting as of December 31, Year 2, based on *Internal Control – Integrated Framework Issued by the Committee of Sponsoring Organizations of the Treadway Commission (COSO).*

Signature   <---------- May be signed, typed, or printed
City and State or Country <---------- Location of audit
Date   <---------- No earlier than the date on which the auditor has obtained sufficient appropriate evidence

23.   The auditor should **modify the standard report** on internal control in any of the following circumstances:

    a.   A **material weakness** requires an **adverse opinion**.

        1)   The report must include the definition of a material weakness.

    b.   Elements of management's annual report on internal control are incomplete or improperly presented.

    c.   The scope of the engagement is restricted.

    d.   The auditor decides to refer to the report of other auditors as the basis, in part, for the auditor's own report.

    e.   Other information is contained in management's annual report on internal control.

    f.   Management's annual certification under Section 302 of the Sarbanes-Oxley Act is misstated.

24.   The PCAOB's **AS No. 4**, *Reporting on Whether a Previously Reported Material Weakness Continues to Exist*, addresses management requests to the auditor to provide a new opinion on whether a material weakness(es), which caused an adverse opinion, has been remediated.

    a.   The auditor is allowed to reaudit the control based on management's assertion that the deficiency has been corrected and to provide an opinion relative to the control.

    b.   Similar standards apply to the new engagement as for the initial reporting engagement on internal control.

Stop and review! You have completed the outline for this subunit. Study multiple-choice questions 19 through 28 beginning on page 326.

9.4 SERVICE ORGANIZATIONS (AU 324 AND AT 801)

Background

AU 324 was originally adopted to address issues related to both the user auditor and the service auditor. However, the AU standards are relevant to the audit of financial statements, while the service auditor is charged with issuing reports on internal control. Since this function is an attestation service, AT 801, *Reporting on Controls at a Service Organization*, was recently adopted. AU 324 provides guidance for the user auditor's use of the reports, while AT 801 addresses the service auditor's preparation of the reports.

---

1.   These standards apply to a financial statement audit of an entity that uses another organization's services as part of its own information system ("outsourcing").

2.   A service organization's services are part of the client's information system if they have an effect on

    a.   Initiation of transactions
    b.   Accounting records, supporting information, and specific accounts
    c.   Processing from initiation to inclusion of transactions in the statements
    d.   The process used to prepare statements, including estimates and disclosures

3.   The standard concerns

    a.   Factors to be considered by an auditor whose client uses a service organization to process certain transactions.

    b.   Guidance to auditors who issue reports on the processing of transactions by a service organization for use by other auditors.

4.   The **user organization (user)** is an entity that is a user of a service organization and whose financial statements are being audited.

5.   The **user auditor** is the auditor of the user organization.

6.   The **service organization** is an entity that provides services to user organizations.

7.   The **service auditor** is an auditor who reports on the processing of transactions by a service organization.

8.   The **report on controls implemented** is the service auditor's report on (a) a service organization's description of its internal controls, (b) whether they were suitably designed to achieve specified control objectives, and (c) whether they had been implemented as of a specific date.

9.   The **report on controls implemented and tests of operating effectiveness** is the service auditor's report on (a) a service organization's description of its internal controls; (b) whether they were suitably designed; (c) whether they had been implemented; and (d) whether the controls tested were operating with sufficient effectiveness to provide reasonable, but not absolute, assurance that the related objectives were achieved.

10. The significance of the **service organization's controls** depends primarily on the transactions it processes for the user and the degree of interaction between its activities and those of the user.

   a.   When the user initiates transactions and the service organization executes and processes such transactions, **the degree of interaction is high**. In this case, the user may be able to implement effective controls for those transactions.

   b.   When the service organization initiates, executes, and processes the user's transactions, **the degree of interaction is lower**, and the user may not be able to implement effective controls.

11. **Planning the Audit**

   a.   An auditor should obtain an understanding of the components of internal control to assess the risks of material misstatement and design further procedures. This understanding may extend to controls implemented not only by the client but also by service organization.

   b.   Sufficient information about the nature of the services that are part of the user's information system and the service organization's controls may be available from many sources. Examples are the contract between the parties or the reports of service auditors, internal auditors, or regulators.

   c.   If sufficient information is not available, the user auditor may

      1)   Request information, through the client, from the service organization.

      2)   Visit the service organization and perform necessary procedures.

      3)   Request that a service auditor be engaged to perform procedures and provide a report.

12. **Assessing the User's Control Risk**

   a.   The user auditor assesses control risk for, among other assertions, those affected by service organization activities.

      1)   This process may allow the user auditor to identify controls that, if effective, will result in an assessment of control risk as **low or moderate**.

      2)   These controls may be implemented by the user or the service organization.

   b.   If relevant controls are **implemented at the service organization**, the user auditor should obtain evidence of their **operating effectiveness** by doing at least one of the following:

      1)   Performing tests of the controls (a) at the service organization or (b) implemented by the user (e.g., tests of the user's sample reperformance of service organization processing)

2) Obtaining (a) a service auditor's report on controls implemented and tests of operating effectiveness or (b) a report on agreed-upon procedures describing tests of controls

c. A **service auditor's report** on the effectiveness of controls may be intended for two or more user auditors.

1) Thus, the user auditor should determine whether the tests and results described are

a) **Relevant to significant assertions** in the user's statements and

b) Provide **appropriate evidence** to support the assessment of control risk.

13. The results of **substantive procedures** performed by **service auditors** may be used by the user auditor as part of the evidence to support the opinion on the financial statements.

14. The user auditor should make **inquiries** concerning the service auditor's **professional reputation**.

15. The user auditor may request **agreed-upon procedures**.

16. The user auditor **should not refer to the service auditor's report** as a basis, in part, for his/her own opinion. The service auditor was not responsible for examining any portion of the user's statements.

17. **Responsibilities of Service Auditors**

a. The engagement differs from an audit of financial statements, but the service auditor should follow applicable GAAS. Thus, (s)he should follow the general standards and the relevant field work and reporting standards.

b. The service auditor should be independent of the service organization (and should include the term "independent" in the title of the report) but not of each user.

c. If the service auditor becomes aware of errors, fraud, or illegal acts that may affect the user, (s)he should determine from management of the service organization whether the information has been communicated to the users. If not, the service auditor should inform those charged with governance of the service organization. If (s)he is not satisfied with the response, the service auditor may consider resigning.

d. **Reports on Controls Implemented**

1) These reports may be relevant to the user auditor's understanding of internal control, but they do not permit the user auditor to assess control risk at a low or moderate level. The report expressing an opinion on a description of the controls implemented includes the following:

a) A reference to the aspects of the service organization covered

b) A description of the service auditor's procedures

c) Identification of the party stating the control objectives

d) A statement of purposes of the engagement

e) A disclaimer of opinion on operating effectiveness

f) An opinion on whether the service organization's description fairly presents, in all material respects, the relevant aspects of the controls implemented at a specific date and whether they were suitably designed to provide reasonable assurance that the control objectives would be achieved if complied with satisfactorily

g) A statement of inherent limitations

h) Identification of the parties for whom the report is intended

e.   **Reports on Controls Implemented and Tests of Operating Effectiveness**

1)   These reports may be relevant to a user auditor in obtaining understanding and determining the effectiveness of internal control. They may allow the user auditor to assess control risk **at a low or moderate level**.

2)   The report expressing an opinion on a description of the controls implemented and tests of operating effectiveness includes all the components of a report on controls implemented (modified as appropriate), except for the disclaimer of opinion and the following:

a)   A reference to a description of tests of specified service organization controls designed to obtain evidence about their operating effectiveness. The description should include the controls that were tested, the control objectives, the tests applied, and the results of the tests. The description should include an indication of the nature, timing, and extent of the tests, as well as sufficient detail to enable a user auditor to determine the effect of such tests on his/her assessment of control risk.

b)   A statement of the period covered by the service auditor's report on the operating effectiveness of the specified controls.

c)   The service auditor's opinion on whether the controls that were tested were operating with sufficient effectiveness to provide reasonable, but not absolute, assurance that the related control objectives were achieved during the period specified.

d)   A statement that no the opinion is expressed on control objectives not listed in the description of tests performed.

e)   A statement that the effectiveness and significance of the service organization's controls are dependent on their interaction with factors present at individual user organizations.

f)   A statement that the service auditor has performed no procedures to evaluate the effectiveness of controls at individual user organizations.

3)   Regardless of the type of report issued, the service auditor should obtain **written representations** from the service organization's management about (a) its responsibility for the controls; (b) the appropriateness of specified control objectives; (c) the fairness of the description of relevant controls; (d) implementation of controls at a given date; (e) the suitability of the design of controls; (f) disclosures of changes in controls since the last examination; (g) subsequent events; (h) disclosures of fraud, illegal acts, or uncorrected errors; and (i) disclosures of design deficiencies.

18. **Reports**

a.   The service organization must prepare a **description of its system**. It includes

1)   The nature of the service to users.
2)   How the service is provided.
3)   Controls over the service.
4)   Control objectives.

b.   The service auditor may provide two types of **examination** reports.

1)   A **type 1 report** expresses an opinion on (a) the fair presentation of the description and (b) whether the controls are **suitably designed**.

a)   Suitable design means the controls can attain the control objectives if they operate effectively.

2)   A **type 2 report** expresses not only the type 1 opinions but also an opinion on whether the controls were **operating effectively** (meeting the control objectives).

c. Management must give the service auditor a **written assertion** about (1) the fair presentation of the system description and (2) the suitability of the design of controls (type 1) and their operating effectiveness (type 2).

1) The system description and the opinion on it address the **period** covered by the tests of operating effectiveness (type 2).

Stop and review! You have completed the outline for this subunit. Study multiple-choice questions 29 through 32 beginning on page 328.

QUESTIONS

9.1 Communicating Internal Control Related Matters Identified in an Audit (AU 325)

1. An auditor's written communication of internal control related matters identified in an audit would be addressed to "those charged with governance," which would include the

A. Board of directors.

B. Director of internal auditing.

C. Chief financial officer.

D. Chief accounting officer.

Answer (A) is correct. *(CPA, adapted)*
REQUIRED: The recipient of the auditor's written communication of internal control related matters identified in an audit.
DISCUSSION: In many organizations, governance is provided by the board of directors (and its related audit committee). However, the communication may be made to individuals at an equivalent level of authority and responsibility if the organization does not have a board.

2. Which of the following matters would an auditor most likely consider to be a significant deficiency or material weakness to be communicated to those charged with governance?

A. Management's failure to renegotiate unfavorable long-term purchase commitments.

B. Recurring operating losses that may indicate going concern problems.

C. Evidence of a lack of objectivity by those responsible for accounting decisions.

D. Management's current plans to reduce its ownership equity in the entity.

Answer (C) is correct. *(CPA, adapted)*
REQUIRED: The significant deficiency or material weakness.
DISCUSSION: Failures in internal control include deficiencies in internal control design and failures in the operation of internal control. An example of the second type is evidence of "undue bias or lack of objectivity by those responsible for accounting decisions" (AU 325).
Answer (A) is incorrect. Management's failure to renegotiate unfavorable long-term purchase commitments is not a failure in internal control over financial reporting. Answer (B) is incorrect. Recurring operating losses that may indicate going concern problems is not a failure in internal control over financial reporting. Answer (D) is incorrect. Management's current plans to reduce its ownership equity in the entity is not a failure in internal control over financial reporting.

3. During consideration of internal control in a financial statement audit, an auditor is **not** obligated to

A. Search for significant deficiencies in the operation of internal control.

B. Understand the internal control environment.

C. Determine whether the control activities relevant to audit planning have been implemented.

D. Perform procedures to understand the design of internal control.

Answer (A) is correct. *(CPA, adapted)*
REQUIRED: The task not required during the auditor's consideration of the internal control.
DISCUSSION: The auditor should obtain an understanding of internal control and assess the risk of material misstatement to plan the audit. The limited purpose of this consideration does not include the search for significant deficiencies or material weaknesses.
Answer (B) is incorrect. The auditor should obtain an understanding of the five components of internal control. Answer (C) is incorrect. Obtaining the understanding of controls relevant to audit planning includes performing procedures to provide sufficient knowledge of the design of the relevant controls pertaining to the internal control components. It also includes determining whether they have been implemented. Answer (D) is incorrect. The understanding also includes knowledge about whether relevant controls have been implemented.

4. Which of the following issues related to internal control over financial reporting should be communicated in writing to management and those charged with governance?

I.   Control deficiencies
II. Significant deficiencies
III. Material weaknesses

    A. I, II, and III.

    B. II and III only.

    C. III only.

    D. None.

Answer (B) is correct. *(Publisher, adapted)*
    REQUIRED: The issues communicated to management and those charged with governance.
    DISCUSSION: Only those control deficiencies considered as significant deficiencies or material weaknesses should be communicated in writing to management and those charged with governance. A control deficiency exists when the design or operation of a control does not allow management or employees, in the normal course of performing their assigned functions, to prevent or detect misstatements on a timely basis. A significant deficiency is a deficiency, or a combination of deficiencies, in internal control that is less severe than a material weakness, yet important enough to merit attention by those charged with governance. A material weakness is a deficiency, or combination of deficiencies, in internal control, such that there is a reasonable possibility that a material misstatement of the entity's financial statements will not be prevented, or detected and corrected on a timely basis.

5. Management may already know of the existence of significant deficiencies or material weaknesses in internal control. Which of the following is a true statement about the auditor's communication in this situation?

    A. The auditor should communicate these control failures orally, but need not communicate them in writing.

    B. The auditor need not communicate these control failures if they represent a conscious decision by management to accept that degree of risk.

    C. The auditor need not communicate these control failures if they had been communicated in prior periods.

    D. The auditor should communicate these control failures in writing regardless of conditions or management's decisions.

Answer (D) is correct. *(Publisher, adapted)*
    REQUIRED: The true statement about communication of control failures.
    DISCUSSION: AU 325 indicates that the auditor's responsibility is to communicate in writing significant deficiencies and material weaknesses regardless of management decisions or other conditions related to the control failures. These should be communicated each period upon completion of the audit of the financial statements.

6. Under the AICPA's auditing standards, which of the following statements about an auditor's communication of significant control deficiencies is true?

    A. A significant control deficiency previously communicated during the prior year's audit that remains uncorrected causes a scope limitation.

    B. An auditor should perform tests of controls on significant control deficiencies before communicating them to the client.

    C. An auditor's report on significant control deficiencies should include a restriction on the use of the report.

    D. An auditor should communicate significant control deficiencies after tests of controls, but before commencing substantive tests.

Answer (C) is correct. *(CPA, adapted)*
    REQUIRED: The true statement about the auditor's communication of significant control deficiencies.
    DISCUSSION: A communication of significant control deficiencies should (1) state that the purpose of the audit was to report on the financial statements, not to provide assurance on internal control; (2) give the definition of significant control deficiencies and material weaknesses; and (3) state that the report is intended solely for the information and use of those charged with governance, management, and others within the organization (or specified regulatory agency) and is not intended to be and should not be used by anyone other than the specified parties.
    Answer (A) is incorrect. Although a significant deficiency previously communicated requires continued communication in the following year, it does not necessarily cause a limitation of the scope of the audit. Answer (B) is incorrect. Tests of controls are performed on internal control, not on significant deficiencies. Answer (D) is incorrect. Significant control deficiencies should be reported at the conclusion of the audit. However, they may be communicated during the audit as well if this information is considered useful to the client.

7. An auditor's written communication issued on significant deficiencies and material weaknesses relating to an entity's internal control observed during a financial statement audit should

A. Include a brief description of the tests of controls performed in searching for material weaknesses.

B. Indicate that the significant deficiencies and material weaknesses should be disclosed in the annual report to the entity's shareholders.

C. Include a paragraph describing management's assertion concerning the effectiveness of internal control.

D. Indicate that the audit's purpose was to report on the financial statements and not to provide assurance on internal control.

Answer (D) is correct. *(CPA, adapted)*
REQUIRED: The content of an auditor's written communication about significant deficiencies and material weaknesses.
DISCUSSION: The communication should state that the purpose of the audit was to express an opinion on the financial statements, not to express an opinion on the effectiveness of the entity's internal control over financial reporting.
Answer (A) is incorrect. The written communication should not describe the tests performed by the auditor. Answer (B) is incorrect. The communication should not be reported to shareholders in the annual report. Answer (C) is incorrect. Management need not make assertions relative to the effectiveness of internal control in the audited financial statements.

8. Which of the following statements is true about the auditor's communication of a material weakness in internal control?

A. A weakness that management refuses to correct should be included in a separate paragraph of the auditor's report on the financial statements.

B. A weakness previously communicated during the prior year's audit that has not been corrected need not be communicated again in writing.

C. Suggested corrective action for management's consideration concerning a material weakness need not be communicated to the client.

D. The auditor should test the controls that constitute a material weakness before communicating it to the client.

Answer (C) is correct. *(CPA, adapted)*
REQUIRED: The true statement about the communication of a material internal control weakness.
DISCUSSION: Although the auditor should communicate material weaknesses to management and those charged with governance, suggested corrective action need not be communicated.
Answer (A) is incorrect. A weakness that management refuses to correct is not, by itself, sufficient to require a separate explanatory paragraph. Answer (B) is incorrect. Regardless of whether those charged with governance acknowledged their understanding and consideration of the weakness, the auditor must communicate it again. Answer (D) is incorrect. The auditor should communicate material weaknesses of which (s)he becomes aware. Testing controls is not a prerequisite of the communication.

9. Which of the following statements is true about an auditor's communication of internal control related matters identified in an audit?

A. The auditor may issue a written report to the audit committee representing that no significant deficiencies were identified.

B. Significant deficiencies need not be recommunicated each year if the audit committee has acknowledged its understanding of such deficiencies.

C. Significant deficiencies may not be communicated in a document that contains suggestions regarding activities that concern other topics, such as business strategies or administrative efficiencies.

D. The auditor may choose to communicate significant internal control related matters during the course of the audit but still should communicate in writing upon completion of the audit.

Answer (D) is correct. *(CPA, adapted)*
REQUIRED: The true statement about an auditor's communication of control related matters in an audit.
DISCUSSION: Timely communication of control related matters may be desirable. Hence, the auditor has the option of making an interim communication before conclusion of the engagement. The timing of the communication is determined by the significance of the matters noted and the urgency of corrective action. However, a written communication should be made at the end of the audit.
Answer (A) is incorrect. AU 325 prohibits issuance of a report declaring that no significant deficiencies were noted. But a written communication stating that no material weaknesses were identified may be given if required by a governmental agency. Answer (B) is incorrect. Control related matters may be known to management, and their existence may reflect a decision to accept the risk because of cost or other considerations. However, the auditor should make a written communication identifying the deficiencies. Answer (C) is incorrect. Items beneficial to the client may be communicated even though they are not related to internal control.

10. The development of constructive suggestions to a client for improvements in its internal control is a

A. Task addressed by the auditor only during a special engagement.

B. Requirement as important as assessing control risk.

C. Requirement of the auditor's consideration of internal control.

D. Desirable by-product of an audit engagement.

Answer (D) is correct. *(CPA, adapted)*
    REQUIRED: The true statement about constructive suggestions to a client for improvements in its internal control.
    DISCUSSION: During an audit, the auditor may become aware of matters related to internal control that may be of interest to management and those charged with governance. Those matters meeting the definition of significant deficiencies or material weaknesses in internal control should be communicated. However, the auditor may identify other matters and report them for the benefit of management or others.
    Answer (A) is incorrect. At a minimum, the auditor should communicate significant deficiencies and material weaknesses in an audit. Answer (B) is incorrect. Constructive suggestions are not necessary, but the auditor should assess the risk of material misstatement (inherent risk and control risk). Answer (C) is incorrect. Constructive suggestions are not necessary.

9.2 The Auditor's Communication with Those Charged with Governance (AU 380)

11. An auditor would **least** likely initiate a discussion with a client's audit committee concerning

A. The methods used to account for significant unusual transactions.

B. The maximum dollar amount of misstatements that could exist without causing the financial statements to be materially misstated.

C. Indications of fraud and illegal acts committed by a corporate officer that were discovered by the auditor.

D. Disagreements with management as to accounting principles that were resolved during the current year's audit.

Answer (B) is correct. *(CPA, adapted)*
    REQUIRED: The item least likely to be discussed with the audit committee.
    DISCUSSION: The auditor is responsible for determining the levels of materiality appropriate in the audit of a client's financial statements. Only the general nature of materiality need be discussed.
    Answer (A) is incorrect. Methods used to account for significant unusual transactions is an item communicated to those charged with governance. Answer (C) is incorrect. Indications of fraud and illegal acts is an item communicated to those charged with governance. Answer (D) is incorrect. Disagreements with management is an item communicated to those charged with governance.

12. Which of the following statements is true about an auditor's communication to those charged with governance?

A. Any matters communicated to those charged with governance also should be communicated to the entity's management.

B. The auditor is required to inform those charged with governance about misstatements discovered by the auditor and not subsequently corrected by management.

C. Disagreements with management about the application of accounting principles are required to be communicated in writing to those charged with governance.

D. Issues previously reported to those charged with governance are required to be communicated to the audit committee after each subsequent audit.

Answer (B) is correct. *(CPA, adapted)*
    REQUIRED: The true statement about an auditor's communication to those charged with governance.
    DISCUSSION: The matters to be discussed with those charged with governance include the auditors' responsibility under GAAS; significant accounting policies; sensitive accounting estimates; audit adjustments, including not only adjustments having a significant effect on financial reports but also uncorrected misstatements pertaining to the latest period presented that were determined by management to be immaterial; the quality of the accounting principles used by management; other information in documents containing audited statements; auditor disagreements with management, whether or not satisfactorily resolved; management's consultations with other accountants; issues discussed with management prior to the auditors' retention; and any serious difficulties the auditors may have had with management during the audit (AU 380).
    Answer (A) is incorrect. Certain information should be communicated to those charged with governance, not management. Answer (C) is incorrect. Communication with those charged with governance may be oral or written. Answer (D) is incorrect. Communication of recurring matters ordinarily need not be repeated.

13. Which of the following statements is true about an auditor's communication with those charged with governance?

   A. This communication is required to occur at the same time as the auditor's report on the financial statements is issued.

   B. This communication should include management changes in the application of significant accounting policies.

   C. Any significant matter communicated to those charged with governance also should be communicated to management.

   D. Audit adjustments proposed by the auditor, whether or not recorded by management, need not be communicated to those charged with governance.

Answer (B) is correct. *(CPA, adapted)*
   REQUIRED: The true statement about an auditor's communication with those charged with governance.
   DISCUSSION: The auditor should communicate to those charged with governance, among other things, management's selection of and changes in significant accounting policies or their application. The auditor should also determine that those charged with governance are informed about the methods used to account for significant unusual transactions and the effects of significant accounting policies in controversial or emerging areas. Moreover, in an SEC engagement, the auditor should discuss the quality of the auditee's accounting principles as applied in its financial reports (AU 380).
   Answer (A) is incorrect. The communication should take place on a timely basis. Answer (C) is incorrect. The communication is required to be made only to those with oversight authority. Answer (D) is incorrect. Audit adjustments, whether or not recorded, should be communicated to those charged with governance.

14. Which of the following statements is true about an auditor's communication with those charged with governance?

   A. This communication should include disagreements with management about audit adjustments, whether or not satisfactorily resolved.

   B. If matters are communicated orally, it is necessary to repeat the communication of recurring matters each year.

   C. If matters are communicated in writing, the report is required to be distributed to both the audit committee and management.

   D. This communication is required to occur after the auditor's report on the financial statements is issued.

Answer (A) is correct. *(CPA, adapted)*
   REQUIRED: The true statement about an auditor's communication with those charged with governance.
   DISCUSSION: The matters to be discussed with those charged with governance include the auditors' responsibility under GAAS; significant accounting policies; sensitive accounting estimates; audit adjustments; the quality of the accounting principles used by management; other information in documents containing audited statements; auditor disagreements with management, whether or not satisfactorily resolved; management's consultations with other accountants; issues discussed with management prior to the auditors' retention; and any serious difficulties the auditors may have had with management during the audit.
   Answer (B) is incorrect. The oral or written communication of recurring matters ordinarily need not be repeated. Answer (C) is incorrect. Communications with management are neither required nor precluded. Answer (D) is incorrect. The communication is to be made on a timely basis.

15. Which of the following is true about the auditor's communication with those charged with governance?

   A. It should be explained that the auditor is responsible for the fairness of the financial statements.

   B. The communication should be a two-way discourse between the auditor and those charged with governance.

   C. Specific audit procedures should be described to those charged with governance.

   D. The auditor should limit the communication to only those issues required to be communicated.

Answer (B) is correct. *(Publisher, adapted)*
   REQUIRED: The true statement about the auditor's communication with those charged with governance.
   DISCUSSION: Two-way communication is expected and should provide those charged with governance an overview of the audit process and of the auditor's responsibilities. It should also allow the auditor to obtain information relevant to the audit.
   Answer (A) is incorrect. It should be discussed that management is responsible for the fairness of the financial statements. Answer (C) is incorrect. The description of specific audit procedures could compromise the audit. Answer (D) is incorrect. Nothing precludes the auditor from communicating other information to those charged with governance.

16. Which of the following matters should an auditor communicate to those charged with governance?

A. The basis for assessing control risk at a low level.

B. The process used by management in formulating sensitive accounting estimates.

C. The auditor's preliminary judgments about materiality levels.

D. The justification for performing substantive procedures at interim dates.

Answer (B) is correct. *(CPA, adapted)*
　REQUIRED: The communication that should be made.
　DISCUSSION: Certain management estimates are particularly sensitive because they are significant to the financial statements, and future events affecting them may differ from current judgments. Those charged with governance should be informed about the process used in formulating sensitive estimates and the basis for the auditor's conclusions concerning their reasonableness (AU 380).
　Answer (A) is incorrect. The basis for assessing control risk need not be communicated to those charged with governance. Answer (C) is incorrect. The preliminary judgments about materiality need not be communicated to those charged with governance. Answer (D) is incorrect. The reasons for interim procedures need not be communicated to those charged with governance.

17. During the planning phase of an audit, an auditor is identifying matters for communication to those charged with governance. The auditor most likely would ask management whether

A. There was significant turnover in the accounting department.

B. It consulted with another CPA firm about installing a new computer system.

C. There were changes in the application of significant accounting policies.

D. It agreed with the auditor's selection of fraud detection procedures.

Answer (C) is correct. *(CPA, adapted)*
　REQUIRED: The issue relative to communication with those charged with governance.
　DISCUSSION: The auditor should determine that those charged with governance are informed about the initial selection of and changes in significant accounting policies or their application. Moreover, the auditor should discuss the quality of the auditee's accounting principles as applied in its financial reports (AU 380).
　Answer (A) is incorrect. The auditor would be concerned about significant turnover in the accounting department in the assessment of risk, but the matter is not likely of sufficient concern to justify disclosure to those charged with governance. Answer (B) is incorrect. The auditor would communicate the consultation with other CPAs about accounting and auditing matters, not about choice of a new computer system. Answer (D) is incorrect. The auditor need not seek approval from management of audit procedures.

18. In an audit engagement, should an auditor communicate the following matters to those charged with governance?

	Auditors' Judgments About the Quality of the Client's Accounting Principles	Issues Discussed with Management Prior to the Auditor's Retention
A.	Yes	Yes
B.	Yes	No
C.	No	Yes
D.	No	No

Answer (A) is correct. *(CPA, adapted)*
　REQUIRED: The matter(s), if any, to be communicated to those charged with governance.
　DISCUSSION: The matters to be discussed with those charged with governance include the quality of the accounting principles used by management. Management is normally a participant in the discussion. Matters covered may include the consistency of principles and their application; the clarity and completeness of the statements; and items significantly affecting representational faithfulness, verifiability, and neutrality. However, objective criteria have not been developed to permit consistent evaluation of the application of principles to a given entity's statements. Thus, the discussion should address the unique circumstances of the auditee. Furthermore, in any audit engagement, the auditor and those charged with governance should discuss any major issues discussed with management in connection with the initial or recurring retention of the auditors, for example, issues concerning the application of accounting principles and auditing standards.

9.3 Reporting on an Entity's Internal Control

19. Firms subject to the reporting requirements of the Securities Exchange Act of 1934 are required by the Foreign Corrupt Practices Act of 1977 to maintain satisfactory internal control. Moreover, the Sarbanes-Oxley Act of 2002 requires that annual reports include (1) a statement of management's responsibility for establishing and maintaining adequate internal control and procedures for financial reporting, and (2) management's assessment of their effectiveness. The role of the registered auditor relative to the assessment made by management is to

    A. Express an opinion on the assessment.

    B. Report clients with unsatisfactory internal control to the SEC.

    C. Express an opinion on whether the client is subject to the Securities Exchange Act of 1934.

    D. Determine whether management's report is complete and properly presented.

Answer (D) is correct. *(Publisher, adapted)*
REQUIRED: The role of the auditor relative to the assessment by the management of internal control and procedures for financial reporting.
DISCUSSION: According to PCAOB AS No. 5, the auditor must express (or disclaim) an opinion on the effectiveness of internal control. Additionally, if the auditor determines that elements of management's annual report on internal control over financial reporting are incomplete or improperly presented, the auditor should modify his or her report to describe the reasons for this determination.
Answer (A) is incorrect. According to PCAOB AS No. 5, the auditor must express (or disclaim) an opinion on internal control but not management's assessment. Answer (B) is incorrect. The auditor's report on internal control is issued in conjunction with the audit report on the financial statements. Answer (C) is incorrect. Issuers must report to the SEC, but the auditor need not express an opinion on whether the client is subject to the Securities Exchange Act of 1934.

20. Which of the following best describes a CPA's responsibility to report on an issuer's (public company's) internal control over financial reporting?

    A. To examine the effectiveness of its internal control.

    B. To identify and communicate control deficiencies to the board of directors.

    C. To report on the expected benefits of the entity's internal control.

    D. To provide constructive advice to the entity on its internal control.

Answer (A) is correct. *(CPA, adapted)*
REQUIRED: The best description of an auditor's responsibility to report on an issuer's internal control over financial reporting.
DISCUSSION: The auditor's objective is to express an opinion on whether internal control is effective, in all material respects, based on the control criteria.
Answer (B) is incorrect. Identifying and communicating significant deficiencies and material weaknesses to the board of directors is secondary to the responsibility to express an opinion on internal controls. Answer (C) is incorrect. The opinion expressed by the CPA should not extend into the future. Answer (D) is incorrect. Consulting engagements do not result in the expression of an opinion.

21. The auditor of an issuer must express an opinion on the effectiveness of internal control. The opinion should be expressed

	As of a Specified Date	For a Specified Period of Time
A.	Yes	Yes
B.	Yes	No
C.	No	Yes
D.	No	No

Answer (B) is correct. *(CPA, adapted)*
REQUIRED: The applicability of a report on an examination of the effectiveness of internal control.
DISCUSSION: The auditor would provide an opinion about whether material weaknesses existed as of the date specified in management's assessment. This is typically the date of the end of the fiscal period.

22. An auditor is auditing internal control in conjunction with the audit of financial statements for an issuer. The auditor is considering the appropriate materiality level for planning the audit of internal control. Relative to the materiality level for the audit of the financial statements, materiality levels for the audit of internal control are

    A. Larger.

    B. Smaller.

    C. The same.

    D. Cannot determine.

Answer (C) is correct. *(Publisher, adapted)*
REQUIRED: The level of materiality appropriate for planning an audit of internal control.
DISCUSSION: AS No. 5 indicates that the auditor should use the same materiality considerations in the audit of internal control over financial reporting that (s)he would use in planning the audit of annual financial statements.
Answer (A) is incorrect. The materiality levels should be the same. Answer (B) is incorrect. The materiality levels should be the same. Answer (D) is incorrect. The materiality levels for the audit of internal control are based on those for the financial statement audit.

23. In gaining an understanding of an issuer's internal control, an auditor does all the following **except**

A. Inspect documents.

B. Observe employees.

C. Perform a walkthrough of the transaction process.

D. Send confirmations to customers.

Answer (D) is correct. *(Publisher, adapted)*
REQUIRED: The procedure least useful in gaining an understanding of controls.
DISCUSSION: Confirmations to customers are substantive procedures used to test the existence assertion. They are not useful in gaining an understanding of controls.
Answer (A) is incorrect. Inspection of documents provides insight into the application of internal controls, such as approvals and oversight. Answer (B) is incorrect. The auditor observes the application of specific controls by employees in gaining an understanding of the controls. Answer (C) is incorrect. A walkthrough of the system relevant to financial reporting allows the auditor to view the application of the controls in various stages of the process.

24. The audit of internal control over financial reporting should test

	Design Effectiveness	Operating Effectiveness
A.	Yes	Yes
B.	Yes	No
C.	No	Yes
D.	No	No

Answer (A) is correct. *(Publisher, adapted)*
REQUIRED: The required testing of internal control in an audit.
DISCUSSION: The auditor should test design effectiveness by determining whether the controls, if they are operated as prescribed by persons with the necessary authority and competence to perform the control effectively, (1) satisfy the control objectives and (2) can effectively prevent or detect errors or fraud that could result in material misstatements in the financial statements. The auditor should test the operating effectiveness of a control by determining whether (1) the control is operating as designed and (2) the person performing the control possesses the necessary authority and competence to perform the control effectively.

25. In an examination of internal control over financial reporting, which deficiencies in control should be communicated in writing to those charged with governance?

A. All deficiencies.

B. Only material weaknesses.

C. Only significant deficiencies.

D. Both material weaknesses and significant deficiencies.

Answer (D) is correct. *(Publisher, adapted)*
REQUIRED: The deficiencies in control required to be communicated in writing to those charged with governance.
DISCUSSION: The auditor should communicate, in writing, to management and to those charged with governance all material weaknesses and significant deficiencies identified during the audit. The written communication should be made prior to the report release date. The auditor also should communicate to management, in writing, all lesser deficiencies in internal control and inform those charged with governance when such a communication has been made.
Answer (A) is incorrect. Material weaknesses and significant deficiencies should be communicated. Answer (B) is incorrect. Significant deficiencies also should be communicated. Answer (C) is incorrect. Material weaknesses also should be communicated.

26. During the audit of internal controls integrated with the audit of the financial statements, the auditor discovered a material weakness in internal control. The auditor most likely will express a(n)

A. Adverse opinion on internal control.

B. Qualified opinion on internal control.

C. Unqualified opinion on internal control.

D. Disclaimer of opinion on internal control.

Answer (A) is correct. *(Publisher, adapted)*
REQUIRED: The type of opinion expressed because of discovery of a material weakness.
DISCUSSION: Material weaknesses are significant control deficiencies that result in more than a remote chance that a material misstatement will result in the financial statements. A material weakness requires the auditor to express an adverse opinion on the effectiveness of internal control.
Answer (B) is incorrect. A qualified opinion (or disclaimer of opinion) is expressed if there is a scope limitation. Answer (C) is incorrect. An unqualified opinion is not expressed if a material weakness exists. Answer (D) is incorrect. Disclaimer of opinion (or qualified opinion) is expressed if there is a scope limitation.

27. Management of an issuer subject to SEC requirements requests the auditor to report on whether a previously reported material weakness in internal control continues to exist. The request comes 3 months after the annual audited financial statements and report on internal control were released.

A. The audited financial statements and report on internal control have been released, and no report may be issued on subsequent information.

B. The auditor may accept the engagement if (s)he withdraws the original report.

C. The auditor may accept the engagement if management provides a statement that the identified material weakness no longer exists.

D. The auditor may accept the engagement but must wait until the next year's audit to report the remediation of the internal control weakness.

Answer (C) is correct. *(Publisher, adapted)*
REQUIRED: The circumstances in which an auditor of an issuer may report on whether a material weakness still exists.
DISCUSSION: PCAOB AS No. 4 applies to engagements tailored solely to report on whether a previously reported material weakness continues to exist. Such an engagement is voluntary and may be performed as of any reasonable date selected by management. To perform such an engagement, the auditor should receive a written report from management that the identified material weakness no longer exists as of the date specified. The auditor then applies appropriate procedures to assess whether remediation has been accomplished.
Answer (A) is incorrect. The auditor may perform the engagement. Answer (B) is incorrect. The previous reports are not withdrawn. Answer (D) is incorrect. The report may be issued as soon as the auditor has concluded whether the material weakness has been remediated.

28. A practitioner is conducting an integrated examination of internal control with the audit of a nonissuer's financial statements. She is using a "top-down approach," which means she will first

A. Focus on entity-level controls and work down to significant accounts.

B. Communicate material weaknesses and significant deficiencies to those charged with governance.

C. Determine the type of opinion in the report that will be expressed.

D. Apply substantive procedures to test financial statement assertions.

Answer (A) is correct. *(Publisher, adapted)*
REQUIRED: The meaning of top-down approach.
DISCUSSION: The top-down approach to evaluating internal control would begin at the financial statement level by understanding overall risks focusing on entity-level controls and work down to significant accounts. Examples of entity-level controls are controls (1) related to the control environment, (2) over management override, (3) to monitor results of operations, (4) over the period-end financial reporting process, and (5) to monitor other controls.
Answer (B) is incorrect. Communication is at the end of the examination when findings would be available. Answer (C) is incorrect. The type of opinion to be expressed cannot be determined until the examination is completed. Answer (D) is incorrect. Substantive procedures are used to test financial statement assertions, not internal controls.

9.4 Service Organizations (AU 324 and AT 801)

29. AU 324, *Service Organizations*, applies to a financial statement audit of an entity that uses services of another organization as part of its information system. For this purpose, the user auditor may need to obtain the service auditor's report. Which of the following is a true statement about a service auditor's report?

A. It provides the user auditor with assurance regarding whether control procedures have been implemented at the user organization.

B. It should include an opinion.

C. If it proves to be inappropriate for the user auditor's purposes, (s)he must personally perform procedures at the service organization.

D. A user auditor need not inquire about the service auditor's professional reputation.

Answer (B) is correct. *(Publisher, adapted)*
REQUIRED: The true statement about a service auditor's report regarding internal control.
DISCUSSION: A service auditor's report should be helpful in providing a sufficient understanding to plan the audit of the user organization. The service auditor's report may express an opinion on the fairness of the description of the controls implemented at the service organization and whether they were suitably designed. If the service auditor also has tested controls, the report may express an opinion on the operating effectiveness of the controls.
Answer (A) is incorrect. A service auditor's report is helpful to the user auditor in obtaining an understanding of internal control at the service organization, but it does not provide assurance regarding conditions at the user organization. Answer (C) is incorrect. Audit procedures at the service organization may be applied by the service auditor at the request of (and under the direction of) the user auditor. Answer (D) is incorrect. The user auditor should inquire about the service auditor's professional reputation.

30. Computer Services Company (CSC) processes payroll transactions for schools. Drake, CPA, is engaged to report on CSC's controls implemented as of a specific date. These controls are relevant to the schools' internal control, so Drake's report will be useful in providing the schools' independent auditors with information necessary to plan their audits. Drake's report expressing an opinion on CSC's controls implemented as of a specific date should contain a(n)

A. Description of the scope and nature of Drake's procedures.

B. Statement that CSC's management has disclosed to Drake all design deficiencies of which it is aware.

C. Opinion on the operating effectiveness of CSC's controls.

D. Paragraph indicating the basis for Drake's assessment of control risk.

Answer (A) is correct. *(CPA, adapted)*
REQUIRED: The item in a service auditor's report on controls implemented.
DISCUSSION: The report expressing an opinion on the description of controls implemented includes (1) a reference to the aspects of the service organization covered, (2) a description of the service auditor's procedures, (3) identification of the party stating the control objectives, (4) a statement of purposes of the engagement, (5) a disclaimer of opinion on operating effectiveness, (6) an opinion on whether the service organization's description fairly presents the controls implemented, (7) a statement of inherent limitations, and (8) the parties for whom the report is intended.
Answer (B) is incorrect. The service auditor need not state whether management has disclosed all design deficiencies. Answer (C) is incorrect. The report on controls implemented does not contain an opinion on operating effectiveness. Answer (D) is incorrect. The report contains no assessment of control risk, only an opinion on the controls implemented.

31. Lake, CPA, is auditing the financial statements of Gill Co. Gill uses the EDP Service Center, Inc. to process its payroll transactions. EDP's financial statements are audited by Cope, CPA, who recently issued a report on EDP's internal control. Lake is considering Cope's report on EDP's internal control in assessing control risk on the Gill engagement. What is Lake's responsibility concerning making reference to Cope as a basis, in part, for Lake's own opinion?

A. Lake may refer to Cope only if Lake is satisfied as to Cope's professional reputation and independence.

B. Lake may refer to Cope only if Lake relies on Cope's report in restricting the extent of substantive procedures.

C. Lake may refer to Cope only if Lake's report indicates the division of responsibility.

D. Lake may not refer to Cope under the circumstances above.

Answer (D) is correct. *(CPA, adapted)*
REQUIRED: The reference, if any, in an auditor's report to a service auditor's report on internal control.
DISCUSSION: The service auditor was not responsible for examining any portion of the user organization's financial statements. Hence, the user auditor should not refer to the service auditor's report as a basis in part for his/her own opinion on those financial statements (AU 324).
Answer (A) is incorrect. Although the user auditor should make inquiries about the service auditor's professional reputation and consider the service auditor's independence, no reference to the service auditor should be made in the user auditor's report. Answer (B) is incorrect. The user auditor should not refer to the service auditor's report even if (s)he uses that report in assessing control risk and in determining the nature, timing, and extent of substantive procedures. Answer (C) is incorrect. The user auditor should not divide responsibility with the service auditor.

32. Payroll Data Co. (PDC) processes payroll transactions for a retailer. Cook, CPA, is engaged to issue a report on PDC's internal controls implemented as of a specific date. These controls are relevant to the retailer's internal control, so Cook's report may be useful in providing the retailer's independent auditor with information necessary to plan a financial statement audit. Cook's report should

A. Contain a disclaimer of opinion on the operating effectiveness of PDC's controls.

B. State whether PDC's controls were suitably designed to achieve the retailer's objectives.

C. Identify PDC's controls relevant to specific financial statement assertions.

D. Disclose Cook's assessed level of control risk for PDC.

Answer (A) is correct. *(CPA, adapted)*
REQUIRED: The components of a service auditor's report.
DISCUSSION: Service auditors may (1) report on controls implemented or (2) report on controls implemented and tests of operating effectiveness. The report limited to controls implemented should include a disclaimer of an opinion related to operating effectiveness of the controls.
Answer (B) is incorrect. The report should state whether PDC's controls were suitably designed to provide reasonable assurance of achieving the specified control objectives of the service organization. Answer (C) is incorrect. Specific controls relevant to specific financial statement assertions need not be identified in the service auditor's report. Answer (D) is incorrect. The assessed level of control risk is not disclosed.

Use the additional questions in Gleim **CPA Test Prep Online** to create Test Sessions that emulate Prometric!

9.5 PRACTICE SIMULATION

| | Auditing and Attestation
Testlet 4 of 4 | Time Remaining
1 hour - 30 minutes | Unsplit | Split Horiz | Split Vertical | Spreadsheet | Calculator | Exit |

DIRECTIONS

Note: If you believe you have encountered a software malfunction, report it to the test center staff immediately.

Navigation

To navigate from task to task, use the controls at the bottom of the screen. Click on the **Next** button to advance to the next task, or the **Previous** button to go to the previous task. To go directly to any task, click on its number.

| ⚑ = Reminder | | Directions | 1 ▽ | 2 ▽ | 3 ▽ | 4 ▽ | 5 ▽ | 6 ▽ | 7 ▽ | | ◀ Previous | Next ▶ |

If you would like a reminder to revisit a task, or want to indicate that you are finished with it, click on the reminder flag below the task number. To clear the flag, click on it again. Reminder flags are for your use only – they do not contribute to your score.

Tabs

In this part of the examination, you will be asked to complete various tasks. Every task has one or more **Work Tabs**. Some tasks have one or more **Information Tabs**, others may have none. Every task has a **Help** tab.

If a task has **Information Tabs**, you may use the information in them to complete your responses in the **Work Tabs**.

| Corporate Gain and Basis | Authoritative Literature | Help |

      Work tab   **Information tab**   **Help tab**

Work Tabs:

- **Work Tabs** are identified with a pencil icon. This is where your responses are expected.
- Each task has one or more **Work Tabs**.
- **Work Tabs** contain directions for completing the task – be sure to read these directions carefully.
- The **Work Tab** name in the example above is for illustration only – yours will differ.
- You must complete all of the **Work Tabs** in each task to receive full credit.

Information Tabs:

- The Authoritative Literature will be provided in all tasks in the AUD, FAR, and REG sections for your reference.
- Your simulation may have one or more additional **Information Tabs**. Like the Authoritative Literature tabs, **Information Tabs** do not have a pencil icon.
- If your task has additional **Information Tabs**, go through each to familiarize yourself with the task content.

Help Tab:

- The **Help Tab** provides assistance with the exam software that is used in this task. For example, if the task is to compose a memorandum, **Help** will provide information about the word processor.

The Toolbar

The toolbar at the top of the screen shows the amount of time remaining for you to complete the tasks. In addition, the following tools are available. Note that only the Exit button is displayed when Directions are visible - the others will appear when you begin the tasks.

Click on these buttons to split or unsplit the screen. You can split the screen vertically or horizontally.

Click on this button to display the calculator; click on it again to hide the calculator. To move the calculator, click on the calculator title bar and drag the calculator to the desired location.

Click on this button to use the spreadsheet; click on it again to hide the spreadsheet. To move the spreadsheet, click on the the spreadsheet title bar and drag the spreadsheet to the desired location.

Click on this button to go on to the next part of the examination. You must complete all of the tasks to receive full credit. Once you click on **Exit** and confirm the action, you will NOT be able to return to this testlet.

| ⚑ = Reminder | | Directions | 1 ▽ | 2 ▽ | 3 ▽ | 4 ▽ | 5 ▽ | 6 ▽ | | ◀ Previous | Next ▶ |

Identification of Significant Deficiencies and Material Weaknesses | Authoritative Literature | Help

Indicate by checking the appropriate box whether each of the following issues would be considered a significant deficiency or material weakness under AU 325, *Communicating Internal Control Related Matters Identified in an Audit*.

Issues	Yes	No
1. Inadequate provisions for the safeguarding of assets		
2. Failure of management to provide the auditor with personal financial statements		
3. Intentional override of controls		
4. Unqualified personnel		
5. Write-off of customer accounts determined to be bad debts		
6. Separation of the accounting function from the finance function		
7. Undisclosed related party transactions		
8. Failure of management to provide confidential information to competitors		
9. Lack of objectivity by accounting decision makers		
10. Failure of management to maximize profits		

▼ = Reminder   Directions | 1 | 2 | 3 | 4 | 5 | 6 | ◀ Previous   Next ▶

Communication with Those Charged with Governance | Authoritative Literature | Help

Certain matters unrelated to internal control should be communicated to those responsible for oversight of the financial reporting and disclosure process. In this case, it is the audit committee for Stone Co. Indicate in the shaded column below whether the item should be communicated or need not be communicated.

Item	Answer
1. Auditor's responsibility under GAAS.	
2. Auditor's responsibility to select GAAP.	
3. Management judgments and accounting estimates.	
4. Management's consultation with other accountants.	
5. Specific audit procedures used by the auditor.	
6. Disagreements the auditor had with management.	
7. Difficulties encountered in performing the audit.	
8. Recommendations to promote certain managers.	

Choices

A) Yes

B) No

▼ = Reminder   Directions | 1 | 2 | 3 | 4 | 5 | 6 | ◀ Previous   Next ▶

Land & Hale, CPAs, are auditing the financial statements of Stone Co., a nonissuer, for the year ended December 31, Year 1. Edwin Land, the engagement supervisor, anticipates expressing an unqualified opinion on May 20, Year 2. Ed Wood, an assistant on the engagement, drafted the auditor's communication of internal control related matters that Land plans to send to Stone's board of directors on May 30, Year 2. Land reviewed Wood's draft and indicated in the *Supervisor's Review Notes* that Wood's draft contained deficiencies.

Independent Auditor's Communication on Internal Control Related Matters

To Management and the Board of Directors:

In planning and performing our audit of the financial statements of Stone Co. as of and for the year ended December 31, Year 1, in accordance with auditing standards generally accepted in the United States of America, we considered Stone Co.'s internal control over financial reporting (internal control) as a basis for designing our auditing procedures for the purpose of expressing our opinion on the financial statements and for the purpose of expressing an opinion on the effectiveness of the Company's internal control.

Our consideration of internal control was for the limited purpose described in the preceding paragraph and can be expected to identify all deficiencies in internal control that might be significant deficiencies or material weaknesses. As discussed below, we identified certain deficiencies in internal control that we consider to be significant deficiencies.

A deficiency in internal control exists when the design or operation of a control does not allow the auditors, in the normal course of performing their assigned functions, to prevent or detect misstatements on a timely basis. A "significant deficiency" is a deficiency, or a combination of inconsequential deficiencies, in internal control that is less severe than a material weakness, yet important enough to merit attention by those charged with governance.

We consider the following deficiencies to be significant deficiencies in internal control: (1) failure to safeguard assets, particularly inventory stored at remote locations; and (2) failure to reconcile subsidiary ledgers to control accounts on a timely basis.

This communication is intended solely for the information and use of management and the Board of Directors of Stone Co. and is not intended to be and should not be used by anyone other than these specified parties.

Land & Hale, CPAs
May 30, Year 2

-- Continued on next page --

| Deficiencies | Authoritative Literature | Help | -- **Continued** |

Indicate in the shaded column whether Land is correct or incorrect in his criticisms of Wood's draft.

Potential Deficiencies	*Answer*
In the first paragraph:	
1. The communication should not refer to "our audit of the financial statements."	
2. The communication should indicate that providing assurance is not the purpose of the consideration of internal control.	
3. The communication should refer to "conformity with generally accepted accounting principles."	
In the second paragraph:	
4. The communication should not refer to deficiencies because such a reference is inconsistent with the expression of an unqualified opinion on the financial statements.	
5. The statement "can be expected to identify all deficiencies" is inappropriate.	
In the third paragraph:	
6. The definition of a control deficiency need not be presented because the communication is about significant deficiencies.	
7. The phrase "does not allow the auditors, in the normal course of performing their assigned functions, to prevent or detect misstatements on a timely basis" is not appropriate.	
8. The term "inconsequential" should not be used.	
9. The communication should define a "material weakness."	
In the fourth paragraph:	
10. The report should state that significant deficiencies were identified but should not identify them.	
11. The communication need not suggest corrective actions to be taken by the client.	
In the final paragraph:	
12. The restriction on the communication's use is inappropriate because other parties ordinarily would receive the communication.	
13. The communication should indicate whether the financial statement audit resulted in an unqualified opinion.	
14. The communication should indicate that the auditor is not responsible for updating the communication for events or circumstances occurring after the date of the communication.	
Dating the report:	
15. The communication may not be dated after the auditor's report on the financial statements.	

Choices
Correct
Incorrect

| Internal Control Communication | Authoritative Literature | Help |

You have been asked by the audit partner to draft a letter to the client on internal-control-related matters. You were informed that the written communication regarding significant deficiencies and material weaknesses identified during an audit of financial statements should include certain statements.

For each of the statements in the table below, select from the list provided the appropriate disposition of each statement in regard to the letter to the client on internal-control-related matters. Each choice may be used once, more than once, or not at all.

Statements	Disposition
1. State that the purpose of the audit was to express an opinion on the financial statements, and to express an opinion on the effectiveness of the entity's internal control over financial reporting.	
2. Identify, if applicable, items that are considered to be material weaknesses.	
3. State that the auditor is not expressing an opinion on the effectiveness of internal control.	
4. Include the definition of the term significant deficiency.	
5. Include the definition of the term material weakness, where relevant.	
6. State that the author is expressing an unqualified opinion on the effectiveness of internal control.	
7. State that the communication is intended solely for management and external parties.	
8. Identify the matters that are considered to be significant deficiencies.	

Choices
A) Included
B) Excluded
C) Included, but only with client management's approval

Reporting on Internal Control | Authoritative Literature | Help

At 501, *An Examination of an Entity's Internal Control over Financial Reporting*, applies when the service is provided to nonissuers. In accordance with AT 501, a standard report expressing an unqualified opinion contains certain language. Indicate in the shaded column whether each item is appropriate for a standard report.

Report Content	Answer
1. "We conducted our audits...standards of the Public Company Accounting Oversight Board."	
2. "In our opinion, management's assertion that W Company maintained effective internal control over financial reporting..."	
3. "We also have audited, in accordance with auditing standards generally accepted in the United States of America, the *[identify financial statements]*..."	
4. "Our examination included...testing and evaluating the design but not the operating effectiveness of internal control..."	
5. "In our opinion, W Company maintained, in all material respects, effective internal control over financial reporting..."	
6. "We have audited W Company's internal control...based on generally accepted auditing standards."	
7. "Our responsibility is to express an opinion on management's assertion based on our examination."	
8. "Because of its inherent limitations, internal control over financial reporting may not prevent or detect and correct misstatements."	
9. "Those standards require that we plan and perform the audit to become assured that it is probable that internal control was effective in all material respects."	
10. "An entity's internal control over financial reporting is a process effected by the audit committee, management, and auditors, designed to provide reasonable assurance..."	

Choices

A) Include
B) Exclude

Research | Authoritative Literature | Help

A client is considering using a service organization to process its payroll. Research and cite the appropriate auditing standard that identifies the auditor's consideration of the client's use of the service organization.

Title	Section	Paragraph

Title Choices						
AU	PCAOB	AT	AR	ET	BL	VS
CS	QC	PR	TS	PFP	CPE	

Unofficial Answers

1. Identification of Significant Deficiencies and Material Weaknesses (10 Gradable Items)

1. <u>Yes.</u> Inadequate provision for the safeguarding of assets is a control weakness that should be communicated to those charged with governance.

2. <u>No.</u> The auditor would not request personal financial statements from management.

3. <u>Yes.</u> Intentional override of controls is a control weakness that should be communicated to those charged with governance.

4. <u>Yes.</u> The existence of unqualified personnel is a control weakness that should be communicated to those charged with governance.

5. <u>No.</u> The write-off of bad debts is a normal event that does not suggest a control weakness.

6. <u>No.</u> The accounting function should be separated from the finance function in a well-designed control system.

7. <u>Yes.</u> The existence of undisclosed related party transactions is a condition that indicates a control weakness that should be communicated to those charged with governance.

8. <u>No.</u> Management would not be expected to provide confidential information to competitors.

9. <u>Yes.</u> Lack of objectivity by accounting decision makers is a control weakness that should be communicated to those charged with governance.

10. <u>No.</u> The auditor is concerned with the fairness of the financial statements, not the maximization of profits.

2. Communication with Those Charged with Governance (8 Gradable Items)

1. <u>A) Yes.</u> The auditor's responsibility under GAAS should be communicated to those responsible for oversight of the financial reporting and disclosure process.

2. <u>B) No.</u> It is management's responsibility to select GAAP.

3. <u>A) Yes.</u> Management judgments and accounting estimates should be communicated to those responsible for oversight of the financial reporting and disclosure process.

4. <u>A) Yes.</u> Management's consultation with other accountants is an issue that should be communicated to those responsible for oversight of the financial reporting and disclosure process.

5. <u>B) No.</u> The specific audit procedures used by the auditor should not be communicated, but should be documented in the working papers.

6. <u>A) Yes.</u> Disagreements the auditor had with management should be communicated to those responsible for oversight of the financial reporting and disclosure process.

7. <u>A) Yes.</u> Difficulties encountered in performing the audit should be communicated to those responsible for oversight of the financial reporting and disclosure process.

8. <u>B) No.</u> It is management's responsibility to judge which managers should be promoted.

3. Deficiencies (15 Gradable Items)

1. <u>Incorrect.</u> The communication should indicate that the purpose of the audit was to report on the financial statements and not to provide assurance on internal control.

2. <u>Correct.</u> The communication should indicate that internal control was considered for the purpose of planning the audit but not to express an opinion on the effectiveness of internal control.

3. <u>Incorrect.</u> The communication relates to control deficiencies, not whether the financial statements are in conformity with GAAP.

4. <u>Incorrect.</u> The purpose is to communicate significant deficiencies and material weaknesses. Thus, it is appropriate to refer to control deficiencies in the communication.

5. <u>Correct.</u> The AICPA's illustrative written communication states that the consideration of internal control "was not designed to identify all deficiencies that might be significant deficiencies or material weaknesses."

6. <u>Incorrect.</u> The AICPA's illustrative written communication states the definition of a control deficiency to place significant deficiencies in the correct context.

7. <u>Correct.</u> The phrase should refer to "management or employees," not to "the auditors."

8. <u>Correct.</u> The definition of significant deficiency does not include the term "inconsequential."

9.   <u>Correct.</u> The communication defines "material weakness" and, if relevant, "significant deficiency."

10. <u>Incorrect.</u> The specific significant deficiencies should be listed in the communication.

11. <u>Correct.</u> The AICPA's illustrative written communication is silent as to corrective action.

12. <u>Incorrect.</u> The communication is intended for use by management, those charged with governance, and others within the organization. If the entity must provide such a communication to a governmental authority, it should specifically refer to that authority. Moreover, it is not intended to be used and should not be used by anyone other than these specified parties.

13. <u>Incorrect.</u> The communication need not identify the type of opinion that was expressed on the financial statements.

14. <u>Incorrect.</u> The communication should not contain a statement about the auditor's responsibility for updating the communication. The auditor has no such obligation.

15. <u>Incorrect.</u> The communication is best made at the audit report release date, but it should be made no later than 60 days after the audit report release date.

4. Internal Control Communication (8 Gradable Items)

1.   <u>B) Excluded.</u> The purpose of the consideration of internal control in a financial statement is to plan the audit.

2.   <u>A) Included.</u> The letter should identify any issues that are considered to be material weaknesses.

3.   <u>A) Included.</u> The letter should state that the auditor is not expressing an opinion on the effectiveness of internal control.

4.   <u>A) Included.</u> The letter should include the definition of the term significant deficiency.

5.   <u>A) Included.</u> The letter should include the definition of a material weakness if any were reported.

6.   <u>B) Excluded.</u> The consideration of internal control in a financial statement audit provides no assurance on internal control.

7.   <u>B) Excluded.</u> The letter should state that the communication is intended solely for management and those charged with governance and not to external parties.

8.   <u>A) Included.</u> The letter should identify the matters that are considered to be significant deficiencies.

5. Reporting on Internal Control (10 Gradable Items)

1.   <u>B) Exclude.</u> The standard report for a nonissuer should state that AICPA standards were followed, not PCAOB standards.

2.   <u>A) Include.</u> The standard report expresses an opinion on either management's assertion or directly on the effectiveness of internal control.

3.   <u>A) Include.</u> The standard report should reference the client's financial statements that were audited.

4.   <u>B) Exclude.</u> The examination of internal control includes testing both the design and operating effectiveness of internal control.

5.   <u>A) Include.</u> The standard report expresses an opinion on either management's assertion or directly on the effectiveness of internal control.

6.   <u>B) Exclude.</u> The standard report should state that the examination was conducted in accordance with AICPA Statements on Standards for Attestation Engagements.

7.   <u>A) Include.</u> The standard report should state that the auditor's responsibility is to express an opinion on management's assertion about the effectiveness of internal control.

8.   <u>A) Include.</u> The standard report should include a caveat concerning inherent limitations.

9.   <u>B) Exclude.</u> The standard report should indicate that the practitioner obtained reasonable assurance about the effectiveness of internal control.

10. <u>B) Exclude.</u> Auditors do not participate in the establishment of a client's internal control.

6. Research (1 Gradable Item)

Answer: 324.01

AU Section 324 – *Service Organizations*

Introduction and Applicability

.01   This section provides guidance on the factors an independent auditor should consider when auditing the financial statements of an entity that uses a service organization to process certain transactions. This section also provides guidance for independent auditors who issue reports on the processing of transactions by a service organization for use by other auditors. However, guidance for service auditors is now provided by AT 801 (see Subunit 9.4).

Gleim Simulation Grading

Task	Correct Responses		Gradable Items		Score per Task
1	_____	÷	10	=	_____
2	_____	÷	8	=	_____
3	_____	÷	15	=	_____
4	_____	÷	8	=	_____
5	_____	÷	10	=	_____
Research	_____	÷	1	=	_____

	Total of Scores per Task	_____
÷	Total Number of Tasks	6
	Total Score	_____ %

Use **CPA Gleim Online** and **Simulation Wizard** to practice more task-based simulations in a realistic environment.

STUDY UNIT TEN
EVIDENCE -- OBJECTIVES AND NATURE

(11 pages of outline)

The primary purpose of the collection of evidence is to test management's **assertions** related to the balances and disclosures reported on the financial statements. The **sufficiency and appropriateness** of evidence are judged by the auditor based on the acceptable level of **detection risk**. This judgment is based on (1) the level to which the auditor wishes to restrict the **risk of material misstatement (RMM)** and (2) the assessments of **inherent risk** and **control risk**.

10.1 NATURE AND SUFFICIENCY (AU 326 AND AS NO. 15)

 You should recognize that the collection and documentation of evidence are keys to the audit. Be sure to understand these processes and, if necessary, review the role of management assertions that were addressed in Study Unit 1, Subunit 2.

1. The following is the third standard of field work:

   The auditor must obtain sufficient appropriate audit evidence by performing audit procedures to afford a reasonable basis for an opinion regarding the financial statements under audit.

2. **Audit evidence** is all information used by the auditor in arriving at the conclusion on which the audit opinion is based.

   a. **Accounting records** include

      1) Initial entries (manual or electronic).
      2) Supporting records. Examples are (a) checks, (b) EFTs, (c) invoices, (d) contracts, (e) the general and subsidiary ledgers, (f) journal entries, (g) worksheets, (h) spreadsheets, and (i) reconciliations.

   b. **Other information** includes (1) minutes of meetings; (2) confirmations; (3) industry analysts' reports; (4) comparable data about competitors; (5) controls manuals; and (6) information obtained by the auditor from inquiries, observation, and inspection.

   c. The auditor typically relies on **persuasive**, rather than convincing, evidence.

   d. The auditor may consider the **cost** of obtaining evidence and its usefulness. However, the difficulty and cost of obtaining evidence are not valid reasons for omitting tests.

3. **Nature of Assertions**

   a. Financial statements implicitly or explicitly include management's **assertions** about the fair presentation of information, that is, about its recognition, measurement, presentation, and disclosure. Most auditor work consists of obtaining and evaluating evidence about management's assertions.

   b. See Study Unit 1, Subunit 2, for the AICPA's and the PCAOB's **assertions models**.

4. **Sufficient Appropriate Audit Evidence**

    a. **Sufficiency** is the measure of the **quantity** of evidence.

        1) The greater the RMM, the more evidence required.
        2) The higher the quality of evidence, the less evidence required.

    b. **Appropriateness** is the measure of the **quality** of evidence. It is the **relevance** and **reliability** of evidence. Evidence is generally **more reliable** when

        1) Obtained from knowledgeable independent sources **outside the entity**.
        2) Generated under **effective internal controls**.
        3) Obtained **directly by the auditor**.
        4) It exists in **documentary form** (in any medium).
        5) It consists of **original documents** (rather than photocopies).

5. **Audit Procedures for Obtaining Audit Evidence**

    a. **Risk assessment procedures** are used to obtain an understanding of the entity and its environment, including internal control. Obtaining the understanding permits the auditor to assess the RMMs at the **financial statement** and **relevant assertion** levels.

    b. **Tests of controls** test the operating effectiveness of controls in preventing or detecting material misstatements at the relevant assertion level (see Study Unit 8). They are required in the following two circumstances:

        1) When the auditor's risk assessment is based on an expectation of the operating effectiveness of controls
        2) When substantive procedures alone do not provide sufficient appropriate evidence

    c. **Substantive procedures** are used to detect material misstatements at the relevant assertion level. They include (1) **tests of detail** of transaction classes, account balances, and disclosures, and (2) substantive **analytical procedures**.

        1) They should be performed for **all** relevant assertions about each material (a) transaction class, (b) account balance, and (c) disclosure.

6. **Types of Audit Procedures**

    a. The auditor should use the following, singly or in combination, as risk assessment procedures, tests of controls, or substantive procedures:

        1) **Inspection of records or documents** is the examination of records or documents, whether internal or external, in paper, electronic, or other media.
        2) **Inspection of tangible assets** is the physical examination of assets to test existence. It accompanies observation of inventory counts.
        3) **Observation** is looking at a process or procedure being performed.
        4) **Inquiry** is seeking information from knowledgeable persons.
        5) **Confirmation** is obtaining a representation about information or an existing condition directly from a third party (see Subunit 10.2).
        6) **Recalculation** is checking mathematical accuracy.
        7) **Reperformance** is the independent execution of procedures or controls.
        8) **Analytical procedures** are evaluations of financial data made by a study of plausible relationships among both financial and nonfinancial data (see Study Unit 3, Subunit 5).

7. **Electronic Environments**

    a. Some information may exist only in electronic form or only at a certain moment (or period) of time.

        1) For example, transactions in **electronic commerce** may occur solely by exchange of electronic messages.

        2) Moreover, **image processing systems** may convert documents to electronic images with no retention of source documents.

    b. The auditor's responses may include

        1) Performing audit procedures using **computer-assisted audit techniques (CAATs)**

        2) Requesting the entity to retain certain information

        3) Performing audit procedures at the moment when information exists

8. **Direction of Testing**

    a. In essence, the auditor collects evidence that the economic events of the entity are fairly reflected in the financial statement assertions. The diagram below illustrates (1) how those events flow to the assertions and (2) the direction of testing for the completeness, existence, and occurrence assertions.

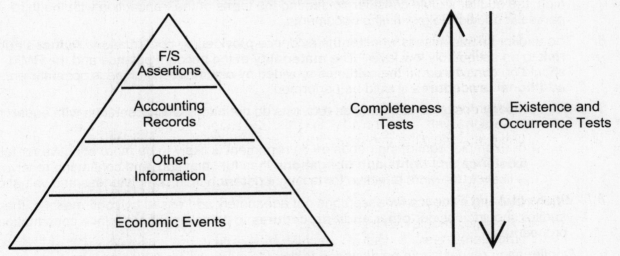

Figure 10-1

    b. For example, to test for completeness that all sales were recorded, an auditor might select a sample of shipping documents (economic event of a sale) and trace them through the recording process to determine that they were included in the sales account. To test that recorded sales occurred, the auditor might select a sample of recorded sales from the sales account and vouch them back through the records to determine that shipments to customers were made.

Stop and review! You have completed the outline for this subunit. Study multiple-choice questions 1 through 10 beginning on page 350.

10.2 THE CONFIRMATION PROCESS (AU 330)

1. **Confirmation** "is the process of obtaining and evaluating a direct communication from a third party in response to a request for information about a particular item affecting financial statement assertions." This process includes the following:

    a. Selecting items for confirmations
    b. Designing the request
    c. Communicating the request to the appropriate third party
    d. Obtaining the response
    e. Evaluating the information, or lack of it, provided by the third party about the audit objectives, including its reliability

2. The auditor uses the audit risk assessment to determine the **appropriate audit procedures**, including confirmation.

3. The greater the **assessed RMM**, the greater the assurance to be provided by substantive procedures. Thus, confirmation might be used when a more effective procedure is needed instead of or in conjunction with tests directed toward documents or parties within the entity.

4. If the entity has entered into an **unusual or complex transaction** and the assessed RMM is high, the auditor should consider confirming the terms of the transaction with the third parties in addition to examining documents.

5. The auditor should assess whether the evidence provided by confirmations **reduces audit risk** to an acceptably low level. The **materiality** of the account balance and the RMM should be considered. If the evidence provided by confirmations alone is not sufficient, **additional procedures** should be performed.

6. Even properly designed confirmation requests do not address all assertions with equal effectiveness.

    a. For example, confirming goods on consignment is likely to be more effective for testing **existence** and **rights and obligations** than for valuation, and confirming receivables is likely to be more effective for testing **existence** than completeness and valuation.

7. When obtaining evidence for assertions not adequately addressed by confirmations, the auditor should consider **other audit procedures** to complement or replace confirmation procedures.

8. Confirmation requests can be designed to provide evidence for the **completeness** assertion. Their effectiveness in this regard depends on whether the auditor selects items from an appropriate population, for example, a list of vendors when accounts payable are confirmed.

    a. However, some confirmations are not designed to elicit evidence on completeness. Thus, the Standard Form to Confirm Account Balance Information with Financial Institutions (bank confirmation) does not provide assurance about information not listed on the form.

9. **Designing Confirmation Requests**

    a. The auditor should exercise an appropriate level of **professional skepticism** throughout the confirmation process.
    b. Requests should be specific to particular **audit objectives**.
    c. The **assertions** addressed and the factors likely to affect the reliability of the confirmations should be considered.

d.   The following **factors affecting the design** of the request directly relate to the **reliability** of the evidence obtained:

   1)   The form of the request
   2)   Prior experience on the audit or similar engagements
   3)   The nature of information being confirmed
   4)   The intended respondent

e.   The **positive confirmation** requests a reply regardless of whether the respondent agrees with the information stated. It may ask the respondent to state whether (s)he agrees with the information given or request that the recipient fill in an account balance (termed a **blank form**) or provide other information.

   1)   Positive forms provide evidence only when responses are received from the recipients.

   2)   Blank forms mitigate the risk that the recipients of a positive confirmation request will sign and return the request without verifying the information.

f.   The **negative confirmation** requests the recipient to respond only if (s)he disagrees with the information stated.

   1)   Negative forms are used to reduce audit risk to an acceptable level when (a) the assessed RMM is low, (b) a large number of small balances is involved, and (c) the auditor has no reason to believe that the recipients are unlikely to consider them.

   2)   The auditor should investigate relevant information provided on negative confirmations that have been returned to determine its effect on the audit. For example, given a pattern of misstatements, the auditor should reconsider the assessed RMM and consider the effect on planned procedures.

   3)   **Unreturned negative confirmation requests** rarely provide significant evidence about assertions other than existence.

      a)   An unreturned negative confirmation request provides some evidence of existence because it has not been returned marked *Return to Sender* with an indication that the addressee is unknown. However, it provides no explicit evidence that the intended recipient verified the information.

g.   The auditor may consider information from **prior years' audits** or **audits of similar entities** when determining the effectiveness and efficiency of using confirmations.

h.   When designing requests, the auditor should consider the **types of information** respondents will most likely confirm. The nature of the information may directly affect the reliability of the evidence obtained and the response rate.

   1)   Understanding the substance of the client's arrangements and transactions with third parties is fundamental to determining the information to be confirmed. The auditor also should consider

      a)   Requesting confirmation of the terms of unusual agreements or transactions as well as the amounts

      b)   Ascertaining whether oral modifications have been made to agreements

i.   The auditor should direct the confirmation request to a **knowledgeable third party**.

   1)   Information about the respondent's competence, knowledge, motivation, ability, willingness to respond, objectivity, or freedom from bias may affect the design of the request and the evaluation of the results, including the determination as to whether other procedures are necessary.

10. **Performing Confirmation Procedures**

    a.   The auditor should control confirmation requests and responses during the performance of procedures.

    b.   **Control** means direct communication between the intended recipient and the auditor to minimize possible bias because of interception and alteration of the requests or responses.

    c.   When **responses other than mailed written communications** (e.g., fax responses) are received, additional evidence may be required to support their validity. For example, the auditor may wish to verify the sources by calling the purported senders or by having the sender mail the original confirmation directly to the auditor.

        1)   **Oral confirmations** should be documented in the audit documentation, and if the information in the oral confirmations is significant, the auditor should request that written confirmation be sent directly to the auditor.

    d.   When using **positive confirmations**, the auditor should usually **follow up** with a second and, if applicable, a third request to parties who did not respond.

11. **Alternative Procedures**

    a.   When the auditor has not received replies to positive confirmation requests, (s)he should apply alternative procedures to the nonresponses to reduce audit risk to an acceptably low level.

    b.   The **omission of alternative procedures** may be warranted when

        1)   The auditor has not identified unusual qualitative factors or systematic characteristics related to the nonresponses.

        2)   Given testing for overstatement, treating the aggregate nonresponses as 100% misstatements would not affect the auditor's decision about whether the financial statements are materially misstated.

    c.   The nature of alternative procedures varies with **the account and the assertion**.

12. The auditor should evaluate the evidence provided by confirmations and alternative procedures to determine whether sufficient appropriate evidence has been obtained about all the applicable financial statement assertions.

    a.   If the evidence gathered is not sufficient and appropriate, the auditor should request additional confirmations or extend other tests.

13. **Confirmation of Accounts Receivable**

    a.   **Accounts receivable** are the entity's claims against customers arising from the sale of goods or services in the normal course of business.

        1)   They include the loans of a financial institution.

    b.   Confirmation of accounts receivable is a **generally accepted auditing procedure**. The presumption is that the auditor will confirm accounts receivable unless

        1)   They are immaterial;

        2)   Confirmation would be ineffective; or

        3)   The assessed RMM is low, and that level, together with the evidence expected to be obtained from other tests of details or substantive analytical procedures, is sufficient to reduce audit risk to an acceptably low level.

    c.   An auditor who has not requested confirmations in the examination of accounts receivable should **document** how (s)he overcame this presumption.

    d.   Confirmation of accounts receivable also is addressed in Study Unit 11.

Stop and review! You have completed the outline for this subunit. Study multiple-choice questions 11 through 18 beginning on page 352.

10.3 AUDIT DOCUMENTATION (AU 339 AND AS NO. 3)

1. Audit documentation **(working papers) must** be prepared to provide a clear understanding of the work performed (including the nature, timing, extent, and results of audit procedures performed), the audit evidence obtained and its source, and the conclusions reached. Audit documentation provides the principal support for

    a. The representation that the audit is in accordance with GAAS
    b. The opinion expressed

2. The auditor should document

    a. Who performed the audit work and the date such work was complete.
    b. Who reviewed specific audit documentation and the date of such review.

3. Audit documentation serves **other purposes**, including

    a. Assisting the audit team to plan and perform the audit
    b. Assisting new auditors to understand the work performed
    c. Assisting audit supervisors
    d. Demonstrating the accountability of the audit team
    e. Retaining a record of matters of continuing significance to future audits
    f. Assisting inspectors, peer reviewers, and quality control reviewers
    g. Assisting a successor auditor

4. Documentation should be assembled into an **audit file**. It should enable an **experienced auditor** to understand

    a. The procedures performed under GAAS or other requirements
    b. The results and evidence obtained
    c. Significant conclusions
    d. That the accounting records agree with the audited information

5. The **form, content, and extent** of documentation are determined by the following:

    a. Risk of material misstatement of an assertion related to an account, a class of transactions, or disclosure
    b. Extent of judgment involved in performing the work and evaluating the results
    c. Nature of the auditing procedures
    d. Significance of the evidence obtained
    e. Nature and extent of exceptions identified
    f. Need to document a conclusion or the basis for a conclusion not readily determinable from other documentation of the work

6. **Tickmarks** are used to document work performed and issues uncovered during the field work. A legend should define the tickmarks used on that working paper. For example, the mark # next to the sum of a column of numbers may be defined in the legend as "# -- Footed the column." The same tickmark may be used on different working papers to mean different things as long as it is defined in the legend on that page.

7. Each page in the working paper should be given a **unique reference number** that identifies its use and location. For example, working paper "C-1" may be for Cash in Bank. These are also used to cross-reference information on other working papers.

8. **Examples of documentation** include (a) audit plans, (b) analyses, (c) memoranda, (d) confirmations, (e) letters of representation, (f) abstracts or copies of documents (e.g., copies of contracts), (g) schedules, and (h) commentaries. Documentation may be on paper or electronic or other media (e.g., tapes, disks, or film).

    a. A **working trial balance** is ordinarily used to record the year-end ledger balances prior to audit. Reclassifications and adjustments are accumulated on the trial balance to reflect the final audited balances.

    b.   **Lead schedules** are summaries of detailed schedules. For example, a cash lead schedule may summarize findings recorded on the cash in bank, petty cash, and count-of-cash-on-hand detail schedules.

    c.   **Permanent files** are schedules, documents, and records with continuing audit significance for a specific client. These may include the articles of incorporation, bylaws, and contracts.

    d.   **Current files** include schedules and analyses that relate to the current year under audit. For example, results of substantive tests, such as confirmations and inventory observation and test counts, are kept in the current files.

9.   **Significant audit findings or issues** to be documented include the following:

    a.   Identification of items tested to determine the operating effectiveness of **controls** or to perform **tests of details** that consist of inspection of documents or confirmations

        1)   The source of the items and the specific selection criteria should be stated, for example, those for a particular type of sample.

    b.   Selection, application, and consistency of application of GAAP, for example,

        1)   Accounting for complex or unusual transactions or
        2)   Treatment of estimates and uncertainties (and any related assumptions).

    c.   Evidence that the financial statements or disclosures may be materially misstated

    d.   Evidence of a need to revise the assessments of RMMs and the responses to them

    e.   Difficulty in applying necessary auditing procedures

    f.   Other findings that could result in modification of the report

    g.   Audit adjustments

Background

Rules over the preparation and maintenance of audit documentation were augmented after claims that documents may have been shredded and evidence destroyed in the Enron case.

---

10.   The auditor should complete the assembly of the final audit file **within 60 days following the report release date (documentation completion date)**.

    a.   The auditor must not delete or discard audit documentation after the documentation completion date.

    b.   The auditor may add to the audit file after the documentation completion date but must include the reason for the addition, who made the addition, and the date of the addition.

11.   **Ownership and Confidentiality**

    a.   Audit documentation is the **property of the auditor**.

    b.   Copies of documentation may be made available to the client if the validity and independence of the audit are not undermined.

    c.   The auditor should retain audit documentation for a period of time sufficient to meet the needs of his or her practice and to satisfy any applicable legal or regulatory requirements for records retention, but **not less than 5 years** from the report release date.

    d.   An auditor should take reasonable steps to preserve the **confidentiality** of documented client information, including prevention of unauthorized access.

12. **Sarbanes-Oxley Act of 2002**

    a.   The act provides further documentation guidance for registered public accountants. The PCAOB's Auditing Standard No. 3, *Audit Documentation*, which applies to audit engagements and reviews of interim financial information of issuers, reflects these considerations.

    b.   Audit documentation must contain sufficient information to enable an **experienced auditor**, having no previous connection with the engagement, to understand the work performed and conclusions reached and to determine who performed and reviewed the work and the relevant dates.

        1)   Audit documentation must not only support final conclusions but also must include auditor-identified information about significant findings and issues that is inconsistent with or contradicts the auditor's final conclusions.

    c.   The auditor must identify all **significant findings or issues** in an **engagement completion document**.

    d.   Audit documentation must be retained for **at least 7 years** from the report release date.

    e.   A complete and final set of audit documentation should be assembled for retention as of a date **(the documentation completion date)** not more than **45 days** after the report release date.

    f.   Audit documentation must **not** be deleted or discarded after the documentation completion date. However, information may be added.

    g.   AS No. 3 does not address the issue of whether audit documentation is the property of the auditor. AS No. 3 also is silent on the confidentiality of audit documentation.

    NOTE: The PCAOB adopted as interim ethics standards only the AICPA's provisions in its *Code of Professional Conduct* on integrity and objectivity. Thus, Conduct Rule 301, *Confidential Client Information*, is not a PCAOB standard.

13. Still **other documentation standards** may apply, for example, those of the SEC regarding retention of memoranda, communications (sent or received), other documents, and records related to engagements.

Stop and review! You have completed the outline for this subunit. Study multiple-choice questions 19 through 29 beginning on page 355.

10.4 THE COMPUTER AS AN AUDIT TOOL

1. **Computer-Assisted Audit Techniques**

    a.   Many auditors use personal computers (PCs) to perform audit functions more efficiently and effectively. For this purpose, auditors must select tasks appropriate for personal computer capabilities and the software for those tasks. The uses of software by the auditor are called computer-assisted audit techniques (CAATs).

    b.   **Advantages of CAATs**

        1)   The auditor can work independently of the auditee.
        2)   The confidentiality of auditor procedures can be maintained.
        3)   Audit work does not depend on the availability of auditee personnel.
        4)   The auditor has access to records at remote sites.

    c.   **Disadvantages of CAATs**

        1)   The auditor must have a working understanding of the computer system, e.g., a complicated database system (may also be an advantage).
        2)   Supervisory review may be more difficult.

d. **Audit procedures** include the following:

1) Directly accessing the entity's database (interrogation)
2) Scanning files for certain types of records, items, etc.
3) Building and using predictive models to identify high-risk areas
4) Applying statistical sampling item selection and analysis routines
5) Using input/output routines to provide hard copy and to reformat data (extraction)
6) Preparing financial statements and other reports with spreadsheet routines
7) Illustrating analyses with graphs and other pictorial displays
8) Writing customized audit plans
9) Storing audit plans, routines, and results electronically
10) Implementing other types of audit procedures and analyses electronically
11) Preparing and storing audit documentation
12) Communicating data through networks
13) Using specialized audit software to, among other things, compare source code with object code to detect unauthorized program changes, analyze unexecuted code, or generate test data
14) Embedding code in the entity's programs to routinely extract/select certain transactions or details to be recorded in a file accessible only by the auditor
15) Employment of expert systems software to automate the knowledge and logic of experts in a certain field to help an auditor with decision making and risk analysis

2. **Generalized Audit Software (GAS)**

a. GAS is useful for both **tests of controls** and **substantive procedures**. It is software that is written to interface with many different client systems.

b. GAS may be used to perform **audit tasks** such as the following:

1) Sampling and selecting items (e.g., confirmations)
2) Testing extensions, footings, and calculations
3) Examining records (e.g., accounts receivable for amounts in excess of credit limits)
4) Summarizing and sorting data
5) Performing analytical procedures (e.g., comparing inventory records with transaction details)
6) File access and file reorganization

c. **Advantages of GAS**

1) It is independent of the client's programs and personnel. Thus, information can be accessed without detailed knowledge of the client's hardware and software.
2) Less computer expertise is needed compared with writing original programs.
3) It can run on a variety of systems.

d. **Disadvantages of GAS**

1) Some software packages may process only sequential files.
2) Modifications may be necessary for a specific audit.
3) Audit software cannot examine items not in machine-readable form.
4) It has limited application in an online, real-time system.

e. A discussion of the test data approach, parallel simulation, and integrated test facilities was presented in Study Unit 8, Subunit 3.

    f.   The leading GAS software packages are currently Audit Command Language (ACL®) and Interactive Data Extraction and Analysis (IDEA™) software. These software packages, designed specifically for use in auditing, perform the following **major functions**:

1) Aging. An auditor can test the aging of accounts receivable.
2) Duplicate identification. Duplicate data can be organized by data field and subsequently identified.
3) Exportation. Data can be transferred to other software.
4) Extraction. Data can be extracted for exception analysis.
5) Gap identification. Gaps in information can be automatically noted.
6) Joining and merging. Two separate data files can be joined or merged to combine and match information.
7) Sampling. Samples of the data can be prepared and analyzed.
8) Sorting. Information can be sorted by any data field.
9) Stratification. Large amounts of data can be organized by specific factors, thereby facilitating analysis.
10) Summarization. Data can be organized to identify patterns.
11) Total fields. Totals for numeric fields can be quickly and accurately calculated.

3. **Artificial Intelligence (AI).** AI is computer software designed to perceive, reason, and understand.

    a.   Business applications of AI are called **expert systems**. Expert systems in taxation, financial accounting, managerial accounting, and auditing have long been in use in major CPA firms.

1) An expert system is **interactive**. It asks a series of questions and uses knowledge gained from a human expert to analyze answers and make a decision.
2) Expert systems allow auditors and accountants to perform their duties in less time and with more uniformity. The result is that different decision makers are more likely to reach the same conclusions given the same set of facts.
3) An expert system can be used to (a) choose an audit plan, (b) select a test sample type and size, (c) determine the level of misstatement, (d) perform analytical procedures, and (e) make a judgment based on the findings.

    b.   **Neural networks** are another form of AI. The software learns from experience because it changes its knowledge database when informed of mistakes.

    c.   An expert system imitates a human expert and relies on many programmed rules, but a neural network has a generalized learning capacity.

4. **Specialized Audit Software**

    a.   Specialized audit software is written to fulfill a specific set of audit tasks. The purposes and users of the software are well defined before the software is written.

    b.   Auditors develop specialized audit software for the following reasons:

1) Unavailability of alternative software
2) Functional limitations of alternative software
3) Efficiency considerations
4) Increased understanding of systems
5) Opportunity for easy implementation
6) Increased auditor independence and prestige

Stop and review! You have completed the outline for this subunit. Study multiple-choice questions 30 through 36 beginning on page 358.

QUESTIONS

10.1 Nature and Sufficiency (AU 326 and AS No. 15)

1. Which of the following statements concerning audit evidence is true?

A. To be appropriate, audit evidence should be either persuasive or relevant, but it need not be both.

B. The measure of the quantity and quality of audit evidence lies in the auditor's judgment.

C. The difficulty and expense of obtaining audit evidence concerning an account balance is a valid basis for omitting the test.

D. A client's accounting records can be sufficient audit evidence to support the financial statements.

Answer (B) is correct. *(CPA, adapted)*
REQUIRED: The true statement about audit evidence.
DISCUSSION: AU 326 indicates that the measure of the quantity and quality of such evidence for audit purposes lies in the judgment of the auditor. Unlike legal evidence, audit evidence is not circumscribed by rigid rules. In determining whether evidence is appropriate and sufficient, the auditor must make many judgments about issues such as relevance, objectivity, timeliness, and the existence of corroboration.
Answer (A) is incorrect. To be appropriate, audit evidence must be both persuasive and relevant. Moreover, an auditor usually must rely on evidence that is persuasive rather than convincing. Answer (C) is incorrect. Although the cost of obtaining evidence and its usefulness should be rationally related, the matter of difficulty and expense is not itself a valid basis for omitting a test. Answer (D) is incorrect. Accounting records must be supported by corroborating information.

2. Audit procedures are designed to obtain evidence about relevant assertions. Which of the following is a **false** statement about audit procedures?

A. The relationship between audit procedures and relevant assertions should be one-to-one.

B. Audit procedures should be developed in light of assertions about the financial statement components.

C. Selection of procedures should depend upon the understanding of internal control.

D. The auditor should resolve any substantial doubt about any of management's material financial statement assertions.

Answer (A) is correct. *(Publisher, adapted)*
REQUIRED: The false statement about audit procedures.
DISCUSSION: Some procedures may relate to more than one assertion, and multiple procedures may address a single assertion.
Answer (B) is incorrect. Assertions should be considered when the auditor designs procedures. Answer (C) is incorrect. The understanding of internal control and the assessed RMM affect the nature, timing, and extent of substantive procedures. Answer (D) is incorrect. The auditor must refrain from forming an opinion until (s)he has gathered sufficient appropriate evidence to remove any substantial doubt about a material assertion. Otherwise, (s)he must modify the opinion or disclaim an opinion.

3. The objective of tests of details of transactions performed as substantive procedures is to

A. Comply with generally accepted auditing standards.

B. Attain assurance about the reliability of the accounting system.

C. Detect material misstatements at the relevant assertion level.

D. Evaluate whether management's policies and procedures operated effectively.

Answer (C) is correct. *(CPA, adapted)*
REQUIRED: The objective of tests of details.
DISCUSSION: Substantive procedures are (1) tests of the details of transaction classes, balances, and disclosures and (2) substantive analytical procedures. They are performed to detect material misstatements at the relevant assertion level. The auditor performs substantive procedures as a response to the related assessment of the RMM (AU 318).
Answer (A) is incorrect. The auditor may use a variety of techniques and is not required to use tests of the details of transactions to comply with GAAS. Answer (B) is incorrect. Tests of controls test the operating effectiveness of internal control. Internally generated audit evidence is generally more reliable when relevant controls are effective. Answer (D) is incorrect. Tests of controls are used to determine whether policies or procedures operated effectively.

4. In determining whether transactions have been recorded, the direction of the audit testing should begin from the

A. General ledger balances.

B. Adjusted trial balance.

C. Original source documents.

D. General journal entries.

Answer (C) is correct. *(CPA, adapted)*
REQUIRED: The direction of testing to determine whether transactions have been recorded.
DISCUSSION: Determining whether transactions have been recorded is a test of the completeness assertion. Thus, beginning with the original source documents and tracing the transactions to the appropriate accounting records determines whether they were recorded.

5. A retail entity uses electronic data interchange (EDI) in executing and recording most of its purchase transactions. The entity's auditor recognizes that the documentation of the transactions will be retained for only a short period of time. To compensate for this limitation, the auditor most likely would

A. Increase the sample of EDI transactions to be selected for cutoff tests.

B. Perform tests several times during the year, rather than only at year-end.

C. Plan to make a 100% count of the entity's inventory at or near year-end.

D. Decrease the assessed risk of material misstatement for the existence or occurrence assertion.

Answer (B) is correct. *(CPA, adapted)*
    REQUIRED: The auditor's response to limited retention time of documentation supporting EDI transactions.
    DISCUSSION: Accounting records and other evidence may be available only in electronic form. For example, if EDI is used, purchase, shipping, billing, cash receipt, and cash payment transactions often occur by exchange of electronic messages instead of source documents. In an image processing system, documents are scanned and converted into electronic form for storage purposes, and the source documents may not be retained. Thus, electronic evidence may exist at a given moment in time, but it may not be retrievable after a specified period if files are changed and no backups exist. Consequently, the auditor should consider the time during which information is available to determine the nature, timing, and extent of substantive tests and tests of controls. For example, the auditor may change the timing of audit tests by performing them several times during the year instead of only at year-end.
    Answer (A) is incorrect. Increasing the sample of transactions does not compensate for the lack of documentation. Answer (C) is incorrect. Inventory is not the only affected balance. Answer (D) is incorrect. The auditor would likely increase the assessed risk of material misstatement for the existence or occurrence assertion in light of this information.

6. Audit evidence can come in different forms with different degrees of persuasiveness. Which of the following is the **least** persuasive type of evidence?

A. Bank statement obtained from the client.

B. Test counts of inventory made by the auditor.

C. Prenumbered purchase order forms.

D. Correspondence from the client's attorney about litigation.

Answer (C) is correct. *(CPA, adapted)*
    REQUIRED: The least persuasive type of evidence.
    DISCUSSION: When documentation, such as purchase order forms, is prepared solely by client personnel, its persuasiveness will be less than that prepared by the auditor or an independent party. Ordinarily, the most reliable documentation is created outside the entity and has never been within the client's control.
    Answer (A) is incorrect. Although a bank statement obtained from the client has been within the client's control, it is an externally generated document and is preferable to an internally prepared document. Answer (B) is incorrect. In principle, evidence is more likely to be reliable when it consists of the auditor's direct personal knowledge. Answer (D) is incorrect. Correspondence from the client's attorney about litigation is externally generated and therefore preferable to an internally generated document.

7. Which of the following generalizations does **not** relate to the reliability of audit evidence?

A. The more effective internal control, the more assurance it provides about the accounting data and financial statements.

B. An auditor's opinion, to be economically useful, is formed within reasonable time and based on evidence obtained at a reasonable cost.

C. Evidence obtained from independent sources outside the entity is more reliable than evidence secured solely within the entity.

D. The independent auditor's direct personal knowledge, obtained through observation and inspection, is more reliable than information obtained indirectly.

Answer (B) is correct. *(CPA, adapted)*
    REQUIRED: The generalization not relating to the reliability of audit evidence.
    DISCUSSION: Appropriate evidence is both reliable and relevant. Ordinarily, evidence obtained from independent sources, developed under effective internal control, or generated through the auditor's personal experience is presumed to be the most reliable (AU 326). However, cost-benefit considerations relate to the sufficiency, not the reliability, of evidence.
    Answer (A) is incorrect. The more effective the controls, the more assurance they provide about the reliability of the accounting data and financial statements. Answer (C) is incorrect. Evidence obtained from independent sources outside an entity provides greater assurance of reliability than evidence secured solely within the entity. Answer (D) is incorrect. The auditor's direct knowledge is usually more reliable than information obtained indirectly.

8. Accounting records alone do not provide sufficient appropriate evidence on which to base an opinion on the financial statements. Thus, the auditor should obtain other information. Which of the following is other information in this context?

A. Worksheets supporting cost allocations.

B. Confirmations of accounts receivable.

C. General and subsidiary ledgers.

D. Journal entries.

Answer (B) is correct. *(Publisher, adapted)*
REQUIRED: The example of other information.
DISCUSSION: Other information includes minutes of meetings; confirmations; and information obtained from inquiry, observation, and inspection. It includes information developed by or available to the auditor that permits valid reasoning (AU 326). Answer (A) is incorrect. Worksheets supporting cost allocations are examples of accounting records. Answer (C) is incorrect. General and subsidiary ledgers are examples of accounting records. Answer (D) is incorrect. Journal entries are examples of accounting records.

9. Which statement about audit evidence is invalid?

A. The auditor is seldom convinced beyond all doubt with respect to all aspects of the statements being audited.

B. The auditor would not undertake a procedure that would provide persuasive evidence only.

C. The auditor evaluates the degree of risk involved in deciding the kind of evidence to gather.

D. The auditor evaluates the usefulness of the evidence against the cost to obtain it.

Answer (B) is correct. *(Publisher, adapted)*
REQUIRED: The invalid statement about audit evidence.
DISCUSSION: In most cases, audit evidence that is obtained to afford a reasonable basis for an opinion is necessarily persuasive rather than convincing. The cost of obtaining convincing evidence may outweigh the benefits. Nevertheless, the difficulty and expense of testing an item are not in themselves a valid basis for omitting an audit procedure if no appropriate alternative exists (AU 326).
Answer (A) is incorrect. The auditor is seldom persuaded beyond all doubt given the high cost of absolute certainty. Answer (C) is incorrect. The auditor should assess the risk of material misstatement before determining the kind and amount of evidence necessary to form an opinion. Answer (D) is incorrect. The auditor may consider the cost and usefulness of evidence.

10. Each of the following might, by itself, form a valid basis for an auditor to decide to omit a test **except** for the

A. Difficulty and expense involved in testing a particular item.

B. Assessment of the risk of material misstatement at a low level.

C. Assessment of inherent risk at a low level.

D. The immateriality of the item under audit.

Answer (A) is correct. *(CPA, adapted)*
REQUIRED: The consideration that is not a valid reason for omission of an audit test.
DISCUSSION: The auditor may consider the relationship between the cost and usefulness of audit evidence. However, the difficulty and expense of performing a procedure are not in themselves valid reasons for omitting it if no appropriate alternative exists (AU 326).
Answer (B) is incorrect. The lower the RMM, the higher the acceptable detection risk and the greater the justification for omitting a substantive procedure. Answer (C) is incorrect. A test might be omitted if the susceptibility to error and fraud is slight. Answer (D) is incorrect. If an item is immaterial, it may not need to be tested.

10.2 The Confirmation Process (AU 330)

11. In which of the following circumstances would the use of the negative form of accounts receivable confirmation most likely be justified?

A. A substantial number of accounts may be in dispute, and the accounts receivable balance arises from sales to a few major customers.

B. A substantial number of accounts may be in dispute, and the accounts receivable balance arises from sales to many customers with small balances.

C. A small number of accounts may be in dispute, and the accounts receivable balance arises from sales to a few major customers.

D. A small number of accounts may be in dispute, and the accounts receivable balance arises from sales to many customers with small balances.

Answer (D) is correct. *(CPA, adapted)*
REQUIRED: The circumstances in which negative accounts receivable confirmations are most likely justified.
DISCUSSION: AU 330 indicates that negative confirmation requests may be used to reduce audit risk to an acceptable level when (1) the assessed risk of material misstatement is low, (2) a large number of small balances is involved, and (3) the auditor has no reason to believe that the recipients of the requests are unlikely to give them consideration.

12. Auditors may use positive or negative forms of confirmation requests. An auditor most likely will use

   A. The positive form to confirm all balances regardless of size.

   B. The negative form for small balances.

   C. A combination of the two forms, with the positive form used for trade balances and the negative form for other balances.

   D. The positive form when the assessed risk of material misstatement is acceptably low and the negative form when it is unacceptably high.

Answer (B) is correct. *(CPA, adapted)*
   REQUIRED: The true statement about the use of positive and negative confirmations.
   DISCUSSION: The negative confirmation asks for a response only when the debtor disagrees. The negative form may be used when the assessed risk of material misstatement is low, many small balances are involved, and the auditor has no reason to believe that recipients are unlikely to give confirmations their consideration (AU 330). A combination of the two forms is often used.
   Answer (A) is incorrect. The negative form is often used, e.g., when many small balances are involved. Answer (C) is incorrect. The nature of the balances does not dictate the form used. Answer (D) is incorrect. The positive form is used when the assessed risk of material misstatement is high.

13. Which of the following strategies most likely could improve the response rate of the confirmation of accounts receivable?

   A. Including a list of items or invoices that constitute the account balance.

   B. Restricting the selection of accounts to be confirmed to those customers with relatively large balances.

   C. Requesting customers to respond to the confirmation requests directly to the auditor by fax or email.

   D. Notifying the recipients that second requests will be mailed if they fail to respond in a timely manner.

Answer (A) is correct. *(CPA, adapted)*
   REQUIRED: The strategy most likely to improve confirmation response rates.
   DISCUSSION: According to AU 330, the auditor should consider what respondents are most readily able to confirm so as to improve the response rate and the competence of the evidence obtained. Thus, some customers may use a voucher system that makes it more convenient to respond to individual invoices rather than the total balance.
   Answer (B) is incorrect. Although the auditor will likely focus on the larger balances, this emphasis is not likely to improve the response rate. Answer (C) is incorrect. When responses other than written communications mailed to the auditor (e.g., email or faxes) are received, additional evidence may be required to support their validity, for example, verifying the response by a telephone call to the purported sender. Answer (D) is incorrect. Notifying the recipients that second requests will be mailed if they fail to respond in a timely manner is threatening. It may reduce the response rate.

14. Which of the following statements is correct concerning the use of negative confirmation requests?

   A. Unreturned negative confirmation requests rarely provide significant explicit evidence.

   B. Negative confirmation requests are effective when detection risk is low.

   C. Unreturned negative confirmation requests indicate that alternative procedures are necessary.

   D. Negative confirmation requests are effective when understatements of account balances are suspected.

Answer (A) is correct. *(CPA, adapted)*
   REQUIRED: The true statement about negative confirmation requests.
   DISCUSSION: Unreturned negative confirmation requests rarely provide significant evidence about assertions other than certain aspects of existence. Additionally, unreturned negative confirmations do not provide explicit evidence that the intended parties received the requests and verified the information provided.
   Answer (B) is incorrect. When desired detection risk is low, positive confirmations are more effective. Answer (C) is incorrect. The auditor assumes the account is fairly stated when negative confirmations are not returned, thus indicating alternative procedures are not necessary. Answer (D) is incorrect. Positive confirmations are more effective when understatements of account balances are suspected.

15. An auditor decides to use the blank form of accounts receivable confirmation rather than the traditional positive form. The auditor should be aware that the blank form may be **less** efficient because

A. Subsequent cash receipts need to be verified.

B. Statistical sampling may not be used.

C. A higher assessed level of detection risk is required.

D. More nonresponses are likely to occur.

Answer (D) is correct. *(CPA, adapted)*
REQUIRED: The disadvantage of a blank form confirmation request.
DISCUSSION: The blank form of accounts receivable confirmation requests the recipient to complete the confirmation by providing the balance due to the client. This procedure may require more effort by the recipient and thus limit response rates. Accordingly, the auditor may have to perform alternative procedures (AU 330).
Answer (A) is incorrect. Verification of subsequent cash receipts is an alternative procedure performed when the response rate is too low. Answer (B) is incorrect. Statistical sampling may be used with any form of confirmation. Answer (C) is incorrect. Detection risk is the risk that a material misstatement may not be detected. It is a function of the effectiveness, not the efficiency, of an auditing procedure and its application by the auditor. The blank form of positive confirmation tends to reduce detection risk.

16. The confirmation of customers' accounts receivable rarely provides reliable evidence about the completeness assertion because

A. Many customers merely sign and return the confirmation without verifying its details.

B. Recipients usually respond only if they disagree with the information on the request.

C. Customers may not be inclined to report understatement errors in their accounts.

D. Auditors typically select many accounts with low recorded balances to be confirmed.

Answer (C) is correct. *(CPA, adapted)*
REQUIRED: The reason confirmations rarely provide evidence about completeness.
DISCUSSION: Confirmations do not address all assertions with equal effectiveness. For example, confirmations of accounts receivable do not necessarily provide reliable evidence about the completeness assertion because customers may not report understatement errors. Also, confirmations may not be designed to provide assurance about information not given in the request forms.
Answer (A) is incorrect. A customer ordinarily confirms the balance, not its details. Moreover, many confirmation requests do not contemplate a response unless the customer disagrees with the entity's recorded amount. Answer (B) is incorrect. Positive confirmations ask the customer to return the confirmation whether it is correct or not. Answer (D) is incorrect. Auditors typically select accounts with material balances. The existence assertion is normally tested by confirmation.

17. In confirming accounts receivable, an auditor decided to confirm customers' account balances rather than individual invoices. Which of the following most likely will be included with the client's confirmation letter?

A. An auditor-prepared letter explaining that a nonresponse may cause an inference that the account balance is correct.

B. A client-prepared letter reminding the customer that a nonresponse will cause a second request to be sent.

C. An auditor-prepared letter requesting the customer to supply missing and incorrect information directly to the client.

D. A client-prepared statement of account showing the details of the customer's account balance.

Answer (D) is correct. *(CPA, adapted)*
REQUIRED: The nature of a confirmation of an accounts receivable balance.
DISCUSSION: A confirmation must be requested by the client because the receiving party has no relationship with the client's auditor. In confirming the customer's account balance, display of the details of the balance will likely help the customer in reconciling the amount and may increase response rates. The auditor, however, will send the request directly to the customer, who will be requested to send the response directly to the auditor.
Answer (A) is incorrect. The request should come from the client. Answer (B) is incorrect. No threats should be included in a confirmation. Answer (C) is incorrect. The response should go directly to the auditor.

18. To reduce the risks associated with accepting email responses to requests for confirmation of accounts receivable, an auditor most likely would

   A. Request the senders to mail the original forms to the auditor.

   B. Examine subsequent cash receipts for the accounts in question.

   C. Consider the email responses to the confirmations to be exceptions.

   D. Mail second requests to the email respondents.

Answer (A) is correct. *(CPA, adapted)*
   REQUIRED: The most likely method of reducing the risks associated with email responses to confirmation requests.
   DISCUSSION: When responses other than written communications mailed to the auditor (e.g., email or faxes) are received, additional evidence may be required to support their validity. For example, the auditor may wish to verify the sources by calling the purported senders or by having the senders mail the original confirmations directly to the auditor.
   Answer (B) is incorrect. Subsequent collections provide evidence as to valuation once the existence assertion has been tested using confirmations. Answer (C) is incorrect. The responses, if from bona fide debtors, are not exceptions. Answer (D) is incorrect. The respondents should still have the original requests.

10.3 Audit Documentation (AU 339 and AS No. 3)

19. Audit documentation

   A. Provides the principal support for the auditor's report.

   B. Satisfies the auditor's responsibilities concerning the *Code of Professional Conduct*.

   C. Monitors the effectiveness of the CPA firm's quality control procedures.

   D. Documents the level of independence maintained by the auditor.

Answer (A) is correct. *(CPA, adapted)*
   REQUIRED: The purpose of audit documentation.
   DISCUSSION: Documentation provides the principal support for (1) the representation in the audit report about compliance with GAAS and (2) the opinion expressed in the audit report (or the assertion that an opinion cannot be expressed).
   Answer (B) is incorrect. Although audit documentation is required to be prepared for each engagement by GAAS, it is not specifically required by the *Code of Professional Conduct*. Answer (C) is incorrect. The creation of audit documentation to satisfy quality control standards is a secondary purpose. Answer (D) is incorrect. The auditor must be independent to perform an audit. An auditor either is or is not independent.

20. Which of the following factors would **least** likely affect the form, content, and extent of audit documentation?

   A. The risk of material misstatement.

   B. The extent of exceptions identified.

   C. The nature of the auditing procedures.

   D. The medium in which it is recorded and maintained.

Answer (D) is correct. *(CPA, adapted)*
   REQUIRED: The least likely factor affecting the form, content, and extent of audit documentation.
   DISCUSSION: The medium used to prepare and maintain the audit documentation, e.g., paper or magnetic disk, does not affect its nature and extent. The form, content, and extent of documentation are determined by (1) the risk of material misstatement, (2) the extent of judgment involved in performing the work and evaluating the results, (3) the nature of the auditing procedures, (4) the significance of the evidence obtained, (5) the nature and extent of exceptions identified, and (6) the need to document a conclusion or the basis for a conclusion.

21. An auditor ordinarily uses a working trial balance resembling the financial statements without notes, but containing columns for

   A. Cash flow increases and decreases.

   B. Risk assessments and assertions.

   C. Reclassifications and adjustments.

   D. Reconciliations and tick marks.

Answer (C) is correct. *(CPA, adapted)*
   REQUIRED: The columns contained on a working trial balance in the audit documentation.
   DISCUSSION: A working trial balance is ordinarily used to record the year-end ledger balances prior to audit in the audit documentation. Reclassifications and adjustments are accumulated on the trial balance to reflect the final audited balances.
   Answer (A) is incorrect. Cash flow increases or decreases are reflected on the client's statement of cash flows. Answer (B) is incorrect. Risk assessments and relevant assertions are determined in the planning stage of the audit and reflected in the audit documentation. Answer (D) is incorrect. The working trial balance has no column for either reconciliations or tick marks.

22. The audit working paper that reflects the major components of an amount reported in the financial statements is the

A. Interbank transfer schedule.

B. Carryforward schedule.

C. Supporting schedule.

D. Lead schedule.

Answer (D) is correct. *(CPA, adapted)*
REQUIRED: The working paper that reflects the major components of a reported amount.
DISCUSSION: Lead schedules help to eliminate detail from the auditor's working trial balance by classifying and summarizing similar or related items that are contained on the supporting schedules. A lead schedule contains the detailed accounts from the general ledger making up the line item total in the financial statements; e.g., the cash account in the financial statements might consist of petty cash, cash-general, cash-payroll, etc.
Answer (A) is incorrect. An interbank transfer schedule is a working paper prepared for several days before and after the end of the period to determine that both parts of these transactions are recorded in the same period. Answer (B) is incorrect. A carryforward schedule is a continuing schedule of an account with a balance carried forward for several years. Answer (C) is incorrect. Supporting schedules provide details aggregated in the lead schedule.

23. In creating lead schedules for an audit engagement, a CPA often uses automated audit documentation software. What client information is needed to begin this process?

A. Interim financial information, such as third quarter sales, net income, and inventory and receivables balances.

B. Specialized journal information, such as the invoice and purchase order numbers of the last few sales and purchases of the year.

C. General ledger information, such as account numbers, prior-year account balances, and current-year unadjusted information.

D. Adjusting entry information, such as deferrals and accruals and reclassification journal entries.

Answer (C) is correct. *(CPA, adapted)*
REQUIRED: The client information needed to begin the creation of lead schedules.
DISCUSSION: Lead schedules are summaries of detailed schedules. To create these summaries, general ledger information is needed. A lead schedule contains the detailed accounts from the general ledger making up the line item total. For example, a cash lead schedule may summarize findings recorded on the cash in bank, petty cash, and count-of-cash-on-hand detail schedules.
Answer (A) is incorrect. Interim information is used in review engagements of interim financial information. Answer (B) is incorrect. Specific transactions are reflected in detailed audit documentation and results are summarized on lead schedules. Answer (D) is incorrect. Specific transactions are reflected in detailed audit documentation, and results are summarized on lead schedules.

24. Which of the following documentation is required for an audit in accordance with generally accepted auditing standards?

A. A flowchart or an internal control questionnaire that evaluates the effectiveness of the entity's internal controls.

B. A list of alternative procedures that were considered but not used in the audit.

C. An indication that the accounting records agree or reconcile with the financial statements.

D. The manner in which management considered trivial errors discovered in the audit.

Answer (C) is correct. *(CPA, adapted)*
REQUIRED: The audit documentation required by GAAS.
DISCUSSION: Audit documentation should enable an experienced auditor to understand that the accounting records agree or reconcile with the financial statements or other audited information (AU 339). It also should enable an experienced auditor to understand the nature, timing, extent, and results of the procedures performed and the significant conclusions.
Answer (A) is incorrect. Although an auditor must document that a sufficient understanding of internal control has been obtained, GAAS do not require a flowchart or questionnaire. Answer (B) is incorrect. Procedures not employed need not be documented. Answer (D) is incorrect. Errors judged as trivial need not be considered by management.

25. The current file of the auditor's audit documentation ordinarily should include

A. A flowchart of the internal control procedures.

B. Organization charts.

C. A copy of the financial statements.

D. Copies of bond and note indentures.

Answer (C) is correct. *(CPA, adapted)*
REQUIRED: The item included in the current file of the auditor's audit documentation.
DISCUSSION: The current file of the auditor's audit documentation includes all working papers applicable to the current year under audit. A copy of the financial statements must be included in the current file because the amounts included in these statements are the focus of the audit.
Answer (A) is incorrect. A flowchart of the internal control procedures would be included in the permanent file. Answer (B) is incorrect. Organization charts would be included in the permanent file. Answer (D) is incorrect. Copies of bond and note indentures would be included in the permanent file.

26. Which of the following statements concerning audit documentation is **false**?

A. An auditor may support an opinion by other means in addition to audit documentation.

B. The form of audit documentation should be designed to meet the circumstances of a particular engagement.

C. Audit documentation is the property of the client.

D. Audit documentation should show that the auditor has obtained an understanding of internal control.

Answer (C) is correct. *(CPA, adapted)*
REQUIRED: The false statement about audit documentation.
DISCUSSION: Audit documentation is the property of the auditor. Copies of documentation may be made available to the client if the validity and independence of the audit are not undermined.
Answer (A) is incorrect. Audit documentation provides the principal support for the auditor's opinion and for compliance with GAAS, but additional means may be used to support an opinion. Answer (B) is incorrect. The form, content, and extent of audit documentation vary with the circumstances. Answer (D) is incorrect. Audit documentation should enable an experienced auditor to understand the nature, timing, and extent of procedures performed to comply with GAAS. For example, the auditor should document the understanding of the components of internal control (AU 314).

27. Although the quantity and content of audit documentation vary with each engagement, an auditor's permanent files most likely include

A. Schedules that support the current year's adjusting entries.

B. Prior years' accounts receivable confirmations that were classified as exceptions.

C. Documentation indicating that the audit work was adequately planned and supervised.

D. Analyses of capital stock and other owners' equity accounts.

Answer (D) is correct. *(CPA, adapted)*
REQUIRED: The component of the permanent section of audit documentation.
DISCUSSION: The permanent section of audit documentation usually contains copies of important company documents. They may include the articles of incorporation, stock options, contracts, and bylaws; the engagement letter, which is the contract between the auditor and the client; analyses from previous audits of accounts of special importance to the auditor, such as noncurrent debt, PP&E, and equity; and information concerning internal control, e.g., flowcharts, organization charts, and questionnaires.
Answer (A) is incorrect. Schedules that support the current year's adjusting entries are not carried forward in the permanent file. They are unlikely to have continuing significance. Answer (B) is incorrect. Prior years' accounts receivable confirmations that were classified as exceptions are not carried forward in the permanent file. They are unlikely to have continuing significance. Answer (C) is incorrect. Documentation indicating that the audit work was adequately planned and supervised is always included in the current files.

28. Which of the following statements is most accurate regarding sufficient and appropriate documentation?

A. Accounting estimates are **not** considered sufficient and appropriate documentation.

B. Sufficient and appropriate documentation should include evidence that the audit working papers have been reviewed.

C. If additional evidence is required to document significant findings or issues, the original evidence is **not** considered sufficient and appropriate and therefore should be deleted from the working papers.

D. Audit documentation is the property of the client, and sufficient and appropriate copies should be retained by the auditor for at least 5 years.

Answer (B) is correct. *(CPA, adapted)*
REQUIRED: The most accurate statement regarding sufficient and appropriate documentation.
DISCUSSION: Proper planning and supervision are required in an audit. Supervision is evidenced on working papers by reviewing and approving the work performed and the conclusions reached.
Answer (A) is incorrect. Accounting estimates are part of the financial statements, not audit documentation. The auditor should evaluate management's estimates and document the conclusions, however. Answer (C) is incorrect. Additional evidence may be required to support a finding and should be added. However, once the documentation completion date has passed, the auditor should not delete any documentation from the working papers. Answer (D) is incorrect. Audit documentation is the property of the auditor.

29. The auditor is required to retain audit documentation

    A. For a period to satisfy applicable legal or regulatory requirements.

    B. For as long as the client remains a client and continues to pay audit fees on a timely basis.

    C. In perpetuity.

    D. For a period to be agreed upon in the engagement letter.

Answer (A) is correct. *(Publisher, adapted)*
REQUIRED: The retention period for audit documentation.
DISCUSSION: AICPA standards require the auditor to retain audit documentation for a period sufficient to meet the needs of his/her practice and to satisfy any applicable legal or regulatory requirements, but not less than 5 years. The PCAOB's AS No. 3, *Audit Documentation*, implements the requirement of the Sarbanes-Oxley Act of 2002 that registered public accounting firms, when performing engagements under PCAOB standards, retain audit documentation for 7 years from the audit report release date.
Answer (B) is incorrect. The auditor must retain the audit documentation beyond the date the auditor is succeeded by a new auditor. Answer (C) is incorrect. Audit documentation need not be maintained in perpetuity. Answer (D) is incorrect. The auditor determines the retention period necessary to meet his/her needs subject to legal and regulatory requirements.

10.4 The Computer as an Audit Tool

30. The two requirements crucial to achieving audit efficiency and effectiveness with a personal computer are selecting

    A. The appropriate audit tasks for personal computer applications and the appropriate software to perform the selected audit tasks.

    B. The appropriate software to perform the selected audit tasks and audit procedures that are generally applicable to several clients in a specific industry.

    C. Client data that can be accessed by the auditor's personal computer and audit procedures that are generally applicable to several clients in a specific industry.

    D. Audit procedures that are generally applicable to several clients in a specific industry and the appropriate audit tasks for personal computer applications.

Answer (A) is correct. *(CPA, adapted)*
REQUIRED: The two requirements necessary to achieve audit efficiency and effectiveness using a personal computer.
DISCUSSION: The question relates to using the computer as an audit tool. To use a personal computer for this purpose effectively and efficiently, the auditor must have the appropriate hardware and software.
Answer (B) is incorrect. Selection of standardized procedures for the industry does not relate directly to the efficient and effective use of a personal computer. Answer (C) is incorrect. Access to the client's records and selection of standardized audit procedures pertain more to the use of generalized audit software to perform substantive tests than to using the personal computer as an audit tool. Answer (D) is incorrect. Selection of standardized procedures for the industry does not relate directly to the efficient and effective use of a personal computer.

31. A primary advantage of using generalized audit software packages to audit the financial statements of a client that uses a computer system is that the auditor may

    A. Consider increasing the use of substantive tests of transactions in place of analytical procedures.

    B. Substantiate the accuracy of data through self-checking digits and hash totals.

    C. Reduce the level of required tests of controls to a relatively small amount.

    D. Access information stored on computer files while having a limited understanding of the client's hardware and software features.

Answer (D) is correct. *(CPA, adapted)*
REQUIRED: The advantage of using generalized audit software (GAS).
DISCUSSION: These packages permit the auditor to audit through the computer; e.g., to extract, compare, analyze, and summarize data; and to generate output for use in the audit. Although generalized audit software requires the auditor to provide certain specifications about the client's records, computer equipment, and file formats, a detailed knowledge of the client's system may be unnecessary because the audit package is designed to be used in many environments.
Answer (A) is incorrect. The auditor is required to apply analytical procedures in the planning and overall review phases of the audit. Answer (B) is incorrect. Self-checking digits and hash totals are application controls used by clients. Answer (C) is incorrect. Audit software may permit far more comprehensive tests of controls than in a manual audit.

32. An auditor would **least** likely use computer software to

A. Construct parallel simulations.

B. Access data files.

C. Prepare spreadsheets.

D. Assess risk.

Answer (D) is correct. *(CPA, adapted)*
REQUIRED: The task least likely to be done with computer software.
DISCUSSION: The auditor is required to obtain an understanding of the entity and its environment, including its internal control, and to assess the risk of material misstatement to plan the audit. This assessment is a matter of professional judgment that cannot be accomplished with a computer.
Answer (A) is incorrect. Parallel simulation involves using an auditor's program to reproduce the logic of the client's program. Answer (B) is incorrect. Computer software makes accessing client files much faster and easier. Answer (C) is incorrect. Many audit spreadsheet programs are available.

33. Which of the following is an engagement attribute for an audit of an entity that processes most of its financial data in electronic form without any paper documentation?

A. Discrete phases of planning, interim, and year-end fieldwork.

B. Increased effort to search for evidence of management fraud.

C. Performance of audit tests on a continuous basis.

D. Increased emphasis on the completeness assertion.

Answer (C) is correct. *(CPA, adapted)*
REQUIRED: The engagement attribute for auditing in an electronic environment.
DISCUSSION: The audit trail for transactions processed in electronic form may be available for only a short period of time. The auditor may conclude that it is necessary to time audit procedures so that they correspond to the availability of the evidence. Thus, audit modules may be embedded in the client's software for this purpose.
Answer (A) is incorrect. This engagement attribute would be appropriate for any type of client. Answer (B) is incorrect. Processing transactions in electronic form does not inherently increase the risk of management fraud. Answer (D) is incorrect. No inherent additional concern arises about the completeness assertion as a result of processing transactions in electronic form.

34. A bank implemented an expert system to help account representatives consolidate the bank's relationships with each customer. The expert system will be used to

A. Calculate balances.

B. Update accounts.

C. Make decisions.

D. Collect loans.

Answer (C) is correct. *(Publisher, adapted)*
REQUIRED: The purpose of an expert system.
DISCUSSION: An expert system relies on a computer's ability to make decisions in a human way. It asks a series of questions and uses knowledge gained from a human expert to analyze answers and make a decision.

35. Using personal computers in auditing may affect the methods used to review the work of staff assistants because

A. Supervisory personnel may not have an understanding of the capabilities and limitations of personal computers.

B. Audit documentation may not contain readily observable details of calculations.

C. The audit field work standards for supervision may differ.

D. Documenting the supervisory review may require assistance of consulting services personnel.

Answer (B) is correct. *(CPA, adapted)*
REQUIRED: The reason using personal computers may affect the review of the work of staff assistants.
DISCUSSION: With the introduction of computers, accountants have been able to perform fewer manual calculations. Usually, the necessary numbers are entered into computer spreadsheets, and the answer is produced. Thus, the use of computers makes the review of a staff assistant's work different from that needed when the calculations are done manually.
Answer (A) is incorrect. Supervisors of the audit staff typically have the skills to evaluate the appropriate use of personal computers. Answer (C) is incorrect. The audit field work standards for supervision are the same whether or not a computer is used. Answer (D) is incorrect. Audit staff typically have skills appropriate for the use of personal computers in documenting the work product of the audit.

36. Specialized audit software

A. Is written to interface with many different client systems.

B. May be written while its purposes and users are being defined.

C. Requires the auditor to have less computer expertise than generalized audit software.

D. May be written in a procedure-oriented language.

Answer (D) is correct. *(Publisher, adapted)*

REQUIRED: The true statement regarding specialized audit software.

DISCUSSION: Specialized audit software is written to fulfill a specific set of audit tasks. The purposes and users of the software are well defined before the software is written. Auditors develop specialized audit software for the following reasons:

1. Unavailability of alternative software
2. Functional limitations of alternative software
3. Efficiency considerations
4. Increased understanding of systems
5. Opportunity for easy implementation
6. Increased auditor independence and prestige

Answer (A) is incorrect. Generalized audit software is written to interface with many different client systems. Answer (B) is incorrect. The purposes and users of this software must be defined before it is written. Answer (C) is incorrect. Generalized audit software purchased "off the shelf" requires less computer expertise than specialized software created by the auditor.

Use the additional questions in Gleim **CPA Test Prep Online** to create Test Sessions that emulate Prometric!

10.5 PRACTICE SIMULATION

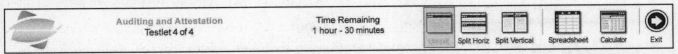

| | Auditing and Attestation
Testlet 4 of 4 | Time Remaining
1 hour - 30 minutes | Unsplit | Split Horiz | Split Vertical | Spreadsheet | Calculator | Exit |

DIRECTIONS

Note: If you believe you have encountered a software malfunction, report it to the test center staff immediately.

Navigation

To navigate from task to task, use the controls at the bottom of the screen. Click on the **Next** button to advance to the next task, or the **Previous** button to go to the previous task. To go directly to any task, click on its number.

| ▼ = Reminder | | Directions | 1 2 3 4 5 6 7 | ◄ Previous Next ► |

If you would like a reminder to revisit a task, or want to indicate that you are finished with it, click on the reminder flag below the task number. To clear the flag, click on it again. Reminder flags are for your use only – they do not contribute to your score.

Tabs

In this part of the examination, you will be asked to complete various tasks. Every task has one or more **Work Tabs**. Some tasks have one or more **Information Tabs**, others may have none. Every task has a **Help** tab.

If a task has **Information Tabs**, you may use the information in them to complete your responses in the **Work Tabs**.

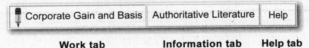

| ✎ Corporate Gain and Basis | Authoritative Literature | Help |
| Work tab | Information tab | Help tab |

Work Tabs:
- **Work Tabs** are identified with a pencil icon. This is where your responses are expected.
- Each task has one or more **Work Tabs**.
- **Work Tabs** contain directions for completing the task – be sure to read these directions carefully.
- The **Work Tab** name in the example above is for illustration only – yours will differ.
- You must complete all of the **Work Tabs** in each task to receive full credit.

Information Tabs:
- The Authoritative Literature will be provided in all tasks in the AUD, FAR, and REG sections for your reference.
- Your simulation may have one or more additional **Information Tabs**. Like the Authoritative Literature tabs, **Information Tabs** do not have a pencil icon.
- If your task has additional **Information Tabs**, go through each to familiarize yourself with the task content.

Help Tab:
- The **Help Tab** provides assistance with the exam software that is used in this task. For example, if the task is to compose a memorandum, **Help** will provide information about the word processor.

The Toolbar

The toolbar at the top of the screen shows the amount of time remaining for you to complete the tasks. In addition, the following tools are available. Note that only the Exit button is displayed when Directions are visible - the others will appear when you begin the tasks.

 Click on these buttons to split or unsplit the screen. You can split the screen vertically or horizontally.

 Click on this button to display the calculator; click on it again to hide the calculator. To move the calculator, click on the calculator title bar and drag the calculator to the desired location.

Click on this button to use the spreadsheet; click on it again to hide the spreadsheet. To move the spreadsheet, click on the the spreadsheet title bar and drag the spreadsheet to the desired location.

 Click on this button to go on to the next part of the examination. You must complete all of the tasks to receive full credit. Once you click on **Exit** and confirm the action, you will NOT be able to return to this testlet.

| ▼ = Reminder | | Directions | 1 2 3 4 5 | ◄ Previous Next ► |

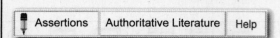

For each of the following, select from the list provided the category to which each assertion belongs. Each choice may be used once, more than once, or not at all.

Assertions	Answer		Choices
1. All transactions and accounts that should be present in the financial statements are included.			A) Rights and obligations
			B) Classification and understandability
2. The recorded sales transactions transpired during the current year.			C) Completeness
			D) Occurrence
3. The components of the financial statements are properly described and disclosed.			E) Valuation and allocation
4. Assets reported are owned by the entity, and the liabilities are the obligations of the entity as of year end.			
5. All assets, liabilities, revenues, and expenses have been included in the financial statements at the appropriate amounts.			

⏷ = Reminder   Directions   1 2 3 4 5   ◀ Previous   Next ▶

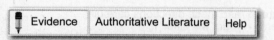

For each of the following items relating to audit evidence, select from the list provided the term with which it is most likely associated. Each term may be used once, more than once, or not at all.

Evidence-Related Item	Answer		Terms
1. Test count of inventory			A) Assertion
2. Ownership rights			B) Accounting record
3. Payroll register			C) Information technology
4. Control manual			D) Materiality
5. Completeness			E) Test of the details of a balance
6. Measure of importance			F) Other information
7. Tracing a purchase into the ledger			G) Test of the details of a transaction
8. Confirmation of an accounts receivable			
9. Occurrence			
10. Minutes of meetings			

⏷ = Reminder   Directions   1 2 3 4 5   ◀ Previous   Next ▶

| Confirmation Process | Authoritative Literature | Help |

Check the shaded box to the right of each correct statement about the confirmation process.

Statement	Correct
1. A confirmation is the process of obtaining and evaluating a direct communication from the client.	
2. Confirmations provide primary evidence concerning the existence assertion.	
3. Positive confirmation requests a reply regardless of whether the respondent agrees with the information stated.	
4. The client should control the confirmations during the process to ensure that they are mailed properly.	
5. When using negative confirmations, the auditor should send a second request if the first is not returned.	
6. A fax could be considered a confirmation if received from an appropriate party.	
7. Confirmation of accounts receivable need not be performed if the balance is immaterial.	
8. An auditor never sends a third confirmation request if previous requests have not been answered.	
9. The auditor uses the audit risk assessment to determine the appropriate form and extent of confirmations.	
10. The auditor can use information from the audits of similar entities in determining the expected effectiveness of the use of confirmations.	

| Documentation Deficiencies | Authoritative Literature | Help |

The following Accounts Receivable – Confirmation Statistics working paper (indexed B-3) was prepared by an audit assistant during the calendar year Year 1 audit of Lewis County Water Co., Inc., a continuing audit client. The engagement supervisor is reviewing the working paper.

Lewis County Water Co., Inc.
ACCOUNTS RECEIVABLE – CONFIRMATION STATISTICS
12/31/Yr 1

| | Index | B-3 |

	Accounts		Dollars	
	Number	Percent	Amount	Percent
Confirmation Requests Positives	54	2.7%	$ 260,000	13.0%
Negatives	140	7.0%	20,000	10.0%
Total sent	194	7.0%	280,000	23.0%
Accounts selected/client asked us not to confirm	6	0.3%		
Total selected for testing	200	10.0%		
Total accounts receivable at 12/31/Yr 1, confirm date	2,000	100.0%	$2,000,000 √ ♦	100.0%
RESULTS				
Replies received through 2/25/Yr 2				
Positives – no exception	44 C	2.2%	180,000	9.0%
Negatives – did not reply or replied "no exception"	120 C	6.0%	16,000	.8%
Total confirmed without exception	164	8.2%	196,000	9.8%
Differences reported and resolved, no adjustment				
Positives	6 Φ	.3%	30,000	1.5%
Negatives	12	.6%	2,000	.1%
Total	18 ‡	.9%	32,000	1.6%
Differences found to be potential adjustments				
Positives	2 CX	.1%	10,000	.5%
Negatives	8 CX	.4%	2,000	.1%
Total – .6% adjustment, immaterial	10	.5%	12,000	.6%
Accounts selected/client asked us not to confirm	6	.3%		

Tickmark Legend

√   Agreed to accounts receivable subsidiary ledger
♦   Agreed to general ledger and lead schedule
Φ   Includes one related party transaction
C   Confirmed without exception, W/P B-4
CX   Confirmed with exception

Overall conclusion – The potential adjustment of $12,000 or .6% is below the materiality threshold. Thus, the accounts receivable balance is fairly stated.

-- Continued on next page --

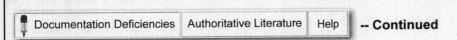

-- **Continued**

Indicate which of the below statements about the deficiencies in the working paper that the engagement supervisor should discover are correct and which are incorrect. Assume that the accounts were selected for confirmation on the basis of a sample that was properly planned and documented on working paper B-2.

Statements about Deficiencies	Answer
1. The working paper was not initialed and dated by the audit assistant.	
2. Negative confirmations not returned can be considered to be accounts "confirmed without exception."	
3. All confirmations are accounted for.	
4. There is no documentation of alternate procedures, possible scope limitation, or other working paper reference for the six accounts selected for confirmation that the client asked the auditor not to confirm.	
5. The dollar amount and percent of the six accounts selected for confirmation that the client asked the auditor not to confirm are properly omitted from the "Dollars" columns for the "Total selected for testing."	
6. The "Dollars–Percent" for "Confirmation Requests–Negatives" is correctly calculated at 10%.	
7. There is no indication of follow-up or cross-referencing of the account confirmed–related party transaction.	
8. The tickmark "‡" is used but is not explained in the tickmark legend.	
9. There is no explanation of the 10 differences aggregating $12,000.	
10. The overall conclusion reached is appropriate.	
11. There is no notation that a projection from the sample to the population was made.	
12. There is no reference to second requests.	
13. Cross-referencing is incomplete for the 12 "Differences reported and resolved, no adjustment."	

Choices
A) Correct
B) Incorrect

▼ = Reminder   Directions   1 2 3 [4] 5   ◀ Previous   Next ▶

Research | Authoritative Literature | Help

Research and cite the appropriate auditing standard that includes (1) illustrative assertions about account balances and (2) examples of substantive procedures for the existence assertion for inventories of a manufacturer.

Title	Section	Paragraph

Title Choices

AU	PCAOB	AT	AR	ET	BL	VS
CS	QC	PR	TS	PFP	CPE	

▼ = Reminder   Directions   1 2 3 4 [5]   ◀ Previous   Next ▶

Unofficial Answers

1. Assertions (5 Gradable Items)

1.   <u>C) Completeness.</u> The completeness assertion relates to whether the account balance contains all the transactions for the reporting period.

2.   <u>D) Occurrence.</u> The occurrence assertion relates to whether the transactions in the statements transpired.

3.   <u>B) Classification and understandability.</u> The classification and understandability assertion relates to proper descriptions and classifications in the financial statements, including appropriate notes.

4.   <u>A) Rights and obligations.</u> The rights and obligations assertion relates to whether the client has ownership rights to the assets and has obligations for the reported liabilities.

5.   <u>E) Valuation and allocation.</u> The valuation and allocation assertion relates to whether the assets, liabilities, and capital accounts are reported in accordance with GAAP and whether proper allocations have been made (e.g., depreciation).

2. Evidence (10 Gradable Items)

1.   <u>E) Test of the details of a balance</u> is the term most associated with a test count of inventory.

2.   <u>A) Assertion</u> is the term most associated with ownership rights.

3.   <u>B) Accounting record</u> is the term most associated with payroll register.

4.   <u>F) Other information</u> is the term most associated with a control manual.

5.   <u>A) Assertion</u> is the term most associated with completeness.

6.   <u>D) Materiality</u> is the term most associated with measure of importance.

7.   <u>G) Test of the details of a transaction</u> is the term most associated with tracing a purchase into the ledger.

8.   <u>E) Test of the details of a balance</u> is the term most associated with confirmation of an accounts receivable.

9.   <u>A) Assertion</u> is the term most associated with occurrence.

10.   <u>F) Other information</u> is the term most associated with minutes of meetings.

3. Confirmation Process (10 Gradable Items)

1.   This statement is <u>not correct</u> because a confirmation is the process of obtaining and evaluating a direct communication from a third party in response to a request for information about a particular item.

2.   This statement is <u>correct</u>.

3.   This statement is <u>correct</u>.

4.   This statement is <u>not correct</u> because the auditor should control the confirmations during the process to ensure that they are mailed properly.

5.   This statement is <u>not correct</u> because, when negative confirmations are sent, the recipient is only to respond if (s)he disagrees with the information stated.

6.   This statement is <u>correct</u>.

7.   This statement is <u>correct</u>.

8.   This statement is <u>not correct</u> because, when positive confirmations are sent, the auditor should usually follow up with a second and, if applicable, a third request to parties who did not respond.

9.   This statement is <u>correct</u>.

10.   This statement is <u>correct</u>.

4. Documentation Deficiencies (13 Gradable Items)

1.   <u>A) Correct.</u> The box in the upper right-hand corner of the working paper would typically contain the initials of the assistant and date the working paper was completed.

2.   <u>B) Incorrect.</u> The unreturned negative confirmations did not necessarily confirm the accounts because there can be other reasons that the confirmations were not returned.

3.   <u>B) Incorrect.</u> There were 200 confirmations selected for testing. The working paper reports: 164 total confirmed without exception, 18 total no adjustment, 10 total with adjustment, and 6 that client requested not to be confirmed. This totals 198, leaving 2 that are not accounted for.

4.   <u>A) Correct.</u> The auditor should perform alternative procedures to determine the existence of those 6 accounts. The conclusions from those procedures should be documented in the working papers.

5. B) Incorrect. The 6 accounts should be included and, based on alternative procedures, should be used to project the findings to the population.

6. B) Incorrect. This should be $20,000/$2,000,000, or 1%.

7. A) Correct. Although the difference in amount is noted as resolved, related party transactions typically require disclosure in the financial statements. This should also be resolved in the working paper.

8. A) Correct. There is no reference to the tickmark in the tickmark legend.

9. A) Correct. The $12,000 potential adjustment is based on the sample of 10% of the population dollars. This should be projected to the population, and any issues should be resolved in the working papers.

10. B) Incorrect. The working paper, as presented, does not appear to support the conclusion that the account is fairly stated. The sample was not projected to the population; thus, the fairness cannot be determined.

11. A) Correct. The sample should be projected to the population.

12. A) Correct. It is unlikely that all positive confirmations were returned on the first request. In any case, the auditor should address the issue that either all confirmations were returned based on the first request or second requests were used.

13. A) Correct. The working paper should describe the issues and how they were resolved or reference another working paper providing the information.

5. Research (1 Gradable Item)

Answer: 318.Appendix

AU 318 - *Performing Audit Procedures in Response to Assessed Risks and Evaluating the Audit Evidence Obtained*

APPENDIX

ILLUSTRATIVE FINANCIAL STATEMENT ASSERTIONS AND EXAMPLES OF SUBSTANTIVE PROCEDURES
ILLUSTRATIONS FOR INVENTORIES OF A MANUFACTURING COMPANY

A1. This appendix illustrates the use of assertions in designing substantive procedures and does not illustrate tests of controls. The following examples of substantive procedures are not intended to be all-inclusive, nor is it expected that all of the procedures would be applied in an audit. The particular substantive procedures to be used in each circumstance depend on the auditor's risk assessment and tests of controls.

Illustrative Assertions About Account Balances	*Examples of Substantive Procedures*
Existence	
Inventories included in the balance sheet physically exist.	• Physical examination of inventory items. • Obtaining confirmation of inventories at locations outside the entity. • Inspection of documents relating to inventory transactions between a physical inventory date and the balance sheet date.
Inventories represent items held for sale or use in the normal course of business.	• Inspecting perpetual inventory records, production records, and purchasing records for indications of current activity. • Reconciling items in the inventory listing to a current computer-maintained sales catalog and subsequent sales and delivery reports using computer-assisted audit techniques (CAATs). • Inquiry of production and sales personnel. • Using the work of specialists to corroborate the nature of specialized products.

Gleim Simulation Grading

Task	Correct Responses		Gradable Items		Score per Task
1	_____	÷	5	=	_____
2	_____	÷	10	=	_____
3	_____	÷	10	=	_____
4	_____	÷	13	=	_____
Research	_____	÷	1	=	_____

Total of Scores per Task _____

÷ Total Number of Tasks   5

Total Score _____ %

Use **CPA Gleim Online** and **Simulation Wizard** to practice more task-based simulations in a realistic environment.

STUDY UNIT ELEVEN
EVIDENCE -- THE SALES-RECEIVABLES-CASH CYCLE

(9 pages of outline)

The primary purpose of the collection of evidence is to test relevant assertions about the transaction classes, balances, and disclosures in the financial statements. The auditor uses these assertions as a basis for assessing risks of material misstatement (RMMs) and designing and performing further audit procedures. Many audit procedures performed in accordance with the risk assessment are intended to detect overstatement of sales, receivables, and cash. The purpose of this study unit is to develop a comprehensive audit plan for the sales-receivables-cash cycle. This plan includes the customary procedures assuming no unusual risks. Some of the CPA questions that follow the study outlines in this study unit concern special risks that require modification of the audit plan. The candidate should consider those questions and problems and practice modification of audit plans to address special risks.

The approach to audit plan development described in the outlines may be used in answering CPA exam questions. Application of the AICPA's assertions model (CAVE CROC is the mnemonic for the assertions -- see Study Unit 1, Subunit 2) ensures that all assertions are tested. However, other formats for presentation of the steps are acceptable, for example, application of the PCAOB's assertions model also addressed in Study Unit 1, Subunit 2.

11.1 SUBSTANTIVE TESTING OF SALES AND RECEIVABLES

1. **Accounts receivable** are the entity's claims against customers that have arisen from the sale of goods or services in the normal course of business or from a financial institution's loans.

2. **Revenues** result from an entity's ongoing major or central operations, for example, sales of goods or services.

   a. Testing assertions about accounts receivable also results in evidence relevant to the assertions about sales revenues. Thus, testing for the completeness of receivables tests the completeness of sales. A credit to sales ordinarily is accompanied by a debit to receivables, an entry that is recorded in the sales journal. **Special journals** record a large volume of similar items. Entries not suitable for one of the special journals are recorded in the **general journal**.

   b. **SEC Staff Accounting Bulletin (SAB) 101** provides guidance for the reporting of revenue in financial statements filed with the SEC, including the criteria for revenue recognition. SAB 101 follows current GAAP but applies them to transactions not addressed in the authoritative literature.

   c. Special consideration of sales-related accounts follows the next section.

3. **Testing relevant assertions.** The following is a standard audit plan for sales and receivables that tests relevant assertions (CAVE CROC).

   a. **Completeness.** Do sales and receivables reflect all recordable transactions for the period?

      1) Compare (reconcile) the total recorded amounts in the **subsidiary ledger** with the accounts receivable amount recorded in the **general ledger**.

      2) **Analytical procedures.** Use the appropriate sources of data (e.g., prior experience, budgets prepared by management at the beginning of the period, nonfinancial data, industry information, and interrelationships) to develop expectations to compare with management's presentations. Calculate and compare ratios for the current period, for example, the **accounts receivable turnover ratio** (net credit sales ÷ average accounts receivable), with those of prior periods and industry norms.

      3) Account for the **numerical sequence** of sales-related documents, such as sales orders, shipping documents, and invoices.

      4) Compare **shipping documents** with sales invoices and journal entries to test whether the related sales were recorded at the time of sale.

   b. **Accuracy.** Have transactions and events been recorded appropriately?

      1) Obtain a **management representation letter** that includes assertions relating to sales and receivables.

      2) Evaluate management's disclosures about **reportable operating segments** and related information, including products and services, geographic areas, and major customers.

   c. **Valuation and allocation.** Are accounts receivable measured in accordance with GAAP, e.g., net realizable value (gross accounts receivable – allowance for uncollectible accounts)?

      1) **Age the accounts receivable.** Classify the receivables by age, and compare percentages within classifications with those of the prior year.

      2) **Trace subsequent cash receipts.** Cash receipts after the balance sheet date provide the best evidence of collectibility. By the end of the field work, the auditor should be able to judge the likely collections of the outstanding balances and determine whether the allowance for uncollectibles is sufficient to properly measure the year-end balance of receivables.

      3) Review delinquent customers' **credit ratings**. This procedure provides evidence for assessing collectibility.

   d. **Existence.** Are the accounts receivable valid assets?

      1) **Confirm accounts receivable** (also tests the rights and valuation assertions).

         a) Confirmation of accounts receivable is a generally accepted auditing procedure. Moreover, confirmation at year end provides greater assurance than at an interim date. The auditor will confirm accounts receivable unless (1) they are immaterial, (2) confirmation would be ineffective, or (3) RMM based on other procedures is judged to be sufficiently low.

         b) An auditor who has not confirmed accounts receivable should **document** how (s)he overcame this presumption.

         c) Confirming receivables may detect lapping because the entity's and customer's records of lapped accounts will differ. **Lapping** is the theft of a cash payment from one customer concealed by crediting that customer's account when a second customer makes a payment.

d) Confirmation also may detect an **improper cutoff**. The client might have held open the sales journal after year end and improperly recorded sales and receivables for the period under audit rather than for the subsequent period. In this case, responses to confirmations would indicate that amounts owed by debtors at year end are smaller than the recorded amounts.

e) A **negative confirmation** contains the recorded balance of the receivable. The debtor is requested to respond only if the amount is incorrect. A **positive confirmation** requests the debtor to respond whether the amount is incorrect or not. The **blank form** of a positive confirmation requests that the debtor fill out the amount owed to the entity being audited.

f) When customers fail to answer a **second request** for a positive confirmation, the accounts may be in dispute, uncollectible, or fictitious. The auditor should then apply alternative procedures (examination of subsequent cash receipts, shipping documents, and other client documentation of existence) to obtain evidence about the validity of nonresponding accounts.

g) The auditor should be convinced that confirmations received via email, fax, telephone, or other electronic media were sent by the debtor and not from an imposter.

2) **Vouch recorded accounts receivable to shipping documents.** Because shipment of goods is typically the event creating the sale and receivable, vouching recorded receivables to shipping documents, such as bills of lading, tests for existence.

e. **Cutoff.** Have transactions been recorded in the proper period?

1) **Sales cutoff test.** Test to determine that a sale and receivable were recorded when title passed to the customer, which often occurs when goods are shipped (i.e., when terms are **FOB shipping point**). Shipping documents are traced to the accounting records for several days prior to and after year end to determine proper recognition in the appropriate period. This test detects inflated sales.

2) **Cash receipts cutoff test.** Test the recording of the receipts of cash and the associated reduction in accounts receivable. Inspection and tracing of the items on the **daily remittance list** for several days prior to and after year end provides evidence of proper recording.

f. **Rights and obligations.** Does the entity have the right to collect receivables?

1) **Inquiries of management.** Consider the motivation and opportunity for factoring or selling the receivables, and inquire of management as to whether such transactions have occurred.

2) **Track cash receipts** to determine that the entity is collecting and depositing the proceeds into bank accounts it controls.

3) Determine whether sales have been made with a **right of return** and what the expected and actual returns are after year end.

g. **Occurrence.** Did sales occur?

1) **Vouch a sample of recorded sales** to customer orders and shipping documents. Large and unusual sales should be included in the sample selected for testing. This test is useful for detecting overstatements.

h. **Classification and understandability.** Are sales and receivables appropriately described and disclosures fairly and clearly expressed?

   1) **Inspect the income statement** to determine that sales are reported as a revenue, minus returns and allowances. **Inspect the balance sheet** to determine that accounts receivable are presented as a current asset, minus the allowance for uncollectible accounts.

   2) **Evaluate note disclosures** to determine that **accounting policies** are disclosed (e.g., accounts receivable should be presented at net realizable value). **Pledges of accounts receivable** should be disclosed. Any significant sales or receivables transactions with **related parties** also should be disclosed.

4. **Testing Relevant Assertions about Related Accounts**

   a. **Sales returns and allowances.** The auditor should test all assertions. But if the risk of material misstatement is low, the primary tests will address the existence and occurrence assertions. Was there a proper authorization for the return of goods, and were those goods actually returned?

      1) The auditor ordinarily tests the **documentation** that supports the return. This procedure determines whether proper **authorization** exists, and the credit to the customer's account was supported by a receiving report representing the return of goods.

   b. **Write-off of bad debts.** If the risk of material misstatement is relatively low, the audit plan for accounts receivable described above should provide sufficient appropriate evidence. However, if controls are ineffective, for example, if the accounting function (the accounts receivable bookkeeper) is allowed to approve write-offs, the auditor will perform specific procedures to reduce detection risk to an acceptably low level.

      1) Thus, the auditor might decide to attempt to confirm the receivables previously written off. If the write-offs were legitimate, most requests will be marked *Return to Sender* because the debtors will probably not be in business.

Stop and review! You have completed the outline for this subunit. Study multiple-choice questions 1 through 21 beginning on page 377.

11.2 SUBSTANTIVE TESTING OF CASH

1. **Cash** includes cash on hand, demand accounts, and other asset accounts held in financial institutions.

2. Substantive testing of cash addresses assertions related to the **balance sheet**.

3. **Testing Relevant Assertions**

   a. **Completeness.** Does the balance at the end of the accounting period reflect all cash transactions?

      1) For cash **receipts**, trace the **daily remittance list** to the last validated deposit ticket for the period. For cash **disbursements**, determine the **last check written** for the period, and trace the effect to the accounting records. Determine that all outstanding checks have been listed on the **bank reconciliation**.

      2) Use of **analytical procedures** is not typically as effective for cash as for most other accounts because it is a managed account. However, the auditor may be able to use management's budget, prepared at the beginning of the period, as an expectation with which to compare the year-end balance.

b. **Accuracy.** Has cash been recorded accurately?

    1) Compare a sample of daily remittance lists with deposits, journal entries, and ledger postings.

c. **Valuation and allocation.** Is cash valued in accordance with GAAP?

    1) U.S. currency has low inherent risk relative to this assertion. However, special circumstances, such as holdings of foreign currency, may require additional testing.

d. **Existence.** Does cash exist? Because **inherent risk** is high for cash, most audit procedures are directed toward existence.

    1) **Count cash on hand.**

        a) Control all cash and negotiable securities to protect against substitution.

        b) Determine that all received checks are payable to the client.

        c) Determine that all received checks are endorsed "For Deposit Only into Account Number XXXX."

    2) **Bank confirmation.** The AICPA *Standard Form to Confirm Account Balance Information with Financial Institutions* is used for specific deposits and loans.

        a) A confirmation is **requested by the client**, but it should be **sent by the auditor** to any bank with which the client has had business during the period.

        b) The form confirms the account name and number, interest rate, and balance for deposits.

        c) For **direct liabilities on loans**, the form confirms account number/ description, balance, due date, interest rate, date through which interest is paid, and description of collateral.

        d) To confirm other transactions and written or oral arrangements, such as contingent liabilities, lines of credit, compensating balances, and security agreements, auditors send a **separate letter signed by the client** to an official responsible for the financial institution's relationship with the client.

        e) The standard form (and separate letter) is designed to substantiate only the information that is stated on the confirmation request. Thus, the auditor should be aware that the standard form is **not** intended to elicit evidence about the **completeness assertion**.

            i) Nevertheless, the standard form requests any additional information about other deposit and loan accounts that may have come to the attention of the financial institution.

    3) **Bank reconciliation.** Inspect or prepare bank reconciliations for each account.

        a) A bank reconciliation verifies the **agreement** of the bank statements obtained directly from the institution and the amount of cash reported in the financial statements. These amounts should be equal after adjustment for deposits in transit, outstanding checks, bank charges, etc.

STANDARD FORM TO CONFIRM ACCOUNT
BALANCE INFORMATION WITH FINANCIAL INSTITUTIONS

ORIGINAL
To be mailed to accountant

CUSTOMER NAME
_____

Financial
Institution's   [
Name and
Address

                 [   ]

We have provided to our accountants the following information as of
the close of business on _____, 20 _____,
regarding our deposit and loan balances. Please confirm the
accuracy of the information, noting any exceptions to the information
provided. If the balances have been left blank, please complete this
form by furnishing the balance in the appropriate space below.*
Although we do not request or expect you to conduct a
comprehensive, detailed search of your records, if, during the process
of completing this confirmation, additional information about other
deposit and loan accounts we may have with you comes to your
attention, please include such information below. Please use the
enclosed envelope to return the form directly to our accountants.

1. At the close of business on the date listed above, our records indicated the following deposit balance(s):

ACCOUNT NAME	ACCOUNT NO.	INTEREST RATE	BALANCE*

2. We were directly liable to the financial institution for loans at the close of business on the date listed above as follows:

ACCOUNT NO./ DESCRIPTION	BALANCE*	DATE DUE	INTEREST RATE	DATE THROUGH WHICH INTEREST IS PAID	DESCRIPTION OF COLLATERAL

_____   _____
(Customer's Authorized Signature)   (Date)

The information presented above by the customer is in agreement with our records. Although we have not conducted a comprehensive,
detailed search of our records, no other deposit or loan accounts have come to our attention except as noted below.

_____   _____
(Financial Institution Authorized Signature)   (Date)

_____
(Title)

EXCEPTIONS AND/OR COMMENTS

Please return this form directly to our accountants: [   ]

*Ordinarily, balances are intentionally left blank if they are not   [   ]
available at the time the form is prepared.

Approved 1990 by American Bankers Association, American Institute of Certified Public Accountants, and Bank Administration
Institute. Additional forms available from: AICPA - Order Department, P.O. Box 1003, NY, NY 10108-1003   D451 5951

EXAMPLE OF LETTER TO CONFIRM OTHER FINANCIAL INSTITUTION INFORMATION

[Date]
Financial Institution Official
First United Bank
Anytown, USA 00000

Dear Financial Institution Official:

In connection with an audit of the financial statements of [name of customer] as of [balance sheet date] and for the [period] then ended, we have advised our independent auditors of the information listed below, which we believe is a complete and accurate description of our contingent liabilities, including oral and written guarantees, with your financial institution. Although we do not request nor expect you to conduct a comprehensive, detailed search of your records, if during the process of completing this confirmation additional information about other contingent liabilities, including oral and written guarantees, between [name of customer] and your financial institution comes to your attention, please include such information below.

Name of Maker	Date of Note	Due Date	Current Balance
Interest Rate	Date Through Which Interest Is Paid	Description of Collateral	Description of Purpose of Note

Information related to oral and written guarantees is as follows:

_____

_____

_____

Please confirm whether the information about contingent liabilities presented above is correct by signing below and returning this directly to our independent auditors [name and address of CPA firm].

Sincerely,

[name of customer]

By: _____
(Authorized Signature)

Dear CPA Firm:

The above information listing contingent liabilities, including oral and written guarantees, agrees with the records of this financial institution. Although we have not conducted a comprehensive, detailed search of our records, no information about other contingent liabilities, including oral and written guarantees, came to our attention. [Note exceptions below or in an attached letter.]

_____

_____

_____

_____
(Name of Financial Institution)

By: _____   _____
(Officer and Title)   (Date)

4) **Cutoff bank statement.** It should be requested directly from the bank for the period 7 to 10 days after year end. Use this statement to test reconciling items on the year-end bank reconciliation, e.g., deposits in transit and outstanding checks.

   a) Search for checks written before year end but **not listed as outstanding** on the bank reconciliation. These checks are often evidence of **kiting**, a fraud resulting from an improper recording of a bank transfer.

      i) To cover a shortage of cash (cash is recorded in the accounting records but not in the bank's records), an employee writes a check just prior to year end on the disbursing bank but does not record the disbursement in the accounting records in the current year. Furthermore, the check also does not appear as a disbursement on the year-end statement issued by the disbursing bank because it would not have cleared. However, the receipt is recorded by the receiving bank (at least as a deposit in transit), thereby covering the shortage. In the short term, the cash balance will appear to reconcile.

      ii) To uncover the fraud, the auditor should match the returned checks written prior to year end listed on the cutoff bank statement with the outstanding checks listed on the bank reconciliation for the disbursing bank. Because the kited check was not recorded, it will not be listed as outstanding.

   b) Consider the **number of checks returned** listed on the cutoff bank statement. This procedure may provide evidence of window dressing, that is, trying to improve the **current ratio**. The client may write checks to pay current liabilities but not mail them until the next accounting period.

5) **Schedule of interbank transfers.** Preparing this schedule can help detect errors in transfers but may not be effective to detect kiting if a disbursement has not been recorded. For this procedure to be effective, the auditor should be assured that all transfers have been identified.

6) **Proof of cash.** When internal control over a transaction process is not effective, a proof of cash may be prepared. It provides direct evidence that amounts recorded by the bank (beginning and ending balances, deposits, and disbursements) reconcile with amounts recorded by the entity for a period of time, typically a month.

e. **Cutoff.** Have transactions been recorded in the proper period?

   1) Inspect and trace the daily remittance lists for several days prior to and after year end.

   2) Identify and trace the last check written for the year into the records.

f. **Rights and obligations.** Does the entity have ownership right to the cash?

   1) In most cases, risks related to ownership are low, and few specific procedures are applied. However, confirmations related to the existence assertion provide evidence for the rights and obligations assertion. Inquiries of management are also appropriate.

g. **Occurrence.** Did the cash transactions occur?

   1) **Vouch** a sample of recorded cash receipts to accounts receivable and customer orders.

   2) Vouch a sample of recorded cash disbursements to approved vouchers.

    h. **Classification and understandability.** Is cash appropriately described and are disclosures fairly and clearly expressed?

        1) **Inquire of management about disclosure.** Include references to cash in the management representation letter.

        2) Determine that **restricted cash** (e.g., sinking funds and compensating balances) is reported in the noncurrent asset section of the balance sheet.

        3) **Assess statement of cash flows.**

            a) Determine proper presentation: direct or indirect method.

            b) Reconcile information with income statement and balance sheet presentations.

            c) Examine elements of statement of cash flows classifications: operating activities, investing activities, and financing activities.

        4) Evaluate financial statement note disclosures.

Stop and review! You have completed the outline for this subunit. Study multiple-choice questions 22 through 31 beginning on page 384.

QUESTIONS

11.1 Substantive Testing of Sales and Receivables

1. Which of the following comparisons would be most useful to an auditor in evaluating the results of an entity's operations?

  A. Prior-year accounts payable to current-year accounts payable.

  B. Prior-year payroll expense to budgeted current-year payroll expense.

  C. Current-year revenue to budgeted current-year revenue.

  D. Current-year warranty expense to current-year contingent liabilities.

Answer (C) is correct. *(CPA, adapted)*
    REQUIRED: The best comparison for evaluating the results of operations.
    DISCUSSION: Revenues result from an entity's ongoing major or central operations. These operations reflect numerous activities and affect many accounts. Consequently, comparing current-year revenue with the budgeted current-year revenue provides evidence as to the completeness of revenue. Revenue is a broad measure of the effects of the entity's main activities and is a primary component of the results of operations.
    Answer (A) is incorrect. The change in accounts payable is too narrow a measure to be useful in this evaluation. Answer (B) is incorrect. Payroll expense is too narrow a measure to be useful in this evaluation. Answer (D) is incorrect. The relationship of warranty expense with contingent liabilities is too narrow a measure to be useful in this evaluation.

2. An auditor most likely would limit substantive audit tests of sales transactions when the risk of material misstatement is assessed as low for the existence and occurrence assertions concerning sales transactions and the auditor has already gathered evidence supporting

  A. Opening and closing inventory balances.

  B. Cash receipts and accounts receivable.

  C. Shipping and receiving activities.

  D. Cutoffs of sales and purchases.

Answer (B) is correct. *(CPA, adapted)*
    REQUIRED: The evidence related to the existence and occurrence assertions for sales transactions.
    DISCUSSION: Cash receipts and accounts receivable have a direct relationship with sales. A cash sale results in a debit to cash and a credit to sales. A sale on account results in a debit to accounts receivable and a credit to sales. Thus, evidence related to cash receipts and accounts receivable provides assurances about sales.
    Answer (A) is incorrect. The opening and closing inventory balances do not directly affect the sales transactions. Answer (C) is incorrect. Although shipping activities are related to sales, receiving activities are not. Answer (D) is incorrect. Although cutoffs of sales provide evidence as to sales transactions, cutoffs of purchases do not.

3. If the objective of a test of details is to detect overstatements of sales, the auditor should compare transactions in the

A. Cash receipts journal with the sales journal.

B. Sales journal with the cash receipts journal.

C. Source documents with the accounting records.

D. Accounting records with the source documents.

Answer (D) is correct. *(CPA, adapted)*
   REQUIRED: The appropriate test to detect overstatement of sales.
   DISCUSSION: Overstatements of sales likely result from entries with no supporting documentation. The proper direction of testing is to sample entries in the sales account and vouch them to the shipping documents. The source documents represent the valid sales.
   Answer (A) is incorrect. The cash receipts journal and the sales journal are books of original entry, not source documents. Answer (B) is incorrect. The cash receipts journal and the sales journal are books of original entry, not source documents. Answer (C) is incorrect. The proper direction of testing is from the accounting records to the source documents.

4. Tracing shipping documents to prenumbered sales invoices provides evidence that

A. No duplicate shipments or billings occurred.

B. Shipments to customers were properly invoiced.

C. All goods ordered by customers were shipped.

D. All prenumbered sales invoices were accounted for.

Answer (B) is correct. *(CPA, adapted)*
   REQUIRED: The evidence provided by tracing shipping documents to prenumbered sales invoices.
   DISCUSSION: The direction of testing to determine that shipments to customers were properly invoiced is from the shipping documents to the sales invoices.
   Answer (A) is incorrect. Tracing a sample of customer orders to the shipping documents provides evidence about duplicate shipments. Answer (C) is incorrect. Tracing sales orders to shipping documents provides evidence that all goods ordered by customers were shipped. Answer (D) is incorrect. Accounting for all the numbered invoices provides assurance that no invoices were lost or misplaced.

5. An auditor most likely would review an entity's periodic accounting for the numerical sequence of shipping documents and invoices to support management's financial statement assertion of

A. Occurrence.

B. Rights and obligations.

C. Valuation and allocation.

D. Completeness.

Answer (D) is correct. *(CPA, adapted)*
   REQUIRED: The assertion supported by reviewing the numerical sequence of shipping documents and invoices.
   DISCUSSION: The completeness assertion concerns whether all transactions (or assets, liabilities, and equity interests) that should be recorded are recorded. Testing the numerical sequence of shipping documents and invoices is a means of detecting omitted items.
   Answer (A) is incorrect. The occurrence assertion addresses whether recorded transactions have occurred and pertain to the entity. Answer (B) is incorrect. The rights and obligations assertion concerns whether assets are the rights of the entity and liabilities are obligations at a given date. Answer (C) is incorrect. The valuation and allocation assertion concerns whether assets, liabilities, and equity interests have been included at appropriate amounts.

6. An entity's financial statements were misstated over a period of years because large amounts of revenue were recorded in journal entries that involved debits and credits to an illogical combination of accounts. The auditor could most likely have been alerted to this fraud by

A. Scanning the general journal for unusual entries.

B. Performing a revenue cutoff test at year end.

C. Tracing a sample of journal entries to the general ledger.

D. Examining documentary evidence of sales returns and allowances recorded after year end.

Answer (A) is correct. *(CPA, adapted)*
   REQUIRED: The procedure to detect misstatement of revenue as a result of illogical entries.
   DISCUSSION: The general journal is a book of original entry used for transactions not suitable for recording in the special journals (sales, purchases, cash receipts, cash disbursements). Entries involving unusual combinations of accounts are more likely to appear in the general journal than in one of the special journals, which are designed to record large numbers of similar items. For example, credit sales (debit accounts receivable, credit sales) are entered in the sales journal.
   Answer (B) is incorrect. A revenue cutoff is a test of the timing of recognition. Moreover, it applies to transactions at year end only. Answer (C) is incorrect. Tracing journal entries will only test whether recorded transactions were posted to the ledger. Answer (D) is incorrect. This procedure applies to year-end transactions only.

7. Which of the following might be detected by an auditor's review of the client's sales cutoff?

    A. Excessive goods returned for credit.

    B. Unrecorded sales discounts.

    C. Lapping of year-end accounts receivable.

    D. Inflated sales for the year.

Answer (D) is correct. *(CPA, adapted)*
    REQUIRED: The condition that might be detected by review of the client's sales cutoff.
    DISCUSSION: Sales cutoff tests are designed to detect the client's manipulation of sales. By examining recorded sales for several days before and after the balance sheet date and comparing them with sales invoices and shipping documents, the auditor may detect the recording of a sale in a period other than that in which title passed.
    Answer (A) is incorrect. Sales returns are not examined in the sales cutoff test. Answer (B) is incorrect. Examination of cash receipts would reveal unrecorded discounts. Answer (C) is incorrect. Lapping may be detected by the confirmation of customer balances and tracing amounts received according to duplicate deposit slips to the accounts receivable subsidiary ledger.

8. An audit client sells 15 to 20 units of product annually. A large portion of the annual sales occur in the last month of the fiscal year. Annual sales have not materially changed over the past 5 years. Which of the following approaches would be most effective concerning the timing of audit procedures for revenue?

    A. The auditor should perform analytical procedures at an interim date and discuss any changes in the level of sales with senior management.

    B. The auditor should inspect transactions occurring in the last month of the fiscal year and review the related sale contracts to determine that revenue was posted in the proper period.

    C. The auditor should perform tests of controls at an interim date to obtain audit evidence about the operational effectiveness of internal controls over sales.

    D. The auditor should review period-end compensation to determine if bonuses were paid to meet earnings goals.

Answer (B) is correct. *(CPA, adapted)*
    REQUIRED: The most effective audit procedure given the timing of revenue.
    DISCUSSION: Tests of the details of transactions at year end would be most effective given that a small number of transactions make up total sales. Also, since most occur in the last month of the year, a particular concern would be establishing that management made proper cutoff.
    Answer (A) is incorrect. Since most sales occur at year end, interim analytical procedures would not likely prove effective. Answer (C) is incorrect. Although internal controls are important, given the small number of transactions, substantive tests would be most effective. Answer (D) is incorrect. Firms often pay bonuses as incentives to meet objectives.

9. Which of the following most likely would give the most assurance concerning the valuation assertion about accounts receivable?

    A. Vouching amounts in the subsidiary ledger to details on shipping documents.

    B. Comparing receivable turnover ratios with industry statistics for reasonableness.

    C. Inquiring about receivables pledged under loan agreements.

    D. Assessing the allowance for uncollectible accounts for reasonableness.

Answer (D) is correct. *(CPA, adapted)*
    REQUIRED: The procedure providing the most assurance about the valuation of accounts receivable.
    DISCUSSION: Assertions about valuation concern whether balance sheet components have been included at appropriate amounts. One such assertion is that trade accounts receivable are stated at net realizable value (gross accounts receivable minus allowance for uncollectible accounts). Hence, assessing the allowance provides assurance about the valuation of the account.
    Answer (A) is incorrect. Vouching amounts in the subsidiary ledger to details on shipping documents provides evidence about the occurrence assertion for transactions. Answer (B) is incorrect. Comparing receivable turnover ratios with industry statistics for reasonableness provides evidence about completeness. Answer (C) is incorrect. Inquiring about receivables pledged under loan agreements pertains to presentation and disclosure assertions.

10. An auditor's purpose in reviewing credit ratings of customers with delinquent accounts receivable most likely is to obtain evidence concerning relevant assertions about

A. Classification and understandability.

B. Existence.

C. Rights and obligations.

D. Valuation and allocation.

Answer (D) is correct. *(CPA, adapted)*
REQUIRED: The assertion about which evidence is provided by reviewing credit ratings of delinquent customers.
DISCUSSION: Assertions about valuation and allocation concern whether balance sheet components have been included at appropriate amounts. Determining the realizable value of accounts receivable includes assessing whether the client's allowance for uncollectibility is reasonable. Reviewing the credit ratings of delinquent customers provides evidence for that purpose.
Answer (A) is incorrect. The assertion about classification and understandability concerns whether financial statement components are properly classified, described, and disclosed. Answer (B) is incorrect. The existence assertion concerns whether assets, liabilities, and equity interests exist. Answer (C) is incorrect. The rights and obligations assertion concerns whether assets are the rights of the entity and liabilities are obligations.

11. For the fiscal year ending December 31, previous year and the current year, Justin Co. has net sales of $1,000,000 and $2,000,000; average gross receivables of $100,000 and $300,000; and an allowance for uncollectible accounts receivable of $30,000 and $50,000, respectively. If the accounts receivable turnover and the ratio of allowance for uncollectible accounts receivable to gross accounts receivable are calculated, which of the following best represents the conclusions to be drawn?

A. Accounts receivable turnovers are 10.0 and 6.6, and the ratios of uncollectible accounts receivable to gross accounts receivable are 0.30 and 0.16, respectively. Examine allowance for possible overstatement of the allowance.

B. Accounts receivable turnovers are 10.0 and 6.7, and the ratios of uncollectible accounts receivable to gross accounts receivable are 0.30 and 0.17, respectively. Examine allowance for possible understatement of the allowance.

C. Accounts receivable turnovers are 14.3 and 8.0, and the ratios of uncollectible accounts receivable to gross accounts receivable are 0.42 and 0.20, respectively. Examine allowance for possible overstatement of the allowance.

D. Accounts receivable turnovers are 14.3 and 8.0 and the ratios of uncollectible accounts receivable to gross accounts receivable are 0.42 and 0.20, respectively. Examine allowance for possible understatement of the allowance.

Answer (B) is correct. *(CPA, adapted)*
REQUIRED: The appropriate conclusions from the accounts receivable turnover and the ratio of the allowance for uncollectible accounts receivable to gross accounts receivable.
DISCUSSION: The accounts receivable turnover equals sales divided by average gross receivables. Thus, it equals 10.0 ($1,000,000 ÷ $100,000) and 6.7 ($2,000,000 ÷ $300,000) for the prior year and current year, respectively. The ratio of allowance for uncollectible accounts receivable to gross accounts receivable is .30 ($30,000 ÷ $100,000) for the prior year and .17 ($50,000 ÷ $300,000) for the current year. The gross accounts receivable tripled in the second year, yet the allowance for uncollectible accounts receivable increased by only 67%. This could be an indication that the allowance for uncollectible accounts receivable is understated.
Answer (A) is incorrect. The gross accounts receivable tripled in the second year, yet the allowance for uncollectible accounts receivable only went up by 67%. This could be an indication that the allowance for uncollectible accounts receivable is understated, not overstated. Answer (C) is incorrect. Net accounts receivable was used to calculate these ratios. Answer (D) is incorrect. Net accounts receivable was used to calculate these ratios.

12. AU 330, *The Confirmation Process*, defines confirmation as "the process of obtaining and evaluating a direct communication from a third party in response to a request for information about a particular item affecting financial statement assertions." The assertions for which confirmation of accounts receivable balances provides primary evidence are

A. Completeness and valuation.

B. Valuation and rights and obligations.

C. Rights and obligations and existence.

D. Existence and completeness.

Answer (C) is correct. *(CPA, adapted)*
REQUIRED: The assertions tested by confirming receivables.
DISCUSSION: Confirmation by means of direct (independent) communication with debtors is the generally accepted auditing procedure for accounts receivable. Properly designed requests may address any assertion in the financial statements, but they are most likely to be effective for the existence and rights and obligations assertions. Thus, confirmation provides evidence that receivables are valid, that the client has ownership of the accounts and the right of collection, and that the debtor has the obligation to pay.
Answer (A) is incorrect. Confirmation is not effective for the completeness assertion. It is unlikely to detect unrecorded accounts. Answer (B) is incorrect. Confirmation is less effective for the valuation assertion than for the existence and rights and obligations assertions. Answer (D) is incorrect. Confirmation is less effective for the completeness assertion than for the existence and rights and obligations assertions.

13. An auditor confirms a representative number of open accounts receivable as of December 31 and investigates respondents' exceptions and comments. By this procedure, the auditor would be most likely to learn of which of the following?

A. One of the cashiers has been covering a personal embezzlement by lapping.

B. One of the sales clerks has not been preparing charge slips for credit sales to family and friends.

C. One of the computer control clerks has been removing all sales invoices applicable to his account from the data file.

D. The credit manager has misappropriated remittances from customers whose accounts have been written off.

Answer (A) is correct. *(CPA, adapted)*
REQUIRED: The fraud most likely to be detected by confirming receivables.
DISCUSSION: Lapping is the theft of a cash payment from one customer concealed by crediting that customer's account when a second customer makes a payment. When lapping exists at the balance sheet date, the confirmation of customer balances will probably detect the fraud because the customers' and entity's records of lapped accounts will differ.
Answer (B) is incorrect. If a charge slip has not been prepared, no accounts receivable balance will exist to be confirmed. Answer (C) is incorrect. If a sales invoice is not processed, no account balance will appear in the records. Answer (D) is incorrect. Once the account has been written off, the account is no longer open.

14. An auditor suspects that a client's cashier is misappropriating cash receipts for personal use by lapping customer checks received in the mail. In attempting to uncover this embezzlement scheme, the auditor most likely would compare the

A. Dates checks are deposited per bank statements with the dates remittance credits are recorded.

B. Daily cash summaries with the sums of the cash receipts journal entries.

C. Individual bank deposit slips with the details of the monthly bank statements.

D. Dates uncollectible accounts are authorized to be written off with the dates the write-offs are actually recorded.

Answer (A) is correct. *(CPA, adapted)*
REQUIRED: The procedure to detect lapping.
DISCUSSION: Lapping involves recording current cash payments on accounts receivable as credits to prior customers' accounts to conceal a theft of cash. Comparing the date that a customer's check was deposited with the date a record was made to reduce the balance determines whether the deposit was made prior to the recording date.
Answer (B) is incorrect. The total cash received and deposited for any one day will reconcile when lapping occurs. Answer (C) is incorrect. The total cash received and deposited for any one day will reconcile when lapping occurs. Answer (D) is incorrect. Lapping does not involve unauthorized write-offs.

15. An auditor who has confirmed accounts receivable may discover that the sales journal was held open past year end if

A. Positive confirmations sent to debtors are not returned.

B. Negative confirmations sent to debtors are not returned.

C. Most of the returned negative confirmations indicate that the debtor owes a larger balance than the amount being confirmed.

D. Most of the returned positive confirmations indicate that the debtor owes a smaller balance than the amount being confirmed.

Answer (D) is correct. *(Publisher, adapted)*
REQUIRED: The result of confirmation indicating that the sales journal was held open past year end.
DISCUSSION: When the majority of the returned positive confirmations indicate smaller balances at year end than those in the client's records, the client may have held open the sales journal after year end. Thus, the client debited customers' accounts for the period under audit rather than for the subsequent period. The effect is to overstate sales and receivables.
Answer (A) is incorrect. The failure to receive replies to positive confirmations may cause the auditor concern about the existence assertion. Answer (B) is incorrect. The failure to return negative confirmations provides some evidence about the existence assertion. Answer (C) is incorrect. Replies indicating balances larger than those confirmed suggest that the sales journal was closed prior to year end.

16. During the process of confirming receivables as of December 31, Year 1, a positive confirmation was returned indicating the "balance owed as of December 31 was paid on January 9, Year 2." The auditor would most likely

A. Determine whether there were any changes in the account between January 1 and January 9, Year 2.

B. Determine whether a customary trade discount was taken by the customer.

C. Reconfirm the zero balance as of January 10, Year 2.

D. Verify that the amount was received.

Answer (D) is correct. *(CPA, adapted)*
REQUIRED: The auditor action when a confirmation response states that the year-end balance was paid.
DISCUSSION: Responses to confirmations that involve significant differences are investigated by the auditor. Others are delegated to client employees with a request that explanations be given to the auditor. Such differences often arise because of recent cash payments. In that event, the auditor should trace remittances to verify that stated amounts were received.
Answer (A) is incorrect. The auditor wishes to confirm a year-end balance, not transactions in the subsequent period. Also, the reply does not suggest a discrepancy in the account. Answer (B) is incorrect. The auditor is more concerned with confirming the balance due at year end than with whether a customer took a discount. Answer (C) is incorrect. Reconfirmation is not required.

17. An auditor confirmed accounts receivable as of an interim date, and all confirmations were returned and appeared reasonable. Which of the following additional procedures most likely should be performed at year end?

A. Send confirmations for all new customer balances incurred from the interim date to year end.

B. Resend confirmations for any significant customer balances remaining at year end.

C. Review supporting documents for new large balances occurring after the interim date, and evaluate any significant changes in balances at year end.

D. Review cash collections subsequent to the interim date and the year end.

Answer (C) is correct. *(CPA, adapted)*
REQUIRED: The year-end procedure most likely performed after receivables were confirmed at an interim date.
DISCUSSION: If incremental RMM can be controlled, procedures to cover the remaining period ordinarily include (1) comparing information at the interim date with information at the balance sheet date to identify and investigate unusual amounts (e.g., new large balances) and (2) other analytical procedures or tests of details.
Answer (A) is incorrect. Sampling is normally used in confirming receivables. Answer (B) is incorrect. Second confirmation requests are normally not sent when initial confirmations were returned. Answer (D) is incorrect. Verification of subsequent collections is an alternative procedure used when the response rate to confirmations is low.

18. To reduce the risks associated with accepting fax responses to requests for confirmations of accounts receivable, an auditor most likely would

A. Examine the shipping documents that provide evidence for the existence assertion.

B. Verify the sources and contents of the faxes in telephone calls to the senders.

C. Consider the faxes to be nonresponses and evaluate them as unadjusted differences.

D. Inspect the faxes for forgeries or alterations and consider them to be acceptable if none are noted.

Answer (B) is correct. *(CPA, adapted)*
REQUIRED: The procedure to reduce the risk of accepting false confirmations by fax.
DISCUSSION: Because establishing the source of a fax is often difficult, the auditor should ensure that the confirmations returned by fax are genuine. One way is to verify the sources by following up with telephone calls to the senders.
Answer (A) is incorrect. The purpose of the confirmation is to test the existence of the receivable by direct communication with the debtor. Answer (C) is incorrect. A fax is considered a valid response if the source can be verified. Answer (D) is incorrect. Faxes may not be signed. Furthermore, the auditor is unlikely to be qualified to recognize forgeries.

19. Cooper, CPA, is auditing the financial statements of a small rural municipality. The receivable balances represent residents' delinquent real estate taxes. Internal control at the municipality is ineffective. To determine the existence of the accounts receivable balances at the balance sheet date, Cooper would most likely

A. Send positive confirmation requests.

B. Send negative confirmation requests.

C. Examine evidence of subsequent cash receipts.

D. Inspect the internal records such as copies of the tax invoices that were mailed to the residents.

Answer (A) is correct. *(CPA, adapted)*
REQUIRED: The best procedure to determine the existence of accounts receivable given ineffective internal control.
DISCUSSION: The presumption that the auditor will request confirmation of receivables cannot be overcome unless the receivables are not material, confirmation is unlikely to be effective, or the assessed risk of material misstatement is low. None of these conditions apply. Thus, the auditor should confirm the receivables. However, negative confirmations are not used unless the assessed risk of material misstatement is low. Because control risk for the municipality is high, the auditor should send positive confirmation requests.
Answer (B) is incorrect. A negative confirmation does not require a reply if the balance is in agreement. Hence, it decreases the reliability of the evidence. Answer (C) is incorrect. This procedure relates more to the valuation of accounts. Answer (D) is incorrect. Replies to positive confirmation requests constitute independent external evidence that is more persuasive than that derived from inspection of internally generated documents.

20. When an auditor does **not** receive replies to positive requests for year-end accounts receivable confirmations, the auditor most likely would

A. Inspect the allowance account to verify whether the accounts were subsequently written off.

B. Increase the assessed level of detection risk for the valuation and completeness assertions.

C. Send the customer a second confirmation.

D. Increase the assessed level of inherent risk for the revenue cycle.

Answer (C) is correct. *(CPA, adapted)*
REQUIRED: The auditor action when positive confirmation requests are not returned.
DISCUSSION: When first requests for positive confirmation are not returned, the auditor should consider a second request. The request will be signed by the client and ask the debtor to respond directly to the auditor.
Answer (A) is incorrect. It is premature to conclude that the account is uncollectible. Answer (B) is incorrect. The auditor must collect sufficient appropriate evidence to achieve the desired level of detection risk. It would be inappropriate to increase the level of risk. Answer (D) is incorrect. Inherent risk is independent of control risk, detection risk, or the audit process.

21. Which of the following procedures would an auditor most likely perform for year-end accounts receivable confirmations when the auditor did **not** receive replies to second requests?

A. Review the cash receipts journal for the month prior to year end.

B. Intensify the study of internal control concerning the revenue cycle.

C. Increase the assessed level of detection risk for the existence assertion.

D. Inspect the shipping records documenting the merchandise sold to the debtors.

Answer (D) is correct. *(CPA, adapted)*
   REQUIRED: The most appropriate audit procedure when customers fail to reply to second request forms.
   DISCUSSION: When customers fail to answer a second request for a positive confirmation, the accounts may be in dispute, uncollectible, or fictitious. The auditor should then apply alternative procedures (examination of subsequent cash receipts, shipping documents, and other client documentation of existence) to obtain evidence about the validity of nonresponding accounts (AU 330).
   Answer (A) is incorrect. Previous collections cannot substantiate year-end balances. Answer (B) is incorrect. Nonresponse to a confirmation request is not proof of ineffective controls. Nonresponses do occur and are expected. Answer (C) is incorrect. Control risk and inherent risk are assessed, but detection risk is not. However, the acceptable level of detection risk may be decreased if the assessment of inherent risk or control risk is increased as a result of nonresponses to confirmation requests.

11.2 Substantive Testing of Cash

22. The best evidence regarding year-end bank balances is documented in the

A. Cutoff bank statement.

B. Bank reconciliations.

C. Interbank transfer schedule.

D. Bank deposit lead schedule.

Answer (B) is correct. *(CPA, adapted)*
   REQUIRED: The best source of evidence regarding year-end bank balances.
   DISCUSSION: A bank reconciliation verifies the agreement of the bank statements obtained directly from the institution and the amount of cash reported in the financial statements. These amounts should be equal after adjustment for deposits in transit, outstanding checks, bank charges, etc. Thus, a bank reconciliation documents direct (primary) evidence of the year-end bank balance.
   Answer (A) is incorrect. The cutoff bank statement covers a brief period after the end of the period. Answer (C) is incorrect. Only the record of transfer activity between banks is recorded on this schedule. Answer (D) is incorrect. The bank deposit lead schedule contains details supporting the cash amount in the working trial balance, but it is the bank reconciliation that supports the amounts in the lead schedule.

23. Which of the following sets of information does an auditor usually confirm on one form?

A. Accounts payable and purchase commitments.

B. Cash in bank and collateral for loans.

C. Inventory on consignment and contingent liabilities.

D. Accounts receivable and accrued interest receivable.

Answer (B) is correct. *(CPA, adapted)*
   REQUIRED: The information confirmed on one form.
   DISCUSSION: The AICPA *Standard Form to Confirm Account Balance Information with Financial Institutions* is used by auditors to confirm the deposit balance held by the bank for a client. In addition, this confirmation requests loan information, such as a description of the collateral securing the loan.
   Answer (A) is incorrect. A confirmation of accounts payable balances requests information about purchase commitments. Answer (C) is incorrect. Inventory on consignment is confirmed by a form sent to the consignee holding the inventory, and contingent liabilities are confirmed by a form sent to an official responsible for a financial institution's relationship with the client. Answer (D) is incorrect. A confirmation of accounts receivable does not provide information about interest that is owed to the client.

24. An auditor ordinarily sends a standard confirmation request to all banks with which the client has done business during the year under audit, regardless of the year-end balance. A purpose of this procedure is to

   A. Provide the data necessary to prepare a proof of cash.

   B. Request that a cutoff bank statement and related checks be sent to the auditor.

   C. Detect kiting activities that may otherwise not be discovered.

   D. Seek information about other deposit and loan amounts that come to the attention of the institution in the process of completing the confirmation.

Answer (D) is correct. *(CPA, adapted)*
   REQUIRED: The reason confirmations are sent to all banks used by the client.
   DISCUSSION: The AICPA *Standard Form to Confirm Account Balance Information with Financial Institutions* is used to confirm specifically listed deposit and loan balances. Nevertheless, the standard confirmation form contains this language: "Although we do not request or expect you to conduct a comprehensive, detailed search of your records, if, during the process of completing this confirmation, additional information about other deposit and loan accounts we may have with you comes to your attention, please include such information below."
   Answer (A) is incorrect. The information for a proof of cash is in the month-end bank statement. Answer (B) is incorrect. A cutoff bank statement is for some period subsequent to the balance sheet date. Answer (C) is incorrect. The auditor should compare the returned checks in the cutoff bank statement with those listed as outstanding on the bank reconciliation, as well as prepare a bank transfer schedule for a few days before and after the balance sheet date.

25. The usefulness of the standard bank confirmation request may be limited because the bank employee who completes the form may

   A. Not believe that the bank is obligated to verify confidential information to a third party.

   B. Sign and return the form without inspecting the accuracy of the client's bank reconciliation.

   C. Not have access to the client's cutoff bank statement.

   D. Be unaware of all the financial relationships that the bank has with the client.

Answer (D) is correct. *(CPA, adapted)*
   REQUIRED: The reason for the limited usefulness of the standard bank confirmation request.
   DISCUSSION: According to AU 330, the standard form is designed to substantiate only the information that is stated on the confirmation request. Thus, the auditor should be aware that the standard form is not intended to elicit evidence about the completeness assertion. The individual completing the form may not be aware of all the financial relationships that the bank has with the client.
   Answer (A) is incorrect. The client requests the information from the bank, and the bank must provide that information. Answer (B) is incorrect. The bank is not responsible for the accuracy of the client's bank reconciliation. Answer (C) is incorrect. The cutoff bank statement is not necessary to complete the form.

26. An independent auditor asked a client's internal auditor to assist in preparing a standard financial institution confirmation request for a payroll account that had been closed during the year under audit. After the internal auditor prepared the form, the controller signed it and mailed it to the bank. What was the major flaw in this procedure?

   A. The internal auditor did not sign the form.

   B. The form was mailed by the controller.

   C. The form was prepared by the internal auditor.

   D. The account was closed, so the balance was zero.

Answer (B) is correct. *(CPA, adapted)*
   REQUIRED: The flaw in the confirmation request to a financial institution regarding a closed payroll account.
   DISCUSSION: The AICPA *Standard Form to Confirm Account Balance Information with Financial Institutions* is used for specific deposits and loans. A confirmation is signed (requested) by the client, but it should be sent by the auditor. Thus, the auditor should control confirmation requests and responses. Control means direct communication between the intended recipient and the auditor to minimize possible bias of the results because of interception and alteration of the requests or responses (AU 330).
   Answer (A) is incorrect. The internal auditor need not sign the form. Answer (C) is incorrect. The auditor may request direct assistance from the internal auditors when performing an audit. Answer (D) is incorrect. The auditor must still obtain evidence about the account even though it has been closed.

27. An auditor should test bank transfers for the last part of the audit period and first part of the subsequent period to detect whether

   A. The cash receipts journal was held open for a few days after year end.

   B. The last checks recorded before year end were actually mailed by year end.

   C. Cash balances were overstated because of kiting.

   D. Any unusual payments to or receipts from related parties occurred.

Answer (C) is correct. *(CPA, adapted)*
   REQUIRED: The reason for testing bank transfers at year end.
   DISCUSSION: Kiting is the recording of a deposit from an interbank transfer in the current period while failing to record the related disbursement until the next period. It is a fraud that exploits the lag (float period) between the deposit of a check in one account and the time it clears the bank on which it is drawn. To detect kiting, the auditor should examine a schedule of bank transfers for a period covering a few days before and after the balance sheet date. For the procedure to be effective, however, the auditor should be assured that all transfers have been identified.
   Answer (A) is incorrect. A cutoff bank statement should be examined to determine whether the cash receipts journal was held open for a few days after year end. Answer (B) is incorrect. A cutoff bank statement should be examined to determine whether the last checks recorded before year end were actually mailed by year end. Answer (D) is incorrect. Unusual payments to or receipts from related parties can occur at any time of the year.

Questions 28 and 29 are based on the following information. The following was taken from the bank transfer schedule prepared during the audit of Fox Co.'s financial statements for the year ended December 31, Year 1. Assume all checks are dated and issued on December 30, Year 1.

Check No.	Bank Accounts		Disbursement Date		Receipt Date	
	From	To	Per Books	Per Bank	Per Books	Per Bank
101	National	Federal	Dec. 30	Jan. 4	Dec. 30	Jan. 3
202	County	State	Jan. 3	Jan. 2	Dec. 30	Dec. 31
303	Federal	American	Dec. 31	Jan. 3	Jan. 2	Jan. 2
404	State	Republic	Jan. 2	Jan. 2	Dec. 31	Jan. 2

28. Which of the following checks might indicate kiting?

   A. #101 and #303.

   B. #202 and #404.

   C. #101 and #404.

   D. #202 and #303.

Answer (B) is correct. *(CPA, adapted)*
   REQUIRED: The checks that might indicate kiting.
   DISCUSSION: Kiting is the recording of a deposit from an interbank transfer in the current period while failing to record the related disbursement until the next period. It is a fraud that exploits the lag (float period) between the deposit of a check in one account and the time it clears the bank on which it is drawn. Checks #202 and #404 may indicate kiting. They were recorded as receipts on the books in the current period. However, they were recorded as disbursements on the books in the next year.
   Answer (A) is incorrect. Checks #101 and #303 were recorded as received after year end. Answer (C) is incorrect. Check #101 was recorded as received after year end. Answer (D) is incorrect. Check #303 was recorded as received after year end.

29. Which of the following checks illustrate deposits/transfers in transit at December 31, Year 1?

   A. #101 and #202.

   B. #101 and #303.

   C. #202 and #404.

   D. #303 and #404.

Answer (B) is correct. *(CPA, adapted)*
   REQUIRED: The checks indicating deposits/transfers in transit.
   DISCUSSION: A deposit/transfer in transit is one recorded in the entity's books as a receipt by the balance sheet date but not recorded as a deposit by the bank until the next period. Check #101 is a deposit/transfer in transit because the check was recorded in the books before the end of the year but not recorded by either bank until January. Check #303 is also a deposit/transfer in transit, because the check was deducted from Federal's balance in December, but it was not added to American's balance until January.
   Answer (A) is incorrect. Check #202 was recorded in the books after the balance sheet date. Answer (C) is incorrect. Checks #202 and #404 were recorded in the books after the balance sheet date. Answer (D) is incorrect. Check #404 was recorded in the books after the balance sheet date.

30. Which of the following cash transfers results in a misstatement of cash at December 31, Year 1?

| Bank Transfer Schedule | | | |
| Disbursement | | Receipt | |
Recorded in Books	Paid by Bank	Recorded in Books	Received by Bank
A. 12/31/Yr 1	1/4/Yr 2	12/31/Yr 1	12/31/Yr 1
B. 1/4/Yr 2	1/5/Yr 2	12/31/Yr 1	1/4/Yr 2
C. 12/31/Yr 1	1/5/Yr 2	12/31/Yr 1	1/4/Yr 2
D. 1/4/Yr 2	1/11/Yr 2	1/4/Yr 2	1/4/Yr 2

Answer (B) is correct. *(CPA, adapted)*
REQUIRED: The interbank cash transfer that indicates an error in cash cutoff.
DISCUSSION: An error in cash cutoff occurs if one half of the transaction is recorded in the current period and one half in the subsequent period. Inspection of the Recorded in Books columns indicates the transfer was recorded as a receipt on 12/31/Yr 1 but not as a disbursement until 1/4/Yr 2. This discrepancy is an error in cutoff called a kite, and it overstates the cash balance.

31. Which of the following procedures would an auditor most likely perform in auditing the statement of cash flows?

A. Compare the amounts included in the statement of cash flows to similar amounts in the prior year's statement of cash flows.

B. Reconcile the cutoff bank statements to verify the accuracy of the year-end bank balances.

C. Vouch all bank transfers for the last week of the year and first week of the subsequent year.

D. Reconcile the amounts included in the statement of cash flows to the other financial statements' balances and amounts.

Answer (D) is correct. *(CPA, adapted)*
REQUIRED: The procedure useful in auditing the statement of cash flows.
DISCUSSION: The information presented on a statement of cash flows is taken from the income statement and balance sheet. Indeed, a reconciliation of net income and net operating cash flow is required to be presented. Thus, reconciliation of amounts in the statement of cash flows with other financial statements' balances and amounts is an important procedure in the audit of the statement of cash flows.
Answer (A) is incorrect. Analytical procedures for cash are not effective. Cash is a managed account. Answer (B) is incorrect. Reconciling the cutoff bank statements to verify the accuracy of year-end bank balances is an appropriate procedure to audit the cash account but not necessarily the statement of cash flows. Answer (C) is incorrect. Vouching all bank transfers for the last week of the year and the first week of the subsequent year is effective for detecting cutoff misstatements, such as those arising from kiting, but not for auditing the statement of cash flows.

Use the additional questions in Gleim **CPA Test Prep Online** to create Test Sessions that emulate Prometric!

11.3 PRACTICE SIMULATION

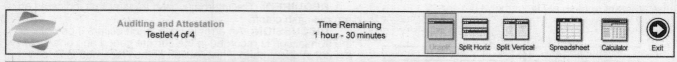

	Auditing and Attestation Testlet 4 of 4	Time Remaining 1 hour - 30 minutes					
			Unsplit	Split Horiz	Split Vertical	Spreadsheet	Calculator	Exit

DIRECTIONS

Note: If you believe you have encountered a software malfunction, report it to the test center staff immediately.

Navigation

To navigate from task to task, use the controls at the bottom of the screen. Click on the **Next** button to advance to the next task, or the **Previous** button to go to the previous task. To go directly to any task, click on its number.

▼ = Reminder		Directions	1	2	3	4	5	6	7		◀ Previous	Next	▶

If you would like a reminder to revisit a task, or want to indicate that you are finished with it, click on the reminder flag below the task number. To clear the flag, click on it again. Reminder flags are for your use only – they do not contribute to your score.

Tabs

In this part of the examination, you will be asked to complete various tasks. Every task has one or more **Work Tabs**. Some tasks have one or more **Information Tabs**, others may have none. Every task has a **Help** tab.

If a task has **Information Tabs**, you may use the information in them to complete your responses in the **Work Tabs**.

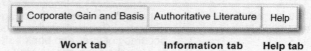

Corporate Gain and Basis	Authoritative Literature	Help
Work tab	Information tab	Help tab

Work Tabs:
- **Work Tabs** are identified with a pencil icon. This is where your responses are expected.
- Each task has one or more **Work Tabs**.
- **Work Tabs** contain directions for completing the task – be sure to read these directions carefully.
- The **Work Tab** name in the example above is for illustration only – yours will differ.
- You must complete all of the **Work Tabs** in each task to receive full credit.

Information Tabs:
- The Authoritative Literature will be provided in all tasks in the AUD, FAR, and REG sections for your reference.
- Your simulation may have one or more additional **Information Tabs**. Like the Authoritative Literature tabs, **Information Tabs** do not have a pencil icon.
- If your task has additional **Information Tabs**, go through each to familiarize yourself with the task content.

Help Tab:
- The **Help Tab** provides assistance with the exam software that is used in this task. For example, if the task is to compose a memorandum, **Help** will provide information about the word processor.

The Toolbar

The toolbar at the top of the screen shows the amount of time remaining for you to complete the tasks. In addition, the following tools are available. Note that only the Exit button is displayed when Directions are visible - the others will appear when you begin the tasks.

Click on these buttons to split or unsplit the screen. You can split the screen vertically or horizontally.

Click on this button to display the calculator; click on it again to hide the calculator. To move the calculator, click on the calculator title bar and drag the calculator to the desired location.

Click on this button to use the spreadsheet; click on it again to hide the spreadsheet. To move the spreadsheet, click on the the spreadsheet title bar and drag the spreadsheet to the desired location.

Click on this button to go on to the next part of the examination. You must complete all of the tasks to receive full credit. Once you click on **Exit** and confirm the action, you will NOT be able to return to this testlet.

▼ = Reminder		Directions	1	2	3	4	5	6		◀ Previous	Next	▶

Audit Procedures and Management Assertions	Authoritative Literature	Help

Select from the list provided the assertion that is most likely tested by each of the audit procedures. Each choice may be used once, more than once, or not at all.

Audit Procedures	Answer		Assertion Choices
1. The auditor reviewed delinquent customers' credit ratings.			A) Completeness
2. The auditor confirmed accounts receivable.			B) Rights and obligations
3. The auditor tested sales transactions at year end to determine that they were recorded in the proper period.			C) Valuation and allocation
4. The auditor accounted for the numerical sequence of sales orders.			D) Existence
5. The auditor vouched the recorded accounts receivable to shipping documents.			E) Classification and understandability
6. The auditor determined that accounts receivable was presented on the balance sheet as a current asset.			F) Cutoff
7. The auditor aged the accounts receivable.			
8. The auditor inquired of management about the possibility that the receivables had been sold or factored.			
9. The auditor reconciled the total receivables from the subsidiary ledger to the balance in the general ledger.			
10. The auditor determined that a note was included describing any sales to related parties.			

Bank Confirmation | Authoritative Literature | Help

For each of the following items, indicate by checking the appropriate box whether the information is typically included on the AICPA *Standard Form to Confirm Account Balance Information with Financial Institutions* (Bank Confirmation) sent by the auditor to all the banks that a client has done business with during the year.

Items of Information	Included	Not Included
1. A place for the signature of the auditor		
2. The following statement: "Please use the enclosed envelope to return the form directly to the auditor."		
3. An area on the form for the bank to list any outstanding checks		
4. An area on the form for a deposit balance to be placed		
5. A place for the signature of the bank official		
6. An area on the form to describe any collateral for loans		
7. A statement on the form that requests the bank to be alert for any fraudulent transactions		
8. The following statement: "Although we do not request or expect you to conduct a comprehensive, detailed search..."		
9. An area on the form for the bank to note exceptions or comments		
10. A statement on the form that requests the bank to keep the information confidential		

▼ = Reminder   Directions   1 2 3 4 5 6   ◀ Previous   Next ▶

| Accounts Receivable | Authoritative Literature | Help |

Indicate by checking the appropriate box which of the following substantive procedures are likely to be performed in an audit of accounts receivable.

Procedures	Yes	No
1. Count cash on hand		
2. Send second requests for all unanswered positive confirmation requests		
3. Perform alternative auditing procedures for unanswered second confirmation requests		
4. Confirm direct liabilities on loans		
5. Reconcile and investigate exceptions reported on the confirmations		
6. Project the results of the sample confirmation procedures to the population and evaluate the confirmation results		
7. Obtain a cutoff bank statement		
8. Determine whether any accounts receivable are owed by employees or related parties		
9. Test the cutoff of sales, cash receipts, and sales returns and allowances		
10. Prepare schedule of interbank transfers		
11. Evaluate the reasonableness of the allowance for doubtful accounts		
12. Perform analytical procedures		
13. Prepare a bank reconciliation		
14. Identify differences, if any, between the book and tax basis for the allowance for doubtful accounts and related expense		

You are collecting evidence in your audit of a client's cash receipts and cash disbursements. To properly test management's assertions about the balances in the financial statements, you are preparing to perform substantive testing of the cash cycle.

The following is a bank reconciliation prepared by your client, who has a September 30 year end:

General Company
Bank Reconciliation
1st National Bank of U.S. Bank Account
September 30, Year 1

Balance per bank				$28,375
Deposits in transit				
	9/29/Year 1		$4,500	
	9/30/Year 1		1,525	6,025
				34,400
Outstanding checks				
	# 988	8/31/Year 1	2,200	
	#1281	9/26/Year 1	675	
	#1285	9/27/Year 1	850	
	#1289	9/29/Year 1	2,500	
	#1292	9/30/Year 1	7,225	(13,450)
				20,950
Customer note collected by bank				(3,000)
Error: Check #1282, written on 9/26/Year 1				
for $270, was erroneously charged by bank				
as $720; bank was notified on 10/2/Year 1				450
Balance per books				$18,400

Assume the following:

- The client prepared the bank reconciliation on 10/2/Year 1.
- The bank reconciliation is mathematically accurate.
- The auditor received a cutoff bank statement dated 10/7/Year 1 directly from the bank on 10/11/Year 1.
- The 9/30/Year 1 deposit in transit, outstanding checks #1281, #1285, #1289, and #1292, and the correction of the error regarding check #1282 appeared on the cutoff bank statement.
- The auditor assessed the risk of material misstatement for cash as high.

-- Continued on next page --

Bank Reconciliation	Authoritative Literature	Help	**-- Continued**

Based on the bank reconciliation, select from the list provided one or more procedures (as indicated) for each of the following items that the auditor most likely should perform to gather sufficient, competent, and relevant evidence. Each choice may be used once, more than once, or not at all.

Item	Answer(s)				
1. Balance per bank – **select 2 procedures**					
2. Deposits in transit – **select 5 procedures**					
3. Outstanding checks – **select 5 procedures**					
4. Customer note collected by bank – **select 1 procedure**					
5. Error – **select 2 procedures**					
6. Balance per books – **select 1 procedure**					

Choices
A) Trace to cash receipts journal.
B) Trace to cash disbursements journal.
C) Compare with 9/30/Year 1 general ledger.
D) Confirm directly with bank.
E) Inspect bank credit memo.
F) Inspect bank debit memo.
G) Ascertain reason for unusual delay.
H) Inspect supporting documents for reconciling item not appearing on cutoff statement.
I) Trace items on the bank reconciliation to cutoff statement.
J) Trace items on the cutoff statement to bank reconciliation.

Cutoff	Authoritative Literature	Help

During the course of the Year 2 audit of the Chester Co., the auditor discovered potential cutoff problems that may or may not require adjusting journal entries. For each of the potential cutoff problems indicated below, complete the required journal entries.

To prepare each entry,

- Select from the list provided the appropriate account name. If no entry is needed, select "No entry required." An account may be used once or not at all for each entry.
- Enter the corresponding debit or credit amount in the appropriate column.
- Round all amounts to the nearest dollar.
- All rows may not be required to complete each entry.

1. The company shipped merchandise held in inventory at $75,000 FOB destination on December 23, Year 2, and recorded the sale and relief of inventory on that date. The customer received the merchandise on December 31, Year 2. The merchandise has a profit margin of 10%. Record the necessary Year 2 adjustments, if any.

Account Name	Debit	Credit

2. The company shipped merchandise held in inventory at $45,000 to a consignee on December 24, Year 2, and recorded the sale and the relief of inventory on that date. The consignee had not sold the merchandise as of January 5, Year 3. The merchandise has a profit margin of 10%. Record the necessary Year 2 adjustments, if any.

Account Name	Debit	Credit

Account Names Choices

- Accounts payable
- Accounts receivable
- Accrued liabilities
- Accumulated depreciation
- Cash
- Cost of goods sold
- Income tax expense
- Interest expense
- Inventory
- Operating expenses
- Other assets
- Other income
- Property and equipment
- Sales
- Stockholders' equity
- No entry required

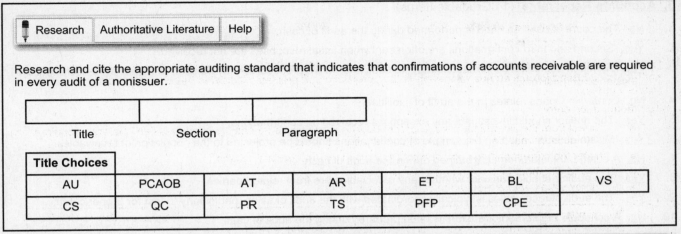

Research | Authoritative Literature | Help

Research and cite the appropriate auditing standard that indicates that confirmations of accounts receivable are required in every audit of a nonissuer.

Title	Section	Paragraph

Title Choices

AU	PCAOB	AT	AR	ET	BL	VS
CS	QC	PR	TS	PFP	CPE	

▼ = Reminder | Directions | 1 2 3 4 5 **6** | ◀ Previous Next ▶

Unofficial Answers

1. Audit Procedures and Management Assertions (10 Gradable Items)

1. <u>C) Valuation and allocation.</u> Considering delinquent accounts and credit ratings relates to the valuation of accounts receivable.

2. <u>D) Existence.</u> Confirmation is a primary test of existence.

3. <u>F) Cutoff.</u> Evaluating transactions for the recording in the proper accounting period at year end tests cutoff.

4. <u>A) Completeness.</u> Accounting for all documents in a sequence is a test of completeness.

5. <u>D) Existence.</u> Vouching is a primary test of existence.

6. <u>E) Classification and understandability.</u> Considering the presentation of items on the balance sheet is a test of classification.

7. <u>C) Valuation and allocation.</u> Aging of accounts receivable to consider collectibility relates to the valuation assertion.

8. <u>B) Rights and obligations.</u> The possibility of factoring receivables relates to ownership (rights) issues.

9. <u>A) Completeness.</u> Reconciling the subsidiary ledger with the general ledger helps determine if transactions failed to be recorded.

10. <u>E) Classification and understandability.</u> Disclosures in notes to the financial statements relate to the understandability assertion.

2. Bank Confirmation (10 Gradable Items)

1. <u>Not included</u> on confirmation.

2. <u>Included</u> on confirmation.

3. <u>Not included</u> on confirmation.

4. <u>Included</u> on confirmation.

5. <u>Included</u> on confirmation.

6. <u>Included</u> on confirmation.

7. <u>Not included</u> on confirmation.

8. <u>Included</u> on confirmation.

9. <u>Included</u> on confirmation.

10. <u>Not included</u> on confirmation.

3. Accounts Receivable (14 Gradable Items)

1.   <u>No.</u> The count of cash on hand is performed during the audit of cash.

2.   <u>Yes.</u> Second and third confirmations are often sent when initial responses are not received.

3.   <u>Yes.</u> Although additional confirmations may be sent, alternative procedures may be used to gather evidence about the existence of receivables.

4.   <u>No.</u> Confirming loans relates to the audit of liabilities.

5.   <u>Yes.</u> The auditor should investigate any exceptions received on confirmations.

6.   <u>Yes.</u> Misstatements based on the sample of confirmations should be projected to the population of receivables.

7.   <u>No.</u> A cutoff bank statement is obtained during the audit of cash.

8.   <u>Yes.</u> The auditor should consider whether any receivables are from related parties.

9.   <u>Yes.</u> The audit of receivables is typically coordinated with the audit of sales, particularly to test for proper cutoff.

10. <u>No.</u> A schedule of interbank transfers is often prepared during the audit of cash.

11. <u>Yes.</u> In considering the valuation of receivables, the auditor tests the reasonableness of the allowance for doubtful accounts.

12. <u>Yes.</u> Analytical procedures should be performed by developing expectations about the receivables balance.

13. <u>No.</u> The preparation of a bank reconciliation would be performed during the audit of cash.

14. <u>Yes.</u> The auditor would normally identify differences, if any, between the book and tax basis for the allowance for doubtful accounts and related expense.

4. Bank Reconciliation (16 Gradable Items)

1)   <u>D) Confirm directly with bank, and I) Trace items on the bank reconciliation to cutoff statement.</u> The balance per bank should be confirmed directly with the bank using a "Standard Form to Confirm Account Balance Information with Financial Institutions." Moreover, the cutoff bank statement gives the balance per bank at September 30, Year 1.

2)   <u>A) Trace to cash receipts journal, G) Ascertain reason for unusual delay, H) Inspect supporting documents for reconciling item not appearing on cutoff statement, I) Trace items on the bank reconciliation to cutoff statement, and J) Trace items on the cutoff statement to bank reconciliation.</u> Each deposit should be supported by an entry in the cash receipts journal. The 9/29/Year 1 deposit in transit should be investigated to determine the reason for the delay. It should have been reported on the cutoff bank statement. The deposits in transit on the bank reconciliation should be compared with items in the cutoff bank statement to test for their existence. In addition, a test should be performed in the opposite direction. The deposits in transit on the cutoff bank statement should be compared with items in the bank reconciliation to test the completeness of the deposits in transit.

3)   <u>B) Trace to cash disbursements journal, G) Ascertain reason for unusual delay, H) Inspect supporting documents for reconciling item not appearing on cutoff statement, I) Trace items on the bank reconciliation to cutoff statement, and J) Trace items on the cutoff statement to bank reconciliation.</u> Each check should be supported by an entry in the cash disbursements journal. Check #988 should be investigated to determine the reason for its delay in clearing and to determine why it did not appear on the cutoff bank statement. Outstanding checks on the bank reconciliation should be compared with the cutoff bank statement to test the existence of the outstanding checks. In addition, a test should be performed in the opposite direction. Outstanding checks on the cutoff bank statement should be compared with the bank reconciliation to test for the completeness of the listed outstanding checks.

4)   <u>E) Inspect bank credit memo.</u> The problem involves reconciling the balance per bank to the balance per books. The proceeds of the customer note collected by the bank increased the balance per bank, so the amount of the note must be subtracted to arrive at the balance per books. The amount collected on the note can be verified by inspecting the bank's credit memo. The bank credited the customer's account (a liability to the bank) when it collected the proceeds of the note.

5)   <u>E) Inspect bank credit memo, and I) Trace items on the bank reconciliation to cutoff statement.</u> The credit memo issued in October should be inspected and the credit given to the customer for $450 should be compared with the cutoff bank statement.

6)   <u>C) Compare to 9/30/Year 1 general ledger.</u> The balance per books should be compared with the 9/30/Year 1 cash balance in the general ledger.

5. Cutoff (7 Gradable Items)

1. No entry required.

2.
Inventory	$45,000	
Cost of goods sold		$45,000
Sales	$50,000	
Accounts receivable ($45,000 ÷ 0.9 = $50,000)		$50,000

6. Research (1 Gradable Item)

Answer: 330.34

AU Section 330 -- *The Confirmation Process*

Confirmation of Accounts Receivable

.34 For the purpose of this section, *accounts receivable* means:

a. The entity's claims against customers that have arisen from the sale of goods or services in the normal course of business, and

b. A financial institution's loans.

Confirmation of accounts receivable is a generally accepted auditing procedure. As discussed in paragraph .06, it is generally presumed that evidence obtained from third parties will provide the auditor with higher-quality audit evidence than is typically available from within the entity. Thus, there is a presumption that the auditor will request the confirmation of accounts receivable during an audit unless one of the following is true:

- Accounts receivable are immaterial to the financial statements.
- The use of confirmations would be ineffective.
- The auditor's combined assessed level of inherent and control risk is low, and the assessed level, in conjunction with the evidence expected to be provided by analytical procedures or other substantive tests of details, is sufficient to reduce audit risk to an acceptably low level for the applicable financial statement assertions. In many situations, both confirmation of accounts receivable and other substantive tests of details are necessary to reduce audit risk to an acceptably low level for the applicable financial statement assertions.

Gleim Simulation Grading

Task	Correct Responses		Gradable Items		Score per Task
1	___	÷	10	=	___
2	___	÷	10	=	___
3	___	÷	14	=	___
4	___	÷	16	=	___
5	___	÷	7	=	___
Research	___	÷	1	=	___

Total of Scores per Task		___
÷ Total Number of Tasks		6
Total Score		___ %

Use **CPA Gleim Online** and **Simulation Wizard** to practice more task-based simulations in a realistic environment.

Success stories!

I used Gleim Review materials to prepare for the CPA Exam. I'm happy to report I was able to pass the four sections on the first try. I couldn't have done that without the Gleim products. They were extremely helpful. The guides were well written and organized, and addressed virtually every topic I faced on the actual exams. Also, on the rare occasion I encountered trouble with the software, your technical support staff provided a quick solution. And they were pleasant to deal with on the phone.

- Dave Loverud

The Gleim products helped me pass all four sections of the CPA exam on my first attempt within one testing window. The exam was exactly like the practice tests in both form and content. I would highly recommend Gleim to anyone taking the CPA exam.

- Bela Toledo

Thank you for the effective role you played in preparing me to take the CPA exam. I was very nervous, but your program enabled me to pass each section the first time. Your customer service was always there to help when I needed it. I am grateful for the way Gleim regularly updates its materials. Your materials helped me get an 83 in FAR, 84 in REG and BEC, and an 88 in AUD. The best part of it is that your program was very cost-effective, an important consideration for a young college student. Keep up the good work!

- Grant Ropp

I have used Gleim CPA Review and I am glad I did. The benefits of using Gleim were that it was an online program hence accessible anywhere and anytime, the break down of topics made it easier to manage study and focus, and there were sufficient questions coupled with a good format. I will recommend CPA to my friends.

- Mohamed Abdullahi, CPA

STUDY UNIT TWELVE
EVIDENCE --
THE PURCHASES-PAYABLES-INVENTORY CYCLE

(6 pages of outline)

The primary purpose of the collection of evidence is to test relevant assertions about the transaction classes, balances, and disclosures in the financial statements. The auditor uses these assertions as a basis for assessing risks of material misstatement (RMMs) and designing and performing further audit procedures. In general, most testing in the inventory-acquisition process is applied to accounts payable and inventory, with a focus on the likelihood of understatement of accounts payable and overstatement of inventory. Evidence about the debit in the payables transaction (i.e., inventory in a perpetual system and purchases in a periodic system) is gathered when the credit (accounts payable) is tested. The interrelationship is apparent in the opposite direction as well. As the debit is tested, evidence about the credit also is produced. The objective of this study unit is to develop a comprehensive audit plan for the accounts payable and inventory accounts. This plan includes the customary procedures assuming no unusual risks. Some of the questions at the end of this study unit concern special risks that require modification of the audit plan. The candidate should consider those questions and problems and practice the modification of programs to address special risks.

The approach to audit plan development described in the outlines may be used in answering CPA exam questions. Application of the AICPA's assertions model (CAVE CROC is the mnemonic for the assertions -- see Study Unit 1, Subunit 2) ensures that all assertions are tested. However, other formats for presentation of the procedures are acceptable, for example, application of the PCAOB's assertion model also addressed in Study Unit 1, Subunit 2.

12.1 SUBSTANTIVE TESTING OF ACCOUNTS PAYABLE AND PURCHASES

1. Testing assertions about accounts payable provides evidence about **purchases** and ultimately **cost of goods sold**. Purchases obviously result in ending inventory, but because inventory is a significant item on the balance sheet, a separate audit plan is typically developed for the account. An audit plan for inventory follows this section.

    a. Candidates should understand the interrelationship of these accounts and the overlap of the audit procedures.

2. **Accounts payable**, sometimes termed trade payables, represent the most significant current liability of most firms.

3. **Testing Relevant Assertions.** The following is a standard audit plan for accounts payable and purchases that tests relevant assertions (CAVE CROC):

    a. **Completeness.** Do the balances contain all transactions for the period? (This is typically the major detection risk for the auditor in testing payables.)

        1) **Reconcile** the accounts payable ledger with the general ledger control account. Compare the total recorded amounts in the subsidiary ledger with the amount recorded in the general ledger.

        2) **Analytical procedures.** The auditor should use appropriate sources of data (e.g., prior experience, budgets prepared by management at the beginning of the period, nonfinancial information, industry data, and interrelationships) to form expectations with which to compare management's presentations. Ratios may be calculated and used (e.g., the **accounts payable turnover ratio**). Unexpected findings should be investigated.

        3) **Trace subsequent payments** to recorded payables. A primary test is to match the payments (checks) issued after year end with the related payables. Checks should be issued only for recorded payables. Any checks that cannot be matched are likely indications of **unrecorded liabilities**.

            a) Management may be motivated to delay recording of liabilities to improve the current ratio. However, unrecorded accounts payable must still be paid, and financial statements that fail to report all liabilities at year end are misstated.

        4) **Search for unvouchered payables.** The accounts payable function prepares and records a voucher (with a debit to purchases and a credit to accounts payable) when all the supporting documentation is assembled. The auditor should search the suspense files for unmatched documents to determine whether relevant documents have been lost, misplaced, or misfiled.

            a) A **suspense file** contains transactions, the classification and treatment of which are in doubt, for example, because of missing documents.

            b) For example, a requisition, receiving report, and invoice may be held by the accounts payable department, but no voucher should be prepared or entry made if the purchase order has not been matched with the other documents. This situation results in an unrecorded liability.

    b. **Accuracy.** Have the amounts been recorded appropriately?

        1) Obtain a management **representation letter** with assertions related to purchases and payables.

        2) Compare the general ledger balances to the balances on the financial statements.

    c. **Valuation and allocation.** Are accounts payable measured in accordance with GAAP? GAAP require that debts be stated at the amount necessary to satisfy the obligation.

        1) Detection risk for this assertion is reduced if the other assertions are tested in accordance with GAAS. The valuation or allocation assertion is interrelated with those for **existence and completeness**.

    d. **Existence.** Do the recorded accounts payable represent valid liabilities at the balance sheet date?

        1) **Confirmation** is not a generally accepted auditing procedure because it is not likely to disclose unrecorded payables. Normally, the auditor can become satisfied as to the existence of recorded payables using evidence available directly from the client.

        a)   If confirmation is undertaken, small and zero balances should be sampled as well as larger balances. The auditor should use the **activity in the account** as a basis for selection. That is, if orders are placed with a vendor on a consistent basis, a confirmation should be sent to that vendor regardless of the recorded balance due at year end.

        b)   The **blank form of positive confirmations** should be used. It requests that the balance due be provided by the creditor (e.g., the vendor).

e.   <u>C</u>utoff. Have transactions been recorded in the proper period?

   1)   **Purchases cutoff test.** Determine that all goods for which title has passed to the client at year end are recorded in inventory and accounts payable.

        a)   Goods shipped **FOB shipping point** by the vendor should be recorded in the period of shipment to the client. Thus, receipts for several days after year end should be evaluated to determine whether the goods should be recorded in the current year.

        b)   Goods shipped **FOB destination** by the vendor should be recorded in the period received by the client. Receiving documents are traced to the accounting records by the auditor for several days prior to and after year end to determine proper recognition of inventory and accounts payable.

   2)   **Cash disbursements cutoff test.** Test the recording of cash disbursements and the associated reduction in accounts payable. Inspecting the last check written and tracing it to the accounts payable subsidiary ledger will provide evidence of proper recording.

f.   **Rights and obligations.** Does the balance of accounts payable reflect the liability of this entity? Because the risk is relatively low that management would report liabilities of others, the procedures testing this assertion are not as consequential as those for other assertions.

   1)   **Inquiries.** Obtain management representations about the nature of the recorded payables.

g.   <u>O</u>ccurrence. Did purchases occur?

   1)   **Vouch recorded payables to documentation.** A sample of recorded payables should be reconciled with documentary support (e.g., requisitions, purchase orders, receiving reports, and approved invoices).

h.   **<u>C</u>lassification and understandability.** Are purchases and payables appropriately described and disclosures fairly and clearly expressed?

   1)   **Inspect the financial statements.** Accounts payable should be presented as a current liability on the balance sheet. Purchases should be used in the determination of cost of sales for the income statement.

   2)   **Evaluate note disclosures.** Any unusual significant transactions or events should be described by management in the notes (e.g., significant accounts payable to related parties).

Stop and review! You have completed the outline for this subunit. Study multiple-choice questions 1 through 13 beginning on page 405.

Background

Recent auditing standards emphasize the importance of understanding their clients and their businesses. Ironically, this has long been an issue with auditing inventory. Auditors have been frequently fooled by their clients about the amount or value of inventory because clients have more knowledge than the auditor. This is particularly true of certain types of inventory, for example, bulk or liquid inventory, high-tech products, or manufactured parts. Current auditing standards require some physical contact (observe and test count) with the inventory in an attempt to mitigate the risks associated with existence of inventory, but auditors still face significant risks.

12.2 SUBSTANTIVE TESTING OF INVENTORY

1. The primary purpose of the collection of evidence for inventory is to test management's assertions about the presentation of the balance and disclosures in the financial statements.

2. **Inventory** consists of the goods held for resale by the client and is presented as a current asset on the balance sheet.

3. **Testing Relevant Assertions.** The following is a standard audit plan that tests relevant assertions (CAVE CROC) about the inventory balance:

   a. **Completeness.** Does the inventory balance contain all inventory owned by the entity at year end?

      1) **Analytical procedures.** The calculation of amounts and ratios and their comparison with expectations can identify unusual findings indicative of misstatements.

         a) The **inventory turnover ratio** (cost of sales ÷ average or ending inventory) should be compared with that of the prior period and industry averages.

         b) **Vertical analysis** (e.g., the percentage of inventory to total assets), using industry information, can identify unusual conditions.

         c) Information from the client's previously prepared **budgets** can provide the basis for expectations.

         d) **Nonfinancial information** (e.g., the volume, in boxes or pounds) may provide expectations about the flow of inventory as well as sales and receivables.

   b. **Accuracy.** Have the amounts been recorded appropriately?

      1) Compare the general ledger balance to the balance on the financial statements.

   c. **Valuation and allocation.** Is inventory recorded at **lower of cost or market**?

      1) **Compare recorded costs with current cost to replace the goods.** Current vendor price lists should be compared with recorded inventory costs to determine that current prices are not less than recorded costs.

      2) **Calculate the turnover ratio.** An applicable analytical procedure is to calculate the inventory turnover ratio for the individual inventory items. Excessive inventory results in small turnover ratios and provides evidence of potentially obsolete items.

      3) **Test costs of manufactured items.** Manufactured goods should be costed to include direct materials, direct labor, and an allocation of overhead. The overhead allocation rate should be tested for reasonableness.

d. **Existence.** Does the inventory exist at a given date?

1) **Observation** of inventories is a generally accepted auditing procedure (AU 331, *Inventories*). The auditor must observe and make test counts but is not responsible for taking inventory.

a) If the entity uses the **periodic inventory method**, test counts should be made at or very close to year end because the counted inventory value is used to calculate cost of sales.

b) If the entity uses the **perpetual inventory method**, counts may be made at interim dates if records are well kept. If the RMM is high, inventory counts should be done at year end.

i) The client may use methods, including **statistical sampling**, that are sufficiently reliable to make an annual count of all items unnecessary. The auditor must be assured these methods are reasonable and statistically valid and have been properly applied. Observations and test counts must still be performed.

c) Observations should encompass all **significant inventory locations**.

i) The auditor must observe and make test counts even if inventory is taken by **independent specialists** (i.e., businesses that perform inventory counts as their service).

2) The client's plan for taking inventory should make effective use of, and exercise control over, **prenumbered inventory tags** and **summary sheets**.

a) The plan should include provisions for handling receipts and shipments during the count.

b) Goods not owned by the client, such as goods held on consignment, should be separated.

c) Appropriate instructions and supervision should be given to employees conducting the count.

3) **Performing tests of the count** should include the following:

a) Observing employees following the plan

b) Assuring that all items are tagged

c) Observing employees making counts and recording amounts on tags

d) Determining that tags and inventory summary sheets are controlled

e) Making test counts, comparing test counts with amounts recorded on the tags and summary sheets, and reconciling amounts with records

f) Being alert for empty boxes, empty squares (i.e., boxes stacked to suggest the block of boxes is solid when the middle does not contain boxes), and inventory defects (e.g., damaged or dirty items)

g) Establishing a cutoff by documenting the last receiving report and shipping document

4) The performance of procedures should be **documented**.

5) The auditor should confirm or investigate inventories held in **public warehouses**.

a) The auditor ordinarily obtains confirmation by direct communication with the custodian. When a significant portion of current or total assets is held in a public warehouse, the auditor should consider testing the client's procedures by (1) evaluating the warehouseman, (2) obtaining an independent accountant's report on the warehouser's internal control, (3) visiting the warehouse and observing physical counts, and (4) investigating the use of warehouse receipts (e.g., whether they are being used for collateral). The auditor should confirm with lenders the details of any pledged receipts.

e. **Cutoff.** Have transactions been recorded in the proper period?

1) **Purchases and sales cutoff tests**. Test recording of transactions subject to the terms (FOB shipping point or FOB receiving point) of both purchase and sale of inventory.

f. **Rights and obligations.** Does the entity own the inventory reported on the balance sheet?

1) **Vouch recorded purchases to documentation.** Vouch a sample of recorded inventory items to payment records. Payment vouchers for inventory should have supporting documentation (e.g., requisition, purchase order, receiving report, and vendor invoice) and canceled checks (if payment has been made).

2) **Consider the industry or client practices for consigned goods.** The nature of the client or industry suggests the possibility of consignment transactions (e.g., the client has held or shipped consigned goods in the past). The auditor should review the client's correspondence, evaluate sales and receivables records, and consider the results of vouching purchases to detect unrecognized consignment activity.

a) For example, if the client has inappropriately recorded consignment shipments as sales, the auditor most likely will find a pattern of large sales on account and many small, periodic cash receipts for the receivables.

g. **Occurrence.** Did the inventory transactions occur?

1) Vouch a sample of recorded purchases to documentation.
2) Vouch a sample of recorded cost of sales to documentation.

h. **Classification and understandability.** Are inventories properly displayed as current assets, and has cost of sales been properly reflected in the income statement? Have adequate disclosures been made concerning inventory measurement, cost flow assumptions, and significant transactions, such as pledging of inventory?

1) **Read financial statements.** The auditor should read the financial statements to determine that accounts are properly reflected and notes adequately informative.

2) **Inquire of management.** The auditor should inquire of management about (a) consigned goods, (b) major purchase commitments, (c) pledging of inventory, and (d) other significant transactions or events.

3) Obtain a **management representation letter** that includes assertions relating to inventory and cost of sales.

Stop and review! You have completed the outline for this subunit. Study multiple-choice questions 14 through 25 beginning on page 409.

QUESTIONS

12.1 Substantive Testing of Accounts Payable and Purchases

1. Which of the following is a substantive procedure that an auditor most likely would perform to verify the existence and valuation assertions about recorded accounts payable?

A. Investigating the open purchase order file to ascertain that prenumbered purchase orders are used and accounted for.

B. Receiving the client's mail, unopened, for a reasonable period of time after year end to search for unrecorded vendor's invoices.

C. Vouching selected entries in the accounts payable subsidiary ledger to purchase orders and receiving reports.

D. Confirming accounts payable balances with known suppliers who have zero balances.

Answer (C) is correct. *(CPA, adapted)*
REQUIRED: The substantive procedure for the existence and valuation assertions about recorded accounts payable.
DISCUSSION: Vouching a sample of recorded accounts payable to purchase orders and receiving reports provides evidence that the obligations exist at a given date. The purchase orders evidence the initiation of the transactions, and the receiving reports indicate that goods were received and that liabilities were thereby incurred. Thus, these documents provide evidence that amounts are owed to others, that the transactions occurred, and that the liabilities have been included at appropriate amounts.
Answer (A) is incorrect. Ascertaining that prenumbered documents are used and accounted for relates most directly to the completeness assertion. Answer (B) is incorrect. Searching for unrecorded liabilities relates most directly to completeness. Answer (D) is incorrect. Confirming payables with known suppliers having zero balances is a procedure for detecting unrecorded liabilities. Thus, it relates most directly to completeness.

2. To determine whether accounts payable are complete, an auditor performs a test to verify that all merchandise received is recorded. The population of documents for this test consists of all

A. Payment vouchers.

B. Receiving reports.

C. Purchase requisitions.

D. Vendors' invoices.

Answer (B) is correct. *(CPA, adapted)*
REQUIRED: The population of documents for a test to verify that all merchandise received is recorded.
DISCUSSION: The population to be tested consists of receiving reports. An accounts payable record should be available for each receiving report.
Answer (A) is incorrect. A payment voucher is prepared for each account payable. A payment voucher would not exist for an unrecorded payable. Answer (C) is incorrect. The goods requisitioned may not have been ordered. If ordered, they may not have been received. Hence, a payable may not exist for each requisition. Answer (D) is incorrect. A vendor's invoice does not provide evidence that the goods have been received and a liability incurred. Thus, a payable need not exist for every vendor's invoice.

3. When performing a substantive test of a random sample of cash disbursements, an auditor is supplied with a photocopy of vendor invoices supporting the disbursements for one particular vendor rather than the original invoices. The auditor is told that the vendor's original invoices have been misplaced. What should the auditor do in response to this situation?

A. Increase randomly the number of items in the substantive test to increase the reliance that may be placed on the overall test.

B. Reevaluate the risk of fraud and design alternate tests for the related transactions.

C. Increase testing by agreeing more of the payments to this particular vendor to the photocopies of its invoices.

D. Count the missing original documents as misstatements, and project the total amount of the error based on the size of the population and the dollar amount of the errors.

Answer (B) is correct. *(CPA, adapted)*
REQUIRED: The auditor's response to finding a photocopy of an invoice in support of a disbursement.
DISCUSSION: Several issues should cause the auditor to be suspicious. First, how could the client lose the original? Second, how did the client obtain a photocopy if the original was lost? Finally, and most importantly, photocopies are much less credible given the ease with which they can be altered. Thus, the auditor should reevaluate the risk of fraud.
Answer (A) is incorrect. The auditor should resolve this issue. The change in audit plan depends on the disposition of this transaction. Answer (C) is incorrect. More tests of this vendor may be in order, but the auditor should insists on obtaining originals of the documents. Answer (D) is incorrect. This may or may not be a misstatement. However, the transaction could be fraudulent with much broader implications.

4. An auditor performs a test to determine whether all merchandise for which the client was billed was received. The population for this test consists of all

A. Merchandise received.

B. Vendors' invoices.

C. Canceled checks.

D. Receiving reports.

Answer (B) is correct. *(CPA, adapted)*
    REQUIRED: The population for a test to determine whether all merchandise for which the client was billed was received.
    DISCUSSION: Vendors' invoices are the billing documents received by the client. They describe the items purchased, the amounts due, and the payment terms. The auditor should trace these invoices to the related receiving reports.
    Answer (A) is incorrect. Testing merchandise received will not detect merchandise billed but not received. Answer (C) is incorrect. Tracing canceled checks to the related receiving reports tests whether goods paid for, not goods billed, were received. Answer (D) is incorrect. Tracing receiving reports to vendors' invoices tests whether all goods received were billed.

5. In auditing accounts payable, an auditor's procedures most likely will focus primarily on the relevant assertion about

A. Existence.

B. Classification and understandability.

C. Completeness.

D. Valuation and allocation.

Answer (C) is correct. *(CPA, adapted)*
    REQUIRED: The assertion that is the focus of an audit of accounts payable.
    DISCUSSION: The primary audit risk for accounts payable is understatement of the liability. Thus, the auditor will most likely focus on the completeness assertion.
    Answer (A) is incorrect. The existence assertion concerns whether liabilities exist at a given date. The audit risk for accounts payable is not great for that assertion. Answer (B) is incorrect. The risk of inappropriate classification and understandability on the financial statements is not as great as the risk that some items are not included. Answer (D) is incorrect. The risk that accounts payable are not measured in accordance with GAAP is less than the risk that the balance may not be complete.

6. Which of the following procedures would an auditor most likely perform in searching for unrecorded liabilities?

A. Trace a sample of accounts payable entries recorded just before year end to the unmatched receiving report file.

B. Compare a sample of purchase orders issued just after year end with the year-end accounts payable trial balance.

C. Vouch a sample of cash disbursements recorded just after year end to receiving reports and vendor invoices.

D. Scan the cash disbursements entries recorded just before year end for indications of unusual transactions.

Answer (C) is correct. *(CPA, adapted)*
    REQUIRED: The procedure most likely to detect unrecorded liabilities.
    DISCUSSION: The greatest risk in the audit of payables is that unrecorded liabilities exist. Omission of an entry to record a payable is an error or fraud that is more difficult to detect than an inaccurate or false entry. The search for unrecorded payables should include (1) examining cash disbursements made after the balance sheet date and comparing them with the accounts payable trial balance, (2) sending confirmations to vendors with small and zero balances, and (3) reconciling payable balances with vendors' documentation.
    Answer (A) is incorrect. Sampling from known accounts payable provides little evidence of unrecorded liabilities. Answer (B) is incorrect. A sample of purchase orders issued after year end is expected to be recorded in the subsequent year, not in the current year. Answer (D) is incorrect. Payments in the current year represent satisfied liabilities, not unrecorded liabilities.

7. An auditor's purpose in reviewing the renewal of a note payable shortly after the balance sheet date most likely is to obtain evidence concerning relevant assertions about

A. Existence.

B. Classification and understandability.

C. Completeness.

D. Valuation and allocation.

Answer (B) is correct. *(CPA, adapted)*
    REQUIRED: The auditor's purpose in reviewing the renewal of a note payable shortly after year end.
    DISCUSSION: Events such as the renewal of the note payable do not require adjustment of the financial statements but may require disclosure (AU 560). Accordingly, the auditor should determine that the renewal had essentially the same terms and conditions as the recorded debt at year end. A significant change may affect the classification of notes payable (e.g., as current or noncurrent), the understandability of the statements, and the required disclosures.

8. Which of the following procedures would an auditor **least** likely perform before the balance sheet date?

    A. Confirmation of accounts payable.

    B. Observation of merchandise inventory.

    C. Assessment of the risk of material misstatement.

    D. Identification of related parties.

Answer (A) is correct. *(CPA, adapted)*
    REQUIRED: The audit procedure least likely to be performed prior to the balance sheet date.
    DISCUSSION: The most important assertion about accounts payable is completeness, which is best tested at year end. For example, the auditor may examine subsequent cash payments to determine whether the related payables are not recorded. Although confirmation is not a generally accepted auditing procedure, it may be useful in detecting unrecorded payables if the auditor's sample includes vendors where the risk of understatement is high, e.g., regular vendors with zero or low recorded balances.
    Answer (B) is incorrect. Observation of inventory at an interim date is more likely when controls are effective. It is also more likely when the year-end balances of the particular transaction classes or account balances that might be selected for interim examination are reasonably predictable with respect to amount, relative significance, and composition (AU 318). In these circumstances, substantive analytical procedures performed with regard to the remaining period are more likely to be effective. Answer (C) is incorrect. The auditor may assess risks prior to year end. Answer (D) is incorrect. The auditor may identify related parties prior to year end.

9. When using confirmations to provide evidence about the completeness assertion for accounts payable, the appropriate population most likely is

    A. Vendors with whom the entity has previously done business.

    B. Amounts recorded in the accounts payable subsidiary ledger.

    C. Payees of checks drawn in the month after the year end.

    D. Invoices filed in the entity's open invoice file.

Answer (A) is correct. *(CPA, adapted)*
    REQUIRED: The appropriate population when confirmations of accounts payable are used to test the completeness assertion.
    DISCUSSION: When sending confirmations for accounts payable, the population of accounts should include small and zero balances as well as large balances. The auditor should use the activity in the account as a gauge for sample selection. That is, if orders are placed with a vendor on a consistent basis, a confirmation should be sent to that vendor regardless of the recorded balance due.
    Answer (B) is incorrect. The auditor, in testing the completeness assertion, is concerned with balances that have not been recorded or invoices that have not been filed. Answer (C) is incorrect. The payees of checks are not an appropriate population for the confirmation process. Payments in the month after year end do not necessarily reflect year-end liabilities. Answer (D) is incorrect. The auditor, in testing the completeness assertion, is concerned with balances that have not been recorded or invoices that have not been filed.

10. An auditor suspects that certain client employees are ordering merchandise for themselves over the Internet without recording the purchase or receipt of the merchandise. When vendors' invoices arrive, one of the employees approves the invoices for payment. After the invoices are paid, the employee destroys the invoices and the related vouchers. In gathering evidence regarding the fraud, the auditor most likely would select items for testing from the file of all

    A. Cash disbursements.

    B. Approved vouchers.

    C. Receiving reports.

    D. Vendors' invoices.

Answer (A) is correct. *(CPA, adapted)*
    REQUIRED: The file tested to determine whether checks are being issued for unauthorized expenditures.
    DISCUSSION: The best procedure to test whether any checks have been issued without supporting vouchers, purchase orders, and receiving reports is to select an appropriate sample of canceled checks (cash disbursements) and trace them to the related supporting documentation.
    Answer (B) is incorrect. The approved vouchers relating to the fraudulent transactions have been destroyed and therefore could not be chosen for audit. Answer (C) is incorrect. The receipt of the merchandise is not recorded. Answer (D) is incorrect. The vendors' invoices relating to the fraudulent transactions have been destroyed and therefore could not be chosen for audit.

11. Tests designed to detect purchases made before the end of the year that have been recorded in the subsequent year most likely would provide assurance about the relevant assertion regarding

A. Valuation and allocation.

B. Existence.

C. Cutoff.

D. Classification and understandability.

Answer (C) is correct. *(CPA, adapted)*
REQUIRED: The purpose of an audit procedure.
DISCUSSION: The cutoff assertion is that transactions and events have been recorded in the proper period. To determine that all goods for which title has passed to the client at year end are recorded in inventory and accounts payable, a purchases cutoff test is appropriate.
Answer (A) is incorrect. The procedure does not directly test the assertion of valuation and allocation. Answer (B) is incorrect. The procedure does not directly test the assertion of existence. Answer (D) is incorrect. The procedure does not directly test the assertion of classification and understandability.

12. An internal control narrative indicates that an approved voucher is required to support every check request for payment of merchandise. Which of the following procedures provides the greatest assurance that this control is operating effectively?

A. Select and examine vouchers and ascertain that the related canceled checks are dated no later than the vouchers.

B. Select and examine vouchers and ascertain that the related canceled checks are dated no earlier than the vouchers.

C. Select and examine canceled checks and ascertain that the related vouchers are dated no earlier than the checks.

D. Select and examine canceled checks and ascertain that the related vouchers are dated no later than the checks.

Answer (D) is correct. *(CPA, adapted)*
REQUIRED: The procedure giving the greatest assurance that approved vouchers support check requests.
DISCUSSION: Payment vouchers bearing the required approvals should be supported by a properly authorized purchase requisition, a purchase order executing the transaction, a receiving report indicating all goods ordered have been received in good condition, and a vendor invoice confirming the amount owed. To determine that check requests are valid, the appropriate audit procedure is therefore to compare checks and the related vouchers. The direction of testing should be from a sample of checks to the approved vouchers. If the date of a voucher is later than the date of the related check, the inference is that a check was issued without proper support.
Answer (A) is incorrect. Tracing from vouchers to canceled checks does not give assurance that all checks are supported by approved vouchers. This test will not detect canceled checks unsupported by approved vouchers, although it will permit comparison of the dates of the respective documents.
Answer (B) is incorrect. Tracing from vouchers to canceled checks does not give assurance that all checks are supported by approved vouchers. This test will not detect canceled checks unsupported by approved vouchers, although it will permit comparison of the dates of the respective documents.
Answer (C) is incorrect. The checks should be dated no earlier than the vouchers. Each voucher should be dated earlier than (or have the same date as) the related check.

13. When performing procedures to test assertions about purchases, an auditor vouches a sample of entries in the voucher register to the supporting documents. Which relevant assertion would this procedure most likely support?

A. Completeness.

B. Occurrence.

C. Valuation and allocation.

D. Classification.

Answer (B) is correct. *(CPA, adapted)*
REQUIRED: The assertion tested by vouching.
DISCUSSION: A voucher signifies a liability. Its issuance is recorded in the voucher register after comparison of the vendor's invoice with the purchase requisition, purchase order, and receiving report. The direction of testing is an important consideration in addressing the RMM. Selecting a sample of recorded entries in the voucher register to vouch to the supporting documentation provides evidence that the transactions occurred.
Answer (A) is incorrect. Sampling recorded transactions to vouch to supporting documents does not test for unrecorded transactions. Answer (C) is incorrect. Sampling recorded transactions provides evidence regarding the amount owed and whether the entry reflects an obligation of the company, but it most directly supports the existence assertion. Answer (D) is incorrect. Sampling recorded transactions provides evidence regarding the amount owed but little evidence that the transactions have been recorded in the proper accounts.

12.2 Substantive Testing of Inventory

14. The element of the audit-planning process most likely to be agreed upon with the client before implementation of the audit strategy is the determination of the

A. Evidence to be gathered to provide a sufficient basis for the auditor's opinion.

B. Procedures to be undertaken to discover litigation, claims, and assessments.

C. Pending legal matters to be included in the inquiry of the client's attorney.

D. Timing of inventory observation procedures to be performed.

Answer (D) is correct. *(CPA, adapted)*
REQUIRED: The element of audit planning most likely agreed upon with the client before implementation.
DISCUSSION: The client is responsible for taking the physical inventory. The auditor is responsible for observing this process and performing test counts. The audit procedures are contingent upon management's plans. Thus, the auditor must coordinate the collection of this evidence with management.
Answer (A) is incorrect. The evidence to be gathered is a matter of professional judgment to be determined solely by the auditor. Answer (B) is incorrect. The procedures performed to discover litigation, claims, and assessments are matters of professional judgment to be determined solely by the auditor. Answer (C) is incorrect. Pending legal matters to be included in the inquiry of the client's attorney are matters of professional judgment to be determined solely by the auditor.

15. When auditing inventories, an auditor would **least** likely verify that

A. All inventory owned by the client is on hand at the time of the count.

B. The client has used proper inventory pricing.

C. The financial statement presentation of inventories is appropriate.

D. Damaged goods and obsolete items have been properly accounted for.

Answer (A) is correct. *(CPA, adapted)*
REQUIRED: The procedure not performed in an audit of inventories.
DISCUSSION: An auditor does not expect all inventory to which the auditee has title to be on hand at the date of the count. Some purchased goods may still be in transit at that time. Also, some inventory may be on consignment or in public warehouses although properly included in the count.
Answer (B) is incorrect. The auditor should test relevant assertions about valuation of inventory. Answer (C) is incorrect. The auditor should test relevant assertions about presentation in the financial statements. Answer (D) is incorrect. The auditor should test relevant assertions about valuation of inventory.

16. A client maintains perpetual inventory records in quantities and in dollars. If the assessed risk of material misstatement is high, an auditor would probably

A. Apply gross profit tests to ascertain the reasonableness of the physical counts.

B. Increase the extent of tests of controls relevant to the inventory cycle.

C. Request the client to schedule the physical inventory count at the end of the year.

D. Insist that the client perform physical counts of inventory items several times during the year.

Answer (C) is correct. *(CPA, adapted)*
REQUIRED: The auditor's action if the RMM for inventory is high.
DISCUSSION: If the RMM is high, a more timely audit procedure may be necessary, and extending the results of work done on an interim basis to year end might be inappropriate. Thus, observation of inventory at year end should provide the best evidence as to existence.
Answer (A) is incorrect. Comparing the gross profit test results with the prior year's results provides evidence about sales and cost of goods sold but not inventory. Answer (B) is incorrect. If the auditor believes control is unlikely to be effective, resulting in a high RMM, more effective substantive tests should be performed. Answer (D) is incorrect. The risk is that year-end inventory is misstated.

17. To gain assurance that all inventory items in a client's inventory listing schedule are valid, an auditor most likely would vouch

A. Inventory tags noted during the auditor's observation to items listed in the inventory listing schedule.

B. Inventory tags noted during the auditor's observation to items listed in receiving reports and vendors' invoices.

C. Items listed in the inventory listing schedule to inventory tags and the auditor's recorded count sheets.

D. Items listed in receiving reports and vendors' invoices to the inventory listing schedule.

Answer (C) is correct. *(CPA, adapted)*
REQUIRED: The step to provide assurance that all inventory items in a client's inventory listing are valid.
DISCUSSION: Validity relates to the existence assertion. To determine that the items exist, the direction of testing should be from the schedule to the inventory tags and ultimately to the auditor's count sheet.
Answer (A) is incorrect. Tracing tags to the inventory listing schedule should provide evidence of completeness. That is, all items counted are included on the listing sheet. Answer (B) is incorrect. Tracing inventory tags to receiving reports and vendors' invoices should provide information useful in determining whether inventory was recorded at cost. Answer (D) is incorrect. Tracing inventory items on receiving reports and vendors' invoices to the inventory listing schedule is not an effective test. Many items received are sold by the inventory date.

18. An auditor selected items for test counts while observing a client's physical inventory. The auditor then traced the test counts to the client's inventory listing. This procedure most likely obtained evidence concerning the relevant assertion about

A. Rights and obligations.

B. Completeness.

C. Existence.

D. Valuation.

Answer (B) is correct. *(CPA, adapted)*
REQUIRED: The assertion relevant to tracing test counts to the client's inventory listing.
DISCUSSION: Tracing the details of test counts to the final inventory schedule assures the auditor that items in the observed physical inventory are included in the inventory records. The auditor should compare the inventory tag sequence numbers in the final inventory schedule with those in the records of his/her test counts made during the client's physical inventory.
Answer (A) is incorrect. The reconciliation of the test counts with the inventory listing does not provide assurance that the inventory is owned by the client. Answer (C) is incorrect. Although the observation of inventory provides evidence as to existence, specifically tracing test counts to the inventory listing provides evidence of completeness. Answer (D) is incorrect. The valuation assertion is tested by determining whether inventory items are included in inventory at lower of cost or market.

19. While observing a client's annual physical inventory, an auditor recorded test counts for several items and noticed that certain test counts were higher than the recorded quantities in the client's perpetual records. This situation could be the result of the client's failure to record

A. Purchase discounts.

B. Purchase returns.

C. Sales.

D. Sales returns.

Answer (D) is correct. *(CPA, adapted)*
REQUIRED: The transaction class not recorded when test counts are greater than recorded quantities.
DISCUSSION: Failure to record sales returns for goods returned to the physical inventory will result in test counts greater than the quantities reported by the perpetual inventory system.
Answer (A) is incorrect. Purchase discounts relate to the measurement of inventory, not to the quantity. Answer (B) is incorrect. Failure to record purchase returns results in lower quantities in the physical inventory than in the perpetual records. Answer (C) is incorrect. Failure to record sales results in lower quantities in the physical inventory than in the perpetual records.

20. Which of the following audit procedures probably would provide the most reliable evidence concerning the entity's assertion of rights and obligations related to inventories?

A. Trace test counts noted during the entity's physical count to the entity's summarization of quantities.

B. Inspect agreements to determine whether any inventory is pledged as collateral or subject to any liens.

C. Select the last few shipping advices used before the physical count and determine whether the shipments were recorded as sales.

D. Inspect the open purchase order file for significant commitments that should be considered for disclosure.

Answer (B) is correct. *(CPA, adapted)*
REQUIRED: The procedure providing the most reliable evidence of rights and obligations related to inventories.
DISCUSSION: Testing the assertion of rights and obligations for inventories determines that the entity has legal title or similar rights to the inventories. Typically, the auditor examines paid vendors' invoices, consignment agreements, and contracts.
Answer (A) is incorrect. Tracing test counts to the summary of quantities tests the assertion of completeness. Answer (C) is incorrect. Examining purchase transactions at year end tests the assertion of cutoff. Answer (D) is incorrect. Determining whether commitments should be disclosed tests the assertions about statement classification and understandability.

21. To measure how effectively an entity employs its resources, an auditor calculates inventory turnover by dividing average inventory into

A. Net sales.

B. Cost of goods sold.

C. Operating income.

D. Gross sales.

Answer (B) is correct. *(CPA, adapted)*
REQUIRED: The calculation of the inventory turnover ratio.
DISCUSSION: Inventory turnover equals cost of goods sold divided by average inventory. It provides a measure of how many times inventory requires replacement.

22. An auditor most likely would analyze inventory turnover rates to obtain evidence concerning relevant assertions about

    A. Existence.

    B. Rights and obligations.

    C. Classification and understandability.

    D. Valuation and allocation.

Answer (D) is correct. *(CPA, adapted)*
    REQUIRED: The assertion about which analysis of inventory turnover rates provides evidence.
    DISCUSSION: Assertions about valuation and allocation address whether (1) assets, liabilities, and equity interests are included in the financial statements at appropriate amounts and (2) resulting adjustments are properly recorded. An examination of inventory turnover pertains to identifying slow-moving, excess, defective, and obsolete items included in inventories (AU 326 and AU 318). This audit procedure tests the valuation and allocation assertion.
    Answer (A) is incorrect. Analysis of inventory turnover does not test existence. Answer (B) is incorrect. Analysis of inventory turnover does not test whether the entity has rights to the inventory. Answer (C) is incorrect. The classification and understandability assertion concerns whether financial information is properly presented and described and disclosures are clear.

23. An auditor most likely would make inquiries of production and sales personnel concerning possible obsolete or slow-moving inventory to support the relevant assertion about

    A. Valuation and allocation.

    B. Rights and obligations.

    C. Existence.

    D. Classification and understandability.

Answer (A) is correct. *(CPA, adapted)*
    REQUIRED: The assertion tested when considering obsolete or slow-moving inventory.
    DISCUSSION: The valuation and allocation assertion is directed towards whether inventory is recorded at lower of cost or market. The discovery of slow-moving, excess, defective, or obsolete inventory suggests that the cost of inventory be written down to market.

24. An auditor concluded that no excessive costs for an idle plant were charged to inventory. This conclusion most likely related to the auditor's objective to obtain evidence about the relevant assertions regarding inventory, including presentation and disclosure and

    A. Valuation and allocation.

    B. Completeness.

    C. Occurrence.

    D. Rights and obligations.

Answer (A) is correct. *(CPA, adapted)*
    REQUIRED: The assertion related to the conclusion that no excessive costs for an idle plant were inventoried.
    DISCUSSION: Inventory should properly include the costs of direct labor, direct materials, and manufacturing overhead. Thus, to be properly measured, an appropriate amount of manufacturing overhead should be charged to inventory. Costs of an idle plant should not be included in manufacturing overhead.

25. Which of the following auditing procedures most likely would provide assurance regarding a manufacturing entity's relevant assertions about inventory valuation?

    A. Testing the entity's computation of standard overhead rates.

    B. Obtaining confirmation of inventories pledged under loan agreements.

    C. Reviewing shipping and receiving cutoff procedures for inventories.

    D. Tracing test counts to the entity's inventory listing.

Answer (A) is correct. *(CPA, adapted)*
    REQUIRED: The procedure that provides assurance about a manufacturing entity's inventory measurement.
    DISCUSSION: Manufactured goods should be recorded at cost, including direct materials, direct labor, and an allocation of overhead. The overhead allocation rate should be tested for reasonableness.
    Answer (B) is incorrect. Obtaining confirmation of inventories pledged under loan agreements tests the assertion of rights and obligations. Answer (C) is incorrect. Reviewing shipping and receiving cutoff procedures tests the assertion of cutoff. Answer (D) is incorrect. Tracing test counts to the inventory listing tests the assertion of completeness.

Use the additional questions in Gleim **CPA Test Prep Online** to create Test Sessions that emulate Prometric!

12.3 PRACTICE SIMULATION

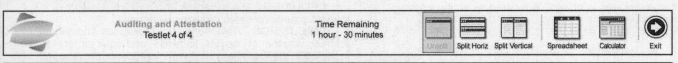

DIRECTIONS

Note: If you believe you have encountered a software malfunction, report it to the test center staff immediately.

Navigation

To navigate from task to task, use the controls at the bottom of the screen. Click on the **Next** button to advance to the next task, or the **Previous** button to go to the previous task. To go directly to any task, click on its number.

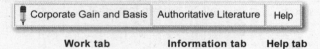

If you would like a reminder to revisit a task, or want to indicate that you are finished with it, click on the reminder flag below the task number. To clear the flag, click on it again. Reminder flags are for your use only – they do not contribute to your score.

Tabs

In this part of the examination, you will be asked to complete various tasks. Every task has one or more **Work Tabs**. Some tasks have one or more **Information Tabs**, others may have none. Every task has a **Help** tab.

If a task has **Information Tabs**, you may use the information in them to complete your responses in the **Work Tabs**.

	Corporate Gain and Basis	Authoritative Literature	Help
	Work tab	**Information tab**	**Help tab**

Work Tabs:
- **Work Tabs** are identified with a pencil icon. This is where your responses are expected.
- Each task has one or more **Work Tabs**.
- **Work Tabs** contain directions for completing the task – be sure to read these directions carefully.
- The **Work Tab** name in the example above is for illustration only – yours will differ.
- You must complete all of the **Work Tabs** in each task to receive full credit.

Information Tabs:
- The Authoritative Literature will be provided in all tasks in the AUD, FAR, and REG sections for your reference.
- Your simulation may have one or more additional **Information Tabs**. Like the Authoritative Literature tabs, **Information Tabs** do not have a pencil icon.
- If your task has additional **Information Tabs**, go through each to familiarize yourself with the task content.

Help Tab:
- The **Help Tab** provides assistance with the exam software that is used in this task. For example, if the task is to compose a memorandum, **Help** will provide information about the word processor.

The Toolbar

The toolbar at the top of the screen shows the amount of time remaining for you to complete the tasks. In addition, the following tools are available. Note that only the Exit button is displayed when Directions are visible - the others will appear when you begin the tasks.

 Click on these buttons to split or unsplit the screen. You can split the screen vertically or horizontally.

 Click on this button to display the calculator; click on it again to hide the calculator. To move the calculator, click on the calculator title bar and drag the calculator to the desired location.

 Click on this button to use the spreadsheet; click on it again to hide the spreadsheet. To move the spreadsheet, click on the the spreadsheet title bar and drag the spreadsheet to the desired location.

 Click on this button to go on to the next part of the examination. You must complete all of the tasks to receive full credit. Once you click on **Exit** and confirm the action, you will NOT be able to return to this testlet.

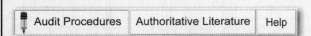

Select from the list provided the appropriate audit procedure for each description.

Description	Answer
1. An auditor independently executes procedures or controls that were originally performed as part of the entity's internal control.	
2. An auditor examines written information relating to transactions and balances, such as shipping and receiving forms, to establish ownership of inventory.	
3. An auditor obtains acknowledgments in writing from third parties of transactions or balances, such as inventory in public warehouses or on consignment.	
4. An auditor recomputes certain amounts, such as the multiplication of quantity times price, to determine inventory amounts.	
5. An auditor questions client personnel about events and conditions, such as obsolete inventory.	
6. An auditor physically examines an item to establish its existence.	
7. An auditor watches the performance of some process or procedure, such as a client's annual inventory count.	

Choices

A) Observation

B) Reperformance

C) Inspection of tangible assets

D) Inquiry

E) Confirmation

F) Inspection of records or documents

G) Recalculation

▼ = Reminder   Directions   1 2 3 4 5 6   ◀ Previous   Next ▶

Audit Procedures and Relevant Assertions	Authoritative Literature	Help

Select from the list provided the appropriate assertions for each audit procedure. Choose the assertion most likely being tested by the procedure. Each choice may be used once, more than once, or not at all.

Audit Procedure	Answer	Choices
1. The auditor determined that pledged inventory was identified.		A) Completeness
2. The auditor confirmed goods held by the client in a public warehouse.		B) Accuracy
3. The auditor performed a test at year end to assure all purchase transactions for the year were included in the proper period.		C) Valuation and allocation
4. The auditor accounted for the numerical sequence of purchase orders.		D) Existence
5. The auditor vouched the transactions to record payables to receiving documents.		E) Cutoff
6. The auditor determined that accounts payable was presented on the balance sheet as a current liability.		F) Rights and obligations
7. The auditor observed the taking of the physical inventory.		G) Occurrence
8. The auditor performed an analytical procedure comparing the relationship of inventory balances with recent purchases, production, and sales.		H) Classification and understandability
9. The auditor obtained representations from management about the amounts included on the financial statements for recorded transactions involving sales and purchases of inventory.		
10. The auditor compared recorded inventory costs with replacement costs.		

| Testing Inventory Cutoff | Authoritative Literature | Help |

The auditor tests the cutoff of inventory and determines whether it should be included in the final balance of the client. The client may ship and receive inventory based on a variety of shipping terms. Indicate by checking the appropriate box whether the inventory should be included in the 12/31/Year 1 balance of inventory for your client based on the following descriptions. Check "Yes" to include the inventory and "No" to exclude the inventory.

Descriptions	Yes	No
1. A shipment was made on 12/30/Year 1 to a customer FOB receiving point. The shipment was received by the customer on 1/3/Year 2.		
2. A shipment was made on 12/29/Year 1 to a customer FOB shipping point. The shipment was received by the customer on 12/31/Year 1.		
3. A shipment was received from a vendor on 1/4/Year 2. It was shipped from the vendor FOB shipping point on 1/2/Year 2.		
4. A shipment was received from a vendor on 1/4/Year 2. It was shipped from the vendor FOB shipping point on 12/29/Year 1.		
5. A shipment was received from a vendor on 1/6/Year 2. It was shipped from the vendor FOB receiving point on 12/29/Year 1.		
6. A shipment was made on 12/28/Year 1 to a customer FOB receiving point. The shipment was received by the customer on 12/31/Year 1.		
7. A shipment was made on 1/2/Year 2 to a customer FOB shipping point. The shipment was received by the customer on 1/3/Year 2.		
8. A shipment was received from a vendor on 12/31/Year 1. It was shipped from the vendor FOB receiving point on 12/30/Year 1.		

| Unrecorded Liabilities | Authoritative Literature | Help |

In conducting the audit procedures for the search for unrecorded liabilities, the materiality/scope for this area was assessed by the auditors at $6,000. Adjustments are only recorded for items equal to or exceeding materiality.

For the items reflected in the following check register, which are not recorded in the accounts payable subsidiary ledger at December 31, Year 2, determine whether each potential liability is recorded in the proper accounting period and also determine the amount that should be journalized, if any. If no action is required, you must enter $0.

For each of the check numbers in the table below, select from the lists provided (1) whether any action or adjustment is required and (2) the dollar value of the required adjustment. Each selection may be used once, more than once, or not at all.

Check Register

Vendor	Check #	Check Date	Amount	Nature of the Expenses
Water World Distributors, Inc.	1333	1/6/Yr 3	$3,500	Water coolers in office and warehouse delivered 12/31/Yr 2
Daniel Breen, Esquire	1334	1/6/Yr 3	$6,000	Corporate legal services for December Year 2
Telephone Services, Inc.	1335	1/8/Yr 3	$6,500	December Year 2 telephone and computer services
Payroll processing -- Paychecks	1336	1/10/Yr 3	$25,500	Bi-weekly payroll (12/25/Yr 2 - 1/7/Yr 3)
Pitt Ohio Trucking Company	1337	1/10/Yr 3	$45,601	Trucking services 12/4/Yr 2 - 1/3/Yr 3, deliveries made evenly throughout the period
Petty cash	1338	1/17/Yr 3	$2,002	Replenish petty cash box
Smith's Forklift Repairs	1339	1/22/Yr 3	$11,000	Received new fork lift on 12/29/Yr 2, ordered on 12/18/Yr 2
Glenn's Glass Distribution Center	1340	1/23/Yr 3	$12,230	Specialty goods ordered 12/20/Yr 2, delivered 12/31/Yr 2
Payroll processing -- Paychecks	1341	1/24/Yr 3	$25,500	Bi-weekly payroll (1/8/Yr 3 - 1/15/Yr 3)
Daniel Breen, Esquire	1342	2/6/Yr 3	$6,800	Corporate legal services for January Year 3

Check #	Adjustment Needed?	Amount
1. 1333		
2. 1334		
3. 1335		
4. 1336		
5. 1337		
6. 1338		
7. 1339		
8. 1340		
9. 1341		
10. 1342		

List for Adjustment Needed
i) No action required
ii) Adjustment

List for Amount
A) $0
B) $2,002
C) $2,970
D) $3,500
E) $4,413
F) $6,000
G) $6,500
H) $6,800
I) $7,650
J) $9,900
K) $11,000
L) $12,230
M) $12,750
N) $25,500
O) $41,188
P) $45,601

| Audit Adjustments | Authoritative Literature | Help |

The year under audit is Year 2.

During the course of the Year 2 audit of the company, the auditor discovered the following situations that may or may not require an adjusting journal entry. Each audit finding is independent of any of the other findings. Select from the list provided the account or accounts included in the adjusting journal entry, if required, to correct the audit finding. Accounts may be used once, more than once, or not at all.

Audit Finding	Adjusting Journal Entry		Accounts
	Dr.	Cr.	A) Cash
1. The bank's confirmation reply regarding the company's line of credit indicated that the December Year 2 interest was unpaid at year end. Accruals for monthly interest expense have been made for 11 months in Year 2 by the company.			B) Accounts receivable
			C) Other current assets
			D) Property and equipment
			E) Accounts payable
2. Employee overtime pay for hours worked before year end, but paid in the following year, were not recorded in Year 2.			F) Accrued liabilities
			G) Common stock
3. In the last week of Year 2, the company recorded revenue for services rendered to some clients in Year 3.			H) Revenues
			I) Allowance for doubtful accounts
4. During Year 2, a former client sued the company for inappropriate work. Legal counsel has advised that it is "reasonably possible" that the company will be assessed damages. An amount can be estimated.			J) Operating expenses
			K) Interest expense
			L) Other income
			M) Accumulated depreciation
5. At the end of Year 2, a major customer filed for bankruptcy.			N) Disclosure but no entry required
			O) No entry or disclosure required

▼ = Reminder   Directions   1 2 3 4 [5] 6   ◀ Previous   Next ▶

| Research | Authoritative Literature | Help |

Research and cite the appropriate auditing standard that describes what an auditor should consider when evaluating the results of confirmations.

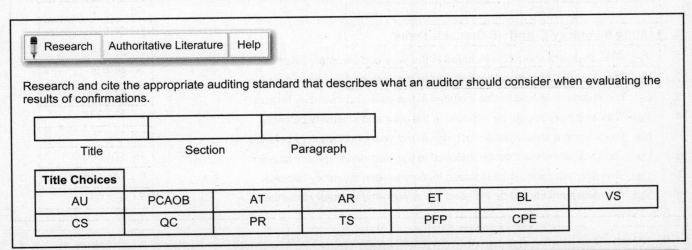

Title	Section	Paragraph

Title Choices						
AU	PCAOB	AT	AR	ET	BL	VS
CS	QC	PR	TS	PFP	CPE	

▼ = Reminder   Directions   1 2 3 4 5 [6]   ◀ Previous   Next ▶

Unofficial Answers

1. Audit Procedures (7 Gradable Items)

1.   B) Reperformance. Reperformance is independently executing procedures or controls that were originally performed as part of the entity's internal control.

2.   F) Inspection of records or documents. Inspection of records or documents includes the examination of written information.

3.   E) Confirmation. Confirmations are communications, typically in writing, with third parties requesting information.

4.   G) Recalculation. Recalculations are computations of mathematical accuracy.

5.   D) Inquiry. Inquiries are questions, typically posed to management and others with information of interest to the auditor.

6.   C) Inspection of tangible assets. Inspection of tangible assets includes physically examining an item to establish its existence.

7.   A) Observation. Observation means watching activities or procedures. It provides the auditor with direct personal knowledge.

2. Audit Procedures and Relevant Assertions (10 Gradable Items)

1.   F) Rights and obligations is the assertion being tested when the auditor determines that pledged inventory was identified. Thus, another party has rights in the inventory.

2.   D) Existence is the assertion being tested when the auditor confirmed goods held by the client in a public warehouse.

3.   E) Cutoff is the assertion being tested when the auditor performed a purchases test to ensure that all purchase transactions for the year were included in the proper period.

4.   A) Completeness is the assertion being tested when the auditor accounted for the numerical sequence of purchase orders.

5.   G) Occurrence is the assertion being tested when the auditor vouched transactions to record payables to receiving documents.

6.   H) Classification and understandability is the assertion being tested when the auditor determined that accounts payable was presented on the balance sheet as a current liability.

7.   D) Existence is the assertion being tested when the auditor observed the taking of the physical inventory.

8.   A) Completeness is the assertion being tested when the auditor performed an analytical procedure comparing the relationship of inventory balances with recent purchases, production, and sales.

9.   B) Accuracy is the assertion about transactions that is tested when the auditor obtains representations from the client about sales and purchases of inventory.

10.   C) Valuation and allocation is the assertion being tested when the auditor compared recorded inventory costs with replacement costs.

3. Testing Inventory Cutoff (8 Gradable Items)

1.   Yes. The shipment should be included in the year-end inventory balance.

2.   No. The shipment should not be included in the year-end inventory balance.

3.   No. The shipment should not be included in the year-end inventory balance.

4.   Yes. The shipment should be included in the year-end inventory balance.

5.   No. The shipment should not be included in the year-end inventory balance.

6.   No. The shipment should not be included in the year-end inventory balance.

7.   Yes. The shipment should be included in the year-end inventory balance.

8.   Yes. The shipment should be included in the year-end inventory balance.

4. Unrecorded Liabilities (10 Gradable Items)

1. <u>i) No action required; A) $0.</u> Although the purchase is for Year 2, the amount of $3,500 is below the materiality limit.

2. <u>ii) Adjustment; F) $6,000.</u> The services are for Year 2, and the amount is equal to the materiality limit.

3. <u>ii) Adjustment; G) $6,500.</u> The services are for Year 2, and the amount is greater than the materiality limit.

4. <u>ii) Adjustment; M) $12,750.</u> One half of the total amount, which is material, is accrued in Year 2.

5. <u>ii) Adjustment; O) $41,188.</u> The total amount is for 31 days, 28 of which were in December, Year 2.
    Thus, 28/31 × $45,601 is $41,188, which is greater than the materiality limit.

6. <u>i) No action required; A) $0.</u> The amount is below the materiality limit, and there is no indication that the transaction relates to Year 2.

7. <u>ii) Adjustment; K) $11,000.</u> The asset was received in Year 2, and the amount is greater than the materiality limit.

8. <u>ii) Adjustment; L) $12,230.</u> The assets were received in Year 2, and the amount is greater than the materiality limit.

9. <u>i) No action required; A) $0.</u> The services were received in Year 3.

10. <u>i) No action required; A) $0.</u> The services were received in Year 3.

5. Audit Adjustments (5 Gradable Items)

1. <u>K) Interest expense; F) Accrued liabilities.</u> The interest expense accrual for December would require recording.

2. <u>J) Operating expenses; F) Accrued liabilities.</u> The wages accrued for December would require recording.

3. <u>H) Revenues; B) Accounts receivable.</u> The revenue recorded, but not earned, for December would be reversed.

4. <u>N) Disclosure but no entry required; N) Disclosure but no entry required.</u> Since the contingent amount was not "probable," it requires only note disclosure in the financial statements.

5. <u>I) Allowance for doubtful accounts; B) Accounts receivable.</u> Since it is unlikely that the customer receivable will be collected, it would be written off to allowance for doubtful accounts.

6. Research (1 Gradable Item)

Answer: 330.33

AU Section 330 -- *The Confirmation Process*

Evaluating the Results of Confirmation Procedures

.33 After performing any alternative procedures, the auditor should evaluate the combined evidence provided by the confirmations and the alternative procedures to determine whether sufficient evidence has been obtained about all the applicable financial statement assertions. In performing that evaluation, the auditor should consider (a) the reliability of the confirmations and alternative procedures; (b) the nature of any exceptions, including the implications, both quantitative and qualitative, of those exceptions; (c) the evidence provided by other procedures; and (d) whether additional evidence is needed. If the combined evidence provided by the confirmations, alternative procedures, and other procedures is not sufficient, the auditor should request additional confirmations or extend other tests, such as tests of details or analytical procedures.

Gleim Simulation Grading

Task	Correct Responses		Gradable Items		Score per Task
1	_____	÷	7	=	_____
2	_____	÷	10	=	_____
3	_____	÷	8	=	_____
4	_____	÷	10	=	_____
5	_____	÷	5	=	_____
Research	_____	÷	1	=	_____

	Total of Scores per Task	_____
÷	Total Number of Tasks	6
	Total Score	_____ %

Use **CPA Gleim Online** and **Simulation Wizard** to practice more task-based simulations in a realistic environment.

STUDY UNIT THIRTEEN
EVIDENCE --
OTHER ASSETS, LIABILITIES, AND EQUITIES

(10 pages of outline)

The objective of this study unit is to develop comprehensive audit plans for accounts not previously considered. Each plan includes the customary procedures assuming no unusual risks. Some of the questions at the end of this study unit concern special risks that require modification of the audit plans. The candidate should consider these questions and practice the modification of audit plans and procedures to address special risks.

The approach to audit plan development described in the outlines may be used in answering CPA exam questions. Application of the AICPA's assertions model (CAVE CROC is the mnemonic for the assertions -- see Study Unit 1, Subunit 2) ensures that all assertions are tested. However, other formats for presentation of the procedures are acceptable, for example, application of the PCAOB's assertions model also addressed in Study Unit 1, Subunit 2.

13.1 SUBSTANTIVE TESTING OF PROPERTY, PLANT, AND EQUIPMENT

1.   **Scope**

   a.   The following balances are included in this audit plan:

      1)   Buildings, equipment, improvements, and vehicles including associated depreciation expense, repairs and maintenance, and accumulated depreciation

      2)   Land

      3)   Capital leases and associated amortization expense

2.   **Testing Relevant Assertions.** The following is a standard audit plan for property, plant, and equipment that tests relevant assertions (CAVE CROC):

   a.   **Completeness.** Are all transactions affecting property, plant, and equipment for the period reflected in the balance?

      1)   **Perform analytical procedures.** The five sources of information for analytical procedures (see Study Unit 3, Subunit 5) can be used to develop expectations. Typical ratios include rate of return on plant assets and plant assets to total assets.

      2)   **Reconcile subsidiary and general ledgers.** The client will usually maintain records for individual assets or classes of assets. The subsidiary records, including cost, current depreciation expense, and accumulated depreciation, should reconcile with the general ledger and the amounts to be included on the financial statements.

         a)   A schedule of fixed assets is typically prepared from the subsidiary records to be used in testing and is included in the audit documentation.

3) **Analyze repairs and maintenance.** The auditor should vouch significant debits from the repairs and maintenance expense account to determine whether any should have been capitalized.

    a) Vouching additions to property, plant, and equipment also tests the completeness assertion because debits may have been for non-capital items.

b. **Accuracy.** Have the amounts for the specific accounts been recorded appropriately?

    1) Include amounts and classifications in the management representation letter.

c. **Valuation and allocation.** Are balances of property, plant, and equipment reported in accordance with GAAP (historical cost – accumulated depreciation)?

    1) **Inspect records of purchases.** The purchase of fixed assets should result in payments. Vouching the entries to the payment records supports the rights and obligations assertion as well as the valuation assertion.

    2) **Vouch additions and disposals.** These are tests of the details of transactions. In a continuing audit, the prior year's balance of property, plant, and equipment is an audited balance. If the auditor tests the details of the transactions that changed the balance, (s)he has made significant progress in obtaining evidence about the valuation assertion (as well as other assertions such as completeness and existence).

    3) **Test depreciation.** Fixed assets (except certain nondepreciable assets such as land) are usually measured at cost minus accumulated depreciation. The depreciation methods and their application should be tested to determine that they are generally accepted and applied consistently.

d. **Existence.** Do the assets reflected in property, plant, and equipment exist at the balance sheet date?

    1) **Inspect plant additions.** The focus is on additions to property, plant, and equipment.

        a) The auditor vouches a sample from the recorded asset additions by examining the supporting documents and inspecting the physical assets. Testing in the opposite direction, i.e., by tracing from the supporting documentation to the general ledger, does not provide evidence that recorded assets exist.

        b) Initial audits require inspection of significant assets reflected in the beginning balance as well as additions.

e. **Cutoff.** Have transactions relating to property, plant, and equipment been recorded in the proper period?

    1) **Test the cutoff.** Additions and disposals near year end should be tested to ensure recording in the proper periods.

f. **Rights and obligations.** Does the entity have ownership rights in the reported property, plant, and equipment?

    1) **Examine titles and leases.** Certain property (e.g., autos and trucks) should have certificates of title. For leased assets, contracts should allow the auditor to determine whether leases have been properly recorded as either capital or operating leases.

2) **Inspect insurance policies.** The entity should insure its assets. Vouching the recorded assets to insurance policies supports the rights assertion.

    a) When liens are placed on equipment or property, the lienholder often requires that the assets be insured and that the lienholder be named as the beneficiary. Hence, the policy is likely to be held by the lienholder even though the client is required to pay the premiums.

3) **Inspect property tax records.** Many states assess property tax on certain fixed assets. Payment of taxes is evidence that the client has rights in the assets.

g. **Occurrence.** Did the transactions relating to property, plant, and equipment occur?

1) The auditor should test the authorization, execution, recording, and custody aspects of a sample of transactions.

h. **Classification and understandability.** Is the balance of property, plant, and equipment reflected on the balance sheet in the noncurrent section? Are adequate disclosures presented for methods of depreciation, commitments of assets, and capital lease terms?

1) **Read financial statements.** The auditor should determine that property, plant, and equipment is presented as a noncurrent asset. Depreciable assets and land should be reported at cost minus accumulated depreciation and cost, respectively. Notes to the financial statements should describe classes of assets, lease agreements, depreciation methods, and any property mortgaged or used as collateral for loans.

2) **Make inquiries of management about disclosures and other reporting issues.** Significant items should be included in the management representation letter.

Stop and review! You have completed the outline for this subunit. Study multiple-choice questions 1 through 9 beginning on page 431.

13.2 SUBSTANTIVE TESTING OF INVESTMENTS (AU 332)

1. **Scope**

a. The following balances are included in this audit plan:

1) **Noncurrent items.** These include (a) capital stock or other equity interests reported using the fair value or equity methods, (b) bonds and similar debt instruments, (c) loans and advances that are essentially investments, and (d) goodwill.

2) **Current items.** These include trading, held-to-maturity, and available-for-sale securities classified as current.

3) **Derivatives and hedges.** A derivative is an unperformed contract that results in cash flow between two counterparties based on (derived from) the change in some other indicator of value. Hedges are defensive strategies to protect an entity against the risk of adverse price or interest rate movements on certain assets, liabilities, or anticipated transactions.

4) **Revenues** generated from investments.

b. The appropriate classification of investments depends on management's **intent** in purchasing and holding the investment, on the entity's actual investment activities, and, for certain debt securities, on the entity's **ability** to hold the investment to maturity. The auditor should obtain an understanding of the process used by management to classify investments before determining the nature, timing, and extent of further audit procedures.

c. Special attention is given to derivatives and hedges in the standards. AU 332, *Auditing Derivative Instruments, Hedging Activities, and Investments in Securities*, provides guidance for planning and performing audit procedures to test assertions about these activities. This guidance applies to all debt and equity securities, including equity-based investments.

   1) An auditor may require **special skill or knowledge** regarding some assertions, for example, an understanding of GAAP for derivatives or of the measurement and disclosure issues for derivatives.

   2) The **assessment of inherent risk** for derivatives and securities depends on such factors as

      a) Their complexity,
      b) Management's objectives,
      c) Whether the transactions involve a cash exchange,
      d) The extent of the entity's experience with derivatives and securities,
      e) Whether a derivative is embedded in a host contract,
      f) External matters (credit risk, market risk, hedging ineffectiveness, legal risk, etc.),
      g) The entity's reliance on the expertise of outsiders, and
      h) Assumptions required by GAAP.

   3) The **assessment of control risk** requires considering whether controls, including those of service organizations, have been implemented that provide for

      a) Independent approval and monitoring of derivatives activities,
      b) Senior management's attention to situations in which limits are exceeded and divergences occur from approved derivatives strategies, and
      c) Reconciliations over the full range of derivatives.

   4) The **design of substantive procedures based on the risk assessments** addresses specific assertions about derivatives and securities. Examples are (a) confirmations with issuers, holders, or counterparties; (b) confirmation of settled and unsettled transactions; (c) physical inspection of contracts and other documentation; (d) analytical procedures; and (e) evaluation of whether presentation and disclosure requirements have been met, such as classification of securities and reporting of changes in fair value in either earnings or other comprehensive income.

      a) The auditor should determine whether **hedging activities** have been carried out in accordance with GAAP.

      b) The auditor also should gather evidence about **management's intent and ability**, for example, to (1) hold debt securities to maturity, (2) exercise significant influence over an equity-based investee, (3) enter into a forecasted transaction, or (4) dispose of securities classified as trading in the near term.

      c) Furthermore, the auditor should obtain written **management representations** confirming various aspects of derivatives and securities transactions.

2. **Testing Relevant Assertions.** The following is a standard audit plan for investments that tests relevant assertions (CAVE CROC):

   a. **Completeness.** Are all transactions affecting investments for the period reflected in the balance?

     1) **Perform analytical procedures.** Prior-period amounts held should be compared with current amounts. The expected return on investments held can be compared with actual recorded amounts.

     2) **Reconcile the subsidiary ledger with the control accounts.** The auditor should prepare a schedule from the subsidiary ledger and reconcile the amounts with the balances in the general ledger and financial statements.

     3) **Evaluate contracts and agreements.** The auditor should determine whether all securities, derivatives, and hedges have been identified and reported.

   b. **Accuracy.** Have the balances for specific accounts been recorded appropriately?

     1) **Recalculate interest revenue.** The auditor should determine that interest revenue, based on stated rates for recorded investments, has been properly recorded.

   c. **Valuation and allocation.** Are balances reported in accordance with GAAP?

     1) **Vouch recorded amounts for trading securities and available-for-sale securities to market quotations if available.** When market quotations are unavailable, the auditor can obtain fair-value estimates from broker-dealers and other third-party sources who derive the fair value of a security by using modeling or a similar technique. The auditor should evaluate the appropriateness of the valuation models and the variables and assumptions used in the model (AU 332).

     2) **Determine that unrealized gains and losses (changes in fair value) are properly accounted for.** Unrealized gains and losses on trading securities are included in earnings. Unrealized gains and losses on available-for-sale securities are reported in other comprehensive income until realized. (An exception is provided for all or part of the unrealized gain or loss on an available-for-sale security designated as hedged in a fair-value hedge.)

     3) **Vouch recorded costs for held-to-maturity securities to market quotations.** The entity should measure these securities at amortized cost only if it has the positive intent and ability to hold them to maturity. The auditor also should recalculate the premium or discount.

     4) **Determine that transfers between categories of investments are at fair value.**

     5) **Inspect relevant records and documents and make appropriate inquiries about nontemporary declines in fair value.** Individual available-for-sale or held-to-maturity securities may suffer a nontemporary decline in fair value below their cost basis. The securities should be written down to fair value reflecting the new cost basis, and the amount of the write-down should be included in earnings.

     6) **Obtain audited financial statements from the investees if investments are accounted for by the equity method.** The investment accounts should be based on percentage ownership in the investee and reported income or loss of the investee.

     7) **Evaluate goodwill for potential impairments.** If management cannot provide evidence to support the value, it should be written off.

   d. **Existence.** Do investments reported at the balance sheet date exist?

1) **Physically inspect and count securities in the client's possession.** Serial numbers should be recorded and compared with the entity's records. Inspection and counting also should be performed when counting other liquid assets (e.g., cash). The client's representative should be available to acknowledge that the securities have been returned intact.

2) **Confirm securities.** Confirmation requests may be made to the issuer, custodian, counterparty, or broker-dealer for unsettled transactions.

e. **Cutoff.** Have transactions relating to investments been recorded in the proper period?

1) **Test the cutoff.** The auditor should test transactions made near year end to ensure they are reflected in the proper period.

f. **Rights and obligations.** Does the entity own the reported investments?

1) **Trace dividend and interest revenue.** The auditor should determine that revenue has been properly recorded.

g. **Occurrence.** Did the transactions relating to investments occur?

1) **Vouch recorded costs to documentation.** The cost of recorded securities can be established by comparing recorded amounts with broker invoices, canceled checks, and other evidence of purchase.

h. **Classification and understandability.** Are balances related to investments reflected on the balance sheet in the current or noncurrent section depending on management expectations?

1) **Read financial statements.** Determine that individual trading, available-for-sale, and held-to-maturity securities are reported as current or noncurrent as appropriate. Determine whether derivatives, hedges, and other financial instruments are adequately described in the notes to the financial statements.

2) **Make inquiries of management about intentions to dispose of investments.** Classification often is based on the actions of management. The responses should be documented in the management representation letter. Also, the auditor should consider whether investment activities corroborate or conflict with management's stated intent.

Stop and review! You have completed the outline for this subunit. Study multiple-choice questions 10 through 19 beginning on page 433.

13.3 SUBSTANTIVE TESTING OF NONCURRENT DEBT

1. **Scope**

a. The following balances are included in this audit plan:

1) Noncurrent notes payable, mortgages payable, and bonds payable
2) Related interest expense

2. **Testing Relevant Assertions.** The following is a standard audit plan for noncurrent debt that tests relevant assertions (CAVE CROC):

a. **Completeness.** Are all transactions affecting noncurrent debt reflected in the balances for the period?

1) **Perform analytical procedures.** Prior-period amounts recorded should be compared with current amounts. A key procedure to detect unrecorded debt is to recalculate interest expense based on recorded debt and compare it with recorded interest expense. Significant unexpected interest expense recorded in the general ledger suggests the existence of unrecorded debt. The debt-to-equity ratio, which equals total liabilities divided by total equity, can also be calculated and compared with previous periods.

        2) **Reconcile the subsidiary ledger with the control accounts.** The auditor should prepare a schedule from the subsidiary ledger and reconcile the amounts with the balances in the general ledger and financial statements.

  b. **Accuracy.** Have the balances for specific accounts been recorded appropriately?

        1) **Make inquiries of management.** Questions about the sources and uses of the recorded debt may be addressed to management.

  c. **Valuation and allocation.** Are balances reported in accordance with GAAP?

        1) **Vouch recorded debt to debt instruments.** Bonds should be recorded at their face amounts, with separate recognition of premium or discount. Debt due in the next year should be reclassified as current (also a classification issue).

        2) **Test amortization.** Recorded debt premium or discount should be recalculated to determine that it is being amortized using appropriate GAAP (the interest method).

  d. **Existence.** Does noncurrent debt reported at the balance sheet date exist?

        1) **Confirm debt.** Debt is confirmed with investment bankers, lenders, and bond trustees. Noncurrent notes payable may be confirmed directly with the holders of the notes. See Study Unit 11, Subunit 2, for the AICPA Standard Form to Confirm Account Balance Information with Financial Institutions.

  e. **Cutoff.** Have transactions relating to noncurrent debt been recorded in the proper period?

        1) **Test the cutoff.** Consider transactions near year end.

  f. **Rights and obligations.** Does the entity owe the noncurrent debt?

        1) **Evaluate existing agreements.** The auditor should obtain evidence that the debt is the obligation of the auditee.

        2) **Examine any bond trust indenture.** The auditor should obtain evidence that the client is meeting the conditions of the contract and is in compliance with the law. Thus, the client should have obtained an attorney's opinion. The indenture contains information about contractual arrangements with bondholders, such as (a) the face amount of the bonds, (b) interest rates, (c) payment dates, (d) descriptions of collateral, (e) provisions for conversion or retirement, (f) trustee duties, and (g) sinking-fund requirements.

  g. **Occurrence.** Did the transactions relating to noncurrent debt occur?

        1) **Review contracts and agreements.** Debt transactions should be supported by appropriate documentation identifying (a) interest rates, (b) payment dates, (c) collateral, and (d) other terms.

  h. **Classification and understandability.** Are balances properly reflected in the balance sheet, is interest expense properly reported on the income statement, and are adequate disclosures provided?

        1) **Evaluate financial statements.** Determine that noncurrent and current debt are properly classified.

        2) **Inspect disclosures.** Appropriate disclosures should be made about the terms of the debt and collateral securing the debt.

Stop and review! You have completed the outline for this subunit. Study multiple-choice questions 20 and 21 on page 436.

13.4 SUBSTANTIVE TESTING OF EQUITY

1. **Scope**

   a. The following typical balances for a corporation are included in this audit plan:

      1) Common and preferred stock
      2) Additional paid-in capital
      3) Retained earnings
      4) Treasury stock
      5) Accumulated other comprehensive income

2. **Testing Relevant Assertions.** The following is a standard audit plan for equity that tests relevant assertions (CAVE CROC):

   a. **Completeness.** Are all transactions affecting equity included in the balances for the period?

      1) **Perform analytical procedures.** Prior-period amounts recorded should be compared with current amounts.
      2) **Reconcile the subsidiary ledger with the control accounts.** The auditor should prepare a schedule from the subsidiary ledger and reconcile the amounts with the balances in the general ledger and financial statements.

   b. **Accuracy.** Have the balances for the specific accounts been recorded appropriately?

      1) The auditor should inquire of management about the actions, activities, and balances related to equity.

   c. **Valuation and allocation.** Are balances reported in accordance with GAAP?

      1) **Trace entries to equity accounts.** The closing entries should be tested to determine that net income has been closed to retained earnings. Any designations (appropriations) of retained earnings should be traced to the related account.
      2) **Test sales of treasury stock.** "Gains" or "losses" on the sale of treasury stock are recognized directly in the equity section of the balance sheet, not in earnings.

   d. **Existence.** Do the shares reported as outstanding or treasury stock exist at the balance sheet date?

      1) **Confirm shares issued and outstanding with the registrar and transfer agent.** The auditor should have direct communication with external parties responsible for contact with the shareholders to request information about the number of shares issued and outstanding and payment of dividends.
      2) **Inspect stock certificates held in treasury.** Treasury stock should be counted.
      3) **Inspect stock certificate book.** If the client keeps its own stock records, the shares outstanding and stubs should be reconciled.

   e. **Cutoff.** Have transactions relating to equity been recorded in the proper period?

      1) The auditor should consider whether transactions near year end have been recognized in the proper period.

   f. **Rights and obligations.** Do equity balances reflect owners' interests?

      1) **Inspect the articles of incorporation and bylaws of the corporation.** These documents provide evidence about the legal status of the shareholders and their relationship(s) to the entity. The auditor should include copies in the working papers.

g. <u>Occurrence.</u> Did the transactions relating to equity occur?

   1) **Vouch entries to supporting documents.** Documentation should exist for each equity transaction.

h. **Classification and understandability.** Are balances appropriately presented and are adequate disclosures provided?

   1) **Read minutes of meetings of the board of directors.** Authorizations of actions relate to equity (e.g., issuances of additional shares, purchases or sales of treasury shares, and declarations of dividends) should be documented in the minutes. Many of these issues have implications for disclosure.

   2) **Inspect disclosures about treasury stock.** The auditor should determine the proper use of the method (cost or par value) to report treasury stock.

   3) **Search for restrictions.** Restrictions on retained earnings may arise from loans, agreements, or state law. The auditor should determine that disclosure is appropriate.

Stop and review! You have completed the outline for this subunit. Study multiple-choice questions 22 through 24 on page 437.

13.5 SUBSTANTIVE TESTING OF PAYROLL

1. **Scope**

  a. The following balances are included in this audit plan:

    1) Payroll expense
    2) Inventories (for manufacturing firms)
    3) Accrued payroll and vacation
    4) Payroll tax liability
    5) Pension costs and other post-employment benefit (OPEB) costs

  b. Payroll processing has traditionally included controls that have allowed the auditor to assess the RMM at a low level and thereby reduce the audit effort devoted to substantive testing. Most entities recognize that the benefits of controls exceed the costs related to the payroll processing system.

    1) One key control is a division of duties that includes the establishment of a **separate human resources department**. This control separates authorization from record keeping by the payroll department.

2. **Testing Relevant Assertions.** The following is a standard audit plan for payroll and related accounts that tests relevant assertions (CAVE CROC):

  a. **Completeness.** Are all transactions affecting payroll reflected in the balances for the period?

    1) **Perform analytical procedures.** The auditor should compare current expense with expectations from prior periods and management-prepared budgets from the beginning of the period with actual results. Total hours worked should be used to develop an expectation for total payroll expense. This expectation is compared with recorded expense. Industry percentages for labor-related ratios also should be compared with the client's results.

    2) **Reconcile payroll tax expense with payroll tax returns** (income tax, FICA, and unemployment taxes).

  b. **Accuracy.** Have the balances for specific accounts been recorded appropriately?

    1) **Make inquiries** of management. Questions include those relating to the reporting and disclosure of contractual arrangements with officers, union contracts, and pension and OPEB agreements.

c. **Valuation and allocation.** Are balances reported in accordance with GAAP?

    1) **Trace costs to inventories (for manufacturing firms).** The auditor should determine that they contain direct labor costs.

    2) **Recalculate pension and OPEB costs.** Appropriate amounts should have been recorded and funded based on the appropriate agreements.

d. **Existence.** Do the accounts and balances exist at the balance sheet date?

    1) **Observe the distribution of paychecks.** A surprise observation of the distribution will provide assurance that only bona fide employees are being paid.

e. **Cutoff.** Have transactions relating to payroll been recorded in the proper period?

    1) **Test payroll cutoff.** Amounts to be accrued for the period should be recalculated from the last payroll date to year end. Also, amounts should have been recorded as payroll expense and accrued payroll.

f. **Rights and obligations.** Are the assets (capitalized in inventory), expenses, and payables those of the entity?

    1) **Inspect canceled checks.** These checks indicate payment to employees, government, and others relating to payroll.

g. **Occurrence.** Did the transactions relating to payroll occur?

    1) **Vouch a sample of employee transactions.** These should be sampled from the payroll-related balances and compared with the supporting documentation, including approved time cards, time tickets, and notations in the human resources records. The purpose is to verify that employees worked the number of hours for which they were paid.

h. **Classification and understandability.** Are payroll costs properly reflected as an expense in the income statement (or properly allocated to inventory and cost of sales for manufacturing firms)? Are liabilities properly displayed as current or noncurrent on the balance sheet, and are disclosures presented adequately?

    1) **Read the financial statements and disclosures.** The auditor should determine the appropriate presentation of balances. Disclosures should include a description of accounting policies and pension-related transactions.

You have completed Study Units 11 through 13, which address the auditor's response to the assessment of material misstatement by applying substantive procedures. You should understand the relationship between management's assertions about the transactions, balances, and disclosures and the auditor's tests of the assertions. If you are having difficulty understanding this relationship or the role of management's assertions, review Study Unit 1, Subunit 2, which defines the assertions and the auditor's responsibility. Even if you have a solid understanding, a refreshed look at that material will likely help you.

Stop and review! You have completed the outline for this subunit. Study multiple-choice questions 25 through 30 beginning on page 438.

QUESTIONS

13.1 Substantive Testing of Property, Plant, and Equipment

1. Which of the following combinations of procedures would an auditor most likely perform to obtain evidence about fixed asset additions?

A. Inspecting documents and physically examining assets.

B. Recomputing calculations and obtaining written management representations.

C. Observing operating activities and comparing balances with prior-period balances.

D. Confirming ownership and corroborating transactions through inquiries of client personnel.

Answer (A) is correct. *(CPA, adapted)*
REQUIRED: The combination of procedures most likely to obtain evidence about fixed asset additions.
DISCUSSION: The auditor's direct observation of fixed assets is one means of determining whether additions have been made. Tracing to the detailed records determines whether additions have been recorded. Inspection of deeds, lease agreements, insurance policies, invoices, canceled checks, and tax notices may also reveal additions.
Answer (B) is incorrect. Recomputations are based on recorded amounts and will not reveal unrecorded additions. Answer (C) is incorrect. Analytical procedures may not detect additions offset by disposals. Answer (D) is incorrect. The auditor must become aware of additions before confirming ownership or corroborating transactions.

2. In testing plant and equipment balances, an auditor may inspect new additions listed on the analysis of plant and equipment. This procedure is designed to obtain evidence concerning relevant assertions about

	Existence	Classification and Understandability
A.	Yes	Yes
B.	Yes	No
C.	No	Yes
D.	No	No

Answer (B) is correct. *(CPA, adapted)*
REQUIRED: The relevant assertion(s), if any, tested by inspection of new additions of plant and equipment.
DISCUSSION: Assertions about existence address whether assets or liabilities of the entity exist at a particular date. Assertions about classification and understandability concern whether financial statement components are appropriately presented, described, and disclosed (AU 326). Thus, inspection by the auditor provides direct evidence that new plant and equipment assets exist but is irrelevant to the classification and understandability assertions. Reading the financial statements and related notes provides evidence about these assertions.

3. A weakness in internal control over recording retirements of equipment may cause an auditor to

A. Inspect certain items of equipment in the plant and trace those items to the accounting records.

B. Review the subsidiary ledger to ascertain whether depreciation was taken on each item of equipment during the year.

C. Trace additions to the "other assets" account to search for equipment that is still on hand but no longer being used.

D. Select certain items of equipment from the accounting records and locate them in the plant.

Answer (D) is correct. *(CPA, adapted)*
REQUIRED: The procedure performed as a result of ineffective control over equipment retirements.
DISCUSSION: Failure to record retirements results in overstating equipment in the subsidiary records because the physical assets are not in the entity's possession. Thus, vouching items from the accounting records by locating the physical assets they represent provides evidence of whether retirements are unrecorded.
Answer (A) is incorrect. The test is in the wrong direction to discover the failure to record retirements. Answer (B) is incorrect. Depreciation should not be taken on equipment that is no longer in possession of the entity. Answer (C) is incorrect. Equipment should be in the equipment account, not other assets. Thus, a search of additions to other assets provides no evidence of retirements to equipment.

4. Determining that proper amounts of depreciation are expensed appropriately provides assurance concerning relevant assertions about valuation and allocation and

A. Accuracy.

B. Completeness.

C. Rights and obligations.

D. Occurrence.

Answer (A) is correct. *(CPA, adapted)*
REQUIRED: The assertions tested by consideration of the amounts of depreciation that are expensed.
DISCUSSION: The accuracy and the valuation and allocation assertions are concerned with whether amounts have been recorded appropriately. Testing depreciation expense involves testing accuracy as well as valuation and allocation.

5. In performing a search for unrecorded retirements of fixed assets, an auditor most likely would

    A. Inspect the property ledger and the insurance and tax records, and then tour the client's facilities.

    B. Tour the client's facilities, and then inspect the property ledger and the insurance and tax records.

    C. Analyze the repair and maintenance account, and then tour the client's facilities.

    D. Tour the client's facilities, and then analyze the repair and maintenance account.

Answer (A) is correct. *(CPA, adapted)*
    REQUIRED: The step performed in a search for unrecorded retirements of fixed assets.
    DISCUSSION: In a search for unrecorded retirements, that is, a test of the completeness assertion, the auditor should first determine from the property ledger what assets are recorded and then tour the facilities to determine whether those assets are physically present. The completeness assertion addresses whether all transactions that should be presented (e.g., retirements) are included in the statements. However, in this case, the completeness assertion is closely related to the existence assertion.
    Answer (B) is incorrect. Touring the facilities and then inspecting the property ledger and insurance and tax records tests to determine whether existing assets are recorded. Answer (C) is incorrect. Analyzing the repair and maintenance account provides evidence as to whether capital assets have been inappropriately expensed. Answer (D) is incorrect. Analyzing the repair and maintenance account provides evidence as to whether capital assets have been inappropriately expensed.

6. Which of the following explanations most likely would satisfy an auditor who questions management about significant debits to the accumulated depreciation accounts?

    A. The estimated remaining useful lives of plant assets were revised upward.

    B. Plant assets were retired during the year.

    C. The prior year's depreciation expense was erroneously understated.

    D. Overhead allocations were revised at year end.

Answer (B) is correct. *(CPA, adapted)*
    REQUIRED: The explanation for significant debits to the accumulated depreciation accounts.
    DISCUSSION: Plant assets retired during the year should be removed from the records. The removal will result in a credit to plant assets and a debit to the related accumulated depreciation.
    Answer (A) is incorrect. Revision of useful lives upward does not affect accumulated depreciation at the time of the change. Answer (C) is incorrect. If depreciation expense is erroneously understated, credits to accumulated depreciation are expected. Answer (D) is incorrect. Revision of overhead allocations is a change in estimate affecting subsequent transactions only.

7. When auditing prepaid insurance, an auditor discovers that the original insurance policy on plant equipment is not available for inspection. The policy's absence most likely indicates the possibility of a(n)

    A. Insurance premium due but not recorded.

    B. Deficiency in the coinsurance provision.

    C. Lien on the plant equipment.

    D. Understatement of insurance expense.

Answer (C) is correct. *(CPA, adapted)*
    REQUIRED: The likely reason an insurance policy is not available for inspection.
    DISCUSSION: When liens are placed on equipment or property, the lienholder often requires that the assets be insured and that the lienholder be named as the beneficiary. Hence, the policy is likely to be held by the lienholder even though the client is required to pay the premiums.
    Answer (A) is incorrect. The premium has been paid and recorded as prepaid insurance. Answer (B) is incorrect. Coinsurance provisions require that the policy holder maintain coverage of a certain percentage of the value of the property (often 80-90%). Answer (D) is incorrect. The issue is not the recording of insurance, but the physical existence of the policy.

8. An auditor analyzes repairs and maintenance accounts primarily to obtain evidence in support of the relevant assertion that all

    A. Noncapitalizable expenditures for repairs and maintenance have been recorded in the proper period.

    B. Expenditures for property and equipment have been recorded in the proper period.

    C. Noncapitalizable expenditures for repairs and maintenance have been properly charged to expense.

    D. Expenditures for property and equipment have not been charged to expense.

Answer (D) is correct. *(CPA, adapted)*
    REQUIRED: The reason an auditor analyzes repairs and maintenance expense.
    DISCUSSION: The auditor should vouch significant debits from the repairs and maintenance expense account to determine whether any should have been capitalized.
    Answer (A) is incorrect. An improper cutoff of repairs and maintenance expenses is not typically a major risk. Answer (B) is incorrect. The repairs and maintenance expense accounts are not the appropriate sources of evidence regarding the cutoff of expenditures for property and equipment. Answer (C) is incorrect. Vouching additions to plant, property, and equipment provides evidence of whether any expense has been inappropriately charged as a capital item.

9. In auditing intangible assets, an auditor most likely would review or recompute amortization and determine whether the amortization period is reasonable in support of the relevant financial statement assertion of

    A. Valuation and allocation.

    B. Existence.

    C. Completeness.

    D. Rights and obligations.

Answer (A) is correct. *(CPA, adapted)*
    REQUIRED: The assertion tested in examining intangible assets and recomputing amortization.
    DISCUSSION: Amortization is an allocation process that the auditor tests by recomputing the amortization based upon the recorded assets and the useful lives.
    Answer (B) is incorrect. The existence assertion is that intangible assets exist. Answer (C) is incorrect. The completeness assertion is that the intangible assets that should be recorded are recorded. Answer (D) is incorrect. The rights and obligations assertion is that the entity controls the rights to the assets.

13.2 Substantive Testing of Investments (AU 332)

10. Which of the following pairs of accounts would an auditor most likely analyze on the same working paper?

    A. Notes receivable and interest income.

    B. Accrued interest receivable and accrued interest payable.

    C. Notes payable and notes receivable.

    D. Interest income and interest expense.

Answer (A) is correct. *(CPA, adapted)*
    REQUIRED: The pairs of accounts that an auditor most likely analyzes on the same working paper.
    DISCUSSION: The auditor analyzes information and presents the analysis for related accounts on the same working paper. Notes receivable and interest on them are such related accounts.
    Answer (B) is incorrect. Interest receivable and interest payable are independent of one another and are not likely to be analyzed on the same working paper. Answer (C) is incorrect. Notes payable and notes receivable are independent of one another and are not likely to be analyzed on the same working paper. Answer (D) is incorrect. Interest income and interest expense are independent of one another and are not likely to be analyzed on the same working paper.

11. An auditor would most likely verify the interest earned on bond investments by

    A. Vouching the receipt and deposit of interest checks.

    B. Confirming the bond interest rate with the issuer of the bonds.

    C. Recomputing the interest earned on the basis of face amount, interest rate, and period held.

    D. Testing internal controls relevant to cash receipts.

Answer (C) is correct. *(CPA, adapted)*
    REQUIRED: The method most likely used to verify bond interest earned.
    DISCUSSION: The audit plan for long-term investments includes making an independent computation of revenue (such as dividends and interest). For example, the auditor may use information from bond certificates (interest rates, payment dates, issue date, and face amount) to recalculate bond interest earned. This amount includes uncollected accruals.
    Answer (A) is incorrect. Vouching the receipt and deposit of interest checks does not consider accrued interest. Answer (B) is incorrect. Confirming the rate would not, by itself, verify interest earned, which must be recomputed. Answer (D) is incorrect. Verification of interest earned requires substantive testing, not tests of controls.

12. An auditor is testing the reasonableness of dividend income from investments in issuers. The auditor most likely would compute the amount that should have been received and recorded by the client by

    A. Reading the details of the board of directors' meetings.

    B. Confirming the details with the investees' registrars.

    C. Electronically accessing the details of dividend records on the Internet.

    D. Examining the details of the client's most recent cutoff bank statement.

Answer (C) is correct. *(CPA, adapted)*
    REQUIRED: The procedure for testing dividend income.
    DISCUSSION: Standard investment advisory services publish dividend records for all listed stocks. They show amounts and payment dates for dividend declarations and permit the auditor to independently recompute the client's reported dividend income.
    Answer (A) is incorrect. Reading the details of the board of directors' meetings may provide the auditor with evidence about the significant events of the entity, but not about the reasonableness of dividend income. Answer (B) is incorrect. Evidence about dividend income from investments in issuers can be obtained more efficiently from publicly available sources. Answer (D) is incorrect. Cutoff bank statements provide evidence about the client's deposits and disbursements made shortly after year end, not about investment income.

13. In performing a count of negotiable securities, an auditor records the details of the count on a security count worksheet. What other information is usually included on this worksheet?

A. An acknowledgment by a client representative that the securities were returned intact.

B. An analysis of realized gains and losses from the sale of securities during the year.

C. An evaluation of the client's internal control concerning physical access to the securities.

D. A description of the client's procedures that prevent the negotiation of securities by just one person.

Answer (A) is correct. *(CPA, adapted)*
REQUIRED: The information usually included on a security count worksheet.
DISCUSSION: A securities count worksheet should include a record of all the significant information from the securities, such as names, amounts, and interest rates. Also, to ensure a clear chain of custody, it should contain an acknowledgment by a client representative that the securities were returned intact when the count was complete.

14. A client has a large and active investment portfolio that is kept in a bank safe-deposit box. If the auditor is unable to count the securities at the balance sheet date, the auditor most likely will

A. Request the bank to confirm to the auditor the contents of the safe-deposit box at the balance sheet date.

B. Examine supporting evidence for transactions occurring during the year.

C. Count the securities at a subsequent date and confirm with the bank whether securities were added or removed since the balance sheet date.

D. Request the client to have the bank seal the safe-deposit box until the auditor can count the securities at a subsequent date.

Answer (D) is correct. *(CPA, adapted)*
REQUIRED: The procedure most likely performed when the auditor cannot count securities at the balance sheet date.
DISCUSSION: Securities should be inspected simultaneously with the verification of cash and the count of other liquid assets to prevent transfers among asset categories for the purpose of concealing a shortage. If this procedure is not possible but the securities are kept by a custodian in a bank safe-deposit box, the client may instruct the custodian that no one is to have access to the securities unless in the presence of the auditor. Thus, when the auditor finally inspects the securities, (s)he may conclude that they represent what was on hand at the balance sheet date.
Answer (A) is incorrect. The bank does not have access to the contents of the client's safe-deposit box. Answer (B) is incorrect. Supporting evidence for transactions occurring during the year is not a substitute for inspection of the securities. Answer (C) is incorrect. The bank does not have access to the contents of the client's safe-deposit box.

15. An auditor testing long-term investments would ordinarily use analytical procedures to ascertain the reasonableness of the

A. Existence of unrealized gains or losses.

B. Completeness of recorded investment income.

C. Classification as available-for-sale or trading securities.

D. Valuation of trading securities.

Answer (B) is correct. *(CPA, adapted)*
REQUIRED: The use of analytical procedures when an auditor tests long-term investments.
DISCUSSION: The auditor may develop expectations regarding the completeness assertion for recorded investment income from stocks by using dividend records published by standard investment advisory services to recompute dividends received. Interest income from bond investments can be calculated from interest rates and payment dates noted on the certificates. Income from equity-based investments can be estimated from audited financial statements of the investees. Thus, applying an expected rate of return to the net investment amount may be an effective means of estimating total investment income.
Answer (A) is incorrect. Unrealized gains or losses are dependent on the fair values of specific securities and cannot be calculated based on plausible relationships among the data. Answer (C) is incorrect. Available-for-sale securities may meet the definition of current assets. Answer (D) is incorrect. Individual trading securities may meet the definition of current assets.

16. In confirming with an outside agent, such as a financial institution, that the agent is holding investment securities in the client's name, an auditor most likely gathers evidence in support of relevant financial statement assertions about existence or occurrence and

    A. Valuation and allocation.

    B. Rights and obligations.

    C. Completeness.

    D. Classification and understandability.

Answer (B) is correct. *(CPA, adapted)*

    REQUIRED: The assertion tested by confirming investments to determine if they are in the client's name.

    DISCUSSION: Confirmations may be designed to test any financial statement assertion (AU 330). However, a given confirmation request does not test all assertions equally well. For example, if the issue is whether securities are being held in the client's name by an outside agent, the completeness assertion with regard to the investment account is not adequately addressed by a confirmation request. Other agents may be holding securities for the client. Moreover, the agent may be holding other securities not specified in the request. Thus, the request tends to be most effective for testing the existence (whether the assets exist at a given date) assertion and the rights (whether the client has a specified ownership interest in the assets) assertion.

17. An auditor inspects a client's investment records to determine that any transfers between categories of investments have been properly recorded. The primary purpose of this procedure is to obtain evidence concerning relevant financial statement assertions about

    A. Rights and obligations, and existence.

    B. Valuation and allocation, and rights and obligations.

    C. Existence or occurrence, and classification and understandability.

    D. Classification and understandability, and valuation and allocation.

Answer (D) is correct. *(CPA, adapted)*

    REQUIRED: The assertions tested by inspecting reclassification of investments.

    DISCUSSION: Auditing standards state that assertions about classification and understandability address whether the presentation, description, and disclosure of financial information are in conformity with GAAP. For example, GAAP require that a debt security be reclassified as available for sale if the entity (1) does not have the positive intent and ability to hold it to maturity but (2) does not intend to sell it in the near term. Inspecting the client's records just prior to and just after year end could help the auditor determine whether investment classifications are appropriate. Assertions about valuation address whether reported amounts conform with GAAP. Classification affects valuation. For example, held-to-maturity securities are measured at cost, and available-for-sale and trading securities are measured at fair value. Thus, inspecting transfers between categories also helps determine whether the investments are recorded at proper amounts (AU 332).

18. To test the valuation assertion when auditing an investment accounted for by the equity method, an auditor most likely would

    A. Inspect the stock certificates evidencing the investment.

    B. Examine the audited financial statements of the investee company.

    C. Review the broker's advice or canceled check for the investment's acquisition.

    D. Obtain market quotations from financial newspapers or periodicals.

Answer (B) is correct. *(CPA, adapted)*

    REQUIRED: The procedure to test the valuation assertion for an equity-based investment.

    DISCUSSION: The equity method recognizes undistributed income arising from an investment in an investee. Under the equity method, investor income is recorded as the investee reports income. Consequently, the audited financial statements of the investee provide the auditor with the undistributed income from the investee.

    Answer (A) is incorrect. Inspection of stock certificates provides evidence about existence, not valuation. Answer (C) is incorrect. Reviewing the broker's advice or canceled check provides evidence about rights. Answer (D) is incorrect. Equity-based investments are not accounted for at fair value.

19. Auditors may need to plan and perform auditing procedures for financial statement assertions about derivatives and hedging activities. Which of the following substantive procedures most clearly tests the completeness assertion about derivatives?

A. Assessing the reasonableness of the use of an option-pricing model.

B. Determining whether changes in the fair value of derivatives designated and qualifying as hedging instruments have been reported in earnings or in other comprehensive income.

C. Requesting counterparties to provide information about them, such as whether side agreements have been made.

D. Physically inspecting the derivative contract.

Answer (C) is correct. *(Publisher, adapted)*
REQUIRED: The substantive procedure that most clearly tests the completeness assertion about derivatives.
DISCUSSION: An audit of the completeness assertion addresses whether balances and transactions related to derivatives and hedging activities that should be recorded are recorded. A substantive procedure for the completeness assertion about derivatives and hedging activities is a request to the counterparty to a derivative for information about it, for example, whether an agreement exists to repurchase securities sold or whether side agreements have been made.
Answer (A) is incorrect. Assessing the reasonableness of the use of an option-pricing model tests the valuation assertion. Answer (B) is incorrect. Determining whether changes in the fair value of derivatives designated and qualifying as hedging instruments have been reported in earnings or in other comprehensive income tests the classification and understandability assertion. Answer (D) is incorrect. Physically inspecting the derivative contract tests the existence assertion.

13.3 Substantive Testing of Noncurrent Debt

20. An audit plan for noncurrent debt should include steps that require

A. Examining bond trust indentures.

B. Inspecting the accounts payable subsidiary ledger.

C. Investigating credits to the bond interest income account.

D. Verifying the existence of the bondholders.

Answer (A) is correct. *(CPA, adapted)*
REQUIRED: The procedure to be included in the audit plan for noncurrent debt.
DISCUSSION: The bond trust indenture contains information about contractual arrangements made with bondholders, such as (1) the face amount of the bonds, (2) interest rates, (3) payment dates, (4) descriptions of collateral, (5) provisions for conversion or retirement, (6) trustee duties, and (7) sinking fund requirements. The auditor should examine any bond trust indenture to determine that the client is meeting the conditions of the contract and is in compliance with the law.
Answer (B) is incorrect. Accounts payable are current liabilities, not noncurrent debt. Answer (C) is incorrect. Credits to bond interest income do not pertain to noncurrent debt (income relates to investments, not debt). Answer (D) is incorrect. The existence of bondholders is implied by the reporting of bonded debt.

21. In auditing for unrecorded noncurrent bonds payable, an auditor most likely will

A. Perform analytical procedures on the bond premium and discount accounts.

B. Examine documentation of assets purchased with bond proceeds for liens.

C. Compare interest expense with the bond payable amount for reasonableness.

D. Confirm the existence of individual bondholders at year end.

Answer (C) is correct. *(CPA, adapted)*
REQUIRED: The appropriate procedure for testing noncurrent bonds payable.
DISCUSSION: The recorded interest expense should reconcile with the outstanding bonds payable. If interest expense appears excessive relative to the recorded bonds payable, unrecorded noncurrent liabilities may exist.
Answer (A) is incorrect. Performing analytical procedures on bond premium and discount are not likely to uncover unrecorded payables. Answer (B) is incorrect. The examination of documentation related to asset additions is considered in the audit of assets, not bonds payable. Answer (D) is incorrect. The greatest risk is that the bonds payable balance is not complete.

13.4 Substantive Testing of Equity

22. During an audit of a company's equity accounts, the auditor determines whether restrictions have been imposed on retained earnings resulting from loans, agreements, or state law. This audit procedure most likely is intended to verify relevant assertion about

- A. Existence.
- B. Completeness.
- C. Valuation and allocation.
- D. Classification and understandability.

Answer (D) is correct. *(CPA, adapted)*
REQUIRED: The assertion that the auditor tests relative to restrictions on retained earnings.
DISCUSSION: The classification and understandability assertion concerns the appropriate presentation and description of financial information and the clarity of disclosures. Hence, when restrictions have been placed on retained earnings, the auditor should determine that they are properly disclosed in the financial statements.
Answer (A) is incorrect. Restrictions on retained earnings have little relevance to the existence assertion. Answer (B) is incorrect. Restrictions on retained earnings have little relevance to the completeness assertion. Answer (C) is incorrect. Restrictions on retained earnings have little relevance to the valuation assertion.

23. An auditor usually obtains evidence of a company's equity transactions by reviewing its

- A. Minutes of board of directors meetings.
- B. Transfer agent's records.
- C. Canceled stock certificates.
- D. Treasury stock certificate book.

Answer (A) is correct. *(CPA, adapted)*
REQUIRED: The source of evidence about equity transactions.
DISCUSSION: Equity transactions are typically few in number and large in amount. They require authorization by the board of directors. Thus, an auditor reviews the minutes of the board meetings to identify transactions.
Answer (B) is incorrect. Although the auditor might confirm certain transactions with the client's transfer agent, the agent's records are not typically made available to the auditor. Answer (C) is incorrect. Canceled stock certificates represent only those shares that were retired. Answer (D) is incorrect. Treasury stock records include only those transactions involving reacquisition and resale of the entity's own stock.

24. When a client's company does not maintain its own stock records, the auditor should obtain written confirmation from the transfer agent and registrar concerning

- A. Restrictions on the payment of dividends.
- B. The number of shares issued and outstanding.
- C. Guarantees of preferred stock liquidation value.
- D. The number of shares subject to agreements to repurchase.

Answer (B) is correct. *(CPA, adapted)*
REQUIRED: The information confirmed by the transfer agent and registrar.
DISCUSSION: The independent stock registrar is a financial institution employed to prevent improper issuances of stock, especially over-issuances. The transfer agent maintains detailed shareholder records and facilitates transfer of shares. Both are independent and reliable sources of evidence concerning total shares issued and outstanding.
Answer (A) is incorrect. The payment of dividends is confirmed, but dividend restrictions are found in the articles of incorporation, bylaws, and minutes of directors' and shareholders' meetings. Answer (C) is incorrect. Guarantees of preferred stock liquidation value are not made by the transfer agent and registrar. Answer (D) is incorrect. The number of shares subject to agreements to repurchase is not the concern of the transfer agent and registrar.

13.5 Substantive Testing of Payroll

25. An auditor vouched data for a sample of employees in a payroll register to approved clock card data to provide assurance that

A. Payments to employees are computed at authorized rates.

B. Employees work the number of hours for which they are paid.

C. Separation of duties exist between the preparation and distribution of the payroll.

D. Internal controls relating to unclaimed payroll checks are operating effectively.

Answer (B) is correct. *(CPA, adapted)*
REQUIRED: The purpose of vouching payroll register information to approved clock card data.
DISCUSSION: To test that payroll events actually occurred, an auditor vouches a sample of employee transactions recorded in the payroll-related balances to supporting documentation, including approved time cards, time tickets, and notations in personnel records. The purpose is to verify that employees work the hours for which they are paid.
Answer (A) is incorrect. The auditor compares the pay rates used in calculating payments to employees with the authorized rates in the personnel files to determine whether they were authorized. Answer (C) is incorrect. The auditor tests separation of duties by inquiry and observation. Answer (D) is incorrect. The auditor observes the activities of the treasurer to determine whether unclaimed payroll checks were being properly controlled.

26. When the risk of material misstatement is assessed as low for assertions related to payroll, substantive tests of payroll balances most likely would be limited to applying analytical procedures and

A. Observing the distribution of paychecks.

B. Footing and crossfooting the payroll register.

C. Inspecting payroll tax returns.

D. Recalculating payroll accruals.

Answer (D) is correct. *(CPA, adapted)*
REQUIRED: The audit procedure for payroll when the RMM is low.
DISCUSSION: When controls are judged to be effective, the auditor's procedures are typically limited to analytical procedures and testing for completeness and cutoff of the year-end accruals.
Answer (A) is incorrect. The auditor considers the observation of the distribution of the paychecks if the RMM is high. Answer (B) is incorrect. Effective controls should provide assurance of proper reporting. Analytical procedures also should indicate likely misstatements. Answer (C) is incorrect. Effective controls should provide assurance of proper reporting. Analytical procedures also should indicate likely misstatements.

27. An auditor most likely would perform substantive tests of details on payroll transactions and balances when

A. Cutoff tests indicate a substantial amount of accrued payroll expense.

B. The assessed risk of material misstatement relative to payroll transactions is low.

C. Analytical procedures indicate unusual fluctuations in recurring payroll entries.

D. Accrued payroll expense consists primarily of unpaid commissions.

Answer (C) is correct. *(CPA, adapted)*
REQUIRED: The situation in which the auditor most likely will perform tests of details on payroll transactions and balances.
DISCUSSION: The auditor should evaluate significant unexpected differences revealed by analytical procedures. The first step is to reconsider the methods and factors used in developing the expectations and to make inquiries of management. If a suitable explanation is not received, additional procedures to investigate the differences are necessary.
Answer (A) is incorrect. A substantial amount of accrued payroll expense is not an abnormal condition. Answer (B) is incorrect. A low assessed RMM may permit the auditor to devote less effort to substantive tests. Answer (D) is incorrect. The existence of unpaid earned commissions provides no indication of a misstatement.

28. In auditing payroll when control risk is assessed as low, an auditor most likely will

A. Verify that checks representing unclaimed wages are mailed.

B. Trace individual employee deductions to entity journal entries.

C. Observe entity employees during a payroll distribution.

D. Compare payroll costs with entity standards or budgets.

Answer (D) is correct. *(CPA, adapted)*
REQUIRED: The procedure most likely performed during the audit of payroll.
DISCUSSION: Comparing payroll costs with budgeted amounts is a standard analytical procedure that is performed in most audits of payroll.
Answer (A) is incorrect. Checks representing unclaimed wages should be maintained by the CFO until claimed by the appropriate employees. Answer (B) is incorrect. The individual employee deductions do not result in entity journal entries, but cumulative journal entries record the sum of the payroll. Answer (C) is incorrect. Observation of payroll distribution is not necessary when the RMM is low.

29. An auditor most likely increases substantive tests of payroll when

A. Payroll is extensively audited by the state government.

B. Payroll expense is substantially higher than in the prior year.

C. Overpayments are discovered in performing tests of details.

D. Employees complain to management about too much overtime.

Answer (C) is correct. *(CPA, adapted)*
REQUIRED: The situation in which the auditor most likely will extend substantive tests of payroll.
DISCUSSION: During the application of substantive tests, the auditor may decide to extend the tests when unexpected findings (e.g., overpayments) are made. The purpose is to determine the extent of any fraud.
Answer (A) is incorrect. When payroll is audited by external parties, the auditor may decide to do less testing in the area. Answer (B) is incorrect. Although an analytical procedure in the planning stage might suggest more testing, the question indicates that substantive tests have already begun. Answer (D) is incorrect. Employees' concern about too much overtime is not likely to affect the auditor's testing of the payroll.

30. Which of the following circumstances most likely will cause an auditor to suspect an employee payroll fraud scheme?

A. There are significant unexplained variances between standard and actual labor cost.

B. Payroll checks are disbursed by the same employee each payday.

C. Employee time cards are approved by individual departmental supervisors.

D. A separate payroll bank account is maintained on an imprest basis.

Answer (A) is correct. *(CPA, adapted)*
REQUIRED: The circumstance most likely to cause the auditor to suspect an employee payroll fraud scheme.
DISCUSSION: Analytical procedures, such as variance analysis, alert the auditor when actual results were not anticipated. Thus, the auditor should consider the possibility that payroll is fraudulently overstated.
Answer (B) is incorrect. The payroll checks should be disbursed by the paymaster each pay period. Answer (C) is incorrect. Supervisors should approve individual time cards. Answer (D) is incorrect. A separate payroll account using an imprest basis provides additional control over payroll.

Use the additional questions in Gleim **CPA Test Prep Online** to create Test Sessions that emulate Prometric!

13.6 PRACTICE SIMULATION

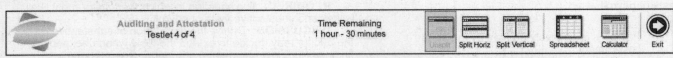

Auditing and Attestation
Testlet 4 of 4

Time Remaining
1 hour - 30 minutes

Unsplit | Split Horiz | Split Vertical | Spreadsheet | Calculator | Exit

DIRECTIONS

Note: If you believe you have encountered a software malfunction, report it to the test center staff immediately.

Navigation

To navigate from task to task, use the controls at the bottom of the screen. Click on the **Next** button to advance to the next task, or the **Previous** button to go to the previous task. To go directly to any task, click on its number.

= Reminder   Directions 1 2 3 4 5 6 7   ◀ Previous   Next ▶

If you would like a reminder to revisit a task, or want to indicate that you are finished with it, click on the reminder flag below the task number. To clear the flag, click on it again. Reminder flags are for your use only – they do not contribute to your score.

Tabs

In this part of the examination, you will be asked to complete various tasks. Every task has one or more **Work Tabs**. Some tasks have one or more **Information Tabs**, others may have none. Every task has a **Help** tab.

If a task has **Information Tabs**, you may use the information in them to complete your responses in the **Work Tabs**.

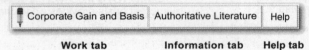

Corporate Gain and Basis | Authoritative Literature | Help

Work tab   Information tab   Help tab

Work Tabs:
- **Work Tabs** are identified with a pencil icon. This is where your responses are expected.
- Each task has one or more **Work Tabs**.
- **Work Tabs** contain directions for completing the task – be sure to read these directions carefully.
- The **Work Tab** name in the example above is for illustration only – yours will differ.
- You must complete all of the **Work Tabs** in each task to receive full credit.

Information Tabs:
- The Authoritative Literature will be provided in all tasks in the AUD, FAR, and REG sections for your reference.
- Your simulation may have one or more additional **Information Tabs**. Like the Authoritative Literature tabs, **Information Tabs** do not have a pencil icon.
- If your task has additional **Information Tabs**, go through each to familiarize yourself with the task content.

Help Tab:
- The **Help Tab** provides assistance with the exam software that is used in this task. For example, if the task is to compose a memorandum, **Help** will provide information about the word processor.

The Toolbar

The toolbar at the top of the screen shows the amount of time remaining for you to complete the tasks. In addition, the following tools are available. Note that only the Exit button is displayed when Directions are visible - the others will appear when you begin the tasks.

Unsplit | Split Horiz | Split Vertical

Click on these buttons to split or unsplit the screen. You can split the screen vertically or horizontally.

Calculator

Click on this button to display the calculator; click on it again to hide the calculator. To move the calculator, click on the calculator title bar and drag the calculator to the desired location.

Spreadsheet

Click on this button to use the spreadsheet; click on it again to hide the spreadsheet. To move the spreadsheet, click on the the spreadsheet title bar and drag the spreadsheet to the desired location.

Exit

Click on this button to go on to the next part of the examination. You must complete all of the tasks to receive full credit. Once you click on **Exit** and confirm the action, you will NOT be able to return to this testlet.

= Reminder   Directions 1 2 3 4 5 6   ◀ Previous   Next ▶

| Relevant Assertions and Substantive Audit Procedures | Authoritative Literature | Help |

Select from the list provided the most likely assertion being tested with each audit procedure in the table below. Each choice may be used once, more than once, or not at all.

Substantive Audit Procedure	Answer
1. The auditor tested the equipment balance by evaluating large debits recorded in repairs and maintenance to determine whether any should have been capitalized.	
2. The auditor tested depreciation related to equipment to determine that it is generally accepted and applied consistently.	
3. The auditor examined titles related to vehicles reported in the equipment account.	
4. The auditor determined that equipment was displayed in the noncurrent asset category on the balance sheet.	
5. The auditor applied an analytical procedure to noncurrent debt by comparing the current year's balance with that of the previous year.	
6. The auditor examined purchase transactions for equipment for several days before and after year end to determine that they were recorded in the proper year.	
7. The auditor reconciled the amounts of debt in the subsidiary ledger with the total in the general ledger account.	
8. The auditor confirmed shares of common stock issued and outstanding with the registrar and transfer agent of the client.	
9. The auditor determined that restrictions on the issuance of dividends were properly described in the financial statement notes.	
10. The auditor determined that the loss associated with the sale of treasury stock was appropriately calculated.	

Relevant Assertion
A) Completeness
B) Accuracy
C) Valuation and allocation
D) Existence
E) Cutoff
F) Rights and obligations
G) Occurrence
H) Classification and understandability

Indicate by checking the appropriate box whether each statement about the audit of securities is correct or incorrect. None of the statements relate to securities being held as a hedge.

Statement	Correct	Incorrect
1. The auditor should determine that trading securities are recorded at cost at the balance sheet date.		
2. The auditor should determine that the client has both the positive intent and ability to hold held-to-maturity securities.		
3. The auditor should determine that available-for-sale securities are measured at fair value.		
4. The auditor expects a client to classify common stock as held-to-maturity.		
5. The auditor should determine that a transfer from the held-to-maturity to the trading category is made at fair value.		
6. The auditor should consider obtaining audited financial statements from an investee if investments are accounted for by the equity method.		
7. The auditor typically concludes that market quotations are the best evidence of fair-value estimates.		
8. The auditor expects premium or discount for available-for-sale securities to be amortized.		
9. The auditor expects to find a nontemporary decline in the value of held-to-maturity securities reflected in current earnings.		
10. The auditor should determine that holding gains on an available-for-sale security are included in other comprehensive income.		

Relevant Assertions | Authoritative Literature | Help

This question has a multiple-choice format that requires you to select the correct response from a drop-down list. Write the answer in the shaded column next to the audit assertion.

Items 1 through 10 represent relevant financial statement assertions for the investments, accounts receivable, and property and equipment accounts. Select from the list provided the substantive audit procedure that primarily addresses each relevant assertion. Select only one procedure for each assertion. Each procedure may be selected only once or not at all.

Relevant Assertions for Investments	Answer
1. Investments are properly presented and described.	
2. Recorded investments represent investments actually owned at the balance sheet date.	
3. Available-for-sale securities are properly measured at fair value at the balance sheet date.	

Substantive Procedures – Investments

A) Trace investment transactions to minutes of the board of directors' meetings to determine that transactions were properly authorized.

B) Obtain positive confirmations as of the balance sheet date of investments held by independent custodians.

C) Determine that any other-than-temporary impairments of the price of investments have been properly recorded.

D) Verify that available-for-sale securities are properly classified as current or noncurrent.

Relevant Assertions for Accounts Receivable	Answer
4. Accounts receivable represent amounts owed to the entity up to the balance sheet date.	
5. The entity has a legal right to all accounts receivable at the balance sheet date.	
6. Accounts receivable are stated at net realizable value.	
7. Accounts receivable are properly presented and described in the financial statements.	

Substantive Procedures – Accounts Receivable

A) Review the aged trial balance for significant past-due accounts.

B) Review the accounts receivable trial balance for amounts due from officers and employees.

C) Perform sales cutoff tests to obtain assurance that sales transactions and corresponding entries for inventories and cost of goods sold are recorded in the same and proper period.

D) Review loan agreements for indications of whether accounts receivable have been factored or pledged.

Relevant Assertions for Property and Equipment	Answer
8. The entity has a legal right to property and equipment acquired during the year.	
9. Recorded property and equipment represent assets that actually exist at the balance sheet date.	
10. Net property and equipment are properly measured at the balance sheet date.	

Substantive Procedures – Property and Equipment

A) Review the provision for depreciation expense and determine that depreciable lives and methods used in the current year are consistent with those used in the prior year.

B) Physically examine all major property and equipment additions.

C) Examine deeds and title insurance certificates.

Working Paper Deficiencies	Authoritative Literature	Help

The following noncurrent debt working paper (indexed K-1) was prepared by client personnel and audited by AA, an audit assistant, during the calendar year Year 2 audit of American Widgets, Inc., a continuing audit client. The engagement supervisor is reviewing the working papers thoroughly.

Index	K-1	
	Initials	Date
Prepared by	AA	3/22/Yr. 3
Approved by		

American Widgets, Inc.
WORKING PAPERS
December 31, Year 2

Lender	Interest Rate	Payment Terms	Collateral	Balance Year 1	Year 2 Borrowings	Year 2 Reductions	Balance 12/31/Yr. 2	Interest Paid to	Accrued Interest Payable 12/31/Yr. 2	Comments
⊕ First Commercial Bank	12%	Interest only on 25th of month, principal due in full 1/1/Yr. 6 no prepayment penalty	Inventories	$ 50,000 √	$300,000 A 1/31/Yr. 2	$100,000 ⊕ 6/30/Yr. 2	$ 250,000 CX	12/25/Yr. 2	$2,500 NR	Dividend of $80,000 paid 9/2/Yr. 2 (WP N-3) violates a provision of the debt agreement, which thereby permits lender to demand immediate payment; lender has refused to waive this violation
⊕ Lender's Capital Corp.	Prime plus 1%	Interest only on last day of month, principal due in full 3/5/Yr. 4	2nd Mortgage on Park St. Building	100,000 √	50,000 A 2/29/Yr. 2	—	200,000 C	12/31/Yr. 2	—	Prime rate was 8% to 9% during the year
⊕ Gigantic Building & Loan Assoc.	12%	$5,000 principal plus interest due on 5th of month, due in full 12/31/Yr. 13	1st Mortgage on Park St. Building	720,000 √	—	60,000 ⊖	660,000 C	12/5/Yr. 2	5,642 R	Reclassification entry for current portion proposed (See RJE-3)
⊕ J. Lott, majority stockholder	0%	Due in full 12/31/Yr. 5	Unsecured	300,000 √	—	100,000 N 12/31/Yr. 2	200,000 C	—	—	Borrowed additional $100,000 from J. Lott on 1/7/Yr. 3
				$1,170,000 √ F	$350,000 F	$260,000 F	$1,310,000 T/B F		$8,142 T/B F	

Interest costs from noncurrent debt

Interest expense for year	$ 281,333	T/B
Average loan balance outstanding	$1,406,667	R

Five year maturities (for disclosure purposes)

Year end	12/31/Yr. 3	$ 60,000
	12/31/Yr. 4	260,000
	12/31/Yr. 5	260,000
	12/31/Yr. 6	310,000
	12/31/Yr. 7	60,000
	Thereafter	360,000
		$1,310,000

Tickmark Legend

F   Readded, foots correctly
C   Confirmed without exception, W/P K-2
CX   Confirmed with exception, W/P K-3
NR   Does not recompute correctly
A   Agreed to loan agreement, validated bank deposit ticket, and board of directors authorization, W/P W-7
⊖   Agreed to canceled checks and lender's monthly statements
N   Agreed to cash disbursements journal and canceled check dated 12/31/Yr. 2, clearing 1/8/Yr. 3
T/B   Traced to working trial balance
√   Agree to 12/31/Yr. 1 working papers
⊘   Agreed interest rate, term, and collateral to copy of note and loan agreement
⊕   Agreed to cancelled check and board of directors' authorization, W/P W-7

Overall Conclusions

Noncurrent debt, accrued interest payable, and interest expense are correct and complete at 12/31/Yr. 2

-- Continued on next page --

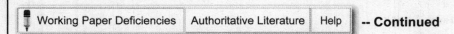

-- **Continued**

Indicate by checking the appropriate box whether the statements about potential deficiencies or issues in the working paper are true or false.

Deficiencies	True	False
1. The working paper will be approved by the supervisor as presented.		
2. There is no indication of any follow-up on the identified error in the accrued interest payable computation.		
3. There is no indication whether the confirmation exception was resolved.		
4. The loan with the unwaived violation of a provision of the debt agreement is misclassified as noncurrent.		
5. The liability activities of Lender's Capital Corp. and the working paper totals do not crossfoot.		
6. Interest is appropriately imputed on the 0% stockholder loan.		
7. The high average interest rate was noted and investigated.		
8. The working paper does not support the overall conclusions expressed.		
9. The tickmark "R" is used but not explained in the tickmark legend.		
10. Collateral is listed on the working paper.		

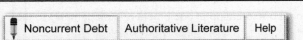

Noncurrent Debt   Authoritative Literature   Help

Select from the list provided the substantive audit procedure that most effectively tests each assertion about noncurrent debt.

Assertion	Answer
1. Occurrence	
2. Cutoff	
3. Accuracy	
4. Classification and understandability	
5. Valuation and allocation	
6. Completeness	
7. Existence	
8. Rights and obligations	

Substantive Procedure
A) Inspect disclosures
B) Perform analytical procedures
C) Request information from SEC
D) Trace dividend revenue
E) Test amortization
F) Make inquiries of management
G) Consider year-end transactions
H) Examine bond indentures
I) Vouch to contracts
J) Confirm debt
K) Recalculate interest revenue

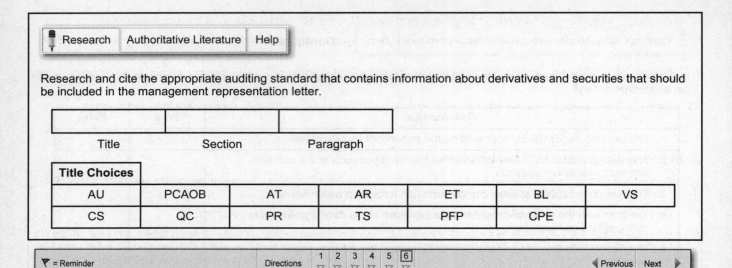

Research and cite the appropriate auditing standard that contains information about derivatives and securities that should be included in the management representation letter.

Title	Section	Paragraph

Title Choices

AU	PCAOB	AT	AR	ET	BL	VS
CS	QC	PR	TS	PFP	CPE	

▼ = Reminder   Directions   1 2 3 4 5 [6]   ◄ Previous   Next ►

Unofficial Answers

1. Relevant Assertions and Substantive Audit Procedures (10 Gradable Items)

1. A) Completeness. Evaluating large debits recorded in repairs and maintenance to determine whether any should have been capitalized tests the completeness assertion for the equipment balance.

2. C) Valuation and allocation. Testing depreciation to determine that the methods are generally accepted and applied consistently relates primarily to the valuation and allocation assertion.

3. F) Rights and obligations. Examining titles related to vehicles reported in the equipment account relates to ownership (rights).

4. H) Classification and understandability. The proper balance sheet presentation of equipment relates primarily to the classification assertion.

5. A) Completeness. Analytical procedures primarily test the completeness assertion.

6. E) Cutoff. Examining purchase transactions for equipment for several days before and after year end to determine that they were recorded in the proper year tests cutoff.

7. A) Completeness. Reconciling the amounts of debt in the subsidiary ledger with the total in the general ledger account is a primary test of completeness.

8. D) Existence. Confirmations primarily test the existence assertion.

9. H) Classification and understandability. Determining that restrictions on the issuance of dividends were properly described in the financial statement notes relates primarily to the assertion of understandability.

10. B) Accuracy. Verifying calculations primarily tests the accuracy assertion.

2. Audit of Investments (10 Gradable Items)

1. Incorrect. The auditor should determine that trading securities are recorded at fair value at the balance sheet date.

2. Correct. The auditor should determine that the client has both the positive intent and ability to hold held-to-maturity securities.

3. Correct. The auditor should determine that available-for-sale securities are measured at fair value.

4. Incorrect. The auditor expects a client to classify common stock of other entities as trading or available-for-sale securities.

5. Correct. The auditor should determine that a transfer from the held-to-maturity to trading category is made at fair value.

6. Correct. The auditor should consider obtaining audited financial statements from an investee if investments are accounted for by the equity method.

7. <u>Correct.</u> The auditor typically concludes that market quotations are the best evidence of fair-value estimates.

8. <u>Incorrect.</u> The auditor expects amortization of premium or discount for available-for-sale securities only if they are debt securities.

9. <u>Correct.</u> The auditor expects to find a nontemporary decline in the value of held-to-maturity securities reflected in current earnings.

10. <u>Correct.</u> The auditor should determine that holding gains on an available-for-sale security are included in other comprehensive income.

3. Relevant Assertions (10 Gradable Items)

1. <u>D)</u> Classification of available-for-sale securities relates to the assertion about proper presentation and description of investments (the classification and understandability assertion).

2. <u>B)</u> Confirmations are most effective for the existence and rights and obligation assertions.

3. <u>C)</u> Impairment of investments means that fair value is less than the recorded amount. If available-for-sale securities are subject to an other-than-temporary impairment, their cost basis is written down, and the change is included in earnings, not in other comprehensive income. The valuation and allocation assertion about assets is that (a) they are reported at appropriate amounts and (b) adjustments are appropriately recorded.

4. <u>C)</u> Cutoff tests determine that all transactions occurring during a period are recorded in that period. Thus, they address the cutoff assertion.

5. <u>D)</u> Pledging receivables as security for a loan or selling receivables means that rights have been conveyed to a creditor or a buyer, respectively. Accordingly, reviewing loan agreements tests the rights and obligations assertion about balances.

6. <u>A)</u> Aging of receivables analyzes the probability of collection of receivables and is therefore related to the valuation and allocation assertion about balances. Accounts receivable should be reported at net realizable value.

7. <u>B)</u> Accounts receivable should be presented as a current asset with any significant issues disclosed. One required disclosure is the existence of related party transactions. Thus, material amounts due from officers and employees should be disclosed.

8. <u>C)</u> Deeds and title insurance provide evidence supporting the rights and obligations assertion about balances.

9. <u>B)</u> Physical examination of property provides strong evidence supporting the existence assertion about balances. The auditor usually inspects all major additions of property recorded during the period.

10. <u>A)</u> Property and equipment (except land) should be recorded at cost and depreciated over their useful lives. The auditor reviews depreciation procedures during the testing of the valuation and allocation assertion about balances.

4. Working Paper Deficiencies (10 Gradable Items)

1. <u>False.</u> Working papers should be subject to supervisory review, and there appear to be significant deficiencies.

2. <u>True.</u> Tickmark NR indicates that the amount does not compute correctly, but the working paper provides no additional information.

3. <u>True.</u> Although tickmark CX refers to working paper K-3, it does not indicate whether the exception was resolved.

4. <u>True.</u> The lender has refused to waive the right to demand payment, so this debt should be reclassified as current.

5. <u>True.</u> The beginning balance of Year 2 of $100,000 plus new borrowings in Year 2 of $50,000 equals $150,000, not $200,000.

6. <u>False.</u> The deficiency is that interest is not appropriately imputed.

7. <u>False.</u> The high rate ($281,333 ÷ $1,406,667 = 20%) apparently was not investigated.

8. <u>True.</u> Because of the unresolved issues, it does not appear appropriate to state that the amounts are "correct and complete."

9. <u>True.</u> The tickmark R was used on the working paper but not defined in the tickmark legend.

10. <u>False.</u> Collateral is appropriately listed.

5. Noncurrent Debt (8 Gradable Items)

1. <u>I) Vouch to contracts.</u> Vouching from the recording of debts back to contracts tests whether the transactions occurred.

2. <u>G) Consider year-end transactions.</u> Considering year-end transactions to determine if they were recorded in the proper period tests cutoff.

3. <u>F) Make inquiries of management.</u> Inquires to management help the auditor determine if accuracy in recording was achieved.

4. <u>A) Inspect disclosures.</u> Note disclosures in the financial statements relate directly to the understandability assertion.

5. <u>E) Test amortization.</u> Testing amortization is related to the valuation and allocation assertion.

6. <u>B) Perform analytical procedures.</u> Analytical procedures are used primarily to test completeness.

7. <u>J) Confirm debt.</u> Confirmations are used primarily to text existence.

8. <u>H) Examine bond indentures.</u> Examining bond indentures (contracts) relates to the rights and obligations of the parties.

6. Research (1 Gradable Item)

Answer: 332.58

AU Section 332 -- *Auditing Derivative Instruments, Hedging Activities, and Investments in Securities*

Management Representations

.58   Section 333, *Management Representations*, provides guidance to auditors in obtaining written representations from management. The auditor ordinarily should obtain written representations from management confirming aspects of management's intent and ability that affect assertions about derivatives and securities, such as its intent and ability to hold a debt security until its maturity or to enter into a forecasted transaction for which hedge accounting is applied. In addition, the auditor should consider obtaining written representations from management confirming other aspects of derivatives and securities transactions that affect assertions about them.

Gleim Simulation Grading

Task	Correct Responses		Gradable Items		Score per Task
1	_____	÷	10	=	_____
2	_____	÷	10	=	_____
3	_____	÷	10	=	_____
4	_____	÷	10	=	_____
5	_____	÷	8	=	_____
Research	_____	÷	1	=	_____

Total of Scores per Task	_____
÷ Total Number of Tasks	6
Total Score	_____%

Use **CPA Gleim Online** and **Simulation Wizard** to practice more task-based simulations in a realistic environment.

STUDY UNIT FOURTEEN
EVIDENCE -- KEY CONSIDERATIONS

(11 pages of outline)

This study unit presents a number of topics related to the collection of evidence. Of these issues, inquiry of the client's lawyer, an entity's ability to continue as a going concern, and client representations have been tested most consistently on recent exams. All topics presented here are likely subjects of future multiple-choice questions.

14.1 INQUIRY OF A CLIENT'S LAWYER CONCERNING LITIGATION, CLAIMS, AND ASSESSMENTS (AU 337)

1. Management is responsible for adopting policies and procedures to identify, evaluate, and account for **litigation, claims, and assessments (LCA)**.

   a. The applicable accounting principles are those relevant to contingencies.

2. The auditor should **obtain evidence** relevant to the following:

   a. Circumstances indicating an uncertainty as to possible loss from LCA
   b. The period in which the underlying cause for legal action occurred
   c. The probability of an unfavorable outcome
   d. The amount or range of potential loss

3. The **auditor's procedures** include the following:

   a. Inquiring about, and discussing with management, the policies and procedures for identifying, evaluating, and accounting for LCA.

   b. Obtaining from management a description and evaluation of LCA at period end, and from then to the date the information is provided, including an identification of matters referred to legal counsel.

      1) The auditor also should obtain assurances from management, ordinarily in writing, that all such matters required to be disclosed by GAAP have been disclosed.

   c. Examining documents in the client's possession (e.g., correspondence and invoices from lawyers).

   d. Obtaining assurance from management, usually in writing, that it has disclosed all unasserted claims that the lawyer has advised them are probable of assertion and that must be disclosed in accordance with GAAP.

   e. Applying related procedures. An audit normally includes procedures undertaken for other purposes that might also produce evidence about LCA. The following are some examples:

      1) Reading minutes of meetings of shareholders, directors, and appropriate committees held during and subsequent to the period being audited
      2) Reading contracts, loan agreements, leases, correspondence from governmental agencies, and similar documents
      3) Obtaining information about guarantees from bank confirmations
      4) Inspecting other documents for possible guarantees by the client

f.   Requesting the client's management to send a **letter of audit inquiry** to lawyers with whom management consulted. An auditor usually cannot make legal judgments.

4. **Inquiry of a Client's Lawyer**

a.   A **letter of audit inquiry** to the client's lawyer is the auditor's primary means of obtaining corroboration of the information provided by management. Evidence provided by **inside counsel** may corroborate this information. However, it does not substitute for information not provided by **outside counsel**.

b.   The **letter of audit inquiry** includes the following:

1) Identification of the entity and its subsidiaries and the date of the audit

2) A management list (or a request by management that the lawyer prepare a list) that describes and evaluates **pending** or **threatened** LCA with respect to which the lawyer has devoted substantive attention on behalf of the entity

a) For each matter, the lawyer should be requested either to provide the following information or comment on disagreements with management:

i)   The nature of the matter, the progress of the case, and the entity's intended action

ii) The probability of an unfavorable outcome and an estimate, if possible, of the amount or range of loss

iii) Omission of any pending or threatened LCA from management's list

3) A management list that describes and evaluates **unasserted** claims and assessments that (a) management considers to be probable and (b) have at least a reasonable possibility of an unfavorable outcome, with respect to which the lawyer has devoted substantive attention on behalf of the entity

a) Also included is a request that the lawyer comment on those matters that are the basis for disagreements with management.

4) A client statement that the client understands that the lawyer will advise the client when an unasserted claim or assertion with respect to which (s)he has provided legal services requires the client to disclose or consider disclosure in accordance with GAAP

a) The letter of audit inquiry should request the lawyer to confirm this understanding.

5) A request that the lawyer explain any limitation on his/her response

c.   An example of the text of a letter of audit inquiry to the client's lawyer is presented on the next page.

d.   Inquiry need not be made about **immaterial matters** if the client and the auditor have an understanding about the limits of materiality.

5. **Limitations on the Scope of a Lawyer's Response**

a.   A lawyer may limit the response to matters to which **substantive attention** has been given.

b.   A lawyer's response may be limited to matters considered **individually or collectively material** if the lawyer and auditor have reached an understanding on the limits of materiality for that purpose.

1) These limits are not limits on the audit scope.

c.   A lawyer's **refusal to furnish the information requested** in an inquiry letter, either in writing or orally, is a limitation on the audit scope sufficient to preclude an unqualified opinion. The auditor ordinarily disclaims an opinion.

d.   A lawyer may not be able to reach a conclusion about some matters because of **inherent uncertainties**.

EXAMPLE – Illustrative Text for a Letter of Audit Inquiry to Client's Lawyer

In connection with an audit of our financial statements at (balance sheet date) and for the (period) then ended, management of the Company has prepared and furnished to our auditors (name and address of auditors) a description and evaluation of certain contingencies, including those set forth below involving matters with respect to which you have been engaged and to which you have devoted substantive attention on behalf of the Company in the form of legal consultation or representation. These contingencies are regarded by management of the Company as material for this purpose (management may indicate a materiality limit if an understanding has been reached with the auditor). Your response should include matters that existed at (balance sheet date) and during the period from that date to the date of your response.

Pending or Threatened Litigation (excluding unasserted claims)

[Ordinarily, the information would include the following: (1) the nature of the litigation, (2) the progress of the case to date, (3) how management is responding or intends to respond to the litigation (for example, to contest the case vigorously or to seek an out-of-court settlement), and (4) an evaluation of the likelihood of an unfavorable outcome and an estimate, if one can be made, of the amount or range of potential loss.] Please furnish to our auditors such explanation, if any, that you consider necessary to supplement the foregoing information, including an explanation of those matters as to which your views may differ from those stated and an identification of the omission of any pending or threatened litigation, claims, and assessments or a statement that the list of such matters is complete.

Unasserted Claims and Assessments (considered by management to be probable of assertion and that, if asserted, would have at least a reasonable possibility of an unfavorable outcome)

[Ordinarily, management's information would include the following: (1) the nature of the matter, (2) how management intends to respond if the claim is asserted, and (3) an evaluation of the likelihood of an unfavorable outcome and an estimate, if one can be made, of the amount or range of potential loss.] Please furnish to our auditors such explanation, if any, that you consider necessary to supplement the foregoing information, including an explanation of those matters as to which your views may differ from those stated.

We understand that whenever, in the course of performing legal services for us with respect to a matter recognized to involve an unasserted possible claim or assessment that may call for financial statement disclosure, if you have formed a professional conclusion that we should disclose or consider disclosure concerning such possible claim or assessment, as a matter of professional responsibility to us, you will so advise us and will consult with us concerning the question of such disclosure and the FASB's applicable requirements regarding accounting for contingencies. Please specifically confirm to our auditors that our understanding is correct.

Please specifically identify the nature of and reasons for any limitation on your response.

[The auditor may request the client to inquire about additional matters, for example, unpaid or unbilled charges or specified information on certain contractually assumed obligations of the company, such as guarantees of indebtedness of others.]

[The letter would be signed by the client.]

Stop and review! You have completed the outline for this subunit. Study multiple-choice questions 1 through 9 beginning on page 460.

14.2 SUBSEQUENT EVENTS (AU 560)

1. Subsequent events are material events or transactions that occur **after the balance sheet date, but prior to the issuance of the financial statements**, that require adjustment of or disclosure in the statements.

2. **Types of Subsequent Events**

    a. One type consists of events **providing additional evidence about conditions at the balance sheet date** and affecting the estimates in the statements. An example is a loss on an uncollectible receivable as a result of a customer's bankruptcy after the balance sheet date.

        1) The financial statements should be **adjusted** for any changes in estimates resulting from such events.

b. A second type consists of events **providing evidence about conditions that arose subsequent to the balance sheet date**. Some of these events require **disclosure but not adjustment**.

1) Examples include the following:

a) Sale of a bond or stock issue

b) Purchase of a business

c) Settlement of litigation when the claim arose after the balance sheet date

d) Loss of plant or inventories as a result of fire or flood

e) Losses on receivables resulting from conditions (e.g., a customer's major casualty) arising after the balance sheet date

2) Some events of the second type may be so significant that the most appropriate form of disclosure is to supplement the historical statements with **pro forma financial data**.

c. Subsequent events affecting the **realization of assets** such as receivables and inventories or the **settlement of estimated liabilities** ordinarily require adjustment. They usually are the culmination of conditions that existed over a relatively long time.

3. **Auditing Procedures in the Subsequent Period**

a. The subsequent period is the period **between the balance sheet date and the report date** with which the auditor must be concerned in completing the audit.

b. Specific procedures applied to transactions occurring after the balance sheet date include the examination of data to

1) Ensure proper cutoffs and

2) Gather information to aid the auditor in the evaluation of the assets and liabilities as of the balance sheet date.

c. The following procedures should be performed at or near the **completion of field work**:

1) Reading the latest **interim financial statements** and comparing them with the financial statements being reported on.

2) Discussing with responsible executives

a) Whether the interim statements were prepared on the same **basis** as the statements being reported on

b) Whether any substantial **contingent liabilities or commitments** existed at the dates of the balance sheet or the inquiry

c) Whether any **significant change** occurred in capital stock, noncurrent debt, or working capital prior to the date of inquiry

d) Whether any **unusual adjustments** were made during the subsequent period

e) The current status of items that were accounted for on the basis of tentative, preliminary, or inconclusive data

3) Reading the available **minutes** of meetings of shareholders, directors, and appropriate committees.

4) Obtaining a letter of audit inquiry from client's **legal counsel** about litigation, claims, and assessments.

5) Obtaining a **letter of representations**, dated as of the date of the auditor's report, from appropriate officials as to whether any subsequent events occurred. This is one of several written representations obtained from the client. Representations are discussed in Subunit 14.4.

6) Making any inquiries or performing any procedures the auditor deems necessary to dispose of questions resulting from the foregoing procedures, inquiries, and discussions.

Stop and review! You have completed the outline for this subunit. Study multiple-choice questions 10 through 15 beginning on page 462.

14.3 SUBSEQUENT DISCOVERY OF FACTS EXISTING AT THE DATE OF THE AUDITOR'S REPORT (AU 561)

1. After the **date of the report**, the auditor is **not obligated** to make further inquiries or perform other procedures with respect to the audited financial statements unless **new information** that may affect the report comes to the auditor's attention.

    a. This information may be of such a **nature** and from such a **source** that the auditor would have investigated it had it come to his/her attention during the audit. In these circumstances, (s)he should determine whether the information is **reliable** and whether the facts **existed at the report date**.

2. If the auditor decides that action should be taken to prevent **future reliance** on the report, (s)he should advise the **client** to make appropriate **disclosures**. These should be made to persons who are known to be currently relying or who are likely to rely on the financial statements and the related report.

3. When the client makes the appropriate disclosures, one of the following should be done:

    a. If the effect of the subsequently discovered information can be **promptly determined**, revised statements and an auditor's report should be reissued as soon as possible.

        1) Reasons for the revision should be stated in a note and referred to in the report.

    b. When **issuance** of statements for a **subsequent period** is imminent, appropriate disclosure can be made in those statements.

    c. When the effect on the statements of the subsequently discovered information **cannot be determined** without a prolonged investigation, persons who are known to be relying or who are likely to rely on the statements and the related report should be **notified** by the client.

4. If the client **refuses to make disclosures**, the auditor should notify each member of the board of the refusal and of the auditor's intent to **prevent future reliance** upon the report. The steps the auditor should take include the following:

    a. Notifying the **client** that the report must no longer be associated with the financial statements

    b. Notifying applicable **regulatory agencies** that the report should no longer be relied upon

    c. Notifying each person **known to be relying** on the statements that the report should no longer be relied upon

        1) In many instances, the auditor will be unable to notify shareholders or investors at large, whose identities ordinarily are unknown. Notification to a regulatory agency will usually be the only practicable method of disclosure.

Stop and review! You have completed the outline for this subunit. Study multiple-choice questions 16 through 20 beginning on page 464.

14.4 MANAGEMENT REPRESENTATIONS (AU 333)

1. **Reliance on Management Representations**

   a. The independent auditor must obtain **written representations** from management as a part of an audit in accordance with GAAS.

   b. Management representations are part of the audit evidence but **do not substitute for** necessary auditing procedures.

   c. The representation letter acknowledges **management's responsibility** for the assertions made in the financial statements.

   d. Written representations from management ordinarily

      1) Confirm oral representations given to the auditor,
      2) Document the continuing appropriateness of the representations, and
      3) Reduce the possibility of misunderstandings.

   e. The auditor often applies auditing procedures specifically designed to **corroborate** written representations.

2. **Obtaining Written Representations**

   a. The specific representations obtained will depend on the circumstances. However, the **sample representation letter** on the next page, which is taken from AU 333, contains many items typically covered.

   b. Although addressed to the auditor, the letter is **drafted by the auditor**. It should be signed by client personnel.

   c. The letter assumes that no matters require specific disclosure to the auditor. If such matters exist, they should be indicated by listing them following the representation, referring to accounting records or financial statements, etc.

Background

The example representation letter in the auditing standards is a one-page document. It basically affirms management's responsibilities to the auditor and for the fairness of the financial statements. In practice, management representation letters are often much longer than the AICPA's example letter. Many CPA firms require management to affirm each key assertion for each major account as well as the other affirmations from the example letter. This should not be too surprising since the word representation has the same meaning as assertion.

---

   d. Representations may be limited to matters that are considered either **individually or collectively material** to the financial statements, provided management and the auditor have reached an understanding on the limits of materiality for this purpose.

      1) These limits do not apply to fraud, communications from regulatory agencies, or to representations not directly related to financial statement amounts.

   e. The auditor may determine, based on the circumstances, that **other matters** should be specifically included among the written representations.

   f. If the auditor reports on a **subsidiary's statements**, (s)he may want to obtain representations from the parent.

   g. The auditor may want to obtain written representations from **other individuals**, for example, about the completeness of the minutes of meetings from the person responsible for the minutes.

   h. Written representations should be

      1) Addressed to the auditor.
      2) Dated as of the date of the audit report.
      3) Signed by responsible and knowledgeable members of management. The **CEO** and **CFO** usually should sign the representations.

ISA Difference

The ISAs state that management's representations should include disclosure to the auditor of its **assessment of the risk of material misstatement due to fraud.**

EXAMPLE – Management Representation Letter

Date of Auditor's Report
To Independent Auditor [Named]

We are providing this letter in connection with your audit(s) of the [identification of financial statements] of [name of entity] as of [dates] and for the [periods] for the purpose of expressing an opinion as to whether the [consolidated] financial statements present fairly, in all material respects, the financial position, results of operations, and cash flows of [name of entity] in conformity with accounting principles generally accepted in the United States of America. We confirm that we are responsible for the fair presentation in the [consolidated] financial statements of financial position, results of operations, and cash flows in conformity with generally accepted accounting principles.

Certain representations in this letter are described as being limited to matters that are material. Items are considered material, regardless of size, if they involve an omission or misstatement of accounting information that, in the light of surrounding circumstances, makes it probable that the judgment of a reasonable person relying on the information would be changed or influenced by the omission or misstatement.

We confirm, to the best of our knowledge and belief, as of [date of auditor's report], the following representations made to you during your audit(s).

1. The financial statements referred to above are fairly presented in conformity with accounting principles generally accepted in the United States of America.

2. We have made available to you all –

   a. Financial records and related data.

   b. Minutes of the meetings of stockholders, directors, and committees of directors, or summaries of actions of recent meetings for which minutes have not yet been prepared.

3. There have been no communications from regulatory agencies concerning noncompliance with or deficiencies in financial reporting practices.

4. There are no material transactions that have not been properly recorded in the accounting records underlying the financial statements.

5. We believe that the effects of the uncorrected financial statement misstatements summarized in the accompanying schedule are immaterial, both individually and in the aggregate, to the financial statements taken as a whole.

6. We acknowledge our responsibility for the design and implementation of programs and controls to prevent and detect fraud.

7. We have no knowledge of any fraud or suspected fraud affecting the entity involving –

   a. Management,
   b. Employees who have significant roles in internal control, or
   c. Others if the fraud could have a material effect on the financial statements.

8. We have no knowledge of any allegations of fraud or suspected fraud affecting the entity received in communications from employees, former employees, analysts, regulators, short sellers, or others.

9. The company has no plans or intentions that may materially affect the carrying value or classification of assets and liabilities.

10. The following have been properly recorded or disclosed in the financial statements:

    a. Related-party transactions, including sales, purchases, loans, transfers, leasing arrangements, and guarantees, and amounts receivable from or payable to related parties.

    b. Guarantees, whether written or oral, under which the company is contingently liable.

    c. Significant estimates and material concentrations known to management that are required to be disclosed in accordance with the FASB's guidance for presentation of certain significant risks and uncertainties. [Significant estimates are estimates at the balance sheet date that could change materially within the next year. Concentrations refer to volumes of business, revenues, available sources of supply, or markets or geographic areas for which events could occur that would significantly disrupt normal finances within the next year. This guidance is outlined in *CPA Review: Financial*.]

11. There are no –

    a. Violations or possible violations of laws or regulations whose effects should be considered for disclosure in the financial statements or as a basis for recording a loss contingency.

    b. Unasserted claims or assessments that our lawyer has advised us are probable of assertion and must be disclosed in accordance with the FASB's guidance applicable to accounting for contingencies.

    c. Other liabilities or gain or loss contingencies that are required to be accrued or disclosed.

12. The company has satisfactory title to all owned assets, and there are no liens or encumbrances on such assets nor has any asset been pledged as collateral.

13. The company has complied with all aspects of contractual agreements that would have a material effect on the financial statements in the event of noncompliance.

[Add additional representations that are unique to the entity's business or industry.]

To the best of our knowledge and belief, no events have occurred subsequent to the balance-sheet date and through the date of this letter that would require adjustment to or disclosure in the aforementioned financial statements.

[Name of Chief Executive Officer and Title]   [Name of Chief Financial Officer and Title]

3. **Scope Limitations**

    a. Management's refusal to provide written representations is a scope limitation that **precludes an unqualified opinion**. The auditor should also consider the effects of the refusal on his/her ability to rely on other representations.

    b. If the auditor is precluded from performing necessary procedures regarding a material matter, even though management has made representations about the matter, the scope limitation requires the auditor to qualify the opinion or disclaim an opinion.

4. **SEC Requirements**

    a. **CEOs** and **CFOs** must certify to the SEC that annual and quarterly reports filed in accordance with the Securities Exchange Act of 1934 contain no material misstatements.

5. **Other Pronouncements**

    a. The PCAOB's AS No. 5 **requires** that an audit of an **issuer's internal control** over financial reporting be integrated with the financial statement audit. The AICPA's AT 501 provides for the **optional** performance of a similar service for a **nonissuer**. Additional representations should include the following:

        1) That management is responsible for establishing and maintaining effective internal control over financial reporting.

        2) That management has evaluated internal control, specified the control criteria, and stated its assertion about the effectiveness of internal control.

        3) That management has disclosed to the auditor all deficiencies in internal control.

        4) That deficiencies identified and communicated to those charged with governance during previous engagements have been resolved and that unresolved deficiencies have been identified.

Stop and review! You have completed the outline for this subunit. Study multiple-choice questions 21 through 28 beginning on page 466.

14.5 AUDITOR'S CONSIDERATION OF AN ENTITY'S ABILITY TO CONTINUE AS A GOING CONCERN (AU 341)

1. The auditor must evaluate whether a **substantial doubt** exists about an entity's ability to continue as a **going concern** for a reasonable period.

    a. Continuation as a going concern is assumed in financial reporting absent significant contrary information. Such information relates to the inability to continue to meet obligations as they fall due without, for example, one of the following:

        1) Substantial disposal of assets outside the ordinary course of business
        2) Debt restructuring
        3) Externally forced revisions of operations

    b. The standard does not apply to an audit of financial statements prepared on the **liquidation basis**.

        1) It applies to audits of financial statements prepared in accordance with GAAP or a comprehensive basis other than GAAP (excluding the liquidation basis).

2. The auditor must "evaluate whether there is substantial doubt about the entity's ability to continue as a going concern for a reasonable period of time, not to exceed **one year beyond the date of the financial statements** being audited" (hereafter, the term "substantial doubt" will be used when referring to this quoted language).

    a. The evaluation is based on relevant conditions and events as of the date of the report.

        1) Necessary information is obtained by applying the auditing procedures planned and performed to test the assertions in the financial statements.

b. The **process of evaluation** is as follows:

1) The auditor considers whether the results of normal auditing procedures identify **conditions and events** that, in the aggregate, indicate that substantial doubt could exist (hereafter, simply "conditions and events").

a) Additional information about the conditions and events, as well as evidence supporting information that mitigates the substantial doubt, may need to be gathered.

2) If the auditor believes a **substantial doubt exists**, (s)he should obtain information about **management's plans** to mitigate the effect of such conditions or events and assess the likelihood that the plans will be effective.

3) The auditor then determines **whether (s)he has a substantial doubt**.

a) If so, (s)he should

i) Consider the adequacy of disclosure about the going concern issue.

ii) Include an explanatory paragraph (after the opinion paragraph) in the audit report. Also, a disclaimer of an opinion is possible.

b) If not, (s)he should still consider the need for disclosure, but need not include an explanatory paragraph in the audit report.

c. The entity's **failure to continue as a going concern**, even within the year after the date of the statements, does not, in itself, indicate inadequate auditor performance.

1) Thus, omission of the reference to substantial doubt provides no assurance of continuation as a going concern.

3. **Audit Procedures**

a. Procedures need not be designed solely to identify conditions and events because typical audit procedures should be sufficient. Such procedures may include the following:

1) Analytical procedures
2) Review of subsequent events
3) Review of compliance with debt and loan agreements
4) Reading minutes of meetings of shareholders, the board, and committees
5) Inquiry of legal counsel about litigation, claims, and assessments
6) Confirmation with related and third parties of arrangements for financial support

4. **Conditions and Events**

a. The significance of conditions and events depends on the circumstances, and some may be significant only in conjunction with others. Such conditions and events include the following:

1) **Negative trends**, e.g., (a) recurring operating losses, (b) working capital deficiencies, (c) negative cash flows from operations, and (d) poor key financial ratios

2) **Financial difficulties**, e.g., (a) default on loans, (b) unpaid dividends, (c) denial of normal trade credit by suppliers, (d) debt restructuring, (e) noncompliance with statutory capital requirements, and (f) the need to seek new financing or to dispose of substantial assets

3) **Internal matters**, e.g., (a) labor difficulties, (b) substantial dependence on the success of one project, (c) uneconomic long-term commitments, and (d) the need to revise operations significantly

4) **External matters**, e.g., (a) litigation, legislation, or similar matters jeopardizing operating ability; (b) loss of a key franchise, license, or patent; (c) loss of a principal customer or supplier; and (d) an uninsured or underinsured catastrophe, such as a drought, earthquake, or flood

5. **Management's Plans**

    a.   Given substantial doubt, the auditor should (1) consider management's plans for responding to the adverse effects of the conditions and events, (2) obtain information about the plans, and (3) consider the likelihood that the adverse effects will be mitigated and the plans can be effectively implemented.

    b.   These considerations may include the following:

        1)   **Disposing of assets**

            a)   Restrictions such as those in loan agreements or interests held by other parties (e.g., mortgages or security interests)

            b)   Marketability of the assets to be sold

            c)   Direct or indirect effects

        2)   **Borrowing money or restructuring debt**

            a)   Availability of debt financing, including credit arrangements, such as lines of credit, factoring of receivables, or sale-leasebacks

            b)   Arrangements to restructure or subordinate debt or to guarantee loans to the entity

            c)   Existing restrictions on borrowing or the sufficiency of available collateral

        3)   **Reducing or delaying expenditures**

            a)   Feasibility of plans to reduce overhead or administrative expenses, postpone maintenance or R&D, or lease rather than purchase

            b)   Direct or indirect effects

        4)   **Increasing ownership equity**

            a)   Feasibility of such plans, including arrangements to obtain capital

            b)   Arrangements to reduce dividends or accelerate cash receipts from affiliates or other investors

    c.   The elements of plans that are particularly significant to overcoming the adverse effects should be identified and procedures performed to obtain evidence about them, for example, about the ability to obtain **additional financing**.

    d.   **Prospective financial information (PFI)** may be important to management's plans, and the auditor should request such information and consider the adequacy of support for significant underlying **assumptions**.

        1)   Special attention should be given to assumptions that are

            a)   Material,

            b)   Especially sensitive or susceptible to change, and

            c)   Inconsistent with historical trends.

        2)   The auditor should have knowledge of the entity, its business, and its management. The auditor should

            a)   Read the PFI and assumptions.

            b)   Compare PFI for prior periods with results and for the current period with results to date.

        3)   If the effects of certain factors are not reflected in the PFI, the auditor should discuss them with management and, if necessary, request revision.

6. **Financial Statement Effects**

    a.   After considering management's plans, the auditor may decide that a substantial doubt exists and should consider the possible effects on the statements and the **adequacy of disclosure.**

b.   Information disclosed may include the following:

1)   The conditions and events on which the substantial doubt is based, their possible effects, and management's evaluation of their significance and of any mitigating factors

2)   Possible discontinuance of operations

3)   Management's plans, including PFI

a)   The information need not meet guidelines for PFI, and the consideration need not go beyond that required by GAAS.

4)   Information about recoverability or classification of recorded assets or the amounts or classification of liabilities

c.   The auditor may decide, primarily because of the consideration of management's plans, that the substantial doubt is mitigated. (S)he then should consider **disclosure** of (1) the principal conditions and events that led to the substantial doubt; (2) their possible effects; and (3) any mitigating factors, including management's plans.

7.   **Effects on the Auditor's Report**

a.   If the auditor has a substantial doubt, the audit report should include an **explanatory paragraph** following the opinion paragraph (described more fully in Study Unit 17, Subunit 3). The wording of the auditor's conclusion should include the phrases **"substantial doubt"** and **"going concern."**

b.   If disclosure is inadequate, the auditor may modify the opinion.

c.   Also, the auditor is **not precluded from disclaiming an opinion** in cases involving **uncertainties**.

8.   **Documentation**

a.   If the auditor has a substantial doubt (even if that doubt is mitigated by management actions), the following should be documented in the working papers:

1)   The conditions or events causing the belief

2)   The important elements of management's plans to overcome the problem considered by the auditor

3)   The auditing procedures performed and evidence obtained

4)   The auditor's conclusions, including any effects on the financial statements or disclosures and any effect on the audit report

9.   **Communications**

a.   An auditor who has a substantial doubt should communicate the following to **those charged with governance**:

1)   Nature of identified conditions and events

2)   Financial statement effects

3)   Adequacy of disclosure

4)   Audit report effects

ISA Difference

The ISAs state that management is responsible for assessing the ability to continue as a going concern. The auditor's responsibility is to evaluate the assessment. When events or conditions that may cast significant doubt on the entity's ability to continue as a going concern have been identified, the ISAs indicate that the auditor should obtain **written representations** from management regarding its plans for future action. These documents would be included in the management representation letter (See Subunit 14.4). While AICPA standards require the auditor to evaluate going concern for a reasonable period not to exceed 1 year beyond the financial statements, the ISAs require consideration of going concern issues extending to **at least**, but not limited to, **1 year**.

Stop and review! You have completed the outline for this subunit. Study multiple-choice questions 29 through 32 beginning on page 468.

QUESTIONS

14.1 Inquiry of a Client's Lawyer Concerning Litigation, Claims, and Assessments (AU 337)

1. The primary source of information to be reported about litigation, claims, and assessments is the

    A. Client's lawyer.

    B. Court records.

    C. Client's management.

    D. Independent auditor.

Answer (C) is correct. *(CPA, adapted)*
    REQUIRED: The primary source of information to be reported about litigation, claims, and assessments.
    DISCUSSION: According to AU 337, "Management is responsible for adopting policies and procedures to identify, evaluate, and account for litigation, claims, and assessments as a basis for the preparation of financial statements in conformity with generally accepted accounting principles." The auditor should discuss with management its policies and procedures for identifying and evaluating these issues.
    Answer (A) is incorrect. The client's lawyer is the auditor's primary source of evidence to corroborate the information furnished by management. Answer (B) is incorrect. The auditor does not ordinarily examine court records. Answer (D) is incorrect. The auditor collects evidence to support management's assertions about litigation, claims, and assessments.

2. Which of the following procedures would best detect a liability omission by management?

    A. Inquiry of senior support staff and recently departed employees.

    B. Review and check mathematical accuracy of financial statements.

    C. Review articles of incorporation and corporate bylaws.

    D. Review purchase contracts and other legal documents.

Answer (D) is correct. *(CPA, adapted)*
    REQUIRED: The procedure to detect a liability omission by management.
    DISCUSSION: The auditor's search for unrecorded liabilities should include reading contracts, loan agreements, leases, correspondence from governmental agencies, and any legal documents in the client's possession.
    Answer (A) is incorrect. The support staff and departed employees do not likely have knowledge about devious actions of management. Answer (B) is incorrect. The omitted liabilities would not be included in the financial statements. Answer (C) is incorrect. The articles of incorporation and the bylaws will not address litigation or liabilities.

3. A lawyer's response to an auditor's inquiry concerning litigation, claims, and assessments may be limited to matters that are considered individually or collectively material to the client's financial statements. Which parties should reach an understanding on the limits of materiality for this purpose?

    A. The auditor and the client's management.

    B. The client's audit committee and the lawyer.

    C. The client's management and the lawyer.

    D. The lawyer and the auditor.

Answer (D) is correct. *(CPA, adapted)*
    REQUIRED: The parties responsible for setting materiality limits for litigation inquiries.
    DISCUSSION: A lawyer's response to an auditor's inquiry about litigation, claims, and assessments may be limited to those that are considered individually or collectively material to the financial statements, provided the lawyer and auditor have reached an understanding on the limits of materiality for this purpose (AU 337).
    Answer (A) is incorrect. An inquiry (versus the response) need not be made about items considered immaterial, provided the auditor and client have an understanding about the limits of materiality for this purpose. Answer (B) is incorrect. The auditor must judge whether items are material relative to the financial statements. Answer (C) is incorrect. The auditor must judge whether items are material relative to the financial statements.

4. Which of the following parties should make an inquiry of a client's lawyer?

    A. The auditor.

    B. The stockholders.

    C. Client management.

    D. The auditor's attorney.

Answer (C) is correct. *(CPA, adapted)*
    REQUIRED: The party(ies) who should make an inquiry of a client's lawyer.
    DISCUSSION: A letter of audit inquiry to a client's lawyer is the auditor's primary means of corroborating information furnished by management about litigation, claims, and assessments. Evidence obtained from the client's legal department may provide the needed corroboration, but it does not substitute for information that outside counsel may refuse to furnish. Thus, the auditor must ask client management to send a letter of audit inquiry to a lawyer with whom management consulted. Without the client's consent, the lawyer may not respond (AU 337).

5. The primary reason an auditor requests letters of inquiry be sent to a client's attorneys is to provide the auditor with

A. The probable outcome of asserted claims and pending or threatened litigation.

B. Corroboration of the information furnished by management about litigation, claims, and assessments.

C. The attorneys' opinions of the client's historical experiences in recent similar litigation.

D. A description and evaluation of litigation, claims, and assessments that existed at the balance sheet date.

6. A client is a defendant in a patent infringement lawsuit against a major competitor. Which of the following items would **least** likely be included in the attorney's response to the auditor's letter of inquiry?

A. A description of potential litigation in other matters or related to an unfavorable verdict in the patent infringement lawsuit.

B. A discussion of case progress and the strategy currently in place by client management to resolve the lawsuit.

C. An evaluation of the probability of loss and a statement of the amount or range of loss if an unfavorable outcome is reasonably possible.

D. An evaluation of the ability of the client to continue as a going concern if the verdict is unfavorable and maximum damages are awarded.

7. Which of the following statements extracted from a client's lawyer's letter concerning litigation, claims, and assessments most likely would cause the auditor to request clarification?

A. "I believe that the possible liability to the company is nominal in amount."

B. "I believe that the action can be settled for less than the damages claimed."

C. "I believe that the plaintiff's case against the company is without merit."

D. "I believe that the company will be able to defend this action successfully."

Answer (B) is correct. *(CPA, adapted)*
REQUIRED: The primary reason an auditor requests letters of audit inquiry to be sent to a client's attorneys.
DISCUSSION: AU 337 notes that a letter of audit inquiry to a client's lawyer is the auditor's primary means of obtaining corroboration of information furnished by management about litigation, claims, and assessments.
Answer (A) is incorrect. Management provides information about the probable outcome of asserted claims and impending or threatened litigation. Answer (C) is incorrect. The auditor is concerned with current litigation, not recent similar litigation. Answer (D) is incorrect. Management provides a description and evaluation of litigation, claims, and assessments that existed at the balance sheet date. The letter of audit inquiry provides corroboration of that information.

Answer (D) is correct. *(CPA, adapted)*
REQUIRED: The items least likely included in the attorney's response to the auditor's letter of inquiry.
DISCUSSION: An inquiry letter response from the client's attorney will normally include information or comment about each pending or threatened litigation, claim, or assessment. The lawyer should address the progress of the case, describe the action the company plans to take, evaluate the likelihood of an unfavorable outcome, and estimate (if possible) the range of any potential loss. The lawyer does not have the expertise or information to make a judgment about the client's going concern issue. The auditor normally makes that judgment.
Answer (A) is incorrect. An evaluation of the probability of loss and a statement of the amount or range of loss if an unfavorable outcome is reasonably possible would be included in the attorney's response letter. Answer (B) is incorrect. A discussion of case progress and the strategy currently in place by client management to resolve the lawsuit would be included in the attorney's response letter. Answer (C) is incorrect. An evaluation of the probability of loss and a statement of the amount or range of loss if an unfavorable outcome is reasonably possible would be included in the attorney's response letter.

Answer (B) is correct. *(CPA, adapted)*
REQUIRED: The lawyer's statement most likely causing an auditor's request for clarification.
DISCUSSION: The letter of audit inquiry requests, among other things, that the lawyer evaluate the likelihood of unfavorable outcomes of pending or threatened litigation, claims, and assessments. It also requests that the lawyer estimate, if possible, the amount or range of potential loss (AU 337). Thus, the auditor is concerned about the amount of the expected settlement as well as the likelihood of the outcome.
Answer (A) is incorrect. The lawyer's statement that the amount of possible liability will not be material states an amount or range of loss. Answer (C) is incorrect. The lawyer has stated that no liability is expected. Answer (D) is incorrect. The lawyer has stated that no liability is expected.

8. The scope of an audit is **not** restricted when an attorney's response to an auditor as a result of a client's letter of audit inquiry limits the response to

A. Matters to which the attorney has given substantive attention in the form of legal representation.

B. An evaluation of the likelihood of an unfavorable outcome of the matters disclosed by the entity.

C. The attorney's opinion of the entity's historical experience in recent similar litigation.

D. The probable outcome of asserted claims and pending or threatened litigation.

Answer (A) is correct. *(CPA, adapted)*
REQUIRED: The appropriate limitations on the lawyer's response to the auditor's inquiry.
DISCUSSION: AU 337 states that two limitations on the lawyer's response will not be considered scope limitations. The response may be limited to matters to which the lawyer has given substantive attention on behalf of the client in the form of legal consultation or representation. Also, if the lawyer and auditor have reached an understanding as to the limits of materiality, the response may be limited to matters that are individually or collectively material.
Answer (B) is incorrect. An evaluation of the likelihood of an unfavorable outcome of the matters disclosed by the entity is just one matter covered in a letter of audit inquiry. Answer (C) is incorrect. A response should be made regarding all material litigation, claims, and assessments to which the lawyer has given substantive attention. Answer (D) is incorrect. The probable outcome of asserted claims and pending or threatened litigation is just one matter covered in a letter of audit inquiry.

9. The refusal of a client's attorney to provide information requested in an inquiry letter generally is considered

A. Grounds for an adverse opinion.

B. A limitation on the scope of the audit.

C. Reason to withdraw from the engagement.

D. Significant deficiency in internal control.

Answer (B) is correct. *(CPA, adapted)*
REQUIRED: The nature of the refusal of a client's attorney to provide information requested.
DISCUSSION: A lawyer's refusal to furnish the information requested in an inquiry letter either in writing or orally is a limitation on the scope of the audit sufficient to preclude an unqualified opinion.
Answer (A) is incorrect. A scope limitation never leads to an adverse opinion. Answer (C) is incorrect. The refusal is not immediate grounds for withdrawal from an engagement. The auditor should attempt to become satisfied by alternative means. Answer (D) is incorrect. Consideration of internal control is related to the client, not the client's attorney.

14.2 Subsequent Events (AU 560)

10. Which of the following procedures should an auditor ordinarily perform regarding subsequent events?

A. Compare the latest available interim financial statements with the financial statements being audited.

B. Send second requests to the client's customers who failed to respond to initial accounts receivable confirmation requests.

C. Communicate material weaknesses in internal control to the client's audit committee.

D. Review the cutoff bank statements for several months after the year end.

Answer (A) is correct. *(CPA, adapted)*
REQUIRED: The subsequent events procedure.
DISCUSSION: Subsequent events procedures include (1) reading the latest interim statements and comparing them with the statements being reported on; (2) inquiring about and discussing with management various financial and accounting matters; (3) reading the minutes of directors', shareholders', and committee meetings; (4) obtaining a letter of representations from management; (5) inquiring of client's legal counsel; and (6) performing any further procedures deemed necessary.
Answer (B) is incorrect. Second confirmation requests would not disclose subsequent events. Answer (C) is incorrect. Communication of material weaknesses is not a subsequent events procedure. Answer (D) is incorrect. Cutoff bank statements are requested from banks 7 to 10 days after year end. They are used to verify the client's bank reconciliations.

11. An auditor should be aware of subsequent events that provide evidence concerning conditions that did not exist at year end but arose after year end. These events may be important to the auditor because they may

A. Require adjustments to the financial statements as of the year end.

B. Have been recorded based on preliminary accounting estimates.

C. Require disclosure to keep the financial statements from being misleading.

D. Have been recorded based on year-end tests for asset obsolescence.

Answer (C) is correct. *(CPA, adapted)*
REQUIRED: Why the auditor should be aware of subsequent events.
DISCUSSION: One type of subsequent event provides evidence about conditions that arose after the balance sheet date. The auditor should evaluate these events to determine whether disclosure is necessary for proper understanding of the financial statements.
Answer (A) is incorrect. Because the event did not relate to conditions that existed at the balance sheet date, the financial statements should not be adjusted. Answer (B) is incorrect. Because the event happened after year end, it would not have been recorded. Answer (D) is incorrect. Because the event happened after year end, it would not have been recorded.

12. Which of the following procedures would an auditor most likely perform to obtain evidence about the occurrence of subsequent events?

A. Recomputing a sample of large-dollar transactions occurring after year end for arithmetic accuracy.

B. Investigating changes in equity occurring after year end.

C. Inquiring of the entity's legal counsel concerning litigation, claims, and assessments arising after year end.

D. Confirming bank accounts established after year end.

Answer (C) is correct. *(CPA, adapted)*
REQUIRED: The auditing procedure for the subsequent events period.
DISCUSSION: Procedures applied after the balance sheet date should include the examination of data to determine that proper cutoffs have been made and to evaluate assets and liabilities as of the balance sheet date. The auditor also should perform procedures with respect to the subsequent events period to ascertain whether events have occurred that may require adjustment or disclosure essential to fair presentation of the financial statements. Such procedures include obtaining a letter of audit inquiry from the client's legal counsel (AU 560).
Answer (A) is incorrect. Testing the arithmetic accuracy of known events does not generate evidence about the occurrence of other subsequent events. Answer (B) is incorrect. The auditor should inquire of officers and other executives as to significant changes in equity, but an investigation of such changes is less likely than the inquiry of legal counsel. Answer (D) is incorrect. A bank account established after year end is not an asset that existed at the balance sheet date.

13. Which of the following procedures would an auditor most likely perform in obtaining evidence about subsequent events?

A. Determine that changes in employee pay rates after year end were properly authorized.

B. Recompute depreciation charges for plant assets sold after year end.

C. Inquire about payroll checks that were recorded before year end but cashed after year end.

D. Investigate changes in noncurrent debt occurring after year end.

Answer (D) is correct. *(CPA, adapted)*
REQUIRED: The procedure likely to be performed in obtaining evidence about subsequent events.
DISCUSSION: Procedures that should be performed on or near the completion of the field work include investigating any significant change in capital stock, noncurrent debt, or working capital. Events related to these accounts may require revision in the year-end financial statements or disclosures in the notes.
Answer (A) is incorrect. Changes in employee pay rates are not typically considered important subsequent events. Answer (B) is incorrect. Depreciation charges for a given period do not change as a result of sale of plant assets in the subsequent period. Answer (C) is incorrect. The times when employee paychecks are cashed are not typically considered important subsequent events.

14. Zero Corp. suffered a loss that would have a material effect on its financial statements on an uncollectible trade account receivable due to a customer's bankruptcy. This occurred suddenly due to a natural disaster 10 days after Zero's balance sheet date but 1 month before the issuance of the financial statements. Under these circumstances,

	The Financial Statements Should Be Adjusted	The Event Requires Financial Statement Disclosure, but No Adjustment	The Auditor's Report Should Be Modified for a Lack of Consistency
A.	Yes	No	No
B.	Yes	No	Yes
C.	No	Yes	Yes
D.	No	Yes	No

Answer (D) is correct. *(CPA, adapted)*
REQUIRED: The effect on the financial statements and the auditor's report.
DISCUSSION: Certain subsequent events may provide additional evidence about conditions at the date of the balance sheet and affect estimates inherent in the preparation of statements. These events require adjustment by the client in the financial statements at year end. Other subsequent events provide evidence about conditions not existing at the date of the balance sheet but arising subsequent to that date and affecting the interpretation of the year-end financial statements. These events may require disclosure but do not require adjustment of the financial statement balances. Thus, in this case, the financial statements should not be adjusted, but disclosure should be made. The auditor's report is unaffected.
Answer (A) is incorrect. The financial statements are not adjusted and the matter is disclosed. Answer (B) is incorrect. The financial statements are not adjusted, the matter is disclosed, and the auditor's report is not affected. Answer (C) is incorrect. The auditor's report is not affected.

15. Which of the following procedures would an auditor most likely perform to obtain evidence about the occurrence of subsequent events?

A. Confirming a sample of material accounts receivable established after year end.

B. Comparing the financial statements being reported on with those of the prior period.

C. Investigating personnel changes in the accounting department occurring after year end.

D. Inquiring as to whether any unusual adjustments were made after year end.

Answer (D) is correct. *(CPA, adapted)*
REQUIRED: The subsequent events procedure.
DISCUSSION: Procedures performed at or near the completion of field work normally include inquiring of management as to (1) whether the interim statements were prepared on the same basis as the statements being reported on, (2) whether any substantial contingent liabilities or commitments existed at the date of the balance sheet, (3) whether any significant change had occurred in equity, (4) whether any unusual adjustments had been made during the subsequent period, and (5) the current status of items that were accounted for on a basis of tentative, preliminary, or inconclusive data.
Answer (A) is incorrect. The auditor confirms receivables represented on the balance sheet at year end. Answer (B) is incorrect. This analytical procedure is performed at the beginning of the audit. Answer (C) is incorrect. Personnel changes after year end do not typically relate to the recording of subsequent events.

14.3 Subsequent Discovery of Facts Existing at the Date of the Auditor's Report (AU 561)

16. After the issuance of a nonissuer's financial statements, the client decided to sell the shares of a subsidiary that accounts for 30% of its revenue and 25% of its net income. The auditor should

A. Determine whether the information is reliable and, if determined to be reliable, request that revised financial statements be issued.

B. Notify the entity that the auditor's report may no longer be associated with the financial statements.

C. Describe the effects of this subsequently discovered information in a communication with persons known to be relying on the financial statements.

D. Take no action because the auditor has no obligation to make any further inquiries.

Answer (D) is correct. *(CPA, adapted)*
REQUIRED: The auditor's responsibility for an event occurring after the issuance of a nonissuer's financial statements.
DISCUSSION: AU 561 states, "After the date of the report, the auditor has no obligation to make any further or continuing inquiry or perform any other auditing procedures with respect to the audited financial statements covered by that report, unless new information that may affect the report comes to his/her attention."
Answer (A) is incorrect. Determining whether the information is reliable and requesting that revised statements be issued would be appropriate if the auditor had subsequently discovered facts existing at the date of the report. Answer (B) is incorrect. Notifying the entity that the report may no longer be associated with the financial statements would be appropriate if the auditor had subsequently discovered facts existing at the date of the report. Answer (C) is incorrect. Communicating the effects of subsequently discovered information to persons known to be relying on the statements would be appropriate if the auditor had subsequently discovered facts existing at the date of the report.

17. After the date of the audit report, an auditor has no obligation to make continuing inquiries or perform other procedures concerning the audited financial statements, **unless**

A. Information that existed at the report date and may affect the report comes to the auditor's attention.

B. Management of the entity requests the auditor to reissue the auditor's report in a document submitted to a third party that contains information in addition to the basic financial statements.

C. Information about an event that occurred after the end of field work comes to the auditor's attention.

D. Final determinations or resolutions are made of contingencies that had been disclosed in the financial statements.

Answer (A) is correct. *(CPA, adapted)*
REQUIRED: The basis for the obligation to perform procedures after the date of the report.
DISCUSSION: Although the auditor may need to extend subsequent events procedures when public companies make filings under the Securities Act of 1933 (AU 711), (s)he ordinarily need not apply any procedures after the date of the report. But the auditor may become aware of information that (1) relates to the financial statements previously reported on, (2) (s)he did not know at the date of the report, and (3) is of such a nature and from such a source that (s)he would have investigated if it had come to light during the audit. In this case, the auditor should, as soon as practicable, determine whether the information is reliable and whether the facts existed at the date of the report (AU 561).
Answer (B) is incorrect. Additional audit procedures are ordinarily not necessary prior to reissuing a report. Answer (C) is incorrect. The subsequent event must have occurred prior to the date of the auditor's report (ordinarily, the date of the completion of field work) for the auditor to have additional responsibilities. Answer (D) is incorrect. The auditor has no continuing responsibility to monitor disclosed contingencies.

18. Which of the following events occurring after the issuance of the financial statement most likely would cause the auditor to make further inquiries about previously issued financial statements?

   A. An uninsured natural disaster occurs that may affect the entity's ability to continue as a going concern.

   B. A contingency is resolved that had been disclosed in the audited financial statements.

   C. New information is discovered concerning undisclosed lease transactions of the audited period.

   D. A subsidiary is sold that accounts for 25% of the entity's consolidated net income.

Answer (C) is correct. *(CPA, adapted)*
   REQUIRED: The event occurring after the issuance of the financial statement most likely resulting in further inquiries.
   DISCUSSION: The auditor may become aware of information that (1) relates to prior financial statements, (2) was not known to him/her at the date of the report, and (3) (s)he would have investigated if it had been discovered during the audit. In this case, the auditor should undertake to determine whether the information is reliable and whether the facts existed at the report date (AU 561).
   Answer (A) is incorrect. An event occurring after the date of the report need not be considered by the auditor if it would not affect the report. Answer (B) is incorrect. The auditor need not consider final determinations or resolutions of contingencies that were disclosed in the financial statements or that resulted in a departure from the auditor's standard report. Answer (D) is incorrect. An event occurring after the date of the report need not be considered by the auditor if it would not affect the report.

19. Soon after Boyd's audit report was issued, Boyd learned of certain related party transactions that occurred during the year under audit. These transactions were not disclosed in the notes to the financial statements. Boyd should

   A. Plan to audit the transactions during the next engagement.

   B. Recall all copies of the audited financial statements.

   C. Determine whether the lack of disclosure would affect the auditor's report.

   D. Ask the client to disclose the transactions in subsequent interim statements.

Answer (C) is correct. *(CPA, adapted)*
   REQUIRED: The step taken when the auditor discovers previously unknown facts existing at the report date.
   DISCUSSION: The auditor should, as soon as practicable, undertake to determine whether the information is reliable and whether the facts existed at the date of the report. If these criteria are met, the auditor must take appropriate action if the report would have been affected and if (s)he believes persons who are currently relying or likely to rely on the statements would consider the information important (AU 561).
   Answer (A) is incorrect. The auditor must take more immediate action. Answer (B) is incorrect. Recall of the audited financial statements is not feasible. However, client revision of the statements and notice to appropriate parties may be necessary. Answer (D) is incorrect. Issuance of revised statements is preferable but only if the auditor has determined that the original statements are affected.

20. On February 25, a CPA issued an auditor's report expressing an unqualified opinion on financial statements for the year ended January 31. On March 2, the CPA learned that on February 11, the entity incurred a material loss on an uncollectible trade receivable as a result of the deteriorating financial condition of the entity's principal customer that led to the customer's bankruptcy. Management then refused to adjust the financial statements for this subsequent event. The CPA determined that the information is reliable and that there are creditors currently relying on the financial statements. The CPA's next course of action most likely would be to

   A. Notify the entity's creditors that the financial statements and the related auditor's report should no longer be relied on.

   B. Notify each member of the entity's board of directors about management's refusal to adjust the financial statements.

   C. Issue revised financial statements and distribute them to each creditor known to be relying on the financial statements.

   D. Issue a revised auditor's report and distribute it to each creditor known to be relying on the financial statements.

Answer (B) is correct. *(CPA, adapted)*
   REQUIRED: The actions of an auditor related to an event discovered subsequent to the issue of the financial statements.
   DISCUSSION: If the auditor decides that action should be taken to prevent future reliance on the report, (s)he should advise the client to make appropriate disclosures to persons who are known to be currently relying or who are likely to rely on the financial statements and the related report. However, if the client fails to take appropriate action, the auditor, who has determined the information's reliability and creditors' reliance on the statements, should notify each member of the board of the refusal. Absent a satisfactory settlement, the auditor should notify the client that the report must no longer be associated with the statements. The auditor also should notify appropriate regulatory agencies and each person known to be relying on the financial statements that the auditor's report should no longer be relied on.
   Answer (A) is incorrect. The board of directors should be notified first. Answer (C) is incorrect. The auditor has no authority to revise management's financial statements. Answer (D) is incorrect. The auditor should not revise the report, but subsequently notify those relying on the report that it is no longer valid.

14.4 Management Representations (AU 333)

21. Which of the following documentation is required for an audit in accordance with generally accepted auditing standards?

    A. An internal control questionnaire.

    B. An organization chart.

    C. A planning memorandum or checklist.

    D. A management representation letter.

Answer (D) is correct. *(CPA, adapted)*
    REQUIRED: The requirement of an audit made in accordance with GAAS.
    DISCUSSION: AU 333 requires that the auditor obtain certain written representations from management. The written representations corroborate information received orally from management but do not substitute for the procedures necessary to afford a reasonable basis for the opinion.

22. A purpose of a management representation letter is to reduce

    A. Audit risk to an aggregate level of misstatement that could be considered material.

    B. An auditor's responsibility to detect material misstatements only to the extent that the letter is relied on.

    C. The possibility of a misunderstanding concerning management's responsibility for the financial statements.

    D. The scope of an auditor's procedures concerning related party transactions and subsequent events.

Answer (C) is correct. *(CPA, adapted)*
    REQUIRED: The purpose of a management representation letter.
    DISCUSSION: Management's written representations confirm representations given to the auditor, indicate and document their continuing appropriateness, and reduce the possibility of misunderstanding about the subject matter of the representations. That subject matter includes management's acknowledgment of responsibility for the financial statements.

23. Which of the following statements ordinarily is included among the written management representations obtained by the auditor?

    A. Management acknowledges that there are no material weaknesses in internal control.

    B. Sufficient evidential matter has been made available to permit the expression of an unqualified opinion.

    C. Guarantees for which the company is potentially liable have been properly recorded or disclosed.

    D. Management acknowledges responsibility for illegal actions committed by employees.

Answer (C) is correct. *(Publisher, adapted)*
    REQUIRED: The statement included among written management representations.
    DISCUSSION: AU 333 lists the concerns ordinarily addressed in management representation letters, if applicable. The list includes disclosure of "guarantees, whether written or oral, under which the entity is contingently liable."
    Answer (A) is incorrect. Representations about internal control are not among those listed in AU 333. Answer (B) is incorrect. The auditor judges the sufficiency of evidence. Answer (D) is incorrect. Assuming illegal acts have occurred, management will rarely acknowledge responsibility for employees' behavior. However, the letter should make representations to the auditor about actual or possible violations of laws or regulations whose effects should be considered for disclosure or as a basis for a contingent loss.

24. To which of the following matters would an auditor **not** apply materiality limits when obtaining specific written management representations?

    A. Disclosure of compensating balance arrangements involving restrictions on cash balances.

    B. Information concerning related party transactions and related amounts receivable or payable.

    C. The absence of errors and unrecorded transactions in the financial statements.

    D. Fraud involving employees with significant roles in internal control.

Answer (D) is correct. *(CPA, adapted)*
    REQUIRED: The matter to which an auditor would not apply materiality limits.
    DISCUSSION: Management's representations may be limited to matters that are considered individually or collectively material on the condition that management and the auditor have reached an understanding concerning the limits of materiality. Such limitations do not apply to certain representations not directly related to amounts in the financial statements, e.g., acknowledgment of responsibility for fair presentation, availability of records, and knowledge of fraud or suspected fraud affecting the entity involving (1) management, (2) employees with significant roles in internal control, or (3) others if the fraud could materially affect the statements (AU 333).
    Answer (A) is incorrect. Materiality limits apply to disclosure of compensating balance arrangements involving restrictions on cash balances. Answer (B) is incorrect. Materiality limits apply to information concerning related party transactions and related amounts receivable or payable. Answer (C) is incorrect. Materiality limits apply to the absence of errors and unrecorded transactions in the financial statements.

25. An auditor finds several errors in the financial statements that the client prefers not to correct. The auditor determines that the errors are not material in the aggregate. Which of the following actions by the auditor is most appropriate?

A. Document the errors in the summary of uncorrected errors, and document the conclusion that the errors do **not** cause the financial statements to be misstated.

B. Document the conclusion that the errors do **not** cause the financial statements to be misstated, but do **not** summarize uncorrected errors in the audit documentation.

C. Summarize the uncorrected errors in the working papers, but do **not** document whether the errors cause the financial statements to be misstated.

D. Do **not** summarize the uncorrected errors in the audit documentation, and do **not** document a conclusion about whether the uncorrected errors cause the financial statements to be misstated.

Answer (A) is correct. *(CPA, adapted)*
REQUIRED: The most appropriate auditor action for discovered errors not corrected and not material in the aggregate.
DISCUSSION: The auditor should document this conclusion in the audit documentation. Additionally, the management representation letter should have an accompanying schedule that lists all discovered errors that were not corrected by management. The letter should include a sentence stating "We believe that the effects of the uncorrected financial statement misstatements summarized in the accompanying schedule are immaterial both individually and in the aggregate, to the financial statements taken as whole."

26. Which of the following expressions most likely would be included in a representation letter by management of an issuer?

A. No events have occurred subsequent to the balance sheet date that require adjustment to, or disclosure in, the financial statements.

B. There are no significant deficiencies identified during the prior-year's audit of which the audit committee of the board of directors is unaware.

C. We do not intend to provide any information that may be construed to constitute a waiver of the attorney-client privilege.

D. Certain computer files and other required evidence may exist only for a short period of time and only in computer-readable form.

Answer (A) is correct. *(CPA, adapted)*
REQUIRED: The expression most likely found in a management representation letter.
DISCUSSION: A management representation letter confirms management's oral and written representations to the auditor (1) about matters in the financial statements and (2) in response to specific inquiries. The auditor should obtain written representations from management to indicate and document their continued validity and reduce possible misunderstandings. Obtaining the letter is a required procedure to gather evidence in an audit in accordance with GAAS, but it does not substitute for other procedures. Information concerning subsequent events is a common matter covered in the letter (AU 333).
Answer (B) is incorrect. The representations from management of an issuer should include whether significant control deficiencies and material weaknesses identified and communicated to those charged with governance during previous engagements have been resolved. The board should be aware of all previous issues. Answer (C) is incorrect. A statement that the client does not intend to provide information that may be interpreted as a waiver of the attorney-client privilege may be made in a communication to the auditor, but it is not a customary element of the representation letter. Disclosure of a part of a privileged communication to the attorney may constitute a waiver as to the entire communication (AU 337C). Answer (D) is incorrect. The statement that certain computer files and other required evidence may exist only for a short period of time and only in computer-readable form is a description of the nature of evidence, not a common management representation.

27. To which of the following matters would materiality limits **not** apply in obtaining written management representations?

A. The availability of minutes of shareholders' and directors' meetings.

B. Losses from purchase commitments at prices in excess of market value.

C. The disclosure of compensating balance arrangements involving related parties.

D. Reductions of obsolete inventory to net realizable value.

Answer (A) is correct. *(CPA, adapted)*
REQUIRED: The matter to which materiality limits do not apply when obtaining written management representations.
DISCUSSION: The availability of minutes to shareholders' meetings and directors' meetings is independent of amounts in the financial statements. Thus, materiality limits do not apply.
Answer (B) is incorrect. Losses from purchase commitments relate to dollar amounts to which the materiality judgment applies. Answer (C) is incorrect. Disclosure of compensating balances relates to dollar amounts to which the materiality judgment applies. Answer (D) is incorrect. Reduction of obsolete inventory to net realizable values relates to dollar amounts to which the materiality judgment applies.

28. Key Co. plans to present comparative financial statements for the years ended December 31, Year 1 and Year 2, respectively. Smith, CPA, audited Key's financial statements for both years and plans to report on the comparative financial statements on May 1, Year 3. Key's current management team was not present until January 1, Year 2. What period of time should be covered by Key's management representation letter?

A. January 1, Year 1, through December 31, Year 2.

B. January 1, Year 1, through May 1, Year 3.

C. January 1, Year 2, through December 31, Year 2.

D. January 1, Year 2, through May 1, Year 3.

Answer (B) is correct. *(CPA, adapted)*
REQUIRED: The dates to be covered by a management representation letter.
DISCUSSION: Because the auditor is concerned with events occurring through the date of his or her report that may require adjustment to or disclosure in the financial statements, the representations should be made as of the date of the auditor's report. Moreover, if current management was not present during all periods covered by the auditor's report, the auditor should nevertheless obtain written representations from current management on all such periods (AU 333).

14.5 Auditor's Consideration of an Entity's Ability to Continue as a Going Concern (AU 341)

29. Which of the following auditing procedures most likely would assist an auditor in identifying conditions and events that may indicate substantial doubt about an entity's ability to continue as a going concern?

A. Inspecting title documents to verify whether any assets are pledged as collateral.

B. Confirming with third parties the details of arrangements to maintain financial support.

C. Reconciling the cash balance per books with the cutoff bank statement and the bank confirmation.

D. Comparing the entity's depreciation and asset capitalization policies to other entities in the industry.

Answer (B) is correct. *(CPA, adapted)*
REQUIRED: The audit procedure that may identify conditions indicating substantial doubt about an entity's continuation as a going concern.
DISCUSSION: The procedures typically employed to identify going concern issues include (1) analytical procedures, (2) review of subsequent events, (3) review of compliance with debt and loan agreements, (4) reading minutes of meetings, (5) inquiry of legal counsel, and (6) confirmation with related and third parties of arrangements for financial support.
Answer (A) is incorrect. Searching for pledged assets is related to disclosure issues. Answer (C) is incorrect. Reconciling the cash balance with cutoff bank statements and the bank confirmation tests the existence of cash. Answer (D) is incorrect. This comparison might identify conditions needing additional consideration but would not provide evidence about going concern issues.

30. Which of the following conditions or events most likely would cause an auditor to have substantial doubt about an entity's ability to continue as a going concern?

A. Significant related-party transactions are pervasive.

B. Usual trade credit from suppliers is denied.

C. Arrearages in preferred stock dividends are paid.

D. Restrictions on the disposal of principal assets are present.

Answer (B) is correct. *(CPA, adapted)*
REQUIRED: The event or condition causing substantial doubt about an entity's ability to continue as a going concern.
DISCUSSION: Auditors should evaluate whether substantial doubt exists about an entity's ability to continue as a going concern. The evaluation is based on procedures planned and performed to obtain evidence about the management assertions embodied in the financial statements. An auditor should examine (1) negative trends, (2) indications of possible financial difficulties, (3) internal problems, and (4) external problems. Denial of normal trade credit by suppliers is an indication of possible financial difficulty.
Answer (A) is incorrect. Related-party transactions are common. They do not indicate an internal problem or financial difficulty. Answer (C) is incorrect. The payment of arrearages in preferred stock dividends is a sign of financial strength. Answer (D) is incorrect. Restrictions on the disposal of assets concern the liquidity of the assets. They do not raise a question as to the ability of the entity to continue operations.

31. Cooper, CPA, believes there is substantial doubt about the ability of Zero Corp. to continue as a going concern for a reasonable period of time. In evaluating Zero's plans for dealing with the adverse effects of future conditions and events, Cooper most likely will consider, as a mitigating factor, Zero's plans to

A. Discuss with lenders the terms of all debt and loan agreements.

B. Strengthen internal controls over cash disbursements.

C. Purchase production facilities currently being leased from a related party.

D. Postpone expenditures for research and development projects.

Answer (D) is correct. *(CPA, adapted)*
REQUIRED: The managerial action that will mitigate adverse effects of future conditions and events.
DISCUSSION: Once an auditor has identified conditions and events indicating that substantial doubt exists about an entity's ability to continue as a going concern, the auditor should consider management's plans to mitigate their adverse effects. The auditor should consider plans to dispose of assets, borrow money or restructure debt, reduce or delay expenditures, and increase equity.
Answer (A) is incorrect. Discussion with lenders is not a sufficient action to mitigate the circumstances. Answer (B) is incorrect. Internal control improvements do not increase cash flows or postpone expenditures. Answer (C) is incorrect. The purchase of facilities may exacerbate the company's problems.

32. When an auditor concludes there is substantial doubt about a continuing audit client's ability to continue as a going concern for a reasonable period of time, the auditor's responsibility is to

A. Express a qualified or adverse opinion, depending upon materiality, due to the possible effects on the financial statements.

B. Consider the adequacy of disclosure about the client's possible inability to continue as a going concern.

C. Report to the client's audit committee that management's accounting estimates may need to be adjusted.

D. Reissue the prior year's auditor's report and add an explanatory paragraph that specifically refers to "substantial doubt" and "going concern."

Answer (B) is correct. *(CPA, adapted)*
REQUIRED: The auditor's action given substantial doubt about a client's ability to continue as a going concern.
DISCUSSION: After considering (1) identified conditions and events in the aggregate that raise going-concern issues and (2) management's plans for coping with their adverse effects, the auditor may conclude there is substantial doubt about the entity's ability to continue as a going concern for a reasonable period of time. In that case, the auditor should consider the possible effects on the financial statements and the adequacy of disclosure. The auditor also should include an explanatory paragraph in the report.
Answer (A) is incorrect. An auditor may still express an unqualified opinion and refer to the going concern issue in an explanatory paragraph. Answer (C) is incorrect. Going concern considerations are independent of the accounting estimates that may need adjustment. Answer (D) is incorrect. The prior year's audit report should not be changed. The auditor's opinion on the prior year has not been altered.

Use the additional questions in Gleim **CPA Test Prep Online** to create Test Sessions that emulate Prometric!

14.6 PRACTICE SIMULATION

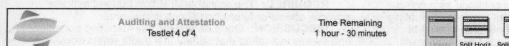

| | Auditing and Attestation
Testlet 4 of 4 | Time Remaining
1 hour - 30 minutes | Unsplit | Split Horiz | Split Vertical | Spreadsheet | Calculator | Exit |

DIRECTIONS

Note: If you believe you have encountered a software malfunction, report it to the test center staff immediately.

Navigation

To navigate from task to task, use the controls at the bottom of the screen. Click on the **Next** button to advance to the next task, or the **Previous** button to go to the previous task. To go directly to any task, click on its number.

| ⚐ = Reminder | | Directions | 1 2 3 4 5 6 7 | | ◄ Previous   Next ► |

If you would like a reminder to revisit a task, or want to indicate that you are finished with it, click on the reminder flag below the task number. To clear the flag, click on it again. Reminder flags are for your use only – they do not contribute to your score.

Tabs

In this part of the examination, you will be asked to complete various tasks. Every task has one or more **Work Tabs**. Some tasks have one or more **Information Tabs**, others may have none. Every task has a **Help** tab.

If a task has **Information Tabs**, you may use the information in them to complete your responses in the **Work Tabs**.

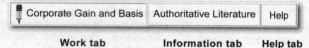

| | Corporate Gain and Basis | Authoritative Literature | Help |
| | Work tab | Information tab | Help tab |

Work Tabs:

- **Work Tabs** are identified with a pencil icon. This is where your responses are expected.
- Each task has one or more **Work Tabs**.
- **Work Tabs** contain directions for completing the task – be sure to read these directions carefully.
- The **Work Tab** name in the example above is for illustration only – yours will differ.
- You must complete all of the **Work Tabs** in each task to receive full credit.

Information Tabs:

- The Authoritative Literature will be provided in all tasks in the AUD, FAR, and REG sections for your reference.
- Your simulation may have one or more additional **Information Tabs**. Like the Authoritative Literature tabs, **Information Tabs** do not have a pencil icon.
- If your task has additional **Information Tabs**, go through each to familiarize yourself with the task content.

Help Tab:

- The **Help Tab** provides assistance with the exam software that is used in this task. For example, if the task is to compose a memorandum, **Help** will provide information about the word processor.

The Toolbar

The toolbar at the top of the screen shows the amount of time remaining for you to complete the tasks. In addition, the following tools are available. Note that only the Exit button is displayed when Directions are visible - the others will appear when you begin the tasks.

 Click on these buttons to split or unsplit the screen. You can split the screen vertically or horizontally.

 Click on this button to display the calculator; click on it again to hide the calculator. To move the calculator, click on the calculator title bar and drag the calculator to the desired location.

 Click on this button to use the spreadsheet; click on it again to hide the spreadsheet. To move the spreadsheet, click on the the spreadsheet title bar and drag the spreadsheet to the desired location.

 Click on this button to go on to the next part of the examination. You must complete all of the tasks to receive full credit. Once you click on **Exit** and confirm the action, you will NOT be able to return to this testlet.

| ⚐ = Reminder | | Directions | 1 2 3 4 5 6 | | ◄ Previous   Next ► |

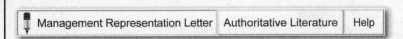

Check the box to the right of each statement that is typically included in the management representation letter obtained by the auditor.

Statement	Included
1. The company is not independent with regard to the financial statements.	
2. The company approved all estimates made by the auditor in the financial statements.	
3. The company has made available to the auditor all minutes of the meetings of the board of directors.	
4. All information in the notes to the financial statements is the representation of the auditor.	
5. The company has no plans that may materially affect the carrying amount of assets or liabilities.	
6. The company has no knowledge of alleged fraud or suspected fraud.	
7. All items included in this letter are assumed to be immaterial.	
8. Related party transactions have been properly disclosed in the financial statements.	
9. No events have occurred subsequent to the balance-sheet date that would require disclosure in the financial statements.	
10. The company has recorded no transactions with a negative effect on earnings.	

Select from the list provided the best description of each statement that deals with the auditor's evaluation of whether the client is a going concern. Each choice may be used once, more than once, or not at all.

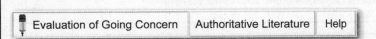

Statement	Answer
1. Restructuring existing debt to attain more favorable conditions	
2. Negative trends in earnings	
3. Inquiry of legal counsel	
4. Review of subsequent events	
5. Resolve any substantial doubt	
6. Delay expenditures	
7. Loss of a key patent	
8. Accelerate cash receipts from affiliates	
9. Document findings	
10. Gathering evidence for relevant assertions about going concern	

Choices
A) A procedure performed by the auditor
B) A purpose of the auditor's procedures
C) An expectation of the client
D) A condition or event that will cause the auditor concern
E) A management plan to address adverse effects of conditions or events

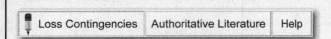

Check the box to the right of each audit procedure below that should be performed when testing for loss contingencies relating to litigation, claims, and assessments.

Audit Procedure	Perform
1. Read minutes of meetings of shareholders, directors, and committees.	
2. Inquire of officials at the courthouse in the county of the client.	
3. Read contracts, loan agreements, leases, and other documents.	
4. Read client correspondence with taxing and other governmental agencies.	
5. Read client correspondence with insurance and bonding companies.	
6. Read legal briefs of all suits filed against competitors of the client.	
7. Read confirmation replies for information concerning guarantees.	
8. Obtain from management or inside general counsel a description and evaluation of litigation, claims, and assessments.	
9. Obtain representation letters from all staff and professional employees of the client.	
10. Obtain an analysis of professional fee expenses and review supporting invoices for indications of contingencies.	
11. Inquire of SEC officials concerning reported violations creating claims or assessments.	
12. Request the client's management to prepare for transmittal a letter of inquiry to those lawyers consulted by the client concerning litigation, claims, and assessments.	
13. Determine that the financial statements include proper accruals and disclosures of contingencies.	
14. Obtain written or oral assurance from the audit committee that the financial statements include all accruals and disclosures required by the FASB's guidance applicable to accounting for contingencies.	

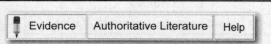

Indicate by checking the appropriate box whether each statement is true or false.

Statement	True	False
1. The primary source of information to be reported about litigation, claims, and assessments is the court records.		
2. Assessing control at a low level is not required to have a reasonable basis for extending audit conclusions from an interim date to the balance sheet date.		
3. Inquiry (versus a response) need not be made about items considered immaterial, provided the auditor and client have an understanding about the limits of materiality for this purpose.		
4. The auditor's communication with those charged with governance must be in writing.		
5. The observation of inventory is the procedure that is least likely to be performed before the balance sheet date.		

Misstatements | Authoritative Literature | Help

The year under audit is Year 2.

During the audit of accounts payable, you detected misstatements previously undetected by the client. All misstatements were related to Year 2. For each of the liability misstatements shown below, select from the lists provided the most appropriate item.

- In Column I, select the audit procedure that was most likely used to detect the misstatement.
- In Column II, select the internal control that most likely could prevent or detect this type of misstatement in the future.

Audit procedures and internal controls may be selected once, more than once, or not at all.

Misstatement	Column I Audit Procedure Used to Detect Misstatement	Column II Internal Control that Could Prevent or Detect Misstatement in the Future
1. An accounts payable clerk misplaces year-end invoices for raw materials that were received on December 21, Year 2, and therefore liabilities were not recorded.		
2. The company tends to be careless in recording payables in the correct period.		
3. The company has the same person approving pay requests and preparing checks.		
4. The company's receiving department misplaces receiving reports for purchases of raw materials at year end and therefore liabilities were not recorded.		

Column I Selection List
A) From the January Year 3 cash disbursements journal, select payments and match to corresponding invoices.
B) Review the cash disbursements journal for the month of December Year 2.
C) On a surprise basis, review the receiving department's filing system, and test check quantities entered on December Year 2 receiving reports to packing slips.
D) Identify open purchase orders and vendors' invoices at December 31, Year 2, and investigate their disposition.
E) Request written confirmation from the accounts payable supervisor that all vendor invoices have been recorded in the accounts payable subsidiary ledger.
F) Investigate unmatched receiving reports dated prior to January 1, Year 3.
G) Compare the balances for selected vendors at the end of Year 2 and Year 1.
H) Determine that credit memos received 10 days after the balance sheet date have been recorded in the proper period.
I) Select an unpaid invoice and ask to be walked through the invoice payment process.

Column II Selection List
A) The purchasing department supervisor forwards a monthly listing of matched purchase orders and receiving reports to the accounts payable supervisor for comparison to a listing of vouched invoices.
B) The accounts payable supervisor review a monthly listing of open purchase orders and vendors' invoices for follow up with the receiving department.
C) Copies of all vendor invoices received during the year are filed in an outside storage facility.
D) All vendor invoices are reviewed for mathematical accuracy.
E) On a daily basis, the receiving department independently counts all merchandise received.
F) All vendor invoices with supporting documentation are canceled when paid.
G) At the end of each month, the purchasing department confirms terms of delivery with selected vendors.
H) Separate the functions of accounts payable and cash disbursements.
I) A clerk is responsible for matching purchase orders with receiving reports and making certain they are included in the proper month.

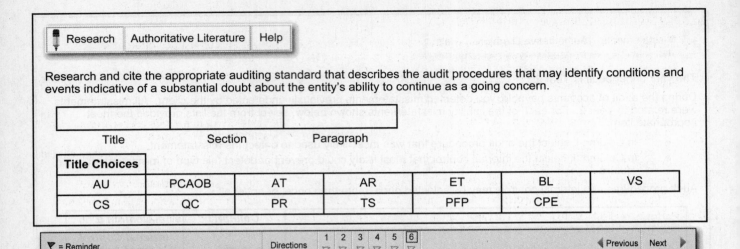

Research and cite the appropriate auditing standard that describes the audit procedures that may identify conditions and events indicative of a substantial doubt about the entity's ability to continue as a going concern.

Title	Section	Paragraph

Title Choices

AU	PCAOB	AT	AR	ET	BL	VS
CS	QC	PR	TS	PFP	CPE	

▼ = Reminder   Directions   1 2 3 4 5 [6]   ◀ Previous   Next ▶

Unofficial Answers

1. Management Representation Letter (10 Gradable Items)

1. <u>Not included.</u> There is no statement concerning the client's independence in the management representation letter.

2. <u>Not included.</u> Management, not the auditor, develops the estimates used in the financial statements.

3. <u>Included.</u> The letter should include a representation that the company has made available to the auditor minutes of all meetings that might affect the audit.

4. <u>Not included.</u> All information in the notes to the financial statements is the representation of management.

5. <u>Included.</u> The letter should state that the company has no plans that may materially affect the carrying amount of assets or liabilities.

6. <u>Included.</u> The letter should state that the company has no knowledge of alleged or suspected fraud.

7. <u>Not included.</u> Items included in the letter are assumed to be material.

8. <u>Included.</u> The letter should state that related party transactions have been properly disclosed in the financial statements.

9. <u>Included.</u> The letter should state that no events have occurred subsequent to the balance-sheet date that would require disclosure in the financial statements.

10. <u>Not included.</u> Many recorded transactions, for example expenses, would have a negative impact on earnings.

2. Evaluation of Going Concern (10 Gradable Items)

1. <u>E) A management plan to address adverse effects of conditions or events.</u> Restructuring existing debt to attain more favorable conditions is a management plan to address adverse effects of conditions or events.

2. <u>D) A condition or event that will cause the auditor concern.</u> Negative trends in earnings is a condition that will cause the auditor concern.

3. <u>A) A procedure performed by the auditor.</u> Inquiry of legal counsel is a procedure performed by the auditor to learn about uncertainties that could lead going concern issues.

4. <u>A) A procedure performed by the auditor.</u> A review of subsequent events is a procedure performed by the auditor to learn about going concern issues.

5. <u>B) A purpose of auditor's procedures.</u> A purpose of the auditor's procedures is to resolve any substantial doubt about going concern.

6. <u>E) A management plan to address adverse effects of conditions or events.</u> Delaying expenditures is a management plan to address adverse effects of conditions or events.

7. <u>D) A condition or event that will cause the auditor concern.</u> The loss of a key patent is an event that will cause the auditor concern.

8. <u>E) A management plan to address adverse effects of conditions or events.</u> Accelerating cash receipts from affiliates is a management plan to address adverse effects of conditions or events.

9. <u>A) A procedure performed by the auditor.</u> Documenting findings is a procedure completed by the auditor.

10. <u>B) A purpose of auditor's procedures.</u> A purpose of the auditor's procedures is to gather evidence for relevant assertions about going concern.

3. Loss Contingencies (14 Gradable Items)

1. Perform. Minutes of the meetings of the board of directors, shareholders, and various committees often provide evidence about unusual events giving rise to potential contingencies.

2. Do not perform. Inquiring of local officials is not a normal procedure. However, in certain instances the auditor may find it necessary to gather evidence from public records.

3. Perform. Contracts, agreements, and leases often contain provisions that commit the client to contingencies.

4. Perform. Correspondence with governmental agencies should be read and evaluated for numerous reasons (e.g., potential violations of laws or regulations, taxes or fees due, and claims or assessments on property).

5. Perform. Insurance companies and bonding agencies often insure clients against potential losses. These losses should be identified and evaluated relative to potential financial reporting requirements.

6. Do not perform. Reading all legal briefs for suits filed against the client's competitors is not feasible or necessary.

7. Perform. Confirmations may disclose certain guarantees offered to customers that would create contingent liabilities.

8. Perform. AU 337 states that the auditor should obtain from management a description and evaluation of litigation, claims, and assessments that existed at the date of the balance sheet being reported on.

9. Do not perform. AU 337 requires the auditor to obtain written representations from management, usually the chief executive officer and chief financial officer. The auditor would not normally obtain written representations from all client staff.

10. Perform. Professional fees (for example, fees paid to lawyers) should be evaluated to determine their purpose. Often, the services are in relation to contingencies.

11. Do not perform. Normally, the auditor will not inquire of SEC officials. However, written correspondence, available from the client, should be evaluated by the auditor.

12. Perform. AU 337 states that a letter of audit inquiry to the client's lawyer is the auditor's primary means of obtaining corroboration of the information furnished by management concerning litigation, claims, and assessments.

13. Perform. The auditor should consider the accounting treatment for each contingency, and determine that the financial statements are consistent with that treatment.

14. Do not perform. It is management's responsibility, not the audit committee's, to assure that appropriate accounting treatment is accorded contingencies.

4. Evidence (5 Gradable Items)

1. False. The primary source of information about litigation, claims, and assessments is management.

2. True. Evidence from interim work can be used without the reliance on internal control. However, the auditor often finds that the ability to rely on controls is helpful in the evaluation of the evidence.

3. True. Items that are immaterial, by definition, are not important to the auditor.

4. False. If the communication is not in writing, the auditor should document the communication in the working papers.

5. False. Observation of inventory may be accomplished at interim if the client uses a perpetual system and the inventory is well maintained.

5. Misstatements (8 Gradable Items)

	Column I	Column II
1.	F)	A)
2.	A)	I)
3.	I)	H)
4.	D)	B)

1. F) Investigate unmatched receiving reports dated prior to January 1, Year 3. Receiving reports should be matched with purchase orders and vendor invoices as support for a payment voucher. Investigating unmatched documents would uncover the failure to prepare a voucher.

    A) The purchasing department supervisor forwards a monthly listing of matched purchase orders and receiving reports to the accounts payable supervisor for comparison to a listing of vouched invoices. Comparing an independent listing of matched purchase orders and receiving reports with vouched invoices would detect a lost document in accounts payable.

2. A) From the January Year 3 cash disbursements journal, select payments and match to corresponding invoices. A cutoff test that evaluates transactions recorded at or near year end would detect transactions recorded in the improper period.

    I) A clerk is responsible for matching purchases orders with receiving reports and making certain they are included in the proper month. Having an employee responsible for making certain that transactions are recorded in the proper period would be a control to help ensure proper cutoff.

3.   I) Select an unpaid invoice and ask to be walked through the invoice payment process. A walkthrough of the process would allow the auditor to identify weaknesses in the system.

H) Separate the functions of accounts payable and cash disbursements.. Separation of the approval and custody functions is a control to mitigate risks in a payment system.

4.   D) Identify open purchase orders and vendors' invoices at December 31, Year 2, and investigate their disposition. To detect missing or lost receiving reports, the auditor should identify open purchase orders and vendors' invoices at December 31, Year 2, and investigate their disposition.

B) The accounts payable supervisor review a monthly listing of open purchase orders and vendors' invoices for follow up with the receiving department. A useful control would be to have the accounts payable supervisor review a monthly listing of open purchase orders and vendors' invoices for follow-up with the receiving department.

6. Research (1 Gradable Item)

Answer: 341.05

AU Section 341 – *The Auditor's Consideration of an Entity's Ability to Continue as a Going Concern*

.05   It is not necessary to design audit procedures solely to identify conditions and events that, when considered in the aggregate, indicate there could be substantial doubt about the entity's ability to continue as a going concern for a reasonable period of time. The results of auditing procedures designed and performed to achieve other audit objectives should be sufficient for that purpose. The following are examples of procedures that may identify such conditions and events:

- Analytical procedures
- Review of subsequent events
- Review of compliance with the terms of debt and loan agreements
- Reading of minutes of meetings of stockholders, board of directors, and important committees of the board
- Inquiry of an entity's legal counsel about litigation, claims, and assessments
- Confirmation with related and third parties of the details of arrangements to provide or maintain financial support

Gleim Simulation Grading

Task	Correct Responses		Gradable Items		Score per Task
1	_____	÷	10	=	_____
2	_____	÷	10	=	_____
3	_____	÷	14	=	_____
4	_____	÷	5	=	_____
5	_____	÷	8	=	_____
Research	_____	÷	1	=	_____

	Total of Scores per Task	_____
÷	Total Number of Tasks	6
	Total Score	_____ %

Use **CPA Gleim Online** and **Simulation Wizard** to practice more task-based simulations in a realistic environment.

STUDY UNIT FIFTEEN
EVIDENCE -- SAMPLING

(19 pages of outline)

The first subunit defines terms, describes the purpose of and approach to sampling, and presents the basic concepts traditionally tested on the CPA exam. A study of these fundamentals is an effective way to prepare for most sampling-related questions. Periodically, however, more comprehensive questions are asked, including those requiring basic calculations or the consideration of tables.

The remaining three subunits contain study materials related to more extensive questions and simulations. They describe, in more detail, specific sampling techniques and provide several examples. Although more comprehensive than the first subunit, they are not intended to be an exhaustive treatment of sampling. These sections are based on concepts that have been tested in the past or are likely to be tested on future CPA exams and are discussed in the AICPA Audit Guide, *Audit Sampling* (2008).

15.1 SAMPLING FUNDAMENTALS (AU 350)

We cannot predict what will be on the exam you take. We can give you some facts to allow you to make some decisions about your study. Sampling is included in the CSO's Area III -- Auditing and Attestation: Performing Audit Procedures and Evaluating Evidence, which is reported to make up between 16% and 20% of the exam. In that Area, "perform audit sampling" is one of 24 topics listed as those subject to testing. When the exam was disclosed, sampling questions normally accounted for about 3% to 4% of the questions, but occasionally more. Many, if not most, of those questions could have been answered by a solid understanding of the material in Subunit 1. Understand all you can about the exam and your strengths and weaknesses, and then decide how much time to invest in more specialized issues of sampling.

1. **Audit Sampling**

    a. Audit sampling applies an audit procedure to fewer than 100% of the items under audit for the purpose of drawing a conclusion about a characteristic of a balance or transaction class (the population sampled). Sampling may be statistical or nonstatistical.

        1) **Judgment (nonstatistical) sampling** uses the auditor's subjective judgment to determine the sample size (number of items examined) and sample selection (which items to examine). This subjectivity is not always a weakness. The auditor, based on other audit work, may be able to test the most material and risky transactions and emphasize the types of transactions subject to high risk of material misstatement.

        2) **Statistical (probability or random) sampling** provides an objective method of determining sample size and selecting the items to be examined. Unlike judgment sampling, it also provides a means of quantitatively assessing **precision** (how closely the sample represents the population) and **reliability** (confidence level, which is the percentage of times the sample will adequately reflect the population).

          a)   **Random-based selection** is the primary characteristic of statistical sampling. It includes (1) random sampling, (2) stratified random sampling, (3) monetary-unit sampling, and (4) systematic sampling.

          b)   Statistical sampling helps the auditor design an efficient sample, measure the sufficiency of the evidence obtained, and evaluate the sample results. The **third standard of field work** requires auditors to obtain sufficient appropriate evidence. Sufficiency is the measure of the quantity of evidence. Thus, it relates to the design and size of the sample. Statistical sampling permits the auditor to measure **sampling risk** and therefore to design more efficient samples (i.e., the minimum samples necessary to provide sufficient appropriate evidence).

    b.   Statistical sampling is applicable to both **tests of controls** (attribute sampling) and **substantive testing** (variables sampling).

    c.   The auditor expects the sample to be **representative of the population**. Thus, the sample should have the same characteristics (e.g., control deviation rate or average amount) as the population, and a conclusion can be drawn from the sample about the population.

2.   Audit risk includes both uncertainties due to sampling and uncertainties due to factors other than sampling. These aspects of audit risk are sampling risk and nonsampling risk, which are discussed next.

3.   **Sampling Risk**

    a.   Sampling risk is the probability that a properly drawn sample may not be representative of the population. The conclusions from the sample may differ from those made if all the items in the population are examined.

    b.   Moreover, sampling risk is **inversely related** to sample size. As the sample increases, sampling risk decreases.

        1)   The auditor controls sampling risk by specifying the acceptable level when developing the sampling plan.

    c.   For **tests of controls**, sampling risk has the following aspects:

        1)   The **risk of assessing control risk too low** is the risk that the assessed level of control risk based on the sample is less than the true operating effectiveness of internal control (recall that control risk is the risk that controls do not prevent or detect material misstatements on a timely basis). In other words, it is the risk that the actual control risk is greater than that indicated by the sample. This risk relates to audit **effectiveness** and could cause **audit failure**.

           a)   This risk also is termed a Type II error or Beta risk.

        2)   The **risk of assessing control risk too high** is the risk that the assessed level of control risk based on the sample is greater than the true operating effectiveness of internal control. In other words, it is the risk that actual control risk is less than that indicated by the sample. This risk relates to audit **efficiency** and is likely to result in **greater audit effort**.

           a)   The auditor's overassessment of control risk may lead to an unnecessary extension of substantive procedures.

           b)   This risk also is termed a Type I error or Alpha risk.

    d.   For **substantive tests** of details, sampling risk has the following aspects:

        1)   The **risk of incorrect acceptance** is the risk that the sample supports the conclusion that the recorded account balance is not materially misstated when it is materially misstated.

           a)   This risk relates to audit **effectiveness** and could cause **audit failure**.

           b)   This risk also is termed a Type II error or Beta risk.

2)   The **risk of incorrect rejection** is the risk that the sample supports the conclusion that the recorded account balance is materially misstated when it is not materially misstated. This risk relates to audit **efficiency** and is likely to result in **greater audit effort**.

   a)   After an incorrect rejection, it is likely that (1) the client will assert the fairness of the balance, (2) the auditor will perform additional procedures, and (3) the fairness of the balance will be affirmed. However, if the cost and effort of selecting additional sample items are low, a higher risk of incorrect rejection may be acceptable.

   b)   This risk also is termed a Type I error or Alpha risk.

e.   The following table is helpful in understanding sampling risk:

	Tests of Controls (Attribute Sampling)	Tests of Details (Variables Sampling)
Type I	Risk of assessing control risk too high *Audit efficiency*	Risk of incorrect rejection *Audit efficiency*
Type II	Risk of assessing control risk too low *Audit failure*	Risk of incorrect acceptance *Audit failure*

f.   The **confidence level**, also termed the reliability level, is the complement of the applicable sampling risk factor. Thus, for a test of controls, if the allowable risk of assessing control risk too low is 5%, the auditor's desired confidence level is 95% (100% − 5%). For a substantive procedure, if the risk of incorrect rejection is 5%, the auditor's desired confidence level is 95% (100% − 5%).

4.   **Nonsampling Risk**

a.   Nonsampling risk concerns all aspects of audit risk not caused by sampling, such as the auditor's application of inappropriate procedures or his/her inability to recognize misstatements or control deviations.

b.   Adequate **planning and supervision**, among other things, decrease nonsampling risk.

5.   **Basic Steps in a Statistical Plan**

a.   **Determine the objectives of the plan.**

   1)   For a test of controls, an example is to conclude that control is reasonably effective.

   2)   For a substantive procedure, an example is to conclude that a balance is not misstated by more than an immaterial amount.

b.   **Define the population.** This step includes defining the sampling unit and considering the completeness of the population.

   1)   For tests of controls, it includes defining the period covered.
   2)   For substantive procedures, it includes identifying individually significant items.

c.   **Determine acceptable levels of sampling risk** (e.g., 5% or 10%).

d.   **Calculate the sample size** using tables or sample-size formulas.

   1)   In some cases, it is efficient to divide the population into subpopulations or strata. The primary objective of **stratification** is to minimize variability. Because the variance within each subpopulation or stratum is lower than in the population as a whole, the auditor may sample a smaller number of items while holding the allowance for sampling risk (precision) and the confidence level constant.

2) For example, when auditing sales revenue, an auditor could divide the population into strata of dollar increments. The auditor could test transactions under $500, between $501 and $2,000, and $2,001 and above.

e. **Select the sampling approach**, e.g., random number, systematic, or block.

1) In **random sampling**, each item in the population has an equal and nonzero probability of selection. Random selection is usually accomplished by generating random numbers from a random number table or computer program and tracing them to associated documents or items in the population.

2) **Systematic sampling** begins with selecting a random start and then taking every n^{th} item in the population. The value of n is computed by dividing the population by the number of sampling units. The random start should be in the first interval. Because the sampling technique only requires counting in the population, no correspondence between random numbers and the items in the population is necessary as in random number sampling. A systematic sampling plan assumes the items are arranged randomly in the population. If the auditor discovers that this is not true, a random selection method should be used.

EXAMPLE

If the population contains 8,200 items and a sample of 50 is required, every 164th item is selected (8,200 ÷ 50). After a random start in the first interval (1 to 164), every additional 164th item is selected. For example, if the 35th item were the first selected randomly, the next would be the 199th (35 + 164). The next item would be the 363rd (199 + 164). The process would be continued until the 50 items were identified.

---

3) **Block sampling** (cluster sampling) randomly selects groups of items as the sampling units rather than individual items. An example is the inclusion in the sample of all cash payments for May and September. One possible drawback is that the variability of items within the blocks may not be representative of the variability within the population. The advantage of block sampling is that it avoids the need to assign random numbers to individual items in the population. Instead, blocks (clusters) are randomly selected.

f. **Take the sample.** The auditor selects the items to be evaluated.

g. **Evaluate the sample results.** The auditor draws conclusions about the population.

h. **Document the sampling procedures.** The auditor prepares appropriate working papers.

6. **Sample Size**

a. In general, the sample size is dependent on

1) The **population size**. As the population size increases, the sample increases but at a decreasing rate.

2) The **acceptable risk** (1 – the confidence level). The smaller the acceptable risk, the larger the sample size.

3) The **variability in the population**. The more variability in the population, measured by the standard deviation for variables sampling or the expected deviation rate for attribute sampling, the larger the sample size.

4) The **tolerable misstatement** for variables sampling or the **tolerable deviation rate** for attribute sampling. The smaller the acceptable misstatement amount or deviation rate, the larger the sample size.

7. **Overview of Attribute Sampling**

   a. Attribute sampling is used to test the effectiveness of controls (tests of controls).

EXAMPLE

The auditor desires to test the effectiveness of the approval process of purchase orders. (S)he selects a sample of purchase orders from the population of all purchase orders issued during the year and inspects each one in the sample for the required approval.

---

   b. The failure (deviation) rate in the application of the control in the sample is used to project the failure rate to the whole population.

   c. By specifying a tolerable deviation rate, a preliminary estimate of the population failure rate, and the risk of assessing control risk too low, the auditor can determine the appropriate sample size by consulting a table.

8. **Primary Methods of Variables Sampling**

   a. Variables sampling applies to dollar values or other quantities in contrast with the binary propositions tested by attribute sampling (see Subunit 15.2).

   b. **Mean-per-unit** averages the audit amounts of the sample items and multiplies the average by the number of items in the population to estimate the population amount. An allowance for sampling risk (achieved precision at the desired level of confidence based on the normal distribution) is then calculated.

   c. **Difference estimation** (of population misstatement) (1) determines differences between the audit and recorded amounts of items in the sample, (2) adds the differences, (3) calculates the mean difference, and (4) multiplies the mean by the number of items in the population. An allowance for sampling risk (achieved precision at the desired level of confidence based on the normal distribution) is then calculated.

      1) **Ratio estimation** is similar to difference estimation except that it estimates the population misstatement by multiplying the recorded amount of the population by the ratio of the total audit amount of the sample items to their total recorded amount.

   d. **Monetary-unit sampling (MUS)**, also known as probability-proportional-to-size (PPS) or dollar-unit sampling (DUS), uses the dollar or another monetary unit as the sampling unit. MUS is appropriate for testing account balances (typically assets) for overstatement when some items may be far larger than others in the population. In effect, it stratifies the population because the larger account balances have a greater chance of being selected. MUS is most useful if few misstatements are expected.

      1) Also, the method does not require the use of a measure of dispersion (e.g., standard deviation) to determine sample size or interpret the results.

Stop and review! You have completed the outline for this subunit. Study multiple-choice questions 1 through 9 beginning on page 496.

15.2 STATISTICAL SAMPLING IN TESTS OF CONTROLS (ATTRIBUTE SAMPLING)

1. **Attribute sampling** tests binary, yes/no, or error/nonerror questions. It is used to test the effectiveness of controls because it can estimate a rate of occurrence of control deviations in a population.

   a. Attribute sampling requires the existence of evidence indicating performance of the control being tested (e.g., a control indicating that the purchasing agent has signed all purchase orders before sending them to the vendor). It is most helpful for a large population of documentary evidence. In general, the performance of any task that leaves evidence of its execution is suitable for attribute sampling. In such cases, the auditor can form conclusions about the population by examining a sample.

b.   The following are examples of activities subject to controls that may be tested using attribute sampling:

1)   Billing
2)   Voucher processing
3)   Payroll
4)   Inventory pricing

2.   **Steps for Testing Controls**

a.   **Define the objectives of the plan.** The auditor should clearly state what is to be accomplished, for example, to determine that the deviation rate from an approval process for a transaction is at an acceptable level.

b.   **Define the population.** The population is the focus of interest. The accountant wants to reach conclusions about all the items (typically documents) in the population.

1)   The **sampling unit** is the individual item that will be included in the sample. Thus, the population may consist of all the transactions for the fiscal year. The sampling unit is each document representing a transaction and containing the required evidence that a control procedure was performed (e.g., an approval signature).

c.   **Define the deviation conditions.** The characteristic indicative of performance of a control is the attribute of interest, for example, the supervisor's signature of approval on a document. Careful definition of the attribute is important so that deviations (departures) from the control may be determined and the sample items properly evaluated. For example, is it acceptable for another person to sign for the supervisor during vacation periods, and must the signature be in a certain place on the form for it to be considered approved?

d.   **Determine the sample size.** Four factors determine the necessary sample size: (1) the allowable risk of assessing control risk too low, (2) the tolerable deviation rate, (3) the expected population deviation rate, and (4) population size. Tables ordinarily are used to calculate the appropriate sample size based on these factors. Tables 1 and 2 on the next page are derived from Appendix A of the AICPA Audit Guide, *Audit Sampling* (2008).

1)   **Allowable risk of assessing control risk too low.** This risk has an inverse effect on sample size. The higher the allowable risk, the smaller the sample size. The usual risk specified by auditors is 5% or 10%. The auditor can specify other levels of risk, but the tables most often presented use only these two.

2)   **Tolerable deviation rate.** This is the maximum rate of deviations from the prescribed control that the auditor is willing to accept without altering the planned assessed level of control risk. Deviations increase the likelihood of misstatements in the accounting records but do not always cause misstatements.

a)   If the auditor cannot tolerate any deviations, sampling is inappropriate, and the whole population must be investigated.

3)   **Expected population deviation rate.** An estimate of the deviation rate in the current population is necessary to determine the appropriate sample size. This estimate can be based on the prior year's findings or a pilot sample of approximately 30 to 50 items.

a)   The expected rate should be less than the tolerable rate. Otherwise, tests of the control should be omitted.

Table 1 -- Sample Sizes for Tests of Controls -- 5% Risk of Assessing Control Risk Too Low

Expected Population Deviation Rate	Tolerable Deviation Rate								
	2%	3%	4%	5%	6%	7%	8%	9%	10%
0.00%	149	99	74	59	49	42	36	32	29
.25	236	157	117	93	78	66	58	51	46
.50	*	157	117	93	78	66	58	51	46
.75	*	208	117	93	78	66	58	51	46
1.00	*	*	156	93	78	66	58	51	46
1.25	*	*	156	124	78	66	58	51	46
1.50	*	*	192	124	103	66	58	51	46
1.75	*	*	227	153	103	88	77	51	46
2.00	*	*	*	181	127	88	77	68	46
2.25	*	*	*	208	127	88	77	68	61
2.50	*	*	*	*	150	109	77	68	61
2.75	*	*	*	*	173	109	95	68	61
3.00	*	*	*	*	195	129	95	84	61
3.25	*	*	*	*	*	148	112	84	61
3.50	*	*	*	*	*	167	112	84	76
3.75	*	*	*	*	*	185	129	100	76
4.00	*	*	*	*	*	*	146	100	89
5.00	*	*	*	*	*	*	*	158	116
6.00	*	*	*	*	*	*	*	*	179

Table 2 -- Results Evaluation for Tests of Controls -- Upper % Limits at 5% Risk of Assessing Control Risk Too Low

Sample Size	Actual Number of Deviations Found										
	0	1	2	3	4	5	6	7	8	9	10
25	11.3	17.7	*	*	*	*	*	*	*	*	*
30	9.6	14.9	19.6	*	*	*	*	*	*	*	*
35	8.3	12.9	17.0	*	*	*	*	*	*	*	*
40	7.3	11.4	15.0	18.3	*	*	*	*	*	*	*
45	6.5	10.2	13.4	16.4	19.2	*	*	*	*	*	*
50	5.9	9.2	12.1	14.8	17.4	19.9	*	*	*	*	*
55	5.4	8.4	11.1	13.5	15.9	18.2	*	*	*	*	*
60	4.9	7.7	10.2	12.5	14.7	16.8	18.8	*	*	*	*
65	4.6	7.1	9.4	11.5	13.6	15.5	17.5	19.3	*	*	*
70	4.2	6.6	8.8	10.8	12.7	14.5	16.3	18.0	19.7	*	*
75	4.0	6.2	8.2	10.1	11.8	13.6	15.2	16.9	18.5	20.1	*
80	3.7	5.8	7.7	9.5	11.1	12.7	14.3	15.9	17.4	18.9	*
90	3.3	5.2	6.9	8.4	9.9	11.4	12.8	14.2	15.5	16.9	18.2
100	3.0	4.7	6.2	7.6	9.0	10.3	11.5	12.8	14.0	15.2	16.4
125	2.4	3.8	5.0	6.1	7.2	8.3	9.3	10.3	11.3	12.3	13.2
150	2.0	3.2	4.2	5.1	6.0	6.9	7.8	8.6	9.5	10.3	11.1
200	1.5	2.4	3.2	3.9	4.6	5.2	5.9	6.5	7.2	7.8	8.4

4) **Population size.** The total number of sampling units in the population should be known. However, the sample size is relatively insensitive to size changes in large populations. For populations over 5,000, a standard table (e.g., Table 1, which assumes a large population) can be used. Use of the standard tables (based on the assumption of large populations) for sampling plans based on a smaller population size is a conservative approach because the sample size will be overstated. Hence, the risk of assessing control risk too low is not affected.

   a) A change in the size of the population has a very small effect on the required sample size when the population is large.

EXAMPLE

Assume the risk of assessing control risk too low is 5%, the tolerable rate is 6%, the expected population deviation rate is 2.5%, and the population size is over 5,000. Given these data, the sample size determined from Table 1 is 150. This is the intersection of the 6% Tolerable Deviation Rate column and the 2.50% Expected Population Deviation Rate row.

---

e. **Perform the sampling plan.** A random sample should be taken. Each item in the population should have an equal and nonzero change of being selected. A random number table or a computer program can be used to identify the items to be selected if a correspondence can be established between the random number and the item in the population.

   1) A statistical consideration is whether to use sampling **with** or **without** replacement. The tables are designed for sampling with replacement, which results in a conservative sample size because a slightly larger sample size than necessary will be indicated. However, in practice, auditors normally sample without replacement. No additional evidence is obtained by choosing the same item more than once.

   2) Sampling without replacement means that a population item cannot be selected again after it is selected in the sampling process.

f. **Evaluate and document sample results.** The steps include calculating the sample deviation rate and determining the achieved upper deviation limit.

   1) **Sample deviation rate.** The number of deviations observed is divided by the sample size to determine the sample deviation rate. This rate is the best estimate of the population deviation rate. For example, if three deviations were discovered in a sample of 150, the auditor's best estimate of the population deviation rate is 2% (3 ÷ 150). The auditor cannot state with certainty that the sample rate is the population rate because the sample may not be representative of the population. However, (s)he can state at a specified confidence level that the deviation rate is not likely to be greater than a specified upper limit.

   2) **Achieved upper deviation limit.** The achieved upper deviation limit is based on the sample size and the number of deviations discovered. See Table 2 on the previous page. The intersection of the sample size and the number of deviations indicates the upper achieved deviation limit. Accordingly, if the auditor discovers three deviations in a sample of 150, (s)he can state at a 95% confidence level (the complement of a 5% risk of assessing control risk too low) that the true occurrence rate is not greater than 5.1%.

      a) The difference between the achieved upper deviation limit determined from a standard table and the sample rate is the allowance for sampling risk (achieved precision) and in the example is 3.1% (5.1%-2%).

      b) When the sample deviation rate exceeds the expected population deviation rate, the achieved upper deviation limit will exceed the tolerable rate at the given risk level. In that case, the sample does not support the planned assessed level of control risk.

      c) When the sample deviation rate does not exceed the expected population deviation rate, the achieved upper deviation limit will not exceed the tolerable rate at the given risk level. Thus, the sample supports the planned assessed level of control risk. This is the case in the example. The sample deviation rate (2%) does not exceed the expected population rate (2.5%); thus, the achieved upper deviation limit (5.1%) does not exceed the tolerable rate (6%).

    3) Each deviation should be analyzed to determine its nature, importance, and probable cause. Obviously, some are much more significant than others. Sampling provides a vehicle for forming a conclusion concerning the overall population but should not be used as a substitute for good judgment.

3. **Analysis of Results**

    a. The following presentation has become a popular method for testing sampling concepts related to tests of controls. It is used to explain how to analyze the information. A variety of questions can be answered based on the analysis.

    b. The table below depicts the possible combinations of the sample results and the true state of the population.

Auditor's Estimate Based on Sample Results	True State of Population	
	Deviation rate is less than tolerable rate.	Deviation rate exceeds tolerable rate.
Deviation rate is less than tolerable rate.	I. Correct	III. Incorrect
Deviation rate exceeds tolerable rate.	II. Incorrect	IV. Correct

    c. The following definitions and explanations should be understood:

      1) The true state of the population is the actual rate of deviations in the population.

      2) If the true deviation rate is less than the tolerable rate, the auditor should have an expectation of the effectiveness of the control tested.

      3) If the true deviation rate exceeds the tolerable rate, the auditor should not have an expectation of the effectiveness of the control tested.

      4) The auditor's estimate based on the sample is the auditor's conclusion about the deviation rate in the population based on taking and evaluating a sample.

      5) Cell I represents a correct decision to have an expectation of the effectiveness of the control tested. The population actually has a deviation rate less than the tolerable rate.

      6) Cell II represents an incorrect decision not to have an expectation of the effectiveness of the control tested. The population has an acceptable deviation rate. But, because of sampling risk, the sample indicates that the population deviation rate is greater than the tolerable rate. This error will compel the auditor to expand substantive testing even though the control is effective. Thus, it relates to the efficiency rather than the effectiveness of the audit.

        a) This is a Type I error or Alpha risk.

      7) Cell III represents an incorrect decision (and a critical one) to have an expectation of the effectiveness of the control tested. The population has a greater than acceptable deviation rate, but the sample indicates that the deviation rate is less than the tolerable rate. Because the auditor expects the control to have some degree of effectiveness, substantive testing would be reduced and an audit failure could result.

        a) This is a Type II error or Beta risk.

8) Cell IV represents a correct decision not to have an expectation of the effectiveness of the control tested. The population has an unacceptable deviation rate, and the sample properly reflects this condition.

d. A CPA exam question may take a variety of forms, but the following is representative:

1) As a result of tests of controls, the auditor assesses control risk too high and thereby increases substantive testing. This is illustrated by which situation? Answer: Cell II.

Stop and review! You have completed the outline for this subunit. Study multiple-choice questions 10 through 22 beginning on page 498.

15.3 CLASSICAL VARIABLES SAMPLING (MEAN-PER-UNIT)

1. **Sampling for Substantive Testing**

a. Sampling for substantive testing provides evidence about whether a financial statement assertion about an account balance is materially misstated, for example, accounts receivable. The amount is expected to represent the true balance of the receivables, which is not known (and will never be known without a 100% audit). By taking a sample and drawing a conclusion about the population, the auditor either supports or rejects the reported number.

b. The following are examples:

1) Is management's recorded balance of accounts receivable measured at net realizable value?

2) Is management's recorded balance of inventory measured at lower of cost or market?

2. **Steps for Mean-per-Unit Sampling**

a. **Define the objectives of the plan.** The auditor intends to estimate the carrying amount of the population, for example, an accounts receivable balance.

b. **Define the population and the sampling unit.** This is the balance or class of transactions and the supporting detail under audit.

EXAMPLE

The population consists of 4,000 accounts receivable with a reported carrying amount of $3,500,000. Each customer account is a sampling unit.

 The material immediately following is rather technical. However, it is not likely that you will need to know the formula for the sample size. The AICPA Audit Guide, *Audit Sampling* (2008), notes that, "...because auditors usually use computer programs to determine appropriate sample sizes for classical variables sampling, they generally do not need to apply the mathematical formulas to use these methods; however, knowledge of the assumptions and computational routines can assist auditors in understanding these methods..." We present the formula and an example to help you understand the relationship of the factors.

c. **Determine the sample size.** The following is the sample size formula for mean-per-unit variables sampling:

$$n = \left[\frac{C \times S \times N}{A}\right]^2$$

If: n = Sample size

C = Confidence coefficient or number of standard deviations related to the required confidence level (1 – the risk of incorrect rejection)

S = Standard deviation of the population (an estimate based on a pilot sample or from the prior year's sample)

N = Number of items in the population

A = Allowance for sampling risk. This allowance is a total. In some representations, the allowance (precision) is stated in the denominator on a per-item basis (A ÷ N), and N would not be included in the formula.

1) The **allowance for sampling risk**, also termed the **precision or confidence interval**, is an interval around the sample statistic that is expected to include the true balance of the population at the specified confidence level. When using classical variables sampling, the allowance for sampling risk is calculated based on the normal distribution.

   a) This allowance is a function of the **tolerable misstatement** or the maximum misstatement that may exist without causing the financial statements to be materially misstated. Tolerable misstatement should not exceed the auditor's **preliminary judgments about materiality**.

   b) The allowance for sampling risk is established as a function of materiality to control the risk of incorrect acceptance. C in the formula is based on the risk of incorrect rejection, but the more important risk to the auditor is that of incorrect acceptance.

      i) The allowance for sampling risk equals the product of tolerable misstatement and a ratio determined in accordance with Table 3 below. This ratio is based on the allowable risk of incorrect acceptance and the risk of incorrect rejection, both of which are specified by the auditor.

Table 3 -- Ratio of Desired Allowance for Sampling Risk to Tolerable Misstatement				
Risk of Incorrect Acceptance	Risk of Incorrect Rejection (Two Sided)			
	.20	.10	.05	.01
.01	.355	.413	.457	.525
.025	.395	.456	.500	.568
.05	.437	.500	.543	.609
.075	.471	.532	.576	.641
.10	.500	.561	.605	.668
.15	.533	.612	.653	.712
.20	.603	.661	.700	.753
.25	.653	.708	.742	.791
.30	.707	.756	.787	.829
.35	.766	.808	.834	.868
.40	.831	.863	.883	.908
.45	.907	.926	.937	.953
.50	1.000	1.000	1.000	1.000

2)   The confidence coefficient, C, is derived from probability theory and is based on the risk of incorrect rejection.

Risk of Incorrect Rejection	Confidence Level	Confidence Coefficient
20%	80%	1.28
10%	90%	1.64
5%	95%	1.96
1%	99%	2.58

EXAMPLE

The number of sampling units is 4,000, the estimated population standard deviation is $125 based on a pilot sample, and the number of standard deviations related to the desired 90% confidence level (10% risk of incorrect rejection) is 1.64. Assuming tolerable misstatement of $100,000 and a risk of incorrect acceptance of 5%, the planned allowance for sampling risk (desired precision) can be determined using Table 3. The intersection of the 10% risk of incorrect rejection and 5% risk of incorrect acceptance is .500. The result is a $50,000 allowance for sampling risk ($100,000 tolerable misstatement × .500).

Thus, the sample size is

$$n = \left[\frac{C \times S \times N}{A} \right]^2$$

$$= \left[\frac{1.64 \times \$125 \times 4,000}{\$50,000} \right]^2$$

$$= 268.96 \text{ or } 269$$

d.   **Select the sample, execute the plan, and evaluate and document the results.**

1)   Randomly select and audit the accounts, e.g., send confirmations.
2)   Calculate the average confirmed accounts receivable amount (assume $880).
3)   Calculate the sample standard deviation (assume $125).
4)   Evaluate the sample results.

a)   The best estimate of the population balance equals the average accounts receivable amount based on the sample times the number of items in the population. Thus, the amount estimated is determined as follows:

$$Estimated\ balance = Average\ sample\ amount \times Items\ in\ population$$

$$= \$880 \times 4,000$$

$$= \$3,520,000$$

b)   The calculated allowance for sampling risk (achieved precision) is determined by solving the sample size formula for A.

$$A = \frac{C \times S \times N}{\sqrt{n}}$$

$$= \frac{1.64 \times \$125 \times 4,000}{\sqrt{269}}$$

$$= \$820,000 \div 16.4 = \$50,000$$

         i)   C, S, and N have the same values used to calculate the original sample size, n. Hence, the allowance for sampling risk, A, will be the same as planned, or $50,000. A will be different only when the standard deviation, S, of the sample differs from the estimate used to calculate n. This difference can result in changes in the levels of risk faced by the auditor, but these issues are beyond the scope of the materials presented here (and are usually not covered on the CPA exam).

     c)   The audit conclusion is that the auditor is 90% confident that the true balance is $3,520,000 plus or minus $50,000, an interval of $3,470,000 to $3,570,000. If the carrying amount was $3,500,000, the auditor cannot reject the hypothesis that it is not materially misstated.

Stop and review! You have completed the outline for this subunit. Study multiple-choice questions 23 through 27 beginning on page 502.

15.4 MONETARY-UNIT SAMPLING (MUS)

1.   The **monetary-unit-sampling (MUS)** approach to variables sampling is distinct from the classical approach. It is a hybrid method that uses attribute sampling methods to estimate monetary amounts. MUS is based on the Poisson distribution, which is used in attribute sampling to approximate the binomial distribution.

2.   MUS uses a monetary unit (e.g., a dollar) as the sampling unit. The classical approach uses items themselves (e.g., invoices, checks, etc.) as the sampling units.

    a.   MUS gives each monetary unit in the population an equal chance of selection. As a practical matter, however, the auditor does not examine an individual monetary unit but uses it to identify an entire transaction or balance to audit (the logical sampling unit).

    b.   MUS is appropriate for account balances that may include only a few overstated items, such as may be expected in inventory and receivables.

        1)   MUS is useful only for tests of **overstatements** (e.g., of assets) because a **systematic selection** method is applied (every n^{th} monetary unit is selected). Accordingly, the larger the transaction or balance, the more likely it will be selected. This method is inappropriate for testing a population (e.g., liabilities) when understatement is the primary audit consideration.

    c.   MUS is used to reach a conclusion regarding the probability of overstating an account balance by a specified monetary amount.

3.   **Advantages** of MUS include the following:

    a.   The largest items are selected for testing (i.e., the population is stratified).

    b.   It is ideal for testing for overstatement.

    c.   Small sample sizes may be considered, especially when no misstatements are expected.

    d.   It is relatively easy to apply, especially if no misstatements are discovered.

    e.   The sample size and sample evaluation can be calculated without dependence on the estimated variation (standard deviation) of the population.

    f.   The sample selection process may begin even before the complete population is available for testing.

4. **Disadvantages** of MUS include the following:

    a. Items with zero or negative balances have no chance of selection.
    b. It is useful only for detecting overstatement errors.
    c. Sample sizes become relatively large if a significant amount of misstatement is expected.
    d. The calculated allowance for sampling risk tends to be overstated when a significant amount of misstatement is found in the sample.

        1) This is an inherent limitation of MUS.

5. **Steps for MUS**

    a. The steps in MUS are similar to those of other sampling methods:

        1) Determine the objective of the plan.
        2) Define the population and sampling unit.
        3) Determine the sampling interval and sample size.
        4) Select the sample.
        5) Execute the sampling plan.
        6) Evaluate and document the results.

Two examples are provided here, one simple and one more complex. It is probably more important that you understand the uses of MUS, the advantages and disadvantages of MUS, and the steps involved in the process than the illustrations presented here. The formulas and factors are specified; do not be concerned about how they were derived. Try to follow the logic and concepts rather than the details.

6. **Simple Example**

   a. Below is a simple example of the application of MUS. This example is then extended to the case in which overstatement errors are detected.

EXAMPLE – Simple

The following assumptions apply in an audit of Seminole, Inc.:

- The auditor's objective is to test the assertion that the $900,000 accounts receivable balance is fairly stated. Tolerable misstatement is $35,000.
- The population contains 900,000 sampling units and over 1,000 individual accounts receivable (logical sampling units), all with debit balances.
- The risk of incorrect acceptance specified by the auditor is 5%. Thus, the auditor desires to be 95% confident that the recorded balance is not overstated by more than $35,000.

The **sample size** is determined by the following formula:

$$Sample\ size = Recorded\ amount\ of\ population \div Sampling\ interval$$

The **sampling interval (SI)** is a function of the risk of incorrect acceptance and **tolerable misstatement (TM)**. SI is determined by dividing tolerable misstatement by a **confidence factor (CF)** associated with the risk level.

$$SI = TM \div CF$$

The following are CFs taken from Appendix C of the AICPA Audit Guide, *Audit Sampling* (2008):

Risk of Incorrect Acceptance	CF
5%	3.00
10%	2.31
15%	1.90

Because the risk of incorrect acceptance is 5%, the CF is 3.00. Thus, the SI is

$$SI = TM \div CF$$
$$= \$35,000 \div 3.00$$
$$= \$11,667$$

The sample size (n) is

$$n = Recorded\ amount\ of\ population \div SI$$
$$= \$900,000 \div \$11,667$$
$$= 77$$

The auditor uses **systematic sampling** (discussed in the extension of the example that follows) to select 77 dollars (actually 77 account balances) to audit.

If **no misstatements are discovered**, the auditor can form the following conclusion: "I am 95% confident that the recorded accounts receivable balance of $900,000 is not overstated by more than $35,000." There is still a 5% risk that the account balance is overstated by more than $35,000.

The **allowance for sampling risk** (also known as precision or confidence interval) is $35,000. Because the sample contains no misstatements, the conclusion is that the population has no misstatements. But, because the sample may not be perfectly representative of the population, an allowance for sampling risk must be considered. Thus, the more accurate conclusion is that the auditor is 95% confident that the misstatements are not greater than the allowance for sampling risk.

Given that the allowance for sampling risk is less than or equal to the TM, the objective of the audit test has been met.

---

7.   Extended Example

a.   The Seminole, Inc., example is extended below and on the next three pages to consider **anticipated misstatements** and to demonstrate the extrapolation of the sample results to the population when misstatements are discovered in the sampling units.

EXAMPLE – Extended

Objective, population, and sampling unit. In this example, the basic information remains the same. However, the auditor anticipates misstatements in the population to be $10,000 based on the prior audit.

Determining the sampling interval and sample size. When no misstatements are expected, the SI equals TM divided by the CF. However, any anticipated misstatements must be considered in the determination of the SI. Moreover, the **anticipated misstatement (AM)** must be multiplied by an **expansion factor (EF)** appropriate for the risk of incorrect acceptance. The revised SI calculation is given below. The CF is the same as when no overstatements are expected.

$$SI = [TM - (AM \times EF)] \div CF$$

The following are EFs taken from Appendix C of the AICPA Audit Guide, *Audit Sampling* (2008):

Risk of Incorrect Acceptance	EF
5%	1.6
10%	1.5
15%	1.4

Accordingly, the revised SI is

$$SI = [TM - (AM \times EF)] \div CF$$
$$= [\$35,000 - (\$10,000 \times 1.6)] \div 3.00$$
$$= \$6,333$$

As before, the sample size is calculated as

$$Sample\ size = Recorded\ amount\ of\ population \div SI$$
$$= \$900,000 \div \$6,333$$
$$= 142$$

The effects of changes in the factors in the sample size formula should be understood. For example, the greater the auditor's allowable risk of incorrect acceptance, the smaller the sample size. Also, the larger the anticipated misstatement, the larger the sample size.

Selecting the sample. The SI is used to select logical sampling units (in this example, accounts receivable) from the population.

A monetary unit (in this example, a dollar) identifies a logical sampling unit. If every 6,333rd cumulative dollar is selected from the population of $900,000, the sample will consist of 142 items. The auditor therefore should start randomly between $1 and $6,333. Given a random start at the 2,733rd cumulative dollar, the sample will include the following:

- The first dollar selected will be $2,733.
- The next dollar will be $9,066 ($2,733 + $6,333).
- The third dollar will be $15,399 ($9,066 + $6,333).
- The fourth dollar will be $21,732 ($15,399 + $6,333).
- Each subsequent dollar will equal the prior dollar selected plus $6,333.

-- Continued on next page --

Extended Example Continued

Table 4 below demonstrates the selection process. When the **cumulative balance** is equal to or greater than the dollar selected, the account is selected because it contains the sampling unit. If an account contains two or more logical sampling units, for example, an account receivable of $15,000, it is selected, but it is given no special consideration. The ultimate sample of logical sampling units may contain fewer items than the calculated n.

Table 4 -- Systematic Selection				
Customer Number	A/R Recorded Amount	Cumulative Balance	Dollar Selected	Recorded Amount of Sample Item
001	$ 2,000	$ 2,000		
002	1,225	3,225	2,733	1,225
003	3,500	6,725		
004	2,500	9,225	9,066	2,500
005	10,000	19,225	15,399	10,000
006	915	20,140		
etc.	etc.	etc.	etc.	etc.
Total	$900,000			

-- Continued on next page --

Extended Example Continued

Executing the sampling plan. The auditor performs procedures on the sampled items (e.g., confirming the accounts). The auditor identifies **overstatement** errors. (Any **understatement** errors require special consideration, but the issue is beyond the scope of this outline.)

Evaluating and documenting the results. The evaluation process depends on whether any misstatements are found in the sample. The following summarizes that process:

- Project the misstatement from the sample to the population.
- Determine the allowance for sampling risk.

$$Allowance\ for\ sampling\ risk\ =\ Basic\ precision\ (BP)\ +\ Incremental\ allowance\ (IA)$$

- Calculate the upper misstatement limit (UML).

$$UML\ =\ Projected\ misstatement\ +\ Allowance\ for\ sampling\ risk$$

If **no overstatement errors** are discovered, the UML equals BP because

- The projected misstatement to the population is $0.
- The allowance for sampling risk equals BP (i.e., the IA is $0).

The calculation for **BP** is

$$BP\ =\ SI\ \times\ CF$$

Assuming no misstatements are found, BP (and the UML) is

$$BP\ =\ \$6,333\ \times\ 3.00$$
$$=\ \$18,999$$

The conclusion is that the auditor is 95% confident that the balance of accounts receivable is not overstated by more than $18,999. This amount is within the TM of $35,000. Moreover, $18,999 is the allowance for sampling risk.

If **some overstatement errors** are discovered, the evaluation process is more involved but follows that presented above.

Project the sample results to the population if misstatements are discovered. Table 5 below illustrates the projection of misstatements to the population.

Tainting. Because each selected dollar represents a group of dollars (the SI), the percentage of misstatement in the logical sampling unit (the account selected) is the percentage of misstatement in the SI. This is termed tainting. However, if the recorded amount of a logical sampling unit (the account selected) **equals or exceeds** the SI, the projected misstatement is the actual misstatement for the SI, and no tainting is calculated.

For each logical sampling unit with a recorded amount (RA) **less than** the SI, calculate the **tainting percentage**.

$$Tainting\ \%\ =\ \frac{(RA\ -\ AA)}{RA}\quad Where:\quad AA\ =\ Audit\ amount$$

$$Projected\ misstatement\ =\ SI\ \times\ Tainting\ \%$$

Add the individual projected misstatements to determine the projected population misstatement.

Table 5 -- Calculation of Projected Misstatement				
Recorded Amount	Audit Amount	Tainting % = (RA – AA) ÷ RA	SI	Projected Misstatement
$ 1,000	$ 800	20%	$6,333	$ 1,267
10,000	6,000	N/A	N/A	4,000
300	0	100%	6,333	6,333
$11,300	$6,800			$11,600

The first and third projected misstatements equal the tainting percentage times SI because the RA of the logical unit sampled is less than the SI. The second projected misstatement included is the actual misstatement. The RA of the logical unit sampled is greater than the SI. The total projected misstatement to the population is $11,600, but the allowance for sampling risk must be added to derive the UML.

-- Continued on next page --

Extended Example Continued

Calculate the **allowance for sampling risk** and the UML.

Allowance for sampling risk has two components: BP and IA.

BP is the same as when no misstatements are found (i.e., SI × CF).

IA is based on projected misstatements related to logical sampling units less than SI. (The misstatements related to logical sampling units greater than SI are not considered in the calculation of IA in Table 5.)

Projected misstatements are ranked by size (but only for misstatements related to logical sampling units less than SI). Each projected misstatement is multiplied by a factor that gives greater weights to the larger amounts. The first few factors for the 5% risk of incorrect acceptance, sufficient to calculate the allowance for sampling risk for this example, are presented in Table 6 below. Each factor equals the incremental change in the confidence factor minus one. Given a 5% risk of incorrect acceptance, the confidence factors for 0, 1, 2, and 3 misstatements are 3.00, 4.75, 6.30, and 7.76, respectively.

In this example, two misstatements are related to logical sampling units less than the SI of $6,333.

The ranked projected misstatements are multiplied by the factors from Table 6 and added to determine IA in Table 7.

Table 6 -- Misstatement Factors 5% Risk of Incorrect Acceptance		
Misstatement Number	Change in Confidence Factor	Change in CF – 1.0
1	1.75 (4.75 – 3.00)	.75
2	1.55 (6.30 – 4.75)	.55
3	1.46 (7.76 – 6.30)	.46
etc.	etc.	etc.

Table 7 -- Calculation of the IA		
Ranked Projected Misstatements	Factor	Incremental Allowance
$6,333	.75	$4,750
1,267	.55	697
Total IA (rounded)		$5,447

The allowance for sampling risk is the sum of BP and IA.

$$\text{Allowance for sampling risk} = \$18,999 + \$5,447$$
$$= \$24,446$$

The total projected misstatement (PM) plus the allowance for sampling risk equals the upper misstatement limit (UML).

$$\text{UML} = \text{PM} + \text{Allowance for sampling risk}$$
$$= \$11,600 + \$24,446$$
$$= \$36,046$$

The **auditor's conclusion** is that (s)he is 95% confident that the balance of accounts receivable is not overstated by more than $36,046. However, TM is only $35,000. Thus, the auditor cannot conclude within the acceptable level of risk that the balance is fairly presented. (The auditor would likely require the client to make adjustments downward to the account before presentation on the balance sheet.)

Stop and review! You have completed the outline for this subunit. Study multiple-choice questions 28 through 32 beginning on page 504.

QUESTIONS

15.1 Sampling Fundamentals (AU 350)

1. An advantage of statistical over nonstatistical sampling methods in tests of controls is that the statistical methods

   A. Afford greater assurance than a nonstatistical sample of equal size.

   B. Provide an objective basis for quantitatively evaluating sample risks.

   C. Can more easily convert the sample into a dual-purpose test useful for substantive testing.

   D. Eliminate the need to use judgment in determining appropriate sample sizes.

Answer (B) is correct. *(CPA, adapted)*
   REQUIRED: The advantage of statistical over nonstatistical sampling methods.
   DISCUSSION: The results of statistical (probability) sampling are objective and subject to the laws of probability. Hence, sampling risk can be quantified and controlled, and the degree of reliability desired (the confidence level) can be specified. Sampling risk is the risk that the sample selected does not represent the population.
   Answer (A) is incorrect. A nonstatistical method may permit the auditor to test the most material and risky transactions and therefore may provide equal or greater assurance. However, that assurance cannot be quantified. Answer (C) is incorrect. Statistical sampling provides no advantage for converting to dual-purpose testing. Answer (D) is incorrect. Sample size is subject to judgments about the sampling plan factors.

2. An advantage of statistical sampling over nonstatistical sampling is that statistical sampling helps an auditor to

   A. Minimize the failure to detect errors and fraud.

   B. Eliminate the risk of nonsampling errors.

   C. Reduce the level of audit risk and materiality to a relatively low amount.

   D. Measure the sufficiency of the evidential matter obtained.

Answer (D) is correct. *(CPA, adapted)*
   REQUIRED: The advantage of statistical sampling over nonstatistical sampling.
   DISCUSSION: Statistical sampling helps the auditor to design an efficient sample, to measure the sufficiency of the evidence obtained, and to evaluate the sample results. The third standard of field work requires auditors to obtain sufficient appropriate evidence. Sufficiency relates to the design and size of the sample.
   Answer (A) is incorrect. In some circumstances, professional judgment may indicate that nonstatistical methods are preferable to minimize the failure to detect errors and fraud. Answer (B) is incorrect. Statistical sampling is irrelevant to nonsampling errors. Answer (C) is incorrect. Statistical sampling is irrelevant to materiality. Moreover, nonstatistical methods may be used to reduce audit risk.

3. The likelihood of assessing control risk too high is the risk that the sample selected to test controls

   A. Does not support the auditor's planned assessed level of control risk when the true operating effectiveness of internal control justifies such an assessment.

   B. Contains misstatements that could be material to the financial statements when aggregated with misstatements in other account balances or transactions classes.

   C. Contains proportionately fewer deviations from prescribed internal controls than exist in the balance or class as a whole.

   D. Does not support the tolerable misstatement for some or all financial statement assertions.

Answer (A) is correct. *(CPA, adapted)*
   REQUIRED: The condition under which the auditor would assess control risk too high.
   DISCUSSION: According to AU 350, one aspect of sampling risk in performing tests of controls is the risk of assessing control risk too high. It is the risk that the assessed level of control risk based on the sample is greater than the true operating effectiveness of the control.
   Answer (B) is incorrect. Substantive procedures are directed towards misstatements in assertions. Answer (C) is incorrect. If the sample deviation rate is lower than the population rate, the auditor may assess control risk too low. Answer (D) is incorrect. Substantive procedures are directed towards misstatements in assertions.

4. A principal advantage of statistical methods of attribute sampling over nonstatistical methods is that they provide a scientific basis for planning the

    A. Risk of assessing control risk too low.

    B. Tolerable rate.

    C. Expected population deviation rate.

    D. Sample size.

Answer (D) is correct. *(CPA, adapted)*
    REQUIRED: The item for which statistical methods provide a scientific basis for planning.
    DISCUSSION: Statistical theory permits the auditor to measure sampling risk and to restrict it to an acceptable level. Statistical methods determine the sample size that will accomplish the auditor's objectives.
    Answer (A) is incorrect. The risk of assessing control risk too low is the risk of believing a control is effective when it is not. Answer (B) is incorrect. The tolerable rate is a function of the auditor's judgment about the planned assessed level of control risk and the desired degree of assurance to be provided by the evidence, not of the statistical methods used. Answer (C) is incorrect. The expected population deviation rate prior to sampling is a function of auditor judgment.

5. While performing a test of details during an audit, the auditor determined that the sample results supported the conclusion that the recorded account balance was materially misstated. It was, in fact, not materially misstated. This situation illustrates the risk of

    A. Incorrect rejection.

    B. Incorrect acceptance.

    C. Assessing control risk too low.

    D. Assessing control risk too high.

Answer (A) is correct. *(CPA, adapted)*
    REQUIRED: The risk of erroneously concluding that a balance is materially misstated.
    DISCUSSION: An auditor is concerned with two aspects of sampling risk in performing substantive tests of details: the risk of incorrect acceptance and the risk of incorrect rejection. The second is the risk that the sample supports the conclusion that the recorded account balance is materially misstated when it is not materially misstated.
    Answer (B) is incorrect. The risk of incorrect acceptance is the risk that an auditor will erroneously conclude that a balance is not materially misstated. Answer (C) is incorrect. The risk of assessing control risk too low is an aspect of sampling risk in performing tests of controls. Answer (D) is incorrect. The risk of assessing control risk too high is an aspect of sampling risk in performing tests of controls.

6. An auditor may decide to increase the risk of incorrect rejection when

    A. Increased reliability from the sample is desired.

    B. Many differences (audit value minus recorded value) are expected.

    C. Initial sample results do not support the planned level of control risk.

    D. The cost and effort of selecting additional sample items are low.

Answer (D) is correct. *(CPA, adapted)*
    REQUIRED: The reason to increase the risk of incorrect rejection.
    DISCUSSION: The risk of incorrect rejection is the risk that the sample supports the conclusion that the recorded account balance is materially misstated when it is not. This risk relates to the efficiency, not the effectiveness, of the audit. Incorrect rejection ordinarily results in the application of additional procedures that finally lead the auditor to the proper conclusion. If the cost and effort of selecting additional sample items are low, a higher risk of incorrect rejection may be acceptable.
    Answer (A) is incorrect. An increase in the desired reliability (confidence level) for a substantive test of details requires a decrease in the risk of incorrect rejection. This risk is the complement of the confidence level for a substantive test of details. Answer (B) is incorrect. If many differences are expected, the account balance is more likely to be materially misstated and incorrect rejection is less likely. Answer (C) is incorrect. The risk of incorrect rejection is associated with substantive testing. Control risk is associated with tests of controls.

7. In statistical sampling methods used in substantive testing, an auditor most likely would stratify a population into meaningful groups if

    A. Monetary-unit sampling (MUS) is used.

    B. The population has highly variable recorded amounts.

    C. The auditor's estimated tolerable misstatement is extremely small.

    D. The standard deviation of recorded amounts is relatively small.

Answer (B) is correct. *(CPA, adapted)*
    REQUIRED: The condition under which the auditor would stratify a population.
    DISCUSSION: The primary objective of stratification is to reduce the effect of high variability by dividing the population into subpopulations. Reducing the effect of the variance within each subpopulation allows the auditor to sample a smaller number of items while holding precision and the confidence level constant.
    Answer (A) is incorrect. MUS automatically stratifies the population. Answer (C) is incorrect. When the tolerable misstatement is extremely small, the auditor will take relatively large sample sizes. Answer (D) is incorrect. When the standard deviation of recorded amounts is relatively small, the auditor would consider the population in total when selecting samples.

8. An auditor is performing substantive tests of pricing and extensions of perpetual inventory balances consisting of a large number of items. Past experience indicates numerous pricing and extension errors. Which of the following statistical sampling approaches is most appropriate?

A. Unstratified mean-per-unit.

B. Monetary-unit.

C. Stop or go.

D. Ratio or difference estimation.

Answer (D) is correct. *(CPA, adapted)*
REQUIRED: The appropriate sampling method for substantive tests of pricing and extensions of perpetual inventory balances.
DISCUSSION: Difference estimation of population misstatement involves (1) determining the differences between the audit and carrying amounts for items in the sample, (2) adding the differences, (3) calculating the mean difference, and (4) multiplying the mean by the number of items in the population. An allowance for sampling risk also is calculated. Ratio estimation is similar except that it estimates the population misstatement by multiplying the carrying amount of the population by the ratio of the total audit value of the sample items to their total carrying amount. It has been demonstrated that ratio or difference estimation is both reliable and efficient when small misstatements predominate and they are not skewed.
Answer (A) is incorrect. Unstratified mean-per-unit requires sample sizes that may be too large to be cost effective. Answer (B) is incorrect. MUS may result in a larger sample size than a classical variables sampling approach when the estimated misstatement is relatively large. Answer (C) is incorrect. Stop-or-go sampling is an attribute sampling mode. It is appropriate when few deviations are expected. The method is not applicable in these circumstances.

9. The use of the ratio estimation sampling technique is most effective when

A. The calculated audit amounts are approximately proportional to the client's carrying amounts.

B. A relatively small number of differences exist in the population.

C. Estimating populations whose records consist of quantities but not carrying amounts.

D. Large overstatement differences and large understatement differences exist in the population.

Answer (A) is correct. *(CPA, adapted)*
REQUIRED: The most effective use of ratio estimation sampling.
DISCUSSION: Ratio estimation calculates the population misstatement by multiplying the carrying amount of the population by the ratio of the total audit amount of the sample items to their total carrying amount. The precision is determined by considering the variances of the ratios of carrying amount to audited amount. Thus, the more homogeneous the ratios, the smaller the precision.
Answer (B) is incorrect. The population of differences must be fairly large for ratio estimation to be useful. Answer (C) is incorrect. Each audited amount must have a carrying amount so that a ratio may be calculated. Answer (D) is incorrect. The ratios are important to the process, not the specific amounts of the population.

15.2 Statistical Sampling in Tests of Controls (Attribute Sampling)

10. Which of the following combinations results in a decrease in sample size in an attribute sample?

	Allowable Risk of Assessing Control Risk Too Low	Tolerable Rate	Expected Population Deviation Rate
A.	Increase	Decrease	Increase
B.	Decrease	Increase	Decrease
C.	Increase	Increase	Decrease
D.	Increase	Increase	Increase

Answer (C) is correct. *(CPA, adapted)*
REQUIRED: The combination that results in a decrease in size in an attribute sample.
DISCUSSION: To determine the sample size for a test of controls, the auditor considers (1) the tolerable rate of deviations from the control being tested, (2) the expected actual rate of deviations, and (3) the allowable risk of assessing control risk too low. An increase in the allowable risk of assessing control risk too low, an increase in the tolerable rate, and a decrease in the expected rate each has the effect of reducing the required sample size.

11. In determining the number of documents to select for a test to obtain assurance that all sales returns have been properly authorized, an auditor should consider the tolerable rate of deviation from the control activity. The auditor should also directly consider the

I. Likely rate of deviations
II. Allowable risk of assessing control risk too high

    A. I only.

    B. II only.

    C. Both I and II.

    D. Either I or II.

Answer (A) is correct. *(CPA, adapted)*
    REQUIRED: The factor(s) in determining sample size.
    DISCUSSION: The factors necessary to determine sample size in an attribute sampling plan for a large population include the tolerable deviation rate, the acceptable risk of assessing control too low, and the expected deviation rate.

12. In planning a statistical sample for a test of controls, an auditor increased the expected population deviation rate from the prior year's rate because of the results of the prior year's tests of controls and the overall control environment. The auditor most likely would then increase the planned

    A. Tolerable deviation rate.

    B. Allowance for sampling risk.

    C. Risk of assessing control risk too low.

    D. Sample size.

Answer (D) is correct. *(CPA, adapted)*
    REQUIRED: The effect of an increase in the expected population deviation rate.
    DISCUSSION: To determine the sample size for a test of controls, the auditor considers (1) the tolerable rate of deviations, (2) the expected actual rate of deviations, and (3) the allowable risk of assessing control risk too low. An increase in the expected rate has the effect of increasing the degree of assurance to be provided by the sample and therefore increasing the planned sample size.
    Answer (A) is incorrect. The tolerable rate is a function of the planned assessed level of control risk and the degree of assurance sought from the evidence. It does not necessarily increase with the expected population deviation rate. Answer (B) is incorrect. The allowance for sampling risk is the difference between the calculated upper deviation rate and the sample rate. According to standard tables, it increases as the actual number of deviations found increases. Answer (C) is incorrect. The risk of assessing control risk too low is specified by the auditor. It does not necessarily increase with the expected rate.

13. Which of the following statements is true concerning statistical sampling in tests of controls?

    A. As the population size increases, the sample size should increase proportionately.

    B. Deviations from specific control activities increase the likelihood of misstatements but do not always cause misstatements.

    C. There is an inverse relationship between the expected population deviation rate and the sample size.

    D. In determining the tolerable rate, an auditor considers detection risk and the sample size.

Answer (B) is correct. *(CPA, adapted)*
    REQUIRED: The true statement concerning statistical sampling in tests of controls.
    DISCUSSION: Deviations from a specific control increase the risk of misstatements in the accounting records but do not always result in misstatements. Thus, deviations from a specific control at a given rate ordinarily result in misstatements at the financial statement level at a lower rate.
    Answer (A) is incorrect. As population size increases, the required sample size increases at a decreasing rate. Answer (C) is incorrect. The relationship between the expected population deviation rate and the required sample size is direct. Answer (D) is incorrect. The tolerable rate depends on the planned assessed level of control risk and the assurance to be provided by the evidence in the sample.

14. For which of the following audit tests would an auditor most likely use attribute sampling?

    A. Making an independent estimate of the amount of a LIFO inventory.

    B. Examining invoices in support of the valuation of fixed asset additions.

    C. Selecting accounts receivable for confirmation of account balances.

    D. Inspecting employee time cards for proper approval by supervisors.

Answer (D) is correct. *(CPA, adapted)*
    REQUIRED: The appropriate use of attribute sampling.
    DISCUSSION: The auditor uses attribute sampling to test the effectiveness of controls. Attribute sampling enables the auditor to estimate the occurrence rate of deviations and to determine its relation to the tolerable rate. Thus, a control, such as proper approval of time cards by supervisors, can be tested for effectiveness using attribute sampling.
    Answer (A) is incorrect. Variables sampling is useful in estimating the amount of inventory. Answer (B) is incorrect. Examining invoices in support of the valuation of fixed asset additions is a substantive test for which variables sampling is appropriate. Answer (C) is incorrect. The selection of accounts receivable for confirmation is a substantive test.

15. An auditor should consider the tolerable rate of deviation when determining the number of check requests to select for a test to obtain assurance that all check requests have been properly authorized. The auditor should also consider

	The Average Dollar Value of the Check Requests	The Allowable Risk of Assessing Control Risk Too Low
A.	Yes	Yes
B.	Yes	No
C.	No	Yes
D.	No	No

16. Which of the following statements is true concerning statistical sampling in tests of controls?

A. The population size has little or no effect on determining sample size except for very small populations.

B. The expected population deviation rate has little or no effect on determining sample size except for very small populations.

C. As the population size doubles, the sample size also should double.

D. For a given tolerable rate, a larger sample size should be selected as the expected population deviation rate decreases.

17. What is an auditor's evaluation of a statistical sample for attributes when a test of 50 documents results in three deviations if the tolerable rate is 7%, the expected population deviation rate is 5%, and the allowance for sampling risk is 2%?

A. Modify the planned assessed level of control risk because the tolerable rate plus the allowance for sampling risk exceeds the expected population deviation rate.

B. Accept the sample results as support for the planned assessed level of control risk because the sample deviation rate plus the allowance for sampling risk exceeds the tolerable rate.

C. Accept the sample results as support for the planned assessed level of control risk because the tolerable rate minus the allowance for sampling risk equals the expected population deviation rate.

D. Modify the planned assessed level of control risk because the sample deviation rate plus the allowance for sampling risk exceeds the tolerable rate.

Answer (C) is correct. *(CPA, adapted)*
   REQUIRED: The issue(s), if any, to consider in determining the size of a sample in a test of controls.
   DISCUSSION: Tests of controls, such as tests whether check requests have been properly authorized, are binary in nature. The auditor determines whether the control has been applied. Dollar amounts are irrelevant in this form of testing. However, in sampling, the auditor must consider the acceptable risk of assessing control risk too low to determine sample size. The auditor also must estimate a population deviation rate.

Answer (A) is correct. *(CPA, adapted)*
   REQUIRED: The true statement about statistical sampling.
   DISCUSSION: A change in the size of the population has a very small effect on the required sample size when the population is large. Tables are available for smaller population sizes providing appropriate smaller sample sizes.
   Answer (B) is incorrect. The expected population deviation rate is a variable in the sample size formula. Answer (C) is incorrect. The population size and the sample size are not proportionate. Answer (D) is incorrect. A lower expected population deviation rate results in a smaller sample size.

Answer (D) is correct. *(CPA, adapted)*
   REQUIRED: The evaluation of an attribute sample given the deviations in the sample, sampling risk, tolerable rate, and expected rate.
   DISCUSSION: The sample has a 6% (3 ÷ 50) deviation rate. The auditor's achieved upper deviation limit is 8% (6% + the 2% allowance for sampling risk). The allowance for sampling risk may be calculated from a standard table as the difference between the upper deviation limit and the sample rate. However, the allowance is given. Thus, the true deviation rate could be as large as 8% and exceed the tolerable rate. Accordingly, the auditor should revise the planned assessed level of control risk for the relevant assertions and possibly alter the nature, timing, and extent of substantive tests (AU 350).
   Answer (A) is incorrect. The precision interval is constructed around the sample rate, not the tolerable rate. Answer (B) is incorrect. A deviation rate that may be as large as 8% is a reason for revising the planned assessed level of control risk. Answer (C) is incorrect. The sample deviation rate, which is the best estimate of the true rate, must not be ignored.

18. The risk of incorrect acceptance and the likelihood of assessing control risk too low relate to the

A. Effectiveness of the audit.

B. Efficiency of the audit.

C. Preliminary estimates of materiality levels.

D. Tolerable misstatement.

Answer (A) is correct. *(CPA, adapted)*
REQUIRED: The true statement about the risks of incorrect acceptance and assessing control risk too low.
DISCUSSION: If an account balance is erroneously accepted as fairly stated based upon a sample, additional audit work and the chances of exposing the mistake will probably be minimal. However, rejection of a fairly stated balance typically results in further audit investigation and ultimately the acceptance of the balance. Similarly, assessing control risk too low leads to an unjustified reduction in substantive testing, thereby decreasing the effectiveness of the audit. Assessing control risk too high results in an unneeded increase in substantive testing but most likely will not decrease the ultimate audit effectiveness.
Answer (B) is incorrect. These risks relate to effectiveness. Answer (C) is incorrect. Preliminary judgments about materiality are considered when planning a sample for a substantive procedure. The risk of assessing control risk too low relates directly to tests of controls. Answer (D) is incorrect. The tolerable misstatement is considered when planning a sample for a substantive procedure. The risk of assessing control risk too low relates directly to tests of controls.

Questions 19 and 20 are based on the following information. An auditor desired to test credit approval on 10,000 sales invoices processed during the year. The auditor designed a statistical sample that would provide 1% risk of assessing control risk too low (99% confidence) that not more than 7% of the sales invoices lacked approval. The auditor estimated from previous experience that about 2.5% of the sales invoices lacked approval. A sample of 200 invoices was examined, and seven of them were lacking approval. The auditor then determined the achieved upper deviation limit to be 8%.

19. In the evaluation of this sample, the auditor decided to increase the level of the preliminary assessment of control risk because the

A. Tolerable rate (7%) was less than the achieved upper deviation limit (8%).

B. Expected deviation rate (7%) was more than the percentage of errors in the sample (3.5%).

C. Achieved upper deviation limit (8%) was more than the percentage of errors in the sample (3.5%).

D. Expected deviation rate (2.5%) was less than the tolerable rate (7%).

Answer (A) is correct. *(CPA, adapted)*
REQUIRED: The reason for increasing the preliminary assessment of control risk.
DISCUSSION: The sample results support the planned assessed level of control risk only if the achieved upper deviation limit is equal to or less than the tolerable rate. The achieved upper deviation limit is a value that may be derived from a standard table based on the actual deviations, the specified risk, and the sample size. In this case, it signifies that the auditor is 99% confident that not more than 8% of the invoices lacked approval. Hence, the sample does not support the planned assessed level of control risk.
Answer (B) is incorrect. The expected rate is 2.5%. Answer (C) is incorrect. By definition, the achieved upper deviation limit equals the sample deviation rate plus an allowance for sampling risk. Answer (D) is incorrect. The expected rate from the sampling plan is not used in the evaluation of the sample.

20. The allowance for sampling risk was

A. 5.5%

B. 4.5%

C. 3.5%

D. 1%

Answer (B) is correct. *(CPA, adapted)*
REQUIRED: The allowance for sampling risk.
DISCUSSION: The allowance for sampling risk equals the achieved upper deviation limit (8%) minus the sample deviation rate (7 ÷ 200 = 3.5%), or 4.5%.

21. The diagram below depicts the auditor's estimated maximum deviation rate compared with the tolerable rate and also depicts the true population deviation rate compared with the tolerable rate.

True State of Population

Auditor's Estimate Based on Sample Results	Deviation rate is less than tolerable rate.	Deviation rate exceeds tolerable rate.
Maximum deviation rate is less than tolerable rate.	I. Correct	III. Incorrect
Maximum deviation rate exceeds tolerable rate.	II. Incorrect	IV. Correct

As a result of testing controls, the auditor assesses control risk too high and increases substantive testing. This is illustrated by situation

A. I.

B. II.

C. III.

D. IV.

Answer (B) is correct. *(CPA, adapted)*
REQUIRED: The situation that involves assessing control risk too high.
DISCUSSION: The risk of assessing control risk too high (situation II) is one aspect of sampling risk in testing controls. According to AU 350, it "is the risk that the assessed level of control risk based on the sample is greater than the true operating effectiveness of the control." Thus, the risk is that the control is actually more effective than indicated by the sample. Like the risk of incorrect rejection in substantive testing, the risk of assessing control risk too high is a form of alpha (Type I) error. Alpha error concerns the efficiency, not the effectiveness, of the audit. It ordinarily leads to application of further audit procedures and ultimate arrival at the correct conclusion.
Answer (A) is incorrect. In situation I, the auditor would properly assess control risk at a low level. Answer (C) is incorrect. In situation III, the sample might lead to assessing control risk too low. Answer (D) is incorrect. In situation IV, the auditor would properly assess control risk at a high level.

22. In addition to evaluating the frequency of deviations in tests of controls, an auditor should also consider certain qualitative aspects of the deviations. The auditor most likely would give broader consideration to the implications of a deviation if it was

A. The only deviation discovered in the sample.

B. Identical to a deviation discovered during the prior year's audit.

C. Caused by an employee's misunderstanding of instructions.

D. Initially concealed by a forged document.

Answer (D) is correct. *(CPA, adapted)*
REQUIRED: The aspect of a deviation requiring broader consideration.
DISCUSSION: The discovery of a fraud ordinarily requires broader consideration than the discovery of an error. The discovery of an initially concealed forged document raises concerns because it indicates that the integrity of employees may be in doubt.
Answer (A) is incorrect. A single error discovered in a sample may not cause major concern. Answer (B) is incorrect. Errors are often repetitive. Discovery of an identical deviation in a subsequent year is not unusual. Answer (C) is incorrect. A misunderstanding is an error rather than a fraud and does not necessarily arouse concern.

15.3 Classical Variables Sampling (Mean-per-Unit)

23. An auditor examining inventory most likely would use variables sampling rather than attributes sampling to

A. Identify whether inventory items are properly priced.

B. Estimate whether the dollar amount of inventory is reasonable.

C. Discover whether misstatements exist in inventory records.

D. Determine whether discounts for inventory are properly recorded.

Answer (B) is correct. *(CPA, adapted)*
REQUIRED: The purpose in an audit of inventory of using variables sampling rather than attribute sampling.
DISCUSSION: Variables sampling is used by auditors to estimate quantities or dollar amounts in substantive testing. Attribute sampling applies to tests of controls and is used to estimate a deviation rate (occurrence rate) for a population. Thus, an auditor who wants to estimate whether the dollar amount of inventory is reasonable uses variables sampling.
Answer (A) is incorrect. An auditor who wants to determine whether inventory items are properly priced uses attribute sampling, as an item is either properly priced or not. Answer (C) is incorrect. An auditor who wants to discover whether misstatements exist in inventory records uses attribute sampling. Answer (D) is incorrect. An auditor who wants to determine whether discounts for inventory are properly recorded uses attribute sampling, as an item is either properly recorded or not.

24. Which of the following statements is true concerning the auditor's use of statistical sampling?

A. An auditor needs to estimate the dollar amount of the standard deviation of the population to use classical variables sampling.

B. An assumption of monetary-unit sampling is that the underlying accounting population is normally distributed.

C. A classical variables sample needs to be designed with special considerations to include negative balances in the sample.

D. The selection of zero balances usually does not require special sample design considerations when using monetary-unit sampling.

Answer (A) is correct. *(CPA, adapted)*
REQUIRED: The true statement concerning statistical sampling.
DISCUSSION: Variables sampling is used to estimate the amount of misstatement in, or the value of, a population. In auditing, this process entails estimating the monetary value of an account balance or other accounting total. The estimated population standard deviation is used in the sample size formula for variables estimation. Hence, it should be stated in dollar terms.
Answer (B) is incorrect. MUS is based on the Poisson distribution, which approximates the binomial distribution, not the normal distribution. Answer (C) is incorrect. Classical variables samples do not require special design considerations for negative balances. Answer (D) is incorrect. MUS is not designed to deal with understatements or negative values without special modifications.

25. When planning a sample for a substantive test of details, an auditor should consider tolerable misstatement for the sample. This consideration should

A. Be related to the auditor's business risk.

B. Not be adjusted for qualitative factors.

C. Be related to preliminary judgments about materiality levels.

D. Not be changed during the audit process.

Answer (C) is correct. *(CPA, adapted)*
REQUIRED: The true statement about the consideration of tolerable misstatement.
DISCUSSION: When planning a sample for a substantive procedure, the auditor should consider how much monetary misstatement in the related account balance or class of transactions may exist without causing the financial statements to be materially misstated. This maximum misstatement is the tolerable misstatement for the sample. It is used in audit planning to determine the necessary precision and sample size. Tolerable misstatement, combined for the entire audit plan, should not exceed the auditor's preliminary judgments about materiality (AU 350).
Answer (A) is incorrect. The auditor's business risk is irrelevant. Answer (B) is incorrect. Qualitative factors should be considered, for example, the nature and cause of misstatements and their relationship to other phases of the audit. Answer (D) is incorrect. If sample results suggest that planning assumptions were incorrect, the auditor should take appropriate action.

26. An auditor is determining the sample size for an inventory observation using mean-per-unit estimation, which is a variables sampling plan. To calculate the required sample size, the auditor usually determines the

	Variability in the Dollar Amounts of Inventory Items	Risk of Incorrect Rejection
A.	Yes	Yes
B.	Yes	No
C.	No	Yes
D.	No	No

Answer (A) is correct. *(CPA, adapted)*
REQUIRED: The factor(s), if any, used to determine a mean-per-unit sample size.
DISCUSSION: Four factors are considered in determining the sample size for mean-per-unit estimation. Those factors include (1) the population size, (2) an estimate of population variation (the standard deviation), (3) the risk of incorrect rejection (its complement is the confidence level), and (4) the tolerable misstatement (the desired allowance for sampling risk is a percentage thereof, and this percentage is a function of the risk of incorrect rejection and the allowable risk of incorrect acceptance).

27. How would an increase in tolerable misstatement and an increase in assessed level of control risk affect the sample size in a substantive test of details?

	Increase in Tolerable Misstatement	Increase in Assessed Level of Control Risk
A.	Increase sample size	Increase sample size
B.	Increase sample size	Decrease sample size
C.	Decrease sample size	Increase sample size
D.	Decrease sample size	Decrease sample size

Answer (C) is correct. *(CPA, adapted)*
REQUIRED: The effects of increases in tolerable misstatement and the assessed level of control risk.
DISCUSSION: An increase in tolerable misstatement or the level of materiality decreases the sample size necessary to collect sufficient appropriate audit evidence. An increase in the assessed level of control risk increases the assurance to be provided by substantive procedures and therefore the necessary sample size.

15.4 Monetary-Unit Sampling (MUS)

28. Which of the following statements is true concerning monetary-unit sampling (MUS), also known as probability-proportional-to-size sampling?

A. The sampling distribution should approximate the normal distribution.

B. Overstated units have a lower probability of sample selection than units that are understated.

C. The auditor controls the risk of incorrect acceptance by specifying that risk level for the sampling plan.

D. The sampling interval is calculated by dividing the number of physical units in the population by the sample size.

Answer (C) is correct. *(CPA, adapted)*
REQUIRED: The true statement about MUS.
DISCUSSION: MUS is one technique whereby the auditor can measure and control the risks associated with observing less than 100% of the population. The auditor can quantify and measure the risk of accepting a client's recorded amount as fair when it is materially misstated.
Answer (A) is incorrect. MUS is most closely associated with the Poisson distribution. Answer (B) is incorrect. As the size of the units in the population increases, so does the probability of selection. Answer (D) is incorrect. The sampling interval is calculated by dividing the total dollars, not units, in the population by the sample size. Every n^{th} dollar is then selected after a random start.

29. In a monetary-unit sample with a sampling interval of $10,000, an auditor discovered that a selected account receivable with a recorded amount of $5,000 had an audited amount of $4,000. If this were the only misstatement discovered by the auditor, the projected misstatement of this sample is

A. $1,000

B. $2,000

C. $5,000

D. $10,000

Answer (B) is correct. *(CPA, adapted)*
REQUIRED: The projected misstatement of the monetary-unit sample.
DISCUSSION: MUS is a commonly used method of statistical sampling for tests of details of balances because it provides a simple statistical result expressed in dollars. Given that only one misstatement was detected, the projected misstatement for this sample is the product of the tainting percentage and the sampling interval. The tainting percentage is calculated as the difference between the recorded amount and the audited amount, divided by the recorded amount. In this sample, the tainting percentage is 20% [($5,000 – $4,000) ÷ $5,000]. Multiplying this number by the sampling interval results in a projected misstatement based on the sample of $2,000 ($10,000 × 20%).

30. Which of the following most likely would be an advantage in using classical variables sampling rather than monetary-unit sampling?

A. An estimate of the standard deviation of the population's recorded amounts is not required.

B. The auditor rarely needs the assistance of a computer program to design an efficient sample.

C. Inclusion of zero and negative balances usually does not require special design considerations.

D. Any amount that is individually significant is automatically identified and selected.

Answer (C) is correct. *(CPA, adapted)*
REQUIRED: The advantage of using classical variables sampling rather than MUS.
DISCUSSION: MUS is most useful if few misstatements are expected, and overstatement is the most likely kind of misstatement. One disadvantage of MUS is that it is designed to detect overstatements. It is not effective for estimating understatements. The smaller the item, the less likely it will be selected in the sample, but the more likely the item is understated.
Answer (A) is incorrect. The sample size formula for estimation of variables includes the standard deviation of the population. Answer (B) is incorrect. A computer program is helpful in many sampling applications. Answer (D) is incorrect. In classical variables sampling, every item has an equal and nonzero probability of selection.

Questions 31 and 32 are based on the following information.

An auditor has been assigned to take a monetary-unit sample of a population of vouchers in the purchasing department. The population has a total recorded amount of $300,000. The auditor believes that a maximum misstatement of $900 is acceptable and would like to have 95% confidence in the results. (The confidence factor at 95% and zero misstatements = 3.00.) Additional information is provided in the opposite column.

Table of First 10 Vouchers in Population

Voucher #	Balance	Cumulative Balance
1	$100	$ 100
2	150	250
3	40	290
4	200	490
5	10	500
6	290	790
7	50	840
8	190	1,030
9	20	1,050
10	180	1,230

31. Given a random start of $50 as the first dollar amount, what is the number of the fourth voucher to be selected, assuming that the sample size will be 1,000?

A. 4

B. 6

C. 7

D. 8

Answer (D) is correct. *(Publisher, adapted)*
REQUIRED: The number of the fourth voucher selected using MUS.
DISCUSSION: The vouchers have a recorded amount of $300,000, and 1,000 items are to be sampled, so every 300th dollar will be chosen. Given a random start of $50, the vouchers containing the 50th, 350th, 650th, and 950th dollars will be selected. The cumulative amount of the first eight vouchers is $1,030. Accordingly, voucher 8 should be the fourth voucher audited because it contains the 950th dollar.
Answer (A) is incorrect. Voucher 4 contains the 350th dollar and should be the second voucher selected. Answer (B) is incorrect. Voucher 6 contains the 650th dollar and should be the third voucher selected. Answer (C) is incorrect. Voucher 7 should not be selected.

32. In examining the sample, one overstatement was detected causing an extension of $270 to the tolerable misstatement. Assuming a sample size of 1,000 and assuming that the maximum dollar amount of overstatement, if no misstatements were found, was established to be $900 before the sampling analysis, what conclusion can the auditor now make from the sampling evidence?

A. (S)he is 95% confident that the dollar amount of overstatement in the population of vouchers is between $900 and $1,170.

B. (S)he is 95% confident that the dollar amount of overstatement in the population of vouchers exceeds $1,170.

C. (S)he is 95% confident that the dollar amount of overstatement in the population of vouchers is less than $1,170.

D. An insufficient number of misstatements were detected to warrant a conclusion.

Answer (C) is correct. *(Publisher, adapted)*
REQUIRED: The conclusion from the audit evidence given an extension of tolerable misstatement.
DISCUSSION: Had the auditor detected no misstatements in the sample, (s)he could have been 95% confident that the dollar amount of overstatement in the balance was less than $900. Given discovery of an overstatement causing an extension to the tolerable misstatement of $270, the auditor can conclude with 95% confidence that the overstatement is less than $1,170 ($900 + $270).
Answer (A) is incorrect. The auditor is 95% confident that the overstatement is less than $1,170. Answer (B) is incorrect. The auditor is 95% confident that the overstatement is less than $1,170. Answer (D) is incorrect. A conclusion is warranted even if no misstatements were found.

Use the additional questions in Gleim **CPA Test Prep Online** to create Test Sessions that emulate Prometric!

15.5 PRACTICE SIMULATION

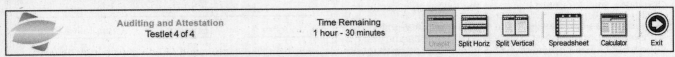

Auditing and Attestation	Time Remaining	Unsplit Split Horiz Split Vertical Spreadsheet Calculator Exit
Testlet 4 of 4	1 hour - 30 minutes	

DIRECTIONS

Note: If you believe you have encountered a software malfunction, report it to the test center staff immediately.

Navigation

To navigate from task to task, use the controls at the bottom of the screen. Click on the **Next** button to advance to the next task, or the **Previous** button to go to the previous task. To go directly to any task, click on its number.

▼ = Reminder   Directions 1 2 3 4 5 6 7   ◀ Previous   Next ▶

If you would like a reminder to revisit a task, or want to indicate that you are finished with it, click on the reminder flag below the task number. To clear the flag, click on it again. Reminder flags are for your use only – they do not contribute to your score.

Tabs

In this part of the examination, you will be asked to complete various tasks. Every task has one or more **Work Tabs**. Some tasks have one or more **Information Tabs**, others may have none. Every task has a **Help** tab.

If a task has **Information Tabs**, you may use the information in them to complete your responses in the **Work Tabs**.

Corporate Gain and Basis	Authoritative Literature	Help
Work tab	Information tab	Help tab

Work Tabs:
- **Work Tabs** are identified with a pencil icon. This is where your responses are expected.
- Each task has one or more **Work Tabs**.
- **Work Tabs** contain directions for completing the task – be sure to read these directions carefully.
- The **Work Tab** name in the example above is for illustration only – yours will differ.
- You must complete all of the **Work Tabs** in each task to receive full credit.

Information Tabs:
- The Authoritative Literature will be provided in all tasks in the AUD, FAR, and REG sections for your reference.
- Your simulation may have one or more additional **Information Tabs**. Like the Authoritative Literature tabs, **Information Tabs** do not have a pencil icon.
- If your task has additional **Information Tabs**, go through each to familiarize yourself with the task content.

Help Tab:
- The **Help Tab** provides assistance with the exam software that is used in this task. For example, if the task is to compose a memorandum, **Help** will provide information about the word processor.

The Toolbar

The toolbar at the top of the screen shows the amount of time remaining for you to complete the tasks. In addition, the following tools are available. Note that only the Exit button is displayed when Directions are visible - the others will appear when you begin the tasks.

Unsplit   Split Horiz   Split Vertical

Click on these buttons to split or unsplit the screen. You can split the screen vertically or horizontally.

Calculator

Click on this button to display the calculator; click on it again to hide the calculator. To move the calculator, click on the calculator title bar and drag the calculator to the desired location.

Spreadsheet

Click on this button to use the spreadsheet; click on it again to hide the spreadsheet. To move the spreadsheet, click on the the spreadsheet title bar and drag the spreadsheet to the desired location.

Exit

Click on this button to go on to the next part of the examination. You must complete all of the tasks to receive full credit. Once you click on **Exit** and confirm the action, you will NOT be able to return to this testlet.

▼ = Reminder   Directions 1 2 3 4 5 6   ◀ Previous   Next ▶

Define and Differentiate Types of Sampling Techniques | Authoritative Literature | Help

Select from the list provided the sampling technique that best fits each sampling explanation. Each choice may be used once, more than once, or not at all.

Sampling Explanations	Answer
1. The larger the item in the population, the more likely it will be included in the sample.	
2. Replace(s) the need for the use of judgment by the auditor.	
3. Use(s) the average amount of sampled items to estimate the amount of the population.	
4. Use(s) results from a portion of the population to draw an inference about the total population.	
5. Allow(s) the auditor to measure and control the risk of accepting a materially misstated balance.	
6. Require(s) the auditor to estimate the population standard deviation to determine the appropriate sample size.	
7. Is (are) equally useful for selecting samples and drawing inferences about asset and liability balances.	
8. Eliminate(s) the need for the auditor to consider materiality.	
9. Automatically stratify(ies) the population during sample selection.	
10. Require(s) documentation of results in the working papers.	

Sampling Choices
A) Classical variables or mean-per-unit (MPU) sampling only
B) Monetary-unit sampling only
C) Both MPU and monetary-unit sampling
D) Neither MPU nor monetary-unit sampling

Attribute Sampling | Authoritative Literature | Help

Baker, CPA, was engaged to audit Mill Company's financial statements for the year ended September 30, Year 1. After obtaining an understanding of Mill's internal control, Baker decided to obtain evidence about the suitability of the design, and the operating effectiveness, of the controls over Mill's shipping and billing functions. During the prior years' audits Baker used nonstatistical sampling, but for the current year Baker used a statistical sample in the tests of controls to eliminate the need for judgment.

Baker wanted to assess the risk of material misstatement based on the expectation that controls are operating effectively. Accordingly, a tolerable rate of deviation or acceptable upper precision limit (UPL) of 20% was established. To estimate the population deviation rate and the achieved UPL, Baker decided to apply a systematic sampling technique of attribute sampling that would use a population expected error rate of 3% for the 8,000 shipping documents, and decided to defer consideration of allowable risk of assessing control risk too low until evaluating the sample results. Baker used the tolerable rate, the population size, and the expected population error rate to determine that a sample size of 100 would be sufficient. When it was subsequently determined that the actual population was about 10,000 shipping documents, Baker did not increase the sample size.

Baker's objective was to ascertain whether Mill's shipments had been properly billed. Baker took a sample of 100 invoices by selecting the first 25 invoices from the first month of each quarter. Baker then compared the invoices with the corresponding prenumbered shipping documents.

When Baker tested the sample, eight errors were discovered. Additionally, one shipment that should have been billed at $10,443 was actually billed at $10,434. Baker considered this $9 to be immaterial and did not count it as an error.

In evaluating the sample results, Baker made the initial determination that a reliability level of 95% (risk of assessing control risk too low of 5%) was desired and, using the appropriate statistical sampling table, determined that for eight observed deviations from a sample size of 100, the achieved UPL was 14%. Baker then calculated the allowance for sampling risk to be 5%, the difference between the actual sample deviation rate (8%) and the expected error rate (3%). Baker reasoned that the actual sample deviation rate (8%) plus the allowance for sampling risk (5%) was less than the achieved UPL (14%). Thus, the sample supported the operating effectiveness of the controls.

Indicate whether each listed statement about Baker's procedures is correct or incorrect.

Statements	Answer
1. Statistical sampling eliminates the need for professional judgment.	
2. The tolerable rate of deviation or acceptable upper precision limit (UPL) is acceptable (20%) if Baker plans to rely on internal control.	
3. Systematic sampling is an appropriate sampling technique in this attribute sampling application.	
4. The sampling technique employed is not systematic sampling.	
5. The increase in the population size has little or no effect on determining sample size.	
6. Baker properly deferred consideration of the allowable risk of assessing control risk too low.	
7. The population from which the sample was chosen (invoices) was the wrong population.	
8. The sample selected was randomly selected.	
9. The difference of an immaterial amount should have been treated as an error.	
10. The allowance for sampling risk was properly calculated.	
11. Baker's reasoning concerning the decision that the sample supported the effectiveness of the controls was erroneous.	

List
A) Correct
B) Incorrect

PPS Sampling | Authoritative Literature | Help

Mead, CPA, was engaged to audit Jiffy Co.'s financial statements for the year ended August 31, Year 1. Mead is applying sampling procedures.

During the prior years' audits, Mead used classical variables sampling in performing tests of controls on Jiffy's accounts receivable. For the current year, Mead decided to use probability-proportional-to-size (PPS) sampling (also known as monetary-unit sampling) in confirming accounts receivable. PPS sampling uses each account in the population as a separate sampling unit. Mead expected to discover many overstatements but presumed that the PPS sample still would be smaller than the corresponding size for classical variables sampling.

Mead reasoned that the PPS sample would automatically result in a stratified sample because each account would have an equal chance of being selected for confirmation. Additionally, the selection of negative (credit) balances would be facilitated without special considerations.

Mead computed the sample size using the risk of incorrect acceptance, the total recorded book amount of the receivables, and the number of misstated accounts allowed. Mead divided the total recorded book amount of the receivables by the sample size to determine the sampling interval. Mead then calculated the standard deviation of the monetary amounts of the accounts selected for evaluation of the receivables.

Mead's calculated sample size was 60, and the sampling interval was determined to be $10,000. However, only 58 different accounts were selected because two accounts were so large that the sampling interval caused each of them to be selected twice. Mead proceeded to send confirmation requests to 55 of the 58 customers. Three selected accounts each had insignificant recorded balances under $20. Mead ignored these three small accounts and substituted the three largest accounts that had not been selected in the sample. Each of these accounts had balances in excess of $7,000, so Mead sent confirmation requests to those customers.

The confirmation process revealed two differences. One account with an audited amount of $3,000 had been recorded at $4,000. Mead projected this to be a $1,000 misstatement. Another account with an audited amount of $2,000 had been recorded at $1,900. Mead did not count the $100 difference because the purpose of the test was to provide assurance that the account was not materially overstated.

In evaluating the sample results, Mead determined that the accounts receivable balance was not overstated because the sum of the projected misstatement and the allowance for sampling risk was less than tolerable misstatement.

Check the appropriate box to indicate which statements about sampling procedures are correct and which are incorrect.

Item	Correct	Incorrect
1. Classical variables sampling is designed for tests of controls.		
2. PPS sampling uses each account in the population as a separate sampling unit.		
3. PPS sampling is not efficient if many misstatements are expected. The sample size can become larger than the corresponding sample size for classical variables sampling as the expected amount of misstatement increases.		
4. Each account does not have an equal chance of being selected. The probability of selection of the accounts is proportional to the accounts' monetary amounts.		
5. PPS sampling requires no special consideration for negative (credit) balances.		
6. Tolerable misstatement was not considered in calculating the sample size.		
7. Expected (anticipated) misstatement was not considered in calculating the sample size.		
8. The standard deviation of the monetary amounts is required for PPS sampling.		
9. The three selected accounts with insignificant balances should not have been ignored or replaced with other accounts.		
10. The account with the $1,000 difference (recorded amount of $4,000 and audited amount of $3,000) was incorrectly projected as a $1,000 misstatement. Projected misstatement for this difference was actually $2,500 [($1,000 ÷ $4,000) × $10,000 interval].		
11. The difference in the understated account (recorded amount of $1,900 and audited amount of $2,000) could have been omitted from the calculation of projected misstatement given the purpose of the test.		
12. The reasoning concerning the decision that the receivable balance was not overstated was erroneous.		

| MUS Sample Size | Authoritative Literature | Help |

Edward Prince, CPA, has decided to use monetary-unit sampling, sometimes called probability-proportional-to-size sampling, in the audit of a client's accounts receivable. Few, if any, overstatements are expected.

Confidence Factors for Misstatements
Risk of Incorrect Acceptance

# of Misstatements	1.00%	5.00%	10.00%	15.00%	20.00%
0	4.61	3.00	2.31	1.90	1.61
1	6.64	4.75	3.89	3.38	3.00
2	8.41	6.30	5.33	4.72	4.28
3	10.05	7.76	6.69	6.02	5.52
4	11.61	9.16	8.00	7.27	6.73

Other information for the current year's audit is outlined below:

Tolerable misstatement	$15,000
Risk of incorrect acceptance	5%
Number of misstatements allowed	0
Recorded amount of accounts receivable	$300,000

Use the current year's audit information to calculate the sampling interval and the sample size. Enter in the table below the proper amounts as given or calculated.

1.	Confidence factor	
2.	Tolerable misstatement	
3.	Sampling interval	
4.	Recorded amount	
5.	Sample size	

| MUS Evaluation | Authoritative Literature | Help |

Keith, CPA, used monetary-unit sampling, sometimes called probability-proportional-to-size sampling, in the audit of a client's accounts receivable.

Other information for the current year's audit is outlined below:

| Tolerable misstatement | $20,000 |
| Recorded amount of accounts receivable | $200,000 |

Keith found the three misstatements listed below. Given this information, calculate the total projected misstatement. Enter the appropriate amounts in the shaded cells in the table below.

	Recorded Amount	Audit Amount	Tainting	Sampling Interval	Projected Misstatement
1st Error	$400	$320	1.	$1,000	4.
2nd Error	$500	$0	2.	$1,000	5.
3rd Error	$3,000	$2,500	3.	$1,000	6.
				Total Projected	7.

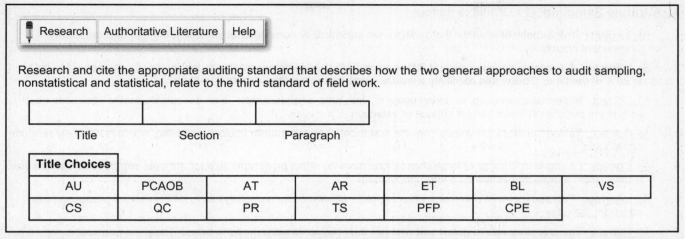

Research and cite the appropriate auditing standard that describes how the two general approaches to audit sampling, nonstatistical and statistical, relate to the third standard of field work.

Title	Section	Paragraph

Title Choices

AU	PCAOB	AT	AR	ET	BL	VS
CS	QC	PR	TS	PFP	CPE	

⚐ = Reminder   Directions   1 2 3 4 5 **6**   ◀ Previous   Next ▶

Unofficial Answers

1. Define and Differentiate Types of Sampling Techniques (10 Gradable Items)

1. <u>B) Monetary-unit sampling only.</u> In monetary-unit sampling, the probability of selection is related to size of the item.

2. <u>D) Neither MPU nor monetary-unit sampling.</u> As noted in AU 350, "Evaluating the appropriateness of evidence is solely a matter of auditing judgment and is not determined by the design and evaluation of an audit sample."

3. <u>A) Classical variables or mean-per-unit (MPU) sampling only.</u> MPU sampling determines the average amount of sampled items (total audited amount of the sample ÷ number of items in the sample) and then multiplies this average by the number of items in the population to estimate the population amount.

4. <u>C) Both MPU and monetary-unit sampling.</u> AU 350 states, "Audit sampling is the application of an audit procedure to less than 100 percent of the items within an account balance or class of transactions for the purpose of evaluating some characteristic of the balance or class."

5. <u>C) Both MPU and monetary-unit sampling.</u> By using statistical theory, the auditor can quantify sampling risk to assist him/herself in limiting it to a level (s)he considers acceptable.

6. <u>A) Classical variables or mean-per-unit (MPU) sampling only.</u> MPU sampling requires the auditor to estimate the population's standard deviation to determine the sample size and evaluate the results. Monetary-unit sampling, however, does not require the use of the population standard deviation.

7. <u>A) Classical variables or mean-per-unit (MPU) sampling only.</u> Monetary-unit sampling is appropriate only for accounts subject to the risk of overstatement (e.g., assets). Because the focus of liability accounts is ordinarily on the risk of understatement, monetary-unit sampling does not meet the objectives for liabilities.

8. <u>D) Neither MPU nor monetary-unit sampling.</u> The auditor must quantify the amount considered material for either sampling method. The amount considered material is one of the factors used in calculating the appropriate sample size.

9. <u>B) Monetary-unit sampling only.</u> Because monetary-unit sampling increases the probability of selecting large items, it effectively stratifies the population.

10. <u>C) Both MPU and monetary-unit sampling.</u> All important evidence and conclusions should be documented in the working papers, regardless of what tools or techniques are used by the auditor.

2. Attribute Sampling (11 Gradable Items)

1. B) Incorrect. Regardless of whether the auditor uses statistical or nonstatistical sampling, the use of professional judgment is necessary.

2. B) Incorrect. A tolerable deviation rate of 20% means that it would be acceptable to the auditor for the control to fail up to 20% of the time. This would not likely allow the auditor to rely on the control.

3. A) Correct. Systematic sampling, or taking every n^{th} item after a random start, is an acceptable method because each item in the population has an equal chance of selection.

4. A) Correct. Taking the first 25 invoices from the first month of each quarter is block sampling, which is not likely random in this case.

5. A) Correct. Changes in the size of large populations have no effect on sample size for attribute sampling as sample size is taken from a table that assumes a large population

6. B) Incorrect. The auditor must determine an acceptable allowance for sampling risk to determine the proper sample size from the table.

7. A) Correct. The objective was to determine whether the shipments were properly billed. Thus, the population should be the shipping documents. The shipping documents would be traced to the invoices to determine if all shipments were properly billed.

8. B) Incorrect. Block sampling typically does not result in a random sample because each item does not have an equal chance of selection.

9. A) Correct. In determining failure rate in a control, attribute sampling does not consider the materiality of the error, only that an error has taken place. However, the auditor would be concerned about the qualitative nature of the errors as well as estimating the deviation rate of the control.

10. B) Incorrect. In evaluating the sample, the achieved allowance for sampling risk is calculated as the upper precision limit (UPL) less the sample rate. Thus, based on the values provided, it would be 14% – 8%, or 6%.

11. A) Correct. The comparison should be made between the tolerable rate of 20% and the UPL of 14. Although likely not justified given the high tolerable rate, since the UPL was less than the tolerable rate, the auditor would rely on the control.

3. PPS Sampling (12 Gradable Items)

1. Incorrect. Classical variables sampling is a method to help the auditor conclude whether quantities and amounts are fairly stated.

2. Incorrect. PPS uses each dollar in the population as a sampling unit. Once the sampling unit is selected, the account in which the dollar is found is identified for audit and called the logical sampling unit.

3. Correct. A weakness in PPS is that when many misstatements are expected, the sample sizes become large and the method is inefficient.

4. Correct. Although each dollar has an equal chance of being selected, the dollar selected is more likely to be in very large accounts than in very small accounts. Thus, the large accounts have a proportionately greater chance of being included in the sample.

5. Incorrect. Since zero or negative balances technically have no sampling units (dollars), they need special consideration in the sampling plan.

6. Correct. Tolerable misstatement or materiality must be considered in PPS to calculate the sample size.

7. Correct. Expected misstatement must be considered in PPS to calculate the sample size (although expected misstatement can be estimated at zero).

8. Incorrect. An advantage of PPS is that the standard deviation of the population need not be estimated.

9. Correct. All accounts selected for audit should be included in the analysis.

10. Correct. Misstatements less than the sampling interval must be projected to the population. Thus, the sampling unit was misstated (tainted) by 25% ($1,000 ÷ $4000), and projecting this to the sampling interval for which it represents of $10,000 results in a projected misstatement of $2,500.

11. Correct. Since the purpose of the test was to gather evidence that the account was not overstated, by ignoring understatement errors in the projection of potential overstatement, the auditor is being conservative.

12. Incorrect. In forming a conclusion, if the sum of the projected misstatement plus the allowance for sampling risk is equal to or less than the tolerable misstatement, the conclusion that the account is not materially overstated is supported.

4. MUS Sample Size (5 Gradable Items)

1. The risk of incorrect acceptance is 5% and 0 misstatements are allowed. Thus, the confidence factor is 3.00.

2. The tolerable misstatement is $15,000.

3.
$$Sampling\ Interval = \frac{Tolerable\ Misstatement}{Confidence\ Factor}$$

$$= \frac{\$15,000}{3.00}$$

$$= \$5,000$$

4. The recorded amount is $300,000.

5.
$$Sample\ Size = \frac{Recorded\ Amount}{Sampling\ Interval}$$

$$= \frac{\$300,000}{\$5,000}$$

$$= 60$$

5. MUS Evaluation (7 Gradable Items)

1. ($400 − $320) ÷ $400 = 20% tainted
2. ($500 − $0) ÷ $500 = 100% tainted
3. The recorded amount is greater than the sampling interval. Thus, the projected misstatement equals the actual misstatement.
4. $1,000 × 20% = $200
5. $1,000 × 100% = $1,000
6. $3,000 − $2,500 = $500
7. $200 + $1,000 + $500 = $1,700

6. Research (1 Gradable Item)

Answer: 350.04

AU Section 350 -- *Audit Sampling*

.04   The third standard of field work states, "The auditor must obtain sufficient appropriate audit evidence by performing audit procedures to afford a reasonable basis for an opinion regarding the financial statements under audit." Either approach to audit sampling, when properly applied, can provide sufficient audit evidence.

Gleim Simulation Grading

Task	Correct Responses		Gradable Items		Score per Task
1	_____	÷	10	=	_____
2	_____	÷	11	=	_____
3	_____	÷	12	=	_____
4	_____	÷	5	=	_____
5	_____	÷	7	=	_____
Research	_____	÷	1	=	_____

Total of Scores per Task		_____
÷ Total Number of Tasks		6
Total Score		_____ %

STUDY UNIT SIXTEEN
REPORTS --
OPINIONS AND DISCLAIMERS

(13 pages of outline)

This study unit presents interrelated reporting issues. Subunit 2 should be studied carefully. Most reporting guidance is based on the standard audit report, which, in its unmodified form, expresses an unqualified opinion on financial statements. For example, the other subunits of this study unit and all of Study Unit 17 outline the requirements for modifications of the standard report. Special reports, covered in Study Unit 18, are adapted from the standard report. Many matters considered in Study Unit 19 relate to standard reporting issues. Governmental audit reports, covered in Study Unit 20, are variations of the standard report.

The following summarizes the information included in the various auditors' reports expressing an opinion (disclaiming an opinion) on financial statements. Scan it now and then revisit it after you complete Study Units 16 and 17. The "[Extra Paragraph]" included in a report expressing an unqualified opinion is addressed in Study Unit 17.

Report Paragraph	Auditor's Opinion			
	Unqualified	Qualified	Adverse	Disclaimer
1st	Introduction	Introduction	Introduction	Introduction/No Opinion
2nd	Scope	Scope	Scope	Reason for No Scope
3rd	Opinion	Scope Limitation/ GAAP Departure	GAAP Departure	Disclaimer
4th	[Extra Paragraph]	Opinion	Opinion	---

16.1 GAAS -- THE REPORTING STANDARDS

1. **First Standard of Reporting**

   a. *The auditor must state in the auditor's report whether the financial statements are presented in accordance with generally accepted accounting principles (GAAP).**

   *An auditor also may express (or disclaim) an opinion on whether the financial statements conform with a comprehensive basis of accounting other than GAAP.

   b. According to a currently effective AICPA pronouncement, GAAP encompass the conventions, rules, and procedures necessary to define accepted accounting practice at a particular time. They include not only broad guidelines of general application, but also detailed practices and procedures. Thus, GAAP provide standards by which to measure financial presentations (AU 411).

   c. Financial statements should

   1) Apply GAAP that are appropriate in the circumstances.
   2) Include adequate disclosure.
   3) Classify and summarize information so that it is neither too detailed nor too condensed.
   4) Reflect underlying events and transactions within an acceptable range.

2. **U.S. GAAP – Nongovernmental Entities**

   a. The report should identify the country of origin of GAAP, for example, accounting principles generally accepted in the United States of America or U.S. generally accepted accounting principles

      1) The **FASB Accounting Standards Codification**™ is the source of authoritative guidance issued by the FASB. It applies to **public and nonpublic** nongovernmental entities.

      2) **SEC registrants** also must follow **SEC** pronouncements.

      3) If authoritative guidance does not apply to a transaction or event, the entity considers GAAP for **similar** transactions or events.

         a) The entity then considers **nonauthoritative** guidance, for example, (1) widely recognized and prevalent practices, (2) Concepts Statements, (3) International Financial Reporting Standards, and (4) pronouncements of regulators.

   b. **Conduct Rule 203** prohibits expression of an opinion that financial statements are in conformity with GAAP if they contain a material departure from a principle issued by the body designated by the AICPA Council to establish such principles (e.g., the FASB).

      1) However, an exception is permitted when the auditor can demonstrate that, because of unusual circumstances, the statements would otherwise have been **misleading**.

      2) Given these circumstances, and if no other basis for modifying the opinion exists, the CPA may express an unqualified opinion.

         a) But (s)he must describe in a **separate paragraph** of the report the departure, its effects, and the reasons compliance with GAAP would have been misleading.

      3) The client should **disclose** the departure and the effects in a note to the financial statements.

3. **Second Standard of Reporting**

   a. *The auditor must identify in the auditor's report those circumstances in which such principles have not been consistently observed in the current period in relation to the preceding period.*

   b. The user has the right to expect that changes in the account balances have resulted from transactions, not changes in principle.

   c. Management has the responsibility to disclose the effects of changes.

   d. The auditor's report should include an additional paragraph whenever a material change in principle has occurred.

4. **Third Standard of Reporting**

   a. *When the auditor determines that informative disclosures are not reasonably adequate, the auditor must so state in the auditor's report.*

   b. Presenting statements in conformity with GAAP includes adequate disclosure of material matters related to the form, arrangement, and content of the statements and notes.

      1) If management omits information required by GAAP, the auditor should provide the necessary disclosures in the report, if practicable, and express a qualified or adverse opinion (AU 431).

5. **Fourth Standard of Reporting**

    a. *The auditor must either express an opinion regarding the financial statements, taken as a whole, or state that an opinion cannot be expressed, in the auditor's report. When the auditor cannot express an overall opinion, the auditor should state the reasons therefor in the auditor's report. In all cases where an auditor's name is associated with financial statements, the auditor should clearly indicate the character of the auditor's work, if any, and the degree of responsibility the auditor is taking, in the auditor's report.*

    b. The objective of the fourth standard is to prevent misinterpretation of the **degree of responsibility** the auditor is assuming when his/her name is **associated with financial statements**.

        1) An accountant may be associated with financial statements of a **public entity** (an **issuer** as defined in federal securities law) that (s)he has not audited or reviewed. If the accountant is aware that his/her name is to be included in a **client-prepared written communication of an issuer** containing financial statements that have not been audited or reviewed, (s)he should request that either

            a) His/her name not be included in the communication, or

            b) The financial statements be marked as unaudited and that a notation be included to the effect that (s)he does not express an opinion on them (AU 504).

        2) The statement in the **introductory paragraph** of the standard report about **management's responsibility** should not be elaborated upon in the standard report or referenced to management's report.

            a) Such a modification might lead users to the erroneous belief that the auditor is giving assurances about **management's representations** concerning matters discussed in the management report.

    c. **"Taken as a whole,"** as referred to in the fourth standard of reporting, applies equally to a complete set of financial statements, to an individual financial statement, and to financial statements for different periods presented comparatively.

        1) The auditor may express an unqualified opinion on one financial statement and express a qualified or adverse opinion or disclaim an opinion on another if indicated by the circumstances.

    d. The auditor's report is customarily issued in connection with an entity's **basic financial statements**. Each financial statement audited should be specifically identified in the introductory paragraph of the auditor's report.

        1) If the basic financial statements include a separate **statement of changes in equity**, it should be identified in the introductory paragraph of the report but need not be reported on separately in the opinion paragraph. Such changes are part of the presentation of financial position, results of operations, and cash flows.

Stop and review! You have completed the outline for this subunit. Study multiple-choice questions 1 through 5 beginning on page 528.

16.2 THE AUDITOR'S STANDARD REPORT (AU 508)

 We recommend that you memorize the standard audit report. You will not be required to draft a report on the exam, but questions often relate to how the report will change based on client issues and audit findings. You do not want to be struggling with the normative language while trying to consider what changes should be made. It will serve you well to have a firm grasp of the report. Following the example report presented below, we give you a break-down of the format to help you recall the parts of the report.

1.   The standard report on **comparative financial statements** is as follows:

EXAMPLE – Standard Audit Report

Independent Auditor's Report

To: <----------- Addressed to the Board of Directors and/or Shareholders

We have audited the accompanying balance sheets of X Company as of December 31, Year 2 and Year 1, and the related statements of income, retained earnings, and cash flows for the years then ended. These financial statements are the responsibility of the Company's management. Our responsibility is to express an opinion on these financial statements based on our audits.

We conducted our audits in accordance with auditing standards generally accepted in the United States of America. Those standards require that we plan and perform the audit to obtain reasonable assurance about whether the financial statements are free of material misstatement. An audit includes examining, on a test basis, evidence supporting the amounts and disclosures in the financial statements. An audit also includes assessing the accounting principles used and significant estimates made by management, as well as evaluating the overall financial statement presentation. We believe that our audits provide a reasonable basis for our opinion.

In our opinion, the financial statements referred to above present fairly, in all material respects, the financial position of X Company as of [at] December 31, Year 2 and Year 1, and the results of its operations and its cash flows for the years then ended in conformity with accounting principles generally accepted in the United States of America.

Signature   <----------- May be signed, typed, or printed

Date   <----------- Date that sufficient appropriate audit evidence was obtained

---

2.   **Paragraphs in the Standard Report**

   a.   **Introductory or opening.** The introductory paragraph identifies the financial statements and period(s) under audit and describes the responsibilities of management and the auditor. It contains three sentences:

   1)   We have audited . . . .
   2)   Statements . . . responsibility . . . management.
   3)   Our responsibility . . . opinion.

   b.   **Scope.** The scope paragraph describes the nature of the audit. It contains five sentences:

   1)   Conducted . . . GAAS.

      a)   The PCAOB's AS No. 1, *References in Auditors' Reports to the Standards of the Public Company Accounting Oversight Board,* requires the report of a client subject to the **Sarbanes-Oxley Act** (issuers) to refer to "the standards of the Public Company Accounting Oversight Board (United States)" rather than to GAAS.

      b)   Clients not subject to the act (nonissuers) also may voluntarily follow the PCAOB standards.

         i)   In this case, the auditors of such clients may indicate in the scope paragraph that the audit was conducted using **both sets of standards**.

      c)   Furthermore, the report on an audit of a nonissuer may contain language to clarify that expression of an opinion on internal control is **not** required. Such an engagement does not require performance of procedures sufficient to express an opinion on the effectiveness of internal control over financial reporting.

        d) An auditor also may indicate that the audit was conducted in accordance with U.S. GAAS and **another set of auditing standards**, e.g., International Standards on Auditing issued by the International Auditing and Assurance Board.

    2) Standards . . . reasonable assurance.

    3) Audit . . . examining on a test basis.

    4) Audit . . . assessing principles and significant estimates by management.

    5) We believe . . . reasonable basis.

  c. **Opinion.** The opinion paragraph presents the auditor's conclusion. It contains one sentence:

    1) In our opinion, the financial statements . . . present fairly . . . GAAP.

        a) An auditor also may report on general purpose financial statements presented in conformity with **International Financial Reporting Standards (IFRSs)** issued by the International Accounting Standards Board.

3. **Types of Reports**

  a. **Unqualified Opinion**

    1) An unqualified opinion states that the financial statements present fairly, in all material respects, the financial position, results of operations, and cash flows of the entity in conformity with GAAP.

  b. **Explanatory Language Added to the Auditor's Standard Report**

    1) Certain circumstances, although not affecting the auditor's unqualified opinion, may require that the auditor add an explanatory paragraph (or other explanatory language) to the report. See Study Unit 17.

  c. **Qualified Opinion**

    1) A qualified opinion states that, **except for** the effects of the matter(s) to which the qualification relates, the financial statements present fairly, in all material respects, the financial position, results of operations, and cash flows of the entity in conformity with GAAP.

  d. **Adverse Opinion**

    1) An adverse opinion states that the financial statements do not present fairly the financial position, results of operations, or cash flows of the entity in conformity with GAAP.

  e. **Disclaimer of Opinion**

    1) A disclaimer of opinion states that the auditor does not express an opinion on the financial statements.

4. **Additional Considerations**

  a. If only **single-year financial statements** are presented, the report is adjusted to refer only to those statements.

  b. Unless otherwise required, an **explanatory paragraph** may precede or follow the opinion paragraph in the auditor's report.

ISA Difference

ISAs expand in the audit report the descriptions of the responsibilities of management and the auditor. Additionally, the report should name the country or jurisdiction where the auditor practices. The jurisdiction may specify the language or report layout that the auditor uses, but the report should indicate that ISA standards were followed only if the jurisdictional standards were congruent with the ISAs.

Stop and review! You have completed the outline for this subunit. Study multiple-choice questions 6 through 12 beginning on page 529.

16.3 ADDRESSING AND DATING THE REPORT (AU 508 AND AU 530)

1. The auditor's report should be addressed to the entity whose statements are being audited or to its board of directors or shareholders. If the client is an unincorporated entity, the report should be addressed as circumstances dictate, e.g., to the partners or the proprietor.

   a. If an auditor is retained to audit the financial statements of an entity that is **not the client**, the report customarily is addressed to the client and not to the board of directors or shareholders of the entity whose financial statements are being audited (AU 508).

ISA Difference

The circumstances of the engagement determine how the report is addressed.

---

2. **The Date of the Report**

   a. The date of the audit report is no earlier than the date on which the auditor has obtained sufficient appropriate evidence to support the opinion. This date is important because the user has a right to expect that the auditor has performed certain procedures to detect subsequent events that would materially affect the financial statements through the date of the report.

      1) The auditor is ordinarily not responsible for making inquiries or carrying out any audit procedures after the date of the report.

   b. When a **subsequent event** disclosed in the financial statements occurs after the date of the report but before the issuance of the related financial statements, the auditor may use **dual dating**. (S)he may use the original date of the report except for the matters affected by the subsequent event, which would be assigned the appropriate later date.

      1) In that case, the auditor's responsibility for events after the original date of the report would be limited to the specific event.

      2) If the auditor is willing to accept responsibility to the later date and accordingly extends subsequent events procedures to that date, the auditor may choose the later date as the date for the entire report.

   c. Use of the original date in a **reissued report** removes any implication that records, transactions, or events after such date have been audited or reviewed. The auditor will thus have no responsibility to carry out procedures relating to the period between original issuance and reissuance.

      1) An exception exists for filings under the Securities Act of 1933. This is covered in AU 711.

ISA Difference

The statements may be amended for facts discovered after the report date but prior to the issuance of the statements. The auditor should issue a new report dated no earlier than the approval of the amended statements, with procedures extended to that date.

Stop and review! You have completed the outline for this subunit. Study multiple-choice questions 13 through 17 beginning on page 531.

16.4 QUALIFIED OPINIONS (AU 508)

1. **Reasons for Qualifying the Opinion**

   a. A qualified opinion may be based on a lack of sufficient appropriate evidence, restrictions on the audit's scope, or a material departure from GAAP.

   b. Financial statements may be fairly presented **except for** the effects of a certain matter. If the opinion is qualified because of such effects, all substantive reasons should be disclosed in one or more separate explanatory paragraph(s) **preceding** the opinion paragraph.

      1) The opinion paragraph should contain qualifying language and refer to the explanatory paragraph.

      2) It should include the word "except" or "exception" in a phrase such as "except for" or "with the exception of."

      3) "Subject to," "with the foregoing explanation," and similar phrases lack clarity and forcefulness and shall **not** be used.

      4) Notes are part of the statements, and language such as "fairly presented when read in conjunction with Note 1" should **not** be used because of the likelihood of misunderstanding.

2. **Scope Limitations**

   a. An unqualified opinion requires the application of all procedures the auditor considers necessary in the circumstances.

   b. Scope restrictions leading to a qualified opinion or a disclaimer may be imposed by the client or by circumstances, for example, by the

      1) Timing of the work,

      2) Inability to obtain sufficient appropriate evidence, or

      3) Inadequacy of the accounting records.

   c. Whether to **qualify the opinion or disclaim an opinion** depends on the assessment of the importance of the omitted procedure(s).

      1) This assessment will be affected by the nature and magnitude of the potential effects of the matters in question and their significance to the statements.

   d. Some **common scope restrictions** relate to the inability to observe inventory, confirm accounts receivable, or obtain audited statements of an investee.

      1) When significant restrictions are imposed by the **client**, the auditor usually should **disclaim an opinion**.

   e. When a qualified opinion results from a **scope limitation or insufficient evidence**, the situation is described in an explanatory paragraph preceding the opinion paragraph and referred to in the scope and opinion paragraphs.

      1) The scope limitation or insufficiency of evidence is not explained in a note to the statements because the description is the responsibility of the auditor.

   f. The wording in the opinion paragraph should indicate that the qualification pertains to the **possible effects** on the financial statements and not to the scope limitation itself.

   g. In a report in which the opinion is qualified because of a scope limitation pertaining to an investment in a foreign affiliate, the

      1) Introductory paragraph is unchanged.

      2) Scope paragraph is unchanged except that it begins with the clause:

         Except as discussed in the following paragraph, . . .

3) Explanatory paragraph and the qualifying language and reference in the opinion paragraph are as follows:

EXAMPLE – Language to Qualify an Audit Report for a Scope Limitation

We were unable to obtain audited financial statements supporting the Company's investment in a foreign affiliate stated at $___ and $___ at December 31, Year 2 and Year 1, respectively, or its equity in earnings of that affiliate of $___ and $___, which is included in net income for the years then ended as described in Note X to the financial statements; nor were we able to satisfy ourselves as to the carrying value of the investment in the foreign affiliates or the equity in its earnings by other auditing procedures.

In our opinion, except for the effects of such adjustments, if any, as might have been determined to be necessary had we been able to examine evidence regarding the foreign affiliate investment and earnings, the financial statements referred to in the first paragraph above present fairly....

---

h. **Other Scope Limitations**

1) If the notes to the statements contain **unaudited information** that should be audited, such as a material share of an investee's earnings recognized using the equity method, the auditor should apply the procedures (s)he deems necessary.

2) If the procedures cannot be applied, (s)he should qualify the opinion or disclaim an opinion because of a scope limitation.

3) If the disclosures, for example, the pro forma effects of a business combination or of a subsequent event, are not necessary to fair presentation, they may be identified as "unaudited" or "not covered by the auditor's report." Thus, the event or transaction would be audited but not the related pro forma disclosures.

   a) With regard to a **material subsequent event** requiring disclosure, however, the only options are to dual date the report or date the report as of the date of the subsequent event and extend subsequent events procedures to that date.

ISA Difference

Unless required by statute, an auditor does not accept an engagement if its terms indicate a **limitation of its scope** that may necessitate a **disclaimer**.

---

3. **Limited Reporting Engagements**

   a. The auditor may report on **one basic financial statement** and not on the others.
   b. These engagements do not involve scope limitations but rather limited reporting objectives.
   c. If an auditor reports on the **balance sheet only**, (s)he may express an opinion on the balance sheet only.
   d. References in the **introductory and opinion paragraphs** of the report are made only to those statements being audited.

4. **Departures from GAAP**

   a. A material departure from GAAP results in a **qualified (or an adverse) opinion**. The basis for modifying the opinion is stated in the report.
   b. The materiality of the effects of a departure involves qualitative as well as quantitative judgments. The following are examples:

      1) Significance of an item to an entity (e.g., inventories to a manufacturer)
      2) Pervasiveness (e.g., whether it affects numerous items)
      3) Effect on the statements as a whole

c. In addition to the substantive reasons for qualifying the opinion, the **explanatory paragraph(s)** should disclose the **principal effects** of the subject matter of the qualification, if practicable.

    1) If the effects are not reasonably determinable, the report should so state.

    2) The paragraph should precede the opinion paragraph.

    3) The explanatory paragraph(s) may be shortened by referring to relevant disclosures made in a note to the statements.

    4) In a report in which the opinion is qualified because of a departure from GAAP,

        a) The introductory and scope paragraphs are unchanged.

        b) The explanatory paragraph and the qualifying language and reference in the opinion paragraph are as follows:

EXAMPLE – Language to Qualify an Audit Report for a Departure from U.S. GAAP

The Company has excluded, from property and debt in the accompanying balance sheets, certain lease obligations that, in our opinion, should be capitalized in order to conform with U.S. generally accepted accounting principles. If these obligations were capitalized, property would be increased by \$___ and \$___, long term debt by \$___ and \$___, and retained earnings by \$___ and \$___. Additionally, net income would be increased (decreased) by \$___ and \$___, and earnings per share would be increased (decreased) by \$___ and \$___, respectively, for the years then ended.

In our opinion, except for the effects of not capitalizing certain lease obligations as discussed in the preceding paragraph, the financial statements referred to above present fairly, in all material respects, the financial position of X Company as of December 31, Year 2 and Year 1, and the results of its operations and its cash flows for the three years then ended in conformity with accounting principles generally accepted in the United States of America.

---

        c) If disclosures are made in a note to the financial statements, the separate paragraph might read as follows:

EXAMPLE – Separate Paragraph Referencing a Note Describing a Departure from U.S. GAAP

As more fully described in Note X to the financial statements, the Company has excluded certain lease obligations from property and debt in the accompanying balance sheets. In our opinion, U.S. generally accepted accounting principles require that such obligations be included in the balance sheets.

---

d. **Inadequate Disclosure**

    1) If the financial statements, including the notes, omit disclosures required by GAAP, a qualified (or adverse) opinion should be expressed. The omitted information should be provided by the auditor in the report, if practicable, unless the omission is permitted by a specific auditing standard.

    2) In a report qualified for inadequate disclosure,

        a) The introductory and scope paragraphs are unchanged.

        b) The explanatory paragraph and the qualifying language and reference in the opinion paragraph are as follows:

EXAMPLE – Language to Qualify an Audit Report for Inadequate Disclosure

The Company's financial statements do not disclose (describe the nature of the omitted disclosures). In our opinion, disclosure of this information is required by U.S. generally accepted accounting principles.

In our opinion, except for the omission of the information discussed in the preceding paragraph, the financial statements referred to above present fairly....

---

    3) If the statements of financial position and results of operations are issued **without a statement of cash flows**, the omission normally requires a qualified opinion.

    4) The auditor need not prepare and include in the report a basic financial statement omitted by management, such as a statement of cash flows.

5) In a report qualified for omission of the statement of cash flows,

    a) The introductory and scope paragraphs are unchanged except that the first does not mention the statement of cash flows.

    b) The explanatory and opinion paragraphs are as follows:

EXAMPLE – Language to Qualify an Audit Report for Failure to Present a Statement of Cash Flows

The Company declined to present a statement of cash flows for the years ended December 31, Year 2 and Year 1. Presentation of such statement summarizing the company's operating, investing, and financing activities is required by U.S. generally accepted accounting principles.

In our opinion, except that the omission of a statement of cash flows results in an incomplete presentation as explained in the preceding paragraph, the financial statements referred to above present fairly, in all material respects, the financial position of X Company as of December 31, Year 2 and Year 1, and the results of its operation for the years then ended in conformity with accounting principles generally accepted in the United States of America.

---

e. **Inappropriate Accounting Changes**

1) A qualified opinion (or, if the effect of the change is sufficiently material, an adverse opinion) should be expressed if one of the following applies:

    a) A newly adopted accounting principle is not generally accepted.

    b) The method of accounting for the effect of the change is not in conformity with GAAP.

    c) Management's justification for the change is not reasonable.

2) In a report qualified for lack of a reasonable justification for an accounting change,

    a) The introductory and scope paragraphs are unchanged.

    b) The explanatory paragraph and the qualifying language and reference in the opinion paragraph are as follows:

EXAMPLE – Language to Qualify an Audit Report for Inappropriate Change in Accounting Principle

As disclosed in Note X to the financial statements, the Company adopted, in Year 2, the first-in, first-out method of accounting for its inventories, whereas it previously used the last-in, first-out method. Although use of the first-in, first-out method is in conformity with generally accepted accounting principles, in our opinion, the Company has not provided reasonable justification, as required by generally accepted accounting principles, for making this change.

In our opinion, except for the change in accounting principles discussed in the preceding paragraph....

---

    c) In effect, both a change in accounting principle and a departure from GAAP results. The explanatory paragraph in the previous example meets the requirements for a consistency paragraph when simply a change in GAAP is encountered (see Study Unit 17, Subunit 2). Hence, a separate consistency paragraph following the opinion paragraph (as normally required for acceptable changes) is not necessary.

3) Whenever an accounting change results in a qualified or adverse opinion for the year of change, the possible effects should be considered in reporting on financial statements for **subsequent years**.

    a) If the statements for the year of change are presented and reported on with a subsequent year's statements, the report should disclose the **auditor's reservations** about the earlier statements.

    b) The **continued use** of an **unacceptable accounting principle** may have a material effect in a subsequent year. The auditor should express a qualified (or an adverse) opinion, depending on the materiality of the departure.

c) If an entity departs from GAAP by accounting for a change **prospectively rather than by retrospective application**, the subsequent year's statements could improperly include a material debit or credit that requires a qualified (or an adverse) opinion.

d) If reasonable justification for a change to an otherwise acceptable principle has not been provided, the auditor should continue to express the exception regarding the year of change as long as the statements are presented and reported on.

  i) The opinion on the subsequent years' statements need not express an exception to adoption of the principle. Hence, if such a change was made in Year 1 and comparative statements for Year 1, Year 2, and Year 3 are presented and reported on, the change will be a basis for a qualified opinion on the Year 1, but not the Year 2 and Year 3, statements.

Stop and review! You have completed the outline for this subunit. Study multiple-choice questions 18 through 31 beginning on page 533.

16.5 ADVERSE OPINIONS (AU 508)

1. An **adverse opinion** is expressed when, in the judgment of the auditor, the financial statements taken **as a whole** are not presented fairly in conformity with GAAP.

2. The auditor should include in a separate explanatory paragraph(s) **preceding the opinion paragraph** all substantive reasons for the adverse opinion and the principal effects of its subject matter, if practicable. If the effects are not reasonably determinable, a statement to that effect should be included.

3. **Example of an Adverse Opinion**

  a. The introductory and scope paragraphs are unchanged.

  b. The opinion paragraph should directly refer to a separate paragraph disclosing the basis for the adverse opinion.

  c. The following are the explanatory and opinion paragraphs (in this example, the departures from GAAP are described in two explanatory paragraphs):

EXAMPLE – Language to Express an Adverse Opinion for Departures from GAAP

As discussed in Note X to the financial statements, the Company carries its property, plant, and equipment accounts at appraisal values and provides depreciation on the basis of such values. Further, the company does not provide for income taxes with respect to differences between financial income and taxable income arising because of the use, for income tax purposes, of the installment method of reporting gross profit from certain types of sales. U.S. generally accepted accounting principles require that property, plant, and equipment be stated at an amount not in excess of cost, reduced by depreciation based on such amount, and that deferred income taxes be provided.

Because of the departures from U.S. generally accepted accounting principles identified above, as of December 31, Year 2 and Year 1, inventories have been increased $___ and $___ by inclusion in manufacturing overhead depreciation in excess of that based on cost; property, plant, and equipment, less accumulated depreciation, is carried at $___ and $___ in excess of an amount based on cost to the company; and deferred income taxes of $___ and $___ have not been recorded; resulting in an increase of $___ and $___, in retained earnings and in appraisal surplus of $___ and $___, respectively. For the years ended December 31, Year 2 and Year 1, cost of goods sold has been increased $___ and $___, respectively, because of the effects of depreciation accounting referred to above and deferred income taxes of $___ and $___ have not been provided, resulting in an increase in net income of $___ and $___, respectively.

In our opinion, because of the effects of the matters disclosed in the preceding paragraphs, the financial statements referred to above do not present fairly, in conformity with accounting principles generally accepted in the United States of America, the financial position of X Company as of December 31, Year 2 and Year 1, or the results of its operations and its cash flows for the years then ended.

Stop and review! You have completed the outline for this subunit. Study multiple-choice questions 32 through 34 on page 537.

Background
As you study disclaimers, you will discover a variety of reporting forms and formats. This is due to the fact that, as issues relating to the need for disclaimers arose, they were dealt with based on prevailing thought at the time. You will also see a different format in the compilation report (Study Unit 18), as it too includes a disclaimer. Attempt to understand the various uses of disclaimers, and note that the overarching principle is that the accountant is accepting no responsibility for the fairness of the financial statements.

16.6 DISCLAIMERS OF OPINION (AU 508 AND AU 504)

1. **Scope Limitation**

   a. The disclaimer states that the auditor does not express an opinion on the financial statements.

   b. It is appropriate when the auditor has not performed an audit sufficient in scope to enable him/her to form an opinion.

   c. A disclaimer is not appropriate when the auditor believes material departures from GAAP exist.

   d. It should **not include a scope paragraph** describing the nature of the audit.

   e. A separate paragraph

      1) Provides reasons that the audit did not comply with GAAS

      2) States that the scope was not sufficient to warrant the expression of an opinion

      3) Does not identify the procedures performed

      4) Discloses any other reservations the auditor has regarding fair presentation in accordance with GAAP (e.g., that the auditor concludes that land is at appraised value rather than cost)

   f. The title is "Independent Auditor's Report."

EXAMPLE – Disclaimer of Opinion Due to a Scope Limitation
Independent Auditor's Report
To: <----------- Addressed to owner or party who engaged accountant
We were engaged to audit the accompanying balance sheets of X Company as of December 31, Year 2 and Year 1, and the related statements of income, retained earnings, and cash flows for the years then ended. These financial statements are the responsibility of the Company's management. [OMIT **"Our responsibility..."**]
[Scope paragraph of standard report should be omitted.]
The Company did not make a count of its physical inventory in Year 2 or Year 1, stated in the accompanying financial statements at $___ as of December 31, Year 2, and at $___ as of December 31, Year 1. Further, evidence supporting the cost of property and equipment acquired prior to December 31, Year 1, is no longer available. The Company's records do not permit the application of other auditing procedures to inventories or property and equipment.
Since the Company did not take physical inventories and we were not able to apply other auditing procedures to satisfy ourselves as to inventory quantities and the cost of property and equipment, the scope of our work was not sufficient to enable us to express, and we do not express, an opinion on these financial statements.
Signature   <----------- May be signed, typed, or printed
Date   <----------- Date of completion of engagement

2. **Piecemeal Opinion**

   a. A piecemeal opinion is an expression of opinion as to certain identified items. It is not appropriate when the auditor has disclaimed an opinion or expressed an adverse opinion on the statements taken as a whole because it would overshadow or contradict the report issued.

3. **Accountant is Associated with the Unaudited Financial Statements of an Issuer**

   a. A disclaimer should be attached to the financial statements of an issuer when an accountant is **associated** with those statements and has **not audited or reviewed them**.

      1) Association means that the accountant has consented to the use of his/her name in a report, document, or written communication containing the statements. It also may mean that the accountant has submitted financial statements that (s)he prepared or assisted in preparing.

      2) An accountant might become associated by performing consulting services for a nonaudit client, for example, structuring a purchase transaction for a new subsidiary.

   b. Each page of the financial statements should be **marked as unaudited**.

   c. The accountant has **no responsibility** to apply any procedures beyond reading the statements for obvious material misstatements. Any **procedures** that may have been performed should **not be described**.

   d. Any reservations known to the accountant regarding fair presentation in accordance with GAAP (e.g., that management has elected to omit substantially all of the disclosures) should be disclosed.

   e. The report has no title or salutation.

   f. The following is an example of a disclaimer on unaudited financial statements of an issuer:

EXAMPLE – Disclaimer of Opinion When Associated with an Issuer, Nonaudit Client's Financial Statements

The accompanying balance sheet of X Company as of December 31, Year 1, and the related statements of income, retained earnings, and cash flows for the year then ended were not audited by us and, accordingly, we do not express an opinion on them.

Signature

Date

---

4. **Accountant Is Not Independent of an Issuer**

   a. An accountant **must not express an opinion** when (s)he is not independent.

   b. The reasons for the lack of an opinion should not be described.

   c. Each page of the financial statements should be marked as unaudited.

   d. Any procedures that may have been performed should not be described.

   e. Any reservations known to the accountant regarding fair presentation in accordance with GAAP (e.g., that management has elected to omit substantially all of the disclosures) should be disclosed.

   f. The report has no title or salutation.

   g. The following is an example of a disclaimer on financial statements of an issuer when the accountant is not independent.

EXAMPLE – Disclaimer of Opinion When Not Independent with an Issuer, Nonaudit Client's Financial Statements

We are not independent with respect to XYZ Company, and the accompanying balance sheet as of December 31, Year 1, and the related statements of income, retained earnings, and cash flows for the year then ended were not audited by us and, accordingly, we do not express an opinion on them.

Signature

Date

Stop and review! You have completed the outline for this subunit. Study multiple-choice questions 35 through 40 beginning on page 538.

QUESTIONS

16.1 GAAS -- The Reporting Standards

1. For a particular entity's financial statements to be presented fairly in conformity with GAAP, it is **not** required that the principles selected

   A. Be appropriate in the circumstances for the particular entity.

   B. Reflect transactions in a manner that presents the financial statements within a range of acceptable limits.

   C. Present information in the financial statements that is classified and summarized in a reasonable manner.

   D. Be applied on a basis consistent with those followed in the prior year.

Answer (D) is correct. *(CPA, adapted)*
   REQUIRED: The item not required for statements to be in conformity with GAAP.
   DISCUSSION: A lack of consistency does not preclude fair presentation in accordance with GAAP. For example, if the entity changes from one generally accepted accounting principle to another and the auditor concurs with the change, a reference in the auditor's report is required, but the financial statements will conform with GAAP.
   Answer (A) is incorrect. The accounting principles should be appropriate in the circumstances. Answer (B) is incorrect. The financial statements should reflect the underlying transactions and events in a manner that presents the financial position, results of operations, and cash flows stated within a range of acceptable limits (AU 411). Answer (C) is incorrect. The information presented in the financial statements should be classified and summarized in a reasonable manner; that is, it should be neither too detailed nor too condensed.

2. For an entity's financial statements to be presented fairly in conformity with generally accepted accounting principles, the principles selected should

   A. Be applied on a basis consistent with those followed in the prior year.

   B. Be approved by the Auditing Standards Board or the appropriate industry subcommittee.

   C. Reflect transactions in a manner that presents the financial statements within a range of acceptable limits.

   D. Match the principles used by most other entities within the entity's particular industry.

Answer (C) is correct. *(CPA, adapted)*
   REQUIRED: The requirement for an entity's financial statements to be presented fairly in conformity with GAAP.
   DISCUSSION: The auditor's judgments about GAAP include whether the financial statements reflect the underlying transactions and events in a manner that presents the financial position, results of operations, and cash flows stated within a range of acceptable limits, that is, limits that are reasonable and practicable to attain in financial statements (AU 411).
   Answer (A) is incorrect. Lack of consistency does not preclude fair presentation. Answer (B) is incorrect. The Auditing Standards Board issues auditing standards, not GAAP. Answer (D) is incorrect. GAAP should meet the test of general acceptance and need not be the most prevalent used in the industry.

3. The fourth standard of reporting requires the auditor's report to contain either an expression of opinion regarding the financial statements taken as a whole or an assertion to the effect that an opinion cannot be expressed. The objective of the fourth standard is to prevent

   A. Misinterpretations regarding the degree of responsibility the auditor is assuming.

   B. An auditor from reporting on one basic financial statement and not the others.

   C. An auditor from expressing different opinions on each of the basic financial statements.

   D. Restrictions on the scope of the audit, whether imposed by the client or by the inability to obtain evidence.

Answer (A) is correct. *(CPA, adapted)*
   REQUIRED: The overall purpose of the fourth standard of reporting.
   DISCUSSION: The fourth standard of reporting states, "In all cases in which an auditor's name is associated with financial statements, the report should contain a clear-cut indication of the character of the auditor's work, if any, and the degree of responsibility the auditor is taking." The objective of this standard is to prevent misinterpretations of the degree of responsibility the auditor is assuming when his/her name is associated with financial statements.
   Answer (B) is incorrect. Limited reporting engagements are permissible. Answer (C) is incorrect. The requirement to report on the financial statements "taken as a whole" applies equally to a complete set and to a single statement. Thus, an unqualified opinion may be expressed on one statement, and a qualified or adverse opinion or a disclaimer may be expressed on another if warranted. Answer (D) is incorrect. Standards cannot prevent scope limitations imposed by the client or by the inability to obtain evidence.

4. Green, CPA, is aware that Green's name is to be included in the interim report of National Company, a publicly held entity. National's quarterly financial statements are contained in the interim report. Green has not audited or reviewed these interim financial statements. Green should request that

I.   Green's name not be included in the communication.

II. The financial statements be marked as unaudited, with a notation that no opinion is expressed on them.

A. I only.

B. II only.

C. Both I and II.

D. Either I or II.

Answer (D) is correct. *(CPA, adapted)*
    REQUIRED: The request(s) that an accountant should make when (s)he is associated with financial statements of an issuer that (s)he has not audited or reviewed.
    DISCUSSION: If the accountant is aware that his/her name is to be included in a client-prepared written communication of an issuer containing financial statements that have not been audited or reviewed, (s)he should request either (1) that his/her name not be included in the communication or (2) that the financial statements be marked as unaudited, with a notation included to the effect that (s)he does not express an opinion of them (AU 504).

5. An annual shareholders' report includes audited financial statements and contains a management report asserting that the financial statements are the responsibility of management. Is it permissible for the auditor's report to refer to the management report?

A. No, because the reference may lead to the belief that the auditor is providing assurances about management's representations.

B. No, because the auditor has no responsibility to read the other information in a document containing audited financial statements.

C. Yes, provided the reference is included in a separate explanatory paragraph of the auditor's report.

D. Yes, provided the auditor reads the management report and discovers no material misrepresentation of fact.

Answer (A) is correct. *(CPA, adapted)*
    REQUIRED: The true statement about a reference in the auditor's report to the management report.
    DISCUSSION: According to an Interpretation of AU 508, such a modification of the standard report may lead users to the erroneous belief that the auditor is giving assurances about management's representations concerning matters discussed in the management report. The statement in the introductory paragraph about management's responsibility should not be elaborated upon in the standard report or referenced to management's report.
    Answer (B) is incorrect. The auditor should read the other information (AU 550). Answer (C) is incorrect. No reference should be made in the auditor's report. Answer (D) is incorrect. No reference should be made in the auditor's report.

16.2 The Auditor's Standard Report (AU 508)

6. How are management's responsibility and the auditor's responsibility represented in the standard auditor's report?

	Management's Responsibility	Auditor's Responsibility
A.	Explicitly	Explicitly
B.	Implicitly	Implicitly
C.	Implicitly	Explicitly
D.	Explicitly	Implicitly

Answer (A) is correct. *(CPA, adapted)*
    REQUIRED: The representation of the responsibilities of management and the auditor in the standard audit report.
    DISCUSSION: The introductory paragraph of the independent auditor's report explicitly states, "These financial statements are the responsibility of the Company's management. Our responsibility is to express an opinion on these financial statements based on our audit" (AU 508).

7. Under the AICPA standards, which paragraphs of an auditor's standard report on financial statements should refer to generally accepted auditing standards (GAAS) and generally accepted accounting principles (GAAP)?

	GAAS	GAAP
A.	Opening	Scope
B.	Scope	Scope
C.	Scope	Opinion
D.	Opening	Opinion

Answer (C) is correct. *(CPA, adapted)*
REQUIRED: The paragraphs in the auditor's standard report that refer to GAAS and GAAP.
DISCUSSION: The auditor's report should contain a clear-cut indication of the character of the auditor's work, if any, and state the degree of responsibility assumed. Under the AICPA standards, GAAS are referred to only in the scope paragraph because they relate to the nature of the audit. The opinion paragraph contains an opinion as to whether the statements as a whole are fairly presented, in all material respects, in conformity with GAAP. Neither GAAS nor GAAP are mentioned in the introductory (opening) paragraph, which identifies the financial statements audited and describes the responsibilities of management and of the auditor (AU 508).

8. Which of the following statements is a basic element of the auditor's standard report?

A. The disclosures provide reasonable assurance that the financial statements are free of material misstatement.

B. The auditor evaluated the overall internal control.

C. An audit includes assessing significant estimates made by management.

D. The financial statements are consistent with those of the prior period.

Answer (C) is correct. *(CPA, adapted)*
REQUIRED: The statement that is an element of the auditor's standard report.
DISCUSSION: The auditor's standard report includes the statement, "An audit also includes assessing the accounting principles used and significant estimates made by management, as well as evaluating the overall financial statement presentation."

9. The existence of audit risk is recognized by the statement in the auditor's standard report that the auditor

A. Obtains reasonable assurance about whether the financial statements are free of material misstatement.

B. Assesses the accounting principles used and also evaluates the overall financial statement presentation.

C. Realizes some matters, either individually or in the aggregate, are important, while other matters are not important.

D. Is responsible for expressing an opinion on the financial statements, which are the responsibility of management.

Answer (A) is correct. *(CPA, adapted)*
REQUIRED: The statement that relates to the element of audit risk.
DISCUSSION: AU 312 indicates that the existence of audit risk is recognized by the statement in the auditor's standard report that the auditor obtained reasonable assurance about whether the financial statements are free of material misstatement. Audit risk is the risk that the auditor expresses an inappropriate audit opinion when the financial statements are materially misstated. Audit risk exists because the assurance is not absolute.
Answer (B) is incorrect. The statement about assessing accounting principles relates to the first standard of reporting. Answer (C) is incorrect. Materiality is mentioned in the standard audit report, but a statement defining materiality is not. Answer (D) is incorrect. The statement about the responsibilities of the auditor and management does not pertain to audit risk.

10. For a nonissuer that does not receive governmental financial assistance, an auditor's standard report on financial statements generally would **not** refer to

A. Significant estimates made by management.

B. An assessment of the entity's accounting principles.

C. Management's responsibility for the financial statements.

D. The entity's internal control.

Answer (D) is correct. *(CPA, adapted)*
REQUIRED: The reference not made in the auditor's standard report.
DISCUSSION: Although the auditor has obtained an understanding of internal control and assessed the risk of material misstatement, the standard auditor's report for a nonissuer does not refer to internal control.
Answer (A) is incorrect. The report states that "an audit also includes assessing the accounting principles used and the significant estimates made by management, as well as evaluating the overall financial statement presentation" (AU 508). Answer (B) is incorrect. The report states that "an audit also includes assessing the accounting principles used and the significant estimates made by management, as well as evaluating the overall financial statement presentation" (AU 508). Answer (C) is incorrect. The introductory paragraph states, "These financial statements are the responsibility of the company's management" (AU 508).

11. When single-year financial statements are presented, an auditor ordinarily would express an unqualified opinion in an unmodified report if the

A. Auditor is unable to obtain audited financial statements supporting the entity's investment in a foreign affiliate.

B. Entity declines to present a statement of cash flows with its balance sheet and related statements of income and retained earnings.

C. Auditor wishes to emphasize an accounting matter affecting the comparability of the financial statements with those of the prior year.

D. Prior year's financial statements were audited by another CPA whose report, which expressed an unqualified opinion, is not presented.

Answer (D) is correct. *(CPA, adapted)*
REQUIRED: The conditions under which an unqualified opinion would be expressed in an unmodified report.
DISCUSSION: When single-year financial statements are presented, the auditor's reporting responsibility is limited to those statements. If the prior year's financial statements are not presented for comparative purposes, the current-year auditor should not refer to the prior year's statements and the report thereon. Furthermore, the failure to present comparative statements is not a basis for modifying the opinion or the report.
Answer (A) is incorrect. An inability to obtain audited financial statements supporting an entity's investment in a foreign affiliate is a scope limitation requiring either a qualified opinion or a disclaimer of opinion. Answer (B) is incorrect. If the entity declines to present a statement of cash flows, the auditor should express a qualified opinion. Answer (C) is incorrect. Adding an additional paragraph to emphasize a matter results in a modified report.

12. Which of the following representations does an auditor make explicitly and which implicitly when expressing an unqualified opinion?

	Conformity with GAAP	Adequacy of Disclosure
A.	Explicitly	Explicitly
B.	Implicitly	Implicitly
C.	Implicitly	Explicitly
D.	Explicitly	Implicitly

Answer (D) is correct. *(CPA, adapted)*
REQUIRED: The explicit and implicit representations an auditor makes when expressing an unqualified opinion.
DISCUSSION: The opinion paragraph of the standard auditor's report explicitly states whether the financial statements are in conformity with GAAP. The third standard of reporting states, "When the auditor determines that informative disclosures are not reasonably adequate, the auditor must so state in the auditor's report." Thus, adequacy of disclosure is implicit in the standard report.

16.3 Addressing and Dating the Report (AU 508 and AU 530)

13. March, CPA, is engaged by Monday Corp., a client, to audit the financial statements of Wall Corp., a company that is not March's client. Monday expects to present Wall's audited financial statements with March's auditor's report to 1st Federal Bank to obtain financing in Monday's attempt to purchase Wall. In these circumstances, March's auditor's report would usually be addressed to

A. Monday Corp., the client that engaged March.

B. Wall Corp., the entity audited by March.

C. 1st Federal Bank.

D. Both Monday Corp. and 1st Federal Bank.

Answer (A) is correct. *(CPA, adapted)*
REQUIRED: The addressee of an auditor's report when the auditee is not the client.
DISCUSSION: If an auditor is retained to audit the financial statements of an entity that is not his/her client, the report customarily is addressed to the client and not to the board of directors or shareholders of the entity whose financial statements are being audited.
Answer (B) is incorrect. The report would be addressed to the client, not to the entity being audited. Answer (C) is incorrect. The report would not be addressed to the intended user of the financial statements but to the client who engaged the CPA. Answer (D) is incorrect. The report would not be addressed to the intended user of the financial statements but to the client who engaged the CPA.

14. In May Year 3, an auditor reissues the auditor's report on the Year 1 financial statements at a continuing client's request. The Year 1 financial statements are not restated, and the auditor does not revise the wording of the report. The auditor should

A. Dual-date the reissued report.

B. Use the release date of the reissued report.

C. Use the original report date on the reissued report.

D. Use the current-period auditor's report date on the reissued report.

Answer (C) is correct. *(CPA, adapted)*
REQUIRED: The date of a reissued report.
DISCUSSION: Under AU 530, use of the original date in a reissued report removes any implication that records, transactions, or events after such date have been audited or reviewed. The auditor will thus have no responsibility to carry out procedures relating to the period between original issuance and reissuance (but see AU 711 regarding filings under the Securities Act of 1933).
Answer (A) is incorrect. The report is dual-dated only if it has been revised since the original reissue date. Answer (B) is incorrect. Using the release date of the reissued report implies that additional audit procedures have been applied. Answer (D) is incorrect. Use of the current report date implies that the report has been updated for additional audit procedures applied between the original issue date and the current auditor's report date.

15. An auditor issued an audit report that was dual-dated for a subsequent event occurring after the date of the auditor's report but before issuance of the related financial statements. The auditor's responsibility for events occurring subsequent to the original report date was

A. Limited to the specific event referenced.

B. Limited to include only events occurring before the date of the last subsequent event referenced.

C. Extended to subsequent events occurring through the date of issuance of the related financial statements.

D. Extended to include all events occurring since the original report date.

Answer (A) is correct. *(CPA, adapted)*
REQUIRED: The auditor's responsibility for events occurring subsequent to the original report date when the report is dual-dated.
DISCUSSION: Subsequent to the original report date, the auditor is responsible only for the specific subsequent event for which the report was dual-dated. (S)he is responsible for other subsequent events only up to the original report date (AU 530).
Answer (B) is incorrect. The auditor's post report date responsibility extends only to the specified subsequent event. Answer (C) is incorrect. The date(s) of the report determines the auditor's responsibility. Answer (D) is incorrect. The auditor's post report date responsibility extends only to the specified subsequent event.

16. Wilson, CPA, completed the field work of the audit of Abco's December 31, Year 1, financial statements on March 6, Year 2. On this date, Wilson obtained sufficient appropriate audit evidence to support the opinion. A subsequent event requiring adjustment of the Year 1 financial statements occurred on April 10, Year 2, and came to Wilson's attention on April 24, Year 2. The subsequent event occurred prior to the issuance of the related financial statements. If the adjustment is made without disclosure of the event, Wilson's report ordinarily should be dated

A. March 6, Year 2.

B. April 10, Year 2.

C. April 24, Year 2.

D. Using dual dating.

Answer (A) is correct. *(CPA, adapted)*
REQUIRED: The date of the report if the statements are adjusted for a subsequent event without disclosure.
DISCUSSION: If a subsequent event requiring adjustment occurs after the date of the report and prior to the issuance of the related financial statements, and the event comes to the auditor's attention, the statements should be adjusted or the opinion should be modified or a disclaimer issued. When the adjustment is made without disclosure, the report should be dated no earlier than the date on which the auditor obtained sufficient appropriate audit evidence to support the opinion (AU 530).
Answer (B) is incorrect. When a subsequent event of the type requiring adjustment is not disclosed, the related financial statements should usually be dated no earlier than the date on which the auditor obtained sufficient appropriate audit evidence to support the opinion. Answer (C) is incorrect. When a subsequent event of the type requiring adjustment is not disclosed, the related financial statements should usually be dated no earlier than the date on which the auditor obtained sufficient appropriate audit evidence to support the opinion. Answer (D) is incorrect. Dual dating is not permitted when the subsequent event is not disclosed.

17. On August 13, a CPA dated the audit report on financial statements for the year ended June 30. On August 27, an event came to the CPA's attention that should be disclosed in the notes to the financial statements. The event was properly disclosed by the entity, but the CPA decided not to dual-date the auditor's report and dated the report August 27. Under these circumstances, the CPA was taking responsibility for

A. All subsequent events that occurred through August 27.

B. Only the specific subsequent event disclosed by the entity.

C. All subsequent events that occurred through August 13 and the specific subsequent event disclosed by the entity.

D. Only the subsequent events that occurred through August 13.

Answer (A) is correct. *(CPA, adapted)*
REQUIRED: The responsibility assumed by dating the audit report as of the date of a subsequent event requiring disclosure.
DISCUSSION: Subsequent events are material events or transactions that occur after the balance sheet date but prior to the issuance of the financial statements. They require adjustment or disclosure in the financial statements. If the auditor dates the report August 27, the auditor is assuming responsibility for all subsequent events that occurred through August 27.
Answer (B) is incorrect. When the report is dual-dated, the auditor's subsequent-events responsibility is for only the specific subsequent event disclosed by the entity. Answer (C) is incorrect. Dating the report August 27 makes the auditor responsible for all subsequent events occurring from June 30th through August 27th. Answer (D) is incorrect. Dating the report August 27 makes the auditor responsible for all subsequent events occurring from June 30th through August 27th.

16.4 Qualified Opinions (AU 508)

18. Which of the following phrases should be included in the opinion paragraph when an auditor expresses a qualified opinion?

	When Read in Conjunction with Note X	With the Foregoing Explanation
A.	Yes	No
B.	No	Yes
C.	Yes	Yes
D.	No	No

Answer (D) is correct. *(CPA, adapted)*
REQUIRED: The phrase(s) used in a qualified opinion.
DISCUSSION: According to AU 508, the auditor should use a phrase such as "with the exception of" or "except for" to qualify an opinion. Wording such as "with the foregoing explanation" is neither clear nor forceful enough and is unacceptable. Moreover, the notes are part of the financial statements, and a reference such as "when read in conjunction with Note X" in the opinion paragraph is likely to be misunderstood.

19. An auditor may reasonably express a "subject to" qualified opinion for

	Lack of Consistency	Departure from Generally Accepted Accounting Principles
A.	Yes	Yes
B.	Yes	No
C.	No	Yes
D.	No	No

Answer (D) is correct. *(CPA, adapted)*
REQUIRED: The type of opinion that uses the phrase "subject to."
DISCUSSION: The phrase "subject to" should not be used in any report. It is not clear or forceful enough (AU 508).

20. An auditor may express a qualified opinion under which of the following circumstances?

	Lack of Sufficient Appropriate Audit Evidence	Restrictions on the Scope of the Audit
A.	Yes	Yes
B.	Yes	No
C.	No	Yes
D.	No	No

Answer (A) is correct. *(CPA, adapted)*
REQUIRED: The circumstances in which the auditor may express a qualified opinion.
DISCUSSION: A qualified opinion is expressed because of a departure from GAAP, a lack of sufficient appropriate evidence, or a restriction on the scope of the audit. AU 508 states that the auditor may be required to qualify the opinion or disclaim an opinion because of scope restrictions, whether imposed by the client or by circumstances, such as the timing of the work, the inability to obtain sufficient appropriate audit evidence, or an inadequacy in the records.

21. Morris, CPA, suspects that a pervasive scheme of illegal bribes exists throughout the operations of Worldwide Import-Export, Inc., a new audit client. Morris notified the audit committee and Worldwide's legal counsel, but neither could assist Morris in determining whether the amounts involved were material to the financial statements or whether senior management was involved in the scheme. Under these circumstances, Morris should

A. Express an unqualified opinion with a separate explanatory paragraph.

B. Disclaim an opinion on the financial statements.

C. Express an adverse opinion on the financial statements.

D. Issue a special report regarding the illegal bribes.

Answer (B) is correct. *(CPA, adapted)*
REQUIRED: The auditor action when (s)he cannot determine the amounts involved in illegal acts or the extent of management's involvement.
DISCUSSION: If an auditor is precluded from applying necessary procedures or, after applying extended procedures, (s)he is unable to determine whether fraud or illegal acts may materially affect the statements, (s)he should disclaim or qualify an opinion. When the auditor cannot determine the role of management in the events, the auditor ordinarily should disclaim an opinion.
Answer (A) is incorrect. An unqualified opinion is not justified. Answer (C) is incorrect. An adverse opinion would be expressed only when the financial statements are not presented fairly. Answer (D) is incorrect. Special reports as defined in AU 623 are not issued on such topics.

22. When qualifying an opinion because of an insufficiency of audit evidence, an auditor should refer to the situation in the

	Opening (Introductory) Paragraph	Scope Paragraph
A.	No	No
B.	Yes	No
C.	Yes	Yes
D.	No	Yes

Answer (D) is correct. *(CPA, adapted)*
    REQUIRED: The effect on the auditor's report when qualified because of an insufficiency of evidence.
    DISCUSSION: When an opinion is qualified for a scope limitation, the introductory paragraph is unchanged. The scope paragraph is unchanged except that it begins with the clause, "Except as discussed in the following paragraph." An explanatory paragraph is added, followed by the opinion paragraph with appropriate qualifying language (AU 508).

23. An auditor decides to express a qualified opinion on an entity's financial statements because a major inadequacy in its computerized accounting records prevents the auditor from applying necessary procedures. The opinion paragraph of the auditor's report should state that the qualification pertains to

A. A client-imposed scope limitation.

B. A departure from generally accepted auditing standards.

C. The possible effects on the financial statements.

D. Inadequate disclosure of necessary information.

Answer (C) is correct. *(CPA, adapted)*
    REQUIRED: The wording in the opinion paragraph when the opinion is qualified because of a scope limitation.
    DISCUSSION: AU 508 states that, when an auditor qualifies his/her opinion because of a scope limitation, the wording in the opinion paragraph should indicate that the qualification pertains to the possible effects on the financial statements and not to the scope limitation itself.
    Answer (A) is incorrect. The qualification should not pertain to the scope limitation. Answer (B) is incorrect. The auditor apparently has followed GAAS in the conduct of the audit. Answer (D) is incorrect. The lack of sufficient appropriate evidence does not constitute inadequate disclosure.

24. An auditor did not observe a client's taking of beginning physical inventory and was unable to become satisfied about the inventory by means of other auditing procedures. Assuming no other scope limitations or reporting problems, the auditor could express an unqualified opinion on the current year's financial statements for

A. The balance sheet only.

B. The income statement only.

C. The income and retained earnings statements only.

D. All of the financial statements.

Answer (A) is correct. *(CPA, adapted)*
    REQUIRED: The financial statement(s) for which the auditor can express an unqualified opinion.
    DISCUSSION: A scope restriction, e.g., on the observation of inventories, may prevent the auditor from obtaining the evidence required to support an unqualified opinion. If (s)he cannot become satisfied regarding inventory, a qualified opinion or a disclaimer of opinion must be expressed, depending on the importance of the omitted procedure. Because the balance sheet reports only the ending inventory balance, the auditor can express an unqualified opinion on it alone, assuming (s)he is satisfied with the ending balance.

25. When an issuer refuses to include in its audited financial statements any of the segment information that the auditor believes is required, the auditor should express a(n)

A. Unqualified opinion with a separate explanatory paragraph emphasizing the matter.

B. Qualified opinion because of inadequate disclosure.

C. Adverse opinion because of a significant uncertainty.

D. Disclaimer of opinion because of the significant scope limitation.

Answer (B) is correct. *(CPA, adapted)*
    REQUIRED: The effect on the report of the client's failure to include required segment information.
    DISCUSSION: The auditor's standard report on financial statements prepared in conformity with GAAP implicitly applies to segment information included in those statements. The auditor should not refer to segment information unless the audit reveals a related material misstatement or omission or was subject to a scope limitation. Under AU 508, if material information is not included that the auditor believes should be disclosed, the auditor should modify the opinion for inadequate disclosure and include the omitted information in the audit report, if practicable.
    Answer (A) is incorrect. Inadequate disclosure requires an opinion modification if it is material in relation to the financial statements taken as a whole. Answer (C) is incorrect. A material uncertainty would typically result in an additional paragraph in the auditor's report but not an opinion modification. Answer (D) is incorrect. Inadequate disclosure does not constitute a scope limitation.

26. In which of the following situations would an auditor ordinarily choose between expressing a qualified opinion or an adverse opinion?

  A. The auditor did not observe the entity's physical inventory and is unable to become satisfied about its balance by other auditing procedures.

  B. Conditions that cause the auditor to have substantial doubt about the entity's ability to continue as a going concern are inadequately disclosed.

  C. There has been a change in accounting principles that has a material effect on the comparability of the entity's financial statements.

  D. The auditor is unable to apply necessary procedures concerning an investor's share of an investee's earnings recognized in accordance with the equity method.

Answer (B) is correct. *(CPA, adapted)*
REQUIRED: The situation ordinarily involving a choice between a qualified opinion and an adverse opinion.
DISCUSSION: When the auditor concludes that there is substantial doubt about an entity's ability to continue as a going concern for a reasonable period of time, (s)he should include an explanatory paragraph (following the opinion paragraph) in the auditor's report to describe the uncertainty. By itself, this doubt does not require a departure from an unqualified opinion. However, if the entity's disclosures about the issue are inadequate, the departure from GAAP may result in a qualified or an adverse opinion.
Answer (A) is incorrect. A scope limitation requires the auditor to choose between a qualified opinion or a disclaimer of opinion. Answer (C) is incorrect. A justified change in accounting principle requires the auditor to add an explanatory paragraph to the standard report but not to depart from an unqualified opinion. Answer (D) is incorrect. A scope limitation requires the auditor to choose between a qualified opinion or a disclaimer of opinion.

27. In which of the following situations would an auditor ordinarily choose between expressing a qualified opinion or an adverse opinion?

  A. The auditor did not observe the entity's physical inventory and is unable to become satisfied as to its balance by other auditing procedures.

  B. The financial statements fail to disclose information that is required by generally accepted accounting principles.

  C. The auditor is asked to report only on the entity's balance sheet and not on the other basic financial statements.

  D. Events disclosed in the financial statements cause the auditor to have substantial doubt about the entity's ability to continue as a going concern.

Answer (B) is correct. *(CPA, adapted)*
REQUIRED: The situation in which an auditor would choose between expressing a qualified opinion or an adverse opinion.
DISCUSSION: Departures from GAAP, including inadequate disclosures, may result in either a qualified or an adverse opinion. The auditor must exercise judgment as to the materiality of the departure, weighing factors such as dollar magnitude, significance to the entity, pervasiveness of misstatements, and impact on the statements taken as a whole (AU 508). If the departure from GAAP is not sufficiently material to require an adverse opinion, the auditor should express a qualified opinion.
Answer (A) is incorrect. A scope limitation is not a basis for an adverse opinion. Answer (C) is incorrect. A limited reporting engagement may result in the expression of an unqualified opinion. Answer (D) is incorrect. Substantial doubt about the entity's ability to continue as a going concern would normally result in the addition of a paragraph to the end of the report.

28. If an issuer releases financial statements that purport to present its financial position and results of operations but omits the statement of cash flows, the auditor ordinarily will express a(n)

  A. Disclaimer of opinion.

  B. Qualified opinion.

  C. Review report.

  D. Unqualified opinion with a separate explanatory paragraph.

Answer (B) is correct. *(CPA, adapted)*
REQUIRED: The reporting responsibility when the statement of cash flows is omitted.
DISCUSSION: GAAP require presentation of a statement of cash flows if statements of financial position and income are issued. Thus, the omission of the cash flow statement is normally a basis for qualifying the opinion. If the statements fail to disclose information required by GAAP, the auditor should provide the information in the report, if practicable. However, the auditor is not required to prepare a basic financial statement. Accordingly, (s)he should qualify the opinion and explain the reason in a separate paragraph (AU 508).
Answer (A) is incorrect. A departure from GAAP is not a basis for a disclaimer. Answer (C) is incorrect. The auditor has been engaged to conduct an audit. Answer (D) is incorrect. Inadequate disclosure is the basis for an opinion modification.

29. Harris, CPA, has been asked to audit and report on the balance sheet of Fox Co. but not on the statements of income, retained earnings, or cash flows. Harris will have access to all information underlying the basic financial statements. Under these circumstances, Harris may

A. Not accept the engagement because it would constitute a violation of the profession's ethical standards.

B. Not accept the engagement because it would be tantamount to rendering a piecemeal opinion.

C. Accept the engagement because such engagements merely involve limited reporting objectives.

D. Accept the engagement but should disclaim an opinion because of an inability to apply the procedures considered necessary.

Answer (C) is correct. *(CPA, adapted)*
REQUIRED: The action taken when a CPA has been asked to audit and report on the balance sheet only.
DISCUSSION: An auditor may report on one basic financial statement and not on the others. These engagements do not involve scope limitations, but rather limited reporting objectives.
Answer (A) is incorrect. The auditor may conduct an audit in accordance with GAAS. Answer (B) is incorrect. An auditor will express an opinion on the balance sheet; thus, it is not a piecemeal opinion. Answer (D) is incorrect. The audit is not subject to a scope limitation.

30. When management does **not** provide reasonable justification for a change in accounting principle, and it presents comparative financial statements, the auditor should express a qualified opinion

A. Only in the year of the accounting principle change.

B. Each year that the financial statements initially reflecting the change are presented.

C. Each year until management changes back to the accounting principle formerly used.

D. Only if the change is to an accounting principle that is not generally accepted.

Answer (B) is correct. *(CPA, adapted)*
REQUIRED: The year(s) or circumstance in which an unjustified accounting change requires a qualified opinion.
DISCUSSION: If management has not provided reasonable justification for a change, the new principle is not generally accepted, or the method of accounting for the effect of the change does not conform with GAAP, the auditor should express a qualified or an adverse opinion in the report for the year of change and add (an) explanatory paragraph(s) preceding the opinion paragraph. Also, the auditor should continue to express the exception with respect to the financial statements for the year of change as long as they are presented and reported on (AU 508).

31. An auditor concludes that a client's illegal act, which has a material effect on the financial statements, has not been properly accounted for or disclosed. Depending on the materiality of the effect on the financial statements, the auditor should express either a(n)

A. Adverse opinion or a disclaimer of opinion.

B. Qualified opinion or an adverse opinion.

C. Disclaimer of opinion or an unqualified opinion with a separate explanatory paragraph.

D. Unqualified opinion with a separate explanatory paragraph or a qualified opinion.

Answer (B) is correct. *(CPA, adapted)*
REQUIRED: The opinion(s) expressed when an illegal act has not been properly accounted for or disclosed.
DISCUSSION: When an illegal act having a material effect on the financial statements has been detected but not properly reported, the auditor should insist upon revision of the financial statements. Failure to revise the statements precludes an unqualified opinion. Depending on the pervasiveness of the misstatement, the auditor should express either a qualified opinion or an adverse opinion.
Answer (A) is incorrect. A disclaimer of opinion is inappropriate. The auditor has concluded that the statements are materially misstated. Answer (C) is incorrect. A disclaimer of opinion is inappropriate. The auditor has concluded that the statements are materially misstated. Answer (D) is incorrect. An unqualified opinion is inappropriate for materially misstated financial statements.

16.5 Adverse Opinions (AU 508)

32. In which of the following circumstances would an auditor be most likely to express an adverse opinion?

A. Information comes to the auditor's attention that raises substantial doubt about the entity's ability to continue as a going concern.

B. The chief executive officer refuses the auditor access to minutes of board of directors' meetings.

C. Tests of controls show that the entity's internal control is so poor that it cannot be relied upon.

D. The financial statements are not in conformity with the FASB Codification guidance regarding the capitalization of leases.

Answer (D) is correct. *(CPA, adapted)*
REQUIRED: The basis for an adverse opinion.
DISCUSSION: An adverse opinion is expressed "when, in the auditor's judgment, the financial statements taken as a whole are not presented fairly in conformity with GAAP." The FASB Accounting Standards Codification is authoritative with regard to GAAP.
Answer (A) is incorrect. Substantial doubt about the entity's ability to continue as a going concern requires an explanatory paragraph following the opinion paragraph, not an adverse opinion. Answer (B) is incorrect. A client-imposed scope limitation ordinarily results in a disclaimer of opinion. Answer (C) is incorrect. Lack of an expectation of the effectiveness of internal control may affect the nature, timing, and extent of substantive procedures but is not a basis for an adverse opinion. Ineffective internal control does not, by itself, indicate that the financial statements are not fairly presented.

33. An auditor's report includes the following statement: "The financial statements do not present fairly the financial position, results of operations, or cash flows in conformity with U.S. generally accepted accounting principles." This auditor's report was most likely issued in connection with financial statements that are

A. Inconsistent.

B. Based on prospective financial information.

C. Misleading.

D. Affected by a material uncertainty.

Answer (C) is correct. *(CPA, adapted)*
REQUIRED: The nature of the financial statements on which the quoted report was issued.
DISCUSSION: The language quoted states an adverse opinion. The essence of an adverse opinion is that the statements reported on, taken as a whole, are not fairly presented in accordance with GAAP (AU 508). The financial statements should be based on principles having general acceptance that are appropriate in the circumstances. If financial statements fail to meet the standards, they are misleading.
Answer (A) is incorrect. An inconsistency, by itself, results in no modification of the standard opinion paragraph. Answer (B) is incorrect. The accountant's standard examination report on a financial forecast or projection refers to guidelines for the presentation of a forecast (or projection) established by the AICPA, not to GAAP (AT 301). Answer (D) is incorrect. A material uncertainty, if properly disclosed, does not require modification of the report.

34. When an auditor expresses an adverse opinion, the opinion paragraph should include

A. The principal effects of the departure from generally accepted accounting principles.

B. A direct reference to a separate paragraph disclosing the basis for the opinion.

C. The substantive reasons for the financial statements being misleading.

D. A description of the uncertainty or scope limitation that prevents an unqualified opinion.

Answer (B) is correct. *(CPA, adapted)*
REQUIRED: The matter included in the opinion paragraph when an adverse opinion is expressed.
DISCUSSION: When an adverse opinion is expressed, the opinion paragraph should include a direct reference to a separate paragraph that discloses the basis for the adverse opinion. This paragraph should precede the opinion paragraph and state (1) all the substantive reasons for the adverse opinion and (2) the principal effects of the subject matter of the adverse opinion, if practicable (AU 508).
Answer (A) is incorrect. The principal effects of the subject matter of the adverse opinion, if practicable, should be stated in the explanatory paragraph. Answer (C) is incorrect. All the substantive reasons for the adverse opinion should be stated in the explanatory paragraph. Answer (D) is incorrect. An adverse opinion is not expressed as a result of an uncertainty or scope limitation.

16.6 Disclaimers of Opinion (AU 508 and AU 504)

35. Under which of the following circumstances would a disclaimer of opinion **not** be appropriate?

A. The auditor is unable to determine the amounts associated with an employee fraud scheme.

B. Management does not provide reasonable justification for a change in accounting principles.

C. The client refuses to permit the auditor to confirm certain accounts receivable or apply alternative procedures to verify their balances.

D. The chief executive officer is unwilling to sign the management representation letter.

Answer (B) is correct. *(CPA, adapted)*
REQUIRED: The circumstances under which a disclaimer of opinion is inappropriate.
DISCUSSION: When management does not provide reasonable justification for a change in accounting principles, a qualified or adverse opinion should be expressed. This failure is a departure from generally accepted accounting principles.
Answer (A) is incorrect. When the auditor is unable to determine amounts associated with an employee fraud scheme, the standards suggest that a disclaimer is appropriate.
Answer (C) is incorrect. Refusal to permit access to evidence results in scope limitations that necessitate a disclaimer.
Answer (D) is incorrect. Unwillingness to sign a management representation letter results in scope limitations that necessitate a disclaimer.

36. When disclaiming an opinion because of a client-imposed scope limitation, an auditor should indicate in a separate paragraph why the audit did not comply with generally accepted auditing standards. The auditor should also omit the

	Scope Paragraph	Opinion Paragraph
A.	No	Yes
B.	Yes	Yes
C.	No	No
D.	Yes	No

Answer (D) is correct. *(CPA, adapted)*
REQUIRED: The paragraph(s), if any, omitted from a disclaimer.
DISCUSSION: When a significant client-imposed scope limitation exists, the auditor ordinarily disclaims an opinion. If an opinion is disclaimed, the introductory and opinion paragraphs are modified and the scope paragraph is omitted.

37. Due to a scope limitation, an auditor disclaimed an opinion on the financial statements taken as a whole, but the auditor's report included a statement that the current asset portion of the entity's balance sheet was fairly stated. The inclusion of this statement is

A. Not appropriate because it may tend to overshadow the auditor's disclaimer of opinion.

B. Not appropriate because the auditor is prohibited from reporting on only one basic financial statement.

C. Appropriate provided the auditor's scope paragraph adequately describes the scope limitation.

D. Appropriate provided the statement is in a separate paragraph preceding the disclaimer of opinion paragraph.

Answer (A) is correct. *(CPA, adapted)*
REQUIRED: The suitability of a statement in an auditor's disclaimer concerning whether an element was stated fairly.
DISCUSSION: Piecemeal opinions (expressions of an opinion as to certain identified items in a financial statement) should not be expressed when the auditor has disclaimed an opinion or has expressed an adverse opinion on the financial statements taken as a whole because piecemeal opinions tend to overshadow or contradict a disclaimer of opinion or an adverse opinion (AU 508).
Answer (B) is incorrect. The auditor may report on one basic financial statement and not on the others. Such a limited reporting engagement is acceptable. Answer (C) is incorrect. A piecemeal opinion is inappropriate in this circumstance. Answer (D) is incorrect. A piecemeal opinion is inappropriate in this circumstance.

38. When an independent CPA assists in preparing the financial statements of an issuer but has not audited or reviewed them, the CPA should issue a disclaimer of opinion. In such situations, the CPA has no responsibility to apply any procedures beyond

    A. Ascertaining whether the financial statements are in conformity with GAAP.

    B. Determining whether management has elected to omit substantially all required disclosures.

    C. Documenting that internal control is not being relied on.

    D. Reading the financial statements for obvious material misstatements.

Answer (D) is correct. *(CPA, adapted)*
    REQUIRED: The procedure applied by a CPA to an issuer's financial statements that (s)he has assisted in preparing.
    DISCUSSION: AU 504 states that the accountant has no responsibility to apply any procedures beyond reading the financial statements for obvious material misstatements. Any procedures applied should not be described.
    Answer (A) is incorrect. An audit is conducted to determine whether the financial statements are in conformity with GAAP. Answer (B) is incorrect. The disclaimer is modified if the accountant concludes on the basis of facts known to him/her that the unaudited financial statements do not conform with GAAP. Lack of adequate disclosure is a departure from GAAP. Answer (C) is incorrect. The CPA need not consider internal control or assess the risk of material misstatement and has no responsibility for documentation related to these activities.

39. Park, CPA, was engaged to audit the financial statements of Tech Co., a new client, for the year ended December 31, Year 1. Park obtained sufficient audit evidence for all of Tech's financial statement items except Tech's opening inventory. Due to inadequate financial records, Park could not verify Tech's January 1, Year 1, inventory balances. Park's opinion on Tech's Year 1 financial statements most likely will be

	Balance Sheet	Income Statement
A.	Disclaimer	Disclaimer
B.	Unqualified	Disclaimer
C.	Disclaimer	Adverse
D.	Unqualified	Adverse

Answer (B) is correct. *(CPA, adapted)*
    REQUIRED: The appropriate opinion on each financial statement when the auditor cannot verify opening inventory.
    DISCUSSION: The auditor may report on one basic financial statement and not on the others. Because the balance sheet presents information at a specific moment in time, the auditor should be able to become satisfied regarding the balances presented at year end. However, beginning inventory enters materially into the determination of the statements of income, retained earnings, and cash flows. Thus, the auditor will probably not be able to form an opinion as to the fairness of these statements and should issue a disclaimer on them.

40. A CPA concludes that the unaudited financial statements on which the CPA is disclaiming an opinion are not in conformity with generally accepted accounting principles (GAAP) because management has failed to capitalize leases. The CPA suggests appropriate revisions to the financial statements, but management refuses to accept the CPA's suggestions. Under these circumstances, the CPA ordinarily would

    A. Express limited assurance that no other material modifications should be made to the financial statements.

    B. Restrict the distribution of the CPA's report to management and the entity's board of directors.

    C. Issue a qualified opinion or adverse opinion depending on the materiality of the departure from GAAP.

    D. Describe the nature of the departure from GAAP in the CPA's report and state the effects on the financial statements, if practicable.

Answer (D) is correct. *(CPA, adapted)*
    REQUIRED: The appropriate action when the CPA suggests revisions to the financial statements but management refuses to accept them.
    DISCUSSION: An accountant associated with unaudited financial statements may discover a material departure from GAAP. The accountant should disclose the departure in the disclaimer, including its effects if they have been determined by management or by the accountant's procedures.
    Answer (A) is incorrect. A disclaimer should provide no assurance. Answer (B) is incorrect. The disclaimer should not be restricted in use. Answer (C) is incorrect. A disclaimer of opinion is necessary when the CPA has not audited the statements.

Use the additional questions in Gleim **CPA Test Prep Online** to create Test Sessions that emulate Prometric!

16.7 PRACTICE SIMULATION

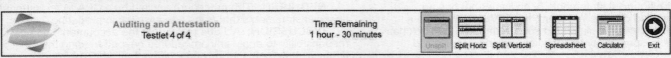

	Auditing and Attestation Testlet 4 of 4	Time Remaining 1 hour - 30 minutes							

Unsplit | Split Horiz | Split Vertical | Spreadsheet | Calculator | Exit

DIRECTIONS

Note: If you believe you have encountered a software malfunction, report it to the test center staff immediately.

Navigation

To navigate from task to task, use the controls at the bottom of the screen. Click on the **Next** button to advance to the next task, or the **Previous** button to go to the previous task. To go directly to any task, click on its number.

▼ = Reminder   Directions [1 2 3 4 5 6 7]   ◀ Previous Next ▶

If you would like a reminder to revisit a task, or want to indicate that you are finished with it, click on the reminder flag below the task number. To clear the flag, click on it again. Reminder flags are for your use only – they do not contribute to your score.

Tabs

In this part of the examination, you will be asked to complete various tasks. Every task has one or more **Work Tabs**. Some tasks have one or more **Information Tabs**, others may have none. Every task has a **Help** tab.

If a task has **Information Tabs**, you may use the information in them to complete your responses in the **Work Tabs**.

Corporate Gain and Basis	Authoritative Literature	Help
Work tab	Information tab	Help tab

Work Tabs:

- **Work Tabs** are identified with a pencil icon. This is where your responses are expected.
- Each task has one or more **Work Tabs**.
- **Work Tabs** contain directions for completing the task – be sure to read these directions carefully.
- The **Work Tab** name in the example above is for illustration only – yours will differ.
- You must complete all of the **Work Tabs** in each task to receive full credit.

Information Tabs:

- The Authoritative Literature will be provided in all tasks in the AUD, FAR, and REG sections for your reference.
- Your simulation may have one or more additional **Information Tabs**. Like the Authoritative Literature tabs, **Information Tabs** do not have a pencil icon.
- If your task has additional **Information Tabs**, go through each to familiarize yourself with the task content.

Help Tab:

- The **Help Tab** provides assistance with the exam software that is used in this task. For example, if the task is to compose a memorandum, **Help** will provide information about the word processor.

The Toolbar

The toolbar at the top of the screen shows the amount of time remaining for you to complete the tasks. In addition, the following tools are available. Note that only the Exit button is displayed when Directions are visible - the others will appear when you begin the tasks.

Unsplit   Split Horiz   Split Vertical

Click on these buttons to split or unsplit the screen. You can split the screen vertically or horizontally.

Calculator

Click on this button to display the calculator; click on it again to hide the calculator. To move the calculator, click on the calculator title bar and drag the calculator to the desired location.

Spreadsheet

Click on this button to use the spreadsheet; click on it again to hide the spreadsheet. To move the spreadsheet, click on the the spreadsheet title bar and drag the spreadsheet to the desired location.

Exit

Click on this button to go on to the next part of the examination. You must complete all of the tasks to receive full credit. Once you click on **Exit** and confirm the action, you will NOT be able to return to this testlet.

▼ = Reminder   Directions [1 2 3 4 5 6]   ◀ Previous Next ▶

Your firm has many clients and many audit reporting obligations. The audits of most clients result in a standard report. The following draft represents the standard report that you contemplate for your nonissuers.

Independent Auditor's Report

To: The Board of Directors

We have (1) the accompanying balance sheet of X Company as of December 31, Year 1, and the (2) statements of income, retained earnings, and cash flows for the year then ended. These financial statements are the responsibility of (3). Our responsibility is to express an opinion on these financial statements based on our audit.

We conducted our audit in accordance with U.S. (4). Those standards require that we plan and perform the audit to obtain (5) assurance about whether the financial statements are (6) misstatement. An audit includes examining, on a (7) basis, evidence supporting the amounts and disclosures in the financial statements. An audit also includes (8) the accounting principles used and significant estimates made by (9), as well as evaluating the overall financial statement presentation. We believe that our audit provides (10) basis for our opinion.

In our opinion, the financial statements referred to above present fairly, (11) the financial position of X Company as of its operations and its cash flows for the year then ended in conformity with U.S. (12).

Signature
Date

Each of the rows in the table below corresponds to a number in the Independent Auditor's Report above. Indicate by checking the appropriate box which word or phrase should be included in the standard report.

Correct Word or Phrase	**A**	**B**
1. A) Examined B) Audited		
2. A) Related B) Accompanying		
3. A) The auditor B) The entity's management		
4. A) Generally accepted auditing standards B) Generally accepted accounting principles		
5. A) Reasonable B) Absolute		
6. A) Free of B) Free of material		
7. A) Sample B) Test		
8. A) Examining B) Assessing		
9. A) Management B) The auditor		
10. A) An absolute B) A reasonable		
11. A) In all respects B) In all material respects		
12. A) Generally accepted auditing standards B) Generally accepted accounting principles		

Each of the following is a phrase from a paragraph in an auditor's report. Assume that, except for the information indicated in the phrase, the report would have been a standard audit report. Select from the list provided the most likely report type for each phrase. Each choice may be used once, more than once, or not at all.

Phrase	Answer
1. In our opinion, except for the omission of the statement of cash flows ...	
2. ... the scope of our work was not sufficient to enable us ...	
3. As discussed in Note 12, the Company changed its method of computing depreciation.	
4. We are not independent with respect to XYZ company ...	
5. ... except for the effects of not capitalizing certain lease obligations as discussed in the preceding paragraph ...	
6. ... based on our audit and the report of other auditors ...	
7. ... for the year then ended were not audited by us ...	
8. ... raises substantial doubt about its ability to continue as a going concern.	
9. ... presents fairly, in all material respects ...	
10. ... In our opinion, except for the effects of such adjustments, if any, ...	

Choices
A) Unqualified
B) Qualified
C) Adverse
D) Disclaimer

Reporting Standards | Authoritative Literature | Help

Three of the reporting standards relate to the issues of application of GAAP, consistency of GAAP, and disclosure. Select from the list provided which phrases should complete each statement about these standards. Each phrase may be used only once.

First standard of reporting - application of GAAP
The auditor must state in the auditor's report [1] _____ [2] _____.

Second standard of reporting - consistency of GAAP
The auditor must identify in the auditor's report [3] _____ [4] _____ [5] _____ [6] _____.

Third standard of reporting - disclosure
When the auditor determines that informative disclosures [7] _____ [8] _____ [9] _____.

Phrases
A) are not reasonably adequate
B) in relation to the preceding period
C) those circumstances
D) whether the financial statements are presented
E) the auditor must so state
F) those circumstances in which such principles
G) observed in the current period
H) in accordance with GAAP
I) in the auditor's report
J) have not been consistently

The auditor's report below was drafted by a staff accountant of Jones & Jones, CPAs, at the completion of the audit engagement on the financial statements of Adams Mining, Inc., for the year ended December 31, Year 2. It was submitted to the engagement partner who reviewed matters thoroughly and concluded that a qualified opinion should be expressed because Adams is a defendant in a lawsuit alleging infringement of certain mining rights. The outcome of this material uncertainty cannot be reasonably estimated and is fully disclosed in the consolidated financial statements.

The financial statements for the year ended December 31, Year 1, are to be presented for comparative purposes. Jones & Jones previously examined these statements and expressed a qualified opinion because of an inability to obtain sufficient appropriate audit evidence supporting management's assertions about the aforementioned lawsuit.

On January 1, Year 3, Adams acquired a new subsidiary, Harris Coal, Inc. Disclosure of this subsequent event was properly made in Note T to the consolidated financial statements.

To the Board of Directors of Adams Mining, Inc.:

   We have audited the consolidated balance sheets of Adams Mining, Inc., and subsidiaries as of December 31, Year 2 and Year 1, and the related consolidated statements of income, retained earnings, and cash flows for the years then ended. We did not audit the financial statements of Ford Realty, Inc., a consolidated subsidiary. These statements were examined by King & Co., CPAs, whose report has been furnished to us, and is not presented separately herein. Our opinion, insofar as it relates to the amounts included for Ford Realty, is based solely upon the report of King.

   We planned and performed the audit to obtain reasonable assurance about whether the financial statements are free of material misstatement. An audit includes examining, on a test basis, evidence supporting the amounts and disclosures in the financial statements. An audit also includes assessing the accounting principles used, as well as evaluating the overall financial statement presentation. We believe that our audits and the report of other auditors provide a reasonable basis for our opinion.

   Due to the complex nature and magnitude of the Company's mineral holdings, we retained the geological engineering firm of Silver & Gold to attest to the value of the Company's mining inventory and mineral reserves. As a result, the specialist's findings fully support the related representations in the consolidated financial statements.

   In our opinion, subject to the effects on the consolidated financial statements of a lawsuit in which the Company is a defendant alleging infringement of certain mining rights, the consolidated financial statements referred to above present fairly the financial position as of December 31, Year 2, and the results of operations for the year then ended, in conformity with accounting principles generally accepted in the United States of America.

Jones & Jones, CPAs
April 10, Year 3, except
for Note T as to which
the date is January 31, Year 3

-- Continued on next page --

| Report Deficiencies | Authoritative Literature | Help | -- **Continued** |

Indicate by checking the appropriate box which statements below are deficiencies in the auditor's report. Be sure to consider which paragraph each statement refers to.

Deficiencies	True	False
Introductory Paragraph		
1. The paragraph does not state whether the statements are in conformity with GAAP.		
2. The paragraph does not state that the audit was in accordance with GAAS.		
3. The magnitude of the portions of the financial statements audited by the other auditor is not disclosed in the paragraph.		
4. The other auditor should not be named unless the other auditor's report is presented together with that of the principal auditor.		
5. The responsibility of management is not stated.		
6. The responsibility of the auditor is not stated.		
Scope Paragraph		
7. The paragraph does not state that the audit was according to U.S. GAAS.		
8. No reference is made to tests of accounting records and other necessary procedures.		
9. Assessing significant accounting estimates is not mentioned.		
Separate Paragraph		
10. Emphasis of a matter is not appropriate unless the opinion is modified.		
11. Reference to the specialist should not be made if the auditor does not modify the opinion as a result of the findings of the specialist.		
12. All the substantive reasons for the qualified opinion are not disclosed in a separate explanatory paragraph.		
Opinion Paragraph		
13. A "subject to" qualification is not a proper form of reporting.		
14. Reference to the other auditor is not made in the opinion paragraph.		
15. The company whose financial statements were audited is not identified in the opinion paragraph.		
16. The draft does not refer to both years (Year 1 and Year 2) in the opinion paragraph.		
17. The paragraph does not refer to cash flows.		
18. The opinion paragraph does not refer to the consistent application of generally accepted accounting principles.		
19. The country of origin of GAAP should not be given.		
Date		
20. Dual dating should not be used when a subsequent event occurs before field work is completed.		

For the year ended December 31, Year 2, Friday & Co., CPAs (Friday), audited the financial statements of Johnson Company and expressed an unqualified opinion on the balance sheet only. Friday did not observe the taking of the physical inventory as of December 31, Year 1, because that date was prior to their appointment as auditors. Friday was unable to satisfy themselves regarding beginning inventory by means of other auditing procedures, so they did not express an opinion on the other basic financial statements that year.

For the year ended December 31, Year 3, Friday expressed an unqualified opinion on all the basic financial statements and satisfied themselves as to the consistent application of generally accepted accounting principles. The field work was completed on March 11, Year 4; the partner-in-charge reviewed the working papers and signed the auditor's report on March 18, Year 4. The report on the comparative financial statements for Years 3 and 2 was delivered to Johnson on March 21, Year 4.

Below is Friday's auditor's report that was submitted to Johnson's board of directors on the comparative financial statements for Years 3 and 2. Indicate whether the paragraph represents a proper form of reporting by checking the appropriate box.

Independent Auditor's Report	Yes	No
To the Board of Directors of Johnson Company:		
1. We have audited the accompanying balance sheets of Johnson Company as of December 31, Year 3 and Year 2, and the related statements of income, retained earnings, and cash flows for the years then ended. These financial statements are the responsibility of the Company's management. Our responsibility is to express an opinion on these financial statements based on our audits.		
2. Except as discussed in the following paragraph, we conducted our audits in accordance with auditing standards generally accepted in the United States of America. Those standards require that we plan and perform our audit to obtain reasonable assurance about whether the financial statements are free of material misstatement. An audit includes examining, on a test basis, evidence supporting the amounts and disclosures in the financial statements. An audit also includes assessing the accounting principles used and significant estimates made by management, as well as evaluating the overall financial statement presentation. We believe that our audits provide a reasonable basis for our opinion.		
3. We did not observe the taking of the physical inventory as of December 31, Year 1, because that date was prior to our appointment as auditors for the Company, and we were unable to satisfy ourselves regarding inventory quantities by means of other auditing procedures. Inventory amounts as of December 31, Year 1, enter into the determination of net income and cash flows for the year ended December 31, Year 2.		
4. Because of the matter discussed in the preceding paragraph, the scope of our work was not sufficient to enable us to express, and we do not express, an opinion on the results of operations and cash flows for the year ended December 31, Year 2.		
5. In our opinion, the balance sheets of Johnson Company as of December 31, Year 3 and Year 2, and the related statements of income, retained earnings, and cash flows for the year ended December 31, Year 3, present fairly, in all material respects, the financial position of Johnson Company as of December 31, Year 3 and Year 2, and the results of its operations and its cash flows for the year ended December 31, Year 3, in conformity with accounting principles generally accepted in the United States of America.		

Friday & Co., CPAs
March 11, Year 4

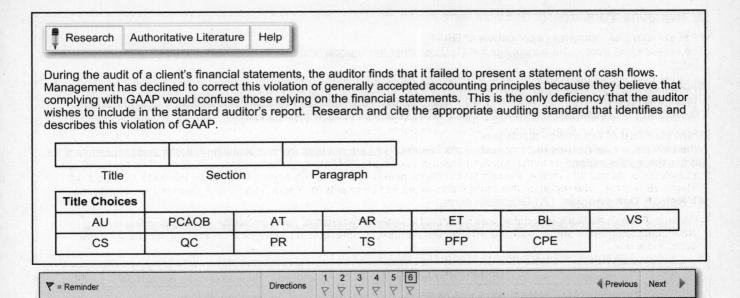

Unofficial Answers

1. Standard Report (12 Gradable Items)

1. **B) Audited.** The standard report uses the term audited.
2. **A) Related.** The statements of income, retained earnings, and cash flows are related to the balance sheet of the entity.
3. **B) The entity's management.** The financial statements are the responsibility of management.
4. **A) Generally accepted auditing standards.** The audit is conducted in accordance with U.S. GAAS.
5. **A) Reasonable.** Reasonable, not absolute, assurance should be obtained by the auditor.
6. **B) Free of material.** The financial statements are expected to be free of material misstatement. The auditor need not be concerned with immaterial matters.
7. **B) Test.** Audit evidence is examined on a test basis.
8. **B) Assessing.** The accounting principles used are assessed to determine that they are appropriate in the circumstances.
9. **A) Management.** Management is responsible for the estimates and other assertions in the financial statements.
10. **B) A reasonable.** The audit provides a reasonable basis for the opinion expressed. An auditor is seldom convinced beyond all doubt with respect to all aspects of the statements audited.
11. **B) In all material respects.** The opinion that the financial statements are presented fairly is subject to the limitation of materiality.
12. **B) Generally accepted accounting principles.** The financial statements should be in conformity with U.S. GAAP.

2. Audit Opinions (10 Gradable Items)

1. **B) Qualified.** A qualified report uses the language "except for" or "with the exception of."
2. **D) Disclaimer.** A scope limitation that does not allow the auditor to collect sufficient appropriate evidence results in a disclaimer.
3. **A) Unqualified.** Reference to a change in accounting principle is a paragraph added to the end of an unqualified report.
4. **D) Disclaimer.** Lack of independence by the auditor results in a disclaimer of opinion.
5. **B) Qualified.** A qualified report uses the language "except for" or "with the exception of."
6. **A) Unqualified.** A reference to other auditors is a division of responsibility that does not affect the opinion on the financial statements.
7. **D) Disclaimer.** Financial statements that were not audited require a disclaimer of opinion.
8. **A) Unqualified.** Reference to going concern is a paragraph added to the end of an unqualified report.
9. **A) Unqualified.** An unqualified opinion states that the financial statements are presented fairly.
10. **B) Qualified.** A qualified report uses the language "except for" or "with the exception of."

3. Reporting Standards (9 Gradable Items)

First standard of reporting - application of GAAP

The auditor must state in the auditor's report [1] <u>D) whether the financial statements are presented</u> [2] <u>H) in accordance with GAAP</u>.

Second standard of reporting - consistency of GAAP

The auditor must identify in the auditor's report [3] <u>F) those circumstances in which such principles</u> [4] <u>J) have not been consistently</u> [5] <u>G) observed in the current period</u> [6] <u>B) in relation to the preceding period</u>.

Third standard of reporting - disclosure

When the auditor determines that informative disclosures [7] <u>A) are not reasonably adequate</u> [8] <u>E) the auditor must so state</u> [9] <u>I) in the auditor's report</u>.

4. Report Deficiencies (20 Gradable Items)

1. <u>False.</u> This is not a deficiency because the introductory paragraph should not include an opinion on the financial statements.

2. <u>False.</u> The scope paragraph should refer to U.S. GAAS.

3. <u>True.</u> The division of responsibility with other auditors should be quantified in the introductory paragraph.

4. <u>True.</u> The name of the other auditors should not be included unless their report is presented.

5. <u>True.</u> The sentence "These financial statements are the responsibility of the Company's management" should be included in the introductory paragraph.

6. <u>True.</u> The sentence "Our responsibility is to express an opinion on these financial statements based on our audits" should be included in the introductory paragraph.

7. <u>True.</u> The scope paragraph should refer to U.S. GAAS.

8. <u>False.</u> The scope paragraph should include the sentence "An audit includes examining, on a test basis, evidence supporting the amounts and disclosures in the financial statements."

9. <u>True.</u> The scope paragraph should include the sentence "An audit also includes assessing the accounting principles used and significant estimates made by management, as well as evaluating the overall financial statement presentation."

10. <u>False.</u> The auditor can choose to add a paragraph to emphasize a matter without modifying the opinion.

11. <u>False.</u> If the reference helps the reader understand the nature of the report, then the reference is appropriate.

12. <u>True.</u> The issue that caused the qualification in the opinion should be identified in a separate paragraph preceding the opinion paragraph.

13. <u>True.</u> The term "subject to" should not be used as qualifying language in a report.

14. <u>True.</u> Reference to the other auditors should be made in the introductory, scope, and opinion paragraphs.

15. <u>True.</u> The opinion paragraph should reference the client's name.

16. <u>True.</u> The opinion should specifically identify the years for which the opinion applies.

17. <u>True.</u> The opinion should refer the statement of cash flows.

18. <u>False.</u> The opinion paragraph is silent as to consistency.

19. <u>False.</u> The country of origin of the accounting standards should be identified in the opinion paragraph.

20. <u>True.</u> Dual dating is used when the disclosure of an event is between the completion of the field work and the issuance of the financial statements.

5. Scope Issues (5 Gradable Items)

1. <u>Yes.</u> The paragraph represents a proper introductory paragraph for the report on the financial statements.

2. <u>Yes.</u> The paragraph represents a proper scope paragraph for the report on the financial statements.

3. <u>Yes.</u> The paragraph represents a proper separate paragraph preceding the opinion paragraph.

4. <u>Yes.</u> The paragraph represents a proper disclaimer on the results of operations and cash flows for Year 2.

5. <u>Yes.</u> The paragraph represents a proper opinion paragraph on the noted financial statements.

6. Research (1 Gradable Item)

Answer: 508.44

AU Section 508 -- *Reports on Audited Financial Statements*

.44 The Company declined to present a statement of cash flows for the years ended December 31, Year 2 and Year 1. Presentation of such statement summarizing the Company's operating, investing, and financing activities is required by accounting principles generally accepted in the United States of America.

Gleim Simulation Grading

Task	Correct Responses		Gradable Items		Score per Task
1	___	÷	12	=	___
2	___	÷	10	=	___
3	___	÷	9	=	___
4	___	÷	20	=	___
5	___	÷	5	=	___
Research	___	÷	1	=	___

Total of Scores per Task ___

÷ Total Number of Tasks 6

Total Score ___%

Use **CPA Gleim Online** and **Simulation Wizard** to practice more task-based simulations in a realistic environment.

STUDY UNIT SEVENTEEN
REPORTS -- OTHER MODIFICATIONS

(13 pages of outline)

This study unit covers explanatory language added to the auditor's report. These modifications normally do not affect the auditor's opinion on the financial statements. They permit the users of the financial statements and readers of the auditor's report to better understand the responsibility assumed by the auditor. They also provide information about the client's financial statements that the auditor considers important. The following summarizes these modifications:

1. Auditor's opinion is based in part on the report of another auditor -- Modify all three paragraphs, but do not add an additional paragraph.

2. A material accounting change affects consistency -- Add an additional paragraph.

3. Substantial doubt exists about the entity's ability to continue as a going concern -- Add an additional paragraph.

4. The auditor changes the opinion for a prior period when reporting on current statements in comparative form -- Add an additional paragraph.

5. Predecessor auditor's report for a prior period is not presented when reporting on current financial statements in comparative form -- Add sentence to introductory paragraph.

6. A matter needs to be emphasized -- Add an additional paragraph.

17.1 PART OF AUDIT PERFORMED BY OTHER INDEPENDENT AUDITORS (AU 543)

1. **Principal Auditor's Judgments**

    a. The auditor must make **professional judgments** about whether (s)he may serve as principal auditor and use the work and reports of other independent auditors.

       1) These parties have audited the financial statements of one or more subsidiaries, divisions, branches, components, or investments included in the financial statements presented.

    b. When **other auditors** have performed a **significant part of the audit**, the auditor must decide whether his/her participation is sufficient to justify serving as the principal auditor. The auditor should consider the following:

       1) The materiality of the portion of the financial statements (s)he has audited
       2) His/her knowledge of the overall financial statements
       3) The importance of the components (s)he audited

    c. If the auditor decides to serve as the principal auditor, (s)he must then decide **whether to refer** to the audit of the other auditor.

       1) If the principal auditor assumes responsibility for the other's work, no reference should be made.
       2) If responsibility is not assumed, the report should refer to the audit of the other auditor and should indicate clearly the **division of responsibility.**
       3) The other auditor remains responsible for his/her work and report.

2. **Decision Not to Refer**

    a. If the principal auditor becomes satisfied as to the **independence and professional reputation** of the other auditor and the audit performed, (s)he may be able to express an opinion **without referring to the other auditor**. In that case, stating that part of the audit was made by another auditor might cause misinterpretation of the responsibility assumed.

    b. The principal auditor may take this position when the

        1) Other auditor is an associated or correspondent firm whose work is acceptable
        2) Other auditor was retained by the principal auditor who guided and controlled the work
        3) Principal auditor becomes satisfied as to the work of the other auditor
        4) Portion of the statements audited by the other auditor is not material

    c. In an audit of an issuer under the PCAOB's AS No. 3, the principal auditor must, before the report release date, obtain, review, and retain an engagement completion document and other documents from the other auditor. For example, these other documents should include

        1) Sufficient information about findings that contradict audit conclusions;
        2) A list of significant fraud risk factors and the auditor's response;
        3) A schedule of audit adjustments, significant deficiencies, and weaknesses in internal control; and
        4) Reconciling information about amounts audited by the other auditor.

ISA Difference

International standards address the issue of other auditors in ISA 600, *Special Considerations – Audits of Group Financial Statements (Including the Work of Component Auditors)*. This standard makes it clear that the group engagement partner is required to be satisfied that those performing the group audit engagement, including component auditors, collectively have the appropriate capabilities and competence. The group engagement partner is also responsible for the direction, supervision, and performance of the group audit engagement and whether the auditor's report that is issued is appropriate in the circumstances. As a result, the auditor's report on the group financial statements **shall not refer to a component auditor**, unless required by law or regulation to include such reference.

---

3. **Decision to Refer**

    a. The principal auditor may decide to refer to the audit of the other auditor because

        1) It may be **impracticable** for the principal auditor to review the other's work or perform the other procedures necessary to become satisfied about the other's audit.
        2) The financial statements of a component audited by another auditor may be **material** in relation to the total.

    b. When the audit of the other auditor is referred to, the report should indicate clearly, in the **introductory, scope, and opinion paragraphs**, the **division of responsibility**. The report also should disclose the magnitude of the audit of the other auditor, e.g., in dollar amounts or percentages of total assets, total revenues, or other appropriate criteria, whichever provides the clearest disclosure.

    c. The other auditor may be **named** if (s)he gives express permission and provided his/her report is presented.

    d. Reference to the other auditor is **not a qualification** of the opinion.

EXAMPLE – Audit Report Referring to Other Auditors

<u>Independent Auditor's Report</u>

To: <--------------- Board of Directors or Shareholders

We have audited the consolidated balance sheet of X Company and subsidiaries as of December 31, Year 2, and the related consolidated statements of income, retained earnings, and cash flows . . . **We did not audit the financial statements of B Company, a wholly owned subsidiary, which statements reflect total assets and revenues constituting 20% and 22%, respectively, of the related consolidated totals. Those statements were audited by other auditors whose report has been furnished to us, and our opinion, insofar as it relates to the amounts included for B Company, is based solely on the report of the other auditors.**

We conducted our audit . . . We believe the audit **and the report of the other auditors** provides a reasonable basis for our opinion.

In our opinion, based on our audit **and the report of the other auditors**, the consolidated financial statements referred to above present fairly, in all material respects, . . .

Signed   <------------ May be signed, typed, or printed

Date   <------------ No earlier than the date on which the auditor has obtained sufficient appropriate evidence

---

4. **Procedures**

   a. Whether or not the principal auditor refers to the audit of the other auditor, (s)he should inquire about the **professional reputation** and **independence** of the other auditor and coordinate their activities.

   b. The following are examples of appropriate procedures:

      1) Making inquiries as to the professional reputation and standing of the other auditor to the AICPA, state societies, other practitioners, bankers, etc., unless known to the principal auditor

      2) Obtaining a representation from the other auditor that (s)he is independent

      3) Communicating with the other auditor to determine that (s)he is aware of

         a) Reliance upon, and possible reference to, his/her report

         b) Applicable GAAP, GAAS, and regulatory requirements

         c) The need for a review of uniformity of accounting practices and the elimination of interentity transactions and balances

5. **Additional Procedures Under Decision Not to Refer**

   a. When the principal auditor decides not to refer to the audit of the other auditor, (s)he should consider

      1) Visiting the other auditor, and discussing the audit procedures followed and the results

      2) Reviewing the audit plans and audit documentation of the other auditor

      3) Making supplemental tests of accounts

6. **Equity-Method Investments**

   a. An auditor who uses another auditor's report to report on an **investor's** equity in underlying net assets and its share of earnings or losses and other transactions of the **investee** is effectively a principal auditor using the work and reports of other auditors.

7. **Departure of Other Auditor's Report from Standard Report**

   a. If the report of the other auditor is other than a standard report, the principal auditor should decide whether the reason for the departure **requires recognition** in his/her report.

   b. If the reason for the departure is **not material** and the other auditor's report is **not presented**, the principal auditor need not refer in the report to such departure.

Stop and review! You have completed the outline for this subunit. Study multiple-choice questions 1 through 5 beginning on page 564.

17.2 CONSISTENCY OF APPLICATION OF GAAP (AU 420 AND PCAOB AS NO. 6)

To a greater extent than any other topic in the Auditing section of the exam, accounting changes integrate the accounting and auditing literature. The auditor must know the accounting treatment of an accounting change to understand how it affects the audit report. (This information is also useful for the Financial section of the exam.) Try to understand the big picture first, and then focus on the more subtle issues. Question number 3 in this study unit's simulation, "Accounting Changes," was derived from a prior CPA exam question and is very enlightening on this particular topic. After you study the material, try the question. If you do well, you probably understand the issues. If you do not do well, you probably should do more work. However, be reasonable in your expectations, as few candidates will get all of the answers correct on the first attempt.

1.   **Comparability vs. Consistency**

   a.   "**Comparability** is the qualitative characteristic that enables users to identify and understand similarities in, and differences among, items" (SFAC 8). For example, auditors are concerned with whether one set of financial statements is comparable with another, e.g., from one period to the next or within each period.

      1)   Many matters affect comparability, such as (a) accounting changes, (b) errors (misstatements), (c) changes in classification, and (d) events or transactions substantially different from those previously accounted for.

   b.   "**Consistency** refers to the use of the same methods for the same items, either from period to period within a reporting entity or in a single period across entities" (SFAC 8). Thus, users of financial statements have an expectation of consistent application of accounting principles from one period to the next. The **second standard of reporting** is applicable:

      The auditor must identify in the auditor's report those circumstances in which such principles have not been consistently observed in the current period in relation to the preceding period.

      1)   Accordingly, an entity should not make voluntary changes in accounting principles unless they can be justified as **preferable** (an improvement in accounting).

2.   **Reporting on Inconsistency**

   a.   A change in an accounting principle or in the method of its application having a material effect on comparability of the financial statements is a departure from the consistency standard. It is described in an **explanatory paragraph (following the opinion paragraph)** stating the nature of the change and referring to a financial statement note that discusses the change in detail.

   b.   The auditor is deemed to concur with the change unless (s)he takes exception to it by modifying the opinion because of a departure from GAAP. Thus, the auditor should evaluate whether

      1)   The new principle is generally accepted,
      2)   The method of accounting for the change conforms with GAAP,
      3)   Disclosures are adequate, and
      4)   The new principle is preferable.

   c.   A lack of consistency, by itself, is not a basis for expressing a qualified or an adverse opinion or disclaiming an opinion.

    d.   The following is an explanatory paragraph (following the opinion paragraph) for a change in principle:

EXAMPLE – **Paragraph Added to Audit Report for a Change in Principle Inseparable from a Change in Estimate**

As discussed in Note X to the financial statements, the Company changed its method of computing depreciation in Year 3.

---

    e.   An explanatory paragraph of this kind is required to be included as long as the year of the change is presented and reported on.

        1)   An exception is a change in principle in the first year reported on for which it is **impracticable** to make a cumulative effect adjustment. An example is a change from FIFO to LIFO. In such a case, the principle has been applied consistently in the comparative statements because the beginning balance in the year of change equals the ending FIFO balance for the prior year. Thus, the paragraph may be subsequently omitted.

            a)   If the change is accounted for by **retrospective application**, the explanatory paragraph is required only in the year of the change. All periods presented will be comparable in subsequent years.

    f.   In **first-year audits**, the auditor should extend procedures to gather evidence about consistency between the current and the preceding year. Given consistency, no report modification is necessary.

        1)   If the auditor is unable to gather evidence, a scope limitation results that may not allow an opinion to be expressed on the results of operations and statement of cash flows.

3.   In general, accounting standards require preparers of financial statements to make them as useful as possible. Thus, changes in prior-period statements presented comparatively may be needed.

4.   GAAP define an **accounting change** as a change in an accounting principle, an accounting estimate, or the reporting entity. An accounting change does **not** include a correction of an accounting error in previously issued financial statements.

    a.   A **change in accounting principle** occurs when an entity (1) adopts a generally accepted principle different from the one previously used, (2) changes the **method** of applying a generally accepted principle, or (3) changes to a generally accepted principle when the principle previously used is no longer generally accepted.

        1)   **Retrospective application** is required for a change in principle. Exceptions are made when it is impracticable to determine the cumulative effect or the period-specific effects of the change.

            a)   Retrospective application requires that carrying amounts of balances at the beginning of the first period reported be adjusted for the **cumulative effect** of the new principle on all periods not reported. All periods reported must be individually adjusted for the **period-specific effects** of applying the new principle.

            b)   It may be **impracticable** to determine the **cumulative effect** of applying a new principle to any prior period. In that case, the new principle is applied as if the change had been made prospectively at the earliest date practicable.

            c)   It may be practicable to determine the cumulative effect of applying the new principle to all prior periods. However, determining the period-specific effects on all prior periods presented may be impracticable. In these circumstances, cumulative-effect adjustments should be made to the beginning balances for the first period to which the new principle can be applied.

   b.   The effects of a **change in accounting estimate** should be accounted for in the period of change and any future periods affected.

        1)   A **change in estimate inseparable from (effected by) a change in principle** is accounted for as a change in estimate. An example is a change in a method of **depreciation, amortization, or depletion** of long-lived, nonfinancial assets. However, because the change relates to a principle, the explanatory paragraph should be added to the auditor's report.

   c.   A **change in reporting entity** is retrospectively applied to interim and annual statements. It results when (1) consolidated or combined statements are presented in place of statements of individual entities, (2) consolidated statements include subsidiaries different from those previously included, or (3) combined statements include entities different from those previously included.

        1)   A change in reporting entity does not result from a **transaction or event**, e.g., a business combination or consolidation of a variable interest entity.

5.   An **accounting error** results from (a) a mathematical mistake, (b) a mistake in the application of GAAP, or (c) an oversight or misuse of facts existing when the statements were prepared. A change to a generally accepted accounting principle from one that is not is an error correction rather than an accounting change.

   a.   An accounting error related to a prior period is reported as a **prior-period adjustment** by restating the prior-period statements. Restatement requires the same accounting adjustments as retrospective application of a new principle.

        1)   Prior-period adjustments reported in **single-period statements** are adjustments of the opening balance of retained earnings.

        2)   If **comparative statements** are presented, corresponding adjustments should be made to the amounts of net income (and its components) and retained earnings balances (and other affected balances) for all periods reported.

6.   The following table describes various changes and how they are reflected in the current and prior years' statements. All shaded items are changes in principle requiring an additional consistency paragraph at the end of the report. The bottom portion includes matters that affect comparability and have accounting implications but do not require modification of the report **unless the accounting departs from GAAP**. Disclosure is usually by notes to the financial statements.

	Factor	Current Year's Financial Statements	Prior Years' Financial Statements
A D D P A R A G R A P H	1. Change in Principle • GAAP to GAAP, including changes in Presentation of Cash Flows (Items Treated as Cash Equivalents) • Non GAAP to GAAP (Correction of Error in Principle)	In comparative statements, adjustment for periodic-specific effects and disclosure. In single-period statements, adjustments for cumulative effect on beginning balances, and period-specific effects Prior-Period Adjustment and Disclosure	Retrospectively Apply Restate
	2. Change in Reporting Entity Not from a Transaction or Event (e.g., presenting consolidated statements instead of individual company statements)	Prior-Period Adjustment and Disclosure	Retrospectively Apply
	3. Change in Estimate Effected by a Change in Principle	Disclosure (Accounted for as a Change in Estimate)	Prospectively Apply
D O N O T A D D P A R A G R A P H	1. Correction of Error Not Involving Principle (PCAOB AS No. 6 requires an additional paragraph for issuers)	Prior-Period Adjustment and Disclosure	Restate
	2. Change in Accounting Estimate	Disclosure	Prospectively Apply
	3. Change in Classification	Disclosure	Adjustment Permitted
	4. Different (New) Transactions	None	Not Applicable
	5. Changes Not Material to Current but May Affect Future Financial Statements	None	Not Applicable
	6. Change in Reporting Entity from a Transaction or Event (e.g., a business combination)	Disclosure	Not Applicable

Stop and review! You have completed the outline for this subunit. Study multiple-choice questions 6 through 13 beginning on page 565.

17.3 UNCERTAINTIES AND GOING CONCERN (AU 508 AND AU 341)

1. **Uncertainties**

   a. A matter involving an uncertainty (including a contingency) is **expected to be resolved** at a future date. At that time, conclusive evidence about its outcome is expected to become available. If the auditor concludes that sufficient appropriate evidence supports the relevant assertions about the nature of an uncertainty, an unqualified opinion ordinarily is expressed. (However, the auditor may add a paragraph to emphasize a matter.)

ISA Difference

The auditor considers modifying the report by including a paragraph for a **significant uncertainty** other than a going concern issue.

---

   b. The auditor must distinguish between situations involving uncertainties that require no opinion modification and those that require modification because of a scope limitation or departure from GAAP. An uncertainty, by itself, does not require such a modification.

   1) **Uncertainties and Scope Limitations**

      a) A scope limitation occurs when sufficient appropriate evidence about the relevant assertions regarding the uncertainty does or did exist but was unavailable, for example, because of record retention policies or a client-imposed restriction.

      b) Although sufficient appropriate evidence about the outcome of an uncertainty cannot be expected to exist at the time of the audit, **management** must analyze relevant existing conditions and their effects, and the auditor must assess whether the evidence is sufficient to support the analysis. A scope limitation arises when the auditor is prevented from making that assessment and results in a qualification or disclaimer.

   2) **Uncertainties and Departure from GAAP**

      a) Departures from GAAP result in a qualified or an adverse opinion when

         i) Disclosure is inadequate.

         ii) Inappropriate accounting principles or unreasonable estimates cause the statements to be materially misstated.

2. **Going Concern**

   a. The auditor's consideration of an entity's ability to continue as a going concern was described in Study Unit 14. If the auditor concludes that substantial doubt exists, an additional paragraph should be added to the end of the auditor's standard report.

   b. But the auditor is not precluded from disclaiming an opinion.

   c. The auditor's explanatory paragraph should include the terms **substantial doubt** and **going concern**.

   d. In the explanatory paragraph, the auditor should **not use conditional language** such as, "If the company is unable to obtain refinancing, there may be substantial doubt about the company's ability to continue as a going concern."

EXAMPLE – Paragraph Added to Audit Report Expressing Substantial Doubt about Going Concern

The accompanying financial statements have been prepared assuming that the Company will continue as a going concern. As discussed in Note X to the financial statements, the Company has suffered recurring losses from operations and has a net capital deficiency that raises **substantial doubt** about its ability to continue as a **going concern**. Management's plans in regard to these matters are also described in Note X. The financial statements do not include any adjustments that might result from the outcome of this uncertainty.

e. If **disclosures are inadequate**, the departure from GAAP may result in a qualified or an adverse opinion.

f. Substantial doubt arising in the current period does not imply that such doubt existed in the prior period and should not affect the report on the prior-period statements.

g. If substantial doubt existed at the date of prior-period statements and **that doubt has been removed** in the current period, the explanatory paragraph in the report for the prior period should not be repeated.

ISA Difference

If a **material uncertainty** about going concern exists, the auditor evaluates whether the statements clearly state the existence of the material uncertainty creating a going concern issue. The statements should describe the events and conditions resulting in the significant doubt about the entity's ability to continue as a going concern and management's related plans.

Stop and review! You have completed the outline for this subunit. Study multiple-choice questions 14 through 22 beginning on page 568.

17.4 COMPARATIVE FINANCIAL STATEMENTS (AU 508)

1. **Reports**

    a. The phrase "financial statements taken as a whole" in the **fourth reporting standard** applies to current-period and prior-period statements presented comparatively.

    b. Thus, a **continuing auditor** should **update the report** for the prior period(s) presented.

        1) If audit firms merge and the new firm becomes the **auditor of a former client** of one of the merged firms, the new firm may accept responsibility as a continuing auditor. The new firm may indicate that a merger took place and name the firm that was merged with it.

            a) Otherwise, the guidance on reports of predecessor auditors should be followed.

        2) An updated report is **not a reissuance** of a previous report. The updated report considers information from the audit of the current-period statements and is issued with the report on those statements.

        3) A continuing auditor need not report if only **summarized comparative information** of the prior period(s) is presented. For example, state and local governmental units and not-for-profit entities often present total-all-funds information rather than information by individual funds.

            a) If the client **requests an opinion on the prior period(s)**, the auditor should consider whether the information contains sufficient detail for a fair presentation. To avoid modification of the report, additional columns or separate detail by fund will usually be needed.

    c. Ordinarily, the report on comparative statements should be **dated** as of the date the auditor obtained sufficient appropriate evidence for the most recent audit.

    d. During the audit, the auditor should be alert for circumstances or events **affecting the prior-period statements** presented and should consider their effects when updating the report.

2. The report applies to **individual financial statements**, so an auditor may (a) express a qualified or an adverse opinion, (b) disclaim an opinion, or (c) include an explanatory paragraph for one or more statements for one or more periods while issuing a **different report on the other statements**. The following are examples of such reports:

    a. Standard report on the prior-year financial statements and a qualified opinion on the current-year financial statements

        1) The introductory and scope paragraphs are unchanged.

        2) The following are the explanatory paragraph and the modification of the opinion paragraph:

EXAMPLE – Language to Qualify the Opinion on the Current Financial Statements

The Company has excluded, from property and debt in the accompanying Year 3 balance sheet, certain lease obligations that were entered into in Year 3 which, in our opinion, should be capitalized in order to conform with U.S. generally accepted accounting principles. If these lease obligations were capitalized, property would be increased by $_____, noncurrent debt by $_____, and retained earnings by $_____ as of December 31, Year 3; net income, basic earnings per share, and diluted earnings per share would be increased (decreased) by $_____, $_____, and $_____, respectively, for the year then ended.

In our opinion, except for the effects on the Year 3 financial statements of not capitalizing certain lease obligations as described in the preceding paragraph . . .

---

    b. Standard report on the current-year financial statements with a disclaimer of opinion on the prior-year statements of income, retained earnings, and cash flows

        1) The introductory paragraph is unchanged.

        2) The scope paragraph is modified by adding the following clause:

> Except as explained in the following paragraph . . .

        3) The following are the explanatory and opinion paragraphs:

EXAMPLE – Language to Disclaim an Opinion on Selected Statements

We did not observe the taking of the physical inventory as of December 31, Year 1, since that date was prior to our appointment as auditors for the Company, and we were unable to satisfy ourselves regarding inventory quantities by means of other auditing procedures. Inventory amounts as of December 31, Year 1, enter into the determination of net income and cash flows for the year ended December 31, Year 2.

Because of the matter discussed in the preceding paragraph, the scope of our work was not sufficient to enable us to express, and we do not express, an opinion on the results of operations and cash flows for the year ended December 31, Year 2.

In our opinion, the balance sheets of ABC Company as of December 31, Year 3 and Year 2, and the related statements of income, retained earnings, and cash flows for the year ended December 31, Year 3, present fairly....

---

3. **Opinion on Prior-Period Statements Different from Previous Opinion**

    a. An auditor may become aware of circumstances or events affecting the statements of a prior period and should consider them when updating the report.

    b. For example, if the opinion was modified because of a departure from GAAP and the statements are **restated** in the current period to conform with GAAP, the updated report should indicate the restatement and express an **unqualified opinion**. An explanatory paragraph(s) **preceding** the opinion paragraph should disclose

        1) All substantive reasons for the different opinion

        2) The date of the previous report

        3) The type of opinion previously expressed

        4) The circumstances or events that resulted in a different opinion

        5) That the updated opinion differs from the previous opinion

c.   The following is a possible explanatory paragraph:

EXAMPLE – Language to Change a Previously Expressed Opinion

In our report dated March 1, Year 3, we expressed an opinion that the Year 2 financial statements did not fairly present financial position, results of operations, and cash flows in conformity with U.S. generally accepted accounting principles: (1) the Company carried its property, plant, and equipment at appraisal values, and provided for depreciation on the basis of such values, and (2) the Company did not provide for deferred income taxes with respect to differences between income for financial reporting purposes and taxable income. As described in Note X, the Company has changed its method of accounting for these items and has restated its Year 2 financial statements to conform with U.S. generally accepted accounting principles. Accordingly, our present opinion on the Year 2 financial statements, as presented herein, is different from that expressed in our previous report.

---

d.   The introductory, scope, and opinion paragraphs are the same as in the standard report.

4.   **Report of Predecessor Auditor**

a.   A predecessor auditor ordinarily may **reissue** the report for a prior period at the **request of the former client** if satisfactory arrangements are made to perform this service and certain procedures are performed.

b.   A predecessor auditor's report may not be reissued in certain circumstances, e.g., because the CPA is no longer in public practice.

5.   **Reissuance of Predecessor Auditor's Report**

a.   Before reissuing (or consenting to reuse of) the report, the predecessor auditor should consider whether the report is still appropriate given the **current form or presentation** of the prior-period statements and any **subsequent events.**

b.   The predecessor auditor should perform the following **procedures**:

1)   Read the current-period statements

2)   Compare the prior-period statements reported on with those to be presented comparatively

3)   Obtain a representation letter from the auditor

a)   The letter should state whether the audit revealed matters that might materially affect, or require disclosure in, the prior-period statements.

4)   Obtain a representation letter from management

a)   The letter should state whether (1) new information indicates that previous representations should be modified, and (2) any events have occurred subsequent to the balance sheet date of the latest prior-period statements reported on by the predecessor that would require adjustment to, or disclosure in, those financial statements.

c.   The predecessor auditor may wish to consider the matters described in Subunit 17.1 but, in the reissued report, should not refer to the report or to the work of the auditor.

d.   Events or transactions **subsequent to the date of the previous report** that may affect the report require the predecessor auditor to make inquiries and perform other necessary procedures, such as reviewing the relevant portions of the auditor's documentation.

1)   If the predecessor auditor revises the report, (s)he should follow the guidance in this subunit about changing the prior opinion.

e.   A predecessor auditor's knowledge of the former client is limited. Thus, (s)he should use the **date of the previous report** to avoid implications that (s)he has examined records, transactions, or events after that date.

1)   If the report is revised or the statements are restated, the report should be **dual-dated**.

6.   **Predecessor Auditor's Report Not Presented**

a.   The introductory paragraph of the auditor's report should state the following:

1)   That the prior-period statements were audited by another auditor

a)   But the auditor should not name the predecessor auditor unless the predecessor's practice was acquired by, or merged with, that of the auditor.

2)   The date of the predecessor's report

3)   The type of report issued by the predecessor

4)   If a standard report is not issued, the substantive reasons for not doing so

b.   Example of an auditor's unqualified report when the predecessor's report is not presented:

1)   The following language is added to the standard introductory paragraph (as the last sentence) for a report on the Year 3 statements:

EXAMPLE – **Language Added to Introductory Paragraph of Auditor's Report to Refer to Predecessor's Report**

The financial statements of ABC Company as of December 31, Year 2, were audited by other auditors whose report dated March 31, Year 3, expressed an unqualified opinion of those statements.

---

2)   The scope paragraph is unchanged.

3)   The first line of the opinion paragraph is revised as follows:

> In our opinion, the Year 3 financial statements referred to above . . . .

c.   If the predecessor did not issue a standard report, the auditor should describe the nature of, and reasons for, the explanatory paragraph added to that report or the opinion qualification. The following is an example of the wording added to the introductory paragraph:

EXAMPLE – **Language Added to Introductory Paragraph of Auditor's Report to Refer to Predecessor's Modified Report**

The financial statements of ABC Company as of December 31, Year 2, were audited by other auditors whose report dated March 1, Year 3, on those statements included an explanatory paragraph that described the change in the Company's method of computing depreciation discussed in Note X to the financial statements.

---

d.   If the statements have been restated, the introductory paragraph should indicate that a predecessor reported on them before restatement. Also, if the auditor becomes satisfied as to the propriety of the restatement, (s)he may include the following paragraph in the report:

EXAMPLE – **Language Added to Introductory Paragraph of Auditor's Report to Express Opinion on Restatement of Prior Year's Financial Statements**

We also audited the adjustments described in Note X that were applied to restate the Year 2 financial statements. In our opinion, such adjustments are appropriate and have been properly applied.

---

7. **Misstatement of Statements Audited by a Predecessor**

   a. If the auditor believes that statements reported on by the predecessor auditor need revision, the auditor should request that the **client inform the predecessor** and arrange for the three parties to resolve the matter.

   b. At the meeting, the auditor should disclose any information that the predecessor may need to consider.

      1) AU 561 discusses the procedures to be followed by an auditor who subsequently discovers facts that existed at the date of the report.

8. **Comparative Presentation of Unaudited Prior-Year Statements with Audited Current-Year Statements**

   a. In these circumstances, the audit report on comparative statements presented in documents **filed with the SEC** should not refer to the unaudited statements, which should be clearly marked as **unaudited**.

   b. In all other cases, the unaudited statements (that may have been reviewed or compiled) also should be clearly marked to indicate their status, and either (1) the report on the prior period should be **reissued** (AU 530), or (2) the report on the current period should include as a separate paragraph a description of the **responsibility assumed** for the prior-period statements (AU 504).

Stop and review! You have completed the outline for this subunit. Study multiple-choice questions 23 through 31 beginning on page 571.

17.5 EMPHASIS OF A MATTER (AU 508)

1. A matter regarding the financial statements may be emphasized in a **separate paragraph without modifying the opinion**. But phrases such as "with the foregoing explanation" should not be included in the opinion paragraph. Matters emphasized may include the following:

   a. The information that the entity is part of a larger enterprise
   b. Significant related party transactions
   c. An important subsequent event
   d. An accounting matter (other than a change in principle) affecting comparability

2. The following is an example of a separate paragraph that emphasizes a matter:

EXAMPLE – Separate Paragraph Emphasizing a Matter

Company A is a subsidiary of Company ABC, and the financial statements reported on here are a component part of the consolidated financial statements of Company ABC reported on by other auditors.

ISA Difference

The ISAs prefer that an **emphasis of a matter paragraph** be included after the opinion paragraph. It generally does **not** state that emphasis of a matter is not a basis for qualifying the opinion.

Stop and review! You have completed the outline for this subunit. Study multiple-choice questions 32 and 33 on page 574.

QUESTIONS

17.1 Part of Audit Performed by Other Independent Auditors (AU 543)

1. An auditor may issue the standard audit report when the

- A. Auditor refers to the findings of a specialist.
- B. Financial statements are derived and condensed from complete audited financial statements that are filed with a regulatory agency.
- C. Financial statements are prepared on the cash receipts and disbursements basis of accounting.
- D. Principal auditor assumes responsibility for the work of another auditor.

Answer (D) is correct.   *(CPA, adapted)*
REQUIRED: The situation in which an auditor may issue the standard audit report.
DISCUSSION: If the principal auditor can become satisfied regarding the independence and professional reputation of, and the audit performed by, the other auditor, (s)he may be able to express an opinion on the financial statements taken as a whole without referring to the audit of the other auditor. If (s)he assumes responsibility for the work of the other auditor, a standard report is appropriate (AU 543).
Answer (A) is incorrect. The auditor does not refer to a specialist in the standard audit report. Answer (B) is incorrect. An auditor is not permitted to report on condensed statements in the same manner as (s)he reported on the complete statements. Answer (C) is incorrect. A special report may be appropriate.

2. Pell, CPA, decides to serve as principal auditor in the audit of the financial statements of Tech Consolidated, Inc. Smith, CPA, audits one of Tech's subsidiaries. In which situation(s) should Pell refer to Smith's audit?

I. Pell reviews Smith's audit documentation and assumes responsibility for Smith's work but expresses a qualified opinion on Tech's financial statements.

II. Pell is unable to review Smith's audit documentation; however, Pell's inquiries indicate that Smith has an excellent reputation for professional competence and integrity.

- A. I only.
- B. II only.
- C. Both I and II.
- D. Neither I nor II.

Answer (B) is correct.   *(CPA, adapted)*
REQUIRED: The situations, if any, in which a principal auditor refers to another auditor's audit.
DISCUSSION: Once the principal auditor is able to become satisfied as to the independence and professional reputation of the other auditor, (s)he may decide to refer to the other auditor's audit. It may be impracticable for the principal auditor to review the other auditor's work or to use other procedures that (s)he deems necessary to obtain satisfaction as to the other auditor's audit. Such a reference indicates a division of responsibility between the auditors. The reference to the other auditor does not prohibit an unqualified opinion. If the principal auditor accepts responsibility for the other auditor's audit, (s)he should not state in the report that another auditor performed part of the audit. Such a reference might lead to misinterpretation of the degree of responsibility assumed. The type of opinion expressed is not relevant to the decision to make reference (AU 543). Under international standards (ISAs), the auditor must be satisfied that the evidence supports the opinion and cannot refer to other (component) auditors.

3. Which of the following procedures would the principal auditor most likely perform after deciding to make reference to another CPA who audited a subsidiary of the entity?

- A. Review the working papers and the audit plans of the other CPA.
- B. Visit the other CPA and discuss the results of the other CPA's audit procedures.
- C. Make inquiries about the professional reputation and independence of the other CPA.
- D. Determine that the other CPA has a sufficient understanding of the subsidiary's internal control.

Answer (C) is correct.   *(CPA, adapted)*
REQUIRED: The procedure most likely to be performed after deciding to refer to another auditor.
DISCUSSION: When the principal auditor decides to divide reporting responsibility and to refer to another auditor, (s)he should inquire about the professional reputation and independence of the other auditor to one or more of the following: the AICPA, a state society, a local chapter, or a foreign auditor's corresponding professional organization; other practitioners; credit grantors; or other appropriate sources (AU 543). Under international standards (ISAs), the auditor must be satisfied that the evidence supports the opinion and cannot refer to other (component) auditors.
Answer (A) is incorrect. If the principal auditor decides not to divide responsibility and not refer to the other auditor's audit in the report, (s)he should consider reviewing the working papers and audit plans of the other auditor. Answer (B) is incorrect. If the principal auditor decides not to divide responsibility and not refer to the other auditor's audit in the report, (s)he should consider visiting the other auditor. Answer (D) is incorrect. If the principal auditor decides to refer to the audit of the other auditor, (s)he does not accept responsibility for the other auditor's work and need not test it.

4. In which of the following situations would a principal auditor least likely make reference to another auditor who audited a subsidiary of the entity?

A. The other auditor was retained by the principal auditor and the work was performed under the principal auditor's guidance and control.

B. The principal auditor finds it impracticable to review the other auditor's work or otherwise be satisfied as to the other auditor's work.

C. The financial statements audited by the other auditor are material to the consolidated financial statements covered by the principal auditor's opinion.

D. The principal auditor is unable to be satisfied as to the independence and professional reputation of the other auditor.

Answer (A) is correct. *(CPA, adapted)*
REQUIRED: The situation in which a principal auditor is least likely to refer to another auditor.
DISCUSSION: According to AU 543, the principal auditor normally does not refer to another auditor when the other auditor is an associate or correspondent firm whose work is acceptable to the principal auditor or when the other auditor was retained by the principal auditor and the work was performed under the principal auditor's guidance and control.
Answer (B) is incorrect. If the principal finds it impracticable to review the work of the other auditor, the other auditor will likely be referred to in the principal auditor's report. Answer (C) is incorrect. The more material the items audited by the other auditor, the more likely reference will be made in the principal auditor's report. Answer (D) is incorrect. When the auditor cannot become satisfied about the independence and professional reputation of the other auditor, the opinion should be qualified or an opinion should be disclaimed.

5. The introductory paragraph of an auditor's report contains the following: "We did not audit the financial statements of EZ, Inc., a wholly owned subsidiary, which statements reflect total assets and revenues constituting 27% and 29%, respectively, of the related consolidated totals. Those statements were audited by other auditors whose report has been furnished to us, and our opinion, insofar as it relates to the amounts included for EZ, Inc., is based solely on the report of the other auditors." These sentences

A. Indicate a division of responsibility.

B. Assume responsibility for the other auditor.

C. Require a departure from an unqualified opinion.

D. Are an improper form of reporting.

Answer (A) is correct. *(CPA, adapted)*
REQUIRED: The effect of the quoted language.
DISCUSSION: The quoted language is from an introductory paragraph provided as an example in AU 543 of appropriate reporting of the decision to refer to the work of another auditor. It meets the requirement that the reference indicate clearly the division of responsibility. However, under international audit standards (ISAs), the auditor must accept responsibility for the work of other (component) auditors and cannot divide responsibility with (i.e., refer to) other auditors in the report.
Answer (B) is incorrect. The statement attempts to divide responsibility, so the principal auditor does not assume responsibility for the other auditor. Answer (C) is incorrect. A division of responsibility does not preclude an unqualified opinion. Answer (D) is incorrect. The wording is standard.

17.2 Consistency of Application of GAAP (AU 420 and PCAOB AS No. 6)

6. In the first audit of a client, an auditor was not able to gather sufficient evidence about the consistent application of accounting principles between the current and the prior year, as well as the amounts of assets or liabilities at the beginning of the current year. This was due to the client's record retention policies. If the amounts in question could materially affect current operating results, the auditor would

A. Be unable to express an opinion on the current year's results of operations and cash flows.

B. Express an adverse opinion on the financial statements because of a client-imposed scope limitation.

C. Withdraw from the engagement and refuse to be associated with the financial statements.

D. Specifically state that the financial statements are not comparable to the prior year due to an uncertainty.

Answer (A) is correct. *(CPA, adapted)*
REQUIRED: The effect on the report of insufficient evidence about beginning balances and consistency of GAAP.
DISCUSSION: The second standard of reporting states, "The auditor must identify in the auditor's report those circumstances in which such principles have not been consistently observed in the current period in relation to the preceding period." An auditor must be able to identify accounting changes that affect consistency. When an auditor is unable to gather evidence about the consistent application of accounting principles due to the client's failure to retain the information, the auditor will be unable to express an opinion on the results of operations and cash flows. The auditor may, however, be able to become satisfied as to the ending balances reported on the balance sheet.
Answer (B) is incorrect. A disclaimer of opinion on the income statement and statement of cash flows is appropriate when the audit is not sufficient to permit the formation of an opinion. Answer (C) is incorrect. No ethical or other reason is given to justify withdrawal. Answer (D) is incorrect. Any potential lack of comparability is not due to an uncertainty.

7. The following explanatory paragraph was included in an auditor's report to indicate a lack of consistency:

> As discussed in note T to the financial statements, the company changed its method of computing depreciation in Year 1.

How should the auditor report on this matter if the auditor concurred with the change?

	Type of Opinion	Location of Explanatory Paragraph
A.	Unqualified	Before opinion paragraph
B.	Unqualified	After opinion paragraph
C.	Qualified	Before opinion paragraph
D.	Qualified	After opinion paragraph

8. For which of the following events would an auditor issue a report that omits any reference to consistency?

- A. A change in the method of accounting for inventories.
- B. A change from an accounting principle that is not generally accepted to one that is generally accepted.
- C. A change in the useful life used to calculate the provision for depreciation expense.
- D. Management's lack of reasonable justification for a change in accounting principle.

9. When there has been a change in accounting principles, but the effect of the change on the comparability of the financial statements is not material, the auditor should

- A. Refer to the change in an explanatory paragraph.
- B. Explicitly concur that the change is preferred.
- C. Not refer to consistency in the auditor's report.
- D. Refer to the change in the opinion paragraph.

Answer (B) is correct. *(CPA, adapted)*
REQUIRED: The proper reporting of a lack of consistency.
DISCUSSION: AU 508 states that a change in accounting principles or in the method of their application having a material effect on comparability requires the auditor to refer to the change in an explanatory paragraph of the report. However, no opinion modification is necessary if the auditor concurs with the change. A change in depreciation method is a change in principle inseparable from a change in estimate. Because a change in principle is involved, an explanatory paragraph is required. The paragraph should follow the opinion paragraph, identify the nature of the change, and refer to a note that discusses the change.

Answer (C) is correct. *(CPA, adapted)*
REQUIRED: The event not requiring a reference to consistency in the auditor's report.
DISCUSSION: A change in an accounting estimate that is not inseparable from a change in an accounting principle, for example, in the useful life of an asset, is not a change that affects consistency. This change is accounted for prospectively and requires disclosure in a note to the financial statements if it affects several future periods. It is not referred to in the auditor's report (AU 420).
Answer (A) is incorrect. A change in the method of accounting for inventory, for example, from FIFO to LIFO, is a change in accounting principle. Such a change affects consistency and requires an explanatory paragraph in the auditor's report. Answer (B) is incorrect. A correction of an error in principle is a change affecting consistency. It is accounted for as a correction of an error, and it requires an explanatory paragraph in the auditor's report. Answer (D) is incorrect. Lack of justification for a change in accounting principle requires the auditor to express a qualified or adverse opinion. The middle paragraph explaining the reasons for the opinion modification contains all the information needed in a paragraph on consistency, so a separate paragraph following the opinion paragraph is not necessary (AU 508).

Answer (C) is correct. *(CPA, adapted)*
REQUIRED: The reference, if any, in the auditor's report to a change in accounting principle not considered material.
DISCUSSION: The standard report implies that comparability between or among periods has not been materially affected by changes in accounting principles because either no change has occurred, or a change in principles or in the method of their application was made, but its effect on comparability is not material (AU 508). Moreover, changes not material to the current financial statements that may be material to future statements require no reference in the auditor's report (AU 420).
Answer (A) is incorrect. An additional paragraph is added following the opinion paragraph only if the change is material. Answer (B) is incorrect. The auditor should not refer to consistency when the effect on comparability is immaterial. Answer (D) is incorrect. The auditor should refer to the change in the opinion paragraph only if (s)he modifies the opinion.

10. When an entity changes its method of accounting for income taxes, which has a material effect on comparability, the auditor should refer to the change in an explanatory paragraph added to the auditor's report. This paragraph should identify the nature of the change and

A. Explain why the change is justified under generally accepted accounting principles.

B. Describe the cumulative effect of the change on all periods prior to those presented.

C. State the auditor's explicit concurrence with or opposition to the change.

D. Refer to the financial statement note that discusses the change in detail.

Answer (D) is correct. *(CPA, adapted)*
REQUIRED: The content of an explanatory paragraph added because of a change in an accounting principle.
DISCUSSION: When a change in accounting principle has a material effect on comparability, the auditor should add an explanatory paragraph after the opinion paragraph that identifies the nature of the change and refers the reader to the note in the financial statements that discusses the change in detail.
Answer (A) is incorrect. The auditor's concurrence with the change is implicit unless (s)he modifies the opinion. Answer (B) is incorrect. The cumulative effect of a change is described in the financial statements, not the audit report. Answer (C) is incorrect. The auditor's concurrence with the change is implicit unless (s)he modifies the opinion.

11. When the auditor concurs with a change in accounting principle that materially affects the comparability of the comparative financial statements, the auditor should

	Concur Explicitly with the Change	Express a Qualified Opinion	Refer to the Change in an Explanatory Paragraph
A.	No	No	Yes
B.	Yes	No	Yes
C.	Yes	Yes	No
D.	No	Yes	No

Answer (A) is correct. *(CPA, adapted)*
REQUIRED: The appropriate report when the auditor concurs with a change in accounting principle.
DISCUSSION: A material change in accounting principle raises a consistency issue. Thus, a report with a separate explanatory paragraph is required. Unless the change is unjustified, however, it does not require a modification of the opinion. Thus, a qualified opinion is not appropriate. Furthermore, an auditor does not concur explicitly with the change in the report. An explanatory paragraph suffices.

12. Digit Co. uses the FIFO method of costing for its international subsidiary's inventory and LIFO for its domestic inventory. Under these circumstances, the auditor's report on Digit's financial statements should express an

A. Unqualified opinion.

B. Opinion qualified because of a lack of consistency.

C. Opinion qualified because of a departure from GAAP.

D. Adverse opinion.

Answer (A) is correct. *(CPA, adapted)*
REQUIRED: The effect on the report of using different inventory methods for two business segments.
DISCUSSION: A difference between the accounting principles used by two segments of an entity does not raise a consistency issue. The second standard of reporting concerns the consistent observation of principles in the current period in relation to the preceding period. Thus, the use of LIFO for one segment and FIFO for another does not, by itself, affect comparability. Assuming that the use of different methods is appropriate, an unqualified opinion is not precluded, and no explanatory paragraph relevant to consistency needs to be added to the report.

13. An entity changed from the straight-line method to the declining-balance method of depreciation for all newly acquired assets. This change has no material effect on the current year's financial statements but is reasonably certain to have a substantial effect in later years. If the change is disclosed in the notes to the financial statements, the auditor should issue a report with a(n)

A. Qualified opinion.

B. Explanatory paragraph.

C. Unqualified opinion.

D. Consistency modification.

Answer (C) is correct. *(CPA, adapted)*
REQUIRED: The report issued when a change in principle has no material effect on the current year's statements.
DISCUSSION: A change in depreciation method is a change in accounting principle inseparable from a change in estimate. If it has no material effect on the current financial statements but is reasonably certain to have a substantial effect in future years, the change should be disclosed but need not be recognized in the report (AU 420).
Answer (A) is incorrect. By itself, an accounting change does not result in a qualified opinion. Answer (B) is incorrect. If an accounting change has no material effect on the current financial statements but is likely to affect future financial statements, the auditor need not modify the report. Answer (D) is incorrect. If an accounting change has no material effect on the current financial statements but is likely to affect future financial statements, the auditor need not modify the report.

17.3 Uncertainties and Going Concern (AU 508 and AU 341)

14. An auditor most likely would express an unqualified opinion and would not add explanatory language to the report if the auditor

A. Wishes to emphasize that the entity had significant transactions with related parties.

B. Concurs with the entity's change in its method of computing depreciation.

C. Discovers that supplementary information required by FASB has been omitted.

D. Believes that there is a remote likelihood of a material loss resulting from an uncertainty.

Answer (D) is correct. *(CPA, adapted)*
REQUIRED: The condition under which an explanatory paragraph is not added to the report.
DISCUSSION: Normally, an uncertainty does not require the auditor to add a paragraph to the report.
Answer (A) is incorrect. Emphasis of a matter is accomplished with an additional paragraph added to the auditor's report. Answer (B) is incorrect. A change in the depreciation method is a change in estimate inseparable from a change in principle. The change in principle requires an additional paragraph describing the lack of consistency. Answer (C) is incorrect. AU 558 requires the auditor to add an additional paragraph when supplementary information that is required by FASB or GASB has been omitted.

15. Management believes and the auditor is satisfied that a material loss probably will occur when pending litigation is resolved. Management is unable to make a reasonable estimate of the amount or range of the potential loss but fully discloses the situation in the notes to the financial statements. If management does not make an accrual in the financial statements, the auditor should express a(n)

A. Qualified opinion due to a scope limitation.

B. Qualified opinion due to a departure from GAAP.

C. Unqualified opinion with an explanatory paragraph.

D. Unqualified opinion in a standard auditor's report.

Answer (D) is correct. *(CPA, adapted)*
REQUIRED: The auditor's reporting consideration of a material loss that is probable but not subject to estimation.
DISCUSSION: If the auditor concludes that sufficient appropriate evidence supports management's assertions about the nature of a matter involving an uncertainty, an unmodified report is ordinarily appropriate.
Answer (A) is incorrect. Inability to make a reasonable estimate of the potential loss is not a scope limitation. Answer (B) is incorrect. No departure from GAAP has occurred. An accrual of the loss contingency is not required in these circumstances, and full disclosure has been made. Answer (C) is incorrect. No basis for including an additional paragraph to the report is given.

16. Tech Company has disclosed an uncertainty arising from pending litigation. The auditor's decision to express a qualified opinion rather than an unqualified opinion most likely would be determined by the

A. Lack of sufficient appropriate evidence.

B. Inability to estimate the amount of loss.

C. Entity's lack of experience with such litigation.

D. Lack of insurance coverage for possible losses from such litigation.

Answer (A) is correct. *(CPA, adapted)*
REQUIRED: The basis for expressing a qualified opinion.
DISCUSSION: By definition, sufficient appropriate evidence regarding the outcome of an uncertainty cannot be expected to exist at the time of an audit. However, management must analyze existing conditions, including uncertainties, and their financial statement effects. The auditor must therefore determine whether appropriate evidence is sufficient to support these analyses. If, as a result of a scope limitation, sufficient appropriate evidence is not available to the auditor to make this determination, a qualification or disclaimer of opinion is appropriate.
Answer (B) is incorrect. An inability to estimate the amount of loss is neither a scope limitation nor a departure from GAAP and does not justify an opinion qualification. Answer (C) is incorrect. The entity's lack of experience with such litigation is neither a scope limitation nor a departure from GAAP and does not justify an opinion qualification. Answer (D) is incorrect. The lack of insurance is neither a scope limitation nor a departure from GAAP and does not justify an opinion qualification.

17. When an auditor concludes that substantial doubt exists about an entity's ability to continue as a going concern for a reasonable period of time, the auditor's responsibility is to

A. Prepare prospective financial information to verify whether management's plans can be effectively implemented.

B. Project future conditions and events for a period of time not to exceed 1 year following the date of the financial statements.

C. Express a qualified or adverse opinion, depending on materiality, because of the possible effects on the financial statements.

D. Consider the adequacy of disclosure about the entity's possible inability to continue as a going concern.

Answer (D) is correct. *(CPA, adapted)*
REQUIRED: The auditor's responsibility given a substantial doubt about an entity's ability to continue as a going concern.
DISCUSSION: If the auditor reaches this conclusion after identifying conditions and events that create such doubt and after evaluating management's plans to mitigate their effects, (s)he should consider the adequacy of disclosure and include an explanatory paragraph (after the opinion paragraph) in the report that includes the words "substantial doubt" and "going concern." If disclosure is inadequate, the departure from GAAP requires modification of the opinion. By itself, however, the substantial doubt does not require a modified opinion paragraph or a disclaimer of opinion.
Answer (A) is incorrect. The auditor should consider management's plans but need not prepare prospective financial information. Answer (B) is incorrect. The auditor is not responsible for predicting future conditions or events. Answer (C) is incorrect. The opinion is not modified solely for a going concern issue.

18. In which of the following circumstances would an auditor most likely add an explanatory paragraph to the standard report while expressing an unqualified opinion?

A. The auditor is asked to report on the balance sheet but not on the other basic financial statements.

B. There is substantial doubt about the entity's ability to continue as a going concern.

C. Management's estimates of the effects of future events are unreasonable.

D. Certain transactions cannot be tested because of management's records retention policy.

Answer (B) is correct. *(CPA, adapted)*
REQUIRED: The situation most likely resulting in an explanatory paragraph and an unqualified opinion.
DISCUSSION: If the auditor reaches this conclusion after identifying conditions and events that create such doubt and after evaluating management's plans to mitigate their effects, (s)he should consider the adequacy of disclosure and include an explanatory paragraph (after the opinion paragraph) in the report. The auditor must use language in the explanatory paragraph that includes the words "substantial doubt" and "going concern." By itself, however, the substantial doubt is not a basis for modifying the opinion.
Answer (A) is incorrect. An auditor may be asked to report on one financial statement. In that event, (s)he may appropriately express an unqualified opinion without adding an explanatory paragraph. Answer (C) is incorrect. The statements are not fairly presented if material estimates included in them are unreasonable. An unqualified opinion could not then be expressed. Answer (D) is incorrect. A qualification or disclaimer of opinion is appropriate when the scope of the audit is limited.

19. An auditor's report included the following paragraph relative to a client's going concern:

The accompanying financial statements have been prepared assuming that the Company will continue as a going concern. If the Company is not able to renew the contract described in Note X, there may be substantial doubt about the company's ability to continue as a going concern.

Which of the following statements is true?

A. The paragraph should not refer to a note to the financial statements.

B. The report should not contain conditional language.

C. The report should refer to a qualification of the opinion.

D. The report should not use the phrase "substantial doubt."

Answer (B) is correct. *(Publisher, adapted)*
REQUIRED: The true statement about a going concern paragraph.
DISCUSSION: The report should not contain conditional language. "If the Company is not able to renew the contract..." is not permissible language.
Answer (A) is incorrect. The report may refer to a note that describes the issues. Answer (C) is incorrect. The opinion should not be qualified for a going concern doubt. Rather, an additional paragraph should be included in the report. Answer (D) is incorrect. The report should include the phrases "substantial doubt" and "going concern."

20. Green, CPA, concludes that there is substantial doubt about JKL Co.'s ability to continue as a going concern. If JKL's financial statements adequately disclose its financial difficulties, Green's auditor's report should

	Include an Explanatory Paragraph Following the Opinion Paragraph	Specifically Use the Words "Going Concern"	Specifically Use the Words "Substantial Doubt"
A.	Yes	Yes	Yes
B.	Yes	Yes	No
C.	Yes	No	Yes
D.	No	Yes	Yes

Answer (A) is correct. *(CPA, adapted)*
REQUIRED: The effects of a substantial doubt about an entity's ability to continue as a going concern.
DISCUSSION: When a substantial doubt exists about an entity's ability to continue as a going concern, the auditor should consider the adequacy of disclosure and include an explanatory paragraph (after the opinion paragraph) in the report. The auditor must use language in the explanatory paragraph that includes the words "substantial doubt" and "going concern."

21. Kane, CPA, concludes that there is substantial doubt about Lima Co.'s ability to continue as a going concern for a reasonable period of time. If Lima's financial statements adequately disclose its financial difficulties, Kane's auditor's report is required to include an explanatory paragraph that specifically uses the phrase(s)

	"Possible Discontinuance of Operations"	"Reasonable Period of Time, Not to Exceed One Year"
A.	Yes	Yes
B.	Yes	No
C.	No	Yes
D.	No	No

Answer (D) is correct. *(CPA, adapted)*
REQUIRED: The phrase(s), if any, required to be included in a paragraph describing a substantial doubt about a firm's ability to continue as a going concern.
DISCUSSION: The auditor has a substantial doubt about the firm's ability to continue as a going concern for a reasonable period of time. Accordingly, the auditor should include an explanatory paragraph at the end of the report. This paragraph should include the terms "substantial doubt" and "going concern." The specific phrases included in the question are not required.

22. An auditor concludes that there is substantial doubt about an entity's ability to continue as a going concern for a reasonable period of time. If the entity's disclosures concerning this matter are adequate and no other issues prevail, the audit report may include a

	Disclaimer of Opinion	Qualified Opinion
A.	Yes	Yes
B.	No	No
C.	No	Yes
D.	Yes	No

Answer (D) is correct. *(CPA, adapted)*
REQUIRED: The nature of the report given a substantial going concern doubt.
DISCUSSION: By itself, a substantial doubt about an entity's ability to continue as a going concern does not require a modification of the opinion paragraph. Hence, a qualified opinion would be inappropriate. However, nothing precludes the auditor from disclaiming an opinion in these circumstances.

17.4   Comparative Financial Statements (AU 508)

23. Mead, CPA, had substantial doubt about Tech Co.'s ability to continue as a going concern when reporting on Tech's audited financial statements for the year ended June 30, Year 1. That doubt has been removed in Year 2. What is Mead's reporting responsibility if Tech is presenting its financial statements for the year ended June 30, Year 2, on a comparative basis with those of Year 1?

A. The explanatory paragraph included in the Year 1 auditor's report should not be repeated.

B. The explanatory paragraph included in the Year 1 auditor's report should be repeated in its entirety.

C. A different explanatory paragraph describing Mead's reasons for the removal of doubt should be included.

D. A different explanatory paragraph describing Tech's plans for financial recovery should be included.

Answer (A) is correct. *(CPA, adapted)*
    REQUIRED: The effect on an updated report when substantial doubt about the auditee's ability to continue as a going concern has been removed.
    DISCUSSION: AU 341 indicates that the explanatory paragraph included in the previous report should not be repeated in subsequent reports if the doubt has been resolved.
    Answer (B) is incorrect. The doubt has been resolved, and the current report should not repeat the explanatory paragraph. Answer (C) is incorrect. The reasons for the removal of doubt need not be included. Answer (D) is incorrect. The paragraph should be removed, and a different explanatory paragraph describing the plans for financial recovery is not necessary.

24. How does an auditor make the following representations when issuing the standard auditor's report on comparative financial statements?

	Examination of Evidence on a Test Basis	Consistent Application of Accounting Principles
A.	Explicitly	Explicitly
B.	Implicitly	Implicitly
C.	Implicitly	Explicitly
D.	Explicitly	Implicitly

Answer (D) is correct. *(CPA, adapted)*
    REQUIRED: The required representations when issuing the standard auditor's report on comparative financial statements.
    DISCUSSION: The scope paragraph of the standard auditor's report on comparative statements explicitly states, "An audit includes examining, on a test basis, evidence supporting the amounts and disclosures in the financial statements." Changes in the application of accounting principles are recognized in the audit report by a separate explanatory paragraph. However, when GAAP have been consistently observed, the standard report makes no mention of consistency (AU 508). Thus, consistency is implicit when no explanatory paragraph is included.

25. When a predecessor auditor reissues the report on the prior period's financial statements at the request of the former client, the predecessor should

A. Indicate in the introductory paragraph of the reissued report that the financial statements of the subsequent period were audited by another CPA.

B. Obtain a representation letter from the auditor but not from management.

C. Compare the prior period's financial statements that the predecessor reported on with the financial statements to be presented for comparative purposes.

D. Add an explanatory paragraph to the reissued report stating that the predecessor has not performed additional auditing procedures on the prior period's financial statements.

Answer (C) is correct. *(CPA, adapted)*
    REQUIRED: The procedure performed by the predecessor auditor before reissuing a report.
    DISCUSSION: AU 508 requires the predecessor auditor to perform certain procedures before reissuing a report on prior-period financial statements. (S)he must read the current period's financial statements and compare the prior and current financial statements. Moreover, the predecessor auditor must obtain a representation letter from the auditor stating whether (s)he has discovered matters having a material effect on, or requiring disclosure in, the statements reported on by the predecessor auditor. Finally, the predecessor auditor must obtain a representation letter from management confirming past representations and stating whether post-balance-sheet events require adjustment to or disclosure in the financial statements.
    Answer (A) is incorrect. The reissued report should not refer to another auditor. Answer (B) is incorrect. The predecessor auditor should obtain a representation letter from the auditor and from management. Answer (D) is incorrect. The report should not be modified unless the auditor's previous conclusions have changed.

26. When reporting on comparative financial statements, an auditor ordinarily should change the previously expressed opinion on the prior year's financial statements if the

    A. Prior year's financial statements are restated to conform with generally accepted accounting principles.

    B. Auditor is a predecessor auditor who has been requested by a former client to reissue the previously issued report.

    C. Prior year's opinion was unqualified and the opinion on the current year's financial statements is modified due to a lack of consistency.

    D. Reporting entity has changed as a result of the sale of a subsidiary.

Answer (A) is correct. *(CPA, adapted)*
    REQUIRED: The event that causes an auditor to change a previously expressed opinion.
    DISCUSSION: If the previous opinion was modified because of a departure from GAAP, but the prior year's statements were restated to remove the basis for the modification, the updated report should express an unqualified opinion.
    Answer (B) is incorrect. The predecessor's report normally should be reissued with the original report date without revision, if the report is still appropriate. Answer (C) is incorrect. A change in accounting principle in the current period has no effect on the opinion expressed in the prior year. Answer (D) is incorrect. A change in the reporting entity resulting from a transaction or event, for example, a purchase or disposition of a business unit, does not require inclusion in the audit report of an explanatory paragraph about consistency (AU 420). Furthermore, such a transaction or event in the current year is not a circumstance that affects the prior period's statements. Thus, it presents no basis for modifying the opinion expressed on those statements.

27. The predecessor auditor, who is satisfied after properly communicating with the current auditor, has reissued a report because the audit client desires comparative financial statements. The predecessor auditor's report should

    A. Refer to the report of the current auditor only in the scope paragraph.

    B. Refer to the work of the current auditor in the scope and opinion paragraphs.

    C. Refer to both the work and the report of the current auditor only in the opinion paragraph.

    D. Not refer to the report or the work of the current auditor.

Answer (D) is correct. *(CPA, adapted)*
    REQUIRED: The true statement about reference to the current auditor in a reissued report.
    DISCUSSION: A predecessor auditor who has been asked to reissue his/her report should (1) read the current-period statements, (2) compare the statements (s)he reported on with other statements to be presented comparatively, (3) obtain a representation letter from the auditor, and (4) obtain a representation letter from management. The predecessor auditor also may wish to consider the professional reputation and standing of the auditor and other matters discussed in AU 543. However, the reissued report should not refer to the report or work of the auditor.

28. Jewel, CPA, audited Infinite Co.'s prior-year financial statements. These statements are presented with those of the current year for comparative purposes without Jewel's auditor's report, which expressed a qualified opinion. In drafting the current year's auditor's report, Crain, CPA, the current auditor, should

I.   Not name Jewel as the predecessor auditor

II. Indicate the type of report issued by Jewel

III. Indicate the substantive reasons for Jewel's qualification

    A. I only.

    B. I and II only.

    C. II and III only.

    D. I, II, and III.

Answer (D) is correct. *(CPA, adapted)*
    REQUIRED: The matter(s) included in an auditor's report.
    DISCUSSION: The auditor should state in the introductory paragraph that the prior year's financial statements were audited by another auditor but should not give the name of the predecessor auditor. (S)he should give the date and the type of report and, if the report was modified, the reasons for modification. If the predecessor auditor expressed a qualified opinion, the nature of and the reasons for the opinion qualification should be described.

29. In auditing the financial statements of Star Corp., Land discovered information leading Land to believe that Star's prior-year financial statements, which were audited by Tell, require substantial revisions. Under these circumstances, Land should

   A. Notify Star's audit committee and shareholders that the prior year's financial statements cannot be relied on.

   B. Request Star to reissue the prior year's financial statements with the appropriate revisions.

   C. Notify Tell about the information and make inquiries about the integrity of Star's management.

   D. Request Star to arrange a meeting among the three parties to resolve the matter.

Answer (D) is correct. *(CPA, adapted)*
REQUIRED: The auditor's action when financial statements from a prior period require revision.
DISCUSSION: Because the prior year's financial statements appear to require restatement, the auditor should discuss the matter with the predecessor auditor. (S)he should communicate any information that the predecessor auditor may need to meet the responsibilities imposed by AU 561, *Subsequent Discovery of Facts Existing at the Date of the Auditor's Report*. AU 315 states that a meeting of the three parties should be requested.
Answer (A) is incorrect. The auditor need not notify shareholders. Answer (B) is incorrect. The financial statements should not be revised until the parties have discussed the matter. Answer (C) is incorrect. The auditor should request that the client communicate with the prior auditor.

30. When unaudited financial statements are presented in comparative form with audited financial statements in a document filed with the Securities and Exchange Commission, such statements should be

	Marked as "Unaudited"	Withheld until Audited	Referred to in the Auditor's Report
A.	Yes	No	No
B.	Yes	No	Yes
C.	No	Yes	Yes
D.	No	Yes	No

Answer (A) is correct. *(CPA, adapted)*
REQUIRED: The treatment of unaudited statements presented comparatively with audited statements in a document filed with the SEC.
DISCUSSION: AU 504 states, "When unaudited financial statements are presented in comparative form with audited statements in documents filed with the Securities and Exchange Commission, such statements should be clearly marked as 'unaudited' but should not be referred to in the auditor's report."

31. When unaudited financial statements of a nonissuer are presented in comparative form with audited financial statements in the subsequent year, the unaudited financial statements should be clearly marked to indicate their status and

I. The report on the unaudited financial statements should be reissued.

II. The report on the audited financial statements should include a separate paragraph describing the responsibility assumed for the unaudited financial statements.

   A. I only.

   B. II only.

   C. Neither I nor II.

   D. Either I or II.

Answer (D) is correct. *(CPA, adapted)*
REQUIRED: The appropriate reporting when unaudited financial statements are presented in comparative form with audited financial statements.
DISCUSSION: When unaudited financial statements are presented comparatively with audited statements in a document not filed with the SEC, the statements that have not been audited should be clearly marked to indicate their status. Moreover, either (1) the report on the prior period should be reissued, or (2) the report on the current period should include as a separate paragraph an appropriate description of the responsibility assumed for the financial statements of the prior period. If the statements are filed with the SEC (i.e., when the filer is an issuer), the unaudited statements must not be referred to in the auditor's report (AU 504).
Answer (A) is incorrect. Alternative II is allowed. Answer (B) is incorrect. Alternative I is allowed. Answer (C) is incorrect. Either form of recognition is appropriate.

17.5 Emphasis of a Matter (AU 508)

32. An auditor includes a separate paragraph in an otherwise unmodified report to emphasize that the entity being reported on had significant transactions with related parties. The inclusion of this separate paragraph

A. Is considered an "except for" qualification of the opinion.

B. Violates generally accepted auditing standards if this information is already disclosed in notes to the financial statements.

C. Necessitates a revision of the opinion paragraph to include the phrase "with the foregoing explanation."

D. Is appropriate and would not negate the unqualified opinion.

Answer (D) is correct. *(CPA, adapted)*
REQUIRED: The effect of a separate paragraph in an otherwise unmodified report.
DISCUSSION: A matter regarding the financial statements may be emphasized in a separate paragraph without modifying the auditor's opinion on the financial statements. Matters to be emphasized might include that the entity is a component of a larger enterprise or that it has had significant related party transactions. Subsequent events and accounting matters affecting comparability (e.g., a divestiture) are other matters suitable for this treatment.
Answer (A) is incorrect. If the opinion were modified with an "except for" qualification, the opinion would not be "otherwise unmodified." Answer (B) is incorrect. The auditor can emphasize a matter without violating GAAS. Answer (C) is incorrect. The phrase "with the foregoing explanation" would create doubt as to whether the report was intended to be qualified.

33. An auditor includes an explanatory paragraph in an otherwise unmodified report to emphasize that the financial statements are not comparable with those of prior years because of a court-ordered divestiture that is already fully explained in the notes to the financial statements. The inclusion of this paragraph

A. Should be followed by a consistency modification in the opinion paragraph.

B. Requires a revision of the opinion paragraph to include the phrase "with the foregoing explanation."

C. Is not appropriate and may confuse the readers or lead them to believe the report was qualified.

D. Is appropriate and would not negate the unqualified opinion.

Answer (D) is correct. *(CPA, adapted)*
REQUIRED: The effect on the report of including an explanatory paragraph to emphasize a matter.
DISCUSSION: An auditor may emphasize a matter in an explanatory paragraph and express an unqualified opinion. Matters to be emphasized might include that the entity is a component of a larger enterprise, or that it has had significant related party transactions. Accounting matters affecting comparability, other than a change in principle, and subsequent events are other matters suitable for this treatment (AU 508). Thus, a divestiture is appropriate for emphasis because it affects comparability. However, a change in the reporting entity resulting from a transaction or event or the creation, cessation, or complete or partial purchase or disposition of a subsidiary or other business unit, does not require that an explanatory paragraph about consistency be included in the auditor's report (AU 420).
Answer (A) is incorrect. A change in the reporting entity as a result of a divestiture does not require a consistency modification of any part of the report. Moreover, lack of consistency, by itself, does not justify an opinion modification. Answer (B) is incorrect. The phrase "with the foregoing explanation" is an inappropriate form of reporting. Answer (C) is incorrect. Confusion is avoided by not modifying the opinion paragraph.

Use the additional questions in Gleim **CPA Test Prep Online** to create Test Sessions that emulate Prometric!

17.6 PRACTICE SIMULATION

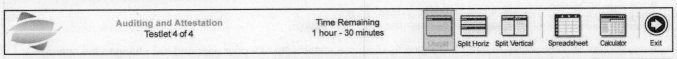

	Auditing and Attestation Testlet 4 of 4	Time Remaining 1 hour - 30 minutes	Unsplit	Split Horiz	Split Vertical	Spreadsheet	Calculator	Exit

DIRECTIONS

Note: If you believe you have encountered a software malfunction, report it to the test center staff immediately.

Navigation

To navigate from task to task, use the controls at the bottom of the screen. Click on the **Next** button to advance to the next task, or the **Previous** button to go to the previous task. To go directly to any task, click on its number.

▼ = Reminder		Directions	1	2	3	4	5	6	7		◀ Previous	Next ▶
			▽	▽	▽	▽	▽	▽	▽			

If you would like a reminder to revisit a task, or want to indicate that you are finished with it, click on the reminder flag below the task number. To clear the flag, click on it again. Reminder flags are for your use only – they do not contribute to your score.

Tabs

In this part of the examination, you will be asked to complete various tasks. Every task has one or more **Work Tabs**. Some tasks have one or more **Information Tabs**, others may have none. Every task has a **Help** tab.

If a task has **Information Tabs**, you may use the information in them to complete your responses in the **Work Tabs**.

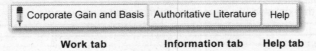

	Corporate Gain and Basis	Authoritative Literature	Help

Work tab	**Information tab**	**Help tab**

Work Tabs:

- **Work Tabs** are identified with a pencil icon. This is where your responses are expected.
- Each task has one or more **Work Tabs**.
- **Work Tabs** contain directions for completing the task – be sure to read these directions carefully.
- The **Work Tab** name in the example above is for illustration only – yours will differ.
- You must complete all of the **Work Tabs** in each task to receive full credit.

Information Tabs:

- The Authoritative Literature will be provided in all tasks in the AUD, FAR, and REG sections for your reference.
- Your simulation may have one or more additional **Information Tabs**. Like the Authoritative Literature tabs, **Information Tabs** do not have a pencil icon.
- If your task has additional **Information Tabs**, go through each to familiarize yourself with the task content.

Help Tab:

- The **Help Tab** provides assistance with the exam software that is used in this task. For example, if the task is to compose a memorandum, **Help** will provide information about the word processor.

The Toolbar

The toolbar at the top of the screen shows the amount of time remaining for you to complete the tasks. In addition, the following tools are available. Note that only the Exit button is displayed when Directions are visible - the others will appear when you begin the tasks.

Click on these buttons to split or unsplit the screen. You can split the screen vertically or horizontally.

Click on this button to display the calculator; click on it again to hide the calculator. To move the calculator, click on the calculator title bar and drag the calculator to the desired location.

Click on this button to use the spreadsheet; click on it again to hide the spreadsheet. To move the spreadsheet, click on the the spreadsheet title bar and drag the spreadsheet to the desired location.

Click on this button to go on to the next part of the examination. You must complete all of the tasks to receive full credit. Once you click on **Exit** and confirm the action, you will NOT be able to return to this testlet.

▼ = Reminder		Directions	1	2	3	4	5		◀ Previous	Next ▶
			▽	▽	▽	▽	▽			

An auditor has become aware of events affecting the financial statements of a prior year and has changed the opinion from unqualified to qualified. Indicate by checking the appropriate box whether the current year's report on the comparative financial statements should address each of the issues below.

Issue	Yes	No
1. The audit procedure used to discover the event causing the change of opinion in the auditor's report.		
2. The date of the previous auditor's report.		
3. The substantive reason for the change of opinion in the auditor's report.		
4. The type of opinion previously expressed.		
5. Indication that the updated opinion differs from that previously expressed.		
6. The reason the auditor did not discover the event in the previous year.		
7. Management's response to the change of opinion.		
8. Identification of the event that caused the change of opinion.		
9. The effect that the change of opinion will likely have on future periods.		
10. The date that the event that caused the change of opinion was discovered.		

A new staff auditor has drafted the paragraph below, which is intended to be added to the audit report of JKL Company about going concern issues. For each of the statements below, indicate whether it is true or false by checking the appropriate box.

> The accompanying financial statements have been prepared assuming that the JKL Company will continue as a going concern. As discussed in Note X to the audit report, JKL Company has suffered recurring losses from operations and has a net capital deficiency. If these losses continue, there will be some doubt about its ability to continue as a going concern. Management has plans to deal with these issues. The financial statements do not include any adjustments that might result from the outcome of this uncertainty.

Statement	True	False
1. The paragraph should be placed after the opinion paragraph of the auditor's report.		
2. It is appropriate to include a note in the audit report.		
3. The phrase "If these losses continue" is appropriate.		
4. The phrase "some doubt" should be replaced with "substantial doubt."		
5. Management's plans to deal with the issues should have a reference to a note that discusses them.		
6. The phrase "continue as a going concern" should be replaced with the phrase "remain profitable."		
7. The phrase "any adjustments that might result" is inappropriate.		
8. If the auditor was satisfied with the plans that management has to deal with the uncertainly, no paragraph need be added to the audit report.		
9. The auditor's going concern reference in the audit report is an opinion qualification.		
10. The auditor should follow up in months following the issuance of the report to keep it updated for new information about the going concern issues.		

The second standard of reporting applies to various types of accounting changes. It states, "The auditor must identify in the auditor's report those circumstances in which such principles have not been consistently observed in the current period in relation to the preceding period." Assume that the following changes have a material effect on the financial statements for the current year.

Three answers are required for each of the eight accounting changes.

- In column 1, fill in the letter of the type of change [A) through H)] that best matches each accounting change.
- In column 2, write M) if any modification is required in the auditor's report as it relates to the second standard of reporting or write N) if no modification is required.
- In column 3, write R) if the accounting change should be retrospectively applied to the prior year's financial statements presented in comparative form with the current year's statements. Also write R) if restatement is required. Write S) if no retrospective application or restatement is necessary.
- Assume that all changes are practicable unless otherwise indicated.
- Each choice may be used once, more than once, or not at all.

1	2	3	Accounting Changes
			1. A change from the completed-contract method to the percentage-of-completion method of accounting for long-term construction contracts
			2. A change in the estimated useful life of previously recorded fixed assets based on newly acquired information
			3. Correction of a mathematical error in inventory pricing made in the prior period
			4. A change from prime costing to full absorption costing for inventory measurement
			5. A change from presentation of statements of individual companies to presentation of consolidated statements
			6. A change in the method of depreciation
			7. A change to including the employer share of FICA taxes as *Retirement Benefits* on the income statement from including it with *Other Taxes*
			8. A change from the FIFO method of inventory pricing to the LIFO method of inventory pricing when it is impracticable to determine the cumulative effect on the period prior to the period of change

1) Types of Changes
A) Change in accounting estimate
B) Change from GAAP to GAAP
C) Correction of an error in principle
D) Change in reporting entity
E) Change in accounting estimate inseparable from change in principle
F) Change in classification
G) Correction of an error not involving a principle
H) New and different transactions

2) Modification Choices
M) Modification Required
N) No Modification Required

3) Restatement Choices
R) Retrospective Application or Restatement Required
S) No Retrospective Application or Restatement Required

Other Independent Auditors | Authoritative Literature | Help

The CPA firm's partner in charge is reviewing a draft of a paragraph that is intended to go into an audit report. The paragraph describes the use of an audit report prepared by other independent auditors on a client's subsidiary in forming an opinion on the client's statements. The draft is as follows:

> We did not audit the financial statements of D Company, which is a wholly owned subsidiary. Those statements were prepared by other auditors, and our opinion is based solely on the report of the other auditors.

This question is presented in a check-the-box format. Indicate which of the following statements about the draft paragraph are true or false by checking the appropriate box.

Statement	True	False
1. The paragraph is a qualification of the audit opinion.		
2. It is appropriate to divide responsibility with other auditors in a report.		
3. The proposed paragraph will be presented in the scope paragraph of the audit report.		
4. The paragraph should give the percentages or amounts audited by the other auditors.		
5. The paragraph should state that the financial statements were audited by other auditors.		
6. It is acceptable to base the audit opinion solely on the report of other auditors.		
7. The paragraph should indicate the date of the other auditor's report.		
8. The other auditor's name must appear in the paragraph.		
9. The principal auditor's report should refer to the other auditor in the opinion paragraph of the report as well as in the draft paragraph.		
10. The paragraph should state whether the principal auditor concurs with the opinion of the other auditor.		

▼ = Reminder   Directions   1 2 3 [4] 5   ◀ Previous   Next ▶

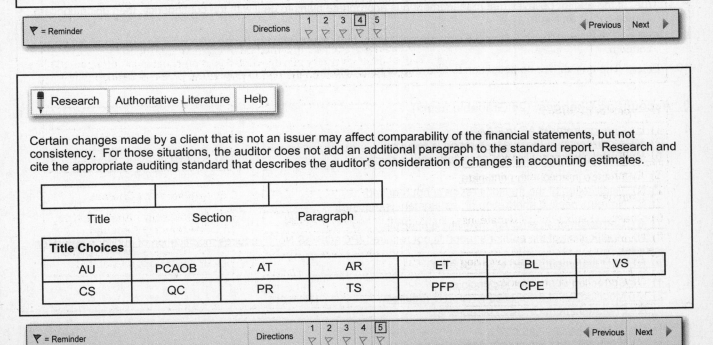

Research | Authoritative Literature | Help

Certain changes made by a client that is not an issuer may affect comparability of the financial statements, but not consistency. For those situations, the auditor does not add an additional paragraph to the standard report. Research and cite the appropriate auditing standard that describes the auditor's consideration of changes in accounting estimates.

Title	Section	Paragraph

Title Choices

AU	PCAOB	AT	AR	ET	BL	VS
CS	QC	PR	TS	PFP	CPE	

▼ = Reminder   Directions   1 2 3 4 [5]   ◀ Previous   Next ▶

Unofficial Answers

1. Change of Opinion from Previous Year (10 Gradable Items)

1. <u>No.</u> The procedure used to discover the event should not be disclosed in the audit report.

2. <u>Yes.</u> A paragraph should be added to the current year's report that describes the issues, including the date of the previous report.

3. <u>Yes.</u> A paragraph should be added to the current year's report that describes the issues, including the substantive reason for the change in the previous year's opinion.

4. <u>Yes.</u> A paragraph should be added to the current year's report that describes the issues, including the type of opinion previously expressed.

5. <u>Yes.</u> A paragraph should be added to the current year's report that describes the issues, including that the updated opinion differs from that previously expressed.

6. <u>No.</u> The reason the auditor did not discover the event in the previous year should not be disclosed in the report.

7. <u>No.</u> No comments or responses from management should be included in the report.

8. <u>Yes.</u> A paragraph should be added to the current year's report that describes the issues, including a description of the event causing the change in opinion.

9. <u>No.</u> The report should not forecast the future effects of the change in opinion.

10. <u>No.</u> The date that the event that caused the change of opinion was discovered should not be disclosed in the report.

2. Going Concern (10 Gradable Items)

1. <u>True.</u> An additional paragraph identifying going concern issues should follow the opinion paragraph.

2. <u>False.</u> Notes are used for disclosures in financial statements, not audit reports.

3. <u>False.</u> It is not acceptable to include a contingent statement in a going concern paragraph.

4. <u>True.</u> The phrase "substantial doubt" should be used in the paragraph.

5. <u>True.</u> More detail should be provided about management's plans and that is typically provided in a note to the financial statements.

6. <u>False.</u> The phrase "continue as a going concern" is appropriate to use in the paragraph.

7. <u>False.</u> The phrase "any adjustments that might result" is appropriate to use in the paragraph.

8. <u>True.</u> If the auditor believes that management has appropriate plans to deal with the contingency, then going concern should not be an issue.

9. <u>False.</u> The opinion that the financial statements present fairly is not affected by the additional paragraph about going concern.

10. <u>False.</u> The auditor has no obligation to follow up or to update the report for new information about going concern.

3. Accounting Changes (24 Gradable Items)

1. <u>1) B) Change from GAAP to GAAP.</u>
    <u>2) M) Modification of the auditor's report is required.</u>
    <u>3) R) Retrospective application or restatement is required.</u>

2. <u>1) A) Change in accounting estimate.</u>
    <u>2) N) Modification of the auditor's report is not required.</u>
    <u>3) S) No retrospective application or restatement is required.</u>

3. <u>1) G) Correction of an error not involving a principle.</u>
    <u>2) N) Modification of the auditor's report is not required (PCAOB AS No. 6 requires modification of auditor's report for issuers).</u>
    <u>3) R) Prior statements need to be restated.</u>

4. <u>1) C) Correction of an error in principle.</u>
    <u>2) M) Modification of the auditor's report is required.</u>
    <u>3) R) Prior statements need to be restated.</u>

5. <u>1) D) Change in reporting entity.</u>
    <u>2) M) Modification of the auditor's report is required.</u>
    <u>3) R) Retrospective application is required.</u>

6.   1) E) Change in accounting estimate inseparable from change in principle.
      2) M) Modification of the auditor's report is required.
      3) S) No retrospective application or restatement is required.

7.   1) F) Change in classification.
      2) N) Modification of the auditor's report is not required.
      3) S) No retrospective application or restatement is required.

8.   1) B) Change from GAAP to GAAP.
      2) M) Modification of the auditor's report is required.
      3) S) No retrospective application or restatement is required.

4. Other Independent Auditors (10 Gradable Items)

1.   False. The paragraph is a division of reporting responsibility.

2.   True. It is acceptable for a principal auditor to divide responsibility with other auditors.

3.   False. This statement would be included in the introductory paragraph. However, the other auditors are also mentioned in the scope and opinion paragraph.

4.   True. The statement should include the percentages or dollar amounts audited by other auditors.

5.   True. The paragraph should state that the financial statements were audited, not prepared, by other auditors.

6.   False. It is appropriate to base the opinion on the portion of the financial statements audited by other auditors solely on their work, but not the whole opinion.

7.   False. The statement need not indicate the date of the other auditor's report.

8.   False. The other auditor's name should not appear unless that report is also presented.

9.   True. The other auditor is mentioned in the introduction, scope, and opinion paragraphs.

10.   False. The principal auditor would not include a statement about concurrence with the other auditor's opinion.

5. Research (1 Gradable Item)

Answer: 420.15

AU Section 420 -- *Consistency of Application of Generally Accepted Accounting Principles*

Change in Accounting Estimate

.15 Accounting estimates (such as service lives and salvage values of depreciable assets and provisions for warranty costs, uncollectible receivables, and inventory obsolescence) are necessary in the preparation of financial statements. Accounting estimates change as new events occur and as additional experience and information are acquired. This type of accounting change is required by altered conditions that affect comparability but do not involve the consistency standard. The independent auditor, in addition to becoming satisfied with respect to the conditions giving rise to the change in accounting estimate, should determine that the change does not include the effect of a change in accounting principle. Provided the auditor is so satisfied, she or he need not comment on the change in the report. However, an accounting change of this type having a material effect on the financial statements may require disclosure in a note to the financial statements.

Gleim Simulation Grading

Task	Correct Responses		Gradable Items		Score per Task
1	_____	÷	10	=	_____
2	_____	÷	10	=	_____
3	_____	÷	24	=	_____
4	_____	÷	10	=	_____
Research	_____	÷	1	=	_____

Total of Scores per Task	_____
÷ Total Number of Tasks	5
Total Score	_____ %

Use **CPA Gleim Online** and **Simulation Wizard** to practice more task-based simulations in a realistic environment.

STUDY UNIT EIGHTEEN
REVIEW, COMPILATION, AND SPECIAL REPORTS

(21 pages of outline)

Review and compilation services are provided in conjunction with the dissemination of financial statements. These services are not as comprehensive as an audit (which provides positive assurance that financial statements are presented fairly in accordance with GAAP). Those performed with respect to unaudited financial statements (except for reviews of interim financial information subject to AU 722) are governed by Statements on Standards for Accounting and Review Services (SSARSs), which are codified as AR 60, 80, 90, etc. AR 80 and AR 90 are the basic pronouncements on compilations and reviews and are outlined in the first two subunits.

Regardless of the service provided, the CPA should establish an **understanding with the entity**, preferably in writing, describing the nature and limitations of the services to be performed and the report to be issued. The understanding also should provide that the engagement is not intended to detect errors, fraud, or illegal acts. The CPA must be **independent** to perform a review but need not be independent to perform a compilation.

The effective study of **special reports** requires little additional effort. The basis of virtually all special reports is the standard, three-paragraph audit report (one more reason to memorize the standard audit report). Several of these reports have been tested on the exam. Most often, statements prepared on a cash basis (an other comprehensive basis of accounting, or OCBOA) have been the subject of questions. In general, if an auditor can form an opinion on the fairness of (1) financial information prepared on an OCBOA; (2) specified elements, accounts, or items; or (3) information presented in other formats, the auditor can express an opinion on the fairness of the presentation.

18.1 COMPILATION (AR 80)

1. A compilation is a service with the objective of assisting management in presenting financial information in the form of financial statements **without undertaking to obtain or provide any assurance.**

   a. Although a compilation is not an assurance engagement, it is considered an attest engagement because it falls under that set of standards.

2. A compilation differs significantly from a review or an audit of financial statements. As codified by AR 80, a compilation can be contrasted with a review and an audit as follows:

Compilation	Review	Audit
No Assurance	Limited Assurance	Positive Assurance

   a. A compilation does not contemplate performing inquiries, analytical procedures, or other procedures performed in a review.

   b. Additionally, a compilation does not contemplate (1) obtaining an understanding of the entity's internal control; (2) assessing fraud risk; (3) testing accounting records by obtaining sufficient appropriate audit evidence through inspection, observation, and confirmation; or (4) examining source documents.

   c. Compilations are typically performed for nonissuers.

3. The accountant should establish an **understanding** with management regarding the services to be performed for compilation engagements and should document the understanding through a written communication with management (e.g., an **engagement letter**).

4. **Understanding of the Entity and Industry**

   a. The accountant should possess an understanding of the industry in which the client operates, including the accounting principles and practices generally used in the industry. This understanding should be sufficient to enable the accountant to compile financial statements that are appropriate in form for an entity operating in that industry.

      1) Lack of knowledge **does not prevent the accountant from accepting a compilation engagement** for an entity in an industry with which the accountant has no previous experience. It does, however, place upon the accountant a responsibility to obtain the required level of knowledge.

   b. The accountant should obtain knowledge about the client, including an understanding of the client's business and accounting principles and practices used by the client.

      1) The accountant should obtain an understanding of the accounting principles and practices used by the client in **measuring, recognizing, recording, and disclosing** all significant accounts and disclosures in the financial statements.

5. **Compilation Procedures**

   a. **Reading the financial statements.** Before submission of the statements to the client or others, the accountant **should read the financial statements** and consider whether such financial statements appear to be appropriate in form and free from obvious material errors.

   b. **Other compilation procedures.** The accountant is **not required to make inquiries or perform other procedures** to verify, corroborate, or review information supplied by the entity. However, the accountant may have made inquiries or performed other procedures.

      1) The results of such inquiries or procedures, knowledge gained from prior engagements, or the financial statements on their face may cause the accountant to become aware that information supplied by the entity is **incorrect, incomplete, or otherwise unsatisfactory** or that fraud or an illegal act may have occurred.

         a) The accountant should request that management consider the effect of these matters on the financial statements and communicate the results of such consideration to the accountant.

         b) If the entity refuses to provide additional or revised information, the accountant should **withdraw** from the engagement.

6. **Documentation.** The accountant should prepare documentation (working papers) in connection with each compilation engagement to include

   a. The **engagement letter** documenting the understanding with the client
   b. Any **findings or issues** that, in the accountant's judgment, are significant
   c. Communications, whether oral or written, to the appropriate level of management regarding **fraud or illegal acts** that come to the accountant's attention

7. **Standard Compilation Report**

   a. The standard compilation report contains three paragraphs. (We recommend that you study the following report to understand its components and the general wording and use of each paragraph.)

EXAMPLE

Accountant's Compilation Report

To the Owners of XYZ Company:

I (we) have compiled the accompanying balance sheet of XYZ Company as of December 31, 20XX, and the related statements of income, retained earnings, and cash flows for the year then ended. I (we) have not audited or reviewed the accompanying financial statements and, accordingly, do not express an opinion or provide any assurance about whether the financial statements are in accordance with accounting principles generally accepted in the United States of America.

Management (owners) is (are) responsible for the preparation and fair presentation of the financial statements in accordance with accounting principles generally accepted in the United States of America and for designing, implementing, and maintaining internal control relevant to the preparation and fair presentation of the financial statements.

My (our) responsibility is to conduct the compilation in accordance with Statements on Standards for Accounting and Review Services issued by the American Institute of Certified Public Accountants. The objective of a compilation is to assist management in presenting financial information in the form of financial statements without undertaking to obtain or provide any assurance that there are no material modifications that should be made to the financial statements.

Signature of accounting firm or accountant   <---------- May be manual, stamped, electronic, or typed

Date   <---------- Date of completion of review procedures

---

    b.   Each page of the financial statements should include the statement "See accountant's compilation report."

    c.   Financial statements prepared in accordance with an other comprehensive basis of accounting (OCBOA) are not considered appropriate in form unless the financial statements include

        1)   A description of the OCBOA, including a summary of significant accounting policies and a description of the primary differences from generally accepted accounting principles (GAAP). The effects of the differences need not be quantified.

        2)   Informative disclosures similar to those required by GAAP.

8.   **Reporting on Financial Statements That Omit Substantially All Disclosures**

    a.   An entity may request the accountant to compile financial statements that omit substantially all the disclosures required by an applicable financial reporting framework. The accountant may compile such financial statements provided that the omission of substantially all disclosures is not, to his/her knowledge, undertaken with the intention of misleading those who might reasonably be expected to use such financial statements.

    b.   When reporting on financial statements that omit substantially all disclosures, the accountant should include in the compilation report after the paragraph describing the accountant's responsibility a paragraph with the following elements:

        1)   A statement that management has elected to omit substantially all the disclosures

        2)   A statement that if the omitted disclosures (and statement of cash flows, if applicable) were included in the financial statements, they might influence the user's conclusions about the company's financial position, results of operations, and cash flows

        3)   A statement that the financial statements are not designed for those who are not informed about such matters

    c.   When the entity wishes to include disclosures about only a few matters in the form of notes to the financial statements, such disclosures should be labeled "Selected Information – Substantially All Disclosures Required by Accepted Accounting Principles Generally Accepted in the United States of America Are Not Included."

9.   **Reporting When the Accountant Is Not Independent**

    a.   When the accountant is issuing a report on a compilation of financial statements for an entity from which (s)he is not independent, the accountant's **report should be modified**. The accountant should indicate his/her lack of independence in a **final paragraph** of the accountant's compilation report.

        1)   For example, such a disclosure might be

> I am (We are) not independent with respect to XYZ Company.

    b.   The accountant **may disclose the reason(s)** that his/her independence is impaired. For example, such a disclosure might be

> I am (We are) not independent with respect to XYZ Company as of and for the year ended December 31, 20XX, because I (a member of the engagement team) had a direct financial interest in XYZ Company.

        1)   If the accountant elects to disclose a description about the reasons his/her independence is impaired, the accountant should ensure that **all reasons** are included in the description.

10.   When the compiled financial statements are not expected to be used by a third party, the accountant **is not required to issue a compilation report**. The accountant should include a reference on each page of the financial statements restricting their use, such as "Restricted for management's use only," or "Solely for the information and use by the management of [name of entity] and not intended to be and should not be used by any other party."

11.   The accountant may **emphasize a matter** in the compilation report. Such explanatory information should be presented in a **separate paragraph** of the accountant's report.

    a.   Emphasis paragraphs are **never required**; they may be added solely at the accountant's discretion.

    b.   Examples of matters that the accountant may wish to emphasize are

        1)   Uncertainties

        2)   That the entity is a component of a larger business enterprise

        3)   That the entity has had significant transactions with related parties

        4)   Unusually important subsequent events

        5)   Accounting matters, other than those involving a change or changes in accounting principles, affecting the comparability of the financial statements with those of the preceding period

    c.   Because an emphasis-of-matter paragraph should not be used in lieu of management disclosures, the accountant should not include an emphasis paragraph in a compilation report on financial statements that omit substantially all disclosures unless the matter is disclosed in the financial statements.

12.   **Departures from GAAP or Other Applicable Financial Reporting Framework**

    a.   If the accountant concludes that modification of the standard report is appropriate because of a departure from GAAP, the departure should be **disclosed in a separate paragraph** of the report, including disclosure of the effects of the departure on the financial statements if such effects have been determined by management or are known as the result of the accountant's procedures.

        1)   The accountant is not required to determine the effects of a departure if management has not done so, provided that the accountant states in the report that such determination has not been made.

EXAMPLE -- Language to Modify Report for a Departure from GAAP

During our compilation, I (we) did become aware of a departure (certain departures) from accounting principles generally accepted in the United States of America that is (are) described in the following paragraph:

As disclosed in Note X to the financial statements, accounting principles generally accepted in the United States of America require that land be stated at cost. Management has informed me (us) that the company has stated its land at appraised value and that, if accounting principles generally accepted in the United States of America had been followed, the land account and stockholders' equity would have been decreased by $500,000.

---

    b. If the accountant believes that modification of the standard report is not adequate to indicate the deficiencies in the financial statements as a whole, the accountant should **withdraw** from the compilation engagement and provide no further services with respect to those financial statements.

        1) There is **no adverse** compilation report.

        2) The accountant may wish to consult with his/her legal counsel upon withdrawal.

13. **General-Use and Restricted-Use Reports**

    a. The term **general use** applies to accountants' reports that are not restricted to specified parties. Accountants' reports on financial statements prepared in conformity with an applicable financial reporting framework ordinarily are not restricted regarding use. However, nothing in this section precludes the accountant from restricting the use of any report.

    b. The term **restricted use** applies to accountants' reports intended only for one or more specified third parties.

        1) The need for restriction on the use of a report may result from a number of circumstances, including, but not limited to, the purpose of the report and the potential for the report to be misunderstood when taken out of the context in which it was intended to be used.

    c. The accountant should restrict the use of a report when the subject matter of the report or the presentation being reported on is based on measurement or disclosure criteria contained in contractual agreements or regulatory provisions that are not in conformity with an applicable financial reporting framework.

    d. If the accountant issues a single combined report covering both (1) subject matter or presentations that require a restriction on use to specified parties and (2) subject matter or presentations that ordinarily do not require such a restriction, the use of such a single combined report **should be restricted** to the specified parties.

    e. The accountant should consider informing the client that restricted-use reports are not intended for distribution to nonspecified parties, regardless of whether they are included in a document containing a separate general-use report.

    f. An accountant's restricted-use report should contain a **separate paragraph at the end of the report** that states the restriction.

14. **An Entity's Ability to Continue as a Going Concern**

    a. During the performance of compilation procedures, evidence or information may come to the accountant's attention indicating that an uncertainty may exist about the entity's ability to continue as a going concern for a reasonable period of time, not to exceed 1 year beyond the date of the financial statements being compiled (referred to as a **reasonable period of time**). In those circumstances, the accountant should request that management consider the possible effects of the going concern uncertainty on the financial statements, including the need for related disclosure.

    b. After management communicates to the accountant the results of its consideration of the possible effects on the financial statements, the accountant should consider the reasonableness of management's conclusions, including the adequacy of the related disclosures, if applicable.

   c.   If the accountant determines that management's conclusions are unreasonable or the disclosure of the uncertainty regarding the entity's ability to continue as a going concern is not adequate, a deviation from GAAP (or other framework) has occurred, and (s)he should follow the guidance in item 12. of this subunit.

   d.   The accountant may emphasize an uncertainty about an entity's ability to continue as a going concern, provided that the uncertainty is disclosed in the financial statements.

15. **Subsequent Events**

   a.   If the accountant learns of subsequent events that could affect the financial statements, (s)he should request that management consider the possible effects, including the adequacy of any related disclosure, if applicable.

   b.   If the accountant determines that the subsequent event is not adequately accounted for in the financial statements or disclosed in the notes, (s)he should follow the guidance in item 12. of this subunit.

16. **Subsequent Discovery of Facts Existing at the Date of the Report**

   a.   After the date of the accountant's compilation report, the accountant has no obligation to perform other compilation procedures with respect to the financial statements unless new information comes to his/her attention. However, when the accountant becomes aware of information that relates to financial statements previously reported on by him/her, but that **was not known** to the accountant at the date of the report (and that is of such a nature and from such a source that the accountant would have investigated it had it come to his/her attention during the course of the compilation), the accountant should, as soon as practicable, undertake to determine whether the information is reliable and whether the facts existed at the date of the report.

   b.   The accountant should **discuss the matter** with his/her client at whatever management levels the accountant deems appropriate and request cooperation in whatever investigation may be necessary. In addition to management, the accountant may deem it appropriate to discuss the matter with those charged with governance.

   c.   When the accountant has concluded that action should be taken to prevent further use of the accountant's report or the financial statements, the accountant should advise his/her client to make appropriate disclosure of the newly discovered facts and their impact on the financial statements to persons who are known to be currently using or who are likely to use the financial statements.

   d.   If the client refuses to make the suitable disclosures, the accountant should notify the appropriate personnel at the highest levels within the entity, such as the manager (owner) or those charged with governance, of such refusal and of the fact that, in the absence of disclosure by the client, the accountant should take steps to prevent further use of the financial statements and the accountant's report.

17. When the basic financial statements are accompanied by information presented for **supplementary** analysis purposes, the accountant should clearly indicate the degree of responsibility, if any, (s)he is taking with respect to such information.

18. **Fraud and Illegal Acts**

   a.   When evidence or information comes to the accountant's attention during the performance of compilation procedures that **fraud or an illegal act** may have occurred, that matter should be brought to the attention of the **appropriate level of management**. The accountant need not report matters regarding illegal acts that are clearly inconsequential.

   b.   The communication may be oral or written. If the communication is oral, the accountant should document it.

    c.   When matters regarding fraud or an illegal act involve an owner of the business, the accountant should consider **resigning** from the engagement.

    d.   The disclosure of any evidence or information that comes to the accountant's attention during the performance of compilation procedures that fraud or an illegal act may have occurred to parties other than the client's senior management (or those charged with governance, if applicable) ordinarily **is not part of the accountant's responsibility** and, ordinarily, would be precluded by the accountant's ethical or legal obligations of confidentiality. However, the accountant should recognize that in the following circumstances, a duty to disclose to parties outside of the entity may exist:

        1)   To comply with certain legal and regulatory requirements

        2)   To a successor accountant when the successor decides to communicate with the predecessor accountant in accordance with AR 400, Communications Between Predecessor and Successor Accountants, regarding acceptance of an engagement to compile or review the financial statements of a nonissuer

        3)   In response to a subpoena

    e.   Because potential conflicts between the accountant's ethical and legal obligations for confidentiality of client matters may be complex, the accountant may wish to consult with legal counsel before discussing matters with parties outside the client.

Stop and review! You have completed the outline for this subunit. Study multiple-choice questions 1 through 10 beginning on page 604.

18.2 REVIEW (AR 90)

1.   The **objective** of a review is to express **limited assurance** that no material modifications should be made to the statements for them to conform with the applicable financial reporting framework (typically GAAP, but may be an other comprehensive basis of accounting, or OCBOA). A review is significantly less in scope than an audit. (See table in item 2. in Subunit 18.1.)

    a.   AR 90 typically relates to a review of annual financial statements of nonissuers.

    b.   Alternatively, reviews of interim (e.g., quarterly) financial statements for issuers follow AU 722. (See Study Unit 19, Subunit 1.)

2.   A review does not contemplate (a) obtaining an understanding of the entity's internal control; (b) assessing fraud risk; (c) testing accounting records by obtaining sufficient appropriate audit evidence through inspection, observation, and confirmation; (d) examining source documents (for example, canceled checks or bank images); or (e) performing other procedures ordinarily performed in an audit. Accordingly, in a review, the accountant does not obtain assurance that (s)he will become aware of all significant matters that would be disclosed in an audit. Therefore, a review is designed to provide only limited assurance.

3.   The accountant should establish an **understanding** with management regarding the services to be performed for review engagements and should document the understanding through a written communication with management (e.g., an **engagement letter**).

4.   **Nature of Review Evidence**

    a.   Procedures should be designed to accumulate review evidence that will provide a **reasonable basis** for obtaining **limited assurance** that there are no material modifications that should be made to the financial statements in order for the statements to be in conformity with the applicable financial reporting framework (e.g., GAAP).

b.   Review evidence obtained through the performance of **analytical procedures** and **inquiry** will ordinarily provide the accountant with a reasonable basis for obtaining limited assurance. However, the accountant should perform **additional procedures** if the accountant determines that such procedures are necessary to obtain limited assurance that the financial statements do not need modification.

c.   The accountant should obtain **written representations** from management.

5.   **Understanding of the Entity and Industry**

a.   The accountant should possess an understanding of the industry in which the client operates, including the accounting principles and practices generally used in the industry, sufficient to determine the specific nature, timing, and extent of review procedures to be performed.

b.   The requirement that the accountant possess a level of knowledge of the industry in which the entity operates **does not prevent the accountant from accepting a review engagement** for an entity in an industry with which the accountant has no previous experience. It does, however, place upon the accountant a responsibility to obtain the required level of knowledge through additional research and study.

c.   The accountant should obtain knowledge about the client sufficient to assist the accountant with determining the specific nature, timing, and extent of review procedures to be performed. That knowledge should include the following:

1)   An understanding of the client's business
2)   An understanding of the accounting principles and practices used by the client

d.   The accountant's understanding of an **entity's business** is ordinarily obtained through experience with the entity or its industry and inquiry of the entity's personnel.

e.   The accountant may obtain an understanding of the **accounting policies and procedures** used by management through inquiry, the review of client-prepared documents, or experience with the client.

6.   **Designing and Performing Review Procedures**

a.   The accountant should design and perform **analytical procedures** and make **inquiries** and perform other procedures based on

1)   His/her understanding of the industry,
2)   His/her knowledge of the client, and
3)   The risk of material misstatement.

b.   The accountant should focus procedures in those areas where (s)he believes there are increased risks of misstatements.

7.   **Analytical Procedures**

a.   **Analytical procedures** involve comparisons of expectations developed by the accountant to the client's recorded amounts or ratios. The accountant develops such expectations by identifying and using **plausible relationships** that are reasonably expected to exist based on the accountant's understanding of the industry in which the client operates and knowledge of the client. Following are five sources of information for developing expectations:

1)   Financial information for **comparable prior period(s)**, giving consideration to known changes
2)   **Anticipated results**, for example, budgets or forecasts
3)   **Relationships** among elements of financial information within the period
4)   Information regarding the **industry** in which the client operates
5)   Relationships of financial information with relevant **nonfinancial information**

    b.   Analytical procedures may be performed at the **financial statement level** or at the **detailed account level**. Those at the financial statement level typically provide evidence of the "big picture." For example, the accountant may question whether the size of the warehouse is sufficient to hold the entire reported inventory. Alternatively, detailed information, for example, a month-to-month comparison of the prior year's receivable with the current year's, provides evidence of potential account balance misstatement.

    c.   If analytical procedures identify fluctuations or relationships that are inconsistent with other relevant information or that **differ from expected values** by a significant amount, the accountant should investigate these differences first by questioning management and then by performing other procedures as necessary in the circumstances.

8.   **Inquiries and Other Review Procedures**

    a.   The accountant should consider

        1)   **Inquiring** of members of management who have responsibility for financial and accounting matters concerning

            a)   Whether the financial statements have been prepared in conformity with the applicable financial reporting framework (e.g., GAAP)

            b)   The entity's accounting principles and practices and the methods followed in applying them

            c)   The entity's procedures for recording, classifying, and summarizing transactions and accumulating information for disclosure in the financial statements

            d)   Unusual or complex situations that may have an effect on the financial statements

            e)   Significant transactions occurring or recognized near the end of the reporting period

            f)   The status of uncorrected misstatements identified during the previous engagement

            g)   Questions that have arisen in the course of applying the review procedures

            h)   Events subsequent to the date of the financial statements that could have a material effect on the financial statements

            i)   Their knowledge of any fraud or suspected fraud affecting the entity involving management or others

            j)   Significant journal entries and other adjustments

            k)   Communications from regulatory agencies

            l)   Actions taken at meetings of shareholders, the board of directors, committees of the board of directors, or comparable meetings that may affect the financial statements

        2)   **Reading** the financial statements to consider, on the basis of information coming to the accountant's attention, whether the financial statements appear to conform with the applicable financial reporting framework

        3)   **Obtaining reports** from other accountants, if any, who have been engaged to audit or review the financial statements of significant components of the reporting entity, its subsidiaries, and other investees

    b.   The accountant ordinarily **is not required to corroborate management's** responses with other evidence; however, the accountant should consider the reasonableness and consistency of management's responses in light of the results of other review procedures and the accountant's knowledge of the client's business and the industry in which it operates.

9. **Incorrect, Incomplete, or Otherwise Unsatisfactory Information**

   a. During the performance of review procedures, the accountant may become aware that information coming to his/her attention is incorrect, incomplete, or otherwise unsatisfactory. In such instances, the accountant should request that management consider the effect of these matters on the financial statements and communicate the results of its consideration to the accountant.

      1) If the accountant believes the financial statements may be materially misstated, the accountant should **perform additional procedures** deemed necessary to obtain limited assurance that no material modifications should be made to the financial statements in order for the statements to be in conformity with the applicable financial reporting framework.

      2) If the accountant concludes that the financial statements are materially misstated, the accountant should modify the report, as discussed in item 17. of this subunit.

   b. The accountant may perform reconciliations, confirmations, tests of details, or other procedures to gain the evidence to provide limited assurance. AR 90, however, does not specifically identify required additional procedures but expects the accountant to use appropriate judgment.

10. **Written representations are required** from management **(a management representations letter)** for all financial statements and periods covered by the accountant's review report.

    a. If current management was not present during all periods covered by the accountant's report, the accountant should nevertheless obtain written representations from current management for all such periods.

    b. The specific written representations obtained by the accountant will depend on the circumstances of the engagement and the nature and basis of presentation of the financial statements.

    c. Because the accountant is concerned with events occurring through the date of the report that may require adjustment to or disclosure in the financial statements, management's representations set forth in the management representation letter should be made as of the **date of the accountant's review report.**

    d. The letter should be signed by those members of management whom the accountant believes are responsible for and knowledgeable about (directly or through others in the organization) the matters covered in the representation letter. Normally, the **chief executive officer** and **chief financial officer** or others with equivalent positions in the entity should sign the representation letter.

11. **Documentation in a Review Engagement**

    a. The accountant **should prepare documentation** (working papers) in sufficient detail to provide a clear understanding of the work performed (including the nature, timing, extent, and results of review procedures performed), the review evidence obtained and its source, and the conclusions reached.

    b. Documentation

       1) Provides the principal support for the representation in the accountant's review report that the accountant performed the review in accordance with SSARS

       2) Provides the principal support for the conclusion that the accountant is not aware of any material modifications that should be made to the financial statements in order for them to be in conformity with the applicable financial reporting framework

    c.   The form, content, and extent of documentation depend on the circumstances of the engagement, the methodology and tools used, and the accountant's professional judgment. The accountant's documentation should include

        1)   The engagement letter

        2)   The analytical procedures performed

        3)   The significant matters covered in the accountant's inquiry procedures and the responses thereto

        4)   Any findings or issues that, in the accountant's judgment, are significant (for example, the results of review procedures that indicate the financial statements could be materially misstated, including actions taken to address such findings, and the basis for the final conclusions reached)

        5)   Significant unusual matters that the accountant considered during the performance of the review procedures, including their disposition

        6)   Communications, whether oral or written, to the appropriate level of management regarding fraud or illegal acts that come to the accountant's attention

        7)   The management representation letter

12. **Standard Report**

    a.   The accountant's objective in reporting on the financial statements is **to prevent misinterpretation of the degree of responsibility** the accountant is assuming when his/her name is associated with the financial statements.

    b.   When the accountant has **no reservations** providing limited assurance on the financial statements, (s)he issues a standard report.

    c.   **Each page** of the financial statements reviewed by the accountant should include a reference, such as "**See Independent Accountant's Review Report.**"

    d.   The following is an example of the standard review report. (We recommend that you study the report to understand its components and the general wording and use of each paragraph.)

EXAMPLE

Independent Accountant's Review Report

To the Owners of XYZ Company:

I (We) have reviewed the accompanying balance sheet of XYZ Company as of December 31, 20XX, and the related statements of income, retained earnings, and cash flows for the year then ended. A review includes primarily applying analytical procedures to management's (owners') financial data and making inquiries of company management (owners). A review is substantially less in scope than an audit, the objective of which is the expression of an opinion regarding the financial statements as a whole. Accordingly, I (we) do not express such an opinion.

Management (owners) is (are) responsible for the preparation and fair presentation of the financial statements in accordance with accounting principles generally accepted in the United States of America and for designing, implementing, and maintaining internal control relevant to the preparation and fair presentation of the financial statements.

My (our) responsibility is to conduct the review in accordance with Statements on Standards for Accounting and Review Services issued by the American Institute of Certified Public Accountants. Those standards require me (us) to perform procedures to obtain limited assurance that there are no material modifications that should be made to the financial statements. I (We) believe that the results of my (our) procedures provide a reasonable basis for my (our) report.

Based on my (our) review, I am (we are) not aware of any material modifications that should be made to the accompanying financial statements in order for them to be in conformity with accounting principles generally accepted in the United States of America.

Signature of accounting firm or accountant   <---------- May be manual, stamped, electronic, or typed

Date   <---------- Date of completion of the review procedures

13. When the accountant is unable to perform the inquiry and analytical procedures (s)he considers necessary or the client does not provide the accountant with a representation letter, the review will be incomplete.

   a. An incomplete review does not provide an adequate basis for issuing a review report. In such a situation, the accountant should consider the effect on the engagement and report.

   b. A typical response would be to withdraw from the engagement.

   c. The accountant may wish to consult with his/her legal counsel in those circumstances.

14. The accountant may be asked to issue a review report on one financial statement, such as a balance sheet, and not on other related financial statements, such as the statements of income, retained earnings, and cash flows. The accountant may do so if the scope of his/her inquiry and analytical procedures has not been restricted.

15. Financial statements prepared in accordance with an OCBOA are not considered appropriate in form unless the financial statements include

   a. A description of the OCBOA, including a summary of significant accounting policies and a description of the primary differences from GAAP. The effects of the differences need not be quantified.

   b. Informative disclosures similar to those required by GAAP.

16. The accountant may **emphasize a matter** disclosed in the financial statements.

   a. Such explanatory information should be presented in a **separate paragraph** of the accountant's report.

   b. Emphasis paragraphs are never required; they may be added solely at the accountant's discretion.

   c. The following are examples of matters that the accountant may wish to emphasize:

      1) Uncertainties

      2) That the entity is a component of a larger business enterprise

      3) That the entity has had significant transactions with related parties

      4) Unusually important subsequent events

      5) Accounting matters, other than those involving a change or changes in accounting principles, affecting the comparability of the financial statements with those of the preceding period

17. **Departures from the Applicable Financial Reporting Framework**

   a. An accountant who is engaged to review financial statements may become aware of a departure from the applicable financial reporting framework (e.g., failure to follow GAAP or include adequate disclosure) that is material to the financial statements.

      1) If the financial statements are not revised, the accountant should **consider whether modification of the standard report is adequate** to disclose the departure.

      2) If the accountant concludes that modification of the standard report is appropriate, an **"except for" modification** should be included with the departure disclosed in a separate paragraph of the report, including disclosure of the effects of the departure on the financial statements if such effects have been determined by management or are known as the result of the accountant's procedures.

      3) The accountant is not required to determine the effects of a departure if management has not done so, provided that the accountant states in the report that such determination has not been made.

4) The following is an example of the modification of the conclusion paragraph with the additional explanatory paragraph:

EXAMPLE -- Language to Modify Review Report for a Departure from GAAP

Based on my (our) review, **with the exception of the matter(s) described in the following paragraph(s)**, I am (we are) not aware of any material modifications that should be made to the accompanying financial statements in order for them to be in conformity with accounting principles generally accepted in the United States of America.

As disclosed in note X to the financial statements, accounting principles generally accepted in the United States of America require that inventory cost consist of material, labor, and overhead. Management has informed me (us) that the inventory of finished goods and work in process is stated in the accompanying financial statements at material and labor cost only, and that the effects of this departure from accounting principles generally accepted in the United States of America on financial position, results of operations, and cash flows have not been determined.

---

   b. If the accountant believes that modification of the standard report is not adequate to indicate the deficiencies in the financial statements as a whole, the accountant should **withdraw** from the review engagement and provide no further services with respect to those financial statements. The accountant may wish to consult with his/her legal counsel in those circumstances.

18. **General-Use and Restricted-Use Reports**

   a. The term **general use** applies to accountants' reports that are not restricted to specified parties.

     1) Accountants' reports on financial statements prepared in conformity with an applicable financial reporting framework **ordinarily are not restricted** regarding use.

     2) However, nothing in this section precludes the accountant from restricting the use of any report.

   b. The term **restricted use** applies to accountants' reports intended only for one or more specified third parties.

     1) The need for restriction on the use of a report may result from a number of circumstances, including, but not limited to, the purpose of the report and the potential for the report to be misunderstood when taken out of the context in which it was intended to be used.

   c. The accountant should restrict the use of a report when the subject matter of the accountant's report or the presentation being reported on is based on measurement or disclosure criteria contained in contractual agreements or regulatory provisions that are not in conformity with an applicable financial reporting framework.

19. **An Entity's Ability to Continue as a Going Concern**

   a. During the performance of review procedures, evidence or information may come to the accountant's attention indicating that there may be an uncertainty about the entity's ability to **continue as a going concern** for a reasonable period of time, not to exceed 1 year beyond the date of the financial statements being reviewed (referred to as a **reasonable period of time**).

     1) In those circumstances, the accountant should request that **management consider the possible effects** of the going concern uncertainty on the financial statements, including the need for related disclosure.

     2) After management communicates to the accountant the results of its consideration of the possible effects on the financial statements, the accountant should consider the reasonableness of management's conclusions, including the adequacy of the related disclosures, if applicable.

3) If the accountant determines that management's conclusions are **unreasonable** or the disclosure of the uncertainty regarding the entity's ability to continue as a going concern is **not adequate**, (s)he should determine if modification of the standard report (include an "except for" with a separate paragraph) is appropriate to convey the departure.

4) If the accountant believes that modification of the standard report is not adequate to indicate the deficiencies in the financial statements as a whole, the accountant should **withdraw** from the review engagement. The accountant may wish to consult with his/her legal counsel in those circumstances.

b. The accountant may emphasize an uncertainty about an entity's ability to continue as a going concern, provided that the uncertainty is disclosed in the financial statements.

20. **Subsequent Events**

a. The accountant may identify evidence or information about a subsequent event that has a material effect on the reviewed financial statements.

1) The accountant should request that management consider the possible effects on the financial statements, including the adequacy of any related disclosure, if applicable.

2) If the accountant determines that the subsequent event is not adequately accounted for in the financial statements or disclosed in the notes, the accountant should determine if a modified report is appropriate or whether the accountant should withdraw from the engagement.

b. The accountant may emphasize a subsequent event, provided that the event is disclosed in the financial statements.

21. **Subsequent Discovery of Facts Existing at the Date of the Report**

a. After the date of the accountant's review report, the accountant has **no obligation to perform other review procedures** with respect to the financial statements unless **new information** comes to his/her attention. However, when the accountant becomes aware of information that relates to financial statements previously reported on by him/her but that **was not known** to the accountant at the date of the report (and that is of such a nature and from such a source that (s)he would have investigated it had it come to his/her attention during the course of the review), the accountant should, as soon as practicable, undertake to determine whether the information is reliable and whether the facts existed at the date of the report.

1) The accountant should discuss the matter with his/her client at whatever management or governance levels the accountant deems appropriate and request cooperation in whatever investigation may be necessary.

b. The accountant should **perform the additional procedures** deemed necessary to obtain limited assurance that no material modifications should be made to the financial statements in order for the statements to be in conformity with the applicable financial reporting framework.

c. When the accountant has concluded that action should be taken to prevent further use of the report or the financial statements, (s)he should advise the client to make appropriate disclosure of the newly discovered facts and their impact on the financial statements to persons who are known to be currently using or who are likely to use the financial statements. When the client undertakes to make appropriate disclosure, the method used and the disclosure made will depend on the circumstances but should be made as expeditiously as possible.

d. If the **client refuses** to make the appropriate disclosures (this is expected to be a rare event) the accountant should notify the appropriate personnel at the highest levels within the entity, such as the manager (owner) or those charged with governance, of such refusal and of the fact that, in the absence of disclosure by the client, the accountant should take steps to prevent further use of the financial statements and the accountant's report.

22. **Supplementary Information**

a. When the basic financial statements are accompanied by information presented for supplementary analysis purposes, the accountant should clearly indicate the degree of responsibility, if any, (s)he is taking with respect to such information.

b. When the accountant has reviewed the basic financial statements, an explanation should be included in the review report or in a separate report on the other data.

c. The report should state that the review has been made for the purpose of expressing a conclusion that there are no material modifications that should be made to the financial statements in order for them to be in conformity with the applicable financial reporting framework.

23. **Fraud and Illegal Acts**

a. When evidence or information comes to the accountant's attention during the performance of review procedures that **fraud or an illegal act** may have occurred, that matter should be brought to the attention of the appropriate level of management.

1) The accountant need not report matters regarding illegal acts that are clearly **inconsequential**.

2) When matters regarding fraud or an illegal act involve senior management, the accountant should report the matter to an individual or group at a higher level within the entity, such as the manager (owner) or those charged with governance.

b. The communication may **be oral or written**. If the communication is oral, the accountant **should document** it.

c. When matters regarding fraud or an illegal act involve an owner of the business, the accountant should consider **resigning** from the engagement. Additionally, the accountant should consider consulting with his/her legal counsel whenever any evidence or information comes to his/her attention during the performance of review procedures that fraud or an illegal act may have occurred, unless such illegal act is clearly inconsequential.

d. The disclosure of any evidence or information that comes to the accountant's attention during the performance of review procedures that fraud or an illegal act may have occurred to parties other than the client's senior management (or those charged with governance, if applicable) ordinarily is not part of the accountant's responsibility and, ordinarily, would be precluded by the accountant's ethical or legal obligations of confidentiality. The accountant should recognize, however, that in the following circumstances, a duty to disclose to parties outside of the entity may exist:

1) To comply with certain legal and regulatory requirements

2) To a successor accountant when the successor decides to communicate with the predecessor accountant regarding acceptance of an engagement to compile or review the financial statements of a nonissuer

3) In response to a subpoena

e. Because potential conflicts between the accountant's ethical and legal obligations for confidentiality of client matters may be complex, the accountant may wish to consult with legal counsel before discussing fraud or illegal matters with parties outside the client.

Stop and review! You have completed the outline for this subunit. Study multiple-choice questions 11 through 25 beginning on page 607.

Before you move on to the additional considerations for compilation and review, make sure you have given the basics sufficient consideration. The AICPA Content Specification Outlines indicate that 12% to 16% of the auditing exam will be based on accounting and review services. This is a considerable percentage given the relatively small amount of material. We have provided a number of task-based simulations on this topic at the end of the study unit to help you assess your knowledge.

18.3 OTHER CONSIDERATIONS FOR COMPILATIONS AND REVIEWS

1. **Change in the Engagement**

    a. An accountant may be asked to change the engagement from a higher level of service (**audit** or review) to a lower level of service (**review or compilation**).

    b. The request may result from (1) a change in circumstances affecting the entity's requirements; (2) a misunderstanding as to the nature of one of the services; or (3) a scope restriction, whether imposed by the client or circumstances.

    c. Before an accountant engaged to perform a **higher level** of service agrees to change to a **lower level**, the following should be considered:

        1) The reason for the entity's request, particularly the implications of a scope restriction, whether imposed by the entity or by circumstances

        2) The additional effort required to complete the original engagement

        3) The estimated additional cost to complete the original engagement

    d. A **change in circumstances** that affects the entity's requirement for the service or a misunderstanding about the **nature of a service** is ordinarily a reasonable basis for requesting a change in the engagement.

    e. In considering the implications of a **scope restriction**, the accountant should evaluate the possibility that the information affected may be incorrect, incomplete, or otherwise unsatisfactory.

        1) But, if an accountant has been prohibited by the entity from contacting the entity's legal counsel, (s)he ordinarily is precluded from issuing a review or compilation report.

        2) If the entity in an **audit or review** engagement that has been changed to a **review or compilation** does not provide a signed representation letter, the accountant is not permitted to issue a review report and ordinarily is precluded from issuing a compilation report.

    f. If the **cost to complete** the higher level of service is insignificant, the accountant should consider the propriety of accepting a change.

    g. The **report on the changed engagement** should **not** mention the following:

        1) The original engagement
        2) Any auditing or review procedures performed
        3) Scope limitations that led to the changed engagement

2. **Consideration of Fraud and Illegal Acts**

    a. Neither a compilation nor a review requires the practitioner to apply procedures specifically directed toward the detection of fraud or illegal acts.

    b. However, if a fraud or illegal act is suspected, the practitioner should communicate the matter (unless it is clearly inconsequential) to an appropriate level of management.

3. **AR 200, *Reporting on Comparative Financial Statements***

    a. Much of the guidance on reporting on comparative statements given in AU 508, *Reports on Audited Financial Statements*, also applies.

    b. A continuing accountant who performs the **same or higher level of service** for the current period should update his/her report for the prior period.

    1) A continuing accountant who performs a **lower level of service** should either include a separate paragraph describing the responsibility assumed for the financial statements of the prior period or reissue the previous report.

  c. Compiled financial statements that **omit substantially all of the disclosures** required by GAAP are not comparable with financial statements that include such disclosures. Accordingly, the accountant ordinarily should not issue a report on comparative financial statements when statements for one or more, but not all, of the periods presented omit substantially all of the disclosures required by GAAP.

  d. Before **reissuing** a compilation or review report, a predecessor accountant should consider whether the report is still appropriate. The predecessor should (1) read the current financial statements and successor's report, (2) compare the prior-period financial statements with the current statements, and (3) obtain a representation letter from the successor.

4. **AR 300, *Compilation Reports on Financial Statements Included in Certain Prescribed Forms***

  a. An alternative form of the standard compilation report is used when a prescribed form or related instructions call for departure from GAAP by specifying a **measurement principle** not in conformity with GAAP or **failing to require disclosures** in accordance with GAAP.

  b. The presumption is that the information required in a prescribed form is sufficient to meet the **needs of the body** that designed or adopted the form.

  c. In the standard report on statements included in such a form, the accountant should indicate that the statements are in a prescribed form and that **they may differ** from those presented in accordance with GAAP, but (s)he need not describe the differences in the report.

5. **AR 400, *Communications Between Predecessor and Successor Accountants***

  a. The successor **may decide to communicate** with the predecessor before accepting a review or compilation engagement.

    1) In an audit, the communication is required.

  b. The predecessor is required to **respond promptly and fully** on the basis of known facts.

  c. Both accountants, however, must have the entity's **specific consent** to disclose confidential information.

  d. Most other provisions of AU 315, *Communications between Predecessor and Successor Auditors* (which is discussed in Study Unit 3), are applicable to these communications.

  e. A successor who believes the statements reported on by the predecessor **may require revision** must request that the client communicate this information to the predecessor.

6. **AR 600, *Reporting on Personal Financial Statements Included in Written Personal Financial Plans***

  a. An accountant may submit a written personal financial plan containing unaudited personal financial statements to a client without complying with the requirements of AR 80 if the accountant

    1) Has an understanding with the client about its use,

    2) Has no reason to believe that the financial statements will be used to obtain credit or for any other purpose except the financial plan, and

    3) Attaches a report describing the engagement.

Stop and review! You have completed the outline for this subunit. Study multiple-choice questions 26 through 32 beginning on page 611.

18.4 SPECIAL REPORTS (AU 623)

1.   Special reports may be issued on

  a.   Financial statements that are prepared in conformity with a comprehensive basis of accounting other than generally accepted accounting principles (OCBOA).

  b.   Specified elements, accounts, or items of a financial statement.

  c.   Compliance with aspects of contractual agreements or regulatory requirements related to audited financial statements.

  d.   Financial presentations to comply with contractual agreements or regulatory provisions.

  e.   Financial information presented in prescribed forms or schedules that require a prescribed form of auditor's report.

2.   **Financial Statements**

  a.   GAAS are applicable when an auditor audits and reports on any financial statement.

  b.   A **financial statement** is "a presentation of financial data, including notes, derived from accounting records and intended to communicate an entity's economic resources or obligations at a moment in time or the changes therein for a period of time in conformity with a comprehensive basis of accounting."

  c.   In addition to the **basic financial statements**, the following financial presentations are considered to be financial statements for reporting purposes:

   1)   Statement of assets and liabilities that does not include owners' equity
   2)   Statement of revenue and expenses
   3)   Summary of operations
   4)   Statement of operations by product lines
   5)   Statement of cash receipts and disbursements

3.   **Financial Statements Prepared in Conformity with an Other Comprehensive Basis of Accounting (OCBOA)**

  a.   An OCBOA is one of the following and would require a special report:

   1)   A basis of accounting that the reporting entity uses to comply with the requirements or financial reporting provisions of a **regulatory agency**, for example, a basis of accounting used by insurers under the rules of a state insurance commission

   2)   A basis of accounting used for **tax purposes**

   3)   The **cash basis** and modifications of the cash basis having substantial support, such as recording depreciation on fixed assets or accruing income taxes

   4)   A definite set of **criteria having substantial support** that is applied to all material items, for example, the price-level basis

  b.   The differences between the standard audit report and a **special report** on statements prepared on an OCBOA are described below and on the next page.

   1)   The **specific financial statements** being audited (identified in the introductory paragraph) may differ from the traditional statements.

   2)   A paragraph is added **before the opinion paragraph** that

    a)   States the basis of presentation and refers to the note to the financial statements that describes the basis.

    b)   Discloses that the basis of presentation is a comprehensive basis of accounting other than GAAP.

3) In the opinion paragraph, the auditor should express an opinion (or disclaim an opinion) on whether the financial statements are presented fairly, in all material respects, **in conformity with the basis of accounting described**.

4) If the financial statements are in accordance with the requirements or reporting provisions of a **regulatory agency**, a paragraph should be added designating the report as a **restricted-use report** because it must state that it is intended solely for the information and use of the specified parties who are identified in the report (AU 532).

c. Unless the statements meet the conditions for presentation in conformity with an OCBOA, the auditor should use the standard form of the audit report modified appropriately for the **departures from GAAP** (i.e., express a qualified or adverse opinion).

d. Terms such as **balance sheet**, **statement of financial position**, **statement of income**, **statement of operations**, and **statement of cash flows** or other similar unmodified titles are understood to apply only to statements in conformity with GAAP (i.e., accrual basis). Consequently, the auditor should consider whether the financial statements that (s)he is reporting on are **suitably titled**.

1) If the statements are not suitably titled, the auditor should qualify the opinion.

e. **Appropriate OCBOA titles** include the following:

1) Balance sheet -- cash basis
2) Statement of assets and liabilities arising from cash transactions
3) Statement of assets, liabilities, and capital -- income tax basis
4) State of revenue collected and expenses paid
5) Statement of revenues and expenses -- income tax basis
6) Statement of income -- statutory basis
7) Statement of operations -- income tax basis

f. The following is an example of reporting on a statement prepared on the cash basis: (The modifications made to the standard audit report are in bold.)

EXAMPLE

Independent Auditor's Report

To: <---------- Addressed to the Board of Directors, Stockholders, or Owner

We have audited the **accompanying statements of assets and liabilities arising from cash transactions of XYZ Company as of December 31, Year 2 and Year 1, and the related statements of revenue collected and expenses paid for the years then ended**. These financial statements are the responsibility of the Company's management. Our responsibility is to express an opinion on these financial statements based on our audits.

We conducted our audits in accordance with auditing standards generally accepted in the United States of America. Those standards require that we plan and perform the audit to obtain reasonable assurance about whether the financial statements are free of material misstatement. An audit includes examining, on a test basis, evidence supporting the amounts and disclosures in the financial statements. An audit also includes assessing the accounting principles used and significant estimates made by management, as well as evaluating the overall financial statement presentation. We believe that our audits provide a reasonable basis for our opinion.

As described in Note X, these financial statements were prepared on the basis of cash receipts and disbursements, which is a comprehensive basis of accounting other than generally accepted accounting principles.

In our opinion, the financial statements referred to above present fairly, in all material respects, **the assets and liabilities arising from cash transactions of XYZ Company as of December 31, Year 2 and Year 1, and its revenue collected and expenses paid during the years then ended, on the basis of accounting described in Note X.**

Signature <---------- May be signed, typed, or printed

Date <---------- No earlier than the date on which the auditor has obtained sufficient appropriate evidence

---

ISA Difference

Under the ISAs, any special purpose audit report should include the **auditor's address**.

---

4. **Evaluating the Adequacy of Disclosure in Financial Statements Prepared in Conformity with an OCBOA**

   a. The auditor should apply essentially the same criteria as applied to financial statements prepared in conformity with GAAP.

   b. The financial statements should include, in the accompanying notes, a **summary of significant accounting policies** that discusses the basis of presentation and describes how it differs from GAAP. However, the effects of the differences need not be quantified.

5. **Specified Elements, Accounts, or Items of a Financial Statement**

   a. An independent auditor may issue a **special report** that expresses an opinion on one or more specified elements, accounts, or items of a financial statement, which may be presented in the report or in an accompanying document.

   1) Examples of the elements, accounts, or items that may be reported on based on an audit include rentals, royalties, receivables, a profit participation, or a provision for income taxes.

   b. The auditor should plan and perform the audit and prepare the report with a view to the purpose of the engagement. With the exception of the **first standard of reporting** (conformity with GAAP), the 10 GAAS apply.

   c. The engagement may be undertaken separately or in conjunction with an audit of the financial statements.

   d. The measurement of **materiality** must relate to each element, account, or item because the auditor expresses an opinion on each element, etc., covered by the report.

   1) For example, if the auditor expresses an opinion of the fairness of a client's current assets, the materiality of each account (i.e., cash, accounts receivable, etc.) that constitutes current assets would be judged relative to current assets.

   2) Thus, an audit of a specified element, etc., is ordinarily more extensive than the consideration of the same information in an audit of the financial statements.

   3) The auditor must become satisfied that elements, etc., interrelated with those on which (s)he expresses an opinion have been considered.

   e. If expressing an opinion on specified elements, etc., is equivalent to expressing a **piecemeal opinion** on the financial statements, an auditor who has expressed an **adverse opinion or disclaimed an opinion** on those statements should avoid such reporting.

   1) However, an auditor may nevertheless be able to express an opinion in these circumstances if a **major portion** of the financial statements is not involved. For example, an auditor who has disclaimed an opinion on the financial statements may be able to express an opinion on the accounts receivable balance. However, the report would be presented separately.

   2) If the preparation of the element, account, or item complies with the requirements or provisions of a contract or agreement that results in a presentation not in conformity with GAAP or an OCBOA, a **restricted-use report** is necessary (AU 532).

6. **Compliance with Aspects of Contractual Agreements or Regulatory Requirements Related to Audited Financial Statements**

    a. Entities may be required by contractual agreements, such as bond indentures and certain types of loan agreements, or by regulatory agencies to furnish **special reports** by independent auditors on compliance.

        1) For example, loan agreements usually impose on borrowers a variety of covenants involving matters such as (a) payments into sinking funds, (b) payments of interest, (c) maintenance of current ratios, (d) restrictions of dividend payments, and (e) the use of proceeds from sales of property. They also usually require audited financial statements.

    b. Reports based upon compliance with aspects of contractual agreements or regulatory provisions should be provided in conjunction with an **ordinary audit** of financial statements.

    c. The report envisioned provides **negative assurance** that may be given in a separate paragraph(s) in the audit report on the financial statements or in a separate report.

        1) But this assurance should not be given unless **an audit** of the statements has been made and should not extend to any covenants relating to matters that have not been subjected to audit procedures in the audit (AU 623).

ISA Difference

The ISAs permit **expression of an opinion**.

---

    d. A **restricted-use report** is required (AU 532).

7. **Financial Presentations to Comply with Contractual Agreements or Regulatory Provisions**

    a. These statements **may not constitute a complete presentation** but may otherwise be prepared in conformity with GAAP or an OCBOA. An audit of these statements results in an **opinion** being expressed by the auditor.

        1) An example is a schedule of gross income and certain expenses of a real estate operation that excludes interest, depreciation, and income tax expense but is otherwise in conformity with GAAP.

    b. The special-purpose presentation may be prepared on a basis that results in a presentation **not in conformity with GAAP or an OCBOA**.

        1) For example, an acquisition agreement may require the acquired entity to prepare statements in which certain assets are reported at a valuation basis stated in the agreement.

    c. The auditor's **special report** should include a paragraph that restricts the use of the report to those knowledgeable of the agreements or provisions (see AU 532).

8. **Financial Information Presented in Prescribed Forms or Schedules that Require a Prescribed Form of Auditor's Report**

    a. **Printed forms** designed by the bodies with which they will be filed often prescribe the wording of the auditor's report. Many are unacceptable to auditors because they conflict with reporting standards.

    b. When a report form calls upon an auditor to make an unjustified assertion, (s)he should reword the form or attach a separate report (AU 623).

Stop and review! You have completed the outline for this subunit. Study multiple-choice questions 33 through 41 beginning on page 614.

QUESTIONS

18.1 Compilation (AR 80)

1. Statements on Standards for Accounting and Review Services (SSARSs) require an accountant to report when the accountant has

   A. Typed client-prepared financial statements, without modification, as an accommodation to the client.

   B. Provided a client with a financial statement format that does not include monetary amounts, to be used by the client in preparing financial statements.

   C. Proposed correcting journal entries to be recorded by the client that change client-prepared financial statements.

   D. Prepared, through the use of computer software, financial statements to be used by third parties.

Answer (D) is correct. *(CPA, adapted)*
   REQUIRED: The situation in which an accountant must issue a report.
   DISCUSSION: The accountant should not consent to the use of his/her name in association with unaudited financial statements of a nonissuer to be used by third parties unless (1) the auditor has compiled or reviewed the financial statements in compliance with SSARSs, or (2) the financial statements are accompanied by an indication that the accountant has not compiled or reviewed the statements and that the accountant assumes no responsibility for them (i.e., issue a disclaimer).
   Answer (A) is incorrect. Typing or reproducing client-prepared financial statements, without modification, as an accommodation to a client does not constitute a submission of financial statements. Answer (B) is incorrect. Without monetary amounts, the presentation is not a financial statement. Answer (C) is incorrect. Journal entries are not a financial statement.

2. An accountant should not compile unaudited financial statements for management of a nonissuer unless, at a minimum, the accountant

   A. Assists in adjusting the books of account and preparing the trial balance.

   B. Types or reproduces the financial statements.

   C. Complies with the Statements on Standards for Accounting and Review Services.

   D. Applies analytical procedures to the financial statements.

Answer (C) is correct. *(CPA, adapted)*
   REQUIRED: The action required of an accountant who compiles unaudited financial statements for management of a nonissuer.
   DISCUSSION: The accountant should not compile unaudited financial statements of a nonissuer to the client or others unless, as a minimum, (s)he complies with the standards set forth in AR 80 applicable to compilation engagements.
   Answer (A) is incorrect. Assisting in adjusting the books of account and preparing the trial balance is not a compilation service. Answer (B) is incorrect. Typing or reproducing client-prepared financial statements, without modification, is not a compilation service. Answer (D) is incorrect. Application of analytical procedures is not required by the standards for compilations.

3. When engaged to compile the financial statements of a nonissuer, an accountant should possess a level of knowledge of the entity's accounting principles and practices. This most likely will include obtaining a general understanding of the

   A. Stated qualifications of the entity's accounting personnel.

   B. Design of the entity's internal controls that have been implemented.

   C. Risk factors relating to misstatements arising from illegal acts.

   D. Internal control awareness of the entity's senior management.

Answer (A) is correct. *(CPA, adapted)*
   REQUIRED: The knowledge acquired to perform a compilation.
   DISCUSSION: To perform a compilation, the accountant should possess an understanding of the nature of the entity's business, its accounting records, the qualifications of its accounting personnel, and the content and accounting basis of the financial statements.
   Answer (B) is incorrect. The consideration of internal control is not necessary to perform compilation services. Answer (C) is incorrect. No assessment of risk or application of auditing procedures is required in a compilation. Answer (D) is incorrect. The consideration of internal control is not necessary to perform compilation services.

4. When compiling a nonissuer's financial statements, an accountant is **least** likely to

A. Perform analytical procedures designed to identify relationships that appear to be unusual.

B. Read the compiled financial statements and consider whether they appear to include adequate disclosure.

C. Omit substantially all of the disclosures required by generally accepted accounting principles.

D. Issue a compilation report on one or more, but not all, of the basic financial statements.

Answer (A) is correct. *(CPA, adapted)*
REQUIRED: The procedure least likely to be performed in a compilation.
DISCUSSION: In a compilation engagement, the accountant is not required to make inquiries or perform analytical or other procedures to verify, corroborate, or review information supplied by the entity. However, analytical procedures are necessary in review and audit engagements.
Answer (B) is incorrect. The accountant should read the compiled statements and consider whether they are free from obvious material errors, including inadequate disclosure. Answer (C) is incorrect. A compilation may omit substantially all disclosures required by GAAP provided the omission is clearly indicated in the report and, to the accountant's knowledge, is not undertaken with an intent to mislead. Answer (D) is incorrect. An accountant may be asked and is permitted to issue a compilation report on one or more, but not all, of the basic financial statements.

5. Which of the following should **not** be included in an accountant's standard report based upon the compilation of an entity's financial statements?

A. A statement that a compilation is limited to presenting in the form of financial statements information that is the representation of management.

B. A statement that the compilation was performed in accordance with Statements on Standards for Accounting and Review Services issued by the AICPA.

C. A statement that the accountant has not audited or reviewed the statements.

D. A statement that the accountant does not express an opinion but provides only limited assurance on the statements.

Answer (D) is correct. *(CPA, adapted)*
REQUIRED: The statement not made in the standard compilation report.
DISCUSSION: A compilation report does not express an opinion or any other form of assurance (AR 80). A review report may provide limited (negative) assurance.
Answer (A) is incorrect. The report should include a statement that a compilation is limited to presenting in the form of financial statements information that is the representation of management. Answer (B) is incorrect. The report should include a statement that the compilation was performed in accordance with the SSARSs. Answer (C) is incorrect. The report should include a statement that the accountant has not audited or reviewed the statements.

6. Compiled financial statements of a nonissuer intended for third-party use should be accompanied by a report stating that

A. The scope of the accountant's procedures has not been restricted in testing the financial information that is the representation of management.

B. The accountant assessed the accounting principles used and significant estimates made by management.

C. The accountant does not express an opinion or any other form of assurance on the financial statements.

D. A compilation consists principally of inquiries of entity personnel and analytical procedures applied to financial data.

Answer (C) is correct. *(CPA, adapted)*
REQUIRED: The language included in a compilation report.
DISCUSSION: A compilation report contains a disclaimer stating that the accountant has not audited or reviewed the financial statements and does not express an opinion or any other form of assurance on them.
Answer (A) is incorrect. A compilation does not entail testing the financial information. Answer (B) is incorrect. A financial statement audit, not a compilation, involves assessing the accounting principles used and the estimates made by management. Answer (D) is incorrect. A review, not a compilation, consists principally of inquiries and analytical procedures.

7. When an accountant attaches a compilation report to a nonissuer's financial statements that omit substantially all disclosures required by GAAP, the accountant should indicate in the compilation report that the financial statements are

A. Not designed for those who are uninformed about the omitted disclosures.

B. Prepared in conformity with a comprehensive basis of accounting other than GAAP.

C. Not compiled in accordance with Statements on Standards for Accounting and Review Services.

D. Special-purpose financial statements that are not comparable to those of prior periods.

Answer (A) is correct. *(CPA, adapted)*
REQUIRED: The statement in a report on a compilation omitting substantially all GAAP disclosures.
DISCUSSION: When disclosures are omitted, a paragraph is added to the standard compilation report stating that management has elected to omit substantially all disclosures required by GAAP and that, if the omissions were included, they might influence the users' conclusions.
Answer (B) is incorrect. The basis of accounting is not at issue. Answer (C) is incorrect. A compilation in accordance with SSARSs is not inconsistent with omission of GAAP disclosures. Answer (D) is incorrect. Financial statements that omit disclosures are not special-purpose.

8. An accountant may compile a nonissuer's financial statements intended for third-party use that omit all of the disclosures required by GAAP only if the omission is

I.   Clearly indicated in the accountant's report

II. Not undertaken with the intention of misleading the financial statement users

A. I only.

B. II only.

C. Both I and II.

D. Either I or II.

Answer (C) is correct. *(CPA, adapted)*
REQUIRED: The situation in which an accountant may compile a nonissuer's financial statements that omit all of the disclosures required by GAAP.
DISCUSSION: An accountant may accept an engagement to compile financial statements that omit substantially all disclosures required by GAAP, provided the omission is clearly indicated in the report and is not, to his/her knowledge, undertaken with the intention of misleading those who might reasonably be expected to use such financial statements (AR 80).

9. Which of the following representations does an accountant make implicitly when issuing the standard report for the compilation of a nonissuer's financial statements?

A. The accountant is independent with respect to the entity.

B. The financial statements have not been audited.

C. A compilation consists principally of inquiries and analytical procedures.

D. The accountant does not express any assurance on the financial statements.

Answer (A) is correct. *(CPA, adapted)*
REQUIRED: The implicit representation in a standard compilation report.
DISCUSSION: Although an accountant who lacks independence is not precluded from issuing a compilation report, (s)he should specifically disclose the lack of independence. Thus, the standard report is silent with respect to independence.
Answer (B) is incorrect. A compilation explicitly states that the financial statements have not been audited. Answer (C) is incorrect. A compilation does not include application of inquiry and analytical procedures. Answer (D) is incorrect. A compilation explicitly states that no assurance is expressed.

10. Miller, CPA, is engaged to compile the financial statements of Web Co., a nonissuer, in conformity with the income tax basis of accounting. If Web's financial statements do **not** disclose the basis of accounting used, Miller should

A. Disclose the basis of accounting in the accountant's compilation report.

B. Clearly label each page "Distribution Restricted--Material Modifications Required."

C. Issue a special report describing the effect of the incomplete presentation.

D. Withdraw from the engagement and provide no further services to Web.

Answer (A) is correct. *(CPA, adapted)*
REQUIRED: The effect on a compilation report of failure to disclose the basis of accounting used.
DISCUSSION: Although the accountant is expected to perform no procedures, if (s)he is aware of misapplications of GAAP or the absence of required disclosures, (s)he should disclose that information in the compilation report.
Answer (B) is incorrect. Each page of the financial statements should contain the statement, "See Accountant's Compilation Report." Answer (C) is incorrect. A special report is issued in conjunction with an audit. Answer (D) is incorrect. The accountant need not withdraw from the engagement.

18.2 Review (AR 90)

11. Which of the following should be the first step in reviewing the financial statements of a nonissuer?

A. Comparing the financial statements with statements for comparable prior periods and with anticipated results.

B. Completing a series of inquiries concerning the entity's procedures for recording, classifying, and summarizing transactions.

C. Obtaining a general understanding of the entity's organization, its operating characteristics, and its products or services.

D. Applying analytical procedures designed to identify relationships and individual items that appear to be unusual.

Answer (C) is correct. *(CPA, adapted)*
REQUIRED: The first step in reviewing the financial statements of a nonissuer.
DISCUSSION: In a review, the auditor expresses limited assurance concerning the financial statements. In performing the review, the auditor should first obtain an understanding of the entity and the entity's industry. This will provide a foundation for completing the review.
Answer (A) is incorrect. Comparing the financial statement with statements for comparable prior periods and with anticipated results is an analytical procedure, which is performed after obtaining an understanding of the business. Answer (B) is incorrect. Completing a series of inquiries concerning the entity's procedures for recording, classifying, and summarizing transactions is performed after obtaining an understanding of the entity's business. Answer (D) is incorrect. Applying analytical procedures designed to identify relationships and individual items that appear to be unusual is done after obtaining an understanding of the business.

12. In reviewing the financial statements of a nonissuer, an accountant is required to modify the standard review report for which of the following matters?

	Inability to Assess the Risks of Material Misstatement Due to Fraud	Discovery of Significant Deficiencies in the Design of the Internal Control
A.	Yes	Yes
B.	Yes	No
C.	No	Yes
D.	No	No

Answer (D) is correct. *(CPA, adapted)*
REQUIRED: The accountant's responsibility in a review engagement.
DISCUSSION: A review does not involve obtaining an understanding of internal control or assessing risk. It also does not involve testing accounting records and responses to inquiries by obtaining corroborating evidence or other tests ordinarily performed in an audit (AR 90). Thus, an auditor must specifically identify and assess the risks of material misstatement due to fraud (AU 316) and must perform procedures to evaluate the effectiveness of the design of controls (AU 314). Because a review consists of making inquiries, applying analytical procedures, and obtaining management representations, the review report need not be modified for the matters specified in the question.

13. Which of the following procedures should an accountant perform during an engagement to review the financial statements of a nonissuer?

A. Communicating control deficiencies discovered during the assessment of control risk.

B. Obtaining a client representation letter from members of management.

C. Sending bank confirmation letters to the entity's financial institutions.

D. Examining cash disbursements in the subsequent period for unrecorded liabilities.

Answer (B) is correct. *(CPA, adapted)*
REQUIRED: The procedure performed in a review.
DISCUSSION: A review primarily consists of inquiries, analytical procedures, and management representations. In addition, the accountant must obtain a sufficient knowledge of the accounting principles and practices of the entity's industry and an understanding of the entity's business. The representations from management should encompass all statements and periods to be covered by the report. The representation letter should be signed by the current managers (usually the CEO and CFO or the equivalent) responsible for, and knowledgeable about, the matters covered (AR 90).
Answer (A) is incorrect. Significant deficiencies and material weaknesses must be communicated in an audit, not a review. Answer (C) is incorrect. Confirmations to financial institutions are normally sent in an audit, not a review. Answer (D) is incorrect. Tests of details, e.g., tests of subsequent payments, are performed in an audit, not a review.

14. Which of the following procedures is usually performed by the accountant in a review engagement of a nonissuer?

A. Sending a letter of inquiry to the entity's lawyer.

B. Comparing the financial statements with statements for comparable prior periods.

C. Confirming a significant percentage of receivables by direct communication with debtors.

D. Communicating control deficiencies discovered during the consideration of internal control.

Answer (B) is correct.   *(CPA, adapted)*
REQUIRED: The procedure performed by the accountant in a review engagement.
DISCUSSION: An accountant should perform inquiries of company personnel, apply analytical procedures, and obtain written representations in a review engagement. Among the analytical procedures identified in AR 90 is the comparison of the financial statements with statements for comparable prior periods and with anticipated results.
Answer (A) is incorrect. AR 90 does not require that inquiries be made of an entity's lawyer. Answer (C) is incorrect. AR 90 does not require the confirmation of receivables. Answer (D) is incorrect. A review engagement does not contemplate obtaining an understanding of internal control.

15. Which of the following inquiry or analytical procedures ordinarily are performed in an engagement to review a nonissuer's financial statements?

A. Analytical procedures designed to test the accounting records by obtaining corroborating evidence.

B. Inquiries concerning unusual or complex situations that may have an effect on the financial statements.

C. Analytical procedures designed to test relevant assertions regarding continued existence.

D. Inquiries of the entity's attorney concerning contingent liabilities.

Answer (B) is correct.   *(CPA, adapted)*
REQUIRED: The inquiries or analytical procedures ordinarily performed during a review.
DISCUSSION: These procedures include inquiries to members of management with responsibility for financial and accounting matters that concern, among other things, unusual or complex situations that may affect the financial statements.
Answer (A) is incorrect. A review does not contemplate gathering corroborating evidence. Answer (C) is incorrect. A review does not contemplate the application of procedures concerning assertions regarding continued existence. Answer (D) is incorrect. AR 90 does not require that inquiries be made of the entity's attorney.

16. Which of the following statements is true concerning both an engagement to compile and an engagement to review a nonissuer's financial statements?

A. The accountant does not contemplate obtaining an understanding of internal control.

B. The accountant must be independent in fact and appearance.

C. The accountant expresses no assurance on the financial statements.

D. The accountant should obtain written management representations.

Answer (A) is correct.   *(CPA, adapted)*
REQUIRED: The true statement about both compilations and reviews.
DISCUSSION: A compilation requires the accountant to have a general understanding of the business, the form of its accounting records, the qualifications of its personnel, the accounting basis of the statements, and their form and content. A review is a higher level of service that also requires the accountant to perform inquiry and analytical procedures as a basis for providing limited assurance. However, neither a compilation nor a review contemplates obtaining an understanding of internal control and assessing control risk.
Answer (B) is incorrect. An accountant must be independent with respect to a review but not a compilation engagement. Answer (C) is incorrect. No expression of assurance is contemplated in a compilation, but limited assurance is expressed as a result of a review. Answer (D) is incorrect. Written management representations are required in a review but not in a compilation engagement.

17. Financial statements of a nonissuer that have been reviewed by an accountant should be accompanied by a report stating that a review

    A. Provides only limited assurance that the financial statements are fairly presented.

    B. Includes examining, on a test basis, information that is the representation of management.

    C. Includes primarily applying analytical procedures to management's financial data and making inquiries of company management.

    D. Does not contemplate obtaining corroborating evidential matter or applying certain other procedures ordinarily performed during an audit.

Answer (C) is correct. *(CPA, adapted)*
    REQUIRED: The statement included in the review report.
    DISCUSSION: The first paragraph of the review report contains a sentence stating, "A review includes primarily applying analytical procedures to management's financial data and making inquiries of company management."
    Answer (A) is incorrect. The report states that the accountant is not aware of material modifications that should be made to the financial statements for them to be in conformity with GAAP. Answer (B) is incorrect. A review engagement does not include examining information that is the representation of management. Answer (D) is incorrect. The report does not contain an explicit description of the difference between an audit and a review.

18. An accountant who reviews the financial statements of a nonissuer should issue a report stating that a review

    A. Is substantially less in scope than an audit.

    B. Provides limited assurance that internal control is functioning as designed.

    C. Provides only limited assurance that the financial statements are fairly presented.

    D. Is substantially more in scope than a compilation.

Answer (A) is correct. *(CPA, adapted)*
    REQUIRED: The statement included in an accountant's review report.
    DISCUSSION: According to AR 90, financial statements reviewed by an accountant should be accompanied by a report stating that a review is substantially less in scope than an audit, the objective of which is the expression of an opinion regarding the financial statements taken as a whole, and, accordingly, no such opinion is expressed.
    Answer (B) is incorrect. A review does not contemplate obtaining an understanding of internal control. Answer (C) is incorrect. The report should state that the accountant is not aware of any material modifications that should be made to the financial statements in order for them to be in conformity with GAAP. Answer (D) is incorrect. The report does not mention a compilation.

19. Financial statements of a nonissuer that have been reviewed by an accountant should be accompanied by a report stating that

    A. The scope of the inquiry and analytical procedures performed by the accountant has not been restricted.

    B. All information included in the financial statements is the representation of the management of the entity.

    C. A review includes examining, on a test basis, evidence supporting the amounts and disclosures in the financial statements.

    D. A review is greater in scope than a compilation, the objective of which is to present financial statements that are free of material misstatements.

Answer (B) is correct. *(CPA, adapted)*
    REQUIRED: The true statement included in an accountant's report based upon a review.
    DISCUSSION: According to AR 90, the second paragraph of the standard report should state, "Management is responsible for the preparation and fair presentation of the financial statements in accordance with accounting principles generally accepted in the United States of America and for designing, implementing, and maintaining internal control relevant to the preparation and fair presentation of the financial statements."
    Answer (A) is incorrect. The report does not need to state that the scope of the inquiry and analytical procedures performed by the accountant has not been restricted. Answer (C) is incorrect. An audit, not a review, includes examining, on a test basis, evidence supporting the amounts and disclosures in the financial statements. Answer (D) is incorrect. The standard review report does not mention a compilation.

20. An accountant's standard report on a review of the financial statements of a nonissuer should state that the accountant

A. Does not express an opinion or any form of limited assurance on the financial statements.

B. Is not aware of any material modifications that should be made to the financial statements for them to conform with GAAP.

C. Obtained reasonable assurance about whether the financial statements are free of material misstatement.

D. Examined evidence, on a test basis, supporting the amounts and disclosures in the financial statements.

Answer (B) is correct. *(CPA, adapted)*
REQUIRED: The statement in a standard review report.
DISCUSSION: The standard review report states, "Based on my review, I am not aware of any material modifications that should be made to the accompanying financial statements in order for them to be in conformity with accounting principles generally accepted in the United States of America" (AR 90).
Answer (A) is incorrect. A review provides limited assurance. Answer (C) is incorrect. An audit provides reasonable assurance about whether the financial statements are free of material misstatement. Answer (D) is incorrect. An audit involves gathering sufficient appropriate evidence to support the amounts and disclosures in the financial statements.

21. During an engagement to review the financial statements of a nonissuer, an accountant becomes aware that several leases that should be capitalized are not capitalized. The accountant considers these leases to be material to the financial statements. The accountant decides to modify the standard review report because management will not capitalize the leases. Under these circumstances, the accountant should

A. Express an adverse opinion because of the departure from GAAP.

B. Express no assurance of any kind on the entity's financial statements.

C. Emphasize that the financial statements are for limited use only.

D. Disclose the departure from GAAP in a separate paragraph of the accountant's report.

Answer (D) is correct. *(CPA, adapted)*
REQUIRED: The modification to a review report for a departure from GAAP.
DISCUSSION: When a departure from GAAP precludes an unmodified review report, and modification of the standard report is sufficient to disclose the departure, the accountant should add an additional paragraph to the report disclosing the departure, including its effects on the financial statements if they have been determined by management or are known as the result of the accountant's procedures.
Answer (A) is incorrect. Unless an audit has been conducted, an opinion may not be expressed. If modification of the report is not adequate to indicate the deficiencies, the auditor should withdraw from the engagement. Answer (B) is incorrect. The accountant provides limited assurance in a review report. Answer (C) is incorrect. A review report need not be limited in distribution.

22. Baker, CPA, was engaged to review the financial statements of Hall Company, a nonissuer. Evidence came to Baker's attention that indicated substantial doubt as to Hall's ability to continue as a going concern. The principal conditions and events that caused the substantial doubt have been fully disclosed in the notes to Hall's financial statements. Which of the following statements best describes Baker's reporting responsibility concerning this matter?

A. Baker is not required to modify the accountant's review report.

B. Baker is not permitted to modify the accountant's review report.

C. Baker should issue an accountant's compilation report instead of a review report.

D. Baker should express a qualified opinion in the accountant's review report.

Answer (A) is correct. *(CPA, adapted)*
REQUIRED: The accountant's reporting responsibility in a review engagement if (s)he concludes that a substantial doubt exists as to whether the entity is a going concern.
DISCUSSION: AR 90 states that, normally, neither an uncertainty about an entity's ability to continue as a going concern nor an inconsistency in the application of accounting principles should cause the accountant to modify the standard report, provided the financial statements appropriately disclose such matters. Nothing in this statement, however, is intended to preclude an accountant from emphasizing in a separate paragraph of the report a matter regarding the financial statements. Nevertheless, if management's conclusions about a going-concern issue are unreasonable, or if disclosure is inadequate, the accountant must follow the guidance for departures from GAAP.
Answer (B) is incorrect. The accountant may emphasize a matter. Answer (C) is incorrect. If appropriate procedures have been applied and the accountant has formed a conclusion, a review report may be issued. Answer (D) is incorrect. Unless an audit has been conducted, an opinion may not be expressed.

23. Baker, CPA, was engaged to review the financial statements of Hall Company, a nonissuer. During the engagement, Baker uncovered a complex scheme involving client illegal acts and fraud that materially affect Hall's financial statements. If Baker believes that modification of the standard review report is **not** adequate to indicate the deficiencies in the financial statements, Baker should

A. Disclaim an opinion.

B. Express an adverse opinion.

C. Withdraw from the engagement.

D. Express a qualified opinion.

Answer (C) is correct. *(CPA, adapted)*
REQUIRED: The auditor action when modification of the standard review report is not adequate to indicate deficiencies in the financial statements.
DISCUSSION: AR 90 states that, if the accountant believes that modification is not adequate to indicate the deficiencies in the financial statements, (s)he should withdraw from the engagement. The SSARSs do not provide for an adverse review report.

24. Each page of a nonissuer's financial statements reviewed by an accountant should include the following reference:

A. See Accountant's Review Report.

B. Reviewed, No Accountant's Assurance Expressed.

C. See Accompanying Accountant's Notes.

D. Reviewed, No Material Modifications Required.

Answer (A) is correct. *(CPA, adapted)*
REQUIRED: The reference on each page of a nonissuer's financial statements reviewed by an accountant.
DISCUSSION: Each page should include a reference such as "See Accountant's Review Report" (AR 90).
Answer (B) is incorrect. A review report ordinarily expresses limited assurance. Answer (C) is incorrect. Notes are part of the financial statements, not the accountant's report. Answer (D) is incorrect. The review report states that the accountant is not aware of any modifications that should be made other than those indicated in the report.

25. Moore, CPA, has been asked to issue a review report on the balance sheet of Dover Co., a nonissuer. Moore will not be reporting on Dover's statements of income, retained earnings, and cash flows. Moore may issue the review report provided the

A. Balance sheet is presented in a prescribed form of an industry trade association.

B. Scope of the inquiry and analytical procedures has not been restricted.

C. Balance sheet is not to be used to obtain credit or distributed to creditors.

D. Specialized accounting principles and practices of Dover's industry are disclosed.

Answer (B) is correct. *(CPA, adapted)*
REQUIRED: The condition under which an accountant may issue a review report on a single financial statement.
DISCUSSION: An accountant may issue a report on one or more of the financial statements and not on the others. This form of reporting is not considered a limitation on scope but a limited reporting engagement. However, the accountant must not be restricted in the procedures to be applied, which, in a review, consist primarily of inquiries and analytical procedures.
Answer (A) is incorrect. The decision is independent of whether the balance sheet is to be presented in a prescribed form. Answer (C) is incorrect. A reviewed financial statement may be used for any appropriate purpose. Answer (D) is incorrect. A review report may be issued on a comprehensive basis of accounting other than GAAP. The specialized principles, however, need not be disclosed.

18.3 Other Considerations for Compilations and Reviews

26. An accountant began an audit of the financial statements of a nonissuer and was asked to change the engagement to a review because of a restriction on the scope of the audit. If there is reasonable justification for the change, the review report should include reference to the

	Original Engagement That Was Agreed To	Scope Limitation That Caused the Changed Engagement
A.	Yes	Yes
B.	Yes	No
C.	No	Yes
D.	No	No

Answer (D) is correct. *(CPA, adapted)*
REQUIRED: The item(s), if any, that should be referred to in the accountant's review report.
DISCUSSION: AR 90 states that if the accountant concludes, based upon his/her professional judgment, that there is reasonable justification to change the engagement and if (s)he complies with the standards applicable to the changed engagement, (s)he should issue an appropriate review report. The report should not include reference to the original engagement, any auditing procedures that may have been performed, or scope limitations that resulted in the changed engagement.

27. Davis, CPA, accepted an engagement to audit the financial statements of Tech Resources, a nonissuer. Before the completion of the audit, Tech requested Davis to change the engagement to a compilation of financial statements. Before Davis agrees to change the engagement, Davis is required to consider the

	Additional Audit Effort Necessary to Complete the Audit	Reason Given for Tech's Request
A.	No	No
B.	Yes	Yes
C.	Yes	No
D.	No	Yes

Answer (B) is correct. *(CPA, adapted)*
 REQUIRED: The matter(s) considered before changing an engagement from an audit to a compilation.
 DISCUSSION: Before an accountant who was engaged to perform an audit in accordance with GAAS agrees to change the engagement to a compilation or a review, at least the following should be considered: (1) the reason given for the client's request, particularly the implications of a restriction on the scope of the audit, whether imposed by the client or by circumstances; (2) the additional audit effort required to complete the audit; and (3) the estimated additional cost to complete the audit (AR 80).

28. Clark, CPA, compiled and properly reported on the financial statements of Green Co., a nonissuer, for the year ended March 31, Year 1. These financial statements omitted substantially all disclosures required by GAAP. Green asked Clark to compile the statements for the year ended March 31, Year 2, and to include all GAAP disclosures for the Year 2 statements only, but otherwise present both years' financial statements in comparative form. What is Clark's responsibility concerning the proposed engagement? Clark may

A. Not report on the comparative financial statements because the Year 1 statements are not comparable with the Year 2 statements that include the GAAP disclosures.

B. Report on the comparative financial statements, provided the Year 1 statements do not contain any obvious material misstatements.

C. Report on the comparative financial statements, provided an explanatory paragraph is added to Clark's report on the comparative financial statements.

D. Report on the comparative financial statements, provided Clark updates the report on the Year 1 statements that do not include the GAAP disclosures.

Answer (A) is correct. *(CPA, adapted)*
 REQUIRED: The accountant's responsibility when compiled financial statements are presented comparatively but the earlier year's statements omit most disclosures required by GAAP.
 DISCUSSION: Compiled financial statements that omit substantially all of the disclosures required by GAAP are not comparable with financial statements that include such disclosures. Accordingly, the accountant ordinarily should not issue a report on comparative financial statements when statements for one or more, but not all, of the periods presented omit substantially all of the disclosures required by GAAP (AR 200).
 Answer (B) is incorrect. The statements are not considered comparable and should not be reported on. Answer (C) is incorrect. No report should be issued. The statements are not comparable. Answer (D) is incorrect. The statements are not considered comparable and should not be reported on.

29. An accountant has been asked to compile the financial statements of a nonissuer on a prescribed form that omits substantially all the disclosures required by GAAP. If the prescribed form is a standard preprinted form adopted by the company's industry trade association and is to be transmitted only to such association, the accountant

A. Need not advise the industry trade association of the omission of all disclosures.

B. Should disclose the details of the omissions in separate paragraphs of the compilation report.

C. Is precluded from issuing a compilation report when all disclosures are omitted.

D. Should express limited assurance that the financial statements are free of material misstatements.

Answer (A) is correct. *(CPA, adapted)*
 REQUIRED: The accountant's responsibility when (s)he compiles statements on a prescribed form to be transmitted only to the prescribing authority.
 DISCUSSION: An alternative form of the standard compilation report is used when a prescribed form or related instructions call for departure from GAAP by specifying a measurement principle not in conformity with GAAP or failing to require disclosures in accordance with GAAP. The presumption is that the information required in a prescribed form is sufficient to meet the needs of the body that designed or adopted the form. In the standard report on statements included in such a form, the accountant should indicate that the statements are in a prescribed form and that they may differ from those presented in accordance with GAAP, but (s)he need not describe the differences in the report (AR 300).
 Answer (B) is incorrect. This disclosure is unnecessary. Answer (C) is incorrect. The report may be issued in these circumstances. Answer (D) is incorrect. A compilation report expresses no assurance.

30. Gole, CPA, is engaged to review the Year 2 financial statements of North Co., a nonissuer. Previously, Gole audited North's Year 1 financial statements and expressed an unqualified opinion. Gole decides to include a separate paragraph in the Year 2 review report because North plans to present comparative financial statements for Year 2 and Year 1. This separate paragraph should indicate that

A. The Year 2 review report is intended solely for the information of management and the board of directors.

B. The Year 1 auditor's report may no longer be relied on.

C. No auditing procedures were performed after the date of the Year 1 auditor's report.

D. There are justifiable reasons for changing the level of service from an audit to a review.

Answer (C) is correct. *(CPA, adapted)*
REQUIRED: The reference in a separate paragraph in a review report when comparative statements are presented and an audit was performed in the previous year.
DISCUSSION: A continuing accountant who performs a lower level of service should include a separate paragraph describing the responsibility assumed for the financial statements of the prior period or reissue the previous report. The paragraph included in the review report should indicate that no auditing procedures were performed after the date of the original auditor's report.
Answer (A) is incorrect. A review report may be distributed to any user. Answer (B) is incorrect. The previous auditor's report may still be relied upon. Answer (D) is incorrect. No mention of the reasons for the change of service should be made in the review report.

31. Before reissuing a compilation report on the financial statements of a nonissuer for the prior year, the predecessor accountant is required to

A. Make inquiries about actions taken at meetings of the board of directors during the current year.

B. Verify that the reissued report will **not** be used to obtain credit from a financial institution.

C. Review the successor accountant's working papers for matters affecting the prior year.

D. Compare the prior year's financial statements with those of the current year.

Answer (D) is correct. *(CPA, adapted)*
REQUIRED: The procedure necessary before reissuing a compilation report.
DISCUSSION: Before reissuing a report, the predecessor should consider whether the report is still appropriate. The predecessor should read the current financial statement, compare the prior financial statements with the current financial statements, and obtain a letter from the successor requesting any information that might affect the prior financial statements.
Answer (A) is incorrect. Making inquiries about actions taken at BOD meetings is not required to reissue the report. Answer (B) is incorrect. Determining the use of the report is not required to reissue the report. Answer (C) is incorrect. Reviewing the successor accountant's working papers is not required to reissue the report.

32. Kell engaged March, CPA, to submit to Kell a written personal financial plan containing unaudited personal financial statements. March anticipates omitting certain disclosures required by GAAP because the engagement's sole purpose is to assist Kell in developing a personal financial plan. For March to be exempt from complying with the requirements of AR 80, *Compilation of Financial Statements*, Kell is required to agree that the

A. Financial statements will not be presented in comparative form with those of the prior period.

B. Omitted disclosures required by GAAP are not material.

C. Financial statements will not be disclosed to a non-CPA financial planner.

D. Financial statements will not be used to obtain credit.

Answer (D) is correct. *(CPA, adapted)*
REQUIRED: The circumstances under which an accountant may depart from the requirements of AR 80.
DISCUSSION: AR 600, *Reporting on Personal Financial Statements Included in Written Personal Financial Plans*, states that an accountant may submit a written personal financial plan containing unaudited personal financial statements to a client without complying with the requirements of AR 80 if the accountant (1) has an understanding with the client about its use and (2) has no reason to believe that the financial statements will be used to obtain credit or for any other purpose except developing the financial plan.
Answer (A) is incorrect. The financial statements may be presented in comparative form. Answer (B) is incorrect. The exemption is appropriate regardless of the disclosures and their materiality level. Answer (C) is incorrect. The financial plan is likely to be used by the client and potentially a financial planner.

18.4 Special Reports (AU 623)

33. An auditor who conducts an audit in accordance with generally accepted auditing standards and concludes that the financial statements are fairly presented in accordance with a comprehensive basis of accounting other than generally accepted accounting principles (OCBOA), such as the cash basis of accounting, should issue a

A. Special report.

B. Report disclaiming an opinion.

C. Review report.

D. Report expressing a qualified opinion.

Answer (A) is correct. *(CPA, adapted)*
REQUIRED: The report issued on financial statements presented in accordance with an OCBOA.
DISCUSSION: An auditor's judgment (opinion) about the fair presentation of financial statements is applied within an identifiable framework, which is usually provided by GAAP. However, an OCBOA (e.g., cash basis) may sometimes be used. A special report is appropriate for reporting on statements prepared on an OCBOA.
Answer (B) is incorrect. The auditor should not disclaim an opinion if (s)he is able to conclude that the statements are fairly presented. Answer (C) is incorrect. An audit results in a positive opinion. A review results in the expression of limited (negative) assurance. Answer (D) is incorrect. The auditor should not qualify the opinion if (s)he is able to conclude that the statements are fairly presented.

34. When an auditor reports on financial statements prepared on an entity's income tax basis, the auditor's report should

A. Disclaim an opinion on whether the statements were examined in accordance with generally accepted auditing standards.

B. Not express an opinion on whether the statements are presented in conformity with the comprehensive basis of accounting used.

C. Include an explanation of how the results of operations differ from the cash receipts and disbursements basis of accounting.

D. State that the basis of presentation is a comprehensive basis of accounting other than GAAP.

Answer (D) is correct. *(CPA, adapted)*
REQUIRED: The statement in an auditor's report on financial statements prepared on an income tax basis.
DISCUSSION: An auditor may report on financial statements prepared in conformity with an other comprehensive basis of accounting (OCBOA). In addition to an introductory paragraph and a standard scope paragraph, the report should include a separate paragraph (after the scope paragraph) that (1) states the basis of the presentation, (2) refers to a note in the statements explaining the basis chosen, and (3) states that the basis of the presentation is a comprehensive basis other than GAAP. Finally, the auditor should include a paragraph expressing an opinion that the statements are presented fairly in conformity with the OCBOA.
Answer (A) is incorrect. The auditor follows GAAS in the engagement. Answer (B) is incorrect. An opinion is expressed on whether the statements are presented in conformity with the OCBOA. Answer (C) is incorrect. Although a note in the financial statements should explain how the basis of accounting differs from GAAP, the auditor's report need only refer to that note.

35. An auditor's report on financial statements prepared on the cash receipts and disbursements basis of accounting should include all of the following **except**

A. A reference to the note to the financial statements that describes the cash receipts and disbursements basis of accounting.

B. A statement that the cash receipts and disbursements basis of accounting is not a comprehensive basis of accounting.

C. An opinion as to whether the financial statements are fairly presented in conformity with the cash receipts and disbursements basis of accounting.

D. A statement that the audit was conducted in accordance with auditing standards generally accepted in the U.S.

Answer (B) is correct. *(CPA, adapted)*
REQUIRED: The statement not included on an auditor's special report on cash-basis financial statements.
DISCUSSION: A statement indicating that the cash receipts and cash disbursements basis of accounting is a comprehensive basis of accounting other than GAAP (OCBOA) should be included in the auditor's report.
Answer (A) is incorrect. A reference to the note of the financial statements that describes the basis should be included in the auditor's report. Answer (C) is incorrect. An opinion as to whether the financial statements are fairly presented should be included in the auditor's report. Answer (D) is incorrect. A statement that the audit was conducted in accordance with GAAS should be included in the auditor's report.

36. Delta Life Insurance Co. prepares its financial statements on an accounting basis insurance companies use pursuant to the rules of a state insurance commission. If Wall, CPA, Delta's auditor, discovers that the statements are **not** suitably titled, Wall should

    A. Disclose any reservations in an explanatory paragraph and qualify the opinion.

    B. Apply to the state insurance commission for an advisory opinion.

    C. Issue a special statutory basis report that clearly disclaims any opinion.

    D. Explain in the notes to the financial statements the terminology used.

Answer (A) is correct. *(CPA, adapted)*
    REQUIRED: The proper action when statements prepared on an OCBOA are not suitably titled.
    DISCUSSION: Terms such as balance sheet, statement of income, or other unmodified titles are ordinarily understood to apply to statements presented in conformity with GAAP. Consequently, the auditor of statements prepared under an OCBOA should consider whether the statements are suitably titled. If (s)he believes they are not, the auditor should disclose his/her reservations in an explanatory paragraph and qualify the opinion (AU 623).
    Answer (B) is incorrect. AU 623 does not require the auditor to apply to the state insurance commission for an advisory opinion. Answer (C) is incorrect. The opinion should be qualified. Answer (D) is incorrect. The notes are the responsibility of management, not the auditor.

37. A CPA is permitted to accept a separate engagement (**not** in conjunction with an audit of financial statements) to audit an entity's

	Schedule of Accounts Receivable	Schedule of Royalties
A.	Yes	Yes
B.	Yes	No
C.	No	Yes
D.	No	No

Answer (A) is correct. *(CPA, adapted)*
    REQUIRED: The separate engagement(s), if any, a CPA is permitted to accept.
    DISCUSSION: An auditor may be requested to express an opinion on one or more specified elements, accounts, or items of a financial statement. The report should be a special report (AU 623).

38. Field is an employee of Gold Enterprises. Hardy, CPA, is asked to express an opinion on Field's profit participation in Gold's net income. Hardy may accept this engagement only if

    A. Hardy also audits Gold's complete financial statements.

    B. Gold's financial statements are prepared in conformity with GAAP.

    C. Hardy's report is available for use by Gold's other employees.

    D. Field owns a controlling interest in Gold.

Answer (A) is correct. *(CPA, adapted)*
    REQUIRED: The requirement to accept an engagement.
    DISCUSSION: AU 623 states that if a specified element, account, or item is, or is based upon, an entity's net income or stockholders' equity or the equivalent thereof, the auditor should have audited the complete financial statements to express an opinion on the specified element, account, or item.
    Answer (B) is incorrect. The financial statements could be based on an OCBOA. Answer (C) is incorrect. The use of the report may be restricted. An auditor may perform many services that result in restricted-use reports, that is, those intended only for specified parties (see AU 532). Answer (D) is incorrect. Whether Field owns a controlling interest in Gold is irrelevant.

39. An auditor's report is designated a special report when it is issued in connection with

    A. Interim financial information of an issuer that is subject to a limited review.

    B. Compliance with aspects of regulatory requirements related to audited financial statements.

    C. Application of accounting principles to specified transactions.

    D. Limited use prospective financial statements such as financial projection.

Answer (B) is correct. *(CPA, adapted)*
    REQUIRED: The auditor's service that results in a special report.
    DISCUSSION: Entities may be required by contractual agreements (e.g., bond indentures and certain types of loan agreements) or by regulatory agencies to furnish compliance reports by independent auditors. These reports should be issued in conjunction with an ordinary audit. The report envisioned provides negative assurance that may be given in the report on the financial statements or in a separate report. But this assurance should not be given unless an audit has been performed and should not extend to any covenants relating to matters that have not been audited (AU 623).
    Answer (A) is incorrect. Special reports are not issued in connection with reviews of interim financial information. AU 722 discusses the report appropriate for such a review. Answer (C) is incorrect. A report on the application of accounting principles is governed by AU 625. Answer (D) is incorrect. AT 301 applies to projections.

40. An auditor's report issued in connection with which of the following is generally **not** considered to be a special report?

A. Compliance with aspects of contractual agreements unrelated to audited financial statements.

B. Specified elements, accounts, or items of a financial statement presented in a document.

C. Financial statements prepared in accordance with an entity's income tax basis.

D. Financial information presented in a prescribed schedule that requires a prescribed form of auditor's report.

Answer (A) is correct. *(CPA, adapted)*
REQUIRED: The report not considered to be a special report.
DISCUSSION: Special reports are issued in connection with, among other things, compliance with aspects of contractual agreements or regulatory requirements related to audited statements. Such a report provides negative assurance that may be given in the report on the financial statements or in a separate report. But this assurance should not be given unless an audit of the statements has been performed.
Answer (B) is incorrect. A special report may be issued on specified elements, accounts, or items of a financial statement presented in a document. Answer (C) is incorrect. A special report may be issued on financial statements prepared in accordance with an entity's income tax basis. Answer (D) is incorrect. A special report may be issued on financial information presented in a prescribed schedule that requires a prescribed form of auditor's report.

41. Financial information is presented in a printed form that prescribes the wording of the independent auditor's report. The form is not acceptable to the auditor because the form calls for statements that are inconsistent with the auditor's responsibility. Under these circumstances, the auditor most likely would

A. Withdraw from the engagement.

B. Reword the form or attach a separate report.

C. Express a qualified opinion with an explanation.

D. Limit use of the report to the party who designed the form.

Answer (B) is correct. *(CPA, adapted)*
REQUIRED: The auditor action regarding a prescribed report form that is inconsistent with his/her responsibility.
DISCUSSION: Printed forms or schedules to be filed with a regulatory body may prescribe the wording of the auditor's report. However, this language may not conform with professional reporting standards. Consequently, AU 623 states that some report forms can be made acceptable by inserting additional wording; others can be made acceptable only by complete revision. When a printed report form calls upon an independent auditor to make a statement that she or he is not justified in making, the auditor should reword the form or attach a separate report.
Answer (A) is incorrect. The auditor need not withdraw if the report can be modified to be consistent with the auditor's responsibility. Answer (C) is incorrect. The auditor need not express a qualified opinion unless the financial statements were materially misstated. Answer (D) is incorrect. If the audit was in accordance with generally accepted auditing standards, a general-use report may be issued.

Use the additional questions in Gleim **CPA Test Prep Online** to create Test Sessions that emulate Prometric!

18.5 PRACTICE SIMULATION

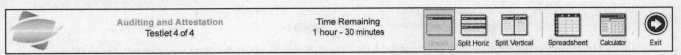

DIRECTIONS

Note: If you believe you have encountered a software malfunction, report it to the test center staff immediately.

Navigation

To navigate from task to task, use the controls at the bottom of the screen. Click on the **Next** button to advance to the next task, or the **Previous** button to go to the previous task. To go directly to any task, click on its number.

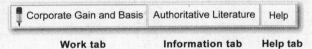

If you would like a reminder to revisit a task, or want to indicate that you are finished with it, click on the reminder flag below the task number. To clear the flag, click on it again. Reminder flags are for your use only – they do not contribute to your score.

Tabs

In this part of the examination, you will be asked to complete various tasks. Every task has one or more **Work Tabs**. Some tasks have one or more **Information Tabs**, others may have none. Every task has a **Help** tab.

If a task has **Information Tabs**, you may use the information in them to complete your responses in the **Work Tabs**.

Corporate Gain and Basis	Authoritative Literature	Help
Work tab	**Information tab**	**Help tab**

Work Tabs:
- **Work Tabs** are identified with a pencil icon. This is where your responses are expected.
- Each task has one or more **Work Tabs**.
- **Work Tabs** contain directions for completing the task – be sure to read these directions carefully.
- The **Work Tab** name in the example above is for illustration only – yours will differ.
- You must complete all of the **Work Tabs** in each task to receive full credit.

Information Tabs:
- The Authoritative Literature will be provided in all tasks in the AUD, FAR, and REG sections for your reference.
- Your simulation may have one or more additional **Information Tabs**. Like the Authoritative Literature tabs, **Information Tabs** do not have a pencil icon.
- If your task has additional **Information Tabs**, go through each to familiarize yourself with the task content.

Help Tab:
- The **Help Tab** provides assistance with the exam software that is used in this task. For example, if the task is to compose a memorandum, **Help** will provide information about the word processor.

The Toolbar

The toolbar at the top of the screen shows the amount of time remaining for you to complete the tasks. In addition, the following tools are available. Note that only the Exit button is displayed when Directions are visible - the others will appear when you begin the tasks.

Click on these buttons to split or unsplit the screen. You can split the screen vertically or horizontally.

Click on this button to display the calculator; click on it again to hide the calculator. To move the calculator, click on the calculator title bar and drag the calculator to the desired location.

Click on this button to use the spreadsheet; click on it again to hide the spreadsheet. To move the spreadsheet, click on the the spreadsheet title bar and drag the spreadsheet to the desired location.

Click on this button to go on to the next part of the examination. You must complete all of the tasks to receive full credit. Once you click on **Exit** and confirm the action, you will NOT be able to return to this testlet.

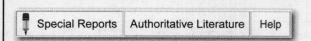

Indicate by checking the appropriate box which of the following statements about an audit engagement resulting in expression of an unqualified opinion on a client's cash-basis financial statements are true and which are false.

Statement	True	False
1. The auditor provides less assurance in the report than for a traditional audit report on GAAP-based statements.		
2. The introductory paragraph identifies management's responsibility relative to the financial statements.		
3. The scope paragraph is unchanged from that of a traditional audit report on GAAP-based statements.		
4. The report should include a separate paragraph stating that the financial statements were prepared on the cash basis.		
5. The auditor should avoid the phrase "present fairly" in the opinion.		
6. The auditor should avoid the phrase "in all material respects" in the opinion.		
7. The report should have the heading "Independent Auditor's Report."		
8. The report should be dated as of the date of the financial statements.		
9. Management should sign the report.		
10. The report should contain a statement limiting its use.		

| | Review Report I | Authoritative Literature | Help |

The following draft of a review engagement report has been submitted by a staff member to the manager for review. The table below contains the comments by the manager about the draft. Indicate by selecting from the list provided whether the original draft is correct, the audit manager's comment is correct, or if neither is correct.

We have reviewed the accompanying balance sheet of ABC Company as of December 31, Year 1, and the related statements of income, retained earnings, and cash flows for the year then ended. A review includes primarily making inquiries of company management. A review is substantially less in scope than an audit, the objective of which is the expression of an opinion regarding the financial statements as a whole. Accordingly, we do not express such an opinion.

Management is responsible for the preparation and fair presentation of the financial statements in accordance with accounting principles generally accepted in the United States of America and for designing, implementing, and maintaining internal control relevant to the preparation and fair presentation of the financial statements.

Our responsibility is to conduct the review in accordance with Statements on Standards for Accounting and Review Services issued by the Auditing Standards Board. Those standards require us to perform procedures to obtain limited assurance that there are no material modifications that should be made to the financial statements. We believe that the results of our procedures provide a reasonable basis for our report.

Based on our examination, we are not aware of any material modifications that should be made to the accompanying financial statements in order for them to be in conformity with accounting principles generally accepted in the United States of America.

Manager's Comments	Answer
1. The report should not refer to the statement of cash flows because a nonissuer does not prepare this statement.	
2. The second sentence in the first paragraph also should refer to analytical procedures.	
3. The third sentence in the first paragraph should state that the review is "substantially greater in scope..."	
4. The last sentence in the first paragraph should be deleted.	
5. The second paragraph should state that the CPA is responsible for the preparation of the fair presentation of the financial statements.	
6. The first sentence in the third paragraph should state that the accounting and review standards are established by the federal government.	
7. The fourth paragraph should state "Based on our study..." rather than "Based on our examination..."	
8. The fourth paragraph should state, "conformity with auditing principles" rather than "conformity with accounting principles."	

Choices
A) The original draft is correct.
B) The manager's comment is correct.
C) Neither the original draft nor the manager's comment is correct.

Items 1 through 15 state unrelated procedures that an accountant may consider performing in separate engagements to review the financial statements of a nonissuer (a review) and to compile the financial statements of a nonissuer (a compilation). Indicate whether or not each procedure is contemplated for a review and a compilation. Make two selections for each item.

Review Choices
A) Procedure is contemplated.
B) Procedure is not contemplated.
Compilation Choices
C) Procedure is contemplated.
D) Procedure is not contemplated.

Procedure	Review A) or B)	Compilation C) or D)
1. The accountant establishes an understanding with the entity regarding the nature and limitations of the services to be performed.		
2. The accountant makes inquiries of management.		
3. The accountant, as the entity's successor accountant, communicates with the predecessor accountant to obtain access to the predecessor's working papers.		
4. The accountant obtains a level of knowledge of the accounting principles and practices of the entity's industry.		
5. The accountant assesses fraud risk.		
6. The accountant performs analytical procedures designed to identify relationships that appear to be unusual.		
7. The accountant obtains an understanding of internal control.		
8. The accountant sends a letter of inquiry to the entity's attorney to corroborate the information furnished by management concerning litigation.		
9. The accountant obtains written representations from management of the entity.		
10. The accountant compares recorded amounts with expectations.		
11. The accountant communicates to the entity's senior management illegal employee acts discovered by the accountant that are clearly inconsequential.		
12. The accountant makes inquiries about events subsequent to the date of the financial statements that would have a material effect on the financial statements.		
13. The accountant modifies the accountant's report for a change in accounting principles that is adequately disclosed.		
14. The accountant submits a hard copy of the financial statements and accountant's report when the financial statements and accountant's report are submitted on a computer disk.		
15. The accountant performs specific procedures to evaluate whether substantial doubt exists about the entity's ability to continue as a going concern.		

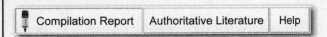

| Compilation Report | Authoritative Literature | Help |

The following report was drafted on October 25, Year 1, by Major, CPA, at the completion of the engagement to compile the financial statements of Ajax Company for the year ended September 30, Year 1. Ajax is a nonpublic entity in which Major's child has a material direct financial interest. Ajax decided to omit substantially all of the disclosures required by GAAP because the financial statements will be for management's use only. The statement of cash flows was also omitted because management does not believe it to be a useful financial statement.

Select from the list provided to indicate which sentences in Major's report on the compiled financial statements contain a deficiency.

To the Board of Directors of Ajax Company:	*Answer*
1. I have compiled the accompanying financial statements of Ajax Company as of September 30, Year 1, and for the year then ended.	
2. I have not audited or reviewed the accompanying financial statements.	
3. Management is responsible for the preparation and fair presentation of the financial statements in accordance with accounting principles generally accepted in the United States of America and for designing, implementing, and maintaining internal control relevant to the preparation and fair presentation of the financial statements.	
4. My responsibility is to conduct the compilation in accordance with accepted standards issued by the American Institute of Certified Public Accountants.	
5. The objective of a compilation is to assist management in presenting financial information in the form of financial statements without undertaking to obtain or provide any assurance that there are no material modifications that should be made to the financial statements.	
6. Management has elected to omit substantially all of the disclosures (and the statement of cash flows) required by generally accepted accounting principles.	
7. If the omitted disclosures and statements were included in the financial statements, they might influence the user's conclusions about the company's financial position, results of operations, and cash flows.	
8. I am not independent with respect to Ajax Company.	
9. This lack of independence is due to my child's ownership of a material direct financial interest in Ajax Company.	
10. This report is intended solely for the information and use of the Board of Directors and management of Ajax Company and should not be used for any other purpose.	

Major, CPA
October 25, Year 1

Choices
Deficient
Not deficient

▼ = Reminder   Directions   1 2 3 [4] 5 6   ◀ Previous   Next ▶

Jordan & Stone, CPAs, audited the financial statements of Tech Co., a nonissuer, for the year ended December 31, Year 1, and expressed an unqualified opinion. For the year ended December 31, Year 2, Tech issued comparative financial statements. Jordan & Stone reviewed Tech's Year 2 financial statements and Kent, an assistant on the engagement, drafted the accountants' review report below. Land, the engagement supervisor, decided not to reissue the prior year's auditor's report, but instructed Kent to include a separate paragraph in the current year's review report describing the responsibility assumed for the prior year's audited financial statements. This is an appropriate reporting procedure.

Land reviewed Kent's draft presented below and indicated in the *Supervisor's Review Notes* below that there were 13 deficiencies in Kent's draft.

We have reviewed and audited the accompanying balance sheets of Tech Co. as of December 31, Year 1 and Year 2, and the related statements of income, retained earnings, and cash flows for the years then ended. A review is substantially less in scope than an audit, the objective of which is the expression of an opinion regarding the financial statements as a whole. Accordingly, we do not express such an opinion.

Management is responsible for the preparation and fair presentation of the financial statements in accordance with accounting principles generally accepted in the United States of America and for designing, implementing, and maintaining internal control relevant to the preparation and fair presentation of the financial statements.

Our responsibility is to conduct the review in accordance with Statements on Standards for Accounting and Review Services issued by the American Institute of Certified Public Accountants. Those standards require us to perform procedures to obtain significant assurance that there are no material modifications that should be made to the financial statements. We believe that the results of our procedures provide a reasonable basis for our report.

Based on our study, we are not aware of any material modifications that should be made to the accompanying financial statements in order for them to be in conformity with accounting principles generally accepted in the United States of America. Because of inherent limitations in a review engagement, this report is intended for the information of management and should not be used for any other purpose.

The financial statements for the year ended December 31, Year 1, were audited by us, and our report was dated March 2, Year 2. We have no responsibility for updating that report for events and circumstances occurring after that date.

Jordan and Stone, CPAs
March 1, Year 3

Items 1. through 13. represent deficiencies noted by Land. For each deficiency, indicate whether Land is correct or incorrect in the criticism of Kent's draft.

Supervisor's Review Notes	Answer	List
1. There should be **no** reference to the prior year's audited financial statements in the first (introductory) paragraph.		A) Correct
2. All the current-year basic financial statements are **not** properly identified in the first (introductory) paragraph.		B) Incorrect
3. A statement should be included in the first paragraph stating that a review includes primarily applying analytical procedures to management's financial data and making inquiries of company management.		
4. In the second paragraph, "fair presentation" should be replaced with "accurate presentation."		
5. There should be **no** reference to the American Institute of Certified Public Accountants in the first (introductory) paragraph.		
6. The phrase "to obtain significant assurance" in the third paragraph should be replaced with "to obtain limited assurance."		
7. The last sentence in the fourth paragraph that begins, "We believe that the results ..." should be deleted.		
8. The fourth paragraph should begin, "Based on our review..."		
9. There should be **no** restriction on the distribution of the accountant's review report in the fourth paragraph.		
10. There should be **no** reference to "material modifications" in the fourth paragraph.		
11. There should be an indication of the type of opinion expressed on the prior year's audited financial statements in the fourth (separate) paragraph.		
12. There should be an indication that **no** auditing procedures were performed after the date of the report on the prior year's financial statements in the fourth (separate) paragraph.		
13. There should be **no** reference to "updating that report for events and circumstances occurring after that date" in the fourth (separate) paragraph.		

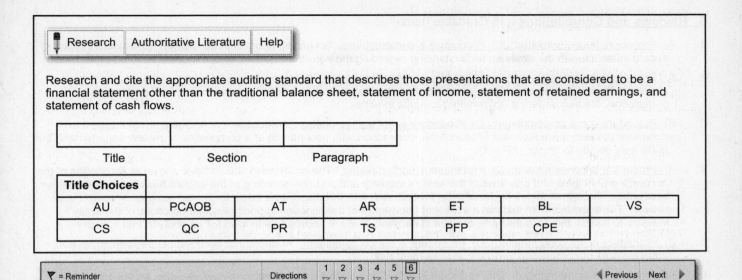

Unofficial Answers

1. Special Reports (10 Gradable Items)

1. <u>False.</u> The same level of assurance, an opinion as to fairness, is presented in special reports as in the audit of GAAP-based financial statements.

2. <u>True.</u> Management's responsibility for the financial statements is presented in the introductory paragraph.

3. <u>True.</u> The scope of the audit for cash-basis financial statements is the same as that for GAAP-based.

4. <u>True.</u> A separate paragraph should be included in the report to explain the basis of reporting.

5. <u>False.</u> The auditor should use the phrase "present fairly" in the opinion if (s)he concludes that the financial statements present fairly on the cash basis.

6. <u>False.</u> The auditor should use the phrase "in all material respects" in the opinion.

7. <u>True.</u> The report should have the heading "Independent Auditor's Report."

8. <u>False.</u> The report should be dated no earlier than when the auditor has gathered sufficient appropriate evidence to support the opinion.

9. <u>False.</u> The auditor should sign the report.

10. <u>False.</u> The report is for general use.

2. Review Report I (8 Gradable Items)

1. <u>A) The original draft is correct.</u> A nonissuer is required to present a statement of cash flows, and the review report should refer to the statement.

2. <u>B) The manager's comment is correct.</u> A review includes inquiries of company personnel and analytical procedures applied to financial data.

3. <u>A) The original draft is correct.</u> The draft is correct as stated.

4. <u>A) The original draft is correct.</u> The draft is correct as stated. A disclaimer is required.

5. <u>A) The original draft is correct.</u> Management is responsible for fair presentation.

6. <u>C) Neither the original draft nor the manager's comment is correct.</u> The report should state that the SSARSs are issued by the American Institute of Certified Public Accountants.

7. <u>C) Neither the original draft nor the manager's comment is correct.</u> The paragraph should begin, "Based on our review..."

8. <u>A) The original draft is correct.</u> The draft is correct as stated.

3. Reviews and Compilations (15 Gradable Items)

1. A) Procedure is contemplated; C) Procedure is contemplated. According to both AR 90 and AR 80, an accountant should establish with the entity an understanding regarding the nature and limitation of the services to be performed.

2. A) Procedure is contemplated; D) Procedure is not contemplated. When performing a review, an accountant must make inquiries of management and, when deemed appropriate, other company personnel. When performing a compilation, the accountant is not required to make inquiries.

3. B) Procedure is not contemplated; D) Procedure is not contemplated. "A successor accountant is not required to communicate with a predecessor accountant in connection with acceptance of a compilation or review engagement, but (s)he may decide to do so" (AR 400).

4. A) Procedure is contemplated; C) Procedure is contemplated. The accountant should have a level of knowledge of the accounting principles and practices of the entity's industry and an understanding of the entity's business to provide the accountant, through inquiries and analytical procedures, with the reasonable basis for limited assurance sought in a review. The accountant should have a level of knowledge of the accounting principles and practices of the entity's industry to enable the accountant to compile statements that are appropriate in form for an entity in that industry.

5. B) Procedure is not contemplated; D) Procedure is not contemplated. Auditors, not accountants performing review engagements or compilation services, assess fraud risk.

6. A) Procedure is contemplated; D) Procedure is not contemplated. In performing review services, an accountant is required to apply analytical procedures to the financial statements, make inquiries of management, and obtain representations from management. In a compilation engagement, an accountant prepares the financial statements of an entity. No assurance is provided; therefore, no analytical procedures are required.

7. B) Procedure is not contemplated; D) Procedure is not contemplated. An auditor should obtain an understanding of internal control. Neither a compilation nor a review contemplates that the accountant will obtain an understanding of internal control.

8. B) Procedure is not contemplated; D) Procedure is not contemplated. During a review engagement, an accountant is required to obtain written representations from management but not to obtain corroborating evidence. Compilation services do not contemplate performing procedures performed in a review, for example, inquiries about information provided by the entity.

9. A) Procedure is contemplated; D) Procedure is not contemplated. When performing a review of an entity's financial statements, the accountant must obtain written representations from responsible and knowledgeable members of management (e.g., the CEO or the CFO or the equivalent). However, compilation services do not contemplate performing procedures performed in a review, for example, obtaining written representations from management.

10. A) Procedure is contemplated; D) Procedure is not contemplated. When reviewing an entity's financial statements, the accountant must perform analytical procedures, which include comparing recorded amounts or ratios with expectations developed by the accountant. Compilation services do not contemplate performing procedures performed in a review, for example, applying analytical procedures.

11. B) Procedure is not contemplated; D) Procedure is not contemplated. The accountant should establish an understanding with the entity, in writing, regarding the services to be performed. The understanding should provide that the accountant will inform the appropriate level of management of any illegal acts that come to his/her attention, unless they are clearly inconsequential.

12. A) Procedure is contemplated; D) Procedure is not contemplated. When performing a review, an accountant must make inquiries of management and, when deemed appropriate, other company personnel. When performing a compilation, the accountant is not required to make inquiries.

13. B) Procedure is not contemplated; D) Procedure is not contemplated. Given proper disclosure, inconsistencies in the application of accounting principles do not normally result in modification of the standard report.

14. B) Procedure is not contemplated; D) Procedure is not contemplated. The form of the financial statements is not important. For example, the copy may be on a computer disk, fax, or other medium.

15. B) Procedure is not contemplated; D) Procedure is not contemplated. In providing compilation and review services, the accountant provides no positive assurance about the financial statements taken as a whole. Hence, these services do not contemplate assessing the entity's ability to continue as a going concern.

4. Compilation Report (10 Gradable Items)

1. <u>Deficient.</u> The report should identify the financial statements that were compiled.

2. <u>Deficient.</u> The report should state that "I have not audited or reviewed the accompanying financial statements and, accordingly, do not express an opinion or provide any assurance about whether the financial statements are in accordance with accounting principles generally accepted in the United States of America."

3. <u>Not deficient.</u> Management's responsibility should be stated in the report.

4. <u>Deficient.</u> The compilation should be conducted in accordance with Statements on Standards for Accounting and Review Services.

5. <u>Not deficient.</u> The objective of a compilation should be stated in the report.

6. <u>Not deficient.</u> It is appropriate to state that management has elected to omit the notes and the statement of cash flows.

7. <u>Not deficient.</u> It is appropriate to state that the disclosures, if made, could influence the financial statement users.

8. <u>Not deficient.</u> It is appropriate in a compilation report to indicate lack of independence.

9. <u>Not deficient.</u> It is appropriate to note the reason for lack of independence in a compilation report.

10. <u>Deficient.</u> The accountant need not limit the use of the report.

5. Review Report II (13 Gradable Items)

1. <u>A) Correct.</u>

2. <u>B) Incorrect.</u>

3. <u>A) Correct.</u>

4. <u>B) Incorrect.</u>

5. <u>B) Incorrect.</u>

6. <u>A) Correct.</u>

7. <u>B) Incorrect.</u>

8. <u>A) Correct.</u>

9. <u>A) Correct.</u>

10. <u>B) Incorrect.</u>

11. <u>A) Correct.</u>

12. <u>A) Correct.</u>

13. <u>A) Correct.</u>

6. Research (1 Gradable Item)
Answer: 623.02

AU Section 623 -- *Special Reports*

Financial Statements Prepared in Conformity with a Comprehensive Basis of Accounting Other than Generally Accepted Accounting Principles

.02   Generally accepted auditing standards are applicable when an auditor conducts an audit of and reports on any financial statement. A financial statement may be, for example, that of a corporation, a consolidated group of corporations, a combined group of affiliated entities, a not-for-profit organization, a governmental unit, an estate or trust, a partnership, a proprietorship, a segment of any of these, or an individual. The term *financial statement* refers to a presentation of financial data, including accompanying notes, derived from accounting records and intended to communicate an entity's economic resources or obligations at a point in time or the changes therein for a period of time in conformity with a comprehensive basis of accounting. For reporting purposes, the independent auditor should consider each of the following types of financial presentations to be a financial statement:

a. Balance sheet
b. Statement of income or statement of operations
c. Statement of retained earnings
d. Statement of cash flows
e. Statement of changes in owners' equity
f. Statement of assets and liabilities that does not include owners' equity accounts
g. Statement of revenue and expenses
h. Summary of operations
i. Statement of operations by product lines

Gleim Simulation Grading

Task	Correct Responses		Gradable Items		Score per Task
1	_____	÷	10	=	
2	_____	÷	8	=	
3	_____	÷	15	=	
4	_____	÷	10	=	
5	_____	÷	13	=	
Research	_____	÷	1	=	

	Total of Scores per Task	_____
÷	Total Number of Tasks	6
	Total Score	_____ %

Use **CPA Gleim Online** and **Simulation Wizard** to practice more task-based simulations in a realistic environment.

STUDY UNIT NINETEEN
RELATED REPORTING TOPICS

(21 pages of outline)

This study unit addresses miscellaneous reporting issues. Subunit 1 applies the field work and reporting standards to a review of interim (e.g., quarterly) financial information of an issuer. The procedures and the report are similar to those of a review of annual statements of nonissuers (see Study Unit 18). Subunits 2 and 3 relate to SEC engagements. The next four subunits (4 through 7) apply to information outside the basic financial statements. Subunit 8 outlines the auditor's responsibilities for financial statements prepared for use in other countries. Subunit 9 discusses the accountant's responsibility when requested to provide an evaluation of, or a conclusion on, how accounting principles will be applied to specific transactions of a particular entity. The general nature of attestation engagements was considered in Study Unit 1. The Statements on Standards for Attestation Engagements are codified in section AT of the professional standards. Covered here are the specific subjects covered in the AT standards.

19.1 INTERIM FINANCIAL INFORMATION (AU 722)

1. Interim financial information (IFI) is financial information for less than a full year or for the 12 months ending on a date other than fiscal year end.

    a. The IFI may be in **statement form**. It also may be in a **condensed form** that is asserted to conform with an **applicable financial reporting framework** (e.g., U.S. GAAP, IFRSs, or an OCBOA).

    b. Before accepting an engagement to review IFI, the accountant should make inquiries of his/her **predecessor** (Study Unit 3).

    c. An accountant may review the IFI of an entity if (1) the latest annual statements are audited, (2) the IFI is prepared using the same applicable financial reporting framework as those statements, and (3) certain other criteria are met.

2. **Review of IFI**

    a. **The objective of a review of IFI** is to enable the accountant to provide **negative assurance**, i.e., to state whether (s)he is aware of any material modifications needed for the IFI to conform with the applicable financial reporting framework.

    b. A review primarily involves performing analytical and inquiry procedures. It does **not** involve (1) testing accounting records and the effectiveness of controls, (2) obtaining corroborating evidence, (3) applying certain other auditing procedures, or (4) becoming aware of all significant matters identified in an audit.

c. Thus, a review is **not** intended to (1) result in expression of an opinion, (2) provide assurance about internal control, or (3) identify significant deficiencies and material weaknesses in internal control (but these should be communicated if identified).

3. **The Understanding with the Client**

a. An understanding with the client should be established regarding the services to be performed.

b. The understanding should be **documented** in a written communication with the client (e.g., an engagement letter).

c. The understanding includes the **objectives and limitations** of the engagement and the **responsibilities** of management and the accountant.

1) Moreover, the understanding should include the **expected form** of the accountant's final communication (e.g., written or oral).

d. **Before acceptance** of the engagement, the accountant should assess management's **ability to acknowledge responsibility** for the sufficiency of controls over preparation of IFI.

1) If management lacks this ability, the engagement should **not be accepted**.

e. **Management's responsibilities** include (1) the IFI, (2) the effectiveness of internal control, (3) compliance with laws and regulations, (4) making information available, (5) providing a **representation letter** at the end of the engagement, and (6) adjusting the IFI for material misstatements.

f. The **accountant's responsibility** is to comply with AICPA standards.

4. **Knowledge of the Business and Controls**

a. The accountant's knowledge of the entity's business and internal controls should be sufficient to (1) identify types of misstatements, (2) consider the likelihood of their occurrence, and (3) select inquiries and analytical procedures. This knowledge must relate to preparation of annual information as well as IFI.

b. Procedures to **update** the accountant's knowledge should include the following:

1) Reading documentation of the prior audit and of prior reviews, with specific consideration of (a) corrected and uncorrected misstatements, (b) identified fraud risks (e.g., management override), and (c) significant matters of continuing interest (e.g., significant deficiencies and material weaknesses)

2) Reading the recent annual information and prior IFI

3) Considering current audit results

4) Inquiring of management about changes in the business or in internal control

5) In an initial review, inquiring of the predecessor accountant and reading his/her documentation (if permitted)

6) Obtaining knowledge of the relevant aspects of the components of internal control relating to annual information and IFI

5. **Review Procedures**

a. **Analytical procedures** should be applied to identify unusual relationships and items. However, the accountant's expectations developed in a review are less precise than in an audit, and management responses generally are not corroborated. The reasonableness and consistency of the responses are considered.

b. The following **inquiries and other procedures** should be performed:

1) Reading the minutes of meetings of shareholders, the board, and committees, and inquiring about the results of meetings for which minutes are unavailable

       2) Obtaining reports of accountants who have reviewed IFI of components of the entity or its investees

          a) If their reports are unissued, inquiries should be made of such accountants.

       3) Inquiring of management about **financial and accounting matters**, such as (a) unusual or complex situations, (b) significant recent transactions, (c) status of uncorrected misstatements, (d) knowledge of fraud, (e) deficiencies in control, (f) significant entries and other adjustments, (g) questions arising from application of review procedures, (h) events subsequent to the date of the IFI, (i) communications from regulators, and (j) preparation of the IFI in conformity with the applicable financial reporting framework

       4) Reconciling the IFI and the accounting records

       5) Reading the IFI to consider, based on information coming to the accountant's attention, whether it conforms with the applicable financial reporting framework

       6) Reading other information in documents containing the IFI

   c. Inquiries about **litigation, claims, and assessments** and **going-concern issues** ordinarily are **not made** unless the accountant becomes aware of reasons for such inquiries.

   d. The accountant **extends procedures** if (s)he believes that the IFI does not conform with the applicable financial reporting framework.

   e. The same accountant usually performs the **audit** of the annual statements and the review of the IFI, and may be able to coordinate them.

   f. The accountant should obtain **written representations from management** about specific matters. See Study Unit 14 for an example representation letter that addresses most of the same matters.

6. **Evaluating Results**

   a. If the accountant becomes aware of **likely misstatements**, (s)he should accumulate them for further evaluation. Misstatements, including inadequate disclosure, are evaluated individually and in the aggregate to determine whether the IFI should be materially modified.

   b. A **scope restriction** may arise from (1) significant deficiencies or material weaknesses in internal control, (2) inability to perform necessary procedures, or (3) the client's failure to provide written representations. The result is an incomplete review, and no report is issued.

7. **Communications**

   a. Possible communications to management and those charged with governance include (1) the inability to complete the review, (2) the need for material modification of IFI, (3) the accountant's awareness of fraud or illegal acts, (4) internal-control-related matters, and (5) certain other matters.

   b. Any discussion of the **quality of the entity's accounting principles** as applied to its interim reports is ordinarily limited to the effects of significant events, transactions, and changes in estimates considered in performing the review.

8. **Report on a Review of IFI**

   a. An accountant ordinarily need not report in writing on a review of IFI. However, the report **should accompany** the IFI if the entity refers to the accountant's **association**. For example, the entity may state in a report, document, or written communication containing the IFI that it has been reviewed by an independent accountant.

1)   The accountant also may decide to issue a written report to prevent a user of the IFI from assuming a higher level of assurance than that provided by a review.

EXAMPLE – **Independent Accountant's Review Report**

We have reviewed the accompanying *[describe the interim financial information or statements reviewed]* of ABC Company and consolidated subsidiaries as of September 30, Year 1, and for the three-month and nine-month periods then ended. These financial statements are the responsibility of the company's management. We conducted our review in accordance with standards established by the American Institute of Certified Public Accountants. A review of interim financial information consists principally of applying analytical procedures and making inquiries of persons responsible for financial and accounting matters. It is substantially less in scope than an audit conducted in accordance with auditing standards generally accepted in the United States, the objective of which is the expression of an opinion regarding the financial information taken as a whole. Accordingly, we do not express such an opinion.

Based on our review, we are not aware of any material modifications that should be made to the accompanying interim financial information for it to be in conformity with *[identify the applicable financial reporting framework, for example, accounting principles generally accepted in the United States of America]*.

---

b.   Each page of the IFI must be clearly **marked as unaudited**.

c.   The accountant **modifies the review report** for material **departures from the applicable financial reporting framework**, including inadequate disclosure. The modification describes the departure and, if practicable, states its effects or provides the necessary information.

Stop and review! You have completed the outline for this subunit. Study multiple-choice questions 1 through 3 on page 648.

19.2 LETTERS FOR UNDERWRITERS AND CERTAIN OTHER REQUESTING PARTIES (AU 634)

1.   **Comfort Letters**

a.   Independent accountants audit financial statements and schedules contained in registration statements filed with the SEC under the **Securities Act of 1933**. Thus, accountants often confer with clients, underwriters, and counsel concerning the accounting and auditing requirements of the act and of the SEC.

b.   In conjunction with the audit, they may issue **comfort letters** for underwriters and certain other requesting parties. Comfort letters are not required by law and are not filed with the SEC, but underwriting agreements often request them.

c.   Accountants are limited in the comments they can make in comfort letters on unaudited financial information. However, underwriters may wish to perform a reasonable investigation of financial and accounting data not **expertized** (covered by an audit report of independent accountants who consent to be named) as a defense under the act.

1)   Accountants may issue comfort letters for other parties, e.g., a party with a **due diligence** defense under the 1933 act who submits either a written attorney's opinion stating that the party has such a defense or a suitable representation letter.

2)   When a party with a due diligence defense requests a comfort letter but does **not** furnish a representation letter, the accountant may **not provide negative assurance** but **may describe procedures performed**.

3)   Because the nature of a reasonable investigation has not been established, only the underwriter can determine what is sufficient.

4)   The assistance provided in a comfort letter is limited. Accountants can comment only on matters to which their expertise is relevant, and the procedures permit the expression of, **at most, negative assurance**.

2. **Format and Content of Comfort Letters**

   a. **Dating.** The letter ordinarily is dated on or shortly before the effective date of the registration statement.

   b. **Addressee.** The letter should not be addressed or given to anyone other than the client and the named underwriters, broker-dealer, intermediary, or buyer or seller.

   c. **Independence.** Accountants customarily make a statement concerning their independence in the letter.

   d. **Compliance with SEC requirements.** A typical comfort letter expresses an opinion on whether audited financial statements and schedules included in the registration statement **comply as to form** in all material respects with the applicable accounting requirements of the act and the related rules and regulations adopted by the SEC.

   e. **Accountants' reports.** Underwriters may request the accountants to repeat in the comfort letter their opinion on the audited financial statements included in the registration statement. Because of the significance of the date of the auditor's report, the accountants should **not repeat their opinion** or give negative assurance about the report.

3. **Comments on Other Matters**

   a. **Unaudited condensed interim financial statements.** Comments in the comfort letter about unaudited condensed interim financial statements appearing in the registration statement should always be in the form of **negative assurance**.

   b. **Knowledge of internal control.** The accountants should have knowledge of the client's internal controls if they comment on (1) unaudited condensed information, (2) capsule information, (3) financial forecasts, (4) changes in capital stock, (5) increases in noncurrent debt, and (6) decreases in selected items. They do not comment on internal control.

   c. **Capsule financial information.** Capsule information is unaudited summarized interim information for subsequent periods used to supplement the audited financial statements or unaudited condensed interim financial information in a **registration statement**. The accountant may give **negative assurance** regarding conformity with GAAP and consistency with the audited financial statements if the capsule information is in accordance with the disclosure requirements of GAAP relating to interim financial reporting and if the accountants have performed a review of the underlying financial statements in accordance with AU 722, *Interim Financial Information*.

   d. **Pro forma financial information.** The accountants should not comment on this information unless they have acquired the appropriate level of knowledge of the accounting and financial reporting practices of the entity, e.g., by auditing or reviewing the historical statements. This topic is covered by AT 401, which is discussed subsequently in this study unit.

   e. **Forecasts.** To apply agreed-upon procedures to a forecast and comment on it in a comfort letter, the accountants must perform **compilation procedures** for a forecast and should attach the report to the comfort letter. Negative assurance on the results of the procedures may **not** be provided.

   f. **Management's discussion and analysis (MD&A).** Comments that attestations are in accordance with AT 701, *Management's Discussion and Analysis,* may be made. No comments on the compliance of the MD&A with the forms required by SEC rules should be made. Furthermore, no comments should be made on nonfinancial data in the MD&A.

g. **Subsequent changes.** Comments on these matters ordinarily concern whether a change has occurred in capital stock, noncurrent debt has increased, or other specified financial statement items have increased/decreased during the change period (the period subsequent to the latest financial statements included in the registration statement). Accountants are usually requested to **read minutes and make inquiries**.

4. **Tables, Statistics, and Other Financial Information**

a. The underwriting agreement may call for a comfort letter commenting on tables, statistics, and other financial information in the registration statement. The accountants should comment only with respect to information

1) Expressed in monetary units (or percentages based on amounts of monetary units) and obtained from records subject to the internal controls of the entity's accounting system

2) Derived directly from the accounting records by analysis or computation

5. **Concluding Paragraph**

a. The comfort letter should conclude with a paragraph stating that the "letter is solely for the information of the addressees and to assist the underwriters" to avoid misunderstanding of the purpose and intended use of the comfort letter.

Stop and review! You have completed the outline for this subunit. Study multiple-choice questions 4 through 8 beginning on page 648.

19.3 FILINGS UNDER FEDERAL SECURITIES STATUTES (AU 711)

1. **Division of Responsibilities**

a. The responsibility for the financial representations contained in documents filed under the federal securities statutes lies with **management**.

b. The **accountant's responsibility** is ordinarily similar to that for other types of reporting, but the statutes specify that responsibility in detail.

1) For example, the Securities Act of 1933 imposes responsibility for false or misleading statements in an effective registration statement.

2) The SEC has a **"whistleblower"** stipulation for fraud informers **other than the auditor**. A whistleblower is defined as a person who provides information to the SEC about a possible violation of securities laws. To be considered for an award, a whistleblower must voluntarily provide the SEC with original information that leads to the SEC obtaining monetary sanctions in excess of $1 million.

c. The independent accountant has a responsibility as an expert when his/her **report is included in a registration statement**. The 1933 act states that no person shall be liable

1) If (s)he, after **reasonable investigation**, had reasonable grounds to believe that the statements in the registration statement were true and that there was no omission to state a material fact required to be stated or necessary to make the statements not misleading.

2) If the part of the registration statement for which (s)he had responsibility did **not fairly represent** his/her statement as an expert or was **not a fair copy** of or extract from his/her report or valuation as an expert.

d. The **standard of reasonableness** is that required of a prudent individual in the management of his/her own property.

e. The independent accountant whose report is included in a registration statement has a statutory responsibility that is determined in light of the **circumstances on the effective date** of the registration statement.

1) A report based on a review of interim financial information is **not deemed to be a report** or **part of the registration statement** for this purpose. The SEC requires that the prospectus contain language to this effect.

2) **Accounting principles** applied must have substantial authoritative support.

3) The SEC requires that registrants obtain reviews of interim financial information by their independent auditors prior to filing **quarterly reports** in Form 10-Q or Form 10-QSB.

f. The independent accountant should be certain that his/her name is not being used in a way indicating his/her responsibility is greater than intended.

2. **Subsequent Events Procedures**

a. To sustain the burden of proof that (s)he has made a reasonable investigation, an auditor should extend his/her subsequent events procedures from the **date of the report up to the effective date of the registration statement**.

b. Following the date of the report, the independent auditor may rely mostly on **inquiries**. The auditor should

1) Apply the normal subsequent events procedures.

2) Read the prospectus and other pertinent portions of the registration statement.

3) Obtain written representations from responsible individuals about whether any events have occurred having a material effect on the audited financial statements or that should be disclosed.

c. An auditor who has audited the financial statements for **prior periods but not for the most recent period** included in the registration statement has a responsibility for material subsequent events affecting the prior period statements.

Stop and review! You have completed the outline for this subunit. Study multiple-choice questions 9 through 11 on page 650.

NOTE: **The following is an overview of the next four subunits: 19.4, 19.5, 19.6, and 19.7.** The candidate should use the table to ensure that the differences among the types of information and the auditor's responsibility are fully understood.

Subunit	AU Section	Type of Information/Example	Accountant's Procedures	Reporting Responsibility
19.4	AU 550	**Other**/CEO's letter included in the annual report	Read for consistency with financial statements.	Add paragraph to audit report only if other information is not consistent with financial statements.
19.5	AU 558	**Required Supplementary**/Oil and gas reserve information	Apply limited procedures.	Add paragraph to audit report only if information is omitted or departs from requirements.
19.6	AU 551	**Supplementary in Relation to Statements**/Schedule of fixed assets	Audit.	Refer to and report on fair presentation in audit report.
19.7	AU 552	**Condensed or Selected**/Summary of financial results	Determine whether stated fairly relative to complete financial statements.	In a separate report, refer to audit report and state conclusion about fairness relative to complete financial statements.

19.4 OTHER INFORMATION IN DOCUMENTS CONTAINING AUDITED FINANCIAL STATEMENTS (AU 550)

1. **Other information** is financial or nonfinancial information (other than the financial statements and the auditor's report) that is included in a document containing audited statements and the auditor's report (excluding RSI).

2. **Auditor's Responsibility**

   a. The auditor's responsibility is to respond appropriately when the other information may undermine the credibility of the statements and the auditor's report.

      1) Thus, the auditor should read (but need not corroborate) the other information to identify **material inconsistencies** with the audited statements.

      2) The auditor also must respond when (s)he becomes aware of a **material misstatement of fact** in the other information.

         a) A misstatement of fact is other information that is unrelated to matters in the audited statements and is incorrectly stated or presented.

            i) When management refuses to correct a material misstatement of fact, the auditor should notify those charged with governance.

   b. If the audited information is presented fairly, the opinion should be unqualified.

      1) If the other information is obtained **prior to the report release date** and needs revision, the auditor should request the client to revise it if it is materially inconsistent. If revision is not made, (s)he should consider

         a) Modifying the report to include an explanatory paragraph,
         b) Withholding use of the report, or
         c) Withdrawing from the engagement.

      2) If a material inconsistency is identified **after the report release date**, and revision is needed, the guidance for subsequent discovery of facts existing at the report date (see Study Unit 14, Subunit 3) applies.

   c. The auditor need not refer to the other information in the audit report.

      1) However, (s)he may **disclaim an opinion** on it.

Stop and review! You have completed the outline for this subunit. Study multiple-choice questions 12 and 13 on page 651.

19.5 REQUIRED SUPPLEMENTARY INFORMATION (RSI) (AU 558)

1. RSI is information that the **designated accounting standard setter** has determined must accompany the basic financial statements.

   a. Thus, **authoritative guidelines** for its **measurement and presentation** have been prescribed.

2. **Procedures.** The auditor should

   a. Inquire about

      1) Whether the RSI is within the guidelines,

      2) Whether methods of measurement or presentation have changed and the reasons for any change, and

      3) Any significant assumptions or interpretations.

   b. Compare the RSI for **consistency** with the basic statements, management's responses to inquiries, and other audit evidence.

   c. Obtain management's **written representations** relevant to its responsibilities for RSI and compliance with guidelines.

3. **Reporting**

    a.   The audit report should include an **explanatory paragraph** referring to the RSI and stating that certain limited procedures were applied. It is presented **after** the opinion paragraph.

    b.   Omission of or a deficiency in the RSI does not affect the **opinion** on the basic statements.

    c.   The auditor need not present the RSI if it is omitted.

EXAMPLE – All RSI Omitted

Management has omitted *[describe the missing required supplementary information]* that *[identify the applicable financial reporting framework (for example, accounting principles generally accepted in the United States of America)]* require to be presented to supplement the basic financial statements. Such missing information, although not a part of the basic financial statements, is required by *[identify designated accounting standard setter]* who considers it to be an essential part of financial reporting for placing the basic financial statements in an appropriate operational, economic, or historical context. Our opinion on the basic financial statements is not affected by this missing information.

Stop and review! You have completed the outline for this subunit. Study multiple-choice questions 14 and 15 beginning on page 651.

19.6 SUPPLEMENTARY INFORMATION IN RELATION TO THE FINANCIAL STATEMENTS AS A WHOLE (AU 551)

1. **Supplementary information (SI)** is presented outside the basic statements and is not necessary for the statements to be fairly presented in accordance with the **applicable financial reporting framework**.

    a.   Examples might include summaries or statistical data extracted from the financial statements.

2. **Conditions**

    a.   An auditor who **is engaged** to report on whether SI is fairly presented in all material respects in relation to the statements as a whole must determine that certain **conditions** are satisfied:

        1)   The SI is derived directly from the **underlying records** used to prepare the statements and relates to the **same period**.

        2)   The auditor is the **principal auditor** of the related statements and did not express an **adverse opinion** or **disclaim an opinion** on them.

        3)   The SI will **accompany** the audited statements.

        4)   Management understands its **responsibilities** for preparing the SI, presenting it with the audit report and the audited statements, and providing **written representations**.

3. **Procedures**

    a.   The following procedures to express an opinion on the SI are performed based on the **materiality level** used for the audit of the statements:

        1)   Inquiring about the purpose of, and criteria for, the SI

        2)   Determining conformity with the criteria

        3)   Understanding methods of preparation

        4)   Reconciling SI with underlying records or the statements

        5)   Inquiring about significant assumptions or interpretations

        6)   Evaluating the appropriateness and completeness of the SI

        7)   Obtaining management's written representations about responsibility for presentation, fairness, methods, assumptions, and interpretations

    b.   The auditor need not perform **subsequent events** procedures on the SI.

4.   **Reporting**

a.   When the **SI and the audited statements** are presented together, the auditor reports on the SI in an explanatory paragraph following the opinion paragraph or in a separate report.

1)   Otherwise, a separate report should be issued.

EXAMPLE – Explanatory Paragraph

Our audit was conducted for the purpose of forming an opinion on the financial statements as a whole. The *[identify accompanying supplementary information]* is presented for purposes of additional analysis and is not a required part of the financial statements. Such information is the responsibility of management and was derived from and relates directly to the underlying accounting and other records used to prepare the financial statements. The information has been subjected to the auditing procedures applied in the audit of the financial statements and certain additional procedures, including comparing and reconciling such information directly to the underlying accounting and other records used to prepare the financial statements or to the financial statements themselves, and other additional procedures in accordance with auditing standards generally accepted in the United States of America. In our opinion, the information is fairly stated in all material respects in relation to the financial statements as a whole.

Stop and review! You have completed the outline for this subunit. Study multiple-choice questions 16 and 17 on page 652.

19.7 REPORTING ON CONDENSED FINANCIAL STATEMENTS AND SELECTED FINANCIAL DATA (AU 552)

1.   This pronouncement applies to the following:

a.   Condensed annual or interim financial statements derived from audited financial statements of an issuer

b.   Selected financial data derived from audited financial statements of an issuer or a nonissuer and presented in a document that includes audited financial statements

2.   **Condensed Financial Statements**

a.   These financial statements are considerably less detailed than complete financial statements. They should be read with the entity's **most recent complete statements** that include all GAAP disclosures.

b.   An **auditor may report** on condensed financial statements but, because they do not constitute a fair presentation, not in the same manner as on the complete statements.

c.   The **auditor's report** should

1)   State that the auditor has audited and expressed an opinion on the complete statements.

2)   Provide the date of the report on the complete statements.

3)   Indicate the type of opinion expressed on the complete statements.

4)   Express an opinion as to whether the information in the condensed statements is fairly stated in all material respects in relation to the complete statements.

d.   If a client names the auditor in a **client-prepared document** and also states that condensed statements have been derived from audited statements, the auditor need not report on the condensed statements if they are included in a document that **contains audited statements**.

e.   Condensed statements of an **issuer** may be presented **comparatively** with **interim information** as of a subsequent date that is accompanied by the **auditor's review report**.

1)   The auditor should report on the condensed statements in each period in a manner appropriate to the service provided.

ISA Difference

Under the ISAs, summarized financial statements should include (1) a clear indication of the nature of the information, (2) a title identifying the audited statements, (3) the addressee, (4) a statement that the summarized statements should be read with the full statements and the audit report on them, and (5) the address of the auditor.

---

3. **Selected Financial Data**

    a. An auditor may report on selected data included in a **client-prepared document containing audited statements**.

    b. Selected financial data are **not** a required part of the basic statements, and management is responsible for determining the specific data to be presented.

    c. The report should be limited to **data derived from audited statements**.

    d. If the selected financial data include other information (such as number of employees or square footage of facilities), the report should **specifically identify** the data on which the auditor is reporting.

    e. The **report** should

       1) State that the auditor has audited and expressed an opinion on the complete statements.

       2) Indicate the type of opinion expressed on the complete statements.

       3) Express an opinion as to whether the information in the selected financial data is fairly stated in all material respects in relation to the complete statements.

    f. In introductory material included in a client-prepared document, an entity might name the auditor and state that the data are derived from financial statements that (s)he audited. This statement does **not** require the auditor to report on the selected data if they are in a document that **contains audited statements**.

Stop and review! You have completed the outline for this subunit. Study multiple-choice questions 18 through 20 on page 653.

19.8 REPORTING ON FINANCIAL STATEMENTS PREPARED FOR USE IN OTHER COUNTRIES (AU 534)

1. An independent auditor practicing in the U.S. may report on the financial statements of a **U.S. entity** prepared in conformity with accounting principles generally accepted in another country for use outside the U.S.

    a. The auditor must clearly understand the purpose and uses of the statements and obtain written representations from management.

    b. If the statements are for general use and the standard report of the foreign country will be used, the auditor must consider any additional legal responsibilities.

    c. However, if the statements are prepared in conformity with **International Financial Reporting Standards** (IFRSs) issued by the International Accounting Standards Board (IASB), **AU 534 does not apply**.

       1) Standard reporting (AU 508) (see Study Units 16 and 17) applies because the IASB is an AICPA-designated standard setter.

2. **General and Field Work Standards**

   a. The auditor's procedures should comply with the **general and field work standards of U.S. GAAS**.

   b. The procedures performed under U.S. GAAS may require modification. For example, accounting principles generally accepted in another country may require that certain assets be revalued to adjust for inflation. The auditor would then need to test the adjustments.

   c. The auditor should understand the other accounting principles.

3. **Compliance with Auditing Standards of Another Country**

   a. The auditor may be requested to apply the auditing standards of the other country. In that case, the auditor should comply with the general and field work standards of that country as well as with U.S. GAAS.

   b. If the statements of a U.S. entity are for general use outside the U.S., the audit may be conducted in accordance with **International Auditing Standards** (IASs) issued by the International Auditing and Assurance Standards Board.

      1) In these circumstances, the auditor follows U.S. GAAS (general and field work standards) and any additional requirements of the IASs.

4. **Reporting Standards**

   a. The auditor may use either a modified U.S.-style report or, as appropriate, the report form of the other country or that provided by IASs.

   b. The auditor may report on financial statements prepared in accordance with U.S. GAAP and financial statements prepared in conformity with accounting principles generally accepted in the other country.

5. **Use Limited to Outside the United States**

   a. A modified U.S.-style report should include the following:

      1) A title including the word **independent**
      2) A statement that the identified statements were **audited**
      3) A reference to the note describing the **basis of presentation**, including identification of the **nationality** of the principles
      4) A statement that the financial statements are the responsibility of management and that the **auditor's responsibility** is to express an opinion based on the audit
      5) A statement that the audit was in accordance with GAAS (and, if appropriate, with the auditing standards of the other country or IASs)
      6) A statement that U.S. standards require the auditor to plan and perform the audit to obtain **reasonable assurance** about whether the financial statements are free of material misstatement
      7) A statement that an audit includes

         a) Examining, on a test basis, evidence supporting the amounts and disclosures in the financial statements
         b) Assessing the **accounting principles** used and **significant estimates** made by management
         c) Evaluating the **overall** financial statement presentation

      8) A statement that the auditor believes that the audit provides a **reasonable basis** for the opinion

9) A paragraph expressing an **opinion** on whether the financial statements are presented fairly, in all material respects, in conformity with the basis of accounting described (including an identification of the country of origin of the accounting principles)

    a) If the statements are **not fairly presented**, the substantive reasons should be disclosed in an additional explanatory paragraph (preceding the opinion paragraph). The opinion paragraph should include modifying language and refer to the explanatory paragraph.

10) If comparative statements are presented, an explanatory paragraph (following the opinion paragraph) that (a) describes any **change in accounting principle** having a material effect on comparability and (b) refers to the note that discusses the change and its effects

11) The **signature** of the auditor's firm

12) The **date** (usually the date the auditor has obtained sufficient appropriate evidence to support the opinion)

6. **Use in the United States**

    a. If the auditor reports on fair presentation in conformity with the **accounting principles generally accepted in another country**, the auditor should use a U.S.-style report, modified because of departures from accounting principles generally accepted in the U.S.

    b. The auditor **may express an opinion** on whether the financial statements are presented in conformity with accounting principles generally accepted in the other country.

Stop and review! You have completed the outline for this subunit. Study multiple-choice questions 21 and 22 on page 654.

19.9 REPORTS ON THE APPLICATION OF ACCOUNTING PRINCIPLES (AU 625)

1. **Applicability**

    a. Management and others may consult with accountants to learn how to apply accounting principles to new transactions and financial products or to increase their knowledge about specific financial reporting issues.

    b. This pronouncement should be applied by an accountant in public practice **(reporting accountant)** when preparing a **written report** on the

        1) Application of accounting principles to **specific transactions**, whether completed or proposed, "involving facts and circumstances of a particular entity."

        2) Type of opinion that may be expressed on a **specific entity's financial statements**.

    c. This pronouncement also applies to **oral advice** believed to be an important factor in the decisions described in b.1) above made by a principal to the transaction.

    d. It does not apply to (1) a **continuing accountant** engaged to report on a specific entity's financial statements, (2) assistance in litigation involving accounting matters or related expert testimony, or (3) professional advice provided to another public accountant.

    e. It also does not apply to (1) position papers (e.g., newsletters, articles, speeches, and texts), (2) lectures and other forms of public presentations, or (3) letters for the public record to professional and governmental standard-setting bodies.

    f. An accountant should not provide a written report on the application of accounting principles to a **hypothetical transaction**.

2. **Performance Standards**

    a. In performing the engagement, the **reporting accountant** should consider the circumstances in which the report or advice is requested, the purpose, and the intended use. Also, the reporting accountant should

        1) Exercise due professional care.
        2) Have adequate technical training and proficiency.
        3) Plan the engagement adequately.
        4) Supervise assistants.
        5) Accumulate sufficient information to provide a reasonable basis for the professional judgment rendered.
        6) Consider the circumstances and purpose of the request for a written report or oral advice and its intended use.
        7) Obtain an understanding of the form and substance of the transaction(s).
        8) Review applicable GAAP.
        9) Consult with other professionals or experts, if appropriate.
        10) Ascertain and consider the existence of creditable precedents or analogies.
        11) Consult with the continuing accountant of the entity to determine all the available relevant facts, including disputes with management.

            a) The reporting accountant should (1) explain to the management of the entity the need for consultation with the continuing accountant, (2) request permission, and (3) request authorization for the continuing accountant to respond fully.

3. **Reporting Standards**

    a. The **addressee** of the accountant's written report is the **requesting entity**. The report should

        1) Briefly describe the engagement and state that it was in accordance with applicable **AICPA standards**.
        2) Identify the specific entity; describe the transaction(s); state the facts, circumstances, and assumptions; and state the source of the information.
        3) Describe the **accounting principle(s)** to be applied, including their country of origin, or the type of opinion to be expressed.

            a) If appropriate, the report should describe the reasons for the conclusions.

        4) State that the responsibility for proper accounting is with the **preparers** of the financial statements, who should consult with their continuing accountant.
        5) State that any difference in the facts, circumstances, or assumptions may change the report.
        6) Contain a separate paragraph at the end of the report **restricting its use** to specified (and identified) parties.

Stop and review! You have completed the outline for this subunit. Study multiple-choice questions 23 and 24 beginning on page 654.

The next 4 subunits cover specific Statements on Standards for Attestation Engagements. These standards relate to services that practitioners provide beyond those on traditional historical financial statements. AT 501 is not included here, as it relates to examining internal control for a nonissuer and was covered in Study Unit 9. Additionally, AT 101, Attest Engagements, was addressed in Study Unit 1. You should do a quick review of these study units while you consider the topics in Subunits 19.10, 19.11, 19.12, and 19.13.

19.10 ENGAGEMENTS TO APPLY AGREED-UPON PROCEDURES (AT 201)

1. **Nature of the Engagement**

   a. An agreed-upon procedures engagement is one in which a practitioner is engaged by a client to issue a report of findings based on specific procedures performed on subject matter.

   b. **Specified parties** assume responsibility for the **sufficiency** of the procedures.

   c. The **report** is in the form of **procedures and findings**, and neither an opinion nor negative assurance should be provided.

   d. The **general, field work, and reporting standards** for attestation engagements apply (Study Unit 1). However, a written assertion is generally not required in an agreed-upon procedures engagement unless specifically required by another attest standard.

2. **Procedures**

   a. **Appropriate procedures** include

      1) Inspection of specified documents for attributes
      2) Confirmation of specific information with third parties
      3) Comparison of documents or schedules with certain attributes
      4) Performance of mathematical computations or sampling

   b. **Inappropriate procedures** include

      1) Mere reading of the work performed by others to describe their findings
      2) Evaluating the competency or objectivity of another party
      3) Obtaining an understanding about a particular subject
      4) General review, checking, or any other overly subjective procedure
      5) Interpreting documents outside the scope of the practitioner's expertise

3. The practitioner may perform an engagement provided that

   a. (S)he is **independent**.

   b. A specified party is responsible for the **subject matter** (or the client has a reasonable basis for providing a written assertion, if required).

   c. The specified parties agree with the practitioner about the **procedures** to be performed.

   d. The specified parties are responsible for the **sufficiency** of the procedures.

   e. Procedures are expected to result in reasonably consistent **findings**.

   f. **Criteria** to be used in the determination of findings are agreed upon.

   g. Reasonably consistent subject matter **measurement** can be expected.

   h. **Evidence** providing a reasonable basis for findings can be collected.

   i. An agreement exists on **materiality** limits for reporting when applicable.

   j. **Use** of the report is restricted to specified parties.

4. To ensure that specified parties take **responsibility for the sufficiency of the procedures**, the practitioner should do one or more of the following:

   a. Communicate directly with, and obtain affirmative acknowledgment from, the parties

   b. Distribute the engagement letter to the specified parties

   c. Distribute a draft of the anticipated report to the specified parties

   d. Consider written requirements of the specified parties

   e. Discuss procedures with appropriate representatives of the specified parties

   f. Review contracts with or correspondence from the specified parties

5.   Attestation **documentation** (working papers) should be prepared.

EXAMPLE – Report on Agreed-Upon Procedures

Independent Accountant's Report on Applying Agreed-Upon Procedures

To the Audit Committee and Managements of ABC, Inc., and XYZ Fund:

We have performed the procedures enumerated below, which were agreed to by the audit committees and managements of ABC, Inc., and XYZ Fund, solely to assist you in evaluating the accompanying Statement of Investment Performance Statistics of XYZ Fund (prepared in accordance with the criteria specified therein) for the year ended December 31, Year 1. XYZ Fund's management is responsible for the statement of investment performance statistics. This agreed-upon procedures engagement was conducted in accordance with attestation standards established by the American Institute of Certified Public Accountants. The sufficiency of these procedures is solely the responsibility of those parties specified in this report. Consequently, we make no representation regarding the sufficiency of the procedures described below, either for the purpose for which this report has been requested or for any other purpose.

[Include paragraphs to enumerate procedures and findings.]

We were not engaged to and did not conduct an examination, the objective of which would be the expression of an opinion on the accompanying Statement of Investment Performance Statistics of XYZ Fund. Accordingly, we do not express such an opinion. Had we performed additional procedures, other matters might have come to our attention that would have been reported to you.

This report is intended solely for the information and use of the audit committees and managements of ABC, Inc., and XYZ Fund and is not intended to be and should not be used by anyone other than these specified parties.

[Signature]
[Date]

Stop and review! You have completed the outline for this subunit. Study multiple-choice questions 25 and 26 on page 655.

19.11 FINANCIAL FORECASTS AND PROJECTIONS (AT 301)

1.   **Prospective Financial Statements (PFSs)**

    a.   PFSs consist of financial forecasts or projections, including summaries of significant assumptions and accounting policies. An accountant must examine, compile, or apply agreed-upon procedures to PFSs if they are, or reasonably might be, expected to be used by another (third) party and if the practitioner

        1)   Submits to the client or others PFSs that (s)he has assembled or assisted in assembling

        2)   Reports on PFSs

    b.   The accountant must be independent to report on an examination or agreed-upon procedures for PFSs. An accountant need not be independent to compile PFSs.

        1)   However, the compilation report should be modified to include a separate paragraph disclosing the lack of independence.

        2)   Additionally, the accountant is not precluded from disclosing the reason(s) that independence is impaired.

2.   A **financial forecast** consists of PFSs that present, to the best of the responsible party's knowledge and belief, an entity's expected financial position, results of operations, and cash flows.

    a.   It is based on the **responsible party's assumptions** reflecting conditions it expects to exist and the course of action it expects to take.

        1)   The responsible party is usually management of the entity, but it may be a party outside the entity, such as a potential acquirer.

b.　It may be expressed in specific monetary amounts as a range or as a single point estimate of forecasted results.　For a range, the responsible party selects key assumptions to form an interval within which it reasonably expects, to the best of its knowledge and belief, the item or items subject to the assumptions to actually fall.

3.　A **financial projection** differs from a forecast.　A projection is based on the responsible party's assumptions reflecting conditions it expects would exist and the course of action it expects would be taken, given one or more **hypothetical assumptions**.　A projection is sometimes prepared to present one or more hypothetical courses of action for evaluation, as in response to a question such as, "What would happen if . . .?"　A projection may be expressed as a point estimate or a range.

4.　PFSs are for **general use** if they are for use by persons with whom the responsible party is not negotiating directly, e.g., in an offering statement of the party's securities.　Only a forecast is appropriate for general use.　All other presentations are for limited use.

a.　General use PFSs should portray expected results to the best of the responsible party's knowledge and belief.

5.　**Limited use** of PFSs means use by the responsible party and those with whom that party is negotiating directly.　Examples are use in a submission to a regulatory body or in negotiations for a bank loan.　These third parties can communicate directly with the responsible party.

a.　Consequently, any type of PFSs that would be useful in the circumstances would be appropriate for limited use.

b.　A projection is appropriate only for limited use.　The reason is that the presentation of a projection is based on one or more hypothetical assumptions.

1)　PFSs are appropriate for general use only if they portray, to the best of the responsible party's knowledge and belief, the expected results.　A hypothetical assumption is a condition or course of action that is not necessarily expected to occur.

6.　**Examinations**

a.　An examination evaluates the preparation of the statements, the support underlying the assumptions, and the presentation of the statements for conformity with AICPA guidelines.

b.　It also involves issuance of a report stating the practitioner's opinion on whether the PFSs conform with AICPA guidelines and whether the assumptions provide a reasonable basis for (1) the forecast or (2) the projection given hypothetical assumptions.

c.　If assumptions that appear to be significant at the time are not disclosed in the presentation, including the summary of assumptions, the practitioner must express an adverse opinion.　Moreover, a practitioner should not examine a presentation that omits all such disclosures.

7.　**Compilations**

a.　A compilation of PFSs, such as a financial forecast, involves (1) assembling, to the extent necessary, the statements based on the responsible party's assumptions; (2) performing required compilation procedures; and (3) issuing a compilation report.

b.　The procedures include reading the statements and considering whether they meet AICPA presentation guidelines and determining that the statements are not obviously inappropriate.

1)　Other procedures consist of inquiries, testing the mathematical accuracy of the computations, and obtaining written representations.　However, these procedures are not required.

      2)   If the accountant inquired or performed procedures before and became aware of incorrect or unsatisfactory information, (s)he should request revised information from the entity. If the entity refuses to provide revised information, the accountant should **withdraw from the engagement**.

  c.   The standard report states that a compilation is limited in scope and does not enable the practitioner to express an opinion or any other form of assurance on the PFSs or the assumptions.

      1)   It adds that a compilation does **not include evaluation of the support** for the assumptions underlying the PFSs.

      2)   A report on a projection also should include a separate paragraph that limits the use of the presentation.

  8.   **Agreed-Upon Procedures**

    a.   A practitioner may accept an engagement to apply **agreed-upon procedures** to PFSs.

    b.   The engagement may be accepted if the practitioner is **independent** and

      1)   The specified parties agree to the procedures and take responsibility for their sufficiency.

      2)   Report use is limited to specified parties.

      3)   The statements include a summary of significant assumptions.

    c.   The report should state that the practitioner did not perform an examination and that other matters might have come to his/her attention if additional procedures had been performed.

      1)   It should also **disclaim an opinion** on conformity with AICPA presentation guidelines, etc.

      2)   The report lists the procedures performed and the related findings. It does not provide positive or limited assurance.

  9.   **Review**

    a.   The standard does not provide for the **review** form of engagement with regard to PFSs. Thus, it does not provide for the expression of limited assurance on them.

Stop and review! You have completed the outline for this subunit. Study multiple-choice questions 27 through 37 beginning on page 656.

19.12 REPORTING ON PRO FORMA FINANCIAL INFORMATION (AT 401)

  1.   Pro forma financial information (PFFI) shows "what the significant effects on historical financial information would have been had a consummated or proposed transaction (or event) occurred at an earlier date." Examples of these transactions include (a) a business combination, (b) disposal of a segment, (c) change in the form or status of an entity, and (d) a change in capitalization.

  2.   An accountant may **examine or review** PFFI if three conditions are met:

    a.   The document containing the PFFI includes or incorporates by reference the complete historical statements for the most recent year available. Moreover, if the PFFI is for an interim period, the document also should include the interim historical information for that period.

    b.   If the PFFI has been examined, the historical financial statements on which it is based have been audited. If the PFFI has been reviewed, the historical financial statements have been audited or reviewed.

    c.   The reporting accountant is appropriately knowledgeable about the accounting and financial reporting practices of each significant part of the combined entity.

3.   A compilation of the historical statements provides no assurance. Accordingly, it would not provide a basis for the accountant to examine or review the PFFI.

4.   The report on an examination should include an opinion (unqualified, qualified, or adverse). It addresses whether (a) management's assumptions provide a reasonable basis for the significant effects attributable to the transaction or event, (b) the pro forma adjustments give appropriate effect to the assumptions, and (c) the pro forma column reflects the proper application of those adjustments to the historical data.

   a.   Scope limitations, reservations about the assumptions or the presentation (including inadequate disclosure), and other matters may lead to modification of the opinion or a disclaimer.

5.   An issuer that discloses a material non-GAAP financial measure (a **pro forma release**) also must disclose the most directly comparable GAAP measure (SEC Regulation G).

Stop and review! You have completed the outline for this subunit. Study multiple-choice questions 38 through 41 beginning on page 659.

19.13 COMPLIANCE ATTESTATION (AT 601)

1.   A practitioner may be asked to provide assurance about the entity's **compliance with specified requirements** (laws, regulations, rules, contracts, or grants). The engagement also may be directed toward the responsible party's **written assertion about compliance**. For example, management might make the assertion: "Z Company complied with the restrictive covenants in paragraph 20 of its Loan Agreement with Y Bank dated January 1, Year 1, as of and for the 3 months ended March 31, Year 1."

   a.   The practitioner also may be asked to provide this type of assurance concerning the **effectiveness of internal control over compliance** with laws, regulations, etc.

2.   The standard provides guidance for engagements related to reporting on compliance with requirements that are either **financial or nonfinancial**.

   a.   The **general, field work, and reporting attestation standards** (AT 50) are applicable to this type of engagement.

   b.   A compliance attestation does **not** provide a legal determination of an entity's compliance.

3.   **Scope of Services**

   a.   A practitioner may perform **agreed-upon procedures** or an **examination**. However, a practitioner should **not** perform a compliance attestation **review** service.

   b.   In an **agreed-upon procedures engagement**, the subject matter (or an assertion about it) consists of (1) compliance with specified requirements, (2) the effectiveness of internal control over compliance, or (3) both.

      1)   The users of the report decide the procedures to be performed by the practitioner and take responsibility for those procedures.

      2)   The practitioner has **no obligation to perform other procedures**. However, if noncompliance comes to the practitioner's attention by other means, such information should be included in the report.

      3)   The practitioner's report should be in the form of procedures and findings but should **not provide negative assurance** about whether an entity is in compliance or whether the responsible party's assertion is fairly stated.

4) The **report**

    a) Has a **title** that includes the word **independent**

    b) Describes the **nature and scope** of the service

    c) **Limits use** to specified parties

    d) Is **signed** by the practitioner

    e) Is **dated** as of the completion of the agreed-upon procedures

c. In an **examination** engagement, the subject matter (or an assertion about it) consists of compliance with specified requirements.

    1) The practitioner gathers evidence to support an opinion on whether an entity is in compliance, in all material respects, based on specified criteria.

    2) The practitioner also may examine the **effectiveness** (or the responsible party's assertion about the effectiveness) **of the entity's internal control over compliance**.

4. **Conditions for Engagement Performance**

a. For an **agreed-upon procedures engagement**, the responsible party should

    1) Accept responsibility for the entity's compliance with specified requirements and the effectiveness of the entity's internal control over compliance.

    2) Evaluate such compliance or effectiveness.

b. For an **examination of the entity's compliance with specified requirements**, sufficient evidence should exist or be capable of development to support management's evaluation. Furthermore, the **responsible party** should

    1) Satisfy the condition in item 4.a.1) above.

    2) Evaluate compliance with specified requirements.

c. To perform a compliance attestation engagement, the practitioner should obtain from the responsible party a **written assertion about compliance**.

5. **Examination Engagement**

a. The purpose is to **express an opinion** on whether an entity is in compliance (or on whether the responsible party's assertion about such compliance is fairly stated), in all material respects, based on the specified criteria. To express an opinion, the practitioner must gather sufficient evidence to **reduce attestation risk** to an acceptably low level. Attestation risk is similar to the audit risk concept used in Statements on Auditing Standards.

b. The practitioner seeks to obtain **reasonable, not absolute, assurance** of compliance.

c. Based on the extent to which (s)he wishes to restrict attestation risk and the assessments of inherent risk and control risk, the practitioner determines the **acceptable level of detection risk**. This level will determine the nature, timing, and extent of the necessary compliance tests.

d. The consideration of **materiality** differs from that in an audit of financial statements in accordance with GAAS. The following should be considered:

    1) The nature of the compliance requirements, which may not be quantifiable in monetary terms

    2) The nature and frequency of noncompliance identified, with appropriate consideration of sampling risk

    3) Qualitative considerations, including the needs and expectations of users

6. **Performing an Examination Engagement**

    a. The practitioner should use **due care** and exercise **professional skepticism** to achieve reasonable assurance that material noncompliance will be detected. The following summarizes the practitioner's **procedures and considerations** in an examination engagement:

        1) Obtain an **understanding** of the specified compliance requirements.

        2) **Plan** the engagement, including the potential use of specialists and internal auditors.

        3) Obtain an **understanding** of the relevant portions of **internal control** over compliance to plan the engagement and to assess control risk. If control risk is to be assessed at a low level, tests of controls must be performed.

        4) Perform **procedures** to provide reasonable assurance of detecting material noncompliance, including obtaining a **written representation letter** from the responsible party.

        5) Consider **subsequent events**. (The requirement is similar to that established by AU 560, *Subsequent Events*, for a financial statement audit.)

        6) Form an **opinion**.

    b. The practitioner's report on an examination should contain **introductory, scope, and opinion paragraphs**.

EXAMPLE – **Standard Report on Compliance with Specified Requirements Based on an Examination**

Independent Accountant's Report

To: <------------ Addressed to Board of Directors or Shareholders

We have examined *[name of entity]*'s compliance with *[list of specified compliance requirements]* during the *[period]* ended *[date]*. Management is responsible for *[name of entity]*'s compliance with those requirements. Our responsibility is to express an opinion on *[name of entity]*'s compliance based on our examination.

Our examination was conducted in accordance with attestation standards established by the American Institute of Certified Public Accountants and, accordingly, included examining, on a test basis, evidence about *[name of entity]*'s compliance with those requirements and performing such other procedures as we considered necessary in the circumstances. We believe that our examination provides a reasonable basis for our opinion. Our examination does not provide a legal determination on *[name of entity]*'s compliance with specific requirements.

In our opinion, *[name of entity]* complied, in all material respects, with the aforementioned requirements for the year ended December 31, Year 1.

Signed   <------------ May be signed, typed, or printed

Date   <------------ Date completed examination

---

7. **Report Modifications**

    a. **Material noncompliance.** When an examination discloses noncompliance with specified requirements that the practitioner believes have a material effect on the entity's compliance, the report should be modified. Depending on materiality, the practitioner should express either a **qualified** (except for) or an **adverse opinion** on compliance. An **explanatory paragraph** (before the opinion paragraph) should be added to the report.

    b. **Scope limitations.** The practitioner should qualify or disclaim an opinion depending on materiality (e.g., if management refuses to provide a written representation letter).

    c. **Report based, in part, on the report of another practitioner.** The practitioner should either refer to the other practitioner or issue the standard report (see the general guidance provided by AU 543, *Part of Audit Performed by Other Independent Auditors*).

Stop and review! You have completed the outline for this subunit. Study multiple-choice questions 42 through 45 beginning on page 660.

QUESTIONS

19.1 Interim Financial Information (AU 722)

1. The objective of a review of interim financial information of an issuer is to provide an accountant with a basis for reporting whether

A. A reasonable basis exists for expressing an updated opinion regarding the financial statements that were previously audited.

B. Material modifications should be made to conform with generally accepted accounting principles.

C. The financial statements are presented fairly in accordance with standards of interim reporting.

D. The financial statements are presented fairly in accordance with generally accepted accounting principles.

Answer (B) is correct. *(CPA, adapted)*
 REQUIRED: The objective of a review of interim financial information.
 DISCUSSION: The review provides the accountant with a basis for reporting whether (s)he is aware of material modifications that should be made for such information to conform with the applicable financial reporting framework. This objective differs significantly from that of an audit, which is to provide a basis for expressing an opinion (AU 722).
 Answer (A) is incorrect. The review of interim financial information does not provide a basis for expressing an opinion. Answer (C) is incorrect. Reporting on whether the statements are fairly presented is the expression of an opinion. Answer (D) is incorrect. Reporting on whether the statements are fairly presented is the expression of an opinion.

2. Which of the following procedures ordinarily should be applied when an independent accountant conducts a review of interim financial information of an issuer?

A. Verify changes in key account balances.

B. Read the minutes of the board of directors' meetings.

C. Inspect the open purchase order file.

D. Perform cutoff tests for cash receipts and disbursements.

Answer (B) is correct. *(CPA, adapted)*
 REQUIRED: The procedure applied in a review of interim financial information.
 DISCUSSION: A review involves (1) establishing an understanding with the client; (2) obtaining knowledge of the entity's business and controls; (3) performing analytical procedures, making inquiries, and applying other limited procedures; (4) obtaining written representations from management; and (5) evaluating the results of procedures. The specific procedures performed include reading the minutes of meetings of shareholders, the board of directors, and committees of the board of directors, and inquiring about the results of meetings for which minutes are unavailable.

3. Which of the following circumstances requires modification of the accountant's report on a review of interim financial information of an issuer?

	Substantial Doubt about the Entity's Ability to Continue as a Going Concern	Inadequate Disclosure
A.	Yes	Yes
B.	No	No
C.	Yes	No
D.	No	Yes

Answer (D) is correct. *(CPA, adapted)*
 REQUIRED: The reasons, if any, for modifying a review report on interim statements.
 DISCUSSION: Modification of the report on a review of interim financial statements is necessary because of departures from the applicable financial reporting framework, including inadequate disclosure. A review of interim financial statements is not intended to identify a going concern issue. But the accountant may become aware of conditions or events indicating a possibility that the entity may not be able to continue as a going concern. In this case, the accountant should inquire of management and consider the adequacy of disclosure. If disclosure is adequate, report modification is not required. Nevertheless, the accountant should include an explanatory paragraph to emphasize the matter.

19.2 Letters for Underwriters and Certain Other Requesting Parties (AU 634)

4. Comfort letters ordinarily are signed by the client's

A. Independent accountants.

B. Underwriters of securities.

C. Audit committee.

D. Senior management.

Answer (A) is correct. *(CPA, adapted)*
 REQUIRED: The persons who sign a comfort letter.
 DISCUSSION: A common condition of an underwriting agreement in connection with the offering for sale of securities registered with the SEC under the Securities Act of 1933 is that the accountants furnish a comfort letter to the underwriters. Hence, the independent accountants sign the comfort letter.

5. Comfort letters ordinarily are addressed to

A. The Securities and Exchange Commission.

B. The intermediary who negotiated the agreement with the client.

C. Creditor financial institutions.

D. The client's audit committee.

Answer (B) is correct. *(CPA, adapted)*
REQUIRED: The addressee of a comfort letter.
DISCUSSION: The letter should not be addressed or given to anyone other than the client and the named underwriters, broker-dealer, intermediary, or buyer or seller. "The appropriate addressee is the intermediary who has negotiated the agreement with the client, and with whom the accountants will deal in discussions regarding the letter" (AU 634).

6. Which of the following matters is covered in a typical comfort letter?

A. Negative assurance concerning whether the entity's internal control activities operated as designed during the period being audited.

B. An opinion regarding whether the entity complied with laws and regulations under Government Auditing Standards and the Single Audit Act.

C. Positive assurance concerning whether unaudited condensed financial information complied with generally accepted accounting principles.

D. An opinion as to whether the audited financial statements comply in form with the accounting requirements of the SEC.

Answer (D) is correct. *(CPA, adapted)*
REQUIRED: The item in a typical letter for underwriters.
DISCUSSION: A typical comfort letter expresses an opinion on whether audited financial statements and schedules "included in the registration statement comply as to form in all material respects with the applicable accounting requirements of the Act and the related published rules and regulations" (AU 634). However, the comfort letter does not state or repeat an opinion about the fairness of presentation of the statements.

7. When an accountant issues to an underwriter a comfort letter containing comments on data that have **not** been audited, the underwriter most likely will receive

A. Positive assurance on supplementary disclosures.

B. Negative assurance on capsule information.

C. A disclaimer on prospective financial statements.

D. A limited opinion of pro forma financial statements.

Answer (B) is correct. *(CPA, adapted)*
REQUIRED: The most likely assurance or lack provided in a comfort letter commenting on unaudited data.
DISCUSSION: According to AU 634, capsule information is unaudited summarized interim information for subsequent periods used to supplement the audited financial statements or unaudited condensed interim financial information in a registration statement. The accountant may give negative assurance regarding conformity with GAAP if (1) the capsule information is in accordance with the disclosure requirements of GAAP regarding interim financial reporting, and (2) the accountants have performed a review of the underlying financial statements in accordance with AU 722, *Interim Financial Information.*
Answer (A) is incorrect. A comfort letter expresses, at most, negative assurance. Answer (C) is incorrect. Prospective statements do not appear in a registration statement. Answer (D) is incorrect. A limited opinion is not a permissible form of reporting.

8. When issuing letters for underwriters, commonly referred to as comfort letters, an accountant may provide negative assurance concerning

A. The absence of any significant deficiencies in internal control.

B. The conformity of the entity's unaudited condensed interim financial information with generally accepted accounting principles (GAAP).

C. The results of procedures performed in compiling the entity's financial forecast.

D. The compliance of the entity's registration statement with the requirements of the Securities Act of 1933.

Answer (B) is correct. *(CPA, adapted)*
REQUIRED: The matter about which an accountant may provide negative assurance in comfort letters.
DISCUSSION: A comfort letter provides negative assurance on whether the unaudited condensed interim financial information included in the registration statement complies as to form in all material respects with the applicable financial reporting framework.
Answer (A) is incorrect. The accountant should have knowledge of the client's internal controls but would not comment on them in the comfort letter. Answer (C) is incorrect. An auditor may not provide any level of assurance on items that the auditor compiled or performed agreed-upon procedures on. Answer (D) is incorrect. Accountants can comment only on matters to which their expertise is relevant. Compliance with aspects of the law is beyond that expertise.

19.3 Filings Under Federal Securities Statutes (AU 711)

9. An independent accountant's report is based on a review of interim financial information. If this report is presented in a registration statement, a prospectus should include a statement clarifying that the

   A. Accountant's review report is not a part of the registration statement within the meaning of the Securities Act of 1933.

   B. Accountant assumes no responsibility to update the report for events and circumstances occurring after the date of the report.

   C. Accountant's review was performed in accordance with standards established by the Securities and Exchange Commission.

   D. Accountant obtained corroborating evidence to determine whether material modifications are needed for such information to conform with GAAP.

Answer (A) is correct. *(CPA, adapted)*
   REQUIRED: The statement in a review report on interim financial information included in a registration statement.
   DISCUSSION: According to AU 711, when an independent accountant has reviewed interim information and his/her report is presented or incorporated by reference in a registration statement, the SEC requires that a prospectus containing a statement about the accountant's involvement clarify that the report "is not a 'report' or 'part' of the registration statement within the meaning of sections 7 and 11 of the Securities Act of 1933." The prospectus should state that reliance on the report should be restricted given the limited procedures applied and that the accountant is not subject to the liability provisions of section 11.
   Answer (B) is incorrect. The registration statement contains audited financial statements. Thus, procedures should be extended from the date of the audit report to the effective date of the filing. Answer (C) is incorrect. The wording suggested by AU 711 is that "the independent public accountants have reported that they have applied limited procedures in accordance with professional standards for a review of such information." Answer (D) is incorrect. Accountants make inquiries and apply analytical procedures to determine whether modifications are needed for financial information to conform with the applicable financial reporting framework. They do not collect corroborating evidence in a review.

10. A registration statement filed with the SEC contains the reports of two independent auditors on their audits of financial statements for different periods. The predecessor auditor who audited the prior-period financial statements generally should obtain a letter of representation from the

   A. Successor independent auditor.

   B. Client's audit committee.

   C. Principal underwriter.

   D. Securities and Exchange Commission.

Answer (A) is correct. *(CPA, adapted)*
   REQUIRED: The party from whom the predecessor auditor should obtain a letter of representation.
   DISCUSSION: An auditor who has audited the financial statements for prior periods but not for the most recent period included in a registration statement has a responsibility for material subsequent events affecting the prior-period statements. Thus, the predecessor auditor who audited the prior-period financial statements generally should obtain a letter of representation from the successor auditor.

11. The Securities and Exchange Commission has authority to

   A. Require auditors to take primary responsibility for information in the financial statements of their public clients.

   B. Deny lack of privity as a defense in third-party actions for gross negligence against the auditors of public companies.

   C. Determine accounting principles for the purpose of financial reporting by companies offering securities to the public.

   D. Require a change of auditors of governmental entities after a given period of years as a means of ensuring auditor independence.

Answer (C) is correct. *(CPA, adapted)*
   REQUIRED: The authority of the SEC.
   DISCUSSION: The SEC has the authority to regulate the form and content of all financial statements, notes, and schedules filed with the SEC, and also the financial reports to shareholders if the company is subject to the Securities Exchange Act of 1934. Accounting principles applied must have substantial authoritative support. The SEC recognizes GAAP and has stated that financial statements conforming to FASB and, in certain cases, IASB standards will be presumed to have substantial authoritative support. However, the SEC reserves the right to substitute its principles for those of the accounting profession.
   Answer (A) is incorrect. Management is responsible for the information in the financial statements. Answer (B) is incorrect. The SEC does not have jurisdiction to determine what defenses may be asserted in an action, based on negligence, brought under state law. Furthermore, lack of privity is never a defense in an action based on gross negligence or fraud. Answer (D) is incorrect. The SEC may not require a change of auditors of governmental entities.

19.4 Other Information in Documents Containing Audited Financial Statements (AU 550)

12. When audited financial statements are presented in a client's document containing other information, the auditor should

A. Perform inquiry and analytical procedures to ascertain whether the other information is reasonable.

B. Add an explanatory paragraph to the auditor's report without changing the opinion on the financial statements.

C. Perform the appropriate substantive auditing procedures to corroborate the other information.

D. Read the other information to determine that it is consistent with the audited financial statements.

Answer (D) is correct. *(CPA, adapted)*
REQUIRED: The auditor's responsibility for other information appearing in a document with audited financial statements.
DISCUSSION: The auditor is obligated to read the other information and consider whether it is materially inconsistent with the audited financial statements or whether it contains a material misstatement of fact.
Answer (A) is incorrect. The auditor has no obligation to perform any procedures to corroborate the other information. Moreover, the auditor need not refer to the other information in the report but may disclaim an opinion on it. Answer (B) is incorrect. The auditor need not add a paragraph unless the other information in the client's document is materially inconsistent with the financial statements and the client has not revised it. Answer (C) is incorrect. The auditor has no obligation to perform any procedures to corroborate the other information.

13. An auditor concludes that there is a material inconsistency in the other information in an annual report to shareholders containing audited financial statements. However, the auditor has not performed procedures to corroborate the other information. If the auditor concludes that the financial statements do **not** require revision but the client refuses to revise or eliminate the material inconsistency, the auditor may

A. Revise the auditor's report to include a separate explanatory paragraph describing the material inconsistency.

B. Express a qualified opinion after discussing the matter with the client's directors.

C. Consider the matter closed because the other information is not in the audited statements.

D. Disclaim an opinion on the financial statements after explaining the material inconsistency in a separate paragraph.

Answer (A) is correct. *(CPA, adapted)*
REQUIRED: The auditor action when the client presents other information with a material inconsistency.
DISCUSSION: If the other information contains a material inconsistency, the auditor should determine whether the statements and the report need revision. If they do not, (s)he should request the client to revise the other information. If revision is not made, (s)he should consider (1) revising the report to include an explanatory paragraph, (2) withholding use of the report, or (3) withdrawing from the engagement. The action taken will depend on the circumstances and the significance of the inconsistency.
Answer (B) is incorrect. The opinion is expressed on the financial statements only. The inconsistency in the other information does not affect that opinion. Answer (C) is incorrect. The auditor may not ignore a material inconsistency in other information. Answer (D) is incorrect. The auditor's decision to disclaim an opinion is not affected by the other information.

19.5 Required Supplementary Information (RSI) (AU 558)

14. If management declines to present required supplementary information, the auditor should express a(n)

A. Adverse opinion.

B. Qualified opinion with an explanatory paragraph.

C. Unqualified opinion without an explanatory paragraph.

D. Unqualified opinion with an explanatory paragraph.

Answer (D) is correct. *(CPA, adapted)*
REQUIRED: The effect on the audit report of the client's failure to disclose RSI.
DISCUSSION: Omission of RSI does not affect the auditor's opinion because such information is not part of the basic financial statements. Instead, the auditor should express an unqualified opinion on the basic financial statements (assuming it is otherwise justified). In the explanatory paragraph, the auditor should state that (1) management omitted the RSI; (2) the RSI is considered to be essential by the designated accounting standard setter, although it is not a part of the basic financial statements; and (3) the audit opinion is unaffected by the omission. The information itself need not be presented by the auditor (AU 558).
Answer (A) is incorrect. The auditor should modify the explanatory paragraph but not change the opinion. Answer (B) is incorrect. The auditor should not change the opinion. Answer (C) is incorrect. The report should include an explanatory paragraph.

15. What is an auditor's responsibility for supplementary information that is outside the basic financial statements but required by the FASB?

A. The auditor has no responsibility for required supplementary information as long as it is outside the basic financial statements.

B. The auditor's only responsibility for required supplementary information is to determine that such information has not been omitted.

C. The auditor should apply certain limited procedures to the required supplementary information and report deficiencies in, or omissions of, such information.

D. The auditor should apply tests of details of transactions and balances to the required supplementary information and report any material misstatements in such information.

Answer (C) is correct. *(CPA, adapted)*
REQUIRED: The auditor's responsibility for RSI outside the basic financial statements but required by the FASB.
DISCUSSION: The FASB (the designated accounting standard setter) regards RSI outside the basic statements as essential to reporting and has established guidelines for its measurement and presentation. Although the auditor has no responsibility to audit this information, (s)he should apply limited procedures and report deficiencies in, or the omission of, such information (AU 558).
Answer (A) is incorrect. The auditor has a responsibility to apply limited procedures to RSI. Answer (B) is incorrect. The application of limited procedures extends beyond determining whether the RSI has been omitted. Answer (D) is incorrect. The auditor is not obligated to apply more than limited procedures.

19.6 Supplementary Information in Relation to the Financial Statements as a Whole (AU 551)

16. Investment and property schedules are presented for purposes of additional analysis in a document outside the basic financial statements. The schedules are not required supplementary information. When the auditor is engaged to report on whether the supplementary information is fairly stated in relation to the audited financial statements as a whole, the measurement of materiality is the

A. Same as that used in forming an opinion on the basic financial statements as a whole.

B. Lesser of the individual schedule of investments or schedule of property by itself.

C. Greater of the individual schedule of investments or schedule of property by itself.

D. Combined total of both the individual schedules of investments and property as a whole.

Answer (A) is correct. *(CPA, adapted)*
REQUIRED: The measure of materiality.
DISCUSSION: When reporting on whether supplementary information is fairly stated in relation to the statements as a whole, the measurement of materiality is the same as that used in forming an opinion on the basic financial statements taken as a whole. Accordingly, the auditor need not apply procedures as extensive as would be necessary to express an opinion on the information taken by itself.

17. The auditor is engaged to report on whether supplementary information is fairly stated in relation to the audited financial statements as a whole. Which of the following best describes the auditor's responsibility for this information if it is outside the basic financial statements and **not** deemed necessary to their fair presentation?

A. The auditor has no reporting responsibility concerning information accompanying the basic financial statements.

B. The auditor should report on the supplementary information only if the auditor participated in its preparation.

C. The auditor must disclaim an opinion on the information if it is supplementary information required by the applicable financial reporting framework.

D. The auditor should not express an opinion on the supplementary information if (s)he disclaimed an opinion on the financial statements.

Answer (D) is correct. *(CPA, adapted)*
REQUIRED: The auditor's reporting responsibility.
DISCUSSION: Supplementary information is presented outside the basic statements and is not deemed necessary for their fair presentation in conformity with the applicable financial reporting framework, e.g., additional details or explanations of items in or related to the statements, consolidating information, statistical data, and historical summaries. The auditor must not express an opinion on the supplementary information if (s)he expressed an adverse opinion or disclaimed an opinion on the audited financial statements. Moreover, the auditor must have served as the principal auditor of those statements.
Answer (A) is incorrect. The auditor was engaged to report on the supplementary information. Answer (B) is incorrect. Management is responsible for preparing the supplementary information. Answer (C) is incorrect. The auditor is not precluded from performing an engagement to express an opinion on RSI. But the opinion on the audited financial statements does not cover RSI absent a specific requirement in the agreement with the client.

19.7 Reporting on Condensed Financial Statements and Selected Financial Data (AU 552)

18. An auditor may report on condensed financial statements that are derived from complete audited financial statements if the

A. Auditor indicates whether the information in the condensed financial statements is fairly stated in all material respects.

B. Condensed financial statements are presented in comparative form with the prior year's condensed financial statements.

C. Auditor describes the additional review procedures performed on the condensed financial statements.

D. Condensed financial statements are distributed only to management and the board of directors.

Answer (A) is correct. *(CPA, adapted)*
REQUIRED: The requirement that permits an auditor to report on condensed financial statements.
DISCUSSION: The report on condensed financial statements should indicate (1) that the auditor has audited and expressed an opinion on the complete financial statements; (2) the date of that report; (3) the type of opinion expressed; and (4) whether, in the auditor's opinion, the information in the condensed statements is fairly stated in all material respects in relation to the complete financial statements.
Answer (B) is incorrect. The condensed statements need not be presented in comparative form. Rather, they should be read in conjunction with the most recent complete financial statements. Answer (C) is incorrect. The auditor need not perform additional review procedures. Answer (D) is incorrect. Distribution of the report is not restricted.

19. In the standard report on condensed financial statements that are derived from an issuer's audited financial statements, a CPA should indicate that the

A. Condensed financial statements are prepared in conformity with another comprehensive basis of accounting.

B. CPA has audited and expressed an opinion on the complete financial statements.

C. Condensed financial statements are not fairly presented in all material respects.

D. CPA expresses limited assurance that the financial statements conform with GAAP.

Answer (B) is correct. *(CPA, adapted)*
REQUIRED: The indication in a standard report on condensed financial statements.
DISCUSSION: The report should state (1) that the auditor has audited and expressed an opinion on the complete statements; (2) the date of that report; (3) the type of opinion expressed; and (4) an opinion as to whether the condensed statements are fairly stated in all material respects in relation to the complete statements (AU 552).
Answer (A) is incorrect. Condensed financial statements are prepared from financial statements prepared in accordance with the applicable financial reporting framework. Answer (C) is incorrect. Condensed financial statements may be fairly presented. Answer (D) is incorrect. The CPA expresses an opinion.

20. An auditor is engaged to report on selected financial data that are included in a client-prepared document containing audited financial statements. Under these circumstances, the report on the selected data should

A. Be limited to data derived from the audited financial statements.

B. Be distributed only to senior management and the board of directors.

C. State that the presentation is a comprehensive basis of accounting other than GAAP.

D. Indicate that the data are not fairly stated in all material respects.

Answer (A) is correct. *(CPA, adapted)*
REQUIRED: The basis of a report on selected data.
DISCUSSION: An auditor may report on selected data included in a client-prepared document containing audited statements. Selected financial data are not a required part of the basic financial statements, and management is responsible for determining the specific data to be presented. The report should be limited to data derived from the audited statements (AU 552).
Answer (B) is incorrect. The report need not be limited in distribution. Answer (C) is incorrect. The selected data are based upon audited financial statements prepared in accordance with the applicable financial reporting framework. Answer (D) is incorrect. The report should state whether the information in the selected financial data is fairly stated in all material respects in relation to the complete statements.

19.8   Reporting on Financial Statements Prepared for Use in Other Countries (AU 534)

21. The financial statements of KCP America, a U.S. entity, are prepared for inclusion in the consolidated financial statements of its non-U.S. parent. These financial statements are prepared in conformity with the accounting principles generally accepted in the parent's country and are for use only in that country. Which is an appropriate report on the financial statements for KCP America's auditor to issue?

I.   A U.S.-style report (unmodified)

II. A U.S.-style report modified to report on the accounting principles of the parent's country

III. The report form of the parent's country

    A.   I only.

    B.   II only.

    C.   II and III only.

    D.   I, II, and III.

Answer (C) is correct.   *(CPA, adapted)*
  REQUIRED: The proper reporting on the financial statements of a U.S. entity prepared for inclusion in the consolidated financial statements of its non-U.S. parent.
  DISCUSSION: According to AU 534, if financial statements prepared in conformity with accounting principles generally accepted in another country are prepared for use only outside the U.S., the auditor may use either a U.S.-style report modified to report on the accounting principles of the other country or, if appropriate, the report form of the other country. An unmodified U.S.-style report is inappropriate because of the departures from GAAP contained in statements prepared in conformity with principles generally accepted in the other country.

22. Before reporting on the financial statements of a U.S. entity that have been prepared in conformity with another country's accounting principles, an auditor practicing in the U.S. should

    A.   Understand the accounting principles generally accepted in the other country.

    B.   Be certified by the appropriate auditing or accountancy board of the other country.

    C.   Notify management that the auditor is required to disclaim an opinion on the financial statements.

    D.   Receive a waiver from the auditor's state board of accountancy to perform the engagement.

Answer (A) is correct.   *(CPA, adapted)*
  REQUIRED: The requirement for reporting on financial statements of a U.S. entity prepared in conformity with another country's accounting principles.
  DISCUSSION: AU 534 states that an independent auditor practicing in the U.S. may report on the financial statements of a U.S. entity prepared in conformity with accounting principles generally accepted in another country. However, the auditor must clearly understand, and obtain written representations from management about, the purpose and uses of the statements. (S)he also must comply with the general and field work standards of U.S. GAAS.
  Answer (B) is incorrect. The accountant needs to be a CPA in the U.S. Answer (C) is incorrect. The accountant may express an opinion on the fairness of the financial statements. Answer (D) is incorrect. No waiver is required to perform this service.

19.9   Reports on the Application of Accounting Principles (AU 625)

23. Blue, CPA, has been asked to report on the application of accounting principles to a specific transaction by an entity that is audited by another CPA. Blue may accept this engagement, but should

    A.   Consult with the continuing CPA to obtain information relevant to the transaction.

    B.   Report the engagement's findings to the entity's audit committee, the continuing CPA, and management.

    C.   Disclaim any opinion that the hypothetical application of accounting principles conforms with generally accepted accounting principles.

    D.   Notify the entity that the report is for general use.

Answer (A) is correct.   *(CPA, adapted)*
  REQUIRED: The proper action of a CPA who accepts an engagement to report on the application of accounting principles.
  DISCUSSION: The reporting accountant should consult with the continuing accountant to determine the available facts relevant to a professional judgment. The reporting accountant should (1) explain to the entity's management the need to consult with the continuing accountant, (2) request permission, and (3) request authorization for the continuing accountant to respond fully (AU 625).
  Answer (B) is incorrect. The accountant's written report should be addressed to the requesting entity (e.g., management or the board). Answer (C) is incorrect. The report should contain a statement describing the appropriate accounting principles to be applied, and, if appropriate, the reasons for the conclusions, not an opinion or a disclaimer. Also, the engagement may not involve reporting on the application of accounting principles to a hypothetical transaction. Answer (D) is incorrect. The use of the report is restricted to specified parties.

24. In connection with a proposal to obtain a new audit client, an accountant in public practice is asked to prepare a report on the application of accounting principles to a specific transaction. The report should include a statement that

  A. The engagement was performed in accordance with Statements on Standards for Accounting and Review Services.

  B. Responsibility for the proper accounting treatment rests with the preparers of the financial statements.

  C. The evaluation of the application of accounting principles is hypothetical and may not be used for opinion-shopping.

  D. The guidance is provided for general use.

Answer (B) is correct. *(CPA, adapted)*
  REQUIRED: The statement included in a report on the application of accounting principles to a specific transaction.
  DISCUSSION: The addressee of the accountant's report is the requesting entity. It should contain (1) a description of the engagement and whether it was in accordance with AICPA standards; (2) a description of the transaction; (3) a description of the accounting principles applied (including their country of origin); (4) a statement that the responsibility for proper accounting is with the preparers of the financial statements; and (5) a statement that any difference in facts, circumstances, or assumptions may change the report (AU 625).
  Answer (A) is incorrect. The engagement is conducted in accordance with applicable AICPA standards. Answer (C) is incorrect. No such language appears in the report. Moreover, such a report may not be provided on a hypothetical transaction. Answer (D) is incorrect. The use of the report is restricted to specified parties.

19.10 Engagements to Apply Agreed-Upon Procedures (AT 201)

25. Negative assurance may be expressed when a practitioner is requested to apply agreed-upon procedures to specified

	Elements of a Financial Statement	Accounts of a Financial Statement
A.	Yes	Yes
B.	Yes	No
C.	No	No
D.	No	Yes

Answer (C) is correct. *(Publisher, adapted)*
  REQUIRED: The report in which negative assurance may be expressed.
  DISCUSSION: The practitioner does not express an opinion or negative assurance. Instead, the practitioner's report on agreed-upon procedures should be in the form of procedures and findings.

26. A practitioner may accept an agreed-upon procedures engagement to calculate the rate of return on a specified investment and verify that the percentage agrees with the percentage in an identified schedule provided that

  A. The practitioner's report does not enumerate the procedures performed.

  B. The practitioner accepts responsibility for the sufficiency of the procedures.

  C. Use of the practitioner's report is restricted.

  D. The practitioner is also the entity's continuing auditor.

Answer (C) is correct. *(CPA, adapted)*
  REQUIRED: The condition of an engagement to apply agreed-upon procedures.
  DISCUSSION: An independent practitioner may accept such an engagement if (1) the specified parties agree to the procedures and take responsibility for their sufficiency, (2) the subject matter is subject to reasonably consistent measurement, (3) evidence is expected to exist providing a reasonable basis for the findings, (4) the use of the report is restricted, and (5) other conditions are met. The report should state that it is intended solely for the information and use of the specified parties and is not intended to be used and should not be used by anyone other than these specified parties.
  Answer (A) is incorrect. The procedures performed must be enumerated. Answer (B) is incorrect. The client or specified parties take responsibility for the sufficiency of the procedures. Answer (D) is incorrect. The practitioner need not be a continuing auditor.

19.11 Financial Forecasts and Projections (AT 301)

27. An examination of a financial forecast is a professional service that involves

    A. Compiling or assembling a financial forecast that is based on management's assumptions.

    B. Restricting the use of the practitioner's report to management and the board of directors.

    C. Assuming responsibility to update management on key events for 1 year after the report's date.

    D. Evaluating the preparation of a financial forecast and the support underlying management's assumptions.

Answer (D) is correct. *(CPA, adapted)*
    REQUIRED: The accountant's responsibility in an examination of a financial forecast.
    DISCUSSION: An examination of a financial forecast entails evaluating the preparation of the statements, the support underlying the assumptions, and the presentation of the statements for conformity with AICPA guidelines (AT 301).
    Answer (A) is incorrect. An examination of a financial forecast involves providing assurance on the representations of management. Answer (B) is incorrect. An examination of a financial forecast need not be limited in its distribution. Answer (C) is incorrect. The practitioner need not assume responsibility to update management on key events after the issuance of the report.

28. Given one or more hypothetical assumptions, a responsible party may prepare, to the best of its knowledge and belief, an entity's expected financial position, results of operations, and cash flows. Such prospective financial statements are known as

    A. Pro forma financial statements.

    B. Financial projections.

    C. Partial presentations.

    D. Financial forecasts.

Answer (B) is correct. *(CPA, adapted)*
    REQUIRED: The prospective statements based on one or more hypothetical assumptions.
    DISCUSSION: Prospective statements include forecasts and projections. The difference between a forecast and a projection is that only the latter is based on one or more hypothetical assumptions, which are conditions or actions not necessarily expected to occur.
    Answer (A) is incorrect. Pro forma statements are essentially historical, not prospective, statements. Answer (C) is incorrect. Partial presentations are not prospective statements. They do not meet the minimum presentation guidelines. Answer (D) is incorrect. Forecasts are based on assumptions about conditions the responsible party expects to exist and the course of action it expects to take.

29. Which of the following statements concerning prospective financial statements is true?

    A. Only a financial forecast would normally be appropriate for limited use.

    B. Only a financial projection would normally be appropriate for general use.

    C. Any type of prospective financial statements would normally be appropriate for limited use.

    D. Any type of prospective financial statements would normally be appropriate for general use.

Answer (C) is correct. *(CPA, adapted)*
    REQUIRED: The true statement about prospective financial statements.
    DISCUSSION: Limited use of prospective financial statements means use by the responsible party and those with whom that party is negotiating directly, e.g., in a submission to a regulatory body or in negotiations for a bank loan. These third parties are in a position to communicate directly with the responsible party. Consequently, AT 100 states, "Any type of prospective financial statements that would be useful in the circumstances would be appropriate for limited use."
    Answer (A) is incorrect. Projections as well as forecasts are appropriate for limited use. Answer (B) is incorrect. Only a forecast is appropriate for general use. Answer (D) is incorrect. Only a forecast is appropriate for general use.

30. Accepting an engagement to examine an entity's financial projection most likely would be appropriate if the projection were to be distributed to

    A. All employees who work for the entity.

    B. Potential shareholders who request a prospectus or a registration statement.

    C. A bank with which the entity is negotiating for a loan.

    D. All shareholders of record as of the report date.

Answer (C) is correct. *(CPA, adapted)*
    REQUIRED: The situation in which acceptance of an engagement to examine a projection is appropriate.
    DISCUSSION: A projection is based on one or more hypothetical assumptions and, therefore, should be considered for limited use only. Limited use of prospective financial statements means use by the responsible party and those with whom that party is negotiating directly. Examples of appropriate use include negotiations for a bank loan and submission to a regulatory body. A projection is inappropriate for distribution to those who will not be negotiating directly with the responsible party.

31. Which of the following is a prospective financial statement for general use upon which a practitioner may appropriately report?

A. Financial projection.

B. Partial presentation.

C. Pro forma financial statement.

D. Financial forecast.

Answer (D) is correct. *(CPA, adapted)*
REQUIRED: The prospective financial statement for general use upon which a practitioner may report.
DISCUSSION: Prospective financial statements are for general use if they are for use by persons with whom the responsible party is not negotiating directly, e.g., in an offering statement of the party's securities. Only a report based on a financial forecast is appropriate for general use.
Answer (A) is incorrect. A projection is appropriate only for limited use. Answer (B) is incorrect. A presentation not in compliance with minimum guidelines is not appropriate for general use. Answer (C) is incorrect. Pro forma statements are essentially historical, not prospective, statements.

32. When a practitioner examines a financial forecast that fails to disclose several significant assumptions used to prepare the forecast, the practitioner should describe the assumptions in the practitioner's report and express

A. An "except for" qualified opinion.

B. A "subject to" qualified opinion.

C. An unqualified opinion with a separate explanatory paragraph.

D. An adverse opinion.

Answer (D) is correct. *(CPA, adapted)*
REQUIRED: The appropriate opinion if a forecast fails to disclose several significant assumptions.
DISCUSSION: An examination results in issuance of a report stating the practitioner's opinion on whether (1) the presentation conforms with AICPA guidelines and (2) the assumptions provide a reasonable basis for the forecast. If significant assumptions are not disclosed in the presentation, including the summary of assumptions, the practitioner must express an adverse opinion. Moreover, a practitioner should not examine a presentation that omits all such disclosures.
Answer (A) is incorrect. Omission of significant assumptions requires an adverse opinion. Other departures from the presentation guidelines, however, may justify a qualified opinion. Answer (B) is incorrect. The language "subject to" is never permissible. Answer (C) is incorrect. An explanatory paragraph is insufficient when significant assumptions are omitted.

33. A practitioner's compilation report on a financial forecast should include a statement that

A. The forecast should be read only in conjunction with the audited historical financial statements.

B. The practitioner expresses only limited assurance on the forecasted statements and their assumptions.

C. There will usually be differences between the forecasted and actual results.

D. The hypothetical assumptions used in the forecast are reasonable in the circumstances.

Answer (C) is correct. *(CPA, adapted)*
REQUIRED: The statement included in a practitioner's compilation report on a financial forecast.
DISCUSSION: The standard report states that a compilation is limited in scope and does not enable the practitioner to express an opinion or any other form of assurance. It adds that there will usually be differences between the forecasted and actual results.
Answer (A) is incorrect. A forecast may stand alone. Answer (B) is incorrect. A compilation provides no assurance. Answer (D) is incorrect. A financial projection, not a financial forecast, contains hypothetical assumptions.

34. Relative to prospective financial statements, a practitioner may not accept an engagement to

A. Perform a review.

B. Perform a compilation.

C. Perform an examination.

D. Apply agreed-upon procedures.

Answer (A) is correct. *(CPA, adapted)*
REQUIRED: The engagement regarding prospective statements that may not be accepted.
DISCUSSION: AT 301 does not provide for the review form of engagement with regard to prospective statements.
Answer (B) is incorrect. A compilation may be performed provided the report does not express any form of assurance. Answer (C) is incorrect. An examination report may express an opinion on presentation in conformity with AICPA guidelines and the reasonableness of assumptions. Answer (D) is incorrect. Application of agreed-upon procedures is permissible.

35. A practitioner has been engaged to apply agreed-upon procedures in accordance with *Statements on Standards for Attestation Engagements* (SSAE) to prospective financial statements. Which of the following conditions must be met for the practitioner to perform the engagement?

A. The prospective financial statement includes a summary of significant accounting policies.

B. The practitioner takes responsibility for the sufficiency of the agreed-upon procedures.

C. The practitioner and specified parties agree upon the procedures to be performed by the practitioner.

D. The practitioner reports on the criteria to be used in the determination of findings.

Answer (C) is correct. *(CPA, adapted)*
REQUIRED: The condition to be met to perform agreed-upon procedures.
DISCUSSION: The following conditions should be met to accept an engagement: (1) The specified parties have participated in determining its nature and scope, and they take responsibility for the adequacy of the procedures; (2) report use is restricted to those parties; and (3) the statements include a summary of significant assumptions.
Answer (A) is incorrect. A summary of significant accounting policies is not required. Answer (B) is incorrect. The specified parties take responsibility for the adequacy of the procedures performed. Answer (D) is incorrect. The practitioner does not report on the criteria to be used in the determination of findings. Rather, the practitioner reports on the findings themselves. (S)he must believe the subject matter to be capable of reasonably consistent evaluation against suitable available criteria.

36. A practitioner's standard report on a compilation of a projection should **not** include a

A. Statement that a compilation of a projection is limited in scope.

B. Disclaimer of responsibility to update the report for events occurring after the report's date.

C. Statement that the practitioner expresses only limited assurance that the results may be achieved.

D. Separate paragraph that describes the limitations on the presentation's usefulness.

Answer (C) is correct. *(CPA, adapted)*
REQUIRED: The item not in a practitioner's standard report on a compilation of a projection.
DISCUSSION: A standard report states that the compilation is limited in scope and does not enable the practitioner to express an opinion or any other form of assurance on the prospective statements. Limited assurance (e.g., based on a review) should not be provided by the practitioner based on any prospective financial statement service.
Answer (A) is incorrect. The report should state that a compilation is limited in scope and does not provide any form of assurance. Answer (B) is incorrect. Every report on prospective financial statements should contain a statement that the practitioner assumes no responsibility to update the report for events and circumstances occurring after the report date. Answer (D) is incorrect. If the practitioner has reservations about the usefulness of the statements (e.g., the statements fail to provide notes), (s)he should so indicate in a separate paragraph.

37. When an accountant compiles a financial forecast, the accountant's report should include a(n)

A. Explanation of the differences between a financial forecast and a financial projection.

B. Caveat that the prospective results of the financial forecast may not be achieved.

C. Statement that the accountant's responsibility to update the report is limited to 1 year.

D. Disclaimer of opinion on the reliability of the entity's internal controls.

Answer (B) is correct. *(CPA, adapted)*
REQUIRED: The statement included in an accountant's compilation report on a financial forecast.
DISCUSSION: The standard report states that a compilation is limited in scope and does not enable the accountant to express an opinion or any other form of assurance. It adds that there will usually be differences between the forecasted and actual results (AT 301).
Answer (A) is incorrect. The standard report does not define a forecast, a projection, or their differences. Answer (C) is incorrect. The practitioner's update responsibility is limited to the date of the report. Answer (D) is incorrect. A compilation engagement does not involve consideration of internal control.

19.12 Reporting on Pro Forma Financial Information (AT 401)

38. A practitioner may report on an examination of pro forma financial information if the related historical financial statements have been

    A. Audited.

    B. Audited or reviewed.

    C. Audited, reviewed, or compiled.

    D. Reviewed or compiled.

Answer (A) is correct. *(Publisher, adapted)*
    REQUIRED: The service provided regarding the historical statements that permits an examination of pro forma financial information.
    DISCUSSION: A practitioner may examine or review pro forma financial information only if certain conditions are met. One of these conditions is that the level of assurance provided on the pro forma financial information be limited to that given on the historical statements. Accordingly, an examination of pro forma financial information, which provides a basis for giving positive assurance, is appropriate only if the historical statements have been audited.
    Answer (B) is incorrect. If the historical statements have been reviewed, only a review of the pro forma financial information would be appropriate. Answer (C) is incorrect. A compilation of the historical statements provides no assurance; thus, it would not provide a basis for the practitioner to examine or review the pro forma statements. Answer (D) is incorrect. A compilation of the historical statements provides no assurance; thus, it would not provide a basis for the practitioner to examine or review the pro forma statements.

39. An accountant has been engaged to examine pro forma adjustments that show the effects on previously audited historical financial statements due to a proposed disposition of a significant portion of an entity's business. Other than the procedures previously applied to the historical financial statements, the accountant is required to

	Reevaluate the entity's internal control over financial reporting	Determine that the computations of the pro forma adjustments are mathematically correct
A.	Yes	Yes
B.	Yes	No
C.	No	Yes
D.	No	No

Answer (C) is correct. *(CPA, adapted)*
    REQUIRED: The procedure(s), if any, applied in an examination of pro forma financial statements.
    DISCUSSION: In an examination of pro forma financial statements, the practitioner's additional procedures include (1) understanding the underlying transaction or event; (2) discussing the assumptions about the transaction or event with management; (3) evaluating whether adjustments are included for all significant effects; (4) gathering sufficient evidence to support the adjustments; (5) evaluating whether the assumptions are sufficiently, clearly, and comprehensively presented; (6) determining that computations are correct and that the pro forma column properly reflects their application to the historical statements; (7) obtaining written management representations; and (8) evaluating the pro forma information to determine whether certain matters (the transaction or event, assumptions, adjustments, and uncertainties) have been properly described and the sources of the historical information have been properly identified. Moreover, in a business combination, the practitioner must obtain a sufficient understanding of each part of the combined entity. However, no evaluation of internal control beyond that done in the engagement is performed with respect to the historical statements.

40. The practitioner's report on an examination of pro forma financial information

    A. Should have the same date as the related historical financial statements.

    B. Should be added to the report on the historical financial statements.

    C. Need not mention the report on the historical financial statements.

    D. May state an unqualified, qualified, or adverse opinion.

Answer (D) is correct. *(Publisher, adapted)*
    REQUIRED: The true statement about the practitioner's report on an examination of pro forma financial information.
    DISCUSSION: The report should include an opinion on whether (1) management's assumptions provide a reasonable basis for the significant effects attributable to the transaction or event, (2) the pro forma adjustments give appropriate effect to the assumptions, and (3) the pro forma column reflects the proper application of those adjustments to the historical data. Scope limitations, uncertainties, reservations about the assumptions or the presentation (including inadequate disclosure), and other matters may lead to modification of the opinion or a disclaimer.
    Answer (A) is incorrect. The report should be dated as of the completion of procedures. Answer (B) is incorrect. The report may appear separately. Moreover, if it is combined with the report on the historical statements, the combined report may need to be dual-dated. Answer (C) is incorrect. The report should refer to the financial statements from which the historical information is derived and state whether they were audited or reviewed.

41. A practitioner's report on a review of pro forma financial information should include a

    A. Statement that the entity's internal control was not relied on in the review.

    B. Disclaimer of opinion on the financial statements from which the pro forma financial information is derived.

    C. Caveat that it is uncertain whether the transaction or event reflected in the pro forma financial information will ever occur.

    D. Reference to the financial statements from which the historical financial information is derived.

Answer (D) is correct. *(CPA, adapted)*
    REQUIRED: The statement that should be included in a review of pro forma financial information.
    DISCUSSION: A practitioner's report on pro forma information should include (1) an identification of the pro forma information, (2) a reference to the financial statements from which the historical financial information is derived and a statement as to whether such financial statements were audited or reviewed, (3) a statement that the review was made in accordance with standards established by the AICPA, (4) a caveat that a review is substantially less in scope than an examination and that no opinion is expressed, (5) a separate paragraph explaining the objective of pro forma financial information and its limitations, and (6) the practitioner's conclusion providing limited assurance.
    Answer (A) is incorrect. The report should not mention internal control. Answer (B) is incorrect. The practitioner should disclaim an opinion on the pro forma financial information. Answer (C) is incorrect. The transaction may already have occurred.

19.13 Compliance Attestation (AT 601)

42. In a compliance attestation engagement,

    A. The field work and reporting but not the general attestation standards apply.

    B. The practitioner may accept an engagement to examine the effectiveness of internal control over compliance only if an assertion about internal control is provided to the practitioner by the client.

    C. The result is a legal determination of an entity's compliance with specified requirements.

    D. The practitioner should accept responsibility for the entity's compliance with the specified requirements.

Answer (B) is correct. *(Publisher, adapted)*
    REQUIRED: The true statement about a compliance attestation engagement.
    DISCUSSION: The written assertion may be provided to the practitioner in a representation letter or may be presented in a separate report that will accompany the practitioner's report.
    Answer (A) is incorrect. The general attestation standards also apply. Answer (C) is incorrect. The report does not provide a legal determination on compliance with specified requirements, but it may be useful to legal counsel or others in making such determinations. Answer (D) is incorrect. The responsible party, typically management, must accept responsibility for compliance.

43. What service(s) may a practitioner perform in a compliance attestation engagement?

	Application of Agreed-Upon Procedures	Examination	Review
A.	Yes	Yes	Yes
B.	No	Yes	Yes
C.	Yes	Yes	No
D.	No	No	Yes

Answer (C) is correct. *(Publisher, adapted)*
    REQUIRED: The service(s) that may be performed in a compliance attestation engagement.
    DISCUSSION: The practitioner may perform agreed-upon procedures as long as the specified users participate in establishing the procedures to be applied and take responsibility for the adequacy of such procedures for their purposes. The practitioner also may conduct an examination in which (s)he gathers evidence to support an opinion. Both types of engagements may be performed with respect to compliance with specified requirements or about the effectiveness of internal control over compliance. However, the standard does not provide for a review engagement.

44. A practitioner's report on agreed-upon procedures related to an entity's compliance with specified requirements should contain

    A. A statement of restrictions on the use of the report.

    B. An opinion about whether management complied with the specified requirements.

    C. Negative assurance that control risk has not been assessed.

    D. An acknowledgment of responsibility for the sufficiency of the procedures.

Answer (A) is correct. *(CPA, adapted)*
    REQUIRED: The statement in a report on a compliance attestation engagement to apply agreed-upon procedures.
    DISCUSSION: The fourth attestation standard of reporting indicates that a report should be restricted to specified parties "when the report is on an attest engagement to apply agreed-upon procedures to the subject matter."
    Answer (B) is incorrect. The report on agreed-upon procedures should be in the form of a summary of procedures and findings, not in the form of an opinion. Answer (C) is incorrect. Negative assurance about whether an entity is in compliance or whether management's assertion is fairly stated is not permitted in reports on applying agreed-upon procedures. Answer (D) is incorrect. The parties who agreed to the procedures are responsible for their sufficiency.

45. Mill, CPA, was engaged by a group of royalty recipients to apply agreed-upon procedures to financial data supplied by Modern Co. regarding Modern's written assertion about its compliance with contractual requirements to pay royalties. Mill's report on these agreed-upon procedures should contain a(n)

    A. Disclaimer of opinion about the fair presentation of Modern's financial statements.

    B. List of the procedures performed (or reference thereto) and Mill's findings.

    C. Opinion about the effectiveness of Modern's internal control activities concerning royalty payments.

    D. Acknowledgment that the sufficiency of the procedures is solely Mill's responsibility.

Answer (B) is correct. *(CPA, adapted)*
    REQUIRED: The statement in a report on a compliance attestation engagement to apply agreed-upon procedures.
    DISCUSSION: The practitioner's report should be in the form of procedures and findings but should not provide negative assurance about whether the entity is in compliance or whether the responsible party's assertion is fairly stated (AT 201).
    Answer (A) is incorrect. The report should not contain a disclaimer of opinion on the fair presentation of Modern's financial statements. However, it should contain a paragraph stating that the independent accountant was not engaged to and did not perform an examination of the financial data regarding the written assertion about compliance with contractual requirements to pay royalties. It also should state that (1) the objective of an examination would have been an expression of opinion on compliance with the specified requirements, and (2) no such opinion is expressed. Answer (C) is incorrect. An agreed-upon procedures engagement typically results in a summary of findings, not an opinion. Answer (D) is incorrect. The specified parties who agreed to the procedures are responsible for their sufficiency.

Use the additional questions in Gleim **CPA Test Prep Online** to create Test Sessions that emulate Prometric!

19.14 PRACTICE SIMULATION

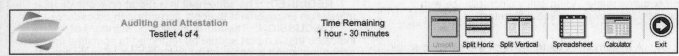

Auditing and Attestation
Testlet 4 of 4

Time Remaining
1 hour - 30 minutes

Unsplit | Split Horiz | Split Vertical | Spreadsheet | Calculator | Exit

DIRECTIONS

Note: If you believe you have encountered a software malfunction, report it to the test center staff immediately.

Navigation

To navigate from task to task, use the controls at the bottom of the screen. Click on the **Next** button to advance to the next task, or the **Previous** button to go to the previous task. To go directly to any task, click on its number.

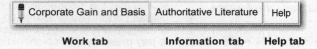

If you would like a reminder to revisit a task, or want to indicate that you are finished with it, click on the reminder flag below the task number. To clear the flag, click on it again. Reminder flags are for your use only – they do not contribute to your score.

Tabs

In this part of the examination, you will be asked to complete various tasks. Every task has one or more **Work Tabs**. Some tasks have one or more **Information Tabs**, others may have none. Every task has a **Help** tab.

If a task has **Information Tabs**, you may use the information in them to complete your responses in the **Work Tabs**.

Corporate Gain and Basis	Authoritative Literature	Help
Work tab	**Information tab**	**Help tab**

Work Tabs:
- **Work Tabs** are identified with a pencil icon. This is where your responses are expected.
- Each task has one or more **Work Tabs**.
- **Work Tabs** contain directions for completing the task – be sure to read these directions carefully.
- The **Work Tab** name in the example above is for illustration only – yours will differ.
- You must complete all of the **Work Tabs** in each task to receive full credit.

Information Tabs:
- The Authoritative Literature will be provided in all tasks in the AUD, FAR, and REG sections for your reference.
- Your simulation may have one or more additional **Information Tabs**. Like the Authoritative Literature tabs, **Information Tabs** do not have a pencil icon.
- If your task has additional **Information Tabs**, go through each to familiarize yourself with the task content.

Help Tab:
- The **Help Tab** provides assistance with the exam software that is used in this task. For example, if the task is to compose a memorandum, **Help** will provide information about the word processor.

The Toolbar

The toolbar at the top of the screen shows the amount of time remaining for you to complete the tasks. In addition, the following tools are available. Note that only the Exit button is displayed when Directions are visible - the others will appear when you begin the tasks.

Click on these buttons to split or unsplit the screen. You can split the screen vertically or horizontally.

Click on this button to display the calculator; click on it again to hide the calculator. To move the calculator, click on the calculator title bar and drag the calculator to the desired location.

Click on this button to use the spreadsheet; click on it again to hide the spreadsheet. To move the spreadsheet, click on the the spreadsheet title bar and drag the spreadsheet to the desired location.

Click on this button to go on to the next part of the examination. You must complete all of the tasks to receive full credit. Once you click on **Exit** and confirm the action, you will NOT be able to return to this testlet.

⚑ = Reminder | | Directions | 1 2 3 4 5 | | ◄ Previous   Next ►

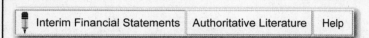

Interim Financial Statements | Authoritative Literature | Help

Check the shaded box to the right of each true statement about an engagement to perform and report on a review of an issuer's interim financial information.

Statement	True
1. The objective of a review of interim financial information is to express an opinion on whether it conforms with the applicable financial reporting framework.	
2. A review primarily involves performing analytical procedures and inquiries.	
3. To perform a review, the the annual statements must have been audited.	
4. To perform a review of interim financial information, the accountant must gain knowledge of the entity's business sufficient to identify types of typical misstatements.	
5. To perform a review of interim financial information, the accountant must obtain an attorney's letter concerning litigation, claims, and assessments.	
6. To perform a review of interim financial information, the accountant should obtain a client representation letter.	
7. A significant scope limitation results in a modified review report.	
8. Each page of the reviewed interim financial information should state "Reviewed by Auditor."	
9. A departure from the applicable financial reporting framework in the financial information may result in a modified review report.	
10. As a result of the review, the accountant should communicate any significant fraud or illegal acts of which (s)he becomes aware to those charged with governance.	

Accountant's Responsibility for Various Types of Information | Authoritative Literature | Help

The accountant will encounter various types of information presented by clients. Listed below are four types of information defined in the standards.

- In column (a), select from List 1 an example of each type of information.
- In column (b), select from List 2 an appropriate procedure for each type of information.

Each choice may be used once, more than once, or not at all.

Type of Information	Example of Information (a)	Accountant's Procedures (b)
1. Other information		
2. Required supplementary		
3. Supplementary on which the auditor is engaged to report		
4. Condensed or selected		

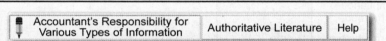

List 1
A) Oil and gas reserve information
B) Schedule of fixed assets
C) Summary of financial results
D) CEO's letter in the annual report

List 2
E) Audit
F) Apply limited procedures
G) Read for consistency with financial statements
H) Determine whether stated fairly relative to complete financial statements

| Comfort Letters | Authoritative Literature | Help |

For each of the following, select from the list provided the appropriate term for each description relating to comments on information other than audited financial statements typically contained in a comfort letter. Each choice may be used once, more than once, or not at all.

Description	Answer	Choices
1. Comments on this information should be in the form of negative assurance.		A) Forecasts
2. The accountants should have this information if they comment on unaudited condensed interim information; capsule information; financial forecasts; or changes in capital stock, increases in noncurrent debt, and decreases in selected items.		B) Capsule financial information
3. This information consists of unaudited summarized interim information for subsequent periods used to supplement the audited financial statements or unaudited condensed interim financial information in a registration statement.		C) Pro forma financial information
4. The accountants should not comment on this information unless they have acquired the appropriate level of knowledge, such as that obtained from auditing or reviewing the historical statements.		D) Subsequent changes
5. To apply agreed-upon procedures, the accountants should perform compilation procedures on this information and should attach the report to the comfort letter.		E) Unaudited condensed interim financial statements
6. Comments that attestations are in accordance with the applicable attestation pronouncement may be made, but no comments on nonfinancial data or the compliance with the forms required by SEC rules should be made.		F) Management's discussion and analysis
7. Comments on these matters ordinarily concern whether a change has occurred in capital stock, noncurrent debt has increased, or other specified financial statement items have increased or decreased during the change period.		G) Knowledge of the client's internal control

---

Prospective Financial Statements | Authoritative Literature | Help

Select from the list provided the true statement about each item related to prospective financial statements.

Statement	Answer		Choices
1. The practitioner can perform a review engagement.		A)	Relates only to a financial forecast
2. Includes one or more hypothetical assumptions.			
3. Appropriate for general use.		B)	Relates only to a financial projection
4. The practitioner can express an opinion.			
5. Includes a set of responsible party's assumptions.		C)	Relates to both a financial forecast and a financial projection
6. Practitioner may issue a report based on agreed-upon procedures.			
7. The practitioner accepts responsibility for the information in the prospective financial statements.		D)	Relates to neither a financial forecast nor a financial projection
8. The practitioner can perform a compilation.			

▼ = Reminder   Directions   1 2 3 [4] 5   ◀ Previous   Next ▶

Research | Authoritative Literature | Help

Research and cite the appropriate auditing standard paragraph that outlines the reporting standards for a U.S.-style report modified to report on financial statements prepared in conformity with accounting principles generally accepted in another country that are intended for use only outside the United States.

Title	Section	Paragraph

Title Choices

AU	PCAOB	AT	AR	ET	BL	VS
CS	QC	PR	TS	PFP	CPE	

▼ = Reminder   Directions   1 2 3 4 [5]   ◀ Previous   Next ▶

Unofficial Answers

1. Interim Financial Statements (10 Gradable Items)

1. <u>Not true.</u> The objective of a review of IFI is to enable the accountant to provide negative assurance, i.e., to state whether (s)he is aware of any material modifications that should be made for the IFI to conform with the applicable financial reporting framework.

2. <u>True.</u> A review engagement primarily involves the use of inquires and analytical procedures.

3. <u>True.</u> An accountant may review the IFI of an entity if (s)he has audited the latest annual statements and the IFI is prepared using the same applicable financial reporting framework as those statements.

4. <u>True.</u> The accountant's knowledge of the entity's business and internal controls should be sufficient to (a) identify types of misstatements, (b) consider the likelihood of their occurrence, and (c) select inquiries and analytical procedures.

5. <u>Not true.</u> A review of IFI does not contemplate communication with the client's attorney.

6. <u>True.</u> The accountant should make appropriate inquires and document the responses in a representation letter.

7. <u>Not true.</u> A scope restriction may arise from (a) significant deficiencies or material weaknesses in internal control, (b) inability to perform necessary procedures, or (c) the client's failure to provide written representations. The result is an incomplete review, and no report is issued.

8. <u>Not true.</u> Each page of the interim financial information should be clearly marked as unaudited.

9. <u>True.</u> The accountant modifies the review report for material departures from the applicable financial reporting framework, including inadequate disclosure. The modification describes the departure and, if practicable, states its effects or provides the necessary information.

10. <u>True.</u> Possible communications to management and those charged with governance include (a) the inability to complete the review, (b) the need for material modification of IFI, (c) the accountant's awareness of fraud or illegal acts, (d) internal-control-related matters, and (e) certain other matters.

2. Accountant's Responsibility for Various Types of Information (8 Gradable Items)

1. (a) <u>D) CEO's letter in the annual report.</u>
    (b) <u>G) Read for consistency with financial statements.</u>

2. (a) <u>A) Oil and gas reserve information.</u>
    (b) <u>F) Apply limited procedures.</u>

3. (a) <u>B) Schedule of fixed assets.</u>
    (b) <u>E) Audit.</u>

4. (a) <u>C) Summary of financial results.</u>
    (b) <u>H) Determine whether stated fairly relative to complete financial statements.</u>

3. Comfort Letters (7 Gradable Items)

1. <u>E) Unaudited condensed interim financial statements.</u> Comments in the comfort letter about unaudited condensed interim financial statements appearing in the registration statement should always be in the form of negative assurance.

2. <u>G) Knowledge of the client's internal control.</u> The accountants should have knowledge of the client's internal controls if they comment on (a) unaudited condensed information, (b) capsule information, (c) financial forecasts, (d) changes in capital stock, (e) increases in noncurrent debt, and (f) decreases in selected items. However, they do not comment on internal control.

3. <u>B) Capsule financial information.</u> Capsule information is unaudited summarized interim information for subsequent periods used to supplement the audited financial statements or unaudited condensed interim financial information in a registration statement.

4. <u>C) Pro forma financial information.</u> The accountants should not comment on pro forma financial information unless they have acquired the appropriate level of knowledge of the accounting and financial reporting practices of the entity, e.g., by auditing or reviewing the historical statements.

5. <u>A) Forecasts.</u> To apply agreed-upon procedures to a forecast and comment on it in a comfort letter, the accountants must perform compilation procedures and should attach the report to the comfort letter. Negative assurance on the results of the procedures may not be provided.

6. <u>F) Management's discussion and analysis.</u> Comments that attestations are in accordance with AT 701, *Management's Discussion and Analysis*, may be made. No comments on the compliance of the MD&A with the forms required by SEC rules should be made. Furthermore, no comments should be made on nonfinancial data in the MD&A.

7. <u>D) Subsequent changes.</u> Comments on subsequent changes ordinarily concern whether a change has occurred in capital stock, noncurrent debt has increased, or other specified financial statement items have increased/decreased during the change period (the period subsequent to the latest financial statements included in the registration statement).

4. Prospective Financial Statements (8 Gradable Items)

1. <u>D) Relates to neither a financial forecast nor a financial projection.</u> Review engagements may not be performed on prospective financial statements.

2. <u>B) Relates only to a financial projection.</u> A financial projection contains one or more hypothetical assumptions.

3. <u>A) Relates only to a financial forecast.</u> Only an examination report for a financial forecast is appropriate for general use.

4. <u>A) Relates only to a financial forecast.</u> Only an examination of a financial forecast results in an opinion by the practitioner.

5. <u>C) Relates to both a financial forecast and a financial projection.</u> Both financial forecasts and projections contain a set of assumptions made by the responsible party.

6. <u>C) Relates to both a financial forecast and a financial projection.</u> Practitioners may perform and report on agreed-upon procedures for both financial forecasts and projections.

7. <u>D) Relates to neither a financial forecast nor a financial projection.</u> The responsible party (typically management) is responsible for the information in the prospective financial statements.

8. <u>C) Relates to both a financial forecast and a financial projection.</u> The practitioner can compile both financial forecasts and projections for limited use.

5. Research (1 Gradable Item)

Answer: 534.09

AU Section 534 -- *Reporting on Financial Statements Prepared for Use in Other Countries*

Reporting Standards -- Use Only Outside the United States

.09 A U.S.-style report modified to report on financial statements prepared in conformity with accounting principles generally accepted in another country that are intended for use only outside the United States should include-

a. A title that includes the word "independent."

b. A statement that the financial statements identified in the report were audited.

c. A statement that refers to the note to the financial statements that describes the basis of presentation of the financial statements on which the auditor is reporting, including identification of the nationality of the accounting principles.

d. A statement that the financial statements are the responsibility of the Company's management and that the auditor's responsibility is to express an opinion on the financial statements based on his/her audit.

e. A statement that the audit was conducted in accordance with auditing standards generally accepted in the United States of America (and, if appropriate, with the auditing standards of the other country).

f. A statement that U.S. standards require that the auditor plan and perform the audit to obtain reasonable assurance about whether the financial statements are free of material misstatement.

g. A statement that an audit includes:

   1) Examining, on a test basis, evidence supporting the amounts and disclosures in the financial statements,
   2) Assessing the accounting principles used and significant estimates made by management, and
   3) Evaluating the overall financial statement presentation.

h. A statement that the auditor believes that his audit provides a reasonable basis for his opinion.

i. A paragraph that expresses the auditor's opinion on whether the financial statements are presented fairly, in all material respects, in conformity with the basis of accounting described. If the auditor concludes that the financial statements are not fairly presented on the basis of accounting described, all substantive reasons for that conclusion should be disclosed in an additional explanatory paragraph (preceding the opinion paragraph) of the report, and the opinion paragraph should include appropriate modifying language as well as a reference to the explanatory paragraph.

j. If the auditor is auditing comparative financial statements and the described basis of accounting has not been applied in a manner consistent with that of the preceding period and the change has had a material effect on the comparability of the financial statements, the auditor should add an explanatory paragraph to his report (following the opinion paragraph) that describes the change in accounting principle and refers to the note to the financial statements that discusses the change and its effect on the financial statements.

k. The manual or printed signature of the auditor's firm.

l. Date.

Gleim Simulation Grading

Task	Correct Responses		Gradable Items		Score per Task
1	_____	÷	10	=	_____
2	_____	÷	8	=	_____
3	_____	÷	7	=	_____
4	_____	÷	8	=	_____
Research	_____	÷	1	=	_____

Total of Scores per Task	_____
÷ Total Number of Tasks	5
Total Score	_____%

Use **CPA Gleim Online** and **Simulation Wizard** to practice more task-based simulations in a realistic environment.

STUDY UNIT TWENTY
GOVERNMENTAL AUDITS

(12 pages of outline)

The first subunit addresses *Government Auditing Standards*, the GAO publication that is fundamental to governmental auditing and is the basis for most of the related questions on recent CPA exams. However, the trend has been to increase the coverage of governmental auditing. Thus, the other subunits provide a more detailed outline of material that is likely to be covered on future exams, including the new AICPA pronouncement on compliance auditing.

20.1 GOVERNMENT AUDITING STANDARDS

1.   The **Government Accountability Office (GAO)** establishes **generally accepted government auditing standards (GAGAS)** and issues *Government Auditing Standards* (the Yellow Book).

   a.   GAGAS pertain to auditors' professional qualifications and the quality of their work, the performance of field work, and the characteristics of meaningful reporting.

   b.   *Government Auditing Standards* contains standards for audits and attestation engagements of government entities, programs, activities, and functions and of government assistance administered by contractors, nonprofit entities, and other nongovernment entities.

2.   **Government Engagements**

   a.   **Financial Audits**

      1)   **Financial statement audits.** These audits are primarily concerned with whether financial statements are presented fairly in all material respects with GAAP or with a comprehensive basis of accounting other than GAAP.

         a)   GAGAS require related reporting on (1) internal control; (2) compliance with laws, regulations, and contract provisions; and (3) fraud and illegal acts.

         b)   The auditor conducting a governmental audit accepts a **greater scope** and assumes **more responsibility** than in an audit of a business entity.

      2)   **Other objectives.** These engagements provide for different levels of assurance and involve various scopes of work. They include

         a)   Special reports for specified elements, accounts, or items of a financial statement

         b)   Reviewing interim financial information

         c)   Issuing letters for underwriters and certain other requesting parties

         d)   Reporting on the processing of transactions by service organizations

         e)   Auditing compliance with regulations relating to federal award expenditures and other governmental financial assistance in conjunction with or as a by-product of a financial statement audit

b. **Attestation Engagements**

1) These engagements involve examining, reviewing, or performing agreed-upon procedures on a subject matter or an assertion about a subject matter and reporting on the results. Examples include reporting on

   a) An entity's internal control over financial or other reporting

   b) An entity's compliance with requirements of specified laws, regulations, rules, contracts, or grants

   c) Management discussion and analysis (MD&A)

   d) Prospective financial statements or performance information

   e) The accuracy or reliability of performance measures

   f) Allowable, reasonable, or final contract cost

   g) The quantity, condition, or valuation of inventory or assets

   h) Results of agreed-upon procedures

c. **Performance Audits**

1) These audits address many objectives, including assessing

   a) Program effectiveness and results,

   b) Economy and efficiency,

   c) Internal control, and

   d) Compliance with legal requirements.

2) They also may provide prospective analyses, guidance, or summary information.

3. **Standards**

a. In the standards for **financial audits**, *Government Auditing Standards* **incorporates AICPA standards of field work and reporting**. However, it states **different** general standards and prescribes **additional** field work and reporting standards.

4. **General Standards**

a. **Independence.** The following is a general standard:

   In all matters relating to the audit work, the audit organization and the individual auditor, whether government or public, must be free from personal, external, and organizational impairments to independence, and must avoid the appearance of such impairments of independence.

1) The rules on **personal impairments** are similar to the AICPA rules. An auditor may not (a) have a **direct** financial interest or **material indirect** financial interest in a client, (b) audit the work of a close family member, (c) seek employment with the audited entity, or (d) be biased. Furthermore, auditors must consider whether performing **nonaudit services** creates a personal impairment. When assessing whether nonaudit services impair independence, the audit organization applies **two overarching principles**:

   a) The audit organization should not provide nonaudit services that involve performing **management functions** or making **management decisions**.

   b) The audit organization should not audit its work or provide nonaudit services that are **significant or material** to the subject matter of audits.

2) **External impairments** occur when auditors are deterred from acting objectively and exercising **professional skepticism** by pressures, actual or perceived, from management or employees of the audited entity or oversight organizations. For example, an external impairment may result from a threat of replacement of the auditor over a disagreement with the contents of the audit report.

3) **Organizational impairments** may be created by the audit organization's place within government or the structure of the audited entity. Government auditors can be presumed to be free from organizational impairments to independence when **reporting externally to third parties** if their audit organization is organizationally independent from the audited entity. A **government internal audit organization** can be presumed to be free from organizational impairments to independence when **reporting internally to management** if the head of the audit organization is (a) accountable to the head or deputy head of the government entity, (b) required to report the results of the audit organization's work to the head or deputy head of the government entity, and (c) located organizationally outside the staff or line management function of the unit under audit.

b. **Professional judgment.** The following is a general standard:

Auditors must use professional judgment in planning and performing audits and attestation engagements and in reporting the results.

c. **Competence.** The following is a general standard:

The staff assigned to perform the audit or attestation engagement must collectively possess adequate professional competence for the tasks required.

1) Every 2 years, each auditor performing work under GAGAS must earn at least 24 hours of CPE directly related to government auditing.

d. **Quality control and assurance.** The following is a general standard:

Each audit organization performing audits or attestation engagements in accordance with GAGAS must:

a. *Establish a system of quality control that is designed to provide the audit organization with reasonable assurance that the organization and its personnel comply with professional standards and applicable legal and regulatory requirements, and*

b. *Have an external peer review at least once every 3 years.*

5. **Field Work Standards**

a. **Auditor communication.** The following is an additional field work standard:

Under AICPA standards and GAGAS, auditors should communicate with the audited entity their understanding of the services to be performed for each engagement and document that understanding through a written communication.

b. **Considering results of previous engagements.** The following is an additional field work standard:

Auditors should evaluate whether the audited entity has taken appropriate corrective action to address findings and recommendations from previous engagements that could have a material effect on the financial statements.

c. **Detecting material misstatements resulting from contract or grant violations or from abuse.** The following is an additional field work standard:

Auditors should design the audit to provide reasonable assurance of detecting misstatements that result from violations of provisions of contracts or grant agreements and could have a direct and material effect on the determination of financial statement amounts or other financial data significant to the audit objectives.

d.   **Developing elements of a finding.** The following is an additional field work standard:

> *Audit findings may involve deficiencies in internal control, fraud, illegal acts, violations of provisions of contracts or grant agreements, and abuse.*

1)   The elements needed for a finding depend on the objectives of the audit but include

a)   **Criteria.** The required or desired state (e.g., law or contract) or expectation with respect to the program or operation.

b)   **Condition.** Condition is a situation that exists.

c)   **Cause.** The cause identifies the reason or explanation for the condition.

d)   **Effect or potential effect.** The effect is a clear, logical link to establish the impact or potential impact of the difference between the situation that exists (condition) and the required or desired state (criteria).

e.   **Audit documentation.** The following is an additional field work standard:

> *Under AICPA standards and GAGAS, auditors should prepare audit documentation that enables an experienced auditor, having no previous connection to the audit, to understand*
>
> *a.   The nature, timing, and extent of auditing procedures performed to comply with GAGAS and other applicable standards and requirements;*
>
> *b.   The results of the audit procedures performed and the audit evidence obtained;*
>
> *c.   The conclusions reached on significant matters; and*
>
> *d.   That the accounting records agree or reconcile with the audited financial statements or other audited information.*

6.   **Reporting Standards**

a.   **Compliance with GAGAS.** The following is an additional reporting standard:

> *Audit reports should state that the audit was performed in accordance with GAGAS.*

b.   **Internal control and compliance with laws, regulations, and contract or grant provisions.** The following summarizes an additional reporting standard:

1)   The report on financial statements (or separate reports) should describe the scope of the auditor's testing of internal control over financial reporting and compliance with laws and regulations and grant or contract provisions. The results of those tests (or an opinion if sufficient work was performed) should be included in the report.

c.   **Deficiencies in internal control, fraud, illegal acts, violations of contracts or grant agreements, and abuse.** The following summarizes an additional reporting standard:

1)   Auditors should report significant deficiencies and material weaknesses in internal control. They also should report fraud and illegal acts that have an effect on the financial statements that is more than inconsequential. They should report material violations of provisions of contracts or grants and material abuse (material either quantitatively or qualitatively).

d.   **Communicating significant matters in the auditor's report.** The following summarizes an additional reporting standard:

1)   Under AICPA standards, auditors may emphasize in the auditor's report significant matters regarding the financial statements. For example, the auditor may express significant concerns or uncertainties about the fiscal sustainability of a government or program.

e. **Reporting on restatement of previously-issued financial statements.** The following summarizes an additional reporting standard:

1) The auditors should essentially follow AU 561, *Subsequent Discovery of Facts Existing at the Date of the Auditor's Report*, if they become aware of new information that might have affected their opinion on previously-issued financial statements.

f. **Reporting views of responsible officials.** The following is an additional reporting standard:

If the auditors' report discloses deficiencies in internal control, fraud, illegal acts, violations of contracts or grant agreements, or abuse, auditors should obtain and report the views of responsible officials concerning the findings, conclusions, and recommendations, as well as planned corrective actions.

g. **Reporting confidential or sensitive information.** The following is an additional reporting standard:

If certain pertinent information is prohibited from public disclosure or is excluded from a report due to the confidential or sensitive nature of the information, auditors should disclose in the report that certain information has been omitted and the reason or other circumstances that make the omission necessary.

h. **Distributing reports.** The following summarizes an additional reporting standard:

1) Audit organizations in government entities should distribute audit reports to those charged with governance, to the appropriate officials of the audited entity, and to the appropriate oversight bodies or organizations requiring or arranging for the audits.

7. **Examples of Reports**

EXAMPLE – Auditor's Unqualified Report on General-Purpose Financial Statements

Independent Auditor's Report

To: <---------- Oversight Body

We have audited the accompanying general-purpose financial statements of City of Example, Any State, as of and for the year ended June 30, Year 1. These general-purpose financial statements are the responsibility of City of Example's management. Our responsibility is to express an opinion on these general-purpose financial statements based on our audit.

We conducted our audit in accordance with auditing standards generally accepted in the United States of America and the standards applicable to financial audits contained in *Government Auditing Standards*, issued by the Comptroller General of the United States. Those standards require that we plan and perform the audit to obtain reasonable assurance about whether the financial statements are free of material misstatement. An audit includes examining, on a test basis, evidence supporting the amounts and disclosures in the financial statements. An audit also includes assessing the accounting principles used and the significant estimates made by management, as well as evaluating the overall financial statement presentation. We believe that our audit provides a reasonable basis for our opinion.

In our opinion, the general-purpose financial statements referred to above present fairly, in all material respects, the financial position of City of Example, Any State, as of June 30, Year 1, and the results of its operations and cash flows of its proprietary fund types and trust funds for the year then ended in conformity with accounting principles generally accepted in the United States of America.

In accordance with *Government Auditing Standards*, we have also issued a report dated *[date of report]* on our consideration of the City of Example's internal control over financial reporting and on our tests of its compliance with certain provisions of laws, regulations, contracts, and grants. That report is an integral part of an audit performed in accordance with *Government Auditing Standards* and should be read in conjunction with this report in considering the results of our audit.

Signature   <---------- May be signed, typed, or printed

Date   <---------- No earlier than the date on which the auditor has obtained sufficient appropriate evidence

EXAMPLE – Auditor's Standard Report on Compliance with Laws and Regulations
(No Material Noncompliance)

Independent Auditor's Report

To: <---------- Oversight Body

We have audited the general-purpose financial statements of City of Example, Any State, as of and for the year ended June 30, Year 1, and have issued our report thereon dated August 15, Year 1.

We conducted our audit in accordance with auditing standards generally accepted in the United States of America and *Government Auditing Standards* issued by the Comptroller General of the United States. Those standards require that we plan and perform the audit to obtain reasonable assurance about whether the financial statements are free of material misstatement.

Compliance with laws, regulations, contracts, and grants applicable to City of Example, Any State, is the responsibility of City of Example, Any State's management. As part of obtaining reasonable assurance about whether the financial statements are free of material misstatement, we performed tests of City of Example, Any State's compliance with certain provisions of laws, regulations, contracts, and grants. However, the objective of our audit of the general-purpose financial statements was not to provide an opinion on overall compliance with such provisions. Accordingly, we do not express such an opinion.

The results of our tests disclosed no instances of noncompliance that are required to be reported herein under *Government Auditing Standards.*

This report is intended solely for the information and use of management, the audit committee, others within the entity, and *[identify legislative or regulatory body]* and is not intended to be and should not be used by anyone other than these specified parties.

Signature   <---------- May be signed, typed, or printed

Date   <---------- No earlier than the date on which the auditor has obtained sufficient appropriate evidence

EXAMPLE – Auditor's Report on Internal Control

Independent Auditor's Report

To: <---------- Oversight Body

We have audited the financial statements of City of Example, Any State, and of and for the year ended June 30, Year 1, and have issued our report thereon dated August 15, Year 1. We conducted our audit in accordance with auditing standards generally accepted in the United States of America and the standards applicable to financial audits contained in *Government Auditing Standards*, issued by the Comptroller General of the United States.

In planning and performing our audit, we considered City of Example, Any State's internal control over financial reporting as a basis for designing our auditing procedures for the purpose of expressing our opinion on the financial statements, but not for the purpose of expressing an opinion on the effectiveness of City of Example's internal control over financial reporting. Accordingly, we do not express an opinion on the effectiveness of internal control over financial reporting.

Our consideration of internal control over financial reporting was for the limited purpose described in the preceding paragraph and would not necessarily identify all deficiencies in internal control over financial reporting that might be significant deficiencies or material weaknesses. However, as discussed below, we identified certain deficiencies in internal control over financial reporting that we consider to be significant deficiencies. A control deficiency exists when the design or operation of a control does not allow management or employees, in the normal course of performing their assigned functions, to prevent or detect misstatements on a timely basis. A significant deficiency is a deficiency, or a combination of deficiencies, in internal control that is less severe than a material weakness, yet important enough to merit attention by those charged with governance. We consider the deficiencies described below to be significant deficiencies in internal control over financial reporting.

[Include paragraphs to describe significant deficiencies.]

A material weakness is a deficiency, or combination of deficiencies, in internal control, such that there is a reasonable possibility that a material misstatement of the entity's financial statements will not be prevented, or detected and corrected on a timely basis. Our consideration of the internal control over financial reporting was for the limited purpose described in the first paragraph of this section and would not necessarily identify all deficiencies in the internal control that might be significant deficiencies and, accordingly, would not necessarily disclose all significant deficiencies that are also considered to be material weaknesses. However, we believe that none of the significant deficiencies described above is a material weakness.

This report is intended solely for the information and use of management, the audit committee, others within the entity, and *[identify the legislative or regulatory body]* and is not intended to be and should not be used by anyone other than these specified parties.

Signature   <---------- May be signed, typed, or printed

Date   <---------- No earlier than the date on which the auditor has obtained sufficient appropriate evidence

Stop and review! You have completed the outline for this subunit. Study multiple-choice questions 1 through 19 beginning on page 680.

20.2 COMPLIANCE AUDITS (AU 801)

1. A **compliance audit** is a program-specific or organization-wide audit of compliance with requirements (laws, rules, regulations, contracts, or grants) that apply to government programs.

   a. It normally is performed with a **financial statement audit**.

2. **Scope**

   a. This guidance applies when an auditor performs a **compliance audit** in accordance with

      1) GAAS,
      2) Financial audit standards in *Government Auditing Standards*, and
      3) A **governmental audit requirement (GAR)** that requires an opinion, generally at the program level.

   b. This guidance does **not** apply to an attestation engagement, including an examination of internal control over reporting.

3. **Management's Responsibilities**

   a. Identifying the entity's government programs and understanding and complying with the compliance requirements
   b. Establishing and maintaining effective controls over compliance
   c. Evaluating and monitoring compliance
   d. Taking necessary corrective action

4. **Audit Objectives**

   a. Obtain sufficient appropriate evidence to form an opinion and report at the level specified in the GAR on whether the entity complied in all material respects with the compliance requirements.
   b. Identify audit and reporting requirements in the GAR that supplement GAAS and *Government Auditing Standards* and perform and report on the related procedures.

5. The auditor, based on professional judgment, **adapts GAAS for a financial statement audit** for use in a compliance audit. But some GAAS do not apply, for example, the requirement for consistent application of GAAP.

6. **Materiality** levels, generally for a government program as a whole, are based on the GAR.

7. **Applicable Compliance Requirements (ACRs)**

   a. Based on the GAR, the auditor determines which government programs and compliance requirements identified by management to test.

8. **The Audit Process**

   a. An audit of compliance typically includes the following steps:

      1) Performing risk assessment procedures
      2) Assessing the risks of material noncompliance **(RMNs)**, which consist of the **inherent risks** and **control risks** of noncompliance
      3) Performing further audit procedures in response to assessed risks
      4) Addressing supplementary audit requirements in the GAR
      5) Obtaining written management representations
      6) Performing subsequent events procedures
      7) Evaluating evidence and forming an opinion
      8) Reporting on compliance
      9) Documenting the audit

9. **Risk Assessment Procedures**

    a.   The auditor should obtain a **sufficient understanding** of the ACRs and the entity's **internal control** over compliance to plan the audit.

    b.   This includes **inquiring** of management about whether findings and recommendations in reports or other communications resulting from previous audits or other monitoring relate to compliance.

10. Based on the results of the risk assessment procedures, the auditor should assess the **RMN**, whether due to fraud or error, for each ACR.

11. **Further Audit Procedures in Response to Assessed Risks**

    a.   If the auditor identifies RMNs that have a **pervasive** effect on compliance, the auditor should develop an **overall response** to such risks.

        1)   For example, the auditor may use more experienced staff or increase supervision.

    b.   The audit should detect intentional and unintentional noncompliance. However, the auditor can obtain only **reasonable assurance** because of

        1)   Performance of sampling procedures
        2)   Use of professional judgment
        3)   Availability of persuasive, not conclusive, evidence
        4)   Inherent limitations of internal control including the potential for collusion of entity employees

    c.   The auditor should perform **further audit procedures**, including **tests of details** (substantive tests) to obtain sufficient appropriate evidence of compliance with each ACR.

        1)   Risk assessment procedures, tests of controls, and analytical procedures alone **are not sufficient** to address RMNs.

        2)   Furthermore, the use of analytical procedures as substantive tests is generally less effective in a compliance audit than in a financial statement audit.

    d.   **Tests of controls** also should be performed if

        1)   The auditor's risk assessment includes an expectation of operating effectiveness of controls related to the ACRs,

        2)   Substantive procedures alone do not provide sufficient appropriate evidence, or

        3)   Tests of controls over compliance are required specifically by the GAR.

12. **Supplementary Audit Requirements**

    a.   The auditor should determine whether audit requirements are specified in the GAR that supplement GAAS and *Government Auditing Standards* and perform the related procedures.

13. **Written Management Representations**

    a.   The auditor should request written representations specific to the entity and the GAR. (These representations parallel those for a financial statement audit and are not repeated here.) Generally, those representations should include

        1)   Acknowledgment of management's responsibility for compliance

        2)   Acknowledgment of management's responsibility for controls over compliance

        3)   Declarations that all evidence has been made available and all instances of noncompliance have been provided to the auditor

14. **Subsequent Events**

    a.   The auditor should perform audit procedures **up to the date of the auditor's report** to obtain sufficient appropriate evidence that all subsequent events related to compliance have been identified.

b. Audit procedures include (1) considering the risk assessment and examples of noncompliance during the subsequent period and (2) inquiring of management.

15. **Evaluating Evidence and Forming an Opinion**

a. The auditor should evaluate the sufficiency and appropriateness of the audit evidence obtained and form an opinion (at the level stated by the GAR) on whether the entity complied, in all material respects, with the ACRs.

b. The auditor evaluates **likely questioned costs** as well as questioned costs and other material noncompliance.

16. **Reporting on Compliance**

a. The auditor may issue a separate report on compliance, or it may be included with a report on internal control over compliance required by the GAR.

b. Given **material noncompliance** with ACRs or a **restriction on the scope** of the audit, the auditor should **modify the report** in accordance with the reporting standards under GAAS.

c. Even without a GAR to report on internal control, the auditor should communicate to management and those charged with governance the identified **significant deficiencies** and **material weaknesses** in internal control over compliance.

1) A material weakness in internal control over compliance arises when a deficiency, or combination of deficiencies, in internal control over compliance is present so that there is a reasonable possibility that material noncompliance with a compliance requirement will not be prevented or detected and corrected on a timely basis.

2) A significant deficiency in internal control over compliance is a deficiency, or a combination of deficiencies, in internal control over compliance that is less severe than a material weakness, yet merits attention by those charged with governance.

d. The following is an example of a separate unmodified report:

EXAMPLE -- Auditor's Report on Compliance

Independent Auditor's Report

To: <---------- Oversight Body

We have audited Example Entity's compliance with the [*identify the applicable compliance requirements or refer to the document that describes the applicable compliance requirements*] applicable to Example Entity's [*identify the government program(s) audited or refer to a separate schedule that identifies the program(s)*] for the year ended June 30, Year 1. Compliance with the requirements referred to above is the responsibility of Example Entity's management. Our responsibility is to express an opinion on Example Entity's compliance based on our audit.

We conducted our audit of compliance in accordance with auditing standards generally accepted in the United States of America; the standards applicable to financial audits contained in *Government Auditing Standards* issued by the Comptroller General of the United States; and [*insert the name of the governmental audit requirement or program-specific audit guide*]. Those standards and [*insert the name of the governmental audit requirement or program-specific audit guide*] require that we plan and perform the audit to obtain reasonable assurance about whether noncompliance with the compliance requirements referred to above that could have a material effect on [*identify the government program(s) audited or refer to a separate schedule that identifies the program(s)*]. An audit includes examining, on a test basis, evidence about Example Entity's compliance with those requirements and performing such other procedures as we considered necessary in the circumstances. We believe that our audit provides a reasonable basis for our opinion. Our audit does not provide a legal determination of Example Entity's compliance with those requirements.

In our opinion, Example Entity complied, in all material respects, with the compliance requirements referred to above that are applicable to [*identify the government program(s) audited*] for the year ended June 30, Year 1.

Signature <---------- May be signed, typed, or printed

Date <---------- No earlier than the date on which the auditor has obtained sufficient appropriate evidence

17. **Documenting the Audit**

    a. The following should be documented by the auditor:

        1) Risk assessment procedures performed, including consideration of internal control

        2) Materiality levels and how they were determined

        3) Responses to the assessed risks

        4) Results of procedures and the conclusions formed

        5) Performance of any supplementary procedures

Stop and review! You have completed the outline for this subunit. Study multiple-choice questions 20 through 24 beginning on page 686.

20.3 FEDERAL AUDIT REQUIREMENTS AND THE SINGLE AUDIT ACT

Background
Prior to 1984, agencies of the federal government that provided awards to state and local governments audited specific grants, contracts, subsidies, etc. This process often resulted in numerous audits of a recipient by various agencies and a wasteful duplication of effort. In other cases, large amounts of federal awards went unaudited.

1. In 1984, Congress passed the Single Audit Act (amended in 1996), which requires one (a single) audit or a **program-specific audit** of a nonfederal entity that expends a certain total amount of federal awards.

    a. A **single audit** is required if the entity expends federal awards under more than one federal program.

    b. Each **federal agency** must, with regard to awards provided by that agency, monitor the use of such awards. Moreover, each **nonfederal agency** must be assigned a single federal agency to assess the quality of audits and provide technical assistance.

    c. **Reporting packages** are delivered to a federal clearinghouse. These packages include financial statements, audit reports, a schedule of expenditures of federal awards, and a corrective action plan.

    d. The **Office of Management and Budget (OMB)** prescribes policies and procedures for the single audit. Those policies and procedures are issued in **OMB Circulars** and **compliance supplements.**

    e. The audit focus is greater for **major programs**, which are selected on the basis of **risk-based criteria** subject to certain limitations based on dollar expenditures.

2. According to the Single Audit Act, the auditor must conduct the audit in accordance with GAGAS. The **scope of the audit** extends to

    a. Expressing or disclaiming an opinion on whether the **financial statements** are presented fairly in all material respects in conformity with GAAP. (This requirement includes reporting on **compliance** with laws and regulations and **internal control** for expenditures not covered explicitly below.)

    b. Expressing or disclaiming an opinion on whether the **schedule of expenditures of federal awards** is presented fairly in all material respects in relation to the financial statements taken as a whole.

    c. Performing procedures to obtain an **understanding of internal control** sufficient to plan the audit to support a low assessed level of control risk for **major programs**, planning **tests of controls** to support that assessment for the assertions relevant to compliance requirements for each major program, and performing **tests of controls**. (Planning and performing tests are not required if the controls are likely to be ineffective.)

1) The **report on internal control** related to the financial statements and major programs should describe the scope of testing and the results of tests, and, if applicable, it should refer to the **schedule of findings and questioned costs**.

2) **Control deficiencies** that are individually or cumulatively material should be identified.

    d. Expressing or disclaiming **an opinion** on whether the **auditee has complied** with laws, regulations, and the provisions of contracts or grants that may have a direct and material effect on each major program.

    e. Following up.

    f. Reporting a schedule of findings and questioned costs.

3. Compliance requirements applicable to awards made by many federal programs are covered in the **Compliance Supplement** to OMB Circular A-133, *Audits of States, Local Governments, and Non-Profit Organizations.* Its focus is on compliance requirements that could have a direct and material effect on a major program.

    a. This supplement lists and describes the **types of compliance requirements** and related **audit objectives and procedures** that should be considered in every audit to which it relates. It also discusses objectives, procedures, and compliance requirements that are specific to **each federal program** included.

4. The Single Audit Act requires nonfederal entities that expend **$500,000 or more of federal awards** in a fiscal year to have a single audit or a program-specific audit.

    a. The single audit replaces any financial audit required under individual federal awards.

    b. The single audit covers the operations of the entire entity, or, at the option of the entity, it may include a **series of audits** of the organizational subunits that expended or administered federal awards.

5. Auditee **management** is responsible for **identifying federal awards** and the **related programs** and preparing a **schedule of the expenditures** of federal awards. The auditee also is responsible for (a) maintaining control over federal programs; (b) complying with laws, regulations, and the provisions of contracts and grants; (c) preparing financial statements; (d) ensuring that required audits are performed and submitted when due; and (e) following up and taking corrective action.

    a. The auditee must submit to the **designated clearinghouse** a data collection form providing information about the auditee, its federal programs, and the results of the audit. Furthermore, the auditee must submit a **reporting package** that includes (1) financial statements, (2) a summary schedule of audit findings, (3) the auditor's reports, and (4) the corrective action plan.

6. The auditor uses a **risk-based approach** in determining which federal programs are major programs. The criteria considered are (a) current and prior audit experience, (b) oversight by federal agencies and pass-through entities, (c) inherent risk, and (d) amounts of federal awards expended.

    a. A federal agency or pass-through entity may request that the auditee have a program audited as a **major program**.

7. The **schedule of audit findings and questioned costs** includes any instances of (a) **known questioned costs** greater than $10,000 or (b) known questioned costs when likely questioned costs exceed $10,000 for compliance requirements for a major program.

    a. Moreover, **likely questioned costs** (a projection) must be considered when evaluating the effects of questioned costs on the audit opinion.

    b. Known questioned costs greater than $10,000 for a **nonmajor program** also should be included.

    c. **Audit findings** should be sufficiently detailed to permit the auditee to prepare a corrective action plan and to take such action.

8. For the purpose of **reporting an audit finding,** the auditor's determination of whether a **deficiency in internal control** is material or whether an **instance of noncompliance** is material is in relation to a **type of compliance requirement** for a major program or an **audit objective** identified in the OMB Circular A-133 Compliance Supplement.

   a. In contrast, materiality is considered in relation to the **financial statements** in an audit under GAAS.

9. Under the Single Audit Act, a federal agency or the U.S. Comptroller General may, upon request, obtain access to the auditor's **working papers** to (a) provide information for a quality review, (b) resolve audit findings, or (c) carry out oversight responsibilities. Access includes the right to obtain copies.

Stop and review! You have completed the outline for this subunit. Study multiple-choice questions 25 through 29 beginning on page 688.

QUESTIONS

20.1 Government Auditing Standards

1. Which of the following bodies issues standards for audits of recipients of federal awards?

A. Governmental Accounting Standards Board.

B. Financial Accounting Standards Board.

C. Government Accountability Office.

D. Governmental Auditing Standards Board.

Answer (C) is correct. *(CPA, adapted)*
REQUIRED: The body that sets standards for audits of federal awards recipients.
DISCUSSION: The federal agency concerned with accounting and auditing standards for U.S. government programs and services is the Government Accountability Office. The GAO issues generally accepted government auditing standards.
Answer (A) is incorrect. The GASB promulgates standards for financial accounting and reporting by state and local governments. Answer (B) is incorrect. The FASB issues standards for financial accounting and reporting by nongovernmental entities. Answer (D) is incorrect. There is no Governmental Auditing Standards Board. The committee of the GAO that issues government auditing standards is the Advisory Council on *Government Auditing Standards*.

2. *Government Auditing Standards* relates to which of the services provided to government entities, programs, activities, and functions?

	Financial Audits	Nonaudit Services	Performance Audits
A.	Yes	Yes	No
B.	Yes	No	Yes
C.	Yes	Yes	Yes
D.	No	No	Yes

Answer (B) is correct. *(Publisher, adapted)*
REQUIRED: The scope of *Government Auditing Standards*.
DISCUSSION: *Government Auditing Standards* relates to financial audits and attestation engagements. Moreover, it relates to performance audits of (1) government entities, programs, activities, and functions and (2) government assistance administered by contractors, nonprofit entities, and other nongovernmental activities. Although GAGAS are not applicable to nonaudit services, they state independence standards that determine whether an auditor may conduct audits.

3. An objective of a performance audit is to determine whether an entity's

A. Performance information is presented fairly.

B. Operational information is in accordance with generally accepted government auditing standards.

C. Financial statements present fairly the results of operations.

D. Specific operating units are functioning economically and efficiently.

Answer (D) is correct. *(CPA, adapted)*
REQUIRED: The objective of a performance audit.
DISCUSSION: Performance audits include economy and efficiency audits. The objectives of these audits are to determine (1) whether the entity is acquiring, protecting, and using its resources economically and efficiently; (2) the causes of any inefficiencies; and (3) whether the entity has complied with laws and regulations concerning matters of economy and efficiency.
Answer (A) is incorrect. Performance information is the subject of attestation engagements. Answer (B) is incorrect. The conduct of the audit and the audit report, not operational information, should be in accordance with *Government Auditing Standards*. Answer (C) is incorrect. Determining whether financial statements present fairly the results of operations is an objective of a financial statement audit.

4. An auditor was engaged to conduct a performance audit of a governmental entity in accordance with *Government Auditing Standards*. These standards do not require the auditor to report

   A. The audit objectives and the audit scope and methodology.

   B. All significant instances of noncompliance and instances of abuse.

   C. The views of the audited program's responsible officials concerning the auditor's findings.

   D. A concurrent opinion on the financial statements taken as a whole.

Answer (D) is correct. *(CPA, adapted)*
   REQUIRED: The action not required of an auditor engaged in a performance audit of a governmental entity in accordance with *Government Auditing Standards*.
   DISCUSSION: Performance audits relate to assessing (1) program effectiveness and results; (2) economy and efficiency; (3) internal control; (4) compliance with legal requirements; or (5) providing prospective analyses, guidance, or summary information. There is no requirement that a financial audit be conducted simultaneously or concurrently with a performance audit.

5. Which of the following statements is a standard applicable to financial statement audits in accordance with *Government Auditing Standards* (the Yellow Book)?

   A. An auditor should report on the scope of the auditor's testing of compliance with laws and regulations.

   B. An auditor should assess whether the entity has reportable measures of economy and efficiency that are valid and reliable.

   C. An auditor should report recommendations for actions to correct problems and improve operations.

   D. An auditor should determine the extent to which the entity's programs achieve the desired results.

Answer (A) is correct. *(CPA, adapted)*
   REQUIRED: The scope of an audit under *Government Auditing Standards*.
   DISCUSSION: According to additional reporting standards for financial statement audits, the report on the financial statements should either (1) describe the scope of the auditor's testing of compliance with laws and regulations and internal controls over financial reporting and present the results of those tests or (2) refer to separate report(s) containing that information. If the scope of the work performed is sufficient, an opinion on internal control and compliance can be expressed. In presenting the results of those tests, auditors should report (1) fraud, (2) illegal acts, (3) other material noncompliance, and (4) significant deficiencies and material weaknesses in internal controls over financial reporting. In some circumstances, auditors should report fraud and illegal acts directly to parties external to the audited entity.
   Answer (B) is incorrect. Economy and efficiency are subjects of performance audits rather than financial audits. Answer (C) is incorrect. Advice may be provided on the correction of problems and the improvement of operations, but the auditor is not required to provide a report. Answer (D) is incorrect. Achievement of desired results is a subject of performance audits rather than financial audits.

6. Which of the following is a documentation requirement that an auditor should follow in a financial statement audit in accordance with *Government Auditing Standards*?

   A. The audit documentation should contain copies of documents examined.

   B. The audit documentation should contain sufficient information to permit another auditor to ascertain the evidence that supports audit conclusions and judgments.

   C. Audit documentation should be considered the personal property of the auditor and should not be shared.

   D. The audit documentation should contain a caveat that all instances of material errors and fraud may not be identified.

Answer (B) is correct. *(CPA, adapted)*
   REQUIRED: The documentation requirement under *Government Auditing Standards*.
   DISCUSSION: *Government Auditing Standards* requires that a record of the auditor's work be retained in the form of audit documentation. According to the additional audit documentation standard for financial statement audits, audit documentation should contain sufficient information to enable an experienced auditor having no previous connection with the audit to ascertain from them the evidence that supports the auditor's significant conclusions and judgments.
   Answer (A) is incorrect. The audit documentation should document the work performed to support significant conclusions and judgments, including descriptions of transactions and records examined that would enable an experienced auditor to examine the same items. However, the auditors are not required to include copies of documents examined or to list detailed information from those documents. Answer (C) is incorrect. Governmental auditors should share their work product to avoid duplication of audit effort. Answer (D) is incorrect. This type of warning is appropriate for the auditor's report, but it need not be stated in the audit documentation.

7. In performing a financial statement audit in accordance with *Government Auditing Standards*, auditors are required to report on the entity's compliance with laws and regulations. This report must

A. Describe the scope of the auditor's testing of compliance.

B. Describe the laws and regulations that the entity must comply with.

C. Express an opinion on overall compliance with laws and regulations.

D. Indicate that the auditors do not possess legal skills and cannot make legal judgments.

Answer (A) is correct. *(CPA, adapted)*
  REQUIRED: The content of a report on compliance with laws and regulations.
  DISCUSSION: According to *Government Auditing Standards*, the report should describe the scope of the auditor's testing of compliance with laws and regulations and internal control over financial reporting. Thus, the report states whether (1) tests provided sufficient evidence to support an opinion on compliance or internal control over financial reporting and (2) such opinions are provided.
  Answer (B) is incorrect. The report need not identify the applicable laws and regulations. Answer (C) is incorrect. The report should identify material instances of noncompliance but need not express an opinion on overall compliance. The report may express an opinion, however, if the scope of the work is sufficient. Answer (D) is incorrect. Auditors are required to provide a report on compliance. However, the auditors must take care not to imply that they have made a determination of illegality.

8. In a financial statement audit in accordance with *Government Auditing Standards*, an auditor must report on the auditor's tests of the entity's compliance with applicable laws and regulations. Thus, the audit must be designed to provide

A. Positive assurance that the internal controls tested by the auditor are operating as prescribed.

B. Reasonable assurance of detecting misstatements that are material to the financial statements.

C. Negative assurance that significant deficiencies in internal control communicated during the audit do not prevent the auditor from expressing an opinion.

D. Limited assurance that internal control designed by management will prevent or detect errors, fraud, and illegal acts.

Answer (B) is correct. *(CPA, adapted)*
  REQUIRED: The design of the audit that satisfies the requirement to report on compliance.
  DISCUSSION: According to the field work standards for financial audits, the auditor should test compliance with applicable laws and regulations. As part of the process, the auditor should design the audit to provide reasonable assurance of detecting errors, fraud, and illegal acts that could have a direct and material effect on the financial statements. The auditor must also be aware of other illegal acts having indirect and material effects.
  Answer (A) is incorrect. The auditor is not required to provide positive assurance on internal control (but may if the scope of testing is sufficient) under *Government Auditing Standards*. The report on compliance (which may be presented separately) must state the scope of the testing and present the results. Answer (C) is incorrect. Auditors identify significant deficiencies but need not provide assurance in the report. Answer (D) is incorrect. Auditors are not required to provide limited assurance on internal control matters. They are, however, required to obtain a sufficient understanding of internal control.

9. When engaged to audit a governmental entity in accordance with *Government Auditing Standards*, an auditor prepares a written report on internal control over financial reporting

A. In all financial audits, regardless of circumstances.

B. Only when the auditor has noted significant deficiencies.

C. Only when requested by the governmental entity being audited.

D. Only when requested by the federal government funding agency.

Answer (A) is correct. *(CPA, adapted)*
  REQUIRED: The true statement about reporting on internal control.
  DISCUSSION: *Government Auditing Standards* imposes more stringent reporting requirements than GAAS. For example, it mandates a written report on internal control over financial reporting in every audit. Furthermore, issuers must report on internal control. In contrast, GAAS require communication only if significant deficiencies or material weaknesses have been observed (AU 325).
  Answer (B) is incorrect. GAAS, not *Government Auditing Standards*, require communication only if significant deficiencies or material weaknesses have been observed. Answer (C) is incorrect. A written report must be prepared in all audits, regardless of circumstances. Answer (D) is incorrect. A written report must be prepared in all audits, regardless of circumstances.

10. Which of the following statements is a standard applicable to financial statement audits in accordance with *Government Auditing Standards* (the Yellow Book)?

A. An auditor should report on the scope of the auditor's testing of internal controls.

B. An auditor should report all instances of fraud, illegal acts, violations of provisions of contracts or grant agreements, and abuse.

C. An auditor should report the views of the public about the auditor's findings.

D. Internal control activities designed to detect or prevent fraud should be reported to the inspector general.

Answer (A) is correct. *(CPA, adapted)*
REQUIRED: The standard for financial statement audits under *Government Auditing Standards.*
DISCUSSION: According to an additional reporting standard for financial statement audits, the report on the financial statements should either (1) describe the scope of the auditor's testing of compliance with laws and regulations and grant or contract provisions and internal controls over financial reporting and present the results of those tests, or (2) refer to separate report(s) containing that information. In presenting the results of those tests, auditors should report (1) fraud, (2) illegal acts, (3) other material noncompliance, and (4) significant deficiencies and material weaknesses in internal controls over financial reporting. In some circumstances, auditors should report fraud and illegal acts directly to parties external to the audited entity.
Answer (B) is incorrect. Auditors should use their professional judgment in determining whether and how to communicate to the audited entity clearly inconsequential instances of (1) fraud, (2) illegal acts, (3) violations of provisions of contracts or grant agreements, or (4) abuse. Answer (C) is incorrect. The views of the public need not be reported. However, the auditor's report may disclose (1) deficiencies in internal control, (2) fraud, (3) illegal acts, (4) violations of provisions of contracts or grant agreements, or (5) abuse. Auditors then should obtain and report the views of responsible officials concerning the findings, conclusions, and recommendations, as well as planned corrective actions. Answer (D) is incorrect. The auditor is not required to comment on the design of the controls to the inspector general.

11. In auditing a not-for-profit entity that receives governmental awards, the auditor has a responsibility to

A. Issue a separate report that describes the expected benefits and related costs of the auditor's suggested changes to the entity's internal control.

B. Assess whether management has identified laws and regulations that have a direct and material effect on the entity's financial statements.

C. Notify the governmental agency providing the awards that the audit is not designed to provide any assurance of detecting errors and fraud.

D. Express an opinion concerning the entity's continued eligibility for the governmental awards.

Answer (B) is correct. *(CPA, adapted)*
REQUIRED: The responsibility of an auditor of a not-for-profit entity that receives governmental awards.
DISCUSSION: Management is responsible for ensuring compliance with laws and regulations. The auditor's responsibility is to understand the possible effects of laws and regulations having direct and material effects on the financial statements and to assess whether management has identified such laws and regulations.
Answer (A) is incorrect. The auditor need not identify the relative costs and benefits related to the client's internal control. However, the auditor must communicate significant deficiencies and material weaknesses. Answer (C) is incorrect. The audit should be designed to provide reasonable assurance of detecting material fraud. Answer (D) is incorrect. The report should express an opinion on the financial statements and present the results of tests of compliance and of internal control over financial reporting. But it does not express an opinion on continued eligibility.

12. In reporting on compliance with laws and regulations during a financial statement audit in accordance with *Government Auditing Standards*, an auditor should include in the auditor's report

A. A statement of assurance that all controls over fraud and illegal acts were tested.

B. Material instances of fraud and illegal acts that were discovered.

C. The materiality criteria used by the auditor in considering whether instances of non-compliance were significant.

D. An opinion on whether compliance with laws and regulations affected the entity's goals and objectives.

Answer (B) is correct. *(CPA, adapted)*
REQUIRED: The issues included in an auditor's report in accordance with *Government Auditing Standards.*
DISCUSSION: An auditor's report, in accordance with *Government Auditing Standards*, should present the results of tests of internal control over financial reporting and compliance with laws and regulations. In presenting these results, the auditor should report (1) fraud, (2) illegal acts, (3) other material noncompliance, and (4) significant deficiencies and material weaknesses in internal control over financial reporting.
Answer (A) is incorrect. No assurance need be provided that all controls over fraud and illegal acts were tested. Answer (C) is incorrect. The materiality criteria need not be reported. Answer (D) is incorrect. No opinion need be expressed.

13. Reporting on internal control under *Government Auditing Standards* differs from reporting under generally accepted auditing standards in that *Government Auditing Standards* requires a

A. Written report describing the entity's internal control activities specifically designed to prevent fraud and illegal acts.

B. Written report included with the audit report on financial statements describing significant deficiencies and material weaknesses in internal control.

C. Statement of negative assurance that the internal control activities not tested have an immaterial effect on the entity's financial statements.

D. Statement of positive assurance that internal control activities designed to detect material errors and fraud were tested.

Answer (B) is correct. *(CPA, adapted)*
REQUIRED: The difference between *Government Auditing Standards* and GAAS regarding reports on internal control.
DISCUSSION: According to the additional standards of reporting for financial audits of governmental entities, the report on the financial statements or a separate report should present the results of tests of compliance with laws and regulations and internal control over financial reporting. This report should present any significant deficiencies and material weaknesses. However, the report need not provide any assurance on internal control design or effectiveness.
Answer (A) is incorrect. *Government Auditing Standards* does not require the auditor to list internal control activities specifically designed to prevent fraud or illegal acts. Answer (C) is incorrect. The auditor is not required to provide a statement of positive or negative assurance regarding internal control. However, positive assurance in the form of an opinion may be provided if the scope of the work is sufficient. Answer (D) is incorrect. The auditor is not required to provide a statement of positive or negative assurance regarding internal control. However, positive assurance in the form of an opinion may be provided if the scope of the work is sufficient.

14. An auditor most likely will be responsible for communicating significant deficiencies in the design of internal controls

A. To a court-appointed creditors' committee when the client is operating under Chapter 11 of the Federal Bankruptcy Code.

B. To shareholders with significant influence (more than 20% equity ownership) when the deficiencies are deemed to be material weaknesses.

C. To the Securities and Exchange Commission when the client is a publicly held entity.

D. To specific legislative and regulatory bodies when reporting under *Government Auditing Standards*.

Answer (D) is correct. *(CPA, adapted)*
REQUIRED: The circumstance in which an auditor is likely responsible for communicating significant deficiencies in internal control.
DISCUSSION: An auditor is required to include significant deficiencies and material weaknesses in internal control over financial reporting in a report prepared under *Government Auditing Standards*. The report is required to be distributed to (1) the appropriate officials of the organization being audited, (2) officials of the organizations requiring or arranging for the audit, (3) other officials who have legal oversight authority or who may be responsible for taking action, and (4) others who may be authorized to receive the report.
Answer (A) is incorrect. Management is responsible for providing audited financial statements to a creditors' committee. Answer (B) is incorrect. The auditor's report is included with the audited financial statements in the annual report, a document that is available to all shareholders. Answer (C) is incorrect. The opinion on internal control of an issuer discloses material weaknesses but not significant deficiencies.

15. When auditing an entity's financial statements in accordance with *Government Auditing Standards* (the Yellow Book), an auditor is required to report on

I. Positive aspects of the program applicable to audit objectives

II. The scope of the auditor's testing of internal controls

A. I only.

B. II only.

C. Both I and II.

D. Neither I nor II.

Answer (B) is correct. *(CPA, adapted)*
REQUIRED: The true statement(s), if any, about reporting under *Government Auditing Standards*.
DISCUSSION: *Government Auditing Standards* imposes more stringent reporting requirements than GAAS. Under GAGAS, the report on the financial statements should describe the scope of the auditor's testing of compliance with laws and regulations and internal control over financial reporting and present the results of those tests or refer to separate reports containing that information. The report on internal control must identify significant deficiencies and material weaknesses but need not provide any assurance on internal control design or effectiveness. Accomplishments of the program, especially those management improvements in one area that may be applicable elsewhere, should be reported in a performance audit, not a financial audit, if they relate to audit objectives.

16. In reporting under *Government Auditing Standards*, an auditor most likely would be required to report a falsification of accounting records directly to a federal inspector general when the falsification is

A. Discovered after the auditor's report has been made available to the federal inspector general and to the public.

B. Reported by the auditor to the audit committee as a significant deficiency in internal control.

C. Voluntarily disclosed to the auditor by low-level personnel as a result of the auditor's inquiries.

D. Communicated by the auditor to the auditee and the auditee fails to make a required report of the matter.

Answer (D) is correct. *(CPA, adapted)*
REQUIRED: The time when an auditor is required to report externally under *Government Auditing Standards.*
DISCUSSION: Under *Government Auditing Standards*, auditors must report fraud and illegal acts directly to parties outside the auditee (for example, to a federal inspector general or a state attorney general) in two circumstances. These requirements are in addition to any legal requirements for direct reporting. First, if auditors have communicated such fraud or illegal acts to the auditee and it fails to report them, the auditors should communicate their awareness of that failure to the auditee's governing body. If the auditee does not make the required report as soon as practicable after the auditor's communication with its governing body, the auditors should report the fraud or illegal acts directly to the external party specified in the law or regulation. Second, management is responsible for taking timely and appropriate steps to remedy fraud or illegal acts that auditors report to it. When fraud or an illegal act involves assistance received directly or indirectly from a government agency, auditors may have a duty to report it directly if management fails to take remedial steps. If auditors conclude that such failure is likely to cause them to depart from the standard report or resign from the audit, they should communicate that conclusion to the auditee's governing body. Then, if the auditee does not report the fraud or illegal act as soon as practicable to the entity that provided the government assistance, the auditors should report directly to that entity.

17. According to the general standards in *Government Auditing Standards*,

A. An audit organization performing audits under GAGAS must have an external peer review every 5 years.

B. The audit organization, but not the auditor, may provide any nonaudit services.

C. Performing nonaudit services creates an external impairment of independence.

D. An audit organization must be free of the appearance of an impairment to independence.

Answer (D) is correct. *(Publisher, adapted)*
REQUIRED: The true statement about the requirements under the general standards.
DISCUSSION: According to the general standard on independence, "In all matters relating to the audit work, the audit organization and the individual auditor, whether government or public, must be free from personal, external, and organizational impairments to independence, and must avoid the appearance of such impairments of independence."
Answer (A) is incorrect. The entity must have an external peer review at least once every 3 years. Answer (B) is incorrect. The audit organization should not (1) provide nonaudit services that involve performing management functions or making management decisions or (2) audit its work or provide nonaudit services that are significant or material to the subject matter of audits. Answer (C) is incorrect. Performing nonaudit services may create a personal impairment of independence.

18. Which of the following statements represents a quality control requirement under government auditing standards?

A. A CPA who conducts government audits is required to undergo an annual external peer review when an appropriate internal quality control system is not in place.

B. A CPA seeking to enter into a contract to perform an audit should provide the CPA's most recent external peer review report to the party contracting for the audit.

C. An external peer review of a CPA's practice should include a review of the working papers of each government audit performed since the prior external quality control review.

D. A CPA who conducts government audits may not make the CPA's external quality control review report available to the public.

Answer (B) is correct. *(CPA, adapted)*
REQUIRED: The quality control requirement under government auditing standards.
DISCUSSION: According to a general standard stated in *Government Auditing Standards*, an audit organization conducting an audit in accordance with these standards must have an appropriate internal quality control system in place and undergo an external peer review at least every 3 years. For example, a CPA seeking to enter into a contract to perform an audit should provide the CPA's most recent external peer review report to the party contracting for the audit.
Answer (A) is incorrect. Organizations conducting audits in accordance with the *Government Audit Standards* should have an external peer review at least once every 3 years. Answer (C) is incorrect. An external peer review consists of evaluating a sample of audits performed and working papers prepared since the last external peer review. Answer (D) is incorrect. Audit organizations should ordinarily make their external peer review reports available to auditors during their work and to appropriate oversight bodies. It is recommended that the report be made available to the public as well.

19. When auditing an entity's financial statements in accordance with *Government Auditing Standards* (the Yellow Book), an auditor is required to report on

I.   Recommendations for actions to improve operations

II. The scope of the auditor's tests of compliance with laws and regulations

    A. I only.

    B. II only.

    C. Both I and II.

    D. Neither I nor II.

Answer (B) is correct. *(CPA, adapted)*
    REQUIRED: The true statement(s), if any, about reporting under *Government Auditing Standards.*
    DISCUSSION: *Government Auditing Standards* imposes more stringent reporting requirements than GAAS. Under GAGAS, the report on the financial statements should either describe the scope of the auditor's testing of compliance with laws and regulations and internal control over financial reporting and present the results of those tests or refer to separate reports containing that information. Auditors should report recommendations for actions to correct problems and to improve operations in a performance audit, not in a financial audit.

20.2 Compliance Audits (AU 801)

20. In a compliance audit, the auditor's primary objective is to

    A. Determine that all instances of noncompliance are discovered and reported.

    B. Test and express an opinion on internal control over compliance.

    C. Obtain sufficient appropriate evidence to form an opinion on compliance.

    D. Provide management with recommendations for improvement over compliance.

Answer (C) is correct. *(Publisher, adapted)*
    REQUIRED: The auditor's primary objective in a compliance audit.
    DISCUSSION: The auditor's objective in a compliance audit is to obtain sufficient appropriate evidence to form an opinion and report at the level specified in the governmental audit requirement on whether the entity complied in all material respects with the applicable compliance requirements.
    Answer (A) is incorrect. Only instances of material noncompliance need be reported on. Answer (B) is incorrect. Although the auditor considers internal control in planning the audit, no opinion is required. Answer (D) is incorrect. An audit of compliance does not require the auditor to provide recommendations for improvement over compliance.

21. In an audit of an entity's compliance with applicable compliance requirements, an auditor obtains written representations from management

    A. Acknowledging its responsibilities for compliance, including disclosure of noncompliance.

    B. Implementation of controls designed to detect all illegal acts.

    C. Expression of positive assurance to the auditor that the entity complied with all applicable compliance requirements.

    D. Employment of internal auditors who can report their findings, opinions, and conclusions objectively.

Answer (A) is correct. *(Publisher, adapted)*
    REQUIRED: The representations obtained from management in a compliance audit.
    DISCUSSION: The auditor obtains written representations from management about its responsibilities for (1) understanding and complying with the compliance requirements and (2) establishing and maintaining controls that provide reasonable assurance that the entity administers government programs in accordance with the compliance requirements. Among other things, the auditor also requests representations that management has disclosed all known noncompliance with the applicable compliance requirements including that subsequent to the period covered by the auditor's report.
    Answer (B) is incorrect. Internal control typically safeguards assets and promotes the reliability of financial statements but, given its inherent limitations, cannot be expected to prevent or detect all illegal acts. Answer (C) is incorrect. In a compliance audit, management does not express an opinion (positive assurance) that it has complied with all applicable compliance requirements. Answer (D) is incorrect. The entity will decide whether to employ internal auditors.

22. What is the risk that an auditor's procedures will lead to an erroneous conclusion that potentially material noncompliance does not exist?

    A. Audit risk of noncompliance.

    B. Inherent risk of noncompliance.

    C. Control risk of noncompliance.

    D. Detection risk of noncompliance.

Answer (D) is correct. *(Publisher, adapted)*
    REQUIRED: The risk that the auditor may erroneously conclude that potentially material noncompliance does not exist.
    DISCUSSION: The detection risk of noncompliance is that the procedures performed to reduce audit risk of noncompliance to an acceptably low level will not detect noncompliance that exists and could be material, either individually or when aggregated, with other instances of noncompliance.
    Answer (A) is incorrect. The audit risk of noncompliance is that the auditor will express an inappropriate audit opinion on the entity's compliance when material noncompliance exists. Answer (B) is incorrect. The inherent risk of noncompliance is the susceptibility of a compliance requirement to noncompliance that could be material, either individually or when aggregated with other instances of noncompliance, before consideration of any related controls over compliance. Answer (C) is incorrect. The control risk of noncompliance is the risk that material noncompliance with a compliance requirement that could occur either individually or when aggregated with other instances of noncompliance, will not be prevented, or detected and corrected, on a timely basis by the entity's internal control over compliance.

23. A material weakness in internal control over compliance arises when

    A. At a minimum, a deficiency is important enough to merit attention by those charged with governance.

    B. A reasonable possibility exists that material noncompliance will not be prevented or timely detected and corrected.

    C. A risk of material noncompliance exists prior to the audit.

    D. The design or operation of a control does not allow management or employees to detect noncompliance in the normal course of their duties.

Answer (B) is correct. *(Publisher, adapted)*
    REQUIRED: The definition of a material weakness.
    DISCUSSION: A material weakness in internal control over compliance arises when a deficiency, or combination of deficiencies, in internal control over compliance is present so that there is a reasonable possibility that material noncompliance with a compliance requirement will not be prevented or detected and corrected on a timely basis.
    Answer (A) is incorrect. A significant deficiency in internal control over compliance is a deficiency, or a combination of deficiencies, in internal control over compliance that is less severe than a material weakness, yet merits attention by those charged with governance. Answer (C) is incorrect. The risk of material noncompliance prior to the audit is the combination of the inherent risk of noncompliance and the control risk of noncompliance. Answer (D) is incorrect. A deficiency in internal control over compliance exists when the design or operation of a control over compliance does not allow management or employees, in the normal course of performing their assigned functions, to prevent or detect and correct noncompliance on a timely basis.

24. When an auditor is performing a compliance audit and identifies pervasive risks of material noncompliance, the auditor should

    A. Withdraw from the engagement.

    B. Develop an overall response to such risks.

    C. Perform additional analytical procedures.

    D. Issue a disclaimer of opinion.

Answer (B) is correct. *(Publisher, adapted)*
    REQUIRED: The auditor's response to pervasive risks of noncompliance.
    DISCUSSION: The auditor should develop an overall response to such risks. For example, the auditor may use more experienced staff or increase supervision.
    Answer (A) is incorrect. The auditor need not withdraw from the engagement and should attempt to mitigate risks by developing an overall response to such risks. Answer (C) is incorrect. The use of analytical procedures to gather substantive evidence is generally less effective in a compliance audit than it is in a financial statement audit. Answer (D) is incorrect. The auditor should attempt to mitigate risks by developing an overall response to such risks.

20.3 Federal Audit Requirements and the Single Audit Act

25. Although the scope of audits of recipients of federal awards in accordance with federal audit regulations varies, audits under the Single Audit Act generally have which of the following elements in common?

A. The auditor is to determine whether the federal financial assistance has been administered in accordance with applicable laws and regulations.

B. The materiality levels are lower and are determined by the government entities that provided the federal awards to the recipient.

C. The auditor should obtain written management representations that the recipient's internal auditors will report their findings objectively without fear of political repercussion.

D. The auditor is required to express both positive and negative assurance that illegal acts that could have a material effect on the recipient's financial statements are disclosed to the inspector general.

Answer (A) is correct. *(CPA, adapted)*
REQUIRED: The common element in federal audit regulations.
DISCUSSION: According to the Single Audit Act, the scope of federal audits may vary, but the auditor must

1. Determine whether the financial statements are presented fairly in all material respects in conformity with GAAP.

2. Determine whether the schedule of expenditures of federal awards is presented fairly in all material respects in relation to the financial statements taken as a whole.

3. With respect to controls over compliance, obtain an understanding of those controls, assess control risk, and perform tests of controls unless the controls are ineffective.

4. Determine whether the nonfederal entity has complied with the provisions of laws, regulations, and contracts or grants that have a direct and material effect on each major program.

5. Report audit findings in a schedule of findings and questioned costs.

   Answer (B) is incorrect. Materiality is determined by the auditor in relation to a type of compliance requirement for a major program or an audit objective identified in the OMB Circular A-133 Compliance Supplement. Answer (C) is incorrect. Although the auditor should obtain written management representations, no specific requirements concerning the entity's internal auditors are stipulated. Answer (D) is incorrect. The auditor is required to report illegal acts but not to provide positive or negative assurance about them.

26. In an audit of compliance with requirements governing awards under major federal programs performed in accordance with the Single Audit Act, the auditor's consideration of materiality differs from materiality under generally accepted auditing standards. Under the Single Audit Act, materiality for the purpose of reporting an audit finding is

A. Calculated in relation to the financial statements taken as a whole.

B. Determined in relation to a type of compliance requirement for a major program.

C. Decided in conjunction with the auditor's risk assessment.

D. Ignored, because all account balances, regardless of size, are fully tested.

Answer (B) is correct. *(CPA, adapted)*
REQUIRED: The materiality determination under the Single Audit Act.
DISCUSSION: Under the Single Audit Act, the emphasis of the audit effort is on major programs related to federal awards administered by nonfederal entities. According to OMB Circular A-133 issued pursuant to the Single Audit Act, the schedule of findings and questioned costs includes instances of material noncompliance with laws, regulations, contracts, or grant agreements related to a major program. The auditor's determination of whether a noncompliance is material for the purpose of reporting an audit finding is in relation to a type of compliance requirement for a major program or an audit objective identified in the OMB Circular A-133 Compliance Supplement. Examples of types of compliance requirements include (1) activities allowed or unallowed; (2) allowable costs/cost principles; (3) cash management; (4) eligibility; (5) matching, level of effort, and earmarking; and (6) reporting.
   Answer (A) is incorrect. In a for-profit financial statement audit, materiality is related to the financial statements taken as a whole. Answer (C) is incorrect. Risk assessment is performed in planning the audit, but once the auditor makes a finding, the decision to report it is contingent on the materiality to the major program. Answer (D) is incorrect. Materiality must be considered in determining the appropriate tests to be applied.

27. Wolf is auditing an entity's compliance with requirements governing a major federal program in accordance with the Single Audit Act. Wolf detected noncompliance with requirements that have a material effect on the program. Wolf's report on compliance should express

   A. No assurance on the compliance tests.

   B. Reasonable assurance on the compliance tests.

   C. A qualified or adverse opinion.

   D. An adverse opinion or a disclaimer of opinion.

Answer (C) is correct. *(CPA, adapted)*
   REQUIRED: The assurance about compliance given noncompliance with material requirements.
   DISCUSSION: Under the Single Audit Act, the auditor should express an opinion on compliance with requirements applicable to a major federal program or state that an opinion cannot be expressed. When the compliance audit detects noncompliance with those requirements that the auditor believes have a material effect on the program, the auditor should express a qualified or adverse opinion. The auditor should state the basis for such an opinion in the report.
   Answer (A) is incorrect. The auditor should express an opinion on compliance. Answer (B) is incorrect. The auditor's report should state that the audit was planned and performed to provide reasonable assurance about whether material noncompliance occurred. Answer (D) is incorrect. A disclaimer is not appropriate when the auditor has detected material noncompliance.

28. A CPA has performed an examination of the general purpose financial statements of Big City. The examination scope included the additional requirements of the Single Audit Act. When reporting on Big City's internal control over the administration of federal awards, the CPA should

   A. Communicate all control deficiencies related to all federal awards.

   B. Express an opinion on the systems used to administer awards under major federal programs and express negative assurance on the systems used to administer awards under nonmajor federal programs.

   C. Communicate significant deficiencies and material weaknesses that are material in relation to a type of compliance requirement for the federal program.

   D. Express negative assurance on the systems used to administer awards under major federal programs and express no opinion on the systems used to administer awards under nonmajor federal programs.

Answer (C) is correct. *(CPA, adapted)*
   REQUIRED: The requirement of a report on internal controls used in administering awards under a federal program.
   DISCUSSION: Under the Single Audit Act, the auditor's determination of whether a deficiency in internal control is a significant deficiency or material weakness is in relation to a type of compliance requirement for a major program or an audit objective identified in the OMB Circular A-133 Compliance Supplement. The auditor also must identify all significant deficiencies and weaknesses.
   Answer (A) is incorrect. Only significant deficiencies and material weaknesses need be communicated. Answer (B) is incorrect. Although an auditor conducting a single audit is required to report on controls that relate to the systems used to administer awards under federal programs, the auditor is not required to provide assurance. Answer (D) is incorrect. Auditors are required to express an opinion (or disclaim an opinion) as to whether the auditee complied with laws, regulations, and the provisions of contracts or grant agreements that could have a direct and material effect on each major program.

29. An auditor is auditing a nonfederal entity's administration of a federal award pursuant to a major program under the Single Audit Act. The auditor is required to

	Obtain Evidence Related to Compliance	Express an Opinion On Compliance
A.	Yes	Yes
B.	Yes	No
C.	No	Yes
D.	No	No

Answer (A) is correct. *(Publisher, adapted)*
   REQUIRED: The auditor's responsibility in a compliance audit.
   DISCUSSION: After an audit of a nonfederal entity that expends federal awards, the audit report on compliance must include an opinion or a disclaimer of opinion as to whether the auditee complied with the applicable compliance requirements, that is, with laws, regulations, rules, and the provisions of contracts or grants. This report also should describe identified noncompliance or refer to an accompanying schedule of noncompliance.

Use the additional questions in Gleim **CPA Test Prep Online** to create Test Sessions that emulate Prometric!

20.4 PRACTICE SIMULATION

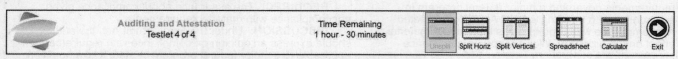

| | Auditing and Attestation Testlet 4 of 4 | Time Remaining 1 hour - 30 minutes | Unsplit | Split Horiz | Split Vertical | Spreadsheet | Calculator | Exit |

DIRECTIONS

Note: If you believe you have encountered a software malfunction, report it to the test center staff immediately.

Navigation

To navigate from task to task, use the controls at the bottom of the screen. Click on the **Next** button to advance to the next task, or the **Previous** button to go to the previous task. To go directly to any task, click on its number.

| ▼ = Reminder | | Directions | 1 2 3 4 5 6 7 | | ◀ Previous Next ▶ |

If you would like a reminder to revisit a task, or want to indicate that you are finished with it, click on the reminder flag below the task number. To clear the flag, click on it again. Reminder flags are for your use only – they do not contribute to your score.

Tabs

In this part of the examination, you will be asked to complete various tasks. Every task has one or more **Work Tabs**. Some tasks have one or more **Information Tabs**, others may have none. Every task has a **Help** tab.

If a task has **Information Tabs**, you may use the information in them to complete your responses in the **Work Tabs**.

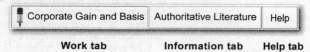

| ✏ Corporate Gain and Basis | Authoritative Literature | Help |

Work tab   Information tab   Help tab

Work Tabs:
- **Work Tabs** are identified with a pencil icon. This is where your responses are expected.
- Each task has one or more **Work Tabs**.
- **Work Tabs** contain directions for completing the task – be sure to read these directions carefully.
- The **Work Tab** name in the example above is for illustration only – yours will differ.
- You must complete all of the **Work Tabs** in each task to receive full credit.

Information Tabs:
- The Authoritative Literature will be provided in all tasks in the AUD, FAR, and REG sections for your reference.
- Your simulation may have one or more additional **Information Tabs**. Like the Authoritative Literature tabs, **Information Tabs** do not have a pencil icon.
- If your task has additional **Information Tabs**, go through each to familiarize yourself with the task content.

Help Tab:
- The **Help Tab** provides assistance with the exam software that is used in this task. For example, if the task is to compose a memorandum, **Help** will provide information about the word processor.

The Toolbar

The toolbar at the top of the screen shows the amount of time remaining for you to complete the tasks. In addition, the following tools are available. Note that only the Exit button is displayed when Directions are visible - the others will appear when you begin the tasks.

Click on these buttons to split or unsplit the screen. You can split the screen vertically or horizontally.

Click on this button to display the calculator; click on it again to hide the calculator. To move the calculator, click on the calculator title bar and drag the calculator to the desired location.

Click on this button to use the spreadsheet; click on it again to hide the spreadsheet. To move the spreadsheet, click on the the spreadsheet title bar and drag the spreadsheet to the desired location.

Click on this button to go on to the next part of the examination. You must complete all of the tasks to receive full credit. Once you click on **Exit** and confirm the action, you will NOT be able to return to this testlet.

| ▼ = Reminder | | Directions | 1 2 3 4 5 | | ◀ Previous Next ▶ |

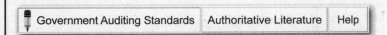

Government Auditing Standards | Authoritative Literature | Help

The auditor's separate report on compliance with laws and regulations was drafted by a staff accountant of Hall & Hall at the completion of the financial statement audit. This audit was in accordance with Generally Accepted Government Auditing Standards (GAGAS). The report contained the following seven statements. It was submitted to the engagement partner who reviewed matters thoroughly and properly concluded that no material instances of noncompliance were identified.

For each of the following seven statements, indicate by selecting from the list provided whether it is an appropriate element of a report on compliance with laws and regulations under GAGAS and, if it is inappropriate, the reason.

Statements	Answers	Choices
1. A statement that the audit was conducted in accordance with GAAS and with *Government Auditing Standards* issued by the Comptroller General of the United States.		A) Appropriate B) Inappropriate because a governmental audit should not refer to GAAS C) Inappropriate because *Government Auditing Standards* is not issued by the U.S. Comptroller General
2. A statement that the auditor's procedures included tests of compliance.		A) Appropriate B) Inappropriate because the auditor's procedures should not include tests of compliance C) Inappropriate because a statement on the auditor's procedures should not be included within the report on compliance
3. A statement that management is responsible for compliance with laws, regulations, contracts, and grants.		A) Appropriate B) Inappropriate because the auditor is responsible for compliance with laws, regulations, contracts, and grants C) Inappropriate because this statement is not required to be included within the report on compliance
4. A statement that the standards require the auditor to plan and to perform the audit to detect all instances of noncompliance with applicable laws and regulations.		A) Appropriate B) Inappropriate because the auditor is required to plan and perform the audit to provide reasonable assurance of detecting all instances of noncompliance having a direct effect on the financial statements, not all instances of noncompliance C) Inappropriate because the auditor is required to plan and perform the audit to detect instances of noncompliance having a direct and material effect on the financial statements, not all instances of noncompliance
5. A statement that the auditor's objective was to provide an opinion on compliance with the provisions of laws and regulations equivalent to that to be expressed on the financial statements.		A) Appropriate B) Inappropriate because expressing an opinion is a lower level of reporting than the positive and negative assurance required by *Government Auditing Standards* C) Inappropriate because the report does not express an opinion

-- Continued on next page --

| Government Auditing Standards | Authoritative Literature | Help | -- Continued |

Statements	Answers	Choices
6. A statement of negative assurance that, with respect to items tested, nothing came to the auditor's attention that caused the auditor to believe that the entity had not complied, in all material respects, with the provisions of laws, regulations, contracts, and grants.		A) Appropriate B) Inappropriate because no assurance should be provided C) Inappropriate because *Government Auditing Standards* requires positive assurance
7. A statement that the report is intended only for the information of the specific legislative or regulatory bodies and that this restriction is intended to limit the distribution of the report.		A) Appropriate B) Inappropriate because *Government Auditing Standards* requires that the report be intended only for the use of management C) Inappropriate because the report is silent as to limiting its distribution

| Independence | Authoritative Literature | Help |

Independence is an important consideration for governmental auditors. *Government Auditing Standards* identifies three types of impairments of auditor independence. Select from the list provided the type of impairment described by the statement. Each choice may be used once, more than once, or not at all.

Statement	Answer	Impairment
1. Auditors are deterred from acting objectively by employees of the audited entity.		A) Personal impairment
2. Auditors should not provide nonaudit services that involve performing management functions of the audited entity.		B) External impairment
3. Auditors are pressured to reduce professional skepticism by an oversight agency of the audited entity.		C) Organizational impairment
4. The impairment that parallels requirements by the AICPA.		
5. Auditors should not have a direct financial interest in the client.		
6. The auditor should be mentally unbiased.		
7. The head of internal auditing does not report results to the head or deputy head of the government entity.		
8. The audit organization should not audit its own work.		

Compliance Issues | Authoritative Literature | Help

Indicate by checking the appropriate box whether each statement below represents potential responsibilities of the auditor, the management of Toxic Waste Disposal Co., Inc., or neither.

Description	Auditor	Management	Neither Management nor the Auditor
1. Ensure compliance with laws and regulations			
2. Consider laws and regulations to plan and perform the audit			
3. Determine whether applicable laws and regulations are fair			
4. Gain an understanding of the possible effects of laws and regulations that may have a direct and material effect on the financial statements			
5. Obtain written representations about laws and regulations			
6. Review minutes of meetings for evidence concerning compliance with laws and regulations			
7. Identify laws and regulations requiring compliance			
8. Suggest new regulations to authorities			
9. Establish internal controls pertaining to compliance with laws and regulations			
10. Provide positive assurance that no laws or regulations have been violated by employees			

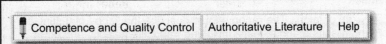

Competence and Quality Control | Authoritative Literature | Help

Indicate by checking the appropriate box whether each of the following statements relating to the competence and quality control for governmental auditors or audit organizations is true or false.

Statement	True	False
1. Each staff auditor must individually possess the professional competence for all the tasks required for the audit of a client.		
2. Each governmental auditor must earn at least 24 hours of governmental CPE every 2 years.		
3. Each audit organization must have a peer review at least once every 2 years.		
4. Each client must establish a quality control system for its auditors.		
5. Each audit organization has the responsibility to ensure that its personnel comply with professional standards.		

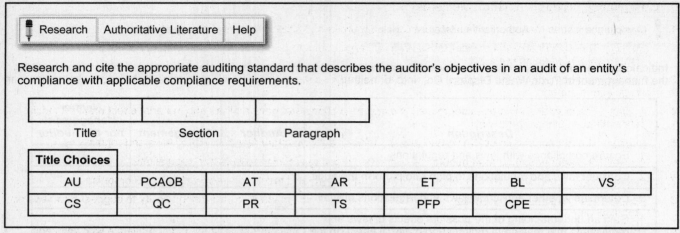

Research | Authoritative Literature | Help

Research and cite the appropriate auditing standard that describes the auditor's objectives in an audit of an entity's compliance with applicable compliance requirements.

| Title | Section | Paragraph |

Title Choices

AU	PCAOB	AT	AR	ET	BL	VS
CS	QC	PR	TS	PFP	CPE	

▼ = Reminder   Directions   1 2 3 4 [5]   ◀ Previous   Next ▶

Unofficial Answers

1. Government Auditing Standards (7 Gradable Items)

1.   <u>A) Appropriate.</u> The second paragraph of the report should indicate that the audit was conducted in accordance with both GAAS and *Government Auditing Standards*.

2.   <u>A) Appropriate.</u> The report should state that the auditor has "performed tests of (name of entity)'s compliance with certain laws, regulations, contracts, and grants."

3.   <u>A) Appropriate.</u> The report states that management is responsible for compliance with laws, regulations, contracts, and grants.

4.   <u>C) Inappropriate because the auditor is required to plan and perform the audit to detect instances of noncompliance having a direct and material effect on the financial statements, not all instances of noncompliance.</u> The report should state that those standards require that we plan and perform the audit to obtain reasonable assurance about whether the financial statements are free of material misstatement.

5.   <u>C) Inappropriate because the report does not express an opinion.</u> The report should describe the scope of testing of compliance with laws and regulations and present the results of those tests, including fraud, illegal acts, and other material noncompliance. It need not express an opinion. However, reporting the scope of testing includes reporting whether the tests provided sufficient evidence to support an opinion and whether the auditor is providing such an opinion.

6.   <u>B) Inappropriate because no assurance should be provided.</u> No assurance on compliance, either positive or negative, need be expressed under *Government Auditing Standards*.

7.   <u>C) Inappropriate because the report is silent as to limiting its distribution.</u> The report states that it is not intended for use by noninformed parties, but it does not limit the distribution of the report.

2. Independence (8 Gradable Items)

1.   <u>B) External impairment.</u> Auditors are deterred from acting objectively by employees of the audited entity.

2.   <u>A) Personal impairment.</u> Auditors should not provide nonaudit services that involve performing management functions of the audited entity.

3.   <u>B) External impairment.</u> Auditors are pressured to reduce professional skepticism by an oversight agency of the audited entity.

4.   <u>A) Personal impairment.</u> The impairment that parallels requirements by the AICPA.

5.   <u>A) Personal impairment.</u> Auditors should not have a direct financial interest in the client.

6.   <u>A) Personal impairment.</u> The auditor should be mentally unbiased.

7.   <u>C) Organizational impairment.</u> The head of the internal auditing does not report results to the head or deputy head of the government entity.

8.   <u>A) Personal impairment.</u> The audit organization should not audit its own work.

3. **Compliance Issues** (10 Gradable Items)

1. <u>Management.</u> It is management's responsibility to ensure compliance with laws and regulations.

2. <u>Auditor.</u> The auditor should consider those laws and regulations that have a direct and material effect on the financial statements in planning the audit.

3. <u>Neither Management nor the Auditor.</u> It is neither the auditor's nor management's responsibility to judge whether laws or regulations are fair.

4. <u>Auditor.</u> The auditor should consider those laws and regulations that have a direct and material effect on the financial statements in planning the audit.

5. <u>Auditor.</u> The auditor should obtain written representations from management concerning laws and regulations.

6. <u>Auditor.</u> The auditor should read minutes of committee meetings relating to laws and regulations.

7. <u>Management.</u> It is management's responsibility to identify laws and regulations applicable to the organization.

8. <u>Neither Management nor the Auditor.</u> It is neither the auditor's nor management's responsibility to suggest new laws or regulations.

9. <u>Management.</u> It is management's responsibility to establish internal controls pertaining to compliance with laws and regulations.

10. <u>Neither Management nor the Auditor.</u> It is neither the auditor's nor management's responsibility to provide positive or negative assurance that no laws or regulations have been violated by employees.

4. **Competence and Quality Control** (5 Gradable Items)

1. <u>False.</u> The staff assigned to perform the audit must collectively possess adequate professional competence required for the audit of a client.

2. <u>True.</u> Each governmental auditor must earn at least 24 hours of governmental CPE every 2 years.

3. <u>False.</u> Each audit organization must have a peer review at least once every 3 years.

4. <u>False.</u> Each audit organization must establish a quality control system.

5. <u>True.</u> Each audit organization has the responsibility to provide for quality control to ensure that its personnel comply with professional standards.

5. **Research** (1 Gradable Item)

Answer: 801.10

<u>AU 801</u> -- *Compliance Auditing*

.10 The auditor's objectives in a compliance audit are to

a. obtain sufficient appropriate audit evidence to form an opinion and report at the level specified in the governmental audit requirement on whether the entity complied in all material respects with the applicable compliance requirements; and

b. identify audit and reporting requirements specified in the governmental audit requirement that are supplementary to GAAS and *Government Auditing Standards*, if any, and perform procedures to address those requirements.

Gleim Simulation Grading

Task	Correct Responses		Gradable Items		Score per Task
1	_____	÷	7	=	_____
2	_____	÷	8	=	_____
3	_____	÷	10	=	_____
4	_____	÷	5	=	_____
Research	_____	÷	1	=	_____

	Total of Scores per Task	_____
÷	Total Number of Tasks	5
	Total Score	_____ %

Use **CPA Gleim Online** and **Simulation Wizard** to practice more task-based simulations in a realistic environment.

The Gleim Team wishes you luck on your exam!

REVIEW CHECKLIST
AUDITING

Your objective is to prepare to pass this section of the CPA exam. It is **not** to do a certain amount of work or spend a certain amount of time with this book or other CPA review material/courses. Rather, you **must**

1. Understand the CPA exam thoroughly -- study *CPA Review: A System for Success* and the Introduction in this book.

2. Understand the subject matter in the 20 study units in this book. The list of subunits in each of the 20 study units (presented below and on the following page) should bring to mind core concepts, basic rules, principles, etc.

3. If you have not already done so, prepare a 1- to 2-page summary of each study unit for your final review just before you go to the exam (do not bring notes into the examination room).

Study Unit 1: Engagement Responsibilities

1.1 Attest Engagements
1.2 Audit Engagements
1.3 Additional Professional Services
1.4 Assurance Services
1.5 Quality Control

Study Unit 2: Professional Responsibilities

2.1 *Code of Professional Conduct*
2.2 Independence
2.3 Integrity and Objectivity
2.4 Professional Standards
2.5 Responsibilities to Clients
2.6 Other Responsibilities
2.7 Other Pronouncements on Professional Responsibilities

Study Unit 3: Risk Assessment

3.1 Pre-Engagement Acceptance Activities
3.2 Planning and Supervision
3.3 Audit Risk and Materiality
3.4 Understanding the Entity and Its Environment
3.5 Analytical Procedures
3.6 Consideration of Fraud in a Financial Statement Audit
3.7 Illegal Acts by Clients

Study Unit 4: Strategic Planning Issues

4.1 The Auditor's Consideration of the Internal Audit Function
4.2 Using the Work of a Specialist
4.3 Related Parties
4.4 Accounting Estimates and Fair Value
4.5 Consideration of Omitted Procedures After the Report Date

Study Unit 5: Internal Control Concepts and Information Technology

5.1 Introduction to Internal Control
5.2 Internal Control Components
5.3 Understanding Internal Control
5.4 Flowcharting
5.5 Internal Control and Information Technology

Study Unit 6: Internal Control -- Sales-Receivables-Cash Receipts Cycle

6.1 Responsibilities/Organizational Structure/Flowcharts
6.2 Controls in a Cash Sale Environment
6.3 Other Sales-Receivables Related Transactions
6.4 Technology Considerations

Study Unit 7: Internal Control -- Purchases, Payroll, and Other Cycles

7.1 Purchases Responsibilities/Organizational Structure/Flowchart
7.2 Purchases Technology Considerations
7.3 Electronic Data Interchange (EDI)
7.4 Payroll Responsibilities/Organizational Structure/Flowchart
7.5 Payroll Technology Considerations
7.6 Other Cycles

Study Unit 8: Responses to Assessed Risks

8.1 Assessing Risks of Material Misstatement
8.2 Auditor's Response to Risks
8.3 Assessing Risk in a Computer Environment

Study Unit 9: Internal Control Communications and Reports

9.1 Communicating Internal Control Related Matters Identified in an Audit
9.2 The Auditor's Communication with Those Charged with Governance
9.3 Reporting on an Entity's Internal Control
9.4 Service Organizations

698

INDEX

CPE EQE RTRP EA CIA CMA CPA

GLEIM CPA REVIEW SYSTEM

Includes: Gleim Online, Review Books, Test Prep Online, Simulation Wizard, Audio Review, Practice Exam, CPA Review: A System for Success booklet, plus bonus Book Bag.

$989.95 x _____ = $_____

Also available by exam section (does not include Book Bag).

GLEIM CMA REVIEW SYSTEM

Includes: Gleim Online, Review Books, Test Prep Software Download, Essay Wizard, Audio Review, Practice Exam, CMA Review: A System for Success booklet, plus bonus Book Bag.

$739.95 x _____ = $_____

Also available by exam part (does not include Book Bag).

GLEIM CIA REVIEW SYSTEM

Includes: Gleim Online, Review Books, Test Prep Software Download, Audio Review, Practice Exam, CIA Review: A System for Success booklet, plus bonus Book Bag.

$824.95 x _____ = $_____

Also available by exam part (does not include Book Bag).

GLEIM EA REVIEW SYSTEM

Includes: Gleim Online, Review Books, Test Prep Software Download, Audio Review, Practice Exam, EA Review: A System for Success booklet, plus bonus Book Bag.

$629.95 x _____ = $_____

Also available by exam part (does not include Book Bag).

GLEIM RTRP REVIEW SYSTEM

Includes: Gleim Online, Question Bank Online, Practice Exam, 15 hours of CE.

$139.95 x _____ = $_____

"THE GLEIM EQE SERIES" EXAM QUESTIONS AND EXPLANATIONS

Includes: 5 Books and *Test Prep Software Download*.

$112.25 x _____ = $_____

Also available by part.

GLEIM ONLINE CPE

Try a FREE 4-hour course at gleim.com/cpe
- Easy-to-Complete
- Informative
- Effective

Contact
GLEIM® PUBLICATIONS
for further assistance:

gleim.com
800.874.5346
sales@gleim.com

SUBTOTAL $_____

Complete your order on the next page

Subject to change without notice.

GLEIM® PUBLICATIONS, INC.

P. O. Box 12848   Gainesville, FL 32604

TOLL FREE:	800.874.5346	
LOCAL:	352.375.0772	
FAX:	352.375.6940	
INTERNET:	gleim.com	
EMAIL:	sales@gleim.com	

Customer service is available (Eastern Time):

8:00 a.m. - 7:00 p.m., Mon. - Fri.

9:00 a.m. - 2:00 p.m., Saturday

Please have your credit card ready, or save time by ordering online!

SUBTOTAL (from previous page) $_____

Add applicable sales tax for shipments within Florida. _____

Shipping (nonrefundable) 14.00

TOTAL $_____

Email us for prices/instructions on shipments outside the 48 contiguous states, or simply order online.

NAME (please print) _____

ADDRESS _____ Apt. _____

(street address required for UPS/Federal Express)

CITY _____ STATE _____ ZIP _____

____ MC/VISA/DISC/AMEX ____ Check/M.O. Daytime Telephone (____) _____

Credit Card No. _____ - _____ - _____ - _____

Exp. ____ / ____ Signature _____
Month / Year

Email address _____

1. We process and ship orders daily, within one business day over 98.8% of the time. Call by 3:00 pm for same day service.

2. Gleim Publications, Inc. guarantees the immediate refund of all resalable texts, unopened and un-downloaded Test Prep Software, and unopened and un-downloaded audios returned within 30 days. Accounting and Academic Test Prep online courses may be canceled within 30 days if no more than the first study unit or lesson has been accessed. In addition, Online CPE courses may be canceled within 30 days if no more than the Introductory Study Questions have been accessed. Accounting Practice Exams may be canceled within 30 days of purchase if the Practice Exam has not been started. Aviation online courses may be canceled within 30 days if no more than two study units have been accessed. This policy applies only to products that are purchased directly from Gleim Publications, Inc. No refunds will be provided on opened or downloaded Test Prep Software or audios, partial returns of package sets, or shipping and handling charges. Any freight charges incurred for returned or refused packages will be the purchaser's responsibility.

3. Please PHOTOCOPY this order form for others.

4. No CODs. Orders from individuals must be prepaid.

Subject to change without notice. 11/12

For updates and other important information, visit our website.

GLEIM
KNOWLEDGE
TRANSFER
SYSTEMS®

gleim.com